The Editors

DONALD STUMP is Professor of English at Saint Louis University. Among his books and edited collections are *Images of Elizabeth I: A Quadricentennial Celebration, Sir Philip Sidney: An Annotated Bibliography of Texts and Criticism (1554–1984),* and *'Hamarita': The Concept of Error in the Western Tradition, Essays in Honor of John M. Crossett.*

SUSAN M. FELCH is Professor of English at Calvin College. Her books include *The Collected Works of Anne Vaughan Lock, Bakhtin and Religion: A Feeling for Faith, The Emmaus Readers,* and *Elizabeth Tyrwhit's Morning and Evening Prayers.*

A NORTON CRITICAL EDITION

ELIZABETH I
AND HER AGE

AUTHORITATIVE TEXTS
COMMENTARY AND CRITICISM

Edited by

DONALD STUMP
SAINT LOUIS UNIVERSITY

SUSAN M. FELCH
CALVIN COLLEGE

W • W • NORTON & COMPANY • *New York* • *London*

W. W. Norton & Company has been independent since its founding in 1923, when William Warder Norton and Mary D. Herter Norton first published lectures delivered at the People's Institute, the adult education division of New York City's Cooper Union. The firm soon expanded its program beyond the Institute, publishing books by celebrated academics from America and abroad. By mid-century, the two major pillars of Norton's publishing program—trade books and college texts—were firmly established. In the 1950s, the Norton family transferred control of the company to its employees, and today—with a staff of four hundred and a comparable number of trade, college, and professional titles published each year—W. W. Norton & Company stands as the largest and oldest publishing house owned wholly by its employees.

Composition by Binghamton Valley Composition
Manufacturing by Courier Companies—Westford Divisions
Book design by Antonina Krass
Production manager: Christine D'Antonio

Library of Congress Cataloging-in-Publication Data
Elizabeth I and her age : authoritative texts, criticism / edited by Donald Stump,
Susan M. Felch.—1st ed.
p. cm.—(A Norton critical edition)
Includes bibliographical references.

ISBN 978-0-393-92822-8 (pbk.)

1. Elizabeth I, Queen of England, 1533–1603—Literary art.   2. Great Britain—Politics
and government–1558–1603—Sources.   3. Great Britain—History—Elizabeth,
1558–1603—Sources.   4. Kings' and rulers' writings, English—History and criticism.
I. Stump, Donald V., 1946– II. Felch, Susan M., 1951–
DA350.E443 2008
942.05'5092—dc22   2008037341

W. W. Norton & Company, Inc., 500 Fifth Avenue, New York, N.Y. 10110
www.wwnorton.com

W. W. Norton & Company Ltd., Castle House, 75/76 Wells Street, London W1T 3QT

1 2 3 4 5 6 7 8 9 0

For my students

The end of reading
is not more books but more life.

Holbrook Jackson

smf

For Eleonore

Quantum in te crescit amor, tantum crescit
pulchritudo; quia ipsa charitas est animae pulchritudo.

St. Augustine
*Homilies on the First
Letter of John* 9.9

ds

Contents

PART FIVE: THE FRENCH MARRIAGE
NEGOTIATIONS (1578–1582)

PART SIX: COURTIERS, ASSASSINS, AND THE DEATH OF MARY STUART (1582–1587)

PART SEVEN: THE SPANISH ARMADA AND ITS AFTERMATH (1588–1592)

Commentary and Criticism 625

Preface

In developing *Elizabeth I and Her Age*, we have sought to create an anthology in which many kinds of writing about the Queen come together naturally and easily. Those who are interested in Renaissance literature will find much to enjoy here, and so will those who like biography, history, women's studies, and cultural studies.

In assembling the selections, our first desire was to understand Elizabeth herself, a ruler who was arguably the most intelligent, adept, and influential English monarch of the modern era. We began with her own words as they have come down to us in speeches, prayers, poems, letters, and proclamations. As we worked our way through her life, period by period, we also gathered works written for her and about her by her contemporaries, and we cast our nets wide. Poets, dramatists, entertainers, councilors, courtiers, ladies in waiting, Parliamentarians, clergymen, liturgists, polemicists, and popular balladeers all have their place. Much of the fascination of the project has come, in fact, from recovering the thoughts and aims of the Queen at various turning points in her reign and seeing the ways in which writers seeking her favor or support actually understood her or were wide of the mark.

The aim in gathering all this material was not simply to look back with antiquarian interest at an extraordinary woman in a remarkable age, compelling as such a backward look might be. We also hoped to recover something of the interplay of eloquent and influential voices that spoke out during important political, cultural, and religious crises that arose during her life—crises that have since had lasting effects on the British Isles, Europe, and the world.

The sheer variety of works required for such a project calls for a range of reading strategies and therefore a somewhat elaborate set of editorial aids. Some works offer a fairly straightforward account of contemporary events; others convey their meanings indirectly, through figures, symbols, allegories, ironies, half-concealed allusions, and myths, and these need to be sorted out and explained. To read any of them well also requires some grasp of the great struggles over religion, the arts, education, politics, governance, nationalism, colonial expansion, and imperial dominance that loomed large in the sixteenth century and that have remained important in the English-speaking world ever since. For that reason, introductions, notes, and glossary entries are somewhat fuller than they might otherwise have been.

When we began work in 1999, we had in mind a much simpler volume of classroom readings, which we expected to be assigned in conjunction with a good biography of Elizabeth, a few longer literary works (such as Edmund Spenser's *Faerie Queene* and Thomas Heywood's two-part play about the Queen, *If You Know Not Me, You Know Nobody*), and a selection of secondary readings. Our own experiences in juggling such resources in class, however, soon made it clear that it would be better to include everything in a single volume, so that connections between biographical material and a full range of readings would be easy to grasp and opportunities to reflect and to discuss important points would not be lost in rummaging through several sources.

It has been a challenge to assemble such a wide-ranging collection of materials, and we could not have done it without a great deal of help. When we began, most of the pageants and entertainments staged before the Queen had not been reprinted since John Nichols assembled them in his 1823 collection *The Progresses and Public Processions of Queen Elizabeth*. Poems of interest were scattered in a variety of nineteenth- and twentieth-century editions, many long out of print and most without adequate introductions or notes. Ballads, broadsides, prayers, sermons, official liturgies, and polemical tracts were even less accessible, requiring us to spin through reels of microfilm or scan through many screens of *Early English Books Online*.

We also encountered a good deal of Latin, and for assistance with the complexities of sixteenth-century England discourse in that language, we turned to one of the foremost experts, Clarence H. Miller, Professor Emeritus of English at Saint Louis University. His renderings of hitherto untranslated passages in the court entertainments lend life and power to the works, and his help in tracking down classical sources and allusions for the notes was invaluable. For his generosity with his time and his learning, we cannot thank him enough.

In locating and drawing primary sources together, modernizing spelling, finding useful secondary literature, resolving questions that came up as we wrote introductions and annotations, and proofreading final copy for the book, we have been blessed with a number of able and efficient research assistants, who were funded through the generosity of Saint Louis University and Calvin College. Our warmest thanks to Janet Gerrard-Willis, Beth Human, Keith Kelly, Tim Moylan, Melissa Mayus, Rebekah Ray Nguyen, Annie Papreck, Chrissie Schicktanz, and Lisa Bont Tjapkes for their unstinting assistance.

We are also grateful to the College of Arts and Sciences of Saint Louis University, Calvin College, the McGregor Foundation, and the Calvin College Alumni Association for providing summer research grants, sabbatical leave support, and foreign travel grants, without which the project would not have been possible. Our thanks, too, to the Saint Louis University Center for Medieval and Renaissance Studies for providing items of computer equipment, to Jamie Schmidt and the reference librarians of Pius XII Library, and to Kathy Struck, Kathy De May, and the librarians of the Hekman Library for their help in locating rare items.

Finally, we wish to thank Margaret Hannay, Carole Levin, Steven May, Janel Mueller, William Oram, Anne Lake Prescott, Mary Beth Rose, and Linda Shenk for their help in looking over our initial plans and in advising and sending materials to us along the way. Without their generosity in offering help and suggestions, the book would have been much poorer than it is.

Introduction

Four centuries after her death, Queen Elizabeth I still holds a special fascination. The daughter of Henry VIII and Anne Boleyn, who was executed for adultery when Elizabeth was not yet three, she was declared a bastard and lost her legal standing as Henry's child. Restored to the royal line of succession in 1544, she was nearly displaced from it again under her brother, Edward VI, and was almost put to death on false suspicion of treason by her sister, Mary I. When Mary died and Elizabeth succeeded to the throne in 1558, only two other women had ever held the office of Queen Regnant in England, and neither had lasted for long. Few thought that Elizabeth could hold onto power unless she married and gave much of her authority over to a husband. For one thing, the role of monarch—which involved being the Commander in Chief of the army, Head of the English Church, and ruler over a court intimately organized around the monarch's private quarters and bedchamber—was fashioned entirely for a man ruling among men. For another, England was only in the earliest stages of becoming a truly Protestant nation, and the enormous cultural dislocations involved in that transformation led to constant (though mostly ineffectual) plotting in France, Spain, and the Papal Court to invade England and restore it to the Catholic fold. It also led discontented English citizens to mount a long string of revolts and assassination plots against the Queen. Yet Elizabeth not only endured, she flourished. What has often been described as the Golden Age in English literature owes much to her love of fine writing and her ability to inspire others to create it. Her leadership was also vital in establishing the Settlement of Religion that still bears her name and the Age of Discovery that launched England as a major sea power and laid the groundwork, for good or ill, of the worldwide British Empire that would reach its zenith three centuries after her death.

This volume sets out to create a composite picture of the Queen and her age, based on early modern sources and supported by modern commentary and criticism. Exploring her character, her education, and her development as a ruler, we also concentrate attention on her place in the great religious, cultural, and political controversies of her time and on her legacy in literature, history, and modern film.

In gathering materials, we have sought to meet two needs not addressed by previous anthologies of Elizabethan literature. One is to satisfy the widespread interest in historical approaches to writers and their works. Since most of the primary texts in the volume are organized by successive periods in the Queen's forty-four-year reign, readers may explore not only the literary and aesthetic qualities of the works, but also the full range of social, religious, and cultural concerns that prompted their creation. The second need is for a convenient anthology that serves the growing numbers of readers interested in the writings of the Queen herself. We include more of her poems, prayers, speeches, letters, and proclamations than any other similar reader, setting them side by side with other works of the period that focus on the same crises, the same controversies, and the same opportunities.

Because the works that offer the most fascinating insights into Elizabeth's life and reign often lie outside the conventional literary canon, the range of authors included here is larger than usual for such an anthology. We include not only works written for and about the Queen by well-known writers but also valuable and interesting selections by less well-known figures, including popular entertainers, balladeers, controversialists, and preachers. A substantial number of the works have never before appeared in a modern scholarly edition, and those that have were dispersed among so many publications that even scholars of the period have not had easy ways to consider them all in relation to one another or in their original historical contexts.

We begin with accounts of the stormy relations between Elizabeth's parents, her birth and early education, and her trials under her brother Edward and her sister Mary (Part One). We then turn to the early years of her reign, which were marked by the establishment of a new, largely Protestant Church of England, entanglement in the First War of Religion in France, and pressure from Parliament for her to marry and produce an heir to the throne (Part Two). Our next focus is on the Queen's troublesome relations with Mary, Queen of Scots, after she was deposed and escaped to England in 1568. Beginning with her trial by an English commission for complicity in the murder of her second husband, Henry Stuart, Earl of Darnley, we take up the dramatic events that followed, including the Rebellion of the Northern Earls, the Pope's excommunication of Elizabeth and call on her subjects not to obey her, and the Ridolfi assassination plot of 1571 (Part Three).

Turning to the middle years of the reign, we concentrate on the growing threat of invasion from Spain and Elizabeth's attempt to form a defensive alliance to protect England by marrying a French prince, and we also take up continued pressure to reform the English Church and Elizabeth's ability, despite such tensions, to maintain her popularity with her subjects (Part Four). Focusing on her intense marriage negotiations with the Duke of Anjou in 1578–82 (Part Five), we then trace the collapse of those plans, the slide into war with Spain in the Netherlands in the mid-1580s, and the renewal of assassination attempts against the Queen, including the Babington plot that led to the execution of Mary Stuart in 1587 (Part Six). After pausing to explore the invasion of the Spanish Armada in 1588 and its importance as a turning point in English history (Part Seven), we take up the painful changes caused by the deaths of many of the Queen's most trusted councilors and friends in the late 1580s and early 1590s and the subsequent appearance of new faces at Court (Part Eight).

We round out our survey of the reign with works related to Tyrone's Rebellion in Ireland, the troubles that subsequently led to Essex's Rebellion, and the Queen's final decline and death in 1603 (Part Nine). Having paused to look back on the most memorable and influential images of the Queen that have survived in later ages (Part Ten), we then survey a selection of reminiscences and histories and biographies of Elizabeth that were published from her lifetime to the middle of the nineteenth century (Part Eleven).

The final section of the anthology (Part Twelve) is devoted to more recent commentary on Elizabeth and to modern criticism on the writers of her age. We begin with studies of Elizabeth herself—her strategies for rule, her decision to remain a virgin monarch, her views and practices in religion, and her own speeches and poems. We then turn to studies of contemporary works about her—the entertainments staged during her summer progresses, the representations of her in the portraits, poetry, drama, and fiction of the period, and some of the rumors and reactions against her that disquieted her reign. We conclude with a study of three twentieth-century depictions of her in popular film.

For those interested in knowing the ways in which Elizabeth developed as a monarch—not only surviving the long train of adversities that confronted her but turning them to account in shaping the course of events for her own age and those that followed—we hope that this collection offers new pleasures, new angles of vision, and new insights.

Editorial Principles

Two principles have guided our selection and editing of copy texts. The first was our intent to recover something of the original effect of the works, which required that they be presented to modern readers in the form in which most Elizabethan readers would have encountered them. For that reason, we generally use first printed editions as copy texts, not manuscripts or later diplomatic editions, even when such texts have greater claims to represent final authorial intent. After all, what was perceived at the time of publication is what shaped the various contemporary political reactions and literary interactions, not what authors intended but did not, for one reason or another, succeed in conveying in print. When contemporary printed editions were not available, we chose later reliable, scholarly editions.

The second principle was to present the material in the most readable form for today's audience. To that end, we have modernized spelling, punctuation, and paragraphing, although we have generally retained original grammar, as, for example, in archaic usage involving singulars and plurals (*other* for *others*). We have, however, modernized archaic possessives of the form "Burghley his horse" ("Burghley's horse"), except where the former is needed to preserve poetic rhythm. Words that the *Oxford English Dictionary* lists separately from their modern equivalents and does not simply note as obsolete spellings are not modernized. Hence, "disgrade" and "brast" are retained, with explanatory glosses, rather than modernized to "degrade" and "burst," but "accompt" and "least" (as in the phrase "least he be discovered") are modernized to "account" and "lest"—though, again, only if rhythms and rhymes in verse are not affected. Apostrophes that substitute for elided vowels have been eliminated and the vowels restored, except in lines of poetry where the rhythm or rhyme would be affected. Although texts, including those from later editions, have been modernized, titles of works printed in the sixteenth and seventeenth centuries and supplied in the notes that list our copy texts are given in the form used by *Early English Books Online*. Since page numbers (when given at all) are not reliable in this period, we supply page signatures.

To remind modern readers of the importance of titles and rank in Elizabethan culture, and to make scanning pages for references to particular people easier, we capitalize titles such as "Queen," "Earl," and "Pope" when they are used in reference to a particular, named person (e.g., "The Queen boxed the Earl's ears."). In the table of contents and in headings above selections, we use the last title attained during Elizabeth's reign (with the exception of Elizabeth herself), as in Sir Philip Sidney or William Cecil, Lord Burghley. In section introductions and explanatory notes, we use titles at the time under discussion.

We capitalize "God," "Lord," etc. whenever the supreme being of a monotheistic religion is intended. We also capitalize pronouns referring to the deity. When the term "god" or "goddess" refers to a divine being from a polytheistic religion, we capitalize the term only when it is used as a personal title, such as "the Goddess of Love," or as the standard title of a specific set of deities, such as "the Muses," "the Graces," or "the Fates." Names of members of general classes of divine beings, such as "nymphs" and "tritons," are not capitalized. Hence, "the Muse of History" and "Sing, ye Graces," but "The sea nymphs rejoiced." Scriptural references are based on the practice in modern Protestant Bibles (e.g., Psalm 51 for Psalm 50, "Have mercy on me"; 1 Chronicles for 3 Kings). All biblical quotations are from the Geneva Bible (1560) unless otherwise noted.

Figures from classical mythology and history and from the Bible are explained in a glossary at the end of the volume rather than in the footnotes.

Illustrations

DIEV ET MON DROIT

The Texts of
ELIZABETH I
AND HER AGE

Part One: The Princess Elizabeth (1533–1558)

HISTORICAL BACKGROUND

On a late Sunday afternoon in the autumn of 1533, worshippers at St. Paul's Cathedral in London or the chapel at Greenwich Palace on the Thames would have heard the words of the *Te Deum*, the ancient Latin hymn of Thanksgiving, floating from the choir: "*Te Deum laudamus; te Dominum confitemur*" ("We praise Thee, O God: we acknowledge Thee to be the Lord"). The singing of the celebratory anthem had been ordered by King Henry VIII. It was the seventh of September and he had once again become a father: the child's name was Elizabeth. Clergy, choir, and common people dutifully offered their praise to God for the new princess, but the bonfires that had been prepared in anticipation of a male heir remained unlit, and the jousting tournament was quietly cancelled. The truncated ceremonies reflected Henry VIII's disappointment in the birth of a daughter who would not, he imagined, continue the Tudor dynasty.

The Tudor royal line had been founded just a generation earlier by Henry VII, Elizabeth's grandfather, who defeated Richard III at Bosworth Field in 1485 and married Richard's niece, Elizabeth of York. The defeat and marriage brought an end to the Wars of the Roses between the houses of Lancaster and York and consolidated Henry's claim to the English throne. Joining the emblematic red rose of his own Lancastrian family with the white rose of Elizabeth's Yorkist clan, Henry VII established the Tudor rose, the pink eglantine, as the symbol of his new dynasty. The hope of Henry VII and Elizabeth of York for a reunified and rejuvenated England was summed up in the name of their first-born son—Arthur—with its invocations of Britain's past glory. But Arthur's death in 1502 elevated his ten-year-old brother, Henry, to the role of heir presumptive and, at the death of Henry VII in 1509, to the throne itself. Within days the teenager married his brother's widow, the Spanish princess Katherine of Aragon, and began to rule as Henry VIII.

The first two decades of Henry VIII's reign were busy both at home and abroad. He fought wars in France and Scotland; regularized the crown's income by imposing a new standard of taxation; coerced the older, landed families into serving his interests; and brought "new men," characterized by intelligence and ambition rather than social standing, into his Court. Cardinal Thomas Wolsey, one of Henry's most powerful councilors, was the son of a butcher; Sir Thomas More, Lord Chancellor from 1529 to 1532, was the son of a lawyer; and Thomas Cranmer, the Archbishop of Canterbury, was a member of the lesser gentry. Henry also proved himself a loyal son of the Roman Catholic Church. He opposed the reformation that Martin Luther had inaugurated in Germany in 1517 and approved laws that banned the importation of Lutheran books into England. So successful were his efforts that Pope Leo X named him "Defender of the Faith" in 1521.

By 1527, however, Henry had grown concerned about the dynastic succession and turned his attention to seeking an annulment from his aging wife. His marriage to Queen Katherine had produced only a single living heir—the Princess Mary—and, after a series of affairs, the King had been drawn to Anne Boleyn, daughter of a gentry family. In 1531, having failed to gain an annulment of his marriage from the Pope, Henry had himself declared Supreme Head of the Church of England and subsequently divorced Katherine and married Anne.

The divorce of Henry from Katherine also meant the divorce of England from the Roman Catholic Church, a move that would have repercussions throughout the rest of the sixteenth century. Immediately, it meant that the senior clergy, such as bishops and heads of religious houses, were forced to recant their oath to the Pope and swear allegiance to the King, not only as their secular ruler but also as Supreme Head of the Church. Many who refused to do so, such as Sir Thomas More and Bishop John Fisher, were executed. The Reformation, then, came to England amid a rather tawdry divorce scandal in an age that did not believe in divorce. When Anne Boleyn was crowned queen on June 1, 1533, her coronation procession elicited only subdued curiosity from the Londoners who lined the streets. Three months later, however, the Princess Elizabeth was born at Greenwich Palace, and to consolidate support for the new marriage and the new Church, her christening at the Chapel of the Observant Friars was a splendid state affair.

Elizabeth's childhood, however, was far from peaceful, glorious, or secure. Even before her mother's execution in 1536, she was kept at a variety of country palaces, mostly in Hertfordshire, including Hatfield, Hertford, and Enfield, only rarely appearing in London or at Court. After Anne Boleyn was charged with committing adultery with her own brother and four other men at Court and was condemned and put to death, Elizabeth was declared a bastard and treated without the deference to which she had become accustomed. Even as a toddler, she sensed the change, reportedly asking, "How hap it yesterday Lady Princess and today but Lady Elizabeth?" a telling comment on her precarious position. Thereafter, she was raised by a series of paid companions. Her first nurse, Lady Margaret Bryan, was followed by her favorite governess, Katherine (Kat) Champernowne Ashley and later by tutors such as William Grindal and Roger Ascham, scholars with pronounced Protestant leanings. In 1543, Elizabeth's fortunes improved. Her father married his sixth and final wife, Katherine Parr, a widow of considerable intellect and character who, like Anne Boleyn, was sympathetic to the Protestant cause. In part at Katherine's urging, Elizabeth was brought back to Court and, through the Act of Succession in 1544, again titled a Princess and placed in the line for the throne. Throughout the remainder of Henry's reign and during the subsequent reign of her brother Edward VI (1547–53), Elizabeth led a relatively peaceful and stable life.

All that changed with Edward's death. In his last days, the young king had attempted to bar his sisters, Mary and Elizabeth, from the succession and to make his cousin Lady Jane Grey "governess" of the realm. After Edward's death, Jane's powerful father-in-law, John Dudley, Duke of Northumberland, arranged for her to be crowned queen, attempting in that way to prevent the ardently Catholic Mary from coming to the throne. The illegality of the move led many to rally to Mary's cause, however, and the hapless Jane reigned for only nine days before she was deposed and Mary brought to the throne. The fact that Northumberland and other Protestants at Court had nearly robbed Mary of the succession made the Queen and others at Court suspicious of Elizabeth's own evangelical proclivities, which had been carefully nurtured by her tutors and by Katherine Parr.

Once Mary's regime was in place, it moved quickly to reestablish Roman Catholicism as the official religion of the realm, leaving Elizabeth in a difficult position. Her response was to conform in public while continuing to practice her Protestant faith in private. In 1554, however, she came under suspicion of involvement in a rebellion led by Sir Thomas Wyatt the Younger and was sent to prison in the Tower of London. Although no evidence to implicate her in treason was ever produced and she was soon released, she was kept under house arrest until November 17, 1558, when her sister fell sick and died, and Elizabeth acceded to the throne.

PARENTAGE AND INFANCY

Elizabeth's mother, Anne Boleyn, was and remains a controversial figure. Her contemporaries were divided in their opinions about the young, dark-eyed woman who had spent her formative years in the French Court, and modern historians have continued the debate. Was she a seductive temptress? a promiscuous witch? a pawn in the high-stakes game of political advantage? an opportunist? a woman in love? a devout religious reformer caught up in the machinations of the Court?

By the time Elizabeth herself came to the throne, the story John Foxe told of Anne Boleyn in his influential history, *Acts and Monuments*, was that of an evangelical or proto-Protestant martyr and saint. Foxe was an Oxford-educated scholar who had converted to Protestantism while still a student and later resigned his fellowship from Magdalen College over matters of religion. He was attached to the English royal family as tutor to the children of the Howard family, the influential clan from which Anne Boleyn, on her mother's side, was descended. When Mary Tudor came to the throne in the 1550s, he joined many other Protestants in fleeing to the Continent to escape persecution. There he began the great project for which he is known, an account of the Christian church that focused on its martyrs. As stories of the persecution of Protestants by Mary Tudor filtered across the channel, Foxe added them to his history, and, when he returned to England after Mary's death, he added yet more documentary evidence from the Marian persecution. John Day, an important London printer, urged Foxe to continue his research and put up the considerable funds needed to publish such a large book. The first edition of the *Acts and Monuments . . . of the Church* (later known as Foxe's *Book of Martyrs*) was printed in 1563, but Foxe continued to expand and revise it throughout his lifetime, with subsequent editions in 1570, 1576, and 1583. By 1571, the work had reached such canonical status in England that an Act of Parliament ordered all cathedral churches to purchase a copy and display it in a public place. The numerous woodcuts ensured that even nonreaders could peruse it to get some sense of England's history as told through the stories of the martyrs.

As Foxe notes, Henry VIII began annulment proceedings against his first wife, Katherine of Aragon, on the grounds that she was his elder brother's widow and so was barred from marrying him by biblical injunctions against incest. Katherine, however, vigorously denied that she had consummated her marriage with Arthur, who was a young teenager at the time. Theologians debated both sides of the issue. Those in favor of Katherine cited the levirate law of Deuteronomy 25.5–10 that a man should marry his brother's widow in order to preserve the family line. Those who supported Henry argued from Leviticus 21.21 that it was forbidden to sleep with your brother's wife. It mattered little that in 1509, when Henry first married Katherine, he had asked for and received a papal dispensation declaring such "incest" no impediment to the match. In 1531, having failed to gain an annulment from the Pope, Henry had himself declared Supreme Head of the Church of England and subsequently carried out the annulment himself.

Foxe argues that the marriage to Anne, which probably took place in November 1532, was crucial to the Reformation because it was she who, through reading

Protestant works imported from France by her brother, Lord Rochford, first took a strong interest in reform, gathered a like-minded circle at court, and won Henry to the cause. Foxe claims that even before their marriage the Pope's "whole power and authority began utterly to be abolished, by the reason and occasion of the most virtuous and noble lady, Anne Boleyn, . . . by whose godly means and most virtuous counsel the King's mind was daily inclined better and better" (1563, p. 508). Foxe also highlights Anne's piety, modesty, and care for the poor and thus rehabilitates her as a virtuous woman rather than a treasonous upstart. In Foxe's account, Anne becomes a fitting parent and role model for the new queen herself.

Although Elizabeth rarely spoke of her mother, she chose Anne Boleyn's motto *Semper eadem* (Always the same) as her own, at times appropriated Anne's badge, which showed a crowned falcon sitting on a stump from which sprang Tudor roses, and around 1575 commissioned a ring that opened to reveal miniature portraits of her mother and herself. She also advanced the careers of her Boleyn relations, elevating Henry Carey to the title of Lord Hunsdon and the rank of Lord Chamberlain and his brother-in-law, Sir Francis Knollys, to her Privy Council.

The baptism of the infant Elizabeth, performed in the Chapel of the Observant Friars at Greenwich, marked the high point of concord in her parents' brief marriage as well as the only time in her youth when she was securely and unambiguously honored. The pomp and circumstance of the ceremony were designed to consolidate the legitimacy and authority of the newly independent English Church as well as to signal Henry's determination that his marriage be recognized. The baptism was performed in a chapel that belonged to clergy who had been particularly outspoken in their criticism of the King's divorce, and the Boleyn family was conspicuously present: Elizabeth's maternal grandfather, Thomas Boleyn, the Earl of Wiltshire, and her uncle, George Boleyn, Lord Rochford, held her train and canopy. The noblest names in England were also in attendance, from Dukes of Norfolk and Suffolk to the Countess of Kent. Agnes Tilney, the elderly dowager Duchess of Norfolk who had been a godmother to the Princess Mary, carried Elizabeth in her arms, and Gertrude Blount, the Marchioness of Exeter who was devoted to Katherine of Aragon, was forced to stand up for Elizabeth as her godmother. The pageantry and promise of Elizabeth's baptism was many years later incorporated into the play *The Famous History of the Life of King Henry the Eighth*, written by William Shakespeare and John Fletcher, which concludes with the christening and with a prophecy by her godfather Thomas Cranmer, Archbishop of Canterbury, that peace and plenty would characterize her reign.

Although Foxe framed his narratives as one who firmly believed that Protestantism represented the true continuing church on earth, he was a thorough historian, who scrupulously gathered letters, eye-witness accounts, court evidence, and other documentary material. His book provides one of the best contemporary historical accounts of the divorce of Queen Katherine, the King's remarriage, the birth and baptism of Princess Elizabeth, Henry's subsequent alienation from Anne, and the charges of adultery that led to her trial and execution in 1536. From this sequence of events came one of Elizabeth's most serious life-long difficulties, namely the King's declaration that she was not his daughter and that, in consequence, she had no legal title to the throne. Her treatment as a bastard, which was not rescinded even after her father restored her rights as a princess through the Act of Succession of 1544, became one of the principal bases upon which Roman Catholics, both at home and abroad, opposed her and denied her right to rule England.

JOHN FOXE

From Acts and Monuments (1583)[†]

[*Henry VIII and Anne Boleyn*]

After the death of Prince Arthur, the Lady Katherine, Princess Dowager and wife to Prince Arthur, by the consent both of her father and of his and also by the advice of the nobles of this realm (to the end her dowry might remain still within the realm), was espoused after the decease of her husband to his next brother, which was this King Henry.[1]

This marriage seemed very strange and hard, for one brother to marry the wife of another. But what can be in this earth so hard or difficult wherewith the Pope, the omnipotent Vicar of Christ, cannot by favor dispense if it please him? The Pope which then ruled at Rome was Pope Julius II, by whose dispensation this marriage, which neither sense of nature would admit nor God's law would bear, was concluded, approved, and ratified and so continued as lawful without any doubt or scruple the space near of twenty years, till about the time that a certain doubt began first to be moved by the Spaniards themselves of the Emperor's[2] Council.

* * *

The King, upon the occasion hereof casting many things in his mind, began to consider the cause more deeply, first with himself, after with certain of his nearest Council, wherein two things there were which chiefly pricked his mind, whereof the one touched his conscience, the other concerned the state of his realm. For if that marriage with his brother's wife stood unlawful by the law of God, then neither was his conscience clear in retaining the mother nor yet the state of the realm firm by succession of the daughter. It happened the same time that the Cardinal which was then nearest about the King had fallen out with the Emperor for not helping him to the Papacy, as ye before have heard, for the which cause he helped to set the matter forward by all practice he might.[3] Thus the King, perplexed in his conscience and careful for the commonwealth and partly also incited by the Cardinal, could not so rest but inquired further to feel what the Word of God and learning would say unto it. Neither was the case so hard, after it began once to come in public question, but that by the Word of God, and the judgments of the best learned clerks, and also by the censure of the chief universities of all Christendom to the number of ten and more, it[4] was soon discussed to be unlawful.

* * *

---

† Copy text: John Foxe, *Actes and monuments of matters most speciall and memorable, happenyng in the Church with an vniuersall history of the same*, Book 8 (London: John Day, 1583; STC 11225), 1049, 1051, 1053, 1054, 1082, 1083.
1. Henry VIII and Katherine were married in June 1509; *Prince Arthur*: eldest son of Henry VII and Elizabeth of York; *Lady Katherine*: Katherine of Aragon, daughter of the Spanish monarchs Ferdinand and Isabella and aunt to Emperor Charles V.
2. Charles V, Duke of Burgundy and Holy Roman Emperor.
3. By supporting the divorce from Katherine, Wolsey took revenge on her nephew, Charles V; *Cardinal*: Cardinal Thomas Wolsey, Henry's Chancellor.
4. Henry's marriage to Katherine; *censure*: judgment.

[In 1530], the King by his ambassadors was advertised that the Emperor and the Pope[5] were both together at Bologna. Wherefore he directed Sir Thomas Boleyn, late created Earl of Wiltshire,[6] and Doctor Stokesley (afterward Bishop of London) and Doctor Lee (afterward Bishop of York) with his message to the Pope's Court, where also the Emperor was. Pope Clement, understanding the King's case and request and fearing what might follow after if learning and scripture here should take place against the authority of their dispensations and moreover doubting the Emperor's displeasure, bore himself strange off from the matter, answering the ambassadors with this delay: that he presently would not define[7] in the case but would hear the full matter disputed when he came to Rome, and according to right he would do justice.

Although the King ought no such service to the Pope to stand to his arbitrament, either in this case or in any other, having both the scripture to lead him and his law in his own hands to warrant him, yet for quietness sake and for that he would not rashly break order (which rather was a disorder indeed), he bore[8] so long as conveniently he might. At length, after long delays and much dissembling, when he saw no hope of redress, he began somewhat to quicken and to look about him what was best both for his own conscience and the stablishment of his realm to do.

No man here doubteth but that all this was wrought, not by man's device, but by the secret purpose of the Lord Himself to bring to pass further things (as afterwards followed) which His divine providence was disposed to work. For else, as touching the King's intent and purpose, he never meant nor minded any such thing as to seek the ruin of the Pope but rather sought all means contrary, how both to stablish the See of Rome[9] and also to obtain the good will of the same See and Court of Rome, if it might have been gotten. And, therefore, intending to sue his divorce from Rome, at the first beginning his device was by Stephen Gardiner, his ambassador at Rome, to exalt the Cardinal of York * * * to be made Pope and universal bishop, to the end that, he[1] ruling that apostolic See, the matter of his unlawful marriage, which so troubled his conscience, might come to a quiet conclusion without any further rumor of the world. Which purpose of his, if it had taken effect as he had devised it and the English Cardinal had once been made Pope, no doubt but the authority of that See had never been exterminate out of England. But God, being more merciful unto us, took a better way than so. For both without and contrary to the King's expectation, He so brought to pass that neither the Cardinal of York was Pope (which should have been an infinite cost[2] to the King), and yet nevertheless the King sped of his purpose too, and that much better than he looked for. For he was rid by lawful divorcement not only from that unlawful marriage which clogged his conscience, but also from the miserable yoke of the Pope's usurped dominion, which clogged the whole realm, and all at one time.

---

5. Clement VII, Giulio de Medici, the nephew of Queen Katherine and the uncle of Catherine de Medici; *advertised*: informed.
6. Anne Boleyn's father.
7. Rule; *bore . . . matter*: distanced himself.
8. That is, waited for a papal annulment; *ought*: owed; *arbitrament*: authoritative ruling; *having both . . . warrant him*: Foxe denies that the popes of Rome ever had the authority to determine such cases for an English king.
9. The seat or authority of the Pope in Rome.
1. Cardinal Wolsey, who was the Cardinal of York.
2. Because Rome would have retained vast Church lands and influence in England.

Thus God's holy providence ruling the matter, as I said, when the King could get no favorable grant of the Pope touching his cause, being so good and honest, he was enforced to take the redress of his right into his own hands, and seeing this Gordian knot[3] would not be loosed at Rome, he was driven against his will (as God would) to play the noble Alexander himself, and with the sword of his princely authority knapped the knot at one stroke clean asunder, loosing, as it were, with one solution infinite questions. For where the doctors and canonists had long disputed and yet could never thoroughly discuss the largeness and fullness of the Pope's two swords, both temporal and spiritual,[4] the King with one sword did so cut off both clean out of England.

* * *

All these things thus being defined and determined in this foresaid Parliament [of 1533], and also being in the same Parliament concluded that no man of what estate, degree, or condition soever hath any power to dispense with God's laws, it was therefore, by the authority aforesaid agreeing with the authority of God's Word, assented that the marriage aforetime solemnized between the King and the Lady Katherine (being before wife to Prince Arthur, the King's brother, and carnally known by him, as is above proved) should be absolutely denied and adjudged to be unlawful and against the law of God and also reputed and taken to be of no value nor effect; and that the separation thereof by Thomas Cranmer, Archbishop of Canterbury, should stand good and effectual to all intents; and also that the lawful matrimony between the King and the Lady Anne, his wife, should be established, approved, and ratified for good and consonant to the laws of Almighty God. And further also, for the establishing of this King's lawful succession, it was fully by the said Parliament adjudged that the inheritance of the crown should remain to the heirs of their two bodies, that is, of the King and Queen Anne, his wife.

* * *

The King, within short time after, proceeded to the marriage of the foresaid lady, Anne Boleyn, mother to our most noble queen now, who without all controversy was a special comforter and aider of all the professors of Christ's gospel, as well of the learned as the unlearned, her life being also directed according to the same as her weekly alms did manifestly declare, who (besides the ordinary of a hundred crowns and other apparel that she gave weekly, a year before she was crowned, both to men and women) gave also wonderful much privy alms to widows and other poor householders continually till she was apprehended.[5] And she ever gave three or four pound at a time to the poor people to buy them kine withal and sent her subalmoner to the towns about where she lay, that the parishioners should

---

3. Gordias, an ancient Greek king, tied an intricate knot of which an oracle declared that whoever untied it would rule Asia. Alexander the Great is said to have cut through it with his sword.
4. Symbols of papal authority in matters earthly as well as divine; *doctors and canonists*: experts in theology and Church law.
5. Arrested. Foxe may mean that Anne followed Christ's instruction to give alms in secret, to be seen by God rather than fellow humans (Matthew 6.2–4); *without all controversy*: beyond all doubt; *ordinary*: usual custom; *a hundred crowns*: about £25, a considerable sum of money at the time; *crowned*: Anne's coronation took place on June 1, 1533; *privy*: secret.

make a bill[6] of all the poor householders in their parish; and some towns received seven, eight, or ten pound to buy kine withal, according as the number of the poor in the towns were. She also maintained many learned men in Cambridge * * * and helped many religious persons out of their cowls.[7]

It hath been reported unto us by divers credible persons which were about this Queen and daily acquainted with her doings concerning her liberal and bountiful distribution to the poor how her Grace carried ever about her a certain little purse, out of the which she was wont daily to scatter abroad some alms to the needy, thinking no day well spent wherein some man had not fared the better by some benefit at her hands. And this I write by the relation of certain noble personages which were chief and principal of her waiting maids about her, specially the Duchess of Richmond by name.[8]

Also concerning the order of her ladies and gentlewomen about her, one that was her silkwoman,[9] a gentlewoman not now alive but of great credit and also of fame for her worthy doings, did credibly report that in all her time she never saw better order amongst the ladies and gentlewomen of the Court than was in this good Queen's days, who kept her maids and such as were about her so occupied in sewing and working of shirts and smocks for the poor that neither was there seen any idleness then amongst them nor any leisure to follow such pastimes as daily are seen nowadays to reign in princes' courts.

Thus the King, being divorced from the Lady Dowager, his brother's wife, married this gracious lady, making a prosperous and happy change for us, being divorced from the foresaid Princess and also from the Pope, both at one time. Notwithstanding, as good and godly purposes are never without some incommodity or trouble following, so it happened in this divorcement that the said Princess, procuring from Rome the Pope's curse, caused both the King and the realm to be interdicted,[1] whereof more is hereafter to be spoken.

[The birth and baptism of Elizabeth]

In the meantime, Queen Anne shortly after her marriage, being great with child, the next year following, which was 1533, after the first divorcement publicly proclaimed, was crowned with high solemnity at Westminster. And not long after her coronation, the seventh day of September, she was brought a bed and delivered of a fair lady, for whose good deliverance Te Deum was sung in all places and great preparation made for the christening.[2]

The Mayor and his brethren, with forty of the chief citizens, were commanded to be present with all the nobles and gentlemen. The King's

6. Census; *ever*: constantly; *kine*: literally cow; more generally meat; *subalmoner*: official who distributed alms or charity.
7. Helped many Roman Catholic monks become Protestant; *Cambridge*: Cambridge University, unlike Oxford, was well known as a center of Protestant thought.
8. Mary Howard, daughter of the third Duke of Norfolk, sister to the poet Henry Howard, Earl of Surrey, and wife of Henry Fitzroy, illegitimate son of Henry VIII and Elizabeth Blount. The Duchess was a patron of Foxe, who also tutored her nephews.
9. Mistress Wilkinson, who brought cloth to the Court and perhaps made clothes for the Queen.
1. Cut off from Catholic offices and privileges, a step just short of excommunication.
2. Held on September 10, 1533, when Elizabeth was three days old; *Te Deum*: Latin hymn of praise, sung as a thanksgiving on special occasions.

palace and all the walls between that and the Friars was hanged with arras and the Friars' church.[3] Also the font was of silver and stood in the midst of the church, three steps high, which was covered with a fine cloth, and divers gentlemen with aprons and towels[4] about their necks gave attendance about it. Over the font hung a fair canopy of crimson satin fringed with gold. About it was a rail covered with say.[5] Between the quire and the body of the church was a close place[6] with a pan of fire to make the child ready in.

These things thus ordered, the child was brought into the hall, and then every man set forward. First the citizens, two and two; then the gentlemen, esquires, and chaplains; next after followed the aldermen and the Mayor alone. Next the Mayor followed the King's Council, then the King's Chapel;[7] then barons, bishops, and earls. Then came the Earl of Essex bearing the covered basins gilt.[8] After him the Marquis of Exeter[9] with the taper of virgin wax. Next him the Marquis Dorset bearing the salt.[1] Behind him the Lady Mary of Norfolk bearing the chrism,[2] which was very rich of pearl and stone. The old Duchess of Norfolk[3] bore the child in a mantle of purple velvet with a long train furred with ermine. The Duke of Norfolk, with his marshal rod, went on the right hand of the said Duchess and the Duke of Suffolk[4] on the left hand. Before them went the officers of arms.[5] The Countess of Kent[6] bore the long train of the child's mantle. Between the Countess and the child went the Earl of Wiltshire on the right hand and the Earl of Derby[7] on the left hand, supporting the said train. In the midst, over the child, was borne a canopy by the Lord Rochford, the Lord Hussey, the Lord William Howard, and the Lord Thomas Howard the Elder.[8]

In this order they came unto the church door, where the Bishop of London[9] met it, with divers abbots and bishops, and began the observances of the sacrament. The Archbishop of Canterbury was godfather and the old

3. Henry VIII had married Katherine of Aragon at this chapel, and the Friars were outspoken against the divorce; *King's palace*: at Greenwich; *and the Friars*: the house of the Observant Friars at Greenwich; *and the Friars' church*: as well as the Friars' church.
4. Ceremonial items for the baptism.
5. A fine-textured cloth.
6. Enclosed room; *quire*: the eastward part of the nave in which the services were held; it was separated from the rest of the church by a screen.
7. Choir; *Next*: After.
8. Gilded; *Earl of Essex*: Henry Bourchier, second Earl of Essex.
9. Henry Courtenay, executed for treason in 1538.
1. Salt was placed in a child's mouth to symbolize deliverance from the corruption of sin and a new taste for good works; *Marquis Dorset*: Henry Grey, third Marquis of Dorset and later Duke of Suffolk through his marriage to Frances Brandon, heiress of Charles Brandon; father to Lady Jane Grey.
2. The container for the oil and balm applied to the child during baptism; *Lady Mary of Norfolk*: Mary Howard; see note 8, page 10.
3. Agnes Tilney, wife of Thomas Howard, second Duke of Norfolk and stepmother to the third Duke and to Elizabeth Howard Boleyn, Anne's mother. In 1516, she had also been godmother to the Princess Mary Tudor.
4. Charles Brandon, friend of Henry VIII and husband of Henry's sister, Mary. Mary had died in June 1533 and Charles married his fourteen-year-old ward, Katherine Willoughby, the same morning Elizabeth was born; *Duke of Norfolk*: Thomas Howard, third Duke of Norfolk and maternal uncle of Anne Boleyn.
5. Heralds.
6. Margaret Dawes Grey, dowager Duchess of Kent and widow of Richard Grey, third Earl of Kent.
7. Edward Stanley, third Earl of Derby; *Earl of Wiltshire*: Anne Boleyn's father, Thomas Boleyn.
8. Son of the second Duke of Norfolk; *Lord Rochford*: Anne Boleyn's brother, George Boleyn; *Lord Hussey*: John Hussey, chamberlain of Mary Tudor's household; *Lord William Howard*: stepbrother of Anne Boleyn's mother, Elizabeth, and father of Charles Howard, Earl of Nottingham, who was to become Elizabeth's Lord Admiral.
9. John Stokesley.

Duchess of Norfolk and the old Marchioness of Dorset,[1] widows, were god-mothers, and the child was named Elizabeth.

After all things were done at the church door, the child was brought to the font and christened. This done, Garter, the chief King of Arms,[2] cried aloud, "God, of His infinite goodness, send prosperous life and long to the high and mighty Princess of England, Elizabeth." Then the trumpets blew, and the child was brought up to the altar and immediately confirmed by the Archbishop, the Marchioness of Exeter[3] being godmother. Then the Archbishop of Canterbury gave to the Princess a standing cup[4] of gold. The Duchess of Norfolk gave to her a standing cup of gold fretted with pearl; the Marchioness of Dorset three gilt bowls, pounced,[5] with a cover; the Marchioness of Exeter three standing bowls, gilt and graven, with a cover. And so, after a solemn banquet ended with hippocras, wafers,[6] and such like in great plenty, they returned in like order again unto the Court with the Princess and so departed.

[*The deaths of the Lady Katherine and of Queen Anne*]

The same year in the which William Tyndale was burned, which was the year of our Lord 1536, in the beginning of the year, first died lady Katherine,[7] Princess Dowager, in the month of January.

After whom, the same year also in the month of May next following, followed the death also of Queen Anne, who had now been married to the King the space of three years. In certain records thus we find that the King, being in his jousts at Greenwich, suddenly with a few persons departed to Westminster, and the next day after, Queen Anne, his wife, was had to the Tower with the Lord Rochford her brother and certain other and, the nineteenth day after, was beheaded. The words of this worthy and Christian lady at her death were these:

"Good Christian people, I am come hither to die. For according to the law and by the law, I am judged to death, and therefore I will speak nothing against it. I am come hither to accuse no man nor to speak anything of that whereof I am accused and condemned to die; but I pray God save the King and send him long to reign over you, for a gentler or a more merciful prince was there never; and to me he was ever a good, a gentle, and sovereign lord. And if any person will meddle of[8] my cause, I require them to judge the best. And thus I take my leave of the world and of you all, and I heartily desire you all to pray for me. O Lord have mercy on me. To God I commend my soul."

And so she kneeled down, saying, "To Christ I commend my soul; Jesu, receive my soul," repeating the same divers times, till at length the stroke was given and her head was stricken off.

---

1. Margaret Wotton, mother of the current Marquis of Dorset, Henry Grey, and grandmother of the Lady Jane Grey; *Archbishop of Canterbury*: Thomas Cranmer.
2. Herald of the College of Arms, which recorded and regulated the use of heraldic emblems.
3. Gertrude Blount, wife of Henry Courtney and a devoted friend of Katherine of Aragon, who did not wish to be godmother to the new princess.
4. A cup with a stem and base.
5. Embossed; *fretted*: richly adorned.
6. Thin, crisp cake often eaten with wine; *hippocras*: wine flavored with spices.
7. Katherine of Aragon; *William Tyndale*: early translator of the Bible into English, burnt at the stake for his work.
8. Concern yourself with.

And this was the end of that godly lady and queen. "Godly" I call her for sundry respects, whatsoever the cause was or quarrel objected against her. First, her last words spoken at her death declared no less her sincere faith and trust in Christ than did her quiet modesty utter forth the goodness of the cause and matter, whatsoever it was. Besides that, to such as wisely can judge upon cases occurrent, this also may seem to give a great clearing unto her: that the King, the third day after, was married in his whites[9] unto another. Certain this was, that for the rare and singular gifts of her mind, so well instructed and given toward God, with such a fervent desire unto the truth and setting forth of sincere religion, joined with like gentleness, modesty, and pity toward all men, there hath not many such queens before her borne the crown of England. Principally this one commendation she left behind her: that, during her life, the religion of Christ most happily flourished and had a right prosperous course.

* * *

This I cannot but marvel: why the Parliament holden this year, that is, the twenty-eighth year of the King (which Parliament three years before had established and confirmed this marriage as most lawful), should now so suddenly and contrary to their own doings repeal and disable the said marriage again as unlawful, being so lawfully before contracted. But more I marvel why the said Parliament, after the illegitimation of the marriage enacted, not contented with that, should further proceed and charge her with such carnal desires of her body as to misuse herself with her own natural brother, the Lord Rochford, and others, being so contrary to all nature that no natural man will believe it.

But in this act of Parliament did lie (no doubt) some great mystery, which here I will not stand to discuss but only that it may be suspected some secret practicing of the papists here not to be lacking, considering what a mighty stop she was to their purposes and proceedings and, on the contrary side, what a strong bulwark she was for the maintenance of Christ's Gospel and sincere religion, which they then in no case could abide. By reason whereof it may easily be considered that this Christian and devout Deborah[1] could lack no enemies amongst such a number of Philistines, both within the realm and without.

* * *

And as touching the King's mind and assent, although at that time, through crafty setters-on, he seemed to be sore bent both against that Queen and to the disinheriting of his own daughter, yet unto that former will of the King so set against her then, I would oppose again the last will of the King,[2] wherein expressly and by name he did accept and by plain ratification did allow the succession of his marriage to stand good and lawful.

Furthermore, to all other sinister judgments and opinions whatsoever can be conceived of man against that virtuous Queen, I object and oppose again (as instead of answer) the evident demonstration of God's favor in maintaining, preserving, and advancing the offspring of her body, the Lady

---

9. White clothes used for ceremonial occasions.
1. Elizabeth, like her mother Anne, would also be compared to the biblical judge Deborah.
2. Expressed in the Act of Succession in 1544.

Elizabeth, now Queen, whom the Lord hath so marvelously conserved from so manifold dangers, so royally hath exalted, so happily hath blessed with such virtuous patience and with such a quiet reign hitherto that neither the reign of her brother Edward nor of her sister Mary to her is to be compared, whether we consider the number of the years of their reigns or the peace-ableness of their state. In whose royal and flourishing regiment we have to behold, not so much the natural disposition of her mother's qualities as the secret judgment of God in preserving and magnifying the fruit and off-spring of that godly Queen.

WILLIAM SHAKESPEARE AND JOHN FLETCHER

From The Famous History of the Life of King Henry the Eighth (1613)[†]

CRANMER: Let me speak, sir,
For heaven now bids me; and the words I utter
Let none think flattery, for they'll find 'em truth.
This royal infant (heaven still move about her),
5   Though in her cradle, yet now promises
Upon this land a thousand thousand blessings,
Which time shall bring to ripeness. She shall be
(But few now living can behold that goodness)
A pattern to all princes living with her
10   And all that shall succeed. Saba[1] was never
More covetous of wisdom and fair virtue
Than this pure soul shall be. All princely graces
That mold up such a mighty piece° as this is,   person
With all the virtues that attend the good,
15   Shall still be doubled on her. Truth shall nurse her,
Holy and heavenly thoughts still° counsel her.   always
She shall be loved and feared. Her own shall bless her;
Her foes shake like a field of beaten corn
And hang their heads with sorrow.
20   Good grows with her.
In her days, every man shall eat in safety
Under his own vine what he plants and sing
The merry songs of peace to all his neighbors.[2]
God shall be truly known, and those about her
25   From her shall read the perfect way of honor,
And by those° claim their greatness, not by blood.   songs of peace
Nor shall this peace sleep with her; but as when

---

† Copy text: William Shakespeare, *Mr. William Shakespeares comedies, histories, & tragedies* (London: Iaggard and Blount, 1623; STC 22273), 231–32 (5.4.14–76, though in some modern editions the scene is 5.5).
1. The Queen of Sheba admired Solomon's wisdom when she visited him in Jerusalem (1 Kings 10).
2. An allusion to the blessed days of the Messiah promised by the biblical prophets and also said to have been experienced during the days of King Solomon (Micah 4.4; 1 Kings 4.25).

The bird of wonder dies, the maiden Phoenix,[3]
Her ashes new create another heir[4]
30 As great in admiration as herself,
So shall she leave her blessedness to one
(When heaven shall call her from this cloud of darkness),
Who from the sacred ashes of her honor
Shall starlike rise, as great in fame as she was,
35 And so stand fixed. Peace, plenty, love, truth, terror,
That were the servants to this chosen infant,
Shall then be his and, like a vine, grow to him.
Wherever the bright sun of heaven shall shine,
His honor and the greatness of his name
40 Shall be and make new nations.[5] He shall flourish
And like a mountain cedar reach his branches
To all the plains about him. Our children's children
Shall see this and bless heaven.
KING: Thou speakest wonders.
45 CRANMER: She shall be, to the happiness of England,
An agéd princess; many days shall see her,
And yet no day without a deed to crown it.[6]
Would I had known no more. But she must die,
She must. The saints must have her. Yet a virgin,
50 A most unspotted lily, shall she pass
To the ground, and all the world shall mourn her.
KING: O Lord Archbishop,
Thou hast made me now a man. Never before
This happy child did I get[7] anything.
55 This oracle of comfort has so pleaséd me
That, when I am in heaven, I shall desire
To see what this child does and praise my Maker.
I thank ye all. To you, my good Lord Mayor,
And you, good brethren, I am much beholding.
60 I have received much honor by your presence,
And ye shall find me thankful. Lead the way, lords.
Ye must all see the Queen, and she must thank ye.
She will be sick else. This day, no man think
'Has[8] business at his house, for all shall stay.
65 This little one shall make it Holy-day.

PRINCESS AND PRODIGY

From 1536, when Anne Boleyn was executed for treason, until 1543, when
Henry VIII married his sixth wife, Katherine Parr, Elizabeth led a precarious
existence. Declared a bastard and excluded from the succession to the throne,

---

3. Also dies.
4. James I, the reigning monarch at the time this play was written.
5. A reference to the English colonies in America.
6. She will do good deeds every day of her life.
7. Beget; Henry had, of course, begotten Princess Mary as well as illegitimate children, but sets them
   aside as of no account.
8. He has.

she was rarely seen at Court. Parr, however, welcomed all three of her stepchildren—Mary, Elizabeth, and the young Edward—and undertook to supervise their education. Parr herself was a woman of considerable intellect and political instinct, who was strongly committed to the establishment of Protestantism in England. She wrote and published devotional works and acted as regent of England when Henry traveled to France. In 1544, Elizabeth who was just eleven years old, completed and presented to her stepmother as a New Year's gift a translation of Marguerite of Navarre's *Le Miroir de L'Âme Péchesse* (*The Mirror of the Sinful Soul*, published in 1531).

Elizabeth's choice of texts was apt: Marguerite, sister of Francis I of France, had been a friend of Anne Boleyn and was, like Katherine, both an author and a powerful patron of early Protestant scholars and clergy. Elizabeth's translation of the *Miroir* not only allowed her to meditate on religion, but also to demonstrate her skill in French, her penmanship, and even her needlework, which graced the elaborately embroidered cover. The translation was prefaced with a letter to Katherine Parr that is still extant in Elizabeth's own handwriting.

In 1548, Elizabeth's translation was published under the English title *A Godly Meditation of the Christian Soul* by one of Parr's protégés, John Bale, a scholar, playwright, and author of polemical tracts; Elizabeth later appointed him a canon (one of the resident clergymen) at Canterbury Cathedral. It is possible that it was Katherine Parr herself who suggested to Bale that he publish Elizabeth's translation. Certainly Katherine promoted other evangelical publishing projects, such as a translation of Erasmus's paraphrases on the New Testament as well as her own devotional writing. Bale made some adjustments to Elizabeth's translation and wrote both a preface and a conclusion to the volume, which was published in Germany. Bale's preface to Elizabeth takes up the question "What is true nobility?" and gives this answer: "True nobility is to love and promote true doctrine and live a godly life." Bale invokes the lessons of the biblical kings of Judah and Israel as exemplars of godly rule, beginning a pattern of exhortation that would follow Elizabeth throughout her life. In the conclusion, Bale moves from biblical to historical exemplars and from male to female rulers. He recounts the virtues of many formidable British queens, beginning in Roman times and continuing to Elizabeth's own grandmother, Elizabeth of York. Yet the final example he invokes is not that of a queen, but rather a martyr and friend of Katherine Parr, Anne Askew, whom Elizabeth herself undoubtedly would have known. The truly noble woman, Bale argues, is not one who inherits a crown but one who is known for her "godly doctrine and deeds of faith." That such things were worth dying for was a belief that Elizabeth was later called on to demonstrate in the face of assassins and foreign rulers bent on restoring England to the Catholic fold.

Bale appended to *A Godly Meditation of the Christian Soul* a metrical version of Psalm 13, probably translated by Elizabeth herself. Although Elizabeth knew Latin and probably read the Vulgate (the traditional Latin translation of the Bible), she also had access to English translations, and she remained throughout her life a proponent of vernacular versions of the Bible. The Great Bible, whose rendering of Psalm 13 is printed below, was the authorized version of her youth, and its translations of the Psalms were later included in the Book of Common Prayer, the liturgical centerpiece of the English Church.

Elizabeth's own skill in languages was developed by her early tutors, William Grindal and Roger Ascham. By the time she became Queen, she was fully fluent in Latin, French, and Italian, understood Spanish without difficulty, and had sufficient proficiency in Greek to write her own prayers in that language. In later years, she spent leisure moments translating ancient Latin texts for pleasure. Her natural ability was honed through Ascham's humanist methods of education, an account of which was published after his death in *The Schoolmaster*. Ascham's system was to have the student translate a classical work from Latin to English, then (without looking) translate it back to Latin again, and finally compare the results with the original. Though tedious, the technique taught the Princess to sense and exploit the nuances of well-ordered words, a skill that would serve her well in later years.

PRINCESS ELIZABETH

Letter of Dedication to Katherine Parr
(December 31, 1544)†

To our most noble and virtuous Queen Katherine, Elizabeth, her humble daughter, wisheth perpetual felicity and everlasting joy.

Not only knowing the affectuous will and fervent zeal the which your Highness hath towards all godly learning as also my duty towards you (most gracious and sovereign Princess), but knowing also that pusillanimity and idleness are most repugnant unto a reasonable creature and that (as the philosopher sayeth) even as an instrument of iron or of other metal waxeth soon rusty unless it be continually occupied, even so shall the wit of a man or woman wax dull and unapt to do or understand anything perfectly unless it be always occupied upon some manner of study (which things considered hath moved so small a portion as God hath lent me to prove what I could do), and therefore have I (as for assay or beginning, following the right notable saying of the proverb aforesaid) translated this little book out of French rhyme into English prose, joining the sentences together as well as the capacity of my simple wit[1] and small learning could extend themselves.

The which book is entitled or named the *Miroir* or *Glass of the Sinful Soul*, wherein is contained how she (beholding and contempling what she is) doth perceive how of herself and of her own strength she can do nothing that good is or prevaileth for her salvation unless it be through the grace of God, whose mother, daughter, sister, and wife[2] by the scriptures she proveth herself to be. Trusting also that, through His incomprehensible love, grace, and mercy, she (being called from sin to repentance) doth faithfully hope to be saved. And although I know that, as for my part which I have wrought in it (as well spiritual as manual), there is nothing done as it should be nor else worthy to come in your Grace's hands, but rather all unperfect and uncorrect, yet do I trust also that, albeit it is like a work which is but new begun and shapen, that the file of your excellent wit and godly learning in the reading of it (if so it vouchsafe your Highness to do) shall rub out, polish, and mend (or else cause to mend) the words (or rather the order of my writing, the which I know in many places to be rude and nothing done as it should be). But I hope that, after to have been in your

---

† Copy text: Cherry MS 36, ff.2r–4v, Bodleian Library, Oxford.
1. Intellect, reason; *affectuous*: passionate; *pusillanimity*: smallness of spirit, timidity; *philosopher*: although "the philosopher" often refers to Aristotle, the proverbial saying here may be from the "heavenly philosopher," Erasmus (May, *Selected Works*, 96); *prove . . . do*: probably an allusion to the parable of the talents (Matthew 25.14–30); *assay*: a first effort.
2. Here Elizabeth echoes the notion of fourfold kinship with God that Marguerite elaborates in the *Miroir*. Texts such as Matthew 12.50 ("Whosoever shall do my Father's will . . . is my brother and sister and mother") and the Song of Songs (whose erotic love language was widely interpreted in spiritual terms), along with many others that Marguerite cites, undergirded such a claim; *contempling*: contemplating.

Grace's hands, there shall be nothing in it worthy of reprehension and that, in the meanwhile, no other (but your Highness only) shall read it or see it, lest my faults be known of many. Then shall they be better excused (as my confidence is in your Grace's accustomed benevolence) than if I should bestow a whole year in writing or inventing ways for to excuse them. Praying God Almighty, the Maker and Creator of all things, to grant unto your Highness the same New Year's Day a lucky and a prosperous year with prosperous issue and continuance of many years in good health and continual joy and all to His honor, praise, and glory. From Ashridge, the last day of the year of our Lord God 1544.

Elizabeth kneeling before the risen Christ.

JOHN BALE

From A Godly Meditation of the Christian Soul (1548)[†]

[*From the Dedicatory Epistle*]

To the right virtuous and Christianly learned young lady Elizabeth, the noble daughter of our late sovereign King Henry VIII, John Bale wisheth health with daily increase of godly knowledge.

Diverse and many (most gracious Lady) have the opinions been among the profane[1] philosophers and Christian divines concerning right nobility and no fewer strifes and contentions for the same.

* * *

John Chrysostom,[2] a man taught and brought up in the Christian philosophy, defineth the true nobility after a far other sort than did the profane writers. He calleth it not with Aristotle a worthiness of progeny,[3] neither yet with Varro an opulency of riches, but a famous renown obtained by long exercised virtue. He is puissant,[4] high, and valiant (saith he) and hath nobil-

---

† Copy text: Marguerite of Navarre, *A godly medytacyon of the christen sowle, concerninge a loue towardes God and hys Christe* ([Wesel: Dirik van der Straten], 1548; *STC* 17320), A2r; A4v–A6v; A7r–A7v; B1r–B1v; E7v–F1r; F2v; F5v–F7r.

1. Secular.

2. Fourth-century church father, often cited by the Protestant reformers; he discusses true nobility in his seven sermons on Lazarus and the Rich Man (see *On Wealth and Poverty*, trans. and intro. Catharine P. Roth [Crestwood, NY: St.Vladimir's Seminary Press, 1984], particularly Sermon 6, pp. 111–12).

3. Derived from noble birth, *Politics* 1283a25–29 (see *The Complete Works of Aristotle. The Revised Oxford Translation*, ed. Jonathan Barnes [Princeton: Princeton UP, 1984], 2:2036).

4. Powerful.

ity in right course that disdaineth to give place to vices and abhorreth to be overcome of them. Doctrine greatly adorneth a man highly born, but a godly endeavor of Christianity beautifieth him most of all.[5] By none other ways have the apostles and martyrs obtained a noble report than by the valiant force of pure doctrine and faith. A gentle heart (saith Seneca) or a stomach that is noble moveth, provoketh, and stirreth only to things honest. No man which hath a noble wit delighteth in things of small value, much less in matters of filthiness or superstition. Chiefly apperteineth it to men and women of sincere nobility to regard the pure doctrine and faith. Unto such hath God promised in the scriptures abundance of temporal things, long life, fortunate children, a kingdom durable, with such other (Deuteronomy 28).

A most worthy conqueror is Gideon, noted in the scriptures for destroying false religion and renewing the kingdom of faith (Judges 6).[6] So is King Asa for removing the male stews from the prelate's abhorring marriage[7] and for putting down idols which his forefathers maintained (1 Kings 15). So is King Jehosaphat for being courageous in the ways of God and for putting down the hill altars and their sacrifices (2 Chronicles 17). So is King Jehu for slaying the idolatrous priests, and for breaking and burning their great god Baal, and for making a jakes of their holy church[8] (2 Kings 10). So is King Hezekiah for cleansing the house of the Lord from all filthiness, afore his time therein occupied (2 Chronicles 29), and for breaking down the brazen serpent and idolatrous images with their altars and sanctuaries (2 Kings 18). So is King Josiah for suppressing religious persons and altar priests, for consuming their jewels and ornaments, and for overthrowing their buggery[9] chambers in the house of the Lord (2 Kings 23). This noble king also destroyed all their carved images; he strewed the dust of them upon their graves that had offered to them and burnt the priests' bones upon their altars, restoring again the laws of the Lord (2 Chronicles 34). Jesus Sirach reporteth of him finally that he wholly directed his heart to the Lord and took away all abominations of the ungodly (Ecclesiasticus 49), besides that[1] is spoken of King David and King Solomon.

Not I only, but many thousands more which will not from henceforth bow anymore to Baal,[2] are in full and perfect hope that all these most highly notable and princely acts will revive and lively flourish in your most noble and worthy brother King Edward VI. Most excellent and godly are his beginnings reported of the very foreign nations calling him (for his virtuous, learned, and godly prudent youth's sake) the second Josiah. Those his wonderful principles in the eyes of the world and no less glorious afore

5. A good life is better even than good doctrine.
6. The biblical judges and kings in the following list are praised for withstanding various manifestations of false religion, all of which are couched in terms of Protestant critiques of Roman Catholic practices.
7. The biblical text says that Asa "took away the whore keepers out of the land" (1 Kings 15.12, Great Bible), but 2 Kings 23.7, which Bale cites below, says that Josiah "broke down the relics of the male stews that were by the house of the Lord." Bale intimates that Roman Catholic prelates and other clergy approved the "marriage" of male prostitutes with their clients; *male stews*: brothels; the reformers frequently accused Roman Catholic priests of sodomy.
8. That is, the temple of Baal; *jakes*: latrine.
9. Heretical, but also with the sense of sexual bestiality or homosexuality.
1. That which.
2. Bale aligns his coreligionist against the false prophets of Baal, that is, the Roman Catholic clergy.

God, thus being to His honor, that eternal, living God continue and prosper to the end, that he may have of them, as had these worthy kings afore
rehearsed, a right noble and famous report. Nobility sought by wicked
enterprises and obtained by the same (as in many afore our days and in
some now of late) is not else but a public and notable infamy and in the end
eternal damnation. Nobility won by the earnest seeking of God's high honor
is such a precious crown of glory as will never perish here nor yet in the
world to come.

*   *   *

Of this nobility have I no doubt (lady most faithfully studious) but that
you are[3] with many other noble women and maidens more in this blessed
age. If question were asked me how I know it, my answer would be this: by
your godly fruit, as the fertile tree is none otherwise than thereby known
(Luke 6). I received your noble book, right fruitfully of you translated out
of the French tongue into English. I received also your golden sentences[4]
out of the sacred scriptures, with no less grace than learning in four noble
languages, Latin, Greek, French, and Italian, most ornately, finely, and
purely written with your own hand. Wonderfully joyous were the learned
men of our city, Murseus, Buscoducinus, Bomelius, Lithodius, and Imannus, as I showed unto them the said sentences, in beholding (as they then
reported) so much virtue, faith, science,[5] and experience of languages and
letters, specially in noble youth and femininity. Through which occasion
there be of them (I know) that cannot withhold their learned hands from
the publishing thereof, to the high praise of God the giver, neither yet from
writing to your worthy Grace for studious continuance in the same.

*   *   *

In your forenamed book, composed first of all by the right virtuous Lady
Margaret, sister sometime to the French King Francis and Queen of
Navarre, and by your noble Grace most diligently and exactly translated
into English, find I most precious treasure concerning the soul. Wherefore
I have added thereunto the title of *A Godly Meditation of the Soul, Concerning a Love towards God and His Christ*. Most lively, in these and such
other excellent facts, express ye the natural emphasis of your noble name:
Elizabeth in the Hebrew is as much to say in the Latin as *Dei mei requies*;
in English, "The rest of my God."[6] Who can think God not to rest in that
heart which sendeth forth such godly fruits? I think none that hath right
discretion. Your pen hath here plenteously uttered the abundance of a godly
occupied heart, like as did the virginal lips of Christ's most blessed mother
when she said with heavenly rejoice, "My soul magnifieth the Lord and my
sprite[7] rejoiceth in God my saver" (Luke 1). Many noble women of fresh[8]

---

3. You belong with the noble ladies mentioned in the previous (omitted) section.
4. The first three sentences translate the first verse of Psalm 14 into Latin, Greek, and French. The
   fourth sentence renders a proverb, "Fear God, honor thy parents, and reverence thy friends" into
   Greek.
5. Knowledge; *Murseus . . . Imannus*: Continental scholars.
6. The metaphoric etymology of Elizabeth's name is drawn from Elishaba, the wife of Aaron, Moses's
   brother (Exodus 6.23) and Elizabeth, the mother of John the Baptist (Luke 1.5) and is interpreted
   to mean "God is fullness" or "God's oath." (Shell, *Elizabeth's Glass*, 320, note 255).
7. Spirit.
8. Other.

literature have been afore time in this region, whose nomenclature or rehearsal of names I intend to show in the end of this book, but none of them were ever yet like to those which are in our age. * * * This one copy of yours have I brought into a number[9] to the intent that many hungry souls by the inestimable treasure contained therein may be sweetly refreshed. The sprite of the eternal Son of God, Jesus Christ, be always to your excellent Grace assistant, that ye may send forth more such wholesome fruits of soul and become a nourishing mother to His dear congregation to their comfort and His high glory.[1] Amen.

Your bound[2] orator,
JOHN BALE

[*From the Conclusion*]

And as touching the portion that my Lady Elizabeth, the King's[3] most noble sister, hath therein, which is her translation, chiefly have she done it for her own exercise in the French tongue, besides the spiritual exercise of her inner soul with God. As a diligent and profitable bee have she gathered of this flower sweetness both ways and of this book consolation in sprite. And thinking that other might do the same, of a most free Christian heart she maketh it here common[4] unto them, not being a niggard over the treasure of God (Matthew 25). The first fruit is it of her young, tender, and innocent labors. For I think she was not full out fourteen years of age at the finishing thereof. She hath not done herein as did the religious and anointed hypocrites in monasteries, convents, and colleges, in sparing their libraries from men studious and in reserving the treasure contained in their books to most vile dust and worms,[5] but like as God hath graciously given it, so do she again most freely distribute it.

Such noble beginnings are neither to be reckoned childish nor babyish, though she were a babe in years that hath here given them. Seldom find we them that in the closing up of their withered age do minister like fruits of virtue. An infinite swarm behold we of old doting bawds and beasts that with consciences laden with sin (as St. Paul reporteth them) taketh every painted stock and stone for their God, besides the small breads that their lecherous chaplains hath blown upon.[6] They shall not be unwise that shall mark herein what commodity it is or what profit might grow to a Christian commonwealth if youth were thus brought up in virtue and good letters. If such fruits come forward in childhood, what will follow and appear when discretion and years shall be more ripe and ancient? A most manifest sign

---

9. Published in multiple copies.
1. As he concludes, Bale applies two powerful images to Elizabeth, who, at this point, is merely a young princess: the image of the Virgin Mary and that of a nursing mother to the church. The latter was a favorite of the reformers to refer to powerful women patronesses; *congregation*: the English Protestant Church.
2. Loyal and subject.
3. Edward VI.
4. Available through publication.
5. Reformers commonly complained that the Roman Catholic Church kept education and the Bible from the common people.
6. A scurrilous allusion to the Roman Catholic doctrine of transubstantiation, by which the sacramental bread is said to become the physical body of Christ during the Latin Mass; *St. Paul reporteth them*: Titus 1.5.

of godliness is it in the friends where youth is thus institute[7] and a token of wonderfully faithful diligence in the studious teachers, tutors, and daily lookers on.

Nobility which she hath gotten of blood in the highest degree, having a most victorious king to her father and a most virtuous and learned king again to her brother, is not in the early spring distained[8] with wanton ignorance, neither yet blemished with the common vices of dissolute youth, but most plenteously adorned with all kinds of languages, learnings, and virtues, to hold it still in right course.

* * *

No realm under the sky hath had more noble women, nor of more excellent graces, than have this realm of England, both in the days of the Britons and since the English Saxons obtained it by valiant conquest.[9]

* * *

Margaret, the noble mother of King Henry the VII, so plenteously minded the preferment of sciences and going forward of learnings that she builded in Cambridge for the same purpose the colleges of Christ and of St. John the Evangelist and gave lands for their maintenance, as Queen Elizabeth[1] did afore to the Queens College there. Long were it to rehearse the exceeding number of noble women which in this land of Britain or realm of England have excelled in beauty, wit, wisdom, science, languages, liberality, policies, heroical force, and such other notable virtues and by reason of them done feats wonderful, either[2] yet to sort out their names and register them one by one which have been married out of the same to emperors, kings, dukes, earls, worthy captains, philosophers, physicians, astronomers, poets, and other of renowned fame and letters, only for their most rare graces and gifts. * * * If they were worthy praise which had these aforenamed virtues single or after a bodily sort only, we must of congruence grant them worthy double honor which have them most plenteously doubled, as now, since Christ's Gospel hath risen, we have beholden them and yet see them still to this day in many noble women, not rising of flesh and blood as in the other, but of that mighty living Spirit of His which vanquished death, hell, and the devil.[3]

Consider yet how strongly that spirit in Anne Askew set them all at naught with all their artillery and ministers of mischief, both upon the rack and also in the fire, whose memory is now in benediction (as Jesus Sirach reporteth of Moses)[4] and shall never be forgotten of the righteous. She, as

7. Taught.
8. Stained.
9. Bale continues with a catalog of learned, political, warrior, and saintly women from early English history, including both Celtic and Anglo-Saxon exemplars. Bale sets Elizabeth among these paragons both as a compliment to her virtue and as an inducement to further feats.
1. Elizabeth of York, wife of Henry VII, mother of Henry VIII, and grandmother of Elizabeth. Bale concludes his survey of noble Englishwomen with Elizabeth's own kin; *Margaret*: Margaret Beaufort, Elizabeth's great-grandmother.
2. Or.
3. If we praise noble women who displayed heroical force and learning in the service of their families or nations, how much more should we honor women who devote themselves to God.
4. Ecclesiasticus 45.1; *Anne Askew*: a kinswoman by marriage to Katherine Parr and a member of the Court, who was tortured on the rack and burned at the stake on July 16, 1546, for denying the doctrine of transubstantiation and for refusing to implicate fellow believers. Bale published a record of her examinations in that same year.

Christ's mighty member, hath strongly trodden down the head of the serpent and gone hence with most noble victory over the pestiferous seed of
that viperous worm of Rome, the gates of hell not prevailing against her.[5]
What other noble women have,[6] it doth now and will yet hereafter appear
more largely by their godly doctrine and deeds of faith.

Mark this present book for one, whose translation was the work of her
which was but a babe at the doing thereof. Mark also the grave sentences
which she giveth forth to the world and laud that living Father of our Lord
Jesus Christ, which hath thus taken His heavenly wisdom from the great
grave seniors, that only are wise in their own conceits, and given it so
largely[7] to children (Matthew 11). That heavenly Lord grant her and other
noble women long continuance in the same to His high pleasure, that like
as they are become glorious to the world by the study of good letters, so may
they also appear glorious in His sight by daily exercise in His divine scriptures, whose nature is in process of time to kindle their minds and inflame
their hearts in the love of Christ, their eternal spouse, as this present book
requireth. So be it.

PRINCESS ELIZABETH

Verse Translation of the Thirteenth Psalm of David (1548)[†]

Fools, that true faith yet never had,
Saith in their hearts, "There is no God."
Filthy they are in their practice;
Of them not one is godly wise.°   *wise in religious matters*
5 From heaven the Lord on man did look
To know what ways he undertook.
All they were vain and went astray;
Not one he found in the right way.
In heart and tongue have they deceit;
10 Their lips throw forth a poisoned bait.
Their minds are mad, their mouths are wode,°   *mad*
And swift they be in shedding blood.
So blind they are, no truth they know;
No fear of God in them will grow.
15 How can that cruel sort be good?
Of God's dear folk, which suck the blood,
On Him rightly shall they not call,[1]
Despair will so their hearts appall.°   *dismay*

5. The woodcut on the title page of Anne Askew's *First Examination* shows a woman holding a Bible
   and a palm of triumph subduing a bearded dragon, or serpent, that wears the triple miter of the
   Pope. Genesis 3.15 prophesies that a descendent of Eve will tread down the serpent who deceived
   her; *as Christ's mighty member*: as a mighty member of Christ's body, the church.
6. Have done.
7. Freely; generously.
† Copy text: Marguerite of Navarre, *A godly medytacyon of the christen sowle, concerninge a loue
   towardes God and hys Christe* ([Wesel: Dirik van der Straten], 1548; *STC* 17320), F7v–F8r.
1. Those who suck the blood of God's people cannot properly call upon God.

At all times God is with the just
20 Because they put in Him their trust.
Who shall, therefore, from Zion give
That health which hangeth in our believe?[2]
When God shall take from His° the smart,°   *His people / affliction*
Then will Jacob rejoice in heart.
25   Praise to God.

THE CHURCH OF ENGLAND

Psalm 13 from the Great Bible (1540)[†]

The fool hath said in his heart, "There is no God." They are corrupt and become abominable in their doings; there is not one that doth good (no not one). The Lord looked down from heaven upon the children of men to see if there were any that would understand and seek after God. But they are all gone out of the way; they are all together become abominable. There is none that doeth good, no not one. Their throat is an open sepulcher; with their tongues they have deceived; the poison of asps is under their lips. Their mouth is full of cursing and bitterness; their feet are swift to shed blood. Destruction and unhappiness is in their ways, and the way of peace have they not known. There is no fear of God before their eyes.

Have they no knowledge, that all are such workers of mischief, eating up my people as it were bread and call not upon the Lord? There were they brought in great fear (even where no fear was), for God is in the generation of the righteous. As for you, ye have made a mock at the council of the poor because he putteth his trust in the Lord. O that the salvation were given unto Israel out of Zion.

When the Lord turneth the captivity of His people, then shall Jacob rejoice and Israel shall be glad.

ROGER ASCHAM

From The Schoolmaster (1570)[‡]

Ye perceive how Pliny teacheth that by this exercise of double translating is learned easily, sensibly, by little and little, not only all the hard congruities of grammar, the choice of aptest words, the right framing of words and sentences, comeliness of figures[1] and forms fit for every matter and proper for every tongue, but that which is greater also. In marking daily and following

2. Depends upon our faith.
† Copy text: *The Byble in Englyshe . . . with a prologe therinto, made by the reuerende father in God, Thomas archbysshop of Cantorbury* (London: Edward Whytchurche, 1540; STC 2070), AA3v. This Psalm is number 13 in the Latin Vulgate, 14 in Protestant Bibles.
‡ Copy text: Roger Ascham, *The scholemaster or plaine and perfite way of teachyng children, to vnderstand, write, and speake, the Latin tong* (London: Iohn Daye, [1570]; STC 832), L2v–L3v.
1. Figures of speech; *double translating*: a humanist pedagogical technique of translating Latin or Greek passages into English and then back into the original language; *congruities*: proprieties, conventions.

diligently thus the steps of the best authors, like invention of arguments, like order in disposition,[2] like utterance in elocution is easily gathered up, whereby your scholar shall be brought, not only to like eloquence, but also to all true understanding and right judgment, both for writing and speaking. * * * And a better and nearer example herein may be our most noble Queen Elizabeth, who never took yet Greek nor Latin grammar in her hand, after the first declining of a noun and a verb, but only by this double translating of Demosthenes and Isocrates daily, without missing every forenoon, and likewise some part of Tully every afternoon for the space of a year or two, hath attained to such a perfect understanding in both the tongues and to such a ready utterance of the Latin, and that with such a judgment as they be few in number in both the universities[3] or elsewhere in England that be, in both tongues, comparable with her Majesty. And to conclude in a short room the commodities of double translation, surely the mind (by daily marking first the cause and matter, then the words and phrases, next the order and composition, after[4] the reason and arguments, then the forms and figures of both the tongues, lastly the measure and compass of every sentence) must needs, by little and little, draw unto it the like shape of eloquence as the author doth use which is read.

THREATS AND IMPRISONMENT

In 1547, Henry VIII died and was succeeded by Elizabeth's younger brother, Edward VI, with whom she remained on friendly terms. Elizabeth herself went to live with Katherine Parr, the dowager Queen, while the care of the young King was divided between his two maternal uncles: Edward Seymour, the Duke of Somerset, was declared the Lord Protector, and Thomas Seymour, his younger brother, claimed the title of Governor of the Royal Person. The ambitious Thomas Seymour soon married Katherine Parr, whom he had long admired, and joined her household at Chelsea. There he began to take playful liberties with the Princess Elizabeth, entering her bedchamber before she rose, teasing and tickling her as she retreated under the bedclothes, and once attempting to kiss her, at which her longtime governess, Kat Ashley, remonstrated and drove him out. On another occasion, at the royal residence of Hanworth, Katherine Parr, who enjoyed her husband's mischief, held Elizabeth down in the garden while he used scissors to cut her gown in pieces. Seymour's flirtatiousness became so scandalous, however, that Elizabeth was sent away to stay with Ashley's sister, Lady Anthony Denny, at Cheshunt, Hertfordshire.

After Parr's death following childbirth in 1548, rumors of a possible marriage between Thomas Seymour and Elizabeth put the Princess in jeopardy and contributed to the charges of treason against Seymour that led to his execution on March 20, 1549. Kat Ashley and the manager of Elizabeth's household, Thomas Parry, were taken to the Tower of London, and Elizabeth herself was entrusted to the supervision of Robert and Elizabeth Tyrwhit at Hatfield House. Elizabeth's letter to the Duke of Somerset in January 1549 reveals her awareness of her precarious position. Although she begins with a humble tone and signs her letter "your assured friend to my little power," Elizabeth is assertive,

---

2. Laying out parts of an argument in an effective order; *like*: similar.
3. Oxford and Cambridge; *declining . . . verb*: laying out of the proper endings for the particular noun or verb in question. *Tully*: Cicero.
4. Thereafter; *short room*: short space.

flatly denying any romantic involvement with Thomas Seymour and asking the Duke to squelch the slanderous reports that she is pregnant with Seymour's child.

Far more serious than the Seymour affair, however, was the potential threat Elizabeth posed to her sister Mary when Edward VI died in 1553. Shortly before his death, John Dudley, the Duke of Northumberland, and Henry Grey, the Duke of Suffolk, had pressured the young King to name Grey's daughter, Lady Jane (who was married to Dudley's son Guildford), as his heir. Although Elizabeth was not party to the machinations that put Lady Jane Grey on the throne for a brief period, the Protestantism she shared with the Dudleys and Greys made her suspect in Mary's eyes.

Among the religious issues most in dispute between Catholics and Protestants were the language of the Bible and the nature of the sacraments. For Roman Catholics, the Latin Vulgate was the Bible of choice; for Protestants, the vernacular English. For Roman Catholics, the wine and bread in the sacrament of the Mass (also known as the Eucharist) were transformed into the blood and body of Christ through a process known as transubstantiation; for most English Protestants, the consecrated elements of the Lord's Supper remained wine and bread, though they believed that Christ, through the Holy Spirit, was truly present in the sacrament. Both Catholics and Protestants viewed one another's practices and beliefs as sacrilegious and blasphemous.

In 1554, when Protestants mounted a major insurrection against Mary, Elizabeth was immediately suspected of involvement and arrested. The facts were these. Late in 1553, Queen Mary negotiated a marriage with Philip II of Spain, soon to be the most powerful Catholic ruler in Europe. To counter this alliance, Sir Thomas Wyatt the Younger raised a force of dissidents in Kent and planned to marry Elizabeth to her cousin, Edward Courtenay, Earl of Devonshire, establishing the two as a Protestant Queen and King of England. Wyatt set up his headquarters at the castle of Rochester and then marched with some 4000 men toward London, expecting to meet with reinforcements. The citizens of London, however, armed themselves to protect the city, and his own supporters melted away. Wyatt surrendered on February 8, and three days later, Mary sent three of her counselors, along with a force of 250 horsemen, to bring Elizabeth to London for interrogation. A month later, still under armed guard and fearful for her life, Elizabeth wrote a letter to Mary protesting her innocence. This letter is remarkable not only for its carefully modulated balance of humility and defiance, but also for its final page. Between the last sentence and her signature, Elizabeth carefully drew eleven diagonal lines to prevent anyone from adding a forged confession of guilt.

Mary, however, was unmoved by her sister's letter. On Palm Sunday, Elizabeth was taken by barge from Hampton Court down the river Thames to the Tower of London, where she was forced to disembark at the entrance known as Traitor's Gate. Refusing to enter by a door reserved for criminals, she sat for a time in the rain rather than go in. Although Wyatt exonerated both Elizabeth and Edward Courtenay at his execution on April 11, Elizabeth was held at the Tower for another month before she was moved to Woodstock to serve a period of house arrest under the watchful eye of Sir Henry Bedingfield. Elizabeth's poems—"Oh Fortune, Thy Wresting Wavering State," " 'Twas Christ the Word," and "No Crooked Leg"– and her prayers from this tense period reflect the conflicts that surrounded her and the fragility of her own personal and political fortunes. It was not until nearly a year later, in April 1555, that Mary acceded to the wishes of her new husband, Philip of Spain, and invited Elizabeth to return to Hampton Court as a sister rather than a prisoner. Although the two met in a dramatic evening audience, they were never truly reconciled, but Elizabeth was allowed to return to her own estate at Hatfield, where she lived until Mary's death.

Although Elizabeth survived Mary's persecutions, others did not. Many Protestants fled to the Continent, and, of those who remained in England, more than three hundred were burned at the stake for their religious beliefs. One of those who perished was Elizabeth's godfather, Archbishop Thomas Cranmer, whose story makes a particularly poignant narrative in Foxe's *Acts and Monuments*. Following Elizabeth's birth, Cranmer had prospered, becoming the architect of the Church of England under Edward VI. Cranmer supervised, and in large measure wrote, both the conservative 1549 and the more reformist 1552 Book of Common Prayer, which prescribed the liturgical practices of the English Church. He also wrote homilies and other important doctrinal treatises. Such a position made him both visible and vulnerable to Mary Tudor, but his unforgivable sin was joining the Duke of Northumberland in the attempt to place Lady Jane Grey on the throne following the death of Edward VI. Cranmer was committed to the Tower of London in September 1553, charged with heresy, brought to Oxford for a theological debate intended to establish his guilt in April 1554, and executed on March 21, 1556.

Given the perils of the time, it is not surprising that, in 1563, John Foxe entitled his account of Elizabeth in this period "The Miraculous Preservation of Lady Elizabeth, now Queen of England, from Extreme Calamity and Danger of Life, in the Time of Queen Mary, Her Sister." Foxe was one of the earliest writers to argue that Elizabeth was a ruler ordained by divine Providence to restore England to the one true faith of the early Church. Although she was technically not a martyr, Foxe cast her sufferings as akin to martyrdom and praised the restraint with which she governed after she came to the throne.

PRINCESS ELIZABETH

Letter to Edward Seymour, Duke of Somerset, Lord Protector (January 28, 1549)[†]

My Lord,

Your great gentleness and goodwill toward me, as well in this thing as in other things, I do understand; for the which, even as I ought, so I do give you most humble thanks. And whereas your Lordship willeth and counseleth me, as a earnest friend, to declare what I know in this matter and also to write what I have declared to Master Tyrwhit,[1] I shall most willingly do it.

I declared unto him first that after that the Cofferer had declared unto me what my Lord Admiral answered for Allen's matter and for Durham Place (that it was appointed to be a mint),[2] he told me that my Lord Admiral did offer me his house for my time being with the King's Majesty. And further said and asked me whether if the Council did consent that I should have my Lord Admiral, whether I would consent to it or no. I answered that

---

[†] Copy text: *Elizabeth I: Collected Works*, ed. Leah S. Marcus, Janel Mueller, and Mary Beth Rose (Chicago and London: University of Chicago Press, 2000), 22–24. Reprinted by permission of the University of Chicago Press. © 2000 by the University of Chicago.

1. Robert Tyrwhit, steward to Katherine Parr and appointed guardian, with his wife Elizabeth Oxenbridge Tyrwhit, of the Princess Elizabeth at Hatfield House; see a prayer for the Queen by Lady Tyrwhit in Part Four.

2. The Bishop of Durham's London palace, which had been promised to Elizabeth as her London residence. Elizabeth was annoyed by reports that it had been appropriated by the government to be used as a mint; *Cofferer*: Thomas Parry, who kept Elizabeth's household accounts; *Lord Admiral*: Thomas Seymour, husband of Katherine Parr, who had died in September 1548, and brother of the Lord Protector; *Allen's matter*: Edmund Allen, Elizabeth's chaplain; it is unclear to what "matter" Elizabeth refers.

I would not tell him what my mind was, and I inquired further of him what he meant to ask me that question or who bade him say so. He answered me and said nobody bade him say so but that he perceived (as he thought) by my Lord Admiral's inquiring whether my patent were sealed or no, and debating what he spent in his house, and inquiring what was spent in my house, that he was given that way rather than otherwise.[3]

And as concerning Kat Ashley, she never advised me unto it but said always (when any talked of my marriage) that she would never have me marry, neither in England nor out of England, without the consent of the King's Majesty, your Grace's, and the Council's, and after the Queen was departed,[4] when I asked of her what news she heard from London, she answered merrily, "They say there that your Grace shall have my Lord Admiral, and that he will come shortly to woo you." And moreover I said unto him that the Cofferer sent a letter hither that my Lord said that he would come this way as he went down to the country. Then I bade her write as she thought best, and bade her show it me when she had done. So she writ that she thought it not best for fear of suspicion, and so it went forth. And my Lord Admiral, after he heard that, asked of the Cofferer why he might not come as well to me as to my sister, and then I desired Kat Ashley to write again (lest my Lord might think that she knew more in it than he) that she knew nothing in it but suspicion. And also I told Master Tyrwhit that, to the effect of the matter, I never consented unto any such thing without the Council's consent thereunto. And as for Kat Ashley or the Cofferer, they never told me that they would practice it.[5]

These be the things which I both declared to Master Tyrwhit and also whereof my conscience beareth me witness, which I would not for all earthly things offend in anything, for I know I have a soul to save as well as other folks have, wherefore I will above all thing have respect unto this same.

If there be any more things which I can remember, I will either write it myself or cause Master Tyrwhit to write it. Master Tyrwhit and others have told me that there goeth rumors abroad which be greatly both against mine honor and honesty,[6] which above all other things I esteem, which be these: that I am in the Tower and with child by my Lord Admiral. My Lord, these are shameful slanders, for the which, besides the great desire I have to see the King's Majesty, I shall most heartily desire your Lordship that I may come to the Court after your first determination,[7] that I may show myself there as I am. Written in haste from Hatfield, this 28 of January.

Your assured friend to my little power,
ELIZABETH

---

3. Seymour signaled his interest in Elizabeth by inquiring about her financial affairs, including the granting of the letters patent for her ownership of Durham Place.
4. After Katherine Parr's death; *Kat Ashley*: Elizabeth's longtime governess.
5. Arrange her marriage with Thomas Seymour.
6. Chastity.
7. As you first suggested.

PRINCESS ELIZABETH

Writings in Captivity

Letter to Mary Tudor (March 17, 1554)[†]

If any ever did try this old saying that a king's word was more than another man's oath, I most humbly beseech your Majesty to verify it in me and to remember your last promise and my last demand that I be not condemned without answer and due proof, which it seems that now I am, for that without cause proved I am by your Council from you commanded to go unto the Tower, a place more wonted[1] for a false traitor than a true subject, which, though I know I deserve it not, yet in the face of all this realm appears that it is proved, which I pray God I may die the shamefullest death that ever any died afore I may mean any such thing. And to this present hour I protest afore God (who shall judge my truth whatsoever malice shall devise) that I never practiced, concealed, nor consented to anything that might be prejudicial to your person any way or dangerous to the state by any mean, and therefore I humbly beseech your Majesty to let me answer afore yourself and not suffer me to trust your counselors, yea, and that afore I go to the Tower (if it be possible), if not afore I be further condemned. Howbeit, I trust assuredly your Highness will give me leave to do it afore I go, for that thus shamefully I may not be cried out on as now I shall be, yea and without cause.

Let conscience move your Highness to take some better way with me than to make me be condemned in all men's sight afore my desert[2] known. Also I most humbly beseech your Highness to pardon this my boldness, which innocency procures me to do, together with hope of your natural kindness, which I trust will not see me cast away without desert (which what it is, I would desire no more of God but that you truly knew, which thing I think and believe you shall never by report know unless by yourself you hear). I have heard in my time of many cast away for want of coming to the presence of their prince, and in late days I heard my Lord of Somerset say that if his brother had been suffered to speak with him, he had never suffered,[3] but the persuasions were made to him so great that he was brought in belief that he could not live safely if the Admiral lived and that made him give his consent to his death. Though these persons are not to be compared to your Majesty, yet I pray God as evil persuasions persuade not one sister again[4] the other, and all for that they have heard false report and not hearkene[d] to the truth known.

---

† Copy text: Public Record Office, State Papers Domestic, Mary I, 11/4/2, fol. 3r. This letter is in Elizabeth's own handwriting.
1. Accustomed; *try*: ascertain the truth of; *and due proof*: Elizabeth inserted these words, probably to strength her claim of innocence.
2. Deserving.
3. Edward Seymour, Duke of Somerset and Lord Protector of Edward VI, executed his younger brother, Thomas Seymour, the Lord Admiral, on March 20, 1549; Elizabeth was suspected of treasonous activities with the younger Seymour; *want*: lack.
4. Against; *as*: that.

Therefore, once again kneeling with humbleness of my heart because I am not suffered to bow the knees of my body, I humbly crave to speak with your Highness, which I would not be so bold to desire if I knew not myself most clear as I know myself most true. And as for the traitor Wyatt, he might peradventure write me a letter, but on my faith I never received any from him, and as for the copy of my letter sent to the French King, I pray God confound me eternally if ever I sent him word, message, token, or letter by any means, and to this my truth I will stand in to my death.⁵

I humbly crave but only one word of answer from yourself.

Your Highness's most faithful subject that hath been from the beginning and will be to my end.

ELIZABETH

[Oh Fortune, Thy Wresting Wavering State] (1555)†

O Fortune, thy wresting,° wavering state	*twisting*
Hath fraught with cares my troubled wit,	
Whose witness this present prison late	
Could bear, where once was joy flown quite.	

5 Thou caused'st the guilty to be loosed
From bands where innocents were enclosed,°   *imprisoned*
And caused the guiltless to be reserved,°   *preserved alive*
And freed those that death had well deserved.°   *fairly won*
But all herein can be naught wrought.
10 So God grant to my foes as they have thought.¹
     Finis. Elisabetha a prisoner, 1555
Much suspected by me, but nothing proved can be.

['Twas Christ the Word] (1554–55?)‡

*Hoc est corpus meum*¹
'Twas Christ the Word that spake it.
The same took bread and brake it,

---

5. Eleven diagonal lines fill the page between the last paragraph and the conclusion of the letter, preventing the insertion of additional words by someone seeking to incriminate the Princess; *write me a letter*: under duress, Wyatt claimed to have sent Elizabeth a letter urging her to leave London; *received*: accepted; *my letter . . . French King*: the copy of a letter Elizabeth had sent to Mary, discovered in the postbag of the French ambassador, was cited as proof of Elizabeth's conspiracy with the King of France.

† Copy text: *Elizabeth I: Collected Works*, ed. Leah S. Marcus, Janel Mueller, and Mary Beth Rose (Chicago and London: University of Chicago Press, 2000), 45–46. Reprinted by permission of the University of Chicago Press. © 2000 by the University of Chicago.

1. Nothing can be done [to me] if God rewards my enemies with the fate they have planned for others.

‡ Copy text: *Elizabeth I: Collected Works*, 47. This poem was attributed to Elizabeth in the seventeenth century, but its earliest attribution (1568) is to D.C., possibly Dr. Richard Cox, one of Elizabeth's tutors (May, *Selected Works*, 330).

1. "This is my body," the words spoken at the distribution of the bread in the Eucharist. The poem reflects the tension between Protestant and Roman Catholic interpretations of what was meant by

And as the Word did make it,
5 So I believe and take it.

QUEEN ELIZABETH

[No Crooked Leg] (1558?)[†]

No crooked leg, no bleared eye,
No part deformed out of kind,°   *nature*
Nor yet so ugly half can be
As is the inward, suspicious mind.

Your loving mistress,
ELIZABETH[1]

Prayers (1554)[‡]

*The Christian prayers of our Sovereign Lady Queen Elizabeth,
which her Grace made in the time of her trouble and imprisonment
in the Tower*

Help me now, O God, for I have none other friends but Thee alone. And suffer me not (I beseech Thee) to build my foundation upon the sands, but upon the rock, whereby all blasts of blustering weather may have no power against me.[1] Amen.

*Another prayer made by her Majesty, when she was in great
fear and doubt of death by murder:*

Grant, O God, that the wicked may have no power to hurt or betray me; neither suffer any such treason and wickedness to proceed against me. For Thou, O God, canst mollify all such tyrannous hearts and disappoint all such cruel purposes. And I beseech Thee to hear me, Thy creature, which am Thy servant and at Thy commandment, trusting by Thy grace ever so to remain. Amen.

---

the words, "This is my body." Catholics believed that the elements of bread and wine in the sacrament of the Mass were transformed into the body and blood of Christ through a process known as transubstantiation. Followers of Zwingli believed that the elements were merely symbols of Christ's death and resurrection. Lutherans believed that Christ was in and among the elements in a mysterious way (consubstantiation). Calvinist or reformed Christians believed that Christ was spiritually, but not bodily, present in the bread and wine. By merely reciting the words of Jesus, the author follows Anne Askew and other early reformers who refused directly to answer the question of whether they believed in transubstantiation.

† Copy text: Royal Library, Windsor Castle, written on the last page of text of a French Psalter. This poem may be dated as late as 1558, soon before Elizabeth's accession.

1. The Psalter was apparently presented as a gift; Elizabeth's signature is completed by a square knot, the personal symbol she used as a princess.

‡ Copy text: Thomas Bentley, *The monvment of matrones conteining seuen seuerall lamps of virginitie*, Lamp 2 (London: H. Denham, 1582; STC 1892), H4r–v.

1. A paraphrase of the parable that concludes Jesus's Sermon on the Mount (Matthew 7.24–27).

JOHN FOXE

From Acts and Monuments[†]

The Life, State, and Story of the Reverend Pastor and Prelate, Thomas Cranmer, Archbishop of Canterbury, Martyr (1583)

Mary, hearing of the death of her brother and shifting for herself, was so assisted by the Commons that eftsoons[1] she prevailed. Who, being established in the possession of the realm, not long after came to London, and after she had caused first the two fathers, the Duke of Northumberland and the Duke of Suffolk,[2] to be executed (as is above remembered), likewise she caused the Lady Jane, being both in age tender and innocent from this crime (after she could by no means be turned from the constancy of her faith), together with her husband to be beheaded.

The rest of the nobles, paying fines, were forgiven, the Archbishop of Canterbury only excepted, who, though he desired pardon by means of friends, could obtain none, insomuch that the Queen would not once vouchsafe to see him, for as yet the old grudges against the Archbishop for the divorcement of her mother[3] remained hid in the bottom of her heart. Besides this divorce, she remembered the state of religion changed, all which was reputed to the Archbishop, as the chief cause thereof.

✻   ✻   ✻

The said Bishop declared afterward to one of Dr. Cranmer's friends that, notwithstanding his attainder of treason, the Queen's determination at that time was that Cranmer should only have been deprived of his archbishopric and have had a sufficient living assigned him, upon his exhibiting of a true inventory, with commandment to keep his house[4] without meddling in matters of religion. But how that was true, I have not to say. This is certain, that not long after this, he was sent unto the Tower and soon after condemned of treason. Notwithstanding, the Queen (when she could not honestly deny him his pardon, seeing all the rest were discharged and specially seeing he, last of all other, subscribed to King Edward's request[5] and that against his own will) released to him his action of treason and accused him only of heresy, which liked the Archbishop right well and came to pass as he wished, because the cause was not now his own but Christ's, not the Queen's but the Church's.

---

† Copy text: John Foxe, *Actes and monuments of matters most speciall and memorable, happenyng in the Church with an vniuersall history of the same*, Book 11 (London: John Day, 1583; STC 11225), 1871, 1883, 1885–88. The 1583 text is somewhat more dramatic than the original 1563 account, although the stories are substantially the same.

1. Soon afterwards; *Mary*: Mary Tudor; *brother*: Edward VI; *shifting for herself*: providing for her own safety; *Commons*: the common people, who refused to support the Lady Jane Grey but rallied around Mary.

2. John Dudley, father of Guildford Dudley, and Henry Grey, father of Lady Jane Grey.

3. The divorce of Henry VIII from Katherine of Aragon.

4. Remain in his home under virtual house arrest; *Bishop*: Nicholas Heath, Bishop of York and Lord Chancellor to Mary Tudor; *attainder*: judgment; *true inventory*: a complete record of his holdings and possessions at the time of his arrest.

5. To make Lady Jane Grey queen; *all the rest were discharged*: other supporters of Lady Jane Grey had been released from prison.

Thus stood the cause of Cranmer, till at length it was determined by the Queen and the Council that he should be removed from the Tower, where he was prisoner, to Oxford, there to dispute with the doctors and divines. And privily, word was sent before to them of Oxford to prepare themselves and make them ready to dispute. And although the Queen and the bishops had concluded before what should become of him, yet it pleased them that the matter should be debated with arguments, that under some honest show of disputation, the murder of the man might be covered; neither could their hasty speed of revengement abide any long delay, and therefore in all haste he was carried to Oxford.

* * *

[After the disputation at Oxford, Cranmer was declared a heretic, deprived of his office as Archbishop, and led out to execution.]

Here then, to be short, when they came to take off his pall[6] (which is a solemn vesture of an archbishop), then said he, "Which of you hath a pall, to take off my pall?" which imported as much as they, being his inferiors, could not disgrade him. Whereunto one of them said, in that they were but bishops, they were his inferiors and not competent judges, but being the Pope's delegates, they might take his pall, and so they did and so proceeding took everything in order from him, as it was put on. Then a barber clipped his hair round about, and the bishop scraped the tops of his fingers where he had been anointed, wherein Bishop Bonner behaved himself as roughly and unmannerly as the other bishop[7] was to him soft and gentle. Whiles they were thus doing, "All this," quoth the Archbishop, "needed not. I had myself done with this gear long ago."

Last of all, they stripped him out of his gown into his jacket and put upon him a poor yeoman beadle's gown, full bare and nearly worn, and as evil favoredly made as one might lightly see, and a townsman's cap on his head, and so delivered him to the secular power.[8]

After this pageant of degradation and all was finished, then spake Lord Bonner, saying to him, "Now are you no Lord anymore." And so whensoever he spake to the people of him (as he was continually barking against him), ever he used this term, "This gentleman here," etc.

And thus, with great compassion and pity of every man, in this evilfavored gown was he carried to prison.

* * *

[While in prison, Cranmer was urged to sign a recantation of his Protestant beliefs, which he did. Despite this abjuration, however, he was brought on March 21, 1556, to St. Mary's Church for the execution sermon, delivered by Dr. Cole, the provost of Eton school.]

Soon after, about nine of the clock, the Lord Williams, Sir Thomas Bridges, Sir John Brown, and the other justices, with certain other noblemen

6. The woolen vestment that signified his office.
7. Cranmer; *Bishop Bonner*: Edmund Bonner, the Bishop of London and, with Stephen Gardiner, one of the arch villains of Foxe's accounts.
8. The state authorities who would conduct the actual execution; *yeoman beadle*: a minor university official; *lightly*: easily or contemptuously; *townsman's cap*: ordinary citizen's hat. Foxe makes much of Cranmer's disrobing, since the clothing that could be worn by various ranks of common, noble, and religious people were strictly regulated by law. It was considered shameful to wear the clothes of social inferiors.

that were sent of the Queen's Council, came to Oxford with a great train of waiting men. Also of the other multitude on every side (as is wont in such a matter) was made a great concourse[9] and greater expectation.

*   *   *

In this so great frequence and expectation, Cranmer at length cometh from the prison Bocardo unto St. Mary's Church (because it was a foul and a rainy day), the chief church in the university, in this order: the Mayor went before; next him the aldermen in their place and degree; after them was Cranmer brought between two friars, which, mumbling to and fro certain psalms in the streets, answered one another until they came to the church door, and there they began the song of Simeon, "*Nunc dimittis*,"[1] and entering into the church, the psalm-saying friars brought him to his standing and there left him. There was a stage set up over against the pulpit of a mean height from the ground, where Cramer had his standing, waiting until Cole made him ready to his sermon.

The lamentable case and sight of that man gave a sorrowful spectacle to all Christian eyes that beheld him. He that late was Archbishop, Metropolitan, and Primate[2] of England, and the King's privy councilor, being now in a bare and ragged gown and ill-favoredly clothed, with an old square cap, exposed to the contempt of all men, did admonish men not only of his own calamity, but also of their state and fortune. For who would not pity his case and bewail his fortune, and might not fear his own chance, to see such a prelate, so grave a councilor, and of so long continued honor, after so many dignities, in his old years to be deprived of his estate, adjudged to die, and in so painful a death to end his life, and now presently from such fresh ornaments[3] to descend to such vile and ragged apparel?

*   *   *

Cranmer, in all this meantime with what great grief of mind he stood hearing this sermon, the outward shows of his body and countenance did better express than any man can declare, one while[4] lifting up his hands and eyes unto heaven and then again for shame letting them down to the earth. A man might have seen the very image and shape of perfect sorrow lively in him expressed. More than twenty several times the tears gushed out abundantly, dropped down marvelously from his fatherly face. They which were present do testify that they never saw in any child more tears than brast[5] out from him at that time, all the sermon while, but especially when he recited his prayer before the people. It is marvelous what commiseration and pity moved all men's hearts that beheld so heavy a countenance and such abundance of tears in an old man of so reverend dignity.

---

9. Large crowd.
1. The Song of Simeon, ironically, begins, "Now lettest thy servant depart in peace" (Luke 2.29, Great Bible); *frequence*: crowd; *Bocardo*: the common jail in Oxford; *rainy day*: the sermon would normally be preached out of doors at the execution site; *degree*: rank; *mumbling . . . streets*: mumbling indicates that they were chanting the psalms in Latin.
2. All three terms—Archbishop, Metropolitan, and Primate—refer to the highest religious position in England.
3. Ecclesiastical clothing.
4. Sometimes.
5. Burst.

Cole, after he had ended his sermon, called back the people, that were ready to depart, to prayers.

"Brethren," said he, "lest any man should doubt of this man's earnest conversion and repentance, you shall hear him speak before you, and therefore I pray you, Master Cranmer, that you will now perform that[6] you promised not long ago, namely, that you would openly express the true and undoubted profession of your faith, that you may take away all suspicion from men and that all men may understand that you are a Catholic indeed."

"I will do it," said the Archbishop, "and with a good will,"[7] who by and by rising up and putting off his cap, began to speak thus unto the people:

"I desire you, well-beloved brethren in the Lord, that you will pray to God for me to forgive me my sins, which above all men, both in number and greatness, I have committed. But among all the rest, there is one offence which of all at this time doth vex and trouble me, whereof in process of my talk you shall hear more in his proper place."

And then, putting his hand into his bosom, he drew forth his prayer, which he recited to the people in this sense.

*   *   *

[After a general prayer of repentance, Cranmer read to the assembly a profession of faith that ended as follows:]

"And now I come to the great thing that so much troubleth my conscience, more than anything that ever I did or said in my whole life, and that is the setting abroad of a writing contrary to the truth, which now here I renounce and refuse as things written with my hand, contrary to the truth which I thought in my heart and written for fear of death and to save my life if it might be; and that is, all such bills and papers which I have written or signed with my hand since my degradation, wherein I have written many things untrue. And forasmuch as my hand offended, writing contrary to my heart, my hand shall first be punished therefore, for may I come to the fire, it shall be first burned.

"And as for the Pope, I refuse him as Christ's enemy and Antichrist, with all his false doctrine.

"And as for the sacrament, I believe as I have taught in my book against the Bishop of Winchester, the which my book teacheth so true a doctrine of the sacrament that it shall stand at the last day before the judgment of God, where the papistical doctrine contrary thereto shall be ashamed to show her face."[8]

Here the standersby were all astonied,[9] marveled, were amazed, did look one upon another, whose expectation he had so notably deceived. Some began to admonish him of his recantation and to accuse him of falsehood.

Briefly, it was a world[1] to see the doctors beguiled of so great an hope. I think there was never cruelty more notably or better in time deluded and

---

6. That which.

7. By "catholic," however, Cranmer means not Roman Catholicism but the universal Christian faith, which Protestants insisted they maintained. As Cranmer stated in his profession of faith: "I believe every article of the Catholic faith, every word and sentence taught by our Savior Jesus Christ, His apostles and prophets, in the New and Old Testaments," (1583, p. 1887) thus neatly substituting biblical for papal authority.

8. Cranmer repudiates his earlier recantation and affirms that he does not believe in the doctrine of transubstantiation; *sacrament*: the Eucharist or Lord's Supper.

9. Stunned.

1. It was a marvel.

The burning of Archbishop Thomas Cranmer.

deceived. For it is not to be doubted but they looked for a glorious victory and a perpetual triumph by this man's retraction. Who, as soon as they heard these things, began to let down their ears,[2] to rage, fret, and fume, and so much the more, because they could not revenge their grief, for they could now no longer threaten or hurt him. For the most miserable man in the world can die but once; and whereas of necessity he must needs die that day, though the papists had been never so well pleased, now being never so much offended with him, yet could he not be twice killed of them.

*   *   *

But when he came to the place where the holy bishops and martyrs of God, Hugh Latimer and Ridley,[3] were burnt before him for the confession of the truth, kneeling down he prayed to God, and not long tarrying in his prayers, putting off his garments to his shirt, he prepared himself to death. His shirt was made long, down to his feet. His feet were bare; likewise his head, when both his caps were off, was so bare that one hair could not be seen upon it.[4] His beard was long and thick, covering his face with marvelous gravity. Such a countenance of gravity moved the hearts both of his friends and of his enemies.

*   *   *

Then was an iron chain tied about Cranmer, whom when they perceived to be more steadfast than that he could be moved from his sentence,[5] they commanded the fire to be set unto him.

2. To become indignant.
3. Hugh Latimer, the Bishop of Worcester, and Nicholas Ridley, the Bishop of London, both members of Katherine Parr's circle, were executed at Oxford on October 16, 1555.
4. As a result of its having been shaved.
5. His final speech repudiating Roman Catholicism.

And when the wood was kindled and the fire began to burn near him, stretching out his arm, he put his right hand into the flame, which he held so steadfast and immovable (saving that once with the same hand he wiped his face), that all men might see his hand burned before his body was touched. His body did so abide the burning of the flame with such constancy and steadfastness that, standing always in one place without moving of his body, he seemed to move no more than the stake to which he was bound. His eyes were lifted up into heaven, and oftentimes he repeated "his unworthy right hand," so long as his voice would suffer him, and using often the words of Stephen,[6] "Lord Jesus, receive my spirit," in the greatness of the flame he gave up the ghost.

The Miraculous Preservation of Lady Elizabeth, now Queen of England, from Extreme Calamity and Danger of Life, in the Time of Queen Mary, her Sister (1563)[†]

That which I have seen and read I trust I may boldly repeat without suspicion, either of feigning or flattery. For so I have read, written, and testified of her Grace, by one both learned and also that can say something in this matter, who in a certain book by him set forth entreating of her Grace's virtuous bringing up (what discreet, sober, and godly women she had about her) namely speaketh of two points in her Grace to be considered: one concerning her moderate and maidenly behavior; the other concerning her training up in learning and good letters, declaring first, for her virtuous moderation of life, that seven years after her father's death, she had so little pride of stomach, so little delight in glistering[1] gazes of the world, in gay apparel, rich attire, and precious jewels, that in all that time she never looked upon those that her father left her and which other ladies commonly be so fond upon, but only once, and that against her will, and moreover, after that, so little gloried in the same that there came neither gold nor stone upon her head till her sister enforced her to lay off her former soberness and bear her company in her glistering gains; yea, and then she so wore it as every man might see that her body bore that which her heart misliked. Wherein the virtuous prudence of this Princess, not reading but following the words of Paul and Peter,[2] well considered true nobility to consist not in circumstances of the body but in substance of the heart; not in such things which deck the body but in that which dignifieth the mind, shining and blazing more bright than pearl or stone, be it never so precious.

Again, the said author, further proceeding in the same matter, thus testifieth that he knew a great man's daughter, receiving from Lady Mary before she was Queen goodly apparel of tinsel, cloth of gold, and velvet laid on with parchment lace of gold, when she saw it, she said, "What shall I do with it?"

---

6. The first Christian martyr (Acts 7); the words Cranmer quotes are from the Great Bible, the translation to which he appended a famous preface, praising the publication of the Bible in English.

† Copy text: John Foxe, *Actes and monuments of these latter and perillous dayes touching matters of the Church* (London: John Day, 1563; STC 11222), 1709 (misnumbered 1710)–1711; 1716. The title is from the 1583 edition of *Acts and Monuments*.

1. Admiring; *one both learned . . . in this matter*: Roger Ascham, humanist scholar appointed to be Elizabeth's tutor in 1548; *pride of stomach*: proud spirit.

2. 1 Timothy 2.9–10 and 1 Peter 3.3–4 include injunctions regarding modest female clothing.

"Marry," said a gentlewoman, "wear it."

"Nay," quoth she, "that were a shame to follow my Lady Mary against God's Word and leave my Lady Elizabeth which followeth God's Word."

Let noble ladies and gentlewomen here learn either to give or to take good example given, and if they disdain to teach their inferiors in well doing, yet let it not shame them to learn of their betters. Likewise also at the coming in of the Scottish Queen, when all the other ladies of the court flourished in their bravery with their hair frowsened, and curled, and double curled, yet she altered nothing but to the shame of them all kept her old maidenly shamefastness.[3]

Let us come now to the second point, declaring how she hath been trained in learning, and that not vulgar and common but the purest and the best which is most commended at these days, as the tongues, arts, and God's Word. Wherein she so exceedingly profited (as the foresaid author doth witness) that being under twenty years of age, she was not in the best kind of learning inferior to those that all their lifetime had been brought up in the universities and were counted jolly[4] fellows. And that you may understand that there hath not been, nor is in her, learning only without nature and knowledge without towardness to practice, I will tell what hath been heard of her first schoolmaster,[5] a man very honest and learned, who reported of her to a friend of his that he learned every day more of her than she of him, which, when it seemed to him a mystery (as indeed it was) and therefore desired to know his meaning therein, he thus expounded it.

"I teach her words," quoth he, "and she me things.[6] I teach her the tongues to speak, and her modest and maidenly life teacheth me words to do. For," sayeth he, "I think she is the best inclined and disposed of any in all Europe."

It seemed to me a goodly commendation of her and a witty saying of him. Likewise, an Italian which taught her his tongue (though that nation lightly praise not out of their own country) said once to the said party that he found in her two qualities which are never lightly yokefellows in one woman, which were a singular wit and a marvelous meek stomach.[7]

If time and leisure would serve to peruse her whole life past, many other excellent and memorable examples of her princely qualities and singular virtues might here be noted, but none, in my mind, more worthy of commendation or that shall set forth the same of her heroical and princely renown more to all posterity than the Christian patience and incredible clemency of her nature, showed in her afflictions and towards her enemies declared. Such was then the wickedness and rage of that time,[8] wherein what dangers and troubles were among the inferior subjects of this realm of England may be easily gathered, when such a Princess of that estate, being both a king's daughter, a queen's sister, and heir apparent to the crown, could not escape without her cross. And therefore, as we have hitherto discoursed the afflictions and persecutions of the other poor members

---

3. Modesty; *Scottish Queen*: Mary de Guise, Mary Stuart's mother; *bravery*: fine clothes; *frowsened*: covered by a curled wig.
4. Excellent.
5. William Grindal, Elizabeth's first tutor; *nature*: natural aptitude; *towardness*: inclination and willingness.
6. The Augustinian and medieval distinction between *verba* and *res*.
7. A fine intelligence and a modest, unvengeful disposition; *lightly praise . . . own country*: seldom praise nonnative speakers.
8. During the reign of Mary Tudor.

of Christ, comprehended in this history before, so likewise I see no cause why the communion[9] of her Grace's afflictions also, among the other saints of Christ, ought to be suppressed in silence, especially seeing the great and marvelous working of God's glory chiefly in this story appeareth above all the rest. And though I should through ingratitude or silence pass over the same, yet the thing itself is so manifest that what Englishman is he which knoweth not the afflictions of her Grace to have been far above the condition of a king's daughter? For there was no more behind to make a very Iphigenia of her but her offering up upon the altar of the scaffold.[1]

In which her storms and tempests, with what patience her Highness behaved herself, although it be best known to them who then being her adversaries had the mewing[2] of her, yet this will I say by the way: that then she must needs be in her affliction marvelous patient, which showeth herself now in this prosperity to be utterly without desire of revenge, or else would she have given some token ere this day of remembrance how she was handled. It was no small injury that she suffered in the Lord Protector's[3] days by certain venomous vipers. But to let that pass, was it no wrong, think you, or small injury that she sustained after the death of King Edward when they[4] sought to defeat both her and her sister from her natural inheritance and right of the crown?

*   *   *

In the month of November and day above written, three years from the death of Stephen Gardiner,[5] followed the death of Queen Mary, as is before declared. After whose departure, the same day which took away the said Queen Mary brought in the same her foresaid sister Lady Elizabeth into the right of the crown of England, who after so long restrainment, so great dangers escaped, such blusterous storms overblown, so many injuries digested, and wrongs sustained, the mighty protection of our merciful God, to our no little safeguard, hath exalted and erected out of thrall[6] to liberty, out of danger to peace and rule, from dread to dignity, from misery to majesty, from mourning to ruling, briefly of a prisoner hath made her a Prince and hath placed her in her throne royal, being placed and proclaimed Queen, with as many glad hearts of her subjects as ever was any king or queen in this realm before her, or ever shall be, I think, hereafter.

[*The Curious Incident of the Goat*] (1583)[†]

And now by the way as digressing, or rather refreshing the reader (if it be lawful in so serious a story to recite a matter incident and yet not impertinent

---

9. Communication.
1. The only thing lacking to make her a true sacrificial offering was her very death.
2. Custody.
3. Edward Seymour, Duke of Somerset, who held Elizabeth under house arrest for accused dalliance with his brother, Thomas Seymour.
4. John Dudley, Duke of Northumberland, and others who sought to disinherit Mary and Elizabeth and place Lady Jane Grey on the throne after the death of Edward VI.
5. Bishop of Winchester, one of the architects of the Marian persecution; *month . . . written*: November 17, 1558.
6. Imprisonment; *digested*: endured.
† Copy text: John Foxe, *Actes and monuments of matters most speciall and memorable, happenyng in the Church with an vniuersall history of the same*, Book 12 (London: John Day, 1583; STC 11225), 2095; an incident from Elizabeth's house arrest at Woodstock, from which the playwright Thomas Heywood later developed a comic episode.

to the same), occasion here moveth, or rather enforceth, me to touch briefly what happened in the same place and time by a certain merry-conceited man, being then about her Grace, who, noting the strait and strange keeping of his lady and mistress by the said Sir Henry Bedingfield (with so many locks and doors, with such watch and ward about her as was strange and wonderful), spied a goat in the ward[1] where her Grace was. And whether to refresh her oppressed mind or to notify her strait handing by Sir Henry, either else[2] both, he took it upon his neck and followed her Grace therewith as she was going into her lodging.

Which, when she saw, she asked him what he would do with it, willing to let it alone.

Unto whom the said party answered, "No, by Saint Mary (if it like your Grace), will I not. For I cannot tell whether he be one of the Queen's friends or no. I will carry him to Sir Henry Bedingfield (God willing) to know what he is."

So leaving her Grace, he went with the goat on his neck and carried it to Sir Henry Bedingfield, who, when he saw him coming with it, asked him half angrily what he had there.

Unto whom the party answered, saying, "Sir," quoth he, "I cannot tell what he is. I pray you examine him, for I found him in the place where my Lady's Grace was walking, and what talk they have had I cannot tell. For I understand him not, but he should seem to me to be some stranger, and I think verily a Welshman, for he hath a white frieze-coat[3] on his back. And forsomuch as I, being the Queen's subject and perceiving the strait charge committed to you of her keeping, that no stranger should have access to her without sufficient license, I have here found a stranger (what he is I cannot tell) in place where her Grace was walking. And therefore for the necessary discharge of my duty, I thought it good to bring the said stranger to you to examine as you see cause."

And so he set him down.

At which his words Sir Henry seemed much displeased and said, "Well, well, you will never leave this gere,[4] I see."

And so they departed.

RETROSPECTIVES ON MARY AND ELIZABETH

The story of Elizabeth in *Acts and Monuments* continued to influence later writers. In 1605, Thomas Heywood dramatized the period following Wyatt's Rebellion in Part One of his immensely popular play *If You Know Not Me, You Know Nobody, or the Troubles of Queen Elizabeth*. Although the dramatist took liberties with his material, particularly by adding comic scenes, he was remarkably faithful to the details of Foxe's original account, drawing a sharp distinction between Mary's Roman Catholicism and Elizabeth's Protestantism. The title page of *Acts and Monuments* highlights this division by portraying the faithful Protestants on God's right hand as those who listen to sermons, read the Bible, praise God in the midst of martyrdom, and are welcomed into

1. The area between the inner and outer walls of the castle, where Elizabeth would walk; *incident*: incidental; *merry-conceited*: witty; *strait*: strict; *watch and ward*: surveillance.
2. Or; *notify*: to draw attention to.
3. Cracked and worn leather coat, such as that worn by peasants.
4. Whim.

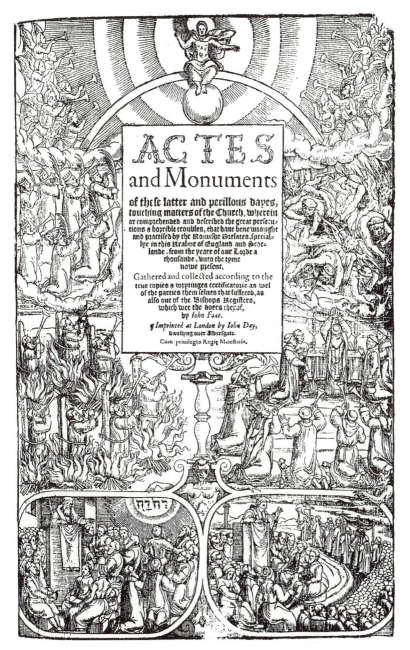

Title-page of John Foxe's *Acts and Monuments* (1563)

heaven in contrast to the Roman Catholics who pray with their beads, go on superstitious pilgrimages, celebrate the Mass, and are denied entry to paradise by a bevy of fallen angels. Heywood does, however, heighten the pathos of Elizabeth's situation, first by stressing her sickness when Mary commands her to return to London for interrogation, then by reiterating her fear of assassination throughout the ordeal, and finally by presenting her as meek and gentle, even when she arrives at the Tower of London, a moment when the real Elizabeth proved less tractable. Philip II, who in Foxe intervenes to help the Princess, is presented even more sympathetically here. Since the play was written in 1605, soon after England had made peace with Spain following two decades of warfare, Heywood may have shaped his treatment of the Spanish King to suit the more irenic mood of his day.

By contrast, Edmund Spenser's treatment of Mary's reign, published in 1590 at the height of the conflict between England and Spain, is far more militant. Book 1 of *The Faerie Queene* draws the reader back to the legendary days of King Arthur, telling tales of knightly quests that are written in a quasi-medieval form of English and laced with allegorical meaning. The hero of the book, the Red Cross Knight, represents Holiness, and his adventures can be interpreted as stages in the long and sometimes painful process by which that virtue is inculcated in the believer. The heroine, Una, who is destined to marry Red Cross, represents the "one true church," the divinely ordained community of faithful people that every Christian is called on to love and defend. Red Cross's task, assigned to him by the Fairy Queen, is to liberate Una and her parents from a dragon (representing Satan, as well as earthly greed and sinfulness), who has seized control of their country ("Eden land") and enslaved its people. Along the way, the hero is captured by two lesser enemies: the enchantress Duessa (the false church, corrupted by worldliness) and her lover, the giant Orgoglio (the sin of pride and love of earthly power). Spenser derives many of his images from the biblical Book of Revelation. Accordingly, Duessa is portrayed as the "whore of Babylon" of Revelation 17–18, riding on a seven-headed beast that calls to mind the seven hills on which Rome was founded and thus raises the specter of the papacy.

In terms of historical allegory, Una also represents the Reformed English Church and its most important defender, Queen Elizabeth; Red Cross stands for the Protestant faction in the English government; Duessa signifies the Catholic Church in England and its royal defender Mary Tudor; and Orgoglio stands for Mary's powerful consort, Philip II. Centrally concerned with the rebellions of the 1550s, in which Sir Thomas Wyatt and others rose up against Mary, Spenser portrays the Red Cross Knight as overwhelmed and tyrannized by Duessa and Orgoglio, and, like the English Protestants of the 1550s, he is rescued with the help of a woman. Learning of the knight's imprisonment from a dwarf and seeking to assist him, Una encounters Arthur and his squire Timias, and they undertake to come to his aid. It is notable that Una herself, representing Elizabeth, cannot conquer Duessa and Orgoglio. Like the Princess of Foxe's "Miraculous Preservation," she is no match for such powerful adversaries. Instead, the rescue is accomplished by the greatest of the ancient English heroes, Prince Arthur, who defeats Orgoglio, unseats Duessa from her Roman beast, releases Red Cross, and sends him off again to fight the dragon. In these actions, Arthur seems to represent the nation of England as a whole, throwing off the tyranny of the Pope and his allies, Philip and Mary, and welcoming the accession of a Protestant Queen.

Among the hopes and expectations that greeted Elizabeth as she exchanged the role of Princess for that of Queen, surely the most prominent were these: that she would settle the "matter of religion" and that, by marrying and bearing children, she would secure the Tudor succession and thereby the peace and stability of England itself. What hopes and expectations Elizabeth herself harbored, her subjects would come to know over the forty-five years of her reign.

THOMAS HEYWOOD

From If You Know Not Me, You Know Nobody, or the Troubles of Queen Elizabeth, Part One (1605)†

Enter SUSSEX *and* LORD CHAMBERLAIN.[1]
SUSSEX: Good morrow, my good Lord Chamberlain.
CHAMBERLAIN: Many good morrows to my good Lord of Sussex.
SUSSEX: Who's with the Queen, my lord?
CHAMBERLAIN: The Cardinal of Winchester, the Lord of Thame,
5   the good Lord Chandos; and besides, Lord Howard, Sir Henry
     Bedingfield,[2] and divers others.
SUSSEX: A word, my lord, in private.

Enter THAME *and* CHANDOS.
CHANDOS: Touching the Queen, my lord, who now sits high,
   What thinks the realm of Philip, th' Emperor's son,[3]
10   A marriage by the Council treated of?
THAME: Pray God 't prove well.
SUSSEX: Good morrow, lords.
THAME: Good morrow, my good Lord of Sussex.
CHANDOS: I cry° your honors' mercy.   beg
15   CHAMBERLAIN: Good morrow to the Lords of Thame and Chandos.
THAME: The like to you, my lord. As you were speaking.[4]

Enter LORD HOWARD *and* SIR HENRY BEDINGFIELD.
BEDINGFIELD: Concerning Wyatt and the Kentish rebels,
   Their overthrow is past, the rebel dukes that sought
   By all means to proclaim Queen Jane, chiefly Northumberland.[5]
20   For Guildford's sake, he forced his brother duke[6] unto that war,
   But each one had his merit.
HOWARD: O, my Lord,
   The law proceeded 'gainst their great offence,
   And 'tis not well, since they have suffered judgment,

---

† Copy text: Thomas Heywood, *If you know not me, You know no bodie; Or, The troubles of Queene Elizabeth* (London: Nathaniel Butter, 1605; STC 13328), A3r–C4v; D3v–D4r; E2v–F4r; G3r–G4r. Heywood closely follows John Foxe's account in *Acts and Monuments*.
1. Sir John Gage, Lord Chamberlain to Mary Tudor and also, according to Foxe, the Constable of the Tower of London; not to be confused with Master Gage, Elizabeth's servant; *Sussex*: Henry Radcliffe, second Earl of Sussex.
2. A staunch supporter of Mary and a member of Parliament; *Cardinal of Winchester*: Stephen Gardiner, Bishop of Winchester and Lord Chancellor to Mary Tudor, but never Cardinal; one of the chief villains of Foxe's and Heywood's accounts; *Lord of Thame*: Sir John Williams, first Baron Thame; *Lord Chandos*: Sir John Brydges, first Baron Chandos; Lieutenant of the Tower of London. *Lord Howard*: William, Lord Howard of Effingham, half-brother to Anne Boleyn's mother; Heywood conflates William with his son, Charles, who probably served at sea during the reign of Mary and became a trusted courtier to Elizabeth.
3. Philip II of Spain, who married Mary in July 1554.
4. Don't let us interrupt you.
5. John Dudley, Duke of Northumberland and father-in-law to Lady Jane Grey.
6. Henry Grey, Duke of Suffolk, father to Lady Jane Grey. *Guildford*: Guildford Dudley, son of John Dudley and husband to Lady Jane Grey.

25   That we should raise° this scandal, being dead: *resurrect*
      'Tis impious, not by true judgment bred.
    SUSSEX: Good morrow, my lord; good morrow, good Sir Henry.
    BEDINGFIELD: Pardon, my lord, I saw you not till now.
    CHAMBERLAIN: Good morrow, good Lord Howard.
30   HOWARD: Your honors. The like to you, my lords.
    THAME: With all my heart, Lord Howard.
    CHAMBERLAIN: Forward, I pray.
    SUSSEX: The Suffolk men,[7] my lord, was to the Queen
      The very stairs by which she did ascend;
35   She's greatly bound unto them for their loves.

        Enter Cardinal of WINCHESTER.
    WINCHESTER: Good morrow, lords. Attend the Queen into the
      presence.[8]
    SUSSEX: Your duties, lords.   *Exeunt omnes.*

        Enter THAME *bearing the purse,* CHANDOS *the mace,* HOWARD *the*
        scepter, SUSSEX *the crown, then the* QUEEN, *after her the Cardinal,*
        SENTLOW, GAGE,[9][*BEDINGFIELD], and attendants.*
    QUEEN: By God's assistance and the power of heaven,
      We are instated in our brother's[1] throne,
40   And all those powers that warred against our right,
      By help of heaven and your friendly aid,
      Dispersed and fled. Here we may sit secure.
      Our heart is joyful, lords, our peace is pure.

        Enter DODDS.[2]
    DODDS: I do beseech your Majesty peruse this poor petition.
45   QUEEN: O Master Dodds, we are indebted to you for your love.
      You stood us in great stead, even in our ebb
      Of fortune, when our hopes were near declined
      And when our state did bear the lowest sail,
      Which we have reason to requite, we know.
50   Read his petition, my good Lord Cardinal.
    DODDS: O gracious Sovereign, let my lord the Duke have the
      Perusing of it or any other that is near your Grace;
      He° will be to our suit an opposite.°   *Winchester / opponent*
    WINCHESTER: And reason,° fellow.   *with reason*
55   Madam, here is a large recital and upbraiding of your Highness's

---

7. During the short-lived Northumberland coup, Mary Tudor fled from Norfolk into Suffolk, where she raised a group of supporters.
8. The presence chamber, where the Queen received visitors.
9. The Lord Chamberlain and the Constable of the Tower, hereafter referred to as Constable or the Lord Constable; *Sentlow:* Sir William St. Loe, keeper of the horse to Edward VI and a supporter of Elizabeth.
1. Edward VI.
2. Foxe mentions Dodds merely as the owner of the house in which Elizabeth stays on her way to the Tower.

sovereignty. The Suffolk men, that lifted you to the throne and here
possessed[3] you, claim your promise you made them about religion.

DODDS: True, gracious Sovereign.

[*To* WINCHESTER] But that we do upbraid your Majesty

60   Or make recital of our deeds forepast
Other than conscience, honesty, and zeal,
By love, by faith, and by our duty bound
To you, the next and true successive heir—
If you contrary this,[4] I needs must say,

65   Your skilless° tongue doth make our well-tuned words   *unskilled*
Jar in the Princess' ears and of our text
You make a wrong construction. Gracious Queen,
Your humble subjects prostrate in my mouth
A general suit.[5] When we first flocked to you,

70   And made first head with you at Framlingham,[6]
'Twas thus concluded: that we, your liegemen,
Should still enjoy our consciences and use that faith°   *Protestantism*
Which in King Edward's days was held canonical.

WINCHESTER: May 't please your Highness note the commons'[7]
insolence:

75   They tie you to conditions and set limits to your liking.

QUEEN: They shall know
To whom their faithful duties thy do owe.
Since they, the limbs, the head would seek to sway,
Before they govern, they shall learn t' obey.

80   See it severely ordered, Winchester.

WINCHESTER: Away with him. It shall be thoroughly scanned,°   *examined*
And you upon the pillory three days to stand.   *Exit* DODDS.

BEDINGFIELD: Has not your sister, gracious Queen, a hand
In these petitions? Well your Highness knows

85   She is a favorite of these heretics.

WINCHESTER: And well remembered. Is 't not probable
That she in Wyatt's expedition
And other insurrection lately quelled
Was a confederate? If your Highness will your own estate preserve,

90   You must foresee fore-danger° and cut off all such   *danger beforehand*
As would your safety prejudice.°   *put in jeopardy*

BEDINGFIELD: Such is your sister,
A mere opposite to us in our opinion; and besides,
She's next successive,° should your Majesty   *heir apparent*

95   Die issueless, which heav'n defend.

OMNES: Which heav'n defend.

BEDINGFIELD: The state of our religion would decline.

---

3. Steadied.
4. If you twist our words to suggest that we are opposed to Queen Mary.
5. Offer a general request as if on bended knee.
6. Castle in Suffolk, where Mary gathered her forces and from which she marched to London on July
    24, 1553; *made first head*: gathered against the opposing force.
7. The common people.

QUEEN: My Lord of Thame and Chandos,
You two shall have a firm commission sealed
100   To fetch our sister, young Elizabeth,
From Ashridge[8] where she lies, and with a band
Of arméd soldiers to conduct her up to London,
Where we will hear her.[9]
SENTLOW: Gracious Queen, she only craves but to behold your face
105   That she might clear herself of all supposéd treasons,
Still protesting she is as true a subject to your Grace
As lives this day.
WINCHESTER: Do you not hear with what a saucy impudence
This Sentlow[1] here presumes?
110   QUEEN: Away with him. I'll teach him know his place,
To frown when we frown, smile on whom we grace.
WINCHESTER: 'Twill be a means to keep the rest in awe,
Making their Sovereign's brow to them a law.
QUEEN: All those that seek our sister's cause to favor,
115   Let them be lodged.[2]
WINCHESTER: Young Courtney, Earl of Devonshire,[3]
Seems chiefly to affect her faction.
QUEEN: Commit him to the Tower,
Till time affords us and our Council breathing space.
A horn within.
120   Whence is that post?°   *message*
QUEEN: Our secretary, unseal them and return
Us present answer of the contents.
[*She speaks to the Lord* CONSTABLE.]
What's the main business?
CONSTABLE: That Philip, Prince of Spain,
125   Son to the Emperor, is safely arrived
And landed at Southampton.
QUEEN: Prepare to meet him, lords, with all our pomp.
HOWARD: Prepare you, lords, with our fair Queen to ride,
And his high princely state let no man hide.
130   QUEEN: Set forward, lords. This sudden news is sweet;
Two royal lovers on the midway meet.   *Exeunt* OMNES.

Enter Master GAGE[4] *and a* GENTLEWOMAN.
GAGE: Good morrow, Mistress. Came you from the Princess?
WOMAN: Master Gage, I did.

---

8. Royal estate in Hertfordshire and one of Elizabeth's childhood homes.
9. In Foxe, those who are sent to fetch Elizabeth are Sir Richard Southwell, Sir John Williams, Sir Edward Hastings, master of the horse, and Sir Thomas Cornwallis, along with 250 horsemen.
1. With a pun on his name: one who is lowly sent.
2. In the Tower of London.
3. Edward Courtenay, Earl of Devonshire and great grandson of Edward IV, released from the Tower in 1553 by Mary and briefly considered as a potential husband, but reimprisoned after involving himself in the Wyatt rebellion.
4. This sympathetic attendant is a creation of Heywood; the Master Gage in Foxe's account who accompanies Elizabeth is a gentleman usher, or chamberlain, to Queen Mary.

GAGE: How fares her Grace?

135   WOMAN: O wondrous crazy,° gentle Master Gage.   *very ill*
Her sleeps are all unquiet and her head
Beats and grows giddy with continual grief.

GAGE: God grant her comfort and release her pain;
So good a lady few on earth remain.

Enter the CLOWN.

140   CLOWN: O arm, arm, arm.

GAGE: How now, what's the matter?

CLOWN: O Lord the house is beset; soldiers are as hot as fire,
Are ready to enter every hole about the house.
For as I was a' th' top of the stack,° the sound of the drum   *of firewood*

145   Hot° me such a box a' th' ear, that I came tumbing down   *Hit*
The stack with a thousand billets° a' th' top on me.   *pieces of wood*
Look about and help, for God's sake.

GAGE: Heaven guard the Princess; grant that all be well.
This drum, I fear, will prove her passing-bell.°   *death knell*

Enter THAME *and* CHANDOS, *with soldiers, drum, etc.*

150   THAME: Where's the Princess?

GAGE: O my honored lords,
(May I with reverence presume to ask)
What means these arms? Why do you thus begirt
A poor weak lady, near at point of death?

155   CHANDOS: Resolve° the Princess; we must speak with her.   *Inform*

WOMAN: My lords, know there is no admittance to her presence
Without the leave first granted from herself.

THAME: Go tell her we must and will.

WOMAN: I'll certify so much.   *Exit Woman.*

160   GAGE: My lords, as you are honorably born,
As you did love her father or her brother,
As you do owe allegiance to the Queen,
In pity of her weakness and low state,
With best of favor her commiserate.

Enter WOMAN.

165   WOMAN: Her Grace entreats you but to stay till morn,
And then your message shall be heard at full.

CHANDOS: 'Tis from the Queen, and we will speak with her.

WOMAN: I'll certify so much.

THAME: It shall not need. Press after her, my lord.

Enter ELIZABETH *in her bed, Doctor* OWEN, *and Doctor* WENDY.⁵

170   ELIZABETH: We are not pleased with your intrusions, lords.
Is your haste such or your affairs so urgent
That suddenly, and at this time of night,
You press on me and will not stay till morn?

---

5. George Owen and Thomas Wendy, royal physicians to Mary Tudor.

THAME: Sorry we are, sweet Lady, to behold you in this sad plight.
175 ELIZABETH: And I, my lords, not glad.
      [*aside*] My heart, O how it beats.
      CHANDOS: Madam, our message and our duty from our Queen
      We come to tender to you. It is her pleasure
      That you the seventh day of this month appear at Westminster.
180 ELIZABETH: At Westminster? My Lords, no soul more glad than I
      To do my duty to her Majesty;
      But I am sorry° at the heart. My heart. O, good   *unwell*
        doctor, raise me.
      O, my heart. I hope, my lords, considering my extremity and
      Weakness, you will dispense a little with your haste.
185 THAME: Doctor Owen and Doctor Wendy,
      You are the Queen's physicians, truly sworn
      On your allegiance, as before her Highness you will answer it.
      Speak. May the Princess be removed with life?
      OWEN: Not without danger, lords, yet without death.
190   Her fever is not mortal; yet you see into what danger
      It hath brought the Princess.
      CHANDOS: Is your opinion so?
      WENDY: My judgment is not deadly, but yet dangerous.
      No sooner shall she come to take the air
195   But she will faint, and, if not well prepared and attended,
      Her life is in much danger.
      THAME: Madam, we take no pleasure to deliver
      So strict a message.
      ELIZABETH: Nor I, my Lords, to hear a message delivered
200   With such strictness. Well, must I go?
      CHANDOS: So says the Queen.
      ELIZABETH: Why then, it must be so.
      THAME: Tomorrow early then you must prepare.
      ELIZABETH: [*aside*] 'Tis many a morrow since my feeble legs
205   Felt this my body's weight; O, I shall faint,
      And if I taste the rawness of the air,
      I am but dead; indeed, I am but dead.
      [*to all*] 'Tis late; conduct these lords unto their chambers
      And cheer them well, for they have journeyed hard,
210   Whilst we prepare us for our morrow's journey.
      CHANDOS: Madam, the Queen hath sent her letter for you.
      ELIZABETH: The Queen is kind, and we will strive with death
      To tender° her our life.   *offer*
      We are her subject and obey her hest.°   *command*
215   Good night. We wish you what we want,°   *lack*
      Good rest.   *Exeunt omnes.*

          Enter QUEEN MARY, PHILIP, *and all the nobles but*
          THAME *and* CHANDOS.
      QUEEN: Thus, in the face of heaven and broad
        eye of all the multitude,
      We give a welcome to the Spanish Prince.

Those plausive° shouts which give you
    entertain°   *applauding / entertainment*
220 Echoes as much to the Almighty's ears,
And there they sound with pleasure and excels
The clamorous trumpets and loud ringing bells.
PHILIP: Thrice excellent and ever gracious Princess,
Doubly famous for virtue and for beauty,
225 We embrace your large-stretched honors with
    the arms of love.
Our royal marriage, treated° first in heaven,   *arranged*
To be solemnized here, both by God's voice
And by our loves' consent, we thus embrace.
Now Spain and England, two populous kingdoms
230 That have a long time been opposed
In hostile emulation,° shall be at one.   *rivalry*
This shall be Spanish England, ours English Spain.
QUEEN: Hark the redoubling echoes of the people.   *Flourish.*
How it proclaims their loves and welcome to this union.
235 PHILIP: Then here before the pillars of the land
We do embrace and make a public contract.
Our souls are joyful. Then bright heavens smile
Whilst we proclaim our new-united style.°   *list of royal titles*
QUEEN: Read, Sussex.
240 SUSSEX: [*reads*] Philip and Mary, by the grace
    of God King and Queen of England, Spain,
    France, and Ireland; King and Queen of
    Naples, Sicily, Lyon, and Aragon; Arch-Duke
    and Duchess of Austria, Burgundy, of Brabant,
245   Zeeland, of Holland; Prince and Princess of
    Sweave; Count and Countess of Habsburg,
    Majorca, Sardinia, of the firm land and the
    main ocean sea; Palatines of Jerusalem, of
    Hainault; Lord and Lady of Friesland, and
250   of the Isles; and Governor and Governess of
    all Africa and Asia.[6]
OMNES: Long live the King and Queen!   *Flourish.*
KING AND QUEEN: We thank you all.
CONSTABLE: When please your Highnesses to
    solemnize this your nuptials?
255 QUEEN: The twenty-fifth day of this month, July.
PHILIP: It likes us well. But, royal Queen, we want°   *lack*
One lady at this high solemnity.
We have a sister called Elizabeth,
Whose virtues and endowments of the mind
260 Hath filled the ears of Spain.

---

6. Heywood's list of titles is more grandiose than that given by Foxe and is probably meant to mock
Mary's pretensions. England, at this date, could not hope to match the extent of Spain's growing
empire; *Brabant*: a province in the Low Countries; *Sweave*: an uncertain location, perhaps Sweden;
Palatines: title equivalent to that of Earl or Count; *Hainault*: Flemish province; *Friesland*: northern
province of the Netherlands; *the isles*: islands located near and belonging to the Netherlands.

WINCHESTER: Great are the causes, now too long to say,
  Why she, my Sovereign, should be kept away.
CONSTABLE: The Lord of Thame and Chandos are returned.

Enter THAME *and* CHANDOS *and* GAGE.

QUEEN: How fares our sister? Is she come along?
265 THAME: We found the Princess sick and in great danger,
  Yet did we urge our strict commission.
  She much entreated that she might be spared
  Until her health and strength might be restored.
CHANDOS: Two of your Highness' doctors we then called
270 And charged them, as they would answer it,
  To tell the truth, if that our journey's toil
  Might be no prejudice unto her life
  Or if we might with safety bring her thence.
  They answered that we might; we did so.
275 Here she is to do her duty to your Majesty.
QUEEN: Let her attend; we will find time to hear her.
PHILIP: But royal Queen, yet for her virtue's sake,
  Deem her offences, if she have offended,
  With all the lenity a sister can.
280 QUEEN: My Lord of Winchester, my Lord of Sussex,
  Lord Howard, Thame, and Chandos,
  Take you commission to examine her
  Of all supposéd crimes. So to our nuptials.
PHILIP: What festival more royal hath been seen
285 Than twixt Spain's Prince and England's royal Queen?   *Exeunt.*

Enter ELIZABETH, *her* GENTLEWOMAN, *and three household servants.*

ELIZABETH: Is not my gentleman usher° yet returned?   chamberlain
WOMAN: Madam, not yet.
ELIZABETH: O God, my fear hath been good physic,°   medicine
  But the Queen's displeasure, that hath cured my body's
    imperfection,
290 Hath made me heart sick, brain sick, and sick even to death.
  What are you?
FIRST SERVANT: Your household officers and humble servants,
  Who, now your house, fair Princess, is dissolved
  And quite broke up, come to attend your Grace.
295 ELIZABETH: We thank you and am more indebted for your loves
  Than we have power or virtue to requite.
  Alas, I am all the Queen's, yet nothing of myself.
  But God and innocence, be you my patrons and defend
    my cause.
  Why weep you, gentlemen?
300 COOKS: Not for ourselves; men are not made to weep
  At their own fortunes. Our eyes are made of fire,
  And to extract water from fire is hard.
  Nothing but such a Princess' grief as yours,
  So good a lady and so beautiful, so absolute a mistress

305	And perfect as you have delivered° been,	*reported*
	Have power to do 't: your sorrow makes us sad.	

ELIZABETH: My innocence yet makes my heart as light
As my front's° heavy. All that heaven sends is welcome.   *face is*
Gentlemen, divide these few crowns amongst you.
310 I am now a prisoner and shall want nothing.
I have some friends about her Majesty
That are providing for me all things, all things,
Aye, even my grave, and being possessed of that,
I shall need nothing. Weep not, I pray.
315 Rather you should rejoice;
If I miscarry in this enterprise and ask you° why,   *you ask*
A virgin and a martyr both I die.

     Enter GAGE.

GAGE: He that first gave you life protect that life
From those that wish your death.
320 ELIZABETH: What's my offence?[7] Who be my accusers?
GAGE: Madam, that the Queen and Winchester best knows.
ELIZABETH: What says the Queen unto my late petition?
GAGE: You are denied that grace;
Her Majesty will not admit you conference.
325 Sir William Sentlow, urging that motion,
Was first committed,° since sent to the Tower.   *imprisoned*
Madam, in brief, your foes are the Queen's friends,
Your friends her foes.
Six of the Council are this day appointed
330 To examine you of certain articles.
ELIZABETH: They shall be welcome. My God, in whom I trust,
Will help, deliver, save, defend the just.

     Enter WINCHESTER, SUSSEX, HOWARD, THAME, CHANDOS, *and* CONSTABLE.

SUSSEX: All forbear this place unless° the Princess.   *except*
WINCHESTER: Madam, we from the Queen are joined in
    full commission
    They sit; she kneels.
335 SUSSEX: By your favor, good my lord, ere you proceed.
Madam, although this place doth tie you to this reverence,
It becomes not you, being a Princess, to deject° your knee.   *bend down*
A chair there.
ELIZABETH: My duty with my fortunes do agree,
340 And to the Queen in you I bend my knee.
SUSSEX: You shall not kneel where Sussex sits in place.
The chamber keeper, a chair there for her Grace.
WINCHESTER: Madam, perhaps you censure hardly°   *strenuously*
That° was enforced in this commission.   *That which*
345 ELIZABETH: Know you your own guilt, my good Lord Chancellor,
That you accuse yourself? I think not so.

---

7. Copy text: My of offence.

I am of this mind: no man is my foe.

WINCHESTER: Madam, I would you would submit unto her Highness.

ELIZABETH: Submit, my Lord of Winchester? 'Tis fit

350   That none but base offenders should submit.

No, no, my lord, I easily spy your drift.

Having nothing whereon you can accuse me,

Do seek to have myself myself betray;

So by myself my own blood should be spilt.

355   Confess submission, I confess a guilt.

THAME: What answer you to Wyatt's late rebellion?

Madam, 'tis thought that you did set them on.

ELIZABETH: Who is 't will say so? Men may much suspect,

But yet, my lord, none can my life detect.

360   I, a confederate with those Kentish rebels?

If I e're saw or sent to them, let the Queen take my head.

Hath not proud Wyatt suffered for his offence?

And in the purging both of soul and body for heaven,

Did Wyatt then accuse Elizabeth?

365   SUSSEX: Madam, he did not.

ELIZABETH: My reverent lord, I know it.

HOWARD: Madam, he would not.

ELIZABETH: O my good lord, he could not.[8]

SUSSEX: The same day Frogmorton[9] was arraigned in the
        Guildhall,

370   It was imposed on him, whether this Princess had a hand

With him or no; he did deny it,

Cleared her fore° his death, yet accused others.°   *before*

ELIZABETH: My God be praised. This is news but of a minute old.

CHANDOS: What answer you to Sir Peter Carew[1] in the west,

375   The western rebels?

ELIZABETH: Ask the unborn infant, see what that will answer,

For that and I are both alike in guilt.

Let not by rigor innocent blood be spilt.

WINCHESTER: Come, Madam, answer briefly to these treasons.

380   ELIZABETH: Treason, Lords? If it be treason to be the daughter

To th' eighth Henry, sister to Edward, and the next of blood unto

My gracious Sovereign, now the Queen, I am a traitor. If not, I

Spit at treason. In Henry's reign, this law could not have stood.

O God, that we should suffer for our blood.

385   CONSTABLE: Madam, the Queen must hear you sing another song,

Before you part with us.

ELIZABETH: My God doth know, I can° no note but truth,   *can speak*

That with heaven's King

One day in choirs of angels I shall sing.

---

8. In Foxe, Wyatt clears both Elizabeth and Edward Courtenay of any involvement in the Rebellion.

9. Frogmorton appears to be a reference to Sir Nicholas Throckmorton, one of the conspirators in the Wyatt Rebellion, who was arraigned on April 17, 1554; he was, however, acquitted.

1. Another conspirator from Devonshire, who had aided Edward VI in putting down the Prayerbook Rebellion in 1549, when English men and women protested the new Book of Common Prayer.

390 WINCHESTER: Then, Madam, you'll not submit?
ELIZABETH: My life I will, but not as guilty.
  My lords, let pale offenders pardon crave;
  If we offend, law's rigor let us have.
WINCHESTER: You are stubborn. Come, let's certify
    the Queen.
395 THAME: Room for the Lords, there. *Exeunt Council.*
ELIZABETH: Thou Power Eternal, innocence's just guide
  That sways the scepter of all monarchies,
  Protect the guiltless from these ravening jaws
  That hideous death presents by tyrant's laws.
400 And as my heart is known to Thee most pure,
  Grant me release or patience to endure.

    Enter GAGE *and* SERVANTS.
GAGE: Madam, we your poor humble servants
  Made bold to press into your Grace's presence
  To know how your cause goes.
405 ELIZABETH: Well, well, I thank my God, well.
  How can a cause go ill with innocence?
  They that to whom wrongs in this world are done
  Shall be rewarded in the world to come.

    Enter the six Councilors.
WINCHESTER: It is the pleasure of her Majesty
410 That you be straight committed to the Tower.
ELIZABETH: The Tower? For what?
WINCHESTER: Moreover, all your household servants we have
    discharged,
  Except this gentleman, your usher, and this gentlewoman.
  Thus did the Queen command,
415 And for your guard, an hundred northern whitecoats
  Are appointed to conduct you thither.
  Tonight unto your chamber; tomorrow early prepare
  You for the Tower. Your barge stands ready
  To conduct you thither. *She kneels.*
420 ELIZABETH: O God, my heart. A prisoner in the Tower?
  Speak to the Queen, my lords, that some other place
  May lodge her sister. That's too vile, too base.
SUSSEX: Come, my lords, let's all join in one petition
  To the Queen that she may not be lodged within the Tower.
425 WINCHESTER: My lord, you know it is in vain,
  For the Queen's sentence is definitive,
  And we must see 't performed.
ELIZABETH: Then to our chamber, comfortless and sad.
  Tomorrow to the Tower, that fatal place,
430 Where I shall never behold the sun's bright face.
SUSSEX: Now God forbid; a better hap° heaven send.   *fortune*
  Thus men may mourn for what they cannot mend.
    Exeunt OMNES.

Enter three whitecoat soldiers with a jack° of beer.   *leather jug*

ONE: Come, my masters, you know your charge. 'Tis now
         About eleven; here we must watch till morning
435   And then carry the Princess to the Tower.
TWO: How shall we spend the time till morning?
THREE: Mass,° we'll drink and talk of our friends.   *By the mass*
TWO: Aye. But, my friend, do not talk of state matters.²
ONE: Not I. I'll not meddle with the state.
440   I hope this a man may say without offence.
         Prithee drink to me.
THREE: With all my hearty faith, this a man might
         Lawfully speak. But now, faith, what wast about to say?
ONE: Mass, I say this: that the Lady Elizabeth is both a lady
445   And Elizabeth, and if I should say she were a virtuous Princess,
         Were there any harm in that?
TWO: No, by my troth, there's no harm in that.
         But beware of talking of the Princess.
         Let's meddle with our kindred; there we may be bold.
450 ONE: Well, sirs, I have two sisters, and the one loves the other
         And would not send her to prison for a million. Is there any harm
         In this? I'll keep myself within compass,° I warrant you,   *proper limits*
         For I do not talk of the Queen; I talk of my sisters.
         I'll keep myself within my compass, I warrant you.
455 THREE: Aye. But sir, that word "sister" goes hardly° down.   *boldly*
ONE: Why, sir, I hope a man may be bold with his own.
         I learned that of the Queen. I'll keep myself within compass,
         I'll warrant you.
TWO: Aye. But sir, why is the Princess committed?
460 ONE: It may be she doth not know herself.
         It may be the Queen knows not the cause.
         It may be my Lord of Winchester does not know.
         It may be so; nothing's unpossible to God.
         It may be there's knavery in monkery:³
465   There's nothing unpossible. Is there any harm in that?
TWO: Shoemaker, you go a little beyond your last.°   *pattern*
ONE: Why, in saying nothing's unpossible to God?
         I'll stand to it. For saying a truth's a truth, I'll prove it.
         For saying there may be knavery in monkery, I'll justify it.
470   I do not say there is, but may be. I know what I know,
         You know what you know, he knows what he knows,
         Marry, we know not what every man knows.
THREE:⁴   My masters, we have talked so long that I think 'tis day.
ONE: I think so, too. Is there any harm in all this?
475 TWO: No harm i' th' world.
THREE: And I think by this time the Princess is ready
         To take her barge.
ONE: Come then, let's go. Would all were well.

---

2. The soldiers are cautious, since speaking ill of the monarch was a punishable offense.
3. Mischief among the monks.
4. Copy text: *Two.*

Is there any harm in all this? But, alas, wishes and tears
480   Have both one property: they show their love that
Want the remedy.[5]   *Exeunt omnes.*

Enter WINCHESTER *and* BEDINGFIELD.

WINCHESTER: Did you not mark what a piteous eye she cast
To the Queen's window as she passed along?
Fain she would have stayed but that I caused
485   The bargemen to make haste and row away.
BEDINGFIELD: The bargemen were too desperate,° my lord,   *careless*
In staying° till the water was so low;   *waiting*
For then, you know, being underneath the bridge,
The barge's stern did strike upon the ground,
490   And was in danger to have drowned us all.
WINCHESTER: Well she hath 'scaped that danger.
Would she but conform herself in her opinion,
She only might rely upon my love
To win her to the favor of the Queen.
495   BEDINGFIELD: But that will never be. This is my censure:°   *judgment*
If she be guilty in the least degree,
May all her wrongs survive and light on her;
If other ways, that she be cleared.
Thus, both ways I wish her down,
500   Or else her state to raise.

Enter SUSSEX, THAME, HOWARD, CHANDOS, *and* GAGE.

SUSSEX: Why doth the Princess keep° her barge so long?   *keep to*
Why lands she not? Someone go see the cause.
GAGE: That shall be my charge, my lord.   *Exit Gage.*
SUSSEX: O me, my lords, her state is wondrous hard.
505   I have seen the day my hand I'd not have lent
To bring my Sovereign's sister to the Tower.
Good my lords, stretch your commission
To do this Princess but some little favor.
CHANDOS: My lord, my lord, let not the love we bear the
510   Princess incur the Queen's displeasure. 'Tis no dallying with
matters of estate. Who dares gainsay the Queen?
SUSSEX: Marry, a° God, not I; no, no, not I.   *to*
Yet who shall hinder these my eyes to sorrow
For her sorrow? By God's marry dear,[6]
515   That the Queen could not, though herself were here.
My lords, my lords, if it were held foul treason
To grieve for her hard usage, by my soul,
My eyes would hardly prove me a true subject.
But 'tis the Queen's pleasure, and we must obey;
520   But I shall mourn, should King and Queen say nay.

---

5. Wishes and tears are alike in that they cannot help the one who is loved.
6. True beloved, with a pun on "Mary dear" and possibly a pun on "deer."

Enter GAGE.

GAGE: My grievéd mistress humbly thus entreats
    For to remove back to the common stairs
    And not to land where traitors put to shore.[7]
    Some difference she entreats your honors make
525   'Twixt crystal fountains and foul, muddy springs,
    'Twixt those that are condemned by the law
    And those whom treason's stain did never blemish.
    Thus she attends your answer and sits still,
    Whilst her wet eyes full many a tear did spill.
530 SUSSEX: Marry, a God, 'tis true, and 'tis no reason. Launch,
    bargeman.
    Good lady land where traitors use to land
    And 'fore her guilt be proved? God's marry, no,
    And° the Queen wills it, that it should be so.   *Even if*
CHANDOS: My Lord, you must look into our commission.
535 No favor's granted; she of force must land.
    'Tis a decree which we cannot withstand.
    So tell her, Master Gage.   *Exit* GAGE.
SUSSEX: As good a lady as e're England bred;
    Would he that caused this woe had lost his head.

Enter GAGE, ELIZABETH, *and* CLARENTIA,[8] *her gentlewoman.*
540 GAGE: Madam, you have stepped too short into the water.
ELIZABETH: No matter where I tread.
    Would where I set my foot there lay my head.
    Land traitor-like? My foot's wet in the flood;
    So shall my heart ere long be drenched in blood.

Enter CONSTABLE.
545 WINCHESTER: Here comes the Constable of the Tower.
    This is your charge.
CONSTABLE: And I receive my prisoner. Come, will you go?
ELIZABETH: Whither, my lord? Unto a grate of iron,
    Where grief and care my poor heart shall environ?
550 I am not well.
SUSSEX: A chair for the Princess.
CONSTABLE: Here's no chair for prisoners.
    Come, will you see your chamber?
ELIZABETH: Then on this stone, this cold stone, I will sit.
555 I needs must say you hardly° me entreat,   *harshly*
    When for a chair this hard stone is my seat.
SUSSEX: My lord, you deal too cruelly with the Princess.
    You knew her father; she's no stranger to you.
THAME: Madam, it rains.
560 SUSSEX: Good lady, take my cloak.
ELIZABETH: No, let it alone. See, gentlemen,
    The piteous heavens weep tears into my bosom.

---

7. Traitor's gate extends directly into the Thames.
8. Susan White Clarenceux, mistress of the robes to Queen Mary; Heywood transposes her into an
    attendant sympathetic to Elizabeth.

On this cold stone I sit, rain in my face,
But better here than in a worser place
565 Where this bad man will lead me.
Clarentia, reach my book. Now lead me where you please;
From° sight of day, or in a dungeon, I shall see to pray.   *Away from*

Exit ELIZABETH, GAGE, CLARENTIA, *and* CONSTABLE.
SUSSEX: Nay, nay, you need not bolt and lock so fast;
She is no starter.° Honorable lords,   *escapee*
570 Speak to the Queen she may have some release.

* * *

[The play next portrays Elizabeth's days in the Tower, then turns to her release
and her period of house arrest at Woodstock.]

Enter WINCHESTER, BEDINGFIELD, *and* THAME.
WINCHESTER: Madam, the Queen, out of her royal bounty,
Hath freed you from the thralldom of the Tower,
And now this gentleman must be your guardian.[9]
ELIZABETH: I thank her. She hath rid me of a tyrant.°   *the Constable*
575 Is he° appointed now to be my keeper?   *Bedingfield*
What is he, lords?
THAME: A gentleman in favor with the Queen.
ELIZABETH: It seems so, by his charge. But tell me, Gage,
Is yet the scaffold standing on Tower Hill,
580 Whereon young Guildford and the Lady Jane did suffer death?[1]
GAGE: Upon my life, it stands not.
ELIZABETH: Lord Howard, what is he?
HOWARD: A gentleman, though of a stern aspect,
Yet mild enough I hope your Grace will find.
585 ELIZABETH: Hath he not, think you, a stretch° conscience,   *lax*
And if my secret murder should be put into his hands,
Hath he not heart, think you, to execute?
HOWARD: Defend it, heaven, and God's almighty hand
Betwixt your Grace and such intendments stand.
590 BEDINGFIELD: Come Madam; will you go?
ELIZABETH: With all my heart. Farewell, farewell,
I am freed from limbo to be sent to hell.   *Exeunt* OMNES.

* * *

[As Elizabeth travels to Woodstock, the common people speak of her goodness,
but having arrived at the decrepit royal estate, she fears murder.]

Enter ELIZABETH, BEDINGFIELD, CLARENTIA, THAME, GAGE, *and* BARWICK.[2]
ELIZABETH: What fearful terror doth assail my heart?
Good Gage, come hither and resolve me true
595 In thy opinion. Shall I outlive this night?

9. Bedingfield will take Elizabeth to the house at Woodstock.
1. Although Guildford was executed on Tower Hill, Lady Jane Grey's death occurred within the
   precincts of the Tower itself.
2. A serving man to Sir Henry Bedingfield.

I prithee, speak.

GAGE: Outlive this night? I pray Madam, why?

ELIZABETH: Then to be plain, this night I look to die.

GAGE: O, Madam, you were born to better fortunes.

600   That God that made you will protect you still
From all your enemies that wish you ill.

ELIZABETH: My heart is fearful.

GAGE: O my honored lord,
As ever you were noble in your thoughts,

605   Speak, shall my lady outlive this night or no?

THAME: You much amaze me, sir, else heav'n forefend.

GAGE: For if we should imagine any plot
Pretending to the hurt of our dear mistress,
I and my fellows, though far unable are

610   To stand against your power, will die together.

THAME: And I with you would spend my dearest blood
To do that virtuous lady any good.
Sir Harry, now my charge I must resign.
The lady's wholly in your custody;

615   Yet use her kindly as she well deserves,
And so I take my leave. Madam, adieu.   *Exit* THAME.

ELIZABETH: My honored lord, farewell. Unwilling I
With grief and woe must continue.
Help me to some ink and paper, good Sir Harry.

620   BEDINGFIELD: What to do, Madam?

ELIZABETH: To write a letter to the Queen, my sister.

BEDINGFIELD: I find not that in my commission.

ELIZABETH: Good jailor, urge not thy commission.

BEDINGFIELD: No jailor, but your guardian, Madam.

625   ELIZABETH: Then reach me pen and ink.

BEDINGFIELD: Madam, I dare not; my commission serves not.

ELIZABETH: Thus have you driven me off, from time to time,
Still urging me with your commission.
Good jailor, be not so severe.

630   BEDINGFIELD: Good Madam, I entreat you, lose that name
Of jailor; 'twill be a by-word to me and my posterity.

ELIZABETH: As often as you name your commission,
So often will I call you jailor.

BEDINGFIELD: Say I should reach you pen, ink, and paper,

635   Who is 't dare bear a letter sent from you?

ELIZABETH: I do not keep a servant so dishonest°   *dishonorable*
That would deny me that.

BEDINGFIELD: Whoever dares, none shall.

GAGE: Madam, impose the letter to my trust.

640   Were I to bear it through a field of pikes,
And in my way ten thousand arméd men ambushed,
I'd make my passage through the midst of them
And perforce bear it to the Queen your sister.

BEDINGFIELD: Body³ of me, what a bold knave's this?

---

3. Copy text: baddy.

645   ELIZABETH: Gage, leave me to myself.
      [*Prays*] Thou ever living Power, that givest all hearts,
      Give to my pen a true persuasive style
      That it may move my impatient sister's ears
      And urge her to compassionate my woe.   *She writes.*

      BEDINGFIELD *takes a book and looks into it.*
650   BEDINGFIELD: What has she written here?   *He reads.*
      "Much suspected by me, nothing proved can be,
      Finis, quoth Elizabeth the prisoner."[4]
      Pray God it prove so. Soft what book 's this?
      Marry a God! What's here, an English Bible?[5]
655   *Sanctum Maria,*[6] pardon this profanation of my heart.
      Water, Barwick, water. I'll meddle with 't no more.
      ELIZABETH: My heart is heavy and my eye[7] doth close.
      I am weary of writing, sleepy on the sudden.
      Clarentia, leave me and command some music
660   In the withdrawing chamber.   *She sleeps.*
      BEDINGFIELD: Your letter shall be forthcoming, lady.
      I will peruse it e're it 'scape me now.   *Exit* BEDINGFIELD.

                      A Dumb Show.

      Enter WINCHESTER, CONSTABLE, BARWICK, *and friars. At the other
      door, two angels. The friar steps to her, offering to kill her; the angels
      drives them back. Exeunt. The angel opens the Bible and puts it in her
      hand as she sleeps. Exeunt angels. She wakes.*
      ELIZABETH: O God, how pleasant was this sleep to me.
      Clarentia, saw'st thou nothing?
665   CLARENTIA: Madam, not I.
      I ne'er slept soundlier for the time.
      ELIZABETH: Nor heardest thou nothing?
      CLARENTIA: Neither, Madam.
      ELIZABETH: Didst thou not put this book into my hand?
670   CLARENTIA: Madam, not I.
      ELIZABETH: Then 'twas by inspiration. Heaven, I trust,
      With His eternal hand will guide the just.
      What chapter's this? "Whoso putteth his trust in the Lord
      Shall not be confounded."[8]
675   My Savior, thanks; on Thee my hope I build.
      Thou lovest poor innocents and art their shield.

      Enter BEDINGFIELD *and* GAGE.

4. In Foxe, this poem is inscribed on a glass window with a diamond (1583, p. 2096).
5. Although English Bibles were no longer illegal, use of a vernacular, rather than Latin, Bible was a
   mark of Protestants throughout the first half of the century. This incident is Heywood's invention,
   as is Elizabeth's dream in the next scene.
6. The ungrammatical Latin invocation to the Virgin Mary marks Bedingfield as an unintelligent
   Roman Catholic.
7. Copy text: heart.
8. Psalm 22.5; the entire Psalm is a plea for protection against surrounding enemies.

BEDINGFIELD: Here have you writ a long excuse, it seems,
  But no submission to the Queen, your sister.
ELIZABETH: Should they submit that never wrought offence?
680 The law will always quit° wronged innocence.   *acquit*
  Gage, take my letter. To the lords commend my humble duty.
GAGE: Madam, I fly
  To give this letter to her Majesty,
  Hoping, when I return,
685 To give you comfort that now sadly mourn.

      Exeunt omnes, praeter° BEDINGFIELD.   *except*
BEDINGFIELD: Aye, do write and send. I'll cross you still.
  She shall not speak to any man alive,
  But I'll o'erhear her. No letter nor no token
  Shall ever have access unto her hands
690 But first I'll see it.
  So like a subject to my Sovereign's state,
  I will pursue her with my deadly hate.

      Enter CLOWN.
CLOWN: O, Sir Harry, you look well to your office.
  Yonder's one in the garden with the Princess.
695 BEDINGFIELD: How, knave, with the Princess? She parted even now.
CLOWN: Aye sir, that's all one, but she no sooner came into the
  Garden, but he leapt o're the wall, and there
  They are together busy in talk, sir.
BEDINGFIELD: Here's for thy pains; thou art an honest fellow.
700 Go, take a guard and apprehend them straight.   *Exit* CLOWN.
  Bring them before me. O this was well found out.
  Now will the Queen commend my diligent care
  And praise me for my service to her Grace.
  Ha, traitors swarm so near about my house?
705 'Tis time to look into 't.
  O well said, Barwick,
  Where's the prisoner?

      Enter CLOWN, BARWICK, *and soldiers, leading of
      a goat, his° sword drawn.*   *Barwick's*
CLOWN: Here he is in a string, my lord.
BEDINGFIELD: Lord bless us, knave, what hast thou there?
710 CLOWN: This is he I told you was busy in talk with the Princess.
  What a° did there, you must get out of him by examination.   *he*
BEDINGFIELD: Why, knave, this is a beast.
CLOWN: So may your worship be, for any thing that I know.
BEDINGFIELD: What art thou, knave?
715 CLOWN: If your worship⁹ does not remember me,
  I hope your worship's crupper¹ doth.
  But if you have anything to say to this honest fellow,

─────────────────────────────

9. Copy text: you worship.
1. Buttocks. The clown has been abusing Bedingfield behind his back.

Who for his gray head and reverent beard is so like,
He may be akin to you.
720 BEDINGFIELD: Akin to me? Knave, I'll have thee whipped.
CLOWN: Then your worship will cry quittance with my
Posteriors for misusing of yours.[2]
BEDINGFIELD: Nay, but dost thou flout me still?   *He beats him. Exeunt.*

Enter WINCHESTER, GRESHAM *with paper;* CONSTABLE *with a pursevant.*[3]
GRESHAM: I pray your honor to regard my haste.
725 WINCHESTER: I know your business, and your haste shall stay.
As you were speaking, my Lord Constable.
CONSTABLE: Whenas the King shall come to seal these writs.
GRESHAM: My lord, you know His Highness's treasure stays°   *is delayed*
And cannot be transported this three months
730 Unless that now your honor seal my warrant.
WINCHESTER: Fellow, what then? This warrant that concerns
The Princess' death shuffle amongst the rest.
He'll ne'er peruse 't.
GRESHAM: [*aside*] How, the Princess' death? Thanks, heaven,
735 By whom I am made a willing instrument her life to save
That may live crowned when thou art in thy grave.   *Exit* GRESHAM.
WINCHESTER: Stand ready, pursevant,
That when 'tis signed
Thou mayest be gone and gallop with the wind.

Enter PHILIP, SUSSEX, *and* GAGE.
740 PHILIP: Our Chancellor, lords. This is our sealing day,
This our state's business. Is our signet there?

Enter HOWARD *and* GRESHAM *as he is sealing.*
HOWARD: Stay your imperial hand! Let not your seal imprint
Death's impress in your sister's heart.
PHILIP: Our sister's heart? Lord Howard, what means this?
745 HOWARD: The Chancellor and that injurious Lord
Can well expound the meaning.
WINCHESTER: [*aside*] O chance accursed. How came he by this notice?
Her life is guarded by the hand of heaven,
And we in vain pursue it.
750 PHILIP: Lord Chancellor, your dealing is not fair.
See, lords, what writs affords itself
To the impress of our seal.
SUSSEX: See, my lord, a warrant for the Princess' death
Before she be convicted. What juggling call you this?
755 See, see for God's sake.
GAGE: And a pursevant, ready to post away with it,
To see it done with speed.
What flinty breast could brook to see her bleed?
PHILIP: Lord Chancellor, out of our prerogative

---

2. Then we'll be even; you'll whip my ass for having made an ass of you.
3. One who serves warrants. *Gresham:* Sir Thomas Gresham, chief financial officer to Mary Tudor
   and later founder of the Royal Exchange.

760   We will make bold to interline[4] your warrant.

SUSSEX: Whose plot was this?

HOWARD: The Chancellor's and my Lord Constable's.

SUSSEX: How was 't revealed?

HOWARD: By this gentleman, Master Gresham, the King's agent here.

765   SUSSEX: He hath showed his love to the King and Queen's Majesties,
     His service to his country, and care of the Princess.

GRESHAM: My duty to them all.

PHILIP: Instead of charging of the sheriffs with her,
     We here discharge her keeper, Bedingfield,

770   And where we should have brought her to the block,
     We now will have her brought to Hampton Court,
     There to attend the pleasure of the Queen.
     The pursevant that should have posted down
     With tidings of her death

775   Bear her the message of her reprievéd life.
     You, Master Gage, assist his speed. A good day's work we ha' made
     To rescue innocence so soon betrayed.

Enter CLOWN *and* CLARENTIA.

CLOWN: Whither go you so fast, Mistress Clarentia?

CLARENTIA: A milking.

780   CLOWN: A milking? That's a poor office for a madam.

CLARENTIA: Better be a milkmaid free than a madam in bondage.
     O hadst thou heard the Princess yesternight,
     Sitting within an arbor all alone to hear a milkmaid sing,
     It would have moved a flinty heart to melt.

785   Weeping and wishing, wishing and weeping,
     A thousand times she with herself debates
     With the poor milkmaid to exchange estates.[5]
     She was a sempster° in the Tower, being a Princess,   *seamstress*
     And shall I, her poor gentlewoman, disdain

790   To be a milkmaid in the country?

CLOWN: Troth, you say true: every one to his fortune,
     As men go to hanging. The time hath been
     When I would ha' scorned to carry coals, but now the
        case is altered;
     Every man as far as his talent will stretch.

Enter a gentlewoman.

795   WOMAN: Where's Mistress Clarentia? To horse, to horse!
     The Princess is sent for to the Court.
     She's gone already. Come, let's after.

CLARENTIA: The Princess gone and I left here behind?
     Come, come, our horses shall outstrip the wind.

800   CLOWN: And I'll not be long after you, for I am sure

---

4. Insert a new line into.
5. Foxe records that Elizabeth, "hearing upon a time, out of her garden at Woodstock, a certain milkmaid singing pleasantly, wished herself to be a milkmaid as she was, saying that her case was better, and life more merrier than was hers, in that state as she was" (1583, p. 2096).

My curtall will carry me as fast as your double
   gelding.⁶   *Exeunt.*

     Enter ELIZABETH *and* GAGE.

ELIZABETH: I wonder, Gage, that we have stayed so long
   So near the Court and yet have heard no news
   From our displeaséd sister. This more affrights me
805   Than my former troubles. I fear this Hampton Court
   Will be my grave.
GAGE: Good Madam, blot such thoughts out of your mind.
   The Lords, I know, are still about your suit,
   And make no doubt, but they will so prevail
810   Both with the King and Queen, that you shall see
   Their heinous anger will be turned to love.

     Enter HOWARD.

HOWARD: Where is the Princess?
ELIZABETH: Welcome, my good Lord Howard. What says
     the Queen?
   Will she admit my sight?⁷
815   HOWARD: Madam, she will; this night she hath appointed
   That she herself in person means to hear you.
   Protract no time, then. Come, let's haste away.   *Exeunt.*

     Enter four torches. PHILIP, WINCHESTER, HOWARD, CHANDOS,
     BEDINGFIELD, *and* ATTENDANTS.

QUEEN: Where is the Princess?
HOWARD: She waits your pleasure at the common stairs.
820   QUEEN: Usher her in by torchlight.
HOWARD: Gentlemen ushers and gentlemen pensioners,⁸ lights
   For the Princess. Attendance, gentlemen.
PHILIP: For her supposed virtues, royal Queen,
   Look on your sister with a smiling brow,
825   And if her fault merit not too much hate,
   Let her be censured with all lenity.
   Let your deep hatred end where it began:
   She hath been too long banished from the sun.
QUEEN: Our favor shall be far 'bove her desert,°   *deserving*
830   And she that hath been banished from the light
   Shall once again behold our cheerful sight.
   You, my lord, shall step behind the arras
   And hear our conference. We'll show her grace,
   For there shines too much mercy in your face.
835   PHILIP: We bear this mind: we errors would not feed,
   Nor cherish wrongs, nor yet see innocents bleed.
QUEEN: Call the Princess.

---

6. My small nag will travel as fast as your large horse.
7. Will she admit me to her presence?
8. Bodyguards.

Exeunt for the PRINCESS. PHILIP *behind the arras. Enter all with*
ELIZABETH.

QUEEN: All forbear this place, except our sister now.   *Exeunt* OMNES.

ELIZABETH: That God that raised you stay you and protect

840   You from your foes and clear me from suspect.

QUEEN: Wherefore do you cry?
       To see yourself so low or us so high?

ELIZABETH: Neither, dread Queen. Mine is a womanish tear,
       In part compelled by joy and part by fear.

845   Joy of your sight these brinish tears have bred,
       For fear of my Queen's frown to strike me dead.

QUEEN: Sister, I rather think they're tears of spleen.

ELIZABETH: You were my sister, now you are my Queen.

QUEEN: Aye, that's your grief.

850   ELIZABETH: Madam, he was my foe and not your friend
       That hath possessed you so. I am as true a
       Subject to your Grace as any lives this day.
       Did you but see
       My heart, it bends far lower than my knee.

855   QUEEN: We know you can speak well. Will you submit?

ELIZABETH: My life, Madam, I will, but not as guilty.
       Should I confess
       Fault done by her that never did transgress?
       I joy to have a sister queen so royal.

860   I would it as much pleased your Majesty,
       That you enjoy a sister that's so true.
       If I were guilty of the least offence,
       Madam, 'twould taint the blood even in your face.[9]
       The treasons of the father, being noble,

865   Unnobles all your children. Let your Grace
       Exact all torture and imprisonment,
       What e're my greatest enemies can devise,
       And they all have done their worst, yet I
       Will your true subject and true sister die.

870   PHILIP: [*behind the arras*] Mirror of virtue and bright nature's pride,
       Pity it had been such beauty should have died.

QUEEN: You'll not submit but end as you begin?

ELIZABETH: Madam, to death I will, but not to sin.

QUEEN: You are not guilty then?

875   ELIZABETH: I think I am not.

QUEEN: I am not of your mind.

ELIZABETH: I would your Highness were.

QUEEN: How mean you that?

ELIZABETH: To think as I think, that my soul is clear.

880   QUEEN: You have been wrong imprisoned then?

ELIZABETH: I'll not say so.

QUEEN: Whate're we think, arise and kiss our hand.
       Say God hath raised you friends.

ELIZABETH: Then God hath kept His promise.

9. If I were guilty, you as my sister would share in that taint.

885 QUEEN: Promise, why?

ELIZABETH: To raise them friends that on His word rely.

Enter PHILIP.

PHILIP: And may the heavens applaud this unity.
Accursed be they that first procured this wrong.
Now by my crown, you ha' been kept down too long.

890 QUEEN: Sister, this night yourself shall feast with me;
Tomorrow for the country. You are free.
Lights for the Princess, conduct her to her chamber.   *Exit* ELIZABETH.

PHILIP: My soul is joyful that this peace is made,
A peace that pleaseth heaven and earth and all,

895 Redeeming captive thoughts from captive thrall.
Fair Queen, the serious business of my father[1]
Is now at hand to be accomplished.
Of your fair sight [I] needs must take my leave;
Return I shall, though parting cause us grieve.

900 QUEEN: Why should two hearts be forced to separate?
I know your business, but believe me, sweet,
My soul divines we never more shall meet.

PHILIP: Yet, fair Queen, hope the best. I shall return,
Who met with joy, though now sadly mourn.

Exeunt ONMES, PHILIP *and* QUEEN.

*   *   *

[In the intervening scenes, Winchester, Cardinal Pole, and the Queen all die,
leaving Elizabeth to be proclaimed the new Queen.]

A Sennet.[2]

Enter four trumpeters; after them SERGEANT TRUMPETER *with a mace;
after him purse-bearer,* SUSSEX *with the crown,* HOWARD *the scepter,*
CONSTABLE *with the cap of maintenance,* CHANDOS *with the sword,*
THAME *with the collar and a George,*[3] *four gentlemen bearing the
canopy over the* QUEEN, *two gentlewomen bearing up her train, six
gentlemen pensioners. The* QUEEN *takes state.*[4]

905 OMNES: Long live, long reign our sovereign.

ELIZABETH: We thank you all.

SUSSEX: The imperial crown I here present your Grace,
With it my staff of office, and my place.

ELIZABETH: Whilst we this crown, so long your place enjoy.

910 HOWARD: Th' imperial scepter here I offer up.

ELIZABETH: Keep it, my Lord, and with it be you High Admiral.[5]

---

1. Emperor Charles V who resigned his throne in the Netherlands to Philip in 1555.
2. Trumpet call.
3. Insignia of the Knights of the Garter; *cap of maintenance:* an insignia of office borne before the
sovereign at her coronation.
4. Is seated on the throne.
5. It was actually William Howard's son, Charles Howard, who was made Elizabeth's Lord Admiral
in 1585; prior to that, from 1558 to 1585, her Lord Admiral was Edward Fiennes de Clinton, first
Earl of Lincoln.

CONSTABLE: This cap of maintenance I present, my state of
     office and my utmost service.
ELIZABETH: Your love we know.
CONSTABLE: Pardon me, gracious Madam. 'Twas not spleen°   *anger*
915   But that allegiance that I owed my queen.
     Madam, I served her truly at that day,
     And I as truly will your Grace obey.
ELIZABETH: We do as freely pardon as you truly serve:
     Only your staff of office we'll displace;
920   Instead of that, we'll owe you greater grace.

        Enter BEDINGFIELD.
BEDINGFIELD: Long live the Queen, long live your Majesty.
     I have rid hard to be the first reporter
     Of these glad tidings first, and° all these here.   *and I find*
SUSSEX: You are in your love as free° as in your care.   *liberal*
925   You're come even just a day after the fair.
ELIZABETH: What's he, my jailor?
BEDINGFIELD: God preserve your Grace.
ELIZABETH: Be not ashamed, man. Look me in the face.
     Who have you now to patronize your strictness on?
930   For your kindness this I will bestow:
     When we have one we would have hardly° used   *harshly*
     And cruelly dealt with, you shall be the man.
     This is a day for peace, not for vengeance fit.
     All your good deeds we'll quit,° all wrongs remit.   *reward*
935   Where we left off, proceed.
CHANDOS: The sword of justice on my bended knee
     I to your Grace present. Heaven bless your reign.
ELIZABETH: This sword is ours; this staff is yours again.
THAME: This garter with the order of the George,
940   Two ornaments unto the crown of England,
     I here present.
ELIZABETH: Possess them still, my lord. What offices bear you?
GAGE: I, Captain of your Highness's pensioners.
BROCKET: I, of your Guard.
945 SERGEANT: I, Sergeant Trumpter, present my mace.
ELIZABETH: Some we intend to raise, none to displace.
     Lord Hunsdon,[6] we will one day find a staff
     To poise° your hand. You are our cousin,   *hold in*
     And deserve to be employed nearer our person.
950   But now to you° from whom we take this staff   *Sussex*
     (Since Cardinal Pole[7] is now deceased and dead),
     To show all malice from our breast is worn,
     Before you let that purse and mace be borne.
     And now to London, lords, lead on the way,
955   Praising that King° that all kings else obey.   *Christ*

6. Henry Carey, son of Mary Boleyn Blount, sister to Anne Boleyn, and rumored to be the son of
   Henry VIII; he was created Lord Chamberlain in 1583.
7. Reginald Pole, the last Roman Catholic Archbishop of Canterbury and chief Councilor to Mary
   Tudor; his death on November 17, 1558, occurred only a few hours after that of his Queen.

Sennet. About the stage in order. The MAYOR *of London meets them.*

MAYOR: I from this city London do present

   This purse and Bible to your Majesty.

   A thousand of your faithful citizens,

   In velvet coats and chains, well mounted, stay

960   To greet their royal Sovereign on the way.

ELIZABETH: We thank you all. But first this book I kiss:

   Thou art the way to honor, thou[8] to bliss.

   An English Bible. Thanks, my good Lord Mayor.

   You of our body and our soul have care.

965   This is the jewel that we still love best;

   This was our solace when we were distressed.

   This book, that hath so long concealed itself,

   So long shut up, so long hid,[9] now, lords, see

   We here unclasp; forever it is free.

970   Who looks for joy, let him this book adore.

   This is true food for rich men and for poor.

   Who drinks of this is certain ne'er to perish.

   This will the soul with heav'nly virtue cherish.

   Lay hand upon this anchor, every soul;

975   Your names shall be in an eternal scroll.

   Who builds on this dwells in a happy state.

   This is the fountain, clear, immaculate.

   That happy issue that shall us succeed

   And in our populous kingdom this book read,

980   For them, as for ourselves, we humbly pray

   They may live long and blest. So lead the way.

Finis.

EDMUND SPENSER

From The Faerie Queene, Book 1 (1590)[†]

[After Arthur attacks Orgoglio, cutting off his left arm
and causing him to howl with pain, Duessa comes
to the giant's aid, riding on a seven-headed beast.]

That when his° dear Duessa heard, and saw   *Orgoglio's*

   The evil stownd° that 'dangered her estate,[1]   *peril*

   Unto his aid she hastily did draw

   Her dreadful beast, who swollen with blood of late[2]

---

8. The Bible; *Thou:* her subjects.

9. Shut up and hidden because it was legally available only in Latin, not English.

† Copy text: Edmund Spenser, *The faerie queene Disposed into twelue bookes, fashioning XII. morall vertues* (London: William Ponsonbie, 1590; STC 23080), G6r–H2r (1.8.12-27).

1. Duessa and the giant are, among things, allegorical figures for Mary Tudor and Philip II. Here Arthur and his squire, Timias, represent English Protestants who rebelled against Mary and Philip during their brief reign.

2. In the book of Revelation, it is the woman who is drunk with the blood of martyrs and saints (Revelation 17.6); *dreadful beast:* the image of the duplicitous Duessa and her steed is derived from the description of the "whore of Babylon," who rides a seven-headed beast and carries a golden cup "full of abominations" (Revelation 17.3–6).

5   Came ramping forth with proud presumptuous gait
       And threatened all his heads like flaming brands.[3]
       But him the Squire made quickly to retrate,°   *retreat*
       Encountering fierce with single° sword in hand,   *only*
       And 'twixt him° and his lord° did like a bulwark stand.   *the beast / Arthur*

10   The proud Duessa, full of wrathful spite
       And fierce disdain to be affronted so,
       Enforced her purple beast with all her might
       That stop° out of the way to overthrow,   *obstacle*
       Scorning the let° of so unequal foe.   *impediment*
15   But nathemore° would that courageous swain   *never more*
       To her yield passage, 'gainst his lord to go,
       But with outrageous strokes did him restrain
       And with his body barred the way atwixt them twain.

     Then took the angry witch her golden cup,
20   Which still she bore, replete with magic arts;[4]
       Death and despair did many thereof sup
       And secret poison through their inner parts,
       Th' eternal bale of heavy wounded hearts;[5]
       Which after charms and some enchantments said,
25   She lightly sprinkled on his° weaker parts.   *the Squire's*
       Therewith his sturdy courage soon was quay'd,°   *quelled*
       And all his senses were with sudden dread dismayed.

     So down he fell before the cruel beast,
       Who on his neck his bloody claws did seize,
30   That life nigh crushed out of his panting breast.
       No power he had to stir nor will to rise.
       That when the careful knight° 'gan well avise,°   *Arthur / to notice*
       He lightly left the foe° with whom he fought   *Orgoglio*
       And to the beast 'gan turn his enterprise,
35   For wondrous anguish in his heart it wrought
       To see his lovéd Squire into such thralldom brought.

     And high advancing his blood-thirsty blade,
       Stroke° one of those deforméd heads so sore   *Struck*
       That of his puissance proud ensample made;
40   His monstrous scalp° down to his teeth it tore,   *the beast's head*
       And that misforméd shape misshapéd more.
       A sea of blood gushed from the gaping wound,
       That her° gay garments stained with filthy gore   *Duessa's*
       And overflowéd all the field around,
45   That° over shoes in blood he waded on the ground.[6]   *So that*

---

3. All seven heads were breathing out fire.
4. Protestants regarded the Roman Catholic doctrine of transubstantiation, according to which the
   bread and wine of the Mass become the body and blood of Christ by a specific process, as belief
   in magic. Duessa's cup represents the chalice used in the Mass.
5. By forcing English Protestants to accept the Mass or be burned for heresy, Mary led many to violate their own consciences, with lasting guilt as the consequence.
6. The blood ran so freely that it covered his feet.

Thereat he° roaréd for exceeding pain,   *the beast*
   That to have heard great horror would have bred,
   And scourging th' empty air with his long train°   *tail*
   Through great impatience of his grievéd head,
50 His gorgeous rider from her lofty stead°   *place*
   Would have cast down and trod in dirty mire
   Had not the giant soon her succoréd,
   Who all enraged with smart and frantic ire,
Came hurtling in full fierce and forced the knight retire.

55 The force, which wont in two to be dispersed,
   In one alone left° hand he° now unites,   *single remaining / Orgoglio*
   Which is through rage more strong than both
      were erst,°   *before*
   With which his hideous club aloft he dights°   *raises*
   And at his foe with furious rigor smites
60 That strongest oak might seem to overthrow.
   The stroke upon his° shield so heavy lights   *Arthur's*
   That to the ground it doubleth him full low.
What mortal wight° could ever bear so monstrous blow?   *man*

And in his fall his shield, that covered was,
65 Did lose his veil by chance and open flew,
   The light whereof, that heaven's light did pass,°   *surpass*
   Such blazing brightness through the air threw
   That eye mote° not the same endure to view.[6]   *might*
   Which when the giant spied with staring eye,
70 He down let fall his arm and soft withdrew
   His weapon huge, that heavéd was on high
For to have slain the man,° that on the ground did lie.   *Arthur*

And eke the fruitful-headed beast, amazed
   At flashing beams of that sunshiny shield,
75 Became stark blind and all his senses dazed,
   That down he tumbled on the dirty field
   And seemed himself as conqueréd to yield.
   Whom when his mistress proud perceived to fall,
   Whiles yet his feeble feet for faintness reeled,
80 Unto the giant loudly she 'gan call,
"O help Orgoglio, help, or else we perish all."

At her so piteous cry was much amoved
   Her champion stout and for to aid his friend
   Again his wonted° angry weapon proved,°   *accustomed / tried*
85 But all in vain, for he has read his end
   In that bright shield, and all their forces spend

---

7. Arthur's shield, described in the previous canto, was made of clear diamond. It shone so brightly that he usually kept it covered, except when pressed in battle. The shield also represents the Word of God that was veiled in the Old Testament law but revealed in Christ (2 Corinthians 3.12–18). Protestants often contrasted their belief in *sola scriptura* (scripture alone), *sola gratia* (grace alone), and *sola fides* (faith alone) with what they regarded as Roman Catholic requirements to follow the "law."

Themselves in vain; for since that glancing sight,
He hath no power to hurt nor to defend,
As where th'Almighty's lightning brand does light,
90   It dims the dazéd ey'n° and daunts the senses quite.   *eyes*

Whom when the Prince, to battle new addressed
And threat'ning high his dreadful stroke did see,
His sparkling blade about his head he blessed
And smote off quite his° right leg by the knee   *Orgoglio's*
95   That° down he tumbled. As an aged tree,   *So that*
High growing on the top of rocky clift
Whose heartstrings with keen steel nigh hewen be,
The mighty trunk, half rent with ragged rift,
Doth roll adown the rocks and fall with fearful drift;°   *impetus*

100   Or as a castle reuréd high and round,
By subtle engines° and malicious slight   *cunning machines*
Is underminéd from the lowest ground
And her foundation forced and, feebled quite,
At last down falls, and with her heapéd height
105   Her hasty ruin does more heavy make
And yields itself unto the victor's might,
Such was this giant's fall, that seemed to shake
The steadfast globe of earth,[8] as° it for fear did quake.   *as if*

The knight then lightly leaping to the prey
110   With mortal steel him smote again so sore,
That headless his unwieldy body lay,
All wallowed in his own foul bloody gore
Which flowéd from his wounds in wondrous store.°   *plentiful supply*
But soon as breath out of his breast did pass,
115   That huge great body, which the giant bore,
Was vanished quite, and of that monstrous mass
Was nothing left, but like an empty bladder was.[9]

Whose grievous fall when false Duessa spied,
Her golden cup she cast unto the ground
120   And crownéd miter[1] rudely threw aside;
Such piercing grief her stubborn heart did wound
That she could not endure that doleful stound°   *sorrow*
But, leaving all behind her, fled away.
The light-foot Squire her quickly turned around,
125   And by hard means enforcing her to stay,
So brought unto his lord, as his deservéd prey.

The royal virgin,[2] which beheld from far,
In pensive plight and sad perplexity,

8. A possible reference to Philip's global empire.
9. Spenser derides Philip's power as King Consort in England as nothing more than hot air and boasting. The allegory reflects not Philip's actual death but the end of his role in English affairs.
1. Pointed hat worn by bishops, here a symbol of Mary's allegiance to the papacy.
2. Una, an allegorical figure for the reformed English Church and here for its most influential adherent, Princess Elizabeth.

The whole achievement of this doubtful war,
130   Came running fast to greet his° victory   *Arthur's*
With sober gladness and mild modesty,
And with sweet joyous cheer him thus bespake:
"Fair branch of *noblesse*,° flower of chivalry,   *nobility*
That with your worth the world amazéd make,
135   How shall I 'quite° the pains ye suffer for my sake?   *requite*

"And you, fresh bud of virtue° springing fast,   *the Squire*
Whom these sad eyes saw nigh unto death's door,
What hath poor virgin for such peril past
Wherewith you to reward? Accept therefore
140   My simple self and service evermore;
And He that high does sit and all things see
With equal eyes their merits to restore°   *reward*
Behold what ye this day have done for me
And what I cannot 'quite, requite with usury."°   *interest*

Part Two: Coronation and the Problems of Legitimacy, Religion, and Succession (1559–1566)

HISTORICAL BACKGROUND

On the morning of November 17, 1558, the highway from London toward Hertfordshire was clogged with courtiers streaming northward from the capital. Among them rode a single horseman who carried a small treasure, Mary Tudor's black enameled betrothal ring. Sir Nicholas Throckmorton was bringing the ring to Elizabeth as confirmation of Mary's death from an abdominal tumor and proof of the princess's accession to the throne of England. The long years of waiting and anxiety were over, as was the ever-present suspicion to which Elizabeth had become accustomed.

It was reported that Elizabeth first heard of her accession while sitting under an oak tree at Hatfield House and that she greeted the report with these words from Psalm 118.23: "This was the Lord's doing, and it is marvelous in our eyes." Given Elizabeth's precarious position in the first years of Mary's reign, her unwitting role in the Wyatt Rebellion, and her sojourn in the Tower of London, such words were indeed appropriate, but it would be a mistake to assume that the news came as a surprise, for the Princess received regular news on the Queen's deteriorating condition from informants at Court. Nor would it be correct to assume that Elizabeth was unprepared to assume the role of queen. She was not a young adolescent under the government of a Lord Protector, as her brother Edward had been at the time of his accession, but rather a twenty-five-year-old woman who was already experienced in handling her own affairs amid political and religious turmoil.

During the reign of Edward VI, Elizabeth had become, according to the terms of her father's will, a wealthy landowner and had later exchanged some of her outlying properties for Hatfield House, which lay a mere twenty miles from London. By 1557, she was beginning to receive delegations of courtiers, both domestic and foreign, who were eager to ingratiate themselves with the heir presumptive, although Mary steadfastly refused to name Elizabeth as her successor until a few days before her own death, despite the 1544 Act of Succession that had reinstated Elizabeth's claim to the throne. At Hatfield, Elizabeth was surrounded by trusted men-of-affairs, including William Cecil, who had been appointed her Surveyor of Lands in 1550, and Nicholas Throckmorton, an outspoken and rigorous Protestant. They and others kept her abreast of developments at Court, despite her infrequent appearances in London.

Elizabeth carefully scripted her movements from the first word of Mary's death to her own coronation on January 15, 1559, in order both to prove her legitimacy and to assure the loyalty of her subjects. Once crowned, she moved quickly to reestablish Protestantism as the state religion and to consolidate her own power. In April 1559, Parliament passed the Act of Supremacy and the Act of Uniformity. The former ratified England's rupture from Roman Catholicism by declaring Elizabeth, not the Pope, as Supreme Governor of the English

Church. The term "Governor" was substituted for "Head" to mollify those who bristled at the notion of a woman as head of the Church. The Act of Uniformity required both clergy and people to conform to the order of worship as found in the newly revised Book of Common Prayer, which, for the most part, followed the Protestant prayerbook established by Edward VI in 1552.

Although religious issues dominated the first years of her reign, another question quickly emerged: who would succeed Elizabeth as England's monarch? For those who still considered Henry VIII's marriage to Anne Boleyn as illegitimate—and these were mainly her Roman Catholic subjects—Elizabeth's own claim to the throne seemed shaky. She herself had been declared a bastard by an act of Parliament in 1536 that banned her from making any claim "as lawful heir" to her father, and, despite the 1544 Act of Succession, the declaration of "bastard" had never been officially revoked. There were also rumbles that her cousin Mary Stuart, the sole surviving child of James V of Scotland and Mary of Guise and the granddaughter of Margaret Tudor, Henry VIII's elder sister, stood closer in the line of succession. Those who wished to see England remain a Roman Catholic nation supported Mary, whose position was strengthened in 1559 when she became Queen of France at the accession of her husband, Francis II, and acquired French claims to the English throne that could be traced to Henry II in the twelfth century. Later, when Mary was suddenly widowed and returned to her native Scotland in August 1561, Elizabeth would be faced with a rival who was now both nearer to home and linked to one of England's traditional enemies, France.

The question of succession was also folded into debates over whom the Queen should marry, debates in which Parliament took a prominent role. Various foreign suitors were proposed, as well as a few Englishmen. Among the latter, none raised more worries than Robert Dudley, the fifth son of John Dudley, Duke of Northumberland, and Jane Guildford and brother-in-law to Lady Jane Grey. Not only was Dudley the son (and grandson) of an executed traitor, but he was already married to Amy Robsart. Dudley had been imprisoned in the Tower in 1554 during Elizabeth's confinement there, and they may have known each other as children. Shortly after her coronation, Elizabeth named Dudley Master of the Horse, a position that gave him frequent access to her since she loved horseback riding and the hunt. In 1560, Amy Robsart Dudley died in a fall at her country house, and although Dudley himself was exonerated, rumors persisted that he had instigated her death. Elizabeth herself did nothing to counteract such reports when, suffering from smallpox in 1562, she named him Protector of England in case of her death. Yet she was careful not to allow Dudley too many liberties, telling him on one occasion, "I will have here but one mistress and no master." When, in 1564, she created him Earl of Leicester, she made it clear that the move was not to make him more eligible to marry her. In fact, she did so in order to offer him as a suitably noble husband to Mary Stuart, hoping to put an Englishman on the Scottish throne. It may not have been a proposal likely to succeed, but it was an ingenious response to an intemperate Scottish rival, an impertinent English suitor, and an importunate Parliament that demanded a marriage.

The opening years of Elizabeth's reign did much to consolidate her position as England's true monarch, although they also brought her first foreign war, a brush with death, and a growing awareness of the magnitude of her responsibilities.

THE NEW QUEEN

Upon receiving word of Mary's death, Elizabeth moved quickly and decisively to consolidate her position as Queen. On November 20 she appointed William Cecil as her Principal Secretary of State. It was a brilliant choice; Cecil was related to Elizabeth's trusted household manager, Thomas Parry, but more importantly, he had already proved himself both a skillful administrator and a survivor. He had served as secretary to Edward Seymour, Duke of Somerset and Lord Protector during the reign of Edward VI, as well as Secretary of State under John Dudley, the Duke of Northumberland who effectively ruled England in the early 1550s, and he had survived the execution of both men for treason. In her formal commission, which has come down to us under the title "Words Spoken by Her Majesty to Master Cecil," Elizabeth noted his reputation for integrity and honest speech, and she commanded him in the future to give "that counsel that you think best," even when such advice might go against her own wishes. It was a command Cecil would heed throughout his long service to the Queen, sometimes to the discomfiture of them both.

That same day Elizabeth also met in the Great Hall at Hatfield House with Mary's Privy Councilors. In her first public speech, "Words Spoken by the Queen to the Lords," Elizabeth claimed her right as the divinely appointed monarch of England, distinguishing between her body natural as an individual woman and her body politic as representative of the state and holding both as subject only to divine, not human, authority. Elizabeth's words to Cecil and to the members of the English nobility were clearly intended to stake her claim as the legitimate Queen whom God had appointed to rule over England.

Elizabeth also gave notice that she would dismiss many who had served on Mary's large and cumbersome Privy Council, which numbered over forty persons at times. In the end, Elizabeth trimmed the Council in half, retaining ten of Mary's men, but none of the clergy. Those she favored included William Herbert, first Earl of Pembroke, and Edward Stanley, third Earl of Derby, who was a staunch Roman Catholic but held too much power in the north of England to be ignored. She chose nine new Councilors, many of whom had served Edward VI but whose Protestantism excluded them from influential positions at Mary's court. Most of the Council members were older, well-seasoned statesmen; Cecil, at thirty-eight, was the most junior but, as Secretary of State, held one of the most powerful positions.

In addition to her Privy Council, Elizabeth made appointments to her Privy Chamber, and here she favored friends and relatives including Kat Ashley, as First Lady of the Bedchamber, and her husband, John, who became Keeper of the Queen's Jewels; Katherine and Philadelphia Carey, granddaughters of her aunt, Mary Boleyn; and Lady Mary Sidney, sister of Robert Dudley, wife of Sir Henry Sidney, and mother of two gifted writers, Philip and Mary, who would themselves become important members of her court. Many of those Elizabeth selected for her government and private staff remained with her throughout their lives, their loyalty a testament to the Queen.

QUEEN ELIZABETH

EARLY SPEECHES

Words Spoken by Her Majesty to Master Cecil[†]

(November 20, 1558)

I give you this charge: that you shall be of my Privy Council and content yourself to take pains for me and my realm. This judgment I have of you: that you will not be corrupted with any manner of gift and that you will be

† Copy text: Public Record Office: State Papers 12/1, fol. 12.

faithful to the state, and that without respect of my private will[1] you will give me that counsel that you think best. And if you shall know anything necessary to be declared to me of secrecy,[2] you shall show it to myself only, and assure yourself I will not fail to keep taciturnity therein, and therefore herewith I charge you.[3]

Words Spoken by the Queen to the Lords (late 1558)[†]

My lords, the law of nature moveth me to sorrow for my sister; the burden that is fallen upon me maketh me over mazed.[1] And yet, considering I am God's creature ordained to obey His appointment, I will thereto yield, desiring from the bottom of my heart that I may have assistance of His grace to be the minister of His heavenly will in this office now committed to me.

And as I am but one body naturally considered, though by His permission a body politic to govern, so I shall desire you all, my lords (chiefly you of the nobility, every one in his degree and power), to be assistant to me that I with my ruling and you with your service may make a good account to Almighty God and leave some comfort to our posterity in earth. I mean to direct all my actions by good advice and counsel, and therefore, considering that divers of you be of the ancient nobility (having your beginnings and estates of my progenitors, kings of this realm, and thereby ought in honor to have the more natural care for maintaining of my estate and this commonwealth), some others have been of long experience in governance (and enabled by my father of noble memory, my brother, and my late sister to bear office), the rest of you being upon special trust lately called to her service only (and trust for your service considered and rewarded), my meaning is to require of you all nothing more but faithful hearts in such service as from time to time shall be in your powers towards the preservation of me and this commonwealth.

And for counsel and advice, I shall accept you of my nobility and such others of you the[2] rest as in consultation I shall think meet and shortly appoint. To the which also, with their advice, I will join to their aid and for ease of their burden others meet for my service. And they which I shall not appoint, let them not think the same for any disability in them but for that I do consider a multitude doth make rather discord and confusion than good counsels. And of my goodwill you shall not doubt, using[3] yourselves as appertaineth to good and loving subjects.

Questions Concerning the Legitimacy of Female Rule

While some Roman Catholics considered Elizabeth a bastard and promoted, at least in private, the accession of Mary Stuart to the throne of England, the

---

1. Personal wishes.
2. That is secret.
3. Impose this commission.
† Copy text: Public Record Office: State Papers 12/1, fol. 12. This speech, given before the Queen's coronation, may have been delivered as early as November 20, 1558, when Elizabeth first met with Mary's Privy Council at Hatfield House.
1. Utterly amazed.
2. Among the.
3. If you use.

question of the legitimacy of a female monarch arose from both Catholic and Protestant quarters. In 1558, shortly before Mary Tudor's death, the Scottish reformer John Knox published *The First Blast of the Trumpet against the Monstrous Regiment of Women*. Knox, who had served as a court preacher for Edward VI and who had been forced to flee to the Continent at the accession of Mary Tudor, directed his blast against three Roman Catholic female rulers: Mary of Guise, Regent of Scotland during Mary Stuart's minority, under whom Knox had served as a galley-slave after being captured by her forces; Mary Tudor, who had burned Protestants at the stake and forced others, including Knox, into exile; and Mary Stuart, who was married to the heir of the French crown and was herself in line to inherit the throne of his native Scotland. Unfortunately, to the dismay of John Calvin and other Protestants, Knox intemperately extended his argument beyond these three "Marys" to include all women monarchs, arguing that it was against nature for women to rule over men. To his credit, Knox allowed that God could ordain a woman to rule, citing the biblical Deborah as his prime example, and when Elizabeth came to the throne only months after the publication of *The First Blast*, Knox suggested that she was just such an exceptional monarch, who ruled under God's authority and with His approval. Elizabeth herself, however, was not mollified, refused Knox entry to England, and only reluctantly supported the Protestant forces in Scotland during the early years of her reign.

In response to Knox, John Aylmer published in 1559 *An Harbor for Faithful and True Subjects against the Late Blown Blast Concerning the Government of Women*. Aylmer's own Protestant credentials were impeccable. He had been tutor to the Lady Jane Grey, had gone into exile rather than live under Mary Tudor, and was later named Bishop of London by Elizabeth. Aylmer defended Elizabeth's legitimacy and the right of women to rule "by the whole consent of nations, by the ordinance of God, and order of law," although he agreed with Knox that women in general were less fit to rule than men and that a wife must submit to her husband, as the "head" of the household. But Aylmer also argued that a female magistrate owes her first allegiance to God and her commonwealth, not to her husband, so that, if needs be, she may "strike [him] with the sword [of state]" and still be a good and obedient wife. Furthermore, Aylmer assured his readers that England was particularly safe in the hands of a woman ruler because safeguards had been established against irrational tyranny: namely, that every English monarch, male or female, was to be governed not by his or her own will but by law, Parliament, and wise councilors.

JOHN KNOX

From The First Blast of the Trumpet Against the Monstrous Regiment of Women (1558)[†]

To promote a woman to bear rule, superiority, dominion, or empire above any realm, nation, or city is repugnant to nature, contumely[1] to God, a thing most contrarious to His revealed will and approved ordinance, and finally it is the subversion of good order, of all equity and justice.

* * *

[†] Copy text: John Knox, *The first blast of the trumpet against the monstruous regiment of women* ([Geneva: J. Poullain and A. Rebul], 1558; *STC* 15070), B1r–7r; E7r–F2r; F7r–F7v; G7r–G8v.
1. A reproach.

And first, where that I affirm the empire of a woman to be a thing repugnant to nature, I mean not only that God by the order of His creation hath spoiled[2] woman of authority and dominion, but also that man hath seen, proved, and pronounced just causes why that it so should be. Man, I say, in many other cases blind, doth in this behalf see very clearly. For the causes be so manifest that they cannot be hid. For who can deny but it repugneth to[3] nature that the blind shall be appointed to lead and conduct such as do see? That the weak, the sick, and impotent persons shall nourish and keep the whole and strong, and, finally, that the foolish, mad, and phrenetic shall govern the discrete and give counsel to such as be sober of mind? And such be all women, compared unto man in bearing of authority. For their sight in civil regiment[4] is but blindness, their strength weakness, their counsel foolishness, and judgment frenzy, if it be rightly considered.

I except such as God, by singular privilege and for certain causes known only to Himself, hath exempted from the common rank of women and do speak of women as nature and experience do this day declare them. Nature, I say, doth paint them forth to be weak, frail, impatient, feeble, and foolish, and experience hath declared them to be unconstant, variable, cruel, and lacking the spirit of counsel and regiment. And these notable faults have men in all ages espied in that kind, for the which not only they have removed women from rule and authority, but also some have thought that men subject to the counsel or empire of their wives were unworthy of all public office. For thus writeth Aristotle in the second of his *Politics*: "What difference shall we put," saith he, "whether that women bear authority or the husbands that obey the empire of their wives be appointed to be magistrates? For what ensueth the one must needs follow the other, to wit, injustice, confusion, and disorder."[5]

*   *   *

I am assuredly persuaded that if any of those men, which illuminated only by the light of nature, did see and pronounce causes sufficient why women ought not to bear rule nor authority, should this day live and see a woman sitting in judgment or riding from Parliament in the midst of men, having the royal crown upon her head, the sword and scepter borne before her in sign that the administration of justice was in her power, I am assuredly persuaded, I say, that such a sight should so astonish them that they should judge the whole world to be transformed into Amazons, and that such a metamorphosis and change was made of all the men of that country as poets do feign was made of the companions of Ulysses, or, at least, that albeit the outward form of men remained, yet should they judge that their hearts were changed from the wisdom, understanding, and courage of men to the foolish fondness[6] and cowardice of women. Yea they further should pronounce that where women reign or be in authority that there must needs vanity be preferred to virtue, ambition and pride to temperance and modesty, and

2. Stripped.
3. Is contrary to.
4. Civil government; *their*: women's.
5. Aristotle, *Politics*, 2.9.1269b (see *The Complete Works of Aristotle*. The Revised Oxford Translation, ed. Jonathan Barnes [Princeton: Princeton UP, 1984], 2:2015).
6. Lack of judgment; *companions of Ulysses*: Knox interprets the changing of Odysseus's men into swine by Circe as a metaphor for the feminization of men ruled by women (see Homer, *The Odyssey*, Book 10).

finally, that avarice, the mother of all mischief, must needs devour equity and justice. But lest that we shall seem to be of this opinion alone, let us hear what others have seen and decreed in this matter. In the rules of the law[7] thus it is written: Women are removed from all civil and public office, so that they neither may be judges, neither may they occupy the place of the magistrate, neither yet may they be speakers for others.

✳ ✳ ✳

Would to God the examples were not so manifest. To the further declaration of the imperfections of women, of their natural weakness and inordinate appetites, I might adduce histories proving some women to have died for sudden joy, some for unpatiency to have murdered themselves, some to have burned with such inordinate lust that, for the quenching of the same, they have betrayed to strangers their country and city; and some to have been so desirous of dominion that, for the obtaining of the same, they have murdered the children of their own sons. Yea and some have killed with cruelty their own husbands and children. But to me it is sufficient (because this part of nature is not my most sure foundation) to have proved that men, illuminated only by the light of nature, have seen and have determined that it is a thing most repugnant to nature that women rule and govern over men. For those that will not permit a woman to have power over her own sons will not permit her (I am assured) to have rule over a realm; and those that will not suffer her to speak in defense of those that be accused, neither that will admit her accusation intended against man, will not approve her, that she shall sit in judgment crowned with the royal crown, usurping authority in the midst of men.

But now to the second part of nature, in the which I include the revealed will and perfect ordinance of God, and against this part of nature, I say, that it doth manifestly repugne[8] that any woman shall reign or bear dominion over man. For God, first by the order of His creation and after by the curse and malediction pronounced against the woman by the reason of her rebellion,[9] hath pronounced the contrary. First, I say that woman in her greatest perfection was made to serve and obey man, not to rule and command him, as Saint Paul doth reason in these words: "Man is not of the woman but the woman of the man. And man was not created for the cause of the woman, but the woman for the cause of man, and therefore ought the woman to have a power upon her head" (that is a coverture in sign of subjection).[1] Of which words it is plain that the Apostle meaneth that woman in her greatest perfection should have known that man was lord above her and, therefore, that she should never have pretended any kind of superiority above him, no more than do the angels above God the Creator or above Christ Jesus their head. So, I say that in her greatest perfection woman was created to be subject to man.

But after her fall and rebellion committed against God, there was put upon her a new necessity, and she was made subject to man by the

7. *De Regulis Juris Antiqui*, 50.17.2; the passage is from a summary of Roman law compiled by command of the Emperor Justinian in 530 C.E., which contributed to the development of English common law.
8. Refute.
9. In Genesis 2–3, Eve is created second but is the first to sin.
1. 1 Corinthians 11.10. Knox quotes early sixteenth-century Bible translations that use the term "power" to indicate a head-covering.

irrevocable sentence of God, pronounced in these words: "I will greatly multiply thy sorrow and thy conception. With sorrow shalt thou bear thy children, and thy will shall be subject to thy man, and he shall bear dominion over thee."[2] Hereby may such as altogether be not blinded plainly see that God, by His sentence, hath dejected[3] all woman from empire and dominion above man. For two punishments are laid upon her, to wit, a dolor, anguish, and pain, as oft as ever she shall be mother, and a subjection of herself, her appetites, and will to her husband and to his will. From the former part of this malediction can neither art, nobility, policy, nor law made by man deliver womankind, but whosoever attaineth to that honor to be mother proveth in experience the effect and strength of God's Word.

But (alas) ignorance of God, ambition, and tyranny have studied to abolish and destroy the second part of God's punishment. For women are lifted up to be heads over realms and to rule above men at their pleasure and appetites.[4] But horrible is the vengeance which is prepared for the one and for the other, for the promoters and for the persons promoted, except they speedily repent. For they shall be dejected from the glory of the sons of God to the slavery of the devil and to the torment that is prepared for all such as do exalt themselves against God. Against God can nothing be more manifest than that a woman shall be exalted to reign above man. For the contrary sentence hath He pronounced in these words: "Thy will shall be subject to thy husband, and he shall bear dominion over thee." As God should say, "Forasmuch as thou hast abused thy former condition and because thy free will hath brought thyself and mankind into the bondage of Satan, I therefore will bring thee in bondage to man. For where before thy obedience should have been voluntary, now it shall be by constraint and by necessity; and that because thou hast deceived thy man,[5] thou shalt therefore be no longer mistress over thine own appetites, over thine own will nor desires. For in thee there is neither reason nor discretion which be able to moderate thy affections, and, therefore, they shall be subject to the desire of thy man. He shall be lord and governor, not only over thy body but even over thy appetites and will." This sentence, I say, did God pronounce against Eve and her daughters, as the rest of the Scriptures doth evidently witness. So that no woman can ever presume to reign above man, but the same she must needs do in despite of God and in contempt of His punishment and malediction.[6]

*　*　*

And now I think it expedient to answer such objections as carnal and worldly men, yea men ignorant of God, use to make for maintenance of this tyranny (authority it is not worthy to be called) and most unjust empire of woman.

First, they do object[7] the examples of Deborah and of Huldah the prophetess, of whom the one judged Israel and the other, by all appearance,

---

2. Genesis 3.16.
3. Overthrown.
4. Knox's particular targets here are three contemporary Catholic women rulers: Mary Tudor; Mary of Guise, the mother of Mary Stuart; and Mary Stuart herself. Warned by John Calvin and other Protestants not to publish a blanket condemnation of all women rulers, his insistence on doing so resulted in Elizabeth's refusal to let him travel to England after her coronation.
5. Eve is held responsible for encouraging Adam to eat of the forbidden fruit in the Garden of Eden.
6. If a woman insists on ruling, she does so in contempt of God's warning and judgment.
7. Raise as an objection.

did teach and exhort. * * * I will descend somewhat deeper into the matter and not fear to affirm that as we find a contrary spirit in all these most wicked women that this day be exalted into this tyrannous authority to the spirit that was in those godly matrons, so I fear not, I say, to affirm that their condition is unlike and that their end shall be divers.[8] In those matrons[9] we find that the spirit of mercy, truth, justice, and of humility did reign. Under them we find that God did show mercy to His people, delivering them from the tyranny of strangers and from the venom of idolatry by the hands and counsel of those women. But in these of our ages we find cruelty, falsehood, pride, covetousness, deceit, and oppression. In them we also find the spirit of Jezebel and Athalia. Under them we find the simple people oppressed, the true religion extinguished, and the blood of Christ's members most cruelly shed. And finally, by their practices and deceit, we find ancient realms and nations given and betrayed into the hands of strangers, the titles and liberties of them taken from the just possessors. Which one thing is an evident testimony how unlike our mischievous Marys be unto Deborah, under whom were strangers chased out of Israel, God so raising her up to be a mother and deliverer to His oppressed people. But (alas) He hath raised up these Jezebels to be the uttermost of His plagues, the which man's unthankfulness hath long deserved. But His secret and most just judgment shall neither excuse them, neither their maintainers, because their counsels be divers.[1]

But to prosecute my purpose, let such as list to defend these monsters in their tyranny prove first that their sovereign mistresses be like to Deborah in godliness and pity and secondarily that the same success doth follow their tyranny which did follow the extraordinary regiment[2] of that godly matron. Which thing although they were able to do (as they never shall be, let them blow till they burst), yet shall her example profit them nothing at all. For they are never able to prove that either Deborah or any other godly woman (having the commendation of the Holy Ghost within the scriptures) hath usurped authority above any realm or nation by reason of their birth and blood. Neither yet did they claim it by right or inheritance, but God by His singular privilege, favor, and grace exempted Deborah from the common malediction given to women in that behalf, and against nature He made her prudent in counsel, strong in courage, happy in regiment,[3] and a blessed mother and deliverer to His people.

* * *

The question is not if women may not succeed to possession, substance, patrimony, or inheritance, such as fathers may leave to their children,[4] for that I willingly grant. But the question is if women may succeed to their fathers in offices and chiefly to that office the executor whereof doth occupy the place and throne of God. And that I absolutely deny and fear not to say: that to place a woman in authority above a realm is to pollute and profane the royal seat, the throne of justice, which ought to be the

---

8. The biblical exemplars Deborah and Huldah differ in their spirits, their reigns, and their final ends from the queens of Knox's own day.
9. Deborah and Huldah.
1. Opposed to that of God; *maintainers*: supporters.
2. Government; *list*: desire.
3. Prosperous in government.
4. Knox himself willed all his possessions to his own daughters.

throne of God and that to maintain them in the same is nothing else but continually to rebel against God.

* * *

Cursed Jezebel of England, with the pestilent and detestable generation of papists, make no little brag and boast that they have triumphed not only against Wyatt[5] but also against all such as have enterprized anything against them or their proceedings. But let her and them consider that yet they have not prevailed against God. His throne is more high than that the length of their horns be able to reach. And let them further consider that in the beginning of this their bloody reign, the harvest of their iniquity was not comen[6] to full maturity and ripeness. No, it was so green (so secret I mean), so covered, and so hid with hypocrisy that some men (even the servants of God) thought it not impossible but that wolves might be changed into lambs and also that the viper might remove her natural venom.

But God, who doth reveal in His time appointed the secrets of hearts and that will have His judgments justified even by the very wicked, hath now given open testimony of her and their beastly cruelty. For man and woman, learned and unlearned, nobles and men of baser sort, aged fathers and tender damsels, and finally the bones of the dead, as well women as men, have tasted of their tyranny. So that now not only the blood of Father Latimer, of the mild man of God the Bishop of Canterbury, of learned and discrete Ridley, of innocent Lady Jane Dudley,[7] and many godly and worthy preachers that cannot be forgotten (such as fire hath consumed and the sword of tyranny most unjustly hath shed) doth call for vengeance in the ears of the Lord God of Hosts, but also the sobs and tears of the poor oppressed, the groanings of the angels, the watchmen of the Lord, yea and every earthly creature abused by their tyranny do continually cry and call for the hasty execution of the same.

I fear not to say that the day of vengeance, which shall apprehend that horrible monster, Jezebel of England, and such as maintain her monstrous cruelty, is already appointed in the counsel of the Eternal, and I verily believe that it is so nigh that she shall not reign so long in tyranny as hitherto she had done, when God shall declare Himself to be her enemy, when He shall pour forth contempt upon her according to her cruelty and shall kindle the hearts of such as sometimes did favor her with deadly hatred against her, that they may execute His judgments. And therefore let such as assist her take heed what they do. For assuredly her empire and reign is a wall without foundation. (I mean the same of the authority of all women.) It hath been underpropped this blind time that is past with the foolishness of people and with the wicked laws of ignorant and tyrannous princes.[8] But the fire of God's Word is already laid to those rotten props (I include the Pope's law with the rest) and presently they burn,[9] albeit we espy not the

---

5. Sir Thomas Wyatt's 1554 uprising, precipitated by Mary Tudor's decision to marry Philip of Spain, resulted in his execution for treason on April 11 of that year; *Jezebel of England*: Mary Tudor.
6. Come.
7. Hugh Latimer, Thomas Cranmer, Archbishop of Canterbury, Nicholas Ridley, and Lady Jane Grey Dudley were among the most prominent Protestants to be executed by Mary Tudor.
8. Such as those of France and Spain.
9. Knox transmutes the fire that burned the Protestant martyrs into the fire of God's wrath, as seen, for instance, in Isaiah 5.24: "Therefore as the flame of fire devoureth the stubble and as the chaff is consumed of the flame, so their root shall be as rottenness and their bud shall rise up like dust, because they have cast off the law of the Lord of Hosts and condemned the word of the Holy One of Israel."

flame. When they are consumed (as shortly they will be, for stubble and dry timber cannot long endure the fire) that rotten wall, the usurped and unjust empire of women, shall fall by itself in despite of all man,[1] to the destruction of so many as shall labor to uphold it. And therefore let all man be advertised,[2] for the trumpet hath once blown.

Praise God, ye that fear Him.

JOHN AYLMER

From An Harbor for Faithful and True Subjects (1559)[†]

Like as sick or feeble bodies cannot abide any great pangs or fits, or old cracked ships any great waves or winds, so disturbed and maimed commonwealths are soon overturned and cast underfoot by sudden and strange mutations. Seeing, therefore, that by frowning fortune and God's wrath for the offenses of the inhabitants, England is of late both in honor and possessions not a little maimed (yea, taking a fall, through the negligence of the nurse half made a cripple),[1] it is necessary for all good men and the duty of all faithful subjects to have an eye to it, that it run not upon the rocks and make shipwreck. And as in great cities great heed is given that, neither by negligence of the citizens nor malice of evil-willers, it be consumed by fire or hurt by any other casualty, so in commonwealths must it be provided that no firebrands of sedition be cast into the houses of men's hearts to impair the obedience of good subjects, to kindle the hearts of the froward,[2] and to destroy honest, godly, and comely order. For man's nature being such as it can hardly be brought to stoop[3] and easily stirred up to disturb, all occasions must be cut off whereby the evil may be encouraged to cast off the yoke of obedience and the simple brought into doubt what they ought to follow.

Happening, therefore, not long ago to read a little book strangely written by a stranger to prove that the rule of women is out of rule and not in a commonwealth tolerable, and weighing at the first what harm might come of it, and feeling at the last that it hath not a little wounded the conscience of some simple[4] and almost cracked the duty of true obedience, I thought it more than necessary to lay before men's eyes the untruth of the argument, the weakness of the proofs, and the absurdity of the whole. In the sifting whereof, I mind to use such modesty that it shall appear to all indifferent men that I seek to defend the cause and not to deface the man, seeing this

---

1. Despite any man's attempt to shore it up.
2. Warned: *man*: men.
† Copy text: John Aylmer, *An harborovve for faithfull and trevve subiectes agaynst the late blowne blaste, concerninge the gouernme[n]t of vvemen. wherin be confuted all such reasons as a straunger of late made in that behalfe, with a breife exhortation to obedience* (Strasborowe [London: John Day], 1559; STC 1005), B1r–2r; C3r–4r; G1r–G1v; G2v–G3v; G4r; H3v.
1. A possible reference to Mephibosheth, the son of Jonathan and grandson of King Saul, crippled after being dropped by his nurse but protected by King David, despite Mephibosheth's claim to the throne (2 Samuel 4.4; 9.1–13).
2. Those who are resistant to government; *casualty*: fatal accident.
3. Submit to authority.
4. Simple people; *little book . . . by a stranger:* John Knox's *The First Blast of the Trumpet Against the Monstrous Regiment of Women.* As a Scotsman and a resident of Geneva, Knox is considered a suspect foreigner.

error rose not of malice but of zeal and by looking more to the present cruelty that then was used than to the inconvenience[5] that after might follow. Wherein surely his doing is somewhat to be pardoned, considering the grief that, like a good member of that body which then suffered, he felt to his great sorrow and trouble. For like as the eye, being full of tears, is the more unable to see, so is the mind full of sorrow much the less able to judge.

As we see in Euripides's Polymestor, (being for his murdering of Polydorus extremely punished of Hecuba and other women who pricked out his eyes with pins, crieth out not only again them that hurt him but against the whole sex that never came near him) and in Hippolytus (who, for the fault of his stepdame Phaedra, curseth the whole kind), so this author seeing the torments of martyrs, the murdering of good men, the imprisonment of innocents, the racking of the guiltless, the banishing of Christ, the receiving of Antichrist, the spoiling of subjects, the maintenance of strangers, the moving of wars, the loss of England's honor, the purchasing of hatred where we had love, the procuring of trouble where we had peace, the spending of treasure where it was needless, and (to be short) all out of joint, he could not but mislike that regiment[6] from whence such fruits did spring. Only in this he was not to be excused (unless he allege ignorance) that he swerved from the *hypothesis* to the *thesis*, that is from the particular question to the general, as though all the government of the whole sex were against nature, reason, right, and law because that the present state then through the fault of the person, and not of the sex, was unnatural, unreasonable, unjust, and unlawful. If he had kept him in that particular person,[7] he could have said nothing too much, nor in such wise, as could have offended any indifferent man.

✳   ✳   ✳

Well, now to the first argument: You say in your minor[8] that the rule of a woman is against nature because the woman is by nature weak, unskillful, and subject to the man, etc. Well, before I answer to these, we must see what is meant by this word "nature," how far it stretcheth, how it must be taken in this proposition, and then how the rule of a woman may agree or not agree with it. Nature is nothing else but a general disposition engraft of God in all creatures for the preservation of the whole and of every kind, or as Seneca saith, "*Quid aliud est natura quam deus et divina ratio toti mundo universisque eius partibus inserta*": "Nature is nothing else but God himself, or a divine order spread throughout the whole world, and engraft in every part of it," as in all fire to be hot, all water moist, all heavy things to move downward, all light things upward, the sun and the moon to run their course, *motus circulari*,[9] etc. Which are so set orders in the substance

---

5. Impropriety and mischief; *indifferent*: unprejudiced; *present cruelty . . . was used*: that of Mary Tudor toward Protestants. Knox was among those forced into exile during her reign.

6. The reign of Mary Tudor; *women*: copy text: weme; possibly the archaic word for womb, but probably a printer's error for women; *pins*: Hecuba's revenge for the death of her son, as narrated in Euripides's play, *Hecuba; curseth . . . kind*: in Euripides's play *Hippolytus*, the hero curses all women after he discovers that his stepmother Phaedra, through the machinations of Aphrodite, has fallen in love with him; *this author*: John Knox.

7. That is, Mary Tudor.

8. Minor premise.

9. In a circular motion; *engraft*: firmly established; *Seneca saith . . . eius partibus inserta*: Lucius Annaeus Seneca (the younger), *On Benefits*, 4.7 (see *Moral Essays*, translated by John W. Basore [Cambridge, MA: Harvard UP, 1935], 2.217).

of every creature as it must needs follow that natural disposition, unless it pleaseth the Creator (who is the Lord of all) to alter those properties which He hath given them by nature, as when He made of the moving water a standing wall, and the fire so to lose his operation that it consumed not the bodies of the three young men that were cast into it,[1] and such like, all which deeds be wonders and miracles and not the work, but the impediment, of nature.

Now if this hath so been engrafted in the nature of all men that no woman should govern, but all women should be subjects, then were there no more to be said: the matter were ended. But because we see by many examples that, by the whole consent of nations, by the ordinance of God and order of law, women have reigned and those not a few; and as it was thought not against nature, therefore it cannot be said that, by a general disposition of nature, it hath been and is denied them to rule. But let us here consider whether it be in a woman against nature to rule, as it is in a stone to move upward or in the fire not to consume. In the stone or in the fire is no manner of aptness, either for the one to go upward or the other to preserve and not destroy, and neither can be done in either without violence and outward force. But in a woman is wit, understanding, and, as Aristotle saith, the same virtues that be in a man, saving that they differ.[2] *Secundum maius et minus*, that is, "more in the man than in the woman." There is the same shape, the same language, and sometime more gifts in them than in the man, as was in Artemisia (as Justinus reporteth) more prowess and wit to rule the army than in the great monarch Xerxes.[3] Only we can pull from them that they be not strong of body or commonly so courageous[4] in mind.

Grant that it is so. Must they therefore be utterly unmeet to rule? Nay, if you said unmeeter than men, we would not much wrestle with you. For as Aristotle saith, the man's rule is *hêgemonikôtera*, that is, "more meet to rule." But to reason thus, women be not so meet as men, *ergo*, it is against nature, is an evil consequent.[5]

*   *   *

The second argument is this: that the scripture forbiddeth that a woman should rule, and therefore it is not tolerable. The proofs be out of the Old Testament. First, that after the fall of Adam through the woman's enticement it was enjoined her and her posterity, as a penance, to be at the beck and commandment of the man. Second, that Isaiah pronounceth as a curse that the rulers for the people's unruliness shall be children and women.[6] Third, that Saint Paul forbiddeth them to speak in the congregation.[7]

---

1. Allusion to the preservation of Daniel's three friends in the fiery furnace of King Nebuchadnezzar (Daniel 3.8–30); *water . . . wall*: allusion to the parting of the Red Sea when the Israelites fled from Egypt (Exodus 14.21–22).
2. Aristotle, *Politics* 3.4.1277b (see *The Complete Works of Aristotle*. The Revised Oxford Translation, ed. Jonathan Barnes [Princeton: Princeton UP, 1984], 2.2027). Aristotle argues that temperance and courage differ, such that a man with no more courage than a woman is thought a coward.
3. Artemisia of Halicarnassus was commended for warning Xerxes I not to engage the Greeks at the Battle of Salamis (480 B.C.E.), during which the Persian king lost his navy (Marcus Junianus Justinus, *Epitome of the Philippic History of Pompeius Trogus*, 2.12).
4. Spirited; *pull from them*: we can only draw from authorities such as Aristotle and Justinus.
5. Bad conclusion to an argument.
6. Isaiah 3.12.
7. 1 Corinthians 14.34–36.

Before that I answer particularly, I must say this to them all in general, that the scripture meddleth with no civil policy further than to teach obedience. And therefore, whatsoever is brought out of the scripture concerning any kind of regiment is without the book,[8] pulled into the game-place by the ears to wrestle whether it will or no. For Christ saith, "*Quis me constituit inter vos iudicem?*"[9] "Who hath made me be betwixt you a judge," as though He should say, mine office is not to determine matters of policy, of succession, and inheritance, for that belongeth to the civil magistrates.

*   *   *

Thus far to the whole in general. Now to each reason in special. Where it is said, *Et ad virum erit conversio vel desiderium tuum*,[1] I might answer it with the common interpretation, which is, "though both in conceiving and bringing forth thy child, thou shalt feel throes and exceeding pangs, yet shalt thou not be able to withdraw thee from thy husband, but shalt give occasion to have more. The pain of the former shall not make thee to avoid the next." This is no evil interpretation, for it answereth[2] in the manner of the pain the quality of the offense. As who should say, "Thou hast enticed thy husband to turn to thy folly; I shall therefore make thee to turn to him, to thine own smart." This place thus interpreted maketh no more for this matter than "*Gloria in excelsis*" doth prove that Saint Peter said Mass. But because some reject this interpretation and we seek not to cavil[3] but to find the truth, therefore I will admit the other, that it maketh for the wife's obedience toward her husband that she must hang upon him as upon her guide, follow his will as the wiser, obey his commandment as her superior, and, to be short, to know him for her head and herself for his subject.

"What? Grant you this? That is enough."

"Yea, I must needs do so, for the truth else and mine own conscience would reprove me."

"How then answer you?"

"Forsooth, as I did before: that she must do all this and more, but *usque ad aras*.[4] So far forth as he commandeth like a husband, like a Christian, and like her head. But if he pass his commission, as if he command that is ungodly, then she may answer him, as Saint Augustine doth the ruler, '*Da veniam imperator tu minaris carcerem, sed deus gehennam*': 'Thou wilt have me obey thy will for fear of thy prison and sword, but I must obey God's will, for fear of his eternal fire and damnation.'[5] If her husband will command her in the public weal, she being the magistrate and not he, she may say to him as the consul said to Fabius, '*Siste lictor*': 'Law, make my husband to obey, for here he is not my head, but my subject.'[6] Yea, if he break any law,

---

8. Without authority; literally, outside the book.
9. Luke 12.14.
1. And your desire shall be turned toward your husband (Genesis 3.16).
2. Matches.
3. Raise frivolous objections, as in the previous suggestion that to use a common phrase found in the Mass makes one a Roman Catholic.
4. Only as far as the hearth; that is, only in the domestic sphere.
5. From Augustine's sermon (12.13) on the godly centurion (Matthew 8 and Luke 7); here Augustine distinguishes between appropriate obedience to civil authority and necessary obedience to God (see Augustine, *Sermons on Selected Lessons of the New Testament*, trans. R.G. MacMullen and ed. Philip Schaff in *A Select Library of the Nicene and Post-Nicene Fathers of the Christian Church*, vol. 6 [Grand Rapids, MI: Eerdmans, 1956], 302); *that is*: that which is.
6. In his marginal note, Aylmer cites Titus Livy's *The History of Rome*, Book 3 on the history of the Decemvirate, the group of ten ruling consuls. Quintus Fabius Vibulanus was a trusted consul who

if it were capital, she might strike with the sword and yet be a wife good enough, for the duty that she oweth to him is not omitted in that she observeth that[7] she oweth to the commonwealth, wherein he is a member contained. But if for her wedlock duty to him she will neglect the commonwealth, then is she a loving wife to him and an evil head to the country."

The second reason out of Isaiah maketh as much as for debarring of young princes' rule (as Joash, Josiah, and our sweet king Edward, as his sister Mary held) as it doth against women, for they be joined together, but indeed it maketh against[8] neither. For Isaiah, being worthily called the Demosthenes of the Hebrews, useth such goodly figures of speaking as all the scripture hath not beside, as in this place: "I will take from you your honorable senators and your wise counselors, and I will give you boys and women, or effeminate persons, to reign over you."[9] Not boys in age but in manners (as Aristotle saith of young men, that to hear philosophy it maketh no matter for their years, but for their manners), not women in sex but in feebleness of wit, and not such as some women be (wiser, better learned, discreeter, constanter, than a number of men) but such as women be of the worst sort: fond, foolish, wanton, flibbertigibbets, tattlers, triflers, wavering, witless, without counsel, feeble, careless, rash, proud, dainty, nice, tale-bearers, eavesdroppers, rumor-raisers, evil-tongued, worse-minded, and, in every wise, doltified with the dregs of the Devil's dung hill, as these minions[1] be. Such shall your senators and rulers be that shall be neither able to rule themselves nor you. No Deborahs, no Judiths, no Esthers, no Elizabeths. For sure where such be, there is no token of God's wrath, which the prophet threateneth here, but of God's favor, whereof we may be assured.

*   *   *

The third reason of this argument is out of Saint Paul, whereby women be forbidden to speak in the congregation, for it is an unseemly thing for them to speak.[2] This is marvelously amplified and urged, as though it were so sound as no fault nor crack could be found in it. This is the Hercules club that beateth all down before it. These be Samson's locks that make him so strong, wherefore there must be taken some pains in the confuting of it. First, therefore, I lay this foundacy[3] on which I laid before, that Saint Paul nor none of the rest of Christ's guard meddle not with civil policy, no further than to teach obedience, nor have no commission thereunto in all the whole scripture. And this being a great matter of policy, yea, the greatest (for

---

later preferred his own advantage to the public good. It was another Fabius, however, Quintus Fabius Maximus Rullianus, the master of the horse and a respected military leader, who was commanded to yield to the authority of the law, as noted in Book 8.32 (see Livy, [*The History of Rome*], trans. B. O. Foster [New York: G. P. Putnams's Sons, 1919–59,] 4.123); '*Siste lictor*': "Stand by, lictor"; the lictors, attendants of the Roman magistrates, were responsible for enforcing their commands.

7. That which.
8. Makes an argument against.
9. Isaiah 3.4–5; 12. Rather than expositing these verses at length, Knox more generally argues that God allows women rulers to reign in order to punish nations for their sins.
1. Women of loose morals; *Aristotle saith . . . their manners*: in the *Nicomachean Ethics* 1.2.1095a, Aristotle argues that immaturity is a matter of character (that is, manners,) not chronological age (see Aristotle, *Complete Works*, 2.1730); *dainty*: lovers of luxury; *nice*: foolish; *doltified*: made dull and stupid.
2. 1 Corinthians 14.34.
3. Foundation.

it containeth the whole) it cannot be within the compass of Paul's commission; and so followeth it, that Paul either in this place meant no such matter as they gather, or if he did, he did it without the compass of his commission, but that is unlike.[4]

* * *

But to what purpose is all this? To declare that it is not in England so dangerous a matter to have a woman ruler, as men take it to be. For, first, it is not she that ruleth but the laws, the executors whereof be her judges appointed by her, her justices of peace and such other officers.

"But she may err in choosing such."

"So may a king, and therefore they have their Council at their elbow, which, by travel abroad, know men how fit or unfit they be for such offices."

Second, she maketh no statutes or laws, but the honorable court of Parliament; she breaketh none, but it must be she and they together or else not. Third, if she should judge in capital crimes, what danger were there in her womanish nature? None at all. For the verdict is the twelve men's, which pass upon life and death, and not hers. Only this belongeth to her ministry: that when they have found treason, murder, or felony, she utter the pain limited[5] in the law for that kind of trespass.

"Yea, but this she cannot do because a woman is not learned in the laws."

"No more is your king, and therefore have they their ministers, which can skill. If they be cruel, wicked, hand-makers,[6] and bribers, it is their fault and not the prince's, unless he know them to be such and wink at it."

THE CORONATION PAGEANTS

Elizabeth's movements from accession to coronation were carefully scripted along the lines of earlier royal ceremonies, including those of Mary Tudor, in order to claim their precedence, assert her own legitimacy, and reassure the nation. On November 23 she left Hatfield House for London, where she stayed at various private houses and in the royal apartments at the Tower of London, which was a fortified palace as well as a prison, before moving to Whitehall Palace for the Christmas season. Her coronation was set for January 15, 1559, the earliest date deemed appropriate by her court astrologer, Dr. John Dee, and on January 12 she moved back to the Tower, as tradition required, in preparation for the festivities.

On the day before her coronation, Elizabeth entered London in a magnificent procession. Riding in a splendidly decorated open litter, she was accompanied by thirty-nine ladies of honor, by a thousand horseman, and by a colorful contingent of royal guards and retainers in crimson jackets, each decorated with her initials and with the white rose of York and the red rose of Lancaster. Processing before her were her household staff and minor court officials, as well as the entire bench of bishops, the titled peers of the realm, and cadres of foreign ambassadors. Her route through London was everywhere decorated with festive hangings and tapestries, which were displayed on gates and walls, homes and shops, fountains and churches.

---

4. Either the apostle Paul did not mean his prohibition against women speaking should extend into civil government, or he spoke outside the authority given him by God, although the latter is unlikely.
5. Punishment required.
6. Those who profit by fraudulent means; *skill*: make judgments.

The parade route took the Queen to eleven stops, including five pageants or stages, from which children addressed speeches to her, musicians played, and symbolic and allegorical figures conveyed sentiments deemed appropriate by the city officials who arranged the festivities. The spectacle was recorded in memorable detail by the principal author of the coronation pageants, the humanist educator Richard Mulcaster. The entertainments, which were published under the title *The Passage of our most Dread Sovereign Lady, Queen Elizabeth, through the City of London to Westminster the Day before her Coronation,* did more than simply glorify the new head of state. They also set out to support her claims to royal authority and legitimacy, to remind her of the virtues of a good ruler, to recognize her as a divinely appointed Protestant

The coronation and the changes brought
by the new queen.

monarch, and to urge her to secure the succession by marrying and bearing children.

The first pageant, entitled "The uniting of the two houses of Lancaster and York," established her royal authority by tracing her paternity back to Henry VII, the Lancastrian who brought peace to England by defeating Richard III, marrying Elizabeth of York, and so ending the Wars of the Roses. The assertion of her legitimacy was made all the more pointed by the fact that the show was staged at the very site where her mother, the disgraced Anne Boleyn, had once watched a pageant during her own installation as Queen.

The last pageant established Elizabeth's legitimacy on religious grounds, likening her to the biblical judge Deborah. It was a telling precedent to cite in establishing the new Queen's right to rule. Not only was Deborah a successful ruler who governed the Old Testament Israelites for forty years, but she was also a judge, a military leader, and a prophet. For English Protestants, the last point was crucial, for Deborah's authority came not from human beings but from God. By treating her as a precedent for Elizabeth, the authors of the pageant implied that the English monarch about to be crowned also spoke for God and ruled by divine right. Perhaps sharing concerns like those of John Aylmer about a young woman's ability to rule on her own, they also suggested her duty to work closely with the Privy Council and the legislative branch by dressing Deborah in Parliament robes and surrounding her with counselors representing the three "estates" into which the English people were traditionally divided: commoners, clergy, and nobility.

The intermediate pageants focused on instructing Elizabeth in the duties of queenship, including the duty to become "the blessed mother of dear children." The second presumed to teach her the virtues proper to a ruler, and the fourth provided her with an English Bible to guide her and cautioned that there were two possible outcomes of her reign, either a well-founded republic or a ruinous one. The third pageant relieved the tone of sober admonition by suggesting that Elizabeth embodied all the virtues set forth by Christ in the Beatitudes and so was an exemplar of Christian righteousness.

Indeed, the most pressing issue after her coronation was to settle the question of exactly what would constitute "Christian righteousness" for her subjects. Elizabeth had already signaled her desire to return England to Protestantism. Soon after her accession, she ordered a bishop at a Christmas Mass not to elevate the bread and wine of the Eucharist, the Catholic ritual by which the consecrated elements are held up before the people as the transfigured body and blood of Christ, and she authorized the Litany, Lord's Prayer, and Creed to be said in English rather than Latin. The procession through London before her coronation, of course, had been replete with Protestant symbolism. The coronation itself, however, followed such traditional rites as the anointing with oil and the singing of a Latin Mass, although the senior bishops recused themselves from participating in the ceremony when Elizabeth again insisted that the elements not be elevated and that the Gospel and Epistle lessons be read in English as well as Latin. Such gestures and disagreements anticipated the religious struggles that Elizabeth would negotiate in the years that lay ahead.

RICHARD MULCASTER

From The Passage of Our Most Dread Sovereign Lady, Queen Elizabeth (1559)[†]

Upon Saturday, which was the fourteenth day of January in the year of our Lord God 1558, about two of the clock at afternoon, the most noble and Christian Princess, our most dread sovereign Lady Elizabeth, by the grace of God Queen of England, France, and Ireland, Defender of the Faith, etc. marched from the Tower[1] to pass through the city of London toward Westminster, richly furnished and most honorably accompanied, as well with gentlemen, barons, and other the nobility of this realm, as also with a notable train of goodly and beautiful ladies, richly appointed. And entering the city was of the people received marvelous entirely, as appeared by the assembly, prayers, wishes, welcomings, cries, tender words, and all other signs which argue a wonderful earnest love of most obedient subjects toward their sovereign. And on the other side, her Grace, by holding up her hands and merry countenance to such as stood far off and most tender and gentle language to those that stood nigh to her Grace, did declare herself no less thankfully to receive her people's good will than they lovingly offered it unto her. To all that wished her Grace well, she gave hearty thanks, and to such as bade God save her Grace, she said again God save them all and thanked them with all her heart, so that on either side there was nothing but gladness, nothing but prayer, nothing but comfort.

The Queen's Majesty rejoiced marvelously to see that so exceedingly showed toward her Grace which all good princes have ever desired, I mean so earnest love of subjects so evidently declared even to her Grace's own person, being carried[2] in the midst of them. The people again were wonderfully ravished with the loving answers and gestures of their Princess, like to the which they had before tried at her first coming to the Tower from Hatfield.[3] This her Grace's loving behavior, preconceived in the people's heads upon these considerations, was then thoroughly confirmed and, indeed, implanted a wonderful hope in them touching her worthy government in the rest of her reign. For in all her passage she did not only show her most gracious love toward the people in general but also privately. If the baser personages had either offered her Grace any flowers or such like as a signification of their good will or moved to her any suit, she most gently, to the common rejoicing of all the lookers on and private comfort of the party, stayed her chariot[4] and heard their requests. So that if a man should say well, he could not

---

[†] Copy text: *The passage of our most drad Soueraigne Lady Quene Elyzabeth through the citie of London to westminster the daye before her coronacion.* 2d ed. (London: Richard Tottill, 1558 [i.e., 1559]; STC 7590). The first edition, which was published in the same year, exists in only one copy and differs in only insignificant details. Though Mulcaster's name is not on the title page, he was paid for "making of the book" and is generally accepted as its author, though Richard Grafton and others helped plan the entertainments.

1. Following tradition, Elizabeth had stayed briefly in the Tower of London before her coronation; *1558*: until 1752, English calendars began the new year on March 25; thus the coronation was regarded as taking place in 1558, though by modern reckoning it was in 1559; *France*: English claims to French territory, particularly in Normandy, went back to the Norman Conquest and the reign of Henry II.

2. In an open litter decorated in yellow cloth of gold lined with white satin and borne by two mules.

3. Royal residence northwest of London where Elizabeth was living when Mary died. The new Queen had been joyously greeted on the road as she traveled to London for her coronation; *tried*: experienced.

4. Litter; *suit*: petition for assistance.

better term the city of London that time than a stage wherein was showed the wonderful spectacle of a noble-hearted princess toward her most loving people and the people's exceeding comfort in beholding so worthy a sovereign and hearing so prince-like a voice, which could not but have set the enemy on fire (since the virtue is in the enemy always commended), much more could not but enflame her natural, obedient, and most loving people, whose weal[5] leaneth only upon her Grace and her government.

Thus, therefore, the Queen's Majesty passed from the Tower till she came to Fenchurch,[6] the people on each side joyously beholding the view of so gracious a lady their queen and her Grace no less gladly noting and observing the same. Near unto Fenchurch was erected a scaffold richly furnished, whereon stood a noise[7] of instruments and a child in costly apparel, which was appointed to welcome the Queen's Majesty in the whole City's behalf. Against which place when her Grace came, of her own will she commanded the chariot to be stayed and that the noise might be appeased till the child had uttered his welcoming oration, which he spake in English meter as here followeth:

O peerless, sovereign Queen, behold what this thy town
Hath thee presented with at thy first entrance here.
Behold with how rich hope she° leadeth thee to thy crown;   *London*
Behold with what two gifts she comforteth thy cheer.°   *countenance*

5   The first is blessing tongues, which many a welcome say,
Which pray thou mayest do well, which praise thee to the sky,
Which wish to thee long life, which bless this happy day,
Which to thy kingdom heaps all[8] that in tongues can lie.

The second is true hearts, which love thee from their root,
10   Whose suit is triumph now and ruleth all the game,[9]
Which faithfulness have won and all untruth driv'n out,
Which skip for joy whenas they hear thy happy name.

Welcome therefore, O Queen, as much as heart can think;
Welcome again, O Queen, as much as tongue can tell.
15   Welcome to joyous tongues and hearts that will not shrink.°   *draw back*
God thee preserve, we pray, and wish thee ever well.

At which words of the last line the whole people gave a great shout, wishing with one assent as the child had said. And the Queen's Majesty thanked most heartily both the City for this her gentle[1] receiving at the first and also the people for confirming the same. Here was noted in the Queen's Majesty's countenance during the time that the child spake, besides a perpetual attentiveness in her face, a marvelous change in look as the child's words touched either her person or the people's tongues and hearts, so that she with rejoicing visage did evidently declare that the words took no less

5. Welfare; *virtue*: of a "prince-like voice."
6. Street leading from the Tower into the city.
7. Consort.
8. Piles up all the blessings.
9. Elizabeth has changed from a suitor to Mary Tudor into triumphant ruler over all the day's festivities.
1. Courteous.

place in her mind than they were most heartily pronounced by the child as from all the hearts of her most hearty citizens. The same verses were fastened up in a table upon the scaffold, and the Latin thereof likewise in Latin verses in another table.[2] * * *

Now, when the child had pronounced his oration and the Queen's Highness so thankfully had received it, she marched forward toward Gracious Street, where, at the upper end before the sign of the Eagle, the City had erected a gorgeous and sumptuous ark,[3] as here followeth.

A stage was made which extended from the one side of the street to the other, richly vaunted with battlements containing three ports, and over the middlemost was advanced three several stages in degrees.[4] Upon the lowest stage was made one seat royal, wherein were placed two personages representing King Henry VII and Elizabeth his wife, daughter of King Edward IV, either of these two princes sitting under one cloth of estate in their seats, no otherwise divided but that the one of them, which was King Henry VII, proceeding out of the House of Lancaster, was enclosed in a red rose and the other, which was Queen Elizabeth, being heir to the House of York, enclosed with a white rose,[5] each of them royally crowned and decently appareled as appertaineth to princes, with scepters in their hands and one vault surmounting their heads, wherein aptly were placed two tables, each containing the title of those two princes. And these personages were so set that the one of them joined hands with the other, with the ring of matrimony perceived on the finger, out of the which two roses sprang two branches gathered into one, which were directed upward to the second stage or degree, wherein was placed one representing the valiant and noble prince, King Henry VIII, which sprung out of the former stock, crowned with a crown imperial, and by him sat one representing the right worthy lady Queen Anne, wife to the said King Henry VIII and mother to our most sovereign lady, Queen Elizabeth that now is, both appareled with scepters and diadems and other furniture[6] due to the state of a king and queen, and two tables surmounting their heads, wherein were written their names and titles. From their feet also proceeded upwards one branch directed to the third and uppermost stage or degree, wherein likewise was planted a seat royal, in the which was set one representing the Queen's most excellent Majesty, Elizabeth, now our most dread sovereign lady, crowned and appareled as the other princes were. Out of the forepart of this pageant was made a standing[7] for a child, which at the Queen's Majesty's coming declared unto her the whole meaning of the said pageant. The two sides of the same were filled with loud noises of music. And all empty places thereof were furnished with sentences concerning unity, and the whole pageant garnished with red roses

---

2. Latin verses omitted; *table*: plaque.
3. Arched entryway; *Gracious*: or Gracechurch; *the Eagle*: a pub. Since there were no street numbers, retail establishments were identified by the images on their signs.
4. Tiers; *ports*: portals.
5. The tableau celebrates the end of the Wars of the Roses (1455–1485), when the houses of York and Lancaster were united in marriage by Henry VII, the first Tudor monarch, and his wife Elizabeth of York, grandparents of Elizabeth I; *cloth of estate*: royal canopy.
6. Furnishings; *crown imperial*: a crown closed at the top by two crossing arches, like that of the Holy Roman Emperor, meaning that its bearer did not owe allegiance to any higher earthly authority. Henry VIII had broken with the Pope and acknowledged no superiors in Europe. In this period, such crowns increasingly implied aspirations to colonial empires, as well. *Queen Anne*: Anne Boleyn, charged with adultery and executed in 1536.
7. Standing place; *pageant*: a temporary structure on which outdoor shows were performed.

and white, and in the forefront of the same pageant in a fair wreath was written the name and title of the same, which was, "The uniting of the two houses of Lancaster and York."

This pageant was grounded upon the Queen's Majesty's name. For like as the long war between the two houses of York and Lancaster then ended when Elizabeth, daughter to Edward IV, matched in marriage with Henry VII, heir to the House of Lancaster, so, since that the Queen's Majesty's name was Elizabeth (and forsomuch as she is the only heir of Henry VIII, which came of both the houses as the knitting up of concord), it was devised that like as Elizabeth was the first occasion of concord, so she, another Elizabeth, might maintain the same among her subjects, so that unity was the end whereat the whole device shot,[8] as the Queen's Majesty's names moved the first ground. This pageant now against the Queen's Majesty's coming was addressed[9] with children representing the forenamed personages, with all furniture due unto the setting forth of such a matter well meant, as the argument declared, costly and sumptuously set forth as the beholders can bear witness.

Now the Queen's Majesty drew near unto the said pageant, and forsomuch as the noise was great by reason of the press of people, so that she could scarce hear the child which did interpret the said pageant, and her chariot was passed so far forward that she could not well view the personages representing the kings and queens above named, she required to have the matter opened unto her and what they signified, with the end of unity and ground of her name,[1] according as is before expressed. For the sight whereof, her Grace caused her chariot to be removed back and yet hardly could she see, because the children were set somewhat with the farthest in. But after that her Grace had understood the meaning thereof, she thanked the City, praised the fairness of the work, and promised that she would do her whole endeavor for the continual preservation of concord, as the pageant did import.

The child appointed in the standing above named to open the meaning of the said pageant spake these words unto her Grace:

The two princes that sit under one cloth of state,
The man in the red rose, the woman in the white,
Henry the Seventh and Queen Elizabeth his mate,
By ring of marriage as man and wife unite.

5   Both heirs to both their bloods, to Lancaster the King,
The Queen to York, in one the two houses did knit,
Of whom as heir to both, Henry the Eighth did spring,
In whose seat his true heir thou, Queen Elizabeth, doth sit.

Therefore as civil war and shed of blood did cease
10 When these two houses were united into one,
So now that jar shall stint° and quietness increase   *conflict shall end*
We trust, O noble Queen, thou wilt be cause alone.

8. Aimed.
9. Prepared; *against*: prior to.
1. She was named for her grandmother.

The which also were written in Latin verses and both drawn in two tables upon the forefront of the said pageant.[2]

*   *   *

These verses and other pretty sentences were drawn in void places of this pageant, all tending to one end: that quietness might be maintained and all dissention displaced, and that by the Queen's Majesty, heir to agreement and agreeing in name with her which tofore[3] had joined those houses, which had been the occasion of much debate and civil war within this realm (as may appear to such as will search chronicles but be not to be touched in this treatise, only declaring her Grace's passage through the city and what provision the City made therefore). And ere the Queen's Majesty came within hearing of this pageant, she sent certain,[4] as also at all the other pageants, to require the people to be silent. For her Majesty was disposed to hear all that should be said unto her.

When the Queen's Majesty had heard the child's oration and understood the meaning of the pageant at large, she marched forward toward Cornhill, alway received with like rejoicing of the people, and there, as her Grace passed by the conduit, which was curiously trimmed against[5] that time with rich banners adorned and a noise of loud instruments upon the top thereof, she espied the second pageant. And because she feared for the people's noise, that she should not hear the child which did expound the same, she inquired what that pageant was ere that she came to it, and there understood that there was a child representing her Majesty's person placed in a seat of government, supported by certain virtues, which suppressed their contrary vices under their feet, and so forth, as in the description of the said pageant shall hereafter appear.

This pageant, standing in the nether end of Cornhill, was extended from the one side of the street to the other, and in the same pageant was devised three gates, all open, and over the middle part thereof was erected one chair, or seat royal, with cloth of estate to the same appertaining, wherein was placed a child representing the Queen's Highness, with consideration had for place convenient for a table which contained her name and title. And in a comely wreath, artificially and well devised with perfect sight and understanding to the people, in the front of the same pageant was written the name and title thereof, which is "The Seat of Worthy Governance," which seat was made in such artificial manner as, to the appearance of the lookers on, the forepart seemed to have no stay, and therefore of force was stayed by lively personages,[6] which personages were in number four, standing and staying

---

2. Latin omitted. Fifteen lines of Latin bearing the heading "Sentences placed therein concerning unity" are substituted for the last stanza of the English poem. This string of pithy sayings may be rendered as follows: "No force can overcome souls in concord. Those who inspire fear when united feel fear when divided. Souls in discord divide, those in concord bind themselves together. By peace small things are made greater, by war great things fall to ruin. Hands bear heavier burdens when joined together. For a kingdom, concord among citizens is like walls of bronze. Those who fight long mourn longer. Warring princes are a plague to their subjects. A prince born to peace is not inclined to arms. Plenty is the daughter of concord, tranquility the granddaughter. A republic divided is exposed to its enemies. Those who hold the same thing, hold it longer. A kingdom divided is easily destroyed. A city united is assailed in vain by force of arms. Consensus everywhere in the world strengthens faith" (translation by Clarence H. Miller).
3. Heretofore; *sentences*: handsomely crafted sayings; *void places*: empty spaces.
4. Certain officials.
5. In preparation for; *conduit*: fountain, from which citizens drew water; *curiously*: ingeniously.
6. Supported by living persons, rather than pillars; *artificially*: artfully; *stay*: support.

the forefront of the same seat royal, each having his face to the Queen and people, whereof every one had a table to express their effects, which are virtues, namely Pure Religion, Love of Subjects, Wisdom, and Justice, which did tread their contrary vices under their feet. That is, to wit, Pure Religion did tread upon Superstition and Ignorance, Love of Subjects did tread upon Rebellion and Insolency, Wisdom did tread upon Folly and Vainglory, Justice did tread upon Adulation and Bribery. Each of these personages according to their proper names and properties had not only their names in plain and perfect writing set upon their breasts easily to be read of all, but also every of them was aptly and properly appareled, so that his apparel and name did agree to express the same person that in title he represented. This part of the pageant was thus appointed and furnished. The two sides over the two side ports had in them placed a noise of instruments, which immediately after the child's speech gave an heavenly melody. Upon the top or uppermost part of the said pageant stood the arms of England totally portraitured with the proper beasts[7] to uphold the same. One, representing the Queen's Highness, sat in this seat crowned with an imperial crown, and before her seat was a convenient place appointed for one child, which did interpret and apply the said pageant as hereafter shall be declared. Every void place was furnished with proper sentences commending the seat supported by virtues, and defacing the vices, to the utter extirpation of rebellion and to everlasting continuance of quietness and peace.

The Queen's Majesty approaching nigh unto this pageant, thus beautified and furnished in all points, caused her chariot to be drawn nigh thereunto that her Grace might hear the child's oration, which was this:

> While that Religion true shall Ignorance suppress
> And with her weighty foot break Superstition's head,
> While Love of Subjects shall Rebellion distress
> And with zeal to the Prince Insolency down tread,
>
> 5 While Justice can Flattering Tongues and Bribery deface,
> While Folly and Vainglory to Wisdom yield their hands,
> So long shall Government not swerve from her right race,
> But Wrong decayeth still and Rightwiseness° up stands.   *Righteousness*
>
> Now all thy Subjects' hearts, O Prince of peerless fame,
> 10 Do trust these Virtues shall máintain up thy throne,
> And Vice be kept down still, the wicked put to shame,
> That good with good may joy, and naught° with naught may moan.   *bad*

Which verses were painted upon the right side of the same pageant, and the Latin thereof on the left side in another table.[8]

---

7. The Queen's coat of arms contained a rampant lion, symbol of royalty, and a dragon, associated with King Arthur and his father, Uther Pendragon, mythical founders of the Tudor dynasty.
8. The Latin version differs from the English and may be rendered "The Queen, who is borne up on high by the proud throne, lovingly presents a picture of the holy prince, one who is supported by Love of Citizens, strengthened by Wisdom, adorned by Justice, and blessed by Religion. Empty Superstition and crudely blatant Ignorance are thrust down, lying under the feet of Pure Religion. The Sovereign's love tames the minds of the unruly and rebellious. The just ruler crushes Flatterers and Devourers of the Royal Household. When a wise person rules the realm, Folly and the substance of her divinity, Vainglory, shall sit in darkness" (translation by Clarence H. Miller).

*   *   *

Beside these verses there were placed in every void room of the pageant, both in English and Latin, such sentences as advanced[9] the seat of governance upholden by Virtue. The ground[1] of this pageant was that, like as by virtues (which do abundantly appear in her Grace) the Queen's Majesty was established in the seat of government, so she should sit fast in the same so long as she embraced Virtue and held Vice under foot. For if Vice once got up the head, it would put the seat of government in peril of falling.

The Queen's Majesty, when she had heard the child and understood the pageant at full, gave the City also thanks there, and most graciously promised her good endeavor for the maintenance of the said virtues and suppression of vices, and so marched on till she came against the great conduit in Cheap,[2] which was beautified with pictures and sentences accordingly against her Grace's coming thither.

Against Soper Lane's end was extended from the one side of the street to the other a pageant which had three gates, all open, over the middlemost whereof were erected three several stages, whereon sat eight children, as hereafter followeth: on the uppermost one child, on the middle three, on the lowest four, each having the proper name of the blessing that they did represent written in a table and placed above their heads. In the forefront of this pageant, before the children which did represent the blessings, was a convenient standing cast out for a child to stand, which did expound the said pageant unto the Queen's Majesty, as was done in the other tofore. Every of these children were appointed and appareled according unto the blessing which he did represent. And on the forepart of the said pageant was written in fair letters the name of the said pageant, in this manner following:

> The eight beatitudes expressed in the fifth chapter of the
> Gospel of St. Matthew, applied to our sovereign lady,
> Queen Elizabeth.

Over the two side ports was placed a noise of instruments. And all void places in the pageant were furnished with pretty sayings, commending and touching the meaning of the said pageant, which was the promises and blessings of Almighty God made to His people. Before that the Queen's Highness came unto this pageant, she required the matter somewhat to be opened unto her that her Grace might the better understand what should afterward by the child be said unto her. Which so was: that the City had there erected the pageant with eight children, representing the eight blessings touched in the fifth chapter of St. Matthew, whereof every one upon just considerations was applied unto her Highness, and that the people thereby put her Grace in mind that as her good doings before had given just occasion why that these blessings might fall upon her, that so, if her Grace did continue in her goodness as she had entered,[3] she should hope for the fruit of these promises, due unto them that do exercise themselves in the blessings, which her Grace heard marvelous graciously and required that

9. Promoted; *room*: space.
1. Allegorical basis.
2. Cheapside, a market area; *against*: beside.
3. Begun.

the chariot might be removed towards the pageant that she might perceive the child's words, which were these, the Queen's Majesty giving most attentive care and requiring that the people's noise might be stayed:

Thou hast been eight times blest, O Queen of worthy fame,
By meekness of thy spirit, when care did thee beset,
By mourning in thy grief, by mildness in thy blame,
By hunger and by thirst, and justice could'st none get,

5   By mercy showed, not felt, by cleanness of thine heart,
By seeking peace always, by persecution wrong.
Therefore, trust thou in God, since He hath helped thy smart,°   *affliction*
That as His promise is, so He will make thee strong.

When these words were spoken, all the people wished that, as the child had spoken, so God would strengthen her Grace against all her adversaries, whom the Queen's Majesty did most gently thank for their so loving wish. These verses were painted on the left side of the said pageant, and other in Latin on the other side.[4]

*   *   *

Besides these, every void place in the pageant was furnished with sentences touching the matter and ground of the said pageant. When all that was to be said in this pageant was ended, the Queen's Majesty passed on forward in Cheapside.

At the Standard in Cheap, which was dressed fair[5] against the time, was placed a noise of trumpets, with banners and other furniture. The cross[6] likewise was also made fair and well trimmed. And near unto the same, upon the porch of Saint Peter's church door, stood the waits[7] of the city, which did give a pleasant noise with their instruments as the Queen's Majesty did pass by, which on every side cast her countenance and wished well to all her most loving people. Soon after that her Grace passed the cross, she had espied the pageant erected at the Little Conduit in Cheap and, incontinent,[8] required to know what it might signify. And it was told her Grace that there was placed Time. "Time?" quoth she, "And Time hath brought me hither." And so forth the whole matter was opened to her Grace, as hereafter shall be declared in the description of the pageant. But in the opening, when her Grace understood that the Bible in English should be delivered unto her by Truth, which was therein represented by a child, she thanked the City for that gift and said that she would oftentimes read over that book, com-

4. Latin omitted. The verses are a loose rendering of the Beatitudes (Matthew 5.3–10): "Those who mourn shall become merry. Those who harbor meek hearts shall harvest many acres of cultivated ground. Those hungering and thirsting for justice shall find themselves filled. It is right for a man who is pure in heart to see God. Whoever has mercy on others, to him will God be merciful. Whoever is a peacemaker, he is the son of God. Whoever suffers for the sake of justice, and has a humble mind, shall receive the kingdom of heaven. The Almighty promised the earth, the sea, and the stars to men of this kind, and each of them shall be blessed" (translation by Clarence H. Miller).
5. Decorated beautifully; *Standard in Cheap*: column beside a public fountain, where people gathered for speeches, proclamations, and executions.
6. One of several large, outdoor crosses erected by Edward I.
7. Musicians employed by the city for public functions.
8. Unable to wait.

manding Sir John Perrot,[9] one of the knights which held up her canopy, to go before and to receive the book. But learning that it should be delivered unto her Grace down by a silken lace, she caused him to stay, and so passed forward till she came against the aldermen in the high end of Cheap tofore the Little Conduit, where the companies of the city ended, which began at Fenchurch and stood along the streets, one by another enclosed with rails hanged with cloths and themselves well appareled with many rich furs and their livery hoods upon their shoulders in comely and seemly manner, having before them sundry persons well appareled in silks and chains of gold as whifflers and guarders of the said companies, beside a number of rich hangings as well of tapestry, arras,[1] cloths of gold, silver, velvet, damask, satin, and other silks, plentifully hanged all the way as the Queen's Highness passed from the Tower through the city. Out at the windows and penthouses[2] of every house did hang a number of rich and costly banners and streamers till her Grace came to the upper end of Cheap.

And there, by appointment, the Right Worshipful Master Randolph Cholmley, Recorder of the City, presented to the Queen's Majesty a purse of crimson satin, richly wrought with gold, wherein the City gave unto the Queen's Majesty a thousand marks in gold, as Master Recorder did declare briefly unto the Queen's Majesty, whose words tended to this end, that the Lord Mayor, his brethren, and commonality[3] of the city, to declare their gladness and good will towards the Queen's Majesty, did present her Grace with that gold, desiring her Grace to continue their good and gracious Queen and not to esteem the value of the gift but the mind of the givers. The Queen's Majesty with both her hands took the purse and answered to him again marvelous pithily, and so pithily that the standers-by, as they embraced entirely her gracious answer, so they marveled at the couching thereof, which was in words truly reported these: "I thank my Lord Mayor, his brethren, and you all. And whereas your request is that I should continue your good lady and Queen, be ye ensured, that I will be as good unto you as ever queen was to her people. No will in me can lack, neither do I trust shall there lack any power. And persuade yourselves that, for the safety and quietness of you all, I will not spare, if need be, to spend my blood. God thank you all."

Which answer of so noble an hearted princess, if it moved a marvelous shout and rejoicing, it is nothing to be marveled at, since both the heartiness thereof was so wonderful and the words so jointly knit.[4] When her Grace had thus answered the Recorder, she marched toward the Little Conduit, where was erected a pageant with square proportion,[5] standing directly before the same conduit, with battlements accordingly. And in the same pageant was advanced two hills or mountains of convenient height. The one of them, being on the north side of the same pageant, was made cragged, barren, and stony, in the which was erected one tree, artificially

---

9. A staunch Protestant, widely regarded as the bastard son of Henry VIII and so Elizabeth's half-brother. She later made him Lord Deputy of Ireland.
1. Tapestries of a style originating in Arras, France; *companies of the city*: organizations of tradesmen responsible for creating the pageants within the city gates; *livery hoods*: hoods worn as signs of office or company affiliation; *whifflers and guarders*: officials employed, respectively, to clear the way and keep order.
2. Projecting roofs over doors and walkways.
3. Citizens below the rank of titled nobility; *Recorder of the City*: London's highest legal officer; *marks*: coins worth roughly two-thirds of a pound sterling each; *brethren*: city officials.
4. Neatly woven.
5. Rather than arches.

made, all withered and dead, with branches accordingly. And under the
same tree, at the foot thereof, sat one in homely and rude[6] apparel,
crookedly and in mourning manner, having over his head in a table, written in Latin and English, his name, which was *Ruinosa Respublica*, a
Decayed Commonweal. And upon the same withered tree were fixed certain tables, wherein were written proper sentences expressing the causes
of the decay of a commonweal. The other hill, on the south side, was made
fair, fresh, green, and beautiful, the ground thereof full of flowers and
beauty, and on the same was erected also one tree very fresh and fair, under
the which stood upright one fresh personage well appareled and appointed,
whose name also was written both in English and in Latin, which was,
Respublica bene instituta, a Flourishing Commonweal. And upon the same
tree also were fixed certain tables containing sentences which expressed
the causes of a flourishing commonweal. In the middle, between the said
hills, was made artificially one hollow place or cave, with door and lock
enclosed, out of the which, a little before the Queen's Highness coming
thither, issued one personage whose name was Time, appareled as an old
man with a scythe in his hand, having wings artificially made, leading a personage of lesser stature than himself, which was finely and well appareled,
all clad in white silk, and directly over her head was set her name and title
in Latin and English, *Temporis filia*, the Daughter of Time,[7] which two so
appointed went forward, toward the south side of the pageant. And on her
breast was written her proper name, which was *Veritas*, Truth, who held a
book in her hand upon the which was written, "*Verbum Veritatis*," the Word
of Truth. And out of the south side of the pageant was cast a standing for
a child which should interpret the same pageant. Against whom, when the
Queen's Majesty came, he spake unto her Grace these words:

This old man with the scythe old Father Time they call,
And her his daughter Truth, which holdeth yonder book,
Whom he out of his rock hath brought forth to us all,
From whence this many years she durst not once out look.

5   The ruthful wight° that sitteth under the barren tree,   *sad creature*
Resembleth to us the form when commonweals decay,
But when they be in state triumphant, you may see
By him in fresh attire that sitteth under the bay.[8]

Now since that Time again his daughter Truth hath brought,
10   We trust, O worthy Queen, thou wilt this Truth embrace,
And since thou understandst the good estate and naught,°   *bad*
We trust wealth thou wilt plant and barrenness displace.

But for to heal the sore and cure that is not seen,
Which thing the book of Truth doth teach in writing plain,

---

6. Coarse, shabby.
7. That "Truth is the daughter of Time" was a Protestant proverb used to justify the emergence of
   Reformed theology after centuries of Catholic teaching. Mary Tudor, a Catholic, had wittily made
   it her own motto, implying that she was again bringing forth Truth after a period of Protestant falsehood under her brother, Edward VI. Here, Mulcaster turns Mary's motto against her, claiming
   Truth again for Elizabeth and the Protestant cause.
8. Bay tree, or laurel, symbol of preeminent excellence and renown.

15 She doth present to thee the same, O worthy Queen,
For that° that words do fly but writing doth remain.   *Meaning*

When the child had thus ended his speech, he reached his book towards the Queen's Majesty which, a little before, Truth had let down unto him from the hill, which by Sir John Perrot was received and delivered unto the Queen. But she, as soon as she had received the book, kissed it and with both her hands held up the same, and so laid it upon her breast, with great thanks to the City therefore. And so went forward towards Paul's Churchyard.[9] The former matter which was rehearsed unto the Queen's Majesty was written in two tables, on either side the pageant eight verses, and in the middest these in Latin. * * * [1] The sentences written in Latin and English upon both the trees, declaring the causes of both estates, were these:

Causes of a ruinous commonweal are these:

Want of the fear of God	Civil disagreement
Disobedience to rulers	Flattering of princes
Blindness of guides	Unmercifulness in rulers
Bribery in magistrates	Unthankfulness in subjects
Rebellion in subjects	

Causes of a flourishing commonweal:

Fear of God	Obedient subjects
A wise prince	Lovers of the commonweal
Learned rulers	Virtue rewarded
Obedience to officers	Vice chastened

The matter of this pageant dependeth of them that went before. For as the first declared her Grace to come out of the house of unity, the second that she is placed in the seat of government stayed[2] with virtue to the suppression of vice, and therefore in the third the eight blessings of Almighty God might well be applied unto her, so this fourth now is to put her Grace in remembrance of the state of the commonweal, which Time with Truth his daughter doth reveal, which Truth also her Grace hath received and therefore cannot but be merciful and careful for the good government thereof. From thence the Queen's Majesty passed toward Paul's Churchyard, and when she came over against Paul's School, a child appointed by the schoolmaster thereof pronounced a certain oration in Latin and certain verses, which also were there written.[3]

[*Translation of the Child's Oration*]

Among many sayings, Plato, that divine philosopher, excellently and wisely handed this observation down to posterity: that a republic will be happiest

---

9. St. Paul's was the cathedral of the city of London.
1. Latin omitted. The verses are a loose translation of the first two stanzas of the English poem on Father Time; *side*: side of.
2. Supported; *house of unity*: the Tudor line, uniting the houses of Lancaster and York.
3. Latin omitted. The translations that follow are by Clarence H. Miller.

if it happens to have a prince who seeks wisdom and is adorned with virtues.[4] Which, if we think truly said (as, indeed, it is most truly said), why should Britain not break out in applause? Why should the people not be overcome with joy and gladness? Nay, why should they not mark this day (as they say) with a white stone?[5] a day on which we have among us a prince such as our ancestors did not see and our descendents will hardly be able to behold again, a prince thoroughly blessed in all the gifts of mind and body. Indeed the gifts of her chaste body are so apparent that there is no lack of language to describe them. Those of her mind, however, are so numerous and so great that it is not even possible to express them in words. To be sure, she is descended from the noblest kings, yet in nobility of virtue and of mind, she outstrips her family. Her breast burns with love of the religion of Christ. By her virtues she will bring light and glory to the people of Britain, and she will defend them with a shield of justice. Most learned in Greek and Latin literature, she stands out for her gifts of intellect. Under such a ruler, piety will thrive, England will flourish, and the Golden Age[6] return. Therefore, people of England, you who are about to receive so much, attend with due honor upon Elizabeth, our most celebrated Queen, destined by Christ Himself to rule this kingdom. Be subject with most willing hearts to her commands, and show yourselves worthy of such a prince. And because boys are not able to perform their duty by strength, but only by prayer, we, the pupils of this school founded by Colet, once Dean of St. Paul's Cathedral,[7] raising our tender palms to heaven, pray to Christ (best and greatest) that your Highness may attain the great age of Nestor, that Christ may cause you to rule over the English with the greatest honor, and that He may make you become the blessed mother of dear children.

[Translation of the Child's Verses]

England, now at length clap your hands, rejoice, re-echo the sound! Life is now at hand, and your protection. Your hope comes, your glory, your light, your perfect splendor. She comes now who brings you genuine assistance. She will hasten to help you in what has gone amiss. She will long to bring back those things that have been lost. All will flourish. Now returns the Golden Age. The good that fell[8] will rise restored. You must, therefore, give yourself over to her in complete faith, for by her accession you will obtain many benefits. You should hail her, then, from the depths of your heart. The salvation of Elizabeth's reign is beyond doubt. She comes a virgin, and may you hope that she will later come accompanied by dear children, that she will come a joyful parent. May Almighty God, who created and rules over heaven and earth, grant this from heaven above.

Which the Queen's Majesty most attentively harkened unto. And when the child had pronounced, he did kiss the oration, which he had there fair written in paper, and delivered it unto the Queen's Majesty, which most

---

4. *Republic* 7.520 (see Plato, *Complete Works*, ed. by John M. Cooper [Indianapolis: Hackett; 1997], 1137).
5. The Romans marked fortunate days with a white stone, unfortunate ones with a black stone.
6. In classical myth, the first age of the world, when all creatures lived in harmony and plenty.
7. John Colet, humanist friend of Sir Thomas More and founder of St. Paul's School.
8. A reference to the decline in England under Mary Tudor and also to the fall of humankind from the perfection of Eden, which is to be restored following the Last Judgment (Revelation 21–22).

gently received the same. And when the Queen's Majesty had heard all that was there offered to be spoken, then her Grace marched toward Ludgate,[9] where she was received with a noise of instruments, the forefront of the gate being finely trimmed up against her Majesty's coming. From thence, by the way as she went down toward Fleet Bridge, one about her Grace noted the City's charge, that there was no cost spared. Her Grace answered that she did well consider the same and that it should be remembered—an honorable answer, worthy a noble prince, which may comfort all her subjects, considering there can be no point of gentleness or obedient love showed toward her Grace which she doth not most tenderly accept and graciously weigh.

In this manner, the people on either side rejoicing, her Grace went forward toward the conduit in Fleet Street, where was the fifth and last pageant erected, in form following. From the conduit, which was beautified with painting, unto the north side of the street was erected a stage embattled with four towers and in the same a square plat rising with degrees, and upon the uppermost degree was placed a chair, or seat royal, and behind the same seat, in curious and artificial manner, was erected a tree of reasonable height and so far advanced above the seat as it did well and seemly shadow the same, without endamaging[1] the sight of any part of the pageant. And the same tree was beautified with leaves as green as art could devise, being of a convenient greatness and containing thereupon the fruit of the date, and on the top of the same tree in a table was set the name thereof, which was a palm tree, and in the aforesaid seat or chair was placed a seemly and meet personage, richly appareled in Parliament robes with a scepter in her hand, as a queen crowned with an open crown,[2] whose name and title was in a table fixed over her head, in this sort: "Deborah, the judge and restorer of the house of Israel (Judges 4)." And the other degrees on either side were furnished with six personages: two representing the nobility, two the clergy, and two the commonality.[3] And before these personages was written in a table, "Deborah, with her estates consulting for the good government of Israel." At the feet of these and the lowest part of the pageant was ordained a convenient room for a child to open the meaning of the pageant. When the Queen's Majesty drew near unto this pageant and perceived, as in the other, the child ready to speak, her Grace required silence and commanded her chariot to be removed nigher that she might plainly hear the child speak, which said as hereafter followeth:

Jabin of Canaan King had long by force of arms
Oppressed the Israelites, which for God's people went.[4]
But God, minding at last for to redress their harms,
The worthy Deborah as judge among them sent.

---

9. Westernmost gate of the city, beyond which lay Westminster.
1. Obstructing; *embattled*: fortified; *square plat . . . degrees*: square surface with ascending platforms.
2. Compare the closed crown worn by the figure representing Elizabeth in the tableau "The Seat of Worthy Governance" at Cornhill. The reason for the contrast is unclear, since Deborah in her Parliament robes is clearly a figure for the Queen.
3. Citizens were traditionally divided into three "estates," or conditions of life: nobility, clergy, and commoners.
4. Which were known as God's people.
5. Not specified in scripture, though the story of Deborah ends with the words "the land had rest forty years" (Judges 5.31).

5 In war she, through God's aid, did put her foes to flight,
   And with the dint of sword the band of bondage brast.°   *broke*
   In peace she, through God's aid, did alway maintain right
   And judgéd Israel till forty years[5] were past.

   A worthy precedent, O worthy Queen, thou hast,
10 A worthy woman judge, a woman sent for stay.°   *support*
   And that the like to us endure alway thou may'st,
   Thy loving subjects will with true hearts and tongues pray.

Which verses were written upon the pageant and the same in Latin also.[6]

*   *   *

The void places of the pageant were filled with pretty sentences concerning the same matter. This ground of this last pageant was that, forsomuch as the next pageant before had set before her Grace's eyes the flourishing and desolate states of a commonweal, she might by this be put in remembrance to consult for the worthy government of her people, considering God oft times sent women nobly to rule among men, as Deborah which governed Israel in peace the space of forty years, and that it behooveth both men and women so ruling to use advice of good counsel. When the Queen's Majesty had passed this pageant, she marched toward Temple Bar.[7] But at St. Dunstan's church, where the children of the hospital[8] were appointed to stand with their governors, her Grace, perceiving a child offered to make an oration unto her, stayed her chariot and did cast up her eyes to heaven, as who should say, "I here see this merciful work toward the poor, whom I must in the midst of my royalty needs remember," and so turned her face toward the child, which in Latin pronounced an oration to this effect: that after the Queen's Highness had passed through the city and had seen so sumptuous, rich, and notable spectacles of the citizens, which declared their most hearty receiving and joyous welcoming of her Grace into the same, this one spectacle yet rested and remained, which was the everlasting spectacle of mercy unto the poor members of Almighty God, furthered by that famous and most noble prince King Henry VIII, her gracious father, erected by the city of London and advanced by the most godly, virtuous, and gracious prince King Edward VI, her Grace's dear and loving brother, doubting nothing of the mercy of the Queen's most gracious clemency by the which they may not only be relieved and helped but also stayed and defended, and therefore incessantly they would pray and cry unto Almighty God for the long life and reign of her Highness, with most prosperous victory against her enemies.

The child, after he had ended his oration, kissed the paper wherein the same was written and reached it to the Queen's Majesty, which received it graciously both with words and countenance declaring her gracious mind toward their relief. From thence her Grace came to Temple Bar, which was dressed finely with the two images of Gotmagot the Albion and Corineus the Briton, two giants big in stature furnished accordingly, which held in their hands, even above the gate, a table wherein was written in Latin verses the effect of

6. Latin omitted.
7. The entrance to Westminster.
8. Christ Hospital, a school for poor boys established by Elizabeth's father.

all the pageants which the city before had erected.[9] * * * Which verses were
also written in English meter in a less table, as hereafter followeth:

Behold here, in one view, thou mayst see all that plain,
O Princess, to this thy people the only stay,
What each-where° thou hast seen in this wide town; again   *everywhere*
This one arch whatsoever the rest contained doth say.

5   The first arch, as true heir unto thy father dear,
Did set thee in the throne where thy grandfather sat.
The second did confirm thy seat as Princess here,
Virtues now bearing sway and vices beat down flat.

The third, if that thou wouldst go on as thou began,
10   Declared thee to be blessed on every side.
The fourth did open Truth, and also taught thee when
The commonweal stood well and when it did thence slide.

The fifth as Deborah declared thee to be sent
From heaven, a long comfort to us thy subjects all.
15   Therefore go on, O Queen, on whom our hope is bent,
And take with thee this wish of thy town as final:

Live long and as long reign, adorning thy country
With virtues, and maintain thy people's hope of thee,
For thus, thus heaven is won; thus must thou[1] pierce the sky.
20   This is by virtue wrought; all other must needs die.

On the south side was appointed by the City a noise of singing children,
and one child richly attired as a poet, which gave the Queen's Majesty her
farewell in the name of the whole City by these words:

As at thine entrance first, O Prince of high renown,
Thou wast presented with tongues and hearts for thy fare,°   *provision*
So now sith thou must needs depart out of this town,
This city sendeth thee firm hope and earnest prayer.

5   For all men hope in thee that all virtues shall reign,
For all men hope that thou none error wilt support,
For all men hope that thou wilt truth restore again,
And mend that° is amiss to all good men's comfort.   *that which*

And for this hope they pray: thou mayst continue long,
10   Our Queen amongst us here, all vice for to supplant,
And for this hope they pray: that God may make thee strong,
As by His grace puissant, so in His truth constant.

9. Latin omitted. *Gotmagot . . . Briton*: according to Geoffrey of Monmouth's *Chronicles* (1.15–16),
   England was founded by two Trojans, Brutus and Corineus, for whom Britain and Cornwall were
   named. In taming the land, Corineus killed all its giants, casting the most famous, Gotmagot (or
   Gogmagog), into the sea (see Geoffrey of Monmouth, *The History of the Kings of Britain*, trans.
   Lewis Thorpe [London: The Folio Society, 1969], 52–55).
1. Copy text: thee.

Farewell, O worthy Queen, and as our hope is sure
That into error's place thou wilt now truth restore,
15   So trust we that thou wilt our sovereign Queen endure
And loving lady stand, from henceforth evermore.

    While these words were in saying, and certain wishes therein repeated for maintenance of truth and rooting out of error, she now and then held up her hands to heavenward and willed the people to say "Amen."

    When the child had ended, she said, "Be ye well assured, I will stand your good Queen." At which saying her Grace departed forth through Temple Bar toward Westminster, with no less shouting and crying of the people than she entered the city with a noise of ordinance which the tower shot off at her Grace's entrance first into Tower Street. The child's saying was also in Latin verses, written in a table, which was hanged up there.[2]

* * *

    Thus the Queen's Highness passed through the city, which, without any foreign person, of itself beautified itself and received her Grace at all places, as hath been before mentioned, with most tender obedience and love, due to so gracious a queen and sovereign lady. And her Grace likewise of her side in all her Grace's passage showed herself generally an image of a worthy lady and governor, but privately these special points were noted in her Grace as signs of a most prince-like courage, whereby her loving subjects may ground a sure hope for the rest of her gracious doings hereafter.

Certain notes of the Queen's Majesty's great mercy,
clemency, and wisdom used in this passage

    About the nether end of Cornhill toward Cheap, one of the knights about her Grace had espied an ancient citizen which wept and turned his head back, and therewith said this gentleman, "Yonder is an alderman,"[3] for so he termed him, "which weepeth and turneth his face backward. How may it be interpreted that he so doth? for sorrow or for gladness?" The Queen's Majesty heard him and said, "I warrant you it is for gladness." A gracious interpretation of a noble courage,[4] which would turn the doubtful to the best. And yet it was well known that, as her Grace did confirm the same, the party's cheer[5] was moved for very pure gladness for the sight of her Majesty's person, at the beholding whereof he took such comfort that with tears he expressed the same.

    In Cheapside her Grace smiled and, being thereof demanded the cause, answered for that she had heard one say, "Remember old King Henry VIII." A natural child, which at the very remembrance of her father's name took so great a joy that all men may well think that, as she rejoiced at his name whom this realm doth hold of so worthy memory, so in her doings she will resemble the same.

2. Latin omitted.
3. Old man.
4. Heart.
5. Countenance.

When the City's charge[6] without partiality, and only the City, was mentioned unto her Grace, she said it should not be forgotten. Which saying might move all Englishmen heartily to show due obedience and entireness[7] to so good a queen, which will in no point forget any parcel of duty lovingly showed unto her.

The answer which her Grace made unto Master Recorder of London, as the hearers know it to be true and with melting hearts heard the same, so may the reader thereof conceive what kind of stomach[8] and courage pronounced the same.

What more famous thing do we read in ancient histories of old time than that mighty princes have gently received presents offered them by base and low personages? If that be to be wondered at, as it is passingly,[9] let me see any writer that in any one prince's life is able to recount so many precedents of this virtue as her Grace showed in that one passage through the city. How many nosegays did her Grace receive at poor women's hands? How oft-times stayed she her chariot when she saw any simple body offer to speak to her Grace? A branch of rosemary[1] given to her Grace with a supplication by a poor woman about Fleet Bridge was seen in her chariot till her Grace came to Westminster, not without the marvelous wondering of such as knew the presenter and noted the Queen's most gracious receiving and keeping the same.

What hope the poor and needy may look for at her Grace's hand, she (as in all her journey continually, so in her hearkening to the poor children of Christ's Hospital with eyes cast up into heaven) did fully declare, as that neither the wealthier estate could stand without consideration had to the poverty, neither the poverty be duly considered unless they were remembered as commended to us by God's own mouth.[2]

As at her first entrance she, as it were, declared herself prepared to pass through a city that most entirely loved her, so she at her last departing, as it were, bound herself by promise to continue good lady and governor unto that city, which by outward declaration did open their love to their so loving and noble prince in such wise as she herself wondered thereat.

But because princes be set in their seat by God's appointing, and therefore they must first and chiefly tender the glory of Him from whom their glory issueth, it is to be noted in her Grace that, forsomuch as God hath so wonderfully placed her in the seat of government over this realm, she in all doings doth show herself most mindful of His goodness and mercy showed unto her, and amongst all other, two principal signs thereof were noted in this passage. First in the Tower, where her Grace, before she entered her chariot, lifted up her eyes to heaven and said,

> O Lord, almighty and everlasting God, I give Thee most hearty thanks that Thou hast been so merciful unto me as to spare me to behold this joyful day. And I acknowledge that Thou hast dealt as wonderfully and as mercifully with me as Thou didst with Thy true and faithful servant

---

6. Share of the day's expenses borne by the local government.
7. Loyalty.
8. Spirit, thought to reside in the diaphragm.
9. Surpassingly.
1. Symbol of remembrance.
2. Matthew 5.3; *poverty*: the poor.

Daniel, Thy prophet, whom Thou deliveredst out of the den from the cruelty of the greedy and raging lions.[3] Even so was I overwhelmed and only by Thee delivered.[4] To Thee, therefore, only be thanks, honor, and praise forever. Amen.

The second was the receiving of the Bible at the Little Conduit in Cheap. For when her Grace had learned that the Bible in English should there be offered, she thanked the City therefore, promised the reading thereof most diligently and, incontinent, commanded that it should be brought. At the receipt whereof, how reverently did she with both her hands take it, kiss it, and lay it upon her breast, to the great comfort of the lookers-on. God will undoubtedly preserve so worthy a prince, which at His honor so reverently taketh her beginning. For this saying is true and written in the book of truth: "He that first seeketh the kingdom of God, shall have all other things cast unto him."[5]

Now therefore all English hearts, and her natural people, must needs praise God's mercy, which hath sent them so worthy a prince, and pray for her Grace's long continuance amongst us.

PRAYERS AND EXHORTATIONS

As Supreme Governor of the newly reestablished Protestant Church, Elizabeth was at the center of religious reform and debate. She quickly brought back the Book of Common Prayer prepared by her martyred godfather, Thomas Cranmer, although it was revised to reflect somewhat more moderate theological positions. Significant changes included a specification that Christ's body and blood was present in the Sacrament—a position consonant, although not identical, with that of both Luther and Calvin, although not with some of the more radical Protestants; allowance for certain rituals such as kneeling at communion; the omission of prayers for deliverance from the tyranny of the Pope; and the addition of several prayers to the Litany, including "A Prayer for the Queen's Majesty." A similar prayer for the Queen was included in "A Form of Prayer to be used in Private Houses Every Morning and Evening." This short set of prose prayers, intended for household use rather than public worship, was appended to the enormously popular collection of versified psalms that became known as the Sternhold and Hopkins Psalter. Many families owned Bibles that were bound with a Book of Common Prayer at the front and a Sternhold and Hopkins Psalter at the back, thus providing them with three essential religious texts in a single volume.

As part of the authorized reorganization of the Church, Elizabeth ordered the sermons that had been composed by Thomas Cranmer for use throughout England during the reign of Edward VI to be reprinted and read in all the churches. *The First Book of Homilies* was so hastily reprinted in 1559, however, that although some of the masculine pronouns have been changed to feminine, not all of the references to "King" have become "Queen," and Elizabeth, like Edward, is still called the "Head of the Church." The homily on obedience, "An Exhortation Concerning Good Order and Obedience to Rulers and Magistrates," is one of the most important for understanding the theological foundation undergirding the role of the English monarch. It celebrates the "most excellent and perfect order" that God has appointed in nature, in individual

---

3. Daniel 6.16–28.
4. A reference to Elizabeth's imprisonment by her sister Mary in 1554 on suspicion of treason.
5. Matthew 6.33.

human beings, and in society and from that order concludes that subjects must obey their sovereign ruler, even if the monarch acts unwisely or unjustly.

In August 1559, Elizabeth authorized visitations to enforce the Act of Uniformity in all the churches of the land. Of some 8000 clergy in England, perhaps as many as 400 refused to conform and were removed from the ministry, including a number of bishops. Many of the vacant bishoprics were filled by men who had spent the years of Mary Tudor's reign on the Continent to avoid persecution. Among these returning exiles were men and women who had lived in Geneva, "the most perfect school of Christ," as one of them described it, and they brought with them a new translation of the Bible into English, which they dedicated to Elizabeth. In their dedicatory letter, the translators cited Deborah, but also urged Elizabeth to follow the example of reforming kings in the Old Testament and to recreate the Church of England as a true "spiritual temple." The Geneva Bible, as it became known, included extensive marginal notes, many of which proffered Protestant interpretations of the biblical text. It was also the first English version to include verse numbers, which allowed readers to find and reference individual scriptural texts more readily. Despite some official resistance, including the printing of the Bishops Bible in 1568 as a countermeasure, the Geneva Bible remained the most popular English Bible until the middle of the seventeenth century.

One of the Genevan exiles who returned late in 1559 was Anne Vaughan Lock, a member of the London merchant class whose parents had both served in the Court of Henry VIII and who was herself a friend of John Knox. In 1560, she published a translation of four *Sermons of John Calvin upon the Song that Hezekiah Made* and appended to them an original set of twenty-six poems based on Psalm 51, the first sonnet sequence printed in English. Lock dedicated her book as a New Year's gift to a fellow exile, Katherine Willoughby Brandon Bertie, the dowager Duchess of Suffolk, but she undoubtedly hoped her offering would also reach the Queen, since it was customary to approach Elizabeth obliquely through one of her courtiers, preferably one placed high enough to have personal access to the monarch. The Duchess was just such a person. As a young teenager, she had been married on Elizabeth's own christening day to the Duke of Suffolk, one of Henry VIII's closest companions, and she later became a staunch friend of William Cecil.

In the dedicatory letter, Lock aligns herself, the Duchess, the biblical King Hezekiah, and (by implication) the Queen as fellow sufferers who must turn to God and His Word for relief and healing. She portrays God as the heavenly physician, John Calvin as the apothecary, and herself as the assistant who places this spiritual medicine of preaching in "an English box" for the benefit of those at Court. The poetic paraphrase of Psalm 51 draws on another royal exemplar, King David, to urge the Queen and the nation toward both individual and national renewal.

An indication of Elizabeth's own personal devotion in this period may be seen in the Latin prayers published under her name in 1563, possibly to commemorate her recovery from a serious case of smallpox in October of the previous year. The *Precationes Privatae*, or private prayers, show the young Queen in postures of gratitude and petition, thanking God for soundness of body and mind and praying for wisdom to guide her people, but they also show her confidence in her role as England's monarch and the seriousness with which she undertook her responsibilities.

THE CHURCH OF ENGLAND

From The Book of Common Prayer (1559)[†]

A Prayer for the Queen's Majesty

O Lord, our heavenly Father, high and mighty, King of Kings, Lord of Lords, the only ruler of princes, which doest from Thy throne behold all the dwellers upon earth, most heartily we beseech Thee with Thy favor to behold our most gracious sovereign lady, Queen Elizabeth, and so replenish her with the grace of Thy Holy Spirit, that she may alway incline to Thy will and walk in Thy way; endue her plenteously with heavenly gifts; grant her in health and wealth long to live; strengthen her, that she may vanquish and overcome all her enemies; and finally, after this life, she may attain everlasting joy and felicity, through Jesus Christ our Lord. Amen.

ANONYMOUS

From A Form of Prayer to be used in Private Houses Every Morning and Evening (1562)[‡]

God save the church universal, our Queen, and realm. God comfort all them that be comfortless. Lord, increase our faith. O Lord, for Christ Thy Son's sake, be merciful to the commonwealths where Thy Gospel is truly preached and harbor granted to the afflicted members of Christ's body, and illuminate, according to Thy good pleasure, all nations with the brightness of Thy Word. So be it.

THE CHURCH OF ENGLAND

From The First Book of Homilies (1559)[†]

From *An Exhortation Concerning Good Order and Obedience to Rulers and Magistrates*

Almighty God hath created and appointed all things in heaven, earth, and waters, in a most excellent and perfect order. In heaven, he hath appointed distinct or several[1] orders and states of archangels and angels. In earth, he

---

† Copy text: *The booke of common prayer and administration of the sacraments* (London: Christopher Barker, 1579; STC 16306.9), B6r. This prayer, first inserted in the 1559 prayerbook, follows the Litany.

‡ Copy text: *The whole booke of Psalmes collected into Englysh metre by T. Starnhold, I. Hopkins, & others* (London: John Day, 1562; STC 2430), Ee1r.

† Copy text: *Certayne sermons appoynted by the Quenes Maiestie to be declared and read, by all persones, vycars, and curates, euery Sonday and holy daye, in theyr Churches: and by her graces aduyse perused a[nd] ouersene, for the better vnderstandyng of the simple people* (London: Richarde Iugge and Iohn Cawvood, 1559; STC 13648), R4r–S1r; S2r–S3r; T1r; T3r–T3v.

1. Separate.

hath assigned and appointed kings, princes, with other governors under them, all in good and necessary order. The water above is kept and raineth down in due time and season. The sun, moon, stars, rainbow, thunder, lightning, clouds, and all birds of the air do keep their order. The earth, trees, seeds, plants, herbs, corn,[2] grass, and all manner of beasts keep themselves in their order. All the parts of the whole year, as winter, summer, months, nights, and days, continue in their order. All kinds of fishes in the sea, rivers, and waters, with all fountains, springs, yea the seas themselves keep their comely[3] course and order.

And man himself also hath all his parts, both within and without, as soul, heart, mind, memory, understanding, reason, speech, with all and singular[4] corporal members of his body, in a profitable, necessary, and pleasant order. Every degree[5] of people in their vocation, calling, and office hath appointed to them their duty and order. Some are in high degree, some in low, some kings and princes, some inferiors and subjects, priests and laymen, masters and servants, fathers and children, husbands and wives, rich and poor, and every one have need of other. So that in all things is to be lauded and praised the goodly order of God, without the which no house, no city, no commonwealth can continue and endure or last. For where there is no right order, there reigneth all abuse, carnal liberty, enormity, sin, and Babelonical confusion.[6] Take away kings, princes, rulers, magistrates, judges, and such estates of God's order, no man shall ride or go by the highway unrobbed, no man shall sleep in his own house or bed unkilled, no man shall keep his wife, children, and possessions in quietness. All things shall be common[7] and there must needs follow all mischief and utter destruction both of souls, bodies, goods, and commonwealths.

But blessed be God that we in this realm of England feel not the horrible calamities, miseries, and wretchedness which all they undoubtedly feel and suffer that lack this godly order. And praised be God that we know the great excellent benefit of God showed towards us in this behalf. God has sent us His high gift, our most dear sovereign lady Queen Elizabeth, with godly, wise, and honorable Council, with other superiors and inferiors in a beautiful order and goodly. Wherefore let us subjects do our bounden duties, giving hearty thanks to God and praying for the preservation of this godly order. Let us all obey, even from the bottom of our hearts, all their godly proceedings, laws, statutes, proclamations, and injunctions, with all other godly orders. Let us consider the scriptures of the Holy Ghost, which persuade and command us all obediently to be subject: first and chiefly, to the Queen's Majesty, Supreme Head over all; and next, to her honorable Council; and to all other noble men, magistrates, and officers, which by God's goodness be placed and ordered. For Almighty God is the only author and provider of this forenamed state and order, as it is written of God in the book of the Proverbs: "Through Me kings do reign; through Me counselors

2. Grain of any sort.
3. Proper.
4. Individual.
5. Social rank.
6. As in the confusion of languages at the biblical Tower of Babel (Genesis 11.1–9); *enormity*: wickedness.
7. Held in common or at the same rank.

make just laws; through Me do princes bear rule and all judges of the earth execute judgment. I am loving to them that love Me."[8]

*   *   *

Forasmuch as God hath created and disposed all things in a comely order, we have been taught in the first part of this sermon concerning good order and obedience that we also ought in all commonwealths to observe and keep a due order and to be obedient to the powers, their ordinances and laws, and that all rulers are appointed of God, for a godly order to be kept in the world. And also how the magistrates ought to learn how to rule and govern according to God's laws. And that all subjects are bounden to obey them as God's ministers, yea although they be evil, not only for fear but also for conscience sake.

And here (good people) let all mark diligently that it is not lawful for inferiors and subjects in any case to resist or stand against the superior powers. For Saint Paul's words be plain, that whosoever withstandeth shall get to themselves damnation; for whosoever withstandeth withstandeth the ordinance of God.[9] Our Savior Christ Himself and His apostles received many and diverse injuries of the unfaithful and wicked men in authority, yet we never read that they or any of them caused any sedition or rebellion against authority. We read oft that they patiently suffered all troubles, vexations, slanders, pangs and pains, and death itself obediently, without tumult or resistance. They committed their cause to Him that judgeth righteously and prayed for their enemies heartily and earnestly. They knew that the authority of the powers was God's ordinance, and therefore both in their words and deeds they taught ever obedience to it and never taught nor did the contrary. The wicked judge Pilate said to Christ, "Knowest thou not that I have power to crucify thee and have power also to loose thee?" Jesus answered, "Thou could'st have no power at all against me, except it were given thee from above."[1] Whereby Christ taught us plainly that even the wicked rulers have their power and authority from God.

And therefore it is not lawful for their subjects by force to withstand them, although they abuse their power; much less then it is lawful for subjects to withstand their godly and Christian princes, which do not abuse their authority but use the same to God's glory and to the profit and commodity[2] of God's people.

*   *   *

These examples being so manifest and evident, it is an intolerable ignorance, madness, and wickedness for subjects to make any murmuring, rebellion, resistance or withstanding, commotion, or insurrection against their most dear and most dread sovereign lord and king,[3] ordained and appointed of God's goodness for their commodity, peace, and quietness. Yet let us believe undoubtedly (good Christian people) that we may not obey kings,

---

8. Proverbs 8.15–17.
9. Romans 13.2.
1. John 19.10–11.
2. Benefit.
3. This sermon was written during the reign of Edward VI; although Elizabeth's name and some female pronouns were inserted in 1559, here, as elsewhere, the original reference to "King" is retained.

magistrates, or any other (though they be our own fathers) if they would command us to do anything contrary to God's commandments. In such a case, we ought to say with the apostles, "We must rather obey God than man."[4] But nevertheless, in that case we may not in any wise withstand violently or rebel against rulers or make any insurrection, sedition, or tumults either by force of arms (or other ways) against the anointed of the Lord or any of His appointed officers. But we must in such case patiently suffer all wrongs and injuries, reserving the judgment of our cause only to God. Let us fear the terrible punishment of Almighty God against traitors or rebellious persons.

✳   ✳   ✳

Thus we learn by the Word of God to yield to our king that[5] is due to our king, that is, honor, obedience, payments of due taxes, customs, tributes, subsidies, love, and fear. Thus we know partly our bounden duties to common authority; now let us learn to accomplish the same. And let us most instantly and heartily pray to God, the only author of all authority, for all them that be in authority according as Saint Paul willeth, writing thus to Timothy in his first epistle: "I exhort therefore that above all things prayers, supplications, intercessions, and giving of thanks be done for all men, for kings and for all that be in authority that we may live a quiet and a peaceable life, with all godliness and honesty, for that is good and accepted or allowable in the sight of God our Savior."[6] Here Saint Paul maketh an earnest and an especial exhortation concerning giving of thanks and prayer for kings and rulers, saying above all things, as he might say, in any wise principally and chiefly, let prayer be made for kings.

Let us heartily thank God for His great and excellent benefit and providence concerning the state of kings. Let us pray for them, that they may have God's favor and God's protection. Let us pray that they may ever in all things have God before their eyes. Let us pray that they may have wisdom, strength, justice, clemency, zeal to God's glory, to God's verity, to Christian souls, and to the commonwealth. Let us pray that they may rightly use their sword and authority for the maintenance and defense of the catholic faith[7] contained in Holy Scripture and of their good and honest subjects and for the fear and punishment of the evil and vicious people. Let us pray that they may faithfully follow the most faithful kings and captains in the Bible: David, Hezekiah, Josiah, and Moses with such other.

And let us pray for ourselves that we may live godly in holy and Christian conversation; so we shall have God of our side. And then let us not fear what man can do against us.[8] So we shall live in true obedience, both to our most merciful King in heaven and to our most Christian Queen in earth; so shall we please God and have the exceeding benefit, peace of conscience, rest, and quietness here in the world. And after this life we shall enjoy a better life, rest, peace, and the everlasting bliss of heaven, which He grant us all that was obedient for us all, even to the death of the cross, Jesus Christ. To whom, with the Father and the Holy Ghost, be all honor and glory, both now and ever. Amen.

---

4. Acts 5.29.
5. That which.
6. 1 Timothy 2.1–3.
7. The orthodox Christian faith, rather than the Roman Catholic faith.
8. Hebrews 13.6; *live godly . . . conversation*: that we may live a godly, holy, and Christian life.

WILLIAM WHITTINGHAM

From The Dedicatory Epistle to the Geneva Bible (April 10, 1560)†

How hard a thing it is and what great impediments let to enterprise[1] any worthy act, not only daily experience sufficiently showeth (most noble and virtuous Queen), but also that notable proverb doth confirm the same, which admonisheth us that all things are hard which are fair and excellent. And what enterprise can there be of greater importance, and more acceptable unto God, or more worthy of singular commendation than the building of the Lord's temple, the house of God, the church of Christ, whereof the Son of God is the head and perfection?[2]

When Zerubbabel went about to build the material temple according to the commandment of the Lord, what difficulties and stays daily arose to hinder his worthy endeavors the books of Ezra and Esdras plainly witness;[3] how that not only he and the people of God were sore molested with foreign adversaries (whereof some maliciously warred against them and corrupted the King's officers and others craftily practiced under pretence of religion) but also at home with domestical enemies, as false prophets, crafty worldlings, faint-hearted soldiers, and oppressors of their brethren, who as well by false doctrine and lies as by subtle counsel, cowardice, and extortion discouraged the hearts almost of all, so that the Lord's work was not only interrupted and left off for a long time, but scarcely at the length with great labor and danger after a sort brought to pass.

Which thing when we weigh aright and consider earnestly how much greater charge God hath laid upon you in making you a builder of His spiritual temple, we cannot but partly fear, knowing the craft and force of Satan, our spiritual enemy, and the weakness and unability of this our nature, and partly be fervent in our prayers toward God that He would bring to perfection this noble work which He hath begun by you. And therefore we endeavor ourselves by all means to aid and to bestow our whole force under your Grace's standard, whom God hath made as our Zerubbabel for the erecting of this most excellent temple, and to plant and maintain His holy Word to the advancement of His glory, for your own honor and salvation of your soul, and for the singular comfort of that great flock which Christ Jesus, the great shepherd, hath bought with His precious blood, and committed unto your charge to be fed both in body and soul.

✳   ✳   ✳

Wherefore great wisdom, not worldly but heavenly, is here required, which your Grace must earnestly crave of the Lord, as did Solomon, to whom God gave an understanding heart to judge his people aright and to

---

† Copy text: *The Bible and Holy Scriptures conteyned in the olde and newe Testament* (Geneva: Rouland Hall, 1560; STC 2093), .˙.2r–3v.
1. Hinder one to undertake.
2. This description of the church draws from 1 Corinthians 3.16–17, 1 Timothy 3.15, Hebrews 3.6, and Ephesians 1.22.
3. Zerubbabel's rebuilding of the Temple after the Babylonian captivity is compared to Elizabeth's restoration of Protestantism in England following Mary Tudor's reign (Ezra 4–5; Nehemiah 6; 1 Esdras 2); *stays*: hindrances.

discern between good and bad. For if God for the furnishing of the old temple gave the spirit of wisdom and understanding to them that should be the workmen thereof, as to Bezaleel, Aholiab, and Hiram, how much more will he endue your Grace and other godly princes and chief governors with a principal Spirit,[4] that you may procure and command things necessary for this most holy temple, foresee and take heed of things that might hinder it, and abolish and destroy whatsoever might impair and overthrow the same?

Moreover, the marvelous diligence and zeal of Jehoshaphat, Josiah, and Hezekiah are by the singular providence of God left as an example to all godly rulers to reform their countries and to establish the Word of God with all speed, lest the wrath of the Lord fall upon them for the neglecting thereof.

*　*　*

Last of all (most gracious Queen) for the advancement of this building and rearing up of the work, two things are necessary. First, that we have a lively and steadfast faith in Christ Jesus, who must dwell in our hearts as the only means and assurance of our salvation. For He is the ladder that reacheth from the earth to heaven; He lifteth up His Church and setteth it in the heavenly places; He maketh us lively stones and buildeth us upon Himself; He joineth us to Himself as the members and body to the head; yea He maketh Himself and His Church one Christ.[5] The next is that our faith bring forth good fruits, so that our godly conversation may serve us as a witness to confirm our election and be an example to all others to walk as appertaineth to the vocation whereunto they are called, lest the Word of God be evil spoken of, and this building be stayed[6] to grow up to a just height, which cannot be without the great provocation of God's just vengeance and discouraging of many thousands through all the world, if they should see that our life were not holy and agreeable to our profession.

For the eyes of all that fear God in all places behold your countries[7] as an example to all that believe, and the prayers of all the godly at all times are directed to God for the preservation of your Majesty. For considering God's wonderful mercies toward you at all seasons, who hath pulled you out of the mouth of the lions, and how that from your youth you have been brought up in the Holy Scriptures,[8] the hope of all men is so increased that they cannot but look that God should bring to pass some wonderful work by your Grace to the universal comfort of His church. Therefore, even above strength you must show yourself strong and bold in God's matters. And though Satan lay all his power and craft together to hurt and hinder the Lord's building, yet be you assured that God will fight from heaven against this great dragon, the ancient serpent, which is called the devil and

---

4. A synonym for the Holy Spirit.
5. 1 Corinthians 12.12; *ladder . . . heaven*: Genesis 28.12 and John 1.51; *lifteth up . . . places*: Ephesians 2.6; *He maketh . . . Himself*: 1 Peter 2.5; *lively*: living; *He joineth . . . head*: Colossians 1.18.
6. Prevented; *conversation*: manner of life; *election*: God's predestination of His own people, a doctrine which was held by all orthodox Christians before the Reformation, but which subsequently became identified particularly with Calvinism; *walk as . . . spoken of*: Ephesians 4.1.
7. Lands, such as Ireland and Scotland as well as England, that Elizabeth claimed to rule.
8. 2 Timothy 3.15; *pulled you . . . lions*: Daniel 6.1–28.

Satan, till He have accomplished the whole work and made His church glorious to Himself, without spot or wrinkle.[9]

* * *

This Lord of Lords and King of Kings, who hath ever defended His, strengthen, comfort and preserve your Majesty, that you may be able to build up the ruins of God's house to His glory, the discharge of your conscience, and to the comfort of all them that love the coming of Christ Jesus our Lord.

ANNE VAUGHAN LOCK

From Sermons of John Calvin upon
the Song that Hezekiah Made (1560)[†]

From The Dedicatory Epistle

To the right honorable and Christian Princess, the Lady Katharine, Duchess of Suffolk.

It often falleth out[1] in experience (my gracious and singular good Lady) that some men, being oppressed with poverty, tossed with worldly adversity, tormented with pain, soreness, and sickness of body, and other such common matters of grief as the world counteth miseries and evils (yet having their minds armed and furnished with prepared patience and defense of inward understanding), all these calamities cannot so far prevail as to make them fall nor yet once stoop into the state of men to be accounted miserable. * * * On the other side, we see some that, flowing in earthly wealth and suffisance, free from fortune's cruelty, healthy in body, and every way to the world's seeming blessed, yet with mind not well instructed, or with conscience not well quieted, even upon such small chances as other can lightly bear are vexed above measure with reasonless extremity.[2]

* * *

So as (to a sick stomach of mind)[3] all bodily matters of delight and worldly pleasures are loathsome and displeasant, as (on the other side) the power of a healthy soul easily digesteth and gathereth good nurture of the hard pains and bitter torments of the body and fortune. He, then, that cureth the sick mind or preserveth it from disease cureth or preserveth not only mind but body also and deserveth so much more praise and thank than the body's physician, as the soul excelleth the body and as the curing or preservation of them both is to be preferred before the cure of the body alone.

But we see daily, when skilful men by art or honest neighbors (having gathered understanding of some special disease and the healing thereof by their own experiment) do apply their knowledge to the restoring of health of any man's body in any corporal sickness, how thankfully it is taken, how

---

9. Ephesians 5.27; *God will fight . . . Satan*: Revelation 12.9.
† Copy text: *The Collected Works of Anne Vaughan Lock*, ed. Susan M. Felch (Tempe: Arizona Center for Medieval and Renaissance Studies/Renaissance English Text Society, 1999), 4–8; 62–71. Copyright Arizona Board of Regents for Arizona State University. Reprinted with permission.
1. Happens.
2. Extreme suffering; *suffisance*: abundance.
3. The stomach is the figurative seat of the emotions.

much the relieved patient accounteth himself bound to him by mean of whose aid and ministration he findeth himself holpen[4] or eased.

What then deserveth he that teacheth such a receipt, whereby health both of body and mind is preserved and whereby, if health be appaired,[5] it may be restored, yea whereby sickness and common miseries continuing shall not have so much power to trouble a man as to make him sick or miserable? This receipt God, the heavenly physician, hath taught; his most excellent apothecary, Master John Calvin, hath compounded; and I, your Grace's most bounden and humble,[6] have put into an English box and do present unto you. My thanks are taken away and drowned by the great excess of duty that I owe you. Master Calvin thinketh his pains recompensed if your Grace or any Christian take profit of it, because how much soever is spent, his store is never the less. And for God, recompensed He cannot be. But how He is continually to be thanked, your Grace's profession of His word, your abiding in the same, the godly conversation[7] that I have seen in you, do prove that yourself do better understand and practice than I can admonish you.

*   *   *

When the believing Christian falleth (as God hath made none to stand whereby they should not need His mercy to raise them when they are fallen), he knoweth whither to reach his hand to be raised up again. Being stung with the sting of the scorpion, he knoweth how with oil of the same scorpion to be healed again; being wounded with the justice of God that hateth sin, he knoweth how with the mercy of the same God that pardoneth sin to have his pain assuaged and hurt amended.[8] He knoweth that whom God hath from eternity appointed to live shall never die, howsoever sickness threaten; no misery, no temptation, no peril shall avail to his everlasting overthrow. He knoweth that his safety is much more surely reposed in God's most steadfast and unchangeable purpose, and in the most strong and almighty hand of the all-knowing and all-working God, than in the wavering will and feeble weakness of man.

This healeth the Christian's sickness, this preserveth him from death, this maketh him to live forever. This medicine is in this little book brought from the plentiful shop and storehouse of God's holy testament, where God's ever-abiding purpose from beyond beginning is set forth, to the everlasting salvation of some and eternal confusion of other. Beside that, this book hath not only the medicine but also an example of the nature of the disease and the mean how to use and apply the medicine to them that be so diseased.

*   *   *

So here this good soul's physician hath brought you where you may see lying before your face the good king Hezekiah,[9] sometime chilling and chattering

---

4. Helped; *skilful men by art*: university-trained, licensed physicians; *honest neighbors*: unlicensed practitioners of medicine, including women.
5. Impaired; *receipt*: recipe or, in this case, a prescription.
6. Humble servant; *compounded*: mixed by an apothecary.
7. Manner of life.
8. Oil of scorpion was a contemporary remedy; throughout the preface Lock shows considerable knowledge of medical practices. She also alludes to the biblical incident where the Israelites are saved from poisonous snake bites by looking at a brass serpent mounted on a pole (Numbers 21.4–9); this brass serpent was later seen as a symbol of salvation (Wisdom of Solomon 16.6–7; John 3.14–15).
9. For accounts of Hezekiah's sickness and recovery see 2 Kings 20.1–11; 2 Chronicles 32.24; and Isaiah 38.

with cold, sometime languishing and melting away with heat, now freezing, now frying, now speechless, now crying out, with other such piteous pangs and passions wrought in his tender afflicted spirit by guilty conscience of his own fault, by terrible consideration of God's justice, by cruel assaults of the tyrannous enemy of man's salvation vexing him in much more lamentable-wise than any bodily fever can work or bodily flesh can suffer. On the other side for his help, you see him sometime throw up his ghastly eyen,[1] staring with horror and scant discerning for pain and for want of the lively moisture to feed the brightness of their sight. You see him sometime yieldingly stretch out, sometime strugglingly throw his weakened legs, not able to sustain his feeble body. Sometime he casteth abroad or holdeth up his white and bloodless hand toward the place whither his soul longeth. Sometime, with falling chaps,[2] he breatheth out unperfect sounds, gasping rather than calling for mercy and help.

These things being here laid open to sight and remaining in remembrance (as the horror and piteous spectacle cannot suffer it to fall out of a Christian tender mind), if we feel ourselves in like anguish, we find that the disease is the same that Hezekiah had and so, by convenience of reason,[3] must by the same mean be healed. Then behooveth us to remember, or to be informed by our diligent physician or charitable neighbor, how we saw Hezekiah healed, whom we imagine in this book to see both dying, revived, and walking after health recovered. There we see the heavenly physician anoint him with the merciful Samaritan's oil, purge the oppressing humours with true repentance, strengthen his stomach with the wholesome conserve[4] of God's eternal decree, and expel his disease, and set him on foot with assured faith of God's mercy, and staying his yet unsteady pace and faltering legs with the sweet promises of God's almighty goodness. So learn we what Physician's help we shall use, and this medicine being offered us, we are bold to take it because we know it will heal us. And being healed, knowing and hearing it confessed that sin was the cause and nourishment of Hezekiah's disease, we learn a new diet and to feed as Hezekiah's Physician and ours appointeth, abstaining from things hurtful, taking things healthful as He prescribeth. So doth the Christian attain his health; so, being attained, he preserveth it for ever.

*   *   *

From *A Meditation of a Penitent Sinner: Written in Manner of a Paraphrase upon the 51st Psalm of David*

The heinous guilt of my forsaken ghost°[5]	*spirit*
So threats,° alas, unto my feebled sprite°	*threatens / weakened spirit*
Deserved death. And (that me grieveth most)	
Still stand[6] so fixed before my dazzled sight	
5 The loathsome filth of my disdainéd° life,	*defiled*

1. Eyes.
2. Jaws.
3. In accordance with reason.
4. Medicine; *Samaritan's oil*: an allusion to the parable of the Good Samaritan (Luke 10.25–37); *humours*: both physical and mental health were thought to be dependent upon a proper balance of the four humours—blood, phlegm, yellow bile, and black bile.
5. The first five prefatory sonnets introduce the psalm by sketching the psychological and spiritual state of David, the royal penitent sinner.
6. The subjects of "stand" are the "filth," "wrath," and "wounds" of the subsequent lines.

The mighty wrath of mine offended Lord
(My Lord, whose wrath is sharper than the knife),
And deeper wounds than double-edged sword,
That, as the dimméd and fordulléd eyen°   eyes
10   (Full fraught with tears and more and more oppressed
With growing streams of the distilléd brine
Sent from the furnace of a grief-full breast)
    Cannot enjoy the comfort of the light
    Nor find the way wherein to walk aright,

15   So I, blind wretch, whom God's inflaméd ire
With piercing stroke hath thrown unto the ground,
Amid my sins still groveling in the mire,
Find not the way that other oft have found,
Whom cheerful glimpse of God's abounding grace
20   Hath oft relieved and oft with shining light
Hath brought to joy out of the ugly place
Where I, in dark of everlasting night,
Bewail my woeful and unhappy case
And fret my dying soul with gnawing pain.
25   Yet blind, alas, I grope about for grace.
While blind for grace, I grope about in vain;
    My fainting breath I gather up and strain,
    "Mercy, mercy," to cry and cry again.

But "Mercy," while I sound with shrieking cry
30   For grant of grace and pardon while I pray,
Ev'n then Despair before my rueful° eye   pitiable
Spreads forth my sin and shame and seems to say,
"In vain thou brayest forth thy bootless° noise   useless
To Him for mercy, O refuséd wight,°   person
35   That hears not the forsaken sinner's voice.
Thy reprobate and foreordainéd sprite,
Fore-damnéd vessel of His heavy wrath
(As self witness of thy beknowing heart
And secret guilt of thine own conscience saith),
40   Of His sweet promises can claim no part.
    But thee, caitiff,° deservéd curse doth draw   wretch
    To hell, by justice, for offended law."

This horror when my trembling soul doth hear
(When marks and tokens of the reprobate,
45   My growing sins, of grace my senseless cheer°   inability to feel grace
Enforce the proof of everlasting hate
That I conceive the heaven's King to bear
Against my sinful and forsaken ghost),
As in the throat of hell I quake for fear.
50   And then in present peril to be lost
(Although my[7] conscience wanteth to reply

7. Copy text: by.

But, with remorse enforcing mine offence,
Doth argue vain° my not availing cry),   *as vain*
With woeful sighs and bitter penitence
55   To Him from whom the endless mercy flows,
I cry for mercy to relieve my woes.[8]

And then, not daring with presuming eye
Once to behold the angry heaven's face,
From troubled sprite° I send confuséd cry   *spirit*
60   To crave the crumbs of all-sufficing grace.[9]
With faltering knee I (falling to the ground,
Bending my yielding hands to heaven's throne),
Pour forth my piteous plaint with woeful sound,
With smoking sighs and oft-repeated groan
65   Before the Lord, the Lord, whom sinner I,
I curséd wretch, I have offended so
That, dreading in His wreakful° wrath to die,   *vengeful*
And damnéd down to depth of hell to go,
     Thus tossed with pangs and passions of despair,
70   Thus crave I mercy with repentant cheer.

                              *   *   *

Have mercy, God, for Thy great mercy's sake,[1]
O God, my God, unto my shame I say,
Being fled from Thee so as I dread to take
Thy name in wretched mouth and fear to pray
75   Or ask the mercy that I have abused.
But God of mercy, let me come to Thee,
Not for justice, that justly am accused,
Which self° word "Justice" so amazeth me   *same*
That scarce I dare Thy mercy sound again.
80   But mercy, Lord, yet suffer me to crave.
Mercy is Thine; let me not cry in vain
Thy great mercy for my great fault to have.
     Have mercy, God; pity my penitence
     With greater mercy than my great offence.

                              *   *   *

85   Show mercy, Lord, not unto me alone,
But stretch Thy favor and Thy pleaséd will,
To spread Thy bounty and Thy grace upon
Zion, for Zion is Thy holy hill,
That Thy Jerusalem with mighty wall
90   May be encloséd under Thy defense
And builded so that it may never fall

---

8. The two main verbs in this sonnet are "quake" and "cry."
9. An allusion to the woman from Syro-Phoenicia who, when her request that Jesus heal her daughter was parried, demanded the crumbs that might fall from the master's table (Matthew 15.21–28;
   Mark 7.24–30).
1. The first and penultimate sonnets of the paraphrased psalm, printed here, are representative of the
   sequence.

By mining° fraud or mighty violence.   *undermining*
Defend Thy church, Lord, and advance it so,
So in despite of tyranny to stand
95 That, trembling at Thy power, the world may know
It is upholden by Thy mighty hand,
    That Zion and Jerusalem may be
    A safe abode for them that honor Thee.

QUEEN ELIZABETH

Prayers from Precationes Privatae (1563)[†]

Collect[1]

Almighty, eternal God, Lord of Lords, King of Kings,[2] from whom comes all power, who set me up as the ruler of Your people and solely through Your mercy brought me to sit on the throne of my father, for my part I am Your handmaiden of not many years, hardly enough for an understanding of Your law. Grant me, I beg you, an understanding heart so that I may know what is acceptable in Your eyes at all times and may be able to judge Your people justly and distinguish right from wrong.[3] Send down from heaven the Spirit of Your wisdom to guide me in all my deeds. Fill my heart with an awareness of Him.[4] Your wisdom gives true knowledge, and from Your mouth come counsel and understanding. May Your grace stand by me, so that I may manage this numerous people of Yours[5] with fairness and justice and may appoint pious, upstanding, and prudent men as Your ministers. Share Your Spirit with them so that I may administer justice with fear of You and no favoring of persons.[6] Give me faithful counselors who out of Your counsel will offer counsel to me and my kingdom. Give me good pastors who will diligently feed with Your Word the sheep you have committed to them. Grant me ministers who will all do their duty to You out of their zeal for justice.

O my God, God of all power and mercy, govern all Your people with Your most Holy Spirit so that they may venerate You, their preeminent prince and their only power, conscientiously and with unspoiled worship, so that in obedience to You they may be peacefully subject to me, their Queen on earth by Your ordination, and so that they may live with one another in mutual peace and harmony. Grant, most loving Father, by the glory of Your name, fullness and continuance of Your tranquillity to all the ranks of this Your kingdom. May they serve one another in charity, may they love and

---

[†] Copy text: *Precationes priuat[ae] Regiae E.R.* ([London: T. Purfoot], 1563; STC 7576.7), C7r–D3v, E2r–E5v. Translation and notes by Clarence H. Miller.
1. A liturgical prayer with a single theme or related themes. It typically begins with a laudatory address to God, proceeds to requests, and ends by invoking the name of one by whom or through whom the prayer is being offered.
2. An echo of 1 Timothy 6.15 and Revelation 19.16.
3. 1 Kings 3.9.
4. An echo of the prayer "Veni sancte spiritus," from the Latin liturgy for Pentecost: "Reple cordis intima / tuorum fidelium" (lines 14–15).
5. 1 Kings 3.9.
6. Acts 10.34.

benefit one another, may all individuals walk in their own callings, piously, justly, and soberly.[7] May I myself preside over each of them, according to Your Word, with solicitude and diligence. Pour forth the Spirit of Your love[8] so that they may be joined together most closely with me and also with one another, as the members of one body.

Do this, O God of all love, that I may administer this kingdom of Yours, not with fear of harshness or the sword, but with regal wrath and the fear of God. Also be with me, O God, highest ruler and governor of all princes, through whom all rulers rule, who possess all fortitude and whose arm extends everywhere, God of peace[9] and harmony, who has chosen me Your handmaiden to rule over Your people so that I may protect them in Your peace. Be with me and preside over me with the Spirit of Your wisdom, so that according to Your will I may preserve and defend Christian peace with all peoples. Bring it about through Christ your Son, who is our peace,[1] that we may all agree together. Confound your enemies with Your powerful hand and Your upraised arm.[2] Give us likewise Your peace, because there is no other to fight for us except You, our God, who alone are strong, preserving Your covenant and Your mercy toward those who walk in Your sight with all their hearts.[3] Turn our hearts to You so that we may walk in all Your ways and keep Your commandments.[4] Under Your sway may all princes rule and all the people obey, so that, with You as our supreme King and protector, we may all serve You in unity of spirit for Your eternal glory. Through Jesus Christ, your Son, our Lord,[5] to whom, together with the Father and the Holy Spirit, be all honor and sovereignty through all ages.

Thanksgiving for Benefits Bestowed

Eternal God, Creator and Maker of all things and likewise most merciful Father of those who trust in You, when I consider how a little while ago I was nothing at all, without a body or a soul, without life or perception or any understanding, and when I was still clay, as it were, in the hands of the potter, so that it was entirely Your decision whether to make me a vessel of honor or of shame,[6] You did not choose that I should be some poor little girl from the lowest level of society, who would lead a wretched life in poverty and squalor, but rather a person sprung from royal parents, royally raised and educated, destined by You for a kingdom; and when I was surrounded and driven hither and thither by the plots of my enemies, You constantly protected and defended me, and having freed me from prison and the danger of death, You endowed me with majesty and royal dominion on earth. Moreover, when I consider how many, not only from the common people but also from the nobility and even from the blood royal, have been afflicted by Your hidden but just judgment, both in the past and also

---

7. Titus 2.12.
8. An echo of the well-known hymn "Veni creator spiritus," line 14: "Infunde amorem cordibus."
9. Philemon 4.9; 1 Thessalonians 5.23; *highest ruler . . . everywhere*: Deuteronomy 4.19; 1 Kings 3.42; 2 Chronicles 6.32.
1. Ephesians 2.14.
2. See Psalm 136.12.
3. 1 Kings 8.23; 2 Chronicles 6.14.
4. 1 Kings 8.58.
5. Romans 7.25; Jude 1.25.
6. Ecclesiasticus 33.13; Romans 9.21.

today—some miserably deformed in body, others much more miserably deprived of all intelligence and intellectual insight, and others by far the most miserably disturbed in mind and reason, all but insane and raving mad—and when I reflect that I, on the other hand, have been endowed with a healthy body, good looks, a mind both sane and sound, and also with uncommon and remarkable prudence (far more than other women), and furthermore with a knowledge and practice of language and literature beyond what is normal in this sex, and finally with all royal gifts worthy of a kingdom, and all this granted to me gratis—then I understand, O most merciful Father, how much more than others I owe to Your kindness, though I have earned no more than others from You. For what could I earn from You before I existed, since I began to exist, and to exist as the person I am, through You and by Your free gift?

O You who endowed, honored, and fitted me out with so many and such great benefits, bestow on me the divine grace of Your Spirit, that I may understand the immensity of Your kindness to me, that I may genuinely acknowledge You as the source of these gifts, that I may be eternally grateful to You, that I may not take pride in any gift as if it came from me, since I have received everything from You, not as if I had earned it, since I have received everything as a free gift beyond merit, beyond desire—grant, I say, that I may understand that this immense generosity of Yours toward me is as much a burden as an honor and that I may remember that, from those to whom You have given much, You will also require much,[7] so that I may always rightly use Your gifts for the just government of Your people and the wholesome administration of the kingdom and Your commonwealth, but especially and above all that I may rightly and constantly use these gifts to Your glory and renown as the giver of these gifts. To whom, together with Your Son Jesus Christ our Savior, and the Holy Spirit, one immortal God, all gratitude, honor, and glory is owed by all, forever and ever.[8] Amen.

QUESTIONS AT HOME AND WARS ABROAD

Although religious issues dominated the first years of Elizabeth's reign, another question quickly emerged: who would succeed Elizabeth as England's monarch? For the next twenty years, that question was folded into debates over whom the Queen would marry, for nearly everyone assumed that she would—indeed must—marry. Even before her succession, various suitors had been proposed, including the Duke of Savoy and Prince Eric of Sweden. But the pressure increased significantly following her coronation. Her brother-in-law, Philip II of Spain, offered for her hand, although without much enthusiasm, and the Swedish prince, now King Eric XIV, continued to press his suit. One of Parliament's first actions was to urge the Queen to marry and bear children, not surprising given that the two previous monarchs had died childless. Elizabeth's tart reply in her first speech before Parliament in February 1559 informed her subjects that God had been a sufficient companion in her life thus far, and she expected that He would "not now of His goodness suffer me to go alone." Furthermore, she warned them that a child born of her

---

7. Luke 12.48. *burden . . . honor*: the wordplay on "onus" (burden) and "honos" (honor) was well known. See, for example, Ovid, *Metamorphoses* 2.634 and *Heroides* 9.31; Marcus Terentius Varro, *De Lingua Latina* 5.73.
8. 1 Timothy 1.17.

Elizabeth presiding over Parliament.

own body might not prove a fit ruler. But her speech was hardly the last word on the matter; throughout the first half of her reign, the issue of her marriage would be raised repeatedly both by Parliament and by her councilors.

In 1563, Elizabeth was particularly annoyed when Alexander Nowell, the Dean of St. Paul's, took advantage of the sermon that opened Parliament to rebuke her for remaining unmarried, asking pointedly, "If your parents had been of your mind, where had you been then?" In her "Answer to the "Commons' Petition that She Marry," she chose a convoluted and elevated style to remind the assembled men that she was their Queen, their savior from the tyranny of Mary Tudor, and their natural "mother," and therefore not a woman to be bullied or hurried into a marriage.

On the matter of religion, it might be argued that Elizabeth achieved (in what became known as the Elizabethan Settlement) a national renewal through the reestablishment of a moderate Protestantism. Many religious people, however, wished the Queen to reform the Church more thoroughly. The publication of sermons other than the official homilies, as well as the printing of many other theological works, spoke to a substantial desire for deepened religious commitment. Such commitment also took on political overtones when the Queen was urged, against her own distaste for foreign wars, to become involved in the advance of international Protestantism. In Scotland to the north, the Presbyterians, led by John Knox and others, were battling Mary of Guise, Mary Stuart's mother, who was acting as Regent in her daughter's stead. Only France's dispatch of troops to Scotland in 1560 and Cecil's threat to resign if Elizabeth failed to support her Protestant co-religionists moved the Queen to send reinforcements. Across the channel, it was the prospect of winning back Calais, an English port in northern France recently lost to French control, that moved Elizabeth to commit troops to the French Protestants, known as Huguenots.

That war quickly turned into a debacle when the Huguenots made peace with the French king and abandoned their allies. Holed up in the port of Newhaven (Le Havre), the English soldiers contracted the plague and began dying at the rate of sixty men a day. When the decimated English troops straggled home, they brought the disease and their despair with them. In an attempt to control both the plague and the public relations disaster occasioned by the retreat, Elizabeth issued a public Proclamation on August 1, 1563. It called on the sick soldiers to keep their distance from their uninfected neighbors and on church and government officials to establish quarantines and provide relief to the returning troops, but it also exonerated the English captain-general, Ambrose Dudley, the Earl of Warwick and Robert Dudley's brother. It was God who had sent the plague, Elizabeth's Proclamation argued, and prudence demanded an orderly withdrawal from France. Elizabeth had learned a valuable, though costly, lesson in the vagaries and expense of war; for the rest of her life she would be reluctant to commit her troops to foreign soil.

QUEEN ELIZABETH

First Speech before Parliament (1559)[†]

Friday the 10th of February. The answer of the Queen's Highness to the petitions proponed[1] unto her by the Lower House concerning her marriage.

As I have good cause, so do I give you all my hearty thanks for the good zeal and loving care you seem to have, as well towards me as to the whole state of your country. Your petition, I perceive, consisteth of three parts, and mine answer to the same shall depend of[2] two.

And to the first part, I may say unto you that from my years of understanding, sith[3] I first had consideration of myself to be born a servitor of Almighty God, I happily chose this kind of life in which I yet live, which I assure you for mine own part hath hitherto best contented myself and I trust hath been most acceptable to God. From the which if either ambition of high estate offered to me in marriage by the pleasure and appointment of my prince (whereof I have some records in this presence, as you our Lord Treasurer well know); or if the eschewing of the danger of mine enemies; or the avoiding of the peril of death, whose messenger or rather

† Copy text: *Elizabeth I: Collected Works*, ed. Leah S. Marcus, Janel Mueller, and Mary Beth Rose (Chicago and London: University of Chicago Press, 2000), 56–58. Reprinted by permission of the University of Chicago Press. © 2000 by the University of Chicago.
1. Proposed.
2. Pertain to.
3. Since.

continual watchman, "the prince's indignation,"[4] was not little time daily before mine eyes, by whose means although I know, or justly may suspect, yet will not now utter; or if the whole cause were in my sister herself, I will not now burden her therewith, because I will not charge the dead. If any of these, I say, could have drawn or dissuaded me from this kind of life, I had not now remained in this estate wherein you see me, but constant have always continued in this determination. Although my youth and words may seem to some hardly to agree together, yet it is most true that at this day I stand free from any other meaning that either I have had in times past or have at this present. With which trade of life[5] I am so thoroughly acquainted that I trust God, who hath hitherto therein preserved and led me by the hand, will not now of His goodness suffer me to go alone.

For the other part, the manner of your petition I do well like of and take in good part, because that it is simple and containeth no limitation of place or person. If it had been otherwise, I must needs have misliked it very much and thought it in you a very great presumption, being unfitting and altogether unmeet for you to require them that may command, or those to appoint whose parts are to desire, or such to bind and limit whose duties are to obey, or to take upon you to draw my love to your liking or frame my will to your fantasies. For a guerdon[6] constrained and a gift freely given can never agree together.

Nevertheless, if any of you be in suspect that[7] (whensoever it may please God to incline my heart to another kind of life), ye may well assure yourselves my meaning is not to do or determine anything wherewith the realm may or shall have just cause to be discontented. And therefore put that clean out of your heads. For I assure you, what credit my assurance may have with you I cannot tell, but what credit it shall deserve to have, the sequel[8] shall declare. I will never in that matter conclude anything that shall be prejudicial to the realm, for the weal, good, and safety whereof I will never shame to spend my life. And whomsoever my chance shall be to light upon, I trust he shall be as careful for the realm and you—I will not say as myself, because I cannot so certainly determine of any other—but at the leastways, by my goodwill and desire, he shall be such as shall be as careful for the preservation of the realm and you as myself.

And albeit it might please Almighty God to continue me still in this mind to live out of the state of marriage, yet it is not to be feared but He will so work in my heart and in your wisdoms as good provision by His help may be made in convenient time, whereby the realm shall not remain destitute of an heir that may be a fit governor, and peradventure more beneficial to the realm than such offspring as may come of me. For although I be never so careful of your well-doings, and mind ever so to be, yet may my issue grow out of kind[9] and become, perhaps, ungracious. And in the end this

4. "The prince's indignation is death," a reference to Proverbs 16.14, had been used to describe Henry VIII, but Elizabeth uses it here to refer to her imprisonment in the Tower by her sister, Mary Tudor; *my prince*: probably Philibert Emmanuel, prince of Piedmont; *Lord Treasurer*: William Paulet, marquis of Winchester [Marcus, Mueller, and Rose's notes].
5. Way of life.
6. Reward or recompense.
7. Of that.
8. Subsequent events.
9. Unnaturally.

shall be for me sufficient: that a marble stone shall declare that a queen, having reigned such a time, lived and died a virgin. And here I end, and take your coming unto me in good part, and give unto you all eftsoons[1] my hearty thanks, more yet for your zeal and good meaning than for your petition.

Answer to the Commons' Petition That She Marry (January 28, 1563)[†]

Williams,[1] I have heard by you the common request of my Commons, which I may well term (me thinketh) the whole realm because they give, as I have heard, in all these matters of Parliament their common consent to such as be here assembled. The weight and greatness of this matter might cause in me, being a woman wanting both wit and memory, some fear to speak and bashfulness besides, a thing appropriate to my sex. But yet the princely seat and kingly throne wherein God (though unworthy) hath constituted me maketh these two causes[2] to seem little in mine eyes, though grievous perhaps to your ears, and boldeneth me to say somewhat in this matter, which I mean only to touch but not presently to answer. For this so great a demand needeth both great and grave advice.

I read of a philosopher (whose deeds upon this occasion I remember better than his name) who always, when he was required to give answer in any hard question of school points, would rehearse over his alphabet before he would proceed to any further answer therein, not for that he could not presently[3] have answered, but have his wits the riper and better sharpened to answer the matter withal. If he, a common man, but[4] in matters of school took such delay the better to show his eloquent tale, great cause may justly move me in this so great a matter, touching the benefit of this realm and the safety of you all, to defer mine answer till some other time, wherein I assure you the consideration of my own safety (although I thank you for the great care that you seem to have thereof) shall be little in comparison of that great regard that I mean to have of the safety and surety of you all.

And though God of late seemed to touch me rather like one that He chastised than one that He punished, and though death possessed almost every joint of me,[5] so as I wished then that the feeble thread of life, which lasted methought all too long, might by Clotho's hand have quietly been cut off; yet desired I not then life (as I have some witnesses here) so much for mine own safety as for yours. For I knew that in exchanging of this reign I should have enjoyed a better reign, where residence is perpetual.

---

1. Again.
† Copy text: Public Record Office: State Papers 12/27, fols. 153v–54r.
1. Thomas Williams, Speaker of the House of Commons.
2. Her marriage and the sucession; *constituted*: appointed and established.
3. Immediately; *philosopher*: in her second speech to Parliament on the matter of Mary Stuart in 1586 (see Part Six), Elizabeth again tells this anecdote, identifying the "philosopher," in one copy, as Caesar Augustus and, in another, as Alcibiades. Since the reference is actually to advice given by Athenadorus to Augustus Caesar in Plutarch's *Moralia*, that man is probably the philosopher she had in mind (see Mears, *The Myth of Elizabeth*, 78); *school points*: matters of academic debate.
4. Merely.
5. Elizabeth here refers to her bout with smallpox in October 1562, a point raised by the petition from the Commons.

There needs no boding of my bane.[6] I know now as well as I did before that I am mortal. I know also that I must seek to discharge myself of that great burden that God hath laid upon me, for of them to whom much is committed, much is required.[7] Think not that I, that in other matters have had convenient[8] care of you all, will in this matter touching the safety of myself and you all be careless. For I know that this matter toucheth me much nearer than it doth you all, who, if the worst happen, can lose but your bodies. But if I take not that convenient care that it behooveth me to have therein, I hazard to lose both body and soul.

And though I am determined in this so great and weighty a matter to defer mine answer till some other time because I will not in so deep a matter wade with so shallow a wit, yet have I thought good to use these few words as well to show you that I am neither careless nor unmindful of your safety in this case (as I trust you likewise do not forget that by me you were delivered whilst you were hanging on the bough ready to fall into the mud, yea to be drowned in the dung), neither yet the promise which you have here made concerning your duties and due obedience (wherewith I assure you, I mean to charge you), as further to let you understand that I neither mislike any of your requests herein nor the great care that you seem to have of the surety and safety[9] of your helps in this matter.

Lastly, because I will discharge some restless heads in whose brains the needless hammers beat with vain judgment that I should mislike this their petition, I say that of the matter and sum thereof I like and allow very well. As to the circumstances, if any be, I mean upon further advice further to answer. And so I assure you all that, though after my death you may have many stepdames, yet shall you never have any a more mother than I mean to be unto you all.

Proclamation on the Return of Soldiers from Newhaven (August 1, 1563)[†]

The Queen's Majesty, considering the return of no small numbers of her faithful subjects, having truly and valiantly served at Newhaven and being many of the same sick or touched with infection of such sickness as reigned there, hath thought meet (because the same numbers shall return to sundry places of her realm, being clear from such contagious sickness) to will and require her said captains and soldiers and every of them to have charitable and neighborly regard to the preservation of their neighbors from infection and to forbear for some season to be conversant with any

---

6. Prediction of my death.
7. Luke 12.48.
8. Fitting.
9. Trustworthiness and protection; *few words . . . show you*: as this sentence unwinds, Elizabeth claims that she is neither careless of their safety, nor forgetful of their promise to obey her, nor angry with their requests; *delivered . . . dung*: a reference to the persecution of Protestants under Mary Tudor, as well as the threat of foreign intervention and monetary problems that Elizabeth inherited upon gaining the throne.
† Copy text: *By the Quene the Quenes Maiestie consyderyng the returne of no small numbers of her faythfull subiectes* (London: Richarde Iugge and Iohn Cawood, [1563]; STC 7959), 2 leaves.

mo[1] than of mere necessity they ought. And for such soldiers as be poor and have any contagious sickness upon them, being no otherwise provided for, her Majesty earnestly requireth, and in God's name chargeth, the principal officers (as well ecclesiastical as civil) of all cities, towns, and parishes where the same poor sick soldiers shall of necessity come, to provide some remote places where the same poor and sick persons may be separated from conversation with other, being whole,[2] and have relief by common provision and alms to be ministered and given by the richer, which, beside that Christian charity requireth it, the same is also requisite and expedient to be done by them which be whole and rich for their own preservation, for otherwise they may feel the sharp hand of God over them for their unmercifulness.

And because no persons should of malice or ignorance have any misliking of such faithful captains and soldiers as shall return to their countries and habitations because the town where they were in garrison is left by composition to the French king (as it was always so intended upon reasonable conditions), it is to be known and understand that there wanted no truth, courage, nor manhood in any one of the said garrison, from the highest to the lowest, who were fully, yea rather as it were obstinately, determined with one full assent to have abidden[3] the whole force of France and their helpers to the uttermost of their lives.

But when it pleased Almighty God, against whose will there is no standing, to permit the said garrison to be visited with so great and incessable plague of infectious mortal sickness as heretofore great, noble armies have been (and thereby forced to yield and decline from their enterprises), it was thought the part and office of Christian wisdom not to tempt the Almighty nor to contend with the inevitable inward mortal enemy of plague, assailing all sorts, as well the strongest as the weakest, the armed as unarmed, the captains as the laborer, neither repulsable by weapon, shot, nor engine; and therefore joining therewith the enemy's offers not unreasonable (proceeding of the opinion which they had conceived by the sundry overthrows given to them by the captains and soldiers of the garrison, that they should never get the town without great effusion of blood on both parts, whereof they had lamentable loss for their part this last year in their civil tumults more than in any wars, as it is esteemed, seven years before) the Queen's Majesty (being advertised that the Constable of France had by messages solicited the Earl of Warwick, her Majesty's Lieutenant, a captain right nobly renowned, to come to some communication for the delivery of the said town with honorable conditions, whereby Christian blood might be saved on both parts, quietness and peace might the rather follow betwixt both the realms) was contented that the said Earl and the Council of that town should not thus lamentably contend and strive any longer with the plague, with the which they had now for the space of five or six months continually fought, leesing daily more and more great numbers thereby, but should (considering he and his company had so nobly acquitted themselves) accord to common with the said Constable; and hearing his conditions to be, as they were reported, honorable (which were a free and quiet

---

1. To live among any more.
2. Who are well; *ecclesiastical as civil*: church and government officials.
3. Withstood; *misliking of*: objection to; *town*: The French port of Le Havre, known to the English as Newhaven; *composition*: as a means of settling a debt by mutual agreement; *wanted*: lacked.

departure in convenient time for the said Lieutenant, captains, soldiers, and people with all their artillery, munitions, ships, vessels, victual,[4] armor, weapon, and goods anywise belonging to her Majesty or to any English person), the said Lieutenant should accord thereunto.

Whereupon the said Lieutenant (being with all the whole garrison of their own disposition of a contrary determination rather to hazard the rest of their lives with the plague and with the assaults of the enemy, whereof they had abidden and repulsed some, than to leave the town by treaty) counseling with the Council and captains there and considering her Majesty's princely mind and intention towards the preservation of her subjects whereof he had charge (being indeed manifestly and inevitably subject still both to the plague and to the enemy's approach by the which they had possessed the entry of the haven and made sundry bulwarks by large breaches saultable and were entered into the ditches), was contented at length to set apart their own great stomachs and by inclining wisdom to open their ears to the Constable's motions and offers, and so by treaty and honorable compact accorded to deliver the town to the French King, after the space of eight days or more if time so required, wherein he[5] might honorably, safely, freely, and warlikely retire by sea the whole garrison under his charge with all manner of riches, artillery, munitions, and other things belonging to any English person. For the doing whereof, being himself hurt in the thigh with a shot at a breach, he committed the principal charge thereof to Sir Hugh Paulet [and] Sir Maurice Denys, knights, and the Knight Marshall Master Randolph,[6] who at this present are therein occupied.

And this is the truth of the just and necessary cause of return of the said Lieutenant, captains, and garrison, such a cause as hath constrained both heathen and Christian emperors to do the like or sometimes things of less advantage to themselves. And, therefore, the courages and activities of the said garrison having been such as the enemies have not let by many means to recommend beyond their accustomed manner, and sithen[7] it cannot be denied but that the plague in the town hath herein brought that to pass that by man's force was either not possible or otherwise not likely, her Majesty doubteth not but all these her true, good, and valiant subjects, having thus served and now returning to their habitations, shall find at this time (as they have well merited) favor, help, and charitable succor according to their estates and, hereafter, honor, love, and praise of their country whilst they live.

Given at Richmond, the first day of August,
the fifth year of her Majesty's reign.
God save the Queen.

4. Provisions, including but not limited to foodstuffs; *enemy's offers not unreasonable*: Christian wisdom and a reasonable offer of retreat from the French motivated the Queen to withdraw her troops; *esteemed*: reckoned; *seven years before*: the Proclamation argues that the French were happy to regain Newhaven without further bloodshed, given their earlier defeats by the English army and the heavy losses both the Huguenot and royalist forces had sustained in their civil war; *Constable of France*: Anne de Montmorency, the commander of the French army; *Earl of Warwick*: Ambrose Dudley, the older brother of Robert Dudley and commander of the English forces at Newhaven; *leesing*: losing; *accord to common*: come to agreement.
5. The Earl of Warwick; *haven*: the port; *saultable*: open to assault; *ditches*: the defensive works surrounding Newhaven; *great stomachs*: courage; *inclining*: submissive; *accorded*: agreed.
6. Edward Randolph was high Marshall of the garrison at Le Havre, under the Earl of Warwick; *being . . . at a breach*: Warwick was severely wounded during the siege and suffered poor health the rest of his life; *Sir Hugh Paulet*: governor of the Island of Jersey in the English Channel; *Sir Maurice Denys*: a soldier from Kent who later died of the plague.
7. Since; *courages*: bravery; *let*: refrained.

ELIZABETH AMONG HER PEOPLE

Elizabeth's visit to the University of Cambridge in August 1564 may have provided welcome relief from questions of international Protestantism, reform of the Church, marriage, and the succession. William Cecil, who among other posts held the Chancellorship of the University, organized the festivities with an eye toward pleasing the Queen. There were lectures, sermons, debates, plays, and a manuscript book of congratulatory poems, as well as banquets and processions. When Cecil suggested that Elizabeth speak to the assembled scholars, she did so in a graceful Latin oration that established her authority as both a Queen and a learned woman, although with a note of self deprecation not found on a similar occasion at Oxford three decades later (see Part Eight).

The Queen had also captured the popular imagination. In a ballad published that same year, although written during Elizabeth's first year as Queen, William Birch likened England to a young lover wooing his beloved "Bessy," a young woman who remained faithful to her intended spouse despite trials and imprisonment. "The Song between the Queen's Majesty and England" melded images of marriage with descriptions of Elizabeth as "a sweet virgin pure" and the "handmaid of the Lord" and in simple rhymes signaled Elizabeth's success: it recognized her as the legitimate heir of Henry VIII; a divinely appointed Protestant monarch; a just and merciful queen; an English ruler whose authority extended to "other lands" as well. It sounded a measure of confidence and hope that was as appropriate in 1564 as it had been when Elizabeth was first proclaimed as Queen.

QUEEN ELIZABETH

Latin Oration at Cambridge University
(August 7, 1564)[†]

Most loyal subjects in this much beloved University of Cambridge, although womanly modesty forbids crude and uncultivated speech in an assemblage of most learned men, nevertheless the intercession of my noblemen and my good will toward the University induce me to speak, however rudely. I am driven to do this by two motivations: the first is the dissemination of learned discourse, which I desire very earnestly and long for very eagerly; the second is the expectation that you all have. So far as the dissemination is concerned, the words of superiors take the place of books for their subjects (as Demosthenes says),[1] and the example of the prince has the force of law. And if this was true in those republics, how much more so in a kingdom. There is no more direct or suitable way to find advancement or to gain my favor than to apply yourselves to your studies (as you have already begun to do), and I pray and beg you to do so.

Now I come to my second motivation. This morning I saw the lavish buildings erected for you by the most noble kings who preceded me on the throne. And when I saw them, I sighed deeply, not unlike Alexander the

---

† Copy text: Bodleian Library, University of Oxford, MS Rawlinson Poetical 85, fols. 37v–38r. Translation by Clarence H. Miller.

1. The Athenian orator Demosthenes, whose works Elizabeth had studied with her tutor, Roger Ascham, argued in *On the Crown* that a ruler's words, as well as his actions, govern the people (see Demosthenes. *The Public Orations of Demosthenes*, trans. Arthur Wallace Pickard [Oxford: Clarendon Press, 1912], 2.47–48).

Great, who, when he read of the many monuments erected by princes, turned to his friend (or rather adviser) and said, "But I have done nothing like this." I have felt this no less than he. But this sorrow of mine, if it is not completely removed, is certainly lessened by the well-known proverb that Rome was not built in a day. I am not yet so old, nor have I reigned for such a long time, but that before I pay my debt to nature (if Atropos does not cut the line of my life sooner than I wish), I will bring forth some renowned and outstanding work, and I will never give up this intention as long as there is still life in my limbs.[2] But if it happens that I must die (and I have no certain knowledge how soon this will come to pass) before I can finish what I now promise, nevertheless after my death I will leave behind some extraordinary work so that I will be well remembered by posterity, and I will motivate others by my example, and will make all of you more devoted to your studies.

But now you see how much difference there is between exceptional learning and mental training that has not been retained. Of the first there are here assembled many quite sufficient examples, but of the latter I have today very unadvisedly made myself and you witnesses, since I have so long detained your learned attention with my barbarous discourse.[3]

That is what I have to say. E. Regina.[4]

WILLIAM BIRCH

A Song between the Queen's Majesty
and England (1564)[†]

ENGLAND: Come over the bourn,° Bessy,   *brook*
            Come over the bourn, Bessy,
            Sweet Bessy, come over to me.[1]
            And I shall thee take
5   And my dear Lady make
            Before all other that ever I see.

BESSY: My think[2] I hear a voice,
            At whom I do rejoice,
            And answer thee now I shall.
10   Tell me, I say,
            What art thou that bids me come away,
            And so earnestly dost me call?

---

2. An echo of Aeneas's promise to remember Dido in *Aeneid*, 4.336 (see Virgil, *Eclogues, Georgics, Aeneid*, 445). The Latin word translated here as "life" is, in the copy text, "*spiritibus*," which does not fit the grammar of the sentence, and is emended to "*spiritus*" [Miller's note]; *bring forth . . . work*: an implicit promise to build another college at Cambridge.
3. Elizabeth's modest disclaimer was undoubtedly meant to draw attention to her fine command of Latin; *here*: copy text: "*tanta hic*," another grammatical problem, emended here to "*hic*."
4. Another manuscript concludes in English, with the disarming remark, "I would to God you had all drunk this night of the river of Lethe, that you might forget all" (British Library MS Sloane 401, fol. 38).
† Copy text: *A songe betwene the Quenes maiestie and Englande* (London: William Pickeringe, [1564]; STC 3079), single sheet.
1. In Shakespeare's *King Lear* (3.6.25–28), Edgar and the Fool sing a bawdy variant of this refrain.
2. Methink.

ENGLAND: I am thy lover fair,
           Hath chose thee to mine heir,
15   And my name is merry England.
           Therefore, come away
           And make no more delay.
      Sweet Bessy, give me thy hand.

BESSY: Here is my hand,
20   My dear lover England.
      I am thine both with mind and heart
           Forever to endure,
           Thou mayst be sure,
      Until death us two depart.

25 ENGLAND: Lady, this long space
           Have I loved thy Grace,
      More than I durst well say,
           Hoping, at the last,
           When all storms were past
30   For to see this joyful day.

BESSY: Yet my lover, England,
           Ye shall understand
      How fortune on me did lower.°   *frown*
           I was tumbled and tossed
35   From pillar to post
      And prisoner in the Tower.

ENGLAND: Dear Lady, we do know
           How that tyrants, not a few,
      Went about for to seek thy blood;
40   An[3] contrary to right,
           They did what they might,
      That now bear two faces in one hood.[4]

BESSY: Then was I carried to Woodstock,
           And kept close under lock,
45   That no man might with me speak.
           And against all reason,
           They accused me of treason,
      And enticingly[5] they did me threat.

ENGLAND: Oh, my lover fair,
50   My dearling and mine heir,
      Full sore for thee I did lament;
           But no man durst speak,

---

3. If.
4. The sign of a hypocrite.
5. Copy text: Tieably or ticably; the unique copy of this poem is badly printed at this point. The word
   is probably formed from "ticen," a Middle English verb meaning to entice, persuade, or seduce.
   Elizabeth's jailors attempted to undermine her confidence with threats.

But they would him threat
And quickly make him repent.

55   BESSY: Then was I delivered their hands,
            But was fain to put in bands
            And good sureties for my forthcoming;[6]
            Not from my house to depart
            Nor nowhere else to start,°   *escape*
60   As though I had been away running.

        ENGLAND: Why, dear Lady, I trow°   *believe*
            Those madmen did not know
            That ye were daughter unto King Harry
            And a princess of birth,
65   One of the noblest on earth,
            And sister unto Queen Mary.

        BESSY: Yes, yet I must forgive
            All such as do live
            If they will hereafter amend.
70   And for those that are gone,
            God forgive them every one
            And His mercy on them extend.

        ENGLAND: Yet, my lover dear,
            Tell me now here,
75   For what cause had ye this punishment?
            For the commons° did not know,   *common people*
            Nor no man would them show
            The chief cause of your imprisonment.

        BESSY: No, nor they themself
80   That would have decayed° my wealth,   *ruined*
            But only by power and abusion.°   *perverse outrages*
            They could not detect me,
            But that they did suspect me
            That I was not of their religion.

85   ENGLAND: O cruel tyrants,
            And also monstrous giants,
            That would such a sweet blossom devour.
            But the Lord, of His might,
            Defended thee in right
90   And shortened their arm and power.

        BESSY: Yet, my lover dear,
            Mark me well here:
            Though they were men of the devil,

---

6. Glad under the circumstances to be imprisoned in a secure place, from which she could not be abducted.

> The scripture plainly saith,
> 95   "All they that be of faith
> Must needs do good against evil."[7]

ENGLAND: Oh, sweet virgin pure!
    Long may ye endure
To reign over us in this land.
100   For your works do accord,
    Ye are the handmaid of the Lord,[8]
For He hath blessed you with His hand.

BESSY: My sweet realm, be obedient
    To God's holy commandment,
105 And my proceedings embrace.
    And for that that is abused
    Shall be better used,
And that within short space.

ENGLAND: Dear Lady and Queen,
110   I trust it shall be seen
Ye shall reign quietly without strife;
    And if any traitors there be
    Of any kind or degree,
I pray God send them short life.

115 BESSY: I trust all faithful hearts
    Will play true subjects' parts,
Knowing me their Queen and true heir by right,
    And that much the rather
    For the love of my father,
120 That worthy prince, King Henry the Eight.

ENGLAND: Therefore, let us pray
    To God both night and day,
Continually and never to cease,
    That He will preserve your Grace
125   To reign over us long space
In tranquility, wealth, and peace.

BOTH: All honor, laud, and praise,
    Be to the Lord God always,
Who hath all princes' hearts in His hands.
130   That by His power and might
    He may guide them aright,
For the wealth of all Christian lands.
    Finis.

                      Quoth William Birch.

    God save the Queen.

---

7. Romans 12.21.
8. An allusion to the Virgin Mary (Luke 1.38).

Part Three: Mary Stuart, the Northern Rebellion, and Protestant Discontent (1567–1571)

HISTORICAL BACKGROUND

The year 1567 opened on a sour note for Queen Elizabeth. She had spent the preceding autumn tussling with Parliament over its desire to see her marry and her desire to raise more money for the Crown. Consequently, the Queen's speech to the closing session of Parliament on January 2 sounded more than a little exasperated: "God forbid that your liberty should make my bondage," she complained. William Cecil, her chief secretary, jotted down a memo listing many of the troublesome issues in the kingdom: "the succession not answered; the marriage not followed; * * * general discontentations; the slender execution of the subsidy [inadequate funds raised by Parliament for the government]; dangers of sedition * * * by persons discontented" (Somerset, *Elizabeth I*, 191).

That Cecil mentioned first the problem of the succession is revealing: Elizabeth was neither married nor had she named an heir, and the thought of *choosing* a monarch, should she die, was unsettling to many of her subjects. Not that Elizabeth had abandoned all expectation of marriage. She continued to dally with the Archduke Charles of Austria, brother of Maximilian, the Holy Roman Emperor, an alliance promoted by Cecil and resisted by Robert Dudley, now the Earl of Leicester, who saw the Archduke as a serious rival to his own matrimonial prospects. Charles's serious commitment to his Roman Catholic faith, however, worried Elizabeth, even after the Archduke promised to hear his masses only in private, for she was keenly aware how little welcome a Catholic co-regent would be to many of her Protestant subjects.

But Elizabeth was soon confronted with even more pressing concerns and none more troubling than those posed by her Scottish cousin, Mary Stuart. By 1568, Mary had come under suspicion of involvement in the murder of her second husband, Henry Stuart, Lord Darnley; had married James Hepburn, the Earl of Bothwell, one of the ringleaders in the conspiracy against Darnley; and had lost her throne. Her infant son, James VI, was installed in her place, and she fled to England, much to Elizabeth's dismay. Although Elizabeth was not unwilling to accept Mary as her successor, and she was eager to maintain her cousin's queenly authority against the peremptory demands of the Scottish nobility, a series of converging events made it impossible for Elizabeth openly to support Mary. A commission of inquiry into the affairs of Mary Stuart, established by the Queen, began work in the northern city of York in October 1568, but was soon moved to Westminster so that the Queen, from her official residence at Hampton Court, could keep a better eye on the proceedings. These were marked by rumors, political maneuverings, and backroom deals. Unbeknownst to the Queen, some of Mary's supporters had begun to urge a marriage between the highest-born English lord, Thomas Howard, fourth Duke of Norfolk, and the Queen of Scots. In the meantime, James Stuart, the Earl of Moray and Mary's half-brother as well as the Regent for her son James, first hinted at and finally revealed a set of incriminating letters purported to have been written by Mary to Bothwell. Enclosed in a small silver box, they came to be known as the "Casket Letters" and, while scholars still debate their authenticity, many Elizabethans accepted them as damning evidence of Mary's adultery with Bothwell and complicity in Darnley's death. To further complicate matters, Elizabeth refused to allow Mary to appear in her own defense; John Lesley, the Bishop of Ross, and Lord Herries, who had been appointed her representatives, then refused to attend the proceedings, and, since no formal defense had been offered or repudiated, no judicial decision could be reached. On January 10, 1569, Elizabeth declared a stalemate and delivered Mary Stuart over to the care of George Talbot, the sixth Earl of Shrewsbury, who with his wife, the formidable Bess of Hardwick, remained Mary's keeper until 1584.

Although the Scottish lords were unhappy with this conclusion to the commission of inquiry, Elizabeth herself was not displeased. She had managed to defuse the tensions in Scotland and exile Mary to a provincial castle and yet not denounce her as a queen. Elizabeth may well have breathed a sigh of relief and given thanks for a providential delivery. If she did so, however, it was premature, for the next crisis of her reign was already brewing. Several earls who lived in the north of England, and whose families had remained staunch Roman Catholics, took advantage of Mary Stuart's presence in England to mount a rebellion against Elizabeth. Although what has become known as the Rebellion of the Northern Earls lasted only four months, it raised fears of a divided England, particularly when Pope Pius V subsequently lent his support to the rebels by issuing an official statement excommunicating Elizabeth from the Roman Catholic Church, denying her legitimacy as Queen, and releasing her subjects from their oath of allegiance to her. The Pope went so far as to threaten excommunication to any English person who obeyed any of her "monitions, mandates, and laws." At the same time, from the other end of the religious spectrum, many Protestants were pressuring Elizabeth to pursue further reforms within the established Church.

So it was that Elizabeth concluded her first dozen years as Queen facing difficulties on many fronts. Although she had managed to avert civil war, it was at the cost of serious reprisals against the northern earls and their supporters. Furthermore, Mary Stuart remained an unwelcome guest within English borders, and Elizabeth's own excommunication from the Roman Catholic Church fueled both real fears for her own safety and the rise of anti-Catholic sentiment. In London and at Court, she was confronted by Protestant activists who wished her to take a stronger hand in guiding the English Church toward a more complete realization of the principles of the Reformation. In these circumstances, she may well have been drawn to the words in a prayer composed for her and published in 1569: "Thou therefore (O endless fountain of all wisdom) send down from Thy holy heaven and from the sovereign throne of Thy majesty Thy wisdom to be ever with me and alway to assist me."

THE MATTER OF MARY STUART

On February 10, 1567, the after-effects of an explosion that rocked Edinburgh reached all the way south to trouble London. The explosion demolished Kirk o'

Field, the house in which Mary Stuart's second husband, Lord Darnley, had been residing. Darnley, a younger cousin of both Elizabeth and Mary Stuart, had married the Scottish Queen just two years earlier, when it became apparent that a match between Robert Dudley, the Earl of Leicester, and Mary, which was favored by Elizabeth, would not be realized. But Mary quickly tired of the immature and debauched Darnley, and many in Scotland and England readily assumed that she had acquiesced in her husband's murder. Furthermore, it was rumored that she had done so in a secret conspiracy with one of her new favorites, James Hepburn, Earl of Bothwell.

Elizabeth was dismayed, not only by the casual way in which Mary was squandering her royal prerogatives but also by the cold-blooded murder of one "so close in blood" and by the rise of Bothwell, who was no friend to the English. Her letter to Mary, written less than two weeks after Darnley's death, began with the curt greeting "Madam" and continued in the same tone, urging Mary to search out and punish the murderers, not fearing "to touch even him whom you have nearest to you if the thing touches him" so that she might show "this to the world: that you are both a noble princess and a loyal wife."

Elizabeth's letter, and similar advice from other royal relatives and advisors, had no effect on Mary Stuart. She allowed herself to be abducted by Bothwell in April and married him on May 15. All this was too much for the Protestant nobles in Scotland, who rose in rebellion, defeated the Queen and her army at Carberry Hill on June 15, forced Bothwell into exile in Denmark, and superintended Mary's abdication on July 24 in favor of her fourteen-month-old son, James VI. Elizabeth's second letter to Mary, written between the Queen of Scot's defeat and her abdication, does not mince words. "How," she asks Mary, "could a worse choice be made for your honor than in such haste to marry such a subject, who (besides other and notorious lacks) public fame hath charged with the murder of your late husband?" Although Elizabeth promised that "whatsoever we can imagine meet for your honor and safety that shall lie in our power, we will perform," her concern was not so much to comfort Mary as to shore up the tattered remnants of the monarchy itself, which was steadily losing power to the Scottish lords.

Following Mary Stuart's abdication, she was held in the Scottish castle of Lochleven, until her daring escape in May 1568, when she fled in a small open boat to England, there to cast herself upon the good graces of Elizabeth. It was to prove a disastrous move for both queens, and the matter of Mary Stuart would loom on Elizabeth's horizon until Mary's execution nearly twenty years later. Over the next several months, Elizabeth's councilors, Mary's defenders, and representatives of the Scottish nobility, led by James Stuart, Regent for the young King James, met to work out the details for an official inquiry into two related issues: Mary's insistence that she had been wrongfully deposed as Queen and the Earl of Moray's claim that she was an accomplice to murder. Elizabeth hoped this judicial proceeding would prove Mary's innocence in the death of Darnley, but it was not to be.

Elizabeth's coat of arms.

Mary Stuart's coat of arms in 1558, showing lions symbolizing her claim to the English monarchy.

In preparation for the trial, John Lesley, the Bishop of Ross and one of Mary's closest advisers, wrote *A Defense of the Honor of the Princess Mary, Queen of Scotland*, which he published in London in 1569. Not only did the Bishop restate Mary's right to the Scottish throne and defend her against charges that she had conspired to murder her second husband, but he also carefully traced her claim to the English throne and took aim against the arguments that the famous Scottish reformer, John Knox, had made a decade earlier in the *First Blast of the Trumpet Against the Monstrous Regiment of Women* (see Part Two). By aligning himself with the right of women to rule and against Knox, whom Elizabeth disliked, Lesley undoubtedly hoped to ingratiate himself and his princess with the English Queen. In his appeal to Elizabeth, Lesley drew upon both the actual and the metaphoric relationship between Elizabeth and Mary. "This Lady and Queen," he told Elizabeth's subjects, "is her most nigh neighbor by place and her nigh cousin and sister by blood. She is a queen." Yet the Bishop immediately softened this argument from equality by casting Mary into a loving and subservient role: "Yea she is, as it were, her daughter both by daughterly reverence she beareth her Majesty and by reason she is of God called to daughter's place in the succession of the crown, if her Majesty fail of issue." To which he added, "And I doubt nothing, if she employ this motherly benefit upon her, but that she shall find her a mindful, thankful, and an obedient daughter." Lesley's appeal for a close relationship between Elizabeth and Mary Stuart, however, did not bear fruit, and Elizabeth continued to hold her cousin in England under house arrest.

QUEEN ELIZABETH

Letters to Mary Stuart (1567)[†]

24 February 1567

Madam:

My ears have been so deafened and my understanding so grieved and my heart so affrighted to hear the dreadful news of the abominable murder of your mad husband and my killed cousin[1] that I scarcely yet have the wits to write about it. And inasmuch as my nature compels me to take his death in the extreme, he being so close in blood,[2] so it is that I will boldly tell you what I think of it.

I cannot dissemble that I am more sorrowful for you than for him. O Madam, I would not do the office of faithful cousin or affectionate friend if I studied rather to please your ears than employed myself in preserving your honor. However, I will not at all dissemble what most people are talking about, which is that you will look through your fingers[3] at the revenging of this deed, and that you do not take measures that touch those who have done as you wished, as if the thing had been entrusted in a way that the murderers felt assurance in doing it. Among the thoughts in my heart, I beseech you to want no such thought to stick[4] at this point. Through all the dealings of the world I never was in such miserable haste to lodge and have in my heart such a miserable opinion of any prince as this would cause me do. Much less will I have such of her to whom I wish as much good as my heart is able to imagine or as you were able, a short while ago, to wish. However, I exhort you, I counsel you, and I beseech you to take this thing so much to heart that you will not fear to touch even him whom you have nearest to you if the thing touches him,[5] and that no persuasion will

---

† Copy text: *Elizabeth I: Collected Works*, ed. Leah S. Marcus, Janel Mueller, and Mary Beth Rose (Chicago and London: University of Chicago Press, 2000), 116–19. Reprinted by permission of the University of Chicago Press. © 2000 by the University of Chicago.
1. Henry Stuart, Lord Darnley, her second husband, who was murdered on February 10, 1567.
2. Darnley, like Mary Stuart herself, was a grandchild of Margaret Tudor, sister to Henry VIII; Mary, however, was descended from Margaret's first marriage to James IV of Scotland while Darnley was descended from Margaret's second marriage to Archibald Douglas, the Earl of Angus.
3. A proverbial saying that means to deceive others (Whiting and Whiting, *Proverbs*, F158).
4. Stand; *want*: permit.
5. A not too subtle reference to James Hepburn, fourth Earl of Bothwell, whom Mary subsequently married on May 15, 1567.

prevent you from making an example out of this to the world: that you are both a noble princess and a loyal wife.

I do not write so vehemently out of doubt that I have, but out of the affection that I bear you in particular. For I am not ignorant that you have no wiser counselors than myself. Thus it is that, when I remember that our Lord had one Judas out of twelve and I assure myself that there could be no one more loyal than myself, I offer you my affection in place of this prudence.[6]

As for the three things that have been communicated to me by Melvin, I understand by all these instructions that you continue to desire greatly to satisfy me and that it will content you to grant the request that my Lord Bedford made you in my name for the ratification of your treaty,[7] which has gone undone for six or seven years. I promise you that I demand it as much for your good as for whatever profit would result to me. About other matters I will not trouble you with a longer letter except to put you in contact with this gentleman[8] and to thank you by this messenger for your good letters, which were and are very agreeable coming from your hands.

Praying the Creator to give you the grace to recognize this traitor and protect yourself from him as from the ministers of Satan, with my very heartfelt recommendations to you, very dear sister.

From Westminster February 24.

23 June 1567

Madam:

It hath been always held for a special principle in friendship that "prosperity provideth but adversity proveth friends,"[9] whereof at this time finding occasion to verify the same with our actions, we have thought meet, both for our profession and your comfort, in these few words to testify our friendship, not only by admonishing you of the worst but to comfort you for the best.

We have understood[1] by your trusty servant Robert Melville such things as you gave him in charge to declare on your behalf concerning your estate, and specially of as much as could be said for the allowance of your marriage.[2] Madam, to be plain with you, our grief hath not been small that in this your marriage so slender consideration hath been had that, as we perceive manifestly, no good friend you have in the whole world can like thereof, and if we should otherwise write or say, we should abuse you. For how could a worse choice be made for your honor than in such haste to

---

6. That is, the "doubt" mentioned at the beginning of the paragraph; *Judas . . . twelve*: Elizabeth implies that, like Christ, Mary is innocent and has simply been betrayed by a Judas figure, Bothwell.
7. The Treaty of Edinburgh, negotiated in 1560, ended the Scottish civil war and prohibited English and French military intervention in Scotland, but Mary Stuart refused to ratify it as long as Elizabeth refused to acknowledge her as the legitimate heir to the English throne; *Melvin*: The Scottish ambassador to England, Sir Robert Melville; *Lord Bedford*: Francis Russell, second Earl of Bedford, a member of the Privy Council and emissary to Scotland who served as Elizabeth's proxy at the baptism of Mary Stuart's son, James.
8. The Earl of Bedford.
9. Latin proverb: "*amicos res opimae pariunt, adverse probant*" (Marcus, Mueller, and Rose's note).
1. Copy text: understand.
2. To Bothwell on May 15; Melville disliked Bothwell and said little to placate Elizabeth on the marriage.

marry such a subject, who (besides other and notorious lacks) public fame hath charged with the murder of your late husband, beside the touching of yourself also in some part, though we trust that in that behalf falsely. And with what peril have you married him that hath another lawful wife alive, whereby neither by God's law nor man's yourself can be his leeful[3] wife, nor any children betwixt you legitimate.

This you see plainly what we think of the marriage, whereof we are heartily sorry that we can conceive no better, what colorable[4] reasons soever we have heard of your servant to induce us. We wish, upon the death of your husband, your first care had been to have searched out and punished the murderers of our near cousin, your husband, which having been done effectually, as easily it might have been in a matter so notorious, there might have been many more things tolerated better in your marriage than now can be suffered to be spoken of. And surely we cannot but for friendship to yourself, besides the natural instinction[5] that we have of blood to your late husband, profess ourselves earnestly bent to do anything in our power to procure the due punishment of that murder against any subject that you have, how dear soever you should hold him. And next thereto, to be careful how your son, the prince, may be preserved, for the comfort of yours and your realm, which two things we have from the beginning always taken to heart and therein do mean to continue, and would be very sorry but you should allow us[6] therein, what dangerous persuasions soever be made to you for the contrary.

Now for your estate: in such adversity as we hear you should be (whereof we could not tell what to think to be true, having a great part of your nobility, as we hear, separated from you), we assure you that, whatsoever we can imagine meet for your honor and safety that shall lie in our power, we will perform the same, that it shall well appear you have a good neighbor, a dear sister, and a faithful friend, and so shall you undoubtedly always find and prove us to be indeed towards you. For which purpose we are determined to send with all speed one of our own trusty servants, not only to understand your state but also thereupon so to deal with your nobility and people as they shall find you not to lack our friendship and power for the preservation of your honor in quietness. And upon knowledge had what shall be further requisite to be done for your comfort and for the tranquility of your realm, we will omit no time to further the same, as you shall well see.

And so we recommend ourselves to you, good sister, in as affectuous[7] a manner as heretofore we were accustomed.

At our manor of Richmond, the 23rd of June, 1567.

---

3. Lawful; *another lawful wife*: Lady Jean Gordon, Bothwell's wife, sued for divorce on April 24.
4. Specious.
5. Instinct.
6. Allow us to continue; *the prince*: soon to be James VI of Scotland and later James I of England; Mary abdicated on July 24 and James was crowned as a Protestant king on July 29 at Stirling parish church.
7. Loving.

BISHOP JOHN LESLEY

From A Defense of the Honor of the Princess Mary, Queen of Scotland (1569)[†]

The author to the gentle reader:

It is not unknown to thee (gentle reader), being an Englishman, what great contention hath of late risen in England, what hot schools and disputations have been kept in many places here touching the right heir apparent of the crown of England,[1] if God call to His mercy our gracious Queen and Sovereign Elizabeth, without issue of her body. Neither hath this stir stood within the list of earnest and fervent talk of each side, but men have gone on farther and have as well by printed as unprinted books done their endeavor[2] to disgrace, blemish, and deface, as much as in them lieth, the just title, claim, and interest of the noble and excellent Lady Mary, Queen of Scotland, to the foresaid crown. Yea they have in uttering their gross ignorance or rather their spiteful malice against her Grace, run so on headlong that they have expressly denied and refused all womanly government. Among other, one of these rash, hot, hasty, and heady companions, hath cast abroad about July last a poisoned, pestiferous pamphlet against the said Queen's claim and interest, wherein he avoucheth also that the civil regiment of women is repugnant both to the law of nature and to the law of God.[3]

It is moreover well known to all England and Scotland what a business and stir there hath been, what earnest, vehement, and violent talk, what false feigned and forged reports and opprobrious slanders have been bruited, as well in the one as in the other realm, against the said virtuous, good, innocent Lady and Queen, by the crafty, malicious drift of her rebellious subjects, who have not only blown abroad and filled men's ears with loathsome and heinous accusations against her Grace touching the slaughter of her late dear husband, but have also (upon this false, slanderous crimination) taken arms against her, imprisoned her, and spoiled her of all manner her costly apparel and jewels, and also bereaved her of her princely and royal authority, intruding themselves into the same under the name and shadow of the young prince, her son.[4]

Touching all these points, ye shall have now, good reader, in this treatise following divided into three books, an answer. And forasmuch as Solomon writeth, and this good Lady so taketh it, that a good name is to be praised and valued above all precious ointments, above all gold and silver, and that the impairing of her honor by these foul and slanderous reports doth touch

---

† Copy text: John Lesley, *A defence of the honour of the right highe, mightye and noble Princesse Marie Quene of Scotlande and dowager of France with a declaration aswell of her right, title & intereste to the succession of the crowne of Englande, as that the regimente of women ys conformable to the lawe of God and nature* (London [actually, Rheims]: Eusebius Dicaeophile [that is, J. Foigny], 1569; STC 15505), †2r–4v; †5r–6r; S8r–S8v; T1v–T2v.

1. Mary Stuart's claim to the English throne came through her grandmother, Margaret Tudor, elder sister of Henry VIII.

2. Done their best; *list*: bounds.

3. An echo of John Knox's *The First Blast of the Trumpet Against the Monstrous Regiment of Women* (see Part Two), which apparently was being re-circulated; *civil regiment*: government.

4. James VI of Scotland and later James I of England; he was proclaimed King by the Scottish nobles in 1567 when he was fourteen months old; *bruited*: reported at large; *innocent*: copy text: innocence; *drift*: intention; *husband*: Lord Darnley, her second husband, who was murdered on February 10, 1567; *crimination*: censure.

and nip her heart nearer than may the loss of any worldly honor (hanging upon her by expectation or that she hath enjoyed or doth presently enjoy) or any other grievous injuries that she hath most wrongfully but most patiently suffered, it is thought good that the defense of her honor should forgo the other two books, whereof the former entreateth, debateth, and discusseth the right title and interest of the said Queen Mary to the succession of this crown of England, declaring her said right and title to be good and lawful by the common law of this realm and the acts of Parliament therein holden, with a full answer of such objections as the adversaries lay forth against her said right by color of[5] the said law or Parliaments. And forasmuch as, with our foresaid new-found doctor,[6] neither common law nor acts of Parliament seem to serve for a sufficient plea but that we are by him driven also to plead by the law of nature and by scripture, we have adjoined in the third book a convenient answer to this fond, fantastical, and dangerous assertion as well to the states of other princes as to the state of his and our gracious Sovereign. Wherein we avouch woman's regiment to be conformable both to the law of God and the law of nature.

Which treatise may seem perchance to some as superfluous, neither I greatly deny it and therefore might and would gladly have spared so much labor and travail, if this little poisoned pamphlet had not many readers and many also favorers and allowers; or if the matter did not so nigh touch even our own gracious and noble Sovereign; or if this lewd assertion were not (as it were by a Samson's post) with the countenance of the law of nature and God's holy Word underpropped; or if that God's holy Word were not nowadays wretchedly applied (God reform it) and licentiously wreathed and wrested to the maintenance of every private man's fancy and folly and as fondly and foolishly credited and embraced also of other fantastical persons; or if this man were the first, or like to be the last, maintainer and setter-forth of such a strange and dangerous paradox; or if there have not already been published and divulged by print English books for the maintenance of the said strange doctrine, which was (if we shall credit the setters-forth of it) first well considered and then advisedly allowed by such persons, as a great multitude of people in many countries do now greatly esteem and honor; or if the danger of this doctrine stretched not to many other great princes and kingdoms; or, to conclude, if the divulgation of this doctrine, stood only in English books and that there were not that have showed their fond fancy therein even in the Latin and most common tongue of all: for these and other causes, we have set in the last book a confutation of this gross and dangerous error whereas also he inveigheth most slanderously against her Highness for the foresaid slaughter with bare-naked but spiteful reproaches and outcries, without any manner of kind or countenance of good proof, we will refer the reader to the foresaid defense of her honor, by the which answer ye shall see her integrity and innocency, and withal[7] that her accusers have in this matter played such a

---

5. By unjustifiable assertions about; *good name . . . gold and silver*: Ecclesiastes 7.1; Proverbs 22.1; *forgo*: precede; *former*: that is, the second book.
6. John Knox.
7. Moreover; *treatise*: the answer to Knox in the third book; *Samson's post*: a kind of mousetrap; *fondly*: foolishly; *fantastical*: irrational; *paradox*: absurd argument.

tragedy against their guiltless Lady and gracious Sovereign as lightly the world hath not heard of the like.

The which their false, slanderous, outrageous, rebellious doings it is hoped that our gracious Queen will well consider and ponder, and will take some convenient order[8] also, as well for the repressing of them as for the restitution of the said Queen Mary into her own realm. And the rather because our said Queen is learned and therefore not ignorant what great commendation and immortal fame many kings have purchased to themselves for such benefit bestowed upon other princes, being in the like distress and extremity.

*   *   *

For this Lady and Queen[9] is her most nigh neighbor by place and her nigh cousin and sister by blood. She is a queen and therefore this were a fit benefit for her relief from a queen. Yea she is, as it were, her daughter, both by daughterly reverence she beareth her Majesty and by reason she is of God called to daughter's place in the succession of the crown, if her Majesty fail of issue. And I doubt nothing, if she employ this motherly benefit upon her, but that she shall find her a mindful, thankful, and an obedient daughter. For of all women in this world, she[1] abhoreth ingratitude. She hath hitherto depended only upon the hope to have help and succor of her Majesty, giving over[2] (partly voluntary, partly at the motion of her Majesty) divers proffers of aid and succor by other mighty and puissant princes, her friends freely to her offered, reposing herself upon the fair and princely promises that her Majesty hath made to her sundry times (as well by letters as by messengers) for her relief, whensoever opportunity should occasion her to crave it. For these and many other considerations, there is good hope, as is aforesaid, that our gracious mistress will take in hand her restitution. Whereupon, I trust, shall follow such farther and entire amity between them both and their realms that the benefit, fruit, and commodity thereof shall plentifully redound, as well to all the posterity of both the said realms hereafter as to us presently.

*   *   *

For these and other considerations,[3] the laws of the realm do not, nor ever did, estrange such princes from the succession of the crown of the realm. Which, by reason of the said natural inclination and benevolence of the one to the other standeth[4] with the law of God and nature and with all good reason. And therefore your conclusion is against God's law, nature, and all good reason, whereby you full ungodly, unnaturally, and unreasonably do conclude an exclusion of the Queen of Scotland (pretending her to be a stranger) to that right that God, nature, and reason, and the true hearts of all good natural Englishmen do call her unto as the dear sister and heir apparent to our noble Queen Elizabeth. The which her said just right, title, and interest we trust we have now fully proved and justified and sufficiently repulsed the sundry objections of the adversaries.

8. Appropriate action; *Queen*: Elizabeth.
9. Mary Stuart.
1. Mary Stuart.
2. Refusing.
3. Lesley's arguments for Mary Stuart's claim as Elizabeth's successor, summarized in the conclusion that follows, derive from the law of God, the law of nature, the laws of England, and good reason.
4. Agrees; *natural inclination . . . other*: Elizabeth's natural love for Mary.

And as these being the principal[5] ought to breed no doubt or scruple in any man (so many other foolish, fond, and fantastical objections, not worthy of any answer that busy quarreling heads do cast forth to disable her right or to disgrace and blemish either her honor or this happy union of both realms), if God shall send it in taking our gracious Sovereign from us without issue (which God forbid), ought much less to move any man. Whose Majesty God long preserve and shield, and bless her if it be His pleasure with happy issue. But if it please Him either to bereave us of her Majesty or her Majesty of all such issue, then yet (that we may not be altogether left desolate and comfortless) this happy union will recompense and supply a great part of this our distress. An happy union I call it, because it shall not only take away the long mortal enmity, the deadly hatred, the most cruel and sharp wars that have so many hundred years been and continued betwixt our neighbors the Scots and us, but shall so entirely consociate and conjoin and so honorably set forth and advance us both and the whole island of Britain as neither tongue can express the greatness of our felicity and happiness nor heart wish any greater.

*   *   *

Then shall we most fortunately see, and most gloriously enjoy, a perfect and entire monarchy of this Isle of Britain or Albion[6] united and incorporated after a most marvelous sort and in the worthy and excellent person of a prince meet and capable of such a monarchy. As in whose person (beside her worthy, noble, and princely qualities) not only the royal and unspotted blood of the ancient and noble kings of Scotland, but of the Normans and of the English kings withal, as well long before as sithens[7] the conquest, yea and of the Britons also, the most ancient inhabitants and lords of this island, do wonderfully and (as it were) even for such a notable purpose, by the great providence of God, most happily concur. The evident truth whereof, the said Queen's pedigree doth most plainly and openly set forth to every man's sight and eye. Then I say, may this noble realm and island be called not Albion only but rather Olbion, that is, fortunate, happy, and blessed. Which happy and blessed conjunction (when it chanceth) if we unthankfully refuse, we refuse our health and welfare and God's good blessing upon us. We refuse our duty to God, who sendeth our duty to the party[8] whom he sendeth, and our duty to our native country to whom he sendeth such a person to be our mistress, and such commodities and honor withal coming thereby (as I have said) to whole Albion, as greater we cannot wish for. And finally we procure and purchase, as much as in us lieth, such disturbance of the commonwealth, such vexations, troubles, and wars as may tend to the utter subversion of this realm.[9] From which dangers God, of his great and unspeakable mercy, defend and preserve us and keep, protect, and defend this realm with our noble Queen Elizabeth and the said Lady Mary, Queen of Scotland, with the nobility and subjects of both the realms in mutual friendship and godly amity, with long prosperous estate and all good quietness. Amen.

5. Most important arguments.
6. Old Roman name for Britain, with an allusion to its white cliffs.
7. Since; *person*: Mary Stuart.
8. Ruler.
9. By noting the dangers to England in advance, we "purchase" and therefore avoid them.

THE REBELLION OF THE NORTHERN EARLS

In January 1569, just as Elizabeth was concluding the commission of inquiry into the affairs of Mary Stuart, Thomas Percy, the Earl of Northumberland, suggested to Don Guerau de Spes, the Spanish ambassador, that the Queen of Scots marry Philip II of Spain. Such an alliance was both reckless and traitorous, as Northumberland, scion of a powerful Roman Catholic family with extensive landholdings in Lincolnshire and other parts of northern England, undoubtedly knew. Although Elizabeth was not privy to Northumberland's proposal, she had grown increasingly concerned about the loyalty of her northern subjects. In the meantime, Thomas Howard, the Duke of Norfolk, was pursuing plans to take Mary Stuart as his own wife. Unwisely, he delayed telling Elizabeth or asking her permission, and when in September 1569 she finally learned of the plan and confronted him, he confessed. Facing the full force of her wrath, he left the Court without her permission and fled northward to his country house of Kenninghall in Norfolk.

Northumberland and Charles Neville, Earl of Westmoreland, who was the head of another powerful northern family and the husband of Jane Howard, Norfolk's sister, sensed an opportune moment. They immediately contacted Norfolk, encouraging him to join with them in a rebellion against the Queen. Although Norfolk was tempted, he decided to return to London and throw himself upon the Queen's good graces. She, in turn, incarcerated him in the Tower of London on October 8 and the next day instructed Thomas Radcliffe, the Earl of Sussex and her representative in the North, to take an oath of allegiance from Northumberland and Westmoreland. Although for a brief time it seemed that disaster had been averted, on November 9, the church bells in the north were rung in a prearranged signal, and the Northern Rebellion officially began.

On November 24 the Queen issued a *Proclamation Against the Earl of Northumberland*. Calm and judicious in its tone, the Proclamation began by outlining events in the North, emphasizing the measured steps taken by the government to reduce rumors and induce the earls to maintain their loyalty to the crown. It concluded, however, by accusing them of open rebellion, "contrary to the natural property of nobility," against God, the Queen, and their native country, and it called on all good subjects "to employ their whole powers to the preservation of common peace (which is the blessing of Almighty God) and speedily to apprehend and suppress all manner of persons that shall by any deed or word show themselves favorable to this rebellious enterprise."

Rebels attempting to assassinate the Queen.

The Rebellion itself quickly collapsed, and, although sporadic fighting continued through February 1570, the army began its retreat on the same day the Proclamation was issued. Elizabeth, however, was in no mood to be conciliatory. On February 20, the day after the final defeat of the Northern army by Lord Hunsdon, she wrote an uncompromising letter to Mary Stuart reminding her cousin of her own beneficence—"even I was the principal cause to save your life"—and castigating her for ingratitude. But the pith of the letter lay in her warning that Mary cease from treasonous activities such as "your contrary late dealings by your ministers to engender and nourish troubles in my realm, to bolden my subjects to become rebels, to instruct and aid them how to continue in the same, and in the end to make invasions into my realm." Nor was Elizabeth's warning without teeth: she put John Lesley, the bearer of Mary's letter to her, under house arrest and concluded that, unless Mary gave assurance of her loyalty, she, Elizabeth, would "be forced to change my course and, not with such remissness as I have used towards offenders." More to the point, in the aftermath of the Northern Rebellion, she executed over 700 rebels and confiscated property from the offending nobility. Although the Earl of Northumberland escaped for a time, he and the Duke of Norfolk were executed in 1572, the latter for his involvement in subsequent plots to further Mary Stuart's claim to the English throne. Westmoreland fled to the Netherlands, where he remained in exile.

In an extraordinary stroke of bad timing, Pope Pius V issued a bull of excommunication just six days after the defeat of the Northern army, in which he formally declared Elizabeth to be a heretic and outcast from the Roman Catholic Church. Although he intended the bull to support the Earls of Northumberland and Westmoreland, it arrived too late to aid the Northern Rebellion. Indeed, most of England remained unaware of its existence until May 25, when a copy was nailed to the gate of the Bishop of London's palace. Yet it was destined to shape affairs in England for the remainder of Elizabeth's reign. Far from being merely a religious document, it boldly stated that "all her subjects are declared absolved from the Oath of Allegiance and every other thing due unto her whatsoever." Couched as it was in such inflammatory language, it is no surprise that the document was immediately countered by outraged Protestants. The translator and playwright Thomas Norton lost no time comparing the rhetorical "bull" to a monstrous bovine. His *A Disclosing of the Great Bull* developed the classical story of Pasiphae's unnatural copulation with a bull and the birth of the Minotaur into an allegory of treason: Pasiphae became Roman Catholic nobles such as Northumberland and Westmoreland; the bull, the papacy; Dedalus, who brought Pasiphae and the bull together, was the Roman Catholic clergy; his son, Icarus, all those disloyal Englishmen who refused to honor the Queen; and the Minotaur the bull of excommunication itself.

Although such derision of the Pope may have amused and heartened English Protestants, the entire affair posed considerable difficulties for their Roman Catholics neighbors, who now had either to demonstrate dual loyalty—both to the Pope as Supreme Head of the Catholic Church and to Elizabeth as their secular governor—or else to choose between these two allegiances. John Felton, who first posted the bull in May, refused to acknowledge Elizabeth as Queen and was tortured and executed. Most Catholics, however, quietly continued to be both Roman Catholics and loyal English citizens, a stance that would become more difficult to maintain as Elizabeth's reign continued.

QUEEN ELIZABETH

Proclamation against the Earl of Northumberland (November 24, 1569)[†]

By the Queen.

The Queen's Majesty was sundry-wise about the latter end of this summer informed of some secret whisperings in certain places of Yorkshire and the bishopric of Durham that there was like to be shortly some assemblies of lewd people[1] in those parts, tending to a rebellion. Whereof, because at the first the informations contained no evident or direct cause of proof, therefore her Majesty had the less regard thereto until, upon certain conventions and secret meetings of the Earls of Northumberland and Westmoreland (with certain persons of suspected behavior), the former reports were renewed, and thereof also the said two earls were in vulgar speeches[2] from place to place expressly noted to be the authors.

Whereupon the Earl of Sussex, Lord President of her Majesty's Council in those north parts, gave advertisement of the like bruits,[3] adding nevertheless (to his knowledge) there was no other matter in deed but lewd rumors, suddenly raised and suddenly ended. And yet shortly after he sent for the said two earls, with whom he conferred of those rumors, who, as they could not deny but that they had heard of such, yet (as it now afterward appeareth) falsely then dissembling, they protested themselves to be free from all such occasions, offering to spend[4] their lives against any that should break the peace, and so much trusted by the said Lord President upon their oaths, they were licensed not only to depart but had power given them to examine the causes of the said bruits.

Nevertheless, the fire of their treasons which they had covered was so great as it did newly burst out mo[5] flames. Whereupon her Majesty (being always loath to enter into any open mistrust of any of her nobility, and, therefore, in this case desirous rather to have both the said earls cleared from such slanders and her good people that lived in fear of spoil to be quieted) commanded the Lord President to require the said two earls in her Majesty's name to repair[6] to her. Whereupon the said Lord President (as it seemed), having then discovered somewhat further of their evil purposes, did only at the first write to them to come to him to consult upon matters appertaining to that council, whereunto they made dilatory and frivolous answers; and so being once again more earnestly required, they more flatly denied. And last of all, her Majesty sent her own private letters of commandment to them to repair to her presence, all which notwithstanding, they refused to come.

---

† Copy text: *By the Queene* (London: Richarde Iugge and Iohn Cawood, 1569; STC 8021), single sheet.
1. The common people, but also with the implication of ruffians; *sundry-wise*: in various ways.
2. Speeches given in English to incite the common people; *conventions*: assemblies; *Earls of Northumberland and Westmoreland*: Thomas Percy and Charles Neville, heads of two of the most important families in the north of England.
3. Reports; *Earl of Sussex*: Thomas Radcliffe, Lord Lieutenant of the North and previously Lord Lieutenant of Ireland; *gave advertisement*: warned.
4. Give up.
5. More.
6. Come.

And having, before the delivery of her Majesty's letters to them, assembled as great numbers as they could (which were not many, for that the honester sort did refuse them), they did enter into an open and actual rebellion, arming and fortifying themselves rebelliously in all warlike manner, and have invaded houses and churches and published proclamations in their own names to move her Majesty's subjects to take their parts, as persons that mean of their own private authority to break and subvert laws, threatening the people that if they cannot achieve their purposes, then strangers[7] will enter the realm to finish the same. And with this they add that they mean no hurt to her Majesty's person, a pretense always first published by all traitors. And as for reformation of any great matter,[8] it is evident they be as evil chosen two persons (if their qualities be well considered) to have credit as can be in the whole realm.

And now her Majesty (manifestly perceiving in what sort these two earls being both in poverty, the one having but a very small portion of that which his ancestors had and lost and the other having almost his whole patrimony wasted, do go about through the persuasion of a number of desperate persons associated as parasites with them to satisfy their private lack and ambition, which cannot be by them compassed without covering at the first certain high treasons against the Queen's Majesty's person and the realm, long hidden by such as have hereto provoked them with the cover of some other pretended general enterprises) hath thought good that all her good, loving subjects should speedily understand how in this sort the said two earls, contrary to the natural property of nobility (which is instituted to defend the prince, being the head, and to preserve peace), have thus openly and traitorously entered into the first rebellion and breach of the public blessed peace of this realm that hath happened (beyond[9] all former examples) during her Majesty's reign, which now hath continued above eleven years, an act horrible against God the only giver of so long a peace and ungrateful to their sovereign Lady, to whom they two particularly have heretofore made sundry professions of their faith, and lastly, most unnatural and pernicious to their native country that hath so long enjoyed peace and now by their only malice and ambition is to be troubled in that felicity.

And herewith also her Majesty chargeth all her good subjects to employ their whole powers to the preservation of common peace (which is the blessing of Almighty God) and speedily to apprehend and suppress all manner of persons that shall by any deed or word show themselves favorable to this rebellious enterprise of the said two earls or any their associates (who as her Majesty hath already willed and commanded to be by the foresaid Earl of Sussex, her Lieutenant General in the north, published rebels and traitors against her crown and dignity), so doth her Majesty by these presents, for avoiding of all pretenses of ignorance, reiterate and eftsoons[1] notify the same to her whole realm, with all their adherents and favorers, to be traitors and so to be taken and used to all purposes (not doubting but this admonition and knowledge given shall suffice for all good subjects to

7. A reference to the Spanish troops from the Low Countries under the command of General Alba, whom the northern earls hoped would come to fortify their own position; *invaded . . . churches*: in particular, to destroy English Bibles and prayerbooks at Durham Cathedral on November 14 and to restore Roman Catholic worship.
8. As to the hope for any radical change.
9. Excluding; *compassed*: devised.
1. Likewise; *these presents*: this present document.

retain themselves in their duties), and to be void from all seducing by these foresaid rebels and traitors, or their adherents and favorers (whatsoever their pretenses shall be made or published by themselves) or such as have not the grace of God to delight and live in peace but to move uproars to make spoil of the goods and substances of all good people, the true proper fruits of all rebellions and treasons.

Given at the castle of Windsor, the 24 day of November 1569, in the twelfth year of her Majesty's reign.

God save the Queen.

QUEEN ELIZABETH

Letter to Mary Stuart (February 20, 1570)[†]

Madam:

I have well considered of your earnest, long letter delivered to me by the Bishop of Ross, who in the principal matters of the said letter was able by reason of his sundry conferences heretofore had with me to have either stayed you before your writing from such unquietness of mind as your letter representeth, or at the least upon the sending of the same to have satisfied you with assurance of more goodwill and care of you on my part than it seemeth by your letter you have by bruits[1] and by untrue suggestions conceived of me. Wherein because I find myself somewhat wronged, yet for this present I set it by, as imputing a great part thereof to others, who to gain with you outwardly make a gain of your favor to bring you in doubt of me, that have in your greatest dangers been your only approved friend and, when all ways are attempted, must be the chief pillar of your stay.[2] And thus bold am I at this present to declare mine ability to do you good above all other your friends, seeing it seemeth nobody else of those whom you trust doth you in remembrance thereof. But considering since the sending of your letter I have had just cause to deny to the Bishop of Ross such freedom of access either to me or to others as he hath had, whereby you may get advice from him, I have thought good with this mine own letter to impart somewhat to you whereby you may deliver yourself of such vain fears as others wish you in, and not be bitten with sharper griefs than your own doings hath or may nourish within your heart. Wishing nevertheless, howsoever your conscience may herein trouble you for your unkindness towards me and my state, yet that God may instruct you to consider your former dealings and direct you sincerely and unfeignedly either to make me and my realm amends for things past, or if that cannot be in your power, yet to make your intentions manifestly appear to me how I and my states of my realm may be hereafter assured, that for my goodwill both past and to come no cause may ensue on the part of you and yours to the just offense of me and my realm. And in so doing or intending you may surely quiet your

---

† Copy text: *Elizabeth I: Collected Works*, ed. Leah S. Marcus, Janel Mueller, and Mary Beth Rose (Chicago and London: University of Chicago Press, 2000), 120–25. Reprinted by permission of the University of Chicago Press. © 2000 by the University of Chicago. Emendations to the damaged manuscript, placed in square brackets in the copy text, are here regularized.
1. Reports; *Bishop of Ross*: John Lesley, one of Mary's chief counselors; *stayed*: prevented.
2. Support.

mind and conscience and be free from all suspicions that either flatterers or evil-disposed persons seek to nourish in you.

In your letter I note a heap of confused, troubled thoughts, earnestly and curiously uttered to express your great fear and to require of me comfort, concerning both which many kinds of speeches are diversely expressed and dispersed in your letter, that if I had not consideration that the same did proceed from a troubled mind, I might rather take occasion to be offended with you than to relent to your desires. For what can be said more unworthy of my former goodwill than in express words to doubt, without cause given by me, that any inventions of such whom you call your enemies with the aid of any whom you name your secret evil-willers about me (of which sort truly I know none) should be able to induce me to consent to anything that might touch your life, or for what respect of any of my doings past to you, Madam, or to any other of meaner estate—yea to any of mine own subjects?

Need you to press me with the remembrance that I should not violate my word nor the laws of amity, of hospitality and parentage and such like, neither recompense your affections and fiance[3] put in me, with any cruel conclusion? Or what example is there extant of my actions to move you to remember unto me that those to whom favor hath been promised ought not to be treated as an enemy if the same be not first thereof advertised? For as you also write, a mortal enemy will not assail his contrary without defiance before he strike him, and so forth you pass with divers speeches, which because they are through your whole letter so full of passions, I of compassion will leave[4] to represent them to your eyes. And will rather by some short remembrance of my former actions, full of goodwill, induce you to believe and trust rather to me in all your difficulties than lightly to credit either bruits of the brainless vulgar or the viperous backbiters of the sowers of discord.

Good Madam, what wrong did I ever seek to you or yours in the former part of my reign, when you know what was sought against me, even to the spoil of my crown from me? Did I invade your country and take or detain any part thereof, as all the world knoweth I might, and as any king or queen of my condition, being so wronged, might with justice and honor have done? But therein my natural inclination to you overcame myself. Did I, when I might have, sell or put to ransom the whole army of the French that were sent into Scotland on your behalf to invade my realm and to oppress my crown? Did I not, I say, friendly send them home into France in my own ships? Yea, did I not victual them and lend them money? Was I not content to accord with your ambassadors (authorized by you and your husband)[5] to remit all injuries past, to my great damage and charges? And what moved me thereto but my natural inclination towards you, with whom I desired to live as a neighbor and a good sister? After this, how patiently did I bear with many vain delays in not ratifying the treaty accorded by your own commission? Whereby I received no small unkindness, beside that manifest cause of suspicion that I might not hereafter trust to any your treaties.

Then followed a hard manner of dealing with me, to entice my subject and near kinsman the Lord Darnley, under color of private suits for lands, to come into your realm, to proceed in treaty of marriage with him without my knowledge, yea to conclude the same without my assent or liking. And

3. Confidence.
4. Cease.
5. Her first husband, Francis II of France.

how many unkind parts accompanied that fact by receiving of my subjects that were base renegades and offenders at home and enhancing them to places of credit against my will, with many such like, I will leave, for that the remembrance of them cannot but be noisome[6] unto you. And yet all these did I (as it were) suppress and overcome with my natural inclination of love towards you, and did afterward gladly, as you know, christen[7] your son, the child of my said kinsman that had before so unloyally offended me both in marriage with you and in other undutiful usages towards me, his sovereign. How friendly dealt I also by messages to reconcile him (being your husband) and you when others nourished discord betwixt you, who (as it seemed) had more power to work their purposes, being evil to you both, than I to do you good without respect of the evil I had received.

Well I will overpass your hard accidents[8] that followed for lack of following of my counsels. And in your most extremity (when you were a prisoner indeed, not as you have at times noted yourself to be here in my realm, and then sought notoriously by your evil-willers to the danger of your life), how far from my mind was the remembrance of any former unkindness showed to me? Nay, how void was I of respect to the hurt that the world had seen attempted by you to my crown and the security that might have ensued to my state by your death, when I, finding your calamity so great as you were at the pit's brink to have miserably lost your life, did not only entreat for your life but so threatened such as were irritated against you that (I only may say it) even I was the principal cause to save your life. And now, Madam, if these my actions were at any time laid before your eyes or in your ears when malicious persons incense you with mistrust of me, I know you would reject their whispering tales or false writings and messages and deal plainly with me, and not only be thankful for my good deeds, but would discover to me such pernicious persons as, to advance their own evil, seek to make you the instrument of inward troubles and rebellions in my realm. Whereof you see how frustrate their purposes be by the goodness of Almighty God, who rewardeth my sincere and good meaning with His blessings of peace, notwithstanding the vehement labors both of foreigners and domestics to trouble my state with wars.

If I should now enter into the accidents happened since flying for your succor out of Scotland into my realm, as well of your manner of coming and your usages sithen that time, as of my benefits towards you, being that you have been charged with such heinous facts offensive to God and to the world, I should exceed the length of a letter and percase[9] overmuch oppress you with remembrance of my goodwill, an argument that I delight not to touch where so little hath been deserved. It must suffice to remember you how favorably I dealt in the trial of your great cause to stay from any open publication of the facts,[1] how I have forborne to fortify your son's title by open act, being by the states of your realm according to the laws of the same a crowned king, otherwise than for the conservation of the mutual peace betwixt the people of both the realms hath been thought very necessary and could not be avoided. But if I should remember to you your

6. Troublesome; *unkind*: unnatural and offensive.
7. Act as a godmother for.
8. Mishaps or, more strongly, disasters.
9. By chance; *flying . . . realm*: on May 16, 1568, after escaping from Lochleven Castle; *sithen*: since.
1. Incriminating evidence of Mary's adultery with James Bothwell and collusion in the murder of her husband, Lord Daraley.

contrary late dealings by your ministers to engender and nourish troubles in my realm, to bolden my subjects to become rebels, to instruct and aid them how to continue in the same, and in the end to make invasions into my realm, I should percase move you to continue in your fear. From the which at this time of compassion I seek to deliver you, and indeed do earnestly wish you not only to be free from the fear expressed in your letters, but that you would minister to me hereafter a plain probation[2] and a demonstration how I may be assured of some contrary course, both by yourself and your ministers, in answering with some like fruits of goodwill as mine hath been abundant. For otherwise surely both in honor and reason, not only for myself but for my people and my countries, I must be forced to change my course and, not with such remissness as I have used towards offenders, endanger myself, my state, and my realm.

And so for this time I think good, though the matter of your letter might have ministered to me occasion of more writing, to end. And to conclude, I have thought good to assure you that the restraining of the Bishop of Ross,[3] your minister at this time, hath proceeded of many reasonable and necessary causes, as hereafter you shall understand, and not of any mind particularly to offend you, as the proof shall well follow, requiring you not to conceive hereby otherwise of me but that very necessity hath thereto urged me. And though he may not come to me, yet may you use your former manner in writing to me as you shall find meet. To the which you shall receive answers as the causes shall require, though he be not at the liberty which heretofore he had, otherwise than my favorable usage did provoke him. And so, Madam, with my very hearty commendations, I wish you continuance of health, quietness of mind, and your heart's desire, to the honor of Almighty God and contentation[4] of your best friends, amongst whom in good right I may compare with any howsoever.

POPE PIUS V

The Bull of Excommunication against Elizabeth (February 25, 1570)[†]

A sentence declaratory of our holy lord, Pope Pius Quintus,
against Elizabeth, Queen of England, and the heretics adhering unto her.
Wherein also all her subjects are declared absolved from
the Oath of Allegiance
and every other thing due unto her whatsoever,
and those which from henceforth obey her are innodated
with the anathema.[1]

Pius Bishop, servant to God's servants, for a future memorial of the matter.

2. Demonstrative proof.
3. John Lesley was being held under house arrest by Edmund Grindal, the Bishop of London.
4. Satisfaction.
† Copy text: William Camden, *The historie of the life and reigne of . . . Elizabeth, late Queene of England* (London: Benjamin Fisher, 1630; STC 4500.5), Aa4r–Bb1r; *Regnans in Excelsis*, the papal bull or edict, translated by Robert Norton from the Latin.
1. Excommunication from the Church; *Pope Pius Quintus*: Michele Ghislieri, elected Pope in 1566; *innodated*: included.

He that reigneth on high, to Whom is given all power in heaven and in earth, committed one holy Catholic and apostolic church, out[2] of which there is no salvation, to one alone upon earth, namely to Peter, the chief of the apostles, and to Peter's successor, the Bishop of Rome, to be governed in fullness of power. Him alone He made prince over all people and all kingdoms, to pluck up, destroy, scatter, consume, plant, and build, that he may contain the faithful that are knit together with the band of charity in the unity of the Spirit and present them spotless and unblameable to their Savior.[3] In discharge of which function, we which are by God's goodness called to the government of the aforesaid church do spare no pains, laboring with all earnestness that unity and the Catholic religion (which the Author thereof hath for the trial of His children's faith and for our amendment suffered to be punished with so great afflictions) might be preserved uncorrupt.

But the number of the ungodly hath gotten such power that there is now no place left in the whole world which they have not assayed to corrupt with their most wicked doctrines, amongst others Elizabeth, the pretensed[4] Queen of England, the servant of wickedness, lending thereunto her helping hand, with whom, as in a sanctuary, the most pernicious of all have found a refuge. This very woman, having seized on the kingdom and monstrously usurping the place of Supreme Head of the Church in all England and the chief authority and jurisdiction thereof, hath again brought back the said kingdom into miserable destruction, which was then newly reduced[5] to the Catholic faith and good fruits.

For having by strong hand inhibited the exercise of the true religion (which Mary, the lawful Queen of famous memory had by the help of this See restored, after it had been formerly overthrown by Henry VIII, a revolter therefrom) and following and embracing the errors of heretics, she hath removed the royal Council consisting of the English nobility and filled it with obscure men, being heretics; suppressed the embracers of the Catholic faith; placed dishonest preachers and ministers of impiety; abolished the sacrifice of the Mass, prayers, fastings, choice of meats, unmarried life, and the Catholic rites and ceremonies; commanded books to be read in the whole realm containing manifest heresy and impious mysteries and institutions by herself entertained and observed according to the prescript of Calvin, to be likewise observed by her subjects; presumed to throw bishops, parsons of churches, and other Catholic priests out of their churches and benefices, and to bestow them and other church-livings upon heretics, and to determine of church causes; prohibited the prelates, clergy, and people to acknowledge the Church of Rome or obey the precepts and canonical sanctions thereof; compelled most of them to condescend to[6] her wicked laws and to abjure the authority and obedience of the Bishop of Rome, and to acknowledge her to be sole lady in temporal and spiritual matters, and this by oath; imposed penalties and punishments upon those which obeyed not and exacted them of those which persevered in the unity of the faith and

---

2. Outside.
3. Colossians 1.22; in the biblical text, Christ presents the spotless and blameless church to the Father; *he may contain the faithful*: the Pope may preserve the faithful.
4. Alleged.
5. Brought back.
6. Comply with; *See*: Rome, the seat (See) of the Pope; *choice of meats*: as in the prohibition of meat on Friday and other holy days; *benefices*: positions in the Church that guarantee a certain income; *determine . . . causes*: made judgments in matters before the Church courts.

their obedience aforesaid; cast the Catholic prelates and rectors of churches in prison, where many of them, being spent with long languishing and sorrow, miserably ended their lives.

All which things, seeing they are manifest and notorious to all nations and by the gravest testimony of very many so substantially proved that there is no place at all left for excuse, defense, or evasion, we, seeing that impieties and wicked actions are multiplied one upon another and moreover that the persecution of the faithful and affliction for religion groweth every day heavier and heavier through the instigation and means of the said Elizabeth (because we understand her mind to be so hardened and indurate that she hath not only condemned the godly requests and admonitions of Catholic princes concerning her healing and conversion, but also hath not so much as permitted the nuncios[7] of this See to cross the seas into England), are constrained of necessity to betake ourselves to the weapons of justice against her, not being able to mitigate our sorrow that we are drawn to take punishment upon one to whose ancestors the whole state of all Christendom hath been so much bounden. Being therefore supported with His authority whose pleasure it was to place us (though unable[8] for so great a burden) in this supreme throne of justice, we do out of the fullness of our apostolic power declare the aforesaid Elizabeth, being an heretic and a favorer of heretics, and her adherents in the matters aforesaid to have incurred the sentence of anathema and to be cut off from the unity [of] the body of Christ.

And moreover we do declare her to be deprived of her pretended title to the kingdom aforesaid and of all dominion, dignity, and privilege whatsoever, and also the nobility, subjects, and people of the said kingdom (and all others which have in any sort sworn unto her) to be forever absolved from any such oath and all manner of duty of dominion, allegiance, and obedience, as we also do, by authority of these presents,[9] absolve them and do deprive the same Elizabeth of her pretended title to the kingdom and all other things above said. And we do command and interdict all and every the noblemen, subjects, people, and others aforesaid that they presume not to obey her or her monitions,[1] mandates, and laws, and those which shall do the contrary we do innodate with the like sentence of anathema.

And because it were a matter of too much difficulty to convey these presents to all places wheresoever it shall be needful, our will is that the copies thereof, under a public notary's hand and sealed with the seal of an ecclesiastical prelate or of his court, shall carry altogether the same credit with all people, judicially and extrajudicially, as these presents should do if they were exhibited or showed.[2]

Given at Rome at St. Peter's in the year of the incarnation of our Lord, one thousand five hundreth sixty-nine,[3] the fifth of the Kalends of March and of our Popedom the fifth year.

---

7. Permanent official representatives of the Roman See at a foreign court; *indurate*: obstinate.
8. Unfit.
9. This present written document.
1. Official notices; *interdict*: prohibit.
2. Copy text: of showed.
3. 1570; the new year began on March 25, Lady Day.

THOMAS NORTON

From A Disclosing of the Great Bull (1570)[†]

The monster of whom I told you is no way so fitly to be described as by the old tale of the ancient poets, that seem (as it were) to have foreshowed him in figure,[1] as followeth. Pasiphae, Queen of Crete, not sufficed[2] with men, conceived inordinate, unnatural, and therewith untemperable lust to engender with a bull. Neither regard of virtue, honor, kindness, nature, or shame, in respect of God, her husband, her country, herself, or the whole world, could restrain her violent rage of unclean affection. Yet wist[3] she neither how to woo the bull nor how to apply herself unto him. A mean at length was found to make this unkindly[4] coupling.

There lived then a cunning craftsman, Dedalus, the self-same Dedalus of whom it is famous how he made him wings, wherewith by cunning guiding himself he passed seas and countries at his pleasure. And wings he made also for Icarus his son to fly with him. But the uncunning Icarus, climbing too near the sun's heat, his wings melting, fell into the water and gave name to the sea.[5]

This fine Dedalus, to satisfy the wicked Queen's fervor of lust and to match her and the bull in abominable copulation, framed a cow and so made, covered, and used it with lewd devices and therein so enclosed and placed the good, innocent, and virtuous lady[6] that of the bull she conceived the abomination of the world and in time brought forth the monster Minotaur, half a bull and half a man, fierce, brutish, mischievous, cruel, deformed, and odious.

To shroud this monster from common wonder and yet therewithal to deliver him the food and contentment[7] of his cruelty, the destruction of men, a labyrinth or maze was builded by the same cunning Dedalus, wherein Minotaur, the man-bull or bull-man, lurked, and men passing in thither to him by entanglement of the maze and uncertain error of ways were brought to miserable end, till at length valiant Theseus, furnished with the policy of wise Ariadne, received of her a clue of thread by which, leaving the one end at the entry, he was continually guided and preserved from the deceiving maze and, having slain the monster, by conduct of the same thread safely returned.

The appliance hereof to the experience of our times hath an apt resemblance, not to prove but to show the image of some doings at these days, and therewith by conference not only to sharpen an intentive sight of that which we wink at, but also to raise a just loathing of that whereof by some hurtful impediments we have not discerned or rather not marked[8] the horror.

Lecherous Pasiphae may well be applied to treason in high estates addicted to papistry, forsaking God's ordinance of human royal govern-

---

† Copy text: *A disclosing of the great bull, and certain calues that he hath gotten, and specially the monster bull that roared at my Lord Byshops gate* (London: John Daye, 1570: STC 18679), A3v–B1r; B2r–B4r; B4r–C1v.

1. As an emblematic representation.
2. Satisfied; in the Greek myth, Poseidon causes Pasiphae to desire the bull that Minos, her husband, refused to sacrifice to the god.
3. Knew.
4. Unnatural.
5. According to Greek myth, that part of the Aegean Sea between Turkey and the Greek islands of Patmos and Leros into which Icarus fell was named the Icarian Sea.
6. The author is apparently being satirical.
7. Satisfaction.
8. Sufficiently noted; *appliance*: application; *conference*: comparison; *intentive*: attentive; *hurtful*: prejudicial.

ment.[9] Which, whensoever it happeneth (for hap it may and hath oft so chanced), such treason destroyeth good and natural affection, it kindleth vile and beastly desires, and among all other none comparable in filthiness to the lust of yielding themselves to bear the engendering of the great bull of Bashan or rather of Babylon, the oppression, encumbrance, and tyranny of Rome, the usurpation of the Roman siege,[1] the siege of all abomination.

*   *   *

The Dedalus that must bring the enjoying of this horrible lust to effect is the treason of popish clergy (full of cunning workmanship, as the world hath long had great experience), even the same popish clergy that hath framed to himself wings, not naturally by God's ordinance growing to the body thereof, but made of feathers pulled from temporal princes and from bishops in their own dioceses by usurpation, fastened together by art of simony,[2] and joined to their bodies with the glue of superstitious credulity. With these have they passed lands and seas, climbing and flying in air (that is, upon no steadfast ground) above mountains, trees, and countries (that is, above emperors, kings, just prelates, and commonweals).

The son of this Dedalus (that is, of treason of popish clergy) is Icarus (that is, aspiring treason of subject),[3] which following his father and guide (popish treason), but not so well guiding himself for lack of experience and desiring too suddenly to climb too near the sun, or perhaps mounting with more haste than good speed before his wings were well fastened, or while himself could but yet flutter with them and not perfectly fly, as, God would, his glue melting and his wings dropping away, fell down in his climbing and no doubt will give name to the place where he lighteth for perpetual memory of his undue presumption, surely yet piteously bewailed of papists as Icarus was of Dedalus his father.

This cunning Dedalus (popish treason), to bring this copulation to contentment of the unchaste Pasiphae, encloseth her in a counterfeit cow (that is, such princes or great estates as desire to lie under the bull of Rome, popish clergy turneth into brutish shape to serve brutish lust, maketh them beastly), forsaking the dignity of man and woman's shape, whom God made upright to look to God and God's seat, the heaven, and it maketh them cowishly stoop to earthward without regard of the nature of man, the dignity of kingdoms, the reverent aspect to divinity, or any other manly and reasonable consideration, without any more vigor, agility of soul, and industry to do nobly than is in a cow, a beast indeed profitable for worldly food (as papistry is), but, as most part of beasts be, ready to promiscuous and unchosen copulations, and specially meet for a bull, and among other pretty[4] qualities having one special grace (as one of their own popish doctors preached) to swing away flies with her tail wet in the water (as foolish papists swing away sins and temptations with a holy water sprinkle).

In this beastly likeness, degenerating from manly form and majesty of governance, by Dedalus's workmanship (that is, by popish clergy's traitorous practice) ensued the copulation of a bull and a queen in a cowish shape

---

9. A reference to the Northern Rebellion of 1569.
1. The seat (See) or dominion of Rome; *encumbrance*: copy text: incumbence.
2. The practice of buying and selling church offices and benefices; the name derives from the story of Simon Magus who attempted to buy the Holy Spirit (Acts 8.18–24).
3. All the traditional estates—nobles, clergy, and commoners—are thus indicted.
4. Crafty.

(that is, sodomitical[5] and unnatural mixture of popish usurpation with and upon royal governance in brutish and reasonless form).

Of this engendering is begotten Minotaur, a compounded monster, half a bull and half a man, a beastly cruel body, roaring out with the voice or sound of a bull and words of a man the sense of a devil. The self-same monster bull is he that lately roared out at the bishop's palace gate in the greatest city of England horrible blasphemies against God and villainous dishonors against the noblest queen in the world, Elizabeth, the lawful Queen of England.[6] He stamped and scraped on the ground, flung dust of spiteful speeches and vain curses about him, pushed with his horns at her noble counselors and true subjects, and for pure anger all to bewrayed[7] the place where he stood. And all this stir he kept to make a proof if his horned army of calves would or durst come flinging about him toward midsummer moon.[8]

But he looked so beastly and he raged so vainly that though the whole wood rang of his noise, yet his sire the great bull, his dam the prostitute cow, and his children the foolish calves, were more ashamed of him than the noble lion was afraid of him. And therefore the bull his sire, the cow his dam, and the wisest of his calves fled once again to Dedalus (the treason of popish clergy) for succor and good counsel, by whose good workmanship this mingled monster is closed up in a maze (that is, in uncertainty of vain and false reports) and (as it happeneth in a maze) by ways leading to other places than they seem to tend unto, by crookedness of devices, by spreading into sundry creeks[9] of rumors, to hide whence the bull came or where he lurketh. Even as in the maze of Dedalus it happened, so it cometh to pass that the Minotaur is not found out, and such as enter into the maze (that is, into following of popish reports and devices) entangle themselves so that wandering uncertainly at length they may hap to perish in Dedalus's engine.[1]

*　*　*

The remedy resteth that some Theseus, some noble and valiant counselor, or rather one body and consent of all true and good nobility and counselors, follow the good guiding thread (that is, godly policy delivered them by the virgin whom they serve) and conducted thereby not only may pass without error through the maze and find out the monster Minotaur that roared so rudely, but also destroy him and settle their prince and themselves in safety. So as, Pasiphae duly and deservedly ordered, Dedalus unwinged and banished, his feathers rightly restored, Icarus fair drowned, the cow transformed, the maze dissolved and razed, the monster destroyed, the calves (after the cow perished) sent with Waltham's calf to suck their bull,[2] Theseus may be victorious, the Virgin Lady most honorable, the land quiet, the subjects safe, and God's providence ever justly praised not vainly

---

5. Not only homosexual, but also any sexual activity deemed perverse; *cowish shape*: an allusion to Mary Stuart.
6. A copy of the bull had been nailed to the door of the Bishop of London's palace in St. Paul's churchyard.
7. Divulged to all.
8. The month during which Midsummer Day occurs, often thought to be a time of madness; *calves*: recusants.
9. A secret nook or crevice.
1. Contraption; that is, the maze.
2. A proverbial example of foolishness: Waltham's calf ran nine miles to suck a bull; *ordered*: punished; brought back into submission.

tempted, His kindness thankfully embraced, His name lovingly magnified, His policies wisely followed, His religion zealously maintained.

But till these noble enterprises be achieved, it is not good to be heedless. The monster may be let out of the maze when it pleaseth Pasiphae and Dedalus.

It is good to be awake. Some men be wakened with tickling and some with pinching or pulling by the ear (that is, some with merry resemblances[3] and some with earnest admonitions). Some be raised out of sleep with noise, as by the speech or calling of men, or by brute voices, as the roaring of bulls and noise of beasts (that is, either by advices of them that warn with reason or with the brags and threatenings of the enemies or inklings slipped out of uncircumspect adversaries' mouths). Some be wakened with very whisperings as with secret rumors and intelligences. Some again are so vigilant and careful that the very weight of the cause and pensive thinking of it will scarcely let them sleep at all. But most miserable is their drowsiness, or rather fatal seemeth their sleepiness, that for all the means aforesaid, and specially so lewd and loud roaring of so rude and terrible a bull, cannot be wakened or made to arm and bestir them till the tumult and alarm in the camp, the clinking of armor, the sound of shot and strokes, the tumbling down of tents round about them, the groaning of wounded men dying on every side of them, treason, force, and hostility triumphing in their lustiest rage, and Sinon, that persuaded the safety of the traitorous horse, insulting[4] among them, yea till the very enemy's weapon in their body awake them. Such may hap so to sleep as they may never wake.

Let us all wake in prayer to God. Let us cry louder in sincerity and devotion than the bull is able to roar in treason and blasphemy. Let us pray God to arm our Queen and Council with all wisdom and fortitude and ourselves with all fidelity and manhood,[5] and to repose ourselves upon confidence of their most blessed governance, and ready with our lives and all that we have to follow and serve them.

PROTESTANT PROTESTS AND PRAYERS

If Elizabeth was threatened by the Roman Catholic earls in the north, she was also under pressure from Protestants closer to home. On February 25, 1570, she invited Edward Dering, a rising young Protestant preacher, to deliver what later became known as the "Unruly Heifer" sermon at Court, but instead of basking in praise for dismantling the Northern Rebellion, she heard a lecture on her responsibilities as Supreme Governor of the Church. The preacher was a gifted Greek scholar, a fellow of Christ's College in Cambridge, a reader at St. Paul's Cathedral in London, and soon to be the second husband of Anne Vaughan Lock (see Part Two). Dering reminded the Queen that she owed her present safety not to her own wisdom and might but to God's providential care, which had brought her from prison to the throne, and he urged her to effect further reforms in the English Church, including allowing preachers to speak freely from the pulpit and removing symbols such as the cross and candles from her own chapel. Perhaps carried away by his own rhetoric, but more likely urged by conscience and the

---

3. Stories with a moral purpose.
4. Suddenly assaulting; *traitorous horse*: that devised by Sinon to convey Greek soldiers into ancient Troy and so conquer it.
5. Courage and valor.

support of other London Protestants, Dering then made an audacious move. Drawing on one of Elizabeth's favorite texts, Psalm 44.11, *"Tanquam ovis,* as a sheep appointed to be slain," which the Queen took as a reference to her own trials under Mary Tudor, Dering substituted a verse from Jeremiah and said to Elizabeth: "Take heed you hear not now of the prophet, *"Tanquam indomita iuvenca,* as an untamed and unruly heifer." Understandably, Elizabeth took umbrage at being compared to a cow and promptly cancelled Dering's preaching privileges.

Other Protestants took a more subtle approach, crafting handsome manuscripts and printed books that appealed to Elizabeth's love of learning. John Conway's collection of *Meditations and Prayers* included a complimentary, proverbial acrostic on Elizabeth's name that offered instruction to the Queen: "Remember thy rule / Incline to justice / Grant gifts by deserving / In mercy delight." In an attempt to win back the Queen's favor, Dering himself—along with his new wife, Anne Vaughan Lock, Mildred Cooke Cecil, the wife of William Cecil, and her sisters—produced a beautiful Italian manuscript encyclopedia, the *Giardino cosmografico coltivato,* for presentation at Court, complete with dedicatory poems in several languages. Another encyclopedic compendium, this one of *Christian Prayers and Meditations* that drew on ancient as well as contemporary sources, was issued in 1569 by John Day, the printer who published John Foxe's *Acts and Monuments.* Perhaps because of its frontispiece, which depicted the Queen kneeling at her prayers, the book became known as "Queen Elizabeth's Prayer Book." Its far-ranging ecumenicity may have been designed to link the thirty-six-year-old Protestant English church with fifteen hundred years of Christian devotion. As an indication of the tumults of the late 1560s, the prayer included here sounds an anxious note. Written in the voice of the Queen, it begins with a comparison to the biblical King Solomon but then asks this question: if Solomon was unable to govern his kingdom without the aid of Almighty God, "how much less shall I Thy handmaid, being by kind a weak woman, have sufficient ability to rule these Thy kingdoms of England and Ireland, an innumerable and warlike nation?" Such modesty may have reflected not so much Elizabeth's own sense of inadequacy as the worries of her subjects as they looked anxiously at an England divided by political and religious controversies.

EDWARD DERING

From A Sermon Preached before the Queen's Majesty (February 25, 1570)[†]

[*The "Unruly Heifer" Sermon*]

O Lord, open Thou my lips, and my mouth shall show forth Thy praise.[1]

Psalm 78.70:
"He chose David His servant also and took him from the
sheepfolds, even from behind the ewes great with young took He him, to
feed His people in Jacob and His inheritance in Israel. So he fed
them according to the simplicity of his heart and guided
them by the discretion of his hands."[2]

---

† Copy text: Edward Dering. *A Sermon preached before the Quenes Maiestie* (London: Iohn Awdely, 1570; STC 6700), A2r–A2v; B2r–B3v; C1v; C2v–C3r; E3r–F1v.
1. Psalm 51.15.
2. Psalm 78.70–72; Dering appears to make his own English translations from the Latin Vulgate; his biblical texts are similar, but not identical, to the Geneva Bible version; *simplicity:* sincerity.

The prophet declareth in this psalm how God of His justice, for the great sin of Ephraim, took from that tribe both the tabernacle and the scepter and gave them to the tribe of Judah, whom then, according to His mercy, He had purposed to bless with all perfect happiness.[3] In which we learn not to abuse God's mercies, lest they be taken away from us, as from the tribe of Ephraim they were. And then what helpeth it us that in times past we have been happy? And lest this should happen also unto the tribe of Judah, to fall from God's mercies into His displeasure, the prophet in this place stirreth them up to thankfulness, that they might be found worthy to have continued toward them so great blessings. And this he doth by example of David, in showing both how mercifully God had dealt with him and how obediently David walked before the Lord.

And herein he useth, as it were, three reasons to move them withal. The first is of God's great mercies whence He had called David. The second is of God's intent and purpose whereunto He called him. The third of David's own person, how faithfully and how truly he did execute that whereunto he was called.

*　*　*

There is nothing more effectual to move a son to obedience than to know he hath a loving father. Nothing maketh so trusty the bondservant as to remember he hath a gentle master. Nothing maketh the subject more faithful unto his prince than to feel by good experience his prince's clemency. Nothing joineth man faster in the bond of friendship than to consider well what his friend hath done for him. And let nothing bind our obedience more carefully to the Word and will of God than that He hath so long continued merciful unto us. As sure as the Lord doth live, this is His holy truth. He that cannot be moved with this, he hath not God's Holy Spirit. Poor or rich, bond or free, high or low, noble or of low degree, prince or subject, all is one. The remembrance of God's mercy must make us all thankful, were we never so mighty. This cogitation[4] must banish far from us the pride of a kingdom, to think how God hath raised us from the sheepfolds, whosoever can say thus: "I have been bond, but I am free. I have been in danger, I am in safety. I have been fearful and trembling, I am careless.[5] I have been full of sorrow, now my soul is at rest. I have been in misery, I am in dignity.[6] I have been a prisoner, I am a princess."[7] Believe me, believe me, if the great and goodly cities which he builded not, if the houses full of all manner of gold which he filled not, if the vineyards and olive trees which he planted not, did not make him to forget the Lord, which brought him out of the land of Egypt, out of the house of bondage;[8] if prosperity have not made him drunken, so that he hath banished far from him all sense and understanding, the remembrance of this thing will make him thankful unto Him that hath been thy worker.

Yea, even you that are now a princess of majesty, if you have felt any such alteration, take heed, flee far away from all unthankfulness. If you have

---

3. Samuel, the last judge of Israel and keeper of the Tabernacle, was from the tribe of Ephraim; the great sin was his failure to curb sons who disobeyed God. David was from the tribe of Judah.
4. Reflection.
5. Free from care.
6. A high estate.
7. References to Elizabeth's imprisonment in the Tower and at the royal lodge at Woodstock in 1554 on suspicion of involvement in Wyatt's Rebellion.
8. An allusion to the warning in Deuteronomy 6.10–12.

seen the days in which you have said, "O Lord, I have no friend but thee alone," now that prosperity hath brought unto you a great many of fair countenances, forget not that God who was your only friend in trouble. If in times past you have prayed that you might not build upon the sand to have your house shaken with every blast of wind, now that you have choice of your own ground, take heed, I beseech you, where you lay your foundation.[9] Now that the stern and helm is in your own hand, guide your ship so that the waves do not overrun it. If you have prayed in times past unto God to mollify your enemies' hearts and to bring their cruel practices to nothing, now that you yourself are in safety, be not cruel unto God's anointed and do His prophets no harm. I need not seek far for offences, whereat God's people are grieved; even round about this chapel I see a great many, and God in His good time shall root them out. If you have said sometime of yourself, "*Tanquam ovis*" (as a sheep appointed to be slain), take heed you hear not now of the prophet, "*Tanquam indomita iuvenca*" (as an untamed and unruly heifer).[1] I will not with many words admonish your Majesty, that are wise enough. Only I will say this: return into your own heart and search your reins.[2] And here I set before you the tribunal seat of Christ.[3] If you know these things to be true, discharge the faith you owe; grieve not your quiet conscience, lest it begin to accuse you and the burden of it be greater than you shall be able to bear. If God have defended you mightily, as ever He did David the prophet, discharge your faith with the prophet David and cry in spirit, "*Quid retribuam Domino pro omnibus quae retribuunt mihi?*" (What shall I give unto the Lord, for all those benefits that He bestowed unto me?).[4]

And thus much as God hath given me utterance, I have noted unto you out of the first part of this scripture how that God did choose David from the sheepfold. The Lord give you grace to confess His goodness and show yourselves[5] more thankful for all His benefits.

* * *

The second argument, which I said the prophet used to make the people thankful, was taken of God's intent and purpose, to what end He chose David, and that He showeth in these words: "To feed His people in Jacob, and His inheritance in Israel." These words are very plain and contain so expressly what is the duty of any prince or magistrate that none can be ignorant but he that will not know. For this purpose they are chosen, "To feed God's people in Jacob, and His inheritance in Israel." Whether he be prince and emperor, duke, earl, lord, counselor, magistrate whatsoever, for this

---

9. An allusion to Matthew 7.24–27 where the foolish man builds his house upon the sand, while the wise man builds his upon the rock.
1. *Tanquam indomita iuvencula* (as an untamed calf), Jeremiah 31.18. Dering picks up on Elizabeth's own words to draw a contrast between a passive sheep and an active cow. He changes the masculine *iuvenculus indomitus* of the biblical text to the feminine form, *indomita iuvenca*, translates it as "heifer" rather than "calf," and intensifies the rebuke with the second adjective, "unruly"; "*Tanquam ovis*": as a sheep, Psalm 44.11. See also Isaiah 53.7, quoted in Acts 8.32, in reference to Christ. According to Foxe, Elizabeth used these words in 1554 to signal her servants that she expected to be killed by Mary's men on her way to captivity at Woodstock (John Foxe, *Acts and Monuments* [1563], fol. 1713v).
2. The seat of your affections.
3. 2 Corinthians 5.10.
4. Psalm 116.12.
5. Yourselves is plural to correspond with the royal "we."

purpose he is called, discharge it as well as he will. He must feed God's people in Jacob and His inheritance in Israel.

*   *   *

We will return to our purpose and learn of a princely prophet what is a prince's duty. He must feed Jacob and Israel, that is, kings must be nurse fathers and queens must be nurses unto the church of God. And to this end they must use their authority that God's children may learn virtue and knowledge. For to seek only worldly peace and security, or to make us live at ease here in this wayfaring city, that is rather to feed flesh and blood than to feed Jacob, rather to make happy this worldly fellowship than to instruct Israel. The true Israelite is strong against the Lord and cometh with violence to claim the kingdom of heaven.[6] What helpeth it in this respect to be rich or honorable? "If I had all the riches in the world, yet could I not pay the price of my brother's soul."[7] Or if I had never so much rule and authority, I am not therefore the nearer to make intercession unto God. They are other weapons that must prevail against Satan, and it is another attire that will be accepted for the marriage garment.[8] If we will feed Jacob and Israel, let us lead them to the house of wisdom and train them up in the fear of God.[9] The Lord open the Queen's Majesty's eyes that she may look to this charge. Otherwise, if we lived never so peaceably under her, yet when the Lord shall come to ask account of her stewardship, how she hath fed her fellow servants with the meat appointed them, then she will be found eating and drinking with sinners.[1]

*   *   *

A miserable commonwealth must it needs be, and far separated from God and His mercies, that hath blind leaders who cannot lead themselves.[2] Whoso feareth the Lord will surely look unto it, that he maintain no such offences within his kingdom nor nourish any such sores in the body of his country.

If a man be once called to the ministry, let him attend upon his flock and feed them as his duty bindeth him with the food of life,[3] or let him be removed. Christ said, *"Pasce, pasce, pasce"* (feed, feed, feed).[4] This charge He hath given, even as we love Him, so to see it executed. Say what we will say, and the more we say it the more impudently we shall lie, if we say we love Him while we keep not His commandments.[5] Would to God we were wise to understand it. Christ said, "They are the salt of the earth," and what shall be done with them if they can season nothing? Christ said, "They are the light of the world," and what heap of miseries shall they bring with them if they themselves be dark? Christ said, "They be the watchmen," and what case shall the city be in if they do nothing but sleep and delight in

---

6. A reference to Matthew 11.12, "the kingdom of heaven suffereth violence, and the violent take it by force."
7. Psalm 49.7–8.
8. Revelation 19:7–8; *weapons . . . Satan*: 2 Corinthians 10.4.
9. Proverbs 9.10 and many other verses; *lead . . . wisdom*: Proverbs 9.1.
1. Eating and drinking with sinners is a reference to the final Day of Judgment when such careless behavior will be censured (Matthew 24.36–39).
2. Matthew 15.4; Luke 6.39.
3. 1 Peter 5.2.
4. The charge given to Peter three times after Christ's resurrection (John 21.16–17).
5. 1 John 2.4.

sleeping?[6] Who seeth not these incurable sicknesses that can see anything? They are the pastors,[7] and how hungry must the flock be when they have no food to give them? They are the teachers, and how great is their ignorance where they themselves know nothing? They are the evangelists or messengers of glad tidings; how little hope have they, and what slender faith, whose messengers cannot tell what the Lord saith?

The Lord enlarge within your Majesty the bowels of mercy,[8] that you may once have pity upon your poor subjects.

                                        *   *   *

If I would declare unto your Majesty all the great abuses that are in our ministry, I should lead you along in the Spirit, as God did the prophet Ezekiel, and after many intolerable evils yet I shall still say unto you, "Behold, you shall see mo abominations than these."[9]

I would first lead you to your benefices, and behold some are defiled with impropriations, some with sequestrations, some loaden[1] with pensions, some robbed of their commodities. And yet behold more abominations than these. Look after this upon your patrons,[2] and lo, some are selling their benefices, some farming them, some keep them for their children, some give them to boys, some to serving-men, and very few seek after learned pastors. And yet you shall see more abominations than these. Look upon your ministry, and there are some of one occupation, some of another; some shakebucklers, some ruffians, some hawkers and hunters, some dicers and carders, some blind guides and cannot see, some dumb dogs and will not bark, and yet a thousand mo iniquities have now covered the priesthood.[3] And yet you in the meanwhile that all these whoredoms are committed, you at whose hands God will require it, you sit still and are careless, and let men do as they list.[4] It toucheth not belike your commonwealth and therefore you are so well contented to let all alone. The Lord increase the gifts of His Holy Spirit in you, that from faith to faith you may grow continually till that you be zealous as good King David to work His will. If you know not how to reform this, or have so little counsel (as man's heart is blinded) that you can devise no way, ask counsel at the mouth of the Lord, and His holy will shall be revealed unto you.

To reform evil patrons, your Majesty must strengthen your laws, that they may rule as well high as low. As Esdras said once, so may I say now: "The hands of the princes and rulers are chief in this trespass."[5] If you will have

---

6. Images of salt, light, and watching are found in various passages including Matthew 5.13–14; 24.42–43; Mark 9.49; 13.33–37; and Luke 14.34.
7. With a pun on the Latin *pastor*, shepherd.
8. Compassion; Colossians 3.12.
9. A refrain repeated in Ezekiel 8.6, 13, 15; *in our ministry*: among the clergy; *Ezekiel*: Ezekiel 8.1–4; *mo*: more.
1. Weighed down; *benefices*: positions in the church that guarantee a certain income. The abuses Dering names are ways of pocketing the income without providing spiritual direction or ministry: impropriations (giving church revenues to a layperson); sequestrations (using church revenues to pay personal debts); pensions (charging expenses to church revenues); commodities (selling church goods for cash).
2. Those who held the right to dispose of benefices.
3. Dering is particularly critical of those who enter the ministry but devote their time to leisure pursuits; *shakebucklers*: serving-men.
4. Please.
5. 1 Esdras 9.12–13. The three books of Esdras were considered noncanonical for Protestants but were still printed in Bibles, along with other apocryphal books, as material useful "for the instruction of godly manners."

it amended, you must provide so that the highest may be afraid to offend. To keep back the ignorant from the ministry, whom God hath not called to such a function, take away your authority from the bishops; let them not thus at their pleasure make ministers in their closet, whomsoever it pleaseth them.[6] To stop the inconveniences[7] that grow in the ministry by other who say they are learned and can preach and yet do not (that are, as I said, dumb dogs and will not bark), bridle at the least their greedy appetites, pull out of their mouths these poisoned bones that they so greed- ily gnaw upon. Take away dispensations, pluralities, *tot-quots*, non- residences, and such other sins.[8] Pull down the Court of Faculties,[9] the mother and nurse of all such abominations. I tell you this before God, that quickeneth all things, and before our Lord Jesus Christ, that shall judge the quick and the dead in His appearance and in His kingdom: amend these horrible abuses and the Lord is on your right hand; you shall not be removed forever.[1] Let these things alone, and God is a righteous God; He will one day call you to your reckoning. The God of all glory open your eyes to see His high kingdom, and enflame your heart to desire it.

JOHN CONWAY

From Meditations and Prayers (1571)[†]

E	Encrease knowledge.
L	Let virtue guide.
I	In prayer persevere.
Z	Zealously ask.
5 A	Acknowledge sin.
B	Beware of presumption.
E	Envy no man.
T	Tender[1] the helpless.
H	Hope for heaven.
10 R	Remember thy rule.
E	Encline to justice.
G	Grant gifts by desert.[2]
I	In mercy delight.
N	No flatterers prefer.
15 A	Accept the wise.

---

6. Ministers should be chosen by the church, not by the private wish of a bishop.
7. Improprieties.
8. Dering lists a number of common abuses of the benefice system: dispensations (exemptions from church law); pluralities (holding more than one benefice concurrently); *tot-quots* (licenses to hold as many benefices as one could obtain); nonresidences (not living within the geographic bound- aries of a benefice).
9. An ecclesiastical court that granted licenses to those who were not legally entitled to them.
1. Psalm 16.18, quoted in Acts 2.25; *God . . . kingdom*: 2 Timothy 4.1.
† Copy text: John Conway, *Meditations and praiers gathered out of the sacred letters and vertuous writ- ers* (London: William How, 1571; *STC* 5652), E4r.
1. Care for.
2. Grant privileges only to those who deserve them.

ATTRIBUTED TO QUEEN ELIZABETH

From Christian Prayers and Meditations (1569)[†]

A Prayer for Wisdom to Govern the Realm

Almighty God and King of all kings, Lord of heaven and earth, by Whose ordinance princes have governance of mortal men, whereas the wisest King Solomon plainly confesseth himself unable to govern his kingdom without Thy help and assistance, how much less shall I Thy handmaid, being by kind[1] a weak woman, have sufficient ability to rule these Thy kingdoms of England and Ireland, an innumerable and warlike nation, or how shall I possibly be able to bear the infinite weight of so great a burden, unless Thou (O most merciful Father), as Thou hast of Thine own liberality, without my deserving and against the expectation of many, given me a kingdom and made me to reign, do also in my reigning endue and help me with Thy heavenly grace, without which none, even the wisest among the children of men, can once think a right thought.

Thou therefore (O endless fountain of all wisdom) send down from Thy holy heaven and from the sovereign throne of Thy majesty Thy wisdom to be ever with me and alway to assist me, to watch and labor with me in governing the commonweal and that it may so teach and instruct me, Thy handmaid, that I may discern between good and evil and between right and wrong, that I may ever have willingness, boldness, and power to give deserved punishment to the guilty, lovingly to defend the innocent, liberally to cherish the painful[2] and profitable members of the commonweal.

Finally, without regard of persons, without account of worldly respects, take in hand, execute, and perform that which I shall know to please Thee alone, that when Thou the rightful judge, that shalt require many and great things at their hands to whom many and great things are committed, shalt call us all to a strait[3] reckoning, I be not condemned as guilty of evil governance. But if I, Thy handmaid, by natural frailty, weakness, and want of consideration, shall in anything have swerved from the right way, it may please Thee of Thy great mercy (most sovereign King and most loving Father) for Jesus Christ Thy Son's sake, to pardon me and grant that after this earthly kingdom expired, I may with Thee enjoy the heavenly and everlasting kingdom, through the same Jesus Christ Thy Son, our Lord and Mediator, to whom with Thee and with the Holy Ghost, the only King of all worlds, immortal, invisible, and only wise God, be all honor and glory for ever.[4]

MARY STUART AND THE RIDOLFI PLOT

In the spring of 1571, Parliament, still worried over the loyalty of Roman Catholics, passed bills declaring it treasonous to bring a papal bull into England

---

[†] Copy text: *Christian prayers and meditations in English French, Italian, Spanish, Greeke, and Latine* (London: John Day, 1569; STC 6428), p2v–4v.
1. Nature; *King Soloman . . . assistance*: 2 Chronicles 1.10.
2. Those who suffer pain.
3. Strict, with an allusion to the strait or narrow gate through which one must pass to enter into the way of life (Matthew 7.13); *committed*: Luke 12.48.
4. The concluding formula is taken from 1 Timothy 1.17; *want of consideration*: lack of importance.

or to declare the Queen a heretic, although Elizabeth rejected another proposal to fine those who refused to participate at least once a year in the Protestant rite of the Lord's Supper.

While Parliament brooded over the Pope's intrusion into English affairs, a more serious problem was brewing closer to home. In February 1571, Mary Stuart, annoyed that Elizabeth had not restored her to the Scottish throne, employed Roberto Ridolfi, a Florentine banker and papal agent who had been involved in the Northern Rebellion, to make contacts with Spain and Rome, urging an invasion of England on her behalf. She also wrote to the Duke of Norfolk, who was living under house arrest in London, urging him to join her cause and carry out an earlier promise to marry her. He entertained her overtures. On April 12, a messenger named Charles Baillie, carrying letters written in code from Ridolfi to Norfolk, was arrested in Dover. Although John Lesley, the Bishop of Ross and one of Mary Stuart's most loyal supporters, managed to substitute innocuous missives, the Ridolfi plot began to unravel. By September, Norfolk and several of his men were imprisoned in the Tower of London, and Elizabeth signed a letter authorizing torture of two servants. The next month, Lesley himself was imprisoned and, under threat, exposed the conspiracy between Mary and Norfolk. In June 1572, after several delays, the Queen signed the death warrant for Norfolk, although she could not be persuaded to move against Mary Stuart herself.

The years 1567–71 had been difficult ones. Beset by traitors, pressed by both Catholics and Protestants, and nearly overtaken by the plots of Mary Stuart and her supporters, Elizabeth steeled herself to the harsh measures needed to restore order. Her poem "The Doubt of Future Foes" reveals her determination to use all the means at her command to frustrate the hopes of the "aspiring minds" ranged against her. Reflecting on the early years of her reign, when the sword of state had been so little used that it had grown rusty, she now threatened to wield it freely, cutting off the heads of all who "seek such change and gape for future joy." As the treatment of those detained after the Northern Rebellion and the Ridolfi plot demonstrates, it was not an idle threat.

To many of her Protestant subjects, the change was welcome. Writing a quarter of a century later, Edmund Spenser recalled this period as one of queenly heroism and national reunification. In *The Faerie Queene,* he portrays Elizabeth in the guise of a feisty and indominable warrior-princess named Britomart, who is destined to marry a less than perfectly loyal knight named Artegall, who seems to represent the Protestant faction at the English Court. Britomart first sees Artegall's image in a crystal ball, falls in love, sets out on a dangerous quest to find him, and eventually wins his love. In Book 5, Artegall is taken captive by Radigund, a beautiful Amazon, who, although she strips him of his arms, dresses him in women's clothes, and puts him to work in her kitchen, also falls in love with him, much as Mary courted English noblemen such as Norfolk while she lived in captivity in England. When Britomart hears of Artegall's humiliation, she rides to his rescue, slays Radigund, releases the men of the city from subjection to the Amazons, and installs her future husband as their new ruler.

In the political allegory of the poem, Britomart's troubled relationship with Artegall represents the stages by which Elizabeth was drawn to the Protestant nobility of England during the 1550s, won their affection after she became Queen, discovered that some had secretly fallen into the orbit of Mary Stuart in the late 1560s, confronted them, and eventually restored many to favor in the early 1570s. In these episodes, Artegall seems to be modeled, at least in part, on Robert Dudley, the Earl of Leicester, who, though a favorite of the Queen and an early candidate for her hand, also secretly curried favor with Mary Stuart. After he assisted the Duke of Norfolk in his plot to marry the Scottish Queen, however, Leicester confessed what he had done to Elizabeth, and, just as Artegall was received again by Britomart once the Amazons had been defeated, the Earl and other wavering courtiers were forgiven once the northern rebels had been put down and Norfolk's treachery exposed.

The Amazons themselves represent a constellation of women rulers in the sixteenth century who included Mary Stuart, her mother Mary of Guise, Mary Tudor, Margaret of Parma, and Catherine de Medici—all Roman Catholics whom Spenser, like John Knox before him, regarded as tyrannous and unjust (see Part Two). Both Spenser and Knox recognized as divinely authorized the reign of Elizabeth herself but considered Mary Stuart as lawless and dangerous.

Though modern historians have tempered some of the worst charges brought against Mary during her lifetime, it is well to remember how infamous she was in her own day. Like Radigund, she had lured Englishmen such as Darnley, Norfolk, and the northern earls into her circle, turning them against their rightful queen and spawning lawlessness in two countries. In Spenser's view, the submission of such noblemen to Mary was unmanly, as he suggests by having Artegall and the other male captives wear women's clothes. Artegall's release and return to Britomart is thus, in his view, a recovery of manhood and also a return to the proper collective—and male—authority of the English nobility.

Inset into the story of Britomart and Artegall is a dream vision Britomart has when, on her journey to rescue Artegall, she stops for the night in the temple of the ancient Egyptian goddess Isis. Imagining herself as a priest of Isis, she encounters the goddess's husband, Osiris, represented in his traditional form as a crocodile, who represents Artegall. At first, the crocodile rises up against her. After she quells his aggression with a magic wand, however, the two mate, producing a lion as their offspring. The incident has two main meanings. First, it exalts the virtue of equity (which Spenser associates with Isis and Britomart) as a necessary correction for the imperfections and excesses of legal justice (represented by Osiris and Artegall). The union of the two virtues leads to true justice in so far as mortals can ever attain it. Second, the marriage of Britomart and Artegall represents the ideal union of masculine and feminine. At the opening of the passage, the god Osiris is likened to the sun (bright, but sometimes excessively hot and injurious) and Isis with the moon (dimmer, but also more restrained and gentle). Their union is thus an allegory of a healthy balance attained in marriage between what Spenser saw as inherent tendencies of men toward aggressiveness and of women toward clemency. Each is drawn closer to the golden mean by living with the other. This complex allegory takes us back to the political implications of the story. Not only was Elizabeth widely represented as the goddess of the moon, particularly in the 1580s and 1590s, when Spenser was writing, but she was also revered for her clemency. In Spenser's view, it was the Queen's willingness to use necessary legal force, balanced by her inclination to pardon offenders, that made her the ideal monarch to heal England's bitter divisions.

QUEEN ELIZABETH

Letter to Sir Thomas Smith, Authorizing the Torture of Two Prisoners (September 15, 1571)[†]

To our trusty and right well-beloved counsellor Sir Thomas Smith, Knight, and to our trusty and well-beloved Doctor Wilson, one of the Masters of our Requests.[1]

Received at the Tower the sixteenth day of September at eleven of the clock in the forenoon, 1571.

Elizabeth R   By the Queen.

Right trusty and well beloved, we greet you well, and finding in traitorous attempts lately discovered that neither Barker nor Bannister, the Duke of Norfolk's men, have uttered their knowledge in the under-proceeding[2] of their master and of themselves, neither will discover the same without torture; forasmuch as the knowledge hereof concerneth our surety and estate, and that they have untruly already answered, we will and by warrant hereof authorize you to proceed to the further examination of them upon all points that you can think by your discretions meet for knowledge of the truth. And if they shall not seem to you to confess plainly their knowledge, then we warrant you to cause them both, or either of them, to be brought to the rack[3] and first to move them with fear thereof to deal plainly in their answers. And if that shall not move them, then you shall cause them to be put to the rack, and to feel the taste thereof until they shall deal more plainly or until you shall think meet. And so we remit the whole proceeding to your further discretion, requiring you to use speed herein, and to require the assistance of our Lieutenant of the Tower.

Given under our signet the 15th of September 1571.

The Doubt of Future Foes (1570?)[‡]

The doubt° of future foes exiles my present joy,   *fear*
And wit° me warns to shun such snares as threaten mine annoy.[1]   *reason*

---

† Copy text: *Elizabeth I: Collected Works*, ed. Leah S. Marcus, Janel Mueller, and Mary Beth Rose (Chicago and London: University of Chicago Press, 2000), 127. Reprinted by permission of the University of Chicago Press. © 2000 by the University of Chicago.

1. Thomas Smith, a member of the Privy Counsel, and Thomas Wilson, who was in charge of the Duke of Norfolk's interrogations. Smith resisted the use of torture, but Wilson, who had been imprisoned in Italy and tortured by the Roman Catholic Inquisition, carried out Elizabeth's orders. A Master of Requests received and processed petitions addressed to the monarch.

2. Secretive actions; *traitorous . . . discovered*: not the Northern Rebellion, for which both Barker and the Duke had been previously imprisoned, but the Ridolfi plot, for which they were now in the Tower; *Barker*: William Barker, a member of Parliament, confessed under threat of torture and betrayed Norfolk; he was pardoned in 1574.

3. An instrument of torture; a victim's wrists and ankles were fastened to rollers which, when rotated, stretched the joints and limbs, causing excruciating pain.

‡ Copy text: George Puttenham, *The arte of English poesie* (London: Richard Field; STC 205119.5); Ee2v. The poem exists in different versions in various manuscripts, but this printed version was most widely circulated; for manuscript variants see May, *Selected Works*, 7–9 or Marcus, Mueller, and Rose, *Collected Works*, 133–34.

1. Ruffle my state of mind.

For falsehood now doth flow, and subject° faith doth ebb,   *subjects'*
Which would not be, if reason ruled or wisdom weaved the
   web.

5 But clouds of joys untried° do cloak aspiring minds,   *unattained*
Which turn to rain, of late repent° by course of changéd   *repentance*
   winds.
The top of hope supposed, the root of ruth° will be,[2]   *sorrow*
And fruitless all their grafféd° guiles,[3] as shortly ye shall see.   *grafted*

Then dazzled eyes with pride,[4] which great ambition blinds,
10 Shall be unsealed by worthy wights,° whose foresight   *persons*
   falsehood finds.
The daughter of debate that eke° discord doth sow   *still*
Shall reap no gain where former rule hath taught still[5] peace to
   grow.

No foreign banished wight shall anchor in this port;
Our realm it brooks no stranger's force; let them elsewhere
   resort.
15 Our rusty sword with rest[6] shall first his edge employ
To poll° their tops that seek such change and gape° for   *cut off / long*
   future[7] joy.

EDMUND SPENSER

From The Faerie Queene, Book 5 (1596)[†]

*[Britomart's dream at Isis Church and her rescue of Artegall
from Radigund and the Amazons]*

Naught is on earth more sacred or divine,
   That gods and men do equally adore,
   Than this same virtue° that doth right define.   *justice*
   For th' heavens themselves, whence mortal men implore
5   Right in their wrongs, are ruled by righteous lore°   *law*
   Of highest Jove, who doth true justice deal
   To his inferior gods and evermore
   Therewith contains° his heavenly commonweal,°   *maintains / commonwealth*
The skill whereof to princes' hearts he doth reveal.

10 Well, therefore, did the antique° world invent   *ancient*
   That Justice was a god of sovereign grace,

2. The flower of false hope will become the root of bitterness and sorrow.
3. Implanted treacheries.
4. Eyes dazzled by pride.
5. Always, but also quiet; peace will always grow and quietness will continue to grow; *daughter of debate*: Mary Stuart.
6. Sword that is rusty because of disuse.
7. Copy text: for joy; the manuscripts read "for future joy," which is clearly required by the meter.
† Copy text: Edmund Spenser, *The faerie queene Disposed into twelue bookes, fashioning XII. morall virtues* (London: VVilliam Ponsonbie, 1596; STC 23082), R6v–S4v (5.7. 1–8, 12–44).

And altars unto him and temples lent,
And heavenly honors in the highest place,
Calling him great Osiris, of the race
Of th' old Egyptian Kings, that whilom° were,   *formerly*
With feignéd colors shading° a true case,   *representing*
For that° Osiris, whilst he livéd here,   *Because*
The justest man alive and truest did appear.

His wife was Isis, whom they likewise made
A goddess of great power and sovereignty,
And in her person cunningly did shade
That part of justice which is equity[1]
(Whereof I have to treat here presently),
Unto whose temple whenas Britomart
Arrived, she with great humility
Did enter in, ne° would that night depart;   *nor*
But Talus[2] mote° not be admitted to her part.°   *might / side*

There she receivéd was in goodly wise
Of many priests, which duly did attend
Upon the rites and daily sacrifice,
All clad in linen robes with silver hemmed;
And on their heads, with long locks comely kem'd,°   *combed*
They wore rich miters[3] shapéd like the moon
To show that Isis doth the moon portend,
Like as Osiris signifies the sun.
For that they both like race in equal justice run.[4]

The championess them greeting, as she could,
Was thence by them into the temple led;
Whose goodly building when she did behold,
Borne upon stately pillars, all dispread°   *overspread*
With shining gold and archéd overhead,
She wondered at the workman's passing° skill,   *surpassing*
Whose like before she never saw nor read;°   *imagined*
And thereupon long while stood gazing still,[5]
But thought that she thereon could never gaze her fill.

Thence forth unto the idol they her brought,
The which was framéd all of silver fine,
So well as could with cunning hand be wrought,
And clothéd all in garments made of line,°   *linen*
Hemmed all about with fringe of silver twine.
Upon her head she wore a crown of gold

1. Procedure by which judges took into account special circumstances when judging a crime, thus allowing greater clemency in passing sentence.
2. An iron man, representing the force of the state, which somewhat harshly and crudely enforces the law in Book 5.
3. Pointed hats such as those worn by bishops.
4. Strict legal justice and equity are both necessary and complementary parts of an ideal legal system.
5. Quietly, but also continuously.

To show that she had power in things divine;
And at her feet a crocodile was rolled,
That with her[6] wreathéd tail her middle did enfold.

55 One foot was set upon the crocodile,
      And on the ground the other fast did stand,
      So meaning to suppress both forgéd° guile   *false*
      And open force; and in her other hand,
      She stretchéd forth a long, white, slender wand.
60 Such was the goddess, whom when Britomart
      Had long beheld, herself upon the land
      She did prostrate and with right humble heart
Unto herself° her silent prayers did impart.   *the idol*

To which the idol, as it were inclining,
65   Her wand did move with amiable look,
      By outward show her inward sense° defining.   *intention*
      Who,° well perceiving how her wand she shook,   *Britomart*
      It as a token of good fortune took.
      By this° the day with damp was overcast,   *this time*
70   And joyous light the house of Jove° forsook,   *the sky*
      Which when she saw, her helmet she unlaced[7]
And by the altar's side herself to slumber placed.

                              * * *

There did the warlike maid herself repose
      Under the wings of Isis all that night,
75   And with sweet rest her heavy eyes did close,
      After that long day's toil and weary plight.
      Where whilst her earthly parts with soft delight
      Of senseless sleep did deeply drownéd lie,
      There did appear unto her heav'nly sprite
80   A wondrous vision, which did close imply°   *secretly reveal*
The course of all her fortune and posterity.

Her seemed,° as she was doing sacrifice   *It seemed to her*
      To Isis, decked with miter on her head
      And linen stole° after those priests' guise,   *long robe*
85   All suddenly she saw transfiguréd
      Her linen stole to robe of scarlet red,
      And moon-like miter to a crown of gold[8]
      That even she herself much wonderéd
      At such a change and joyéd to behold
90 Herself adorned with gems and jewels manifold.

---

6. Although feminine here, the crocodile is elsewhere in the dream vision figured as male.
7. Britomart has armed herself as a knight to disguise her gender and protect herself.
8. Under her sister, Mary Tudor, Princess Elizabeth conformed to Catholic practices (symbolized by the bishop's hat or miter). What follows is (among other things) a vision of her future coronation and union with her Protestant supporters, figured in Artegall.

And in the midst of her felicity,
    An hideous tempest[9] seeméd from below
    To rise through all the temple suddenly,
    That from the altar all about did blow
95   The holy fire and all the embers strow°   *scattered*
    Upon the ground, which kindled privily°   *secretly*
    Into outrageous flames un'wares did grow,
    That all the temple put in jeopardy
Of flaming and herself in great perplexity.

100 With that the crocodile, which sleeping lay
    Under the idol's feet in fearless° bower,   *safe*
    Seemed to awake in horrible dismay,
    As being troubled with that stormy stour,°   *turmoil*
    And gaping greedy wide,° did straight devour   *eagerly*
105 Both flames and tempest, with which growen great,
    And swoll'n with pride of his own peerless power,
    He 'gan to threaten her° likewise to eat,   *Britomart*
But that the Goddess with her rod him back did beat.[1]

Though turning all his pride to humbless meek,
110 Himself before her feet he lowly threw,
    And 'gan for grace and love of her to seek.
    Which she accepting, he so near her drew,
    That of his game she soon enwombéd grew,
    And forth did bring a lion of great might
115 That shortly did all other beasts subdue.[2]
    With that she wakéd, full of fearful fright,
And doubtfully dismayed through that so uncouth° sight. *unaccustomed*

So thereupon long while she musing lay,
120 With thousand thoughts feeding her fantasy
    Until she spied the lamp of lightsome day
    Up-lifted in the porch of heaven high.
    Then up she rose, fraught with melancholy,
    And forth into the lower parts did pass,
125 Whereas the priests she found full busily
    About their holy things for morrow Mass[3]
Whom she saluting fair, fair re-saluted was.

But by the change of her uncheerful look,
    They might perceive she was not well in plight° *her circumstances*

---

9. Commonly interpreted as the Northern Rebellion in 1569, which had roots in tensions between northern Catholics and southern Protestants.
1. Some of the Protestants who supported the Queen during the Northern Rebellion came, in the next decade, to be a threat to her as they pressed for more radical church reforms than she would accept.
2. After stormy relations in the 1570s, Elizabeth pleased Protestants when she sent an army to fight Catholic forces in the Netherlands in 1585 and defended England against the Spanish Armada in 1588. The lion is here a symbol of English strength.
3. Spenser frequently uses traditional religious terms, such as "Mass," and only the context indicates whether they are to be taken positively or negatively; here the holiness of the priests is not suspect.

        Or that some pensiveness to heart she took.

130   Therefore, thus one of them, who seemed in sight
        To be the greatest and the gravest wight,
        To her bespake: "Sir Knight, it seems to me
        That thorough° evil rest of this last night,   *through*
        Or ill apaid,° or much dismayed ye be,   *Either discontented*
135 That by your change of cheer° is easy for to see."   *mood*

     "Certes," said she, "sith° ye so well have spied   *since*
        The troublous passion of my pensive mind,
        I will not seek the same from you to hide,
        But will my cares unfold in hope to find
140   Your aid to guide me out of error blind."
        "Say on," quoth he, "the secret of your heart.
        For by the holy vow which me doth bind,
        I am adjured best counsel to impart
To all that shall require my comfort in their smart."

145 Then 'gan she to declare the whole discourse
        Of all that vision which to her appeared,
        As well as to her mind it had recourse.
        All which when he unto the end had heard,
        Like to a weak, faint-hearted man he fared,
150   Through great astonishment of that strange sight;
        And with long locks up-standing, stiffly stared
        Like one adawéd° with some dreadful sprite.   *frightened*
So, filled with heav'nly fury,° thus he her behight:°   *inspired frenzy / addressed*

     "Magnific° virgin, that in quaint° disguise   *Glorious / curious*
155   Of British arms dost mask thy royal blood
        So to pursue a perilous emprise,°   *undertaking*
        How could'st thou ween,° through that disguiséd hood,   *suppose*
        To hide thy state from being understood?
        Can from th' immortal gods ought hidden be?
160   They do thy lineage and thy lordly brood,°   *parentage*
        They do thy sire,[4] lamenting sore for thee,
They do thy love, forlorn in women's thralldom, see.[5]

     "The end whereof, and all the long event,°   *eventual outcome*
        They do to thee in this same dream discover.
165   For that same crocodile doth represent
        The righteous knight that is thy faithful lover,
        Like to Osiris in all just endeavor.
        For that same crocodile Osiris is,
        That under Isis' feet doth sleep forever
170   To show that clemence° oft, in things amiss,   *clemency*
Restrains those stern behests and cruel dooms of his.

---

4. Her father, whom she left behind in order to seek Artegall.
5. The gods see Artegall imprisoned by Radigund and the Amazons.

"That knight shall all the troublous storms assuage
    And raging flames that many foes shall rear
    To hinder thee from the just heritage
175   Of thy sire's crown and from thy country dear.
    Then shalt thou take him to thy lovéd fere°   *spouse*
    And join in equal portion of thy realm,
    And afterwards a son to him shalt bear,
    That lion-like shall show his power extreme.
180 So bless thee God and give thee joyance of thy dream."

All which when she unto the end had heard,
    She much was easéd in her troublous thought,
    And on those priests bestowéd rich reward,
    And royal gifts of gold and silver wrought
185   She for a present to their goddess brought.
    Then taking leave of them, she forward went
    To seek her love where he was to be sought,
    Ne rested till she came without relent
Unto the land of Amazons, as she was bent.

190 Whereof when news to Radigund[6] was brought,
    Not with amaze, as women wonted° be,   *are accustomed to*
    She was confuséd in her troublous thought
    But filled with courage and with joyous glee,
    As glad to hear of arms, the which, now she
195   Had long surcease,° she bade to open bold,[7]   *cessation of war*
    That she the face of her new foe might see.
    But when they of that iron man° had told,   *Talus*
Which late her folk had slain, she bade them forth to hold.[8]

So there without the gate (as seeméd best)
200   She causéd her pavilion be pight;°   *placed*
    In which stout Britomart herself did rest,
    Whiles Talus watchéd at the door all night.
    All night, likewise, they of the town in fright
    Upon their wall good watch and ward did keep.
205   The morrow next, so soon as dawning light
    Bade do away the damp of drowsy sleep,
The warlike Amazon out of her bow'r did peep.

And causéd straight a trumpet loud to shrill,
    To warn her foe to battle soon be pressed,
210   Who long before awoke (for she full ill
    Could sleep all night, that in unquiet breast
    Did closely harbor such a jealous[9] guest)
    Was to the battle whilom ready dight.°   *then already dressed*

---

6. Queen of the Amazons.
7. Open the gates boldly.
8. Keep Britomart and Talus out of the city.
9. Spenser portrays Elizabeth's struggle with Mary Stuart over who will rule England as a quarrel over
  a lover.

Eftsoons that warrioress with haughty crest
215　　Did forth issue, all ready for the fight.
On th' other side her foe appearéd soon in sight.

But ere they rearéd hand, the Amazon
　　Began the strait° conditions[1] to propound　　　　　　　*strict*
　　With which she uséd still to tie her fone°　　　　　　　　*foes*
220　　To serve her so, as she the rest had bound.[2]
　　Which when the other heard, she sternly frowned
　　For high disdain of such indignity
　　And would no longer treat,° but bade them° sound.　　*negotiate /*
　　For her no other terms should ever tie　　　　　　　　*trumpets*
225　Than what prescribéd were by laws of chivalry.[3]

The trumpets sound, and they together run
　　With greedy rage and with their falchions° smote;　　*broad swords*
　　Ne either sought the other's strokes to shun,
　　But through great fury both their skill forgot
230　　And practic° use in arms, ne sparéd not　　　　　　　*cunning*
　　Their dainty parts, which nature had created
　　So fair and tender, without stain or spot,
　　For other uses than they them translated,°[4]　　　　　*adapted*
Which they now hacked and hewed, as if such use they hated,

235　As when a tiger and a lioness
　　Are met at spoiling of some hungry prey,
　　Both challenge it with equal greediness.
　　But first the tiger claws thereon did lay,
　　And therefore, loath to loose her right away,
240　　Doth in defense thereof full stoutly stand;
　　To which the lion strongly doth gainsay°　　　　　　　*counter*
　　That she to hunt the beast first took in hand
And therefore ought it have, wherever she it found.[5]

Full fiercely laid the Amazon about
245　　And dealt her blows unmercifully sore,
　　Which Britomart withstood with courage stout,
　　And them repaid again with double more.
　　So long they fought that all the grassy floor
　　Was filled with blood, which from their sides did flow
250　　And gushéd through their arms, that all in gore
　　They trod and on the ground their lives did strow
Like fruitless seed, of which untimely death should grow.

1. Radigund requires that her opponents agree, if defeated, to be ruled by her.
2. A reference to Mary's claim to be Elizabeth's rightful heir, which made even English Protestants reluctant to oppose her openly, since she might one day be their Queen.
3. Elizabeth never acknowledged Mary's claim to the throne.
4. Neither Mary's supporters nor Elizabeth's were above accusing the Queen they opposed of sexual improprieties.
5. Mary Stuart first claimed the English crown upon the death of Mary Tudor.

At last proud Radigund with fell despite,°   *lethal anger*
    Having by chance espied advantage near,
255   Let drive at her with all her dreadful might
    And thus upbraiding said, "This token bear
    Unto the man whom thou dost love so dear,
    And tell him for his sake thy life thou gavest."
    Which spiteful words she, sore engrievèd to hear,
260   Thus answered: "Lewdly° thou my love depravest,°   *basely / defames*
Who shortly must repent that now so vainly bravest."°   *boasts*

Nath'lesse,° that stroke so cruel passage found   *Nevertheless*
    That, glancing on her shoulder plate, it bit
    Unto the bone and made a grisly wound,
265   That she her shield through raging smart of it
    Could scarce uphold; yet soon she it requit.
    For having force increased through furious pain,
    She her so rudely on the helmet smit
    That it empiercèd to the very brain,
270 And her proud person low prostrated on the plain.

Where being laid, the wrathful Britoness
    Stayed not till she came to herself again,
    But in revenge both of her love's distress
    And her late vile reproach, though vaunted vain,°   *vainly displayed*
275   And also of her wound, which sore did pain,
    She with one stroke both head and helmet cleft.[6]
    Which dreadful sight, when all her° warlike train   *Radigund's*
    There present saw, each one of sense bereft
Fled fast into the town and her sole victor left.

280 But yet so fast they could not home retrate°   *retreat*
    But that swift Talus did the foremost win,
    And pressing through the preace° unto the gate,   *crowd*
    Pell-mell with them at once did enter in.
    There then a piteous slaughter did begin.
285   For all that ever came within his reach,
    He with his iron flail did thresh so thin,
    That he no work at all left for the leach,°   *doctor*
Like to an hideous storm, which nothing may impeach.°[7]   *hinder*

And now by this the noble conqueress
290   Herself came in, her glory to partake;
    Where though revengeful vow she did profess,
    Yet when she saw the heaps which he did make
    Of slaughtered carcasses, her heart did quake
    For very ruth,° which did it almost rive,°   *pity / break*
295   That she his fury willèd him to slake;

6. Some interpret this as the execution of Mary in 1587, but the events that come next fit better Mary's deposition by Elizabeth following the Northern Rebellion. Mary's trial and execution are depicted in the Mercilla episode (5.9.36–5.10.4, included in Part Ten).
7. A reference to the execution of more than 700 insurgents following the Northern Rebellion.

For else he sure had left not one alive,
But all in his revenge of spirit would deprive.

Though when she had his execution stayed,
    She for that iron prison did inquire
300   In which her wretched love was captive laid,
    Which breaking open with indignant ire,
    She entered into all the parts entire.
    Where when she saw that loathly, uncouth sight
    Of men disguised in womanish attire,
305   Her heart 'gan grudge° for very deep despite°   *murmur / anger*
Of so unmanly mask° in misery misdight.°   *disguise / ill-clothed*

At last, whenas to her own love she came,
    Whom like disguise no less deforméd had,
    At sight thereof abashed with secret shame,
310   She turned her head aside, as nothing glad
    To have beheld a spectacle so bad.[8]
    And then too well believed that which tofore°   *before*
    Jealous suspect as true untruly drad,[9]
    Which vain conceit° now nourishing no more,   *thought*
315 She sought with ruth° to salve his sad misfortunes sore.   *pity*

Not so great wonder and astonishment
    Did the most chaste Penelope possess
    To see her lord, that was reported drent°   *drowned*
    And dead long since in dolorous distress,
320   Come home to her in piteous wretchedness
    After long travail of full twenty years,
    That she knew not his favor's likeliness,°   *face's resemblance*
    For° many scars and many hoary hairs,   *Because of*
But stood long staring on him, 'mongst uncertain fears.

325 "Ah, my dear Lord, what sight is this?" quoth she.
    "What May-game hath misfortune made of you?
    Where is that dreadful° manly look? Where be   *awesome*
    Those mighty palms,[1] the which ye wont t' imbrue°   *stain*
    In blood of kings and great hosts to subdue?
330   Could aught° on earth so wondrous change have wrought   *anything*
    As to have robbed you of that manly hue?°   *appearance*
    Could so great courage stoopéd have to aught?
Then farewell, fleshly force; I see thy pride is naught."

Thenceforth she straight into a bow'r him brought
335   And caused him those uncomely weeds° undight,°   *clothes / remove*
    And in their stead for other raiment sought,

8. A reference to the English noblemen who courted favor with Mary Stuart in case she should ever
   become their Queen.
9. Jealous suspicion disloyally had dreaded might be true.
1. Signs of victory.

Whereof there was great store and armors bright
Which had been reft° from many a noble knight   *seized*
Whom that proud Amazon subduéd had
340 Whilst fortune favored her success in fight;
In which whenas she him anew had clad,
She was revived and joyed much in his semblance glad.

So there awhile they afterwards remained,
Him to refresh and her late wounds to heal,
345 During which space she there as Princess reigned,
And changing all that form of commonweal,
The liberty of women did repeal,
Which they had long usurped; and them restoring
To men's subjection, did true justice deal,
350 That all they as a goddess her adoring,
Her wisdom did admire and hearkened to her loring.°[2]   *instruction*

For all those knights, which long in captive shade
Had shrouded been, she did from thralldom free,
And magistrates of all that city made,
355 And gave to them great living° and large fee.°   *income / property*
And that they should forever faithfull be,
Made them swear fealty[3] to Artegall.
Who, when himself now well recur'd° did see,   *restored*
He purposed to proceed, what so° befall,   *whatsoever*
360 Upon his first adventure, which him forth did call.[4]

Full sad and sorrowful was Britomart
For his departure, her new cause of grief,
Yet wisely moderated her own smart,
Seeing his honor, which she tendered° chief,   *cherished*
365 Consisted much in that adventure's prief,°   *trial*
The care whereof and hope of his success
Gave unto her great comfort and relief,
That womanish complaints she did repress
And tempered for the time her present heaviness.

---

2. After Mary's deposition, Elizabeth negotiated the crowning of her young son, James VI, as ruler of
    Scotland, which then became an English ally.
3. Obedience owed by a knight to his lord.
4. Later episodes involving Artegall in Book 5 recount England's wars to subdue Ireland.

Part Four: Changing Alliances (1572–1577)

HISTORICAL BACKGROUND

Shortly after New Year's Day 1572, Sir Thomas Smith, who had negotiated England's treaty with France after the disastrous Newhaven expedition (see Part Two), found himself again at the French court. This time his diplomatic mission was not to conclude a war but to reopen a courtship, for Queen Elizabeth was once more besieged by Parliament and her councilors to marry and secure the succession. That the Queen had no heir was bad enough, but events of the past few years had made her unmarried situation even more worrisome. The Northern Rebellion, the Pope's bull of excommunication, and the Ridolfi plot all underscored the presence of serious enemies inside and outside of England, enemies who might not only go to open war against Elizabeth but also work secretly to assassinate her. In such a climate, it appeared dangerous that Elizabeth had no heir, intolerable that the heir presumptive was still her cousin, Mary Stuart, and imperative to look to Europe for a marriage alliance that would strengthen the Queen's position with potential enemies and provide the possibility of an heir.

The question that confronted Elizabeth, however, was this: should she turn for assistance to France or to Spain? Mary Stuart, around whom the unrest of the previous decade had swirled, was a former Queen of France, but the Ridolfi plot had linked her with Philip II of Spain, Elizabeth's one-time brother-in-law and suitor. Moreover, although both countries were governed by Roman Catholic monarchs, Philip II was seen as closer to the Pope and therefore to the infamous bull of 1570 that had excommunicated Elizabeth and had called on her subjects to renounce her authority. On balance, the Queen decided to take her chances with the French. Thus, on April 19, 1572, Sir Thomas Smith and Sir Francis Walsingham, the resident ambassador in France, concluded the Treat of Blois, which aligned France and England against any "third power," that power being understood by both to be Spain. The ambassadors also began discreetly to explore the possibilities of a French husband for their Queen. When the King's brother Henry, Duke of Anjou, proved recalcitrant, attention turned to a younger sibling, Francis, Duke of Alençon (later to be named the Duke of Anjou when Henry became King and so called later in this volume). Relations with France turned chilly, however, after the simmering unrest between Roman Catholics and the Huguenots (as the French Protestants were known) turned into a late-summer bloodbath on St. Bartholomew's Day in which as many as 10,000 Protestants were killed.

The massacre angered Elizabeth, but there was little to be gained by turning from France to Spain. In 1567, Philip II had sent Fernandez Alvarez de Toledo, Duke of Alva, to the Low Countries to quell the rising Protestant unrest. William, Prince of Orange, was forced into exile and hundreds of Dutch men, women, and children crossed the English Channel to the safe haven of England's coastal cities. Some of them also took to the seas, harrying Spanish ships and looting other vessels that came within their reach. On March 1, 1572, Elizabeth, incensed by these acts of piracy, expelled the "sea beggars" from British ports, whereupon they promptly sailed to the Netherlands, captured the towns of Flushing and Brill, and reactivated the Protestant revolt. Throughout the remainder of her reign, Elizabeth would be plagued by religious and political tensions generated in the Netherlands that extended from the Continent into her Court and Privy Council. For Walsingham and his cohort, Alva's occupation of the Low Countries combined with the St. Bartholomew's Day massacre were ample evidence of a growing international Catholic conspiracy to eradicate Protestantism that should be confronted at all costs. For Robert Dudley, Earl of Leicester, the ongoing war in the Netherlands offered the opportunity to become a general and war hero and thus to enhance his standing with the Queen. When Elizabeth visited his home at Kenilworth during her summer progress of 1575, Dudley crafted the entertainments with an eye toward persuading the Queen to send him to the Low Countries.

Elizabeth herself, however, was reluctant to be drawn into a foreign engagement. It was not just that she had bad memories of the rout at Newhaven, or that she understood how expensive it would be to wage war, or that she found uncongenial the type of Protestantism practiced by the Dutch merchants and townspeople who fueled the revolt in the Netherlands. All this was true; but Elizabeth was also well aware of Spain's military and economic power, backed by nearly a century of global trade and colonization that had made it the center of a worldwide empire. In an open contest between England and Spain, there was little doubt which nation could marshal more resources, and Elizabeth was not eager to challenge the superpower of her day.

Instead, she chose to concentrate on consolidating her power at home, trimming the Privy Council to better suit her needs, reining in Parliament and the bishops of the Church when they overstretched their authority or underestimated hers, and strengthening the ties between herself and her subjects. The summer season offered an excellent opportunity for the latter. After a winter of living in various palaces, Elizabeth and much of her Court would set off into the English countryside for a royal progress. Ordinary folk could catch a glimpse of the Queen as she traveled—her itinerary was published in advance—and selected country houses, towns, and universities provided her with accommodations and entertainments. While such visits were a great honor for those who hosted Elizabeth and her entourage, they also involved considerable expense; nevertheless, both the Queen and her subjects profited from the opportunity to meet face-to-face and to engage in the delicate negotiation of reaffirming and realigning their common bonds.

PROSPECTS OF MARRIAGE AND TROUBLE IN FRANCE

While in France to conclude the Treaty of Blois, Sir Thomas Smith, Elizabeth's special envoy, revived conversations with the Queen Mother, Catherine de Medici, and her eldest son, Charles IX, about Elizabeth's possible marriage to the second son, Henry, Duke of Anjou. Although Henry professed himself to be an ardent Catholic, he had initially agreed to hear Mass only in private if he became Elizabeth's consort, but he now withdrew that concession and with it all serious possibility of marrying Elizabeth. Not to be outmaneuvered, Catherine de Medici suggested to Sir Thomas that Elizabeth consider her third son, Francis, Duke of Alençon (later himself Duke of Anjou). The match did not seem likely. It was not only that the Duke was still a teenager, but also that he was small, with a complexion marred from a bout with smallpox. His christening name, Hercules, had been altered to Francis when it became clear that he would in no way compare with his namesake.

The Queen established in her kingdom.

Elizabeth, however, did not peremptorily dismiss the offer. She was not, after all, actually marrying the young Duke of Alençon but merely entering into a set of complex conversations about the possibility of beginning a courtship. Her first letter to Sir Francis Walsingham in July instructs him in the delicate act of refusing this marriage proposal while maintaining civil relations with the royal family. Elizabeth uses flattering terms—Alençon is said to be full of "excellent virtues and good conditions"—but she stresses that he is far too young to be considered seriously as a marriage partner.

The tone of the second letter to Walsingham, sent in December, is distinctly chillier. And little wonder, for terrible events had taken place in France that made further marriage negotiations unthinkable, at least for the time. On August 22, Admiral Gaspard de Coligny, a prominent Huguenot (French Protestant), was hit by a bullet while walking in Paris. Although he survived the assassination attempt, suspicion fell (correctly as it proved) on the Queen Mother, who was concerned at the undue influence Coligny was wielding as adviser to her eldest son, Charles IX. Coligny himself was in Paris to celebrate the wedding of Charles's sister Marguerite to the Huguenot leader, Prince Henry of Navarre, a marriage that many had hoped would help heal the breach between Catholics and Protestants after years of religious wars. However, during the early morning hours of August 24, as the nuptial festivities continued, French soldiers attacked Protestant leaders; soon a mob formed, and when the violence ended, nearly 4000 Protestants, including Coligny, lay dead in the streets of Paris. Many more were slain throughout France. The Saint

Bartholomew's Day massacre, as it came to be known, sent shock waves through the Protestant world. If the marriage celebrations of a Protestant heir and a Catholic princess, intended to draw rival parties into a national alliance, could go so fatally awry, then hopes for international cooperation seemed dim indeed. More than any other single event, the massacre strengthened the resolve of leading English Protestants, including Sir Francis Walsingham and his ally, Robert Dudley, Earl of Leicester, to keep Catholic Europe at bay. It also encouraged suspicion of foreigners and convinced loyal English men and women of the favored status of their own nation.

Yet such divine favor could not be taken for granted. Throughout Elizabeth's reign, special "Forms of Common Prayer" that supplemented the traditional liturgy from the Book of Common Prayer were issued, often in response to a national crisis. On October 27, just two months after the St. Bartholomew's Day massacre, one such form of prayer enjoined parsons and curates of the Church of England to exhort their parishioners to come to church on Wednesdays and Fridays "with as many of their family as may be spared from their necessary business" to pray for deliverance "during this dangerous and perilous times of the troubles in Christendom." The "Thanksgiving and Prayer for the Queen," taken from this form of prayer, emphasizes the peaceable kingdom of England in contrast to the treacherous battleground of France, just across the channel, and also implores protection for those suffering in other countries. A second prayer "For Deliverance from Enemies" is a collage psalm, compiled entirely of lightly revised verses from the Great Bible's translation of the Psalms, which were used in the prescribed liturgy of the Church. By using only sacred (and therefore authorized) words, such collage prayers minimized the role of the human compositor and presented themselves as divine commentary on contemporary events, in this case the St. Bartholomew's Day massacre.

QUEEN ELIZABETH

Letters to Sir Francis Walsingham (1572)[†]

23 July 1572

To our right trusty and well-beloved Francis Walsingham, Esquire, our ambassador resident with our good brother, the French King.

Elizabeth Regina   By the Queen.

Trusty and well beloved, we greet you well. Where at the being here with us of the Duke of Montmorency, he and de Foix, after other their ordinary matter of ratification of the treaty passed over, did many times very earnestly deal with us, and in like manner with sundry of our Council, to move us to incline to an offer of marriage which the French King and Queen Mother willed them to make to us for the Duke of Alençon; and that we found the matter somewhat strange, considering some things past not in good order, as you know, in the matter of like offer for Monsieur d'Anjou, wherein the said Montmorency and his colleagues labored much to satisfy us, but especially considering the youngness of the years of the Duke of Alençon being compared to ours; so for those respects, although we

---

† Copy text: *Elizabeth I: Collected Works*, ed. Leah S. Marcus, Janel Mueller, and Mary Beth Rose (Chicago and London: University of Chicago Press, 2000), 205–9; 215–17. Reprinted by permission of the University of Chicago Press. © 2000 by the University of Chicago.

could give them no answer of comfort to content them, yet such was their importunacy in reciting of many reasons and arguments to move us not to mislike thereof, in respect as well of the strength of the amity which this amity should give to the continuance of this last league, and consideration as also of the worthiness of the said Duke of Alençon for his excellent virtues and good conditions[1] which they allege to be in him, with sundry other arguments tending to remove the difficulties and to gain our contentation and liking of the said Duke.

And in the end, after their many conferences had both with us as with our Council, when we perceived them very much perplexed to see our strangeness from assenting to their desires and how loath they were to have any flat denial, we were advised to forbear from making of a plain refusal and to expect the return of my Lord Admiral,[2] by whom and by others of his company we might understand what might be further conceived of the personage and conditions of the said Duke. And so our answer to them at their departure was this: that we found such difficulties in this matter, especially for the difference of his age, as presently we could not disgest[3] the same; yet such was the importunacy of our own subjects of all estates to have us to marry as we would forbear to give any such resolute answer as might miscontent the said ambassadors and, as we know, would much grieve our people at this time. And so we would take some further time to be advertised[4] upon the matter, and after one month space we would make a direct answer to the French King, which also we would first communicate to the said Duke of Montmorency to be by him, if he would, delivered over to the said King.

And so with this answer they departed, whereupon after the return of the Lord Admiral, we have considered with him and with some other that were there, by whom we find that indeed the conditions and qualities of the said Duke, as far forth as they could by their observation gather or by report of others understand, were nothing inferior to Monsieur d'Anjou but rather better to be liked. But as to his visage and favor, everybody doth declare the same to be far inferior, and that especially for the blemishes that the smallpox hath wrought therein, so as his young years considered and the doubtfulness of the liking of his favor joined therewith, wherein nobody that hath seen him can otherwise report, although otherwise to all other purposes he is commended before[5] his brother, we cannot indeed bring our mind to like of this offer, specially finding no other greater commodity offered to us with him whereby the absurdity that the general opinion of the world might grow to concerning this our choice, after so many refusals of others of great worthiness, might be counterpoised or in some manner recompensed.

Wherefore, according to our answer made to the said ambassadors, we have determination that you shall in our name say as followeth to Montmorency,

---

1. Good character; moral nature. *Duke . . . passed over*: François, Duke of Montmorency, headed the French delegation sent to England to ratify the Treaty of Blois in April 1572, which established an alliance between France and England. Paul de Foix, formerly French ambassador to England, was another member of the delegation [Marcus, Mueller, and Rose's note]; *French King and Queen Mother*: Charles IX of France and his mother, Catherine de Medici; *Duke of Alençon*: François Hercule, later the duke of Anjou and Elizabeth's long-standing suitor; *Monsieur d'Anjou*: Henry, current duke of Anjou, who would become Henry III in 1574; *league*: the treaty of Blois.
2. Edward Fiennes de Clinton, who had headed the English delegation to Paris for ratification of the Treaty of Blois [Marcus, Mueller, and Rose's note]; *strangeness from assenting*: reluctance to assent.
3. Comprehend or accept.
4. Informed.
5. Above; *visage and favor*: face and appearance.

or if he shall desire that you yourself (considering the answer is not plausible) shall make it to the King, then you shall so do, requiring him to be present and to move the King and his mother to interpret the same to the best, as indeed we mean it plainly[6] and friendly. And then you shall say that we have considered of the matter of the King's offer unto us of Monsieur d'Alençon in marriage, and for the same we do most heartily thank the King and the Queen Mother, knowing manifestly that the same proceedeth of very great goodwill to make a very perfect continuance of the amity lately contracted between us by this last treaty. And considering we have as great desire to have the same amity continued and strengthened, we are very sorry to find so great difficulties in this matter, that should be a principal bond thereof, as we cannot disgest the inconveniences of the same (by reason of the differences of our ages) to assent thereunto. Praying the King and his mother to assure themselves that there is no lack of desire in us to continue (yea, if it might be, to increase) this amity, that maketh us to think of the difficulties in this offer otherwise than we think all others that doth consider thereof[7] and must conceive (which proceedeth almost only of the difference of the age of Monsieur d'Alençon and ourself) a matter that cannot be remedied either by the King's brother, that desireth the match, or by us. So as the lack of not perfecting[8] this manner of bond of amity cannot be justly imputed to either of us, nor to the party himself, of whose conditions and virtues (truly you may say) we hear so well as we cannot but esteem him very much and think him well worthy to have as good fortune by marriage as he or any other might have by us.

And you may say, if so you see cause, although we might have known thus much as concerning his age when the ambassadors were here, and therefore might at that time have given them answer and not thus to have deferred it until this time; yet to satisfy the King therein you shall say that true it is that, although we ourselves were of this mind from the beginning, to think the match inconvenient for his age, yet at the being here of the ambassadors we continually labored by our Council, and also by our estates then assembled in Parliament, in laying before us the necessity of our marriage, both for our own comfort and also for the weal[9] of the realm. And some of them alleging unto us that there could be no such difficulty in this matter of years but the evil opinion that might be conceived thereof in the world to our lack might percase be recompensed with some other matter of advantage to us in our realm, in the sight also of the world, as being overcome with the importunity of their reasons, we did yield to take some further consideration of the matter and to prove whether in some time we could work our mind in the mean season to some other purpose, or whether any such further matter might be offered to which this match as might counterpoise in the judgment of the world the inconvenience[1] of the difference of the age. But so it is that in all this time we can neither find our mind altered nor yet hear of any other thing that might countervail the inconvenience. But so for observing of our promise, and especially because we mean to deal plainly with our good brother and the Queen his mother, we do make

6. Candidly; *plausible*: agreeable.
7. Elizabeth's objection to the match mirrors that of "all others," namely that Anjou is too young for her.
8. Failure to complete.
9. Well-being; *inconvenient*: unsuitable; *Parliament*: both the House of Lords and the House of Commons.
1. Absurdity or unsuitableness; *percase*: perhaps; *prove*: endeavor; *mean season*: intervening time.

them this answer: that surely we cannot find ourselves void of doubt and misliking to accept this offer, which is principally for the difference of years, allowing nevertheless of his worthiness for his virtuous and honorable conditions, as much as we can require in any prince to be our husband. And so we pray the King and his mother that the Duke himself may understand our judgment to be of his worthiness. And for the great goodwill we understand that he hath borne to us, who do assure him that we shall for the same esteem and to him at all times hereafter as well as any other prince of his estate, reserving only the band of love that ought to accompany marriage.

Given under our signet at Theobalds the 23 of July 1572, in the fourteenth year of our reign.

December 1572

*To our trusty and well-beloved Francis Walsingham, Esquire,
our ambassador resident in France.*

Elizabeth R

Trusty and well beloved, we greet you well. There hath been with us Monsieur de Mauvissière with letters from the King, the Queen Mother, and the Duke of Alençon.[2] His credence was in three points: the continuance of the amity, that we should be godmother to the infant, and pursue[3] still to the request of marriage with the Duke of Alençon. To whom we answered first, that as for amity, having it of late by league so straitly made betwixt us, on our behalf we never attempted or minded to attempt anything that should impair it, but rather do study[4] and wish to increase the same if we could.

And therefore, you may say, it is that and the goodwill appertaining to that amity that made us, by you before and now de Mauvissière, to declare what we have heard of our good brother. We are sorry to hear, first, the great slaughter made in France of noblemen and gentlemen, unconvicted and untried, so suddenly (as it is said, at his commandment) did seem with us so much to touch the honor of our good brother as we could not but with lamentation and with tears of our heart hear it of a prince so well allied unto us and in a chain of undissoluble love knit unto us by league and oath. That being after excused by a conspiracy and treason wrought against our good brother's own person, which whether it was true or false, in another prince's kingdom and jurisdiction where we have nothing to do, we minded not to be curious.[5] Yet that we[6] were not brought to answer by law and to judgment before they were executed (those who were found guilty) we do hear it marvelously evil taken and as a thing of a terrible and dangerous example and are sorry that our good brother was so ready to condescend to any such counsel, whose nature we took to be more humane and noble.

But when more was added unto it—that women, children, maids, young infants, and sucking babes were at the same time murdered and cast into the river, and that liberty of execution was given to the vilest and basest sort

---

2. François Hercule, later the duke of Anjou, was still being offered as a husband to Elizabeth; *Monsieur de Mauvissière*: Michael de Castelnau, Sieur de la Mauvissière, the French ambassador [Marcus, Mueller, and Rose's note].

3. Proceed; *credence*: official message; *amity*: the Treaty of Blois; *infant*: daughter of Charles IX and Archduchess Elizabeth of Austria, born in October.

4. Endeavor; *straitly*: closely.

5. To pry.

6. Possibly miscopied for "they" [Marcus, Mueller, and Rose's note].

of the popular,[7] without punishment or revenge of such cruelties done afterwards by law upon those cruel murderers of such innocents—this increased our grief and sorrow in our good brother's behalf, that he should suffer himself to be led by such inhumane counselors. And now sithence it doth appear by all doings, both by the edicts and otherwise, that the rigor is used only against them of the religion Reformed, whether they were of any conspiracy or no, and that contrary to the edict of pacification so oftentimes repeated, they of the Reformed religion are driven either to fly or to die, or to recant or lose their offices, whereby it doth appear by all actions now used by our good brother that his stop[8] and intent doth tend only to subvert that religion that we do profess and to root it out of this realm. At the least, all the strangers[9] of all nations and religions so doth interpret it, as may appear by the triumphs and rejoicing set out as well in the realm of France and other.

Which maketh that it must needs seem very strange, both to us and to all other, that our good brother should require us to be godmother to his dear child, we being of that religion which he doth now persecute and cannot abide within his realm. And if we should believe the persuasions of others and the opinions of all strangers, our friends who be not our subjects, we should not in no wise condescend to any association in that or any other matter. But as we have always hitherto had a special love to our good brother in his younger age and a desire to the conservation of his good estate and quietness (which we have indeed manifestly showed, never seeking any advantage of time against him as peradventure other princes would have done but ever sought to preserve his estate and his subjects of what quality or condition in religion soever they were, exhorting them to unity and concord and with loyal heart to live together in quiet under our good brother without offering injury the one to the other, glad of their agreement and sorry of the division and discord), so the late league of straiter amity made betwixt our good brother and us, to the which he did so frankly and lovingly condescend, or rather procure it at our hands, is so fresh in our memory that we cannot suffer that by us in any jot it should be diminished, but rather increased daily so long as our good brother do show the like unto us. And that maketh us to interpret all things in better part than otherwise by any means they can appear, such is our love to our good brother; and so can we be content to persuade ourselves, for the love that we do bear unto him and for the hope of the continuance in our begun amity, without faintness or dissimulation. And this, for the matter of amity, we said to Mauvissière: we would not be slack in any good office-doing at the request of our good brother. And so, notwithstanding the doubts and impediments before mentioned, we intend to send a worthy personage, a nobleman of our realm, to repair to his Court and to visit the King our good brother, the Queen, and the Queen Mother, and the rest that hath written in our behalf, and to do what office which is required of us as appertaineth, wishing that these spiritual alliances[1] may be to our comforts and conservation of the amity begun betwixt us.

7. Common people.
8. Purpose; *sithence*: since; *pacification*: the Edict of Toleration (1562) allowed Huguenots to worship publicly outside French towns and privately inside them; *Reformed religion*: in particular, the French Calvinists or Huguenots, but more generally Protestants.
9. Foreigners.
1. The spiritual alliance formed by Elizabeth's consenting to be godmother to Charles IX's daughter. Elizabeth sent the Earl of Worcester to represent her, but the baptismal gift, a golden tray, was confiscated by pirates during the Channel crossing.

To the motion of the marriage with the Duke of Alençon, wherein Mau-vissière seemed somewhat earnest, after declaration of inconveniences that might come in that marriage by the diversity of age and religion, which we termed in our talk extreme and in true impediments, we made this final res-olution and answer: that forasmuch that we had given to our ambassador resident there charge to demand and make relation of certain things touch-ing the matter to the King and Queen Mother, to the which you have had no answer but of the Queen Mother in a certain generality, before that we shall have a special answer to them, we cannot well resolve. The which once being done, we shall the better understand what to answer for any other proceedings in that request.

THE CHURCH OF ENGLAND

From A Form of Common Prayer (October 27, 1572)[†]

A Thanksgiving and Prayer for the Preservation of the Queen and the Realm

O God, most merciful Father, who in Thy great mercies hast both given unto us a peaceable princess and a gracious Queen, and also hast very often and miraculously saved her from sundry great perils and dangers, and by her government hast preserved us and the whole realm from manifold mis-chiefs and dreadful plagues, wherewith nations round about us have been and be most grievously afflicted, have mercy upon them, O Lord, and grant us grace, we beseech Thee, for these Thy great benefits, that we may be thankful and obedient unto Thee, to fly from all things that may offend Thee and provoke Thy wrath and indignation against us, and to order our lives in all things that may please Thee, that Thy servant, our sovereign lady, and we Thy people committed to her charge may by Thy protection be con-tinually preserved from all deceipts and violences of enemies and from all other dangers and evils both bodily and ghostly, and by Thy goodness may be maintained in all peace and godliness. Grant this, O merciful Father, for Thy dear Son's sake, our Savior Jesus Christ, to whom with Thee, and the Holy Ghost, one God immortal, invisible, and only wise, be all honor and glory for ever and ever.[1] Amen.

A Prayer for Deliverance from Enemies[2]

Hear our prayer, O Lord, consider our desire; hearken unto us for Thy truth and mercy's sake.[3]

Lord, how are they increased that trouble us; many are they that rise against us.[4]

---

† Copy text: *A fourme of common prayer to be vsed, and so commaunded by auctoritie of the Queenes Maiestie, and necessarie for the present tyme and state* (London: R. Iugge, 1572; STC 16511), B2v–B3v.
1. The final benediction, beginning "one God immortal" is taken from 1 Timothy 1.17; *deceipts*: deceptions; *ghostly*: spiritual.
2. This collage psalm is compiled entirely of lightly revised Bible verses and was said or sung antiphonally, as suggested by the alternation of roman and italic fonts.
3. Psalm 143.1.
4. Psalm 3.1.

The ungodly bend their bows and make ready their arrows within the quiver, that they may shoot at those that call upon the name of the Lord.[5]

They smite down Thy people, O Lord, and trouble Thine heritage.[6]

The dead bodies of Thy servants have they given to be meat unto the fowls of the air and the flesh of Thy saints unto the beasts of the land.[7]

Their blood have they shed like water on every side of Jerusalem, and there was no man to bury them.[8]

And we that live are become an open shame to our enemies, a very scorn and derision unto them that are round about us.[9]

O Lord, why is Thy wrath such against the sheep of Thy pasture? How long wilt thou be angry? Shall Thy jealousy burn like fire forever?[1]

Wherefore should the ungodly say, "Where is now their God? There is now no more help for them in their God."[2]

O remember not our old sins, but have mercy upon us, and that soon, for we are come to great misery.[3]

O let the sorrowful sighing of the prisoners come before Thee, according to the greatness of Thy power. Preserve Thou those seely souls that are appointed to die.[4]

O Lord, think upon the congregation of Thy people, whom Thou hast purchased and redeemed of old. O deliver us and save us for the glory of Thy name.[5]

And our praise shall be of Thee in the great congregation; our vows will we perform in the sight of them that fear Thee.[6]

And all the ends of the world shall remember themselves and be turned unto the Lord, and all the kindreds of the nations shall worship before Him.[7]

Glory be to the Father, and to the Son, and to the Holy Ghost.

As it was in the beginning, is now, and ever shall be, world without end. Amen.[8]

ELIZABETH ON SUMMER PROGRESS

In the midst of international crises, Elizabeth enjoyed the attention and good will, not to mention the flattery, of her own subjects, particularly during her summer progresses. A short poem, "The First Anointed Queen I Am," commemorated the Queen's visit to the coastal town of Rye in Sussex in August 1573. Printed as a cheap broadside on a single sheet of paper that could easily be tacked up on boards and doors, the poem served both to celebrate Elizabeth and to commend the town as a place that she had chosen to visit.

No one knew better how to flatter Elizabeth—or expected greater rewards—than her favorite, Robert Dudley, the Earl of Leicester. When he learned that the Queen planned to visit him at Kenilworth Castle during her summer

5. Psalm 11.2.
6. Psalm 94.5; the marginal gloss in the copy text reads Psalm 104.
7. Psalm 79.2.
8. Psalm 79.3.
9. Psalm 79.4.
1. Psalm 74.1 and Psalm 79.5.
2. Psalm 79.10 and Psalm 3.2; the marginal gloss reads only Psalm 79.
3. Psalm 79.8.
4. Psalm 79.12; *seely*: innocent.
5. Psalm 74.2 and Psalm 79.9; the marginal gloss reads only Psalm 74.
6. Psalm 22.25.
7. Psalm 22.27.
8. The Gloria Patri ("Glory be to the Father . . . Amen") is abbreviated in the copy text.

progress of 1575, Dudley arranged a set of entertainments for his monarch. They were unprecedented in their scale, their variety, and their opulence. For eighteen days in July, Elizabeth was feasted, courted, and lavishly entertained. There were pageants celebrating her arrival, banquets, dances, bearbaitings, outings for hunting, interludes devised to surprise her in the forest, full-dress neoclassical plays, fireworks, mock battles, and even a comic wedding that matched an ill-favored country bride with a lame and bumbling rustic groom. At Kenilworth, Leicester set the standard for royal entertainments for the remainder of the reign.

Two accounts of the entertainments survive. *The Princely Pleasures at Kenilworth Castle*, published by George Gascoigne, includes most of the more elevated, literary shows. *A Letter, Wherein Part of the Entertainment unto the Queen's Majesty at Killingworth Castle in Warwickshire in This Summer's Progress, 1575, Is Signified* purports to be by Robert Laneham (or Langham), a minor court official, and devotes attention to the cruder and more laughable parts, such as the comic wedding and the bear-baiting. David Scott (1977) argues persuasively that Laneham's letter is really by William Patten, a servant of William Cecil, Lord Burghley, Leicester's chief rival at court, and that it is a spoof designed to lampoon Laneham's peculiar spelling habits and mode of speech and to satirize the follies of the Court on summer progress.

Gascoigne was a prolific poet of Leicester's circle who did much to set the fashions in literature in the mid-1570s. He teamed up with George Ferrers (a royal entertainer and former Lord of Misrule, or master of ceremonies for humorous entertainments at Court) as well as with poets who more fully shared his own progressive Protestant views, including Richard Mulcaster (author of the 1559 coronation pageants) and William Hunnis (master of the children's choir in the Queen's chapel). The entertainments they devised turned on several myths. One was that, since the Tudor monarchs were descended from the ancient Britons rather than the Anglo-Saxon invaders of the early Middle Ages, the Queen was of especially venerable ancestry. Both Leicester and Elizabeth had troubled lineages, his father and grandfather having been executed for treason and her mother for adultery. The Tudor monarchs had, moreover, little to show for their royal claims before the time of Elizabeth's grandfather, Henry VII, who came to power by marriage and force of arms at the end of the Wars of the Roses. Both host and royal guest stood to benefit, then, from associations with the glorious, mythic court of King Arthur, here called to mind by entertainments centering on the Lady of the Lake.

Another useful myth was that the Queen had uncanny powers to tame the hearts of her least civilized subjects. There was some truth in this, since she had largely managed to keep the peace in a country recently torn by much religious strife. The entertainments involving the Savage Man and his son underscore

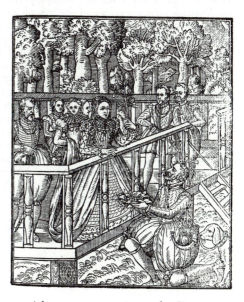

A huntsman reporting to the Queen.

her unusual ability to win the loyalty and obedience of even the most backward and ignorant of the common people.

Although these uses of court mythology were familiar and doubtless pleasant enough to the Queen, two prominent adaptations of neoclassical myth were not so likely to please. One involved the Reformation and its effects on international affairs. As a militant Protestant, Leicester was very much interested in defending his co-religionists on the Continent. Since his fortune came mainly through the cloth trade with the Netherlands, he was an especially outspoken advocate of English intervention against Spain in the Dutch wars of religion. In the Kenilworth entertainments, when the sea gods Triton and Proteus call on the Queen to rescue the Lady of the Lake from forced marriage to the brutal Sir Bruse, the speeches echo Leicester's similar call for England to confront Philip II and other Catholics on the Continent who were threatening to attack the Virgin Queen and to force her nation into the Catholic fold.

Elizabeth was not, however, interested in a dangerous and costly war with Spain, and she had no intention of assigning Leicester the part of commander general in such a project, as he wished. As Susan Frye (1993) suggests, the last-minute cancellation of an elaborate mock battle in which several dozen troops were to rescue the Lady of the Lake may well have been caused by the Queen's displeasure at Leicester's saber rattling.

Other neoclassical elements of the entertainments may have irritated Elizabeth even more. Since her accession, she had been promising to marry and bear a royal heir if a suitor came forth who was acceptable to her and if a match would serve England's national interests. Leicester himself had been an early candidate, though the scandal caused by the death of his wife, Amy Robsart, under mysterious circumstances in 1560 had effectively ended his prospects. As late as 1575, however, he seems to have nursed hopes of marriage, or at least to have found it advantageous to present himself in public as a suitor sufficiently eminent and dear to the Queen to be a serious candidate.

The chief argument for marriage comes in the play that served as the centerpiece of the entertainments, the competition between the goddesses Juno and Diana for the allegiance of the nymph Zabeta. There, the claims of marriage over virginity are clearly meant to carry the day. Though we have no direct evidence that Elizabeth knew in advance the play's import, we do know that, like the mock battle, it was suddenly cancelled, and it may be, as Frye suggests, that the Queen got wind of Leicester's intent to use the play to urge marriage and refused to allow it to be performed. Hence, perhaps, the events that follow: the Queen's hasty departure and the Earl's attempt to make amends by sending Gascoigne to intercept her and offer a speech declaring his "great good will" and urging her to return. If Leicester was attempting to placate an angry Queen, the tactic did not succeed, however; a despairing allegorical figure named Deepdesire, suffering for his love of the "courteous cruel" Zabeta, who has transformed him into a holly bush, called for the Queen to remain at the castle and restore him to his former happy state, but she rode resolutely away. If Elizabeth was happy to receive the adulation of her subjects, she was equally annoyed when they failed to observe the courtesies she had come to expect.

ANONYMOUS

The First Anointed Queen I Am (1573)†

The first anointed Queen I am,
Within this town which ever came.

A saying of each good subject of Rye

O happy town, O happy Rye,
That once in thee the Queen doth lie.
Such joy before was never seen
In Rye as now to lodge the Queen.
5   You fishermen of Rye rejoice
To see your queen and hear her voice.
Now clap your hands, rejoice and sing,
Which never erst° lodged queen ne° king.   *never before / nor*
Rejoice thou town and port of Rye
10   To see thy sovereign's majesty.
What heart hath he that dwells in Rye,
That joys not now as well as I?
O God that givest life and breath,
Preserve our queen Elizabeth.

Vivat Nestorios Elizabetha dies.[1]

GEORGE GASCOIGNE, WILLIAM HUNNIS, GEORGE FERRERS, AND OTHERS

The Princely Pleasures at Kenilworth Castle (July 9–27, 1575)‡

*A brief rehearsal, or rather a true copy, of as much as was
presented before her Majesty[1] at Kenilworth
during her last abode there, as followeth:*

Her Majesty came thither (as I remember) on Saturday, being the ninth of July last past, on which day there met her on the way, somewhat near the castle, Sibylla, who prophesied unto her Highness the prosperous reign that she should continue according to the happy beginning of the same. The order thereof was this: Sibylla, being placed in an arbor in the park near the highway where the Queen's Majesty came, did step out and pronounced as followeth:

---

† Copy text: *The First anointed Queene I am* (London?: J. Allde, 1573; STC 7582.5).
1. The days of Nestor live on in Elizabeth.
‡ Copy text: *The vvhole woorkes of George Gascoigne Esquire: newlye compyled into one volume* (London: Abell Ieffes, 1587, STC 11638), sigs. A1r–C8v. The first edition contained a preface, no longer extant, entitled "The Printer to the Reader" and dated March 26, 1576.
1. Copy text: majesties.

All hail, all hail, thrice happy prince. I am Sibylla, she
Of future chance and after hap,[2] foreshowing what shall be.
As now the dew of heav'nly gifts full thick on you doth fall,
Even so shall virtue more and more augment your years withal.
5   The rage of war, bound fast in chains, shall never stir ne° move,   *nor*
But peace shall govern all your days, increasing subjects' love.
You shall be called the Prince of Peace,[3] and peace shall be your
     shield,
So that your eyes shall never see the broils of bloody field.
If perfect peace then glad your mind, he° joys above the rest   *Leicester*
10 Which doth receive into his house so good and sweet a guest.
And one thing more I shall foretell, as by my skill I know:
Your coming is rejoicéd at ten thousand times and mo.°   *more*
And whiles your Highness here abides, nothing shall rest
     unsought
That may bring pleasure to your mind or quiet to your thought.
15 And so pass forth in peace, O Prince of high and worthy praise.
The God that governs all in all increase your happy days.

This device was invented, and the verses also written,
by Master Hunnis, Master of her Majesty's chapel.

   Her Majesty passing on to the first gate, there stood in the leads and
battlements thereof six trumpeters hugely advanced,[4] much exceeding
the common stature of men in this age, who had likewise huge and monstrous trumpets counterfeited, wherein they seemed to sound. And
behind them were placed certain trumpeters who sounded indeed at her
Majesty's entry. And by this dumb show[5] it was meant that, in the days
and reign of King Arthur, men were of that stature, so that the castle
of Kenilworth should seem still to be kept by Arthur's heirs and their
servants. And when her Majesty entered the gate, there stood Hercules
for porter, who seemed to be amazed at such a presence upon such a
sudden,[6] proffered to stay them, and yet, at last, being overcome by view
of the rare beauty and princely countenance of her Majesty, yielded himself and his charge, presenting the keys unto her Highness with these
words:

What stir, what coil° is here? Come back. Hold! Whither now?   *ruckus*
Not one so stout to stir.[7] What harrying° have we here?   *disturbance*
My friends, a porter, I, no poper[8] here am placed.
By leave perhaps, else not while club and limbs do last.[9]

2. What will come after.
3. A title applied to the Christ in Isaiah 9.6.
4. Highly elevated above the spectators; *in the leads*: at the front.
5. An emblematic show without words.
6. Appearing so suddenly.
7. Let no one be so bold as to move.
8. Obscure, but perhaps a bird running about, with a pun meaning an adherent of the Pope.
9. You may have leave to enter, but otherwise, you shall not proceed while I have a club and limbs to
   oppose you.

5   A garboil° this indeed! What yea,° fair dames, what   *tumult / what indeed*
            yea?
     What dainty darling's here? O God, a peerless pearl.[1]
     No worldly wight, no doubt, some sovereign goddess
            sure.
     Even face, even hand, even eye, even other features
            all,
     Yea beauty, grace, and cheer,° yea port° and majesty,   *countenance / bearing*
10   Show all some heav'nly peer[2] with virtues all beset.
     Come, come, most perfect paragon, pass on with joy
            and bliss.
     Most worthy welcome, goddess guest, whose presence
            gladdeth all.
     Have here, have here both club and keys. Myself my
            ward[3] I yield,
     Even gates and all, yea Lord himself,[4] submit and seek
            your shield.°   *protection*

These verses were devised and pronounced by Master Badger of Oxford,
Master of Art and Beadle[5] in the same university.

When her Majesty was entered the gate and come into the base court,
there came unto her a lady attended with two nymphs, who came all over[6]
the pool, being so conveyed that it seemed she had gone upon the water.
This lady named herself the Lady of the Lake,[7] who spake to her Highness
as followeth:

     Though haste say on,° let suit obtain some stay,[8]   *press on*
            Most peerless Prince, the honor of your kind,
     While that in short my state I do display,
            And yield you thanks for that which now I find,
5   Who erst° have wished that death me hence had fet,°   *at first / fetched*
            If gods not born to die had ought° death any debt.   *owed*

     I am the Lady of this pleasant lake,
            Who since the time of great King Arthur's reign,
     That here with royal court abode did make,
10   Have led a low'ring° life in restless pain,   *gloomy or declining*
     Till now that this your third arrival here[9]
            Doth cause me come abroad and boldly thus appear.

---

1. Elizabeth took pearls as a personal emblem, often wearing jewelry and gowns ornamented with
   them. In the New Testament, the pearl is associated with the Kingdom of God (see Matthew
   13.45–46).
2. One equal in rank with the heavenly powers.
3. Castle.
4. The Earl of Leicester. Though he occupied Kenilworth, it belonged to the Queen.
5. Minor official, who bore a mace in official processions.
6. Who all came across; *base court*: the lower or outer court of a castle, occupied by the servants.
7. Having appeared twice in the reign of King Arthur, the Lady of the Lake was to appear a third time
   at the return of the legendary king, who, according to prophecies, would then restore justice and
   peace to England.
8. Request obtain some pause.
9. The Queen had also visited in 1566 and 1572.

For after him° such storms this castle shook,   *Arthur*
    By swarming Saxons first, who scourged this land,
15 As forth of this my pool I ne'er durst look,
        Though Kenelme, King of Merce,[1] did take in hand,
As sorrowing to see it in deface,
    To rear these ruins up and fortify this place.

For straight by Danes and Normans all this isle
20   Was sore distressed and conqueréd at last,
Whose force this castle felt, and I therewhile
    Did hide my head, and though it straightway past
Unto Lord Sentloe's[2] hands, I stood at bay,
    And never showed myself, but still in keep° I lay.   *confinement*

25 The Earl Sir Mumford's force gave me no heart,
        Sir Edmund Crouchback's state,[3] the Prince's son,
Could not cause me out of my lake to part,
    Nor Roger Mortimer's[4] ruff,° who first begun   *pride*
(As Arthur's heir) to keep the table round,
30   Could not comfort once my heart or cause me come
            on ground.

Nor any owner else, not he that's now[5]
    (Such fear I felt again some force° to feel),   *violence*
Till now the gods do seem themselves t' allow
    My coming forth, which at this time reveal,
35 By number due, that your thrice coming here
        Doth bode thrice happy hope and voids the place
            from fear.
Wherefore I will attend while you lodge here,
    Most peerless Queen, to Court to make resort,
And as my love to Arthur did appear,
40   So shall't to you in earnest and in sport.
Pass on, Madam, you need no longer stand.
    The lake, the lodge, the Lord are yours for to command.

These verses were devised and penned by Master Ferrers,
sometime Lord of Misrule[6] in the Court.

Her Majesty, proceeding towards the inward court, passed on a bridge, the
which was railed in on both sides. And in the tops of the posts thereof were set

1. Mercia, an area in central England.
2. The first of a list of former occupants of Kenilworth Castle. Sentloe was a court figure in the reign
   of Richard I (1157–1199). Mumford (l. 25) has not been identified.
3. Edmund, first Earl of Lancaster and first Earl of Leicester (1245–96), second son of Henry III.
4. First Earl of March (1287–1330), who with Queen Isabella overthrew Edward II and for several
   years dominated England. In 1328, he assembled a Round Table of knights, holding jousts, distributing gifts, and arranging marriages to consolidate his power.
5. The claim, here and elsewhere in the entertainments, that Leicester owned Kenilworth apparently
   displeased Elizabeth. "Robert Laneham's" *Letter* records that, when the Lady of the Lake offered
   her watery abode to the Queen, Elizabeth replied, "we had thought indeed the lake had been ours,
   and do you call it yours now? Well, we will herein commune more with you hereafter" (B4v–B5r).
6. Master of ceremonies for traditional entertainments in which servants became masters and master became servants for a day.

sundry presents and gifts of provision, as wine, corn, fruits, fishes, fowls, instruments of music, and weapons for martial defense. All which were expounded by an actor clad like a poet, who pronounced these verses in Latin:[7]

* * *

[*Translation of the Poet's verses*]

Jupiter, as he watches from the highest peak of Olympus, sees you turning your steps this way, O foremost of queens. No doubt inflamed by the extraordinary image of your beauty and mindful of the fires that have always burned in him from time immemorial, he speaks: "Will the heaven-dwellers so shamefully allow the Queen to enter the castle in this way, deprived of any gift, a castle that she enters so happily?" The other gods hear the voice of the thunderer. Each on his own behalf gives eagerly his special domain: Sylvanus little melodious birds, Pomona her fruit, nourishing Ceres her grain, Dionysus grapes dripping with dew, Neptune fish, Mars his spears and armor. These gifts, powerful Queen, the gods of heaven give. The very Lord of this estate gives himself and the castle of Kenilworth.

These verses were devised by Master Mulcaster, and other verses to the very selfsame effect were devised by Master Patten[8] and fixed over the gate in a frame. I am not very sure whether these or Master Patten's were pronounced by the author, but they were all to one effect.

This speech being ended, she was received into the inner court with sweet music. And so alighting from her horse, the drums, fifes, and trumpets sounded, wherewith she mounted the stairs and went to her lodging.

On the next day, being Sunday, there was nothing done until evening, at which time there were fireworks showed upon the water, the which were both strange and well executed, as sometimes passing under the water a long space, when all men had thought they had been quenched, they would rise and mount out of the water again and burn very furiously until they were utterly consumed.

Now to make some plainer declaration and rehearsal of all these things before her Majesty, on the tenth of July there met her in the forest as she came from hunting one clad like a savage man, all in ivy, who, seeming to wonder at such a presence, fell to quarrelling with Jupiter as followeth:

O thundering Jupiter, which swayest the heav'nly sword,
At whose command all gods must crouch and knowledge
    thee their lord,
Since I, O wretch therewhiles,° am here by thy decree,   *during that time*
Ordainéd thus in savage wise forever more to be,
5 Since, for some cause unknown but only to thy will,
I may not come in stately court but feed in forests still,
Vouchsafe yet, greatest god, that I the cause may know
Why all these worthy lords and peers are here
    assembled so?

---

7. Latin omitted. Translation by Clarence H. Miller.
8. William Patten, a servant of Lord Burghley and Teller of the Exchequer, the likely author of the *Letter* by "Robert Laneham."

Thou know'st, O mighty god, no man can be so base,

10 But needs must mount° if once it° see a spark of   *raise himself / he*
    perfect grace.

And since I see such sights, I mean such glorious dames

As kindle might in frozen breasts a furnace full of flames,

I crave, great god, to know what all these peers might be

And what hath moved these sundry shows which I of late
    did see?

15 Inform me, some good man, speak, speak some courteous
    knight.

They all cry mum.° What shall I do? What sun shall   *refuse to speak*
    lend me light?

Well, Echo, where art thou? Could I but Echo find,

She would return me answer yet by blast of every wind.

Ho, Echo, Echo, ho! Where art thou, Echo, where?

20 Why Echo, friend, where dwell'st thou now? Thou
    wont'st⁹ to harbor here.

                 Echo answered.

                             Echo: Here.

Then tell thou me some news,

For else my heart would burst with grief of truth, it
    cannot choose.

                           Echo: Choose.

25 Choose? Why? But¹ thou me help, I say my heart will break.

And therefore, ev'n of courtesy, I pray thee, Echo, speak.

                            Echo: Speak.

I speak, yes that I will, unless thou be too coy.

Then tell me first what is the cause that all the people joy?

30   *Echo*: Joy.

Joy? Surely that is so, as may full well be seen.

But wherefore do they so rejoice? Is it for king or queen?

                           Echo: Queen.

Queen? What, the Queen of Heaven? They knew her long
    agone.²

35 No, sure some queen on earth whose like was never none.

                            Echo: None.

O then it seems the Queen of England for to be,

Whose graces make the gods to grudge, methinks it should
    be she.

                             Echo: She.

40 And is it she indeed? Then tell me what was meant

By every show that yet was seen. Good Echo, be content.

                          Echo: Content.

What meant the woman first, which met her as she came?

Could she divine of things to come, as sibyls use the same?

45   *Echo*: The same.

9. Are accustomed.
1. Unless.
2. Ago.

The same? What, Sibyl? She which useth not to lie?
Alas, what did that beldame[3] there? What, did she prophesy?
Echo: Prophesy.

O then belike she caused the worthy Queen to know
50 What happy reign she still should hold, since heav'ns ordainéd so.
Echo: So.

And what meant those great men which on the walls were seen?
They were some giants certainly; no men so big have been.
Echo: Have been.

55 Have been? Why then they served King Arthur, man of might,
And ever since this castle kept for Arthur's heirs by right.
Echo: Right.

Well Hercules stood by. Why came he from his dorter?[4]
Or was it eke[5] some monstrous man, appointed for a porter?
60 Echo: A porter.

A porter? Surely then he either was acrazed,
Or else, to see so many men, his spirits were amazed.
Echo: Amazed.

Amazed? So methought. Why did he let them pass
65 And yield his keys? Percase[6] he knew his master's will so was.
Echo: So was.

Well, then did he but well, yet saw I yet a dame
Much like the Lady of the Lake. Perchance so was her name.
Echo: Her name.

70 Alas, and what could she, poor dame distressed, deserve?
I knew her well. Percase she came this worthy queen to serve.
Echo: To serve.

So would I her advise. But what meant all those shifts
Of sundry things upon a bridge? Were those rewards of gifts?
75 Echo: Gifts.

Gifts? What? Sent from the gods as presents from above?
Or pleasures of provision as tokens of true love?
Echo: True love.

And who gave all these gifts? I pray thee, Echo, say.
80 Was it not he who, but of late, this building here did lay?
Echo: Dudley.

Oh, Dudley. So methought. He gave himself and all,
A worthy gift to be received, and so I trust it shall.
Echo: It shall.

85 What meant the fiery flames which through the waves so flew?
Can no cold answers quench desire? Is that experience true?
Echo: True.

Well, Echo, tell me yet, how might I come to see
This comely Queen of whom we talk? O were she now by thee.
Echo: By thee.

---

3. Aged woman.
4. Bedchamber.
5. Also.
6. Perhaps.

90   By me? O were that true, how might I see her face?
     How might I know her from the rest or judge her by her grace?
                         Echo: Her grace.
     Well then, if so mine eyes be such as they have been,
95   Methinks I see, among them all, this same should be the Queen.
                         Echo: The Queen.

     Herewith he fell on his knees[7] and spoke as followeth:

     O Queen, I must confess, it is not without cause,
     These civil people so rejoice that you should give them laws.
     Since I, which live at large, a wild and savage man,
100 And have run out a willful race since first my life began,
     Do here submit myself, beseeching you to serve,°   *to serve you*
     And that you take in worth my will, which can but
          well deserve.
     Had I the learnéd skill which in your head is found,
     My tale had flowed in eloquence where now my words
          are drowned.
105 Had I the beauty's blaze which shines in you so bright,
     Then might I seem a falcon fair, which now am but
          a kite.°   *lesser bird of prey*
     Could I but touch the strings which you so heav'nly
          handle,
     I would confess that fortune then full friendly did me
          dandle.°   *pamper*
     O Queen without compare, you must not think it strange
110 That here amid this wilderness your glory so doth range.
     The winds resound your worth, the rocks record your name.
     These hills, these dales, these woods, these waves,
          these fields pronounce your fame.
     And we which dwell abroad can hear none other news
     But tidings of an English Queen, whom heav'n hath decked
          with hues.
115 Yea, since I first was born, I never joyed so much
     As when I might behold your face, because I see none such.
     And death or dreary dole I know will end my days
     As soon as you shall once depart or wish to go your ways.
     But comely, peerless Prince, since my desires be great,
120 Walk here sometimes in pleasant shade to fend the parching
          heat.
     On Thursday next, think I, here will be pleasant dames,
     Who bet° than I may make you glee with sundry gladsome   *better*
          games.
     Meanwhile, good Queen, farewell. The gods your life prolong.

---

7. "Laneham's" *Letter* records that, at this moment, the savage man broke an uprooted sapling that
he was using for a staff and cast it away as a sign of his submission to the Queen. Unfortunately,
part of it nearly struck her horse on the head, causing it to bolt out of her footman's control. As
soon as it was reined in, she reassured the onlookers by calling out "No hurt. No hurt." The writer
dryly records that her words were "the best part of the play" (C3v–C4r).

And take in worth the wild man's words, for else you do him
    wrong.

Then he bade Echo farewell thus:

125   Echo, likewise farewell. Let me go seek some death.
Since I may see this Queen no more, good grief now stop my
    breath.

> *These verses were devised, penned, and pronounced*
> *by Master Gascoigne, and that (as I have heard credibly*
> *reported) upon a very great sudden.*[8]

    The next thing that was presented before her Majesty was the delivery
of the Lady of the Lake, whereof the sum was this. Triton, in likeness of a
mermaid, came towards the Queen's Majesty as she passed over the
bridge, returning from hunting, and to her declared that Neptune had sent
him to her Highness to declare the woeful distress wherein the poor Lady
of the Lake did remain, the cause whereof was this. Sir Bruse *sans pitié* in
revenge of his cousin Merlin, the prophet, whom for his inordinate lust
she had enclosed in a rock, did continually pursue the Lady of the Lake
and had long sithens surprised her but that Neptune, pitying her distress,
had environed her with waves. Whereupon she was enforced to live always
in that pool, and was thereby called the Lady of the Lake. Furthermore
affirming[9] that, by Merlin's prophecy, it seemed she could never be delivered but by the presence of a better maid than herself. Wherefore, Neptune had sent him right humbly to beseech her Majesty that she would
no more but show herself, and it should be sufficient to make Sir Bruse
withdraw his forces. Furthermore, commanding both the waves to be calm
and the fishes to give their attendance, and this he expressed in verse as
followeth:

The Speech of Triton to the Queen's Majesty.

Muse not at all, most mighty Prince, though on this lake you see
Me, Triton, float that in salt seas among the gods should be.
For look, what Neptune doth command of Triton is obeyed.
And now in charge I am to guide your poor distresséd maid,
5   Who, when your Highness hither came, did humbly yield her lake,
And to attend upon your court did loyal promise make.
But parting hence, that ireful knight, Sir Bruse, had her in chase,
And sought by force her virgin's state full foully to deface.
Yea, yet at hand about these banks his bands be often seen,
10 That neither can she come nor scape, but by your help, O Queen.
For though that Neptune hath so fenced with floods her fortress long,
Yet Mars her foe must needs prevail, his batt'ries are so strong.

---

8. On the spur of the moment.
9. Triton is the one "affirming" the prophecy here and "commanding" the waves at the end of the paragraph; *sans pitié*: without pity (French); *long sithens surprised her*: long since ambushed her.

How then can Diane Juno's force and sharp assaults abide
When all the crew of chiefest gods is bent on Bruse's side?
15 Yea, oracle and prophecy say sure she cannot stand,
Except a worthier maid than she her cause do take in hand.
Lo, here therefore a worthy work, most fit for you alone,
Her to defend and set at large. But you, O Queen, can none.[1]
And° gods decree and Neptune sues, this grant, O peerless Prince.   *If*
20 Your presence only shall suffice her enemies to convince.

Herewith Triton soundeth his trump and spake to the winds, waters, and
fishes, as followeth:

You winds, return into your caves and silent there remain.
You waters wild, suppress your waves and keep you calm and
        plain.
You fishes all and each thing else that here have any sway,
I charge you all, in Neptune's name, you keep you at a stay,
25 Until such time this puissant° prince Sir Bruse hath put to   *powerful*
        flight
And that the maid releaséd be by sovereign maiden's might.

This speech being ended, her Majesty proceeded further on the bridge, and
the Lady of the Lake (attended with her two nymphs) came to her upon
heaps of bull-rushes, according to this former device, and spake as followeth:

What worthy thanks might I, poor maid, express
Or think in heart that is not justly due
To thee, O Queen, which in my great distress
Succors hast sent mine enemies to subdue?
5 Not mine alone but foe to ladies all,
That tyrant Bruse, *sans pitié* whom we call.[2]

Until this day, the lake was never free
From his assaults, and other of his knights,
Until such time as he did plainly see
10 Thy presence dread and fearéd of all wights,°   *creatures*
Which made him yield, and all his bragging bands,
Resigning all into thy princely hands.

For which great grace of liberty obtained,
Not only I but nymphs and sisters all
15 Of this large lake, with humble heart unfeigned,
Render thee thanks and honor thee withal,
And for plain proof how much we do rejoice,
Express the same with tongue, with sound and voice.

---

1. Besides you, O Queen, none can do this.
2. Whom we call "without pity."

From thence her Majesty passing yet further on the bridge, Proteus appeared, sitting on a dolphin's back. And the dolphin was conveyed upon a boat, so that the oars seemed to be his fins. Within the which dolphin a consort of music[3] was secretly placed, the which sounded and Proteus, clearing his voice, sang this song of congratulation, as well in the behalf of the Lady distressed as also in the behalf of all the nymphs and gods of the sea:

The Song of Proteus.

O noble Queen, give ear to this my floating muse,
And let the right of ready will my little skill excuse.
For herdmen of the seas sing not the sweetest notes.
The winds and waves do roar and cry where Phoebus seldom floats.
5 Yet since I do my best in thankful wise to sing,
Vouchsafe, good Queen, that calm consent these words to you may bring.
We yield you humble thanks in mighty Neptune's name,
Both for ourselves and therewithal for yonder seemly dame,
A dame whom none but you deliver could from thrall,
10 Ne none but you deliver us from loit'ring life withal.
She pinéd long in pain, as overworn with woes,
And we consumed in endless care to fend her from her foes.
Both which you set at large, most like a faithful friend.
Your noble name be praised therefore, and so my song I end.

This song being ended, Proteus told the Queen's Majesty a pleasant tale of his delivery and the fishes which he had in charge. The device of the Lady of the Lake also was Master Hunnis's, and surely if it had been executed according to the first invention, it had been a gallant show, for it was first devised that (two days before the Lady of the Lake's delivery) a captain with twenty or thirty shot[4] should have been sent from the Heron House (which represented the Lady of the Lake's castle) upon heaps of bulrushes, and that Sir Bruse, showing a great power upon the land, should have sent out as many or more shot to surprise the said captain, and so they should have skirmished upon the waters in such sort that no man could perceive but that they went upon the waves. At last (Sir Bruse's men being put to flight) the captain should have come to her Majesty at the castle window and have declared more plainly the distress of his mistress and the cause that she came not to the Court, according to duty and promise, to give her attendance, and that thereupon he should have besought her Majesty to succor his mistress, the rather because Merlin had prophesied that she should never be delivered but by the presence of a better maid than herself. This had not only been a more apt introduction to her delivery, but also the skirmish by night would have been both very strange and gallant,[5] and thereupon her Majesty might have taken good occasion to have gone in her barge upon the water for the better executing of her delivery. The verses, as I think, were penned some by Master Hunnis, some by Master Ferrers, and some by Master Goldingham.

3. Company of musicians.
4. Soldiers with firearms.
5. Gorgeous; *strange*: astonishing.

And now you have as much as I could recover hitherto of the devices executed there, the country show excepted and the merry marriage,[6] the which were so plain as needeth no further explication. To proceed then, there was prepared a show to have been presented before her Majesty in the forest, the argument whereof was this:

Diana, passing in chase with her nymphs, taketh knowledge of the country and thereby calleth to mind how (near seventeen years past) she lost in those coasts one of her best-beloved nymphs called Zabeta.[7] She describeth the rare virtues of Zabeta. One of her nymphs confirmeth the remembrance thereof and seemeth to doubt[8] that Dame Juno hath won Zabeta to be a follower of hers. Diana confirmeth the suspicion, but yet, affirming herself much[9] in Zabeta's constancy, giveth charge to her nymphs that they diligently hearken and espy in all places to find or hear news of Zabeta, and so passeth on.

To entertain *intervallum temporis*, a man clad all in moss cometh in, lamenting and declaring that he is the wild man's son which (not long before[1]) had presented himself before her Majesty, and that his father (upon such words as her Highness did then use unto him) lay languishing like a blind man until it might please her Highness to take the film from his eyes.

The nymphs return one after another in quest of Zabeta. At last Diana herself, returning and hearing no news of her, invoketh the help of her father, Jupiter. Mercury cometh down in a cloud, sent by Jupiter to recomfort Diana, and bringeth her unto Zabeta. Diana rejoiceth, and after much friendly discourse, departeth, affying herself in Zabeta's prudence and policy.[2] She and Mercury being departed, Iris cometh down from the rainbow, sent by Juno, persuading the Queen's Majesty that she be not carried away with Mercury's filed[3] speech nor Diana's fair words, but that she consider all things by proof, and then she shall find much greater cause to follow Juno than Diana.

The interlocutors were these:

> Diana, goddess of chastity.
> Castibula, Anamale, Nichalis, Diane's nymphs.
> Mercury, Jove's messenger.
> Iris, Juno's messenger.
> Audax, the son of Silvester.

Actus 1, Scena 1

DIANA, CASTIBULA

[DIANA:]   Mine own dear nymphs, which knowledge° me   *acknowledge*
      your Queen,
And vow like me to live in chastity,

---

6. See the selection below, from the account of the pageants attributed to Robert Laneham.
7. A transparent figure for Elizabeth.
8. Suspect.
9. Affirming that she has much faith.
1. See above the account of the entertainments of July 10; *intervallum temporis*: in the intervening time.
2. Political wisdom; *affying herself*: placing her trust.
3. Polished.

My lovely nymphs, which be as I have been,
Delightful dames and gems of jollity,
5   Rejoicing yet much more to drive° your days   *pursue*
In life at large,° that yieldeth calm content,   *at liberty*
Than willfully to tread the wayward ways
Of wedded state, which is to thralldom bent,
I need not now with curious° speech persuade   *skillful*
10 Your chaste consents in constant vow to stand.°   *remain steadfast*
But yet beware lest Cupid's knights invade,
By sleight, by force, by mouth, or mighty hand,
The stately tower of your unspotted minds.
Beware, I say, lest whiles we walk these woods
15 In pleasant chase of swiftest harts and hinds,
Some harmful hart entrap your harmless moods.
You know these holts,° these hills, these covert places   *woods*
May close convey° some hidden force unseen.   *hide*
You see likewise the sundry gladsome graces,
20 Which in this soil we joyfully have seen,
Are not unlike some court⁴ to keep at hand,
Where guileful tongues, with sweet enticing tales,
Might, Circe like, set all your ships on sand
And turn your present bliss to after bales.°   *griefs*
25 In sweetest flowers the subtle snakes may lurk.
The sugared bait oft hides the harmful hooks.
The smoothest words draw wills to wicked work,
And deep deceits do follow fairest looks.

Hereat pausing and looking about her, she took knowledge of the coast and
proceeded:

But what? Alas. O whither wander we?
30 What chase hath led us thus into this coast?
By sundry signs, I now perceive we be
In Brutus' land, whereof he made such boast,
Which Albion in olden days did hight,°   *was called*
And Britain next by Brute his noble name,
35 Then Hengist's land, as chronicles do write,
Now England short,° a land of worthy fame.   *for short*
Alas, behold how memory breeds moan.
Behold and see how sight brings sorrow in.
My restless thoughts have made me woebegone.
40 My gazing eyes did all this grief begin.
Believe me, nymphs, I feel great grips of grief,
Which bruise my breast, to think how here I lost,
Now long ago, a love to me most lief,°   *dear*
Content you all, her whom I lovéd most.
45 You cannot choose but call unto your mind
Zabeta's name, who twenty years or more

---

4. The woods where the entertainment took place were, in fact, the Queen's Court, since "Court" was
   defined as any place the monarch happened to be.

Did follow me, still° scorning Cupid's kind°   *always / nature*
And vowing so to serve me evermore.
You cannot choose but bear in memory
50   Zabeta, her whose excellency was such,
In all respects of every quality,
As gods themselves those gifts in her did grutch.°   *begrudge*
My sister first, which Pallas hath to name,
Envied Zabeta for her learnéd brain.
55   My sister Venus feared Zabeta's fame,
Whose gleams of grace her beauty's blaze did stain.°   *overshadow*
Apollo dread to touch an instrument
Where my Zabeta chanced to come in place.°   *near him*
Yea, Mercury was not so eloquent,
60   Nor in his words had half so good a grace.
My stepdame Juno, in her glittering guise,
Was nothing like so heav'nly to behold.
Short tale to make, Zabeta was the wight
On whom to think my heart now waxeth cold.
65   The fearful bird oft lets her food down fall
Which finds her nest despoiled of her young,
Much like myself, whose mind such moans appall
To see this soil, and therewithal among,
To think how, now near seventeen years ago,
70   By great mishap I chanced to leese° her here.   *lose*
But my dear nymphs, on hunting as you go,
Look narrowly and hearken everywhere.
It cannot be that such a star as she
Can leese her light for any lowering cloud.
75   It cannot be that such a saint to see
Can long in shrine her seemly self so shroud.
I promise here that she which first can bring
The joyful news of my Zabeta's life
Shall never break her bow nor fret her string.
80   I promise eke that never storm of strife
Shall trouble her. Now, nymphs, look well about.
Some happy eye spy my Zabeta out.

CASTIBULA: O heav'nly Dame, thy woeful words have pierced
The very depth of your forgetful mind,
85   And by the tale which thou hast here rehearsed,
I yet record those heav'nly gifts which shined
Triumphantly in bright Zabeta's deeds.
But therewithal, a spark of jealousy,
With nice conceit,° my mind thus far-forth feeds,   *trick*
90   That she, which always likéd liberty,
And could not bow to bear the servile yoke
Of false suspect,° which mars these lovers' marts,[5]   *suspicion*
Was never won to like that smoldering smoke

---

5. Trades, exchanges. The play glances at the worldly motives for many arranged marriages, particularly among the aristocracy and royalty.

Without some feat that passeth common arts.
95 I dread Dame Juno with some gorgeous gift
Hath laid some snare her fancy to entrap
And hopeth so her lofty mind to lift
On Hymens' bed by height of worldly hap.°   *fortune*

DIANA: My loving nymph, even so fear I likewise,
100 And yet to speak as truth and cause requires,
I never saw Zabeta use the guise
Which gave suspect of such unchaste desires.
Full twenty years I markéd still her mind,
Ne could I see that any spark of lust
105 A loitering lodge within her breast could find.
How so it be (dear nymphs), in you I trust
To hark and mark what might of her betide
And what mishap withholds her thus from me.
High Jove himself my lucky steps so guide
110 That I may once mine own Zabeta see.

Diana with her nymphs proceed in chase,[6] and to entertain time, cometh
in one clad in moss, saying as followeth:

Actus 1, Scena 2

AUDAX *solus*°   *alone*

If ever pity pierced a peerless princess' breast
Or ruthful moan moved noble mind to grant a just request,
Then, worthy Queen, give ear unto my woeful tale,
For needs that son must sob and sigh whose father bides in bale.
5 O Queen, O stately Queen, I am that wild man's son,
Which not long since before you here presuméd for to run,
Who told you what he thought of all your virtues rare.
And therefore ever since (and yet) he pines in woe and care.
Alas, alas, good Queen, it were a cruel deed
10 To punish him which speaks no more but what he thinks indeed.
Especially whenas all men with him consent,
And seem with common voice to prove the pith of his intent.
You heard what Echo said to every word he spake;
You hear the speech of Diana's nymphs and what reports they make;
15 And can your Highness then condemn him to be blind?
Or can you so with needless grief torment his harmless mind?
His eyes, good Queen, be great, so are they clear and gray.
He never yet had pin or web[7] his sight for to decay,
And sure the dames that dwell in woods abroad with us
20 Have thought his eyes of skill enough their beauties to discuss.
For proof your Majesty may now full plainly see,
He did not only see you then, but more he did foresee
What after should betide. He told you that ere long

6. With the hunt.
7. White, opaque film over the eye; cataract.

You should find here bright heav'nly dames would sing the
    self-same song.
25   And now you find it true that he did then pronounce:
Your praises peise° by them a pound which he weighed   *weigh*
    but an ounce.
For sure he is nor blind nor lame of any limb,
But yet because you told him so, he doubts° his eyes   *fears*
    are dim.
And I therefore, his son, your Highness here beseech
30   To take in worth,° as subject's due, my father's simple   *think well of*
    speech.
And if you find some film that seems to hide his eyes,
Vouchsafe, good Queen, to take it off in gracious wonted wise.
He sighing lies and says, "God put mine eyes out clean
Ere choice of change in England fall° to see another queen."   *occur*

Finis Actus 1

Actus 2, Scena 1

ANAMALE *sola*

Would God I either had some Argus eyes
Or such an ear as every tidings hears.
O that I could some subtlety devise
To hear or see what mould[8] Zabeta bears,
5   That so the mood of my Diana's mind
Might rest, by me contented or appeased,
And I likewise might so her favor find,
Whom, goddess like, I wish to have well pleased.
Some courteous wind, come blow me happy news;
10   Some sweet bird, sing and show me where she is;
Some forest god or some of Faunus' crews,
Direct my feet, if so they tread amiss.

Actus 2, Scena 2

NICHALIS *sola*

If ever Echo sounded at request
To satisfy an uncontented mind,
Then Echo now come help me in my quest
And tell me where I might Zabeta find.
5   Speak, Echo, speak. Where dwells Zabeta, where?
Alas, alas, or° she or I am deaf.   *either*
She answered not. Ha? What is that I hear?
Alas, it was the shaking of some leaf.
Well, since I hear not tidings in this place,
10   I will go seek her out in someplace else.
And yet my mind divineth in this case
That she is here, or not far off she dwells.

8. Character or natural disposition.

Actus 2, Scena 3

DIANA with her train°   *attendants*

No news, my nymphs? Well then, I may well think
That carelessly you have of her inquired.
And since from me in this distress you shrink,
While I, meanwhile, my weary limbs have tired,
5   My father Jove, vouchsafe to rue my grief,
Since here on earth I call for help in vain.
O king of kings, send thou me some relief,
That I may see Zabeta once again.

Actus 2, Scena 4

MERCURY, DIANA, and the NYMPHS

[MERCURY:]   O Goddess, cease thy moan. Thy plaints have pierced
    the skies,
And Jove, thy friendly father, hath vouchsafed to hear thy cries.
Yea more he hath vouchsafed, in haste (post haste) to send
Me down from heaven to heal thy harm and all thy miss° to mend.   *loss*
5   Zabeta, whom thou seekest, in heart ev'n yet is thine,
And passingly,⁹ in wonted wise, her virtues still do shine.
But as thou doest suspect, Dame Juno trained a trap
And many a day to win her will hath lulled her in her lap.
For first, these sixteen years, she hath been daily seen
10   In richest realm that Europe hath, a comely, crownéd Queen.
And Juno hath likewise subornéd sundry kings,
The richest and the bravest both that this our age forth brings,
With other worthy wights which sue to her for grace,
And cunningly, with quaint conceits,¹ do plead the lover's case.
15   Dame Juno gives her wealth; Dame Juno gives her ease;
Dame Juno gets her every good that woman's will may please.
And so, in joy and peace, she holdeth happy days,
Not as thou thought'st nor done to death, or won to wicked ways.
For though she find the skill a kingdom for to wield,
20   Yet cannot Juno win her will nor make her once to yield
Unto the wedded life, but still she lives at large
And holds her neck from any yoke, without control of charge.²
Thus much it pleaséd Jove that I to thee should say,
And furthermore, by words expressed, he bade I should not stay,
25   But bring thee to the place wherein Zabeta bides
To prop up so thy staggering mind, which in these sorrows slides.
O Goddess then be blithe, let comfort chase out grief.
Thy heav'nly father's will it is to lend thee such relief.

DIANA: O noble Mercury, doest thou me then assure
30   That I shall see Zabeta's face and that she doeth endure

9. Surpassingly.
1. Clever devices.
2. Without being controlled by responsibilities.

Even yet in constant vow of chaste, unspotted life?
And that my stepdame° cannot yet make her a wedded wife?   *Juno*
If that be so indeed, O Muses, help my voice,
Whom grief and groans have made so hoarse I cannot well rejoice.
35   O Muses, sound the praise of Jove his mighty name,
And you, dear nymphs which me attend, by duty do the same.

Here Diana with her nymphs, assisted by a consort of music unseen, should
sing this song or roundlet[3] following:

O Muses, now come help me to rejoice,
Since Jove hath changed my grief to sudden joy
And since the chance whereof I cravéd choice
40   Is granted me to comfort mine annoy.
          O praise the name of Jove, who promised plain
          That I shall see Zabeta once again.

O gods of woods and goddess Flora eke,°   *also*
Now clear your breasts and bear° a part with me.   *sing*
45   My jewel she, for whom I wont° to seek,   *am accustomed*
Is yet full safe, and soon I shall her see.
          O praise the name of Jove, who promised plain
          That I shall see Zabeta once again.

And you, dear nymphs, who know what cruel care
50   I bear in breast since she from me did part,
May well conceive what pleasures I prepare
And how great joys I harbor in my heart.
          Then praise the name of Jove, who promised plain
          That I shall see Zabeta once again.

55   MERCURY: Come, goddess, come with me. Thy leisures last
          too long,
For now thou shalt her here behold for whom thou
          sing'st this song.
Behold where here she sits, whom thou so long hast
          sought.
Embrace her, since she is to thee a jewel dearly bought.
And I will now return to God in heav'n on high,
60   Who grant you both always to please His heav'nly majesty.

          MERCURY *departeth to heaven.*

[DIANA:]   What, do I dream, or doth my mind but muse?
Is this my lief, my love, and my delight?
Or did this god my longing mind abuse
To feed my fancy with a feignéd sight?
65   Is this Zabeta, is it she indeed?
It is she sure. Zabeta mine, all hail!
And though dame Fortune seemeth you to feed°   *seems to elevate you*

3. A song with a refrain.

With princely port,° which serves for your avail,   *honor*
Yet give me leave to gaze you in the face,
70 Since now, long since, myself yourself did seek,
And be content, for all your stately grace,
Still to remain a maiden always meek.
Zabeta mine, now Queen of high renown,
You know how well I lovéd you always,
75 And long before you did achieve this crown,
You know how well you seemed to like my ways,
Since when, you (won by Juno's gorgeous gifts)
Have left my launds° and closely kept in Court;   *forest glades*
Since when, delight and pleasure's gallant shifts°   *showy devices*
80 Have fed your mind with many a princely sport.
But peerless Queen, sometime° my peerless maid,   *once*
And yet the same as Mercury doth tell,
Had you but known how much I was dismayed[4]
When first you did forsake with me to dwell.
85 Had you but felt what privy pangs I had
Because I could not find you forth again,
I know full well yourself would have been sad
To put me so to proof of pinching pain.
Well, since Dan° Jove, my father, me assures   *Master*
90 That, notwithstanding all my stepdame's wiles,
Your maiden's mind yet constant still endures,
Though well content a queen to be therewhiles,°   *during that time*
And since by prudence and by policy
You win from Juno so much worldly wealth,
95 And since the pillar of your chastity
Still standeth fast, as Mercury me tell'th,
I joy with you and leave it to your choice
What kind of life you best shall like to hold.
And in meanwhile I cannot but rejoice
100 To see you thus bedecked with glistering gold,
To see you have this train of stately dames,
Of whom each one may seem some goddess' peer,
And you yourself, by due desert of fame,
A goddess full, and so I leave you here.
105 It shall suffice that on your faith I trust;
It shall suffice that once I have you seen.
Farewell, not as I would, but as I must.
Farewell, my nymph, farewell my noble Queen.

DIANA *with her train departeth.*

Actus 2, Scena ultima

IRIS *sola*

O lo, I come too late. O why had I no wings
To help my willing feet, which fet° these hasty, frisking flings?   *fetch*

4. Copy text: dismaide, which highlights a pun.

Alas, I come too late. That babbling god is gone,
And Dame Diana fled likewise; here stands the
    Queen alone.
5   Well, since a bootless plaint° but little would   *useless complaint*
    prevail,
I will go tell the Queen my tale. O peerless Prince,
    all hail!
The Queen of Heav'n° herself did send me to control   *Juno*
That tattling traitor Mercury, who hopes to get the goal
By curious filéd° speech, abusing you by art.   *polished*
10   But Queen, had I come soon enough, he should have
    felt the smart.
And you, whose wit excels, whose judgment hath no peer,
Bear not in mind those flattering words which he
    expresséd here.
You know that in his tongue consists his chiefest might.
You know his eloquence can serve to make the crow
    seem white.
15   But come to deeds indeed, and then you shall perceive
Which goddess means your greatest good and which
    would you deceive.
Call you to mind the time in which you did ensue°   *take part in*
Diana's chase° and were not yet a guest of Juno's crew.   *hunt*
Remember all your life before you were a Queen,
20   And then compare it with the days which you since
    then have seen.
Were you not captive caught? Were you not kept in walls?
Were you not forced to lead a life like other wretched
    thralls?
Where was Diana then? Why did she you not aid?
Why did she not defend your state, which were and
    are her maid?
25   Who brought you out of briars? Who gave you rule
    of realms?
Who crownéd first your comely head with princely
    diadems?
Even Juno, she which meant and yet doth mean likewise
To give you more than will can wish or wit can
    well devise.
Wherefore, good Queen, forget Diana's ticing° tale: *enticing*
30   Let never needless dread presume to bring your
    bliss to bale.°   *grief*
How necessary were for worthy queens to wed
That know you well, whose life always in learning
    hath been led.
The country craves consent, your virtues vaunt themself,
And Jove in heav'n would smile to see Diana set on shelf.°   *dismissed*
35   His queen hath sworn, but° you, there shall no   *except*
    mo° be such;   *more*
You know she lies with Jove a nights, and night ravens
    may do much.

Then give consent, O Queen, to Juno's just desire,
Who for your wealth would have you wed and for your
    farther hire°   *reward*
Some empress will you make, she bade me tell you thus.
40   Forgive me, Queen, the words are hers; I come not to discuss.
I am but messenger. But sure she bade me say
That, where you now in princely port have past one pleasant day,
A world of wealth at will you henceforth shall enjoy
In wedded state and, therewithal, hold up from great annoy
45   The staff of your estate.[5] O Queen, O worthy Queen,
Yet never wight felt perfect bliss but such as wedded been.

> *Tam Marti, quam Mercurio.*[6]

This show was devised and penned by Master Gascoigne, and being prepared and ready (every actor in his garment) two or three days together, yet never came to execution. The cause whereof I cannot attribute to any other thing than to lack of opportunity and seasonable weather.[7]

The Queen's Majesty hasting her departure from thence, the Earl commanded Master Gascoigne to devise some farewell worth the presenting, whereupon he himself, clad like unto Sylvanus, god of the woods, and meeting her as she went on hunting, spake *ex tempore*, as followeth:

"Right excellent, puissant, and most happy Princess, whiles I walk in these woods and wilderness (whereof I have the charge), I have often mused with myself that your Majesty being so highly esteemed, so entirely beloved, and so largely endued by the celestial powers, you can yet continually give ear to the counsel of these terrestrial companions and so, consequently, pass your time wheresoever they devise or determine that it is meet for your royal person to be resident. Surely, if your Highness did understand (as it is not to me unknown) what pleasures have been for you prepared, what great goodwill declared, what joy and comfort conceived in your presence, and what sorrow and grief sustained by likelihood of your absence (yea, and that by the whole bench[8] in heaven) since you first arrived in these coasts, I think it would be sufficient to draw your resolute determination forever to abide in this country and never to wander any further by the direction and advice of these peers and counselors, since thereby the heavens might greatly be pleased and most men thoroughly recomforted.

"But because I rather wish the increase of your delights than any way to diminish the heap of your contentment, I will not presume to stay your hunting for the hearing of my needless, thriftless, and bootless discourse. But I do humbly beseech that your Excellency will give me leave to attend you as one of your footmen, wherein I undertake to do you double service, for I will not only conduct your Majesty in safety from the perilous passages which are in these woods and forests but will also recount unto you (if your

---

5. Scepter of your realm.
6. As much to Mars as to Mercury. As his motto suggests, Gascoigne prided himself on being both a soldier and an eloquent writer.
7. For other reasons why the play may have been cancelled, see introduction.
8. Tribunal.

Majesty vouchsafe to hearken thereunto) certain adventures, neither unpleasant to hear nor unprofitable to be marked."

Herewith her Majesty proceeded, and Sylvanus continued as followeth: "There are not yet twenty days passed, most noble Queen, since I have been by the Procurer General[9] twice severally summoned to appear before the great gods in their council chamber, and making mine appearance according to my duty, I have seen in heaven two such exceeding great contrarieties, or rather two such wonderful changes, as draw me into deep admiration and sudden perplexity. At my first coming, I found the whole company of heaven in such a jollity as I rather want skill to express it lively than will to declare it readily. There was nothing in any corner to be seen but rejoicing and mirth, singing, dancing, melody and harmony, amiable regards, plentiful rewards, tokens of love and great good will, trophies and triumphs, gifts and presents (alas, my breath and memory fail me), leaping, frisking, and clapping of hands.

"To conclude, there was the greatest feast and joy that ever eye saw or ear heard tell of since heaven was heaven and the earth began to have his being. And inquiring the cause thereof, Reason, one of the heavenly ushers,[1] told me that it was to congratulate for the coming of your most excellent Majesty into this country. In very deed, to confess a truth, I might have perceived no less by sundry manifest tokens here on earth, for even here in my charge, I might see the trees flourish in more than ordinary bravery, the grass grow greener than it was wont to do, and the deer went tripping (though against[2] their death) in extreme delicacy and delight. Well, to speak of that I saw in heaven, every god and goddess made all preparations possible to present your Majesty with some acceptable gift, thereby to declare the exceeding joy which they conceived in your presence. And I, poor rural god, which am but seldom called amongst them, and then also but slenderly countenanced, yet for my great good will towards your Majesty, no way inferior to the proudest god of them all, came down again with a flea in mine ear and began to beat my brains for some device of some present, which might both bewray[3] the depth of mine affections and also be worthy for so excellent a princess to receive. But whiles I went so musing with myself many (yea, too many) days, I found by due experience that this proverb was all too true: *Omnis mora trahit periculum.*[4] For whiles I studied to achieve the height of my desires, behold, I was the second time summoned to appear in heaven. What? Said I heaven? No no, most comely Queen, for when I came there, heaven was not heaven; it was rather a very hell. There was nothing but weeping and wailing, crying and howling, dole, desperation, mourning and moan. All which I perceived also here on earth before I went up, for of a truth, most noble Princess, not only the skies scowled, the winds raged, the waves roared and tossed, but also the fishes in the waters turned up their bellies, the deer in the woods went drooping, the grass was weary of growing, the trees shook off their leaves, and all the beasts of the forest stood amazed.

"The which sudden change I plainly perceived to be for that[5] they understood above that your Majesty would shortly (and too speedily) depart out

---

9. One who summons others into the presence of the gods.
1. Court attendants.
2. Toward.
3. Reveal; *but slenderly countenanced*: given only slight respect; *with a flea . . . ear*: with my mind obsessed.
4. All delay brings risk.
5. Because.

of this country, wherein the heavens have happily placed you and the whole earth earnestly desireth to keep you. Surely, gracious Queen, I suppose that this late alteration in the skies hath seemed unto your judgment drops of rain in accustomed manner. But if your Highness will believe me, it was nothing else but the very flowing tears of the gods, who melted into moan for your hasty departure.

"Well, because we rural gods are bound patiently to abide the censure of the celestial bench, I thought meet to hearken what they would determine, and for a final conclusion it was generally determined that some convenient messenger should be dispatched with all expedition possible, as well to beseech your Majesty that you would here remain as also further to present you with the proffer of any such commodities and delights as might draw your full consent to continue here for their contentation and the general comfort of men."

Here her Majesty stayed her horse to favor Sylvanus, fearing least he should be driven out of breath by following her horse so fast. But Sylvanus humbly besought her Highness to go on, declaring that if his rude speech did not offend her, he could continue this tale to be twenty miles long, and therewithal protested that he had rather be her Majesty's footman on earth than a god on horseback in heaven, proceeding as followeth:

"Now to return to my purpose, most excellent Queen, when I had heard their deliberation and called unto mind that sundry realms and provinces had come to utter subversion by over great trust given to ambassadors, I (being thoroughly tickled[6] with a restless desire) thought good to plead in person. For I will tell your Majesty one strange property that I have: there are few or none which know my mind so well as myself, neither are there many which can tell mine own tale better than I myself can do. And therefore, I have continually awaited these three days to espy when your Majesty would, in accustomed manner, come on hunting this way.

"And being now arrived most happily into the port of my desires, I will presume to beseech most humbly and to entreat most earnestly that your Highness have good regard to the general desire of the gods, together with the humble petitions of your most loyal and deeply affectionate servants.

"And for my poor part, in full token of my dutiful meaning, I here present you the store of my charge, undertaking that the deer shall be daily doubled for your delight in chase. Furthermore, I will entreat Dame Flora to make it continually spring here with store of redolent and fragrant flowers. Ceres shall be compelled to yield your Majesty competent provision, and Bacchus shall be sued unto for the first fruits of his vineyards. To be short, O peerless Princess, you shall have all things that may possibly be gotten for the furtherance of your delights. And I shall be most glad and triumphant if I may place my godhead in your service perpetually. This tedious tale, O comely Queen, I began with a bashful boldness; I have continued in base eloquence; and I cannot better knit it up than with homely humility, referring the consideration of these my simple words unto the deep discretion of your princely will. And now I will, by your Majesty's leave, turn my discourse into the rehearsal of strange and pitiful adventures.

"So it is, good gracious lady, that Diana passeth oftentimes through this forest with a stately train of gallant and beautiful nymphs, amongst whom

6. Stirred up.

there is one surpassing all the rest for singular gifts and graces. Some call her Zabeta, some other have named her Ahtebasile, some Completa, and some Complacida.[7] Whatsoever her name be, I will not stand upon it.[8] But as I have said, her rare gifts have drawn the most noble and worthy personages in the whole world to sue unto her for grace.

"All which she hath so rigorously repulsed, or rather (to speak plain English) so obstinately and cruelly rejected, that I sigh to think of some their mishaps.[9] I allow and commend her justice towards some others, and yet the tears stand in mine eyes (yea, and my tongue trembleth and faltereth in my mouth) when I begin to declare the distresses[1] wherein some of them do presently remain. I could tell your Highness of sundry famous and worthy persons whom she hath turned and converted into most monstrous shapes and proportions, as some into fishes, some others into fowls, and some into huge stony rocks and great mountains.[2] But because diverse of her most earnest and faithful followers (as also some sycophants) have been converted into sundry of these plants whereof I have charge, I will on show[3] unto your Majesty so many of them as are in sight in these places where you pass.

"Behold, gracious lady, this old oak. The same was many years a faithful follower and trusty servant of hers named Constance,[4] whom when she could by none other means overthrow, considering that no change could creep into his thoughts nor any trouble of passions and perplexities could turn his resolute mind, at length she caused him, as I say, to be converted into this oak, a strange and cruel metamorphosis. But yet the heavens have thus far forth favored and rewarded his long continued service that, as in life he was unmovable, even so now all the vehement blasts of the most raging winds cannot once move his rocky body from his rooted place and abiding. But to countervail this cruelty with a show of justice, she converted his contrary, Inconstancy, into yonder poplar, whose leaves move and shake with the least breath or blast.

"As also she dressed Vainglory in his right colors, converting him into this ash tree, which is the first of my plants that buddeth and the first likewise that casteth leaf. For believe me, most excellent Princess, Vainglory may well begin hastily but seldom continueth long.

"Again, she hath well requited that busy elf Contention, whom she turned into this bramble briar, the which, as your Majesty may well see, doth even yet catch and snatch[5] at your garments and every other thing that passeth by it. And as for that wicked wretch Ambition, she did by good right condemn him into this branch of ivy, the which can never climb on high nor flourish without the help of some other plant or tree, and yet, com-

7. Gentle, peaceful, or pleasing; *Ahtebasile*: Elisabetha spelled backwards; *Completa*: perfect, filled with all good qualities.
8. Insist on settling the matter.
9. In Petrarchan love poetry, the lady is commonly represented as cruel in her rejection of the men who woo her.
1. Copy text: the declare to distresses.
2. Gascoigne imagines Elizabeth as an enchantress who, like the goddess Circe in Homer's *Odyssey*, transforms men into lower forms. Her power is greater, however, since Circe only succeeded in turning men into beasts.
3. Put on show.
4. Although this and other allegorical figures to follow are general human types, their relation to Zabeta suggests that they were also meant to call particular persons to mind. Since Gascoigne's argument is that the Queen is being cruel to Leicester in leaving him, Constancy and the later figure Deepdesire probably have to do with him as an abused but loyal servant and suitor.
5. Copy text: snath.

monly, what tree soever it rise by, it never leaveth to wind about it and straitly to enfold it until it have smoldered[6] and killed it. And by your leave, good Queen, such is the unthankful nature of cankered, ambitious minds that commonly they malign them by whom they have risen and never cease until they have brought them to confusion.[7]

"Well, notwithstanding these examples of justice, I will now rehearse unto your Majesty such a strange and cruel metamorphosis as I think must needs move your noble mind unto compassion. There were two sworn brethren which long time served her, called Deepdesire and Duedesert, and although it be very hard to part these two in sunder, yet is it said that she did long sithens[8] convert Duedesert into yonder same laurel tree. The which may very well be so, considering the etymology of his name, for we see that the laurel branch is a token of triumph in all trophies and given as a reward to all victors, a dignity for all degrees, consecrated and dedicate to Apollo and the Muses as a worthy flower, leaf, or branch for their due deserts. Of him I will hold no longer discourse because he was metamorphosed before my time, for your Majesty must understand that I have not long held this charge, neither do I mean long to continue in[9] it, but rather most gladly to follow your Highness wheresoever you shall be come.

"But to speak of Deepdesire (that wretch of worthies and yet the worthiest that ever was condemned to wretched estate), he was such an one as neither any delay could daunt him, no disgrace could abate his passions, no time could tire him, no water quench his flames, nor death itself could amaze him with terror.

"And yet this strange star, this courteous cruel,[1] and yet the cruelest courteous that ever was, this Ahtebasile, Zabeta, or by what name soever it shall please your Majesty to remember her, did never cease to use imprecation, invocation, conjuration, and all means possible until she had caused him to be turned into this holly bush, and [as] he was in this life and world continually full of compunctions, so is he now furnished on every side with sharp pricking leaves to prove the restless pricks of his privy[2] thoughts. Marry,[3] there are two kinds of holly, that is to say he-holly and she-holly. Now, some will say that she-holly hath no pricks, but thereof I intermeddle not."

At these words her Majesty came by a close[4] arbor made all of holly, and whiles Silvanus pointed to the same, the principal bush shaked. For therein were placed both strange[5] music and one who was there appointed to represent Deepdesire. Silvanus, perceiving the bush to shake, continued thus:

"Behold, most gracious Queen, this holly bush doth tremble at your presence, and therefore I believe that Deepdesire hath gotten leave of the gods to speak unto your excellent Majesty in their behalf, for I myself was present in the council chamber of heaven when Desire was thought a meet messenger to be sent from that convocation unto your Majesty as ambassador.

---

6. Smothered; *leaveth*: ceases; *straitly*: tightly.
7. Ruin; *cankered*: eaten up, as if by cancer.
8. Since.
9. Copy text: it.
1. In Petrarchan love poetry, the lady is often compared with a cold and distant star.
2. Private; *compunctions*: feelings of contrition.
3. To be sure.
4. Enclosed, confined.
5. Unexpected.

And give ear, good Queen. Methinks I hear his voice." Herewith Deepdesire
spake out of the holly bush, as followeth:

Stay, stay your hasty steps, O Queen without compare,
And hear him talk whose trusty tongue consuméd is with care.
I am that wretch Desire, whom neither death could daunt,
Nor dole decay, nor dread delay, nor feignéd cheer enchaunt,
5 Whom neither care could quench nor fancy force to change,
And therefore turned into this tree, which sight percase° seems   *perhaps*
    strange.
But when the gods of heaven and goddesses withal,
Both gods of fields and forest gods, yea, satyrs, nymphs, and all,
Determinéd a dole by course of free consent,
10 With wailing words and mourning notes your parting to lament,
Then thought they meet to choose me, silly wretch Desire,
To tell a tale that might bewray° as much as they require.   *reveal*
And hence proceeds, O Queen, that from this holly tree
Your learnéd ears may hear him speak whom yet you cannot see.
15 But Queen, believe me now, although I do not swear;
Was never grief, as I could guess, which sat their hearts so near
As when they heard the news that you, O royal Queen,
Would part from hence, and that to prove, it may full well be seen.
For mark what tears they shed these five days past and gone.
20 It was no rain, of honesty;[6] it was great floods of moan.
As first, Diana wept such brinish, bitter tears
That all her nymphs did doubt° her death; her face the sign yet bears.   *fear*
Dame Flora fell on ground and bruised her woeful breast.
Yea, Pan did break his oaten pipes; Sylvanus and the rest
25 Which walk amid these woods for grief did roar and cry,
And Jove, to show what moan he made, with thundering
    cracked the sky.
O Queen, O worthy Queen, within these holts° and hills   *woods*
Were never heard such grievous groans nor seen such
    woeful wills.
But since they have decreed that I, poor wretch Desire,
30 In their behalf shall make their moan and comfort thus require,
Vouchsafe, O comely Queen, yet longer to remain
Or still° to dwell amongst us here. O Queen, command again   *always*
This castle and the knight which keeps the same for you,[7]
These woods, these waves, these fowls, these fishes, these deer,
    which are your due.
35 Live here, good Queen, live here. You are amongst your friends.
Their comfort comes when you approach, and when you part, it ends.
What fruits this soil may serve, thereof you may be sure;
Dame Ceres and Dame Flora both will with you still endure.
Diana would be glad to meet you in the chase;
40 Sylvanus and the forest gods would follow you apace.

---

6. In all honesty.
7. See previous note on the ownership of Kenilworth.

Yea, Pan would pipe his part, such dances as he can,
Or else Apollo music make, and Mars would be your man.°   *serving man*
And to be short, as much as gods and men may do,
So much your Highness here may find, with faith and favor too.
45 But if your noble mind, resolvéd by decree,
Be not content by me, Desire, persuaded for to be,
Then bend your willing ears unto my willing note
And hear what song the gods themselves have
    taught me now by rote.
Give ear, good gracious Queen, and so you shall perceive
50 That gods in heaven and men on earth are loath such queens
    to leave.

Herewith the consort of music sounded and Deepdesire sung this song:

Come, Muses, come, and help me to lament.
    Come woods, come waves, come hills, come doleful dales.
Since life and death are both against me bent,
    Come gods, come men, bear witness of my bales.
55 O heav'nly nymphs, come help my heavy heart
    With sighs to see Dame Pleasure thus depart.

If death or dole could daunt a deep desire,
    If privy pangs could counterpeise° my plaint,   *counterbalance*
If tract of time a true intent could tire
60   Or cramps of care a constant mind could taint,
O then might I at will here live and sterve,°   *starve*
    Although my deeds did more delight deserve.

But out,° alas, no gripes° of grief suffice   *out with it / pangs*
    To break in twain this harmless heart of mine,
65 For though delight be banished from mine eyes,
    Yet lives Desire, whom pains can never pine.°   *cause to languish*
O strange effects, I live which seem to die,
    Yet die to see my dear delight go by.

Then farewell, sweet, for whom I taste such sour.
70   Farewell delight, for whom I dwell in dole.
Free will, farewell, farewell my fancy's flower.
    Farewell content, whom cruel cares control.
O farewell life, delightful death farewell.
    I die in heaven, yet live in darksome hell.

This song being ended, the music ceased and Sylvanus concluded thus:

"Most gracious Queen, as it should but evil have beseemed a god to be found fraudulent or deceitful in his speech, so have I neither recounted nor foretold anything unto your Majesty but that which you have now found true by experience. And because the case is very lamentable in the conversion of Deepdesire, as also because they know that your Majesty is so highly favored of the gods that they will not deny you any reasonable request, therefore I do humbly crave in his behalf that you would either be a suitor for him unto the heavenly powers or else but only to give your gracious consent that he may be restored to his pristinate estate.[8] Whereat your Highness may be assured that heaven will smile, the earth will quake, men will clap their hands, and I will always continue an humble beseecher for the flourishing estate of your royal person, whom God now and ever preserve to His good pleasure and our great comfort. Amen."

Tam Marti, quam Mercurio.[9]

FINIS

"ROBERT LANEHAM"

From A Letter, Wherein Part of the Entertainment unto the Queen's Majesty at Killingworth Castle in Warwickshire in This Summer's Progress, 1575, Is Signified (1575)[†]

Wednesday, her Majesty rode into the chase, ahunting again of the *hart of fors*.[1] The deer, after his property, for refuge took the soil, but so mastered by hot pursuit on all parts that he was taken quick[2] in the pool. The watermen held him up hard by the head while, at her Highness's commandment, he lost his ears for a ransom and so had pardon of life.

Thursday, the fourteenth of this July and the sixth day of her Majesty's coming, a great sort of bandogs[3] were there tied in the outer court and thirteen bears in the inner. Whosoever made the panel, there were enough for a quest and one for challenge, and[4] need were. A wight[5] of great wisdom and gravity seemed their foreman to be, had it come to a jury. But it fell out that they were caused to appear there upon no such matter, but only to answer to an ancient quarrel between them and the bandogs in a cause of controversy that hath long depended, been obstinately full often debated with sharp and biting arguments a both sides, and could never be decided, grown now to so marvelous a malice that with spiteful upbraids and uncharitable chafings always they fret, as far as anywhere the tone can hear, see, or smell the tother, and indeed at utter deadly foehood.[6] Many a maimed member (God wot[7]), bloody face, and a torn coat hath the quarrel cost between them, so far likely the less yet now to be appeased as there wants not partakers to back them a both sides.

8. Original place of favor with the Queen; *conversion:* into a holly bush.
9. See above p. 215, note 6.
† Copy text: *A letter whearin part of the entertainment vntoo the Queenz Maiesty at Killingworth Castl in Warwik sheer in this soomerz progress 1575 is signified* ([London: n.p., 1575]; STC 15190.5), C4r–D1v, D2v–E1v. *Killingworth:* Kenilworth.
1. Stag of the red deer.
2. Alive; *property:* nature; *took the soil:* went into the water.
3. Mastiffs.
4. If; *panel:* list of jurymen; the author compares bear-baiting with arguments between prosecution and defense in a trial; *quest:* inquest; *challenge:* appeal.
5. Creature.

Well, sir, the bears were brought forth into the court, the dogs set to them to argue the points even face to face. They had learned counsel also a both parts. What, may they be counted partial that are retained but a tone side?[8] I ween[9] no. Very fierce both tone and tother and eager in argument. If the dog in pleading would pluck the bear by the throat, the bear with traverse would claw him again by the scalp; confess and a list, but avoid a could not that was bound to the bar, and his counsel told him that it could be to him no policy[1] in pleading.

Therefore, thus with fending and proving, with plucking and tugging, scratting and biting, by plain tooth and nail a tone side and tother, such expense of blood and leather was there between them as a month's licking, I ween, will not recover, and yet remain as far out[2] as ever they were.

It was a sport very pleasant of these beasts to see the bear with his pink neyes leering after his enemies' approach, the nimbleness and wait[3] of the dog to take his advantage, and the force and experience of the bear again to avoid the assaults. If he were bitten in one place, how he would pinch in another to get free, that if he were taken once, then what shift, with biting, with clawing, with roaring, tossing, and tumbling, he would work to wind himself from them, and when he was loose, to shake his ears twice or thrice with the blood and the slaver about his fiznamy[4] was a matter of a goodly relief.

As this sport was had a daytime in the castle, so was there abroad at night very strange and sundry kinds of fireworks.

* * *

Now within also, in the meantime, was there showed before her High-ness, by an Italian, such feats of agility—in goings, turnings, tumblings, castings, hops, jumps, leaps, skips, springs, gambols, somersaults, capret-ties, and flights; forward, backward, sidewise, downward, upward, and with such windings, gyrings,[5] and circumflexions—all so lightly and with such easiness as by me in few words it is not expressible by pen or speech, I tell you plain.

* * *

A Sunday, opportunely, the weather brake up again, and after divine ser-vice in the parish church for the Sabbath day and a fruitful sermon there in the forenoon, at afternoon (in worship of this Kenilworth Castle and of God and Saint Kenelm, whose day forsooth by the calendar this was), a solemn bride-ale of a proper couple was appointed, set in order in the tilt-yard, to come and make their show before the castle in the great court, whereas was pight a comely quintain[6] for feats at arms, which when they

---

6. Enmity; *depended*: awaited judgment; *a*: on; *tone*: one; *tother*: other.
7. Knows.
8. Copy text: a to-side; *a*: on.
9. Think.
1. Helpful strategy; *a list*: if he wanted; *bound to the bar*: while being baited, bears were chained to stakes, as defendants in court might be chained to the bar of justice.
2. Distant from their goal; *scratting*: tearing with claws; *a tone side*: copy text: a to-side.
3. Watchfulness; *neyes*: eyes.
4. Physiognomy; *one*: copy text: no.
5. Twistings; *gambols*: dancing leaps; *capretties*: little frolicsome leaps; probably a word coined from the corrupted French *capriot* or Italian *capriccio*.

had done, to march out at the north gate of the castle homeward again into the town.

And thus were they marshaled. First, all the lusty lads and bold bachelors of the parish, suitably every wight with his blue buckram bride-lace upon a branch of green broom ('cause rosemary is scant there) tied on his left arm (for a that side lies the heart) and his alder pole for a spear in his right hand, in martial order ranged on afore, two and two in a rank: some with a hat, some in a cap, some a coat, some a jerkin; some for lightness in his doublet and his hose, clean trussed with a point afore; some boots and no spurs, he spurs and no boots, and he neither nother; one a saddle, another a pad or a panel fastened with a cord, for girths were geason; and these to the number of a sixteen wight riding men and well beseen.[7] But the bridegroom foremost, in his father's tawny worsted jacket (for his friends were fain that he should be a bridegroom before the Queen); a fair strawn hat with a capital crown, steeplewise on his head; a pair of harvest gloves on his hands, as a sign of good husbandry; a pen and inkhorn at his back, for he would be known to be bookish; lame of a leg, that in his youth was broken at football; well beloved yet of his mother, that lent him a new muffler for a napkin that was tied to his girdle for[8] losing. It was no small sport to mark this minion in his full appointment, that through good schoolation became as formal in his action as[9] had he been a bridegroom indeed, with this special grace by the way: that ever as he would have framed him the better countenance, with the worse face he looked.

Well, sir, after these horsemen, a lively morris dance according to the ancient manner: six dancers, Maud Marion,[1] and the fool. Then three pretty puzels, as bright as a breast of bacon, of a thirty-year-old apiece, that carried three special spice-cakes of a bushel of wheat (they had it by measure out of my Lord's bakehouse) before the bride, sizely,[2] with set countenance and lips so demurely simpering as it had been a mare cropping of a thistle. After these, a lovely lubber-worts, freckle-faced, red-headed, clean trussed in his doublet and his hose taken up now indeed by commission, for that he was so loath to come forward, for reverence belike of his new-cut canvas doublet, and would by his good will have been but a gazer, but found to be a meet actor for his office, that was to bear the bride-cup, formed of a

---

6. An upright pole with a cross-beam attached on a pivot to the top. At one end of the beam is a target made of wood and at the other is suspended a bag of sand, which swings around when the target is struck. The quintain was originally used to train knights, who practiced striking the target with their lances and then deftly managing their horses to avoid being struck from behind by the sand bag. By Elizabeth's day, the apparatus was used mainly for amusement; *worship*: honor; *bride-ale*: wedding feast. Since other entertainments at Kenilworth focusing on marriage were never performed, it may be significant that the Queen chose not to attend the mock-celebration; *pight*: pitched.

7. Well furnished; *bride-lace*: a piece of lace around sprigs of rosemary presented to guests at weddings, as scarves were given at funerals; *green broom*: a flowering plant sometimes fashioned into brooms; *rosemary*: an herb symbolizing remembrance, traditionally given at weddings and funerals; *alder pole*: pole made of alder wood; *jerkin*: short, close-fitting jacket; *doublet*: close-fitting, vest-like garment, sometimes with sleeves; *geason*: scarce; *wight*: valiant.

8. To prevent; *worsted*: tightly spun woolen; *fain*: eager. Hence, they persuaded his father to lend his jacket; *napkin*: mufflers were worn by women. Here the scarf is used for a handkerchief or napkin, which contributes to the picture of an effeminate bridegroom.

9. As if; *appointment*: outfit; *schoolation*: another coinage by "Laneham."

1. Maid Marian, a figure in the Robin Hood legend, but also a pun on "maud," which means "old hag"; *morris dance*: grotesque dance done in elaborate costumes associated with that legend.

2. Daintily; a pun since the three maidens were large; *puzels*: pucelles, a term that meant maidens but also courtesans.

sweet sucket barrel, a fair-turned foot set to it, all seemly besilvered and parcel-gilt, adorned with a beautiful branch of broom gaily begilded for rosemary, from which two broad bride-laces of red and yellow buckram,[3] begilded, and gallantly streaming by such wind as there was (for he carried it aloft). This gentle cup-bearer yet had his freckled fiznamy somewhat unhappily infested as he went by the busy flies that flocked about the bride-cup for the sweetness of the sucket that it savored on. But he, like a tall[4] fellow, withstood their malice stoutly (see what manhood may do), beat them away, killed them by scores, stood to his charge, and marched on in good order.

Then followed the worshipful bride, led (after the country manner) between two ancient parishioners, honest townsmen. But a stale stallion and a well spread, (hot as the weather was) God wot,[5] and an ill-smelling was she—a thirty-five year old, of color brown-bay, not very beautiful indeed but ugly, foul, ill-favored—yet marvelous fain of the office because she heard say she should dance before the Queen, in which feat she thought she would foot it as finely as the best. Well, after this bride came there by two and two a dozen damsels for bride-maids that for favor, attire, for fashion and cleanliness, were as meet for such a bride as a treen[6] ladle for a porridge-pot. Mo' (but for fear of carrying all clean)[7] had been appointed, but these few were enough.

As the company in this order were come into the court, marvelous were the martial acts that were done there that day.

The bridegroom, for preeminence, had the first course at the first quintain, brake his spear *treshardiment,* but his mare in his manage did a little so titubate that much ado had his manhood to sit in his saddle and to 'scape the foil[8] of a fall. With the help of his band,[9] yet he recovered himself, and lost not his stirrups (for he had none to his saddle); had no hurt, as it happed, but only that his girth burst, and lost his pen and inkhorn, that he was ready to weep for. But his handkercher, as good hap was, found he safe at his girdle. That cheered him somewhat, and had good regard it should not be filed.[1] For though heat and coolness upon sundry occasions made him sometime to sweat, and sometime rheumatic, yet durst he be bolder to blow his nose and wipe his face with the flappet of his father's jacket than with his mother's muffler. 'Tis a goodly matter when youth is mannerly brought up in fatherly love and motherly awe.

Now, sir, after the bridegroom had made his course, ran the rest of the band a while in some order, but soon after, tag and rag, cut and long tail, where the specialty of the sport was to see how some for his slackness had a good bob with the bag, and some for his haste to topple downright and come tumbling to the post; some striving so much at the first setting out that it seemed a question between the man and the beast whether the

---

3. Coarse linen or cotton fabric; *lubberworts:* an imaginary herb that induces laziness; hence a dull, heavy fellow; *commission:* request; *belike:* apparently; *gazer:* spectator; *barrel:* container for sweets; *parcel-gilt:* partly gilded; *begilded:* decorated, as if with gold.
4. Brave.
5. Knows; *stallion . . . spread:* a prostitute no longer in demand, with a broad rump.
6. Wooden;
7. Except for fear that they would bear down all in their path.
8. Disgrace, but also manure; *treshardiment:* valiantly; *titubate:* totter, stumble.
9. Of groomsmen.
1. Defiled; *regard:* care.

course should be made a horseback or afoot; and put forth with the spurs, then would run his race bias[2] among the thickest of the throng, that down came they together hand over head. Another, while he directed his course to the quintain, his *jument*[3] would carry him to a mare among the people, so his horse as amorous as himself adventurous. Another, too, run and miss the quintain with his staff and hit the board with his head.

Many such gay games were there among these riders, who by and by after, upon a greater courage,[4] left their quintaining and ran one at another. There to see the stern countenance, the grim looks, the courageous attempts, the desperate adventures, the dangerous courses, the fierce encounters, whereby the buff at the man and the counterbuff at the horse, that both sometime came toppling to the ground, by my troth, Master Martin, 'twas a lively pastime. I believe it would have moved some man to a right merry mood, though had it be told him his wife lay a dying.

PRAYERS, ADVICE, AND PRAISE FOR THE QUEEN

Entertainments written for the Queen during her summer progresses were a way for Elizabeth's subjects to show affection and respect for their monarch, but such pageants also provided opportunities to offer her advice. Leicester, for instance, took advantage of Elizabeth's visit to Kenilworth to urge her both to marry and to support the Protestant cause in the Netherlands. Other citizens were concerned about matters of religion closer to home. A dozen years after the Elizabethan Settlement had charted a course for the English Church that preserved traditional liturgical and organizational structures within a Protestant framework, there were some who felt that the Reformation had been insufficiently realized in England. In particular, they were eager to give more authority to local ministers and congregations (a form of church government known as Presbyterianism), rather than to the appointed bishops; to move church services away from the Book of Common Prayer toward the Calvinist form of worship in which many had participated while they were in exile during Mary Tudor's reign; and to educate clergy to become better preachers. A 1572 Parliamentary bill authorizing deviations from the Book of Common Prayer failed, but it fueled discontent among the powerful London churches, sympathetic members of Parliament, and even some Privy Councilors. Within two years, many of the more radical Protestant leaders were in jail, and several died while incarcerated. While some of the hotter heads fired off incendiary pamphlets, others worked more quietly at Court to win the Queen to their reformist views. Elizabeth, for her part, was concerned to maintain the stability of the country and the Church, and she would not, as she would later tell Parliament, "tolerate newfangledness" (see her Speech at the Closing of Parliament in Part Six).

She may, however, have been pleased by a tiny book, *Morning and Evening Prayers, with Divers Psalms, Hymns, and Meditations*, compiled by one of the Queen's former governesses, the Lady Elizabeth Tyrwhit, that was published in 1574. Printed on pages barely one inch wide and two inches high, one copy was bound into a gold enameled cover that could be hung from a chain and worn as a piece of jewelry. It is thought that this exquisite prayerbook was presented

2. Diagonally through the other riders; *tag . . . tail*: references to the differences between the rather undistinguished horses ridden by the bridal party.
3. A stallion (French) or a common beast of burden (English).
4. Purpose, but also heartiness of spirit.

to the Queen herself, and its contents included both traditional prayers that predated the Reformation as well as those that were distinctively Protestant. Tyrwhit's prayer for the Queen mingled entreaty, praise, and advice in a short invocation that called on God to "confound all idolatry and superstition, and set up Thy true and holy religion" in England. But it also urged the Queen toward "all godliness and virtue," and in so doing suggested that Elizabeth herself had a responsibility to maintain God's "true and holy religion."

Edward Hake's *Commemoration of the Most Prosperous Reign of Our Sovereign Elizabeth*, written for the Queen's Accession Day on November 17, was more frankly celebratory. Although it commended Elizabeth for her virginity, it also praised her motherly care over England and her Church. Comparing her to a series of biblical heroes including Esther, Moses, and Elijah, Hake saluted Elizabeth for maintaining the peace and quiet of Protestant England and avoiding the civil wars and tumults raging on the Continent.

England was far from civil war, but some Protestants continued to pressure the Queen to further reform the Church, and Elizabeth worried that religious divisions might create the very "tumults" she and her subjects were anxious to avoid. Her appointment of Edmund Grindal, a Marian exile and collaborator of the martyrologist John Foxe, as Archbishop of Canterbury in 1575 was a conciliatory gesture that brought about a rapprochement among the bishops, the Queen, and the more radical reformers, creating for a short time "a goodly space of quietness," as the historian Josias Nichols would later term it. By late 1576, however, Grindal was under house arrest after refusing to undertake sanctions against ministers who were holding unauthorized meetings to advance the Presbyterian cause. "Although you are a mighty prince," he told Elizabeth, "yet remember that He that dwelleth in heaven is mightier." Other reformers, who were now beginning to be called Puritans, were more diplomatic. James Sanford, an inveterate translator of Latin, French, and Italian texts, prefaced his 1576 edition of Ludovico Guicciardini's *Hours of Recreation* with a sustained panegyric to Queen Elizabeth, comparing her to Plato's philosopher king, Solomon, learned women of the past and present, the Virgin Mary, and even Christ himself. Yet as he praised Elizabeth for her godliness and learning, he situated her, not among her favorite courtiers, but with such exemplary "gentlewomen famous for their learning" as the pious Mildred Cecil, wife of Lord Burghley, and Anne Vaughan Lock—poet, translator, a member of the London reformist community, and wife of the Edward Dering who had preached the infamous "Unruly Heifer" Sermon (see Parts Two and Three).

Nicholas Hilliard, who became Elizabeth's official royal limner or miniature painter in 1572, placed her firmly at Court, however, both in his paintings and his later memoirs. In *A Treatise Concerning the Art of Limning*, Hilliard recounted their conversations about his craft and remarked on her curiosity about, and attentiveness to, the technical aspects of painting.

The exquisite detail of a miniature portrait found its literary counterpart in the intricate lyrics that began to be circulated at Court in increasing numbers throughout the 1570s. Although Richard Tottel had published an anthology of court poetry as early as 1557—his *Songs and Sonnets* was popularly known as "Tottel's Miscellany"—Elizabethan courtier poetry was distinguished by its use of more elegant language and more complicated imagery. It often cast the now middle-aged Elizabeth as the beautiful, aloof, distant lady of the Petrarchan sonnet tradition. The poet took over the role of the young lover, ready to expire at her feet in the throes of unrequited love. Sir Christopher Hatton, to whom Sanford dedicated his translation of *Hours of Recreation*, was Elizabeth's Captain of the Guard and one of the first to address Elizabeth as a Petrarchan lover. In a letter written to her in 1573 while he was on the Continent, he exclaimed, "No death, no, not hell, no fear of death shall ever win of me my consent so far to wrong myself again as to be absent from you one day," and concluded, "Bear with me, my most dear sweet lady. Passion overcometh me" (Brooks, *Hatton*, 96–97).

As the decade went on, other poets would begin to adopt a similar stance. In one such poem, "What Cunning Can Express," Edward de Vere, the Earl of Oxford and son-in-law of William Cecil, portrayed Elizabeth as the unattainable beloved, more pure than the lily of the field, more beautiful than Cynthia, more gracious than the rose, a goddess whose look inspired him to exclaim, "No sweeter life I try, / Than in her love to die." If such exaggeration played the game of flattery with a knowing look, it also cast Elizabeth the woman in the powerful roles of patron, lady, and muse—not in the subservient role of a potential wife. Such lyrics, and the many more that would be produced in the coming years, served to consolidate Elizabeth's power even as they expressed both the desire of her male courtiers to win her favor and (often) their mingled joy and anguish at being thus tied to their Virgin Queen.

LADY ELIZABETH TYRWHIT

From Morning and Evening Prayers (1574)[†]

I do commit to Thy mercy Thy servant, our most gracious Queen, and this realm, beseeching Thee to incline her heart to all godliness and virtue that she may long reign over us in peace and tranquility, to live in Thy fear and call upon Thy holy name, and to be ready at all times to set forth Thy blessed laws and commandments; and that Thou, O omnipotent God, with Thy mighty hand and stretched-out arm wilt confound all idolatry and superstition and set up Thy true and holy religion, that Thy faithful servants may triumph and rejoice in Thee with merry hearts, and sing unto Thy praise that this the mighty hand of God hath brought to pass, and to Thy name give the honor and glory to whom all honor and glory is due for ever. Amen.

EDWARD HAKE

From A Commemoration of the Most Prosperous and Peaceable Reign of Our Gracious and Dear Sovereign Lady Elizabeth (1575)[‡]

No fountain there stands free from filth, no crystal spring runs clear.
Instead of streaming floods of life, deep damps of death are there.
And whilst these woes do wander thus, as foreign coasts have tried,
Thine English people, Lord, dwell safe, with them doth peace abide.
5   With them doth live a loving Queen, who like a mother reigns

† Copy text: Lady Elizabeth Trywhit, *Morning and euening prayers, with diuers psalms himnes and meditations* (London, 1574; STC 24477.5); E8r–F1r.
‡ Copy text: Edward Hake, *A commemoration of the most prosperous and peaceable raigne of our gratious and deere soueraigne lady Elizabeth* (London: William How, 1575; STC 12605), A7v–A8v; C1r–C4v.

And like a chosen sacred imp° immortal glory gains.   *offspring*
Her hands she holds not forth to war, her heart doth rest in peace;
She joys to see her people's wealth and wails their harms'
    increase.
Thy Gospel's sound she sends abroad, she stops no
    wholesome spring;
10 But popish puddles dams she up, which noisome
    humors° bring.   *harmful vapors*
A prince of price,° most worthy praise for Thee and in   *great worth*
    Thy name,
Of all that ever scepter bare, of all that ever came
From English loins to royal seat, I say, none worthy more
Amongst the race of English kings that ever scepter bore.
15 I would contain my fervent muse; ah, Gem, thy name denies.[1]
My praise nor all the poets' pens thy merit can suffice.
And highest King, that welkin wieldest,° if hence Thy   *heaven governs*
    glory come,
That of a virgin Queen whom thou hast set in sacred room,°   *position*
Thy people's peace should be sustained, Thy gospel
    should be spread,[2]
20 Why should my burning° muse lie still? why should   *ardent*
    my pen lie dead?
Is hand of flesh her firmest force? is frowning face her sway?
Doth subtle drifts° draw forth her peace, or vaunting   *schemes*
    glory? Nay.
Of flesh the feeblest seer by kind,[3] of face not Juno's fere,°   *equal*
But mild Susanna in her look and Esther in her cheer.°   *demeanor*
25 The work is Thine, 'tis Thine, Jehov;° no jot begun   *Jehovah*
    by man.
Thou fram'dst her only for Thy praise, by Thee her days began.
All only Thou, Jehovah, Thou has wrought her for Thy praise;
All only Thou hast made her deeds a wonder to our days.

[From the concluding prayer]

*A meditation wherein the godly English giveth thanks to God for the
Queen's Majesty's prosperous government hitherto and prayeth for the
continuance thereof to God's glory.*

Now the eighteenth suns most happily environeth in the firmament
sithence, by the means of a poor vessel of the weaker sex and a silly
maiden, Thou (performing the glorious deliverance of Thy people out of
the thraldom and slavery of Pharaoh and Egypt)[4] didst anoint the King's
daughter with an holy oil, setting a crown of pure gold upon her head

---

1. Your worthy name will not allow the muse to keep silent.
2. If God's glory comes down from heaven, it will be in the form of the virgin Queen who brings peace
and spreads the Christian gospel.
3. In body, the weakest overseer by nature (because she is a woman).
4. The author compares Pharaoh to the Pope, Egypt to the Roman Catholic Church, Moses to Elizabeth, and Israel to England (see Exodus 5–15 for the account of the deliverance from Egypt); *environeth*: have circled; Elizabeth was celebrating her eighteenth Accession Day; *sithence*: since; *silly*:
innocent; frail.

and investing her with the purple and scepter and regal diadem of this realm.

*   *   *

Whiles other lands round about have warred to the destruction of one another, our Moses hath guided us in peace. Whiles other nations, like Egypt, round about hath been plagued by the destroyer from the first born, sitting upon the prince's throne, unto the slave grinding at the handmill,[5] our Moses hath not diminished of her flock. Whiles the firm lands have been overwhelmed by the rage of the seas and waters, our island, having dwelt in peace, in peace hath sent her ships into Ophir[6] for gold and prepared her navy against the danger of the enemy. Whiles Athalia hath murdered her own blood, our Joash hath learned the law of the Lord of Jehoiada.[7] Whiles Ahaz consecrateth his own son in the fire and Samaria eateth her own children on the walls, our Eliza directeth the children of the prophets in their offices.[8] Whiles Jezebel setteth up Baal, and embreweth Ahab with the blood of the prophets and of Naboth, our Elijah gathereth the people of God to Mount Carmel to behold the wonder of the fire of God lighting from heaven upon the sacrifices and replenishing the hearts with joy and tongues with gifts of languages.[9] This is then so worthy an instrument of Thy goodness, and express image of Thy majesty, and the ample matter of this day's celebrity.[1]

*   *   *

[Do] thou plentifully pour of thy principal Spirit upon her and ravish her heart with the flame of the love of Thee and Thy house, with Moses to lead and with Joshua to bring into the land of promise; with Deborah to fight Thy battle and with Jael to knock Sisera of Rome in the temples of his usurped headship to his utter destruction; with David to bring home the ark[2] and with Solomon to finish and consecrate to eternity Thy temple amongst Thy people. On the earth for the time to give largely her foster-milk to Jerusalem, in heaven at the time in the pureness of her virginity to be presented to the Lamb and sing the song of her wedding day with Thy angels and Thy saints,[3] to the praise of Thy glorious majesty, the Father, the Son, and the Holy Ghost, in one eternal deity for ever and ever. Amen.

---

5. The tenth plague, which moved the Pharaoh to release the Israelites, caused the death of each first-born child and animal (Exodus 11–12).
6. *Ophir*: in biblical times, a place in southern Arabia from which products of India were shipped to the West.
7. After the death of her son, Queen Athalia murdered her own grandchildren to secure the throne of Judah; the infant Joash was rescued by his uncle, Jehoiada, and later proclaimed king.
8. Elisha the prophet, an enemy of Ahaz, was the director of a "school" of prophets (2 Kings 4.1; 6.1–7). The author puns on Eliza/Elisha. *Samaria . . . walls*: a reference to the siege of Samaria (also known as Israel) by Benhadad, King of Syria (2 Kings 6.25–29).
9. The author elides the story of Elijah and the prophets of Baal on Mt. Carmel with the coming of the Holy Spirit and the gift of tongues at Pentecost (1 Kings 18; Acts 2); *embreweth*: defiles; stains with blood; *Ahab . . . Naboth*: Queen Jezebel, with her husband Ahab, established the worship of the god Baal in Israel, persecuted the prophets of Jehovah, and arranged the death of Naboth, who owned a vineyard coveted by Ahab (1 Kings 16.29–34, 18–21).
1. Solemn celebration.
2. David's triumphant entry into Jerusalem with the ark of the corenant is recorded in 2 Samuel 6; *principal Spirit*: Holy spirit; see especially translations of Psalm 51.11; *ravish*: fill with ecstasy; *Jael . . . Sisera*: here the author casts Elizabeth as the heroic Jael with the Pope in the role of Sisera.
3. An allusion to the virgins of Revelation 14.4; *foster-milk . . . Jerusalem*: Jerusalem often signifies the church; in a common metaphor, monarchs are the nursing mothers of the church, whose true parent is God.

JAMES SANFORD

From Hours of Recreation, or Afterdinners (1576)[†]

To the right Worshipful Master Christopher Hatton, Esquire,
Captain of her Majesty's guard, and one of the gentlemen
of her Highness's Privy Chamber, long life and felicity.

The divine Plato, prince of philosophers (right Worshipful), saith that then commonwealths should flourish when philosophers were rulers or when princes gave themselves to the study of philosophy. A worthy saying no doubt, and in these days here at home verified. For what prince is recorded better to have governed his commonwealth than our most worthy Queen, to the greatest commendation of her sex? What prince of the ancients, if he now lived, could rule a country, amidst these broils of war, in such great quietness?

* * *

And no doubt we ought to think that we have a prince skillful, not only in Plato's philosophy and all good learning, but also in the heavenly philosophy, for the setting forth whereof the Almighty doth every way bless her and maketh her safe from the bitter spite of them that envy at her prosperous reign and quietness, which God defend from foreign disturbers and such as under the color of friendship may come out of other countries to salute her Majesty, bringing with them workers of mischief and sowers of dissension. The Queen of Sheba went very far to see Solomon and hear his wisdom, and very many in these days have come out of far countries to see the Queen of England endued with Solomon's wisdom.[1] For none, almost, is ignorant that her Highness without interpreter understandeth the ambassadors of diverse countries and so wisely answereth them in their own language that her Council (which excelleth in wisdom) could not say more upon long consultation than her Majesty did on the sudden,[2] which declareth her sharpness of wit, learning, and memory.

Let not antiquity boast of her Muses, of her Sybils, of her Pythia nor the Pythagoreans of their women philosophers. Let not the Socratians brag of Diotima nor Aspasia; nor let the monuments of Greece avaunt[3] of their women poets: Sappho, Corinna, Erinna, Praxilla, Telesilla, Cleobulina, and others. We may now easily believe the Romans that the daughters of Laelius and Hortensius, and Cornelia, mother of the Gracchi, were most eloquent matrons, sith England hath such a learned and eloquent Queen, with ladies also of the same sort. We know this doubtless, we know this, that nature hath not condemned that sex of slowness or dullness. England hath had and hath at this day noble gentlewomen famous for their learning, as

---

[†] Copy text: Lodovico Guicciardini, *Houres of recreation, or afterdinners which may aptly be called The garden of pleasure*, trans. James Sanford (London: Henry Binneman, 1576: STC 12465), A3r–A5r; A7r–A8r.

1. In a neat reversal, Sanford compares Elizabeth not with a woman, the Queen of Sheba, but with King Solomon.
2. Extemporaneously.
3. Boast; *Socratians*: those who follow Socrates.

the right honorable my Lady Burghley, my Lady Russell, my Lady Bacon, Mistress Dering,[4] with others.

*   *   *

As it is a glory to England and a praise to her Majesty to rule with mercy, to set forth God's word, and by wisdom to keep her commonwealth in peace, so contrariwise, it is a foul reproach for other princes abroad to be overcome by a queen in all virtues whilst they rule with tyranny, oppressing godliness and disturbing the common quietness. As Christ our Savior did erst take flesh of a virgin for our sakes, so is to be hoped that, as her Highness hath been a mighty pillar of God's church, she shall also wax mightier in power and spirit, to the utter confusion of Antichrist, and be a peerless virgin in these days that shall do greater things.[5] For besides the goodly endowments of her mind, the Almighty hath given her Highness such a majesty that it hath daunted stout warriors, as it did Marquise Vitelli few years past at Windsor, who was sent from the Spanish king in embassage and greatly desired to see her Grace, for that the golden trump of fame had so much blazed her virtues and gifts of mind (which alone of themselves make one blessed and which also needing no outward help can neither be taken away from any, nor abate with time, nor perish with death) all other things being frail, transitory, and for a time, which, because they are guided by fortune and chance, every man (whether he be rich or wise) is so much the more to be accounted of as he despiseth them, her Majesty, endowed with the gifts of the mind, body and fortune, did (as it appeared, and as he confessed) so much appall him that he said he was never so out of countenance[6] before any other prince as he was in the presence of her Highness. He was known to have been an excellent warrior, and yet the countenance and words of a queen put him almost out of conceit.[7]

*   *   *

Postellus[8] a Frenchman known of many for his learning as well in languages as otherwise, hath written a book (erroneously through some melancholy humor) that as Christ died for mankind, so also that a woman must die for womankind. Belike he dreamed so and so wrote. Aristotle saith, "*Melancholici maximeque vera somni,*" *ut,* melancholy persons have the truest dreams,[9] but they are to be divided (according to such as write of this argu-

---

4. Anne Vaughan Lock (See Part Two), wife of Edward Dering (see Part Three) and mother of Henry Lock (see Part Eight). *Lady Burghley*: Mildred Cooke Cecil, eldest daughter of Ann Fitzwilliams and Sir Anthony Cooke and wife of William Cecil, Lord Burghley. *Lady Russell*: Elizabeth Cooke Hoby Russell, the third Cooke sister and wife successively of Sir Thomas Hoby, translator of *The Courtier*, and John, Lord Russell, heir of the second Earl of Bedford. *Lady Bacon*: Anne Cooke Bacon, the second Cooke sister, wife of Sir Nicholas Bacon, Lord Keeper of the Great Seal, and mother of Sir Francis Bacon.

5. Sanford conflates the images of Elizabeth as both virgin and incarnate savior; *erst*: formerly; *Antichrist*: that is, the Pope.

6. Disconcerted; *Marquise Vitelli*: Chiappino Vitelli, an Italian adventurer and supporter of Mary Stuart; *in embassage*: on a diplomatic mission; *every man . . . despiseth them*: men are more worthy when they despise transitory riches; *appall*: frighten.

7. Presence of mind.

8. The French mystic Guillaume Postel.

9. In *On Divination in Sleep*, Aristotle argued that melancholics are more sensitive to movements in nature, such as those that cause dreams, and hence are more likely to see future events in their dreams (464a30; see *The Complete Works of Aristotle*. The Revised Oxford Translation, ed. Jonathan Barnes [Princeton: Princeton UP, 1984], 1:738–39); *ut*: that is (Latin).

ment) into dreams figurative and dreams showing things to fall out according as they are dreamed or else into mixed dreams. If this be a dream, it must needs be figurative and to be unfolded after their precepts in this sort: death signifieth a quiet life, for they that are dead be at rest. That a woman should die for women signifieth that some rare and godly woman should live and reign in great quietness and preserve a great multitude, as Christ saved all by His death and passion, and to triumph over her enemies as Christ did over death. If this interpretation may agree to any woman alive, our most excellent Queen is she; for doth not her Highness reign in great quietness? Doth she not save many thousands of men, women, and children, fleeing hither for succor?[1] Doth not she triumph over her privy[2] enemies, that envy her quiet state? Hath not she triumphed also over her open enemies? Behold how from error to truth, how from a fable to the verity,[3] I am come.

Some may perchance marvel (right Worshipful) why I continue thus far her Majesty's praises, to whom it may be answered that I am sure your Worship, with others, take pleasure to hear the praises of none so much as of her Majesty, and I delight to write of none so much as of her Grace, who is the best knot in this garden that holdeth Englishmen together, who is the sweetest flower in this garden. God grant that we may long enjoy her with pleasure, not fading as a flower but lasting as a precious jewel or diamond that uneath[4] yieldeth to age. It may be said I flatter. I answer: is it flattery to speak the truth, to confess and put in writing the virtues of a most noble Princess, and to say that the sun giveth light to the world? To flatter is to feign that to be in one which is not, to make one believe that to be in a man which he hath not. Let greater wits enterprise to write of this great matter. As the field of her Highness's praises is very large, so is there a cunning workman required, whose skillful eloquence may better blaze so rare virtues. This finally I hope in God, that as to represent and figure Himself to the world He hath chosen, among stars, the sun; among people, lineages, tongues and nations, the believers; among seeds, the wheat and the bread made thereof; among trees and plants, the vine and his fruit; among flowers, the lily; among birds, the simple dove; among tame beasts, the lamb and sheep; and among the wild, the lion; that He will preserve you from all dangers and grant your Worship long and prosperously to guard that Prince whom the three golden lions passant with the three lilies do represent.[5]

Your worship's most humbly to command,
JAMES SANFORD.

---

1. From religious persecution on the Continent.
2. Secret or hidden.
3. Truth.
4. With difficulty.
5. A reference to the symbols on Elizabeth's coat of arms. The lions symbolize England and the lilies France, where English claims to the throne went back to Henry II; *your Worship*: Christopher Hatton.

NICHOLAS HILLIARD

From A Treatise Concerning the Art of Limning
(ca. 1570s)[†]

This makes me to remember the words also and reasoning of her Majesty when first I came in her Highness's presence to draw, who after showing me how she noted great difference of shadowing in the works and diversity of drawers of sundry nations, and that the Italians, [who] had the name to be cunningest and to draw best, shadowed not, required[1] of me the reason of it, seeing that best to show oneself needeth no shadow of place but rather the open light. To which I granted, [and] affirmed that shadows in pictures were indeed caused by the shadow of the place or coming in of the light as only one way into the place at some small or high window, which many workmen covet to work in for ease to their sight, and to give unto them a grosser line and a more apparent line to be discerned, and maketh the work emboss well, and show very well afar off, which to limning work[2] needeth not, because it is to be viewed of necessity in hand near unto the eye. Here her Majesty conceived the reason and therefore chose her place to sit in for that purpose in the open alley[3] of a goodly garden, where no tree was near nor any shadow at all, save that, as the heaven is lighter than the earth, so must that little shadow that was from the earth. This her Majesty's curious demand hath greatly bettered my judgment, besides diverse other like questions in art by her most excellent Majesty, which to speak or write of were fitter for some better clerk.[4]

EDWARD DE VERE, EARL OF OXFORD

What Cunning Can Express (ca. 1576)[‡]

What cunning can express
The favor° of her face   comeliness, kindness
To whom in this distress
I do appeal for grace?
5   A thousand Cupids fly
About her gentle eye.

From which each throws a dart
That kindleth soft sweet fire
Within my sighing heart,
10   Posséssed by desire.

---

† Copy text: *The First Annual Volume of the Walpole Society, 1911–1912* (Oxford: Walpole Society, 1912), 28–29. This treatise was not published during Elizabeth's reign, and the title was given to the manuscript by George Vertue, its eighteenth-century owner. *Limning*: painting.
1. Copy text: requiring.
2. Here not just painting, but the painting of miniatures; *emboss*: stand out in relief; copy text: imborse.
3. An avenue bordered by trees or bushes; *conceived*: understood.
4. Scholar; *curious*: attentive.
‡ Copy text: *The phoenix nest* (London: Iohn Iackson, 1593; STC 21516), I3v-I4r.

No sweeter life I try
Than in her love to die.

The lily in the field
That glories in his white
15 For pureness now must yield
And render up his right.
    Heav'n pictured in her face
    Doth promise joy and grace.

Fair Cynthia's silver light
20 That beats on running streams
Compares not with her white,
Whose hairs are all sunbeams.
    Her virtues so do shine,
    As day unto my eyne.°   *eyes*

25 With this there is a red
Exceeds the damask rose,[1]
Which in her cheeks is spread,
Whence every favor grows.
    In sky there is no star
30   That she surmounts not far.

When Phoebus from the bed
Of Thetis doth arise,
The morning blushing red
In fair carnation wise,
35   He shows it in her face
    As queen of every grace.

This pleasant lily white,
This tint of roseate red,
This Cynthia's silver light,
40 This sweet fair *dea*° spread,   *goddess*
    These sunbeams in mine eye,
    These beauties make me die.

---

1. Pink rose, symbolic of the Tudor monarchs, who ended the Wars of Roses by uniting the houses of Lancaster (the red rose) and York (the white).

Part Five: The French Marriage Negotiations (1578–1582)

HISTORICAL BACKGROUND

The relative peace that England enjoyed following the Northern Rebellion of 1569 was fragile. By 1578, it had grown precarious. Throughout the reign, Elizabeth had sought to consolidate her authority in Ireland, but rebellion continued to simmer there, breaking out every decade or two into open conflict. When a new round of violence began in 1579, the English strategy was simple: put down the rebels by force of arms and famine, then colonize the area with reliable "New English" settlers—a term used to distinguished them from the "Old English," who had moved into Ireland in the Middle Ages and had local ties that divided their loyalties.

The violence that engulfed much of the southwestern province of Munster in 1579 was led by Gerald Fitzgerald, fifteenth Earl of Desmond. Because he had managed to persuade the Pope and the King of Spain to send a garrison of soldiers to support him, he posed an especially difficult problem for Elizabeth. English forces under Lord Grey de Wilton were dispatched to the town of Smerwick to repulse the foreign invaders, who were holed up in a local fort. Their situation soon became desperate, however, and they agreed to surrender on the assumption that the English would be merciful. They paid a terrible price for their mistake, for though high-ranking officers were held for ransom, 600 common soldiers were put to the sword. Then crops throughout the province were set on fire, causing the starvation of some 30,000 native Irish. With the rebellion broken, Lord Grey opened a large area known as the Munster Plantation to English settlers. Among them were Sir Walter Ralegh and Edmund Spenser. Such tactics only served, however, to harden hostility among the Irish, and by the late 1590s, rebels were again up in arms in Munster, burning many settlers, including Spenser and his family, out of their homes.

At the time of the Desmond Rebellion, trouble was also brewing in Europe. In the latter half of the 1570s, Elizabeth's anxiety over the growing power and hostility of Catholic Spain led to a major reversal of policy. Against the inclinations of Robert Dudley, the Earl of Leicester, and other forward Protestants on her Council, she undertook to ally England with its long-time enemy France by reopening negotiations to marry Francis, Duke of Anjou, the younger brother of King Henry III. Since he was older now than he had been when his mother, Catherine de Medici, had first proposed him as a potential match back in 1572, he was more acceptable to Elizabeth, and since Philip was such a threat, the young prince's desire to practice his Catholicism openly after he was married was set aside as a matter for later negotiation. As early as May 1578, discussions were underway in Paris and signs that an agreement would be reached were favorable. During that summer, the Queen feasted and entertained a delegation of French ambassadors, and the following winter, after Anjou had tried unsuccessfully to gain a foothold in the Netherlands by fighting on the side of

Protestant rebels against the Spanish government, he sent a personal representative to press the negotiations with Elizabeth to a successful conclusion.

That representative, Jean de Simier, Baron de St. Marc, was a man of extraordinary charm and diplomatic adroitness. He pleased the Queen, and she set out to please him by giving feasts and entertainments in his honor and spending hours in his company. Through gifts and letters to his master, she was soon showing every sign of being in love. The question was whether she was in love with the thought of marriage or with Anjou himself. In response to her requirement that he come to woo her in person, the Duke traveled to England in August of 1579, spending ten days in constant company with her. Delighted, she turned in the fall to the serious business of persuading her Council and her people to accept him as her husband.

Neither was won over. Some on the Council, led by William Cecil, Lord Burghley, felt that a marriage would cause Anjou's brother Henry III to ally France with England and so hold Spain at bay, force its king, Philip II, to be more tolerant of Protestantism in the Netherlands, and end the scheming of English Catholics to put Mary Stuart on the throne. Others, however, were opposed, fearing Anjou's Catholicism, distrusting French intentions, and worrying that, if an heir were born of the match, England might one day become a subject state to its ancient enemy. Within the Court and beyond it in London and the countryside, poets, preachers, pamphleteers, and rumor mongers raised a furor of opposition such as Elizabeth had never experienced. When her divided Council could not come to a recommendation, she burst into tears and bitterly reproached them. A week later, they submitted, pledging to support the match if she still wished it, but she knew that their support was tepid. In the face of opposition inside and outside her government, the Queen retreated. Though she allowed negotiations to drag on for some time rather than lose the diplomatic gains that they had given her against Spain, serious thought of marrying Anjou seems to have ended by December 1579.

During the decade that followed, the confrontation with Philip II that she had feared when she began the marriage negotiations gradually worsened. His forces first consolidated their control of the southern provinces of the Netherlands. When the King of Portugal died, Philip claimed the crown for himself and added yet another powerful state to those he already ruled. Spanish and papal forces invaded Ireland for a second time in support of the rebels. From 1580 on, England would be forced to defend itself at greater and greater cost, first by backing Anjou's brief and ineffectual rule as elected Governor of the Protestant states in the Low Countries, then by direct deployment of English forces there, and finally, in 1588, by taking on the mighty navy of Spain in a concerted frontal assault aimed at overthrowing the English government.

THE QUEEN, THE FRENCH AMBASSADORS, AND THE VISIT TO NORWICH

In the summer of 1578, early in the Queen's negotiations to marry the Duke of Anjou, she entertained a delegation of French emissaries, bringing them along on summer progress as her vast train lumbered through the countryside of East Anglia. The most important stop along the way was Norwich, the second-most populous city in England and home of one of the most fervently anti-Catholic populations outside of London. Lying just across the North Sea from the Low Countries, Norwich had become a haven for Dutch Protestants who had fled their homes during the ongoing revolt against Spain that had been raging there since the 1560s. Many citizens of the town were not well disposed to Elizabeth's scheme to marry a Catholic prince, even one such as Anjou who had recently taken the side of the Dutch rebels.

News of the French ambassadors and their purpose seems to have reached Norwich well before the royal party did. In one of the two partial records of the festivities published after the event—the one that appeared under the title *The Joyful Receiving of the Queen's Most Excellent Majesty into Her Highness's City of Norwich*—the French negotiators are mentioned among the onlookers. One can readily imagine the tightrope that the writers and speakers charged with entertaining the Queen were forced to walk. If they openly opposed the match, they risked alienating their royal guest. If they maintained a discreet silence on the subject, they risked offending local Protestants on an issue of great concern to them. The result was something of a muddle, in which anti-Catholic rhetoric was woven cautiously and uneasily into statements of loyal support for the Queen in whatever decision she might choose to make.

In his welcoming speech, for example, the Mayor emphasized the city's Protestant leanings, calling it "most studious of God's glory and true religion." He also, however, offered his backing for any course that was conducive to her Majesty's "health, honor, and pleasure." The mythical figure Gurgunt, said to be one of the early kings of England and the founder of the city, then appeared to remind the Queen of her country's legendary conquest over ancient imperial Rome, likening that victory to Henry VIII's break with modern papal Rome. In good Protestant fashion, Gurgant identified the papacy with the "purple whore" of Babylon in the Book of Revelation. The First Welcoming Pageant then presented the six "causes of this commonwealth," beginning with one that had distinctly anti-Catholic overtones: "God truly preached." In the Second Welcoming Pageant, Bernard Garter, one of the chief writers, made a point that must have been even less welcome to the French ambassadors, calling up figures from the Bible and early English legend to stress Elizabeth's sacred duty to stand up to her enemies abroad. Though he did not specify who those might be, he clearly had the French in mind, for his reference to a struggle that had lasted "twenty winters long" can only refer to the series of military campaigns against France that occupied England between 1558 and 1578. The minister of the Dutch Congregation spoke next, drawing attention to the sufferings of local refugees from Catholic aggression.

The drift so far was against the marriage. In subsequent parts of the entertainments, however, the authors softened their tone. In William Goldingham's Masque of the Gods, for example, Cupid gave the Queen a golden arrow, saying "Shoot but this shaft at king or Caesar he, / And he is thine." The poet might just as well have said a French Duke. Yet even here, the emphasis of the Masque was on the Queen's virginity and her goddess-like immunity to desire. If the Protestants of Norwich hoped for signs that the Queen was willing to heed their concerns and not marry Anjou, they never got them, but neither did the Queen receive much support in her new policy toward the French.

She may not have wanted any. Always a wily negotiator, she knew that to satisfy her own political base among Protestants she needed to persuade Anjou to give up the requirement that he be allowed to practice his Catholic faith openly once they were married. That she decided to take the French ambassadors to Norwich in the first place suggests that she wanted them to experience Protestant opposition at first hand. If anything, her trip was designed to stir up religious tensions. Behind the scenes, agents of the government were scouring the countryside for nonconforming Catholics (known as recusants) who refused to obey laws requiring regular attendance at services in the Church of England. The weekend before the Queen arrived in Norwich, she stayed in the house of a young Catholic of this sort named Edward Rookwood, and while she was there, he was suddenly seized and taken away to jail. A subsequent search of his barn turned up a statue of the Virgin Mary, which the Queen ordered burned in her presence, with people from the surrounding countryside looking on. That summer, her Council also welcomed militant Protestants from the surrounding region to attend royal functions and authorized them to preach again after years of officially silencing them. One wonders what the French made of this show of Protestant unity and anti-Catholic zeal. It certainly made Anjou's demand that he be allowed open practice of his religion seem unrealistic.

The incident with Rookwood may also reveal something about the Queen's tactics in dealing with her own Catholic subjects. That she chose to stay with Rookwood in the first place is surprising, since he was not of the rank normally involved in royal visits and his house was not adequate for her entourage. A letter to the Earl of Shrewsbury by Richard Topcliffe, a government agent assigned to hunt down subversive Catholics, describes the visit in detail, making clear how little Elizabeth liked her accommodations or her host. When they first met, she greeted him amiably. Shortly afterward, however, Thomas Radcliffe, Earl of Sussex, who managed her private chambers, called for Rookwood and had him arrested on grounds that one "excommunicated for papistry" ought never have "durst presume" to come into the Queen's presence. Was the Queen involved in a deliberate effort to entrap Rookwood and make an example of him? Or were Sussex and others on the Council working on their own, using the progress to round up Catholics? The evidence is not entirely clear.

Whatever her involvement, Topcliffe's letter does make clear that simmering religious tensions lay behind much that took place that summer. Whether in responding to offers of marriage or in dealing with Catholic opposition along the Channel Coast, the Queen was forced to consider the danger that Philip of Spain would one day invade England, rouse local Catholics to his side, and overthrow the government. A decade later, he would attempt to do just that.

BERNARD GARTER AND WILLIAM GOLDINGHAM

The Joyful Receiving of the Queen's Most Excellent Majesty into Her Highness's City of Norwich (August 16–22, 1578)[†]

The Epistle Dedicatory

To the right worshipful Sir Owen Hopton, Knight, the Queen's Majesty's Lieutenant of her Highness's Tower of London, Ber[nard] Gar[ter], citizen of London, wisheth health and increase of worship.

Sithens[1] at my return from Norwich, Right Worshipful, you vouchsafed to impart unto me your earnest desire to understand the order and manner how her Majesty was received into that worthy city, I am bold likewise to decipher unto your Worship what occasions offered themselves to me upon the same your request. First appeared to me the majesty of my prince,[2] which beautifieth her kingdom as the bright shining beams of beautiful Phoebus decketh forth the earth, which gladded the hearts of the people there as they no less labored to travel forth to view the excellency of their

---

[†] Copy text: *The ioyfull receyuing of the Queenes most excellent Maiestie into hir Highnesse citie of Norvvich* (London: Henrie Bynneman, 1578; STC 11627).
1. Since.
2. Elizabeth preferred the title "Prince" to "Princess."

sovereign than the true laboring bee enforceth herself in the springtime (when Dame Flora first decketh the soil) to seek their delights, and our profit, amongst the sweet-smelling flowers. Then the abundant clemency of her Highness, receiving the loyal hearts of her loving people in part[3] as good as their meaning deserved, so enflamed their former desires, as every spark kindled a bonfire. The nobility, delighting [in] this harmony, so endeavored to hold in tune every string of this heavenly music as there seemed but one heart in Queen, Council, and commonalty.[4] The Mayor, magistrates, and good citizens employed their study and substance to hold on[5] this happy beginning; the Prince had her pleasure, the nobility their desire, the whole train such entertainment as, for the time of her continuance there, Norwich seemed (if any such there be) a terrestrial paradise. But when the frowning Friday followed which called her Majesty thence, I leave (because I am loth to tell) the dolor that was to the report of them that did see it. These all, Right Worshipful, upon your demand, presented themselves unto me to be uttered, and these (I think) are the things which you desired to hear. And because I doubt not but that there are a great number of your virtuous mind herein, to satisfy both them and you, I have here set forth what my small capacity could collect (touching the premises[6]) during the whole time of her abode there. Accept my rude and rash dealing in this my doing, I beseech you, for that your worshipful request carrieth me to my uttermost limit, wherein though the sudden chop of an unskillful carpenter perhaps disquareth the strong timber of this beautiful frame, yet let the skillful eye of your Worship and other learned readers (to whom I submit me) place the same to the best purpose, and hold my good will as recompense of my fault and bind me to them and you forever. *Vale.*[7]

Your Worship's to command, B. G.

The Receiving of the Queen's Majesty into Her Highness's City of Norwich

On Saturday, being the 16th of August 1578, and in the twentieth year of the reign of our most gracious sovereign, Lady Elizabeth, by the grace of God Queen of England, France, and Ireland, Defender of the Faith, etc., the same our most dread and sovereign lady (continuing her progress in Norfolk) immediately after dinner set forward from Bracon Ash, where she had dined with the Lady Stile,[8] being five miles distant from Norwich towards the same her most dutiful city. Sir Robert Wood, then Esquire and now Knight, Mayor of the same city, at one of the clock the same happy day, set forward to meet with her Majesty in this order: first there rode before him, well and seemly mounted, three score of the most comely young men of the city as bachelors, appareled all in black satin doublets, black hose, black taffeta hats, and yellow bands, and their universal livery was a mandilion[9]

---

3. In response.
4. Common people; *Council*: the Privy Council.
5. Carry on; *study*: minds.
6. Things mentioned before.
7. Farewell; *disquareth*: puts out of square.
8. Elizabeth, Lady Stile, the Catholic wife of Thomas Townsend.
9. Long coat or cassock; *Esquire*: member of the English gentry, in rank just below a knight; *bachelors*: junior members of trade guilds appointed to carry out such ceremonial functions; *doublets*: men's close-fitting upper body garments; *livery*: uniform.

of purple taffeta laid about with silver lace, and so appareled, marched forwards two and two in a rank.

Then one which represented King Gurgunt, sometime King of England, which builded the Castle of Norwich, called *Blanch Floure,* and laid the foundation of the city. He was mounted upon a brave courser and was thus furnished: his body armed, his bases[1] of green and white silk; on his head a black velvet hat with a plume of white feathers. There attended upon him three henchmen in white and green; one of them did bear his helmet, the second his target,[2] the third his staff. After him a noble company of gentlemen and wealthy citizens in velvet coats and other costly furniture,[3] bravely mounted. Then followed the officers of the city, every one in his place. Then Master Sword-bearer with the sword and hat of maintenance.[4] Then Master Mayor and four and twenty aldermen and Master Recorder, all in scarlet gowns, whereof so many as had been mayors of the city and were justices did wear their scarlet cloaks. Then followed so many as had been sheriffs and were no aldermen in violet gowns and satin tippets.[5] Then followed divers other to keep the people from disturbing the array aforesaid.

Thus everything in due and comely order, they all (except Gurgunt, which stayed her Majesty's coming within a flight-shot[6] or two of the city, where the Castle of *Blanch Floure* was in most beautiful prospect) marched forwards to a bridge, called Hartford Bridge, the uttermost limit that way, distant from the city two miles or thereabouts, to meet with her Majesty, who within one hour or little more after their attendance came in such gracious and princely wise as ravished the hearts of all her loving subjects and might have terrified the stoutest heart of any enemy to behold. Whether the majesty of the prince, which is incomparable, or joy of her subjects, which exceeded measure, were the greater I think would have appalled[7] the judgment of Apollo to define. The acclamations and cries of the people to the almighty God for the preservation of her Majesty rattled so loud as hardly for a great time could anything be heard. But at last, as everything hath an end, the noise appeased; and Master Mayor saluted her Highness with the oration following and yielded to her Majesty therewith the sword of the city and a fair standing cup of silver and gilt, with a cover, and in the cup one hundred pounds in gold.[8]

* * *

The Mayor's Oration Englished

If our wish should be granted unto us by the Almighty what human thing we would chiefly desire, we would account nothing more precious, most royal Prince, than that the bright beam of your most chaste eye, which doth so cheer us, might penetrate the secret strait[9] corners of our hearts. Then surely should you see how great joys are dispersed there and how the spirit

---

1. Knee-length skirts.
2. Light, round shield.
3. Apparel.
4. Symbols of high office.
5. Capes or short cloaks.
6. Distance carried by an arrow shot from a bow; *stayed*: waited for.
7. Baffled.
8. Latin version omitted.
9. Concealed; *human*: ordinary or secular, as opposed to divine or supernatural.

and lively blood tickle in our arteries and small veins in beholding thee, the light of this realm (as David was of Israel[1]), now at length, after long hope and earnest petitions, to appear in these coasts. Truly on mine own part, which by your Highness's authority and clemency (with humble thanks be it spoken) do govern this famous city, and on the part of these my brethren and all these people, which by your authority we rule (speaking as they mean and as I myself do think), this only with all our hearts and humble prayers we desire: that we may so find your Majesty gracious and favorable unto us, as you for your part never came to any subjects better welcome than to us your poor subjects here. For most manifest token whereof, we present unto your Majesty here these signs of honor and office,[2] which we received of the most mighty prince Henry IV in the fifth year of his reign, then to us granted in the name of mayor, aldermen, and sheriffs, whereas before time out of mind or mention, we were governed by bailiffs (as they term them), which ever since have been both established and increased with continual privileges of kings and which, by your only clemency (which with immortal thanks we shall never cease to declare), we have now these twenty years enjoyed. And together with those signs, this treasure is a pledge of our good wills and ability, which all, how great or little soever they be, we pour down at your pleasure, that if we have neglected anything in all this course of your most happy reign which becometh most loving, obedient, and well-willing subjects to perform for the preservation of your crown and advancement of your Highness, you may then determine of[3] us and all ours at your most gracious pleasure. But if we have (God being our guide) so ordered the governance of this city that we have kept the same in safety to your Majesty's use and made the people therein (as much as in us lieth) first most studious of God's glory and true religion and next of your Majesty's health, honor, and pleasure, then ask we nothing of you, for that the singular clemency engrafted in your Highness will easily of itself grant that which is requisite for us to obtain. We only therefore desire that God would abundantly bless your Highness with all good gifts of mind and body.

Which oration ended, her Majesty, accepting in good part everything delivered by the Mayor, did thankfully answer him in these words, or very like in effect: "We heartily thank you, Master Mayor and all the rest, for these tokens of goodwill. Nevertheless, princes have no need of money. God hath endowed us abundantly. We come not therefore[4] but for that which in right is our own, the hearts and true allegiance of our subjects, which are the greatest riches of a kingdom; whereof as we assure ourselves in you, so do you assure yourselves in us of a loving and gracious sovereign." Wherewith was delivered to Master Mayor a mace or scepter, which he carried before her to her lodging, which was in the Bishop of Norwich's palace two miles distant from that place. The cup and money was delivered to a gentleman, one of her Majesty's footmen, to carry. The Mayor said to her, "*Sunt hic centum librae puri auri.*"[5] The cover of the cup lifted up, her Majesty said to the footman, "Look to it,

---

1. See 2 Samuel 21.17; *tickle*: thrills, tingles.
2. The sword and hat of maintenance mentioned above.
3. Pass judgment on.
4. For money.
5. "Here are a hundred pounds worth of pure gold."

there is a hundred pound." With that her Highness, with the whole company, marched towards Norwich till they came to a place called the Town Close, distant from the city a good flight-shot, where the party which represented Gurgunt came forth, as in manner is expressed, and was ready to have declared to her Majesty this speech following, but by reason of a shower of rain which came, her Majesty hasted away, the speech not uttered. But thus it was:

Leave off to muse, most gracious Prince of English soil,
What sudden wight° in martial wise approacheth near. *unexpected person*
King Gurgunt I am hight,° King Belin's eldest son, *called*
Whose sire Dunwallo first the British crown did wear,
5 Whom⁶ truthless Gutlack forced to pass the surging seas,
His falsehood to revenge and Denmark land to spoil.
And finding, in return, this place a gallant vent,⁷
This castle fair I built, a fort from foreign soil.
To win a conquest gets renown and glorious name;
10 To keep and use it well deserves eternal fame.
When bruit° through cities, towns, the woods, and dales *rumor*
  did sound
Elizabeth this country, peerless Queen, drew near,⁸
I was found out.⁹ Myself in person, noble Queen,
Did haste before thy face in presence to appear.
15 Two thousand years well nigh in silence lurking still,
Hear why to thee alone this service I do yield.
Besides that, at my city's suit, their founder first
Should gratulate° most this joyful sight in open field, *welcome*
Four special points and rare concurring in us both
20 This special service have reserved to thee alone,
The glory though¹ of each in thee doth far surmount,
Yet great with small compared will like appear anon.²
When doubtful wars the British princes long had wrung,
My grandsire,³ first uniting all, did wear the crown.
25 Of York and Lancaster who did conclude the broils?⁴
Thy grandsire Henry Seventh, a king of great renown.
Mine uncle Brennus eke,° my father⁵ joining hands, *also*
Old Rome did raze and sack, and half consume with fire.
Thy puissant father so new Rome, that purple whore,⁶
30 Did sack and spoil her near of all her glittering tire.° *attire*
Lo, Cambridge schools by mine assignment founded first,
By thee my Cambridge schools⁷ are famous through the
  world.

6. That is, Gurgunt.
7. Outlet to the sea.
8. That Elizabeth drew near this area, peerless Queen.
9. Called for.
1. Though the glory.
2. Will shortly appear similar.
3. Dunwallo.
4. Conflicts. The Wars of the Roses pitted the House of Lancaster against that of York.
5. Belin; *Brennus*: see Brennius in the Glossary.
6. The Whore of Babylon; *puissant father*: Elizabeth's father, Henry VIII, ended papal control by declaring himself Supreme Head of the English Church and confiscating church property; *new Rome*: the Roman Catholic Church.
7. Cambridge University, sixty miles west of Norwich.

I thirty wandering ships of banished men[8] relieved;
The throngs of banished souls that in this city dwell,
35 Do weep for joy and pray for thee with tears untold.
In all these things thou, noble Queen, dost far excel.
But lo, to thee I yield as duty doth me bind
In open field myself, my city, castle, key.
Most happy fathers, kings, in such a daughter queen;
40 Most happy England were, if thou shouldst never die.
Go on, most noble prince, for I must haste away.
My city gates do long their sovereign to receive.
More true thou never couldst, nor loyal, subjects find,
Whose hearts full fast with perfect love to thee do cleave.

Then her Majesty drew near the gates of the city called St. Stephen's Gates, which with the walls there were both gallantly and strongly repaired. The gate itself was thus enriched and beautified. First, the portcullis[9] was new made both timber and iron. Then, the outward side of the gate was thus beautified: the Queen's arms[1] were most richly and beautifully set forth in the chief front of the gate. On the one side thereof, but somewhat lower, was placed the scutcheon of St. George, or St. George's cross; on the other side, the arms of the city; and directly under the Queen's Majesty's arms was placed the falcon, her Highness's badge[2] in due form, and under the same were written these words: "God and the Queen we serve." The inner side of the gate was thus beautified: on the right side was gorgeously set forth the red rose signifying the House of York, on the left side[3] the white rose representing the House of Lancaster. In the midst was the white and red rose united, expressing the union, under the which was placed by descent the arms of the Queen, and under that were written these two verses:

> Division kindled strife,
>   Blest union quenched the flame;
> Thence sprang our noble Phoenix dear,[4]
>   The peerless prince[5] of fame.

And besides that, at this gate, the waits[6] of the city were placed with loud music, who cheerfully and melodiously welcomed her Majesty into the city. And then passed she forward through St. Stephen's Street, where the first pageant was placed, in form following.

The first pageant was in St. Stephen's Parish, in this manner:

It was builded somewhat like the manner of a stage, of forty foot long and in breadth eight foot. From the standing place upward was a bank framed

---

8. Protestant refugees from the Netherlands.
9. Gate.
1. Coat of arms, the heraldic symbols of a royal or noble person or family, which were painted on a shield surmounted by a crest (a scroll or crown bearing a motto).
2. Personal emblem. Elizabeth's was a falcon with a crown and scepter; *the scutcheon of St. George*: shield of the patron saint of England, which bore a red cross on a silver or white background.
3. Copy text: the left the side. The writer also has the roses wrong; white stood for York, red for Lancaster.
4. Elizabeth, in danger of execution during the reign of Mary Tudor, later took the phoenix as a favorite emblem.
5. Supreme embodiment.
6. Players of wind instruments, maintained by the city.

in the manner of a free-stone wall, in very decent and beautiful sort; and in the height thereof were written these sentences, *viz.*[7]

The causes of this commonwealth are,

God truly preached.

Justice duly executed.   The people obedient.

Idleness expelled.   Labor cherished.

Universal concord preserved.

From the standing place downward, it was beautified with painters' work artificially expressing to sight the portraiture of these several looms, and the weavers in them (as it were working) and over every loom the name thereof, *viz.* over the first loom was written, "The weaving of worsted"; over the second, "The weaving of russels"; over the third, "The weaving of darnir"; over the fourth, "The weaving of tuft mockado"; the fifth, "The weaving of lace"; the sixth, "The weaving of taff[et]a"; the seventh, "The weaving of fringe."[8] And then was there the portraiture of a matron and two or three children, and over her head was written these words: "Good nurture changeth qualities."[9] Upon the stage there stood knitting at the one end eight small women children spinning worsted[1] yarn and at the other end as many knitting of worsted yarn hose, and in the midst of the said stage stood a pretty boy richly appareled, which represented the commonwealth of the city. And all the rest of the stage was furnished with men, which made the said several works, and before every man the work indeed; and everything thus in readiness, stayed[2] her Majesty's coming. And when she did come, the child which represented commonwealth did speak to her Highness these words, *viz.*

Most gracious prince, undoubted sovereign Queen,
Our only joy next God and chief defense,
In this small show our whole estate is seen.
The wealth we have we find proceed from thence.
5 The idle hand hath here no place to feed;
The painful wight° hath still to serve his need.   *hard-working person*

Again our seat denies our traffic here;[3]
The sea too near decides us from the rest.[4]
So weak we were within this dozen year
10 As care did quench the courage of the best,
But good advice hath taught these little hands
To rend in twain the force of pining bands.[5]

---

7. That is to say; *free-stone wall*: one in which the stones are fitted together without mortar.
8. Sale of these fabrics was important to the city's economy.
9. Good rearing improves character.
1. Tightly twisted.
2. Awaited; *works*: products.
3. Our location again prevents our trading. In 1568–72 and again in the late 1570s, Norwich suffered disruptions in its lucrative trade with the Netherlands because of tensions with Spain and the Dutch Protestant rebellion.
4. The Channel cuts us off from the rest of the cloth traders (in the Low Countries).
5. To tear in two the bonds that caused us pain.

From combéd wool we draw this slender thread;[6]
From thence the looms have dealing with the same,
15   And thence again in order do proceed
These several works, which skillful art doth frame,
And all to drive Dame Need into her cave
Our heads and hands together labored have.

We bought before the things that now we sell;
20   These slender imps[7] their works do pass° the waves.   *send over*
God's peace and thine we hold and prosper well;
Of every mouth the hands the charges saves.[8]
Thus through thy help and aid of power divine
Doth Norwich live, whose hearts and goods are thine.
Finis. B. G.

This show pleased her Majesty so greatly as[9] she particularly viewed the knitting and spinning of the children, perused the looms, and noted the several works and commodities which were made by these means, and then, after great thanks by her given to the people, marched towards the marketplace, where was made a second device as followeth.

The Second Pageant

The second pageant thwarted the street at the entrance of the market between Master Skinner and Master Quashe, being in breadth two and fifty foot of assize, and was divided into three gates, *viz.* in the midst a main gate and on either side a postern:[1] the main gate in breadth fourteen foot, each postern eight foot, their heights equal to their proportion. Over each postern was as it were a chamber, which chambers were replenished with music.[2] And over all the gates passed a stage of eight foot broad made in the manner of a pageant both curious,[3] rich, and delightful. The whole work, from the pageant downward, seemed to be jasper and marble. In the forefront, towards her Majesty, was the arms of England on the one side[4] the gate, and on the other side the falcon with crown and scepter, which is her own badge. The other side was beautified with the arms of England on the one side the gate and with the crest[5] of England on the other side. The stage or pageant was replenished with[6] five personages appareled like women. The first was the city of Norwich, the second Deborah, the third Judith, the fourth Esther, the fifth Marcia, sometime[7] Queen of England. At the first sight of the Prince, and till her Majesty's coming to the pageant, the musicians which were close in the chambers of the said pageant used their loud music and then ceased,

6. According to a marginal note, the child here points to spinners, weavers, and their products.
7. Children in the pageant, with a pun meaning yarn added to the ends of skeins.
8. The hands at work here save the public the expense of feeding the Dutch refugees.
9. That.
1. Smaller gate; *thwarted*: crossed; *assize*: in size.
2. Provided with musicians.
3. Ingenious; *pageant*: temporary stage.
4. Side of.
5. See p. 245, note 1 on the royal coat of arms.
6. Occupied by.
7. At one time.

wherewith her Highness stayed,[8] to whom the personage representing the
city of Norwich did speak in these words, *viz.*

Whom Fame resounds with thundering trump, which rends the
    rattling skies,
And pierceth to the haughty heavens, and thence descending flies
Through flickering air, and so conjoins the sea and shore together
In admiration of thy grace, good Queen, th' art welcome hither,
5 More welcome than Terpsicore was to the town of Troy.[9]
Sea-faring men by Gemini conceive not half my joy.
Strong Hercules to Theseus was never such delight,
Nor Nisus to Eurialus as I have in this sight.
Penelope did never thirst Ulysses more to see
10 Than I, poor Norwich, hungered have to gain the sight of thee.
And now that these my happy eyes behold thy heav'nly face,
The Lord of Lords I humbly pray to bless thy noble Grace
With Nestor's life, with Sibyl's health, with Croesus' stock and store,
With all good gifts of Solomon, and twice as many more.
15 What should I say? Thou art my joy next God; I have none other,
My princess and my peerless queen, my loving nurse and mother.
My goods and lands, my hands and heart, my limbs and life are thine,
What is mine own in right or thought, to thee I do resign.
Grant then, O gracious sovereign Queen, this only my request,
20 That that which shall be done in me be construed to the best.
And take in part my slender[1] shows, wherein my whole pretence
Is for to please you, Majesty, and end without offence.
So shall I clap my hands for joy and hold myself as rich
As if I had the gold of Ind,[2] and double twice as much.
                Finis. B. G.

Then spake Deborah:

Where princes sitting in their thrones set God before their sight
And live according to His law and guide their people right,
There doth His blessed gifts abound, there kingdoms firmly stand,
There force of foes cannot prevail, nor fury fret the land.
5 Myself, O peerless Prince, do speak by proof of matter past,
Which proof by practice I performed and foiled His foes at last.
For Jabin, King of Canaan, poor Israel did spite,
And meant by force of furious rage to overrun us quite.
Nine hundred iron chariots he brought into the field,
10 With cruel Captain Sisera by force to make us yield.
His force was great, his fraud was more, he fought, we did defend,
And twenty winters long did last this war without an end.[3]

8. Stopped; *close:* enclosed; *used:* played.
9. According to English myth, Britain was named for its founder, the Trojan Brutus, and London was
   the "New Troy," or Troynovant.
1. Insignificant.
2. India.
3. In 1578, Elizabeth, too, had reigned twenty years, most spent in hostile relations with France. The
   passage invites the Queen to imitate Deborah in opposing such foreign powers, defending God's
   "elect," a term favored by Protestants for those of "true" (rather than Roman Catholic) faith.

But He that neither sleeps nor slacks such furies to correct
Appointed me, Deborah, for the judge of His elect
15 And did deliver Sisera into a woman's hand.
I slew them all, and so in rest His people held the land.
So mighty Prince, that puissant Lord hath placed thee here
    to be;
The rule of this triumphant realm alone belong'th to thee.
Continue as thou hast begun, weed out the wicked rout,°   *rabble*
20 Uphold the simple, meek, and good, pull down the proud
    and stout.[4]
Thus shalt thou live and reign in rest, and mighty God shalt
    please,
Thy state be sure, thy subjects safe, thy commonwealth at ease.
Thy God shall grant thee length of life to glorify His name;
Thy deeds shall be recorded in the book of lasting fame.
Finis. B. G.

Then spake Judith:

O flower of grace, O prime of God's elect,
O mighty Queen and finger of the Lord,
Did God sometime° by me, poor wight, correct   *once*
The champion stout that Him and His abhor'd?
5 Then be thou sure thou art His mighty hand
To conquer those which Him and thee withstand.

The rage of foes Bethulia[5] did besiege;
The people faint were ready for to yield.
God aided me, poor widow, ne'ertheless
10 To enter into Holofernes' field
And with this sword by His directing hand
To slay His foe and quiet so the land.

If this His grace were giv'n to me, poor wight,
If widow's hand could vanquish such a foe,
15 Then to a Prince of thy surpassing might,
What tyrant lives but thou mayest overthrow?
Persever then His servant as thou art
And hold for aye° a noble victor's part.   *forever*
Finis B. G.

Then Hester spake:

The fretting heads of furious foes have skill
As well by fraud as force to find their prey.
In smiling looks doth lurk a lot as ill
As where both stern and sturdy streams do sway.[6]

---

4. Arrogant, unyielding.
5. Town guarding a strategic pass into Israel.
6. As where both the rudder and cross currents are pulling the ship of state their way.

5 Thyself, O Queen, a proof hath seen of this
    So well as I, poor Esther, have iwis.°   *certainly*

    As Jabin's force did Israel perplex
    And Holofornes fierce Bethulia besiege,
    So Haman's slights sought me and mine to vex,
10 Yet showed a face a subject to[7] his liege.
    But force, nor fraud, nor tyrant strong can trap
    Those which the Lord in His defense doth wrap.

    The proofs I speak by us have erst° been seen;   *formerly*
    The proofs I speak to thee are not unknown.
15 Thy God thou knowest, most dread and sovereign Queen,
    A world of foes of thine hath overthrown
    And hither now triumphantly doth call
    Thy noble Grace, the comfort of us all.

    Dost thou not see the joy of all this flock?
20 Vouchsafe to view their passing° gladsome cheer.   *exceedingly*
    Be still,° good Queen, their refuge and their rock,   *always*
    As they are thine to serve in love and fear.
    So fraud, nor force, nor foreign foe may stand
    Against the strength of thy most puissant hand.
                     Finis. B. G.

Then spake Marcia:

With long discourse, O puissant Prince, some tract of time we spend.
Vouchsafe yet now a little more, and then we make an end.
The thundering blast of Fame, whereof Dame Norwich first did speak,
Not only shook the air and skies but all the earth did break.
5 It rent up graves and bodies raised; each spirit took his place,
And this alonely word[8] was heard: "Here com'th the pearl of grace;
Here comes the jewel of the world, her people's whole delight,
The paragon of present time and prince of earthly might."
The voice was strange, the wonder more, for when we viewed the earth,
10 Each prince that erst had reignéd here, received again his breath,
And with his breath, a liberty to hold again his place,
If any one amongst us all exceed your noble Grace.
Some comfort every one conceived to catch again his own;[9]
His utmost skill was trimly[1] used to have his virtues known.
15 The plays[2] surpass my skill to tell, but when each one had said,
Apollo did himself appear and made us all dismayed.
"Will you contend with her," quoth he, "within whose sacred breast
Dame Pallas and myself have framed our sovereign seat of rest?
Whose skill directs the Muses nine, whose grace doth Venus stain,[3]

---

7. As if he were subject to.
8. Single statement.
9. His own breath.
1. Cleverly.
2. Diversions, when the princes take turns boasting.
3. Make less beautiful by contrast.

20 Her eloquence like Mercury, like Juno in her train?[4]
     Whose god[5] is that eternal Jove which holds us all in awe?
     Believe me, you exceed the bounds of equity and law."
     Therewith they shrank themselves aside; not one I could espy.
     They couched them in their caves again and there full quiet lie.
25 Yet I that Marcia hight,[6] which sometime ruled this land
     As Queen for thirty-three years space, gat license at his hand,[7]
     And so Gurguntius did, my husband's father dear,
     Which built this town and castle both, to make our homage[8] here,
     Which homage, mighty Queen, accept; the realm and right is thine.
30 The crown, the scepter, and the sword to thee we do resign
     And wish to God that thou mayst reign twice Nestor's years in peace,
     Triumphing over all thy foes to all our joys' increase. Amen.

Finis. B. G.

Herewith she passed under the gate with such thanks as plainly expressed her noble nature, and the musicians within the gate upon their soft instruments used broken music,[9] and one of them did sing this ditty:

From slumber soft I fell asleep,
From sleep to dream, from dream to deep delight.
Each gem the gods had given the world to keep
In princely wise came present to my sight.
5 Such solace then did sink into my mind,
As mortal man on mould° could never find.   *earth*

The gods did strive, and yet their strifes were sweet;
Each one would have a virtue of her own.
Dame Juno thought the highest place most meet
10 For her, because of riches was her throne.
Dame Venus thought by reason of her love
That she might claim the highest place above.

The virgin's state Diana still did praise,
And Ceres praised the fruit of fertile soil,
15 And prudence did Dame Pallas chiefly raise;
Minerva all for eloquence did strive.
They smiled to see their quarreling estate,
And Jove himself decided their debate.

"My sweets," quoth he, "leave off your sugared strife;
20 In equal place I have assigned you all.
A sovereign wight there is that beareth life,
In whose sweet heart I have enclosed you all.
Of England soil she is the sovereign Queen;
Your vigors there do flourish fresh and green."

4. Entourage.
5. Patron deity.
6. Am called.
7. Permission at Jove's hand.
8. Offer their allegiance to Elizabeth.
9. Played music with parts for each instrument.

25   They skipped for joy and gave their frank consent;
       The noise resounded to the haughty sky.
       With one loud voice they criéd all, "Content!"°   *We are contented*
       They clapped their hands, and therewith wakéd I.
       The world and they concluded with a breath°   *shout*
30   And wished long reign to Queen Elizabeth.
                    Finis. B. G.

Herewith she passed through the marketplace, which was goodly garnished, and thence through the other streets, which were trimly decked,
directly to the cathedral church, where *Te Deum* was sung, and after service she went to the Bishop's palace, where her Majesty kept the time she
continued[1] in Norwich. All this was upon Saturday the 16th of August,
1578.

Upon the Monday following, Master Churchyard brought Mercury in a
gallant coach, strangely appareled, into the green-yard[2] under the privy or
bedchamber window, out of the which the Queen's Majesty looked, which
Mercury, in verse made for the purpose, uttered to her Highness that, if it
were her pleasure at any time to take the air abroad, there were devices to
be seen to pleasure her Majesty. And according to that promise, on Tuesday following (for before that day, by means of the weather, she went not
abroad), he performed a very pretty pleasant show before her Highness
without St. Benet's Gates as she went towards Cossie Park to hunt. In
which day the minister of the Dutch church, pronouncing to her Majesty
the oration following, presented the cup therein mentioned, which I esteem
to be worth fifty pounds, very curiously wrought.[3]

                    ✻   ✻   ✻

The Minister of the Dutch Church's Oration in English

The orators, most gracious Queen, which lived in the age of them that
won greatest renown were highly commended for that they could transform
the judges' minds (partly by eloquence and partly by setting down before
their eyes the calamity of the thing and person they spake of) into what disposition them listed.[4] The first part[5] declareth unto us no common facility
of men, in that they were so willing in following and attentive in hearing as
they would suffer themselves to be led by eloquence. The last[6] obtained
great favor amongst all nations whose commonweal was governed in good
order, and far greater amongst the Christians, but greatest of all with thee,
O most excellent Queen, the nurse of Christ's Church, whose mind, obedient to God's Word, the spirit of Christ and zeal of godliness and not this
profane kind of speech hath instructed. The very calamity of godly men and
tears of the afflicted (the tears, I say, of faithful Christians) have thoroughly

---

1. Passed the time that she remained; *Te Deum*: Latin hymn sung to celebrate victory.
2. A grassy yard within the grounds of the Bishop's palace, where sermons were sometimes preached. *Master Churchyard*: Thomas Churchyard, a professional poet and court entertainer.
3. Latin version omitted.
4. Into what attitude they pleased.
5. Willingness to be persuaded by eloquence.
6. Skill in showing "the calamity of the thing."

moved thee to defend and protect the miserable and dispersed members of Christ[7] (object to every kind of injury, before beaten in pieces by a thousand deaths) with the safety and preservation as well of mind as body. For these thy singular benefits of godliness towards us, and that we live under so good a tutor, being magistrate in this the city of Norwich (which thy Majesty hath of clemency granted unto us for a mansion place, which were banished for Christ's religion), and moreover that we find the minds of the people favorable towards us, first we give immortal thanks, not such as we ought but such as we are able, unto God the Father and the Lord, our only savior Jesus Christ, and then unto thee, most merciful Queen. Moreover, it is our humble and yet our only petition to show unto your Majesty the thankfulness of our mind. Behold, therefore, dedicated to your most excellent Majesty not any gift but our mind, no princely jewel but a monument of godliness and posterity, the which we hope will be so much the more acceptable to your Majesty for because the goodness of God towards your Majesty is lively drawn out of the history of the innocent and most godly Joseph, whom neither policy, strength, nor desire of bearing rule, but constant faith, godliness of a Christian heart,[8] and heavenly virtue by God's singular mercy delivered from the bloody conspiracy of his brethren and fear of death, and brought unto high dignity and royal kingdom, to whose brethren that proverbial sentence of the Hebrews is very fitly alluded: "Envy, being the desire of evil things and covetousness of transitory renown, is oftentimes the occasion of man's destruction." But touching the mind of Joseph, the same was endued with such temperance and fortitude that he might be thought no less unjust than wicked that would accuse him so much as with the least affection of revengement, so wholly did he commit himself and all the government of his life (his life, I say, put in hazard in a strange kingdom) unto the providence of God that he seemed to hang off[9] no other thing than the only will of God. But to what end speak I this? Are not these self same things and others their like (O most excellent Queen) by the eyes of all men clearly beholden in thee and the order of thy kingdom?[1] What man (I say), having his wits, can deny these things to be the most happy joy, spiritual crown, and chiefest ornament of Christ's church, and truly of this kingdom the princely beauty and perpetual renown? Thou surely dost follow most holily the mind of Joseph by the singular goodness of God, as well in preserving thy kingdom as in amplifying the kingdom of Christ (O thou most faithful nurse of the church of God). For it is in God only to destroy this man by prosperity (as it seemeth unto man) and advance another by all kinds of adversity and human danger, whom He acknowledgeth as the vessels of His mercy,[2] and so by His goodness, together with the consolation and strength of His spirit, doth bring them to the happiness of eternal life, which our petition that good and merciful God grant may be ratified in establishing your Majesty and governance

---

7. Christians, seen as limbs of the body of Christ.
8. Though Joseph is a patriarch from the Book of Genesis, the minister treats him as having saving knowledge of Christ, a view of certain Old Testament figures with roots in the New Testament (see Hebrews 11); *lively*: with lifelike resemblance.
9. Depend on; *that he might . . . revengement*: anyone who accused Joseph of the least desire for revenge was both unjust and wicked; *hazard . . . kingdom*: Joseph's brothers sold him into slavery in Egypt.
1. Elizabeth resembled Joseph in coming to power despite abuse by her brother Edward VI, who tried to disinherit her, and by her sister Mary Tudor, who imprisoned her; *their like*: like them.
2. See Romans 9.23; *this man*: one particular man.

of your kingdom with spiritual wisdom and understanding, in preserving the same for many years, and in enduing your Majesty's subjects more and more with true knowledge of Him for His son's sake, our Lord Jesus Christ. Amen.

The oration ended, there was a certain monument presented to her princely Majesty, in the upper part whereof was artificially graven the history of Joseph out of Genesis. In the compass[3] thereof was this verse:

> To royal scepters, godliness, Josephus innocent
> Doth take[4] from brothers' bloody hands and murderers' intent.
> So thee, O Queen, the Lord hath led from prison and deceit
> Of thine[5] unto these highest tops of your princely estate.

In the inner part of the same, there was the figure of a serpent interfolding itself, in the midst whereof did sit a dove with this sentence of Christ, Matthew 10.16: "Wise as the serpent and meek as the dove."

The Wednesday towards evening, Master Churchyard was likewise ready upon the water with another device when her Majesty was without the gates towards Mount Surrey, but weather hindered it so as nothing was then done by him. But as she returned homeward, within Bishop's Gate at the hospital door, Master Stephen Limbert, Master of the Grammar School in Norwich, stood ready to render her an oration. Her Majesty drew near unto him and, thinking him fearful, said graciously unto him, "Be not afeared." He answered her again in English: "I thank your Majesty, for your good encouragement," and then with good courage entered into this oration:[6]

* * *

The oration of Stephen Limbert, public schoolmaster,
to the most magnificent Prince, Elizabeth of England,
France,[7] and Ireland Queen, etc. before the
gates of the hospital of Norwich

It is reported, most gracious Queen, that Egypt is watered with the yearly overflowing of Nile and Lydia[8] with the golden stream of Pactolus, which thing is thought to be the cause of the great fertility of these countries. But upon us (and farther, over all England, even in the uttermost borders) many and main rivers of godliness, justice, humility, and other innumerable good things, in comparison of the which gold is vile and naught worth, do most plentifully gush out, and those not from Tmolus[9] or other hills, I know not which, but from that continual and most abundant wellspring of your goodness. And that of those infinite goodnesses I may lightly touch one (for that

---

3. The verse was inscribed around the pictures of Joseph, which were "artificially graven."
4. Advance.
5. Of Elizabeth's kin, particularly her sister Mary, who in 1554 detained her on suspicion of involvement in Wyatt's Rebellion.
6. Latin version omitted.
7. English claims of sovereignty over France go back to the Middle Ages.
8. A region on the western coast of modern-day Turkey.
9. A mountain in Lydia; *main*: large.

neither place, time, nor my faculty doth permit to speak of many), with what praises shall we extol, with what magnificent words shall we express that notable mercy of your Highness, most renowned Queen, and uncredible readiness to relieve the need of poor men, than the which of many virtues none can be more acceptable unto God, as Homer writeth,[1] neither any virtue in a mighty prince more wondered at amongst men. This hospital of poor men is most famous, which will be a monument of princely virtue and beneficence amongst all posterity, instituted by the most mighty King Henry, your Highness's father, confirmed with the Great Seal by the most noble King Edward, your brother, but by your Majesty, which deserveth no less praise, of late notably increased and amplified by the lands and possessions of Cringleford,[2] that you may not now worthily rejoice so much in others' ornaments as your own virtues. For you are said, for your singular wisdom and learning, to have studied that divine law of the most wise Plato, which he left written in the Eleventh Book of *Laws*. Such your great bounty therefore, so exceeding, and incredible mercy, O most virtuous Prince, in what books shall we comprehend? With what duties or with what voice shall we testify the good will of a thankful mind? For when we diligently seek all the most exquisite and curious means of thanksgiving, we cannot so much as attain unto the greatness of this one benefit, by the which we acknowledge ourselves bound and straitly holden[3] to your most royal Majesty. We shall be overcome, even with this one and singular benefit. So much the less hope have we, then, in any point to countervail the huge sea of the rest of thy benefits, which overfloweth on every side as well publicly and generally over all thy subjects as properly and particularly upon this city. We certainly now inhabit and lead our lives in those most happy islands of the which Hesiodus maketh mention, which not only abound with all manner of grain, wool, cattle, and other aids of man's life but much more with the most precious treasure of true religion and the Word of God, in the which only the minds of men have rest and peace. There be that call England another world, which I think may be most true in this our age; for whereas all lands on every side of us are afflicted with most grievous wars and tossed with the floods of dissention, we only, your Highness governing our stern, do sail in a most peaceable haven and, severed from the world of mischiefs, do seem after a sort to be taken up into a heaven of happiness. We, therefore, according to our bounden duty, first give thanks unto God Almighty, unto whose goodness only with thanks we refer all this our happiness, how great soever it be, and pray that He would vouchsafe to make the same proper[4] and perpetual unto us. And afterwards unto your Highness (O most gracious Queen) by whose study, care, and diligence we confess this blessedness to be gotten and so many years preserved unto us.

1. The reference here is probably to a passage in *The Odyssey* where Nausikaa tells her servant girls to help Odysseus as he emerges naked and wretched from the sea (6.207ff.; source identified by James A. Arieti); *uncredible*: incredible.
2. According to the Cringleford Historical Society, after George Redman of Cringleford was executed for leading an insurrection in 1570 to drive immigrants from the Low Countries out of the area, the Crown seized his lands on the outskirts of Norwich. They were then given to the Great Hospital, a charitable institution for the needy.
3. Closely beholden; *curious*: ingenious.
4. Our own.

We are glad in this beholding you, and we rejoice with desire more than may be believed, which as I speak of mine own thought, so also all these subjects of Norwich desire me to say the same in their behalf. And I would to God you could pierce these our breasts with your eyes and thoroughly view the hidden and covered creeks of our minds. Then undoubtedly should you behold an infinite heap of good will closely shut up within, which cannot break out of so narrow straits. All the faith, study,[5] and obedience which are due to so great a prince, as hitherto we have most willingly employed, so will we always most diligently perform the same. And if at any time any chance shall happen (which fortune God turn from us) that the state of thy blessed Majesty or of this flourishing realm should come in danger, or the worthiness thereof be in hazard, we do not only protest the effusion[6] of all our goods and substance, but also the putting forth and brunt of our strengths and bodies therein. Finally we desire and beseech thy Excellency (most renowned Queen) well to accept of this our duty, howsoever it be, proceeding from a singular good will and a most thankful mind, and so to think of us citizens of Norwich that perhaps you have many times come to people more wealthy, but to more joyful never.

Immediately after the beginning of the oration, her Majesty called to her the French ambassadors, whereof there were three, and divers English lords and willed them to hearken, and she herself was very attentive, even until the end thereof. And, the oration ended, after she had given great thanks therefore to Master Limbert, she said to him, "It is the best that ever I heard; you shall have my hand," and pulled off her glove and gave him her hand to kiss, which, before kneeling on his knee, he arose and kissed, and then she departed to the Court without any other show[7] that night but that she sent back to know his name.

The next night, being Thursday, there was an excellent princely masque brought before her after supper by Master Goldingham in the Privy Chamber.[8] It was of gods and goddesses, both strangely and richly appareled.

The first that entered was Mercury.

Then entered two torch-bearers in purple taffeta mandilions[9] laid with silver lace, as all other the torch-bearers were.

Then entered a consort of music, *viz.* six musicians, all in long vestures of white sarcenet[1] girded about them and garlands on their heads, playing very cunningly.

Then two torch-bearers more.

Then Jupiter and Juno.

Then two torch-bearers more.

---

5. Thoughtful commitment.
6. Solemnly promise the bountiful outlay.
7. Appearance.
8. Large room in the Queen's lodgings where she handled state business. Like the Presence Chamber, it varied according to the palace or temporary residence she happened to be in, but one room was always designated by the title.
9. Long coats or cassocks.
1. A soft, silken material.

Then Mars and Venus.
Then two torch-bearers more.
Then Apollo and Pallas.
Then two torch-bearers.
Then Neptune and Diana.
And last cometh Cupid and concludeth the matter.

Thus when they had once marched about the Chamber, Mercury dischargeth his message in these words to the Queen:

The good-meaning Mayor and all his brethren, with the rest, have not rested from praying unto the gods to prosper thy coming hither, and the gods themselves, moved by their unfeigned prayers, are ready in person to bid thee worthily welcome, and I, Mercury, the god of merchants and merchandise, and therefore a favorer of these citizens, being thought meetest and chosen fittest to signify the same. Gods there be also which cannot come, being tied by the time of the year, as Ceres in harvest, Bacchus in wines, Pomona in orchards. Only Hymeneus denieth his good will, either in presence or in person, notwithstanding Diana hath so counter-checked[2] him, therefore, as he shall ever hereafter be at your commandment. For my part, as I am a rejoicer at your coming, so am I a furtherer of your welcome hither, and for this time I bid you farewell.

Then marched they about again, and that done, Jupiter spake to the Queen in this sort and then gave her a riding wand[3] of whales' fin curiously wrought:

Fear not, O Queen, thou art belovéd so,
As subjects true will truly thee defend.
Fear not my power to overthrow thy woe;[4]
I am the god that can each miss amend.
5 Thou doest know great Jupiter am I,
That gave thee first thy happy sovereignty.

I give thee still, as ever thou hast had,
A peerless power unto thy dying day.
I give thee rule to overcome the bad
10 And love to love thy loving subjects aye.°   always
I give thee here this small and slender wand
To show thou shalt in quiet rule the land.

Then Juno spake, whose gift was a purse curiously wrought:

Is Juno rich? No, sure she is not so;
She wants° that wealth that is not wanting here.   lacks
Thy good gets thee friends, my wealth wins many a foe;
My riches rusts, thine shine passing clear.
5 Thou art beloved of subjects far and nigh,
Which is such wealth as money cannot buy.

2. Rebuked.
3. Whip.
4. Doubt not my power to end your troubles.

Farewell, fair Queen, I cannot give thee aught,°   *anything*
Nor take away thy good that is so bound.
Thou canst not give that° I so long have sought,   *that which*
10 Ne can I hold the riches thou hast found.
Yet take this gift, though poor I seem to be,
That thou thyself shalt never poorer be.

Then, after they had marched again about, Mars gave his gift, which was a
fair pair of knives, and said:

Where force doth fiercely seek to foster wrong,
There Mars doth make him make a quick recoil,
Nor can endure that he should harbor long
Where naughty wights manure° in goodly soil.   *bad men flourish*
5 This is the use° that aids the force of war: *custom*
That Mars doth mend that° force doth seek to mar.   *that which*

And though, O Queen, thou beest a Prince of Peace,[5]
Yet shalt thou have me fastly sure° at need   *firmly committed*
The storms of strife and blustering broils to cease,
10 Which foreign foes or faithless friends may breed,
To conquer, kill, to vanquish and subdue,
Such feignéd folk as loves to live untrue.

These words were graven on those knives:

To hurt your foe and help your friend,
These knives are made unto that end.
Both blunt and sharp you shall us find,
As pleaseth best your princely mind.[6]

Then spake Venus, whose gift was a white dove:

In vain, fair Queen, from heaven my coming was
To seek t' amend that° is no way amiss,   *that which*
For now I see thy favor so doth pass[7]
That none but thou, thou only, she it is
5 Whose beauty bids each wight° to look on thee.   *being*
By view they may another Venus see.

Where beauty boasts and favor doth not fail,
What may I give to thee, O worthy wight?
This is my gift: there shall no woe prevail
10 That seeks thy will against thy will's delight.
Not where they will but where it likes thy mind
Accept that friend, if loyal thou him find.[8]

5. A title also applied to Christ (Isaiah 9.6).
6. It is up to her whether to use the sharp or dull edge of the blade.
7. Your attractiveness does so surpass that of others.
8. Perhaps a half-veiled reference to Anjou.

The dove, being cast off, ran directly to the Queen, and being taken up and set upon the table before her Majesty, sat so quietly as if it had been tied.

Then after they had marched again about, Apollo presented his gift, which was an instrument called a bandonet,[9] and did sing to the said instrument this ditty as he played:

> It seemeth strange to see such strangers here,
> Yet not so strange but strangers knows you well.
> Your virtuous thoughts to gods do plain appear,
> Your acts on earth bewrays° how you excel.   *reveals*
> 5 You cannot die; love here hath made your lease,
> Which gods have sent and God say'th shall not cease.
>
>   Virtuous desire desired me to sing
> No subject's suit, though suitors they were all.
> Apollo's gifts are subjects to no king;
> 10 Rare are thy gifts that did Apollo call.
> Then still rejoice, sithens° God and man say so.   *since*
> This is my gift: thou never shalt have woe.

Pallas then speaketh, and presenteth her gift, which was a book of wisdom:

> Most worthy wight, what wouldst thou have of me?
> Thou hast so much thou canst enjoy no more.
> I cannot give that° once I gave to thee,   *that which*
> Nor take away that good I gave before.
> 5 I robbéd was[1] by Nature's good consent
> Against my will, and yet I was content.
>
>   A Pallas thou, a princess I will be;
> I queen of loss, thou goddess which hast got.
> I sometime was, thou only now art she;
> 10 I take, thou gavest that luck that was my lot.
> I give not thee this book to learn thee aught,[2]
> For that I know already thou art taught.

Then, after they had marched again about, Neptune did speak. His gift was a great artificial fish, and in the belly thereof a noble pike, which he threw out before her Majesty.

> What art thou, Queen, that gods do love thee so?
> Who won their wills to be so at thy will?
> How can the world become thy cruel foe?
> How can Disdain or Malice seek to kill?
> 5 Can Sea or Earth devise to hurt thy hap,
> Since thou by gods dost sit in Fortune's lap?
>
>   As Heaven and Earth have vowéd to be thine,
> So Neptune's seas have sworn to drench thy foes.

---

9. Perhaps a bandurion, relative of the lute.
1. By Elizabeth, who now excels Pallas in wisdom.
2. Teach you anything.

As I am god and all the waters mine,
10 Still shalt thou get, but never shalt thou lose.
And since on earth my wealth is naught at all,
Accept good will; the gift is very small.

Diana presented a bow and arrows nocked[3] and headed with silver. Her
speech was this:

Whoever found on earth a constant friend
That may compare with this my virgin Queen?
Whoever found a body and a mind
So free from stain, so perfect to be seen.
5 O heavenly hue, that aptest° is to soil,   *most likely*
And yet dost live from blot of any foil.[4]

Rare is thy gift and given to few or none,
Maliced therefore of some that dare not say.[5]
More shines thy light, for that° I know but one   *because*
10 That any such show to follow[6] on their way.
Thou, thou art she; take thou the only praise
For chastest Dame in these our happy days.

Accept my bow, since best thou dost deserve,
Though well I know thy mind can thee preserve.

Cuipid's speech, his gift an arrow of gold:

Ah ha, I see my mother out of sight;
Then let the boy now play the wag awhile.
I seem but weak, yet weak is not my might;
My boyish wit can oldest folk beguile.
5 Who so doth think I speak this but in jest,
Let me but shoot, and I shall quench his rest.

Mark here my shafts: this all is made of wood,
Which is but soft and breeds but soft goodwill.
Now this is gilt,° yet seems it gold full good   *gold plated*
10 And doth deceive blind loving people still.°   *continually*
But here is one is seldom felt or seen:
This is of gold, meet for the noblest Queen.

Wherefore, Dame fair, take thou this gift of me;
Though some deserve, yet none deserve like you.
15 Shoot but this shaft at king or Caesar,[7] he,
And he is thine, and if thou wilt allow.

---

3. Fitted on the butt-end.
4. Far from seeming blemished by any comparison.
5. Throughout the reign, the Queen suffered rumors that she had engaged in love affairs with Leicester and other favorites and had borne illegitimate children.
6. Make a show of following.
7. Emperor.

It is a gift that many here would crave,
Yet none but thou this golden shaft may have.

There was written upon the shaft

> My color joy, my substance pure,
> My virtue such as shall endure.
>> *Finis.* Goldingham.

Her Majesty received these gifts very thankfully. The gods and goddesses
with the rest of the masque marched about the chamber again and then
departed in like manner as they came in. Then the Queen called to her
Master Robert Wood, the Mayor of Norwich, whom first she heartily
thanked, and took by the hand, and used secret conference, but what
I know not. And thus this delightful night passed to the joy of all which saw
her Grace in so pleasant plight.[8]

The next day, being Friday, in which day the Court removed, the streets
toward St. Benet's Gates were hanged from the one side to the other with
cords made of herbs and flowers, with garlands, coronets, pictures, rich
clothes, and a thousand devices.[9] At the gates themselves, there was a stage
made, very richly appareled with cloth of gold and crimson velvet, whereupon in a close place made thereon for the purpose was placed very sweet
music and one ready to tender her this speech following. The doleful hour
of her departure came; she passed from the Court to those gates with such
countenances, both of her Majesty's part and her subjects', now dolorous,
now cheerful, as plainly showed the loving hearts of both sides. When she
came there, the speech was thus uttered unto her:

Terrestrial joys are tied with slender file;°   *string*
Each happy hap full hastily doth slide.
As summer season lasteth but a while,
So winter storms do longer time abide.
5 Alas, what bliss can any time endure?
Our sunshine day is dashed with sudden shower.

Could tongue express our secret joys of heart,
O mighty Prince, when thou didst come in place?°   *into the city*
No, no, God wot, nor can express the smart
10 Thy subjects feel in this departing case.
But gracious Queen, let here thy grace remain
In gracious wise till thy return again.

In lieu whereof, receive thy subjects' hearts,
In fixéd faith continually thine own,
15 Who ready rest to lose their vital parts
In thy defense when any blast[1] is blown.

---

8. Circumstances.
9. Painted signs bearing symbolic images; *removed*: departed; *coronets*: small crowns; *clothes*: hangings.
1. Of the trumpets of war.

Thou art our Queen, our rock and only stay,[2]
We are thine own to serve by night and day.

    Farewell, O Queen, farewell, O Mother dear;
20 Let Jacob's God thy sacred body guard.
All is thine own that is possessèd here,
And all in all is but a small reward.
For thy great grace, God length thy life like Noe,°   *Noah*
To govern us and eke thy realm in joy. Amen.
        Finis. B. G. and spoken by himself, to whom
        her Majesty said, "We thank you heartily."

Then with the music in the same place was sung this short ditty following, in a very sweet voice:

    What availeth life, where sorrow soaks the heart?
Who feareth death, that is in deep distress?
Release of life doth best abate the smart
Of him whose woes are quite without redress.
5 Lend me your tears, resign your sighs to me,
Help all to wail the dolor which you see.

    What have we done° she will no longer stay?   *done that*
What may we do to hold her with us still?
She is our queen, we subjects must obey.
10 Grant, though with grief, to her departing will.
Conclude we then and sing with sobbing breath,
God length° thy life, O Queen Elizabeth.   *lengthen*
        Finis. B. G.

Then departed her Majesty out of the gates, within a flight-shot or little more whereof Master Churchyard had another show, which I leave to himself to utter because my hope is he will manifest[3] that amongst the rest shortly.

    This finished, her Majesty in princely manner marched towards the confines of the liberties[4] of the city of Norwich, which I suppose almost two miles. Before she came there, Master Mayor brake[5] to my Lord Chamberlain that he was to utter to her Majesty another oration, whereof my Lord seemed to have good liking. But before they came to the said confines, Master Mayor was willed to forbear the utterance of the same (his oration) because it was about seven of the clock, and her Majesty had then five miles to ride. Nevertheless he gave to her Majesty both his orations in writing, which she thanked him for. She also thanked the Mayor, every alderman, and the commoners, not only for the great cheer they had made her, but also for the open households they kept to her Highness's servants and all other. Then she called Master Mayor and made him Knight, and so departing said, "I have laid up in my breast such goodwill as I shall never forget Norwich," and proceeding onward, did shake her riding rod and said, "Farewell, Norwich," with the water standing in her eyes. In which great

---

2. Words usually used of God.
3. That is, print.
4. The district beyond Norwich that was still under the control of the city.
5. Revealed.

goodwill towards us all I beseech God to continue her Majesty with long
and triumphant reign over us all. Amen.[6]

To the sun, covered with clouds, upon Monday, being the 18th of August 1578

In shadowing clouds why art thou closed? O Phoebus bright, retire.
Unspouséd Pallas present is; O Phoebus bright, retire.
The threatening spear is flung far off; doubt[7] not grim Gorgons' ire.
Unarméd Pallas present is; O Phoebus bright, retire.
5 Perhaps thou art afraid, and why? At this so large a light,
Lest that a woman should excel thy beams, O Phoebus bright.
Let not a Queen, a virgin pure, which is and ever was,
O fair Apollo, make thee blush; you both in beauty pass.[8]
O Phoebus, safe and sound return, which banishing the night
10 Bringst back the day, in all the world nothing of like delight.
She, only she, the darkness drave of popery quite away
And by religion hath restored the bright and lightsome day.
O Phoebus with thy beams, which foilst[9] the clouds both blind and black,
The world, in manner all,[1] a thing of like delight doth lack.
15 A thousand dangers and delays the papists had devised
To th' end our Princess should abridge her progress enterprised.[2]
Yet this,[3] our bright and shining sun, cast light through every cloud,
Although in clouds thou art content, Apollo, oft to shroud.
Thou seest our Sun in comely course cuts off each stop and stay;[4]
20 Do thou the like and by thy light drive every cloud away.
In shadowing clouds why art thou closed? O Phoebus bright, retire.
Unspouséd Pallas present is; O Phoebus bright, retire.

By the same:

Her kingdom all by providence Queen Juno doth uphold,
And of Minerva, lady learn'd, is learnéd lore extolled,
And Venus, fair of countenance, hath beauty uncontrolled.
    These sundry gifts of goddesses three Elizabeth possesseth;[5]
5 By providence, her people's peace and comfort she increaseth.
Her learning, learning amplifies; her beauty never ceaseth.
    I did but jest, of 'goddesses' to give them three the name.
This lady mayst thou 'goddess' call, for she deserves the same,
Although she will not undertake a title of such fame.[6]

---

6. We omit the Latin and English texts of parting speeches by the Mayor and by Stephen Limbert
   (which were never delivered) and the Latin versions of the poems "To the sun" and "Her kingdom
   all by providence" (printed below).
7. Fear.
8. Excel. Having begun by claiming that the Queen (figured as Pallas Athena) excels the sun god
   (Phoebus Apollo), the poet now tries to coax the sun into returning from behind the clouds by saying that it excels any earthly beauty and (in lines 13–14) that the world lacks anything comparable.
9. Who sets off by contrast.
1. In a sense, all there is.
2. Cut short her planned summer progress.
3. This source of light, the Queen. Now the poet returns to treating her as superior to Apollo.
4. Hindrance.
5. These lines, suggesting that Elizabeth has all the best qualities of Juno, Minerva, and Venus, echo the
   myth of the Judgment of Paris. (See also the selection from Peele's *Arraignment of Paris* in Part Six).
6. We omit three final items not presented before the Queen: a Latin poem by Stephen Limbert and
   two poems by William Goldingham, one in Greek and the other in Latin.

RICHARD TOPCLIFFE

From A Letter to the Earl of Shrewsbury
(August 30, 1578)[†]

The principal news is her Majesty's good health and well liking her journey since my Lordship's return; for whose Lordship's health her Majesty sayeth she will thank you and my Lady.[1] I did never see her Majesty better received by two countries[2] in one journey than Suffolk and Norfolk now: Suffolk of gentlemen and Norfolk of the meaner sort, with exceeding joy to themselves and well-liking to her Majesty. * * * The next good news (but in accompt the highest): her Majesty hath served God with great zeal and comfortable examples; for by her Council two notorious papists—young Rookwood (the master of Euston Hall, where her Majesty did lie upon Sunday now a fortnight)[3] and one Downes, a gentleman—were both committed, the one to the town prison at Norwich, the other to the country prison there, for obstinate papistry. And seven more gentlemen of worship[4] were committed to several houses in Norwich as prisoners (two of the Lovells, another Downes, one Beningfield, one Parry, and two others not worth memory) for badness of belief.

This Rookwood is a papist of kind newly crept out of his late wardship.[5] Her Majesty, by some means I know not, was lodged at his house, Euston, far unmeet for her Highness but fitter for the blackguard.[6] Nevertheless (the gentleman brought into her Majesty's presence by like device), her excellent Majesty gave to Rookwood ordinary thanks for his bad house and her fair hand to kiss, after which it was braved at.[7] But my Lord Chamberlain, nobly and gravely understanding that Rookwood was excommunicated for papistry, called him before him; demanded of him how he durst presume to attempt her real presence, he unfit to accompany any Christian person; forthwith said he was fitter for a pair of stocks; commanded him out of the Court[8] and yet to attend her Council's pleasure; and at Norwich he was committed. And, to decipher the gentleman to the full, a piece of plate being missed in the Court and searched for in his hay house, in the hay rick such an image of our Lady was there found as for greatness,[9] for gayness and workmanship I did never see a match. And after a sort of country dances ended, in her Majesty's sight the idol was set behind the people,

---

† Copy text: *Illustrations of British History, Biography, and Manners in the Reigns of Henry VIII, Edward VI, Mary, Elizabeth, and James I*, ed. Edmund Lodge. 3 vols. (London: G. Nicol, 1791), 2.187–90. George Talbot, sixth Earl of Shrewsbury, was a northern landowner and Privy Councilor who held Mary Stuart under house arrest at his country manor at Tutbury from 1568 to 1584.
1. Elizabeth Talbot, Countess of Shrewsbury, better known as Bess of Hardwick; *Lordship's return*: the Earl of Leicester, one of Topcliffe's patrons, had been at Buxton taking mineral baths to restore his health and had rejoined Elizabeth a month prior to her arrival in Norwich. Shrewsbury owned the spa at Buxton.
2. Counties.
3. Two weeks ago; *accompt*: account.
4. Reputation.
5. Period when he was a minor and his estate was managed by others.
6. Kitchen servants.
7. Boasted of; *device*: plan, stratagem.
8. Out of the house; wherever the Queen happened to be was regarded as the Court. *Lord Chamberlain*: Thomas Radcliffe, third Earl of Sussex. The Chamberlain managed the monarch's private chambers.
9. Size; *to decipher . . . full*: disclose Rookwood's character fully; *hay rick*: enclosure; *our Lady*: the Virgin Mary.

who avoided.[1] She rather seemed a beast raised upon a sudden from hell by conjuring than the picture[2] for whom it had been so often and long abused. Her Majesty commanded it to the fire, which in her sight by the country folks was quickly done to her content and unspeakable joy of everyone but some one or two who had sucked of the idol's poisonous milk.

Shortly after, a great sort of good preachers, who had been long commanded to silence for a little niceness, were licensed and again commanded to preach, a great and more universal joy to the countries and the most[3] of the Court than the disgrace of the papists. And the gentlemen of those parts, being great and hot Protestants (almost before by policy discredited and disgraced) were greatly countenanced.[4]

I was so happy lately, amongst other good graces, that her Majesty did tell me of sundry lewd popish beasts that have resorted to Buxton from these countries in the south since my Lord did come from thence.[5] Her Majesty doubteth not but you regard them well enough,[6] amongst whom there is a detestable popish priest, one Durham, or Durand, as I remember, at the bath or lurking in those parts after the ladies. Mr. Secretary hath written to your Lordship, as he said, in this his letter here enclosed, to wish your Lordship to apprehend him; to examine him of his coming to the Church; and, upon the least or lightest occasion, to commit him and to certify the lords thereof; and they mean to send for him, as Mr. Secretary said, upon further causes.[7] Hereof he did give me charge to signify your Lordship besides his letter.[8] It had commed[9] to your Lordship's hand ere now but that my best nag, by chance, did break his leg, wherefore I trust your Lordship will pardon me.

Your Lordship countenancing me about Morton is well taken of[1] her Majesty. And surely, my good Lord, I see well if your Lordship did scale the nest of papists that this progress time hath thither shrunk out of these quarters, it would not offend the highest, and that can I well ascertain[2] your Lordship by such speech as I heard and reckons my duty to yourself to tell you. You may find twenty occasions, and none better than if you can learn that they come not there to God's service.[3] For unworthy be they to receive any fruit of God's good blessing under your Lordship's rule (as that bath is) who will not serve God, and shall in that infected place poison others with papistry and disobedience of her Majesty's laws. God knows how he[4] and her Majesty would take it.

1. Drew back.
2. The image or, in the view of many Protestants of the period, the idol shaped in the likeness of Mary.
3. Majority of the members; *a little niceness*: small offense.
4. Given great attention; *gentlemen*: rural landowners; *policy*: the Queen's policy of keeping the most radical Protestants in check by silencing the preachers who inspired them.
5. Since Leicester rejoined the Queen after his visit to the spa at Buxton.
6. Keep them under surveillance as owner of the spa.
7. Other charges; *Mr. Secretary*: Sir Francis Walsingham, Elizabeth's spymaster, who was responsible for maintaining surveillance on those who might threaten the Queen or the state. Since Buxton was near Tutbury, where Mary Stuart was held, and since Mary was an inveterate plotter against the Queen, a suspicious priest there was a matter of concern; *coming to the Church*: all citizens were required to attend services of the Church of England each Sunday; *the lords*: members of the Privy Council.
8. Inform your Lordship as well as give you his letter.
9. Come.
1. Received by; *countenancing . . . Morton*: giving me your approval about Morton, presumably another Catholic apprehended by Topcliffe.
2. Assure; *scale*: scrape away; *shrunk out . . . quarters*: the recusants were apparently going to Buxton to escape Essex, the area being visited by the Queen.
3. Sunday worship.
4. Leicester.

ELIZABETH, ANJOU, AND THE DEBATE AT COURT

After the Norwich entertainments were staged, talks to conclude a marriage between Elizabeth and Anjou went on for more than three years. In August 1579, Anjou himself arrived in England to woo the Queen, and though he left at the end of the month and the Queen required that the visit be kept secret—something that proved impossible and became a joke around London—the stir that the Catholic Duke's intentions aroused among English Protestants was anything but funny. It became such a hot issue that the Queen forbad writers and preachers to address it openly.

Just how serious Elizabeth was in negotiating marriage with the Duke is a matter of debate. Certainly she showed every sign of being in love. Nicknaming him her Frog, she carried a pair of gloves that he had given her wherever she went. She also wrote love letters to Anjou. In one, she confided that there was "no prince in the world to whom I would more willingly yield to be his than to yourself, nor with whom I would pass the years of my life." In another, she thanked him for flowers that he had sent her, "culled by the hand that has the little fingers that I bless a million times," saying, "I have taken care not to lose a leaf or a flower, despite all the other jewels that I have."

Yet the correspondence between them soon showed signs of strain. She was not pleased by his persistent demands that he be allowed to practice his Catholicism publicly in England and that he receive more guarantees of financial support. His requests for a large personal allowance and funding for his military adventures in the Netherlands struck the rather parsimonious Queen as exorbitant. He, in turn, grew increasingly irritated over her constant delays in concluding the negotiations. By the time it became clear to everyone that there would be no marriage, the affectionate tone of her early letters had given way to defensiveness, exasperation, and reproach. In her last letter, written in 1583, she went so far as to compare herself with "the dog who, often beaten, returns to his master."

Even in the early letters, however, it was clear that her love was never so passionate as to tempt her to any course that might harm England or weaken her authority. Near the end of a lengthy second visit from Anjou in 1581–82, she startled her attendants and councilors by taking a ring from her hand and placing it on his, kissing him on the lips and declaring to everyone who was present, "the Duke of Anjou shall be my husband" (Somerset 328). Yet the act was almost certainly a calculated ploy to keep him on her side in the war in the Netherlands. Despite such displays of affection, her last conditions for a marriage treaty were tough, and when he rejected them, she allowed him to depart for the Continent without any further attempt to settle the match.

Elizabeth's strongest ally in the negotiations to marry the Duke of Anjou was William Cecil, Lord Burghley. No one at Court felt more strongly than he that a marriage treaty between England and France was necessary. Having consulted doctors about the Queen's health and her ability to bear children, he pressed her to marry on grounds that were virtually all political: the match would offset the power of Spain, secure a lasting peace in the Netherlands, and promote the cause of international Protes-

The Queen's signature in 1580.

tantism. Surprisingly, however, his best-known statement on the matter, his letter to the Queen regarding her proposed marriage, hardly mentions the international situation. Instead, it appeals to the aging monarch's need for "some partner" to give her "delight, honor, and pleasure." One wonders whether Cecil had read her correctly. Later events suggest that she was quite capable of putting policy before personal honor and desire.

At about the time that Burghley was composing his remarkably personal letter of advice, Philip Sidney was writing a more elaborate "Discourse to the Queen's Majesty" on the same subject. The letter, which opposed the Anjou marriage just as strongly as Burghley's had supported it, bears comparison with John Stubbs's similar but less diplomatic argument in A *Gaping Gulf* (excerpts of which appear later in Part Five). The contrast between the language and the argumentative strategies of an experienced courtier and those of an inexperienced polemicist such as Stubbs are illuminating. Sidney seems to have been recruited to write the letter by members of the militant Protestant faction headed by his uncle, the Earl of Leicester, and his father-in-law, Elizabeth's spymaster, Sir Francis Walsingham. Like them, Sidney knew enough to be discrete. The letter was never published during his lifetime, though it circulated widely in manuscript. Because his family was well placed at Court and he was able to take his concerns directly to the Queen and the inner circles of her government rather than broadcast them to the reading public, he fared better than Stubbs, who was severely punished for his opposition to the match. Sidney retired to his sister's country estate from late 1579 through 1580, and it may be that the Queen sent him away for participating in the political maneuvering surrounding the French marriage. There were other reasons for him to withdraw, however, including discouragement over his lack of advancement and a celebrated quarrel with Edward de Vere, Earl of Oxford, which really did displease Elizabeth. His letter cannot have been welcome, but it may not have led to a breach with the Queen.

QUEEN ELIZABETH

LETTERS TO THE DUKE OF ANJOU AND
CATHERINE DE MEDICI (1579–84)[†]

[Queen Elizabeth to the Duke of Anjou]
ca. December 1579–January 1580

Monsieur,

When I remember that there is no more lawful debt than the word of a just man, nor anything that more binds our actions than a promise, I would forget myself too much in regard to you and my honor if I passed over the term appointed for my answer to the matter that we have long discussed. You are not unaware, my dearest, that the greatest delays consist in doing what our people should rejoice in and applaud. And in so doing, I have used time, which ordinarily accomplishes more than reason does.[1] And having made use of both,[2] I have not refrained from roundly declaring to you what

† Copy text: *Elizabeth I: Collected Works*, ed. Leah S. Marcus, Janel Mueller, and Mary Beth Rose (Chicago and London: University of Chicago Press, 2000), 243–44; 249–50; 253–56; 259–61. Reprinted by permission of the University of Chicago Press. © 2000 by the University of Chicago.
1. Elizabeth has delayed her answer in order to give her subjects more time to approve of the match.
2. Time and reasonable arguments.

I know and you will find true always. I see well that many people go away repenting of having made rash judgments at the first stroke, without having weighed in a better balance the depth of their opinions; I assure myself that some, upon hazard of their own lives, wish not to be so foolishly governed.[3] And nevertheless I promise you on my faith, which has never yet sustained a spot, that the public exercise of the Roman religion sticks so much in their hearts that I will never consent to your coming among such a company of malcontents without your being pleased to consider that the commissioners loosen the strict terms that Monsieur Simier offered us;[4] and because I do not want you to send them unless the cause would thereby be concluded, I entreat you to give great consideration to this, as a thing so hard for the English to bear that you would not be able to imagine it without knowing it.

For my part, I confess that there is no prince in the world to whom I would more willingly yield to be his than to yourself, nor to whom I think myself more obliged, nor with whom I would pass the years of my life, both for your rare virtues and sweet nature, accompanied with so many honorable parts that I cannot recite them for their number nor dare to make mention of them for the length of time that would take me. Such that, if it would please you to consider how sincerity accompanies me in this negotiation from the beginning to the present, I do not fear to present myself before the seat of your just judgment and acquit myself of every wile and dissimulation. I have doubts about our agreements as individuals, being uncertain as much about not complying as not assured that I should consent, seeing the great questions that were then being raised about the nation from which you come, then about the manner of government and several other things which ought not to be written down.[5] And in the which, having used up so many means of making them agreeable,[6] I do not believe I have done hard work but rather huge labor for a whole week! And at this hour I would not deceive you by not placing openly before your eyes how I find the case, and what I think of it, in which I have had so much regard to your ease and contentment as if for my own life or consideration of my state, which would otherwise have moved me to make another answer.[7]

And for conclusion I cannot deny that I do not want this negotiation to trouble you thus any more, that we may remain faithful friends and assured in all our actions, unless it pleases you to make other resolution than the open exercise of religion, and it seems good to you to write me about it or to send some good answer; for I desire nothing that does not content you. There are still some things to be said about your allowance, which I have given in charge to this bearer for him to tell you from well to better,[8] like other things that it will please you with your customary goodness to hear, and to entrust yourself to him as to a faithful man, as you know him to be, and as I have well proved. For which I owe you a million thanks for the

---

3. Some have reconsidered their earlier, foolish judgment against the marriage.
4. Jean de Simier, Baron de St. Marc and Anjou's chief negotiator, had insisted that the Duke openly continue to practice his Roman Catholic faith.
5. Elizabeth doubts whether she would be able to comply with, or even should continue to consent to, their earlier agreements.
6. Making their marriage arrangements agreeable to her subjects.
7. Elizabeth's own regard for Anjou moves her to accept his offers, but honesty compels her to speak plainly about the disapproval of her subjects.
8. Anjou will find her new arrangements for his allowance better to his liking.

honor, favor, and liberality which you have used towards him in his place, for which you have put me under obligation long before now.

I received eight days ago a letter that it pleased you to send me, by which I see that your affection is not diminished by absence nor cools by persuasions, for which I can only return a sincere and immovable goodwill, ready to serve you on all occasions contrary or ill, and such that I will never forsake your fortune but take my part in it. I have never heard any news from you either of France or of the Low Countries or of any other parts since the arrival of Simier, and believe that you doubt too much of a woman's silence[9] or otherwise I would learn less by other means and more by you. For from another place I learn more than it pleases you to communicate to me, as God knows, whom I pray to preserve you in good life and long, with my commendations to my very dear Frog.

[Queen Elizabeth to the Duke of Anjou] 17 March 1581

My dearest,

The honor that you do me is indeed great, sending me often of your letters, but the comfort that I conceive from them exceeds it by much, wishing nothing so much as the continuation of your good opinion in regard to me, thanking you very humbly for the sweet flowers culled by the hand that has the little fingers that I bless a million times. And I promise you that there was never gift better carried, for the verdure[1] stayed as fresh there as if they had been culled in the same instant and showed me in an altogether lively fashion your verdant[2] affection in regard to me. And I hope that I will never give just cause for it to wither at my behest. Monsieur, I have taken care not to lose a leaf or a flower, despite all the other jewels that I have. I entreat you to believe that I cannot express the contentment that this bearer bore to me. And pardon me if he did not return sooner when awaiting my courier, by whom I have received a letter from you in which you put me under infinite obligation, not least by so many honorable offers all full of affection which, however much it is in all, I cannot satisfy it at all, unless I fail to recognize it by all the means that are in my power.[3]

I content myself, Monsieur, that you assure yourself of me[4] as of the most faithful friend that ever prince had. And if you trust to such a rock, all the tempests of the sea will be far from shaking it, nor will any storm on the earth turn it aside from honoring and loving you. There has not been a word written in the intention of separating myself from your good affection, but for this, that you may not be ignorant of all that is done here. But what I ought to think I do not know, unless that you make me obliged to you forever. And I will never think otherwise of you than the same honor and a heap piled high with virtue, as the Creator knows, to whom with my very cordial commendations I pray to grant you all the honor and contentment

---

9. You fear a woman will not be discreet.
1. Greenness.
2. Green and abundant.
3. Elizabeth recognizes and returns Anjou's affection, although she qualifies her response by using double negatives: "I cannot satisfy it at all, unless I fail to recognize it."
4. Trust yourself to me.

in the world, entreating you always to hold me in your good graces. From Westminster this 17 of March.

Your most obliged forever, *Elizabeth R*

[Queen Elizabeth to the Duke of Anjou]
24 May 1582

Copy of the Queen's letter to Monsieur sent from Greenwich by one of his lackeys,[1] *twenty-fourth of May, 1582*

My dearest,

You make me acknowledge that notwithstanding the great affairs and importance of your business, you fail not to console me with the coming of your long writings, and for them, confessing myself infinitely obliged to you, I render you a million thanks. And in reading them I see a mass of affection there containing humors[2] of several qualities. And however much I am not a scholar in natural philosophy nor a good enough physician to make a right distinction of them, still I will take the boldness of enlightening you on the true property of some parts that I set down in the keeping of my memory.

It seems to me that in commemorating the history of the dealings between us, it pleases you to tell me at length of the hazards, losses, and machinations that you have endured for my sake. The which I cannot forget, having them engraved in my soul, where, until its separation from my body, I will not leave[3] to recognize and be pained by them always. Only I entreat you not to forget that all these postponements have not derived from me, my thoughts not having been lacking in respect of our more happy stay in this country, tending not only towards my honor but as well towards your surety.[4] Remove, therefore, my dearest Monsieur, any thought that I stand to blame for the passion of anger that gives you offense, because your constancy should be doubted. I absolve myself of such a doubt, having never said nor thought it, whatever opinion others may have had of it. I care not to offer you so much injury; only by machination do I purge myself of the calumnies[5] imputed to me, in France and elsewhere, of having used subtleties or changefulness in what I promised you. And so much was it wrong that I was to blame that I will not cease to impute it to the person[6] to whom it most pertained.

What I see by your letters written to Pinard has given you an argument for writing in the same fashion with our permission, which seems strange to me, in making a show that I push you to proceed more urgently as much from my doubtfulness as from my haste.[7] O Monsieur, how that touches my

1. Footmen.
2. Fluids in the body (chiefly blood, phlegm, choler, and bile) thought to determine tendencies in the personality as well as physical characteristics.
3. Cease.
4. Safety.
5. Slanderous reports; *machination*: public relations efforts.
6. Anjou himself.
7. Anjou's letters to Pinard suggest that Elizabeth has allowed him to say that she urges him to hurry, knowing that he cannot, as a way to hide her own uncertainty. *Pinard*: Claude Pinard, Secretary of State to Catherine de Medici.

honor, lady that I am! You will think about it at your good leisure; some will laugh about it at their ease. And I feel it to my regret, which lessens notwithstanding when I imagine an end leading to attaining an end to our long enmeshments that redouble so, before the fastening of my bonds that no one will ever know how to unloose them.[8]

You wrote me about having sent me the copies of the letters of the King and the Queen, the which I have not yet seen except a letter to Pinard, which was only written the twelfth of May, a day very distant from the time of your departure from this kingdom; by which I see that you have never mentioned it since your arrival in Flanders.[9] Herein I can justify myself as not having delayed shamelessly, my ambassador having several times made mention of it. And I think that the King will repute me for such a one as goes a-wooing,[1] which will always be a fine reputation for a woman! You can see, if you please, clearly and easily, the hope that I can conceive of a sincere accomplishment of the thing which is resolved with such difficulty, or rather not at all.[2]

If you bring up the subject of money, I am so poor an orator for my profit and like so little to play the housewife that I give charge of this to such as are wiser than I. They have declared everything to Marchaumont,[3] who is of my resolution. To whom I have made request to inform you of it particularly, you being very importunate in this affair, and entreat you with hands clasped to be willing to weigh in a just balance on what foundation I go; and you will see that I do not have less consideration of your greatness and contentation[4] in your enterprises than you yourself would be able to wish.

Receiving your last letter of news sent by the Queen of Navarre,[5] I am only too bound to you by the great joy that you take from it. But for my part, I heard nothing of it by the last audience that my ambassador had with the King, which was the sixth of this month, and believe that my last information will be found too true, since I received it from a good place and am very greatly astonished that you have not yet received it, since I dispatched it to you as soon as the wind permitted. You will pardon me if I do not easily give credit to too good news, for fear that deception will redouble my anxiety. Without being assured of it, I keep myself still from answering to the name by which you conjure me.[6] Only I can tell you that such obligation does not more tie my affection than your merits have already done, which cannot receive increase. And I will make comparison with whomever it may be in having no less affection for you than if the little priest had already performed his office. I will perform in such a sort that you will not justly be able to impute any deficiencies in your behalf.[7]

8. Once married, no one will be able to unloose, or divorce, them; *to my regret . . . redouble so*: Elizabeth's regrets lessen when she imagines their marriage after a long and difficult courtship.
9. Anjou delayed writing to the King and Queen Mother; *King . . . Queen*: Henry III of France and Catherine, the Queen Mother; *departure . . . kingdom*: Anjou wooed the Queen in England from the end of October 1581 until February 1582.
1. Because her ambassador is the only one who presses for letters.
2. Given the difficulties, Elizabeth has little hope of resolving the marriage negotiations.
3. Clausse de Marchaumont, Count de Beaumont, Anjou's principal envoy in England at this time (Marcus, Mueller, and Rose's note).
4. Satisfaction; *weigh in . . . I go*: Elizabeth wishes Anjou to weigh carefully her judicious response to his repeated requests for money.
5. Marguerite de Valois, the sister of Anjou and the wife of Henry of Navarre, who seems to have written positively about Henry III's eagerness to conclude the marriage negotiations.
6. The name, presumably, is "intended wife."
7. From your point of view.

I could dilate[8] on the answer that I sent you by Marchaumont, but I have left that work for him, entreating you to believe that if our marriage were made, I would not take away from it any good for England. If by chance God took me out of this world before having children, if ever I will have any, you are wise to think what good turn I had done them to gain them such good neighbors, if perchance Flanders changed masters and the French governed there. Pardon me this frankness. Do not forget my heart, which I risk a little for you in this matter, more than you will be able to imagine but not more than I already feel. And it rejoices me to have tasted of it more than a fine liquor. But when I remember for whom this is, I console myself so and then am borne up by it. As for the commission that we will give you, I shall not entertain myself with it so far as to understand, if the desire to please you so much occupied the Queen's mind that she understood the King's intention to resemble the sum of your desires (not at all the interpretation that perhaps can be made of it), which to understand. . . . [9]

[Queen Elizabeth to the Duke of Anjou] 10 September 1583

[*Endorsed in Burghley's hand*] *Copy of the Queen's letter to Monsieur, sent by Monsieur de Reaux from Oatlands*[1] *the 10th of September 1583*

Monsieur,

After a long wait to receive some news of you and your affairs, Monsieur de Reaux came to visit me on your behalf, carrying nothing but letters entirely full of affection and assurance of the continuance of the same forever, for which I render you an infinity of thanks, for I have heard of the care that you take for fear of some bad impression that I could conceive of your actions. Then he tired me with language that seemed very strange to me: that you desired to know what will be the aid you will give for the preservation of the Netherlands, saying to me that you are assured by the King that he will aid you the same as I do. My God, Monsieur, how unfortunate you are to believe that this is the way to preserve your friends, by always debilitating[2] them! Whoever they are who have given you the advice on this have thought to make a spot on our friendship, or to break it altogether in order by the same means to achieve their designs and reclaim you to their desire.

Do you not remember at all, Monsieur, against how many friends I have to prepare? Must I think so much of those afar while I neglect the closest? The King, our brother, is he so feeble a prince that he is not able to defend you without another neighbor who has enough on her back, or so weakened as to open a path for assailants? You will not esteem me so unworthy of reigning that I may not fortify myself, indeed, with the sinews of war while waiting too long for courtesy from those who seek my ruin. I am astonished

---

8. Expand.
9. The copy breaks off here; *commission . . . you*: Anjou, who by this time was confined in Antwerp while the Spanish Duke of Parma marched through the Netherlands, constantly petitioned Elizabeth for more support, which she was reluctant to give.
1. A hunting lodge in Surrey; *Monsieur de Reaux*: Anjou's most recent emissary to England.
2. Weakening them with financial burdens.

at the King our brother, who has given me the precedence in fortifying you in so great a need, I having begun before him while he is not lacking in better means by way of less inconvenience. Pardon me, I pray you, that I tell you that this answer is altogether clear: he would[3] do nothing, thinking that I would have little reason for not giving. So much so that if the King will not speak and will not do much more than formerly, such an enterprise will break off very soon; and if it be up to him alone, I think that such is his determination. There is my opinion.

As for you, Monsieur, I see that you are so environed[4] with contrarious persuasions and such differing humors, doubting so much and assuring yourself of nothing, that you do not know where you should well turn, as you have sufficient reason not to. Would to God I were skilled enough in judgment to give you counsel, the best and most assured counsel, and that I had the understanding, as I have the will, to do it. Then rather would I bring it[5] to you than send it. I hope among other things that you will remember that he is well worthy of falling who enters into nets: do not only take advice, think shrewdly. That is enough.

I hear to my great regret that the King, the Queen Mother, even your own, put on me the fault that I have never committed,[6] having always looked to the King to perfect that which I can no longer do more than mention, except to entreat you to do me so much right as to exculpate me even by the sentence of your ministers, who themselves know my innocence in this matter. For I cannot bear such an injury, that they bite and weep at my affection with regard to you. I appeal to the King's ambassador, to Monsieur La Mothe, Marchaumont, and Bacqueville;[7] and as long as God does not permit such a pact, so long will I never cease honoring, loving, and esteeming you like the dog who, often beaten, returns to his master. God keep you from glozing counsels and permit you to follow those who respect[8] you more than themselves.

[Queen Elizabeth to Catherine de Medici, Queen Mother of France, on Monsieur's Death] ca. July 1584

[Addressed] To Madame, my good sister, the Queen Mother[1]

Madame,

If the extremity of my unhappiness had not equaled my grief for his sake and had not rendered me inadequate to touch with pen the wound that my heart suffers, it would not be possible that I would have so forgotten myself as not to have visited you[2] in the company that I make with you in your

3. The King of France prefers to.
4. Surrounded.
5. Her advice.
6. The context suggests that the fault ascribed to her was negotiating the marriage in bad faith; *your own:* your own agents.
7. French emissaries to Elizabeth's court.
8. Think of, honor; *glozing:* falsely flattering.
1. The letter was written after news of Anjou's death reached England.
2. Sent you a letter.

sorrow, which I am sure cannot be greater than my own. For inasmuch as you are his mother, so it is that there remain to you several other children. But for me, I find no consolation except death, which I hope will soon re-unite us. Madame, if you were able to see the image of my heart, you would see the portrait of a body without a soul. But I will trouble you no longer with my plaints, since you have too many of your own. It remains to me at this point to avow and swear to you that I will turn a good part of my love for him towards the King my good brother and you, assuring you that you will find me the most faithful daughter and sister that ever princes had and this for the principal reason that he belonged to you so nearly, he to whom I was entirely dedicated; he to whom, if he had had the divine favor of a longer life, you would have sent more help.[3] Madame, I pray you to give firm credit to this gentleman, who will tell you more amply in my stead my thoughts on your behalf. And believe that I will fulfill them faithfully as if I were your daughter born. As God knows, to whom I pray to give you long life and every consolation.

Your very affectionate sister and cousin,
Elizabeth R

WILLIAM CECIL, LORD BURGHLEY

Letter to the Queen Regarding Her Proposed Marriage (1579)[†]

[*Endorsed*] 1579. *To the Queen's majesty. Advice about her match.*

The clock that stond so long hath now so weighty plummets of favor and courage put on that it striketh still,[1] a clock not to tell how this day passeth only, but how days and time passeth like river streams, whose waves return no more. In so great a matter, it was necessary to consider well what was good, with counsel and leisure, and as good reason and policy to go through with the good when it is determined, except some secret stay that is not within the level of our sights to see.[2] But if your Majesty tarry till all clocks strike and agree of one hour, or tarry till all the oars row the barge, you shall never point the time and you may slip[3] the tide that yet patiently tarryeth for you.

In the beginning, the morning of your time, your Majesty hath taken the sweet dew of pleasure and delight, the temperate air of a quiet and a calm, contented mind, a moisture and a breath as natural to maintain and feed a dainty[4] nature as the most wholesome meat to strengthen and maintain the

---

3. The meagerness of French financial support for Anjou's military endeavors in the Netherlands was a sore point in Elizabeth's dealings with Catherine and Henry III.
† Copy text: *Elizabeth I: Collected Works*, ed. Leah S. Marcus, Janel Mueller, and Mary Beth Rose (Chicago and London: University of Chicago Press, 2000), 240–42. Reprinted by permission of the University of Chicago Press. © 2000 by the University of Chicago.
1. The clock that stood silent is now hung with such favorable weights that it has begun once again to chime.
2. Unless prevented by some unforeseen difficulty.
3. Miss; *till all clocks . . . barge*: the various clocks and oars refer to the diversity of opinions among her counselors; *point*: settle upon; appoint.
4. Excellent.

body. From the beginning, pleasure and content agrees with your nature; long custom makes it not voluntary but necessary. It is not enough then your Majesty reign and to be Queen still, but to reign and rule honored, pleased, and contented, and to have the morning dew all the whole day of your life. Admitting then all reasons of policy and causes removed and answered that persuade and lead you to this match, your Majesty still in your old state to sit sure and rule singly as you did, could you yet then think it morning still?[5] Have you the sweet dew and the temperate air so agreeable and necessary to your nature? No, but either they be quite altered, or if they be not, yet are your senses so full that the satisfaction makes an end of pleasure.

And so in that state (the food of your mind spent and not new provided for), is it mirth, meat or music, honor, duty, and service done by your servants that doth satisfy, if there be not some partner of the delight, honor, and pleasure, and that[6] your Majesty may love and esteem above the rest? Or lives the man and speaks he English that you highly esteem and love at this day? I grant it is enough for some to think upon a good dinner, a supper, a soft bed, a carpet and a cushion, of coin and crowns, and to keep a reckoning.[7] But to some others of more fine spirits, all these not seasoned with the presence of a virtuous, discoursing, and delightful friend have neither taste nor savor. Who[8] might command the whole world and had every necessary and every pleasure provided to her hand without pain or care, and no companion, friend, or servant beloved on whom to bestow favors of that plenty, nor from whom to receive any sign of love and service, should that person live contented and be glad of full dishes, full coffers, and of elbow room? No, since it were no more able to content nature, at least the best natures, than an empty cup were able to slake an extreme thirst. God Himself was not contented alone with perfection and height of all happiness till He made the angels and man to be witnesses and partakers of His felicity. How shall they content you then, Madam, your honor, state, wealth, and delights, if you have not the friend that may content you best and who you find desirous to content you most? For without that person you are alone, though a hundred be about, as well as the person I brought for example that had never a one.

If then I have proved it as necessary your Majesty have content and pleasure as rule and treasure; if I have showed where it is not and where it is, and now prove plainly you may take it if you please, I have then ended my desire, though to no effect beside.[9] Three sorts of people we find against this marriage: one for doubt lest a husband of contrary faith should alter and overthrow the religion; the second sort lest it might be impediment or defeasance[1] of some plot and hope laid and had of a successor to their likings; a third kind for loathness and doubt lest such as have had the highest credit should come down, on whom their suits and

---

5. If all the political reasons in favor of the match are discounted, will you be content to return to your single state?
6. One whom.
7. Account.
8. Whoever.
9. If Cecil has proved to the Queen that she needs a companion and that she is free to marry Anjou, then his task is complete, even if she decides against the alliance.
1. Defeat.

their profits have and do depend. To the first is answered that he[2] shall not have authority nor power to alter religion now used and established. He brings no preachers to persuade; and violently to do it, where shall be his force? Example shall do no hurt, since his chapel door shall be shut. The second sort be unanswerable, and be for their expectation and foresight to be contemned,[3] and for their number and small power to be contemned. The third kind will be satisfied when they see their lovers or their loves take no hurt.

Then may it please your Majesty to peruse on the other side whom ye have with it,[4] and the reckoning I think, Madam, not to be disproved: first, the nobility of all your Council and all other of your Council, either warmly with it or very coldly against it, and yet I hope none against you, howsomever you please to proceed. Next, the whole nobility of England, three or four excepted, who either would come fast on[5] if they saw your Majesty resolute or sit as still as a bird in a dark winter night. All the Protestants of England that love you for yourself could not choose but desire it; the Catholics pray for it, not in hope to have their religion set at liberty, but to have a privy coat[6] against persecution; as for the sort of men that be not earnest in any religion, they follow directly what the prince commandeth and desireth. Add to this strength at home the strength of the neighbor and alliance that be bound in honor and for their own security and better peace to war and wrestle on your side in this quarrel, and if there be a party so wicked and so hardy to disturb the marriage by tumult and by force as they did the Queen your sister's (if you mean to meet at home, as God knows and the reckoning plain, you are ten times so strong), your Majesty might be strongly assisted from thence.[7] But doubt not, Lady, for when lions make a leap, the bears and other beasts lie down. And at least be resolute and know what you may, though you know not what you will; or so your Majesty be quit and out of doubt,[8] it is no matter though all we doubt still. I most humbly beseech your Majesty that as I know you read, so you take order that none read after ye;[9] and for the pain taken in reading and for your last favors, I vow my life and all I have to serve you. And kissing your hands with the humble and earnest affection of my heart, singly and simply yours, I take my leave and ask leave for two days' absence.

2. Anjou.
3. Disregarded or viewed with contempt.
4. Who support the marriage.
5. Favorably support.
6. Coat of mail worn under regular clothes; a Roman Catholic consort to the Queen would provide protection against persecution.
7. That is, from France; *sister's*: Mary's marriage to Philip II of Spain provoked opposition from the English people.
8. Free and without doubt; *or so*: and so if.
9. Cecil puns on the word "read," meaning both to peruse the written page and to interpret. The Queen should make up her own mind and not allow anyone else to overread or misread her intentions.

SIR PHILIP SIDNEY

From A Discourse of Sir Philip Sidney to the Queen's Majesty Touching Her Marriage with Monsieur (1579)[†]

Most feared and beloved, most sweet and gracious Sovereign:

To seek out excuses of this my boldness, and to arm[1] the acknowledging of a fault with reasons for it, might better show I knew I did amiss than any whit diminish the attempt, especially in your judgment who, able lively to discern into the nature of the thing done, it were folly to hope with laying on better colors to make it more acceptable. Therefore, carrying no other olive branches[2] of intercession but the laying myself at your feet, nor no other insinuation either for attention or pardon but the true vowed sacrifice of unfeigned love, I will in simple and direct terms (as hoping they shall only come to your merciful eyes) set down the overflowing of my mind in this most important matter, importing (as I think) the continuance of your safety and (as I know) the joys of my life. And because my words (I confess shallow, but coming from the clear wellspring of most loyal affection) have already delivered unto your gracious ears what is the general sum of my traveling[3] thoughts, herein I will now but only declare what be the reasons that make me think the marriage of Monsieur unprofitable for you. Then will I answer your objections of those fears which might procure so violent a refuge.[4]

The good or evil which might come unto you by it must be considered either according to your state or your person.[5] To your estate, what can be added to the being an absolute born and accordingly respected princess? But as they say the Irishmen are wont to tell them that die, "They are rich, they are fere; what need they to die?"[6] So truly to you, endued with felicities beyond all others (though short of your deserts), a man may well ask, "What maketh you in such a calm to change course, to so healthful a body to apply such a weary medicine? What hope can recompense so hazardous an adventure?" Hazardous indeed, if it were for nothing but the altering a well maintained and well approved trade.[7] For as in bodies natural any sudden change is not without peril, so in this body politic, whereof you are the only head, it is so much the more as there are more humors[8] to receive a hurtful impression.

But hazards are then most to be regarded when the natures of the agent and patient are fitly composed to occasion them.[9] The patient I account

---

[†] Copy text: *The Complete Works of Sir Philip Sidney*, ed. Albert Feuillerat, vol. 3 (Cambridge: Cambridge University Press, 1923), 51–55, 59–60. Although, at the time the work was written, Sidney had not yet been knighted, we use his conventional title, "Sir Philip."
1. Defend.
2. Symbol of peace.
3. Wandering; travailing or laboring.
4. Refuge from Spanish hostility; *of*: against.
5. The monarch was thought to have two bodies: one political (as an embodiment of the nation of England) and the other personal or natural (as a woman).
6. That is, they were better off where they were; *fere*: strong, healthy.
7. Course of action.
8. Bodily fluids—chiefly blood, phlegm, choler, and bile—thought to govern one's physical and psychological makeup.
9. When the natures of the one acting and the one affected are so matched that they give special opportunities for danger.

your realm, the agent Monsieur and his designs. For neither outward accidents do much prevail against a true inward strength, nor inward weakness doth lightly subvert itself without being thrust at by some outward force. Your inward force (for as for your treasure, indeed the sinews of your crown, your Majesty doth best and only know) doth consist in your subjects, generally unexpert in warlike defense and, as they are, divided into two mighty factions, and factions bound upon the never-ending knot of religion. The one[1] is of them to whom your happy government hath granted the free exercise of the eternal truth. With these (by the continuance of time, by the multitude of them, by the principal offices and strengths they hold, and lastly by your dealings both at home and abroad against the adverse party[2]) your estate is so enwrapped as it were impossible for you, without excessive trouble, to put yourself out of the party so long maintained. For such a course once taken is not much unlike to a ship in a tempest, which how dangerously soever it be beaten with waves, yet is there no safety nor succor without it. These, therefore, as their souls live by your happy government, so are they your chief, if not sole, strength. These, howsoever the necessity of human life make them look, yet cannot they look for better conditions than presently they enjoy. These, how their hearts will be galled, if not aliened, when they shall see you take to husband a Frenchman and a papist, in whom, howsoever fine wits may find either further danger or painted excuses, yet very common people will know this: that he is the son of that Jezebel of our age; that his brothers made oblation of their own sister's marriage, the easier to make massacres of all sexes; that he himself, contrary to his promise and against all gratefulness, having had his liberty and principal estate chiefly by the Huguenots' means, did sack La Charité and utterly spoiled Issoire with fire and sword.[3] This, I say, at the first sight giveth occasion to all the truly religious to abhor such a master and so consequently to diminish much of their hopeful love they have long held in you.

The other faction, indeed most rightly to be called a faction, is of the papists, men whose spirits are full of anguish: some being forced to oaths they account damnable, some having their ambition stopped because they are not in the way of advancement, some in prison and disgrace, some whose best friends are banished; practisers, many thinking you an usurper, many thinking the right you had disannulled by the Pope's excommunication, all grieved at the burdenous weight of their consciences; men of great number, of great riches because the affairs of the estate[4] have not lain upon them, of minds united as all men that deem themselves oppressed naturally are. With them I would willingly join all discontented persons such as want

---

1. The Protestant faction.
2. The Roman Catholic faction.
3. In the mid-1570s, Anjou took arms in defense of the Huguenots, but in 1577, he turned on them as part of an agreement with his brother, Henry III, and besieged and destroyed the two Protestant towns mentioned here; *aliened*: alienated; *painted*: deceptive; *Jezebel . . . age*: Catherine de Medici; *oblation*: blood sacrifice; *massacres . . . sexes*: in August 1572, Anjou's brothers, Charles IX and the future Henry III, were involved in the St. Bartholomew's Day massacre. Sidney was present during the slaughter of at least 3000 Huguenots who had come to Paris for the wedding of Anjou's sister to the Protestant leader Henry of Navarre. As many as 7000 more died elsewhere in France.
4. State; *practisers*: conspirators, agents; *Pope's excommunication*: Pope Pius V's bull excommunicating Elizabeth in 1570 denied her right to the English crown and excommunicated any who "dare[d] obey her orders, mandates, and laws" (see Part Four).

or disgrace keepeth lower than they can set their hearts, such as are resolved what they have to look for at your hands, such, as Caesar said, "*quibus opus est bello civili*," and are of Otho's mind, "*malle in acie quam in foro cadere*."[5] Those are men so much the more to be doubted because, as they embrace all estates, so are they commonly of the bravest[6] and wakefulest sort and know the advantage of the world most. This double rank of people, how their minds have stood, the Northern Rebellions[7] and infinite other practices have well taught you, which if it be said they did not prevail, that is true indeed; for if they had prevailed, it were too late now to deliberate. But at this present, they want nothing so much as a head, who shall in effect need but to receive their instructions, since they may do mischief enough only with his countenance.[8] Let the singing man in Henry IV's time, Perkin Warbeck in your grandfather's, but of all, the most lively and proper example is of Lewis, the French King's son in Henry III's time (who having at all no show of title here, yet did half the nobility and more swear direct fealty and vassalage and delivered the strongest holds unto him)[9] be sufficient to prove that occasions give minds scope to stranger things than ever would have been imagined.

If, then, the affectionate have their affections weakened and the discontented have a gap to utter their discontentation, I think it will seem an evil preparative for the patient (I mean your estate) to a greater sickness.

Now for the agent party, which is Monsieur: whether he be not apt to work upon the disadvantage of your estate is to be judged by his will and his power. His will to be as full of light ambition as is possible, besides the French disposition and his own education, his inconstant attempts against his brother, his thrusting himself into the Low County matters (he sometime seeking the King of Spain's daughter, sometime your Majesty) are evident testimonies of a light mind carried with every wind of hope, taught to love greatness any way gotten, and having the motioners and ministers of his mind only such young men as have showed (they think) evil contentment a sufficient ground of any rebellion, whose ages giveth them to have seen no commonwealth[1] but in faction, and divers of them which have defiled their hands with odious murders. With these fancies and such favorites, is it to be hoped for that he will be contained in the limits of your conditions?[2] Since in truth it were strange, he that cannot be content to be second person in France and heir apparent would come to be the second person where he should pretend no way sovereignty. His power, I imagine,

5. "They prefer to fall in battle rather than in the Forum," where their creditors might seize them (Suetonius, *Life of Otho* 5); *quibus . . . civili*: "For whom what is needed is a civil war" to give them a new start (Suetonius, *Divus Julius* 27); *foro*: copy text: *foco*.
6. Boldest; *doubted*: feared, suspected; *embrace all estates*: cultivate people of all classes.
7. Uprisings against the Queen in 1569 by Catholics in the north of England (see Part Three); *double rank of people*: Papists and malcontents.
8. Approval; *want*: lack.
9. The story is told in Holinshed, *Chronicles* (1577) 3.191–92; *singing man*: probably John Maudelen, a chaplain of Richard II who gathered discontented subjects against Richard's successor, Henry IV; *Perkin Warbeck*: executed in 1499 by Henry VII for encouraging conspiracies by claiming to be a son of Edward IV.
1. Sharing in governance; *light*: fickle; *attempts . . . brother*: while defending the Huguenots in the mid-1570s. The Treaty of Beaulieu (1576), which reconciled him with the King, gave him extensive estates and the title Duke of Anjou; *thrusting . . . matters*: in 1578, Protestant rebels in the Netherlands enlisted Anjou to fight with them against their Spanish rulers; *evil contentment*: discontent.
2. Conditions for marriage currently being negotiated.

is not to be despised, since he is to come into a country where the way of evil-doing will be presented unto him, where there needeth nothing but a head to draw together evil-affected limbs, himself a prince of great revenues, of the most populous nation of the world, full of soldiers and such as are used to serve without pay, so they have show of spoil,[3] and without question shall have his brother in such a case ready to help him, as well for old revenges as for to divert him from troubling France and to deliver his own country the sooner from evil humors. Neither is King Philip's marriage herein any example, since that it was between two of one religion, so that he in England stood only upon her strength and had abroad Henry of France ready to impeach any enterprise he would make for his greatness that way.[4] And yet, what events time would have brought forth of that marriage, your most blessed reign hath made vain all such considerations.

But things holding in the state present, I think I may justly conclude that your country, being as well by long peace and fruits of peace as by the poison of division (whereof the faithful shall by this means be wounded and the contrary enabled) made fit to receive hurt, and Monsieur being every way apt to use the occasion to hurt, there can almost happen no worldly thing of more evident danger to your estate royal. For as for your person (indeed the seal of our happiness), what good there may come by it to balance with the loss of so honorable a constancy truly yet I perceive not.

I will not show so much malice as to object the universal doubt of all that race's unhealthfulness; neither will I lay to his charge his ague-like manner of proceeding: sometimes hot, sometimes cold in time of pursuit, which always likely is most fervent.[5] And I will temper my speeches from any other irreverent disgracings of him in particular, though they be never so true. This only will I say: if he do come, he must live here in far meaner reputation than his mind will well brook, having no other royalty to countenance himself with; or else you must deliver him the keys of your kingdom and live at his discretion; or, lastly, he must separate himself,[6] to more dishonor and further discontentment of heart than ever before.

Often have I heard you with protestation say no private pleasure nor self-affection could lead you unto it.[7] But if it be both unprofitable for your kingdom and unpleasant to you, certainly it were a dear purchase of repentance.[8] Nothing can it add unto you but the bliss of children, which I confess were an unspeakable comfort, but yet no more appertaining to him than to any other to whom that height of all good haps were allotted to be your husband. And therefore I think I may assuredly affirm that what good soever can follow marriage is no more his than anybody's, but the evils and dangers are particularly annexed to his person and condition. For as for the enriching of your country with treasure (which either he hath not or hath otherwise to bestow it), or the staying your servants' minds with new expectations

---

3. So long as they may have expectations to share the spoils of war; *evil-affected limbs*: parts of the body politic bent on evil. Sidney often uses imagery of disease in assessing Anjou's likely effects.
4. Henry II of France was Philip's chief adversary in the 1550s; *marriage*: Philip II married Mary Tudor in 1554; *impeach*: impede.
5. At a time when he is first pursuing her, which is always likely to be the most passionate; *object . . . doubt*: raise the widespread English fear; *unhealthfulness*: the French royal family was rumored to suffer from syphilis; *ague-like*: flu-like.
6. Live separate from her; *meaner*: lower.
7. That is, to marriage.
8. An expensive change of heart.

and liberalities (which is more dangerous than fruitful), or the easing your Majesty of your cares (which is as much to say as easing you of being a queen sovereign), I think everybody perceiveth this way either full of hurt or void of help.[9]

*   *   *

Since then it is dangerous for your estate, as well because it (by inward weakness principally caused by division) is fit to receive harm as because he both in will and power is like enough to do harm; since to your person it can no ways be comfortable (you not desiring marriage), and neither to person nor estate he is to bring any more good than anybody,[1] but more evil he may; since the causes that should drive you to this are either fear of that which cannot happen or by this mean cannot be prevented, I do with most humble heart say unto your Majesty that (laying aside this dangerous help), for your standing alone, you must take it as a singular honor God hath done you to be indeed the only protector of His church and yet, in worldly respect, your kingdom very sufficient so to do. If you make that religion upon which you stand to carry the only strength and have abroad those who still maintain the same cause (who, as being as they may,[2] be kept from utter falling), your Majesty is sure enough from your mightiest enemies.

As for this man, as long as he is but Monsieur in might and a papist in profession, he neither can nor will greatly stead[3] you. And if he grow king, his defense will be like Ajax's shield, which weighed down rather than defended[4] those that bare it.

Against contempt at home (if there be any, which I will never believe), let your excellent virtues of piety, justice, and liberality daily, if it be possible, more and more shine. Let some such particular actions be found out (which is easy, as I think, to be done) by which you may gratify all the hearts of your people. Let those in whom you find trust, and to whom you have committed trust in your weighty affairs, be held up in the eyes of your subjects. Lastly, doing as you do, you shall be as you be: the example of princesses, the ornament of your age, the comfort of the afflicted, the delight of your people, the most excellent fruit of all your progenitors, and the perfect mirror to your posterity.

THE WIDENING CONTROVERSY

One of the most alarming incidents in Anjou's courtship of Elizabeth occurred on July 17, 1579, when one of the Queen's oarsmen was seriously injured by a stray bullet shot from a light musket by Thomas Appletree, who was hunting birds along the Thames. Elizabeth was traveling at the time from Greenwich to Deptford by barge, accompanied by her Lord Admiral and the French ambassador, Jean de Simier. At first, authorities suspected an assassination attempt related to the French marriage negotiations. When the truth was discovered, the Queen pardoned Appletree, and life at Court returned to normal. The

9. We omit the refutation of reasons favoring the marriage: fear of standing alone against Spain and of suffering the contempt of her subjects tired of her long reign and anxious that she has no heir.
1. Than any other man might.
2. Whatever condition they may be in.
3. Help.
4. Copy text: defend; *grow*: become.

incident was, however, memorably captured by William Elderton in "A New Ballad, Declaring the Dangerous Shooting of the Gun at the Court." Elderton was the master of a company of comedians and a ballad-writer described by Gabriel Harvey as one of "the very ringleaders of the rhyming and scribbling crew." This ballad, like many others, was printed as a "broadside," that is, a large single sheet of paper sold inexpensively to a large cross-section of the London population.

More troubling to the Queen than a stray bullet on the Thames was a tract by John Stubbs written in August 1579 to protest the French marriage. Its full title—*The Discovery of a Gaping Gulf whereunto England is like to be swallowed by another French marriage, if the Lord forbid not the banns, by letting her Majesty see the sin and punishment thereof*—suggests the polemical tone adopted in the volume. Stubbs, the scion of a well-established Norfolk family, was a graduate of Trinity College, Cambridge, and had worked as a lawyer and a translator. He had militant Protestant sympathies, and his sister was married to Thomas Cartwright, one of the leaders of the early Puritan movement.

Stubbs objected to the French marriage on a number of grounds, including the physical threat posed to the Queen should she become pregnant or contract syphilis, which the English called the "French disease." Primarily, however, he disapproved of a Protestant monarch marrying a Roman Catholic prince and a foreigner because he thought that the Bible forbade such a mixed union and because the match threatened the stability of the English Church. It also raised the specter of a return to a Catholic government should Elizabeth give birth to an heir raised in Anjou's religion. Though his mistrust of the French bordered on the xenophobic, he and other Protestants had reason to fear the Medici family. Catherine and her older sons had orchestrated the betrayal of the Huguenots in the 1572 St. Bartholomew's Day massacre, and Anjou himself had played a leading role in the brutal sacking of the Protestant strongholds of La Charité and Issoire.

On September 20, a month after a thousand copies had been printed and distributed, the Queen issued a proclamation refuting the book and ordering its confiscation. Along with Hugh Singleton, the printer, and William Page, who had helped distribute the work, Stubbs was arrested and tried for seditious writing. On November 3, he and Page were taken to the market place at Westminster, where their right hands were cut off. Warrant for this unusual and dramatic sentence was dredged up from an act passed during the reign of Mary Tudor, and there was considerable disagreement at the time as to whether the punishment was even legal. Stubbs himself appealed to the Queen for mercy, but to no avail. Nevertheless, it is reported that, after his right hand had been stricken off, he swept off his hat with his left and loudly proclaimed, "God save the Queen." Then he fainted. His claim that he had always remained loyal to Queen and country was vindicated by his later life, for he subsequently entered the service of Lord Burghley.

Stubbs was unusual in his boldness. Other opponents of the French marriage were more cautious, taking pains to veil their opinions and avoid his fate. In Philip Sidney's pastoral romance the Old *Arcadia*—so called to distinguish it from a later revision known as the New *Arcadia*—the courtier occasionally called to mind current affairs in England through his fictional narratives. One particularly suggestive analogy appeared in the beast fable "As I My Little Flock." Satirizing the folly of longing for a king, the poem seems to have been directed at Englishmen who, having experienced two reigning queens in a row, were anxious to have a king once again and so were pinning their hopes on Anjou. The poem combines elements of the myth of Prometheus, Aesop's fable of the frogs who asked Jupiter for a king, and the Israelites' unwise petition for a king in the Old Testament (1 Samuel 8.1–22). When Sidney's animals request a strong ruler to keep order, Jove warns them against the idea but ultimately lets them have their way. Making the new creature's spirit of heavenly fire, he requires that each animal contribute an attribute of its own. The lion gives heart, the parrot "ready tongue," the fox craft, the dog flattery, and so on. Before long, however, the new ruler forgets his origins and becomes a tyrant, enslaving the others and killing them for sport.

Sidney may have had in mind here the gifts that Englishmen had showered on Anjou while he was in England and his penchant for turning on his Protestant friends and participating in massacres. The ape calls to mind Anjou's chief emissary, Jean de Simier, whom Elizabeth had nicknamed her "monkey" because his surname called to mind the Latin word for "ape." As his gift, the ape bestows "The instrument of instruments, the hand," perhaps (as Jan van Dorsten has suggested) a reference to the Queen's hand in marriage. Beyond Sidney's immediate concern with the French marriage, however, lay other, deeper issues, particularly the declining power of the English aristocracy. Represented here by the nobler animals, the titled aristocrats had looked on as Elizabeth had bestowed high offices at Court on able commoners such as William Cecil, Sir Francis Walsingham, and Sir Walter Mildmay. In the view of many noblemen, these should have been reserved for men of rank.

In the period 1581–86, after the marriage crisis had passed but while it was still on people's minds, Christopher Marlowe wrote the satiric play *Dido, Queen of Carthage,* which dramatized a love story from the first four books of Virgil's *Aeneid.* Like Elizabeth, the Queen in the play is bent on a strategically advantageous marriage with a foreign prince, one who is more interested in founding an empire for himself across the sea than in settling down with her. Soon after the Trojans suffer shipwreck and come ashore in Carthage, the Queen falls in love with their leader, Aeneas, and similarities between her and the English Queen begin to emerge. The resemblance is never more clear than in the passage excerpted here, which has no analog in Virgil. Taking her Trojan guests on a tour of her portrait gallery, Dido pauses to boast of the many distinguished suitors in the paintings who have come to seek her hand in marriage. As Elizabeth had done with Philip II, the Earl of Leicester, Eric of Sweden, Don Carlos, Anjou's brother Henry, and others, Dido has turned them all away. Shortly after this incident, she and Aeneas go out hunting and are caught in a sudden shower. Forced to seek shelter in a cave, Dido then seduces the rather obtuse and clumsy Trojan only to see him sail off and leave her a short time later. Marlowe's send-up of the Queen's passion for Anjou and the fecklessness and ambition with which he responded was the most unflattering account of the French marriage of the period. Probably for that reason, it was never performed in London but only in the area around Norwich and Ipswich, where large numbers of ardent Protestants would have been more likely to welcome its veiled criticisms of the Queen and her beloved Frenchman.

WILLIAM ELDERTON

A New Ballad, Declaring the Dangerous Shooting of the Gun at the Court (1579)[†]

Weep, weep, still I weep, and shall do till I die,
To think upon the gun was shot at Court so dangerously.

[†] Copy text: William Elderton, *A newe ballade, declaryng the daungerons* [sic] *shootynge of the gunne at the courte* (London: Edward White, [1579]; *STC* 7557.4). Elderton suggested that this ballad be sung to the tune "Sick and Sick."

The seventeen day of July last, at evening toward night,
Our noble Queen Elizabeth took barge for her delight
5 And bade the watermen to row, her pleasure she might take
About the river to and fro, as much as they could make.
    Weep, weep, still I weep, and shall do till I die,
      To think upon the gun was shot at Court so dangerously.

And of her Council, with her Grace, were nobles two or three,
10 As fittest were to be in place, regarding their degree;
The French Ambassador likewise, to common° with her Grace   *to talk*
Of weighty causes sat with her, each one in comely° place.   *proper*
    Weep, weep, etc.

But when her Grace an hour or two had passed to take the air,
15 Returning reading on a book, she said, "Row soft and fair."[1]
Whereby, as God the matter wrought the slackness° and   *slowness*
   the stay,°   *delay*
Softly she passed and nothing thought of gunshot any way.
    Weep, weep, etc.

But all this while upon the Thames in a sculler's boat[2] unknown,
20 A wretched fellow got a gun that was none of his own,
And shot a bullet two or three at random all about,
And gave no great regard to see what time the Queen went out.
    Weep, weep, etc.

But as her Grace came passing by, had giv'n his piece a charge[3]
25 And there out let a bullet fly that hit one in the barge,
A waterman through both his arms as he began to row,
That he cried out upon his harms, whereat the Queen was woe.° *distressed*
    Weep, weep, etc.

Herself in sight and presence by, when that the bullet came,
30 She saw him hurt, she saw him fall, yet shrunk not at the same;
Neither made she any fearful show to seem to be dismayed,
Nor seemed to the Ambassador of anything afraid.
    Weep, weep, etc.

But having such a mighty mind, as passeth tongue to tell,
35 She stepped unto the wounded man and bade him take it well.
His gushing blood could not abash her noble courage then,
But she was readier to give help than all the noble men.
    Weep, weep, etc.

But what her Highness said and did, in that so sudden fear,
40 Hereafter in my sorry tale the substance you shall hear.

---

1. Leisurely and smoothly; *returning reading*: returning to reading.
2. A boat propelled by a pair of sculls, or short oars, rowed by a single person.
3. Loaded the musket.

"Let boats go out and fetch him in," she said, "that this hath done."
And quickly was the person brought that so discharged the gun.
    Weep, weep, etc.

The noble councilors most abroad, to whom these tidings came,
45 Made haste to Court with trembling hearts to think upon the same,
Applauding God upon their knees most humbly in their place,
With tears of joy that bitter bale° had so escaped her Grace.   *evil; death*
    Weep, weep, etc.

His name was Thomas Appletree, of Court a serving man,
50 Which was no little grief to see to his good master then.
He was committed to the jail, at councilors' grave regard,
That they might judge what vilest death were fit for his reward.
    Weep, weep, etc.

With blubbering tears it is no boot° to tell the weeping eyes   *it is no use*
55 That were full woe° of such a shot, where all our safety lies.   *distressed*
The bullet came so near her Grace, within six foot at least,
Was never such a curséd case by such a willful beast.
    Weep, weep, etc.

Wherefore it was decreed and judged, by all the Council grave,
60 That hanging was too good a death for such a wretch to have.
A gibbet was set up in haste, against the Court full nigh,
Where this unhappy Appletree was pointed° for to die.   *appointed*
    Weep, weep, etc.

And on the Tuesday following then, this wicked prisoner came,
65 Well guarded with the Marshal's men to hang upon the same.
His master standing on the bank to hear what he could say,
He humbly fell upon his knees and mercy did him pray.
    Weep, weep, etc.

"Would God thou hadst never served me," quoth he with woeful look.
70 "But God," he said, "forgive it thee, that curséd mark° thou took."   *aim*
And after prayer said and done, on the ladder as he stood,
He took his death before them all; he was a subject good.
    Weep, weep, etc.

And never meant to hurt her Grace, nor any in the barge,
75 Nor meant to shoot in any place to hurt with any charge,
But wished he never had been born, for his good master's sake,
Whom he had made a woeful man and no amends could make.
    Weep, weep, etc.

For troth° it was and truth it is, the Queen and Council know   *truth*
80 Not willingly, though wittingly, he let the bullet go.
Which matter hath been sifted° so, it moveth more   *examined closely*
  her Grace

To let the passion° of it go, the meeklier° in his case.   *effect / the more so*
  Weep, weep, etc.

The Queen that saw this sacrifice, a ready wretch to die,
85 Whose pity pleadeth pardon still, put forth her princely eye:
And sent the Captain of her guard, a councilor grave and wise,
To make the fact and favor known, as he could best devise.
  Weep, weep, etc.

Who gave a thundering peal of grace, the prisoner's fault to show
90 And° all the people in the place what Prince they had to know,   *to*
What courage in her noble Grace in peril did appear
Before the French Ambassador's face in such a sudden fear.
  Weep, weep, etc.

And told again if that mishap had happened on her Grace,
95 The stay° of true religion, how perilous were the case,   *support*
Which might have turned to bloody wars, of strange and
   foreign foes.
Alas, how had we been accursed, our comfort so to lose.
  Weep, weep, etc.

Then of° the mercy of her Grace, her subjects' lives to save,   *for*
100 By whom these twenty years in peace such quiet lives we have,
The tears fell down on every side and aloud the people cry,
"The Almighty long preserve her Grace to govern prosperously."
  Weep, weep, etc.

And last of all he said again, "Mark yet this piteous° queen,   *full of pity*
105 For all this vile unhappy fact, so lewdly° done and seen,   *foolishly; wickedly*
Returns to her inuréd° course, of mercy to forgive,   *habitual*
That this accurséd shall not die but pardons him to live."
  Weep, weep, etc.

And then to hear the people shout and see them clap their hands,
110 Who would have torn his flesh before, being in hangman's hands,
To see the goodness of her Grace, to such great pity bent,
It made the stoniest heart of all astonied° to lament.   *astonished*
  Weep, weep, etc.

The Councilor that the pardon brought, then kneeling on his knee,
115 And every subject as they ought, kneeled as well as he
And said a prayer for her Grace upon the doleful ground,
Whereof the people's sighing sherles[4] above the skies rebound.
  Weep, weep, etc.

All loving subjects learn to know your duties to our Queen
120 By land and water where ye go, that no such deed be seen.

---

4. Cries; literally "shrills," from the Middle English "shrelle" or "shirle."

But pray to God that rules the skies her Highness to defend,
To reign with him perpetually when her Highness's life shall end.
    Weep, weep, still I weep, and shall do till I die,
    To think upon the gun was shot at Court so dangerously.

JOHN STUBBS

From The Discovery of a Gaping Gulf (1579)[†]

In all deliberations of most private actions, the very heathen are wont first
to consider honesty and then profit, some of them also many times not
without some blind regard to a certain divine nature, which they wor-
shiped before the altar of the unknown God.[1] O the strange Christianity
of some men in our age, who in their state consultations have not so much
respect to piety as those first men had to honesty, nor so much regard to
honesty as they had to profit, and are therefore justly given up of the Lord
our God to seek profit where indeed it is not and deceived by their lusts to
embrace a showing and false good instead of that which is the good end
of a wise man.[2] Yea, who neglecting the holy and sure wisdom of God in
His Word, wherein are the only honorable instructions for politics and
honestest rules of governing our houses and own person, do beat their
brains in other books of wicked, vile atheists and set before them the
example of Turkish and Italian practices,[3] whereby the Lord many times
thrusts their hands into the nest of wasps and hornets while they seek the
honey of the sweet bee.

This sickness of mind have the French drawn from those eastern parts
of the world as they did that other horrible disease of the body[4] and, having already too far westward communicated the one contagion, do now seek
notably to infect our minds with the other. And, because this infection
spreads itself after another manner from the first, they have sent us hither
not Satan in body of a serpent but the old serpent in shape of a man, whose
sting is in his mouth and who doth his endeavor to seduce our Eve that she
and we may lose this English paradise, who because she is also our Adam
and sovereign Lord or lordly Lady of this land, it is so much the more dangerous, and therefore he so much the more busily bestirs him.

Now although the truth be that upon further ripping up of this serpen-
tine attempt we shall find the church notably undermined by the Pope, the
very foundations of our commonweal dangerously digged at by the French,
and our dear Queen Elizabeth (I shake to speak) led blindfold as a poor

---

† Copy text: John Stubb, *The discouerie of a gaping gulf vvhereinto England is like to be swallovved
  by another French mariage, if the Lord forbid not the banes, by letting her Maiestie see the sin and
  punishment thereof* ([London: H. Singleton for W. Page], 1579; STC 23400), A2r; A4v; A7v–A8r;
  B3r; B6v; C2r; C7r; C8v–D1v; D8v–E1v; E5v–E6v; F3v.
1. The Athenians are said to have built an altar to the unknown God (Acts 17.23); *wont*: accustomed.
2. A reference to Romans 1.21–24, where those who refuse to honor God are "given up" by Him to
  their own lusts and idolatry; *first men*: the ancients.
3. Earlier in the century, to defeat the power of Spain, France had made an alliance with the Ottoman
  Turks and certain Italian princes; *vile atheists*: probably a reference to Machiavelli, whose politics
  were considered anti-Christian by the English.
4. Syphilis.

lamb to the slaughter, yet should not my fear be so great, knowing her Majesty's wisdom sufficient to teach her in such a matter as this neither to trow a Frenchman nor once hear speak a daily hearer of Mass (for she may know him by his hissing and lisping), but that some English mouths, professing Christ, are also persuaders of the same.[5] And though this ship fraught with England's bane were already under crossed sail with the freshest gale of wind in her stern that can blow in the sky for our best port, yet had we counterpuffs and counterbuffs enough to keep him aloof[6] and to send him back again into the deeps if he had none but only French mariners and only French tackle. But, alas, this ship of unhappy load hath among us and of ourselves (I would not[7] in prince's court) those who with all their might and main help to hale it in, and, as though the blustering winds of our enemy's malice and the broad sails of our sins were not sufficient to give it a speedy passage hither, our own men walk on this shore and lay to their shoulders with fastened lines and cables to draw it in. This is our mischief, this is the swallowing gulf of our bottomless destruction, else might we think ourselves impregnable.

*   *   *

Yet to the end our minds may be the more earnestly stirred up by more particularly weighing the evils of this matter, we will enter into the parts of this practice and gauge the very belly of this great horse[8] of hidden mischiefs and falsehood meant to us. And according as those not half-taught Christians and half-hearted Englishmen which persuade and solicit this French marriage have in their mouths nothing but the church and the commonweal, pretending hereby either against their own conscience or of some other humor that blindeth them to bring great advancement to religion and advantage to the state with many smooth words of I wot what assurance to her Majesty's person, I will likewise draw all my reasons to those chief heads of religion and policy, showing and proving, I hope, that this is a counsel against the church of Christ, an endeavor of no well-advised Englishman, as well in regard of the common state as of her Majesty's good estate, to every of which it is pernicious and capital.[9]

*   *   *

[I]t is a sin, a great and a mighty sin for England, to give one of Israel's daughters to any of Hamor's sons; to match a daughter of God with one of the sons of men; to couple a Christian lady, a member of Christ, to a prince and good-son[1] of Rome, that anti-Christian mother city.

---

5. Led by William Cecil, Lord Burghley, several of the Queen's Protestant counselors, those "English mouths, professing Christ," supported marriage to Anjou; *ripping up*: bringing to notice an unpleasant fact; *lamb . . . slaughter*: a reference to Psalm 44.11, the verse spoken by Elizabeth when she feared for her life during the reign of Mary Tudor; Stubbs draws on old fears to kindle anxiety regarding the Queen's proposed marriage; *trow*: trust.
6. Apart; in nautical terms, to the windward. *bane*: poison; fatal mischief; *crossed sail*: sail with the sign of the cross on it. Stubbs here alludes to Anjou's secret crossing of the English Channel to court Elizabeth in August 1579, which was hindered by storms; *counterpuffs . . . counterbuffs*: counter winds and blows.
7. I would it were not so.
8. An allusion to the Trojan horse.
9. Deadly; *chief heads*: principal topics.
1. Son-in-law; *Hamor's sons*: a reference to the rape of Dinah, the daughter of Jacob, by Shechem, the son of Hamor the Hivite (Genesis 34); *match . . . men*: an allusion to the wickedness before the Great Flood, when the sons of God were married to the daughters of men (Genesis 6.2).

*   *   *

It is more than enough to break the holy ordinance instituted of God, which ought to govern us, without further inquiry of reason or commodity.[2] But as the holiness of His laws is wholesome to us even in this life by obedience, so doth their transgression breed us infinite incommodities. For the end of this holy kind of marriage is our mutual help and upholding one another in the fear of God, which appeareth by the reason of forbidding those unholy marriages, which is lest (saith the Spirit of God) their sons draw your daughters or their daughters your sons from the Lord.[3] Now as the one comes to pass where the order of God is kept, so the contrary effect must justly follow upon neglect, especially if such a marriage be made in a Gospel-like land where the law of God is preached (and contrary to warning given out of God's book). Then without,[4] peradventure all blessing is taken away and the plague followeth. And to teach our politiques[5] by reasonable arguments, what other reasons have the laws of all lands to join like to like in marriage but for the nourishing of peace and love between man and wife and for the well bringing-up of the children in every family, whereby to make them profitable members in some serviceable vocation (considering that families are the seeds of realms and petty parts of commonweals, where, if there be good order, the whole land is well ordered)? And contrary (as in any instrument), if every string or many strings be out of tune, the whole music is marred and whoso will preserve any entire must conserve every part, so if the families be distempered and out of tune, the whole land is disturbed.

*   *   *

But specially the breach of this law of God, in whomsoever private person it lighteth, draweth not only a certain falling away to the goodman or goodwife of the house so ungodly married but a danger also to children, servants, and every retainer of that household, much more manifold is the danger when the honorable Dame and (as in humbleness I may say) the Goodwife of England should be so (which God forbid) unevenly matched. It were more perilous to the overthrow of religion in this faithful household of England than if in one day were consummate the like marriages of a hundred thousand of other her subjects. For the straitest and roundest-going[6] prince shall with much ado keep his people upright, especially in religion. But let the prince lack never so little, and the people will halt right down.[7] The prince's fall is like that of a mighty oak, which bears down with it many arms and branches. Therefore is it often recited in the scripture that Jeroboam fell away from God and all Israel with him again, for the sins of Jeroboam whereby he caused all Israel to sin against the Lord.[8]

2. Convenience or advantage.
3. Deuteronomy 7.3–4.
4. Without warning.
5. Members of a French moderate party, and their sympathizers, who urged compromise as an alternative to continued religious wars. Anjou's brother, Henry III, was a leader of the Politiques.
6 Most thorough and uncompromising; *straitest*: strictest.
7. Fall away immediately.
8. See 1 Kings 12.26–33; 14.14–16, and many other passages that name Jeroboam as the cause of Israel's sin.

* * *

Here is therefore an imp[9] of the crown of France to marry with the crowned nymph of England. It is proved already that his coming shakes the church in England, and how shall he stablish the religion[1] in France? What is France to the church of God and to England for religion's sake? France is a house of cruelty (especially against Christians), a principal prop of the tottering house of Antichrist, and without which our Western Antichrist had been ere this sent to his brother Mohammed into Greece whither he long since sent his masters, the Emperors of Rome.[2] The long and cruel persecutions in France, the exquisite torments, and infinite numbers there put to death do witness how worthy that throne is to be reckoned for one horn of that persecuting beast, the primitive Empire.[3]

* * *

For the Lord's name sake therefore, O Christian Queen Elizabeth, take heed to yourself and to the church of Jesus Christ for which He shed His blood and which He hath shielded under your royal defense. Show yourself a zealous prince for God's Gospel to the end. Foresee, in a tender love to this people committed to your government, the continuance of the truth among them and their posterity. And for so much as in any great plague that can come to this church your Majesty must have your part, being a chief member therein, as by being in the bosom thereof you receive of the graces bestowed among us, have a care even of yourself and for yourself also, we instantly beseech you, to keep this sin far from you by admitting no counsel that may bring it near you, and in that common confession of sins (with the shaking of this rod drives us all to deny some of your delights also), and enter with the whole church into judgment of ourselves that we be not judged of the Lord.[4] And sith[5] the Lord hath used you as a mean to spread and enlarge Christ's kingdom in other churches and to harbor the persecuted Christians in your own kingdom, stop your Majesty's ears against these sorcerers and their enchanting counsels, which seek to stay this happy course of yours and to provoke God's anger against you. Pray against these dangerous tempters and temptations, and know assuredly (to your comfort) that all the faithful of God pray for you, and when you are in your secret most separate closet of prayer, they join with you in spirit.

* * *

[T]he true and natural old English nation never esteemed nor loved the French. They have it sunk so deep and deeply laid up in their heart as the savor wherewith their young shells were seasoned to the sun from grandfather to father, who in teaching them to shoot would have them imagine

9. Royal offspring.
1. The Protestant religion.
2. Protestant polemicists frequently align the papacy, the Holy Roman Empire, and Islam against the supporters of true religion; *Antichrist*: the Pope.
3. A reference to the horned beasts, representing secular kingdoms, from Daniel 8 and Revelation 17, that wage war against God and His people; *persecutions in France*: of the Huguenots.
4 We beseech you to preserve us all from judgment by rejecting those who counsel you to marry Anjou, accepting the loss of marriage with its delights and leading the Church in common confession and repentance; *instantly*: urgently and insistently; *shaking . . . rod*: the threat of a plague, seen as punishment sent by God.
5. Since.

a Frenchman for their butt, that so in shooting they might learn to hate kindly and in hating learn to shoot nearly.[6] Out of this inbred hatred it came that Frenchmen above other aliens bear this addition[7] in some of our ancient chronicles, charters, and statutes to be the ancient enemies of England. And can it be safe that a stranger and Frenchman should as owner possess our Queen, the chief officer in England, our most precious rich treasure, our Elizabeth, Jonah,[8] and ship of good speed, the royal ship of our aid, the highest tower, the strongest hold and castle in the land?

*   *   *

There is another dangerous danger in this foreign French match that ariseth yet far higher, in that he is the brother of childless France. So as if Henry III, now king, should die the morrow after our marriage and Monsieur repair home, as we may be sure he would, into his native country, a larger and better kingdom, then by all likelihood either must our Elizabeth go with him out of her own native country and sweet soil of England (where she is Queen as possessor and inheritor of this imperial crown, with all regal rights, dignities, prerogatives, pre-eminences, privileges, authorities, and jurisdictions of this kingly office and having the kingrick in her own person) into a foreign kingdom, where her writ doth not run[9] and shall be but in a borrowed majesty as the moon to the sun, shining by night as other kings' wives. And so she that hath ruled all this while here shall be there overruled in a strange land by some beldame not without awe perhaps of a sister-in-law.[1] And we, her poor subjects that have been governed hitherto by a natural mother, shall be overlooked[2] at home by some cruel and proud governor. Or else must she tarry here without comfort of her husband, seeing herself despised or not wifelike esteemed and as an eclipsed sun diminished in sovereignty, having such perhaps appointed to "serve her" and "be at her commandment" after the French phrase, which in plain English will govern her and her state.

*   *   *

These dangers, wherein this dangerous practice of marriage wrappeth Queen Elizabeth in her lifetime and her England together alike, will, I doubt not, move those in authority to avoid them and others that are private to pray against them most fervently. But these calamities, alas, end not with this age. For whereas these persuaders lay for a chief ground their certain expecting issue of her Majesty's body upon this match and the commodities thereof ensuing, thereby persuading this strange conceit,[3] I will at once dispatch that reason that might be objected against me and make it a chief argument (for I esteem it my second politic reason) to dissuade

---

6. Well; *butt*: target; *kindly*: naturally.
7. Reputation.
8. Probably a reference to Jonah as a figure of the resurrected Christ (Matthew 12.40); under Mary Tudor, Elizabeth faced death and was politically "resurrected."
9. Her authority carries no weight; *imperial crown*: here, not in the modern sense of a crown to rule over an empire but one entitling her to rule with no empire over her; *kingrick*: kingdom.
1. Any female relative by marriage; *beldame*: grandmother, but with the additional sense of an old, violent woman; a reference here to the powerful Dowager Queen, Catherine de Medici.
2. Governed.
3. Thought; the possibility of a child is an argument in favor of the marriage.

the French marriage especially. If it may please her Majesty to call her faithfulest wise physicians and to adjure them by their conscience towards God, their loyalty to her, and faith to the whole land to say their knowledge simply without respect of pleasing or displeasing any, and that they consider it also as the cause[4] of a realm and of a prince how exceedingly dangerous they find it by their learning for her Majesty at these years to have her first child, yea how fearful the expectation of death is to mother and child, I fear to say what will be their answer. And I humbly beseech her Majesty to inform herself thoroughly even in her love to the whole land, which holds dear her life and peace and which as it hath hitherto dutifully sought her marriage while hope of issue was (desiring it as the chiefest commonwealth good) and with all that fear God (English or stranger) would have rejoiced to see that the reign of Queen Elizabeth might have been drawn forth (as I may say) in her faithful line, yet dare we not now otherwise crave it but so as it might be by such a father as had a sound body and holy soul—and yet not them neither, unless she may first find it[5] to stand with her life and safety.

And when I think more earnestly of this matter, methinks it must needs come first of a very French love to our Queen and land to seek this marriage even now so eagerly at the uttermost time of hope to have issue and at the very point of most danger to her Majesty for childbearing. Whereby they think, if her Majesty have issue, to see either the mother die in childbed (which the Lord forbid) and the land left again, as theirs hath been, to an infant, or else to see both mother and child put in a grave and so the land left a spoil to foreign invasion and as a stack of wood[6] to civil wars.

*　*　*

For let it be that he have issue by her and that none but female only. We have hazarded our kingdom for putting it in the hands of the father, who, under color[7] of some tutorship to his daughter, will have her into France and so either adjoin this land to France or marry her to some French or other stranger at his liking. And all this while we never the near possession of our old right in France,[8] which we so much desired. For the Salic law bars her quite.[9] And though she should come and dwell in England, yet her bringing up being in France, her father will nuzzle her in his own religion, and so she coming home shall strive to stablish Popery as the late Queen of Scots[1] did when she came out of France, whereupon ensued those bloodsheds and red wars, besides the ill-favored examples of the French Court and kings, which we would be loath our English princes shall learn and bring home hither.

If this issue by Monsieur should be a son and but one son, then will he translate[2] his court into France and leave this poor province to the manag-

---

4. Matter of concern.
5. Her marriage; *hope of issue was:* possibility of children was still there; *faithful line:* her lineage might have been extended through her children.
6. Ready to be set afire.
7. Under the pretext.
8. The English still claimed medieval rights to rule large areas of France; *never:* never obtain.
9. The Salic law forbade females to inherit the throne, a fact made much of in Shakespeare's *Henry V*.
1. Mary Stuart; she is "late" not because she is dead, but because she has lost the throne of Scotland; *nuzzle:* educate, nurture.
2. Transfer.

ing of a viceroy. So did the ancient monarchies melt, so did this present empire lose her provinces[3] and is now become less than a kingdom, and so may this ancient kingdom be transferred to a rebellious seed. Such rough plowers do our sins deserve, to plow deep furrows on our backs if the Lord in mercy look not on us.[4]

*   *   *

[H]er Majesty, in whom as two persons or bodies (as they say) do presently fall in consideration (the one, her natural body, such as other private ones have; the other, her body politic or commonweal body which is her body of majesty, incorporate in understanding of the laws) even so several discommodities and hurts are here to fall in consideration also, in respect of these her two bodies, which albeit they be of that nature as nothing can be harmful to one but the same is full of harm to both.[5] Yet have I in speaking of the commonwealth handled also her Majesty's civil body as that which can no more be removed from the commonweal than the head from the body and as that which hath mutual suffering with the commonweal in weal and woe, as hath the head with the body.

*   *   *

Let us then see whether this Prince be a convenable[6] marriage in regard of her private person, who is already proved most unworthy and extremely dangerous for her princely personage.

Here comes first to our remembrance her constant dislike and indisposed mind toward marriage from the flower of her youth, which in all that love her breeds fear of a discontented life if, at these years, she take not her best heed and faithfulest advice in her marriage. This first difficulty on the part of her Majesty offers a second as great a difficulty on the part of his Excellency, that is, that he should hardly be the man, that choice man of choice in all respects, to content both eye and mind.

And if any that persuades this marriage think to have quit[7] himself substantially out of these two difficulties only by a bare objecting of them with referring over to be answered by her Majesty, as in whose heart rests the best knowledge of her disposition to marriage and contentation to this man, such one must be told that he doth not his bounden endeavor, especially if his place give any leave to debate at large with her. In this point, belike, he is to learn of every parent or other whatsoever that hath a loving care of their daughter or dear friend. Who upon a marriage moved will not set them down and rest in saying, "You know whether it be fit for you to marry, and you know whether this man be fit for you and to your liking," but cannot content themselves unless they press to help her with their best advice, laying about to search and inquire whether he be such as they wish? And if they find him otherwise, they lay the matter forth in time and frankly tell it her, lest through their silence or negligence she fall in danger of an ill husband, the greatest cross that may be laid on a poor woman's shoulders.

---

3. English lands in France.
4. A reference to Psalm 129.3, "The plowers plowed upon my back, and made long furrows."
5. Whatever harms the body natural harms the body politic, and vice versa; legally the two bodies were regarded as one; *incorporate . . . laws*: embodied in the eyes of the law.
6. Appropriate.
7. Aquitted.

The same should be much more diligently done in marriage of a queen and her realm, and it is a faithless, careless part to leave her helpless in her choice of the person and personal conditions of her husband to her own only consideration. Which, howsoever sufficient it be, so much the more hath she need of help as the matter is more weighty in her than in common matches.

* * *

This Prince cannot but, either for love or fear, be great with the Guisian duke[8] and, indeed, of very late more than ever. Even when it was said he should come over hither, he was nearly inward and in deep conferences with that Duke, who is to us an enemy by kind and for near consanguinity a fast friend to the late Scottish queen, who is the most hidden and pestilent adversary creature that lives to our Prince and state, the fairest daughter of the Pope and shot anchor[9] of all Papists. For as the Holy League hath tied all these great ones together by oath and their duty to the Pope, whom they will not displease, to hate to the death all religious[1] princes, so have they vowed it in the fourth degree against our Prince, as chief support of religion and in whose life or death (as they think) depends the exercise or not exercise of the Gospel in England and elsewhere.

* * *

Above all the dangers to her Majesty, I would she had one that might every day cry with a loud voice, "TAKE HEED, O ELIZABETH OF ENGLAND, AND BEWARE OF SCOTTISH MARY." The Lord her God defend her from all her popish enemies.

Let other men's squeamish judgments keep them in what temper of suspecting it likes them. I cannot be so blockish but to think that it is more than likely he comes for this Mary, to the end that (whereas if there be any rebellious papists at home, which can do naught for want of a leader, and those fugitive rebels abroad can do nothing unless there be first some hurly-burly in the land) this man may be he where they shall first make head[2] and so grow into a body of rebellion, which afterward they mean to aid with their foreign forces to the destruction of those foolish rebels as well as of us. And though, in truth, without flattery she be inferior to our Queen in all the best gifts, yet may I well enough think that Monsieur will stoop to her as well as King Philip (their old example whom yet again they use even here) did stoop in Flanders and otherwhere, most lowly in that respect and beyond all courtesy even in Queen Mary's life.[3]

* * *

Where is the preservation of religion? Where is the strength and gain to the land? Where is this honor to our kingdom? Even as far from this mar-

---

8. Henri de Lorraine, third Duke of Guise, cousin to Mary Stuart, head of the violently anti-Protestant Catholic League, and architect of the St. Bartholomew's Day massacre; *be great with*: be intimate with.
9. Sheet-anchor; the largest of anchors, used in emergencies, and hence that on which one depends when everything else has failed; the last hope; *nearly inward*: closely associated with; *kind*: nature; *Scottish queen*: Mary Stuart.
1. Protestant.
2. Anjou will become the head of a rebel army; *blockish*: stupid; *he*: Anjou; *this Mary*: Mary Stuart.
3. Mary Tudor; Philip II's relations with Mary Stuart extended to his seeking to marry her to his eldest son, Don Carlos; *she*: Mary Stuart; *King Philip*: Philip II of Spain, husband of Mary Tudor; *otherwhere*: elsewhere.

riage as preservative is from poison, gain from spoil and beggary, and honor from danger of perpetual slavery. I should have been afraid to have spoken thus much had not the strait of this necessity driven me and my words been the words not of a busybody, speaking at all adventures,[4] but of a true Englishman, a sworn liegeman to her Majesty, gathering these necessary consequences by their reasonable causes. And sith the faith of a man is broken sometime as well in not doing or not saying as in doing or saying, I humbly beseech that whatsoever offense anything here said may breed, it be with favor construed by the affection of my heart, which must love my country and Queen though it should cost me my life.

SIR PHILIP SIDNEY

From Arcadia (ca. 1578–80)[†]

[As I My Little Flock on Ister Bank]

The whole company would gladly have taken this occasion of requesting Philisides in plainer sort to discover[1] unto them his estate. Which he willing to prevent (as knowing the relation thereof more fit for funerals than the time of a marriage) began to sing this song he had learned before he had ever subjected his thoughts to acknowledge no master, but a mistress:

As I my little flock on Ister[2] bank
(A little flock, but well my pipe they couthe°)   *knew*
Did piping lead, the sun already sank
Beyond our world, and ere I got my booth[3]
5 Each thing with mantle black the night doth soothe,
    Saving the glow-worm, which would courteous be
    Of that small light oft watching shepherds see.

The welkin° had full niggardly enclosed   *vault of heaven*
In coffer of dim clouds his silver groats,°   *coins*
10 Yclepéd° stars, each thing to rest disposed.   *called*
The caves were full, the mountains void of goats,
The birds' eyes closed, closed their chirping notes.
    As for the nightingale, wood-music's king,
    It August was, he deigned not then to sing.

---

4. Randomly or recklessly; *strait*: constriction.

† Copy text: *The Covntesse of Pembrokes Arcadia* (London: William Ponsonbie, 1593; STC 22540), Kk5v–Ll1v. Since the Old *Arcadia*, for which the poem was originally written, was not found and published until the twentieth century, we print from the New *Arcadia*. Though the poem appears in the 1590 edition, the 1593 is used here because it was more carefully edited and had greater influence on later writers.

1. Reveal; *Philisides*: a representation of Philip Sidney himself, as the name suggests. Having wooed Mira, a figure reminiscent of the Queen (as discussed in Part Ten), he is presented as a melancholy stranger moping among the shepherds, much as Sidney lingered unhappily at his sister Mary's rural estate at Wilton after withdrawing from Court from late 1579 through 1580. He wrote the Old *Arcadia* while he was there. The poem is, fittingly, cast in the form known as rhyme-royal.

2. Danube River in Vienna, where in 1573 and 1574 Sidney visited his long-time mentor, Hubert Languet.

3. Arrived at my shelter.

15 Amid my sheep, though I saw nought to fear,
Yet (for I nothing saw) I fearéd sore.
Then found I which thing is a charge to bear,[4]
As for my sheep I dreaded mickle° more   *much*
Than ever for myself since I was bore.°   *born*
20   I sat me down, for see to go ne could,°   *I could not*
And sang unto my sheep lest stray they should.

The song I sang old Languet had me taught,
Languet, the shepherd best[5] swift Ister knew
For clerkly rede[6] and hating what is naught,°   *bad*
25 For faithful heart, clean hands,[7] and mouth as true.
With his sweet skill my skilless youth he drew
    To have a feeling° taste of Him that sits   *deeply felt*
    Beyond the heaven, far more beyond your wits.

He said the music best thilk° powers pleased   *those*
30 Was jump° concord between our wit and will,   *perfect*
Where highest notes to godliness are raised
And lowest sink not down to jot of ill.
With old true tales he wont° mine ears to fill,   *was accustomed*
    How shepherds did of yore, how now they thrive,
35   Spoiling[8] their flock, or while twixt them they strive.

He likéd me, but pitied lustful youth.
His good strong staff my slipp'ry years upbore.
He still hoped well, because I[9] lovéd truth,
Till forced to part, with heart and eyes e'en sore,
40 To worthy Coreden[1] he gave me o'er.
    But thus in oak's[2] true shade recounted he
    Which now in night's deep shade sheep heard of me.

Such manner time there was (what time I n'ot°)   *know not*
When all this earth, this dam or mould of ours,[3]
45 Was only woned° with such as beasts begot;   *inhabited*
Unknown as then were they that builded towers.
The cattle, wild or tame, in nature's bowers
    Might freely roam or rest, as seeméd° them: *suited*
    Man was not man[4] their dwellings in to hem.

50 The beasts had sure some beastly policy,
For nothing can endure where order n'is.°   *is not*

4. What it is to be charged with a responsibility.
5. The best shepherd that.
6. Learned counsel.
7. An echo of Psalm 24.4.
8. Despoiling, plundering for their own advantage.
9. Copy text: he. Most reliable manuscripts: I.
1. Probably Edward Dyer, Sidney's mentor and friend.
2. Traditional symbol of ruling authority.
3. Mother or soil from which we have sprung.
4. Man did not yet exist.

For once the lion by the lamb did lie;[5]
The fearful hind the léópard did kiss;
Hurtless was tiger's paw and serpent's hiss.
55   This think I well: the beasts with courage clad
    Like senators a harmless empire had.

At which, whether the others did repine
(For envy harb'reth most in feeblest hearts)
Or that they all to changing did incline
60 (As e'en in beasts their dams leave changing parts),[6]
The multitude to Jove a suit imparts,
    With neighing, blaying,° braying, and barking,   *bleating*
    Roaring, and howling for to have a king.

A king, in language theirs, they said they would°   *wanted*
65 (For then their language was a perfect speech).
The birds likewise with chirps and pewing° could,   *plaintive crying*
Cackling and chattering, that of Jove beseech.
Only the owl[7] still warned them not to seech°   *beseech*
    So hastily that which they would repent,
70   But saw they would, and he to deserts went.

Jove wisely said (for wisdom wisely says),
"O beasts, take heed what you of me desire.
Rulers will think all things made them to please,[8]
And soon forget the swink due to their hire.[9]
75 But since you will, part of my heav'nly fire
    I will you lend; the rest yourselves must give,
    That it° both seen and felt may with you live."   *the fire*

Full glad they were, and took the naked sprite,°   *spirit*
Which straight the earth yclothéd in his clay.
80 The lion heart; the ounce° gave active might;   *lynx*
The horse good shape; the sparrow lust to play;
Nightingale voice, enticing songs to say.
    Elephant gave a perfect memory,
    And parrot ready tongue, that to apply.

85 The fox gave craft; the dog gave flattery;
Ass patience; the mole a working thought;
Eagle high look; wolf secret cruelty;
Monkey sweet breath; the cow her fair eyes brought;
The ermine whitest skin, spotted with nought;°   *nothing*
90   The sheep mild-seeming face; climbing, the bear;
    The stag did give the harm-eschewing fear.

---

5. In Isaiah 11.6–8, it is the wolf that lies with the lamb. Such harmony among animals also appears in Ovid's account of the Golden Age (*Metamorphoses* 1.89–112).
6. Their mothers, being more changeable than their fathers, pass down the trait to their offspring.
7. A symbol of wisdom.
8. To please them.
9. The labor they owe for the wealth and power they are given.

The hare her sleights; the cat his melancholy;
Ant industry; and cony° skill to build;   *rabbit*
Cranes order; storks to be appearing holy;
95   Chameleon ease to change; duck ease to yield;
Crocodile tears, which might be falsely spilled.
    Ape[1] great thing gave, though he did mowing° stand,   *making faces*
    The instrument of instruments, the hand.

Each other beast likewise his present brings,
100   And but they drad their prince they oft should want,
They all consented were to give him wings.[2]
And ay° more awe towards him for to plant,   *always*
To their own work° this privilege they grant,   *creation*
    That from thenceforth to all eternity,
105   No beast should freely speak, but only he.

Thus man was made; thus man their lord became,
Who at the first, wanting° or hiding pride,   *lacking*
He did to beasts' best use his cunning frame;
With water drink, herbs meat, and naked hide,[3]
110   And fellow-like let his dominion slide,
    Not in his sayings saying "I" but "we,"
    As if he meant his lordship common be.

But when his seat° so rooted he had found   *authority*
That they now skilled° not how from him to wend,°   *knew / turn away*
115   Then gan° in guiltless earth full many a wound   *he began to make*
Iron to seek,[4] which gainst itself should bend,
To tear the bowels that good corn should send.
    But yet the common dam° none did bemoan   *mother earth*
    Because (though hurt) they never heard her groan.

120   Then gan he[5] factions in the beasts to breed,
Where helping weaker sort, the nobler beasts
(As tigers, leopards, bears, and lions' seed)
Disdained with[6] this, in deserts sought their rests,
Where famine ravin taught their hungry chests,[7]
125   That° craftily he forced them to do ill,   *so that*
    Which being done he afterwards would kill.

For murders done, which never erst° was seen   *at first*
By those great beasts, as° for the weaker's good   *as if*

---

1. Another beast fable of the period, Spenser's *Mother Hubberd's Tale*, also includes an ape, who steals the coat of a lion, emblem of the English monarchy, and uses it to tyrannize over other animals. The ape likely represents Anjou's emissary, Jean de Simier, who sued for Elizabeth's hand in marriage.
2. And except that they feared their prince would fly off, they all would have consented to give him wings.
3. That is, he drank only water, ate only herbs, and, like them, wore nothing.
4. The peace and order of the Ages of Gold and Silver gave way to the artifice, greed, and violence in the Age of Iron (Ovid, *Metamorphoses* 1.89–312).
5. Copy text: the. The best manuscripts: he.
6. Feeling indignant at.
7. Where famine taught them to kill rapaciously.

He chose themselves° his guarders for to been   *the weaker ones*
130 Gainst those of might of whom in fear they stood,
     As horse and dog, not great but gentle blood.
         Blithe° were the common's cattle of the field[8]   *happy*
         Tho° when they saw their foen° of greatness killed.[9]   *Then / foes*

     But they, or° spent or made of slender might,   *either*
135 Then quickly did the meaner cattle find,
     The great beams gone, the house on shoulders light;[1]
     For by and by the horse fair bits did bind;
     The dog was in a collar taught his kind.°   *nature, place*
         As for the gentle° birds, like case might° rue   *noble / they might*
140   When falcon they, and goshawk, saw in mew.°   *cage*

     Worst fell to smallest birds and meanest herd,
     Who now his° own full like his own he used.[2]   *man's*
     Yet first but wool or feathers off he teared,
     And when they were well used to be abused,
145 For hungry throat[3] their flesh with teeth he bruised.
         At length for glutton taste he did them kill,
         At last for sport their silly[4] lives did spill.

     But yet, O man, rage not beyond thy need;
     Deem it no glory[5] to swell in tyranny.
150 Thou art of blood;[6] joy not to see things bleed.
     Thou fearest death; think they are loath to die.
     A plaint of guiltless hurt doth pierce the sky.
         And you, poor beasts, in patience bide your hell,
         Or know your strengths, and then you shall do well.[7]

155 Thus did I sing, and pipe eight sullen° hours   *melancholy*
     To sheep, whom love, not knowledge, made to hear
     Now fancy's fits, now fortune's baleful stours.°   *tumults*
     But then I homewards called my lambkins dear,
     For to my dimméd eyes began t' appear
160   The night grown old, her black head waxen gray,
         Sure shepherd's sign that morn should soon fetch day.

---

8. Cattle that grazed on the commons, the unfenced land available for all to use.
9. Their great enemies killed, or perhaps their enemies killed by someone great.
1. With the great beams gone, the house rested on light (or inadequate) shoulders.
2. He used his own subjects just like his own property.
3. Copy text: teeth. The best manuscripts: throat.
4. Innocent.
5. The best manuscripts: *gloire*. The French term points to Anjou, whom Sidney regarded as a glory-
   seeker and potential tyrant.
6. Made up, in part, of blood—a pun, since Anjou bore the title "Prince of the Blood."
7. Humanists of the period debated citizens' right to oppose tyrannical rulers. Here, Sidney seems to
   endorse resistance but does not commit himself on the far more dangerous question of outright
   rebellion.

CHRISTOPHER MARLOWE

From The Tragedy of Dido, Queen of Carthage
(ca. 1581–86)†

[*Aeneas hears Dido's appeal that he remain in Carthage*]

[DIDO *with her sister* ANNA *and* CUPID,
who is disguised as AENEAS's *son* ASCANIUS]

DIDO:	O dull-conceited° Dido, that till now		*unimaginative*
	Didst never think Aeneas beautiful.[1]		
	But now, for quittance° of this oversight,		*payment*
	I'll make me bracelets of his golden hair;		
5	His glistering eyes shall be my looking-glass,		
	His lips an altar, where I'll offer up		
	As many kisses as the sea hath sands.		
	Instead of music, I will hear him speak;		
	His looks shall be my only library,		
10	And thou, Aeneas, Dido's treasury,		
	In whose fair bosom I will lock more wealth		
	Than twenty thousand Indias can afford.		
	O here he comes. Love, love, give Dido leave		
	To be more modest than her thoughts admit,		
15	Lest I be made a wonder to the world.		

[*Enter* AENEAS *and several of his men:* ACHATES,
SERGESTUS, ILIONEUS, *and* CLOANTHUS]

	Achates, how doth Carthage please your lord?	
ACHATES:	That will Aeneas show your Majesty.	
DIDO:	Aeneas, art thou there?	
AENEAS:	I understand your Highness sent for me.	
20	DIDO: No, but now thou art here, tell me in sooth	
	In what might Dido highly pleasure thee?	
AENEAS:	So much have I received at Dido's hands	
	As without blushing I can ask no more.	
	Yet, Queen of Afric, are my ships unrigged,	
25	My sails all rent in sunder with the wind,	
	My oars broken, and my tackling lost,	
	Yea all my navy split with rocks and shelfs.[2]	
	Nor stern nor anchor have our maimed fleet;	
	Our masts the furious winds struck overboard,	
30	Which piteous wants if Dido will supply,	
	We will account her author of our lives.	
DIDO:	Aeneas, I'll repair thy Trojan ships	
	Conditionally that thou wilt stay with me	

---

† Copy text: Christopher Marlowe, *The tragedie of Dido Queene of Carthage played by the Children of her Maiesties Chappell* (London: Thomas Woodcocke, 1594; STC 17441), C4r–D1v (3.1.82–176).
1. In her early letters, Elizabeth reveals concern over Anjou's looks based on reports that his face was scarred with smallpox.
2. In sailing to England in 1579, Anjou endured dangerous storms.

And let Achates sail to Italy.
35 I'll give thee tackling made of riveled° gold   *tangled*
Wound on the barks of odoriferous trees,
Oars of massy ivory full of holes
Through which the water shall delight to play.
Thy anchors shall be hewed from crystal rocks,
40 Which if thou lose shall shine above the waves;
The masts whereon thy swelling sails shall hang
Hollow pyramids of silver plate;
The sails of folded lawn,° where shall be wrought   *fine linen*
The wars of Troy, but not Troy's overthrow.
45 For ballast, empty Dido's treasury;
Take what ye will, but leave Aeneas here.
Achates, thou shalt be so meanly clad
As sea-born nymphs shall swarm about thy ships[3]
And wanton mermaids court thee with sweet songs,
50 Flinging in favors of more sovereign worth
Than Thetis hangs about Apollo's neck,[4]
So that Aeneas may but stay with me.
AENEAS: Wherefore would Dido have Aeneas stay?
DIDO: To war against my bordering enemies.
55 Aeneas, think not Dido is in love,
For if that any man could conquer me,
I had been wedded ere Aeneas came.
See where the pictures of my suitors hang,
And are not these as fair as fair may be?
60 ACHATES: I saw this man at Troy ere Troy was sacked.
AENEAS: I this in Greece when Paris stole fair Helen.
ILIONEUS: This man and I were at Olympus' games.[5]
SERGESTUS: I know this face; he is a Persian born.
I traveled with him to Etolia.
65 CLOANTHUS: And I in Athens with this gentleman,
Unless I be deceived, disputed once.
DIDO: But speak, Aeneas; know you none of these?
AENEAS: No, madam, but it seems that these are kings.[6]
DIDO: All these, and others which I never saw,
70 Have been most urgent suitors for my love.[7]
Some came in person, others sent their legates,
Yet none obtained me; I am free from all,
And yet, God knows, entangled unto one.
This was an orator and thought by words
75 To compass me, but yet he was deceived;
And this a Spartan courtier vain and wild,
But his fantastic humors pleased not me.

---

3. That is, even dressed in the humblest trappings Dido has to offer, he will attract sea nymphs.
4. Since classical myth contains no such image of Apollo and the sea nymph Thetis, the line may simply be an artful depiction of the sun low over the sea, encircled with mist.
5. The Olympic games, associated with Mount Olympus.
6. Since Aeneas recognized one of the earlier portraits, his words "No, madam" suggest that Dido has turned to a new group comprised of kings.
7. Although Virgil mentions previous suitors for Dido's hand (*Aeneid* 4.35–53), the elaborate catalog that follows is entirely Marlowe's invention.

    This was Alcion, a musician,
    But played he ne'er so sweet, I let him go.
80   This was the wealthy king of Thessaly,
    But I had gold enough and cast him off;
    This Meleager's son, a warlike prince,
    But weapons 'gree not with my tender years.
    The rest are such as all the world well knows,
85   Yet how I swear, by heaven and him I love,
    I was as far from love as they from hate.
    AENEAS: O happy shall he be whom Dido loves.
    DIDO: Then never say that thou art miserable,
    Because it may be thou shalt be my love.
90   Yet boast not of it, for I love thee not,
    And yet I hate thee not. O if I speak,
    I shall betray myself. Aeneas speak.
    We two will go a-hunting in the woods,
95   But not so much for thee (thou art but one)
    As for Achates and his followers.

Exeunt.

SUPPORT FOR THE QUEEN

Not everyone in England was unhappy at the prospect of a French marriage. George Puttenham, who later wrote one of the earliest treatises on the art of poetry, presented the Queen with a series of flattering *Partheniads* as a New Year's gift in the winter of 1579–80. The title means "poems about a virgin" and hints, somewhat playfully, at heroic themes by echoing the title of Homer's *Iliad*. Two of Puttenham's poems seem to support a marriage with Anjou. One figures Elizabeth as a flower, glorious for a time but doomed to fade, and laments her lack of a child to succeed her. The other compares her with a mighty ship and alludes to the lily, or fleur de lis, emblematic of the French crown, concluding that "None but a king or more may her aboard."

    The panegyric to Elizabeth in John Lyly's prose romance *Euphues and His England* is not concerned with marriage and childbearing but simply with Elizabeth's glory as a monarch. Looking back to earlier works that had celebrated her as a mother to her people and a defender of the Gospel against the corrupt teachings of the Catholic Church, it also looked forward to later works such as Spenser's *Faerie Queene*, which celebrated her as a virgin ruler of almost mythic stature. To Lyly, she was a modern Caesar or Alexander, who exemplified not only the classical virtues of magnanimity, courage, wisdom, and justice but also the Christian virtues of faith, love, mercy, and obedience to God. The passage included here is notable for its language. Combining balanced phrases and antitheses, complex syntax modeled on the rhetoric of Cicero, and fantastic comparisons drawn from the animal lore of antiquity and the Middle Ages, Lyly's style (known as Euphuism) became enormously popular in the 1580s. Spreading from the universities to the parlors of London and the royal Court, it set the fashion in polite speech. By the early 1590s, however, when Shakespeare laughingly put it into the mouths of his royal characters in *Love's Labor's Lost*, it was beginning to sound overblown, and it soon disappeared.

    Thomas Blenerhasset's *Revelation of the True Minerva* is a less polished work, though one of considerable charm. For some years stationed as a soldier on the lonely island of Guernsey in the English Channel, Blenerhasset spent his idle hours teaching himself to write poetry. In the process, he devised a lengthy poem of varied content and inventive structure. Framed as an account by an unnamed pilgrim of a book that he found while roaming "all the world to find his heart's desire," it relates the decline of the Olympian deities, the loss of the goddess Minerva (patron of wisdom and defender of Athens), and the quest to find a "true Minerva" to take her place. The search leads all the gods, including the Muses and the Graces, to England, where they find in Elizabeth what they have been seeking. They then take up their ancient role as patrons of human pursuits once again, founding a new Olympus and Parnassus on English soil. This simple plot is ornamented with various short works: a pastoral lament, songs written in inventive meters, and poems devised in curious shapes. Included here are the prophecy that begins the great quest, a characterization of Elizabeth by the god Mercury, and an encomium to her sung by the Muse Clio at the conclusion of the book.

GEORGE PUTTENHAM

From Partheniads (1579)[†]

[*Partheniad* 9, Melpomenê.][1] A very strange and rueful vision presented to the author, the interpretation whereof was left to her Majesty till by the purpose discovered.

In fruitful soil behold a flower sprung,
Distaining[2] gold, rubies, and ivory.
Three buds it bare, three stalks, tender and young,
One more[3] middle earth, one top that touch° the sky,   *touches*
5   Under the leaves, one branches broad and high;
Millions of birds sang shrouded in the shade.
I came anon and saw with weeping eye
Two blossoms fallen, the third began to fade
So as, within the compass of an hour,
10   Sore withered was this noble, dainty flower,
That no soil bred, no land shall lose the like,
Ne° no season or sun or soaking shower   *nor*
Can rear again for prayer ne for mead.°   *reward*
"Woe and alas!" the people cry and shriek,
15 "Why fades this flower and leaves no fruit nor seed?"

Partheniad 10, Calliopê. Another vision happened to the same author, as comfortable and recreative as the former was dolorous.

A royal ship I saw, by tide and by wind,
Single° and sail in sea as sweet as milk.   *set forth*

---

† Copy text: British Library MS Cotton Vespasian E.VIII, fols. 172r–173r.
1. This poem comes after verses marked in the margin "Parthe: 8 Thalia." Since the next poem should be "Parthe: 9" but is, in fact, "Parthe: 10," a heading seems to have been omitted. Given the tragic theme of "A very strange and rueful vision," we have taken the liberty of supplying the missing heading, assuming that it would have been assigned to Melpomenê, Muse of Tragedy.
2. Making seem tarnished by contrast.
3. Rooted in; *Three buds*: Edward VI, Mary I, and Elizabeth.

Her cedar keel, her mast of gold refined,
Her tackle and sails as silver and silk,
5   Her fraught° more worth than all the wares of Ind.°   *cargo / India*
Clear was the coast, the waves were smooth and still,
The skies all calm. Phœbus so bright, he shined;
Æolus in poop° gave her weather° at will;   *stern / wind*
Dan° Neptune steered, while Proteus played his sport   *Master*
10   And Nereus' dainty daughters sang full shrill
To slice° her sails, that they might swell their fill.   *cut across*
Jove from above his pleasant showers poured.
Her flag, it bears the flowers of man's comfort.[4]
None but a king or more may her aboard.
15   O gallant piece,° well will the Lily[5] afford°   *vessel / allow*
Thou strike mizzen° and anchor in his port.   *main sail*

JOHN LYLY

From Euphues and His England (1580)[†]

Two and twenty years hath she born the sword with such justice that neither offenders could complain of rigor nor the innocent of wrong, yet so
tempered with mercy as malefactors have been sometimes pardoned upon
hope of grace and the injured requited to ease their grief, insomuch that in
the whole course of her glorious reign, it could never be said that either the
poor were oppressed without remedy or the guilty repressed without cause,
bearing this engraven in her noble heart: that justice without mercy were
extreme injury and pity without equity[1] plain partiality, and that it is as great
tyranny not to mitigate laws as iniquity to break them.

    Her care for the flourishing of the Gospel hath well appeared, whenas
neither the curses of the Pope (which are blessings to good people) nor the
threatening of kings (which are perilous to a prince) nor the persuasions of
papists (which are honey to the mouth) could either fear her or allure her
to violate the holy league contracted with Christ or to maculate[2] the blood
of the ancient Lamb, which is Christ. But always constant in the true faith,
she hath to the exceeding joy of her subjects, to the unspeakable comfort
of her soul, to the great glory of God, established that religion, the maintenance whereof she rather seeketh to confirm by fortitude than leave off
for fear, knowing that there is nothing that smelleth sweeter to the Lord
than a sound spirit,[3] which neither the hosts of the ungodly nor the horror
of death can either remove or move.

---

4. The fleur-de-lis, lily-shaped symbol of the French monarchy. Elizabeth wore it in her coat of arms
    as a sign of English rulers' claim to the throne of France. Since the fleur-de-lis also marked north
    on compasses, it gave sailors the comfort of knowing their course.
5. The French king, Henry III, who backed the proposed marriage of Elizabeth to Anjou.
† Copy text: *Euphues and his England* (London: Gabriell Cawood, 1580; STC 17070), Ii3v–Ii4v.
1. Equal treatment of all who commit the same offence.
2. Defile; *whenas*: in as much as; *fear*: frighten; *holy league*: in contrast to the Catholic League, a
    mythical union that many Protestants believed had been formed between the Pope and the rulers
    of France, Spain, and other European states as early as the 1560s in order to overthrow Elizabeth.
    In France, an actual league of the same name was led by Henry, Duke of Guise.
3. An allusion to 2 Corinthians 2.15; *that religion*: the form of Protestant religion established in En-
    gland in 1559.

This gospel, with invincible courage, with rare constancy, with hot zeal, she hath maintained in her own countries without change and defended against all kingdoms that sought change, insomuch that all nations round about her threatening alteration, shaking swords, throwing fire, menacing famine, murder, destruction, desolation, she only hath stood like a lamp on the top of a hill, not fearing the blasts of the sharp winds but trusting in His providence that rideth upon the wings of the four winds.[4] Next followeth the love she beareth to her subjects, who no less tendereth them than the apple[5] of her own eye, showing herself a mother to the afflicted, a physician to the sick, a sovereign and mild governess to all.

Touching her magnanimity, her majesty, her estate royal, there was neither Alexander, nor Galba the Emperor, nor any that might be compared with her.

This is she that, resembling the noble Queen of Navarre,[6] useth the marigold for her flower, which at the rising of the sun openeth her leaves and at the setting shutteth them, referring all her actions and endeavors to Him that ruleth the sun. This is that Caesar that first bound the crocodile to the palm tree, bridling those that sought to rein her.[7] This is that good pelican that to feed her people spareth not to rend her own person.[8] This is that mighty eagle that hath thrown dust into the eyes of the hart that went about to work destruction to her subjects, into whose wings although the blind beetle would have crept and so, being carried into her nest, destroyed her young ones, yet hath she with the virtue of her feathers consumed that fly in his own fraud.[9]

✻　✻　✻

Behold, ladies, in this glass a queen, a woman, a virgin, in all gifts of the body, in all graces of the mind, in all perfection of either, so far to excel all men that I know not whether I may think the place too bad for her to dwell among men.

To talk of other things in that court were to bring eggs after apples or, after the setting out of[1] the sun, to tell a tale of a shadow.

But this I say, that all offices are looked to with great care, that virtue is embraced of all, vice hated, religion daily increased, manners reformed, that whoso seeth the place there will think it rather a church for divine service than a court for princes' delight.

This is the glass,[2] ladies, wherein I would have you gaze, wherein I took my whole delight. Imitate the ladies in England, amend your manners, rub

---

4. Psalms 18.10 and 104.3; *nations . . . hill:* Matthew 5.15, 25.1–8.
5. Pupil. The metaphor is several times used in the Bible (for example, Psalm 17.8).
6. Margaret d'Angoulême, wife of Henry II of Navarre. In adolescence, Elizabeth translated a religious work by Margaret under the title *A Godly Meditation of the Christian Soul* (see Part One).
7. A reference to Julius Caesar's conquest of Egypt, here symbolized by tying a crocodile to a date palm. After defeating (or "bridling") Ptolemy XIII, husband of Cleopatra, Caesar elevated her and her brother Ptolemy XIV to rule in his place.
8. Pelicans were thought to feed their young with flesh plucked from their own breasts.
9. In Aesop's *Fables,* a beetle avenges itself on an eagle by entering its nest and rolling its eggs out onto the rocks (1671 edition, p. 86); the detail about the destructive power of eagle feathers is from Pliny 10.4 (Bond, *Complete Works of John Lyly,* 2.535, n. 21). Which of Elizabeth's enemies the hart and the beetle represent is not clear, but Philip II and the Pope seem likely, since one worked against her overtly (by threatening war) and the other covertly (by sending Jesuit priests to England); *eagle . . . hart:* according to Pliny's *Natural History* 10.5, an eagle sometimes kills a stag by rolling on the ground, then perching in the animal's antlers, maddening it by shaking dust in its eyes and so driving it off a cliff (Bond 2.535, n. 19).
1 Describing; *bring . . . apples:* to bring common food after dessert, which in this period was often fruit.
2. Mirror.

out the wrinkles of the mind, and be not curious about the wems[3] in the
face. As for their Elizabeth, sith[4] you can neither sufficiently marvel at her
nor I praise her, let us all pray for her, which is the only duty we can perform and the greatest that we can proffer.

Yours to command,
EUPHUES

THOMAS BLENERHASSET

From A Revelation of the True Minerva (1582)[†]

[Mercury prophesies concerning the kingdom of the true Minerva]

Where arctic pool° with guards[1] doth stand,	*North Sea*
L. and two degrees from land,[2]	
Minerva doth remain,	
Where want° of war and quiet peace	*absence*
5 Hath cloyed the country with increase°	*rising income*
of gold and goodly grain;	
Where Troynovant,[3] where Athens new,	
where noble nymphs do dwell;	
Where many modest Muses be,	
10 e'en such as do excel.	
This great goddess there in throne	
Of highest dignity alone	
doth sit and bear the sway.°	*authority*
Olympus there, Parnassus high;[4]	
15 Parnassus' springs be never dry,	
the ground is green and gay.	
The palm and laurel[5] there doth grow;	
e'en there her biding° is,	*dwelling place*
Out° from the world, yet on the ground,	*Removed*
20 e'en in a place of bliss.	

* * *

[Mercury characterizes the Queen]

Her heav'nly hue,° her more than mortal grace	*form, appearance*
(For virtue may mortal immortal make),	

---

3. Blemishes; *Imitate . . . England*: Euphues, originally from Athens, is addressing ladies on the Continent.
4. Since.
† Copy text: Thomas Blenerhasset, *A reuelation of the true Minerua The effect of this booke. Who on earth be gods: and by what meanes mortall men may bee made immortall* (London: Thomas Wood-coke, 1582; STC 3132), A3v, B4v–C1r, G1r–G1v.
1. Islands. As a captain in the army, Blenerhasset was stationed on Guernsey, one of several Channel Islands located strategically between England and France.
2. Latitude not quite two degrees from land. Mercury's prophetic riddle locates England just off the coast of Europe. "And" here means "if" in the sense "if that much"; hence the marginal note in the copy text: "Lacking a third part."
3. New Troy, a reference to the myth that England was founded by Brutus, the great-grandson of the Trojan warrior Aeneas, who founded ancient Rome.
4. Mount Olympus and Mount Parnassus in Greece, associated with the gods and the Muses.
5. Symbols of victory and of high achievement, particularly in poetry.

Her stately steps, her princely royal race,°   *lineage*
Her majesty makes mortal men to quake;
5   Her dignity doth make the gods to shake.
When earthly eyes her Highness do behold,
They do affirm her form not from the mould.°   *earth*

Over her head, angels with swords in hand;
Betwixt her eyes doth right remorse remain.[6]
10   Before her face the fear of God doth stand;
Solomon's bliss abideth in her brain.[7]
Her ears be stopped° to matters vile and vain;   *closed*
From goodly lips her learnéd tongue doth tell
The way to heav'n, where she no doubt doth dwell.

15   Contented life within her mind doth rest;
Upon her breast doth perfect bliss abide,
And charity° doth sit upon her chest.   *Christian love*
A certain, sure state that cannot slide°   *decline*
Is fixed, as best beseems, fast to her side.
20   Most worthy praise for her virginity,
Diana never half so chaste as she.

Her arm doth rule a mighty realm by right;
Her hand doth give each one his due desert.°   *reward*
To walk in righteous ways is her delight;
25   From perfect path her feet do not depart;[8]
Her steps most straight do show her heav'nly heart.
Under her feet, raging Revenge doth couch,°   *lie in wait*
At her command her valor to avouch.°   *demonstrate*

When treason's spiteful, hid conspiracies
30   They would untwine her worthy-warpéd twist,[9]
These heav'nly angels then with Argus' eyes,
Do force the bloody blade from traitor's fist,
Whose gotten gain is heavy had, I wist.[1]
When foreign foes would reave° her earthly crown,   *steal away*
35   Then black Revenge doth beat their boastings down.

*   *   *

[*The Muse Clio praises Elizabeth as a goddess immune to misfortune*]

Thus she who once was but a mortal queen
And, subject,° sat on Fortune's turning wheel,   *subject to luck*
The greatest goddess now on earth is seen,
Whose high estate can neither roll nor reel,[2]

---

6. Tears flow from the inner corners of her eyes.
7. Solomon asked God for wisdom and was blessed with it (1 Kings 3.5–14).
8. Psalm 119.35.
9 Unravel the worthily woven thread of her life, a reference to the myth of the Fates, who spin, measure out, and cut the thread of life for each person.
1. Whose reward for their treason is dearly bought (at the cost of future punishment), I know.
2. Neither fall (from the height of Fortune's wheel) nor totter unsteadily.

5   Nor Fortune's force shall never hurt her heel,[3]
    For virtue did (and due desert°) advance   *worthiness*
    Her Grace, and not the force of changing chance.
    She is not now as other princes be
    Who live on earth, to every tempest thrall;°   *constrained*
10 Desert hath crowned her with eternity.
    Her godly zeal in seat sempeternal[4]
    Hath set her now; from thence she cannot fall
    But lively live on earth eternally
    And have in heaven heav'nly felicity.

ANJOU'S DEPARTURE AND THE QUEEN'S GRIEF

Long before Anjou's final departure from England in 1582, Elizabeth had come to terms with the political necessity of giving up her last chance at marriage. It may not, however, have been easy. Her poem "Sonetto" ("I Grieve and Dare Not Show My Discontent"), which was probably written in 1582, suggests both distress and the adoption of a public mask to conceal it. As in other relationships with the foreign princes who courted her, however, it is difficult to say how much of the poem was sincere and how much politically calculated. She could hardly, after all, admit to leading the Duke on for her own purposes and then jilting him. Perhaps for a queen, the personal and the political can never be separated.

The Queen at prayer.

Curiously, Elizabeth's prayer book from this period, which was composed during the years when Anjou was actively courting her, betrays nothing of her thoughts or feelings about him. A tiny book, written in her own hand and graced with miniatures of herself and Anjou by Nicholas Hilliard, it was probably a "girdle book" designed to be hung by a chain at the Queen's waist. The prayers echoed liturgies of the Church of

3. An allusion to the Greek warrior Achilles, whose heel was his only vulnerable point.
4. In an everlasting throne.

England, but they were also, at times, intensely personal. Composed in English, French, Italian, Latin, and Greek, they also displayed the Queen's remarkable facility in languages.

QUEEN ELIZABETH

POEM AND PRAYERS (ca. 1579–82)

[I Grieve and Dare Not Show My Discontent]†

I grieve and dare not show my discontent;
    I love, and yet am forced to seem to hate;
I do, yet dare not say I ever meant;
        I seem stark mute, but inwardly do prate.°   *chatter*
5   I am, and not; I freeze, and yet am burned,
           Since from myself another self I turned.

My care is like my shadow in the sun,
    Follows me flying, flies when I pursue it,
Stands and lies by me, doth what I have done;
10   His too familiar care doth make me rue it.[1]
           No means I find to rid him from my breast,
           Till by the end of things it be suppressed.

Some gentler passion[2] slide into my mind,
    For I am soft, and made of melting snow;
15 Or be more cruel, Love, and so be kind.
           Let me or° float or sink, be high or low;   *either*
           Or let me live with some more sweet content,
           Or die, and so forget what love e'er meant.

           Eliza Regina, *upon Monsieur's departure.*

From the Queen's Prayerbook‡

O most glorious King and Creator of the whole world, to whom all things be subject both in heaven and earth and all best princes most gladly obey, hear the most humble voice of Thy handmaid, in this only happy: to be so accepted. How exceeding is Thy goodness and how great mine offenses! Of nothing hast Thou made me, not a worm but a creature according to Thine own image: heaping all the blessings upon me that men on earth hold most happy; drawing my blood from kings and my bringing up in virtue; giving me

---

† Copy text: John Nichols, *The Progresses and Public Processions of Queen Elizabeth* (London: J. Nichols, 1823), 2:346.
1. Rue is a complex pun: My sorrow is so intimate that I pity it, repent of it, have compassion for it.
2. Copy text: passions; best manuscript: passion.
‡ Copy text: *Elizabeth I: Collected Works*, ed. Leah S. Marcus, Janel Mueller, and Mary Beth Rose (Chicago and London: University of Chicago Press, 2000), 311–13; 319–21. Reprinted by Permission of the University of Chicago Press. © 2000 by the University of Chicago.

that more is,[1] even in my youth, knowledge of Thy truth, and in times of most danger, most gracious deliverance; pulling me from the prison to the palace; and placing me a sovereign princess over Thy people of England. And above all this, making me (though a weak woman) yet Thy instrument to set forth the glorious Gospel of Thy dear Son Christ Jesus. Thus in these last and worst days of the world, when wars and seditions with grievous persecutions have vexed almost all kings and countries round about me, my reign hath been peaceable and my realm a receptacle to Thy afflicted Church. The love of my people hath appeared firm and the devices of mine enemies frustrate.[2]

Now for these and other Thy benefits, O Lord of all goodness, what have I rendered to Thee?[3] Forgetfulness, unthankfulness, and great disobedience. I should have magnified Thee; I have neglected Thee. I should have prayed unto Thee; I have forgotten Thee. I should have served Thee; I have sinned against Thee. This is my case.[4] Then where is my hope? If Thou, Lord, wilt be extreme to mark what is done amiss, who may abide it?[5] But Thou art gracious and merciful, long suffering, and of great goodness, not delighting in the death of a sinner.[6] Thou seest whereof I came, of corrupt seed; what I am, a most frail substance; where I live, in the world full of wickedness, where delights be snares, where dangers be imminent, where sin reigneth and death abideth. This is my state. Now where is my comfort?

In the depth of my misery, I know no help, O Lord, but the height of Thy mercy, who hast sent Thine only Son into the world to save sinners. This God of my life and Life of my soul, the King of all comfort, is my only refuge. For His sake, therefore, to whom Thou hast given all power and wilt deny no petition, hear my prayers. Turn Thy face from my sins, O Lord, and Thine eyes to Thy handiwork. Create a clean heart and renew a right spirit within me.[7] Order my steps in Thy Word, that no wickedness have dominion over me;[8] make me obedient to Thy will and delight in Thy law. Grant me grace to live godly and to govern justly, that so living to please Thee and reigning to serve Thee, I may ever glorify Thee, the Father of all goodness and mercy, to whom, with Thy dear Son, my only savior, and the Holy Ghost my sanctifier, three persons and one God, be all praise, dominion, and power, world without end. Amen.

*   *   *

O Lord God, Father everlasting, which reignest over the kingdoms of men and givest them at Thy pleasure, which of Thy great mercy hast chosen me Thy servant and handmaid to feed Thy people and Thine inheritance; so teach me, I humbly beseech Thee, Thy Word and so strengthen me with Thy grace that I may feed Thy people with a faithful and a true heart and rule them prudently with power. O Lord, Thou hast set me on high; my flesh is frail and weak. If I, therefore, at any time forget Thee, touch my heart, O

---

1. That which is more; *not a worm . . . own image*: an inversion of Psalm 22.6, "I am a worm and no man" [Marcus, Mueller, and Rose's note].
2. Have been frustrated.
3. Psalm 116.12.
4. Sum of the matter, but also a legal case; Elizabeth pleads guilty before God.
5. Psalm 130.3.
6. Ezekiel 33.11.
7. Psalm 51.10.
8. Psalm 119.133.

Lord, that I may again remember Thee. If I swell against Thee, pluck me down in my own conceit, that Thou mayest raise me in Thy sight. Grant me, O Lord, a listening ear to hear Thee and a hungry soul to long after Thy Word. Endue me with Thy heavenly Spirit. Give me Thy Spirit of wisdom that I may understand Thee. Give me Thy Spirit of truth, that I may know Thee, Thy feeling[9] Spirit that I may fear Thee, Thy Spirit of grace that I may love Thee, Thy Spirit of zeal that I may hunger and thirst after Thee, Thy persevering Spirit that I may live and dwell and reign with Thee.

I acknowledge, O my King, without Thee my throne is unstable, my seat unsure, my kingdom tottering, my life uncertain. I see all things in this life subject to mutability, nothing to continue still at one stay;[1] but fear and trembling, hunger and thirst, cold and heat, weakness and faintness, sorrow and sickness doth evermore oppress mankind. I hear how ofttimes untimely death doth carry away the mightiest and greatest personages. I have learned out of Thy holy Word that horrible judgment is nigh unto them which walk not after Thy will, and the mighty, swerving from Thy law, shall be mightily tormented. Therefore, sith all things in this world, both heaven and earth, shall pass and perish and Thy Word alone endureth forever, engraft, O most gracious Lord Christ, this Thy Word of grace and life so in my heart that from henceforth I neither follow after feigned comforts in worldly power, neither distract my mind to transitory pleasures, nor occupy my thoughts in vain delights, but that carefully[2] seeking Thee where Thou showest Thyself in Thy Word, I may surely find Thee to my comfort and everlastingly enjoy Thee to my salvation.

Create therefore in me, O Lord, a new heart and so renew my spirit within me that Thy law may be my study, Thy truth my delight, Thy church my care, Thy people my crown, Thy righteousness my pleasure, Thy service my government,[3] Thy fear my honor, Thy grace my strength, Thy favor my life, Thy Gospel my kingdom, and Thy salvation my bliss and my glory. So shall this my kingdom through Thee be established with peace; so shall Thy church be edified with power; so shall Thy Gospel be published with zeal; so shall my reign be continued with prosperity; so shall my life be prolonged with happiness; and so shall myself at Thy good pleasure be translated into immortality.[4] Which, O merciful Father, grant for the merit of Thy Son Jesus Christ, to whom with the Holy Ghost be rendered all praise and glory forever. Amen.

---

9. Powerful.
1. To continue stable.
2. Diligently; *sith . . . forever*: Matthew 24.35; Mark 13.31; Luke 21.33.
3. Thy service that which governs me; *Create . . . within me*: Psalm 51.10; see also Ezekiel 36.26.
4. I shall be transformed into an immortal person; Elizabeth here conflates the classical notion of immortality of the soul with the Christian understanding of the resurrection of the body.

Part Six: Courtiers, Assassins, and the Death of Mary Stuart (1582–1587)

HISTORICAL BACKGROUND

New Year's Day 1582 opened on a familiar ritual, the exchange of gifts at Court, but amidst the silver and clothing and foodstuffs, one gift stood out. It was a decorative anchor set with jewels, enormously expensive, and presented to the Queen by her devoted suitor, the Duke of Anjou. It was, he said, a gift to demonstrate his constant and abiding love. Despite Elizabeth's delight in expensive presents, she must have been more than a little alarmed. For several months she had been encouraging Anjou to set sail for the Netherlands and to take up the fight against Spain, which she was now willing to finance—at least to a degree. Anjou's persistent attentions had alienated both her councilors and her subjects, and she no longer seriously considered marriage to him. When Anjou finally set sail in February from Sandwich, Elizabeth accompanied him to Canterbury for a tearful farewell before returning to London.

Although the Queen was now older, and had dismissed her last serious prospect for marriage, she continued to enjoy the banquets, dances, and witty exchanges with her favorites that characterized life at Court. She also enjoyed her entertainments, particularly the increasingly elaborate festivities held to celebrate her Accession Day on November 17, which included both solemn religious services of thanksgiving as well as tournaments held at the tilt-yard at Whitehall.

There was always much more to Court life, however, than plays and tournaments and dances and sermons. The news from abroad was disturbing. The situation in the Netherlands continued to decline despite Elizabeth's financial support for the rebels. On June 10, 1584, Anjou died, and a month later Prince William of Orange, the Protestant leader in the Netherlands, was assassinated. In light of William's death, Elizabeth's councilors grew increasingly alarmed about her own safety. They were particularly worried about the surreptitious arrival of young Jesuit missionaries, intent on winning England back to the Roman Catholic faith. Although Pope Gregory XIII had moderated the 1570 Bull of Excommunication against Elizabeth so that Catholic subjects were now allowed to recognize her as their Queen, she remained under the judgment of the Roman Catholic Church. Protestants feared that, if pressed, their Catholic neighbors would prefer Church to Queen and aid any rebellion that might arise against the Protestant monarch.

The worries of the Privy Council proved all too real when in 1583 Sir Francis Walsingham, the Queen's Secretary of State, uncovered a plot by two Catholic brothers, Francis and Thomas Throckmorton, to murder Elizabeth and proclaim Mary Stuart as Queen of England. Although English Catholics protested their loyalty to Elizabeth, William Cecil, Lord Burghley, drew up a Bond of Association which many Englishmen signed, pledging to protect their Protestant Queen against any who might seek to harm her. Matters escalated

The Queen enthroned in peace.

when William Parry, a member of Parliament who may have been acting on his own initiative, was arrested on charges of conspiring to kill the Queen. That Parry was a recusant, or closet Catholic, simply fueled the flames of Protestant anger, as did Mary Stuart's subsequent attempts to regain some of her royal prerogatives.

Mary Stuart had now been held under house arrest in England since 1568, and although she had spent many of those years in relative quiet under the guardianship of George Talbot, sixth Earl of Shrewsbury, she was growing restive. In 1586, Mary became involved in a plot with Anthony Babington, a former page in Shrewsbury's household, to kill Elizabeth and regain her own freedom. Although Elizabeth was furious with Mary when the plot was uncovered, she was equally annoyed with her own councilors and Parliament, who used this occasion to urge her to execute Mary. Elizabeth delayed as long as she was able, but on February 1, 1587, she signed the death warrant and a week later, on February 8, Mary Stuart was dead.

In a short five-year span, Elizabeth had said goodbye to her last serious suitor, had received word of his death, and had signed the execution warrant for her own cousin. She had been beset by would-be assassins and come under pressure from members of Parliament and her own Privy Council, and she had seen growing religious divisions among her subjects. Never, perhaps, had one of the prayers composed on her behalf seemed more appropriate: "Be Thou unto me, O Lord, in the daytime a defender and in the night season a place of refuge, that Thou mayest save me." Just ahead, however, lay that "miraculous year," 1588, when Elizabeth would, at least for a short time, reign triumphantly over her enemies.

CUPID AT COURT

Despite her determination not to marry Anjou, Queen Elizabeth recognized that, with his departure, she had bid farewell to the last serious suitor for her hand. The tone of "I Grieve and Dare Not Show My Discontent," included in Part Five and said to have been written upon the Duke of Anjou's departure to the Netherlands, was both melancholy and realistic as the Queen assessed the pressure her public role as monarch put upon her feelings as a woman. Furthermore, as hopes of marriage slipped away, so too did what remained of her youth. Other poems from this period suggest her obsession with the passing of time. "When I was Fair and Young" imagines a conversation with Cupid who, dismissed once too often, refuses now to play the love-game with her. "Now Leave and Let Me Rest" takes a more serious tone. Nature, not Cupid, acts as Elizabeth's teacher, forcing her to recognize that "all fair earthly things / Soon ripe, will soon be rot." As Elizabeth contemplates her own mortality—and approaching fiftieth birthday—she determines to count as "nothing worth" the "pleasant courtly games / That I do pleasure in."

Despite this noble resolution, however, the Queen continued to play the "pleasant courtly games" that also served more serious purposes, such as regulating the behavior of her courtiers. One new favorite who emerged during this time was Sir Walter Ralegh, who first gained her attention during the Desmond Rebellion in Ireland, in which he fought bravely as captain of a modest contingent of troops. In 1580, he traveled to London to bring the Privy Council important documents captured from the papal and Irish soldiers and managed to impress Sir Francis Walsingham and Lord Burghley, with whom he continued to correspond after his return to Ireland. A year later, on another trip to England, he was invited to report to the Queen herself, and he seems to have dazzled her, for in short order she took him into her innermost circle of advisors. It was not long before they became constant companions and their relationship took on amorous overtones.

There is a gradual evolution in feeling in the poems that he wrote to her in the 1580s. From silent love at a distance in "Our Passions Are Most Like to Floods and Streams" and easy delight in her initial favor in "Sweet Are the Thoughts," he progresses to lover's banter in "Calling to Mind Mine Eye Long Went About," which claims that he did everything in his power to keep from falling in love with her. There was, of course, nothing reluctant on either side. Elizabeth advanced Ralegh in every way she could, granting him licenses to tax English trade in wine and wool in ways that soon made him a wealthy man. After gaining a seat in Parliament, he was knighted and given civil and military offices that established him as the unrivaled authority over government affairs in most of southwest England. He also played a major role in England's campaign to counter Spanish dominance in the New World.

In 1587, however, just as he was putting in motion grand schemes to design more potent English warships and to colonize North America, Elizabeth began to cultivate a new companion, the young and headstrong Robert Devereux, second Earl of Essex and the stepson of Robert Dudley. Devoting to him many of the private hours once reserved for Ralegh, she divided her attention in ways that inevitably provoked dissention and rivalry. When Ralegh protested, sending Elizabeth the cautiously worded complaint "Fortune Hath Taken Away My Love," her reply was charming, reassuring—and infuriating. In dismissing his concerns, she began "Ah, silly pug, wert thou so sore afraid?" treating the great naval planner as if he were her bargeman, jealous of a new oarsman in the boat, or (if one prefers the other meaning of "pug" in the period) a small dog sulking at the arrival of a new pet in the household. By 1589, when Ralegh asked permission to retire for a time to his Irish estates, he was despondent and unsure of his future, as we can see in the poem "Like Truthless Dreams."

Many later poets followed Ralegh's lead, addressing Elizabeth as if they were her lovers. These expressions of passion and despondency were, of course, part of an elaborate ritual of artful play and royal praise that had developed in the progress entertainments and pastorals of the 1570s. It would be a mistake to take most works in this vein as confessions of the heart. With Ralegh, however, the well-worn tropes of courtly and Petrarchan love have the vividness of lived experience.

QUEEN ELIZABETH

REFLECTIONS ON LOVE AND GROWING OLDER (ca. 1580s)

[When I Was Fair and Young]†

When I was fair and young, then favor gracéd me;
Of many was I sought, their mistress for to be.
But I did scorn them all and answered them therefore,
"Go, go, go, seek some otherwhere;° importune me no more."   elsewhere

5   How many weeping eyes I made to pine in woe,
How many sighing hearts I have not skill to show.
But I the prouder grew and still this spake therefore:
"Go, go, go, seek some otherwhere; importune me no more."

† Copy text: British Library, Harleian MS 7392 (2) fol. 21v.

Then spake fair Venus' son,° that brave, victorious boy,   *Cupid*
10 Saying, "You dainty dame, for that you be so coy,
I will so pull your plumes as you shall say no more,
'Go, go, go, seek some otherwhere; importune me no more.'"

As soon as he had said, such change grew in my breast
That neither night nor day I could take any rest.
15 Wherefore I did repent that I had said before,
"Go, go, go, seek some otherwhere; importune me no more."

FINIS.

[Now Leave and Let Me Rest]†

1. Now leave and let me rest. Dame Pleasure, be content.
Go choose among the best; my doting° days be spent.   *foolish*
By sundry signs I see thy proffers° are but vain,   *offers*
And wisdom warneth me that pleasure asketh pain;
5   And Nature, that doth know how Time her steps doth try,°   *test*
Gives place to painful woe and bids me learn to die.

2. Since all fair earthly things, soon ripe, will soon be rot,
And all that pleasant springs, soon withered, soon forgot,
And youth that yields men joys that wanton lust desires,
10 In age repents the toys° that reckless youth requires,   *amorous play*
All which delights I leave to such as folly trains
By pleasures to deceive, till they do feel the pains.

3. And from vain pleasures past I fly, and fain would know
The happy life at last whereto I hope to go.
15 For words or wise reports, ne° yet examples gone,   *nor*
'Gan° bridle youthful sports, till age came stealing on.   *Began to*
The pleasant courtly games that I do pleasure in,
My elder years now shames such folly to begin.

4. And all the fancies strange that fond° delight brought forth   *foolish*
20 I do intend to change and count them nothing worth.
For I by proffers vain am taught to know the skill
What might have been forborne° in my young reckless will;   *avoided*
By which good proof I fleet° from will to wit again,   *waver*
In hope to set my feet in surety to remain.

† Copy text: *Elizabeth I: Collected Works*, ed. Leah S. Marcus, Janel Mueller, and Mary Beth Rose
(Chicago and London: University of Chicago Press, 2000), 305–306.

SIR WALTER RALEGH

LOVE POEMS TO THE QUEEN (ca. 1582–89)

[Our Passions Are Most Like to Floods and Streams]†

Our passions are most like to floods and streams;
The shallow murmur, but the deep are dumb.
So when affections yield discourse, it seems
The bottom is but shallow whence they come.
5   They that are rich in words must needs discover
   That they are poor in that which makes[1] a lover.

Wrong not, dear Empress of my heart,
   The merit of true passion
With thinking that he feels no smart
10   That sues for no compassion,
Since if my plaints° serve not to prove   *complaints*
   The conquest of your beauty,
They come not from defect of love
   But from excess of duty.

15 For knowing that I sue to serve
   A saint of such perfection
As all desire, but none deserve,
   A place in her affection,
I rather choose to want° relief   *lack*
20   Than venture the revealing.
When glory recommends the grief,
   Despair distrusts the healing.

Thus those desires that aim too high
   For any mortal lover,
25 When reason cannot make them die,
   Discretion will them cover.
Yet when discretion doth bereave°   *take away*
   The plaints that they should utter,
Then your discretion may perceive
30   That silence is a suitor.

Silence in love bewrays° more woe,   *reveals*
   Than words, though n'er so witty.
A beggar that is dumb, ye know,
   Deserveth double pity.
35 Then misconceive not, dearest heart,
   My true, though secret, passion;

† Copy text: *The Poems of Sir Walter Ralegh: A Historical Edition*, ed. Michael Rudick (Tempe, Ariz.: Arizona Center for Medieval and Renaissance Studies, Renaissance English Texts Society, 1999), 106–108. Copyright Arizona Board of Regents for Arizona State University. Reprinted with permission.
1. Copy text: make.

He smarteth most that hides his smart
    And sues for no compassion.

[Sweet Are the Thoughts]†

Sweet are the thoughts where hope persuadeth hap;[1]
    Great are the joys where heart obtains request;
Dainty the life nursed still° in Fortune's lap.   *continually*
    Much is the ease where troubled minds find rest.
5 These are the fruits that valor doth advance,[2]
    And cuts off dread by hope of happy chance.

Thus hope brings hap but° to the worthy wight;°   *only / person*
    Thus pleasure comes but after hard assay;°   *trial*
Thus Fortune yields in maugre of° her spite;   *despite*
10   Thus happy state is none° without delay.   *not happy*
Then must I needs advance myself by skill
    And live and serve in hope of your goodwill.

[Calling to Mind Mine Eye Long Went About]‡

Calling to mind mine eye long went about
T' entice my heart to seek to leave my breast,
All in a rage, I thought to pull it out,[1]
By whose device I lived in such unrest.
5   What could it say to purchase so° my grace?   *after that*
    Forsooth, that it had seen my mistress' face.

Another time, I likewise call to mind,
My heart was he that all my woe had wrought,
For he my breast, the fort of Love, resigned,
10 When of such wars my fancy never thought.
    What could it say, when I would him have slain?
    But° he was yours and had forgone me clean.[2]   *Only*

At length, when I perceived both eye and heart
Excused themselves as guiltless of mine ill,
15 I found my self was cause of all my smart
And told my self, "My self now slay I will."
    But when I found my self to you was true,
    I loved my self, because my self loved you.

---

† Copy text: *The Poems of Sir Walter Ralegh: A Historical Edition*, ed. Michael Rudick (Tempe, Ariz: Arizona Center for Medieval and Renaissance Studies, Renaissance English Texts Society, 1999), 7. Copyright Arizona Board of Regents for Arizona State University. Reprinted with permission.
1. Where hope persuades us that good fortune is coming.
2. Ralegh's boldness in fighting in Ireland first recommended him to the Queen.
‡ Copy text: *The phoenix nest Built vp with the most rare and refined workes of noble men, woorthy knights, gallant gentlemen, masters of arts, and braue schollers*, ed. R.S. (London: Iohn Iackson, 1593; STC 21516), K4v.
1. An echo of Matthew 5.29: "If thy right eye cause thee to offend, pluck it out."
2. Altogether forsaken me.

[Verse Exchange with the Queen (1587)]†

Ralegh to Elizabeth:

Fortune hath taken away my love,
My life's joy and my soul's heav'n above.
Fortune hath taken thee away, my princess,
My world's joy and my true fantasy's mistress.

5 Fortune hath taken thee away from me;
Fortune hath taken all by taking thee.
Dead to all joys, I only live to woe.
So is Fortune become my fantasy's foe.

In vain, my eyes, in vain ye waste your tears;
10 In vain, my sights,° the smoke of my despairs,   *sighs*
In vain you search the earth and heav'n above.
In vain you search, for Fortune keeps my love.

Then will I leave my love in Fortune's hand;
Then will I leave my love in worldlings' band°   *bondage*
15 And only love the sorrows due to me
(Sorrow, henceforth, that shall my princess be)

And only joy that Fortune conquers kings.
Fortune, that rules the earth and earthly things,
Hath taken my love in spite of virtue's might.
20 So blind a goddess did never virtue right.

With wisdom's eyes had but blind Fortune seen,
Then had my love my love forever been.
But love, farewell. Though Fortune conquer thee,
No fortune, base nor frail, shall alter me.

Per Reginam Waltero Ralegh:[1]

Ah, silly pug,[2] wert thou so sore afraid?
Mourn not, my Wat,[3] nor be thou so dismayed.
It passeth fickle Fortune's power and skill
To force my heart to think thee any ill.
5 No Fortune base, thou sayest, shall alter thee;
And may so blind a witch so conquer me?
No, no, my pug, though Fortune were not blind,

---

† Copy text: *The Poems of Sir Walter Ralegh: A Historical Edition*, ed. Michael Rudick (Tempe, Ariz: Arizona Center for Medieval and Renaissance Studies, Renaissance English Texts Society, 1999), 19–20. Copyright Arizona Board of Regents for Arizona State University. Reprinted with permission.
1. From the Queen to Walter Ralegh.
2. A term of endearment, often applied to dolls or small dogs; also a slang word for a boatman on the Thames. Since Ralegh was small and had large naval ambitions, the Queen's teasing was as apt as it was irritating.
3. Since Ralegh spoke with a Devonshire accent, dropping the letter l in his own first name, the Queen nicknamed him Water, or Wat for short.

Assure thyself she could not rule my mind.
Fortune, I know, sometimes doth conquer kings
10 And rules and reigns on earth and earthly things;
But never think Fortune can bear the sway
If virtue watch and will her not obey.
Ne° chose I thee by fickle Fortune's rede,°   *neither / counsel*
Ne° she shall force me alter with such speed,   *nor*
15 But if° to try this mistress' jest with thee: *unless*
--4

Pull up thy heart, suppress thy brackish tears,
Torment thee not, but put away thy fears;
Dead to all joys and living unto woe,
Slain quite by her that ne'er gave wise man blow,
20 Revive again and live without all dread.
The less afraid, the better thou shalt speed.°   *succeed*

[Like Truthless Dreams, So Are My Joys Expired]†

Like truthless dreams, so are my joys expired,
And past return are all my dandled° days,   *pampered*
My love misled and fancy quite retired,[1]
Of all which past, the sorrow only stays.

5 My lost delights, now clean from sight of land,
Have left me all alone in unknown ways,[2]
My mind to woe, my life in Fortune's hand,
Of all which past, the sorrow only stays.

As in a country strange without companion,
10 I only wail the wrong of death's delays,
Whose sweet spring spent, whose summer well nigh done,
Of all which past, the sorrow only stays.

Whom care forewarns, ere age and winter cold,
To haste me hence to find my fortune's fold.[3]

CELEBRATIONS ON ACCESSION DAY

November 17, the day of Elizabeth's accession to the throne of England in
1558, was celebrated with increasing fervor throughout her reign. Although

4. Although the line drawn here in the manuscript may indicate a lost poetic line rhyming with "thee,"
the Queen has just mentioned an unexpected alteration and introduced the line as "this mistress'
jest." By withdrawing from the poem and then returning, the Queen may be poking fun at Ralegh's
fear that she has abandoned him for good.
† Copy text: *The phoenix nest Built vp with the most rare and refined workes of noble men, woorthy
knights, gallant gentlemen, masters of arts, and braue schollers,* ed. R.S. (London: Iohn Iackson,
1593; STC 21516), K3v.
1. Liking quite withdrawn, a reference to Elizabeth's new favor for Essex.
2. The poem may have been written after Ralegh withdrew from Court and sailed to Ireland to visit
estates that he had recently acquired in Munster on the lands of the defeated rebel Gerald Fitzgerald, Earl of Desmond.
3. Sheep-pen; Ralegh elsewhere calls one of his other country homes "Fortune's fold."

many of the festivities were grand public events, Elizabeth's subjects were also enjoined to pray for the Queen in their homes and thus to raise up a new generation of loyal citizens. Indeed, although public worship services followed the Book of Common Prayer, family worship was encouraged in the home, and many private prayerbooks were published to fill the need for suitable material. One such devotional encyclopedia, Thomas Bentley's *The Monument of Matrons*, includes an Accession Day liturgy cast in the form of a dialogue between a mother and her child. The mother's prayer, following a set of antiphonal versicles, draws on images of ships and sheep, which provided national and scriptural resonances for English subjects surrounded by the sea and still dependent on the wool trade. Bentley's *Monument*, fashioned after John Foxe's famous *Acts and Monuments*, readily aligned such patriotic and religious devotion. Intended as a complete "domestical library" of devotional material, primarily for women but also suitable for men, the *Monument* orbited around the Queen. The second of Bentley's seven sections or "Lamps" opened with Elizabeth's own translation of Margaret of Navarre's *A Godly Meditation of the Inward Love of the Soul towards Christ Our Lord*. The Third Lamp, from which the following excerpts are taken, consisted mainly of psalms, meditations, and prayers suitable for Accession Day, "being the memorable day of her Majesty's most joyful deliverance out of trouble and happy entry to her blessed reign." The various acrostic prayers on her name, Elizabeth Regina, combined piety with the sixteenth-century love of formal structures and visualized verbal puns.

Although Elizabeth must have been pleased when her subjects knelt to pray for her—whether in church, at home, or on the street—she undoubtedly was just as well pleased with the mock-fights that were mounted for her in the tiltyard. Sir Philip Sidney, one of the rising young favorites, was a constant participant in "jousts, triumphs, and other such royal pastimes" at Court, always using his wit to devise "a gallant show." In his pastoral entertainment *The Lady of May*, which was first performed in 1578 during a royal visit to the household of his sister Mary, the Countess of Pembroke, at her country estate at Wilton, the Queen herself was called on to decide which of two young lovers best deserved the hand of the title figure. Most of Sidney's court "devices," however, involved the chivalric tournaments of which Elizabeth was so fond. In 1577, he made his public debut at the Accession Day tilts. On that occasion, Sidney seems to have jousted with her champion, Sir Sidney Lee, an encounter described in his prose romance *Arcadia,* in a passage where Philisides tilts with Lelius. Something of Sidney's strong desire to cut a striking figure at court and his fondness for humorous self-deprecation appears in the passage. Concerned for Sidney's safety, the Queen seems to have bound Lee with a promise to raise his lance on each pass, just missing Sidney's helmet. The move infuriated the young man, who, of course, wanted to show his mettle against the Queen's champion. Sidney's embarrassment was intensified by the presence of Lady Penelope Devereux, looking on from the windows of Whitehall Castle. She would later become the object of his desire in the sonnet sequence *Astrophil and Stella*. Not until 1581 would Sidney have a chance to joust with Lee in earnest at the same festivities, an event also allegorized in *Arcadia* as a joust between Philisides and the "Frozen Knight." From such material, we gain early glimpses of the Accession Day tilts, which were to be expanded, regularized, and elaborated throughout the second half of Elizabeth's reign (as discussed in Part Eight).

The increasing sophistication of the literature surrounding the Accession Day tilts was matched by that of the plays performed at court. Of particular skill and lyricism was George Peele's *Arraignment of Paris*, a retelling of the ancient myth of the origin of the Trojan war. It was staged in 1582–83 by children schooled to sing in the Queen's chapel. In the original myth, three goddesses vie for a golden ball inscribed with the words "For the most fair," choosing the Trojan prince Paris as their adjudicator. Venus bribes the Prince with an offer to give him Helen, the beautiful wife of the Greek king Menelaus, but the Greeks respond by inaugurating the ten-year conflict in which Troy is destroyed. Peele's version replaces Paris's corrupt judgment with the solemn verdict of the goddess Diana. In the final scene, the Goddess of Chastity persuades Venus and Minerva to bestow the prize upon Elizabeth. The play thus contrasts the English Queen, the guardian of peace and concord, with Venus, who enflames desire and provokes strife.

THOMAS BENTLEY

From The Monument of Matrons[†] (1582)

On the seventeenth day of November, commonly called "The Queen's Day"

Sundry forms of Christian prayers and thanksgivings unto God for the preservation of the most virtuous lady Elizabeth, our most dear and dread Sovereign; Queen of England, France, and Ireland; defender of the faith, etc., very necessary to be used, as generally of all faithful subjects continually, so especially of the mother and her daughter upon the seventeenth day of November and every Sabbath and holy day, in honorable remembrance of that joyful Sabbath rest and peace from careful mourning, which that memorable seventeenth day brought to us, the banished exiles of England and persecuted members of Christ, by the most happy entrance of her most royal and excellent Majesty into this her imperial crown and kingdom.[1]

A Psalm[2]

MOTHER: Come, O all you that fear God, come hither, I pray you, and give ear a while and rehearse with me the great benefits that He, the Lord, hath bestowed upon us.[3]

DAUGHTER: For lo, when the most mighty men gathered their power against us and lay in wait for our life, they conspired together to work our destruction, as though the Lord had determined the same and exhorted one another saying, "God hath forsaken them; therefore persecute them now, flying away, and take them, being destitute of all help."[4]

MOTHER: These men, our adversaries I say, wheresoever we removed or went by sea or by land, lay in wait most diligently for us; yea, multitudes

---

[†]   Copy text: Thomas Bentley, *The Monvment of Matrones: conteining seuen seuerall Lamps of Virginitie*, Lamp Three (London: H. Denham, 1582; STC 1892), Fff4r–Fff7r; Bb8v; Dd1r–Dd2v; Jjj2r–Jjj3r.

1.   The biblical Sabbath rest (a complex image that referred to the seventh day of creation, the entry of the Jewish people into their promised land under the leadership of Joshua, and the heavenly rest promised to Christian believers) is here aligned with the joy Protestants felt upon the accession of Elizabeth; *careful:* sorrowful.

2.   Many of the following psalms and prayers are collages, similar in composition to the public thanksgiving included in Part Four, where nearly every word is taken from a biblical passage; key texts are noted below.

3.   Psalm 66.16.

4.   Psalm 71.10–11.

of the cruel enemies did not cease craftily to environ and beset us round about and ran upon us with gaping mouths like raging and roaring lions, of malicious minds to bring us to extremity and to devour us.[5]

DAUGHTER: For Thy sake, O Lord, alone were we killed every day, neither were we in any better condition than sheep appointed of butchers to the slaughter.[6]

MOTHER: Many of us wandered in the waste wilderness and sought strange cities commodious to dwell in, half dead and killed with famine and thirst, overwhelmed with the shadow of death, and, being cast down by the burden of our miseries, lay down flat, cleaving to the earth.[7]

DAUGHTER: The bands of death compassed us round about and bound us; most wicked men like most raging floods made us afraid, environing us round about.[8]

MOTHER: We were snared and cast fast bound with chains into most dark dungeons; yea, we tasted the heat of the fire and the force of the water.[9]

DAUGHTER: Then we called upon the Lord in these extremities. We called upon the Lord, I say, and He heard our voice out of His high palace and, receiving into His ears the cry that we made unto Him, He delivered us from our miseries and distress.[1]

MOTHER: He gathered us home which were scattered, from the east and the west, from the north and south, and brought us from the dungeons of the prisons and darkness of death, breaking the fetters and gyves of iron in pieces.[2]

DAUGHTER: The Lord hath delivered our life from death. He stayed the tears of our eyes and established our feet that they did not fall;[3] He hath brought us out of our distress. Hence have we our light, whereby He causeth us to shine and hath driven away our darkness.[4]

MOTHER: Therefore will we praise Thee, O Lord, among the nations, and will sing lauds unto Thy Majesty.[5] Yea, we will declare Thy power and will show forth Thy praise and mercy early in the morning, because Thou hast defended us and wast our refuge in extreme dangers.[6]

DAUGHTER: O acknowledge and declare ye openly that the Lord is good, for His bounteous goodness is forever.[7] Let all the sincere worshippers of the Lord now confess that His loving kindness is perpetual. Praise ye the Lord.[8]

MOTHER: Glory be to the Father, and to the Son, and to the Holy Ghost.

DAUGHTER: As it was in the beginning, is now, and ever shall be, world without end. Amen.[9]

---

5. Psalm 22.12–13.
6. Psalm 44.22.
7. Psalm 107.4–5 and Psalm 44.25; see also Hebrews 11.37–38 and Psalm 23.4 for the most familiar reference to the "shadow of death."
8. Psalm 18.4.
9. Psalm 18.5.
1. Psalm 18.6.
2. Psalm 107.3, 14; *gyves*: shackles.
3. Psalm 42.2.
4. Psalm 107.14.
5. Psalm 57.9.
6. Psalm 59.16.
7. Psalm 100.5
8. Psalm 106.1
9. Only the opening words of this liturgical formula, known as the *Gloria Patri*, are included in the copy text.

The Versicles.

MOTHER: O Lord, show Thy great mercy upon us miserable sinners.

DAUGHTER: And grant Thine everlasting health and salvation unto us.

MOTHER: O Lord save Elizabeth, our gracious Queen and Governor.

DAUGHTER: Which putteth her only confidence in Thee, O God, her tower.

MOTHER: O send her still continual help from Thy most holy place.

DAUGHTER: And evermore from dangers all, defend Thou her most royal Grace.

MOTHER: O let not the infernal foe have any advantage of her.

DAUGHTER: Nor let the wicked enemy once approach to hurt her.

MOTHER: Endue her ministers alway with righteousness and equity.

DAUGHTER: And make Thou Thy chosen servants full joyfully to praise Thee.

MOTHER: O Lord, save Thy people from all perils and dow[1] them with Thy gifts.

DAUGHTER: And bless Thou Thine inheritance with all Thy bounteous benefits.

MOTHER: In our time, O Lord, give us Thy peace, which passeth all understanding.[2]

DAUGHTER: Because none other God doth fight for us but only Thou, our King.

MOTHER: O soften Thou our hardened hearts, and cleanse our filthy souls from sin.

DAUGHTER: And by Thy spirit and gifts of grace make us a holy life for to begin.[3]

*   *   *

The prayer.

MOTHER: We yield unto Thee, most mighty and merciful Father, immortal thanks for that it hath pleased Thee of Thy mere mercy and fatherly bounty, after the storms of so many troublesome times, to conduct us as upon this day out of banishment and exile into the comfortable port of tranquility by the hand of Thy most gracious servant and our dear sovereign lady, Queen Elizabeth. When we were as sheep wandering astray in the wilderness,[4] Thou ordained'st her Majesty to be our shepherd, to gather us again into Thy sheepfold. When we had been long tossed hither and thither with the outrage and cruel fury of tyrannical persecution, like a poor weather-beaten bark that hath been continually turmoiled and tossed on the perilous surges of the outrageous and swelling seas, finding no sure road nor harbor wherein to rest but continually in danger either to sink into the sands, or to be overwhelmed with waves, or violently to be dashed in pieces against the main[5] rocks, even then, I say, when we despaired utterly of safeguard, standing still in fear of the hazard of everlasting confusion, Thou committed'st the helm to be guided by her Grace's wisdom, who at last conducted us into the haven of this long desired peace and tranquility.

1. Enrich; endow.
2. Philippians 4.7.
3. The first of two alternative prayers is omitted.
4. Psalm 119.176; Isaiah 53.6; Ezekiel 34.6.
5. Mass of.

Therefore, whereas Thou hast placed her in the regal throne to be our David, our Josiah, our Samuel, yea to be our shepherd and ringleader in the way of true holiness and sincere religion, inspire her mind with the manifold blessings of Thy grace, that she may walk all the days of her life in the path of Thy commandments and happily discharge her duty in that stewardship and dispensation[6] which Thou hast committed to her Majesty's hands. Inflame her mind more and more with the love of Thy holy Gospel that all her deeds, thoughts, and practices may tend to the propagation and planting of Thy Word and Christian religion in these her Majesty's dominions. Incline the motions of her virtuous disposition above all things to seek Thine honor and glory; to sow the seeds of the catholic faith[7] abundantly in all places; to cut off the brood of superstition and idolatry; to constitute true preachers of Thy Word; and stablish everywhere Thine holy Gospel and true religion.

Preserve her, most merciful Father (as hitherto Thou hast most miraculously done) from the devilish devices and practices of her enemies that she may have a long and happy reign among us to the advancement of Thy glory and joy and comfort of all us, her subjects. Let her natural disposition continue to her foes terrible; to her subjects amiable; to her offenders merciful; to the virtuous bountiful; indifferent[8] to all men and in all respects partial in no point, neither in causes ecclesiastical nor yet in matters concerning politic government. Assist her, most merciful Father, with the might of Thy heavenly Spirit, to quail the pride of the triple-headed Romish Cerberus,[9] to banish his beggarly ceremonies, to abridge the term of his reign, and finally to cut off and prevent the seeds that continually strive to spring up from abominable superstition and idolatry.

Grant her grace, most merciful Father, to run the remnant of her race in the right path of Thy commandments, declining neither to the right hand nor to the left,[1] but so using all times Thy heavenly Word as the rule and compass to direct her course. Preserve her Grace, most merciful Father, in continual health of body and quietness of mind, that she may be always able to rule the bridle of her high charge and to execute right and justice to all sorts and degrees, to the advancement of Thy glory and the universal commodity[2] of her Majesty's subjects. And finally grant, O most merciful Father, that when it shall please Thee to end the term of her days in this world, Thou wilt make her partaker of the celestial joys which are prepared for them that fear and love Thee since the foundation of the world.[3] Grant this, most merciful Father, for Thy dear Son our Lord Jesus Christ's sake, to whom with Thee and the Holy Ghost, three persons and one God, be all glory, honor, and praise, world without end. Amen.

---

6. Administration; *David . . . Samuel*: in each case, these biblical leaders revived a flagging nation and reestablished, if only briefly, a fading glory; *ringleader*: a chief authority, without the negative connotations of modern usage.
7. Universal faith; here referring to Protestantism rather than Roman Catholicism; *motions*: inward inclinations.
8. Impartial, fair.
9. The three-headed watchdog who guarded the entrance to hell is a reference to the Pope's hat encircled with three crowns, known as a tiara; *Thy heavenly Spirit*: the Holy Spirit.
1. A conflation of Old and New Testament texts that use images of the godly life as running a race (1 Corinthians 9.24–26; Hebrews 12.1) and as not swerving to the right or the left (Proverbs 4.27); *declining*: turning aside.
2. Benefit; *rule the bridle*: govern, as one might a high-spirited horse.
3. Matthew 25.34.

❊   ❊   ❊

*Holy prayers and godly meditations, deciphering in alphabetical form
the royal name of our virtuous Sovereign, Queen Elizabeth, properly to
be used of her Majesty*[4]

E

Engrave Thy laws in the depth of my heart, O Lord, that being instructed
in Thy commandments, I may serve Thee in fear, and rejoice in Thee with
trembling, and take hold upon Thy discipline in all things, lest at any time
Thou become angry and I perish from the right way.[5] Amen.

L

Lord, give me help from my trouble, for vain is the help of man. In Thee
I have strength, and Thou bringest unto nothing those things which trouble
me. Let my soul be subject unto Thee, for from Thee proceedeth my
patience. For Thou art my God and Savior, my Helper, and I will not depart
from Thee. In Thee is my health[6] and my glory. Thou art the God of my
help, and my help is in Thee.[7] Amen.

I

I have broken Thy fold and wandered long as a lost sheep.[8] Let me return,
O Lord, because I have not forgotten Thy commandments. The misdeeds
and ignorances of my tender years remember not, Lord, but according to
Thy mercy have mind on me.[9] For Thy goodness, O Lord, keep my soul and
deliver me; let me not be ashamed, because I have trusted in Thee.[1] Turn
my heaviness into joy, cut off my sack of sorrows, and gird me with gladness that my glory may sing unto Thee,[2] and I shall not be grieved. [Amen.]

Z

Zerubbabel, king of Judah, in the depth of Thy displeasure tasted of Thy
mercy and received by the mouth of Haggai, Thy prophet, sweet comfort
and knowledge of Thy favor and grace. Yea, after Thy determination to
destroy the whole kingdom of the heathen, Thy right hand did preserve
him, and Thine incomparable mercy did choose him for a seal to Thyself.[3]
Lord, this happy king in Thy goodness was but an earthly creature, and
then could he have no righteousness in himself to move such Thy compassion. If it proceeded from the multitude of Thy mercies that surmount
the iniquities of the whole world and that Thou didst only vouchsafe to
behold in him the image of Thyself,[4] bow down Thine eyes, Lord, and

---

4. Only one of the sets of prayers on Elizabeth's name is included here.
5. Psalm 2.12; *Engrave . . . heart:* Jeremiah 31.33.
6. Psalms 42.11; 43.5
7. Many Psalms acknowledge God as helper (cf. Psalms 10.14; 54.4).
8. Isaiah 53.6; *broken:* broken away from.
9. Remember me; *misdeeds . . . Lord:* Psalm 25.7.
1. Psalm 25.2.
2. Psalm 30.11–12.
3. Haggai 2.20–23.
4. God's mercy, which is greater than all the sins of the world, is given not because humans deserve
   it but because they are made in God's image (Genesis 1.27).

behold the selfsame in me. Certify my conscience with remission of my sins that my sorrowful soul may be at rest within me. Send down Thy Holy Spirit to remain with me that I may become with that good king Thy chosen seal and servant, and so grant Thy people that I may with them, and they with me, never deserve further than to taste of Thy rod of favorable correction, but that all my labors and studies may ever bend to the performance of Thy holy will and discharge of my duty. Amen.

A

Arise and illuminate my mind (most benign Savior) that I sleep not at any time in death, lest mine enemies say they have prevailed against me. They which trouble me will be glad if I be cast down, but I have fixed my hope in Thy mercy.[5] Enter not into judgment with Thy servant, for no living creature shall be justified in Thy sight.[6] I will ever look upon the Lord, for He shall be on my right hand that I be not moved. For this my heart is glad and my tongue rejoiceth, yea moreover my flesh shall rest in hope.[7] Amen.

B

Be Thou unto me, O Lord, in the daytime a defender and in the night season a place of refuge, that Thou mayest save me.[8] For Thou art my strength and unto Thee I fly. Lord God, deliver me from the hand of sinners and from the lawbreaker and the wicked-doer, for Thou, Lord, art my patience, Thou art my hope, even from my youth. In Thee I am confirmed, even from my mother's womb. Thou art my protector; in Thee shall be my song for ever and ever.[9] Amen.

E

Ever my tongue shall be telling of Thy rich mercy and wondrous works, O Lord, for Thou hast caused me to pass through fire and water and led me into a fresh place.[1] Thou hast given my soul life and hast not suffered my feet to fall.[2] According to the multitude of my sorrows, Thy comforts have made my soul merry.[3] My soul is like a sparrow taken out of the fowler's snare.[4] Thou hast delivered my life from death and my hands from blood, that I may please Thee, O Lord, in the light of the living.[5] Amen.

T

Thou art just, O Lord, and all Thy commandments be true and all Thy ways mercy, truth, and judgment. And now, Lord, be mindful of me, take not revengement of my sins,[6] remember not mine offences, neither the offences of my fathers, because we have not obeyed Thy precepts. Give me

5. Psalm 13.3–5.
6. Psalm 143.2.
7. Psalm 16.8–9.
8. Psalm 42.8.
9. Psalm 71.4–8.
1. Psalm 66.12; *Ever . . . Lord*: Psalm 35.28.
2. Psalm 66.9.
3. Psalm 94.19.
4. Psalm 91.3.
5. Psalm 56.13.
6. Psalm 25.7.

an heart of understanding and set Thy fear always before mine eyes, that I may be obedient in word, deed, and thought to all that is Thy will.[7] Lord, give unto me the power of Thy Holy Spirit to rule and govern Thy people committed to my charge in all godly fear and knowledge of Thy Word and that I may be unto them an example in all godliness and virtue, to the praise of Thy holy name. Amen.

H

Heal me, Lord, and I shall be healed. Save me, and I shall be saved.[8] My life cleaveth unto the earth. Quicken me according to Thy word.[9] According to Thy mercy relieve me, and I will keep the testimonies of Thy lips.[1] Help me, Lord, so shall I be safe, and I will from henceforth study Thy righteousness.[2] Thy mercies are many, O Lord. According to Thy Word, restore my health.[3] Amen.

✳   ✳   ✳

A prayer to be said mentally or aloud of all true-hearted
English men and women for the Queen's Majesty when
she rideth by them at any time

God save your royal Majesty. The God of gods preserve your noble Grace. Good luck have you with your honor, O you, the fairest among women![4] Ride on, O Queen, according to the great worship and high renown wherewith the King of Kings hath enobled you because of the Word of truth, of meekness and righteousness, which you profess. So shall your right hand teach you terrible things.[5] The Lord Himself be your keeper and preserve you from all evil. The Lord of heaven and earth be your defense on your right hand and on the left. The Lord preserve your going out and your coming in, from this time forth for evermore, so that the sun shall not burn you by day neither the moon by night.[6]

The King of Kings have pleasure in your beauty and make you His daughter, His spouse, and virgin most glorious within. The most mighty Jehovah establish you in His seat of judgment, even in the throne of your father David, that you may become an old mother in Israel. Peace and prosperity be unto them that love your honor, but horror of conscience and confusion of face be unto all those that hate you.[7] For your endurable gifts of God's graces, all people do highly praise you, and for your zeal to Zion, all the world doth honor you. Therefore, for Zion's sake also, we wish you all manner of prosperity. Yea, because of the house of the Lord, which you have reformed, and His religion, which your Grace hath restored, we will continually triumph in His mercy and pray still for the renown of your most royal name

7. Psalm 119.34.
8. Jeremiah 17.14.
9. Psalm 119.25.
1. Psalm 119.146.
2. Psalm 71.12; 14–15.
3. Jeremiah 30.17.
4. Song of Songs 1.8; 5.9; 6.1.
5. Psalm 45.4.
6. Psalm 121.5–8.
7. Psalm 35.4, 26; *Peace . . . honor*: Psalm 122.7.

and majesty, that your fame may more and more be universally spread over the earth and be remembered from one generation to another.

For the Gospel's sake, I say, which your Majesty doth maintain, we will uncessantly[8] praise God for you and with loud voices cry and say, "God save our most gracious Queen Elizabeth. Jesus bless your Highness. The Holy Ghost from heaven comfort and conduct your Majesty in all your ways. Bless our sovereign lady, O blessed Trinity. Heap glory and honor upon Elizabeth, our Queen, O glorious Deity; Bless her sacred Majesty, I say, O God, from this time forth for evermore."

O King of Heaven, receive our Queen; receive and embrace this Thy most glorious virgin and dear daughter, accompanied with her fellow virgins, the princes' daughters, and honorable women, into thy tuition[9] and protection. With joy and gladness, I say, let her, the lively[1] image of Thy princely majesty, be brought safe and unhurt home again unto her ivory palaces and at the last enter into the King's court, her Father's house, where she may enjoy a perpetual crown and everlasting kingdom and rejoice in Thee, her God, her spouse, and her Savior for ever and ever. So shall she and we, her people, give thanks unto Thee, O Lord, world without end. Amen.

SIR PHILIP SIDNEY

From Arcadia (1584–85)[†]

[The Joust Between Philisides and Lelius]

The first that ran was a brave knight whose device was to come in all chained,[1] with a nymph leading him. His *impresa*[2] was. . . . Against him came forth an Iberian whose manner of entering was with bagpipes instead of trumpets, a shepherd's boy before him for a page, and by him a dozen appareled like shepherds for the fashion, though rich in stuff, who carried his lances, which though strong to give a lancely blow indeed, yet so were they colored, with hooks near the morne,[3] that they prettily represented sheep hooks. His own furniture[4] was dressed over with wool so enriched with jewels artificially placed that one would have thought it a marriage between the lowest and the highest. His *impresa* was a sheep marked with pitch, with this word: "Spotted to be known."[5] And because I may tell you out his conceit (though that were not done till the running for that time was

8. Incessantly; continually.
9. Guardianship.
1. Living.
† Copy text: *The Covntesse of Pembrokes Arcadia* (London: William Ponsonbie, 1593; STC 22540), Q4v.
1. As the ending of the passage will make clear, the chains symbolize the promise that Lelius made to his lady (the Queen) not to strike Sidney.
2. Emblem on a shield identifying the knight. It often included a "word" or motto. Sidney left a blank here, intending to add a description later.
3. Lance-head blunted for tilting; *Iberian*: one from Spain or Portugal; *stuff*: apparel.
4. Furnishings, armor.
5. Sidney's own shield bore the image of a sheep branded with a star and bearing the same motto (in Latin). The star alludes to "Astrophil" ("star lover"), Sidney's name for himself in his sonnet sequence *Astrophil and Stella*.

ended) before the ladies departed from the windows, among whom there was one (they say) that was the "star" whereby his course was only directed.[6] The shepherds attending upon Philisides went among them and sang an eclogue, one of them answering another while the other shepherds, pulling out recorders (which possessed the place of pipes[7]), accorded their music to the others' voice. The eclogue had great praise. I only remember six verses. While having questioned one with the other of their fellow shepherd's sudden growing a man-of-arms[8] and the cause of his so doing, they thus said:

> Methought some staves he missed;[9] if so, not much amiss,
> For where he most would hit, he ever yet did miss.
> One said he brake across;[1] full well it so might be,
> 5   For never was there man more crossly crossed[2] than he.
> But most cried, "O, well broke!" O fool full gaily[3] blessed,
> Where failing is a shame and breaking is his best.[4]

Thus I have digressed because his manner liked me well. But when he began to run against Lelius, it had near grown (though great love had ever been betwixt them) to a quarrel. For Philisides breaking his staves with great commendation, Lelius (who was known to be second to none in the perfection of that art) ran ever over his head, but so finely[5] to the skillful eyes that one might well see he showed more knowledge in missing than others did in hitting. For with so gallant a grace his staff came swimming close over the crest of the helmet as if he would represent the kiss, and not the stroke, of Mars. But Philisides was much moved with it while he thought Lelius would show a contempt of his youth, till Lelius (who therefore would satisfy him, because he was his friend) made him know that to such bondage he was for so many courses tied by her whose disgraces to him were graced by her excellency and whose injuries he could never otherwise return than honors.[6]

---

6. Lady Penelope Rich, the real-life Stella ("star") of the sonnets; *conceit*: thought (in devising the *impresa*); *before . . . windows*: the *impresa* was not explained until after the tilting, when the ladies looking on from the windows in Whitehall Palace had gone inside.
7. A more traditional instrument for shepherds.
8. Having asked the attendants about the oddity of a shepherd becoming a knight.
9. Some lances he lacked (to replace those he might break).
1. Broke his lance, not by striking the opponent but by wedging it in front of his body; *One*: copy text: Once; 1590 edition: One.
2. A pun on "cross" in three senses: angry, athwart, and against his will.
3. Derisively.
4. Where breaking his lance is the best he can do.
5. Expertly.
6. Than as honors. The Queen honored Lelius in believing him able to keep his saddle despite his opponent's blows; *satisfy him*: give him an explanation; *to him*: to Lelius, who has had to wear chains and face Philisides without defending himself.

GEORGE PEELE

From The Arraignment of Paris (1584)†

[*The final scene of judgment, in which a golden orb inscribed
"To the fairest" is to be awarded to one of four goddesses:
Juno, Minerva, Venus, or Diana*]

DIANA *describeth the nymph* ELIZA, *a figure of the Queen*

DIANA:	There wones° within these pleasant shady woods—	*dwells*

Where neither storm nor sun's distemperature
Have power to hurt, by cruel heat or cold,
Under the climate of the milder heav'n;
5 Where seldom lights Jove's angry thunderbolt
For favor of that sovereign earthly peer;[1]
Where whistling winds make music 'mong the trees
Far from disturbance of our country gods—
Amidst the cypress springs, a gracious nymph
10 That honors[2] Diane for her chastity
And likes the labors well of Phoebus' groves.

The place Elizium[3] hight,° and of the place   *is called*
Her name that governs there Eliza is,
A kingdom that may well compare with mine.
15 An ancient seat of kings, a second Troy,[4]
Ycompast° round with a commodious sea.   *Encompassed*
Her people are yclepéd° Angeli,[5]   *named*
Or if I miss, a letter is the most.
She giveth laws of justice and of peace,
20 And on her head, as fits her fortune best,
She wears a wreath of laurel, gold, and palm;[6]
Her robes of purple and of scarlet dye,[7]
Her veil of white, as best befits a maid.
Her ancestors live in the House of Fame;
25 She giveth arms of happy victory
And flowers to deck her lions, crowned with gold.[8]
This peerless nymph, whom heav'n and earth beloves,
This paragon, this only, this is she
In whom do meet so many gifts in one,
30 On whom our country gods so often gaze,
In honor of whose name the Muses sing.

---

† Copy text: *The araygnement of Paris, a pastorall. Presented before the Queenes Maiestie, by the Children of her chappell* (London: Henrie Marsh, 1584; STC 19530), E3r–E4v.
1. Probably the earth-god Tellus, a deity comparable in status to Jove (hence "peer").
2. Copy text: honor.
3. A pun on "Elysium," the place reserved for the blessed in the classical underworld.
4. Elizabeth favored Arthurian legends that traced her Welsh lineage back to Brutus, the Trojan who
supposedly settled England and named it New Troy, or Troynovant.
5. A pun on angels and Angles, the Germanic tribe that settled England in the early Middle Ages.
6. All three symbolize highest honor, though the palm also implies victory, gold incorruptibility, and
the laurel achievement in poetry.
7. Colors associated with royalty.
8. Symbol of the British monarchy.

In state, Queen Juno's peer; for power in arms
And virtues of the mind, Minerva's mate;°   *equal*
As fair and lovely as the Queen of Love;
35   As chaste as Diane in her chaste desires.
The same is she, if Phoebe° do no wrong,   *Diana*
To whom this ball in merit doth belong.
PALLAS°:   If this be she whom some Zabeta call,   *Minerva*
To whom thy wisdom well bequeaths the ball,
40   I can remember at her day of birth
How Flora with her flowers strewed the earth,
How every power with heavenly majesty
In person honored that solemnity.
JUNO: The lovely Graces were not far away;
45   They threw their balm for triumph of the day.
VENUS: The Fates against their kind° began a cheerful song   *nature*
And vowed her life with favor to prolong.
Then first 'gan Cupid's eyesight waxen° dim;   *to grow*
Belike° Elisa's beauty blinded him.   *Perhaps*
50   To this fair nymph, not earthly but divine,
Contents it me my honor to resign.
PALLAS: To this fair Queen, so beautiful and wise,
Pallas bequeaths her title in the prize.
JUNO: To her whom Juno's looks so well become,
55   The Queen of Heaven yields at Phoebus' doom.
And glad I am Diana found the art,
Without offence, so well to please desart.°   *reward merit*
DIANA: Then mark my tale: the usual time is nigh,
When wont° the dames of life and destiny[9]   *are accustomed*
60   In robes of cheerful colors to repair°   *approach*
To this renownéd queen, so wise and fair,
With pleasant songs this peerless nymph to greet.
Clotho lays down her distaff at her feet,
And Lachesis doth pull the thread at length;
65   The third[1] with favor gives it stuff° and strength   *fibers*
And, for contrary kind,° affords her leave   *nature*
As her best likes, her web of life to weave.[2]
This time we will attend, and in the meanwhile,
With some sweet song the tediousness beguile.

The music sound and the nymphs within sing or sol-fa[3] with voices
and instruments awhile. Then enter CLOTHO, LACHESIS, *and*
ATROPOS *singing.*

---

9. The Fates.
1. Atropos, who was said to cut each mortal's thread of life at the time destined by the gods.
2. Against nature, Atropos gives Elizabeth control of the length and course of her own life.
3. Use the names of the notes (*do, re, mi, fa, sol*, etc.) in singing.

ATTACKS AND ASSASSINATION ATTEMPTS

Although George Peele had cast Venus as the provoker of strife in his play, in the real world it was Mars, not Venus, who most often stirred up trouble. By the mid-1580s, rebellions, wars, and rumors of war surrounded Elizabeth. 1584 proved to be a disastrous year in the Netherlands, where Elizabeth had recently employed troops. In June, the Duke of Anjou, Elizabeth's "little frog," died, and the following month William of Orange was assassinated. Prince William's murder fueled worries about Elizabeth's safety, particularly because she refused to limit her contact with her subjects or take what some of her Councilors, including Sir Francis Walsingham, considered to be simple precautions. Walsingham and others were especially worried about potential papal plots against Elizabeth, and this anxiety increased as Jesuit missionaries, loyal to the Pope and determined to win England back to the true faith, began to slip into England. In 1581, one of the Jesuit leaders, Edmund Campion, and several other missionaries were captured and executed, and in 1583 Walsingham's spies uncovered a conspiracy between the young Roman Catholics Francis and Thomas Throckmorton and Bernadino de Mendoza, the Spanish ambassador in London, to murder Elizabeth and proclaim Mary Stuart queen. In the aftermath of this event, William Cecil published a pamphlet that argued the government's case against Catholic dissidents, *The Execution of Justice in England for Maintenance of Public and Christian Peace against Certain Stirrers of Sedition and Adherents to the Traitors and Enemies of the Realm.* He also orchestrated a Bond of Association by which Englishmen were encouraged to pledge their arms and their lives to protect Elizabeth. Several thousand signed their names to the document.

Understandably, such actions worried English Catholics, none more so than Cardinal William Allen, who had left England in 1565 to found an English seminary at Douai in the Netherlands and who had organized the first Jesuit mission to England in 1580. In *A True, Sincere, and Modest Defense of English Catholics,* Cardinal Allen argued that Campion and other Jesuits had been illegally detained and executed when the Queen's Councilors became alarmed that the Catholic faith was being "revived in the hearts of the greatest number, noblest, and honestest sort of the realm." Rather than being traitors, he said, Campion and his cohorts were holy martyrs whose public execution should put all Englishmen in mind of the death of the innocent Naboth, orchestrated by King Ahab and Queen Jezebel, the worst of the Old Testament rulers of Israel. In aligning the Queen and her Privy Council with such repellant biblical examples, Allen neatly reversed the imagery with which Elizabeth was familiar: no longer was she a Deborah, a David, a Hezekiah, or an Esther, but the very Jezebel that her own polemicists had declared Rome to be.

The Bond of Association that put English Catholics at risk and so worried Cardinal Allen also worried Elizabeth, since it not only claimed to protect her life, but, should she be killed, also acted to bar from the throne both Mary Stuart and her son, James VI of Scotland. Although Elizabeth had no intention of naming Mary her heir, she was equally keen not to disinherit James, despite her reluctance actually to name him as her successor. Still, the Bond of Association was not a futile or unnecessary gesture, for there was a need to protect Elizabeth from imminent danger, as the Parry incident soon proved.

On March 2, 1585, William Parry, a member of Parliament for Kent, was executed for planning to assassinate the Queen at her palace in Richmond. It was the end to a tumultuous life. Married in turn to two wealthy widows, Parry squandered their fortunes; served as a foreign spy for William Cecil; secretly converted to Roman Catholicism; and was pardoned by the Queen both for assaulting a well-known lawyer and later for objecting to an act of Parliament against Jesuits and other Catholic dissidents. At his trial, Parry was accused of fostering a popish plot against the Queen. He first pled guilty but later proclaimed his innocence. He certainly met with Roman Catholic leaders during his travels on the Continent, but whether or not the assassination plot was condoned by the Pope is uncertain. In 1606, Thomas Heywood wrote a sequel to his enormously popular play on the life of Queen Elizabeth, *If You Know Not Me, You Know Nobody,* in which he dramatized Parry's assassination attempt. In actuality, the scene in the garden included in this section, in which Parry attempts to shoot the Queen but instead stands awestruck and repentant, never took place; the would-be assassin was arrested on the word of a fellow conspirator, Edmund Neville, before he could act against the Queen. Nevertheless, his case became a *cause célèbre* and his execution a further warning to the English Roman Catholics that their loyalty to the Queen was suspect.

One response to the attempted assassination by William Parry was the publication of a special service of public worship, *An Order of Prayer and Thanksgiving for the Preservation of the Queen's Majesty's Life and Safety.* Preachers were enjoined "the next Sunday after the receiving of this order . . . [to] make a sermon of the authority and majesty of princes, according to the Word of God" and to instruct their parishioners "what a grievous and heinous thing it is both before God and man traitorously to seek their destruction, and the shedding of their blood, which are the anointed of God, set up by Him to be the ministers of His justice and mercy to His people." The preachers were also to announce from the pulpit William Parry's confession, a summary of which was included in the printed pamphlet, which declared that the Pope had authorized him to assassinate the Queen and had granted absolution for the murder. The service was to conclude with the printed prayer and the singing of Psalm 21 or "some other Psalm to the like effect." The metrical version of Psalm 21 in the Sternhold and Hopkins Psalter, the standard hymnal for the English Church, began with these words:

> Lord, how joyful is the King in Thy strength and Thy power;
> How vehemently doth he rejoice in Thee, his Savior.
> For Thou hast given unto him his godly heart's desire;
> To him nothing hast Thou denied of that he did require.

Such special services of prayer served both to give Elizabeth's subjects the official version of important, and potentially dangerous, events and to cement their loyalty to the Queen.

CARDINAL WILLIAM ALLEN

From A True, Sincere, and Modest Defense of English Catholics (1584)[†]

Hitherto we have made it clear that divers (contrary to the drift of this libel)[1] have been condemned and put to death either without all law or else only upon new laws by which matter of religion is made treason. Now it followeth, and is next to be considered, whether such other as were accused and appeached[2] of old treasons upon a statute made in the days

---

[†] Copy text: William Allen, *A true, sincere and modest defence, of English Catholiques* ([Rouen: Fr. Parsons' Press, 1584]; STC 373), B1v–B3v.

1. The libel was a pamphlet entitled *The Execution of Justice in England for maintenance of public and Christian peace against certain stirrers of sedition and aherents to the traitors and enemies of the Realm,* probably written by William Cecil and first published in December 1583; *divers:* various Roman Catholics.

2. Charged with the crime.

of Edward III in the twenty-fifth year of his reign were indeed guilty of any such crimes.

The intent of that law is to register divers cases that were to be deemed treason, in which the first and chief is to conspire or compass the death of the sovereign or to levy men-of-arms against him, and thereof can be by open fact convinced.[3] Upon which special clause, Father Campion (good man) and his fellow priests and Catholic brethren were (to the wonder of the world) arraigned, namely indicted: that, at Rome and Rheims the last day of March and May in the twenty-second year of her Majesty's reign, they compassed the Queen's death, the subversion of the state, and invasion of the realm, feigning (for better coloring of the collusion) the foresaid places, days, and times when this conspiracy should be contrived.[4]

Which forgery and false accusation is now so clearly discovered to all Englishmen of any consideration, Protestants and others, that for excuse of that foul, sinful practice they have set out at length to strangers (as they did with like luck before at home) this late libel[5] by which God Almighty, the protector of His saints and our innocency, hath marvelously confounded themselves and justified the cause and conscience of His holy martyrs, as by the declaration following shall appear.

When the *politiques* of our country, pretending to be Protestants, saw the Catholic religion (contrary to their worldly-wise counsels and determinations and against their exquisite diligence and discipline and twenty-years' endeavor, in which time they thought verily to have extinguished the memory of our fathers' faith) to be revived in the hearts of the greatest number, noblest, and honestest sort of the realm (and that neither their strange, violent, and capital laws for the Queen's spiritual superiority against the Pope's pre-eminence, the power of priesthood in absolving penitents, the saying and hearing of Mass, having or wearing of *Agnus Deis* or other external signs of our Society[6] with the Catholic Church of all times and nations, nor the execution of many by death and other penalties and punishment according to the said laws, would serve nor were of force to hold out of England the priests of the Society and seminaries, to whom Christ had given more apostolic spirit, courage, zeal, and success than of so small a beginning was looked for), by whom the Protestants began to fear lest great alteration in religion (whereon they think their new state, that is to say the weal of a very few in comparison, dependeth) might ensue, they thought good by their long exercised wisdom to alter the whole accusation from question of faith and conscience to matter of treason. Which being resolved upon, they went about by divers proclamations, libels, and speeches first to make the people believe that all Catholics, and specially Jesuits and such priests and scholars as were brought up in the seminaries or colleges out of the realm, were traitors. And for their better persuasion gave out one wile that, by the said priests and others in banishment, there was a marvelous confederation of the Pope, King of Spain, Duke of Florence[7] and others for the

---

3. Convicted; *compass*: devise; *levy*: raise up.
4. Edmund Campion and several other Jesuit missionary priests were tried and executed in 1581.
5. *The Execution of Justice in England* was republished in 1584 and translated into Italian, Dutch, Latin, and French.
6. The Jesuits; *politiques*: political operators, so called to align them with a French faction during the Huguenot wars; *Agnus Deis*: small pendants of wax imprinted with the insignia of a lamb bearing a cross or flag and blessed by the Pope.
7. Gregory XIII, Philip II, and Francesco de Medici; *wile*: underhanded stratagem; here, a pamphlet identified in a marginal note as having been published in July 1580.

invasion of the realm. But that being shortly proved nothing, they feigned that the said Jesuits and priests were confederated with the Irish quarrel, and to give more color of somewhat,[8] they sticked not to rack Father Campion extremely for search of that point.

But this fiction failing, they found out another as foul: that the death of the Queen and divers of the Council was contrived (forsooth) in the seminaries of Rome and Rheims, of which conspiracy in fine[9] they resolved to indict them, as they did, and pursued them to death for the same, with such evident partiality, default of justice and equity, as was in that court (once most honorable for justice) never heard or read of before.

Such as pleaded against them to make them odious in judgment discoursed (as this libel now doth) first of the nature and horror of rebellion in general, and then of a rebellion in the North for religion a dozen years before, when the parties there accused were young boys in the schools and universities of the realm; of the Pope's Bull of excommunicating the Queen a good many of years before any of them came over sea or ever saw Pope, Rome, or Rheims (yea, when some of them were yet Protestants in England); they discoursed also of the rebellion in Ireland by Stukely, Sanders, and others, none of which men divers there arraigned ever saw or knew in their lives; of their being made priests by the Pope's authority, and of their obligation and obedience to him being the Queen's enemy, of their authority to absolve and reconcile in England received from him, of their coming in at the same time when they were in arms in Ireland (as though they had not entered their native country and exercised those spiritual functions seven years before[1] or could not then exercise them but in favor of such as took arms against the Queen).

And when these generalities were uttered only to make them odious and amaze the hearers with those that should have to judge of their guiltiness or innocency, the good fathers and priests made just exceptions against such vulgar invectives as could not touch them that there stood in judgment more than any other priest or Catholic in the realm, and many of the points such as they were sure none should have been arraigned of in King Edward III's time (upon whose statute nevertheless the indictment was pretended to be drawn), humbly praying the judge and bench that they would more directly, plainly, and sincerely pass on them for their faith and exercises of the Roman religion (for proof whereof they should not need to seek for so impertinent and far-fetched matter), which they openly professed and desired to die for with all their hearts or, if they would needs proceed against them as for treason in the sense of the old laws of our country, that then it would please them to aggravate[2] no farther to their disadvantage and death either other men's faults or matter of pure religion but to come to the indictment and to the particular charge of every person there arraigned, which was of conspiring the Queen's death. Whereof if they could by any proof or sufficient

---

8. Obtain specious proof.
9. In conclusion.
1. A number of Roman Catholic priests unaffiliated with the Jesuits entered England in the 1570s, one of whom, Cuthbert Mayne, was executed in 1577; *as this libel*: copy text: at this libel; *rebellion . . . before*: on the Northern Rebellion of 1569, see the relevant documents in Part Three; *Bull . . . Queen*: published in 1570; see Part Three; *Stukely . . . others*: Thomas Stukely, a Catholic adventurer known as the Duke of Ireland and reported to be an illegitimate son of Henry VIII, and Nicholas Sanders, a Catholic historian and priest. In 1579, they conspired to land in Ireland a force of Spanish and Italian troops whose mission was to shore up the rebellion of James Fitzmaurice Fitzgerald.
2. Heap up charges; *exceptions*: legal objections; *pass*: pass judgment.

testimony of credible persons convict all or any of them, then their death to be deserved; if not, their innocent blood upon all that should be accessory to the shedding thereof, a crime that crieth for vengeance at God's hand when it is done but by private malice and mischief, but committed in public place of judgment by authority and pretence of law (as in the case of Naboth and of Christ our Master), it is in the sight of God most horrible and never long escapeth public punishment, from the which our Lord God of His mercy save our poor country, even by the prayers of these holy martyrs, for whose blood it is otherwise highly deserved.[3]

THOMAS HEYWOOD

From If You Know Not Me, You Know Nobody, Part Two (1606)[†]

[The Assassination Attempt of William Parry]

Enter three lords.

LORD 1: You are an early riser, my good lord.

LORD 2: The blood of youth that traffics° in the Court   *busies itself*
Must not be sluggish. Your kind remembrance.

LORD 3: My very good lord, we that are stars that wait upon
the train

5   Of such a Cynthia under which we live
Must not be tardy.

LORD 1: You have said true. We are starters in one hour,
And our attendance is to wait° one such a Queen,   *wait upon*
Whose virtue all the world—but to leave that

10   Which every tongue is glad to commune with,
Since Monsieur's first arrival in the land,[1]
The time that he was here and the time since,
What royalty hath been in England's court,
Both princely reveling and warlike sport.

15   LORD 2: Such sports do fitly fit our nation,
That foreign eyes beholding what we are
May rather seek our peace than wish our war.

LORD 3: Heaven bless our Sovereign from her foes' intent.
The peace we have is by her government.

Enter Doctor Parry.

20   LORD 1: Master Doctor Parry.

LORD 2: Good morrow, Master Doctor.

LORD 3: You are an early riser, sir.

---

3. England itself bears responsibility for the blood of these martyrs.
† Copy text: Thomas Heywood, *The Second Part of, If you know not me, you know no bodie* (London: Nathaniel Butter, 1606; STC 13336), H3r–I1v.
1. Anjou spent the winter of 1581–82 in London, courting the Queen.

DOCTOR: My lord, my lord, my very good lord.

LORD 1:   This summer morning makes us covetous

25   To take the profit of the pleasant air.

DOCTOR: 'Tis healthful to be stirring in a morning.

LORD 2: [*Aside*]   It hath pleased the Queen to show him many favors.

LORD 3:   You say but right, and since his last disgrace

(The cause so great it had surely touched his life

30   Had not the Queen been gracious), he seems at Court

A man more gracious in our Sovereign's eye

Than greater subjects.

LORD 2:   She hath given him much preferment,

In greatest place graced him with conference,°   *consulted with him*

35   Asked for him in his absence, and indeed

Made known to us he is one in her regard.

LORD 1:[2]   But did you never hear the cause of his disgrace?

LORD 3:   He did intend the murder of a gentleman,

One Master Hare, here of the Inner Temple,[3]

40   And so far brought his purpose to effect

That Master Hare being private in his chamber,

He,° watching as he thought fit time, broke in upon him.   *Dr. Parry*

But he,° assaulted, so behaved himself   *Master Hare*

That he did guard himself and attached° him;   *seized*

45   From whence he was committed unto Newgate[4]

And at the Sessions,[5] by twelve honest men,

Found guilty of burglary and condemned to die,

And had died, had her Grace not pardoned him.

LORD 2:   She is a gracious Princess unto all.

50   Many she raiseth, wisheth none should fall.

LORD 1: [*To Doctor Parry*]   Fie, Master Doctor,

Your face bears not the habit it was wont,

And your discourse is altered. What's the matter?

DOCTOR: And if my brow be sad or my face pale,

55   They do belie my heart, for I am merry.

LORD 1:   Men being as you are, so great in grace

With such a royal Princess, have no reason.

     Enter a Gentleman.

GENTLEMAN: Room, gentlemen, for my Lord High Steward.

     Enter the Earl of Leicester;[6] all the lords flock after him and exeunt.
                               Manet Parry.[7]

DOCTOR: The discontent desire to be alone.

60   My wishes are made up, for they are gone.

---

2. Copy text: Lord 3.

3. Hugh Hare, one of Parry's creditors; the Inner Temple was one of four Inns of Court, where lawyers and gentlemen were prepared for civil and court life.

4. A London prison.

5. Sessions of the Peace, a court with civil and criminal jurisdiction.

6. Robert Dudley.

7. Parry remains.

Here are no blabs° but this, and this one clock   *tongues*
I'll keep from going with a double lock.°   *his two lips*
Yet it will strike. This day it must be done.
What must be done? What must this engine° do?   *his hand*
65   A deed of treason hath prepared me two.
These two, these two,° why they had life by her,   *his two hands*
And shall these two kill their deliverer,
The life that makes me rise? These once my sin
Had forfeited; her mercy pardoned me.
70   I had been eaten up with worms ere this
Had not her mercy given a life to this.
And yet these hands, if I perform my oath,
Must kill that life that gave a life to both.
I have ta'en the sacrament to do 't, conferred
75   With Cardinal Como[8] about it, and received
Full absolution from his Holiness,[9]
Been satisfied° by many holy fathers   *satisfied in conscience*
During my travels both in France and Italy.
The deed is just and meritorious,
80   And yet I am troubled when I do remember
The excellency of her Majesty,
And I would fain desist, but that I know
How many vows of mine are gone to heaven,
My letters and my promises on earth
85   To holy fathers and grave Catholics,
That I would do 't for good of Catholics.
Then in the garden where this day she walks,
Her graces I will cast behind mine eyes,

                         Enter Gentleman.
And by a subject's hand, a sovereign dies.
90   GENTLEMAN: Clear the way, gentlemen, for the Queen.
Master Doctor Parry.

                         Exit Gentleman.
DOCTOR: O let me see a difference in this man!
Before this Queen (that I am come to kill)
Showed me the gracious eye of her respect
95   And gave me countenance 'mongst greatest earls,
This man was forwarder to thrust me forth
Than now he is humble to accept me in.
If then her Grace hath honored me so much,
How can this hand give her a treacherous touch?°   *stroke or hit*
100   The trumpets speak. Heaven, what shall I do?
Even what hell, and my damned heart, shall thrust me to.

---

8. Parry considered Cardinal Como's letter, written in response to a letter Parry had sent the Pope, as tacit approval of his plans to murder the Queen.
9. Pope Gregory XIII.

Enter Queen, Leicester, and lords.

QUEEN: Fair day, my lords. You are all larks this morning,
Up with the sun; you are stirring early.

LEICESTER: We are all subjects to your Sovereign's light.

105 QUEEN: That you call duty, we accept as love,
And we do thank you, nay we thank you all.
'Tis not to one, but 'tis in general.

LEICESTER: The Queen would walk apart. Forbear, my lords.

DOCTOR: [*Aside*] Now, what makes me shake?
110 Do angels guard her, or doth heaven partake
Her refuge?

QUEEN: In such a garden may a sovereign
Be taught her loving subjects to maintain:
Each plant unto his nature and his worth
115 Having full cherishing, it springeth forth.
Weeds must be weeded out, yet weeded so:
Till they do hurt, let them a° God's name grow.[1]   *in*

DOCTOR: [*Aside*] Now, Queen.

He offers[2] to shoot.

QUEEN: Who's there? My kind friend, Master Doctor Parry?
120 DOCTOR: My most dread Sovereign.

QUEEN: Why do you tremble, Master Doctor? Have you any suit to us?
Shake not at us; we do our subjects love.
Or does thy face show signs of discontent
Through any heavy want oppresseth thee?[3]
125 Though at our Court of Greenwich thou wert crossed
In suing to be master of Saint Katherine's,[4]
To do thee good, seek out a better place.
She'll give thee that, the which hath given thee grace.

DOCTOR: I know your love, dread Queen. [*Aside*] Now.

130 QUEEN: Master Doctor, about the talk we had together
Of English fugitives that seek my life,
You told me of them. I am beholding to you.

DOCTOR: I did no more than duty. [*Aside*] O happy time!

QUEEN: And will they still persist? Do they desire my blood
135 That wake, when I should sleep, to do them good?

DOCTOR: Madam.   [*brandishes his pistol*]

QUEEN: O my Maker! Parry, villain, traitor,
What dost thou with that dag°?   *heavy pistol*

DOCTOR: Pardon, dread Sovereign.

140 QUEEN: "Pardon," thou villain, shows thou art a traitor,
Treason, my lords, treason!

---

1. Let weeds grow, for God's sake, until they do harm; a possible allusion to the parable of the wheat and weeds (Matthew 13.24–30).
2. Raises the pistol briefly.
3. Are you disappointed because you lack something?
4. St. Katherine's Hospital near the Tower of London; Parry asked for this position in January 1584 after he informed the Queen of a plot to murder her and place Mary Stuart on the throne.

Enter the lords.

LEICESTER: Ha, by the blest place of heaven, treason, and we so near?
A traitor with a dag; God's holy mother.
Lords, guard the Queen. Are you not frighted, Madam?
145   I'll play the sergeant to arrest the wretch.[5]
QUEEN: Be not so rash, good Leicester. He's dead already,
Struck with remorse of that he was come to do.
Pray let me speak with him. Say, Master Doctor,
Wherein have I deserved an ill of you,
150   Unless it were an ill in pardoning you.
What have I done toward you to seek my life,
Unless it were in taking you to grace.
DOCTOR: Mercy, dread Queen.
QUEEN: I thank my God, I have mercy to remit
155   A greater sin, if you repent for it. Arise.
LEICESTER: [*Aside*] My lords, what do you mean? Take hence that villain.
Let her alone,[6] she'll pardon him again.
[*To the Queen*] Good Queen, we know you are too merciful
To deal with traitors of this monstrous kind.
160   Away with him to the Tower, then to death;
A traitor's death shall such a traitor have
That seeks his sovereign's life that did him save.
QUEEN: Good Leicester.
LEICESTER: Good Queen, you must be ruled.   *Exeunt.*

THE CHURCH OF ENGLAND

From An Order of Prayer and Thanksgiving for the Preservation of the Queen's Majesty's Life and Safety (1585)[†]

O eternal God and merciful Father, with humble hearts we confess that we are not able either by tongue to utter or in mind to conceive the exceeding measure of Thine infinite goodness and mercy towards us wretched sinners and towards this our noble realm and natural country. Not many years since (when for our unthankful receiving of the heavenly light and truth of Thy Gospel we were justly cast into thralldom and misery and thrust again under the kingdom of darkness, so that our consciences lay groaning under the heavy burdens of error, superstition, and idolatry), even then, even then, O Lord, Thou didst vouchsafe of Thy great goodness, not only without our desert[1] but far beyond our hope and

---

5. In the autumn of 1584, the Earl of Leicester and others had drawn up a Bond of Association, signed by thousands of Englishmen, which promised to protect Elizabeth against assassination attempts, particularly from Roman Catholic subjects.
6. If you let her alone.
† Copy text: *An Order of Praier and Thankes-giving, for the preseruation of the Queenes Maiesties life and salfetie: to be used of the Preachers and Ministers of the Dioces of Winchester* (London: Ralfe Newberie, 1585; STC 16516), A3v–A4v.
1. Deserving; *since*: during the reign of Mary Tudor.

expectation, to preserve for us Thy faithful servant, our gracious prince and sovereign, Queen Elizabeth, and to save her from the jaws of the cruel tigers that then sought to suck her blood and to work to us perpetual tyranny and bondage of conscience.

This Thou didst, O gracious Lord, undoubtedly that she might be to this Thy Church of England a sweet and tender nurse and that this realm, under her happy government, might be a blessed sanctuary and place of refuge for Thy poor afflicted saints, in these dangerous days persecuted and troubled in many countries for the profession of Thy Gospel. Yea, and that this our benefit and their comfort might be the more assured, Thy divine providence from time to time hath many ways mightily and miraculously preserved and kept her from the crafty, cruel, and traitorous devices of her bloody adversaries and the deadly enemies of Thy Gospel, which with barbarous cruelty have sought to extinguish the light thereof by shedding her Majesty's most innocent blood.

But this Thy gracious goodness and mighty providence never so apparently showed itself at any one time as even within these few days, when a traitorous subject (never injured or grieved by her, but sundry times holpen, relieved, and countenanced[2] far above his state and worthiness) had of long time retained a wicked and devilish purpose and often sought occasion and opportunity to lay violent hands upon her royal person and to have murdered her. But still the vigilant eye of Thy blessed providence did either prevent him by some sudden interruption of his endeavor or, by the majesty of her person and princely behavior towards him, didst strike him so abashed that he could not perform his conceived bloody purpose. And at the last, this wretched villainy was by Thy means disclosed and his own tongue opened to confess his detestable and wicked intent.

For this Thy inestimable goodness towards us (O heavenly Father), with humble hearts and minds we thank Thee and bless Thy name for ever and ever. For assuredly if Thou hadst not been now on our side (as the prophet David saith), the whole floods and waves of wickedness had overwhelmed us, and we had been sunk into the bottomless pit of infinite and unspeakable miseries.[3] We beseech Thee therefore (O Lord) that Thou wilt bless us so with Thy grace that we may be rightly and truly thankful to Thee (that is, not in word only but in deed also), daily studying to frame our lives according to the direction of Thy holy Word, which Thou hast sent among us; and that her Majesty, thus feeling the mighty hand of Thy providence fighting for her safety, may more boldly and constantly with an heroical spirit stand in the protection and defense of Thy blessed Church, which by Thy Word thou hast planted among us; and lastly that the cruel spirits of Antichrist that seek the subversion of the Gospel may by the hand of Thy justice feel what it is to set to sale for money the innocent blood of Thine anointed princes, which Thou hast prepared and set up to be the nurses and protectors of Thy truth. Grant this, O heavenly Father, for Jesus Christ's sake, Thy only Son, our Savior, to whom with Thee and the Holy Ghost be given all honor and glory, world without end.

---

2. Helped, raised up, and favored.
3. A sentiment frequently expressed in the psalms; see, for instance, Psalms 18.4 and 32.6.

THE EXECUTION OF MARY STUART

Another response to Parry's assassination attempt was Elizabeth's *Speech at the Closing of Parliament* on 29, March 1585. Although she thanked the lords and commons for their care towards her, as expressed in the Bond of Association, she carefully charted her way between the "Romanists," against whom the Bond was directed, and those who advocated "newfangleness," in other words her increasingly vocal Protestant subjects who urged greater strictness against Catholics. Her pledge "to guide them both by God's holy true rule" was meant to remind them not just of her own piety, but more particularly of her prerogative, as the only anointed and therefore legitimate ruler of England, to make decisions for the country and for herself.

Although Elizabeth fully intended to go her own way, she found her path blocked again and again in the 1580s by her cousin, Mary Stuart. Following the aborted Northern Rebellion a decade earlier, Mary lived for a number of years in relative quiet under the guardianship of George Talbot, the sixth Earl of Shrewsbury. Following the Throckmorton plot, however, she was removed to the more strict keeping of Sir Amias Paulet at Chartley in Staffordshire. Both Mary and Elizabeth made attempts to reconcile Mary with her son, James VI of Scotland: Mary wished to regain her crown—or at least half a crown, shared with James—and Elizabeth was eager for Mary to leave England. But by the middle of 1585, it was clear to everyone that no such reconciliation would take place, and Mary began to cast about for other ways to escape her captivity. Sir Francis Walsingham, ever fearful of plots against the Queen, employed a double agent, Gilbert Gifford, to carry letters between the French embassy and Mary Stuart. Gifford first took the French letters to Walsingham's decoder, Thomas Phelippes, who deciphered their contents. They were then delivered to a local brewer, who conveyed them to Mary by inserting them into barrels of beer, which were opened in turn by her servants in the cellars at Chartley. Messages came back from Mary in the same way, traveling in the empty casks to Phelippes before being delivered to the French embassy. In the meantime, Anthony Babington, who had served as a page in the house of George Talbot and had met the Queen of Scots when he was still a young man, joined a group of English Catholics who were hiding Jesuit missionaries. One of the priests, John Ballard, recruited Babington for a plot to kill Elizabeth and free Mary. In July 1586, Babington wrote Mary of their plans; when she replied, Walsingham arrested Babington, who implicated his fellow conspirators.

Elizabeth, of course, was furious, both at Mary for her perfidy and at Walsingham and her Privy Council for putting her into a serious bind. On the one hand, she recognized that Mary had gone from being a nuisance to posing a full-blown threat, since the Queen of Scots had implicated herself in yet another major plot; on the other hand, Elizabeth had no desire to bring a fellow monarch to trial, let alone to execute her. Nevertheless, on September 25, Mary was brought to Fotheringay Castle in Northamptonshire and on October 14 her trial before a royal commission began. The commissioners declared her guilty of treason on October 25, and in November Parliament began to pressure Elizabeth to sign her cousin's death warrant. In her *First Answer to the New Parliament Concerning Mary Stuart* on November 12, Elizabeth both defended her own reluctance to condemn Mary and professed herself ready to die "if by my death other nations and kingdoms might truly say that this realm had attained an ever-prosperous and flourishing estate." The main point of her speech, however, was to remind Parliament sharply that she had an obligation not to act with undue haste but in such a way that "our proceedings be just and honorable."

In *The Second Answer Made by the Queen's Majesty to Parliament* on November 24, Elizabeth complained that she was being "forced to this proceeding" with the result that the world might well call her a tyrant "when it shall be spread that for the safety of her life a maiden Queen could be content to spill the blood even of her own kinswoman." With her conscience on the rack and her reputation at stake, Elizabeth demanded that Parliament "content yourselves with an answer without answer."

It was a masterful speech, but not one to content either Parliament or the Privy Council. On December 4, Elizabeth allowed a public Proclamation of Mary's impending death to be read, but still refused to sign the death warrant. At last, buffeted by rumors of Mary's impending escape, Elizabeth signed the warrant on February 1, 1587, but did not release it. When William Davison, an inexperienced assistant secretary of state, took it to the Privy Councilors and so set the execution in motion, Elizabeth flew into a rage. Davison was arrested, fined, and confined to the Tower of London. But the warrant had already been sealed and delivered. On February 8, Mary Stuart, the Queen of Scots, was executed at Fotheringay Castle.

Mary's own final letter to Henry III of France, her former brother-in-law, is a poignant defense of her innocence. "The Catholic faith and the assertion of my God-given right to the English crown are the two issues on which I am condemned," she wrote, "and yet I am not allowed to say that it is for the Catholic religion that I die, but for fear of interference with theirs." The ideological battle between Protestants and Catholics was played out not only in her execution, but also in the differing accounts that were written after the event.

A Circumstantial Account of the Execution of Mary, Queen of Scots, written by Robert Wyngfield, gave a Protestant account of Mary's death. Addressed to William Cecil, it was intended to give the Privy Councilors in London an eyewitness description of the proceedings at Fotheringay. Although Wyngfield was perhaps overly concerned with Mary's attire and personal habits, he did report that "without any terror of the place, the persons, or the preparations, she came out of the entry into the hall, [and] stepped up to the scaffold." On the other hand, he viewed with dismay her refusal to listen to Richard Fletcher, the Dean of Peterborough and one of Elizabeth's favorite royal chaplains, who had been sent to preach her execution sermon. Mary told him "with great earnestness, 'Good Master Dean, trouble not yourself anymore about this matter, for I was born in this religion, have lived in this religion, and am resolved to die in this religion.'" Wyngfield's details of Mary's final moments—as she lays aside her crucifix and *Agnus Dei* medal, crosses herself, and prays in Latin—are meant to convey her unrepentant spirit, and his report of her short grey hair, uncovered as the axe separates head from body, underscores her pathetic end. Although the final story of her little dog evokes pity among modern readers, it may have been intended to remind Wyngfield's contemporaries of the biblical Queen Jezebel, whose final humiliation was to have her flesh eaten by dogs (2 Kings 9.36), or it may have been intended to show the folly of the Scottish Queen, who went to her execution with a lapdog concealed beneath her gown.

A Roman Catholic account of Mary Stuart's execution was penned by Adam Blackwood, a Scottish lawyer who lived most of his life in France. Written in French and printed in Paris as part of his *History of Mary, Queen of Scots*, it portrayed Mary as a saint and martyr, who prayed on the scaffold that God would "turn away His anger from the isle of Great Britain, which she did perceive He threatened with scourges for the abominable, willful impiety committed by the inhabitants." In Blackwood's account, Richard Fletcher was not a godly pastor, intent on saving an erring soul at the moment of death, but rather a crude fellow who delighted in ridiculing and persecuting the Queen.

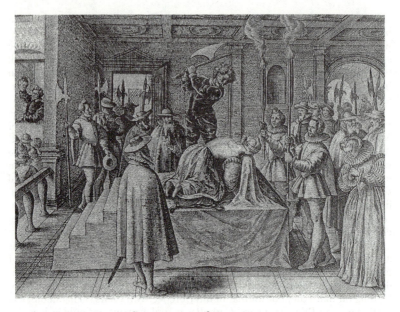

The execution of Mary Stuart.

Mary Stuart, as in most martyr stories, wins out over her persecutors on moral grounds, so that "her hardest-hearted enemies were greatly moved" and were forced to examine their own consciences as to the injustice of such cruel treatment. Despite the partisan biases of Wyngfield and Blackwood's accounts, both provide evidence as to what happened on February 8, 1587, at Fotheringay Castle, and the truth of the matter undoubtedly lies somewhere between the two stories.

Richard Fletcher delivered not only the execution sermon to Mary, but also *A Sermon Preached before the Queen Immediately after the Execution of the Queen of Scots*. In an oration dense with biblical images, he reminded Elizabeth of her own past difficulties, choosing the same image of a sheep led to slaughter that the Queen herself favored and that Edward Dering had so naughtily turned against her years before (see Part Three). With a nod toward the Privy Councilors at whom she was still furious, Fletcher noted "that this hath been as blessed service to you, as even it was to Joseph, to be warned and informed of your enemies' secret maliciousness by the angel of God, by divine and miraculous intelligence." And citing as his central text the command to "arise," he urged Elizabeth to take up her task as preeminent Protestant monarch, leading her Church and her country in "the begun and confirmed course of the Gospel of Christ."

Elizabeth herself, however, refused to take responsibility for Mary Stuart's death, calling it, in a letter to James VI a week after the execution, a "miserable accident." And James himself, in his reply to Elizabeth, pointed out that while he considered her "unspotted," her reputation in Europe had been damaged by what many considered to be a precipitous action. Although he was right and Elizabeth would soon have to confront the greatest military threat of her reign, in the midsummer of 1587 she paused to make peace with the woman who had been her nearest "enemy." With all the pomp and ceremony of a royal funeral, Mary Stuart was laid to rest in Peterborough Cathedral, a queen again in death if not in life.

QUEEN ELIZABETH

Speeches to Parliament (1585–86)

[Speech at the Closing of Parliament (March 29, 1585)][†]

My lords and ye of the Lower House:[1] My silence must not injury the owner so much as to suppose a substitute sufficient to render you the thanks that my heart yieldeth you, not so much for the safekeeping of my life (for which your care appeareth so manifest) as for the neglecting your private future peril, not regarding other way[2] than my present state. No prince herein, I confess, can be surer tied or faster bound than I am with the link of your goodwill and can for that but yield a heart and head to seek forever all your best. Yet one matter toucheth me so near as I may not overskip: religion, the ground on which all other matters ought to take root and, being corrupted, may mar all the tree. And that there be some fault-finders with the order of the clergy, which so may make a slander to myself and the Church (whose over-looker God hath made me, whose negligence cannot be excused if any schisms or errors heretical were suffered), thus much I must say: that some faults and negligences may grow and be (as in all other great charges it happeneth), and what vocation without?[3] All which if you, my lords of the clergy, do not amend, I mind to depose you. Look you, therefore, well to your charges. This may be amended without heedless or open exclamation.

I am supposed to have many studies,[4] but most philosophical. I must yield this to be true: that I suppose few (that be no professors) have read more. And I need not tell you that I am so simple that I understand not, nor so forgetful that I remember not. And yet amongst my many volumes, I hope God's Book hath not been my seldomest lectures, in which we find that which by reason (for my part) we ought to believe: that seeing so great wickedness and griefs in the world, in which we live but as wayfaring pilgrims, we must suppose that God would never have made us but for a better place and of more comfort than we find here. I know no creature that breatheth whose life standeth hourly in more peril for it than mine own, who entered not into my state without sight of manifold dangers of life and crown, as one that had the mightiest and greatest to wrestle with. Then it followeth that I regarded it so much as I left myself behind my care.[5] And so, you see that you wrong me too much (if any such there be) as doubt my coldness in that behalf. For if I were not persuaded that mine were the truth of God's will, God forbid I should live to prescribe it to you.

---

† Copy text: John Stow, *The annales, or a generall chronicle of England* (London: Thomae Adams, 1615; STC 23338), 701–702.
1. Elizabeth addresses both the House of Lords, which included the bishops, and the House of Commons.
2. Anything other; *my silence . . . yieldeth you*: my inclination not to speak must not prevent me from recognizing that no speech by someone else will properly convey my heartfelt thanks; *neglecting . . . peril*: the Privy Council had issued a Bond of Association in 1584, signed by many citizens, which committed the signatories to defend the Queen with their lives and attack any who might seek to depose her.
3. What calling is without such things?
4. I am known as one who studies.
5. Elizabeth has cared more for attaining heaven than for her own safety; *regarded it*: considered the "better place" of heaven.

Take heed lest Ecclesiastes say not too true: "They that fear the hoary frost, the snow shall fall upon them."[6] I see many overbold with God Almighty, making too many subtle scannings of His blessed will, as lawyers do with human testaments. The presumption is so great as I may not suffer it. Yet mind I not hereby to animate Romanists (which what adversaries they be to mine estate is sufficiently known), nor tolerate newfangledness.[7] I mean to guide them both by God's true rule. In both parts be perils, and of the latter, I must pronounce them dangerous to a kingly rule to have every man according to his own censure to make a doom of the validity and privity of his prince's government with a common veil and cover of God's Word, whose followers must not be judged but by private men's exposition.[8] God defend you from such a ruler that so evil would guide you.

Now I conclude that your love and care neither is nor shall be bestowed upon a careless prince, but such as for your good will passeth as little for this world as who careth least, with thanks for your free subsidy (a manifest show of the abundance of your good wills) the which, I assure you, but to be employed to your weal,[9] I could be better pleased to return than receive.

[The First Answer to the New Parliament Concerning Mary Stuart (November 12, 1586)][†]

The bottomless graces and immeasurable benefits bestowed upon me by the Almighty are and have been such as I must not only acknowledge them but admire them, accounting them as well miracles as benefits, not so much in respect of His divine Majesty, with whom nothing is more common than to do things rare and singular, as in regard of our weakness, who cannot sufficiently set forth His wonderful works and graces, which to me have been so many, so diversely folded and embroidered one upon another as in no sort I am able to express them.

And although there liveth not any that may more justly acknowledge themselves infinitely bound unto God than I, whose life He hath miraculously preserved at sundry times (beyond my merit) from a multitude of perils and dangers, yet is not that the cause for which I count myself the deeplyest bound to give Him my humblest thanks or to yield Him greatest recognition, but this which I shall tell you hereafter, which will deserve the name of wonder (if rare things and seldom seen be worthy of account).

---

6. The quotation is not from Ecclesiastes but is an exact English rendering of the Latin Vulgate reading of Job 6.16: "*Qui timent pruinam, irruet super eos nix*" (see Marcus, Mueller, and Rose, *Collected Works*, 182).

7. Elizabeth rejects both Roman Catholicism and the newer Puritan party.

8. Elizabeth warns against the dangers of private Bible study and unauthorized preaching; *doom*: judgment; *privity*: legality or proper business; *with*: under.

9. Benefit; *world . . . least*: such a prince who cares for this world only insofar as it benefits you; *subsidy*: gift.

† Copy text: *The copie of a letter to the Right Honourable the Earle of Leycester* (London: Christopher Barker, 1586; STC 6052), C1r–C4v. The recorder of the speech apologizes in a headnote that "he cannot express [the speech] answerable to the original," a reminder of the difficulty of transcribing speeches before the advent of shorthand.

Even this it is: that as I came to the crown with the willing hearts of my subjects, so do I now, after twenty-eight years' reign, perceive in you no diminution of goodwills, which, if haply I should want, well might I breathe but never think I lived.[1]

And now, albeit I find my life hath been full dangerously sought and death contrived by such as no desert procured,[2] yet am I therein so clear from malice (which hath the property to make men glad at the falls and faults of their foes and make them seem to do for other causes, when rancor is the ground) as I protest it is and hath been my grievous thought that one not different in sex, of like estate, and my near kin should fall into so great a crime. Yea, I had so little purpose to pursue her with any color of malice that, as it is not unknown to some of my lords here (for now I will play the blab), I secretly wrote her a letter upon the discovery of sundry treasons that, if she would confess them and privately acknowledge them by her letters to myself, she never should need be called for them into so public question. Neither did I it of mind to circumvent[3] her, for then I knew as much as she could confess, and so did I write.

And if even yet, now that the matter is made but too apparent, I thought she truly would repent (as perhaps she would easily appear in outward show to do) and that, for her, none other would take the matter upon them, or then we were but as two milkmaids with pails upon our arms, or that there were no more dependency upon us[4] but mine own life were only in danger and not the whole estate of your religion and well doings, I protest (wherein you may believe me, for though I may have many vices, I hope I have not accustomed my tongue to be an instrument of untruth) I would most willingly pardon and remit this offence. Or if by my death other nations and kingdoms might truly say that this realm had attained an ever-prosperous and flourishing estate, I would (I assure you) not desire to live, but gladly give my life to the end my death might procure you a better prince.

And for your sakes it is that I desire to live, to keep you from a worse. For as for me, I assure you, I find no great cause I should be fond to live. I take no such pleasure in it that I should much wish it, nor conceive such terror in death that I should greatly fear it, and yet I say not but, if the stroke were coming, perchance flesh and blood would be moved with it[5] and seek to shun it.

I have had good experience and trial of this world. I know what it is to be a subject, what to be a sovereign, what to have good neighbors and sometime meet evil-willers. I have found treason in trust, seen great benefits little regarded, and instead of gratefulness, courses of purpose to cross.[6]

These former remembrances, present feeling, and future expectation of evils, I say, have made me think an evil is much the better the less while it

1. If I did not have your goodwill, I would scarcely feel alive.
2. My death is undeserved since those who plot against me have no reason to do so.
3. Entrap.
4. If no one else was dependent upon my safety; Elizabeth here uses the royal "we."
5. Would be moved with fear.
6. Instead of being grateful, those whom I have helped have set themselves at cross-purposes with me.

endureth, and so them happiest that are soonest hence[7] and taught me to bear with a better mind these treasons than is common to my sex, yea, with a better heart, perhaps, than is in some men. Which I hope you will not merely impute to my simplicity or want of understanding but rather that I thus conceived that, had their purposes taken effect, I should not have found the blow before I had felt it, and, though my peril should have been great, my pain should have been but small and short. Wherein, as I would be loath to die so bloody a death, so doubt I not but God would have given me grace to be prepared for such an event, chance when it shall, which I refer to His good pleasure.

And now, as touching their treasons and conspiracies, together with the contriver of them, I will not so prejudicate myself and this my realm as to say or think that I might not, without the last statute, by the ancient laws of this land have proceeded against her, which was not made particularly to prejudice her, though perhaps it might then be suspected in respect of the disposition of such as depend that way.[8]

It was so far from being intended to entrap her that it was rather an admonition to warn the danger thereof, but sith it is made and in the force of a law, I thought good, in that which might concern her, to proceed according thereunto rather than by course of common law wherein, if you the judges have not deceived me or that the books[9] you brought me were not false (which God forbid), I might as justly have tried her by the ancient laws of the land.

But you lawyers are so nice in sifting and scanning every word and letter that many times you stand more upon form than matter, upon syllables than sense of the law. For, in the strictness and exact following of common form, she must have been indicted in Staffordshire, have holden up her hand at the bar, and been tried by a jury—a proper course, forsooth, to deal in that manner with one of her estate.[1] I thought it better therefore, for avoiding of these and more absurdities, to commit the cause to the inquisition of a good number of the greatest and most noble personages of this realm, of the judges and others of good account, whose sentence I must approve. And all little enough,[2] for we princes, I tell you, are set on stages in the sight and view of all the world duly observed. The eyes of many behold our actions; a spot is soon spied in our garments, a blemish quickly noted in our doings. It behooveth us, therefore, to be careful that our proceedings be just and honorable.

But I must tell you one thing more, that in this last act of Parliament, you have brought me to a narrow strait, that I must give direction for her death, which cannot be to me but a most grievous and irksome burden. And lest you might mistake mine absence from this Parliament (which I had almost forgotten, although there be no cause why I should willingly come amongst

7. That soonest die; *an evil . . . endureth*: an evil is easier to bear if it lasts only a short time.
8. See Cardinal William Allen's defense in this section where he argues that old laws are used illegitimately to denounce Roman Catholics as traitors; *prejudicate*: judge in advance for; *prejudice her*: the laws were not written especially to condemn Mary; *depend*: lean.
9. Probably law books sent by Parliament; *sith*: since.
1. Elizabeth is, of course, being ironic; *Staffordshire*: the Babington plot was discovered while Mary was residing at Chartley Castle in Staffordshire, under the oversight of Sir Amias Paulet.
2. It is a small enough precaution to try Mary by a royal commission rather than in the common courts.

multitudes, for that amongst many some may be evil), yet hath it not been the doubt of any such danger or occasion that kept me from thence but only the great grief to hear this cause spoken of, especially that such a one of state and kin should need so open a declaration and that this nation should be so spotted with blots of disloyalty. Wherein the less is my grief for that I hope the better part is mine and those of the worse not much to be accounted of, for that in seeking my destruction, they might have spoiled their own souls.

And even now could I tell you that which would make you sorry; it is a secret, and yet I will tell it you, although it is known. I have the property to keep counsel but too well, oftentimes to mine own peril. It is not long since mine eyes did see it written that an oath was taken within few days either to kill me or to be hanged themselves, and that to be performed ere one month were ended. Hereby I see your danger in me[3] and neither can nor will be so unthankful or careless of your consciences as not provide for your safety.

I am not unmindful of your oath made in the Association[4] (manifesting your great goodwills and affections, taken and entered into upon good conscience and true knowledge of the guilt) for safety of my person and conservation of my life, done (I protest to God) before I heard it or ever thought of such a matter, until a great number of hands, with many obligations, were showed me at Hampton Court, signed and subscribed with the names and seals of the greatest of this land, which as I do acknowledge as a perfect argument of your true hearts and great zeal to my safety, so shall my bond be stronger tied to greater care for all your good.

But forasmuch as this matter is rare, weighty, and of great consequence, I think you do not look for any present resolution, the rather for that, as it is not my manner in matters of far less moment to give speedy answer without due consideration, so in this of such importance I think it very requisite with earnest prayer to beseech His divine Majesty so to illuminate my understanding and inspire me with His grace as I may do and determine that which shall serve to the establishment of His church, preservation of your estates, and prosperity of this commonwealth under my charge. Wherein (for that I know delay is dangerous) you shall have with all conveniency our resolution delivered by our message. And whatever any prince may merit of their subjects for their approved testimony of their unfeigned sincerity (either by governing justly, void of all partiality, or sufferance[5] of any injuries done, even to the poorest) that do I assuredly promise inviolably to perform for requital of your so many deserts.

---

3. If I am in danger, you are also in danger.
4. The Bond of Association, signed in 1584.
5. Forbearance.

From The Second Answer Made by the Queen's Majesty (November 24, 1586)[†]

I have strived more this day than ever in my life whether I should speak or use silence. If I speak and not complain, I shall dissemble;[1] if I hold my peace, your labor taken were full vain. For me to make my moan were strange and rare, for I suppose you shall find few that for their own particular will cumber you with such a care.[2] Yet such, I protest, hath been my greedy desire and hungry will: that of your consultation might have fallen out some other means to work my safety (joined with your assurance), than that for which you are become such earnest suitors, as, I protest, I must needs use complaint (though not of you but unto you and of the cause), for that I do perceive by your advices, prayers, and desires, there falleth out this accident: that only my injurer's bane must be my life's surety.[3]

※   ※   ※

And since now it is resolved that my surety cannot be established without a princess's end, I have just cause to complain that I, who have in my time pardoned so many rebels, winked at so many treasons, and either not produced them[4] or altogether slipped them over with silence, should now be forced to this proceeding against such a person. I have besides during my reign seen and heard many opprobrious books and pamphlets against me, my realm, and state, accusing me to be a tyrant. I thank them for their alms. I believe therein their meaning was to tell me news, and news it is to me indeed. I would it were as strange to hear of their impiety. What will they not now say when it shall be spread that, for the safety of her life, a maiden Queen could be content to spill the blood even of her own kinswoman? I may therefore full well complain that any man should think me given to cruelty, whereof I am so guiltless and innocent as I should slander God if I should say He gave me so vile a mind. Yea, I protest, I am so far from it that for mine own life I would not touch her. Neither hath my care been so much bent how to prolong mine as how to preserve both, which I am right sorry is made so hard, yea so impossible.

※   ※   ※

When first I took the scepter, my title made me not forget the Giver and therefore began, as it became me, with such religion as both I was born in, bred in, and I trust shall die in. Although I was not so simple as not to know what danger and peril so great an alteration might procure me, how many great princes of the contrary opinion would attempt all they might against me, and generally what enmity I should breed unto myself (which all I regarded not, knowing that He, for whose sake I did it, might and would defend me), for which it is that, ever since, I have been so dangerously prosecuted as I rather marvel that I am than muse that I should not be,[5]

---

† Copy text: *The copie of a letter to the Right Honourable the Earle of Leycester* (London: Christopher Barker, 1586; STC 6052), D4v–E3r.
1. Hide my true intentions.
2. Few will complain when their own interests are at stake; *make my moan*: complain.
3. My life can be saved only if the one who seeks to injure me is killed; *assurance*: protection; *accident*: result.
4. Brought them into court.
5. Should die; *alteration*: the change from Roman Catholicism to Protestantism.

if it were not God's holy hand that continueth me beyond all other expectation.

Then entered I further into the school of experience, bethinking what it fitted a king to do, and there I saw he scant was well furnished if either he lacked justice, temperance, magnanimity, or judgment. As for the two latter, I will not boast; my sex doth not permit it. But for the two first, this dare I say: amongst my subjects I never knew a difference of person where right was one, nor never to my knowledge preferred for favor whom[6] I thought not fit for worth, nor bent my ears to credit a tale that first was told me, nor was so rash to corrupt my judgment with my censure before I heard the cause. I will not say but many reports might fortune be brought me by such as might hear the case, whose partiality might mar sometime the matter.[7] For we princes may not hear all ourselves. But this dare I boldly affirm: my verdict went ever with the truth of my knowledge. As full well wished Alcibiades's friend that he should not give any answer till he had recited the letters of the alphabet,[8] so have I not used over-sudden resolutions in matters that have touched me full near. You will say that with me, I think.

And therefore, as touching your counsels and consultations, I conceive them to be wise, honest, and conscionable, so provident and careful for the safety of my life (which I wish no longer than may be for your good) that, though I never can yield you of recompense your due, yet shall I endeavor myself to give you cause to think your goodwill not ill bestowed and strive to make myself worthy for such subjects.

And now for your petition, I shall pray you for this present to content yourselves with an answer without answer. Your judgment I condemn not, neither do I mistake your reasons, but pray you to accept my thankfulness, excuse my doubtfulness, and take in good part my answer answerless. Wherein I attribute not so much to mine own judgment, but that I think many particular persons may go before me,[9] though by my degree I go before them. Therefore, if I should say I would not do what you request, it might peradventure be more than I thought, and to say I would do it might perhaps breed peril of that you labor to preserve, being more than in your own wisdoms and discretions would seem convenient, circumstances of place and time being duly considered.

MARY STUART

Letter to Henry III (February 8, 1587)[†]

Royal brother, having by God's will, for my sins I think, thrown myself into the power of the Queen my cousin, at whose hands I have suffered much for almost twenty years, I have finally been condemned to death by her and

6. A person whom; *I never knew . . . one*: I never showed partiality based on the status of a person.
7. Whose bias might corrupt their judgment; *but*: but that.
8. A favorite anecdote, Elizabeth had also referred to Alcibiades, though not by name, in her 1563 answer to the House of Common's petition that she marry (see Part Two). The reference is actually to advice given by Athenadorus to Augustus Caesar in Plutarch's *Moralia* (see Mears, *The Myth of Elizabeth*, 78).
9. May offer sounder advice.
† Copy text: National Library of Scotland, Adv.MS.54.1.1. Translated from the original French. Printed by permission of the Trustees of the National Library of Scotland.

her estates.[1] I have asked for my papers, which they have taken away, in order that I might make my will, but I have been unable to recover anything of use to me, or even get leave either to make my will freely or to have my body conveyed after my death, as I would wish, to your kingdom where I had the honor to be Queen, your sister and old ally.

Tonight, after dinner, I have been advised of my sentence: I am to be executed like a criminal at eight in the morning. I have not had time to give you a full account of everything that has happened, but if you will listen to my doctor and my other unfortunate servants, you will learn the truth and how, thanks be to God, I scorn death and vow that I meet it innocent of any crime, even if I were their subject. The Catholic faith and the assertion of my God-given right to the English crown are the two issues on which I am condemned, and yet I am not allowed to say that it is for the Catholic religion that I die but[2] for fear of interference with theirs. The proof of this is that they have taken away my chaplain, and although he is in the building, I have not been able to get permission for him to come and hear my confession and give me the last sacrament, while they have been most insistent that I receive the consolation and instruction of their minister,[3] brought here for that purpose.

The bearer of this letter[4] and his companions, most of them your subjects, will testify to my conduct at my last hour. It remains for me to beg your most Christian Majesty, my brother-in-law and old ally, who have always protested your love for me, to give proof now of your goodness on all these points: firstly by charity, in paying my unfortunate servants the wages due them—this is a burden on my conscience that only you can relieve; further, by having prayers offered to God for a queen who has borne the title "Most Christian" and who dies a Catholic, stripped of all her possessions.

As for my son,[5] I commend him to you in so far as he deserves, for I cannot answer for him.

I have taken the liberty of sending you two precious stones, talismans against illness, trusting that you will enjoy good health and a long and happy life. Accept them from your loving sister-in-law, who, as she dies, bears witness of her warm feeling for you.

Again I commend my servants to you. Give instructions, if it please you, that for my soul's sake part of what you owe me should be paid and that, for the sake of Jesus Christ to whom I shall pray for you tomorrow as I die, I be left enough to found a memorial mass[6] and give the customary alms.

Wednesday, at two in the morning,
Your most loving and most true sister,
MARY R

---

1. Parliament; *Royal brother*: Henry III of France was the younger brother of Mary's first husband, Francis II.
2. But only.
3. Richard Fletcher, Dean of Peterborough.
4. Probably her personal physician, Doctor Bourgoing.
5. James VI of Scotland.
6. A chantry or endowment to maintain one or more priests to sing a daily mass for the soul of a departed patron.

ROBERT WYNGFIELD

From A Circumstantial Account of the Execution of Mary, Queen of Scots (February 8, 1587)[†]

The said eighth day of February being come and time and place appointed for the execution, the Queen, being of stature tall, of body corpulent, round shouldered, her face fat and broad, double-chinned and hazel-eyed, her borrowed hair auburn, her attire was this: on her head she had a dressing of lawn edged with bone-lace; a pomander chain and an *Agnus Dei* about her neck; a crucifix in her hand; a pair of beads at her girdle with a golden cross at the end of them; a veil of lawn fastened to her caul, bowed out with wire and edged round about with bone-lace; her gown was of black satin printed, with a train and long sleeves to the ground with acorn buttons of tett trimmed with pearl, and short sleeves of satin black cut with a pair of sleeves of purple velvet whole under them; her kirtle whole of figured black satin and her petticoat skirts of crimson velvet; her shoes of Spanish leather with the rough side outward; a pair of green silk garters; her nether stockings worsted color watchet clocked with silver and edged on the top with silver and next her leg a pair of jersey hose white, etc.[1] Thus appareled she departed her chamber and willingly bended her steps towards the place of execution.

* * *

Then with an unappalled countenance, without any terror of the place, the persons, or the preparations, she came out of the entry into the hall, stepped up to the scaffold, being two foot high and twelve foot broad, with rails round about hanged and covered with black, with a low stool, long fair cushion, and a block covered also with black. The stool brought her, she sat down. The Earl of Kent stood on the right hand and the Earl of Shrewsbury[2] on the other; other knights and gentlemen stood about the rails. The commission for her execution was read (after silence made) by Mr. Beale,[3] Clerk of the Council, which done, the people with a loud voice said, "God save the Queen." During the reading of this commission, the said Queen was very silent, listening unto it with so careless a regard as if it had not concerned her at all, nay, rather with so merry and cheerful a countenance as if it had been a pardon from her Majesty for her life and withal used such

---

[†] Copy text: Robert Wyngfield, *A Circumstantial Account of the Execution of Mary, Queen of Scots* in *Clarendon Historical Society Reprints*, Vol. 8 (Clarendon: Clarendon Historical Society, 1886), 256–61.

1. Finely knitted white woolen stockings; presumably the stockings were observed only after Mary was disrobed or when her body was prepared for embalming. After the full description of Mary's elaborate costume, the etcetera may be ironic; *borrowed hair*: her wig; *dressing . . . bone-lace* headpiece made of fine linen and trimmed with linen lace; *pomander chain*: hollow beads containing perfumes that were meant to ward off infections; *Agnus Dei*: a small pendant of wax imprinted with the insignia of a lamb bearing a cross or flag and blessed by the Pope; *beads . . . golden cross*: a rosary; *veil of lawn*: linen veil; *caul*: a close-fitting cap, usually richly ornamented; *tett*: wool; *kirtle*: outer skirt; *figured*: patterned; *nether stockings*: the stockings on her legs; *watchet . . . silver*: made of light blue wool embroidered with silver.
2. George Talbot, sixth Earl of Shrewsbury who, with his wife Bess of Hardwick, had been Mary's jailer from 1569 to 1584; *Earl of Kent*: Henry Grey, sixth Earl of Kent.
3. Robert Beale, clerk of the Privy Council, who acted as Elizabeth's emissary to Mary and carried the death warrant from London to Fotheringay Castle.

a strangeness in her words as if she had not known any of the assembly nor had been anything seen[4] in the English tongue.

Then Master Doctor Fletcher, Dean of Peterborough, standing directly before her without[5] the rails, bending his body with great reverence, uttered this exhortation following:

"Madam, the Queen's most excellent Majesty (whom God preserve long to reign over us) having (notwithstanding this preparation for the execution of justice, justly to be done upon you for your many trespasses against her sacred person, state, and government) a tender care over your soul, which presently departing out of your body must either be separated in the true faith in Christ or perish forever, doth for Jesus Christ offer unto you the comfortable promises of God, wherein I beseech your Grace, even in the bowels[6] of Jesus Christ, to consider these three things: first, your state past and transitory glory; secondly, your condition present of death; thirdly, your estate to come, either in everlasting happiness or perpetual infelicity. For the first, let me speak to your Grace with David the king: forget, Madam, yourself and your own people and your father's house, forget your natural birth, your royal and princely dignity, so shall the King of Kings have pleasure in your spiritual beauty," etc.

"Madam, even now, Madam, doth God Almighty open you a door into a heavenly kingdom. Shut not therefore this passage by the hardening of your heart and grieve not the Spirit of God, which may seal your hope to a day of redemption."[7]

The Queen three or four times said unto him, "Master Dean, trouble not yourself nor me, for know I am settled in the ancient Catholic and Roman religion, and in defense thereof, by God's grace, I mind to spend my blood."

"Then," said Master Dean, "Madam, change your opinion and repent you of your former wickedness. Settle your faith only upon this ground: that in Christ Jesus you hope to be saved."

She answered again and again, with great earnestness, "Good Master Dean, trouble not yourself anymore about this matter, for I was born in this religion, have lived in this religion, and am resolved to die in this religion."

Then the earls, when they saw how far uncomformable she was to hear Master Dean's good exhortations, said, "Madam, we will pray for your Grace with Master Dean that you may have your mind lightened with the true knowledge of God and His Word."

"My lords," answered the Queen, "if you will pray with me, I will even from my heart thank you and think myself greatly favored by you, but to join in prayer with you in your manner, who are not of one religion with me, it were a sin, and I will not."

Then the lords called Master Dean again and bade him say on or what he thought good else. The Dean kneeled and prayed as follows: "Oh most gracious God," etc.

All the assembly, save the Queen and her servants, said the prayer after Master Dean as he spake it, during which prayer the Queen sat upon her

---

4. Had ever been tutored.
5. Outside; *Dean of Peterborough*: Richard Fletcher, later Bishop of London, who also preached a sermon to Elizabeth after the execution; see selection in this section.
6. Seat of compassion.
7. Ephesians 4.30.

stool, having her *Agnus Dei*, crucifix, beads, and an office[8] in Latin. Thus furnished with superstitious trumpery, not regarding what Master Dean said, she began very fastly,[9] with tears and a loud voice, to pray in Latin and in the midst of her prayers, with overmuch weeping and mourning, slipped off her stool and kneeling presently said divers other Latin prayers. Then she rose and kneeled down again, praying in English for Christ's afflicted church, an end of her troubles, for her son, and for the Queen's Majesty, to God for forgiveness of the sins of them in this island. She forgave her enemies with all her heart that had long sought her blood. This done, she desired all saints to make intercession for her to the Savior of the world, Jesus Christ. Then she began to kiss her crucifix and to cross herself, saying these words: "Even as Thy arms, O Jesus Christ, were spread here upon the cross, so receive me, so receive me into the arms of mercy."

Then the two executioners kneeled down unto her, desiring her to forgive them her death. She answered, "I forgive you with all my heart, for I hope this death shall give an end to all my troubles." They, with her two women helping, began to disrobe her, and then she laid the crucifix upon the stool. One of the executioners took from her neck the *Agnus Dei*, and she laid hold of it, saying she would give it to one of her women and withal told the executioner that he should have money for it. Then they took off her chain. She made herself unready[1] with a kind of gladness and smiling, putting on a pair of sleeves with her own hands (which the two executioners before had rudely put off) and with such speed as if she had longed to be gone out of the world. During the disrobing of this Queen, she never altered her countenance, but smiling said she never had such grooms before to make her unready nor ever did put off her clothes before such company.

At length, unattired and unapparalled to her petticoat and kirtle, the two women burst out into a great and pitiful shrieking, crying, and lamentation, crossed themselves and prayed in Latin. The Queen turned towards them, embraced them, and said these words in French, "*Ne criez vous; j'ai prier pour vous*,"[2] and so crossed and kissed them, and bade them pray for her.

Then with a smiling countenance, she turned to her men servants, Melvin,[3] and the rest, crossed them, bade them fare well and pray for her to the last.

One of the women, having a *Corpus Christi* cloth,[4] lapped it up three-corner-wise and kissed it, and put it over the face of the Queen, and pinned it fast upon the caul of her head. Then the two women departed. The Queen kneeled down upon the cushion resolutely and without any token of fear of death, said aloud in Latin the Psalm, "*In Te Domine Confido*."[5] Then groping for the block, she laid down her head, putting her chain[6] over her back with both her hands, which holding there still had been cut off

8. Prayer book with a prescribed set of prayers for each day.
9. Steadfastly.
1. Undressed herself.
2. "Do not weep; I have prayed for you."
3. Andrew Melville, one of her most trusted servants.
4. Cloth that covered the sacrament during the Corpus Christi procession, a feast that celebrated the holy Eucharist.
5. "In you, Lord, I put my trust" (Psalm 11). The psalm continues, "For lo, the wicked bend their bow and make ready their arrows upon the string, that they may secretly shoot at them which are upright in heart."
6. She seems to have put the chain, perhaps to her *Agnus Dei*, back on after disrobing.

had they not been espied. Then she laid herself upon the block most quietly and stretching out her arms and legs cried out, "*In manus tuas, Domine, commendo spiritum meum*"[7] three or four times.

At last while one of the executioners held her straitly[8] with one of his hands, the other gave two strokes with an axe before he did cut off her head and yet left a little gristle behind. She made very small noise, no part stirred from the place where she lay. The executioners lifted up the head and bade, "God save the Queen." Then her dressing of lawn fell from her head, which appeared as grey as if she had been threescore and ten years old, polled[9] very short, her face much altered, her lips stirred up and down almost a quarter of an hour after her head was cut off.

Then said Master Dean, "So perish all the Queen's enemies." The Earl of Kent came to the dead body and with a lower voice said, "Such end happen to all the Queen's and Gospel's enemies."

One of the executioners, plucking off her garters, espied her little dog which was crept under her clothes, which would not be gotten forth but with force and afterwards would not depart from the dead corpse but came and lay between her head and shoulders, a thing much noted. The dog, imbrued in her blood, was carried away and washed, as all things else were that had any blood save those things which were burned. The executioners were sent away with money for their fees, not having any one thing that belonged unto her. Afterwards every one was commanded forth of the hall saving the sheriff and his men, who carried her up into a great chamber made ready for the surgeons to embalm her, and there she was embalmed.

ADAM BLACKWOOD

From History of Mary, Queen of Scots (1587)[†]

The place of execution was in a great parlor, in the midst whereof a scaffold was set up, twelve foot square and two foot high, spread over with black cotton, towards the which her Majesty mounted so nimbly that she seemed to have no fear of death, neither ever changed her countenance. And now being come up, she rested herself a little and presently beginneth to speak to the officers of her cruel cousin Elizabeth, entreating them to permit her to have her almoner[1] to come to her, to comfort her in her God and to receive of him some comfortable instruction, together with the holy sacrament, before her departure out of this vale of misery.

The Earl of Kent[2] answered that he was sorry for her to see her so much given to the superstitions of the times past and that it were better for her to carry the cross of Christ in heart, not in her hand.

---

7. "Into your hands, Lord, I commend my spirit," spoken by Christ as he died (Luke 23.46 quoting Psalm 31.5).
8. Tightly.
9. Clipped.
† Copy text: Adam Blackwood, *Martyre de la Royne d'Escosse* ([Paris]: Chez Iean Nafeild, 1587; *STC* 3107). Translation from *History of Mary Queen of Scots, a Fragment*, [ed. and trans. Alexander Macdonald] (Edinburgh: Maitland Club, 1834), 188–89; 191–94.
1. One who distributes alms, but who might also act as a chaplain.
2. Henry Grey, sixth Earl of Kent.

To whom she replied that it was to little purpose to carry such an object in her hand if the heart were not touched inwardly with earnest motion and remembrance of His bitter death and passion, which He suffered upon the cross for miserable man's sin, that died upon the cross. "I think it," saith she, "a thing most fit for every true Christian to have it to put them in remembrance of their redemption purchased by Christ, but specially they at that time when death threateneth."

✳ ✳ ✳

These were her prayers, being upon her knees upon the scaffold, praying also for the Pope, the kings of France [and] Spain, the Queen of England, and the King of Scotland, her dear son, that God would enlighten them all with His Spirit and direct them in the truth and that He would take pity upon His church militant[3] and turn away His anger from the isle of Great Britain, which she did perceive He threatened with scourges for the abominable, willful impiety committed by the inhabitants.

She thus likewise prayed at her first entry upon the scaffold and after reiterated the same three several times. But the Dean of Peterborough, Doctor Fletcher,[4] did what he could to interrupt her, whom she entreated not to trouble her, for she was fully resolved how to die without any counsel from him or any of his sort. He could give her no further contentment for her soul than she had already, for she did anchor her on Christ, and for the people, they could give her no further comfort. This notwithstanding, the Dean continued in his prayers and she proceeded likewise forward, praying in Latin, lifting up her voice above his so loud that all being present did clearly hear her. She had a golden cross about her neck having the image of our Savior, which prayer being ended, she would have given to one of her maids. But the butcher snatched at it and would not suffer her, albeit her Majesty did earnestly entreat, offering him that her maid should give him thrice the value of it, but no remedy. He would not let her have it.

All being ready, she taketh her last farewell of her maids and kissed them courteously, thanking them for their faithful services, bidding them adieu, and bid them retire themselves quietly, giving them her last blessing and making the sign of the cross over them. But perceiving one of them could not hold but burst forth into tears, she commanded to hold her peace and to keep silence, telling her she had passed[5] her promise that she and the other maid should not be troublesome to her in her death. She bid them both retire themselves soberly and to pray to God for her, now[6] they could do her no more good. This done, she fell down upon her knees, without giving the least sign or demonstration of discontent or fear of death. Her constancy and boldness of spiritual courage, her confidence and assurance of hope of recompense of eternal life of God, in lieu and place of her momentary afflictions, now to be enjoyed of her was such that all the assistants, yea her hardest-hearted enemies, was greatly moved and it was credibly reported of many that were present that amongst all the whole company there was only two or three persons that could withhold weeping, they

---

3. The church militant is a term used for the present-day church, those who are already dead being considered the church triumphant.
4. Richard Fletcher, later Bishop of London.
5. Given.
6. Now that.

esteemed the spectacle so strange, condemning these in their conscience who were the authors of such a cruelty which, in former times, they never heard nor read of the like. She commends finally her soul to the tuition of the Almighty in these words of the psalm, saying often and reiterating the words, "*In manus tuas, Domine, commendo spiritum meum,*"[7] and that with a loud voice, far surmounting the Dean in the ears of the assistants.

In the meanwhile, the butcher gave her a great blow with the axe, whereby he pierced the strings within her head, which he struck not off but at the third blow, to make her martyrdom the more noble, albeit it well is known that not the pain or the punishment but the cause maketh the martyr.[8] After he had done, he hastily snatcheth up the head in his hand and, showing it to the assistants, said, "God save Queen Elizabeth and so befall all the enemies of the Gospel," as though[9] there were no other that favored the Gospel and that lived as the Gospel directed but Elizabeth. But howsoever in outward show, she[1] made a cloak for her wicked life of the sacred Gospel, which thereby she profaned. Yet if her life were weighed in just and even balance, it should be found (if all things were clearly known and censured accordingly) she should become behind and be postponed[2] this holy martyr by many degrees.

After,[3] in derision and contempt, he pulled off her coif and showed her white hairs, with contemptuous words unworthy to be spoken or heard by the mouth or ears of any Christian. He pointed also at the crown of her head to show it to the people because it was newly shaven, which she was constrained to do by reason of a grievous rheum[4] which troubled her often.

The tragedy ended, the poor maids, careful of the honor of their mistress, humbly besought and prayed Paulet, the cruel jailor,[5] that the butcher might have no more ado with their sovereign lady's body and that it might be permitted them to disattire her body when all the people were departed the place, that no further indignity might be offered her sacred Majesty's corpse, seeing all malice, hatred, envy, and contempt of the dead ought to end after their decease. They promised him her apparel and all that was about her and whatsoever besides he would demand in reason, so that he would not anymore come near or handle her sacred body.

But cursed Cerberus, Paulet I mean, commandeth them very rudely to depart the chamber, leaving his hellhound[6] with the corpse to do with what he would. He presently pulleth off her shoes and all the rest of her apparel, which as yet was left about her body, and after, when he had done what he would, the corpse was carried into a chamber next adjoining, fearing the said maids should come to do any charitable good office.

It did increase greatly their desire so to do after they did see their mistress's corpse through a little hole of the chamber wall, which [was] covered

---

7. "Into your hands, Lord, I commend my spirit," spoken by Christ as he died (Luke 23.46 quoting Psalm 31.5).
8. This was a point much insisted upon by both Roman Catholics and Protestants in order to deny the term "martyr" to those who died outside their own faith.
9. Copy text: although.
1. Elizabeth.
2. Put into an inferior position by.
3. Afterward.
4. Salt rheum; eczema.
5. Sir Amias Paulet, her keeper since April 1585, who uncovered the Babington conspiracy.
6. The sheriff.

with cloth. But the woeful corpse was kept a long time in this chamber till it began to corrupt and smell strongly, so that in the end they were constrained to salt it, and to embalm lightly to save charges, and after to wrap it up in a cask of lead, keeping it seven months there before it was interred at Peterborough, where also Katherine of Spain[7] lay buried before.

RICHARD FLETCHER

From A Sermon Preached before the Queen Immediately after the Execution of the Queen of Scots by the Dean of Peterborough (1587)[†]

The angel of the Lord appeared to Joseph in Egypt in a dream, saying, "Arise, and take up the Child and His mother, and return into the land of Israel; for they are dead that sought the Child's life."[1]

*   *   *

The holy Evangelist, having written the birth and the pedigree of Jesus Christ our Savior according to the flesh (together with the clearing of all doubts arising thereupon), hath, as it were in a tragedy, described the falsehood and fury of Herod (the tyrant and enemy to this Christ and Savior of the world), for the escaping of whose cruelty Joseph, his tutor and supposed father, is warned from God by this messenger and angel to arise and convey him into Egypt, as more safe in the house of bondage than in Bethlehem, the house of bread[2] and city of David. What earthly affliction and vexation of spirit must they devour and overcome which have given their heart to the profession and their hand to the plow of the Gospel of Christ? What might he not have hoped for in all peace and felicity that did nourish Christ in his bosom, the riches and treasures of the graces of God? But neither was his entry thereunto free from tribulation, nor his going on void of the vexation of his spirit. What fear and what jealousy was there for Mary, his espoused wife, being found with Child by the Holy Ghost? And when God's oracle had cleared that cloud, and all seemed safe and full of security, what news was it by night to see the same angel again and to hear him cry, "Arise, and take the Child and His mother, and fly into Egypt"?

"*Justus, ut fortis Leo,*"[3] sayeth Solomon. The righteous and innocent man is as bold and courageous as a lion. And why should he fly? Let sinners fly and be confounded that tarry[4] the worm and sting and torment of an evil and guilty conscience. Let Adam fly, that hath broken and transgressed the law and commandment of his good[5] and gracious God and is become

---

7. Katherine of Aragon, first wife of Henry VIII; *charges*: expense.
† Copy text: Cambridge University Library, St. John's College Cambridge MS. I.30, fols. 49v–67v; transcription provided by Peter E. McCullough.
1. Matthew 2.19–20.
2. Bethlehem as the house (Bêt) of bread (lechem) was associated by Christian commentators with Christ as the bread of life; *clearing . . . thereupon*: an angel, in Matthew's gospel, assures a perplexed Joseph that Mary is truly a virgin; *tutor*: guardian.
3. Proverbs 28.1.
4. Prolong.
5. Copy text: godd.

ashamed of himself and his sin. Let Cain, that murderer, fly that had shed the innocent blood of his righteous brother Abel. Let Sheba fly, that traitor that hath blown a trumpet and raised sedition and discharged the subjects from the obedience of David, their true and natural prince. Let Jonah fly, that forsaken his coat and his calling in the ministry of the gospel. Let Onesimus fly, that hath robbed his master and falsified his faith and service to Philemon. *Fugiat impius nemine persequente.*[6] Let the wicked fly when no man pursueth them.

But why should Joseph fly, who is a just man, and Mary, who is a pure and undefiled virgin, and Christ, who is an innocent and lamb without spot? Though the righteous may sometime stand and stay in the testimony of their innocency and simplicity of a dove, yet must they sometime fly in the wisdom of a serpent.[7] It is Christ's own doctrine and heavenly direction, "If they persecute you in one city, fly into another."[8] It is his own example to convey himself from death until his time be come. Learn it of Solomon: "*Qui amat periculum peribit in eo.*"[9] He that loveth danger shall perish in his danger. And of Christ our Savior to use the means of safety offered by God: "For thou shall not tempt the Lord thy God."[1] Well said the subjects of David the King, which serveth likewise in these dangerous days, "David is the strength and candle of Israel. Therefore David may not go forth into battle, into danger, lest David put out the light of Israel."[2] "But is there any treacle,"[3] sayeth the prophet, "at Gilead?" Is therefore any comfort and consolation in Egypt, the old and inveterate furnace of Israel's affliction, whose very name doth carry the note of all tyranny and memorial of this people's misery and captivity? It is all one for God's providence to protect at Memphis in Egypt and at Bethlehem in Jewry. His grace to His servants is wanting in no place. "If I go down into hell," sayeth David, "thou art there."[4]

Deus nunquod deest, et tamen ab iniquose cogitationibus longe est; quia ubi non est per gratiam, adest pro vindictam.[5] God is never wanting, and yet he is far off from the thoughts of the wicked; for where He is not by grace, there is He present in vengeance. If the malice of Jacob's sons sell Joseph into Egypt, there is God present for his promotion. If Lot be in Sodom laden with Sodom's uncleanness, as with a burden, there is an angel for his deliverance. If Daniel be in the lions' den, there is the power of God to hold the lions' jaws. If Elijah be in the wilderness, hungry and harborless, lain down under his juniper bush, weary of his life, there is an angel with bread to recomfort him. If Jeremiah be tossed into the dungeon, there is a blackamoor[6] to help to lift him out. If Peter be in his prison and Paul in his perils and Christ upon His cross, there is an angel to open their passages and a God that will never forsake them in their death.

---

6. Proverbs 28.1.
7. Matthew 10.16.
8. Matthew 10.23.
9. Sirach 3.26.
1. Deuteronomy 6.16, quoted by Christ to Satan during the temptation in the wilderness (Matthew 4.7).
2. 2 Samuel 21.17.
3. Remedy; the Bishops' Bible, the authorized version in Elizabethan churches after 1567, uses "treacle" where other translations use the more familiar "balm" in Gilead (Jeremiah 8.22).
4. Psalm 139.8.
5. Pope Gregory the Great, *Sermons on Ezekiel*, Homily 8.
6. Ebedmelech, an Ethiopian, rescued Jeremiah from the dungeon into which King Zedekiah had thrown him (Jeremiah 38.5–13).

But you are not in Egypt but in Canaan; you are not at Babylon but at Jerusalem, the city and sanctuary of peace, to receive the angel's message and oracle of God for your comfort in all tribulation. *Angeli suis mandavit de te.*[7] God hath given his angels charge over you, to keep you in all your ways, to inspire you with counsel, to arm you with constancy to save yourself and the church of God, and to bring out of Egypt. So did God's angel for Joseph, and so hath he ministered to the safety of God's elect.

To Abraham he appeared once and came again that Sarah might have seed, wherein all the nations of the world might be blessed. To Lot he came in Sodom to carry him to Zoar, the city of his safety. With Tobias he went in his journey into Media and brought him home again to his parents in peace. To Manoah in his sacrifice, to Mary for her conception, to Zechariah and Elizabeth for John the Baptist's birth, to the shepherds for Christ's incarnation, to Christ himself in the wilderness to minister to his hunger, to the disciples in His sepulcher to testify His resurrection, to St. Peter in his prison, and to all the elect for their salvation. What thing is man that God so regardeth him or the son of man that God so visiteth him, to make the excellent spirits[8] created to His blessed and glorious service to watch and to ward for the comfort of dust and ashes?

In which dignity and ministry of holy angels, how hath your kingdom, yourself, and your people been magnified many years? You have been yourself sometime in Egypt and have had experience of trouble and adversity. The plowers plowed upon your back and made long furrows.[9] They led you as a sheep appointed to be slain, and the iron (as that of Joseph) entered into your soul.[1] Wherein what joy and gladness, what comfort and consolation was left to you in Egypt but the guard and tents of the angels of the Lord, without whom it had not failed, as David sayeth, but your soul had been put to silence.[2] What rejoicing had you but the testimony of your innocency sealed unto you by the Holy Ghost? Egypt would have eaten you, but the angel of the Lord delivered you as miraculously as ever he did St. Peter.[3] He smote your enemies in the hinder parts and put them to perpetual shame. He struck you on the side with his right hand when you lay in your prison, and caused a light of honor and glory to shine round about you, and made the fetters of your fear and captivity to fall from your feet. He opened the gate, the iron gate that your enemies would have rampired[4] against your most just and natural succession. The iron gates of foreign princes contrariant to your faith opened themselves wide to receive your amity and society. And if Elisha the prophet had been amongst us to have opened our eyes in our conflicts against Midian and the power of Antichrist striving against us, we should have seen whole legions of angels to have stood for us against all our enemies, whereof as many as we have had yet, *plures nobiscum quem contra nos*[5] (there be more on our side than be against us).

---

7. Psalm 91.11, quoted by Satan to Christ during the latter's temptation in the wilderness (Matthew 4.6).
8. Angels; *What thing . . . visiteth him*: Psalm 8.4 and Job 7.17–18.
9. Psalm 129.3.
1. Genesis 39.20; *led . . . slain*: Psalm 44.11; the verse spoken by Elizabeth to her servants as she was escorted from the Tower of London to Woodstock in 1554 after Wyatt's Rebellion and feared for her life.
2. Psalm 94.17.
3. Acts 12.6–9; *eaten you*: copy text is indistinct.
4. Strengthened.
5. 2 Kings 6.16–17; *Midian*: Syria.

And see yet more the favor and love of God to His children. When Joseph is at rest and laid into his bed and place of forgetfulness, then doth God's angel bring him glad tidings of deliverance. Whether you sleep or wake, you are the Lord's.[6] "I will lay me down and take my rest," sayeth David the King, "for the Lord sustaineth me."[7] Though you do sleep or slumber unto God, yet He that keepeth you doth watch over you.[8] *Lex non venit dormientibus*, say we in our policies. The law and benefit thereof cometh not to them that be asleep, but God's loving kindness cometh even to our bedsides, when we are asleep and think not upon it. And that this hath been as blessed service to you, as even it was to Joseph, to be warned and informed of your enemies' secret maliciousness by the angel of God, by divine and miraculous intelligence, the many detections of their manifold designments have sealed it unto you insomuch that, even in the tents of the King of Aram,[9] it is said as sometime in the days of Elisha the prophet, "Who is it that betrayeth our counsel unto the King of Israel?" the enemies answering themselves, "It is none of thy servants; it is Elisha the prophet."[1] It is the angel of the Lord, the divine instinct[2] of the wisdom of the Holy Ghost. It is the fluttering of the feathers of the wings of the fowls of the air that bewrayeth[3] and betrayeth treacherous treatises in their privy chambers. *Laetentur sancti in gloria, exultent in tubilibque suis.*[4] Let the saints triumph in glory, let them rejoice in their beds, for in their beds shall mercy come unto them.

Therefore, because the angels of God are sent with God's direction into your bedchambers, let them be holy and adorned fit for their celestial presence, not in surfeiting and drunkenness, nor in chambering and wantonness, but as becometh the saints knowing it and saying it with David the King, "Thou art about my bed and about my paths and spiest out all my ways."[5] So shall your bodies and your beds be comely for divine and heavenly spirits to reveal the will of God when Holofernes, being drunken with the blood of grapes and overcome of his lust, shall lie under his canopy and covering of voluptuousness while the sword devoureth him. *Ecce*, behold, behold this, for it is marvelous and memorable and shall be showed to all posterity, when your soul shall be translated,[6] what God Almighty by His angel and Spirit and providence hath done for you in Egypt and in Israel, in wealth and in woe, in prosperity and adversity.

Awake therefore your lute and your harp, your spiritual glee and glory;[7] awake yourself right early and say with that king, "Praise the Lord, O my soul, and all that is within me praise His holy name. Praise the Lord, O my soul, and forget not all His benefits."[8] God hath never forgotten you. He forgot you not in your cradle but was your hope when you hanged upon your mother's breast. He forgot you not when your enemies laid hands

6. 1 Thessalonians 5.10.
7. Psalm 4.8.
8. Psalm 121.3–4.
9. Syria.
1. 2 Kings 6.11–12.
2. Prompting.
3. Exposes.
4. Psalm 149.5.
5. Psalm 139.3; *them*: the bedchambers; *holy . . . wantonness*: Romans 13.13.
6. Taken into heaven.
7. Psalm 57.8.
8. Psalm 103.1–2.

upon the bow, the sword, and the battle. He forgot you not when many dogs came about you to take away your life,[9] your life so precious to God, to angels, and to men. He forgetteth you not yesterday and today to open unto you the conspiracies of your enemies.

Forget you not these mercies and graces of God towards you. You have many provocations to the forgetfulness of them, by reason of the corruption of nature that useth to wax wanton by God's bountifulness. The vines which they planted not, the butter and honey and plenty of Canaan may make a fullness and so a forgetfulness of that God which brought you out of Egypt and the house of bondage.[1] But if you do forget Him and His goodness towards you, then *audi virgam*,[2] bear the rod and hear your punishment: If thou do forget the God of thy salvation and do not remember the God of thy strength, thou shalt sow pleasant plants, but the harvest shall be gone in the day of possession and there shall be desperate sorrow.[3] For the wicked shall be turned into hell and all that forget God. Forget therefore yourself and your father's house, forget your honor and your glory, your scepter and your diadem, and let not your life be precious in your sight to keep in remembrance the benefits and blessings, the mercy and loving kindness of your God and our gracious God towards you.

Thus much of the angel's apparition,[4] and now to the oracle, and first the proposition. *Surge*. Arise, and take the Child and His mother, and return into the land of Israel.

How long Joseph with his charge was in Egypt it is uncertain, but as he had received a charge from the angel to stay and tarry there till he brought him word, so his faith was found constant in waiting for the promise. In all troubles and temptations thus teacheth the Holy Ghost: "O tarry thou the Lord's leisure; be strong and He shall comfort thy heart and put thou thy trust in the Lord."[5] And albeit the strangers of the place, and the manners of the people, and the testimony of his innocency might have provoked him to have attempted and practiced[6] his return, to have set Him up in Israel that should govern Israel by God's decree, yet moveth he not his foot without the warrant and oracle of the angel.

O that our runagates[7] and seedmen of sedition would learn this divinity, that if Israel had banished them with Christ into Egypt, yet not to return and set Him up without the testimony of God and the warrant of the angel. But how far are their spirits from that apostolical piety that was in St. Paul, who, when he had been vowed to death and suffered many evils of his countrymen the Jews, yet in his appeal to Rome for justice he neither prayed vengeance, nor curse, nor excommunication against them, but said most like a meek minister, "I have appealed to Caesar, not that I have ought to accuse my countrymen of."[8] Then as bad as Rome was, it was not the

9. Psalm 22.16.
1. Deuteronomy 6.11–12.
2. Listen, virgin.
3. Isaiah 17.10–11.
4. Appearance.
5. Psalm 27.14.
6. Carried out.
7. Renegades.
8. Acts 25.11.

shop of Vulcan to frame devices to overthrow Christian King James.[9] But you, O most monstrous apostatates, not successors of the apostles, have made it a den of thieves[1] and invention of cruel men, a sanctuary of tyrants, and in one word the receptacle of all the filth and refuse of the world, from whence do leap all these locusts to croak and to cry into the ears of princes and people to prepare them to the battle of the great God.

But let us hear the angel: "Arise, Joseph; why sleepest thou? and look unto thy charge." What need have you to be awaked and stirred up, which have taken upon you the tuition[2] of Christ, the care of His church, and conduct of His people. The thunder and lightnings of Moses upon the mount, the storm and tempest of Elijah in his cave, the mighty wind that came to the apostles in the day of Pentecost, the trumpet that sounded to St. John in his vision, and the cock that crew to St. Peter in his abjuration are all too little to awake you out of the sleep and slumber of your security. How secure was Lot in Sodom, that sink of sin, when the fire and brimstone were even upon his head, till the angel cried, "*Surge.* Arise, and get thee out of Sodom."[3] How dreamed Jacob in the service of Laban, whom God had appointed to great exercises, till God came unto him and said, "Arise, and get thee out of this country."[4] How unprovided was Joshua to the battles of the Lord till God himself called unto him and said, "Arise, get thee over Jordan."[5] How slumbered Jonah under the hatches in the midst of the tempest till the master of the ship awaked him with crying, "Arise, and pray unto thy God."[6] And how sat David, that good king, sorrowing and lamenting after the most righteous and honorable execution of justice that ever was in Israel, till Joab his faithful counselor came unto him and said, "*Surge.* Arise, and speak comfortably to thy servants that have done this thing, which if thou do not, I swear unto thee by God, there will not one man abide with thee this night. Thou wilt lose the hearts and love of all thy faithful subjects, and that will be worse unto thee than all the evil that ever befell thee from thy youth hitherto."[7] And how sat Jerusalem, God's own sanctuary, in darkness and in the shadow of death, till the prophet cometh unto them and said, "*Surge, illuminare Jerusalem.*[8] Arise, Jerusalem, and be lightened with the brightness of the benefits and blessings of the Lord bestowed upon thee." If God still watch for you and He that keepeth Israel doth neither slumber nor sleep; if Jesus Christ be in the garden praying and groaning in spirit before the throne of God with drops of sweat like blood,[9] beware it be not said unto you as unto Peter, James, and John, "Sleep henceforth, and take your rest. Behold the Son of Man is betrayed unto the hands of sinners. Arise, let us go hence."[1]

9. James VI of Scotland, the son of Mary Stuart.
1. Matthew 21.13; Mark 11.17; Luke 19.46, in reference to Jesus's cleansing of the temple; *apostatates*: apostates.
2. Guardianship.
3. Genesis 19.15; *sink*: cesspool.
4. Genesis 31.13.
5. Joshua 1.2.
6. Jonah 1.6.
7. 2 Samuel 19.7; Joab's rebuke to David, mourning the death of his son Absalom, who had mounted a rebellion against his father.
8. Isaiah 60.1.
9. Luke 22.44; *still*: unceasingly; *keepeth . . . sleep*: Psalm 121.4.
1. Matthew 26.45–46.

"Awake thou that sleepest, and stand up from death, and Christ shall give thee light."[2] *Tempus est.* It is time for us to awake out of sin, our sleep. For our salvation, nay, I fear our judgment is nearer than when we believed. Therefore, stir up and awake yourselves with that notable judge of Israel: *Surge, Deborah; surge, Baracke.* Arise, Deborah; arise, Barak.[3] Arise, Prince; arise, Council; and arise, people; and let your enemies be scattered. Let them also that hate you fly before you. And albeit we may say of you, as Tully said of Caesar, *Nullade virtutibus tuis gratior aut admirabilior, aut gratior misericordia tua est.*[4] None of your virtues are either more wonderful or more gracious than your clemency. Yet arise with Moses, the most meek magistrate that ever was upon the earth, and forget your lenity and mercy. If Israel sit down to eat and drink and rise up again to play with vengeance to all idolaters,[5] arise to the perfecting and finishing of the tabernacle. Arise to the succor of all distressed Christians as Deborah from her palm tree to help the Lord against the mighty. "Arise, and take the Child and His mother, and return into the land of Israel." Christ is your charge and God hath made you His nurse, Mary, that fostereth Him. And all that profess Him within your kingdom hath Almighty God committed to your protection, and the adder's brood and the serpents of the wilderness hath sought them to murder them, and they have fled unto you for succor against their enemies. And if you see them naked and do not clothe them, and harborless and do not entertain them, and forsaken and do not receive them,[6] the Egyptians shall succor them, and you shall be forsaken.

Remember what Mordecai said to Esther the Queen, when she hasted not to cross and encounter the designments of Haman the Agagite: "If thou hold thy peace at this occasion, God shall send deliverance by some other means, and thou and thy father's house shall perish. For who doth know whether thou be come to the kingdom for such a time."[7] The more the devil and his instruments do rage against Christ, the more cause you have to arise, and take Him up, and establish Him in Israel. Alas He is not known, nay scarcely heard of in many places of your Israel. Ireland, as that poor woman in the gospel, hath suffered many things many years of many physicians, and still she bleedeth and cannot touch the hem of Christ's vesture, the only means to heal thy malady and thine infirmity.[8] The cold parts towards the pole are frozen in their dregs and the Son of Righteousness hath not shined unto them. Have mercy upon them, as God hath had mercy upon you, that they also may be boughs and branches in the garland of your glory, when they shall rise with you and you with them in the day of God's judgment. Set up Christ in Israel, and your Israel shall prosper. *Et exurget deus,* and God shall rise, and your enemies shall be scattered.

Give me leave, I do most humbly pray and beseech your most Christian Majesty, to stir you up from God the Father to the taking up of Jesus Christ, His Son, to the spreading of His Gospel, to the relieving of His distressed

---

2. Ephesians 5.14.
3. Judges 5.12.
4. Cicero, *Pro Ligario* 12.37 (see Cicero, *The Speeches with an English Translation*, trans. N. H. Watts. [New York: G. P. Putnam's Sons, 1931], 493).
5. 1 Corinthians 10.7.
6. Matthew 25.35–36.
7. Esther 4.14.
8. Luke 8.43–48.

members, to the revenging of the blood of His saints, to the punishing the rebellion of His enemies. It is Christ the babe that hath loved you, and given Himself for you, and made you defender of His faith; that hath set and kept your crown upon your head; that hath gone forth before your armies; that hath (as unto David) given you prosperity and hath preserved you from the peril of the sword; that hath subdued your enemies under your feet and preserved you as the apple of His eye; that hath blessed you in all spiritual blessings in Jesus Christ, our Savior, having made you a saved soul before He made the world; that hath called you to the knowledge of His glorious Gospel[9] when many other monarchies of the world lie bound at Babylon with fetters of infidelity; that hath justified you by faith in His name and sanctified you by washing you in the fountain of regeneration through His most precious blood and shall glorify you with Him if you persevere unto the end, which God Almighty for Jesus Christ's sake grant unto you.

The last thing to be considered of is the reason why Joseph should return with his charge into his native country, *Mortui enim sunt qui quaerebant animam pueri*.[1] For they are dead that sought the Child's life. Herod, the better to compass[2] his cruelty, gave it out that, if Christ could be found, he would come and worship Him. O the subtlety of a serpent, but here the angel of God doth search the heart and reins[3] of an hypocrite and interpreteth the worship of the tyrant. The Spirit of God cannot dissemble[4] the subtleties of men. *Querebat animam pueri*. He sought the Child's life. The worshipping of persecutors is the destruction of the Gospel.

Pleaseth it you that this Mercury and messenger of God,[5] which knoweth the secret of the heart, may likewise expound unto you the barking of Cerberus. Cerberus I do call that faction papal, schismatical, heretical, diabolical, with their several heads. One of Cain (as St. Jude describeth them), full of murder and cruelty. Another of Balaam, given to covetousness and filthy lucre. And the third of Korah, fraught with sedition and conspiracy.[6] Thus they bark and dissemble[7] their hypocrisy: "We are your good subjects; we honor and love and worship you; we will spend our lives and lands at your service and commandment." But the truth is, *quaerunt animam*. They seek your destruction. For there is not a mischief in hand which is not shrouded in their heart, and yet all must be done under the cloak and color of religion and holiness. So Absalom, when he was most full of treason, he pretendeth two things especially: the zeal of religion and the love of justice. For religion, he must go on pilgrimage down to Hebron, to pay his vows and offer his sacrifice. And who must go with him but Abiathar the priest. And what must he carry with him? the Ark of God, the visible testimony of His presence and covenant. But treason is his practice and deposing of his father. The Devil, when he will put out the light, doth not always use his owls and chimeras, black and smeared priests, but hath for that purpose

---

9. 2 Corinthians 4.4; *preserved . . . eye*: Psalm 17.8; *blessed . . . world*: Ephesians 1.3–4.
1. Copy text: *Mortui enim sunt qui caes.*
2. Contrive a plan for.
3. Literally, kidneys, but idiomatically the center of one's emotions.
4. Ignore.
5. The Holy Spirit.
6. Jude 1.11.
7. Disguise.

even angels of light.[8] And when the Church of God is most impugned, then is the cry[9] greatest for the Catholic Church. When Antichrist corrupteth faith and good works, religion and holiness, confession and remission of sins, repentance and satisfaction, prayer and fasting, chastity and obedience, poverty of the spirit and all the parts of a Christian man's duty, then must the names and the virtue of them all be most pretended.

But let this suffice for a caveat against all popish hypocrites: their fawning is but flattery, and their pretended piety nothing else but treachery. *Petunt ingulum.* They seek your life and the life of your child Jesus. It is all their practice to work their designments by all manner of show and means whatsoever: giving of faith, swearing upon books, eating of consecrated hosts, receiving of sacraments, celebrating of marriage, setting forth of triumphs, making of leagues, witnessing at baptism, inviting to feasts, reconciling to God, confession of sins, absolution of priests. All are covered with pretense of holiness and religion, and all to uphold and hold up the Whore of Babylon with all her detestable enormities. But they are dead, *quaerebant.*[1] The text sayeth not only Herod was dead, but the angel said they are dead. What else should the twigs and branches do but wither when the stem is rooted up? One thunderbolt of God threw down Lucifer to hell and after went all his angels.[2] When Joab had smitten Abner, the contriver of that faction Ishbosheth (the competitor of David's crown) *et universus Israel perteritus est.*[3] All that faction in Israel was discomforted. And what should, I beseech you, all the host of those insolent and cruel Assyrians do which lay at the siege of poor Bethulia but fly and be confounded. When Holofernes, their chief captain, lieth headless by the hand of Judith, follow therefore upon them, Uzziah and you elders and men of Bethulia, for God hath delivered them into your hands.[4] It is true. They are dead that sought the Child's life and the life of you all. And God be blessed for it forever, and rejoice for it, you righteous, and give thanks for a remembrance of His holiness.

And *Ulula Moab ad Moab.*[5] Howl, atheist to papist, and traitor to atheist, and one idolater to another. *Ulula Pinae, recidit Cedrus.*[6] Howl you pine trees, your cedar tree is fallen. And you that have made a covenant with God and with His anointed to stand fast as the moon and as the faithful witness in heaven,[7] hear the words of the Lord: "Comfort you, comfort you," sayeth the Lord, "for the Lord shall comfort Zion. He shall comfort her desolations and shall make her desert like paradise and her wilderness like the garden of the Lord. Joy and gladness shall be found in her, praise and the voice of singing."[8] As for the wicked, fear them not. They shall seek Christ and Mary and Joseph; they shall seek your life, but they shall not find it. Herod and his instruments may conspire together and take counsel to take

---

8. 2 Corinthians 11.14.
9. Clamor of support.
1. Those who sought. Copy text: *qui caes.*
2. Isaiah 14.12.
3. 2 Samuel 4.1.
4. Judith 15.4.
5. Isaiah 16.7
6. Zechariah 11.2.
7. Psalm 89.37. In contrast to most poets, Fletcher understands the moon as a symbol of constancy. Unless God commands, neither the sun nor the moon can be moved.
8. Isaiah 51.3.

away your life, but they all shall do no more than the hand and counsel of the Lord shall decree. Who can hinder the sun in the firmament to arise and lighten the world? Even so, no power, no tyranny, nor practice, nor policy can hinder the Son of Righteousness from rising and shining to the comfort of them that shall be saved.[9] Herod hath had his time, his cruelty, and his period and revolution, and his whelps had their course, but they and their seed are eaten up with worms, and Christ doth reign in glory in His church.

O that the kings and princes of the world which cast down their crowns at the feet of the beast and false prophet and spend their days in presenting[1] Christ in His members and their years in fighting against God would understand this: that Christ can no more be crucified but the Gospel must be preached to all nations, and then shall the end come, an end of their pride, an end of their tyranny, an end of the militant state of Christ's church, no more to groan under the weight and burden and edge of the sword. Jesus Christ must be lifted up in the wilderness of this world upon the word of His cross, though Egypt have a Pharaoh, and Iberia a Nicanor, and Asia an Holofernes, and Africa an Antiochus, and Italy an Herod, and Rome a Pilate.[2] The just shall be as the olive, fresh and green, and their horn lifted up as the horn of a unicorn.[3] When the ungodly shall be caught away with a sudden tempest, or consumed with immoderate heat and molten away as the fat of lambs, or be as the untimely fruit of a woman and never see the sun, or gnash with their teeth and consume away (for the desire of the ungodly shall perish), look therefore into Israel again and say with that king, "Return unto thy rest, O my soul, for the Lord hath rewarded thee."[4]

Take up the Son of God, the begun and confirmed course of the Gospel of Christ. Advance the chariot, the triumphant chariot of Justice. Take up yourself in the arms of wise and Christian providence. Gird on your sword upon your thigh, according to your worship and renown. Ride on because of the Word of truth, of meekness and righteousness, and your right hand shall teach you terrible things.[5] The arrows of God and of your government are very sharp and the people shall be subdued unto you, even in the midst among the king's enemies.[6] *Mortui enim sunt.* For they are dead that sought the Child and your life. They are dead and you are alive. Lay up your life then with Christ in God, and no man shall take it out of His hands. But when He shall appear, you shall also appear with Him in glory.[7] Which God the Father, for God the Son's sake, in mercy grant unto you, to whom with the Holy Ghost be all honor and glory forever. Amen. Amen.

Finis.

9. Malachi 4.2.
1. Accusing, with the sense of persecution; *beast . . . prophet*: the enemies of Christ in the book of Revelation.
2. Christ's suffering kingship stands in contrast to the tyrannical rule of the kings of this world; *word of his cross*: possibly "wood of His cross"; *Egypt*: copy text: Celta.
3. A reference to Psalm 92.10; "unicorn" is later translated as "wild ox."
4. Psalm 116.7.
5. Psalm 45.4.
6. Psalm 45.3–5.
7. Colossians 3.4.

QUEEN ELIZABETH

Letter to James VI on the Execution of His Mother
(February 14, 1587)[†]

My dear brother,

I would you knew, though not felt, the extreme dolor that overwhelms my mind for that miserable accident which far contrary to my meaning hath befallen.[1] I have now sent this kinsman of mine,[2] whom ere now it hath pleased you to favor, to instruct you truly of that which is too irksome for my pen to tell you. I beseech you that, as God and many more know how innocent I am in this case, so you will believe me that, if I had bid aught, I would have bid by it.[3] I am not so base minded that fear of any living creature or prince should make me afraid to do that were just or, done, to deny the same. I am not of so base a lineage nor carry so vile a mind; but as not to disguise fits most a king, so will I never dissemble my actions but cause them show even as I meant them. Thus assuring yourself of me that, as I know this was deserved, yet if I had meant it I would never lay it on others' shoulders, no more will I not damnify myself that thought[4] it not. The circumstance it may please you to have of this bearer. And for your part, think you have not in the world a more loving kinswoman nor a more dear friend than myself, nor any that will watch more carefully to preserve you and your estate. And who shall otherwise persuade you, judge them more partial to others than you. And thus in haste, I leave to trouble you, beseeching God to send you a long reign. The 14 of February, 1587.

Your most assured, loving sister and cousin,
ELIZABETH R.

KING JAMES VI

Reply to Elizabeth (March 1587)[‡]

Madame and dearest sister,

Whereas by your letter and bearer, Robert Carey, your servant and ambassador, ye purge yourself of your unhappy fact, as on the one part—considering your rank and sex, consanguinity, and long-professed goodwill to the defunct,[1] together with your many and solemn attestations of your innocency—I dare not wrong you so far as not to judge honorably of your unspotted part therein; so on the other side, I wish that your honorable

† Copy text: *Elizabeth I: Collected Works*, ed. Leah S. Marcus, Janel Mueller, and Mary Beth Rose (Chicago and London: University of Chicago Press, 2000), 296–97. Reprinted by permission of the University of Chicago Press. © 2000 by the University of Chicago.
1. The "accident" is the execution of Mary Stuart, for which Elizabeth refused to claim responsibility.
2. Sir Robert Carey, son of Henry Carey, Lord Hunsdon.
3. If I had commanded her death, I would have abided by my decision [Marcus, Mueller, and Rose's note].
4. Intended.
‡ Copy text: *Elizabeth I: Collected Works*, edited by Leah S. Marcus, Janel Mueller, and Mary Beth Rose (Chicago and London: University of Chicago Press, 2000), 297. Reprinted by permission of the University of Chicago Press. © 2000 by the University of Chicago.
1. The dead Mary Stuart; *consanguinity*: blood relationship.

behavior in all times hereafter may fully persuade the whole world of the same. And as for my part, I look that ye will give me at this time such a full satisfaction in all respects as shall be a mean to strengthen and unite this isle, establish and maintain the true religion, and oblige me to be as of before I was, your most loving . . . [2]

[Postscript] this bearer hath somewhat to inform you of in my name, whom I need not desire you to credit,[3] for ye know I love him.

---

2. The letter is incomplete and unsigned.
3. Believe.

Part Seven: The Spanish Armada and Its Aftermath (1588–1592)

HISTORICAL BACKGROUND

The execution of Mary, Queen of Scots, in 1587 set in motion events that would change the balance of power in Europe forever. In the late 1570s and early 1580s, Philip II of Spain had sent troops to aid rebels against Elizabeth in Ireland and had twice supported schemes to invade England and place Mary Stuart on the throne. He had, however, never been entirely comfortable with the thought of a Scottish Queen with French connections governing England. That and the costs and practical difficulties of a Spanish invasion had prevented him from mounting a frontal attack to change the regime. Shortly before Mary's death, however, she had written to confer on him her claim to the English crown, and as soon as she was dead, Philip began preparations to enforce that claim by force. Informed of his intentions by spies, Elizabeth sent Sir Francis Drake in April 1587 to attack Philip's fleet in the Spanish port of Cadiz. Though the operation led to the capture or destruction of over two dozen enemy vessels and buoyed English spirits, it could only postpone the inevitable. A year later, on May 28, 1588, the most powerful naval fighting force ever assembled left Spain for England.

As the Armada approached the French port of Calais on its way up the English Channel, it sailed in a tight formation shaped like a crescent moon. The plan was for it to join up with a Spanish army stationed in the Netherlands, protect the army as it took barges across the Channel and marched on London, and so bring down the English government. With a combined force of nearly 50,000 men, Philip might very well have been successful had it not been for a flaw in the plan. Faulty communications prevented his commander in the Netherlands, Alexander Farnese, Duke of Parma, from receiving news of the Armada's arrival, and in consequence, he was unable to muster his forces and march to the coast in time for the planned invasion.

Finding no army awaiting him, the commander of the fleet, Alonzo Peréz de Guzmán, Duke of Medina Sidonia, ordered his ships to drop anchor in the unprotected harbor at Calais. There, on July 28, his crews were surprised by the English, who under cover of darkness set a number of their lesser ships ablaze and sent them drifting down the wind into the midst of the Spanish fleet. Fearing that fire would spread and stores of gunpowder explode, the Spanish cut their anchor cables and sailed into the Channel in considerable disarray. Early the following morning, the commanders of the English fleet—Charles, Lord Howard of Effingham, and Sir Francis Drake—caught them at a disadvantage against the coast of Flanders and pounded them with cannon shot. To save his fleet, Medina Sidonia was forced to take advantage of a favorable wind and sail up the Channel toward the North Sea. Though the English gave chase, their gunners were running short of ammunition and their sailors were suffering from a severe outbreak of the plague. Howard decided to break off the engagement and return to port.

It was fortunate that Lord Admiral Howard did not continue the pursuit, for a series of fierce storms soon set in, battering the Spanish fleet as it attempted to sail around the northern coast of Scotland and down along the western shores of Ireland on its way back to Spain. Since many of the ships had been badly mauled by English gunners and were no longer seaworthy, the strong winds and high seas took a terrible toll. Nearly half the force of 130 ships sank or suffered shipwreck on the rocky shores. Such crewmen as washed up in Scotland and Ireland were regarded as invaders and potential catalysts of Catholic rebellion, and local officials took little pity on them, hunting them down and slaughtering them by the hundreds. Officers often fared better, being ransomed and sent back to Spain, but the toll on ordinary seamen was high. Of roughly 30,000 who sailed from Spain, only 10,000 are thought to have survived.

Though the Armada no longer posed a threat once it had passed up the Channel to Scotland, the Queen and her Council had no way to be sure that it would not regroup or that Parma's forces might not find a way to attack on their own. To prevent such eventualities, soldiers under the command of Robert Dudley, Earl of Leicester, continued to muster along the Thames River east of London, ready to defend the capital against any force that might approach from the sea. In early August, Leicester invited the Queen to review the troops at their camp near the town of Tilbury, and she obliged, giving them one of the most stirring and memorable speeches of her reign. Only after she had left the camp did she learn that the Armada had been dispersed and the Spanish plan for an invasion abandoned.

All across England, bells rang and the people celebrated. There was, however, a darker side to the victory. Among the sailors who had fought so well, the outbreak of the plague continued unabated, and to prevent disease from passing to the civilian population, the government quarantined the victors in their ships. Having survived the hazards of war, many in the holds now succumbed to lack of food and unbearable heat, and those who survived were never fully paid the wages that they were promised. It was a sorry end to a glorious affair.

For the Spanish who managed to limp back to their homeland, the outcome was not much better. Though Philip sought to rebuild the Armada and mount another invasion, the English managed to disrupt his plans at every stage, first by mounting a naval blockade of the Netherlands and launching a major (though ultimately fruitless) counterattack on Spanish ports in Portugal, and then by undertaking systematic attacks on Spanish treasure ships sailing from the New World. In 1589 alone, they captured more than ninety, leading one Spanish observer to conclude that the English "[are] become lords and masters of the sea, and need care for no man." (Neale, *Queen Elizabeth*, 338). It was a turning point from which much would follow, including the colonization of America and, in the eighteenth and nineteenth centuries, the growth of a world-wide English empire.

At the time, however, few could see beyond the joy of the moment. With Philip neutralized and Mary Stuart no longer alive to stir up trouble, Elizabeth felt sufficiently secure to resume her summer progresses, setting aside restrictions on her travel that had confined her to London and its immediate environs for most of the 1580s. Yet conditions were not entirely peaceful. In 1589, smoldering hostilities between her Archbishop of Canterbury, John Whitgift, and the most militant of her Protestant subjects broke into the open. Subversive tracts signed with the pseudonym Martin Marprelate began to appear, winning a wide readership by attacking corruption in the Anglican Church, urging the elimination of bishops, and proposing a new system of governance based on Presbyterian models. Although a secret press that had produced the pamphlets was eventually found and destroyed and those thought responsible for it were executed for treason, a battle had been joined that would simmer for half a century, ultimately erupting into the English Civil War. At the time, even the

Queen's most reliable supporters were distressed by her severity toward radical Protestants. Her old advisor Sir Francis Knollys wrote to Lord Burghley, "I do marvel how her Majesty can be persuaded that she is in as much danger of such as are called Puritans as she is of the papists" (Ridley, *Shrewdness*, 302).

Elizabeth also faced a dangerous religious situation in France. In January 1589, Catherine de Medici died, her schemes to secure a glorious and lasting dynasty for her children in shambles. Shortly after her death, her one remaining son, Henry III, made a last attempt to control the religious violence that had afflicted France since the 1560s by arranging the assassination of the leader of the militant Roman Catholic faction, Henry, Duke of Guise. Rather than producing quiet, however, the murder further inflamed sectarian hatred, and a short time later, the King was himself assassinated by a fanatical monk. All this worked to Elizabeth's advantage, since her long-time ally, the great Huguenot general, Henry of Navarre, was now the likely successor to the French crown. Yet complications soon arose. Penniless and at war with his predominantly Catholic subjects, Navarre begged Elizabeth for troops to consolidate his power. When she consented, sending an expeditionary force under the Earl of Essex, Navarre went off with the Earl on other business and frittered away the opportunity for a decisive victory. Enraged, Elizabeth summoned Essex and his forces back to England, leaving Henry to fend for himself. The consequences of her withdrawal of support were lasting, for Henry soon concluded that his situation was hopeless and took a course that would trouble Elizabeth even more than his squandering of her resources. He converted to Roman Catholicism. Nothing, in short—not the elimination of Mary Stuart, the Duke of Guise, or the Spanish Armada—could entirely calm the storms of religious conflict swirling around the Queen.

Prophecies and Provocations

In the English imagination, the year 1588 lingered for generations as the "Wonderful Year." In part, its commemoration was a natural consequence of the heady, bell-ringing joy that accompanied the unexpected retreat of the supposedly "invincible" Armada. To a degree difficult to imagine today, however, the awe was also religious. The motto on the commemorative coin that Elizabeth had struck after the battle said simply "*Afflavit Deus et dissipati sunt*" (God blew and they were scattered). Not only did the fierce storms that struck the Spanish navy seem to many, including Philip himself, signs of divine judgment, but the entire affair fulfilled a series of fifteenth- and sixteenth-century prophecies that foretold calamities of biblical proportions in that very year. Though the extent of actual belief in the oracles is impossible to gauge, they certainly fired the imaginations of the English people.

A fifteenth-century German astronomer named Johann Müller von Königsberg (or Regiomontanus) seems to have set things in motion. As the author of astrological tables used by many of the great navigators, including Columbus and Magellan, he was a writer of considerable authority. Translated out of German, his original prophecy reads,

> Fifteen hundred and eighty-eight
> That is the year I contemplate.
> If then the world do not go under
> There'll else be great events and wonder.
> (trans. Whitehead, *Brags*, 17)

Similar prophecies of the "Wonderful Year" by Cyprian von Leowitz and others circulated widely in England in the 1570s and 1580s. One by the Cambridge scholar Richard Harvey—brother of the more famous Gabriel Harvey—gained particular notoriety because its author had boldly (and incorrectly) forecast similar cataclysms for the year 1583. Although the fiasco damaged Harvey's reputation, it also drew attention to his book and so helped to perpetuate the notion that 1588 was to be a very special year. Although the edition of Raphael Holinshed's *Chronicles of England, Scotland, and Ireland* published in 1587 reports that "The great year of 1588 is more talked of than feared" (Whitehead 19), the prognostications of Harvey and others seem to have caused quite a stir. Elizabeth's Council was so concerned that it sponsored a response to the rumors, John Harvey's *Discursive Problem Concerning Prophecies.*

Religious feeling also played other important roles in the crisis. In June of 1588, for example, Cardinal William Allen printed a broadside entitled *A Declaration of the Sentence and Deposition of Elizabeth,* in which he incited the Queen's Catholic subjects to lend their support to the Spanish invasion. Printed in the Netherlands and smuggled into England, it had the look of an official papal document, leading Lord Burghley to call it "a roaring hellish bull." It was, of course, nothing of the kind, as he well knew, but it did reveal the intentions of Pope Sixtus V, who had been laboring behind the scenes to bring Elizabeth down and purge England of Protestant heresy. The opening paragraph gives a succinct summary of the reasoning behind the invasion from the point of view of the Queen's most militantly Catholic opponents.

CYPRIAN VON LEOWITZ

From Of the End of This World (1564)[†]

[*A Prophecy of the "Wonderful Year" 1588*]

When, after Christ's birth, there be expired
    Of hundreds fifteen years eighty and eight,°   *1588 years*
Then comes the time of dangers to be feared,
    And all mankind with dolors it shall freight.°   *weigh down*
5 For if the world in that year do not fall,
    If sea and land then perish ne decay,[1]
Yet empires all, and kingdoms, alter shall,
    And man to ease himself shall have no way.

RICHARD HARVEY

From An Astrological Discourse (1582)[‡]

[*Another Prophecy*]

That year hath many hundred years ago been specially foretold and much spoken of amongst astrologers, who have, as it were, *unanimi consensu,* prognosticated that either a marvelous fearful and horrible alteration of

---

† Copy text: Cyprian von Leowitz, *Of the ende of this world, the seconde commyng of Christ,* translated by Thomas Rogers (London: Andrew Maunsel, 1577; *STC* 11803a.7), D4r.
1. Neither perish nor decay.
‡ Copy text: Richard Harvey, *An astrological discourse vpon the great and notable coniunction of the tvvo superiour planets, Saturne & Iupiter* (London: Henry Bynneman, 1582; *STC* 12909.7), C6v–C7r.

empires, kingdoms, seignories,[1] and states (together with other wonderful and very extraordinary accidents, as extreme hunger and pestilence, desperate treasons and commotions) shall then fall out to the miserable affliction and oppression of huge multitudes, or else that an utter and final overthrow and destruction of the whole world shall ensue.

CARDINAL WILLIAM ALLEN

From A Declaration of the Sentence and Deposition of Elizabeth, the Usurper and Pretensed Queen of England (1588)[†]

Sixtus V, by God's providence the universal pastor of Christ's flock, to whom by perpetual and lawful succession appertaineth the care and government of the Catholic Church, seeing the pitiful calamities which heresy hath brought into the renowned countries of England and Ireland, of old so famous for virtue, religion, and Christian obedience; and how at this present, through the impiety and perverse government of Elizabeth, the pretensed Queen, with a few her adherents, those kingdoms be brought not only to a disordered and perilous state in themselves but are become as infected members, contagious and troublesome to the whole body of Christendom; and not having in those parts the ordinary means which by the assistance of Christian princes he hath in other provinces to remedy disorders and keep in obedience and ecclesiastical discipline the people, for that Henry VIII, late King of England, did of late years, by rebellion and revolt from the See Apostolic, violently separate himself and his subjects from the communion and society of the Christian commonwealth; and Elizabeth, the present usurper, doth continue the same, with perturbation and peril of the countries about her, showing herself obstinate and incorrigible in such sort that without her deprivation and deposition[1] there is no hope to reform those states nor keep Christendom in perfect peace and tranquility. Therefore, our Holy Father, desiring as his duty is, to provide present and effectual remedy, inspired by God for the universal benefit of His Church, moved by the particular affection which himself and many his predecessors have had to these nations, and solicited by the zealous and importunate instance of sundry the most principal persons of the same, hath dealt earnestly with divers princes, and specially with the mighty and potent King Catholic of Spain—for the reverence which he beareth to the See Apostolic, for the old amity between his house and the Crown of England, for the special love which he hath showed to the Catholics of those places, for the obtaining of peace and quietness in his countries adjoining, for the augmenting and increase of the Catholic faith, and finally for the universal benefit of all Europe—that he will employ those forces which Almighty God hath given him to the deposition of this woman, and correction of her complices so

---

1. Feudal lordships over tenants; *unanimi consensu*: with unanimous consent.
† Copy text: William Allen, *A declaration of the sentence and deposition of Elizabeth, the vsurper and pretensed quene of Englande* [Antwerp: A. Conincx, 1588; STC 22590], single sheet.
1. Without taking away her authority and removing her from the throne; *See Apostolic*: seat of the Pope, the Bishop of Rome.

wicked and noisome to the world, and to the reformation and pacification of these kingdoms, whence so great good and so manifold public commodities[2] are like to ensue.

THE DEFEAT OF THE ARMADA

The course of the action between the English and Spanish navies was traced in several literary works of the period, notably James Aske's poem *Elizabetha Triumphans* and the second part of Thomas Heywood's dramatic retrospective on the life of the Queen, *If You Know Not Me, You Know Nobody*. In Aske's poem, a loosely factual account of the battle has been transformed into the stuff of heroic myth. Classical deities are invoked, sentences swell, and the language rises to epic heights—or nearly does, for the poem cannot entirely sustain its lofty intentions. One of the difficulties is simply that it reduces its principal figures to caricatures, depicting the English as faultless heroes and the Spanish as dehumanized villains. The poet delights in the death of his enemies, jesting over the reunion of the Spanish sailors in the underwater court of the god Neptune. At the end, he also mounts a vitriolic attack on the Pope as the servant of the devil and his agents as blind idolaters, appealing to English recusants to abandon their Catholic faith and return to their former allegiance to the Queen. Nothing shows the depth of partisan feeling in the period more clearly, for though no Englishmen rose up in support of the invasion and most English Catholics remained stoutly loyal, Protestants of the sort that Aske was addressing remained convinced that their neighbors had gone over to the enemy.

Though Heywood's play is less concerned with divisions in the English body politic and is more realistic in its account of the actual battle, it, too, contrasts simplified Spanish villains with noble and resolute English heroes. The plot is that of a cautionary tale designed to illustrate the adage that pride goes before a fall. In the opening scene, which takes place just before the battle, the Spanish commanders gather to deride the pitiful forces arrayed against them, dismissing Elizabeth as a silly woman and her counselors as effeminate weaklings. Their arrogance then receives its just reward when the English prove the braver fighters and the more astute tacticians.

JAMES ASKE

From Elizabetha Triumphans (1588)[†]

[*The Defeat of the Armada*]

That time expired, they fight afresh again
And jointly meet before the Isle of Wight,
Where then began a fierce and greater fight.
There musket-shot, discharged of either fleet,
5 Did fall like hail into the raging seas.
There cross-bars° flew most liberally bestowed,   *expanding projectiles*
Which brake the sides of their late-battered ships,
And there was cast against each other's foe

---

2. Advantages; *importunate instance*: urgent entreaty; *complices*: accomplices; *noisome*: offensive.
† Copy text: James Aske, *Elizabetha triumphans Conteyning the dammed practizes, that the diuelish popes of Rome haue vsed euer sithence her Highnesse first comming to the Crowne* (London: Thomas Gubbin and Thomas Newman, 1588; STC 847), E4r–F2r.

The battle of the Armada, as shown on seventeenth-century
English playing cards.

A thousand balls of wild-fire[1] merciless,
10 By which were sent great store of Spanish ships
To follow those that were to Neptune gone.
And lest the first should troubled be too sore
In coming back to fetch this late-sent train,°   *line of ships*
These meet with them halfway (their looked-for friends),
15 Whence all make haste unto King Neptune's court,
Where they do find such pleasant pleasing friends,
As ne'er they'll to King Philip's palace turn.°   *return*
A world it is to see what messengers
They send to show in what estate they stand,
20 For Spanish felts[2] with Spaniards' dearest blood
Becheckereth the sea with black and red,
As there no white[3] could possibly be seen.
Don Pedro[4] with his ship and company
Did like so ill (the cause I know not why)
25 Of that the news these messengers did bring,
As they do better England's bondage like
Than Neptune's court from whence these lately came.
The other ships, in better case than his,
Do neither like their state, ne° yet his choice,   *nor*
30 But think it best to trust unto their heels.
Wherefore they hoist up all their sails at once
And take their way to Calais haven,[5] whereas
They lie at rode,° with often wishes that   *at anchor*
They were again in Spain from whence they came.
35 Ours, not far off, do rest their toiled corps[6]
Sore overcharged by too, too forwardness
In prosecuting their late quailed° foes.   *overpowered*
Where for their deeds, their well performed deeds,
Lord Thomas Howard, with the Sheffield Lord,[7]
40 And Roger Townsend[8] (forward in those wars),
With Martin Frobisher[9] (not a little known)—
Most worthy gentles newly entertained
By mighty Mavors° from Bellona Queen—   *Mars*
Received from her the gift of knighthood there.[1]

45 Which deed performed, England was not slack
In trying means which might annoy her foes.

1. Balls of substances, such as tar, that were difficult to extinguish.
2. Black woolen hats.
3. Whitecaps on the waves.
4. Don Pedro de Valdés, squadron commander and captain of the first Spanish ship captured in the battle. He surrendered to Sir Francis Drake.
5. Port in northwestern France, across the English Channel from Dover.
6. Body of seamen.
7. Edmund, third Baron Sheffield. A nephew of Lord Admiral Howard, he commanded three ships against the Armada; *Lord Thomas Howard*: later first Earl of Suffolk. The eldest son of the Duke of Norfolk, he had a long and distinguished naval career.
8. Gentleman in the service of Thomas Howard and his family.
9. Privateer and explorer famous for his 1576–78 expeditions to find the Northwest Passage. In 1588, he was a principal tactician in the campaign, commanding one of the four "great ships" of the Elizabethan navy.
1. The four men were knighted at sea by Charles, Lord Howard of Effingham, commander of the English fleet (treated as if he were the god of war), acting on behalf of Elizabeth (depicted as the goddess of war).

For presently a wondrous stratagem
Did then ensue, by her in practice put.
For certain ships of our worst English ships,
50 By Lord Charles Howard, worthy general,
Commanded, were forthwith then set on fire,
Which driven thence through a swift-running stream
Did fall among the Spaniards' roding ships.[2]
At which strange sight they so astonied° were,   *astonished*
55 As they rejoiced that could the cables cut,
Which fastened were unto their anchors cast.
This sudden maze,° which nothing settled wits,[3]   *amazement*
Were chiefest cause of this, their second bane,
For then each ship on other's cables foul
60 And run on rocks to their ensuing loss.
They hoist up sails, and as they thither came,
So hie° they fast unto the Northern Seas.[4]   *hasten*
These thus in flight are chaséd very sore
By General of this our conquering fleet,[5]
65 Who lion-like (sufficéd° near enough   *supplied*
With honor's laud) pursues his flying foes.
And Cumberland, a wondrous forward earl[6]
But new embarked, attaining to this flight,
Did show himself, and showing made them feel
70 His power, not felt before of° Spaniards.   *by*
What shall I say, or what could that her° fleet   *England's*
Perform in better sort than there was done?
Their Spanish foes with all that conquered fleet
(Although they said that English land was theirs,
75 And therefore when they first receivéd word
That then but thirty little English boats
Could be descried, cried oft "*Victoria!*"°)   *victory*
Are sunk, are drowned, are burnt with England's fire,
And grounded lie before the French town's haven.[7]
80 The rest (even then remaining weakly) sail
They know not whither, guided by their fate,
Now chased far beyond this island's bounds.[8]
Our little fleet, our famous General
Doth shame to follow them that will not fight,
85 And therefore turns his course unto his charge,[9]
Still sailing with an happy southern wind
Attains unto the same the Narrow Seas,[1]
Where setting everything in needful sort,

2. Ships lying at anchor.
3. Which did nothing to calm their minds.
4. The North Sea, off the eastern coast of Scotland.
5. Charles, Lord Howard of Effingham.
6. George Clifford, Earl of Cumberland, courtier, privateer, and (after 1590) the Queen's champion in the annual Accession Day jousts at court.
7. The harbor at Calais.
8. Driven by fierce storms, the Spanish fleet passed north of Scotland and down along the western coast of Ireland on its way back to Spain. Many ships were wrecked and their crews killed or captured.
9. His duty to report to the Queen.
1. The Strait of Dover, narrowest part of the English Channel.

    Left then the fleet and hasted to the Court
90 Of his thrice-sacred sovereign, our Queen,
    Whose welcome thither was as his deserts
    And famous deeds perforḿed had deserved.

    Our gracious Queen (for this God's mercy showed
    To her, her land, through conquest over them
95 Who came to seek her death and death of those
    Who steadfast are unto His holy Word)
    Doth yield Him thanks devoutly on her knees
    And wills her subjects throughout all her land
    To fast and pray for this His providence.
100 But Sixtus Quintus, Pope of whorish Rome,
    Hath lost his bulls[2] and hath his soldiers lost,
    With credit[3] cracked, and all in eighty-eight.
    And well I wit what was the cause thereof:
    Belike his saints, himself, and cardinals,
105 With friars, monks, and seminary priests,
    Were all at dice for England's people's goods,
    And quite forgot to fall to morning Mass.
    Or otherwise, they told their beads[4] so oft
    And said so many matins[5] to their gods
110 (Their wooden gods) as that they fell asleep
    And so left off to persevere in prayers;
    Whereby their saints, at that time sleepy too,
    Did likewise nod and sued not to their gods.[6]
    Or lastly thus (which likest° is of all)   *most likely*
115 His silver scant, whereby his crosses few
    And holy-water niggardly bestowed,[7]
    Did scarcely bless his soldiers going forth,
    For which hard dearth the God of heaven (our God)
    Did wash them all within His hallowed seas,
120 Where plenty is of water like the Pope's.[8]
    By which (as by His goodness ever showed
    To England, where His little flock remains,
    With always loss unto the hapless Pope),
    His Holiness, with all deceived by him
125 Or instruments he to that end hath sent,
    May now confess with sore repenting heart
    That long enough they all provoḱed have
    Our loving God to never-ceasing ire.
    But if his father Beelzebub, that fiend,
130 Hath bound the Pope so to his damńed lore

2. Pun meaning male cattle and papal decrees, namely those that Sixtus V promised to Cardinal Allen in 1588. Had the Spanish invasion succeeded, these would have made Allen Papal Legate, with power to reestablish the Roman Catholic Church in England. But the bulls never arrived.
3. Belief in him among the people and ability to cover his debts.
4. Said their rosaries, prayers repeated according to the number of beads on a chain.
5. Morning prayers.
6. Protestants disapproved of prayers to saints, thought by Catholics to intercede with God in their behalf.
7. He, being short of funds, and so unable to buy enough crosses or to sprinkle enough holy water.
8. That is, no more holy; Protestants regarded blessing water to sprinkle on the faithful as a superstitious act.

As that he cannot turn unto the Lord,
Yet Englishmen recusants[9] (ah, I grieve
To term ye so because my countrymen),
Despise his deeds (his mere deceitful deeds)
And turn your hearts unto your sacred Queen,
135 And with your Queen, belovéd of our God,
Turn to God's Word, and shun the devilish Pope.
So God will joy in this His little flock,
And bless this land with still° increasing store,°   *always / abundance*
140 Whereas He now like to a natural sire
Weeps over it, as once He shedded tears
When that he saw Jerusalem he loved.[1]
Which (heavenly God) with three-fold Nestor's years
Giv'n to our Queen, to England's ever joy,
145 Fulfill (I pray) with such convenient speed,
As shall seem good unto Thy holy will.

THOMAS HEYWOOD

From If You Know Not Me, You Know Nobody, Part Two (1606)[†]

[*The Attack and Destruction of the Armada*]

Enter the DUKE OF MEDINA, DON PEDRO, JOHN MARTINUS RICALDUS,[1]
and other Spaniards.

MEDINA: We are where we long wished to be at last,
And now this elephant's burden,[2] our Armada,
Three years an embryon,° is at length produced   *embryo*
And brought into the world to live at sea.
5 *Non sufficit orbis,*[3] our proud Spanish motto
By th' English mocked and found at Carthagen,[4]
Shall it not now take force?
Can England satisfy our avarice,
That worlds cannot suffice? What thinks Don Pedro?
10 PEDRO: Alphonsus Perez Guzman,
Duke of Medina and Sidonia,
And royal General of our great Armada,
I think we come too strong; what's our design
Against a petty island governed by a woman?

---

9. Catholics who refused to convert to Protestantism.
1. A reference to Luke 19.41–44, where Jesus weeps over the coming destruction of Jerusalem.
† Copy text: Thomas Heywood, *If you know not me, you know no body. The second part* (London: Nathanael Butter, 1633; STC 13339), J3v–K4v.
1. John Martinez de Recalde, famous navigator and commander of the Biscayan forces; *Duke of Medina*: Alonso Pérez de Guzmán, seventh Duke of Medina Sidonia and the commander of the Armada; *Don Pedro*: Don Pedro de Valdés, commander of the Andalusian forces.
2. Offspring; a large and cumbersome task.
3. "The world is not enough," motto of Philip II, a reference to his ambition to excel, even beyond his vast worldly domains.
4. Cartegena, a Spanish port in the Caribbean on the northern coast of Columbia, sacked by Sir Francis Drake in 1585.

15   I think, instead of military men
        Garnished with arms and martial discipline,
        She, with a feminine train
        Of her bright ladies, beautifulest and best,
        Will meet us in their smocks, willing to pay
20   Their maidenheads for ransom.
    MEDINA: Thinkest thou so, Don Pedro?
    PEDRO: I therein am confident
      And partly sorry that our King of Spain
      Hath been at charge of such a magazine,[5]
25   When half our men and ammunition
      Might have been spared.
    MEDINA: Thou puttest me now in mind
      Of the Grand Seignior,[6] who (some few years since)
      Whenas° the great Ambassador of Spain   *when*
30   Importuned him for aid against the land
      Styled by the title of the Maiden Isle,
      Calls for a map. Now when the Ambassador
      Had showed him th' Indies, all America,
      Some parts of Asia and Europa, too
35   (Climes° that took up the greatest part o' the card°),   *regions / map*
      And finding England but a spot of earth,
      Or a few acres, if at all, compared
      To our so large and spacious provinces,
      Denies him aid as much against his honor
40   To fight with such a centuple° of odds,   *hundred-fold*
      But gave him this advice: "Were I," said he,
      "As your great King of Spain, out of my kingdoms,
      I'd press[7] or hire so many pioneers°   *foot soldiers*
      As with their spades and mattocks should dig up
45   This wart of earth and cast it in the sea."
      And well, methought, he spake.

                              *   *   *

    MEDINA: John Martinus Ricaldus, you our prime navigator
      Since famed Columbus or great Magellan,
      Give us a brief relation of the strength
50   And potency of this our great Armada,
      Christened by the Pope "The Navy Invincible."
    RICALDUS: Twelve mighty galleons of Portugal;
      Fourteen great ships of Biscay of Castile;
      Eleven tall ships of Andalusia;
55   Sixteen galleons, fourteen of Guipúzcoa;
      Ten sail that run by the name o' th' Eastern Fleet;
      The ships of Urcas, Zaibras, Naples;[8] galleys,

---

5. Spent so much for this store of armaments.
6. The Sultan of the Ottoman Empire.
7. Forcibly recruit or impress into military service.
8. *Urcas, Zabras,* and *Navios* were terms for Spanish ships, here perhaps mistaken for ports of origin.

Great galliasses, fly-boats, pinnaces[9]
Amounting to the number of an hundred
60   And thirty tight, tall sail, the most of them
Seeming like castles built upon the sea.
MEDINA: And what can all their barges, cock-boats, oars,[1]
Small vessels (better to be said to creep
Than sail upon the ocean) do 'gainst these?
65   They are o'ercome already.   *Exeunt*

* * *

Drum and colors.[2]

Enter the EARL OF LEICESTER, SIR ANTHONY BROWNE, *the* EARL OF
HUNSDON *bearing the standard,*[3] QUEEN ELIZABETH *completely armed,
and soldiers.*

QUEEN: A stand.° From London thus far have we marched;   *Halt*
Here pitch our tents. How do you call this place?
LEICESTER: The town you see, to whom these downs belong,
Gives them to° name the plains of Tilbury,   *by*
70   QUEEN: Be this then styled our camp at Tilbury,
And the first place we have been seen in arms
Or thus accoutered. Here we fix our foot,
Not to stir back, were we sure here t' encounter
With all the Spanish vengeance threatened us,
75   Came it in fire and thunder. Know, my subjects,
Your Queen hath now put on a masculine spirit
To tell the bold and daring what they are,
Or what they ought to be. And such as faint,
Teach them, by my example, fortitude.
80   Nor let the best-proved soldier here disdain
A woman should conduct an host of men,
To their disgrace or want of president.[4]
Have you not read of brave Zenobia,
An eastern queen, who faced the Roman legions
85   Even in their pride and height of potency,
And in the field encountered personally
Aurelianus Caesar? Think in me
Her spirit survives, Queen of this western isle,
To make the scornéd name of Elizabeth
90   As frightful and as terrible to Spain
As was Zenobia's to the state of Rome.
O, I could wish them landed and in view
To bid them instant battle, ere march farther
Into my land. This is my vow, my rest:°   *pledge*

---

9. Small, light boats often used as scouts or tenders; *galliasses*: galleys or galleons, large, clumsy ships
built up at stem and stern that could be propelled both by sail and oars; galliasses were a third larger
than galleons and required three hundred galley slaves; *fly-boats*: small, fast sail boats.
1. Rowboats; *barges*: small sailboats; *cock-boats*: small boats often towed behind larger vessels.
2. Regimental flags.
3. The English flag; Robert Dudley, Earl of Leicester, was the Lord General at Tilbury; Sir Anthony
Browne, first Viscount Montagu, came from a Roman Catholic family whose loyalty to Elizabeth
during the Armada attack demonstrated the patriotism of the English Catholics; Henry Carey, Lord
Hunsdon, was Elizabeth's Lord Chamberlain and commander of the land forces.
4. Lack of a leader; or perhaps "precedent," lack of an example.

95   I'll pave their way with this my virgin breast.
LEICESTER: But Madam, ere that day come,
      There will be many a bloody nose and crackéd crown;
      We shall make work for surgeons.
QUEEN: I hope so, Leicester; for you, Sir Anthony Browne,
100   Though[5] your religion and recusancy
      Might in these dangerous and suspicious times
      Have drawn your loyalty into suspense,°   *under suspicion*
      Yet have you herein amply cleared yourself
      By bringing us five hundred men well armed
105   And your own self in person.
SIR ANTHONY: Not only those, but all that I enjoy
      Are at your Highness' service.
QUEEN: Now, Lord Hunsdon,
      The Lord Lieutenant of our force by land
      Under our General, Leicester, what thinkest thou
110   Of their Armada, christened by the Pope
      "The Navy Invincible?"
HUNSDON: That there's a power above both them and us
      That can their proud and haughty menaces
      Convert to their own ruins.
QUEEN: Thinkest thou so, Hunsdon?
115   No doubt it will. Let me better survéy my camp.   *Flourish trumpets*
      Some wine there—a health to all my soldiers.
      Methinks I do not see 'mongst all my troops
      One with a courtier's face—but all look soldier-like.
      Whence came this sound of shot?   *A peal of shot within*
LEICESTER: It seems the navy,
120   Styled by the Pope "The Navy Invincible,"
      Riding along the coast of France and Dunkirk,
      Discovered first by Captain Thomas Fleming,[6]
      Is met and fought with by your Admiral.[7]
QUEEN: Heaven prosper their defense.
125   O, had God made us manlike, like our mind,
      We'd not be here fenced in a mure° of arms,   *wall*
      But ha' been present at these sea alarms.

          Horn.   Enter First Post.°   *messenger*
      Make way there, what's the news?
1 POST: Heaven bless your Majesty,
130   Your royal fleet bids battle to the Spaniard,
      Whose number, with advantage of the wind,
      Gains them great odds; but the undaunted worth
      And well-known valor of your Admiral,
      Sir Frances Drake, and Martin Frobisher,
135   John Hawkins,[8] and your other English captains

---

5. Copy text: Thought.
6. Thomas Fleming sailed into Plymouth Harbor on July 19 to announce the arrival of the Armada.
7. Charles, Lord Howard of Effingham, later Earl of Nottingham.
8. Drake commanded the *Revenge*, Frobisher the *Triumph*, and Hawkins the *Swallow*. With Howard's *Ark Royal*, these were the four royal "great ships" of the English navy.

Takes not away all hope of victory.

QUEEN: Can'st thou describe the manner of the fight
And where the royal navies first encountered?

1 POST: From Dover cliff we might discern them join

140 'Twixt that and Callice;° there the fight begun.   *Calais*
Sir Frances Drake, Vice Admiral, was first,
Gave an onset° to this great Armada of Spain.   *provocation*
The manner thus: with twenty-five sail,
(Those ships of no great burden,° yet well manned,   *tonnage*

145 For in that dreadful conflict few or none
Of your ships royal came within the fight)
This Drake, I say, (whose memory shall live
While this great world he compassed first[9] shall last)
Gave order that his squadrons, one by one,

150 Should follow him some distance, steers his course,
But none to shoot till he himself gave fire.
Forward he steered as far before the rest,
As a good musket can well bear at twice,[1]
And, as a spy, comes to survey their fleet,

155 Which seemed like a huge city built on the sea.
They shot and shot and emptied their broadsides
At his poor single vessel. He sails on,
Yet all this while no fire was seen from him.
The rest behind (longing for action)

160 Thought he had been turned coward that had done
All this for their more safety. He now finding
Most of their present fury spent at him,
Fires a whole tier° at once, and having emptied   *row of guns*
A full broadside, the rest came up to him

165 And did the like undaunted. Scarce the last
Had passed by them, but Drake had cleared the sea.
For ere th' unwieldy vessels could be stirred
Or their late emptied ordnance charged again,
He takes advantage both of wind and tide,

170 And the same course he took in his progress
Doth in his back return keep the same order,
Scouring along as if he would besiege them
With a new wall of fire, in all his squadrons
Leaving no charge° that was not bravely manned,   *position*

175 Insomuch that blood as visibly was seen
To pour out of their portholes in such manner
As, after showers i' the city, spouts spill rain.
And thus Drake bade them welcome. What after happened,
Such a huge cloud of smoke environed us

180 We could not well discover.

QUEEN: There's for thy speed, [*hands him a cup of wine*]
And England ne'er want such a Drake[2] at need.

---

9. Drake circumnavigated the world between 1577 and 1580; Magellan's crew had done so earlier,
   but their commander died before completing the voyage.
1. Twice as far as a good musket can fire.
2. With a double pun on Drake's name as meaning also "dragon" and "cannon."

Enter the Second Post.
Thou art welcome. What canst thou relate
Touching this naval conflict?
185　2 POST:　　Since Drake's first onset, and our fleet retired,
The Spanish navy being linked and chained°　　　*held in tight formation*
Like a half moon or to a full-bent bow,
Attend advantage.° Where 'mongst the rest　　　*wait for the advantage*
Sir Martin Frobisher, blinded with smoke,
190　By chance is fallen into the midst of them,
Still fighting 'gainst extremity of odds,
Where he with all his gallant followers
Are folded in death's arms.
QUEEN:　　　　　　　　If he survive,
He shall be nobly ransomed; if he be dead,
195　Yet he shall live in immortality.
How fares our Admiral?
2 POST:　　　　　　　Bravely directs
And with much judgment. England never bred
Men that a sea fight better managed.
QUEEN:　　It cheers my blood—and if so heaven be pleased
200　For some neglected duty in our self
To punish with loss of these brave spirits, His will be done.
Yet will we pray for them. What says valiant Leicester?
Thou wilt not leave us, wilt thou? Lookest thou pale?
What says old Hunsdon? Nay, I'll speak thy part.
205　Thy hand, old lord; I'm sure I have thy heart.
HUNSDON:　　Both hand and heart.

Enter the Third Post.
QUEEN:　　Before thou speak'st, take that. If he be dead,　　[*hands him wine*]
Our self will see his funeral honoréd.
3 POST:　　I then proceed thus: when the great galleons
210　And galliasses had environed them,
The undaunted Frobisher, though round beset,
Cheered up his soldiers and well manned his fights,
And standing bare-head bravely on the deck
When murdering shot, as thick as April's hail,
215　Swung by his ears, he waved his warlike sword,
Firing at once his tiers on either side
With such a fury that he brake their chains,
Shattered their decks, and made their stoutest ships
Like drunkards reel and tumble side to side.
220　Thus, in war's spite and all the Spaniards' scoff,
He brought both ship and soldiers bravely off.
QUEEN:　　War's spite indeed, and we to do him right
Will call the ship he fought in the *War's Spite*.
Now countrymen, shall our spirits here on land
225　Come short of theirs so much admired at sea?　　*A march³ within.*
If there be any here that harbor fear,

3. Drum beat

We give them liberty to leave the camp
And thank them for their absence.
A march.° Lead on. We'll meet the worst can fall.   *command to march*
230   A maiden Queen is now your general.

> As they march about the stage, SIR FRANCES DRAKE *and* SIR MARTIN
> FROBISHER *meet them with Spanish ensigns*[4] *in their hands and drum
> and colors before them.*

QUEEN: What means those Spanish ensigns in the hands
Of English subjects?
DRAKE: Gracious Queen,
They show that Spaniards' lives are in the hands
Of England's Sovereign.
QUEEN: England's God be praised.
235   But prithee, Drake (for well I know thy name,
Nor will I be unmindful of thy worth),
Briefly rehearse the danger of the battle.
Till Frobisher was rescued, we have heard.
DRAKE: We then retired and, after counsel called,
240   We stuffed eight empty hoys° with pitch and oil,   *small sloops*
And all th' ingredients aptest to take fire,
And sent them where their proud Armada lay.
The Spaniard, now at anchor, thought we had come
For parley and so rode secure. But when
245   They beheld them flame like to so many
Bright bonfires,
Making their fleet an Etna[5] like themselves,
They cut their cables, let their anchors sink,
Burying at once more wealth within the sea
250   Than th' Indies can in many years restore.
Now their high-built and large capacious bottoms°   *vessels*
Being by this means unaccommodated,[6]
Like to so many rough unbridled steeds
Command themselves, or rather are commanded,
255   And hurried where th' inconstant winds shall please.
Some fell on quicksands, others brake on shelves.
Medina, their great grand° and general,   *grandee*
We left unto the mercy of the sea.
Don Pedro, their High Admiral, we took
260   With many knights and noblemen of Spain,
Who are by this time landed at St. Margaret's,[7]
From whence your Admiral brings them up by land,
And at St. James he[8] means to greet your Grace.
QUEEN: Next under heav'n, your valors have the praise.
265   But prithee, Drake, give us a brief relation
Of those ships that in this expedition
Were employed against the Spanish forces.

4. Naval flags.
5. Mount Etna, a volcano on the east coast of Sicily.
6. Without ballast, the ships rode high in the water and were difficult to manage.
7. A suburb of London on the Thames, across from Richmond.
8. Copy text: his.

DRAKE: The *Elizabeth, Jonas, Triumph*, the *White Bear*,
The *Mer Honora*, and the *Victory*;
270   *Ark Ralegh*,[9] *Due Repulse, Garland, War's Spite*,
The *Mary Rose*, the *Bonaventure, Hope*,
The *Lion, Rainbow, Vanguard, Nonpareil*,
Dreadnought, Defiance, Swift-Sure, Anspach,
The *Whale*, the *Scout, Achates*, the *Revenge*.
275   QUEEN: Drake, no more.
Where e'er this navy shall hereafter sail,
O, may it with no less success prevail.
Dismiss our camp and tread a royal march
Toward St. James, where in martial order
280   We'll meet and parley our Lord Admiral.
As for those ensigns, let them be safely kept,
And give commandment to the Dean of Paul's,[1]
He not forget in his next learnéd sermon
To celebrate this conquest at Paul's Cross,[2]
285   And to the audience in our name declare
Our thanks to heaven in universal prayer.
For though our enemies be overthrown,
'Tis by the hand of heaven and not our own.
One sound a call. Now, loving countrymen   *Call.*
290   And fellow soldiers, merited thanks to all.
We here dismiss you and dissolve our camp.
OMNES: Long live, long reign our Queen Elizabeth!
QUEEN: Thanks, general thanks.°   *thanks to all*
Towards London march we to a peaceful throne.
295   We wish no wars, yet we must guard our own.   *Exeunt omnes.*

THE QUEEN AT TILBURY

In the months leading up to the invasion, rumors were constant. When a Latin poem attributed to Philip II made the rounds, listing arrogant demands for abject submission by the Queen, it was quickly followed by a terse and witty reply that made its haughtiness seem foolish. While it is unlikely that either monarch actually had a hand in the Queen's purported verse exchange with Philip II, it must have delighted the English to think so.

Elizabeth's speech to the troops at Tilbury was the most memorable—and the most daring—of her career. Buckling on a silver breastplate over her white, velvet dress and holding up a commander's baton, she announced to her men, "[I am] resolved in the midst and heat of the battle to live and die amongst you all. I know I have the body but of a weak and frail woman, but I have the heart and stomach of a king, and of a king of England too!" The words caught the imagination, not just of those who heard her on that cloudy August day, but of a far wider audience. Lionel Sharp, one of her chaplains, transcribed the speech, quickly arranging for it to be printed and distributed throughout England. So memorable was it that it lingered in popular consciousness for gen-

---

9. Renamed by Elizabeth the *Ark Royal*.
1. Alexander Nowell, long-time Dean of St. Paul's Cathedral in London.
2. Open-air pulpit near the cross in the St. Paul's Cathedral churchyard, used as the forum for public sermons, and surrounded by galleries for dignitaries and benches for commoners.

The Queen in armor treading down the Spanish invaders.

erations. Nearly forty years later, Thomas Cecil's engraving, "Truth Presents the Queen with a Lance," was able to catch people's imaginations by depicting the Queen on horseback, bearing not only a breastplate but also a helmet, sword, and shield. Under her horse's hoofs, Cecil included a serpent, slithering among pieces of cast-off Spanish armor. It served as a symbol of papal falsehood and the defeat as an image of the Truth of Christ triumphing in the person of England's Protestant queen.

Two literary accounts of events at the English camp that day, both apparently written by eyewitnesses, were more accurate if not more restrained. The first, "The Queen's Intent to See Tilbury Camp" by Thomas Deloney, was written in a form suitable for sale to ordinary citizens on the streets of London for a penny. Deloney, a Norwich silkweaver, was a well-known writer of popular ballads and works of fiction. His account is notable for its vivid images of the colorful ceremony when the Earl of Leicester and his subordinate officers and men greeted the Queen. The second, a passage in *Elizabetha Triumphans* by James Aske, is more detailed and adopts a more elevated style, at one point comparing the English with ancient Trojans preparing to do battle with the Greeks. In some passages, the Queen is described as a goddess, in others as Penthesilea, Queen of the Amazons, or as the English heroine Boadicia, or even as the mythic hero Hercules. Although the poem has all the immediacy of a detailed report, its author is surprisingly hesitant to quote the actual words of the Queen. A comparison of his paraphrase of her speech with more reliable versions suggests the extent to which the words that people remember on such occasions are often little more than hazy approximations of those that are actually said.

QUEEN ELIZABETH

WORDS OF DEFIANCE AND INSPIRATION (1588)

[Verse Exchange with Philip II][†]

The King of Spain to Elizabeth:

1. I forbid your army's ling'ring Belgian war.
2. Drake's spoils at Cadiz all must be returned.
3. Rebuild monastic cells your father overthrew,[1]
4. And papal faith entirely restore.

Elizabeth's reply:

1. When Greeks do measure months by the moon,
   Then, Spanish Philip, thy will shall be done.[2]

[Speech to the Troops at Tilbury][‡]

My loving people, we have been persuaded by some that are careful of our safety to take heed how we commit ourself to armed multitudes for fear of treachery, but, I assure you, I do not desire to live to distrust my faithful and loving people. Let tyrants fear. I have always so behaved myself that, under God, I have placed my chiefest strength and safeguard in the loyal hearts and goodwill of my subjects. And therefore I am come amongst you, as you see, at this time not for my recreation and disport but being resolved in the midst and heat of the battle to live or die amongst you all, to lay down for my God, and for my kingdom, and for my people my honor and my blood even in the dust.

I know I have the body but of a weak and feeble woman, but I have the heart and stomach of a king and of a king of England, too, and think foul scorn that Parma or Spain[1] or any prince of Europe should dare to invade the borders of my realm, to which rather than any dishonor shall grow by me, I myself will take up arms, I myself will be your general, judge, and rewarder of every one of your virtues in the field. I know already for your forwardness you have deserved rewards and crowns, and we do assure you in the word of a prince they shall be duly paid you. In the meantime, my Lieutenant General[2] shall be in my stead, than whom never prince commanded a more noble or worthy subject, not doubting but by your obedience to my General, by your concord in the camp, and your valor in the field, we shall shortly have a famous victory over those enemies of my God, of my kingdoms, and of my people.

---

† Copy text: *Elizabeth I: Collected Works*, ed. Leah S. Marcus, Janel Mueller, and Mary Beth Rose (Chicago and London: University of Chicago Press, 2000), 409–10. Reprinted by permission of the University of Chicago Press. © 2000 by the University of Chicago. The lines attributed to Philip are here translated from Latin into English by Clarence H. Miller and Donald Stump. The copy text includes both Elizabeth's Latin reply and a rendering of it into English, which we print here.

1. The monasteries that Henry VIII seized in the 1530s when he dissolved England's allegiance to the Roman Catholic Church.
2. Though the Romans measured months in this way, the Greeks did not.

‡ Copy text: *Cabala, sive, Scrinia sacra mysteries of state & government: in letters of illustrious persons, and great agents.* Part. 1 (London: G. Bedel and T. Collins, 1654; Wing C184), LL2v.

1. The King, Philip II of Spain; *think foul scorn*: think it shameful; *Parma*: Alexander Farnese, Duke of Parma and the Spanish commander in the Netherlands.
2. Robert Dudley, Earl of Leicester.

THOMAS DELONEY

The Queen's Visiting of the Camp at Tilbury (1588)[†]

Within the year of Christ our Lord,
  a thousand and five hundreth full
And eighty-eight by just recórd,
  the which no man may disannul;
5 And in the thirtieth year remaining
  of good Queen Elizabeth's reigning,
A mighty power there was prepared
  by Philip, then the King of Spain,
Against the Maiden Queen of England,
10 which in peace before did reign.

Her royal ships to sea she sent
  to guard the coast on every side,
And seeing how her foes were bent,
  her realm full well she did provide
15 With many thousands so prepared,
  as like was never erst° declared,   *before*
Of horsemen and of footmen plenty,
  whose good hearts full well is seen
In the safeguard of their country
20 and the service of our Queen.

In Essex fair, that fertile soil,
  upon the hill of Tilbury,
To give our Spanish foes the foil
  in gallant camps they now do lie,
25 Where good order is ordained
  and true justice eke° maintained   *also*
For the punishment of persons
  that are lewd° or badly bent.   *wicked*
To see a sight so strange in England
30 'Twas our gracious Queen's intent.

And on the eighth of August, she
  from fair Saint James's[1] took her way
With many lords of high degree
  in princely robes and rich array,
35 And to barge upon the water
  (being King Henry's royal daughter)
She did go, with trumpets sounding
  and with dubbing drums apace,
Along the Thames, that famous river,
40 for to view the camp a space.

---

† Copy text: Thomas Deloney, *The Queenes visiting of the campe at Tilsburie* (London: Edward White, 1588; *STC* 6565), single sheet. Deloney notes that the ballad is to be sung to the tune of Wilson's Wild.
1. St. James's Palace, one of Elizabeth's principal London residences.

When she as far as Gravesend came,
    right over against that pretty town,
Her royal Grace with all her train
    was landed there with great renown.
45 The lords and captains of her forces,
    mounted on their gallant horses,
Ready stood to entertain her,
    like martial men of courage bold.
"Welcome to the camp, dread Sovereign,"
50   thus they said, both young and old.

The bulwarks strong that stood thereby,
    well guarded with sufficient men,
Their flags were spread courageously,
    their cannons were dischargéd then.
55 Each gunner did declare his cunning
    for joy conceivéd of her coming.
All the way her Grace was riding,
    on each side stood arméd men,
With muskets, pikes, and good calivers°   *a light musket*
60   for her Grace's safeguard then.

The Lord General[2] of the field
    had there his bloody ancient° borne.   *insignia*
The Lord Marshal's[3] colors eke
    was carried there, all rent and torn,
65 The which with bullets was so burned
    when in Flanders he sojourned.
Thus in warlike-wise they marched,
    even as soft as foot could fall,
Because her Grace was fully minded
70   perfectly to view them all.

Her faithful soldiers, great and small,
    as each one stood within his place,
Upon their knees began to fall
    Desiring God to save her Grace.
75 For joy whereof her eyes was filled,
    that the water down distilled.
"Lord bless you all, my friends," she said,
    "but do not kneel so much to me."
Then sent she warning to the rest
80   they should not let such reverence be.

Then casting up her princely eyes
    unto the hill with perfect sight,
The ground all covered, she espies,
    with feet of arméd soldiers bright.
85 Whereat her royal heart so leaped,

2. Robert Dudley, Earl of Leicester, who had recently served in the Netherlands as Governor General.
3. Sir John Norris, experienced military commander and Leicester's deputy at Tilbury.

on her feet upright she stepped,
Tossing up her plume of feathers
    to them all as they did stand,
Cheerfully her body bending,
90   waving of her royal hand.

Thus through the camp she passéd quite,
    in manner as I have declared.
At Master Ritche's,[4] for that night,
    her Grace's lodging was prepared.
95 The morrow after her abiding,
    on a princely palfrey riding,
To the camp she came to dinner
    with her lords and ladies all.
The Lord General went to meet her,
100   with his guards of yeomen tall.

The Sergeant Trumpet, with his mace,
    and nine with trumpets after him
Bareheaded went before her Grace
    in coats of scarlet color trim.
105 The King of Heralds, tall and comely,
    was the next in order duly,
With the famous arms[5] of England
    wrought with rich embroidered gold
On finest velvet, blue and crimson,
110   that for silver can be sold.

With maces of clean beaten gold,
    the Queen's two Sergeants then did ride,
Most comely men for to behold,
    in velvet coats and chains beside.
115 The Lord General then came riding
    and Lord Marshal hard beside him.
Richly were they both attired
    in princely garments of great price,
Bearing still their hats and feathers
120   in their hands in comely-wise.

Then came the Queen on prancing steed,
    attired like an angel bright,
And eight brave footmen at her feet,
    whose jerkins° were most rich in sight;   *jackets*
125 Her ladies, likewise of great honor,
    most sumptuously did wait upon her,
With pearls and diamonds brave adorned
    and in costly cauls° of gold;   *netted caps*
Her guards, in scarlet, then rid after
130   with bows and arrows, stout and bold.

4. Elizabeth spent the night of August 8 at Saffron Garden, the house of Edward Ritche.
5. Shield and crest symbolic of the English monarchy.

The valiant captains of the field
    mean space° themselves in order set,   *meanwhile*
And each of them, with spear and shield,
    to join in battle did not let°   *refuse*
135 With such a warlike skill extended,
    as the same was much commended.
Such a battle pitched in England
    many a day hath not been seen.
Thus they stood in order waiting
140   for the presence of our Queen.

At length, her Grace most royally
    received was and brought again
Where she might see most loyally
    this noble host and warlike train.
145 How they came marching all together,
    like a wood in winter's weather.
With the strokes of drummers sounding
    and with trampling horses then,
The earth and air did sound like thunder
150   to the ears of every man.

The warlike army then stood still
    and drummers left their dubbing sound,
Because it was our Prince's will
    to ride about the army round.
155 Her ladies she did leave behind her
    and her guard, which still° did mind her;   *continually*
The Lord General and Lord Marshal
    did conduct her to each place.
The pikes, the colors, and the lances,
160   at her approach, fell down apace.

And then bespake our noble Queen,
    "My loving friends and countrymen:
I hope this day the worst is seen
    that in our wars ye shall sustain.
165 But if our enemies do assail you,
    never let your stomachs° fail you.   *courage*
For in the midst of all your troop,
    we ourselves will be in place
To be your joy, your guide and comfort,
170   even before our enemy's face."

This done, the soldiers all at once
    a mighty shout or cry did give,
Which forcéd from the azure skies
    an echo loud from thence to drive.
175 Which filled her Grace with joy and pleasure,
    and riding then from them by leisure,°   *slowly*
With trumpets' sound most loyally,

   along the Court of Guard she went,
Who did conduct her Majesty
180   unto the Lord Chief General's tent,

Where she was feasted royally
   with dainties of most costly price.
And when that night approachéd nigh,
   Her Majesty, with sage advice,
185 In gracious manner then returnéd
   from the camp where she sojourned,
And when that she was safely set
   within her barge and passed away,
Her farewell then the trumpets sounded
190   and the cannons fast did play.

FINIS

JAMES ASKE

From Elizabetha Triumphans (1588)[†]

[*The Queen at Tilbury*]

Now came the day, the happy blissful day,
Wherein Aurora putting forth her head,
Her curled head with wiry hanging locks
Of brightest silver, whence did newly shine
5 Her clearest streams and never-darkened lights,
The morning gray, wherein the hovering larks
(Whose sweet shrill notes recording° harmony   *singing*
Resound within the heavenly creature's° ears)   *Aurora's*
Did notice give to wretched Phaeton's sire[1]
10 To harness up his fierce and furious steeds
To draw him thence unto his western home,
From whose clear beams, once in his chariot placed,
Did gladsome glimpse,[2] as bright as burnisht gold,
Shine all displayed upon the weighty globe.
15 On this same day, a fair and glorious day,
Came this our Queen (a Queen most like herself[3])
Unto her camp (now made a royal camp),
With all her troop (her court-like stately troop),
Not like to those who couch on stately down,[4]
20 But like to Mars, the god of fearful war,
And heaving oft to skies her warlike hands,

---

† Copy text: James Aske, *Elizabetha triumphans Conteyning the dammed practizes, that the diuelish popes of Rome haue vsed euer sithence her Highnesse first comming to the Crowne* (London: Thomas Gubbin and Thomas Newman, 1588; STC 847), D1v–D2v, D3v, D4r, D4v, E1r–E2r.
1. The sun god, Helios, who with a team draws the sun across the sky in a chariot.
2. Brief flash (subject of "shine" in the next line).
3. The Queen's motto was *Semper eadem* (Always the same).
4. Sleep on feather-beds.

Did make herself Bellona-like renowned.
The Lord Lieutenant[5] notice had thereof,
Who did forthwith prepare to entertain
25 The sacred goddess of this English soil.
The order how thus presently ensues.
On every side of that directest way
From blockhouse where she should be set on land[6]
Unto the outward quarter of the camp,
30 There rankéd were both arméd men and shot,°   cannons
With captains who of them had taken charge
To entertain their sacred general.[7]

*   *   *

The Earl of Leicester, with those officers
Which chosen were to govern in the field,
35 At water-side within the blockhouse stayed,
In readiness there to receive our Queen,
Who, landed now, doth pass along her way.
She thence some way still marching king-like on,
The cannons at the blockhouse were discharged,
40 The drums do sound, the fifes do yield their notes,
And ensigns[8] are displayed throughout the camp.
Our peerless Queen doth by her soldiers pass
And shows herself unto her subjects there.
She thanks them oft for their (of duty) pains,
45 And they again on knees do pray for her.
They couch[9] their pikes and bow their ensigns down,
Whenas their sacred royal Queen passed by,
In token of their loyal-bearéd hearts
To her alone, and none but only she.
50 A troop of brave and warlike horsemen did
(Conducted by Sir Roger Williams, Knight[1])
Meet with the Queen amid the way she came,
The half whereof, which was five hundred horse,
Most stately steeds, made complete° for the field,   fully equipped
55 With neighing sounds and foaméd champing bits,
Betrampling sore the ground whereas° they stood,   where
Attended on her sacred self. The rest,
Five hundred more (in naught to them unlike)
Before her train in stately order marched.
60 These jointly did with twenty hundred men,
Which footmen were, our gracious sovereign guard
Unto the house whereas she lay all night.
Whither once come, the horsemen turnéd back,
But all the rest, with her great sergeant,[2] did
65 Watch there all night, aloof° her royal court.   apart from

5. Robert Dudley, Earl of Leicester.
6. Arriving by boat, Elizabeth stayed in a house near the camp.
7. As commander-in-chief, Elizabeth was the highest of the general officers.
8. Flags designating military units.
9. Lower into fighting position.
1. Under Robert Devereux, Earl of Essex, Williams was the second in command of the cavalry at Tilbury.
2. Sergeant Major, a high-ranking field officer mentioned later in the poem.

The soldiers which placéd were far off
From that same way through which she passed along
Did hollo° oft, "The Lord preserve our Queen!"   *call out*
He happy was that could but see her coach,
70 The sides whereof beset with emeralds
And diamonds, with sparkling rubies red
In checker-wise by strange° invention,   *marvelous*
With curious knots embroideréd with gold,
Cast such a glimpse as if the heavenly place°   *palace*
75 Of Phoebus were by those his foaming steeds
On four round wheels drawn all along that way.
Thrice happy they who saw her stately self,
Who, Juno-like, drawn with her proudest birds,°   *peacocks*
Whose tails do hold her herdman's° hundred eyes,   *Argus's*
80 Passed along through quarters of the camp.

*   *   *

Now by the time that Phoebus had beyoked
His foaming steeds within their harnesses
To draw his bright and never-darkened lights,
The captains of the camp with all their men
85 Did from their quarters with their several charge
Come marching to the place prepared for arms.
When thither come was every officer,
A royal battle° royally was set   *mock battle*
With two most strong and brave battalions.

*   *   *

90 Which warlike show, with that Mars-thund'ring noise,
So ravishéd our princely Sovereign
(Addicted° only then to marshal prowess)³   *Devoted*
As that she doth (her train forbid therefro),⁴
Most bravely mounted on a stately steed,
95 With truncheon in her hand (not used thereto)
And with her none, except her Lieutenant
Accompanied with the Lord Chamberlain,⁵
Come marching towards this her marching fight,
In naught unlike the Amazonian queen,°   *Penthesilea*
100 Who beating down amain° the bloody Greeks   *with full force*
Thereby to grapple with Achilles stout,
Ev'n at the time when Troy was sore besieged.
Ne had that wight° (that thrice puissant wight)   *Hercules*
Who well performed twelve labors passing strange
105 A braver grace encount'ring with his foes
Than this our Queen in that her marching pace.
Thus comes our Queen (our thrice renownéd Queen),
A general beseeming such a camp.
Thus comes our guide, a princely careful guide,

3. Elizabeth had pursued a policy of peace until the mid-1580s.
4. Her attendants ordered to remain behind.
5. Henry Carey, Lord Hunsdon.

110   In warlike sort to see her warring men,
Who couchéd[6] had their strong defensive pikes
As if they were to fight at push thereof.
She nigh them come, they pitch[7] their fore-couched pikes,
And she stands still to see the battle set,
115   With joy to see her men to keep their ranks.
Now Voada,° once England's happy queen,   *Boadicia*
(Through Romans' flight by her constrained to fly,
Who making way amidst the slaughtered corps,
Pursued her foes with honor of the day)
120   With Vodice° her daughter (her too like,   *Voadicia*
Who, urging wounds,[8] with constant courage died)
Are now revived. Their virtues live (I say)
Through this our Queen, now England's happy Queen.

* * *

Her stateliness was so with Jove-showed[9] joined
125   As all there then did jointly joy and fear.
They joyed in that they see their ruler's love,
But feared lest that in aught they should offend
Against herself, the goddess of this land.
Thus causing joy and fear, she passéd thence
130   With cheerful heart, for this her late-viewed sight,
Unto the tent of her Lieutenant there,
Where ready were in readiness each thing
Which could be fit to entertain a Queen.

* * *

When Phoebus' lights were in the middle part
135   'Twixt east and west fast hasting to his home,
Our Sovereign (our sacred, blissful Queen)
Was ready to depart from out her camp,
Against whose coming every captain was
There pressed to show themselves in readiness
140   To do the will of their high general.
There might you see most brave and gallant men,
Who lately were beclad in Mars's clothes,
Enrankéd then in court-like costly suits,
Through whom did pass our Queen most Dido-like
145   (Whose stately heart doth so abound with love,
As thousand thanks it yields unto them all)
To water-side to take her royal barge.
Amidst the way (which was the outward ward
Of that her camp) her Sergeant Major stood
150   Among those squadrons which there then did ward.°   *guard her*
Her eyes were set so earnestly to view°   *look for him*
As, him unseen, she would not pass along,

6. Lowered into fighting position.
7. Order for battle.
8. Urging her soldiers to fight despite wounds.
9. Jove-like presence.

But calls him to her rich-built couch's sides
And thanking him (as oft before she had),
155 Did will him do this message from her mouth,
Deliveréd with full-of-wisdom words,
Which that it may not altogether be
(Through unfit words hewed from a stony wit)
Obliterated to my utter shame,
160 Ye sacred dames, ye seven-fold nymphs,° I mean,   *the Muses*
(Whose thicky groves resound your heavenly words,
Whence every art had first their several names)
Bebathe my temples with those pearl-like drops
Which fall amain° from that your silver stream,   *in abundance*
165 That through your aid my wit, now dulléd sore,
May quickened be with that your flowing art.
Then shall I write in these my lines too rude
Her royal speech (though nothing like her speech),
Which in effect was it that here ensues:

170 "We will them° know that now by proof we see   *the soldiers*
Their loyal hearts to us their lawful Queen,
For sure we are that none beneath the heav'ns
Have readier subjects to defend their right,
Which happiness we count to us as chief.
175 And though of love their duties crave no less,
Yet say to them that we in like regard
And estimate of this their dearest zeal,
If time of need shall ever call them forth
To dare in field their fierce and cruel foes,
180 Will be ourself their noted general.
Ne dear at all to us shall be our life,
Ne palaces or castles huge of stone
Shall hold as then our presence from their view,
But in the midst and very heart of them,
185 Bellona-like, we mean as then to march.
On common lot of gain or loss to both
They well shall see we reck shall then betide.[1]
And as for honor with most large rewards,
Let them not care; they common there shall be.
The meanest man, who shall deserve a mite,
190 A mountain shall for his desert° receive.   *reward*
And this our speech, and this our solemn vow,
In fervent love to those our subjects dear,
Say, Sergeant Major, tell them from ourself,
195 On kingly faith, we will perform it there."

Which said, she bowed her princely body down
And passéd thence unto the water side,
Where once embarged, the roaring cannons were
Discharged, both those which were on Tilb'ry hill

---

1. They will see plainly that we shall reckon the rewards of battle that come due so that every man
has an equal share of the gain or loss, according to his merit and not his rank.

200   And also those which at the blockhouse were.
      And there, even then, the fore° white-mantled air,   *formerly*
      From whence the sun shed forth his brightest beams,
      Did clothe itself with dark and dusky hue,
      And with thick clouds barred Phoebus' gladsome streams
205   From lightning then the earth with glorious show.
      It pours forth showers in great and often drops,
      Signs of the grief for her departure thence.

VICTORY CELEBRATIONS

Following the defeat of the Armada, Elizabeth wrote several works about that great turning point in English history. In a prayer of thanksgiving (published after her death), she took the stance of one of "the weakest sex," thanking God for His "strongest help" against the Spanish and all the other enemies who had threatened her life and the safety of her people during the 1580s. In a letter to James VI written shortly after the main battle in the English Channel, she was more pragmatic. Warning her ally not to allow any of his noblemen to betray her by giving safe harbor to Spanish castaways washed up on Scottish shores, she lashed out at Philip II for his "tyrannical, proud, and brainsick attempt" and predicted that it would lead to his ruin. In a song of triumph sung at a service commemorating the defeat of the Armada that she and the dignitaries of her Court attended at St. Paul's Cathedral on November 24, 1588, we see her in a more exultant mood. Implicitly comparing herself with other great women who sang songs to celebrate God's victories, including the Virgin Mary and the Old Testament heroines Miriam and Deborah, she calls herself God's "turtledove" and rejoices at having witnessed God's miraculous care for His "chosen people" in a time of great trial.

Not only at St. Paul's but also in churches throughout the country, parishioners held services of national thanksgiving. The Queen's official printer, Christopher Barker, published a special Armada Liturgy for use in the Church of England. It consisted of a "psalm" followed by a brief "collect," or prayer, designed to sum up various reflections appropriate to the occasion. For the psalm, the liturgist followed the sixteenth-century practice of gathering relevant scriptural passages and bringing them together in a verbal collage, with marginal notes to refer the reader to the original verses (see also "A Thanksgiving and Prayer" in Part Four). In this case, bits of the Bible were artfully arranged and elaborated to condemn the Spanish and praise the Queen. The liturgy was remarkably forthright in its attacks on the invaders, calling them "men bewitched by the Romish Antichrist, men drowned in idolatries and superstitions." Such liturgies show how closely public worship in the sixteenth century could be intertwined with the politics of nationalism.

Less exalted writers than the Queen and her liturgists also published celebrations of the English victory. A curious example is David Gwyn, who had good reason to rejoice in the outcome of the battle in his poem "In Commendation of Sir Francis Drake." Once a pirate, Gwyn had been taken prisoner by the Spanish and was serving as a galley slave aboard the *Diana* when it engaged the English fleet. Though Gwyn claims that he took advantage of his servile position to spy for the English, he was an adventurer and a self-promoter, and he may well have exaggerated his own exploits in hopes of financial reward. After the Armada had been driven off and he had escaped from the *Diana*, he traveled to Ireland to question Spanish survivors. There, he was accused of mishandling funds and fled rather than stand trial. Shady as his business practices may have been, Gywn reflected the popular adulation that attended heroes such as Sir Francis Drake and Lord Howard of Effingham on their return from the battle.

Once jubilation among the populace had subsided, poets began to elevate Elizabeth in a new way, treating her not only, as before, as a wise and merciful monarch who had brought peace to England and was beloved of her people, but also as a leader of substantial military prowess and international influence. A pillar poem that George Puttenham published in 1589 brought together for this purpose two well-known sources: the writings of the Italian humanist Petrarch, who in his *Triumph of Chastity* had established the pillar as a symbol of upright womanly virtue, and the personal emblem of the Spanish Emperor Charles V, who had symbolized his reign using an image of the Pillars of Hercules (or, as we now call them, either end of the Straits of Gibraltar), topped with royal crowns. Echoing Charles's claim to control the gateway from the Mediterranean, Puttenham's emblem envisioned England as the keeper of a new and greater seaway into the world. The poem proved prophetic since, over the next century, trade routes from Europe through the Netherlands and England to the Americas and the Far East gradually supplanted those centered in Spain.

QUEEN ELIZABETH

THE QUEEN IN VICTORY (1588)

Prayer of Thanksgiving for the Overthrow of the Spanish Navy[†]

Most omnipotent Creator, Redeemer, and Conserver. When it seemed most fit time to Thy worthy providence to bestow the workmanship of this world's globe with Thy rare judgment, Thou didst divide into four singular parts the form of all this mould,[1] which aftertime hath termed elements, all they serving to continue in orderly government of all the mass. Which all, when of Thy most singular bounty and never erst[2] seen care, Thou hast this year made serve for instruments to daunt our foes and to confound their malice. I most humbly, with bowed heart and bended knees, do render my humblest acknowledgements and lowliest thanks. And not the least for that the weakest sex hath been so fortified by Thy strongest help that neither my people need find lack by my weakness nor foreigners triumph at my ruin.

Such hath been Thy unwonted grace in my days, as though Satan hath neither made holiday in practicing for my life and state,[3] yet Thy mighty hand hath overspread both with the shade of Thy wings so that neither hath been overthrown nor received shame but abide with blessing, to Thy most glory and their greatest ignominy. For which, Lord, of Thy mere goodness, grant us grace to be hourly thankful and ever mindful, and if it may please Thee to pardon my request, give us Thy continuance in my days of like goodness that my years never see change of such grace to me, but especially to this my kingdom, which Lord grant (for Thy Son's sake) may flourish many ages after my end. Amen.

---

† Copy text: Thomas Sorocold, *Supplications of saints A booke of prayers* (London: Nicholas Bourne, 1612; STC 22932), N7r–N8v.
1. Earth.
2. Before.
3. Although Satan has not ceased to work against my life and realm.

[Letter to James VI on the Fate of the Armada]†

August 1588

Now may appear, my dear brother, how malice joined with might strikest to make a shameful end to a villainous beginning, for by God's singular favor, having their fleet well beaten in our narrow seas and pressing with all violence to achieve some watering place to continue their pretended invasion, the winds have carried them to your coasts, where I doubt not they shall receive small succor and less welcome, unless those lords[1] (that so traitors-like would belie their own Prince and promise another King relief) in your name be suffered to live at liberty to dishonor you, peril you, and advance some other (which God forbid you suffer them live to do). Therefore I send you this gentleman,[2] a rare young man and a wise, to declare unto you my full opinion in this great cause as one that never will abuse you to serve my own turn, nor will you do aught that myself would not perform if I were in your place.

You may assure yourself that, for my part, I doubt no whit but that all this tyrannical, proud, and brainsick attempt will be the beginning, though not the end, of the ruin of that King that, most unkingly, even in midst of treating[3] peace, begins this wrongful war. He hath procured my greatest glory that meant my sorest wrack, and hath so dimmed the light of his sunshine that who[4] hath a will to obtain shame, let them keep his forces company. But for all this, for yourself's sake, let not the friends of Spain be suffered to yield them force, for though I fear not in the end the sequel, yet if by having them unhelped you may increase the English hearts unto you, you shall not do the worst deed for your behalf.[5] For if aught should be done, your excuse will play the *boiteux* if you make not sure work with the likely men to do it.[6] Look well unto it, I beseech you.

The necessity of this matter makes my scribbling the more speedy, hoping that you will measure my good affection with the right balance of my actions, which to you shall be ever such as I have professed, not doubting of the reciproque of your behalf,[7] according as my last messenger unto you hath at length signified, for the which I render you a million of grateful thanks together for the late general prohibition to your subjects not to foster nor aid our general foe. Of which I doubt not the observation, if the ringleaders be safe in your hands. As knoweth God, who ever have you in His blessed keeping, with many happy years of reign.

Your most assured, loving sister and cousin,

ELIZABETH R

---

†   Copy text: *Elizabeth I: Collected Works*, ed. Leah S. Marcus, Janel Mueller, and Mary Beth Rose (Chicago and London: University of Chicago Press, 2000), 357–58. Reprinted by permission of the University of Chicago Press. Copyright © 2000 by the University of Chicago.
1.   Scottish noblemen who favored a return to Roman Catholicism.
2.   Sir Robert Sidney, the younger brother of Sir Philip Sidney.
3.   Negotiating. Philip had continued peace negotiations with England while preparing for war.
4.   Whoever.
5.   James will benefit himself by helping the English now, perhaps a subtle reference to the possibility of his being named Elizabeth's successor; *yield them force*: let not any in Scotland join the Spanish troops or give them aid; *the sequel*: what might happen next.
6.   If anything is done to help the Spanish, your excuse will be unacceptable unless you suppress the noblemen most likely to aid them; *boiteux*: cripple.
7.   Being confident of your reciprocal natural affection.

[Song on the Armada Victory][†]

A song made by her Majesty and sung before her at her coming from
     Whitehall to Paul's[1] through Fleetstreet in *Anno Domini* 1588.
     Sung in December after the scattering of the Spanish Navy.

Look and bow down Thine ear, O Lord;
From Thy bright sphere behold and see
Thy handmaid and Thy handiwork
Amongst Thy priests, offering to Thee
5 Zeal for incense reaching the skies,
Myself and scepter, sacrifice.[2]

My soul ascend His holy place,
Ascribe Him strength and sing Him praise,
For He refraineth° princes' spirits   *restrains*
10 And hath done wonders in my days.
He made the winds and waters rise
To scatter all mine enemies.

This Joseph's Lord and Israel's God,
The fiery pillar and day's cloud,[3]
15 That saved His saints from wicked men
And drenched the honor of the proud,
And hath preserved in tender love
The spirit of His turtle dove.[4]

Finis.

THE CHURCH OF ENGLAND

From The Armada Liturgy (1588)[†]

A Psalm of Thanksgiving

O come hither and hearken, all ye that fear God, and we will tell you
what He hath done for our souls.[1]

For we may not hide His benefits from our children, and to the generation to come and to all people we will show the praises of the Lord, His
power also, and His wonderful works that He hath done for us.[2]

---

† Copy text: National Maritime Museum, Greenwich, MS SNG/4.
1. St. Paul's Cathedral. Bertrand Whitehead argues that the song, which was set to music by William
   Byrd, was first sung during a commemorative service at St. Paul's on November 24, 1588 (186–92).
2. Rather than incense, Elizabeth offers herself and her queenship as a sacrifice to God (cf. Romans
   12.1).
3. God's presence with the Israelites, when he led them out of slavery in Egypt toward the promised
   land, was manifest in a pillar of cloud by day and a pillar of fire by night (Exodus 13.21).
4. Steven May notes that this may be an allusion to Psalm 74.19, where the psalmist prays that God
   "give not the soul of Thy turtle dove unto the beast" (*Selected Works*, 23).
† Copy text: *A Psalme and Collect of thankesgiuing, not vnmeet for this present time to be said or sung
   in Churches* (London: Christopher Barker, 1588; STC 16520), A2r–A4v.
1. Psalm 66.16; marginal glosses in the copy text do not always correspond exactly to the verses cited.
2. Psalm 78.4.

When the kings and rulers of the earth and nations round about us furiously raged and took counsel together against God and against His anointed,[3]

When men of another devotion than we be (men bewitched by the Romish Antichrist, men drowned in idolatries and superstitions) hated us deadly and were maliciously set against us for our profession of the Word of God and the blessed Gospel of our Savior Christ,[4]

They cast their heads together with one consent; they took their common counsel, and were confederate, and imagined mischief against Thy people, O Lord God.[5]

* * *

They came furiously upon us, as it were roaring and ramping lions, purposing to devour us and to swallow us up.[6] They approached near unto us, even to eat up our flesh.[7]

They said in their hearts, "Let us make havoc of them altogether; let us root them out, that they be no more a people and that the name of England may be no more had in remembrance."[8]

And surely their coming was so sudden (their multitude, power, and cruelty so great) that, had we not believed verily to see the goodness of God and put our trust in His defense and protection, they might have utterly destroyed us.[9]

* * *

The Lord arose, and took the cause (which indeed was His own) into His own hands, and fought against them that fought against us.[1]

The Lord scattered them with His winds; He confounded and disappointed their devices and purposes of joining their powers together against us.[2]

The angel of the Lord persecuted them, brought them into dangerous, dark, and slippery places, where they (wandering long to and fro) were consumed with hunger, thirst, cold, and sickness.[3] The sea swallowed the greatest part of them.[4]

And so the Lord repressed the rage and fury of our cruel enemies (intending nothing but bloodshed and murder), and turned the mischief which they purposed against us upon their own heads, and delivered and saved us, who were as sheep appointed to the shambles and slaughter.[5]

3. Psalm 2.1–2; the anointed in the biblical psalm refers to the King of Israel but here to Elizabeth.
4. Matthew 10.22, 24; *another . . . we be*: Psalm 144.7, which speaks of the enemies of God's people as "strangers"; *Romish Antichrist*: Pope Sixtus V; *idolatries and superstitions*: Psalm 115.4, a reference to idols of silver and gold; *hated us deadly*: Psalm 55.3.
5. Psalm 83.3; a marginal gloss refers to the Council of Trent, which met from 1543 to 1563, and to the Catholic League in France, which was active in the 1580s, both of which solidified the Roman Catholic opposition to Protestantism, the first theologically and the second politically.
6. Psalm 56.1–2; *They came . . . as lions*: Psalms 22.13; 17.12.
7. Psalm 27.2.
8. Psalm 83.4; the marginal gloss acknowledges that the biblical text says "that the name of Israel [not England] may be no more had in remembrance"; *Let them . . . altogether*: Psalm 74.8.
9. Psalms 124.1–3; 94.17; *coming . . . great*: Psalm 55.3; *believed . . . God*: Psalm 27.13.
1. Psalm 35.1; *The Lord . . . hands*: Psalm 10.12,14.
2. Psalms 33.10; 35.4; *The Lord . . . winds*: Psalms 11.6; 18.12–13; 48.7; a storm, rather than the English navy, destroyed much of the Spanish fleet.
3. Such words often describe the persecuted people of God (cf. Psalm 107.4–5), but here are used to depict England's enemy; *angel . . . places*: Psalms 35.5–6; 83.15.
4. Exodus 15.4–5, a reference to the destruction of Pharaoh's army in the Red Sea. Only sixty-seven ships from the Spanish navy and a third of the men survived; many perished in storms off the coasts of Ireland and Scotland.
5. Psalm 44.11, 22; *Lord . . . heads*: Psalms 7.16; 35.8; 9.15–17; 18.17; *shambles*: slaughterhouse or meat market.

This was the Lord's doing, and it is marvelous in our (and in our enemies') sight and in the eyes of all people, and all that see it shall say, "This is the Lord's work."[6]

God is our King of old.[7] The help that is done by sea and by land is His.[8]

It is God that giveth deliverance unto princes, and that rescueth our Queen from the hurtful sword, and saveth her from all dangers and perils.[9]

We will therefore give thanks, whom the Lord hath redeemed and delivered from the hand of the enemy.[1]

✳   ✳   ✳

A Collect of Thanksgiving

We cannot but confess, O Lord God, that the late terrible intended invasion of most cruel enemies was sent from Thee to the punishment of our sins, of our pride, our covetousness, our excess in meats and drinks, our security, our ingratitude, and our unthankfulness towards Thee for so long peace and other Thy infinite blessings continually poured upon us, and to the punishment of other our innumerable and most grievous offences continually committed against Thy divine Majesty. And indeed our guilty consciences looked for (even at that time) the execution of Thy terrible justice upon us, so by us deserved.

But Thou, O Lord God (who knowest all things), knowing that our enemies came not of justice to punish us for our sins committed against Thy divine Majesty (whom they by their excessive wickedness have offended and continually do offend, as much or more than we) but that they came with most cruel intent and purpose to destroy us, our cities, towns, country, and people, and utterly to root out the memory of our nation from off the earth forever, and withal wholly to suppress Thy holy Word and blessed Gospel of Thy dear Son, our Savior Jesus Christ, which they (being drowned in idolatries and superstitions) do hate most deadly and us likewise, only for the profession of the same and not for any offences against Thy divine Majesty or injuries done to themselves.

Wherefore it hath pleased Thee, O heavenly Father, in Thy justice to remember Thy mercies towards us, turning our enemies from us and that dreadful execution which they intended towards us into a fatherly and most merciful admonition of us, to the amendment of our lives, and to execute justice upon our cruel enemies, turning the destruction which they intended against us upon their own heads. For the which the same Thy most gracious protection of us and all other Thy graces (without all our desert) continually and most plenteously poured upon our Church, our Queen, our realm and people of England, we beseech Thee add and pour also the grace of gratitude and thankfulness into our hearts that we (never forgetting but bearing in perpetual memory this Thy merciful protection and deliverance of us from the malice, force, fraud, and cruelty of our enemies and all other Thy benefits most plenteously poured upon us) may enjoy the continuance of Thy fatherly goodness towards our church, our Queen, our realm and people of England, and continually magnify Thy holy and most glorious name; which we do beseech Thee, O heavenly Father, to

6. Psalm 64.9; *This was . . . sight*: Psalm 118.23; *eyes . . . see it*: Psalm 107.42.
7. Psalm 74.12.
8. Psalms 107.23–25; 74.12–13.
9. Psalm 144.10; the marginal gloss notes that the biblical citation is to David rather than to Elizabeth.

grant to us, most unworthy sinners, for the worthiness of Thy dear Son, our Savior Jesus Christ, to whom with Thee and the Holy Ghost, one God of most glorious Majesty, be all honor and glory, world without end. Amen.

DAVID GWYN

In Commendation of Sir Francis Drake
(August 18, 1588)[†]

O noble knight, O worthy wight,
 O prince of navigation,
In martial affairs is thy delight
 for country's preservation.
5 Thy noble fame like Phoebus's trim°   *guise*
 in all the world is spread.
As eclipse the sun and moon doth dim,
 so Spaniards do thee dread.
Thy valiant acts and worthy heart
10 deserves eternal fame;
Thy knowledge and astrology's art
 doth verify the same.
Thy happy course that thou didst run
 unto the western land[1]
15 Did make the Spaniards all to shun
 as fearing of thy hand.
Santo Domingo makes great moan,
 Cartagena eke° doth cry,[2]   *also*
The western isles do greatly groan,
20 thy force hath been so nigh.
Calais likewise doth greatly fear,
 with reason thereunto.
The narrow straits[3] do daily care
 because thou art their foe.
25 Thy enterprise hath been so high
 that Turks could not compare,
Nor with his galleys come so nigh,
 which makes them all to fear.
"The Grand English," they thee do call,
30 "of famous good report."
The Spaniards and the Portingal°   *Portuguese*
 to England will resort
To serve the Queen and thee, good Drake,
 for thy good famous acts.

1. Psalm 107.2.
† Copy text: David Gwyn, *Certaine English verses . . . Presented to the Queenes most excellent Maiestie in the Parke at Saint Iames on Sunday the xviii. of August 1588* (London: Richard Hudson, [1588]; STC 12556), A6v–A8r.
1. Drake's piracy in the New World.
2. In 1585, Drake sacked the Spanish ports of Santo Domingo and Cartagena in the Caribbean, helping push Philip II toward sending the Armada.
3. The Straits of Magellan, through which Drake first sailed in 1578 when he circumnavigated the globe, or perhaps the "narrow seas" off Calais.

35 The Spanish king they will forsake
   with England to compact.
 Thou art so dread as God is feared
   in southern coast and land.
 The Spaniard daily shakes his beard[4]
40   and fears thy mighty hand.
 Therefore, good worthy Drake,
   serve thou thy sovereign Queen,
 And make the Spanish foe to quake
   and English force be seen.
45 For help and aid thou shalt not want,
   thy virtuous Queen is bent;°   *inclined to you*
 Money and victuals is not scant
   and men will not repent.[5]
 If thou wilt follow victory,
50   as first thou didst begin,
 All Protestants will pray for thee
   and for our gracious Queen.
 The Spaniards brag and make great boast,
   as thou dost partly know;
55 A huge great fleet they make in haste,
   as letters mine did show,
 Wherein I writ a warning good
   to thee and to the Queen,
 Rehearsing all both bad and good
60   that in their fleet was seen.
 Also I wrote the sum of men
   as near as I could learn
 And sent it by an Englishman,
   whereby thou might'st discern
65 To know thy foes and what they be,
   all kind of generation,
 The dukes and earls in their degree
   rehearséd by relation.
 Their ships and force I daily wrote
70   and all their preparation;
 To name them all I misséd not,
   as void of desperation.[6]
 And thus, good noble knight,
   my simple verse I end.
75 Unto thy hand, good worthy wight,
   my help I do commend
 And with all English Christian men
   to pray for me, poor Gwyn
 That lieth in bondage and in chain
80   with popish Spanish king.

---

4. Drake was said to have "singed the beard" of the King of Spain, when he attacked Cadiz in 1587 and destroyed nearly thirty Spanish ships.
5. His sailors will not abandon him.
6. While held captive in Spain, Gwyn recklessly spied on and reported the Spanish military buildup, with no concern for his own safety.

GEORGE PUTTENHAM

From The Art of English Poesy (1589)[†]

Her Majesty Resembled to the Crowned Pillar

Ye must read upward.[1]

	Is bliss with immortality.	
	Her trimmest top of all ye see	
	Garnish the crown.	
	Her just renown	
5	Chapter and head.[2]	
	Parts that maintain°	*support*
	And womanhead,°	*womanhood*
	Her maiden reign	
	In- te- gri- ty.	
10	In ho- nor and	
	With ve- ri- ty	
	Her roundness° stand	*honesty*
	Strengthen the state.	
	By their increase	
15	With- out de- bate,	
	Concord and peace	
	Of her sup- port.	
	They be the base	
	With steadfastness,	
20	Virtue and grace	
	Stay and comfort,	
	Of Albion's° rest.	*England's*
	The sound Pillar	
	And seen a- far	
25	Is plainly expressed	
	Tall, stately, and straight,	
	By this no- ble por- trait,	

The Wit and Wisdom of the Queen

In praising Elizabeth, Jane Seager, sister of the court painter William Seager, took an even more ingenious approach than the one employed by Puttenham. In a manuscript book given to the Queen as a New Year's gift in 1589, the writer included ten poems, each with ten lines and each imitating and praising one of the ten Sibyls (or women prophets) of classical antiquity who were said to have foreseen the coming of Christ. In the poem "Libica," reprinted here, the Sibyl in question foretells Christ's special blessing on the Queen, the English

---

[†] Copy text: George Puttenham, *The arte of English poesie* (London: Richard Field, 1589; STC 20519.5), N2v.

1. In giving advice about the form in the same volume, Puttenham recommends lines of six to eight metrical feet for the base and head and four for the shaft. Here, however, he uses three or four feet at the top and bottom and two for the shaft.

2. The capital, often elaborately decorated (or "garnished"), and the plainer topmost piece.

Church, and its people. The book itself is a work of art and learning. Each poem has been transcribed into an early system of shorthand invented by Dr. Timothy Bright, and the entire collection is bound in sumptuous purple fabric, with miniatures painted on glass adorning its front and back covers. Taking virginity as a theme, the poet sees herself, the Sibyls, the Blessed Virgin Mary, and the Queen as members of one enduring community, that of chaste and devout women.

The stress on ingenuity and wisdom also appears in other works presented to the Queen in this period. In July 1591, she traveled to London to visit her Vice Chamberlain, Sir Thomas Heneage. Among the entertainments that he provided was the recitation of a story known as "A Peddler's Tale" by an unknown author. It seems to have served as an elaborate prologue to the usual gift-giving that accompanied such visits, as we can tell from the peddler's remark at the end that he is come "to tell you this idle tale and show you my foolish trifles." In the story itself, he trades in both merchandise and gossip, engaging an unnamed noblewoman in a debate over the wise and foolish uses of the tongue. The lady—whose replies are so swift and penetrating that they daunt the clever peddler—is clearly a figure for the Queen. After disparaging foreigners and praising true religion and good morals, he compliments her and leaves her to give the last word to the assembled guests, which is to serve God sincerely, love their Prince truly, act justly and kindly, and behave honestly. The Queen would have approved.

JANE SEAGER

From The Divine Prophesies of the Ten Sibyls (1589)[†]

To the Queen's Most Excellent Majesty

Sacred Majesty, may it please those most gracious eyen[1] (acquainted with all perfections and above others most excellent) to vouchsafe to make worthy of their princely view the handiwork of a maiden, your Majesty's most faithful subject. It containeth (renowned Sovereign) the divine prophecies of the ten Sibyls (virgins) upon the birth of our Savior Christ by a most blessed virgin, of which most holy faith your Majesty being chief defendress[2] and a virgin also, it is a thing (as it were) preordained of God that this treatise, written by a maiden your subject, should be only devoted unto your most sacred self. The which (albeit I have graced both with my pen and pencil and late practice in that rare art of charactery, invented by Dr. Bright,[3] yet accounting it to lack all grace without your Majesty's most gracious acceptance) I humbly present the same with hearty prayers for your Majesty.

JANE SEAGER

---

† Copy text: British Library MS Add. 10037,1589, fol. 3v.
1. Eyes.
2. One of Elizabeth's official titles was "Defender of the Faith."
3. The shorthand system Seager used was invented by Dr. Timothy Bright, who published *Charactery, An Art of Short, Swift, and Secret Writing by Character* in 1588; *pencil*: a small paintbrush used for miniatures; Seager's manuscript book includes miniatures on the front and back covers.

Libica

Behold, behold, the day shall come whenas°   when
A joyful Prince, shining upon His seed,
His Church with graces shall illuminate
And clear the darkness which through sin was bred.
5 He shall unlock the unclean lips of them
That guilty are, and being true and just,
He shall His people love. But for His foes
They shall not come nor stand before His sight:
He shall indue° with blessings from above   endow
10 The Queen, His Church, the more for our behove.°   necessity

[*Concluding Address "To Queen Elizabeth"*]

Lo, thus in brief (most sacred Majesty)
I have set down whence all these Sibyls were;
What they foretold or saw, we see and hear
And profit reap by all their prophecy.
5 Would God I were a Sibyl to divine°   prophesy
In worthy verse your lasting happiness.
Then only I should be characters[4]
Of that which worlds with wonder might define.
But what need I to wish, when you are such,
10 Of whose perfections none can write too much.

ANONYMOUS

A Peddler's Tale that was Told to Our Majesty's Grace at Sir Thomas Heneage's House in London (July 1, 1591)[†]

Most honorable ladies, whom lords love to please and the world seeks to serve, as it hath pleased you to command me to open my pack, so you must be contented I follow my property, which is like a peddler to utter my words as well as my wares, but the one good cheap (though the other more dear).[1] And yet this light merchandise, fetched but from conceit and vented most by breath, proves more profitable to traffic with than gold of India or the spices of Molucca.[2] I will not meddle with the religious (who are to be reverenced) but the merchant with his oaths, the lawyer with his brawls, the courtier with his flattery will prove this without argument.

---

4. A reference both to letters and to Bright's shorthand system.
† Copy text: Ms. at John Rylands University Library of Manchester. Adapted from Marion Colthorpe's article in *The Reed Newsletter*. Transcription by Marion Colthorpe and Susan M. Felch. See also Marion Colthorpe, "A Pedlar's Tale to Queen Elizabeth I," *Records of Early English Drama* 10.2 (1985): 1–5; this essay was written before a complete version of the Tale was discovered. Heneage was Vice-Chamberlain of the royal household and a member of the Privy Council.
1. One set of goods, his words, are cheap; the other, his merchandise, is expensive; *property*: particular profession.
2. The Spice Islands, located in the eastern archipelago, near India; *conceit*: the imagination of the mind; *vented*: sold.

And I that have passed through a great part of the world (not like a rogue I would be thought, but as a wanderer), I must confess have found [in] all countries, whatsoever be the matter, the tongue makes the man to seem wise when he is not. I saw it in Flanders to show true when he is not; I found it in France [to] seem noble when he is not; I saw it in Spain to show honest when he is not; I proved it in Italy to seem holy when he is not; I found it in Rome—more particulars I will not speak of lest I offend my own country.

But this is very manifest through the whole world: this little busy merchant (this tongue I tell you of) is the readiest utterer I know of wares he is trusted with, whether they be good or bad, true or false, whether they come from the head or from the heart as imaginations and thoughts, devices and determinations with their infinite appurtenances,[3] which prove (I may tell you) full costly things both for the buyer and the seller, the utterer and the receiver. And yet these be the great wares of the world, whereof for the most part the tongue is the merchant.

Which, when I found and withal perceived that nowadays men were more esteemed for their many tongues than their good conditions and it was rather looked how well he could speak than how honest he should be, drawn to care for my profit (which all the world cares for), I cast myself to be a traveler, which belongs to my trade, and to go into divers[4] countries to learn divers languages, thereby to be more acceptable. So passing through many places, I came at last into Greece, the ancient seat both of the best orators and the best philosophers in the world. There, wandering through a wilderness to seek out near the sea where old Athens was situate, I espied suddenly a lady whose looks was to be reverenced more than Pallas as she is pictured. Whom, when I approached and had humbly saluted, I besought to know the way of which I told her I had lost.

"So do many," quoth she, "that seek unknown ways and likewise that follow their own ways. But what brought you hither?"

"My desire," quoth I, "to see and withal to be satisfied."

"No worse guide," quoth she, "upon earth (except it be guided from heaven). Hast thou not seen desire pictured both blind and flying to show his error and his haste, besides unbridled to show how hardly it can be stayed?"[5]

"But, Madam," quoth I, "is this the place where renowned Athens was seated and the wisest men in the world were settled?"

"Men called wise," said she, "had here once some being. But which of them all thinkest thou was the wisest?"

Then thinking to speak wisely, I told her, "Diogenes, that saw nothing in the world whereof he had any need."

"Who need nothing in the world," quoth she, "the world hath no need of, but it most needeth wise men."

Then I reckoned up unto her all the most notable captains and orators of Greece that with their wit and their words bare most rule in the world and most sway with the people.

"What were those," quoth she, "but bubbles, and what are they but dust?"

At last I showed her how Plato and Aristotle were reputed most wise.

"And why?" quoth she. "Because the one wrote of God, which he knew

---

3. Those parts that belong together; *little busy merchant*: See also James 3.5–12, where the tongue is described as a "little member" and a "fire."
4. Several; *good conditions*: good character.
5. How difficult it is to restrain and guide desire.

not, and the other of virtues, which he had not, even as Tully taught his sons the offices which he used not?"

"But, Madam," quoth I, "the books they have left behind them make many both more learned and more wise."

"Some," quoth she, "be more learned but never the more wise, and some more wise but never the more virtuous. And surely philosophers be but as sundry other professors, pretending that they be not. Truth is that they shoot at, and truth is that they miss. I could resemble them to divers[6] but best to lovers and priests: lovers to be constant and priests to be holy. This is their profession and likewise their praise, but how be they found? the one unstable, the other profane."

Then questioning with me of my trade and my travel, finding her so wise [I] began to shrink back, which she perceiving and demanding the cause, I durst not but confess it was both for shame and for fear.

"These be two things," quoth she, "worse becoming a man: such need to be ashamed as care too little for their honesty, and they be found afraid that care too much for their life."

"Madam," quoth I, "I trust to be found none of those. My shame groweth to show what poor occupation I am of and my fear to talk with so wise a lady."

"Wise?" quoth she and smiled. "How can women be wise when all men that live with them be so foolish? Thy fear is very vain and thy shame much worse, to be ashamed of thy trade thou gettest thy living by. There is no occupation evil but that which is evil used. Thou art a peddler and sellest thy trifles very dear, but many greater than thou art sell themselves too good cheap[7] and sometime for naught. But," quoth she, "hadst thou no other errand hither but to seek men that be dead and places that be gone? Athens is so wasted as no man can tell well where it was."

"Yes, Madam," quoth I, "in truth I have gone through many countries, not so much to see the places I knew not as to learn the languages I had not."

"It is not so good," quoth she, "to go abroad to learn languages as to tarry at home and learn wit. And learn this of me: neither vices be lost nor virtues be gotten very much by wandering, though it be, again, there is no places that a man may not get both in. But it is the mind and not the tongue should make a man to be esteemed."

"But Lady," quoth I, "a good tongue is thought one of the best things in the world."

"It is," quoth she, "as it is ordered.[8] But I think tongues be (as men say women be) needful evils."

With this I replied, "Can there be anything, Madam, more needful than to speak well?"

"No," quoth she, "so it be no more than is needful. But to speak well is most rare, to speak wisely most hard, to speak true most honest, and to speak nothing most safe."

"This," quoth I, "I will not forget, both often to think on and to thank your Excellency for."

"Alas," quoth she, "poor fool, what a phrase is this of flattery. There is no excellency but in perfection and no perfection but in heaven."

---

6. I could compare them to many others.
7. At too low a price.
8. Restrained and controlled; see also James 3.2: "If any man sin not in word, he is a perfect man and able to bridle all the body."

"Madam," quoth I, "I meant not to offend you but to thank you."

"And I," quoth she, "meant rather to speak truth than to please you. But because I believe the best of your meaning and think nothing better in the world than to be thankful, to give you more cause I will give you this counsel, not hard, but most needful: leave in time your wandering and return to your natural dwelling. Think, as birds be content with their own nests and conies[9] with their own caves, so should men be with their own countries, where it is best for every man to be that is worthy to be anywhere. There serve God sincerely, love thy Prince truly, do in the world justly, deal with neighbors kindly, and behave thyself honestly. So shalt thou live and die happily."

With this away she went, I think into the air. And I, to follow her advice, came home as fast as I could. And by chance am come hither to tell you this idle tale and show you my foolish trifles, which done I shall depart, wishing well, ladies, to you all and best to the best of you, praying you when you come home and shall think of my tale, to think of it as a cipher that serves for something: that it signify nothing.

A RETURN TO SUMMER PROGRESSES

In the 1590s, after the threat of invasion and assassination had subsided, Elizabeth resumed her rambling journeys into the countryside. During the previous decade, she had confined her travel to relatively safe areas near London. Now, she ventured further abroad to mingle with subjects who rarely had an opportunity to see her. There was special need to reassure them with her presence. The war with Spain dragged on, causing taxes to rise; times were hard, and people were uneasy. Since she was getting old, many worried that she might die and leave her noblemen to battle over her successor. Traveling to the provinces allowed her to address such concerns, gauge the mood of the nation, strengthen bonds with important members of her landed aristocracy, and demonstrate that she was still very much in command.

At first glance, one of the noblemen selected to receive the honor of an extended visit was an odd choice. Edward Seymour, first Earl of Hertford, had a good pedigree; he was the eldest son of Protector Somerset, who had for a time been the most powerful man in the kingdom during the reign of Edward VI. The Earl was also a staunch Protestant, a stance that would normally have recommended him. But in the early 1560s, he had run afoul of Elizabeth by going behind her back to marry Lady Katherine Grey, the younger sister of Lady Jane Grey. Since Katherine was, by some reckonings, next in line to the English throne after Elizabeth herself, to marry her was to position oneself to become the next King of England. When Elizabeth found out what Hertford had done, she was furious. If she had learned one thing from her experiences during the reign of her sister Mary, it was that governing with an attractive successor waiting in the wings was dangerous. For ignoring protocol and placing her in that position without consultation, she sent Hertford and his bride to prison, where they languished for the better part of a decade, first in the Tower of London and then in private households. Only after Katherine died in 1568 was Hertford released. In 1571, Elizabeth remitted some of his fines and allowed him to return to Court, where he performed minor duties over the years. But she never entrusted him with a major post.

To all appearances, he had learned his lesson. He lived quietly on his estates and, for many years, made no further effort to meddle in court politics. The

9. Rabbits.

affair was not entirely settled, however, since Katherine had given birth to two male children, and they now had claims of their own to the crown. Although Elizabeth had refused to acknowledge Seymour's marriage and had taken legal steps to have his sons declared bastards, some at Court still regarded them as rightful successors to the crown. Hertford did well to mind his behavior.

As Elizabeth planned the summer progress of 1591, however, conditions favored a further thaw in relations. In need of wealthy supporters to help balance the budget and wage the ongoing war with Spain, Elizabeth graced Hertford with a visit to his opulent estates at Elvetham. It did not hurt that the Earl had taken as his second wife the sister of the most celebrated military hero of the day, Lord Howard of Effingham, commander of the English navy in the battle against the Spanish Armada. With this connection in mind, Hertford set out to entertain the Queen in ways that stressed his family's glorious past and promising future. Not only were the entertainments at Elvetham unusually lavish and costly—involving the creation of an artificial lake, a fort, a fantastic island, a small ship, and a large array of pavilions and banqueting facilities—but they were also among the most beautifully written of the age. They reflect many of the literary forms developed by the "new poets," whose accomplishments in the last two decades of Elizabeth's reign were among its most important legacies to later generations.

On the first day, Hertford's poets played on the Queen's fondness for mythology by representing her in several classical guises: as Venus, attended by the Graces and the Hours; as Jupiter, visiting the hut of the humble Philemon; as the "Queen of Second Troy"; and as Augusta, ruler of an empire worthy of comparison with ancient Rome. The second and third days' festivities turned to a figure made popular by Sir Walter Ralegh: Elizabeth seen as Cynthia, goddess of the moon and "the wide ocean's empress." Having built an artificial pond in the shape of a crescent moon, Hertford reminded spectators of Lord Howard's exploits by staging a mock battle centered on an island shaped like a ship (which stood for England and its new, light fighting vessels) and one shaped like a snail (which represented Spain, with its more cumbersome galleons). Yet the pageants did not simply represent the nation's new strength as a sea power. In a "Plowman's Song" and a skit about the love of the forest god Sylvanus for the sea nymph Neaera, the unnamed poets who devised the festivities suggested that England's future lay in sorting out the relationship between its traditional strength as a rural agricultural producer and its promise as an up-and-coming center for world sea-trade. On the fourth and final day, the entertainments turned to literary figures for the Queen made fashionable by Edmund Spenser: the shepherdess Eliza and the Fairy Queen.

The festivities accomplished what Hertford had hoped they would, a return to royal favor. Unfortunately, however, his new amity with the Queen was brief. In 1595, having screwed up his courage to petition to have the validity of his marriage to Katherine Grey affirmed and his sons declared legitimate, he was again sent to the Tower. This time, however, his stay was brief, and by 1602, he was back in the Queen's good graces, serving her at the end of his life as Lord Governor of Somerset and Wiltshire.

In the summer of 1592, Elizabeth again set out on progress, this time traveling north and west through Berkshire, Oxfordshire, and Gloucestershire. The journey was notable because, on her return, she stopped in Oxford, making only the third visit to a university of her entire reign. She spent several days listening to lectures and disputations between students (one of which was rather too long, she thought), and in the hours not taken up with such standard classroom activities, she attended a sermon, a "medical demonstration," and the performance of a Roman comedy. The Latin speech to the university that she delivered at her departure was short and pithy, and it had an edge. As befitted an accomplished politician, she began by lowering expectations, apologizing for her poor Latin on the grounds that "the cares of ruling are so weighty that they tend to dull the mind rather than sharpen the memory." She then went on to deliver a polished oration on the duties of subjects to God and their monarch. In tone and approach, it was very different from the speech that she had given nearly thirty years earlier at Cambridge (which appears in Part Two). Not only had her bearing before men of learning changed, but her struggles to overcome social turmoil and religious dissent had clearly altered her assessment of the value— and the dangers—of higher education.

ANONYMOUS

The Entertainment at Elvetham (1591)[†]

The Proem[1]

Before I declare the just time or manner of her Majesty's arrival and entertainment at Elvetham, it is needful (for the reader's better understanding of every part and process in my discourse) that I set down as well the conveniency of the place as also the sufficing, by art and labor, of what the place in itself could not afford on the sudden for receipt of so great a majesty and so honorable a train.[2]

Elvetham House being situate in a park but of two miles in compass or thereabouts, and of no great receipt as being none of the Earl's chief mansion houses, yet for the desire he had to show his unfeigned love and loyal duty to her most gracious Highness, purposing to visit him in this her late progress, whereof he had to understand by the ordinary guess as also by his honorable good friends in Court, near to her Majesty,[3] his Honor with all expedition set artificers a-work, to the number of three hundred, many days before her Majesty's arrival to enlarge his house with new rooms and offices. Whereof I omit to speak how many were destined to the offices of the Queen's household and will only make mention of other such buildings as were raised on the sudden, fourteen score off[4] from the house on a hillside within the said park, for entertainment of nobles, gentlemen, and others whatsoever.

First there was made a room of estate[5] for the nobles and, at the end thereof, a withdrawing place for her Majesty. The outsides of the walls were all covered with boughs and clusters of ripe hazel nuts, the insides with arras, the roof of the place with works[6] of ivy leaves, the floor with sweet herbs and green rushes.

Near adjoining unto this were many offices new builded, as namely spicery, lardery, chandry, wine cellar, ewery,[7] and pantry, all which were

---

† Copy text: *The Honorable Entertainement gieuen to the Queenes Maiestie in Progresse, at Eluetham in Hampshire, by the Right Honorable the Earle of Hertford. 1591* (London: Iohn Wolfe, 1591; *STC* 7583). This is the first of three quartos, all dated 1591.
1. Preface.
2. Company of attendants; *just*: exact; *conveniency*: suitability; *sufficing*: provision; *receipt*: reception.
3. The Earl could only guess at a royal visit on the basis of the announced route and assurances by officials, since the Queen often altered her itinerary at the last minute; *park*: enclosed area of ornamental woods and grassland; *compass*: diameter; *receipt*: capacity.
4. 280 paces away.
5. Large room for state functions.
6. Creations, perhaps painted or carved; *arras*: tapestries.
7. Room for storing pitchers used in washing hands before meals; *chandry*: room for making and storing candles.

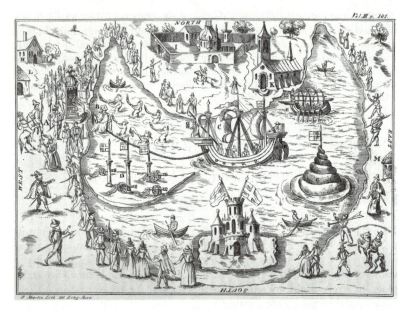

The moon-shaped pond devised for the Elvetham entertainments.

A.   Her Majesty's presence-seat and train.°   *entourage*
B.   Nereus and his followers.
C.   The pinnace of Neaera and her music.
D.   The ship isle.
E.   A boat with music attending on the pinnace of Neaera.
F.   The fort mount.
G.   The snail mount.
H.   The room of estate.
I.   Her Majesty's court.
K.   Her Majesty's wardrobe.°   *private lodging*
L.   The place whence Silvanus and his company issued.°   *came forth*

tiled. Not far off was erected a large hall for entertainment of knights, ladies, and gentlemen of chief account. There was also a several[8] place for her Majesty's footmen and their friends.

Then was there a long bower for her Majesty's guard; another for other officers of her Majesty's house; another to entertain all comers, suitors and such like; another for my Lord's steward,[9] to keep his table in; another for his gentlemen that waited. Most of these foresaid rooms were furnished with tables, and the tables carried[1] twenty-three yards in length.

Moreover, on the same hill, there was raised a great common buttery; a pitcher house; a large pastry with five ovens new built, some of them fourteen foot deep; a great kitchen with four ranges and a boiling place for small boiled meats; another kitchen with a very long range, for the waste,

8. Separate.
9. Official who oversaw and paid the household staff; *comers*: visitors.
1. Extended.

to serve all comers; a boiling house for the great boiler; a room for the scullery;[2] another room for the cook's lodgings. Some of these were covered with canvas and other some with boards.

Between my Lord's house and the foresaid hill where these rooms were raised, there had been made in the bottom, by handy labor, a goodly pond, cut to perfect figure of a half moon.[3] In this pond were three notable grounds where hence to present her Majesty with sports and pastimes. The first was a ship isle, of one hundred foot in length and forty foot broad, bearing three trees orderly set for three masts. The second was a fort, twenty foot square every way and overgrown with willows. The third and last was a snail mount, rising to four circles of green privy hedges,[4] the whole in height twenty foot and forty foot broad at the bottom. These three places were equally distant from the sides of the pond and every one by a just measured proportion distant from other. In the said water were divers boats prepared for music, but especially there was a pinnace full furnished with masts, yards, sails, anchors, cables, and all other ordinary tackling, and with iron pieces and lastly with flags, streamers, and pendants to the number of twelve, all painted with divers[5] colors and sundry devices. To what use these particulars served it shall evidently appear by that which followeth. And therefore I am to request the gentle reader that, when any of these places are briefly specified in the sequel of this discourse, it will please him to have reference to this fore-description, that in avoiding tantilogies[6] or reiterations I may not seem to them obscure, whom I study to please with my plainness.

For proem these may suffice. Now to the matter itself, that it may be *ultimum in executione* (to use the old phrase) *quod primum fuit in intentione*,[7] as is usual to good carpenters, who, intending to build a house, yet first lay their foundation, and square many a post, and fasten many a rafter before the house be set up. What they first purposed is last done. And thus much for excuse of a long foundation to a short building.

The First Day's Entertainment

On the twentieth day of September, being Monday, my Lord of Hertford joyfully expecting her Majesty's coming to Elvetham to supper as her Highness had promised, after dinner, when every other needful place or point of service was established and set in order for so great an entertainment, about three of the clock his Honor seeing all his retinue well mounted and ready to attend his pleasure, he drew them secretly into a chief thicket of the park, where in few words but well couched to the purpose, he put them in mind what quietness and what diligence or other duty they were to use at that present, that their service might first work her Majesty's content, and thereby his honor, and lastly their own credit with increase of his love and favor towards them. This done, my Lord with his train (amounting to the

2. Area for washing and storing dishes, plates, and utensils; *buttery*: place where butts of liquor and other provisions were stored; *pitcher house*: storage house for ale and wine; *pastry*: bakery; *serve all comers*: food left by official guests was dispensed to anyone who wanted it.
3. Symbolic of Elizabeth as the goddess Cynthia.
4. Hedges, made of evergreens, meant to conceal what was within them; *snail mount*: artificial hill shaped like the shell of a snail.
5. Various; *pinnace*: small, light vessel; *yards*: wooden arms from which sails were suspended; *iron pieces*: cannons.
6. Probably a printer's error for "tautologies," or needless repetitions.
7. What is ultimately done in execution is what is initially done in intention.

number of three hundred, and most of them wearing chains of gold[8] about their necks and in their hats yellow and black feathers) met with her Majesty two miles off, then coming to Elvetham from her own house of Odiham four miles from thence. As my Lord in this first action showed himself dutiful, so her Majesty was to him and his most gracious, as also in the sequel. Between five and six of the clock, when her Highness, being most honorably attended, entered into Elvetham Park and was more than half way between the park gate and the house, a poet saluted her with a Latin oration in heroical verse—I mean *veridicus vates*, a soothsaying poet, nothing inferior for truth, and little for delivery of his mind, to an ordinary orator.

This poet was clad in green to signify the joy of his thoughts at her entrance; a laurel garland on his head to express that Apollo was patron of his studies; an olive branch in his hand to declare what continual peace and plenty he did both wish and abode her Majesty; and lastly booted to betoken that he was *vates cothurnatus*[9] and not a loose or low-creeping prophet, as poets are interpreted by some idle or envious ignorants. This poet's boy offered him a cushion at his first kneeling to her Majesty, but he refused it, saying as followeth.[1] Because all our countrymen are not Latinists, I think it not amiss to set this down in English, that all may be indifferently partakers of the poet's meaning.

The Poet's Speech to His Boy Offering Him a Cushion

Now let us use no cushions but fair hearts,[2]
For now we kneel to more than usual saints.

The Poet's Speech to Her Majesty[3]

While at the fountain of the sacred hill,[4]
Under Apollo's lute, I sweetly slept,
'Mongst prophets full possessed with holy fury;[5]
And with true virtue, void of all disdain,
5   The Muses sung, and waked me with these words:
     "Seest thou that English nymph, in face and shape
Resembling some great goddess, and whose beams
Do sprinkle heaven with unacquainted light
While she doth visit Semer's[6] fraudless house,
10   As Jupiter did honor with his presence
The poor thatched cottage where Philemon dwelt?
See thou salute her with an humble voice.
Phoebus and we will let thee lack no verses,
But dare not once aspire to touch her praise,
15   Who like the sun for show, to gods for virtue,

---

8. Symbols of office in the Earl's household.
9. Poet in the high boots (or buskins) of tragedy, associated with lofty speech and action; *abode*: prophesy for.
1. We omit the Latin version of this epigraph and speech.
2. That is, let us kneel inwardly on the cushions of our hearts.
3. This poem—and perhaps the poet's previous speech to his boy refusing the offer of a cushion—are by Thomas Watson, who reworked it in his *Aminta Gaudia*, Éclogue 2.93ff.
4. Mount Parnassus, associated with the worship of Apollo and the Muses.
5. According to Plato, the Muses bring a "divine madness" upon poets like that which inspires prophets (*Phaedrus* 243e–246a).
6. Literary name for Edward Seymour, Elizabeth's host.

Fills all with majesty and holy fear.
More learnéd than ourselves, she ruleth us;
More rich than seas, she doth command the seas;
More fair than nymphs, she governs all the nymphs;
20 More worthy than the gods, she wins the gods."
     Behold, Augusta,[7] thy poor suppliant
Is here at their desire but thy desert.°   *deserving*
O sweet Elisa,[8] grace me with a look
Or from my brows this laurel wreath[9] will fall
25 And I, unhappy, die amidst my song.
Under my person Semer hides himself.[1]
His mouth yields prayers, his eye the olive branch;
His prayers betoken duty, th' olive peace;[2]
His duty argues love, his peace fair rest;
30 His love will smooth your mind, fair rest your body.
This is your Semer's heart and quality,
To whom all things are joys while thou art present,
To whom nothing is pleasing in thine absence.
Behold, on thee how each thing sweetly smiles
35 To see thy brightness glad° our hemisphere.   *gladden*
Night only envies whom fair stars do cross;[3]
All other creatures strive to show their joys.
The crooked-winding kid[4] trips o'er the lawns;
The milk-white heifer wantons with the bull;
40 The trees show pleasure with their quivering leaves,
The meadow with new grass, the vine with grapes,
The running brooks with sweet and silver sound.
Thee, thee (sweet Princess), heav'n, and earth, and floods,
And plants, and beasts salute with one accord,
45 And while they gaze on thy perfections,
Their eyes' desire is never satisfied.
Thy presence frees each thing that lived in doubt.
No seeds now fear the biting of the worm,
Nor deer the toils,[5] nor grass the parching heat,
50 Nor birds the snare, nor corn the storm of hail.
O Empress, O draw forth these days to years,
Years to an age, ages to eternity,
That such as lately joyed to see our sorrows[6]
May sorrow now to see our perfect joys.
55   Behold where all the Graces, Virtue's maids,
And lightfoot Hours, the guardians of heaven's gate,
With joinéd forces do remove those blocks,

---

7. "Consecrated or venerable one," with an implied comparison between Elizabeth and the first emperor of Rome, Caesar Augustus.
8. Literary name for the Queen.
9. Symbol of highest achievement in poetry.
1. That is, I speak for the Earl.
2. As a member of a Catholic family that Elizabeth had punished as recusants, Seymour was anxious to make peace.
3. Only night feels envy when fair stars pass over.
4. Young goat that runs this way and that.
5. Hunting nets.
6. The sorrows of the Earl and his family during their period of disgrace.

Which Envy laid in majesty's high way.
   Come, therefore, come under our humble roof,
60 And with a beck° command what it contains,   *gesture*
For all is thine; each part obeys thy will.
Did not each part obey, the whole should perish.
   Sing songs, fair nymphs, sing sweet triumphal songs;
Fill ways with flowers, and th' air with harmony.

    While the poet was pronouncing this oration, six virgins were behind him busily removing blocks out of her Majesty's way, which blocks were supposed to be laid there by the person of Envy, whose condition is to envy at every good thing, but especially to malice the proceedings of Virtue and the glory of true Majesty. Three of these virgins represented the three Graces and the other three the Hours, which by the poets are feigned to be the guardians of heaven gates. They were all attired in gowns of taffeta sarcenet[7] of diverse colors, with flowery garlands on their heads and baskets full of sweet herbs and flowers upon their arms. When the poet's speech was happily ended and in a scroll delivered to her Majesty (for such was her gracious acceptance that she deigned to receive it with her own hand), then these six virgins, after performance of their humble reverence to her Highness, walked on before her towards the house, strewing the way with flowers and singing a sweet song of six parts to this ditty, which followeth:

The Ditty of the Six Virgins' Song[8]

With fragrant flowers we strew the way
And make this our chief holiday.
For though this clime were blest of yore,
Yet was it never proud before.
5   O beauteous Queen of second Troy,[9]
   Accept of our unfeignéd joy.
Now th' air is sweeter than sweet balm
And satyrs dance about the palm.
Now earth with verdure newly dight°   *clothed*
Gives perfect sign of her delight.
10   O beauteous Queen of second Troy,
   Accept of our unfeignéd joy.

Now birds record° new harmony,   *sing*
And trees do whistle melody.
15 Now every thing that nature breeds
Doth clad itself in pleasant weeds.°   *garments (with pun)*
   O beauty's Queen of second Troy,
   Accept of our unfeignéd joy.

    This song ended with her Majesty's entrance into the house, where she had not rested her a quarter of an hour but from the snail mount and the

7. Fine, lustrous silk.
8. In the anthology *England's Helicon* (1600), the poem is attributed to Thomas Watson.
9. According to popular myth, London was founded by the Trojan Brutus and called "Troynovant," or "New Troy."

ship isle in the pond (both being near under the prospect of her gallery window) there was a long volley of chambers[1] discharged. After this, supper was served in, first to her Majesty and then to the nobles and others. Were it not that I would not seem to flatter the honorable-minded Earl or but that I fear to displease him, who rather desired to express his loyal duty in his liberal bounty than to hear of it again, I could here willingly particulate the store of his cheer[2] and provision, as likewise the careful and kind diligence of his servants, expressed in their quiet service to her Majesty and the nobility and by their loving entertainment to all other, friends or strangers. But I leave the bounty of the one and the industry of the others to the just report of such as beheld or tasted the plentiful abundance of that time and place.

After supper was ended, her Majesty graciously admitted unto her presence a notable consort of six musicians, which my Lord of Hertford had provided to entertain her Majesty withal at her will and pleasure and when it should seem good to her Highness. Their music so highly pleased her that, in grace and favor thereof, she gave a new name unto one of their pavans made long since by Master Thomas Morley, then organist of Paul's Church.[3]

These are the chief points which I noted in the first day's entertainment. Now therefore it followeth that I proceed to the second.

The Second Day's Entertainment

On the next day following, being Tuesday and Saint Matthew's festival, the forenoon was so wet and stormy that nothing of pleasure could be presented her Majesty. Yet it held up a little before dinnertime and all the day after, where otherwise fair sports would have been buried in foul weather.

This day, her Majesty dined with her nobles about her in the room of estate, new builded on the hillside above the pond's head. There sat below her many lords, ladies, and knights. The manner of service and abundance of dainties[4] I omit upon just consideration, as also the ordinance discharged in the beginning of dinner.

Presently, after dinner, my Lord of Hertford caused a large canopy of estate to be set at the pond's head for her Majesty to sit under and to view some sports prepared in the water. The canopy was of green satin, lined with green taffeta sarcenet,[5] every seam covered with a broad silver lace, valenced about and fringed with green silk and silver more than a hand breadth in depth, supported with four silver pillars moveable and decked above head with four white plumes spangled with silver. This canopy being upheld by four of my Lord's chief gentlemen and tapestry spread all about the pond's head, her Majesty, about four of the clock, came and sat under it to expect the issue of some device, being advertised[6] that there was some such thing towards.

At the further end of the pond, there was a bower close built to the brink thereof, out of which there went a pompous[7] array of sea-persons which waded breast high or swam till they approached near the seat of her

1. Small cannons.
2. Hospitality; *particulate*: detail.
3. St. Paul's Cathedral in London; *pavans*: grave and stately dance, often performed in elaborate costumes; *Thomas Morley*: the first great composer of English madrigals.
4. Delicacies.
5. Fine silk; *canopy of estate*: traditional canopy raised over a monarch's throne.
6. Told in advance; *device*: creation or entertainment.
7. Stately.

Majesty. Nereus, the Prophet of the Sea, attired in red silk and having a cornered cap on his curled head, did swim before the rest as their pastor[8] and guide. After him came five tritons breast high in the water, all with grisly[9] heads and beards of diverse colors and fashions, and all five cheerfully sounding their trumpets. After them went two other gods of the sea, Neptune and Oceanus, leading between them that pinnace whereof I spake in the beginning of this treatise.

In the pinnace were three virgins, which with their cornets played Scottish jigs made three parts in one. There was also in the said pinnace another nymph of the sea named Neaera, the old supposed love of Sylvanus, a god of the woods. Near to her were placed three excellent voices to sing to one lute and, in two other boats hard by, other lutes and voices to answer by manner of echo. After the pinnace and two other boats which were drawn after it by other sea gods, the rest of the train followed breast high in the water, all attired in ugly marine suits, and every one armed with a huge wooden squirt[1] in his hand, to what end it shall appear hereafter. In their marching towards the pond all along the middle of the current, the tritons sounded one half of the way, and then, they ceasing, the cornets played their Scottish jigs. The melody was sweet and the show stately.

By the way, it is needful to touch here many things abruptly for the better understanding of that which followeth: first, that in the pinnace are two jewels to be presented her Majesty: the one by Nereus, the other by Neaera; secondly, that the fort in the pond is round environed with armed men; thirdly, that the snail mount now resembleth a monster, having horns full of wildfire continually burning; and lastly, that the god Sylvanus lieth with his train not far off in the woods and will shortly salute her Majesty and present her with a holly scutcheon,[2] wherein Apollo had long since written her praises.

All this remembered and considered, I now return to the sea gods, who having under the conduct of Nereus brought the pinnace near before her Majesty, Nereus made his oration, as followeth. But before he began, he made a privy[3] sign unto one of his train, which was gotten up into the ship isle directly before her Majesty, and he presently did cast himself down, doing a somersault from the isle into the water, and then swam to his company.

The Oration of Nereus to Her Majesty

Fair Cynthia, the wide ocean's empress,[4]
I, wat'ry Nereus, hovered on the coast
To greet your Majesty with this my train
Of dancing tritons and shrill-singing nymphs.
5   But all in vain. Elisa was not there,
For which our Neptune grieved and blamed the star

---

8. Shepherd.
9. Fearsome.
1. Water-gun; *ugly*: repulsive.
2. Plaque shaped like a shield.
3. Secret.
4. Elizabeth rules the seas as the moon-goddess Cynthia governs the tides. The claim rests on the 1588 English defeat of the navy of Philip II, then ruler of the two greatest sea powers of the era, Spain and Portugal.

Whose thwarting influence dashed our longing hope.[5]
Therefore, impatient that this worthless earth
Should bear your Highness' weight and we sea gods
10 (Whose jealous waves have swallowed up your foes,[6]
And to your realm are walls impregnable)
With such large favor seldom time are graced,
I from the deeps have drawn this winding flood,
Whose crescent form figures the rich increase
15 Of all that sweet Elisa holdeth dear.[7]
And with me came gold-breasted India,[8]
Who, daunted at your sight, leapt to the shore,
And sprinkling endless treasure on this isle,
Left me this jewel to present your Grace,
20 For him, that under you doth hold this place.
See where her ship remains, whose silk-woven tackling
Is turned to twigs, and threefold mast to trees,
Receiving life from verdure[9] of your looks
(For what cannot your gracious looks effect?).
25 Yon ugly monster,° creeping from the south   *the Armada*
To spoil these blessed fields of Albion,°   *England*
By self-same beams is changed into a snail,
Whose bullrush horns are not of force to hurt.[1]
As this snail is, so be thine enemies,
30 And never yet did Nereus wish in vain.
That fort did Neptune raise for your defense,
And in this bark,° which gods hale near the shore,   *small boat*
White-footed Thetis sends her music maids
To please Elisa's ears with harmony.
35 Hear them, fair Queen, and when their music ends,
My Triton shall awake the sylvan gods
To do their homage to your Majesty.

This oration being delivered, and withal the present whereof he spake, which was hidden in a purse of green rushes cunningly woven together, immediately the three voices in the pinnace sung a song to the lute with excellent divisions,[2] and the end of every verse was replied by lutes and voices in the other boat somewhat afar off, as if they had been echoes.

The Sea Nymph's Ditty

How haps° that now, when prime° is done,   *does it happen / spring*
Another springtime is begun?

5. The stars were believed to influence affairs on earth. Neptune's hope to see Elizabeth in 1591 was dashed when she decided not visit the sea coast, fearing sudden attack by Spanish forces in the Netherlands.
6. The Spanish Armada was dispersed and nearly half its ships destroyed by a storm.
7. That is, in resembling a waxing moon, Hertford's artificial pond symbolizes Elizabeth's rising fortunes.
8. The West Indies, where Spanish shipping was often plundered by English privateers, to the profit of the Queen and other backers.
9. The power to engender springtime growth.
1. The ponderous warships of the Armada were outmaneuvered by lighter English vessels; *bullrush*: a water plant with weak stalks.
2. Arrangement into parts; *withal*: also.

Our hemisphere is overrun,
With beauty of a second sun.
5   *Echo.* A second sun.

What second sun hath rays so bright
To cause this unacquainted light?
'Tis fair Eliza's matchless grace,
Who with her beams doth bless the place.
    Echo. Doth bless the place.

This song being ended, Nereus commanded the five tritons to sound. Then came Sylvanus with his attendants from the wood, himself attired from the middle downward to the knee in kids' skins with the hair on, his legs, body, and face naked but dyed over with saffron,[3] and his head hooded with a goat's skin, and two little horns over his forehead, bearing in his right hand an olive tree and in his left a scutcheon, whereof I spake somewhat before. His followers were all covered with ivy leaves and bare in their hands bows made like darts. At their reproach[4] near her Majesty, Sylvanus spake as followeth and delivered up his scutcheon, engraven with golden characters, Nereus and his train still continuing near her Highness:

The Oration of Sylvanus

[SYLVANUS.]   Sylvanus comes from out the leafy groves
    To honor her whom all the world adores,
    Fair Cynthia, whom no sooner Nature framed
    And decked with Fortune's and with Virtue's dower,°   dowry
5   But straight admiring what her skill had wrought,
    She broke the mold, that never sun might see
    The like to Albion's Queen for excellence.
    'Twas not the tritons' air-enforcing shell,[5]
    As they perhaps would proudly make their vaunt,°   boast
10   But those fair beams that shoot from majesty
    Which drew our eyes to wonder at thy worth.
    That worth breeds wonder, wonder holy fear,
    And holy fear unfeignéd reverence.
    Amongst the wanton days of Golden Age,[6]
15   Apollo playing in our pleasant shades
    And printing oracles in every leaf,
    Let fall this sacred scutcheon from his breast,
    Wherein is writ, "*Detur dignissimae.*"[7]
    O therefore hold what heaven hath made thy right;
20   I but in duty yield desert° her due.   worthiness
NEREUS.   But see, Sylvanus, where thy love doth sit.

3. Herb yielding a reddish-orange dye.
4. Approach.
5. Shells blown as horns.
6. In classical myth, the first age of the world, when all creatures lived together in peace and plenty.
7. "Let it be given to the most worthy lady." The phrase echoes, and alters, the inscription "To the most beautiful" on the golden ball bestowed in the Judgment of Paris.

SYLVANUS.   My sweet Neaera? Was her ear so near?
　　O set my heart's delight upon this bank,
　　That in compassion of old sufferance
25　She may relent in sight of beauty's queen.
NEREUS.   On this condition shall she come on shore,
　　That with thy hand thou plight a solemn vow
　　Not to profane her undefiled state.[8]
SYLVANUS.   Here, take my hand, and therewithal I vow . . . .
30　NEREUS.   That water will extinguish wanton fire.

Nereus, in pronouncing this last line, did pluck Sylvanus over head and ears into the water, where all the sea gods, laughing, did insult over him. In the meanwhile, her Majesty perused the verses written in the scutcheon, which were these:[9]

　　You surpass the Aeonian Muses[1] and,
　　More beautiful than goddesses of the ocean depths,
　　You excel the nymphs of Idalium.[2]
　　The nymphs of Idalium you excel,
5　　Than goddesses of the ocean depths more beautiful,
　　And the Aeonian Muses you surpass.

Over these verses was this poesy written: *Detur dignissimae.*

　　After that the sea gods had sufficiently ducked Sylvanus, they suffered him to creep to land, where he no sooner set footing but, crying "Revenge, Revenge!" he and his begun a skirmish with those of the water, the one side throwing their darts, and the other using their squirts, and the tritons sounding a point of war. At the last, Nereus parted the fray with a line or two, grounded on the excellence of her Majesty's presence, as being always friend to peace and enemy to war. Then Sylvanus with his followers retired to the woods, and Neaera, his fair love, in the pinnace presenting her Majesty a sea jewel bearing the form of a fan, spake unto her as followeth:

The Oration of Fair Neaera

When Neptune late bestowed on me this bark°　　　　　　　　　boat
And sent by me this present to your Grace,
Thus Nereus sung, who never sings but truth:
"Thine eyes, Neaera, shall in time behold

---

8. As a satyr, Sylvanus is not trustworthy in matters of chastity.
9. For the original Latin poem, we provide a translation by Clarence H. Miller. It is a palindrome, reading virtually the same backward as forward. Scribal error seems likely in the final line (*Pulchrior et divis, ac prior Aöniis*), since reversing the words of the first line is grammatically and metrically correct and makes the palindrome perfect:

　　　　Aöniis prior, et divis es pulchrior alti
　　　　Aequoris, ac nymphis es prior Idaliis.
　　　　Idaliis prior es nymphis, ac aequoris alti
　　　　Pulchrior es divis, et prior Aöniis.

1. Aeonian mountains in Greece, where the springs of Helicon and Aganippe are sacred to the Muses.
2. Mountain city in Cyprus, sacred to Venus.

5 A sea-borne queen worthy to govern kings.
   On her depends the fortune of thy boat,
   If she but name it with a blissful word
   And view it with her life-inspiring beams.
   Her beams yield gentle influence, like fair stars;
10 Her silver-sounding word is prophecy."
   Speak, sacred Sibyl, give some prosperous name,
   That it may dare attempt a golden fleece[3]
   Or dive for pearls and lay them in thy lap.
   For wind and waves and all the world besides,
15 Will make her way whom thou shalt doom° to bliss,   *destine*
   For what is Sibyl's speech but oracle°?   *true prophecy*

Here her Majesty named the pinnace the Bonadventure,[4] and Neaera went on with her speech, as followeth:

Inow° Neaera's bark is fortunate   *now*
And in thy service shall employ her sail
And often make return to thy avail.°   *profit*
O live in endless joy with glorious fame;
Sound trumpets, sound, in honor of her° name.   *Elizabeth's*

Then did Nereus retire back to his bower, with all his train following him in self-same order as they came forth before, the tritons sounding their trumpets one half of the way and the cornets playing the other half. And here ended the second day's pastime, to the so great liking of her Majesty that her gracious approbation thereof was to the actors more than a double reward, and yet, withal, her Highness bestowed a largesse upon them the next day after, before she departed.

The Third Day's Entertainment

On Wednesday morning, about nine of the clock, as her Majesty opened a casement of her gallery window, there were three excellent musicians who, being disguised in ancient country attire, did greet her with a pleasant song of Coridon and Phyllida,[5] made in three parts of purpose. The song, as well for the worth of the ditty as for the aptness of the note thereto applied, it pleased her Highness, after it had been once sung, to command it again and highly to grace it with her cheerful acceptance and commendation.

The Plowman's Song[6]

In the merry month of May,
In a morn by break of day,
Forth I walked by the woodside,
Whéreas° May was in his pride.   *Where*

---

3. Like Jason's ship, the Argo, which bore its crew in search of a ram with golden fleece. Kinney also points out a political meaning, since Philip II's most honored knights were inducted into the Order of the Golden Fleece (*Renaissance Drama* 151, n. 606).
4. Good fortune.
5. Traditional pastoral names for a shepherd and his shepherdess.
6. In *England's Helicon*, this poem is attributed to Nicholas Breton.

5 There I spièd, all alone,
  Phyllida and Coridon.
  Much ado there was, God wot,°   *God knows*
  He would love, and she would not.
  She said, "Never man was true."
10 He said, "None was false to you."
  He said he had loved her long.
  She said, "Love should have no wrong."
  Coridon would kiss her then.
  She said, "Maids must kiss no men,
15 Till they did for good and all."[7]
  Then she made the shepherd call
  All the heav'ns to witness truth:
  Never loved a truer youth.
  Thus with many a pretty oath,
20 Yea and nay, and faith and troth,
  Such as silly° shepherds use   *simple, humble*
  When they will not love abuse,
  Love, which had been long deluded,
  Was with kisses sweet concluded,
25 And Phyllida with garlands gay
  Was made the Lady of the May.[8]

The same day after dinner, about three of the clock, ten of my Lord of Hertford's servants, all Somersetshire men, in a square green court before her Majesty's window did hang up lines, squaring out the form of a tennis court and making a cross line in the middle. In this square they, being stripped out of their doublets, played five to five with the handball at board and cord[9] (as they term it) to so great liking of her Highness that she graciously deigned to behold their pastime more than an hour and a half.

After supper there were two delights presented unto her Majesty: curious fireworks and a sumptuous banquet,[1] the first from the three islands in the pond, the second in a low gallery in her Majesty's privy garden. But I will first briefly speak of the fireworks.

First, there was a peal of a hundred chambers discharged from the snail mount, in counter whereof a like peal was discharged from the ship isle and some great ordinance withal. Then was there a castle of fireworks of all sorts, which played in the fort. Answerable to that there was in the snail mount a globe of all manner of fireworks, as big as a barrel. When these were spent on either side, there were many running rockets upon lines, which passed between the snail mount and the castle in the fort. On either side were many fire wheels, pikes of pleasure, and balls of wildfire,[2] which burned in the water.

---

7. Kissed to seal a promise of marriage.
8. Traditional May Day festivities included parading with green boughs and flowers, crowning a King and Queen of the May, and dancing around a Maypole. A woman recently engaged was often named Queen or Lady of May.
9. Lawn tennis; *doublets*: close-fitting vests or jackets.
1. Dessert course.
2. Material used in warfare that is difficult to extinguish once lit; *pikes of pleasure*: perhaps Roman candles.

During the time of these fireworks in the water, there was a banquet served, all in glass and silver, into the low gallery in the garden from a hillside fourteen score off[3] by two hundred of my Lord of Hertford's gentlemen, every one carrying so many dishes that the whole number amounted to a thousand. And there were, to light them in their way, a hundred torchbearers. To satisfy the curious, I will here set down some particulars in the banquet:

Her Majesty's arms in sugar-work.[4]

The several arms of all our nobility in sugar-work.

Many men and women in sugar-work, and some enforced by hand.[5]

Castles, forts, ordinance, drummers, trumpeters, and soldiers of all sorts in sugar-work.

Lions, unicorns, bears, horses, camels, bulls, rams, dogs, tigers, elephants, antelopes, dromedaries, apes, and all other beasts in sugar-work.

Eagles, falcons, cranes, buzzards, heronshaws,[6] bitterns, pheasants, partridges, quails, larks, sparrows, pigeons, cocks, owls, and all that fly in sugar-work.

Snakes, adders, vipers, frogs, toads, and all kind of worms in sugar-work.

Mermaids, whales, dolphins, congers,[7] sturgeons, pikes, carps, breams, and all sorts of fishes in sugar-work.

All these were standing dishes[8] of sugar-work. The self-same devices were also there all in flat-work.[9] Moreover, these particulars following, and many such like, were in flat sugar-work and cinnamon:

Marchpanes,[1] grapes, oysters, mussels, cockles, periwinkles, crabs, lobsters.

Apples, pears, and plums of all sorts.

Preserves, succades, jellies, leaches, marmalades, pastes, comfits[2] of all sorts.

The Fourth Day's Entertainment

On Thursday morning, her Majesty was no sooner ready and at her gallery window, looking into the garden, but there began three cornets to play certain fantastic dances, at the measure whereof the Fairy Queen came into the garden dancing with her maids about her. She brought with her a garland made in form of an imperial crown.[3] Within the sight of her Majesty, she fixed upon[4] a silver staff and, sticking the staff into the ground, spake as followeth:

3. The great distance—nearly 300 paces—made the torchlit procession of the army of waiters a striking spectacle; *banquet*: here, dessert course.
4. A confection made to look like the royal coat of arms.
5. Produced individually, rather than in molds.
6. Herons.
7. Eels.
8. Upright figures.
9. Confections lying flat.
1. Sweets made from almond paste.
2. Sugarplums; *succades*: sweets made from candied fruit; *leaches*: jellies containing, meat, eggs, fruit, and spices.
3. A crown closed at the top, like that of the Holy Roman Emperor, to indicate that the bearer governed other rulers and owed fealty to no higher earthly authority.
4. Took hold of.

The Speech of the Fairy Queen to Her Majesty

I that abide in places underground,
Aureola, the Queen of Fairyland,
That every night in rings of painted flowers
Turn round and carol out Elisa's name,
5   Hearing that Nereus and the sylvan gods
Have lately welcomed your Imperial Grace,
Opened the earth with this enchanting wand
To do my duty to your Majesty
And humbly to salute you with this chaplet,[5]
10   Given me by Oberon, the Fairy King.
Bright shining Phoebe, that in human shape
Hidest heav'n's perfection, vouchsafe t' accept it.
And I, Aureola, beloved in heaven
(For amorous stars fall nightly in my lap),
15   Will cause that heavens enlarge thy golden days
And cut them short that envy at thy praise.

After this speech, the Fairy Queen and her maids danced about the garland singing a song of six parts, with the music of an exquisite consort wherein was the lute, bandore, base viol, cittern,[6] treble viol, and flute. And this was the fairies' song:[7]

Elisa is the fairest Queen
That ever trod upon this green.
Elisa's eyes are blessèd stars
Inducing peace, subduing wars.
5   Elisa's hand is crystal bright;
Her words are balm, her looks are light.
Elisa's breast is that fair hill
Where Virtue dwells and sacred skill.
O blessèd be each day and hour
10   Where sweet Elisa builds her bower.

This spectacle and music so delighted her Majesty that she desired to see and hear it twice over and then dismissed the actors with thanks and with a gracious largesse, which of her exceeding goodness she bestowed upon them.

Within an hour after, her Majesty departed with her nobles from Elvetham. On the one side of her way as she passed through the park, there was placed, sitting on the pond side, Nereus and all the sea gods in their former attire; on her left hand, Sylvanus and his company; in the way before her, the three Graces and the three Hours, all of them on every side wringing their hands and showing sign of sorrow for her departure. While she beheld this dumb show, the poet made her a short oration, as followeth:

---

5. Garland of flowers or leaves.
6. A kind of guitar strung with wire and played with a quill; *bandore*: instrument resembling a guitar or lute, played to provide a bass line to a cittern.
7. The music was by Edward Johnson (Kinney, *Renaissance Drama* 153, n. 771–80).

The Poet's Speech at Her Majesty's Departure

O see, sweet Cynthia, how the wat'ry gods,
Which joy'd of late to view thy glorious beams,
At this retire° do wail and wring their hands,   *departure*
Distilling from their eyes salt showers of tears
5 To bring in winter with their wet lament.
      For how can summer stay when sun[8] departs?

See where Sylvanus sits and sadly mourns
To think that autumn with his withered wings
Will bring in tempest when thy beams are hence.
10   For how can summer stay when sun departs?

See where those Graces and those Hours of heav'n
Which at thy coming sung triumphal songs,
And smoothed the way, and strewed it with sweet flowers,
Now, if they durst,° would stop it with green boughs,   *dared*
Lest by thine absence the year's pride decay.
15   For how can summer stay when sun departs?

Leaves fall, grass dies, beasts of the wood hang head,
Birds cease to sing, and every creature wails
To see the season alter with this change.
20   For how can summer stay when sun departs?

O either stay or soon return again,
For summer's parting is the country's pain.

After this, as her Majesty passed through the park gate, there was a consort of musicians hidden in a bower, to whose playing this ditty of "Come again" was sung with excellent division[9] by two that were cunning.

O come again, fair Nature's treasure,
Whose looks yield joys exceeding measure.

O come again, heav'n's chief delight,
Thine absence makes eternal night.

5 O come again, world's star-bright eye,
Whose presence doth adorn the sky.

O come again, sweet beauty's sun.
When thou art gone, our joys are done.

Her Majesty was so highly pleased with this and the rest that she openly protested to my Lord of Hertford that the beginning, process, and end of this his entertainment was so honorable as hereafter he should find the

---

8. Traditional metaphor for monarchs, seen as a source of life, growth, and enlightenment to their realms.
9. Fine harmony.

reward thereof in her especial favor, and many and most happy years may her gracious Majesty continue to favor and foster him and all others which do truly love and honor her.

Finis.

QUEEN ELIZABETH

Latin Oration at Oxford University
(September 28, 1592)[†]

Your merits and my gratitude have so captivated my reason that they force me to do what reason itself forbids.[1] The cares of ruling are so weighty that they tend to dull the mind rather than sharpen the memory. Moreover, I am completely out of practice in speaking this language, which I have used so slightly and rarely in thirty-six years that I remember using it not as often as thirty times. But now that the ice is broken, I must either continue or make an end.

It is not the extraordinary and remarkable praise of me (however undeserved); it is not the explications, displays, and evidence of your learning in many fields; it is not the learned and eloquent orations in many and varied styles that move me, but rather something else that is more extraordinary and precious to me, namely your love, such as was never heard of nor written about nor known to the memory of man, which has no parallel in the love of parents or friends or that between a man and a woman (where experience teaches us that faithfulness does not always last). Such love as this could not be eradicated by persuasion, threats, or curses. Indeed, it is not subject to time, which consumes iron and wears down crags; but this love time cannot unbind. These merits of yours are such that, if I could endure forever, I think they would last forever. For them I could not express the gratitude I owe even if I had a thousand tongues instead of one. Only the mind can conceive what it cannot express. In gratitude, accept only my wishes and my advice.

From the beginning of my reign, the first and highest care, solicitude, and watchfulness of my rule has been aimed at protecting my kingdom from both external and internal disturbances, so that what has flourished for so long, through many ages, may not be weakened at my hands. Second to the salvation of my soul, I have taken the kingdom as the sole object of my solicitude. But if I have always been so watchful over the whole kingdom, and if the university itself is thought to be no small part of that kingdom, how could my heedfulness not extend to the university? For its interests, I have always been so careful that there has been no need for any external stimulus of my diligence, since it always stands ready on its own to promote, preserve, and endow this university.

---

† Copy text: *Elizabeth I: Autograph Compositions and Foreign Language Originals*, ed. Leah S. Marcus, Janel Mueller, and Mary Beth Rose (Chicago and London: University of Chicago Press, 2003), 163–65. Translation by Clarence H. Miller.

1. That is, to give a speech in Latin; as Elizabeth notes in the next clause, affairs of state have prevented her from developing her academic prowess.

But as for my advice, listen to this. If you follow it, I do not doubt that it will contribute to the glory of God, to your advantage, and to my own singular joy. In order for this university to be long-lived, care should be taken above all that God be worshipped, not according to all manner of opinion, not according to far-fetched and over-ripe wits, but according to the commands of God's law and mine. For you do not have the sort of ruler who would ever command you to do anything that ought to be considered contrary to a truly Christian conscience. Be sure that I would rather die than do anything, or command anything, that is forbidden by sacred scripture. For if I have always undertaken to care for your bodies, would I be remiss in caring for your souls? God forbid. Would I neglect to care for your souls if neglecting them would place my own soul under judgment? Far from it. Therefore, I advise you not to get ahead of the laws but to follow them, not to argue about whether something better might be prescribed but rather to observe what God's law commands and ours enforces.

Then, too, you should remember that everyone, according to his rank, obeys some superior, not by prescribing what ought to be but by following what is prescribed, keeping in mind that, if your superiors should begin to do something they should not do, they also have a superior who rules over them, who both ought to punish them and desires to do so. Finally, remember to be of one mind, since you know that what is united is stronger, what is divided is weaker, and will quickly fall into ruin.

Part Eight: A Changing Court and Aging Queen (1592–1597)

HISTORICAL BACKGROUND

Following the defeat of the Armada, the balance of power in Europe gradually shifted in England's favor. The war with Spain, however, dragged on until after Elizabeth's death, and the intervening years were for her a time of trouble and loss. Many of her old friends and allies either passed away or betrayed her, and the government was often divided. Without the cadre of seasoned councilors, commanders, and attendants on whom she had so long relied, ruling became more difficult.

The losses came in rapid succession. In the autumn of 1588, Leicester died while traveling to reinvigorate his failing health in the mineral baths at Buxton. It was a devastating loss. Though he and Elizabeth had often quarreled, no man had ever been closer to her. During the preceding summer, they had patched up their differences and were once again spending long evenings together, as they had in happier days. When he died, she locked herself in her chambers and refused to come out. After several days, members of her Council became alarmed and broke down the door, only with some difficulty persuading her to return to her duties at Court.

Other losses followed. First came the death of Sir Walter Mildmay, her Chancellor of the Exchequer, who had played a part in sensitive negotiations with Mary Stuart and was given other important assignments. Next came the death of the chief gentlewoman of her Privy Chamber, Blanch Parry, who had served her faithfully since Elizabeth was a girl. Then came the death of Leicester's brother Ambrose Dudley, Earl of Warwick, followed by that of Sir Francis Walsingham, Elizabeth's long-time Secretary of State and spy-master, and then by that of Sir James Croft, the staunchly Protestant military commander and Privy Councilor on whom she had so often relied. Last came the death of Sir Christopher Hatton, one of her most loyal and intimate friends, who in the 1570s had written fervent love letters to her and in the 1580s had helped to interest her in voyages to the New World. In his final illness, she came to his bedside to nurse him.

Death was not the only kind of loss that befell the Queen in the early 1590s. Unbeknownst to her, Sir Walter Ralegh had been having a love affair with Elizabeth Throckmorton, one of her Maids of Honor, and after a child was conceived, the couple secretly married. When the Queen found out, she was furious and sent them to prison. Though she soon relented, allowing Ralegh to return to government service—and even, some years later, to head up a major voyage of discovery to what is now Guiana—she never fully trusted him again or restored him to his former power. His fall was followed in the middle part of the decade by another, slower decline of even greater moment. The most trusted of her Councilors, William Cecil, Lord Burghley, was growing old, and though he lived until 1598, he was forced to spend more and more time at Theobalds, his country estate, suffering through painful bouts of the gout. As with Hatton, Elizabeth visited him in his last days, feeding him soup with her own hands.

As the 1590s wore on, England also suffered a growing sense of national malaise. The problems confronting the country were not so grave as the plots of Mary Stuart or the attack of the Armada, but they proved more intractable and gradually undermined morale. Strains on the English economy caused by the ongoing war with Spain led to rapid inflation, and expenditures to prop up the Protestants of the Netherlands and France made the situation worse. A series of bad harvests added to the burden on ordinary people, and in 1595 and 1596, bread riots broke out in Oxford and London. Even more insidious were fears of political instability should Elizabeth die. As she passed her sixtieth birthday, she was remarkably fit. Yet neither the auburn wig that she wore nor the cosmetics that she so liberally applied could hide the fact that she was an old woman, with wrinkled skin and teeth blackened from decades of eating sweets. Worries over the civil strife that might ensue should she die without a successor led to renewed pressure to name an heir. On that issue, however, she was adamant, having learned from her own situation during the reign of her sister Mary just how ready men were to form factions against their current ruler as soon as a promising alternative came on the scene.

In dealing with such difficulties, the Queen was forced to rely on new men at Court. The steadiest was Lord Burghley's son Robert Cecil, who had a quick memory, a prodigious capacity for work, something of his father's subtlety as a strategist, and an aptitude for reading the Queen's moods and gaining her assent. She called him her "pygmy," an affectionate reference to his small stature (the result of a childhood accident), and though she never held him in the same esteem as his father, she eventually came to rely on him almost as much. His chief rival for preeminence at Court was Robert Devereux, second Earl of Essex, who was the stepson of Robert Dudley, Earl of Leicester. Handsome, robust, and daring to the point of recklessness, he was everything that Cecil was not. In the late 1580s, he had begun his career at Court by supplanting Ralegh in the Queen's favor. Soon, he had been granted Leicester's old position as Master of the Horse, and he had also begun to cast about for ways to control Walsingham's former post as Secretary of State. Though unsuited to the position himself, he began paying for the services of Walsingham's network of spies in order to obtain the position for one of his followers. Not to be outdone, Cecil created a rival network, hoping to secure the office for himself. Although Elizabeth was aware of the rivalry and probably encouraged it to keep the two men in line, vying for her favor, she does not seem to have realized how dangerous it was to her Court, which gradually polarized around the contenders. After leaving the post unfilled for more than half a decade, she was finally forced to choose, and by then the consequences of disappointing one faction or the other were grave.

In 1596, the crisis came to a head when Elizabeth appointed Essex to join Charles, Lord Howard of Effingham, in command of a major naval operation against Philip II's fleet as it lay at anchor in the Spanish port of Cadiz. Coming on the harbor unexpectedly, the English destroyed several major warships, set fire to the town, and seized a vast quantity of booty. Having distinguished himself in the fighting, Essex returned to London a hero, and many assumed that his desire to gain ascendancy over Cecil would now be realized. The Queen, however, was concerned that a major command of this sort might go to Essex's head and preferred to maintain a balance between his influence and that of Cecil. While Essex was away, she therefore promoted his rival to the long-sought post of Secretary of State, taking the Earl's return from Cadiz as the occasion to inform him of her decision. He was outraged. Rather than putting an end to the infighting at Court, the Queen's decision actually intensified it, sowing seeds of unhappiness and mistrust in Essex that would grow into more serious troubles later on.

For the moment, however, the Queen was satisfied. All the vacant posts at the top of her government were once again in the hands of able men; Philip had received a setback that would deter him from sending a second Armada to attack England; and Essex had earned the acclaim as a national leader for which she had long been grooming him.

BREAKING WITH OLD FAVORITES AND FRIENDS

Other than the deaths of Leicester and Walsingham, the loss that did the most to reshape political realities at Court in the early 1590s was the fall of Sir Walter Ralegh. Elizabeth regarded his clandestine affair and subsequent marriage to Elizabeth Throckmorton not only as a betrayal of trust by one whom she had elevated to high station and large resources, but also as an affront to her honor as a queen. She had been very close to Ralegh, and many of her feelings were doubtless personal, but there were also issues of order and governance involved. Life in the close quarters of the Court was full of temptations, and Elizabeth prided herself on maintaining a high ethical tone among her attendants. They were not to receive the attentions of men without her knowledge, nor were they or her courtiers to marry without her permission. It is not surprising, then, that she committed Ralegh and his wife to the Tower.

What is surprising is Ralegh's response. In a series of poems that includes the cryptic lyric "If Cynthia Be a Queen," a despairing sonnet "My Body in the Walls Captived," and a long reflection on his fall from grace entitled *The Twenty-First and Last Book of the Ocean to Cynthia,* he provides remarkably intimate glimpses of his relationship with the Queen, alternately expressing his love for her and blaming her for her fickleness and cruelty. Though the poems are not dated, most scholars believe that they were written during Ralegh's imprisonment or shortly afterward. The full title of *The Ocean to Cynthia* suggests the existence of earlier "books," but no trace of them has ever been found, and it may be that Ralegh began the poetic account of his long relationship with the Queen at the end, intending to work his way backwards, or perhaps that he simply wanted to stress that the relationship had been long and its ending shockingly final. Whatever the case, the fragment that has come down to us provides a psychological portrait of a man suffering through the humiliation of a sudden and devastating fall from power. As his mind circles over the causes of his misfortune, the crush of painful and confused reflections strains the very bounds of syntax, producing one of the earliest instances of stream-of-consciousness poetry in English. Pronouns are often hard to trace back to their referents, thoughts elaborate and digress, yet such effects are necessary to the experience of loss and recrimination that the poet is seeking to convey.

It seems unlikely that the Queen ever saw any of the poetry that Ralegh composed during this crisis. Prisoners were rarely allowed to address correspondence to the monarch, and the manuscript in which these works are preserved was left among Ralegh's personal papers, where it lay undiscovered and unpublished until the nineteenth century. Judging from his indulgence in long passages of self-justification, however, and from his many appeals to pity, he seems to have hoped that they might somehow reach the Queen and move her to leniency. After an initial, lengthy defense against charges of disloyalty and an assertion of unending love, the unfinished fragment of *The Ocean to Cynthia* turns to the errors that led to his unfortunate liaison and so to the loss of the

Queen's favor. At one point he blames Elizabeth for being the first to withdraw her attentions; at others, he admits his mistake only to complain that she is cruel and her punishment unbearably harsh. Although grief and reproach sometimes give way to expressions of love, as when he terms her "The seat of joys and love's abundance" or "that mass of miracles," such feelings ultimately fade and the poem ends in bitterness and despair. As things actually turned out, however, Ralegh's fall was not as tragic as he supposed. After a few weeks in prison, he was released, and he soon was back at work carrying out important responsibilities in the government. Whatever lapses in honor and loyalty he may have been guilty of, he was simply too important to her projects for Elizabeth to imprison for long. Yet he never regained his former stature or his accustomed intimacy with the Queen, and his wife was banished from the Court for the remainder of the reign.

Besides Ralegh's secret marriage, the personal betrayal in this period that most moved Elizabeth and was hardest for her to forgive was the conversion of Henry of Navarre to the Roman Catholic faith. Having inherited the French throne in 1589, following the assassination of Henry III, he had tried for years to consolidate his power as a Protestant king in a predominantly Roman Catholic country, but to little effect. In 1593, therefore, with the famous comment that "Paris is worth a Mass," he set aside religious conviction and attended Mass at the Cathedral of St. Denis. After applying to the Pope to be absolved from the sin of heresy and waiting some months for an answer, he was formally received into the Catholic Church and at last crowned Henry IV of France. Elizabeth was stunned. Having lost her greatest Huguenot ally just when the fortunes of the Protestants of Europe were looking up, she wrote a letter to Henry IV conveying her horror at his decision. Though she promised to continue praying for him, she saw his act as "iniquitous" and compared it with changing one's father or doing as the biblical figure Esau had done, selling his birthright for a bowl of stew.

It is perhaps no coincidence that, in her leisure hours during these difficult years, the Queen turned to translating Boethius's *Consolation of Philosophy*, a medieval Latin work on the uncertainties of earthly life and the right response of a philosopher to the misfortunes that flesh is heir to. Finished over the course of a few months in 1593, the translation is taut and compressed, like the work of more modern poets. The parts reprinted here begin with images of a great storm at sea, emblem of earthly misfortune, including Boethius's own fall from grace and unjust execution in the sixth century under King Theodoric. Drawing on the teaching of the Stoic philosophers that the mind must not allow itself to be moved by earthly joys or fears, Boethius then turns his thoughts to the divine order that governs the heavens and the earth, setting seasons and bounds, keeping the sea in its proper place, and linking contraries to bring about great goods. Contrasting trust in an eternal Father who loves all His children with reliance on sinful earthly rulers, he finds his ultimate consolation in trusting the all-seeing, all-knowing God who framed the world. In such passages, the translation offers an implicit response to Henry IV, who trusted in Catholic princes rather than in God and transgressed the natural bounds of his own faith.

SIR WALTER RALEGH

POEMS FROM PRISON (ca. 1592)[†]

[If Cynthia Be a Queen]

If Cynthia be a queen, a princess, and supreme,
Keep these° among the rest or say it was a dream,[1]   *these poems*
For those that like expound and those that loathe express
Meanings according as their minds are movéd more or less,
5 For writing what thou art or showing what thou were
Adds to the one disdain, to th' other but despair.[2]
    Thy mind of neither needs, in both seeing it exceeds.[3]

[My Body in the Walls Captived]

My body in the walls captived
Feels not the wounds of spiteful envy,
But my thralléd mind, of liberty deprived,
Fast fettered in her ancient memory,[1]
5 Doth naught° behold but sorrow's dying face.   *nothing*
Such prison erst° was so delightful   *at first*
As it desired no other dwelling place;
But time's effects and destines° despiteful   *destinies*
Have changéd both my keeper and my fare.°   *food*
10 Love's fire and beauty's light I then had store,°   *in abundance*
But now close kept, as captives wonted° are,   *usually*
That food, that heat, that light I find no more.
    Despair bolts up my doors, and I alone
    Speak to dead walls, but those hear not my moan.

From The Twenty-First and Last Book of the Ocean to Cynthia

Suffice it to you,[1] my joys interred,
In simple words that I my woes complain,
You that then died when first my fancy erred,

---

† Copy text: *The Poems of Sir Walter Ralegh: A Historical Edition*, ed. Michael Rudick (Tempe: Arizona Center for Medieval and Renaissance Studies, Renaissance English Texts Society, 1999), 47–65. Reprinted by permission.
1. A reflection of Ralegh's desire to conceal from others his current tumultuous relationship with the Queen.
2. At least on first reading, the meaning seems clear: those that "loathe" Ralegh (line 3) will disdain the poem, and those that "like" him will despair at his predicament.
3. The complexity enters when one considers the possible meanings of "Thy." If he is speaking of himself, the meaning is that he has no need of either disdain for himself or despair over his circumstances since he has more than enough of both. "Thy," however, may also refer to Cynthia, as may "thou" in line 5, and rereading in light of that possibility yields a variety of meanings depending on the attitudes of different "minds" involved (line 4).
1. Fettered in the mind's old memories, but also, perhaps, in memories of her (the Queen).
1. Probably the joys addressed in the next phrase, but perhaps the Queen.

Joys under dust that never live again.
5   If to the living[2] were my muse addressed,
Or did my mind her[3] own spirit still inhold,
Were not my living passion so repressed,
As to the dead the dead did these unfold,[4]
Some sweeter words, some more becoming verse
10   Should witness my mishap in higher kind.°   *in a more exalted genre*
But my love's wounds, my fancy in the hearse,
The idea but resting of a wasted mind,[5]
The blossoms fallen, the sap gone from the tree,
The broken monuments of my great desires—
15   From these so lost what may th' affections° be,   *feelings, desires*
What heat in cinders of extinguished fires?
Lost in the mud of those high-flowing streams
Which through more fairer fields their courses bend,
Slain with self-thoughts,[6] amazed in fearful dreams,
20   Woes without date, discomforts without end,
From fruitful trees I gather withered leaves
And glean the broken ears with miser's hands,
Who sometime did enjoy the weighty sheaves.
I seek fair flowers amid the brinish[7] sand,
25   All in the shade, even in the fair sun days,
Under those healthless trees I sit alone,
Where joyful birds sing neither lovely lays
Nor Philomene° recounts her direful moan.   *the nightingale*
No feeding flocks, no shepherd's company[8]
30   That might renew my dolorous conceit,°   *thought; metaphor*
While happy then,[9] while love and fantasy
Confined my thoughts on that fair flock to wait:
No pleasing streams fast to the ocean wending,
The messengers sometimes of my great woe,
35   But all on earth, as from the cold storms bending,
Shrink from my thoughts in high heavens and below.
O hopeful love, my object and invention,
O true desire, the spur of my conceit,
O worthiest spirit,[1] my mind's impulsion,
40   O eyes transpersant,° my affection's bait,   *penetrating*
O princely form, my fancy's adamant,°   *lodestone, magnet*
Divine conceit, my pain's acceptance,[2]
O all in one, O heaven on earth transparent,
The seat of joys and love's abundance:
45   Out of that mass of miracles,° my muse   *Elizabeth*

2. That is, to living joys.
3. The mind's, or perhaps the Queen's, regarded in line 8 as if she were dead to him.
4. As if the dead were speaking to the dead (Ruddick).
5. Only the idea remaining of a devastated mind.
6. My own thoughts, or thoughts about myself.
7. Salty, as from tears.
8. Late in the poem, Ralegh returns to the image of himself as a despairing shepherd (line 504).
9. As I was once happy.
1. Probably Elizabeth, to whose eyes and "princely form" the next lines seem to refer, but perhaps the spirit of love that impels him.
2. She who accepts my pain.

Gathered those flowers,[3] to her pure senses pleasing;
Out of her eyes (the store of joys) did choose[4]
Equal delights, my sorrows counterpoising.
Her regal looks, my rigorous sighs suppressed;
50 Small drops of joys sweetened great worlds of woes;
One gladsome day a thousand cares redressed.
Whom love defends, what fortune overthrows?
When she did well, what did there else amiss?
When she did ill, what empires could have pleased,
55 No other power effecting woe or bliss?
She gave, she took, she wounded, she appeased.
The honor of her love, love still° devising,   *continually*
Wounding my mind with contrary conceit,
Transferred itself sometime to her aspiring,
60 Sometime the trumpet of her thought's retreat.[5]
To seek new worlds for gold, for praise, for glory,
To try desire, to try love severed far
When I was gone, she sent her memory,
More strong than were ten thousand ships of war,
65 To call me back, to leave great honor's thought,
To leave my friends, my fortune, my attempt,
To leave the purpose I so long had sought,
And hold both cares and comforts in contempt.
Such heat in ice, such fire in frost remained,
70 Such trust in doubt, such comforts in despair,[6]
Much like the gentle lamb, though lately weaned,
Plays with the dug° though finds no comfort there.   *teat*
But as a body violently slain
Retaineth warmth although the spirit be gone,
75 And by a power in nature moves again
Till it be laid below the fatal stone;
Or as the earth, even in cold winter days
Left for a time by her life-giving sun,
Doth by the power remaining of his rays
80 Produce some green, though not as it hath done;
Or as a wheel forced by the falling stream,
Although the course be turned some other way,
Doth for a time go round upon the beam,
Till wanting° strength to move, it stands at stay;°   *lacking / stops*
85 So my forsaken heart, my withered mind,
Widow of all the joys it once possessed,

---

3. Posies of beautiful images, with a commonplace pun on "poesies," or poems.
4. The subject here is still "my muse" (line 45).
5. Though lines 57–60 are obscure, lines 61–68 suggest their meaning. Ralegh was continually devising ways to honor her love of him (by seeking new worlds, etc.), and in the process wounding himself by the "contrary conceit" of sailing away from her and enduring "love severed far" (62). In obeying her, moreover, he sometimes transferred his efforts from seeking her honor to pursuing her more worldly aspirations, and then was forced to obey her trumpet of retreat, leaving "great honor's thought" and other things of value behind (65). In 1592, the Queen called him back to Court during his first voyage to America.
6. The many comparisons heaped up in lines 69–103 all suggest the poet's desire to feel as he did before the Queen abandoned him. The realization that he is unable to do so renders his reflections futile and spiritless; he "writes in the dust" (line 91).

My hopes clean out of sight, with forcéd wind
To kingdoms strange, to lands far off addressed,
Alone, forsaken, friendless on the shore
90 With many wounds, with death's cold pangs embraced,
Writes[7] in the dust as one that could no more,
Whom love, and time, and fortune had defaced,
Of things so great, so long, so manifold,
With means so weak, the soul even then departing,
95 The weal, the woe, the passages of old
And worlds of thoughts described by one last sighing,
As if, when after Phoebus° is descended,   *the sun*
And leaves a light much like the past day's dawning
And every toil and labor wholly ended,
100 Each living creature draweth to his resting,
We should begin by such a parting light
To write the story of all ages past[8]
And end the same before th' approaching night.
Such is again the labor of my mind,
105 Whose shroud, by sorrow woven now to end,
Hath seen that ever-shining sun declined,
So many years that so could not descend[9]
But that the eyes of my mind held her beams,
In every part transferred by love's swift thought;
110 Far off or near, in waking or in dreams,
Imagination strong their luster brought.
Such force her angel-like appearance had
To master distance, time, or cruelty,
Such art to grieve, and after to make glad,
115 Such fear in love, such love in majesty.
My weary limbs her memory embalmed;°   *soothed with balm*
My darkest ways her eyes make clear as day.
What storms so great but Cynthia's beams appeased?
What rage so fierce that love could not allay?
120 Twelve years entire I wasted in this war,[1]
Twelve years of my most happy younger days,[2]
But I in them, and they now wasted are,
Of all which past the sorrow only stays.
So wrote I once[3] and my mishap foretold,
125 My mind still feeling sorrowful success[4]
Even as before a storm the marble cold
Doth by moist tears tempestuous times express.
So felt my heavy mind my harms at hand,

---

7. The subject of the verb here is "mind" (85).
8. The attempt to remember the "worlds of thoughts" that filled his mind during earlier days with the Queen is like trying to write the history of the world in an evening before the light fades. During his last, long imprisonment under James I, Ralegh did, in fact, write *A History of the World* prior to being executed.
9. That for so many years could not so decline.
1. The inner war of contrary feelings.
2. Ralegh initially came to Elizabeth's attention in 1579–80 through his boldness in the Irish wars.
3. In his poem "Like truthless dreams," he had used the line "Of all which past the sorrow only stays."
4. My mind continually feeling that the outcome (of the relationship) would be sorrowful.

Which my vain thought in vain sought to recure;°   *cure again*
130 At middle day my sun seemed under land
When any little cloud did it obscure.
And as the icicles in a winter's day
Whenas the sun shines with unwonted° warm,   *unaccustomed*
So did my joys melt into secret tears,
135 So did my heart dissolve in wasting drops;
And as the season of the year outwears,
And heaps of snow from off the mountain tops
With sudden streams the valleys overflow,
So did the time draw on my more despair.
140 Then floods of sorrow and whole seas of woe
The banks of all my hope did overbear
And drowned my mind in depths of misery.
Sometime I died, sometime I was distract,°   *distracted, mad*
My soul the stage of fancy's° tragedy.   *imagination's*
145 Then furious madness, where true reason lacked,
Wrote what it would and scourged mine own conceit.
O heavy heart, who can thee witness bear?
What tongue, what pen, could thy tormenting treat
But thine own mourning thoughts which present were?
150 What stranger mind believe the meanest° part?   *least*
What altered sense[5] conceive the weakest woe
That tore, that rent, that piercéd thy sad heart?
And as a man distract, with treble might
Bound in strong chains doth strive and rage in vain
155 Till, tired and breathless, he is forced to rest,
Finds by contention but increase of pain
And fiery heat inflamed in swollen breast,
So did my mind in change of passion
From woe to wrath, from wrath return to woe,
160 Struggling in vain from love's subjection.
Therefore, all lifeless and all helpless bound,
My fainting spirits sunk and heart appalled,
My joys and hopes lay bleeding on the ground
That not long since the highest heaven scaled.
165 I hated life and curséd destiny;
The thoughts of passéd times, like flames of hell,
Kindled afresh within my memory
The many dear achievements that befell
In those prime° years and infancy of love,   *first; most perfect*
170 Which to describe were but to die in writing.
Ah, those[6] I sought but vainly to remove,
And vainly shall, by which I perish living,
And° though strong reason hold before mine eyes   *Even*
The images and forms of worlds past,
175 Teaching the cause why all those flames that rise

5. What consciousness, exchanged with mine.
6. The "thoughts of passed times" (166).

From forms external can no longer last
Than that° those seeming beauties hold in prime[7] *that which*
Love's ground, his essence, and his empery,° *imperial might*
All slaves to age and vassals unto time,
180 Of which repentance writes the tragedy.
But this[8] my heart's desire could not conceive,
Whose love outflew the fastest flying time,
A beauty that can easily deceive
Th' arrest of years and creeping age outclimb;
185 A spring of beauties which time ripeth not,
Time, that but works on frail mortality;
A sweetness which woe's wrongs outwipeth not,
Whom love hath chose for his divinity;
A vestal fire that burns, but never wasteth,
190 That loseth naught° by giving light to all, *nothing*
That endless shines eachwhere° and endless lasteth, *everywhere*
Blossoms of pride that can nor vade° nor fall. *fade, disappear*
These were those marvelous perfections,
The parents of my sorrow and my envy,
195 Most deathful and most violent infections;
These be the tyrants that in fetters tie
Their wounded vassals, yet nor kill nor cure
But glory in their lasting misery,
That as her beauties would, our woes should dure.° *endure*
200 These be th' effects of powerful empery.° *imperial power*

Yet have these wounders want,°which want° compassion; *a fault / lack*
Yet hath her mind some marks of human race;
Yet will she be a woman for a fashion;[9]
So doth she please her virtues to deface.
205 And like as that immortal power° doth seat° *Nature / lay down*
An element of waters to allay
The fiery sunbeams that on earth do beat
And temper by cold night the heat of the day,
So hath Perfection, which begat her mind,
210 Added thereto a change of fantasy[1]
And left her the affections of her kind,[2]
Yet free from every evil but cruelty.[3]

---

7. His reason can contemplate previous worlds that have gone out of existence and so understand the Platonic notion that desire ("those flames") for external things can last no longer than the youthful perfection ("prime") of the beauty that excites it. Nonetheless, he cannot remove thoughts of the "infancy of love" for the Queen, which he goes on to assert is, like her beauty, "endless" in its power over him (191).
8. This death brought about by slavery to time.
9. To enjoy the way it looks to others. Ralegh here takes a sardonic tone, noting "some marks" of humanity that still remain in the Queen.
1. Changeableness in the way she imagines and feels about others (her fancy).
2. The emotions of her sex.
3. A trait traditionally ascribed to the woman in Petrarchan love poetry. Ralegh suggests that the divine Perfection that created her mind tempered the cruelty of her sex by making her tend to change her feelings later, softening her harshness (as water cools fire and night cools the heat of day). Having admitted a ray of hope, here, the poet quickly abandons it in the next line, "But leave her praise, speak thou of naught but woe."

But leave her praise, speak thou of naught but woe;
Write on the tale that sorrow bids thee tell;
215 Strive to forget, and care no more to know.
Thy cares are known, by knowing those too well.[4]
Describe her now as she appears to thee,
Not as she did appear in days fordone.°   gone by
In love, those things that were no more may be,
220 For fancy seldom ends where it begun.
And as a stream, by strong hand bounded in
From Nature's course where it did sometime run,
By some small rent or loose part doth begin
To find escape, till it a way hath won,
225 Doth then all unawares in sunder tear
The forcéd bounds and, raging, run at large
In th' ancient channels as they wonted were,[5]
Such is of women's love the careful charge,[6]
Held and maintained with multitude of woes.
230 Of long erections[7] such the sudden fall;
One hour diverts, one instant overthrows,
For which our lives, for which our fortunes thrall°   in bondage
So many years those joys have dearly bought.[8]
Of which, when our fond hopes do most assure,
235 All is dissolved, our labors come to naught,
Nor any mark thereof there doth endure,
No more than when small drops of rain do fall
Upon the parchéd ground, by heat up dried.
No cooling moisture is perceived at all,
240 Nor any show or sign of wet doth bide.
But as[9] the fields clothed with leaves and flowers,
The banks of roses smelling precious sweet,
Have but their beauty's date° and timely hours   natural ending
And then defaced by winter's cold and sleet
245 So far as° neither fruit nor form of flower   With the result that
Stays for a witness what such branches bear,
But as time gave, time did again devour
And change our rising joy to falling care,
So of affection which our youth presented.
250 When she[1] that from the sun reaves° power and light   steals
Did but decline her beams as discontented,
Converting sweetest days to saddest night,
All droops, all dies, all trodden under dust,

4. Your cares are brought home to you by knowing all too well those qualities that characterized her in the past ("change of fantasy," "affections," "cruelty").
5. As they used to be.
6. The troublesome burden of desire.
7. Barriers that men attempt to erect to restrain their desires despite the difficulties ("woes") of doing so. The ironic sexual meaning conveyed by "of long erections such the sudden fall" shows graphically the end of the story and so reinforces the futility of such attempts.
8. For which our lives and our captive fortunes have, for so many years, bought those joys so dearly. The lines admit of other readings, but this seems the most likely.
9. This "as" leads to a corresponding "so" in line 249: as summer's flowering fields are defaced by winter's cold, so [the same may be said] of the affection which our youth presented.
1. Cynthia, the moon-goddess.

The person, place, and passages[2] forgotten,
255 The hardest steel eaten with softest rust,
The firm and solid tree both rent and rotten.
Those thoughts° so full of pleasure and content,   *written thoughts*
That in our absence were affection's food,[3]
Are razéd out° and from the fancy° rent;   *erased / imagination; liking*
260 In highest grace and heart's dear care that° stood   *those that*
Are cast for prey to hatred and to scorn.
Our dearest treasures and our heart's true joys,
The tokens° hung on breast and kindly worn,   *jewels he gave the Queen*
Are now elsewhere disposed° or held for toys.°   *given away / trifles*
265 And those° which then our jealousy removed   *tokens she gave him*
And others for our sakes then valued dear,
The one forgot, the rest are dear beloved,[4]
When all of ours doth strange or vild° appear.   *vile*
Those streams seem standing puddles which before
270 We saw our beauties in, so were they clear.[5]
Belphoebe's course° is now observed no more;   *way of acting*
That fair resemblance weareth out of date.[6]
Our ocean seas are but tempestuous waves
And all things base° that blesséd were of late.   *of little value*
275 And as field wherein the stubble stands
Of harvest past the plowman's eye offends,
He tills again or tears them up with hands
And throws to fire as foiled° and fruitless ends   *trampled*
And takes delight another seed to sow,
280 So doth the mind root up all wonted° thought   *customary*
And scorns the care of[7] our remaining woes.
The sorrows, which themselves for us have wrought,
Are burnt to cinders by new-kindled fires.[8]
The ashes are dispersed into the air;
285 The sighs, the groans of all our past desires
Are clean outworn,[9] as things that never were.

With youth is dead the hope of Love's° return,   *Cupid's*
Who looks not back to hear our after-cries.

---

2. Events, and perhaps also passages in earlier writings.
3. That when I was away sustained her affection. Here and in the lines following, "our" means "my," as "our ocean seas" (274) makes clear. Ralegh is the ocean, and Elizabeth is the changeable moon that controls it.
4. His gifts to her are forgotten, but those ("the rest") that she gave him and he, in jealousy, removed and gave to others are, ironically, still regarded as precious because they came from him.
5. Unclear. If the poet is returning to the notion of written thoughts given to the Queen (lines 257–59), he may mean that the rushing streams of words that he used to describe her, which were so clear and reflected so well his own beauty as a poet and lover, now seem stagnant puddles. In that case, his mention in the next line of his favorite poetic figure for her as the moon goddess Belphoebe or Cynthia would continue his reflections about his writings.
6. The resemblance of Elizabeth to the gentle and peaceful moon (which Ralegh made popular) is dated, since she is now harsh and angry. As the next line suggests, the effect of her anger is to stir up in him (the ocean) tempestuous waves rather than the quiet tides of affection that he once felt.
7. Disdains to be concerned about.
8. Elizabeth's sorrows, which have worked themselves up for Ralegh, are now consumed by new desires (probably those for her new favorite, the Earl of Essex).
9. A continuation of the idea that the relationship has lost its emotional force and its aura of the divine (line 272).

Where he is not, he laughs at those that mourn;
290 Whence he is gone,[1] he scorns the mind that dies;
When he is absent, he believes no words;
When reason speaks, he careless stops his ears;
Whom he hath left, he never grace affords,
But bathes his wings in our lamenting tears.
295 Unlasting passion, soon outworn conceit°   *poetic image (of Cupid)*
Whereon I built and on so dureless° trust.   *transient*
My mind had wounds, I dare not say deceit.
Were I resolved her promise was not just?
Sorrow was my revenge[2] and woe my hate;
300 I powerless was to alter my desire.
My love is not of time or bound to date;
My heart's internal heat and living fire
Would not, or could, be quenched with sudden showers.
My bound respect was not confined to days,
305 My vowéd faith not set to ended hours.[3]
I love the bearing and not bearing sprays,[4]
Which now to others do their sweetness send,
Th' incarnate,° snow-driven white, and purest azure,°   *blood red / blue*
Who[5] from high heaven doth on their fields descend,
310 Filling their barns with grain and towers with treasure.
Erring or never erring, such is love
As, while it lasteth, scorns th' account of those
Seeking but self-contentment to improve,[6]
And hides, if any be, his inward woes,
315 And will not know, while he knows his own passion,
The often and unjust perseverance
In deeds of love and state, and every action
From that first day and year of their joy's entrance.[7]

But I, unblessed and ill-born creature
320 That did embrace the dust her body bearing,[8]
That loved her both by fancy and by nature,
That drew, even with the milk in my first sucking,
Affection from the parent's breast that bare me,[9]
Have found her as a stranger so severe,
325 Improving° my mishap in each degree.[1]   *aggravating*
But love was gone. So would I, my life were.

1. In the place from which Love has departed.
2. Was I convinced her promise was not true? Well, then, sorrow was my only revenge.
3. Not brought to an end when she ended her practice of spending hours with him.
4. I love both branches that bear flowers and those that don't; that is, I do not love Elizabeth only when she offers me political or material gain.
5. Referring to the "sprays" of pink, white, and blue flowers. Ralegh uses the personal "who" rather than "which" because the branch represents Elizabeth.
6. A dig at Essex, who was enriched by the Queen (as was Ralegh).
7. Knowing that his own passion is more worthy, a true lover will not pay any attention to the frequent and unjust honors that his beloved showers so persistently on his rivals when they first begin to feel the joy of her attentions.
8. Ground she walked on.
9. A loving nature derived from his mother.
1. Making my misfortune worse at every stage.

A queen she was to me, no more Belphoebe;
A lion then, no more a milk-white dove;
A prisoner in her breast I could not be;
330 She did untie the gentle chains of love.
Love was no more the love of hiding
All trespass and mischance for her own glory.
It had been such, it was still for th' elect,[2]
But I must be th' example in love's story.
335 This was of all forepast the sad effect.

But thou, my weary soul and heavy thought,
Made by her love a burden to my being,
Dost know my error never was forethought
Or ever could proceed from sense of loving.[3]
340 Of other cause if then it had proceeding,
I leave th' excuse, sith° judgment hath been given;   *since*
The limbs divided, sundered, and a-bleeding[4]
Cannot complain the sentence was uneven.

This° did that nature's wonder, virtue's choice,   *This punishment*
345 The only paragon of time's begetting,[5]
Divine in words, angelical in voice,
That spring of joys, that flower of love's own setting,°   *planting*
Th' idea remaining of those golden ages,[6]
That beauty braving° heavens and earth embalming,[7]   *challenging*
350 Which after° worthless worlds but play on stages.   *afterwards*
Such did'st thou her long since describe, yet sighing
That thy unable spirit could not find aught
In heaven's beauties or in earth's delight
For likeness° fit to satisfy thy thought.   *a comparison*
355 But what hath it availed thee so to write?
She cares not for thy praise, who knows not theirs;[8]
It's now an idle labor and a tale
Told out of time that dulls the hearer's ears,
A merchandise whereof there is no sale.
360 Leave them, or lay them up with thy despairs;
She hath resolved and judged thee long ago;
Thy lines are now a murmuring to her ears,
Like to a falling stream which passing slow
Is wont to nourish sleep and quietness.

---

2. Those she chose in his place, but also with a theological overtone suggesting that she was acting like God, singling out the Chosen and holding him up as an example of godlessness.
3. In this, Ralegh's only reference to his wife, Elizabeth Throckmorton, he denies that he intended to become entangled with her or that he ever loved her.
4. A metaphor based on the punishment for treason, which involved dividing the traitor limb from limb.
5. A reference to the proverb "Truth is the daughter of Time," used at Elizabeth's coronation to celebrate her vindication after her unjust imprisonment under Mary Tudor.
6. In classical myth, the first era in human history, seen as a time of universal peace, plenty, and justice.
7. Bringing balm to.
8. Unclear, but perhaps the "likenesses" to her in poems, such as the present one, that she does not know because Ralegh has never shared them with her.

365 So shall thy painful labors be perused
    And draw on rest, which sometime had regard.[9]
    But those, her cares, thy errors have excused;[1]
    Thy days foredone have had their day's reward.
    So her hard heart, so her estrangéd mind,
370 In which, above the heavens, I once reposed;
    So to thy error have her ears inclined
    And have forgotten all thy past deserving,
    Holding in mind but only thine offense
    And only now affecteth thy depraving,°   *desires thy dishonor*
375 And thinks all vain that pleadeth thy defense.
    Yet greater fancy° beauty never bred,   *liking*
    A more desire the heart-blood never nourished,
    Her sweetness an affection never fed,
    Which more in any age hath ever flourished.
380 The mind and virtue never have begotten
    A firmer love, since love on earth had power,
    A love obscured, but cannot be forgotten,
    Too great and strong for time's jaws to devour,
    Containing such a faith as ages wound not.
385 Care, wakeful ever of her good estate;
    Fear, dreading loss, which sighs and joys not;
    A memory of the joys her grace begat;
    A lasting gratefulness for those comforts past,
    Of which the cordial sweetness cannot die.
390 These thoughts,[2] knit up by faith, shall ever last;
    These time assays,° but never can untie,   *assails*
    Whose life once lived in her pearl-like breast,
    Whose joys were drawn but° from her happiness,   *only*
    Whose heart's high pleasure, and whose mind's true rest,
395 Proceeded from her fortune's blessedness;
    Who was intentive, wakeful, and dismayed
    In fears, in dreams, in feverous jealousy;
    Who long in silence served and obeyed
    With secret heart and hidden loyalty;
400 Which never change to sad adversity,
    Which never age or nature's overthrow,
    Which never sickness or deformity,
    Which never wasting care or wearing woe
    (If subject unto these she could have been),
405 Which never words or wits malicious,
    Which never honor's bait or world's fame
    Achieved by attempts adventurous,

---

9. His poetry, which she once liked, will now put her to sleep.
1. Her preoccupation with cares of state excuse his errors (in seeking love from another woman).
2. "These thoughts" are the subject of a complex, swelling sentence that fills twenty-five lines and
   seems to change focus as it proceeds, the clauses beginning "whose" (392) and "who" (396) coming to refer to Ralegh rather than to his thoughts. The meaning, in outline, is as follows: "My
   thoughts shall ever last, I whose life once lived in her pearl-like breast . . . , who was attentive . . .
   and who long in silence served and obeyed with hidden loyalty, which never a change to sad
   adversity . . . can so dissolve . . . but that the thoughts and memories will cause a relapse of passion
   and so remain the sorrow-sucking bees of my heart."

Or aught° beneath the sun or heaven's frame   *anything*
Can so dissolve, dissever, or destroy
410 The essential love, of no frail parts compounded,
Though of the same now buried be the joy,
The hope, the comfort, and the sweetness ended,
But that the thoughts and memories of these,
Work a relapse of passion and remain
415 Of my sad heart the sorrow-sucking bees.
The wrongs received, the scorns persuade in vain,
And though these medicines work desire to end°   *to end desire*
And are in others the true cure of liking,
The salves that heal love's wounds and do amend
420 Consuming woe and slake our hearty sighing,
They work not so in thy mind's long disease.³
External fancy⁴ time alone recureth,
All whose effects do wear away with ease.
Love of delight, while such delight endureth,
425 Stays by° the pleasure, but no longer stays.   *Remains with*
But in my mind so is her love enclosed
And is thereof not only the best part,
But into it the essence is disposed.⁵
O love, the more my woe, to it thou art
430 Even as the moisture in each plant that grows,
Even as the sun unto the frozen ground,
Even as the sweetness to th' incarnate rose,
Even as the center in each perfect round,
As water to the fish, to men as air,
435 As heat to fire, as light unto the sun.
O love, it is but vain to say thou wear;°   *wear out*
Ages and times cannot thy power outrun.

Thou art the soul of that unhappy mind
Which, being by nature made an idle thought,
440 Began even then to take immortal kind⁶
When first her virtues in thy spirits wrought.°   *had their effects*
From thee, therefore, that mover cannot move⁷
Because it is become thy cause of being,⁸
Whatever error may obscure that love,
445 Whatever frail effect in mortal living,
Whatever passion from distempered heart,
What absence, time, or injuries effect,
What faithless friends or deep dissembled art
Present, to feed her most unkind suspect.°   *suspicion*

---

3. Ralegh's mind is so diseased with love that the usual medicines to cure it ("wrongs" and "scorns" in line 416) do not work.
4. Liking for external beauty.
5. Ralegh's love for Elizabeth is essential, not accidental (involving external appearance or mere delight). It is part and parcel of his mind itself.
6. Take on an immortal nature.
7. Since God is described as the "unmoved mover," the line suggests that she became like God to him, his "cause of being" and the controller of his actions.
8. See lines 426–28 and note.

450 Yet as the air in deep caves underground
    Is strongly drawn when violent heat hath rent
    Great clefts therein till moisture do abound,
    And then the same imprisoned and up-pent
    Breaks out in earthquakes,⁹ tearing all asunder,
455 So in the center of my cloven heart,
    My heart, to whom her beauties wear such wonder,
    Lies the sharp poisoned head of that love's dart,
    Which, till all break and all dissolve to dust,
    Thence drawn it cannot be or therein known.
460 There, mixed with my heart blood, the fretting° rust   gnawing
    The better part hath eaten and outgrown.
    But what of those, or these, or what of aught°   anything
    Of that which was, or that which is, to treat?°   speak of
    What I possess is but the same I sought.
465 My love was false, my labors were deceit,
    Nor less than such they are esteemed to be:
    A fraud bought at the price of many woes;
    A guile, whereof the profits unto me—
    Could it be thought premeditate for those?
470 Witness those withered leaves left on the tree,
    The sorrow-worn face, the pensive mind,
    The external shows what may th' internal be.
    Cold care hath bitten both the root and rind.

    But stay, my thoughts, make end, give fortune way.
475 Harsh is the voice of woe and sorrow's sound;
    Complaints cure not, and tears do but allay
    Griefs for a time, which after more abound.
    To seek for moisture in th' Arabian sand
    Is but a loss of labor and of rest.
480 The links which time did break of hearty bands
    Words cannot knit or wailings make anew.
    Seek not the sun in clouds when it is set
    On highest mountains, where those cedars grew
    Against whose banks the troubled ocean beat
485 And where the marks¹ to find thy hopéd port
    Into a soil far off themselves remove.
    On Sestos' shore, Leander's late resort,
    Hero hath left no lamp to guide her love.
    Thou lookest for light in vain, and storms arise;
490 She sleeps thy death,² that erst° thy danger sighed.   at first
    Strive then no more, bow down thy weary eyes,
    Eyes which to all these woes thy heart have guided.

    She is gone, she is lost. She is found, she is ever fair.
    Sorrow draws weakly where love draws not too.³

9. Elizabethans commonly attributed earthquakes to pent-up "wind" or steam in the bowels of the earth.
1. Landmarks, meaning the mountains and cedars.
2. Sleeps at news of thy death.
3. Sorrow is ineffective unless accompanied by love.

495   Woe's cries sound nothing, but only in love's ear.
     Do then, by dying, what life cannot do.
     Unfold° thy flocks and leave them to the fields   *Release*
     To feed on hills or dales, where likes them best,
     Of what the summer, or the springtime, yields,
500   For love and time hath given thee leave to rest.
     Thy heart, which was their fold, now in decay
     By often storms and winter's many blasts,
     All torn and rent becomes misfortune's prey.
     False hope, my shepherd's staff, now age hath brast.°   *broken*
505   My pipe, which love's own hand gave my desire
     To sing her praises and my woe upon,
     Despair hath often threatened to the fire,
     As vain to keep now all the rest are gone.
     Thus home I draw, as death's long night draws on.
510   Yet every foot,[4] old thoughts turn back mine eyes.
     Constraint me guides as old age draws a stone
     Against the hill, which over-weighty lies
     For feeble arms or wasted strength to move.
     My steps are backward, gazing on my loss,
520   My mind's affection and my soul's sole love
     Not mixed with fancy's chaff or fortune's dross.
     To God I leave it, who first gave it to me,
     And I her gave, and she returned again
     As° it was hers. So let His mercies be   *As if or since*
525   Of my last comforts the essential mean.°   *source*

     But be it so or not, th' effects are past.
     Her love hath end; my woe must ever last.[5]

QUEEN ELIZABETH

WORKS OF SORROW AND CONSOLATION (1593)

[Letter to Henry IV of France][†]

July 1593

    Ah what griefs, O what regrets, O what groanings felt I in my soul at the sound of such news as Morlains has told me![1] My God, is it possible that any worldly respect should efface the terror with which the fear of God threatens us? Can we with any reason expect a good sequel from an act so iniquitous? He

---

4. A pun on poetic feet and those of a traveler.
5. We omit a final brief section of the manuscript headed "The end of the books, and of the Ocean's love to Cynthia, and the beginning of the 22nd book, entreating of sorrow."
† Copy text: *Elizabeth I: Collected Works*, ed. Leah S. Marcus, Janel Mueller, and Mary Beth Rose (Chicago and London: University of Chicago Press, 2000), 370–71. Reprinted by permission of the University of Chicago Press. Copyright © 2000 by the University of Chicago. Henry succeeded to the throne in 1589, but was not actually crowned King until February 1594.
1. Jean de Morlans arrived in London in July to convey the news that Henry of Navarre, now Henry IV of France, had converted to Roman Catholicism; Henry is reported to have said, in his defense, that "Paris is worth a Mass."

who has preserved you many years by His hand—can you imagine that He would permit you to walk alone in your greatest need? Ah, it is dangerous to do evil to make good out of it; I still hope that a sounder inspiration will come to you. However, I will not cease to place you in the forefront of my devotions,[2] that the hands of Esau may not spoil the blessing of Jacob. And where you promise me all friendship and fidelity, I confess I have dearly merited it, and I will not repent it, provided you do not change your Father. Otherwise I will be only a bastard sister, at least not your sister by the Father. For I will always prefer the natural to the adopted, as God best knows. May He guide you in the right path of the best way.

> Your most assured sister, if it be after the old fashion;
> with the new I have nothing to do.

From Translation of Boethius's Consolation of Philosophy[†]

1.7.

Dim° clouds		*Dark*
Sky close,		
Light none		
Can afford.[1]		
5	If rolling seas	
Boistous° south°		*Violent / south wind*
Mix his foam		
Greeny, once		
Like the clearest		
10	Days the water	
Straight (mud		
Stirred up all foul),		
The sight gainsays.°[2]		*obscures*
Running stream		
15	That pours	
From highest hills		
Oft is stayed°		*stopped*
By slaked°		*fallen*
Stone of rock.		
20	Thou, if thou wilt	
In clearest light		
The troth[3] behold,		
By straight line		
Hit in° the path.		*Thrust forward along*
25	Chase° joys,	*Chase away*
Repulse fear,		
Thrust out hope,		

2. Prayers.
† Copy text: *Queen Elizabeth's Englishings of Boethius, De consolatione philosophiae*, ed. Caroline Pemberton (London: Early English Text Society, Original Series 113, 1899), 24, 29, 32, 38, 43.
1. When dark clouds close over the sky, there is no light.
2. If rolling seas, stirred up violently by the south wind, are churned into green foam, the water (which once was clear as the day) becomes obscure with mud.
3. Truth.

Woe not retain.
Cloudy is the mind
30   With snaffle° bound   *bridle*
Where they reign.[4]

2.8.

That world with stable trust
      The changing seasons turns
And divers° seeds° still holds league,°[5]   *contrary / elements / covenant*
      That Phoebus the ruddy day
5   With golden car[6] brings forth,
            That° moon may rule the night,   *So that the*
            Which Hesperus° brought.   *the evening star*
The greedy sea her stream
      In certain limits kept
10   That lawful be not to wide world
            To bank her spacious bounds.[7]
All this whole mould° ties   *earth*
      In ruling earth and sea,
Love ruling heavens.[8]
15   Who° if the reins He slake,°   *Love / loosens*
What so now by love is linked,
            Straight maketh war
And seeks to wrack that work
            Which linkéd faith
20   It quiet motions moved.[9]
He in holy peace doth hold
      The bounded people's pact
And links sacred wedlock
      With chaste goodwill,
25   Who laws his own
      To true associates gives.[1]
O happy humankind,
      If Love your minds
That same that heaven doth rule
30   Might guide.[2]

---

4. For Boethius, a clear mind required the expulsion of both joy and fear, hope and sorrow.
5. The world with constant faithfulness regulates the changing seasons and binds its competing elements together in a harmonious covenant.
6. Phoebus, as the sun-god, was conventionally depicted driving a gold chariot across the sky.
7. The greedy sea keeps its boundaries so as not unlawfully to encroach upon the wide world's boundaries.
8. The whole world is bound by Love (here treated as a name for God) who rules the heavens and also earth and sea.
9. If God loosens His control, that which was harmoniously interconnected by love (namely the quiet, regular motions of the seasons, the contrasting elements, the sun and moon, and the earth and sea) will be disrupted.
1. God also undergirds human covenants and unites marriage with affection, giving His own laws to His faithful friends.
2. O happy humans, if your minds are guided by the same Love that rules the heavens.

3.6.

All humankind on earth
    From like beginning comes;
One Father is of all,
    One only all doth guide.
5 He gave to sun the beams
    And horns on moon bestowed;
He men to earth did give
    And signs° to heaven.   *stars*
He closed in limbs our souls,
10   Fetched from highest seat;[3]
A noble seed therefore brought forth
    All mortal folk.
What crake° you of your stock°   *brag / lineage*
    Or forefathers old?
15 If your first spring and author
    God you view,
No man bastard be,
    Unless with vice the worst he feed
And leaveth so his birth.[4]

4.2

Those which you see as kings
    Sit in the top of highest seat
Flourishing with purple fare,°   *royal pomp*
    Environed with dreadful arms,[5]
5 With ireful° look that threats,   *wrathful*
    For heart's ire scant drawing breath.[6]
If any take from wicked men
    Of false honor the cover,[7]
Within shall° see their lords   *they shall*
10   Straitened gyves° to bear: *confining shackles*
Hither lust them draws;
    Here ire their minds afflicts,
Who stirred raiseth storms;[8]
    Sorrow or the taken° wears,   *captive*
15 Or slipper° hopes torment.[9]   *slippery*
    Wherefore, when one head
So many tyrants bears,

---

3. Boethius believed that souls were created in heaven and then placed into bodies.
4. If you understand that God is your creator, no one is born a bastard, but only makes himself one by persisting in wicked behavior, thereby departing from his divine lineage. In this regard, note Elizabeth's warning to Henry IV in the preceding letter not to abandon his Father and thus bastardize their relationship.
5. Surrounded by dread-inspiring weapons.
6. Threatening with angry looks; so angry, indeed, they don't stop to catch their breath (that is, they are consumed by passion).
7. The cloak of false honor.
8. Here lust entices them; here anger, stirred up into a storm, afflicts their minds.
9. Sorrow either wearies them [as] captives or slippery hopes torment them.

He doth not that° he would,   *that which*
Pressed with so wicked lords.[1]

5.2.

"Clear Phoebus with purest light,"
The honeyed mouth of Homer sings.
Who yet the deep bowels of earth and sea
With weak sight of beams pierce not;
5   Not so of the great world the Framer.[2]
'Gainst Him that all from high doth view,
No weight of earth may resist,
Not night with darkest clouds gainsays.
In moment stroke His mind all sees:[3]
10 What were, what be, what shall befall.
Whom sole alone for that° He all espies,   *because*
Truly thee may Sol° call.[4]   *Sun*

New Faces on Accession Day

Though hardly the greatest of the losses suffered by the Queen in the early 1590s, the retirement of Sir Henry Lee was perhaps the most visible to her people. Having served as her champion in royal tournaments for nearly twenty years, Lee was more than just a skillful jouster. As the founder and principal promoter of the annual Accession Day tilts at Court, he helped to turn an informal tradition of ringing church bells on November 17 into a national holiday so popular that it continued to be observed for more than a century after the Queen's death. Not all the credit, of course, goes to him. After the Rebellion of the Northern Earls, the occasion had become a celebration of the Protestant Queen's triumph over her Catholic enemies, and in towns and villages throughout the country, it was observed with speeches, religious services, parties, banquets, and fireworks. Under Lee's sponsorship, however, the celebration at Court developed into something grander. Knowing the Queen's fondness for the myth that her Tudor ancestors were descended from the royal line of King Arthur, Lee devised festivities that hearkened back to the days of the Round Table, when England was united around a great and charismatic monarch. In mixing heady nationalism with religious devotion and storybook pageantry, the jousts proved enormously popular.

By 1590, even Lee's remarkable strength and stamina was no longer adequate to his position, and he resigned. The retirement ceremony, which was staged before the Queen on Accession Day, was recorded by the military historian William Seagar. It began with curious music and the sudden appearance, as if out of the ground, of a pavilion made of white taffeta, which Seagar identified with the Temple of Vesta in ancient Rome. Three virgin priestesses appeared,

---

1. When a kingly "head" is oppressed with the tyrants of lust, wrath, sorrow, and false hopes, he is not free to do whatever he wishes.
2. Even the bright, clear sun, of which Homer sweetly sang, cannot penetrate the depths of earth and sea with his weak beams, but God the Creator does see all things. Homer praised "clear Phoebus" as the one who sees and hears all things, a description cited by Boethius in the line that immediately precedes this poem (cf. *The Iliad*, trans. Robert Fagles, Book 3, line 331, p. 138; *The Odyssey*, trans. Robert Fagles, Book 11, line 124, p. 253). Boethius, however, draws a contrast between the created sun and the Creator God, granting only to the latter the ability to see all things.
3. God sees all from the single and instantaneous perspective of eternity, not through the lens of time.
4. Because God alone sees all things past, present, and future, you may truly call Him the Sun.

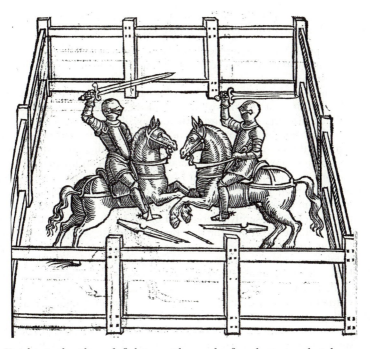

Knights in the tilt-yard, fighting with swords after shattering their lances.

clad in white, presenting gifts to the Virgin Queen. Lee then approached the throne, removing his armor and placing it before a pillar symbolizing the Queen's virtue and imperial might. After kneeling in prayer, he petitioned the Queen to release him from service and to give his office to a younger man, George Clifford, Earl of Cumberland. Although Elizabeth granted his request, allowing him to retire to his rural estate at Woodstock, she was grieved to see her old champion go. Afterwards, she sometimes recalled him to Court to help with ceremonies, and in 1592, she paid him a grand visit during one of her summer progresses.

As older jousters such as Lee retired from the Accession Day tournament, younger ones such as the Earl of Essex and members of his faction and the sons of Elizabeth's Comptroller of the Household, Sir Francis Knollys, vied for the limelight. Honor came partly through strength and skill and partly through ingenious pageantry. Since participants were expected to devise new armaments for themselves and fresh trappings for their attendants for each year's festivities, a good deal of time and money was spent in creating sumptuous outfits and in painting shields with clever *impresas* (emblems inscribed with pithy mottos). Prominent contestants also devised tiltyard speeches for the Queen and entertainments for the evening banquet that concluded the festivities.

The Accession Day tilts of 1595 reveal what the celebration was like at its highest level of development. In a letter to Sir Robert Sidney (brother of Sir Philip), Rowland White describes an entertainment commissioned for the occasion by the Earl of Essex. It began on the field of combat and reached its conclusion later that evening. In it, Essex addressed the Queen as an unrequited lover, much as Sir Christopher Hatton and Sir Walter Ralegh had done in earlier days. The end of White's letter reveals the Court's fascination with topical allegory, for as the characters finished their speeches, the spectators immediately tried to identify them with particular men at Court. White, however, was skeptical, finding no truth in their speculations:

> Some pretty while before he [Essex] came in himself to the tilt, he sent his page with some speech to the Queen, who returned with her Majesty's glove. And when he came himself, he was met with an old hermit, a secretary of state, a brave soldier, and an esquire [or squire]. The first presented him with a book of meditations, the second with political discourses, the third with orations of brave-fought battles, and the fourth was but his own follower, to whom th' other three imparted much of their purpose before his coming in. Another devised with him, persuading him to this and that course of life, according to their inclinations. Comes into the tiltyard (unthought upon) th' ordinary post boy of London, a ragged villain all bemired, upon a poor lean jade, galloping and blowing for life, and delivered the secretary a packet of letters, which he presently offered my Lord of Essex. And with this dumb show our eyes were fed for that time. In th' after supper, before the Queen, they first delivered a well-penned speech to move this worthy knight [Essex] to leave his vain following of love and to betake him to heavenly meditation. But the esquire answered them all and concluded that this knight would never forsake his mistress's love, whose virtue made all his thoughts divine, whose wisdom taught him all true policy, whose beauty and worth were at all times able to make him fit to command armies. The world makes many untrue constructions of these speeches, comparing the hermit and the secretary to two of the lords and the soldier to Sir Roger Williams.[1] But the Queen said that, if she had thought there had been so much said of her, she would not have been there that night, and so went to bed. (Collins, *Letters and Memorials of State*, 1.362)

Few other Accession Day tilts are so fully described in documents of the period. In a colorful, eyewitness poem entitled *Anglicorum Feriae*, the poet and playwright George Peele celebrated the religious importance of the occasion (about which see Part 6) and also, in the selection presented here, detailed the jousting. The collector of emblems and heraldic symbols, Henry Peacham, printed Essex's Accession Day Tournament *Impresa*, adding a poem elaborating on its meaning; and the celebrated essayist, courtier, and advocate of empirical science, Francis Bacon, author of Essex's entertainment *Of Love and Self-Love*, left a copy among his papers.

Bacon's work is particularly elegant and sophisticated, with syntax framed out of carefully balanced clauses and words chosen with an eye to subtleties of meaning and overtone. The entertainment is also funny. It begins with three servants of the villain of the piece, Lady Philauta (Self-Love), strutting and preening themselves on the three branches of human endeavor that they represent: study, warfare, and statesmanship. To refute them, Essex need not appear himself but only send his humble servant, the Squire, who knows more than they do in all their worldly sophistication. The Squire argues that Essex's devotion to Erophilus (Love of Erotic Love) is worth more than anything Self-Love has to offer, since love of Elizabeth leads to truer learning, greater bravery and achievement in battle, and wiser governance.

---

1. Williams, who had distinguished himself fighting in the Netherlands in the 1570s and 1580s and in France in the early 1590s, was Essex's friend, having served under him as, among other things, second in command over the cavalry at Tilbury.

WILLIAM SEAGAR

From Honor, Military and Civil (1602)[†]

[*The Retirement of the Queen's Champion, Sir Henry Lee,
November 17, 1590*]

Here will we remember also (and I hope without envy so may) that these
annual exercises in arms, solemnized the seventeenth day of November,
were first begun and occasioned by the right virtuous and honorable Sir
Henry Lee, Master of her Highness's Armory, and now deservingly Knight
of the most noble order, who, of his great zeal and earnest desire to
eternize the glory of her Majesty's court in the beginning of her happy reign,
voluntarily vowed (unless infirmity, age, or other accident did impeach
him) during his life to present himself at the tilt armed, the day aforesaid
yearly, there to perform in honor of her sacred Majesty the promise he formerly made. Whereupon the lords and gentlemen of the said Court,
incited by so worthy an example, determined to continue that custom
and, not unlike to the ancient knighthood *de la Banda* in Spain, have ever
since yearly assembled in arms accordingly, though true it is that the
author of that custom (being by age overtaken) in the thirty-third year
of her Majesty's reign resigned and recommended that office unto the
right noble George, Earl of Cumberland, the ceremonies of which assig-
nation[1] were publicly performed in presence of her Majesty, her ladies
and nobility, also an infinite number of people, beholding the same as
followeth.

On the seventeenth day of November, *anno* 1590, this honorable gentleman together with the Earl of Cumberland, having first performed their
service in arms, presented themselves unto her Highness at the foot of the
stairs under her gallery window in the tiltyard at Westminster, where at that
time her Majesty did sit, accompanied with the Viscount Turenne,[2] Ambassador of France, many ladies, and the chiefest nobility.

Her Majesty, beholding these armed knights coming toward her, did
suddenly hear a music so sweet and secret,[3] as everyone thereat greatly
marveled. And hearkening to that excellent melody, the earth as it were
opening, there appeared a pavilion made of white taffeta, containing eight
score ells,[4] being in proportion like unto the sacred Temple of the Virgins
Vestal. This temple seemed to consist upon pillars of porphyry,[5] arched like
unto a church. Within it were many lamps burning. Also on the one side
there stood an altar covered with cloth of gold and thereupon two wax candles burning in rich candlesticks; upon the altar also were laid certain
princely presents, which after by three virgins were presented unto her
Majesty. Before the door of this temple stood a crowned pillar embraced by

---

† Copy text: William Seagar, *Honor military, and ciuill* (London: Robert Barker, 1602; STC 22164),
  R3r–R4v.
1. Transfer of responsibilities; *de la Banda: la orden de la banda* was a chivalric order founded by
   Alfonso XI of Castile in 1332; *Earl of Cumberland:* George Clifford, third Earl of Cumberland, privateer and trusted courtier. He remained the Queen's champion until her death.
2. Henry de la Tour d'Auvergne, French General in the Huguenot army of Henry of Navarre.
3. That is, the musicians were concealed from view.
4. Since an ell is forty-five inches, the cloth was about 600 feet long; *taffeta:* fine silk cloth.
5. Red granite or marble; *consist:* stand.

an eglantine[6] tree, whereon there hanged a table and therein written (with letters of gold) this prayer following:

For Eliza., &c.[7]

To you, O pious, powerful, and most blessed virgin,
Vindicator of loyalty, peace, nobility,
To whom God, the stars, and your own virtue
Have assigned the highest station,
After so many years, so many triumphs,
An old man, ready to lay his life at your feet,
Hangs up his sacred arms.
He prays that you have
A tranquil life, imperial dominion, fame,
Eternal fame,
Willing to redeem them with his own blood.
May your pillar be moved beyond
The Pillars of Hercules.
May your crown surpass all crowns
So that the crown which heaven
Bestowed on you at your most happy birth
You may take back to heaven at your most blessed death.
Eternal God, most high and holy,
Hear, O hear, this prayer.

The music aforesaid was accompanied with these verses, pronounced and sung by Master Hales,[8] her Majesty's servant, a gentleman in that art excellent and for his voice both commendable and admirable:

My golden locks time hath to silver turned
(O time too swift, and swiftness never ceasing);
My youth 'gainst age, and age at youth hath spurned,[9]
But spurned in vain. Youth waneth° by increasing.   *diminishes*
Beauty, strength, and youth flowers fading been;
Duty, faith, and love are roots and ever green.

My helmet now shall make an hive for bees,[1]
And lovers' songs shall turn to holy psalms.
A Man at Arms must now sit on his knees
And feed on prayers, that are old age's alms.[2]

---

6. Wild, pink rose. Elizabeth's grandfather, Henry VII, ended the Wars of the Roses by uniting the red rose of Lancaster (his family) with the white rose of York (that of his wife Elizabeth). Eglantine became a symbol of the national unity brought by the Tudors; *pillar*: in Petrarch's *Triumph of Chastity*, a pillar symbolizes sexual continence. In the Sieve Portraits of Elizabeth and elsewhere, columns also imply imperial might. Charles V of Spain used the Pillars of Hercules at Gibraltar with the motto *"Plus Ultra"* ("Beyond the Furthest") as his insignia, symbolizing his dominions beyond the western boundaries of Europe.
7. Translated from the original Latin by Clarence H. Miller.
8. Robert Hales, a singer and lute player favored by the Queen; *verses*: the popular song "My golden locks" has been attributed to Lee himself, though it also appeared in George Peele's *Polyhymnia*.
9. Triumphed over. Lee defeated older knights when he was young and younger knights when he was old.
1. In Lee's retirement, he expected rural pursuits like beekeeping to replace tilting and Court service.
2. Offerings to God.

And so from Court to cottage I depart;
My saint[3] is sure of mine unspotted heart.

And when I sadly sit in homely cell,
I'll teach my swains this carol for a song:
15 "Blest be the hearts that think my Sovereign well;
Cursed be the souls that think to do her wrong."
Goddess, vouchsafe this agéd man his right,
To be your beadsman[4] now, that was your knight.

The gifts which the Vestal maidens presented unto her Majesty were
these: a veil of white, exceeding rich and curiously wrought; a cloak and
safeguard set with buttons of gold, and on them were graven *impresas* of
excellent device.[5] In the loop of every button was a nobleman's badge[6] fixed
to a pillar, richly embroidered.

And here, by way of digression, let us remember a speech which this
noble gentleman used at such time as these buttons were set upon the garment aforesaid: "I would," quoth he, "that all my friends might have been
remembered in these buttons, but there is not room enough to contain
them all; and if I have them not all, then," said he, "those that are left out
may take exception." Whereunto another standing by answered, "Sir, let as
many be placed as can be and cause the last button to be made like the character of '&c.'" "Now, Godamercy, with all my heart," quoth the Knight, "for
I would not have given the *cetera*[7] of my friends for a million of gold."

But to return to the purpose, these presents and prayer being with great
reverence delivered into her Majesty's own hands and he himself disarmed,
offered[8] up his armor at the foot of her Majesty's crowned pillar and, kneeling upon his knees, presented the Earl of Cumberland, humbly beseeching she would be pleased to accept him for her knight, to continue the
yearly exercises aforesaid. Her Majesty graciously accepting of that offer,
this aged knight armed the Earl and mounted him upon his horse. That
being done, he put upon his own person a side coat of black velvet,
pointed[9] under the arm, and covered his head (in lieu of an helmet) with a
buttoned cap of the country fashion.

✻   ✻   ✻

Thus much was the substance (and well near the whole circumstance) of
Sir Henry Lee's last taking of arms, wherein he seemed to imitate the ancient
Romans, who having served a convenient time and claiming the privileges
due to old soldiers (whom they called *Emeriti*) did come into *Campo Mar-
tio*,[1] every man leading his own horse, and there offered his arms unto Mars
in presence of the chief magistrates, which ceremony Scipio, Cassius, the
great Pompey, with many other noble captains, disdained not to do.

---

3. Elizabeth.
4. One devoted to his prayer beads or paid from an endowment to pray for others.
5. Inventiveness; *safeguard*: protective riding skirt; *impresas*: painted images, often with a pithy motto,
    used on knights' shields to identify them.
6. Heraldic device representing a knight's house or lineage.
7. Remainder, with a pun on *et cetera*; *Godamercy*: God have mercy.
8. He offered.
9. Fastened with laces.
1. Field outside ancient Rome used for military training, ceremonies, and monuments.

Summarily, these annual actions have been most nobly performed (according to their times) by one duke, nineteen earls, twenty-seven barons, four Knights of the Garter, and above 150 other knights and esquires.

GEORGE PEELE

From Anglorum Feriae, England's Holidays (1595)[†]

Descend, ye sacred daughters[1] of King Jove.
Apollo, spread thy sparkling wings to mount
And try some lightsome sweet Castalian springs[2]
That warble to their silver-winding waves,
5   Making soft music in their gentle glide.
Clio, the sagest of these sisters nine,
Conduct thy learnéd company to Court,
Eliza's Court, Astræa's earthly heaven;
There take survey of England's emperess,[3]
10 And in her praise tune your heroic songs:
Write, write, you chroniclers of time and fame
That keep Remembrance' golden register
And recommend to Time's eternity[4]
Her honor's height and wonders of her age.

*   *   *

15 Set down the day in characters of gold,
And mark it with a stone as white as milk,[5]
That cheerful, sunny day. Wear eglantine,
And wreaths of roses red and white[6] put on
In honor of that day, you lovely nymphs,
20 And paeans sing and sweet melodious songs;
Along the chalky cliffs of Albion[7]
Lead England's lovely shepherds in a dance
O'er hill and dale, and downs, and daisy-plots,

[†] Copy text: George Peele, *Anglorum feriae, Englandes hollydayes, celebrated the 17th of Novemb. last, 1595, beginninge happyly the 38 yeare of the raigne of our soveraigne ladie Queen Elizabeth* [privately printed, Ipswich: R. Root for Mr. Fitch, 1830?], B1r–B1v, B2r–B2v, D1r–E1r, E1v–E2v, F1v. Since the editor, Mr. Fitch, badly damaged the only extant manuscript by using chemicals to bring out faint passages, his is the best remaining copy text. Undamaged parts of the original reveal, however, that his transcription was meticulous.

1. The Muses. The poem invokes Clio, Muse of History, for its primary inspiration.
2. Spring on Mt. Helicon, sacred to Apollo and the Muses.
3. Empress, a term that, in this period, means primarily that she does not owe obedience to any higher earthly authority but also, increasingly, that she rules other lands besides England.
4. History gives to mortals a form of unending life, metaphorically an eternity in time.
5. In Revelation 2.17, Christ promises a white stone with a secret new name on it to believers who overcome earthly adversity.
6. The Tudor pink rose (eglantine) symbolized the union of the houses of York (white rose) with that of Lancaster (red rose) accomplished when Elizabeth's grandfather, Henry VII, married Elizabeth of York at the end of the Wars of the Roses.
7. The White Cliffs of Dover, symbol of England (Albion).

And be that day England's high holiday;
25 And holidays and high days be they all,
High holidays, days, minutes, months, and hours,
That multiply the number of her years;
Years that for us beget this Golden Age,[8]
Wherein we live in safety under her,
30 Wherein she reigns in honor over us:
So may she long and ever may she so,
Untouched of traitorous hand or treacherous foe!
Her birthday being celebrated thus,
Clio, record how she hath been preserved,
35 Even in the gates of death and from her youth,
To govern England in the ways of truth;
Record heaven's goodness to this gracious Queen,
Whose virtue's peer what age hath ever seen?
    To pass° the story of her younger days   *narrate*
40 And stormy tempest happily o'erblown,
Wherein by mercy and by miracle
She was rescued[9] for England's happiness,
And comfort of the long-afflicted flock
That strayed like scattered sheep scared from the fold.
45 To slip remembrance of° those careful° days,   *recall / sorrowful*
Days full of danger, happy days withal,°   *in spite of that*
Days of her preservation and defense.
Behold the happiest day, the holiday
That young and old and all do celebrate,
50 The day of joy, the day of jollity!
The best of all the days that we have seen
Was wherein she was crownéd England's Queen,
Elizabeth, anointed of the Highest
To sit upon her kingly father's seat,
55 And wear in honor England's diadem,
To sway that massy scepter and that sword
That awed the world in his triumphant hand
And now in her's commands the enemy,
And with dishonor drives the daring foe
60 Back to his den, tired with successless arms,
Wearied with wars by land and wrack by sea.
Muses and Graces, gods and goddesses,
Adorn, adore, and celebrate this day.
The meanest with the mightiest may in this
65 Express his love; for loyalty alike
Blazons affection's force in lord and loon.°   *low-born folk*
    In honor of this happy day, behold
How (high and low, the young and old in years)
England hath put a face of gladness on,

---

8. Elizabeth is frequently represented as Astraea, Goddess of Justice, returned to the earth to restore the peace and justice of the Age of Gold.
9. The copy text reads "reseued," which, if it is not an error, is an archaic form of "received."

70 And court and country carol in her praise,
And in her honor tune a thousand lays!
            With just return of this triumphant day
And prosperous revolution of the same,
Auspiciously beginning many years
75 And golden days and infinite to come,
Passing in number and in happiness
The best that ever earthly prince enjoyed
By suffrance° of the highest King of kings,[1]   *sufferance*
Behold, in honor of this holiday,
80 What pæans loud triumphant London sings,
What holy tunes and sacrifice of thanks
England's metropolis as incense sends.
And in the sound of cymbals, trumps, and shawms°   *oboes*
In honor of his noble mistress' name,
85 To whom his life he owes and offers up,
Lo, London's shepherd,[2] guardian of his flock,
Praiseth the Mighty One of Israel,
And with the strings of his unfeignéd heart
Tunes his true joy for all those days of peace,
90 Those quiet days that Englishmen enjoy
Under our Queen, fair Queen of Brute's New Troy.
            With whom, in sympathy and sweet accord,
All loyal subjects join, and hearts and hands
Lift up to heaven's high throne, and sacrifice
95 Of praises and of hearty prayers send,
Thanksgiving for our blessings and the grace,
The gracious blessings on that day poured down
On England's head, that day whereon this Queen
Inaugured° was and holily installed,   *Consecrated*
100 Anointed of the highest King of kings,
In her hereditary royal right
Successively to sit enthronizéd
And in this general plaudit° and applause   *praise*
And celebration of this joyful day
105 (Wherein pale Envy,° vanquished long ago,[3]   *ill-will*
Gave way to Virtue's great deserts in her
And, wounded with remembrance of her name,[4]
Made hence amain° to murmur that abroad   *speedily*
He durst° not openly disgorge° at home[5]   *Which he dares / vomit*
110 In his own nest, filed° with so foul a bird,°   *defiled / Envy*
And breathe his discontentments over sea[6]
Among those erring fugitives[7] that pine

1. Christ, as exalted in 1 Timothy 6.15 and Revelation 17.14 and 19.16.
2. Richard Fletcher, the bishop or shepherd of London.
3. The Catholic hostility to Elizabeth, which was defeated at home after Mary's death and Elizabeth's
   accession.
4. Unhappy at the thought of Elizabeth's title of Queen.
5. Envy is here seen as bringing forth publications against Elizabeth, which circulated freely abroad
   but could not be published in England because the government censored the press.
6. He dares not breathe his discontentment across the sea, in England.
7. Catholic recusants, who were forbidden by law to practice their faith in England.

At England's prosperous peace and nothing more
Do thirst° than alteration of the state   *desire*
115 And nothing less than our good Queen affect°—   *focus on*
A number of unnatural Englishmen
That curse the day so happy held of us,
Whose base revolt from their allegiance due
To prince and country makes them infamous,
120 Condemned among the Turks and infidels,
False architects of those foul practices[8]
That end in their dishonor and their shame.)
Those bloody stratagems, those traitorous trains
And cruel siege they lay unto her life,[9]
125 Precious in sight of heaven and dear to us,
Her loving and her loyal subjects all,
Whom Jacob's God hath many ways preserved,
Yea, even betwixt the bridge and water's brink,
Saving her, as by miracle, in the fall°   *descending stroke*
130 From Pharaoh's rod and from the sword of Saul.[1]
Lo, in this triumph that true subjects make
(Envied of none but enemies of the truth,
Her enemies, that serves the living Lord
And puts in Him her confidence and trust),
135 Thou, sacred Muse of History,[2] describe
(That all may see how well she is beloved)
What troop of loyal English knights in arms,
Right richly mounted and appointed all
In shining arms accoutered for the war,
140 Small number of a number numberless,
Held jousts in honor of her holiday,
Ready to do their duties and devoir°   *appointed task*
Against the mightiest enemy she hath,[3]
Under what clime soe'er his colors wave,
145 And with keen sword and battle-axe in hand
To wound his crest, whatever foe he be
That any way in her dishonor braves.°   *challenges*
    Among this stirring company of knights,
That at the tilt in fair habiliments°   *apparel*
150 'Gan show themselves, renownéd Cumberland,
Knight of the Crown,[4] in gilded armor dight,°   *dressed*
Mounted at Queen Elizabeth's approach,
Inflamed with honor's fire, and left his hold
Kept by a dragon, laden with fair spoils:[5]

---

8. Plots of assassination and revolt against Elizabeth.
9. They lay their bloody schemes and treasonous plots and their cruel attack against her life.
1. Elizabeth's deliverance from Mary Tudor, as well as from assassination attempts and the Armada, are here compared to Israel's deliverance from Egypt and King David's deliverance from the hand of Saul, his predecessor.
2. Clio, first invoked in line 6.
3. Philip II of Spain, with which England was at war.
4. After the retirement of Sir Henry Lee in 1590, George Clifford, Earl of Cumberland, served as the Queen's personal champion at such tournaments.
5. Cumberland's tent bore the heraldic shields of knights that he had defeated. The dragon, imagined here as guarding the hoard, is a symbol of indomitable strength and of the Tudor monarchs.

155 And there his duty done and large device
     Made by his page known to her Majesty[6]
     (Whose gracious eye reflecting on this earl
     Was like Prometheus' life-infusing fire),[7]
     Behold, he stands impatient of delay,
160 Awaiting there his friendly foe's approach.

* * *

     The first that led,[8] in cheerful colors clad,
     In innocent white and fair carnation,[9]
     Was he whose wisdom in his younger years
     And love to arms make him so far renowned,
165 The noble Earl of Essex and of Ewe.[1]
     His mute approach and action of his mutes°   *silent attendants*
     Said that he was solicited diversely,[2]
     One way to follow war and war's designs,
     And well he may, for skill he can[3] full well
170 Of war's adventures, 'larms,° and stratagems;   *alarms*
     Another way t' apply him to the care
     Of commonweal affairs, and show the way
     To help to underbear° with grave advice   *support*
     The weighty beam whereon the state depends.
175 Well may he this way or the other take,
     And both shall his nobility become;°   *befit*
     The gravity and greatness of the one
     Shall beautify the other's worthiness;
     His senate-robes shall beautify his arms,
180 His chivalry nobilitate his name.
        Then Sussex,[4] seated on his champing steed,
     Dreadful to see and in sad tawny dight,[5]
     Came in as if some angry man of war
     Had charged his lance and put himself in arms
185 Under an eben-tree or blasted yew.[6]
     Such showed his plume, or like in my conceit
     To ravens' feathers by the moon's reflex,°   *reflection*
     Shining where night by day doth take repose.[7]
     Mars in his wrath, sitting upon his drum
190 Devising tragedies, strikes no greater fear
     Into the eyes and hearts of earthly men

6. Having paid his respects before the Queen, Cumberland left his page to explain the symbolic *impresa* or "device" painted on his shield.
7. That is, she inspired courage just by looking into his eyes.
8. Cumberland's first challenger in the jousting.
9. Symbols of purity and love.
1. Robert Devereux possessed two earldoms.
2. Torn between two courses in life.
3. Is able to show.
4. Robert Radcliff, fifth Earl of Sussex, a soldier who later served under Essex at Cadiz. He was detained after Essex's Rebellion in 1601 but no evidence of involvement was found and he was released.
5. Dressed in brownish yellow clothing.
6. He appeared under a banner painted with ebony and yew trees, symbols of melancholy and grief.
7. The feathers on his helmet appeared (or so it seemed to me) like raven's feathers in the dim moonlight before dawn.

Than did, methought, this champion in his way,[8]
Nor in his doings ever man-at-arms
So young of years more forward than this earl,
195 So prone, so puissant, and successful still[9]
In all his courses was this warlike knight.
     Then Bedford and Southampton[1] made up five,
Five valiant English earls. Southampton ran
As Bevis of Southampton;[2] that good knight
200 Had jousted in the honor of the day;
And certes° Bevis was a mighty man,   *truly*
Valiant in arms, gentle and debonair.[3]
And such was young Wriothesley, that came
As if, in duty to his sovereign
205 And honor's race, for° all that he had done,   *despite*
He would be of the noblest over-run.[4]

*   *   *

     In bases and caparisons of cost[5]
Came three redoubted° knights and men-at-arms,   *respected*
Old Knollys'[6] offspring, gallant cavaliers;
210 And such they showed as were King Arthur's knights
He whilom used to feast at Camelot,
Or three of great King Priam's valiant sons
Had left Elysium and the fields of Mars
To celebrate Eliza's holiday:
215 They ran as if three Hectors had made way
To meet Achilles, Ajax, Diomede.
Palline had the eldest branching of his crest;[7]
'Tis hard to say which brother did the best.
     Like Venus' son in Mars's armor clad,
220 Beset with glorious globes and golden flames,
Came Dudley[8] in; nor shall it me become
To dive into the depth of his device;[9]
Rich in his thoughts and valiant in his deeds,
No whit dishonored by his feinting horse,
225 That cowardlike would have held his master back
From honor's goal, ill-natured and ill taught

---

8. Course against opponents in the tilts.
9. So apt, so powerful, so continually successful.
1. Henry Wriothesley, second Earl of Southampton, sometimes identified as the young gentleman of
   Shakespeare's sonnets. He and Edward Russell, third Earl of Bedford, were associates of Essex and
   took part in his rebellion in 1601.
2. Hero of a fourteenth-century chivalric romance.
3. Gracious, affable.
4. He was willing, humbly, to be defeated by greater knights.
5. Expensive chain-mail jousting skirt and saddle-cloth.
6. Sir Francis Knollys, Elizabeth's Comptroller of the Household and Privy Councilor. The three sons
   who jousted were probably William, Robert, and Thomas.
7. Unclear. Perhaps "palline" comes from Italian *pallina* (ball), since the Knollys coat of arms has
   three red stylized roses that, seen from a distance, may have looked like balls. Since these are not
   on the crest (or helmet) and hardly "branch," more likely a fleur-de-lis on the crest was mistaken
   for fronds and "palline" is a mistranscription of "palm," symbol of victory and of Christian pilgrimage. Knollys's eldest son, William, first Earl of Banbury, was Essex's uncle and a member of
   his faction.
8. Sir Robert Dudley, illegitimate son of the Earl of Leicester.
9. Interpret the symbols on his shield.

To fail him foully in so great a presence.
But as an archer with a bendéd bow
The farther from the mark he draws his shaft
230 The farther flies it and with greater force
Wounds earth and air, so did it fare in this;
This lusty runner, thus restrain'd at first,
Now all inflamed, soon having changed his steed
And view'd the person of his princely mistress
235 (Whose radiant beams have[1] power to set on fire
The icy ridge of snowy Rhodope),[2]
Flies like a bullet from a cannon's mouth.
His arméd horse made dreadful harmony
Grating against the rails.[3] So valiantly
240 He jousted that unjust it were in me
Not to admire young Dudley's chivalry.

                              *   *   *

    Long may they run in honor of the day!
Long may she live to do them honor's right,
To grace their sports and them as she hath done,
245 England's Astraea, Albion's shining sun!
And may she shine in beauty fresh and sheen°   *resplendent*
Hundreds of years, our thrice-renownéd queen!
Write, Clio, write; write and record her story,
Dear in heaven's eye, her Court and country's glory.

HENRY PEACHAM

On Essex's Accession Day Tournament *Impresa*, 1595 (1612)[†]

The Accession Day tournament device[1] of the late
Honorable Earl of Essex.

"Par nulla figura dolori."

We eas'ly limn° some lovely Virgin face   *paint, depict*
And can, to life, a landscape represent,
Afford to antiques° each his proper grace,   *people of antiquity*
Or trick out this or that compartement.[2]
5   But with the pencil, who could ere express
    The face of grief and hearty pensiveness?

1. Copy text: and.
2. Mountain range in Greece.
3. Fences between which the knights jousted.
† Copy text: Henry Peacham, *Minerua Britanna or A garden of heroical deuises furnished, and adorned with emblemes and impresa's of sundry natures* (London: Wa: Dight, [1612]; STC 19511), R3r.
1. His *impresa*, the image painted on his shield as a figurative indication of his identity and condition. Often, such figures were accompanied by a motto, here "Par nulla figura dolori," which means "No figure is adequate to represent sorrow."
2. Framed area in which an image can be drawn or painted, as in the emblem below.

For where the mind's with deadly sorrow wounded,
There no proportion can effect delight,
For like a chaos, all within's confounded,
10 Resembling nothing save the face of night,
        Which in his shield this noble Earl did bear,
        The last *impresa* of his grief and care.

FRANCIS BACON

Of Love and Self-Love,
An Accession Day Entertainment (1595)[†]

[The ambassadors of Philaua to Erophilus[1] present their arguments
to Erophilus's squire before the Queen.]

The Squire's Speech in the Tiltyard

Most excellent and most glorious Queen, give me leave, I beseech your
Majesty, to offer my master's complaint and petition: complaint that, coming hither to your Majesty's most happy day, he is tormented with the
importunity of a melancholy, dreaming Hermit; a mutinous, brain-sick Soldier; and a busy, tedious Secretary. His petition is that he may be as free as

---

† Copy text: Sir Francis Bacon, *The Letters and the Life of Francis Bacon Including All His Occasional
  Works*, ed. James Spedding, 7 vols. (London: Longman, Green, Longman, and Roberts, 1862–74),
  2.378–86.[Also treated as vol. 8 in *The Works of Francis Bacon*, ed. James Spedding, Robert Leslie
  Ellis, and Douglas Denon Heath, 14 vols. (London: Longman, Greeen, Longman, and Roberts,
  1857–74)].
1. Love of erotic love, a figure for the Earl of Essex; *Philaua*: self-love, mistress of the Hermit, Soldier, and Statesman, who seek to win Erophilus to their self-serving ways.

the rest and, at least whilst he is here, troubled with nothing but with care how to please and honor you.

The Hermit's Speech in the Presence[2]

Though our ends be diverse, and therefore may be one more just than another, yet the complaint of this Squire is general and therefore alike unjust against us all, albeit he is angry that we offer ourselves to his master uncalled and forgets we come, not of ourselves, but as the messengers of Self love, from whom all that comes should be well taken. He[3] saith, when we come, we are importunate. If he mean that we err in form, we have that of his master, who being a lover useth no other form of soliciting.[4] If he will charge us to err in matter,[5] I for my part will presently prove that I persuade him to nothing but for his own good. For I wish him to leave turning over the book of fortune (which is but a play for children), where there be so many books of truth and knowledge better worthy the revolving, and not fix his view only upon a picture in a little table where there be so many tables of histories, yea to life,[6] excellent to behold and admire. Whether he believe me or no, there is no prison to[7] the prison of the thoughts, which are free under the greatest tyrants. Shall any man make his conceit as an anchor, mured up with the compass[8] of one beauty or person, that may have the liberty of all contemplation? Shall he exchange the sweet traveling through the universal variety for one wearisome and endless round or labyrinth?

Let thy master, Squire, offer his service to the Muses. It is long since they received any into their court. They give alms continually at their gate that many come to live upon, but few have they ever admitted into their palace. There shall he find secrets not dangerous to know, sides and parties not factious to hold, precepts and commandments not penal to disobey. The gardens of love wherein he now playeth himself are fresh today and fading tomorrow, as the sun comforts them or is turned from them. But the gardens of the Muses keep the privilege of the Golden Age;[9] they ever flourish and are in league with Time. The monuments of wit survive the monuments of power; the verses of a poet endure without a syllable lost, while states and empires pass many periods.[1] Let him not think he shall descend, for he is now upon a hill as a ship is mounted upon the ridge of a wave, but that hill of the Muses is above tempests, always clear and calm, a hill of the goodliest discovery[2] that man can have, being a prospect upon all the errors and wanderings of the present and former times. Yea, in some cliff[3] it leadeth the eye beyond the horizon of time and giveth no obscure divinations of times to come. So that if he will indeed lead *vitam vitalem*,[4] a life that

---

2. Area where the Queen received dignitaries and others not part of her inner circle.
3. The squire.
4. That is, as a lover, the Squire's master Erophilus is always importunate in pursuing his desires.
5. The content of our speeches.
6. Painted realistically; *revolving*: process of reflection; *little table*: surface on which to paint or write. In the lover's case, the "picture" is doubtless of the beloved's face.
7. Comparable to.
8. Penned up within the confines; *conceit*: thought, or perhaps a poetic figure (conceived for the beloved).
9. Mythical first era when Saturn ruled the world and human beings lived in peace and plenty.
1. Go through many eras, in contrast to the more enduring "periods" devised by poets, that is, complex sentences with a number of subordinate parts.
2. Vantage point for discovery; *descend*: suffer a fall.
3. One later text reads "as from a cliff."
4. A vital life.

unites safety and dignity, pleasure and merit; if he will win admiration without envy; if he will be in the feast and not in the throng, in the light and not in the heat, let him embrace the life of study and contemplation. And if he will accept of no other reason, yet because the gift of the Muses will enworthy him in his love and, where he now looks on his mistress's outside with the eyes of sense (which are dazzled and amazed), he shall then behold her high perfections and heavenly mind with the eyes of judgment, which grow stronger by more nearly and more directly viewing such an object.

The Soldier's Speech

Squire, the good old man hath said well to you, but I dare say thou wouldst be sorry to leave[5] to carry thy master's shield and to carry his books, and I am sure thy master had rather be a falcon, a bird of prey, than a singing-bird in a cage. The Muses are to serve martial men, to sing their famous actions, and not to be served by them. Then hearken to me.

It is the wars that giveth all spirits of valor not only honor but contentment. For mark whether ever you did see a man grown to any honorable commandment in the wars but, whensoever he gave it over,[6] he was ready to die with melancholy? Such a sweet felicity is in that noble exercise that he that hath tasted it thoroughly is distasted for all other.[7] And no marvel, for if the hunter take such solace in his chase, if the matches and wagers of sport pass away with such satisfaction and delight, if the looker-on be affected with pleasure in the representation of a feigned tragedy, think what contentment a man receiveth when they that are equal to him in nature, from the height of insolency and fury, are brought to the condition of a chased prey, when a victory is obtained whereof the victories of games are but counterfeits and shadows, and when in a lively tragedy a man's enemies are sacrificed before his eyes to his fortune.

Then for the dignity of military profession, is it not the truest and per-fectest practice of all virtues? of wisdom, in disposing those things which are most subject to confusion and accident? of justice, in continual distributing rewards? of temperance, in exercising of the straitest[8] discipline? of fortitude, in toleration of all labors and abstinence from effeminate delights? of constancy, in bearing and digesting the greatest variety of fortune? So that, when all other places and professions require but their several[9] virtues, a brave leader in the wars must be accomplished with all. It is the wars that are the tribunal seat where the highest rights and possessions are decided, the occupation of kings, the root of nobility, the protection of all estates.[1] And lastly, lovers never thought their profession sufficiently graced till they have compared it to a warfare.[2] All that in any other profession can be wished for is but to live happily, but to be a brave commander in the field, death itself doth crown the head with glory. Therefore, Squire, let thy master go with me, and though he be resolved in the pursuit of his love, let him aspire to it by the noblest means. For ladies count it no honor to subdue them with their fairest eyes which will be daunted with the fierce

5. Cease.
6. Ended his career.
7. He that has tasted it deeply loses his taste for everything else.
8. Most strict.
9. Particular.
1. Social classes. In England, there were traditionally three estates: nobility, clergy, and commoners.
2. That is, the battle of the sexes.

encounter of an enemy, and they will quickly discern a champion fit to wear their glove from a page not worthy to carry their *pantofle*.[3] Therefore I say again, let him seek his fortune in the field,[4] where he may either lose his love or find new arguments to advance it.

The Statesman's Speech

Squire, my advice to thy master shall be as a token wrapped up in words, but then will it show itself fair when it is unfolded in his actions. To wish him to change from one humor[5] to another were but as if, for the cure of a man in pain, one should advise him to lie upon the other side but not enable him to stand on his feet. If from a sanguine, delightful humor of love he turn to a melancholy, retired humor of contemplation or a turbulent, boiling humor of the wars, what doth he but change tyrants? Contemplation is a dream, love a trance, and the humor of war is raving. These be shifts[6] of humor but no reclaiming to reason. I debar him not studies nor books to give him store and variety of conceit, to refresh his mind, to cover[7] sloth and indisposition, and to draw to him (from those that are studious) respect and commendation. But let him beware lest they possess not too much of his time, that they abstract not his judgment from present experience nor make him presume, upon knowing much, to apply[8] the less. For the wars, I deny him no enterprise that shall be worthy in greatness, likely in success, or necessary in duty, not mixed with any circumstance of jealousy but duly laid upon him.[9] But I would not have him take the alarm from his own humor but from the occasion, and I would again he should know an employment from a discourting.[1] And for his love, let it not so disarm his heart within as it make him too credulous to favors, nor too tender to unkindnesses, nor too apt to depend upon the heart he knows not. Nay, in his demonstration of love, let him not go too far; for these silly lovers, when they profess such infinite affection and obligation, they tax[2] themselves at so high a rate that they are ever under arrest. It makes their service seem nothing and every cavil or imputation very great.

But what, Squire, is thy master's end?[3] If to make the prince happy he serves, let the instructions to employed men, the relations of ambassadors, the treaties between princes, and actions of the present time be the books he reads. Let the orations of wise princes or experimented[4] counselors in council or Parliament and the final sentences of grave and learned judges in weighty and doubtful causes be the lectures he frequents. Let the holding of affection with confederates without charge, the frustrating of the attempts of enemies without battles, the entitling of the Crown to new pos-

3. Slipper. Ladies gave gloves to inspire knights to fight for them.
4. Field of battle.
5. In Renaissance medical theory, fluids in the body affected mood and behavior. Excess of blood (the sanguine humor) made one cheerful and outgoing, whereas black bile (the melancholy humor) did the opposite and yellow bile made one choleric or easily angered.
6. Changes.
7. Relieve; *debar*: forbid.
8. Apply his knowledge; *abstract not*: do not draw away.
9. Called for by his superiors; *circumstance of jealousy*: occasion of rivalry.
1. Know when he is sent to employ his abilities and when simply to get him away from Court; *alarm*: call to battle
2. Obligate, put themselves in debt to the lady.
3. Goal.
4. Experienced.

sessions without show of wrong, the filling of the prince's coffers without grudging, the appeasing tumults and seditions without violence, the keeping of men in appetite without impatience be the inventions[5] he seeks out. Let policy[6] and matter of state be the chief (and almost the only) thing he intends. But if he will believe Philautia and seek most his own happiness, he must not of them embrace all kinds but make choice and avoid all matter of peril, displeasure, and charge, and turn them over to some novices that know not manacles from bracelets nor burdens from robes.[7] For himself, let him set for matters of commodity and strength, though they be joined[8] with envy. Let him not trouble himself too laboriously to sound into any matter deeply or to execute anything exactly, but let him make himself cunning rather in the humors and drifts of persons than in the nature of business and affairs. Of that, it sufficeth to know only so much as may make him able to make use of other men's wits and to make again a smooth and pleasing report. Let him entertain the proposition of others, and ever rather let him have an eye to the circumstances[9] than to the matter itself, for then shall he ever seem to add somewhat of his own. And besides, when a man doth not forget so much as a circumstance, men do think his wit doth superabound for the substance.[1] In his counsels let him not be confident, for that will rather make him obnoxious to the success; but let him follow the wisdom of oracles, which uttered that which might ever be applied to the event.[2] And ever rather let him take the side which is likeliest to be followed than that which is soundest and best, that everything may seem to be carried by his direction. To conclude, let him be true to himself and avoid all tedious reaches of state that are not merely pertinent to his particular.[3]

And if he will needs pursue his affection[4] and go on his course, what can so much advance him in his own way? The merit of war is too outwardly glorious to be inwardly grateful, and it is the exile of his eye which, looking with such affection upon the picture,[5] cannot but with infinite contentment behold the life. But when his mistress shall perceive that his endeavors are [to] become a true supporter of her, a discharge of her care, a watchman of her person, a scholar of her wisdom, an instrument of her operation, and a conduit of her virtue, this (with his diligences, accesses, humility, and patience) may move her to give him further degrees[6] and approaches to her favor. So that I conclude I have traced[7] him the way to that which hath been granted to some few: *amare et sapere*, to love and be wise.

---

5. Topics of discussion; *charge*: expense, trouble; *appetite*: desire to serve.
6. Political strategy.
7. Chains of enslavement from bracelets bestowed by superiors and burdens of responsibility from robes of honor. Novices fail to recognize the ways in which their superiors manipulate them; *embrace all kinds*: pursue all kinds of policies.
8. Accompanied; *set for . . . strength*: strive for things the bring personal advantage and power.
9. Inessential details.
1. Essential points.
2. Which were so ambiguously worded that they applied no matter what happened; *obnoxious . . . success*: harmful to the outcome he seeks.
3. Own advantage; *reaches*: undertakings.
4. Love of a woman.
5. The woman's picture carried with him to war; *grateful*: welcome (to the woman); *it is . . . his eye*: it is the thing that takes from her his admiring eye.
6. Steps to ascend; *accesses*: demonstrations of diligence and efforts to gain access to her.
7. Shown.

The Reply of the Squire

Wandering Hermit, storming Soldier, and hollow Statesman, the enchanting orators of Philautia, which have attempted by your high charms to turn resolved Erophilus into a statua[8] deprived of action, or into a vulture attending about dead bodies, or into a monster with a double heart: with infinite assurance, but with just indignation and forced patience, I have suffered you to bring in play your whole forces. For I would not vouchsafe to combat you one by one, as if I trusted to the goodness of my breath and not the goodness of my strength, which little needeth the advantage of your severing and much less of your disagreeing.[9]

Therefore, first, I would know of you all what assurance you have of the fruit whereto you aspire. You, father, that pretend to truth and knowledge, how are you assured that you adore not vain chimeras[1] and imaginations? that in your high prospect,[2] when you think men wander up and down, that they stand not indeed still in their place, and it is some smoke or cloud between you and them which moveth, or else the dazzling of your own eyes? Have not many which take themselves to be inward counselors with Nature proved but idle believers, that told us tales which were no such matter?

And, Soldier, what security[3] have you for these victories and garlands which you promise to yourself? Know you not of many which have made provision of laurel for the victory and have been fain to exchange it with cypress[4] for the funeral? of many which have bespoken Fame to sound their triumphs and have been glad to pray her to say nothing of them and not to discover them in their flights?[5]

Corrupt Statesman, you that think by your engines and motions to govern the wheel of Fortune: do you not mark that clocks cannot be long in temper?[6] that jugglers are no longer in request when their tricks and sleights are once perceived? Nay, do you not see that never any man made his own cunning and practice (without religion, honor, and moral honesty) his foundation but he over-built himself and in the end made his house a windfall?[7]

But give ear now to the comparison of my master's condition and acknowledge such a difference as is betwixt the melting hail-stone and the solid pearl. Indeed it seemeth to depend[8] as the globe of the earth seemeth to hang in the air, but yet it is firm and stable in itself. It is like a cube or die-form, which toss it or throw it any way, it ever lighteth upon a square.[9] Is he denied the hopes of favors to come? He can resort to the remembrance of contentments past. Destiny cannot repeal that which is past. Doth he find the acknowledgment of his affection small? He may find the merit of his affection the greater. Fortune cannot have power over that which is within. Nay, his falls are like the falls of Antaeus; they renew his

8. Statue.
9. Setting yourselves apart from one another, much less disputing among yourselves.
1. Phantasms.
2. Lofty place looking down on the world.
3. Guarantee.
4. Symbol of death; *laurel*: symbol of honor.
5. Expose them as they run away; *bespoken*: called for.
6. Tell the time (to act) accurately; *engines and motions*: schemes and actions.
7. Structure collapsed by wind.
8. Hang upon the beloved's will; *it*: his master's condition.
9. Symbol of stability and honesty.

strength. His clouds are like the clouds of harvest,[1] which make the sun break forth with greater force. His wanes and changes are like the moon, whose globe is all light towards the sun[2] when it is all dark towards the world. Such is the excellency of her nature and of his estate.

Attend, you beadsman of the Muses, you take your pleasure in a wilderness of variety, but it is but of shadows.[3] You are as a man rich in pictures, medals, and crystals.[4] Your mind is of the water, which taketh all forms and impressions but is weak of substance. Will you compare shadows with bodies, picture with life, variety of many beauties with the peerless excellency of one? the element of water with the element of fire? And such is the comparison between knowledge and love.

Come out, man of war. You must be ever in noise.[5] You will give laws, and advance force, and trouble nations, and remove landmarks of kingdoms, and hunt men, and pen tragedies in blood, and that which is worst of all, make all the virtues accessary to bloodshed. Hath the practice of force so deprived you of the use of reason as that you will compare the interruption of society with the perfection of society, the conquest of bodies with the conquest of spirits, the terrestrial fire which destroyeth and dissolveth with the celestial fire which quickeneth[6] and giveth life? And such is the comparison between the soldier and the lover.

And as for you, untrue *politique* but truest bondman to Philautia, you that presume to bind occasion and to overwork[7] Fortune, I would ask you but one question: did ever any lady, hard to please or disposed to exercise her lover, enjoin him so hard tasks and commandments as Philautia exacteth of you? while your life is nothing but a continual acting upon a stage, and that your mind must serve your humor, and yet your outward person must serve your end, so as you carry in one person two several servitudes to contrary masters? But I will leave you to the scorn of that mistress whom you undertake to govern—that is, to Fortune, to whom Philautia hath bound you.

And yet, you commissioners of Philautia, I will proceed one degree further. If I allowed both of your assurance and of your values as you have set them, may not my master enjoy his own felicity and have all yours for advantage?[8] I do not mean that he should divide himself in both pursuits, as in your fainting tales towards the conclusion you did yield[9] him, but because all these are in the hands of his mistress more fully to bestow than they can be attained by your addresses, knowledge, fame, and fortune. For the Muses, they are tributary to her Majesty for the great liberties they have enjoyed in her kingdom during her most flourishing reign, in thankfulness whereof they have adorned and accomplished her Majesty with the gifts of all the sisters.[1] What library can present such a story of great actions as her

1. Short storms of autumn.
2. Conventional image for the beloved, shedding the light of her countenance on the lover.
3. According to Plato, the mind contains only inexact reflections of the world, which is itself made up of inexact reflections of the eternal forms conceived in the mind of God; *beadsman . . . Muses*: the Hermit, pictured praying to his goddesses or serving as their messenger. Originally, beadsmen followed an order in their prayers set by a string of beads of various sizes.
4. Images, whether painted, stamped (like the medals of medieval medicine placed on the body to treat disease), or seen as reflections in stones (like crystal balls used in attempts at prophecy and magic).
5. Noise of battle.
6. Conceives.
7. Control; *politique*: politician, political schemer.
8. To boot; *set*: presented.
9. Allow.
1. All nine Muses; *accomplished*: given accomplishments to.

Majesty carrieth in her royal breast by the often return of this happy day?[2] What worthy author or favorite of the Muses is not familiar with her? Or what language wherein the Muses have used to speak is unknown to her?[3] Therefore, the hearing of her, the observing of her, the receiving instructions from her may be to Erophilus a lecture exceeding all dead monuments of the Muses. For[4] Fame, can all the exploits of the war win him such a title as to have the name of favored and selected servant of such a Queen? For Fortune, can any insolent politique promise to himself such a fortune by making his own way as the excellency of her nature cannot deny to a careful, obsequious,[5] and dutiful servant? And if he could, were it equal honor to obtain it by a shop[6] of cunning as by the gift of such a hand?

Therefore, Erophilus's resolution is fixed: he renounceth Philautia and all her enchantments. For her[7] recreation, he will confer with his Muse. For her defense and honor, he will sacrifice his life in the wars, hoping to be embalmed in the sweet odors of her remembrance. To her service will he consecrate all his watchful endeavors and will ever bear in his heart the picture of her beauty, in his actions of her will, and in his fortune of her grace and favor.

The Woman behind the Mask

Some of the most remarkable accounts of Elizabeth from the 1590s are glimpses of her in private life. Sir John Harington, translator of Ariosto's romantic epic *Orlando Furioso*, provided a number of the most intimate and amusing recollections. As the Queen's godson, he enjoyed uncommon access to her and her ladies-in-waiting. When, after inventing an early version of the flush toilet, he was allowed to install it in the royal apartments at Richmond Palace, he used the opportunity to write a witty and scatological work entitled *The Metamorphosis of Ajax*, which took readers into the most private reaches of the royal household. Punning on the name of one of Homer's greatest heroes as well as the common term "jakes," meaning latrine, he was so unabashed in jesting about the matter and so impudent in teasing her female attendants that the Queen banished him from Court. She soon relented, however, and a cousin of his at Court assured him that, "Though her Highness signified displeasure in outward sort, yet did she like the marrow of your book; she hath been heard to say, 'that merry poet, her godson, must not come to [the royal palace at] Greenwich, till he hath grown sober, and leaveth the ladies' sports and frolics'" (McClure, *Letters and Epigrams of Harington*, 18). Harington's volume of *Most Elegant and Witty Epigrams* displays the boyish playfulness for which Elizabeth seems to have liked him. In the poems reprinted here, he cleverly mocks the Pope following the defeat of the Armada, begs the Queen and her attendants to think better of him after publication of the *Metamorphosis*, attacks a writer who had criticized the book, and teases the Queen over her belief in astrology, which occasionally led her to consult a devotee of the occult, Dr. John Dee, before she made major decisions.

The celebrated university wit and playwright John Lyly was similarly bold in representing Elizabeth as a woman rather than as a monarch. Though his prose work *Euphues and His England* (excerpted in Part Five) and his plays *Endymion*

2. Elizabeth's Accession Day.
3. The Queen was proficient in Latin, French, and Italian and had a working knowledge of Greek and German.
4. As for.
5. Attentive, obedient.
6. A storehouse.
7. The Queen's.

and *Midas* contain flattering characterizations of her, he was not above twitting her for faults that he regarded as common to her sex. His late play *The Woman in the Moon*, which was performed before her in the early 1590s, contains two characters who call her to mind, neither of them in terms that are entirely flattering. His goddess Cynthia is associated with fickleness and irrationality as much as with power and light. His character Pandora—another mythological figure often associated with the Queen because, in classical myth, she was the first and most perfect woman—is similarly represented as changeable and irascible. In alluding to Elizabeth's vanity and her tendency to fits of rage, however, he was careful to cover his tracks. The Prologue to the play, reprinted here, treats the work as a mere "dream," subsuming the misconduct of the divine and human characters under the rule of the "only queen" in the play, the wise goddess Nature.

A look behind the scenes at the Queen's private life would not be complete without one of the games available to her in her off hours. The "Square in Verse" was created by Henry Lok, son of the poet Anne Vaughan Lock and her first husband, Henry Lock. A prolific author of devotional verse and a writer of sonnets, he also penned a poetic version of the book of Ecclesiastes. His "Square" is an example of the elaborate visual, verbal, and mathematical puns that many Elizabethans loved and that showcased their ability to devise intricate aesthetic forms.

A last, remarkable glimpse of the woman behind the royal mask in this period comes from a private audience with the French ambassador, André Hurault, Sieur de Maisse. An experienced diplomat, Hurault arrived in England in late November 1597 with the charge of persuading the Queen to join Henry IV in making peace with Philip II of Spain. Hurault preserved his observations of the Queen and her Court in a journal kept during his embassy. The Queen surprised him by having him ushered into her presence when she was not properly dressed to receive a foreign dignitary. Not only was she wearing a light, low-cut gown that she fiddled with in suggestive ways, but her words and demeanor came across—in Hurault's view, at least—as flirtatious. If the report is true, her conduct was all the more surprising because the matter at hand was so serious. The question whether or not to make peace with Spain was dividing the Court, with the faction headed by the Earl of Essex at loggerheads with that dominated by the Secretary of State, Robert Cecil. With so much at stake, one wonders what effect the Queen had in mind in receiving the French ambassador as she did and what his intentions were in recording the interview in such coarse and suggestive terms.

SIR JOHN HARINGTON

From Most Elegant and Witty Epigrams (ca. 1589–98)[†]

Against Pius Quintus,[1] *that Excommunicated Queen Elizabeth*

Are kings your foster fathers, queens your nurses,
O Roman Church?[2] Then why did Pius Quintus

---

† Copy text: Sir John Harington, *The most elegant and witty epigrams of Sir Iohn Harrington, Knight* (London: G.P. for Iohn Budge, 1618; STC 12776), M1r–v, C3r–C4r, D4r.
1. Pope Pius V, who in 1570 issued a bull excommunicating the Queen and all English subjects who continued to obey her. See above, Part Three.
2. A reference to support traditionally given the papacy by European monarchs for the cure of their subjects' souls. The poem goes on to suggest that the Pope is more interested in money than ministry.

With Bashan bulls (not like one *pius intus*[3])
Lay on our sacred Prince unhallowed curses?
5 It is not health of souls but wealth of purses
You seek[4] by such your hell-denouncing threats,
Oppugning° with your chair our Prince's seats,[5]   *Assaulting*
Disturbing our sweet peace; and that which worse is,
You suck out blood and bite your nurse's teats.
10   Learn, learn, to ask your milk, for if you snatch it,[6]
The nurse must send your babes pap with a hatchet.[7]

To the Queen's Majesty, When She Found Fault with Some Particular Matters in Misacmos'[8] Metamorphosis

Dread Sovereign, take this true, though poor, excuse
Of all the errors of Misacmos' Muse:
A hound that of a whelp myself hath bred
And at my hand and table taught and fed,
5 When other curs did fawn and flatter coldly,
Did spring and leap and play with me too boldly;
For which, although my pages check and rate° him,   *scold*
Yet still myself doth much more love than hate him.

To the Ladies of the Queen's Privy Chamber, at the Making of Their Perfumed Privy at Richmond

The book hanged in chains[9] saith thus:
Fair dames, if any took in scorn and spite
Me, that Misacmos' Muse in mirth did write,
To satisfy the sin, lo, here in chains,
5 For aye° to hang, my master he° ordains.   *ever / Harington*
Yet deem the deed to him no derogation,
But doom to this device[1] new commendation,
Sith here you see, feel, smell that this conveyance
Hath freed this noisome° place from all annoyance.   *ill-smelling*
10 Now judge you that the work mock, envy, taunt,

---

3. Pious within, with a pun on the Pope's name; *Bashan bulls*: in Psalm 22.12, traditionally seen as a prophecy of the passion of Christ, the speaker sees himself encircled by "strong bulls of Bashan." The pun here on "bull" suggests that the excommunication of the Queen is as impious as the crucifixion. For more on the bull of 1570 and Protestant reactions to it, see Part Three.
4. Protestants opposed such Catholic practices as the sale of indulgences, which was devised to raise funds for the Church.
5. Plural because Elizabeth claimed to be Queen of several kingdoms, including England, France, Scotland, and Ireland; *chair*: the Pope was said to sit in the throne of St. Peter.
6. A reference to papal support for the 1588 Spanish invasion aimed at overthrowing Elizabeth and restoring England to the Catholic fold.
7. A phrase borrowed from a pamphlet entitled *Pap with a Hatchet* (1589) by John Lyly, part of the so-called Marprelate Controversy over the power of Anglican bishops. The point is that unwanted puppies that have been singled out for the hatchet can be readily located at the teats of their mothers.
8. Harington's pseudonym (meaning "hater of filth") in *The Metamorphosis of Ajax*.
9. Harington seems to have placed a copy of his book in the privy that he had installed in Richmond Palace, attaching it with a chain so that no one could take it. The chain could imply that the book was a felon, imprisoned for offences, or that it was a classic, since the most valued books were often chained to reading desks.
1. Adjudge to Harington's water closet.

Whose service in this place may make most vaunt:[2]
  If us or you to praise it were most meet,°   *fitting*
  You, that made sour, or us, that make it sweet?

Against Linus, a Writer, That Found Fault with the Metamorphosis

Linus, to give to me a spiteful frump,°   *jeer*
Said that my writings savored of the pump,
And that my muse, for want of matter,[3] takes
An argument to write of from the jakes.°   *outhouse*
5 Well, Linus, speak each reader as he thinks,
Though thou of scepters wrat'st,° and I of sinks,° *wrote / drains*
  Yet some will say, comparing both together,
  My wit brings matter thence, thine matter thither.[4] *to it*

Of Soothsaying, to the Queen of England

Might queens shun future mischief by foretelling,
Then among soothsayers 'twere excellent dwelling.
But if there be no means, such harms expelling,
The knowledge makes the grief the more excelling.[5]
5 Well yet, dear Liege, my soul this comfort doth,[6]
  That of these soothsayers very few say sooth.°   *the truth*

JOHN LYLY

From The Woman in the Moon (ca. 1591–95)[†]

Prologus

Our poet, slumb'ring in the Muses' laps,
Hath seen a woman seated in the moon,
A point beyond the ancient theoric,[1]
And as it was, so he presents his dream
5 Here in the bounds of fair Utopia,[2]
Where lovely Nature, being only queen,
Bestows such workmanship on earthly mould°   *soil*
That heavens themselves envy her glorious work.
But all in vain. For (malice being spent)
10 They yield themselves to follow Nature's doom,° *judgment*

---

2. Claim most glory.
3. Lacking material to write about (with a pun on "matter" or excrement).
4. My wit takes matter (i.e., sewage) away from the palace, yours brings matter to it.
5. The grief is worse if one foresees harms but cannot prevent them.
6. Gives itself this comfort.
† Copy text: John Lyly, *The VVoman in the Moone. As it was presented before her Highness* (London: William Iones, 1597; STC 17090), A1v.
1. Theory (here, of astral bodies).
2. England. Lyly borrows the term "Utopia" (Greek for "nowhere") from the supposedly ideal but not entirely attractive state created by Sir Thomas More.

And fair Pandora sits in Cynthia's orb.[3]
This,[4] but the shadow of our author's dream,
Argues the substance[5] to be near at hand,
At whose appearance I most humbly crave
15 That in your forehead she[6] may read content.
If many faults escape in her discourse,[7]
Remember all is but a poet's dream,
The first he had in Phoebus' holy bow'r,
But not the last, unless the first displease.

HENRY LOK

A Square in Verse (1593)[†]

The Square plainly set down:

God hath poured forth rare grace on this isle and
Makes crowned your rule, Queen, in the same so still.[1]
Kings laud this saint fair, that with truth doth stand.
Rule so long time, mild Prince; joy land it will.[2]
For proof you shows,° wise of earth's race whom there   *shows you*
Heavens have upheld, just choice, whom God thus shields.
Your stock of kings (world's rich offspring and fear,[3]
State's fame known far) praise isle which all bliss yields.
Hold God, therefore, sure stay° of all[4] the best   *support*
Blest is your reign. Here builds sweet peace, true rest.

3. In the play, the gods that rule the planets envy Pandora's perfection and cause her to misbehave, but Nature restores her at the end and seats her in "Cynthia's orb."
4. The prologue.
5. The play, but also, perhaps, Cynthia and the Queen herself. According to the 1597 edition, Elizabeth attended a performance at Court.
6. The goddess Cynthia on stage, though also, perhaps, the Queen in the audience.
7. If there are uncorrected faults in Cynthia's speeches.
† Copy text: Henry Lok, *Sundrie sonnets of Christian passions* (London: Richard Field, 1597; STC 16696), I6v–I7r. The square was originally printed in the first edition of the sonnets (1593), but the copy is damaged.
1. In the same nation forever.
2. It will give joy to the land.
3. Object of awe and fear; *stock of kings*: your royal ancestors.
4. Copy text: "and port," although the square itself reads "of all."

E					Ha A	ec[5] B					F
In[6]	God 5	Hath	Poured	Forth	Rare	Grace	On	This	Isle	And 5	Hoc
	Makes	Crowned 4	Your	Rule	Queen	In	The	Same	So 4	Still	
	Kings	Laud	THis 3	Saint	Fair	That	With	Truth 3	Doth	Stand	
	Rule	So	Long	Time 2	Mild	Prince	Joy 2	Land	It	Will	
C Forma	For	Proof	You	Shows	1 Wise	1 Of	Earth's	Race	Whom	There	D Quadrata
	Heavens	Have	Up	Held	Just 1	Choice 1	Whom	God	Thus	Shields	
	Your	Stock	Of	Kings 2	Worlds	Rich	Off- 2	Spring	And	Fear	
	State's	Fame	Known 3	Far	Praise	Isle	Which	ALI 3	Bliss	Yields	
	Hold	God 4	There-	Fore	Sure	Stay	Of	All	The 4	Best	
	Blest 5	Is	Your	Reign	Here	Builds	Sweet	Peace	True	Rest 5	
Vinces					Fir	ma					Signo

The observations of the Square following:[7]

1. A Saint George's cross[8] of two columns, in description of her Majesty, beginning at A and B in the middle (to be read downward) and crossing at C and D (to be read either single or double).

5. *Haec Quadrata Firma Forma* (This square is a strong form).
6. *In Hoc Signo Vinces* (In this sign you will conquer), the motto of the Emperor Constantine, referring to the sign of the cross.
7. For a thorough discussion of this square, see Roche, *Petrarch*, 549–51.
8. A cross composed of an upright and a horizontal bar, crossing each other at the center; thus,

> Rare Queen, fair, mild, wise
> Shows you proof, for
> Heavens have upheld
> Just world's praise sure. Here
> Grace in that Prince
> Of earth's race, whom there
> Shields thus God, whom
> Choice, rich isle, stay builds.

2. A Saint Andrew's cross, beginning at E and read thwartways[9] and ending with F, containing the description of our happy age by her Highness.
3. Two pillars in the right and left side of the square, in verse, reaching from E and F perpendicularly, containing the sum of the whole, the latter column having the words placed counterchangeably[1] to rhyme to the whole square.
4. The first and last two verses,[2] or the third and fourth with seventh and eighth, are sense in themselves, containing also sense of the whole.
5. The whole square of one hundred, containing in itself five squares, the angles of each of them are[3] sense particularly and united depend each on other, beginning at the center.
6. The out-angles are to be read eight several ways in sense and verse.[4]
7. The eight words placed also in the ends of the Saint George's cross are sense and verse, alluding to the whole cross.[5]
8. The two third words in the bend dexter of the Saint Andrew's cross, being the middle from the angles to the center, have in their first letters T. and A. for the author and H. L. in their second for his name, which, to be true, the words of the angles in that square confirm.[6]

---

9. From corner to corner; *Saint Andrew's cross*: a cross in the form of an X; thus, God crowned this time, etc.
1. In alternate lines; thus, God makes kings rule, etc.
2. Lines.
3. Make; *five squares*: nested inside each other so that one reads all the 1's; then all the 2's, and so forth; thus, Wise, of just choice, etc.
4. Each triangular quadrant can be read from base to apex or from apex to base; thus, for example,

> God hath poured forth rare grace on this isle and
> Crowned your rule, Queen, in the same. So
> This saint fair, that with truth
> Time, mild Prince, [give] joy
> of wise.

> Or

> Wise of
> Time, mild Prince, joy [give]
> This saint fair, that with truth
> Crowned your rule, Queen, in the same. So
> God hath poured forth rare grace on this isle. Etc.

5. Thus, Rare race there shields, for heavens here builds.
6. That is, "This truth all known"; *bend dexter*: right-hand side; *name*: the number 3 words on the right-hand side of the St. Andrew's cross: T[he]H[enry]is A[uthor]L[ok]l.

ANDRÉ HURAULT, SIEUR DE MAISSE

A Private Audience with Elizabeth
(December 18, 1597)[†]

On the 8th of December,[1] I did not think to be given an audience for that day and was resolved to make my complaint; but about one hour after noon, there came a gentleman from the Queen who said to me that her Majesty was much grieved that she had not given me audience sooner and that she prayed me to come to her that very hour. He brought me in a coach to take me down to the river where one of the barges awaited me, and we went thence to the gate of the Queen's palace. At our landing there came to seek me a gentleman who spoke very good Italian, called Monsieur Wotton,[2] who told me that her Majesty sent word that I should be very welcome and that she was awaiting me. He had four or five other gentlemen with him. As he led me along, he told me that the whole Court was well satisfied to see me, and that they knew well how greatly I loved their nation, and that in Italy I had done all that I could for them. I told him that I was very sorry that I had not done more and that what had been done was by the command of the King,[3] who wished me in all that concerned the Queen of England to busy myself as much as in his own affairs.

He led me across a chamber of moderate size wherein were the guards of the Queen and thence into the Presence-Chamber, as they call it, in which all present, even though the Queen be absent, remain uncovered.[4] He then conducted me to a place on one side, where there was a cushion made ready for me. I waited there some time, and the Lord Chamberlain,[5] who has the charge of the Queen's household (not as *maitre d'hotel*, but to arrange audiences and to escort those who demand them and especially ambassadors), came to seek me where I was seated. He led me along a passage somewhat dark into a chamber that they call the Privy Chamber,[6] at the head of which was the Queen seated in a low chair, by herself and withdrawn from all the lords and ladies that were present, they being in one place and she in another.

After I had made her my reverence at the entry of the chamber, she rose and came five or six paces towards me, almost into the middle of the chamber. I kissed the fringe of her robe and she embraced me with both hands. She looked at me kindly and began to excuse herself that she had not sooner given me audience, saying that the day before she had been very ill with a gathering[7] on the right side of her face (which I should never have thought, seeing her eyes and face), but she did not remember ever to have

---

† Copy text: André Hurault, *De Maisse; a journal of all that was accomplished by Monsieur de Maisse*, trans. and ed. G. B. Harrison and R. A. Jones ([London]: Nonesuch Press, 1931), 22–26. Copyright © by G. B. Harrison and R. A. Jones and published by the Nonesuch Press, permission of Gerald Duckworth & Co. Ltd.

1. André Hurault, Sieur de Maisse, arrived in England on November 30, 1597, as an ambassador from Henry IV of France. He was charged with persuading Elizabeth to join peace negotiations with Spain.
2. Probably Thomas Wotton.
3. Henry IV of France.
4. Without hats or outer garments; *Presence-Chamber*: the reception hall of the palace.
5. George Carey, Lord Hunsdon.
6. The Queen's private apartment.
7. Swelling; Elizabeth often suffered from toothaches caused by the sweets she loved to eat.

been so ill before. She excused herself because I found her attired in her nightgown and began to rebuke those of her Council who were present, saying, "What will these gentlemen say" (speaking of those who accompanied me) "to see me so attired? I am much disturbed that they should see me in this state."

Then I answered her that there was no need to make excuse on my account, for that I had come to do her service and honor and not to give her inconvenience. She replied that I gave her none and that she saw me willingly. I told her that the King had commanded me to visit her and to kiss her hands on his behalf and charged me to learn the news of her well being and health, which (thanks be to God) I saw to be such as her servants and friends would desire and which I prayed God might continue for long years and in all prosperity and dignity. She stood up while I was speaking, but then she returned to her chair when she saw that I was only speaking of general matters. I drew nearer to her chair and began to deal with her in that wherewithal I had been charged, and because I was uncovered, from time to time she signed to me with her hand to be covered, which I did. Soon after, she caused a stool to be brought, whereon I sat and began to talk to her.

She was strangely attired in a dress of silver cloth, white and crimson, or silver "gauze," as they call it. This dress had slashed sleeves lined with red taffeta and was girt about with other little sleeves that hung down to the ground, which she was forever twisting and untwisting. She kept the front of her dress open, and one could see the whole of her bosom[8] (and passing low), and often she would open the front of this robe with her hands as if she was too hot. The collar of the robe was very high and the lining of the inner part all adorned with little pendants of rubies and pearls, very many but quite small. She had also a chain of rubies and pearls about her neck. On her head she wore a garland of the same material and beneath it a great reddish-colored wig, with a great number of spangles of gold and silver, and hanging down over her forehead some pearls, but of no great worth. On either side of her ears hung two great curls of hair, almost down to her shoulders and within the collar of her robe, spangled as the top of her head.

Her bosom is somewhat wrinkled, as well as [one can see for[9]] the collar that she wears round her neck, but lower down her flesh is exceeding white and delicate, so far as one could see. As for her face, it is and appears to be very aged. It is long and thin, and her teeth are very yellow and unequal compared with what they were formerly, so they say, and on the left side less than on the right. Many of them are missing so that one cannot understand her easily when she speaks quickly. Her figure is fair and tall and graceful in whatever she does; so far as may be, she keeps her dignity, yet humbly and graciously withal.

All the time she spoke, she would often rise from her chair and appear to be very impatient with what I was saying. She would complain that the fire was hurting her eyes, though there was a great screen before it and she six or seven feet away; yet did she give orders to have it extinguished, making them bring water to pour upon it. She told me that she was well pleased to stand up, and that she used to speak thus with the ambassadors who

8. Not her breasts, but her upper chest.
9. Because of.

came to seek her, and used sometimes to tire them, of which they would on occasion complain. I begged her not to overtire herself in any way, and I rose when she did; and then she sat down again, and so did I.

At my departure, she rose and conducted me to that same place where she had come to receive me, and again began to say that she was grieved that all the gentlemen I had brought should see her in that condition, and she called to see them. They made their reverence before her, one after the other, and she embraced them all with great charm and smiling countenance.

Part Nine: Ireland, Rebellion, and the Passing of the Queen (1598–1603)

HISTORICAL BACKGROUND

In the last years of the Queen's life, another dangerous rebellion broke out in northern Ireland. Its leader, Hugh O'Neill, second Earl of Tyrone, was a commander of considerable ability, and in his first major engagement with the English in July 1598, he ambushed and decimated a force of more than 4000 at a place called Yellow Ford. The following autumn, he carried the rebellion south into Munster, where the poet Edmund Spenser and his family managed to escape the burning of their home at Kilcolman Castle only by fleeing through a secret tunnel and seeking refuge in the nearby town of Cork.

When the Queen learned of the slaughter at Yellow Ford, she was outraged, not least because she had recently pardoned Tyrone for other acts against her. In the spring of 1599, she sent Robert Devereux, Earl of Essex, at the head of an army of more than 17,000 to crush the rebellion. Reluctant to engage Tyrone's main force in the north, however, Essex frittered away the main fighting season by taking the army south into Munster. In September, having long ignored direct orders to engage the main body of the rebel army, he arranged a parley with Tyrone at an isolated river crossing and negotiated a truce, going so far as to promise to seek a royal pardon for the Irish earl.

None of this, of course, had been authorized by the Queen, and to stave off her wrath, Essex set off hastily to return to England and talk with her in person. Accompanied by a small band of men including Sir John Harington, he arrived at the palace of Nonesuch early in the morning, still dressed in muddy riding clothes. Bursting into Elizabeth's bedchamber, he cast himself down on his knees and begged for pardon. It was a grave mistake. Not only had he come back against her explicit orders but he had stumbled on her when she was only half dressed. Placing him under house arrest, she appointed a royal commission to investigate his conduct, and though it released him the following summer, it found him guilty of gross insubordination and official misconduct and deprived him of his offices. To a man of his high standing, it was a staggering blow, leaving him without authority or income adequate to cover his many obligations.

His command in Ireland was given over to Charles Blount, Lord Mountjoy, who, after some months spent rebuilding the army, began a ruthless but successful campaign against Tyrone. Inducing widespread starvation by destroying crops and food supplies, Mountjoy built new fortifications and slaughtered many civilians suspected of supporting the insurrection. In December 1601, as Tyrone attempted to join forces with a contingent of Spanish soldiers sent to aid him, Mountjoy surprised him, slaughtering much of his army and scattering the rest. The Spanish were forced to retreat, and the back of the rebellion was broken. Shortly before the Queen died in 1603, she bowed to pressure from her Council and, in return for a peace agreement, granted the rebellious Earl the pardon that Essex had sought for him four years earlier.

Essex, however, did not live to see the victory. In the fall of 1600, still in disgrace and deeply in debt, he began to plot to regain power by capturing the Queen and bringing down the government. The following February, when he put the plan into effect, he expected widespread support among the common people, but when Essex and a band of two hundred supporters who had gathered at his house took to the streets, few joined them, and the insurrection was over in a matter of hours. He and others involved in the plot were quickly tried, convicted of treason, and put to death. Although Elizabeth showed none of the hesitation that had delayed the execution of Mary Stuart, she hated signing the death warrant, feeling that she herself bore some of the blame because she had not properly reined Essex in when signs of willfulness and arrogance first appeared. Two months before her death in 1603, she was still grieving. When Robert Cecil spoke in favor of pardoning the Earl of Tyrone, she rounded on him, demanding how he could ask her to forgive a man who had been seven years a traitor when she had approved the execution of Essex for the treason of a single day. Yet her grief was mixed with anger and indignation. As she told one ambassador, if the Earl had managed to lead his rabble of supporters to Whitehall, she would have come out in person to confront him, "to know which of the two of them ruled."

In the last three years of her life, the Queen remained as acute and fit for rule as ever. Blessed with a robust constitution and committed to spare eating and vigorous hunting, walking, and dancing, she had lived longer than any other English monarch before her. Until the end, she continued her summer progresses, though even her youngest courtiers complained about the hardships they entailed. In the end, her spirit declined before her body. In February 1603, after one of her oldest and most beloved attendants, Katherine Howard, the Countess of Nottingham, died, the Queen sank into a deep depression. Within weeks, her body was failing, and by March 23, she had lost the power of speech. When Robert Cecil came at the request of the Council to ask her preferences for a successor, she was reduced to raising her hand to her head at the mention of James VI. Cecil and others were happy to interpret the gesture as a sign of assent. Afterward, she took evident comfort in the prayers of John Whitgift, the Archbishop of Canterbury, who reported that she showed no interest when he talked of her recovery but squeezed his hand when he spoke of the joys of heaven. Early the next morning, she died, and by ten o'clock, James VI had been proclaimed King in the streets of London.

For two days, the Queen's body lay unattended in Richmond Palace. At her request, it was wound in linen, but the servants skimped on material in order to steal some for their own uses. It was a shameful end. Officials soon bestirred themselves, however, arranging to have the body properly prepared and conveyed by torchlight down the Thames to Whitehall. There, it was sealed in a lead coffin and lay in state for a month, surrounded by her female attendants. The people of England, exhausted by economic hardship and the long wars in the Netherlands and Ireland, were ready for a new monarch and a fresh start. Londoners, however, turned out in great numbers on April 28 for the funeral. At the front of the procession walked two hundred and forty poor women, followed by royal servants and household officers of all titles and ranks. The Queen's coffin, carried on an open wagon, came next, bearing an effigy of her dressed in queenly array. After the wagon came the Master of the Horse, the Lord Admiral, and the Lord Treasurer, and after them the wives and daughters of the nobility. Last of all came the Yeomen of the Guard, with their halberds pointed downwards in a gesture of mourning.

It was, as everyone sensed, the end of an age. Elegies appeared in great numbers, and poets as obscure as Henry Petowe and as famous as William Shakespeare and Michael Drayton remarked on the alteration in the world that her passing had brought about. Shortly after James came to the throne, he revived her Accession Day as a national holiday, and it continued to be widely celebrated for more than a century. As difficulties with her Stuart successors became apparent, people looked back on her with the selective vision of nostalgia. Memories of her long reign gradually turned to myth, helping to shape England's sense of its own identity as an island paradise, a daring but beneficent colonial power, and a land of poets and military heroes.

TYRONE'S REBELLION AND THE FALL OF ESSEX

A late poem by the Earl of Essex, entitled "It Was a Time When Silly Bees Could Speak," suggests something of the trouble brewing between him and the Queen. Comparing himself to a worker bee, Essex complains that all the others in the hive advance when they have served their time, but not he. The drone, who is also the King of the Bees, rebukes him for being unhappy with his lot, noting that the personified figure of Time is the true ruler at Court and remarking scornfully that "Th' art bound to serve the time, the Time not thee." Perhaps Sir Robert Cecil was the drone to whom the poem refers, since he was, along with Essex, the chief power at Court at this time. Evidence in the manuscripts suggests that the poem was written in the summer of 1598, shortly after the Earl became angry with the Queen during a Council meeting about the coming Irish campaign, turned his back on her, and had his ears boxed for his insolence. Enraged that she had hit him, he placed his hand on the hilt of his sword as if to draw on her, and she banished him from Court. He stayed away for two months. Though they reconciled, and she subsequently gave him command of the Irish expedition, the incident was a foretaste of troubles to come.

Following the English defeat at Yellow Ford, Elizabeth issued a proclamation "On Sending the Army into Ireland." Intended as much for the Irish as for the English, it set out to demonstrate the Queen's justice in using force on the rebels and her mercy in offering to spare as many as would put down their arms and accept her authority.

More revealing of realities behind the scenes is Elizabeth's secret correspondence with the commander of the English army in Ireland. In July 1599, she wrote a letter to Essex taking him to task for incompetence and insubordination. Although he had wasted the spring and half the summer in minor skirmishes, achieving only one notable victory (the capture of Cahir Castle), he had nonetheless conferred battlefield knighthoods on many of his supporters and had reported his activities to the Queen as if he were achieving great things. She responded by lashing out at him for making "a bush kern [or peasant] to be accounted so famous a rebel" and for treating an enormous English army as "too little to be employed." Brushing aside the victory at Cahir as a minor action against a "rabble of rogues," she reproached him for his freedom with knighthoods, his promotion of a disgraced courtier (his friend Henry Wriothesley, Earl of Southampton), and his squandering of time and resources in the south.

The letter marks the start of a disastrous decline in Essex's fortunes. Glimpses of its progress appear in the letters and memoirs of Sir John Harington. Famous in his day for his translation of Ludovico Ariosto's Italian romance *Orlando Furioso*, Harington was unequalled in his ability to craft intimate and amusing sketches of personalities at Court. Although his lightheartedness endeared him to the Queen, she never trusted him or gave him a major post, and to lift his fortunes, he was forced to accept command of a company of cavalry and accompany the army into Ireland. Warned by his cousin Robert Markham not to tell amusing anecdotes about his superiors, he seems to have done well there, for Essex knighted him in the field.

The Queen looked less kindly on his exploits, particularly one involving the Earl of Tyrone. Having tagged along with English negotiators for an unauthorized meeting with the famous rebel, Harington had chatted amiably with him, taking the opportunity to read aloud a passage from *Orlando Furioso* and offering a copy to Tyrone's sons. On Harington's return to London, the Queen asked to see a journal that he had kept during the campaign, and having read of the incident with Tyrone, she lashed out at her godson for befriending a rebel. Having learned details of Essex's conduct from the same source, she became enraged, swearing "by God's Son, we were all idle knaves, and the Lord Deputy worse, for wasting our time and her commands in such wise." In his "Brief Notes and Remembrances," Harington tells of a subsequent incident in which Essex pleaded with him to intervene with the Queen on his behalf, behaving so wildly that he seemed "devoid of good reason or right mind," but by then, Harington was too frightened to meddle in the matter. His *Epigrams* suggest bitterness at the subsequent stagnation of his own career at Court, prudent detachment from Essex, and sardonic humor at the Earl's mistakes. It was lucky that the Queen's merry godson drew back when he did, for his former commander was on a course that would soon lead to treason and the gallows.

Although, in hindsight, the rebellion mounted by the Earl in 1601 does not appear to have had much hope of success, it caused Elizabeth and her government considerable concern. Part of the reason for their worry lay in the factions that had developed around Essex and his chief rival, Sir Robert Cecil. Enraged at the loss of his royal offices, the Earl had convinced himself that the cause lay, not in his own folly or even in the anger of the Queen, but in the backbiting of Cecil and Essex's other old rival, Sir Walter Ralegh. The aim of the rebellion was not so much to overthrow the Queen as to wrest her away from them, regain her confidence, and restore Essex to power. In pursuing this scheme, the Earl relied on two main sources of support. One was the people of London, who admired him for his exploits during the 1596 raid on the Spanish port of Cadiz. The other was James VI of Scotland, who because of a long and secret correspondence with Essex had become convinced that Cecil was hostile to him and would oppose any attempt to name him Elizabeth's successor. To counter Cecil, James promised diplomatic support for Essex and the rebellion.

Believing himself in a commanding position, Essex swung into action. In February 1601, he gathered supporters at his house in London, rousing their courage by staging a private performance of Shakespeare's *Richard II*, a play about a nobleman who overthrows the government after being unfairly driven from Court. On the following morning, the Earl and his supporters took to the streets, hoping to raise the people of London and seize the Queen in her quarters at Whitehall Palace. Few citizens heeded the call, and after a brief skirmish with the local militia, the rebels scattered. Essex and a few friends retreated to his house, where they were surrounded and captured.

To the government, the situation remained a matter of concern. The Queen's *Proclamation on the Seizure of the Earls of Essex, Rutland, and Southampton for Rebellion* suggests that, for a time at least, Essex was not the only one who believed in his ability to command popular support. As it happened, no publicity campaign against him was needed. The citizens of London remained loyal to the Queen.

ROBERT DEVEREUX, EARL OF ESSEX

It Was a Time When Silly Bees Could Speak (1598)[†]

It was a time when silly[1] bees could speak,
And in that time I was a silly bee,

[†] Copy text: John Dowland, *The third and last booke of songs or aires Newly composed to sing to the lute, orpharion, or viols* (London: Thomas Adams, 1603; STC 7096), K2v–L1r.
1. Simple, lowly, as well as foolish.

Who fed on Time[2] until my heart 'gan break,
Yet never found the Time would favor me.
5   Of all the swarm I only did not thrive,
Yet brought I wax and honey to the hive.

Then thus I buzzed, when Time no sap would give,
"Why should this blesséd Time to me be dry,
Sith° by this Time the lazy drone doth live,   *Since*
10 The wasp, the worm, the gnat, the butterfly?"
Mated° with grief, I kneeléd on my knees   *Overcome*
And thus complained unto the King of Bees:

"My Liege, gods grant thy time may never end,
And yet vouchsafe to hear my plaint of Time,
15 Which fruitless flies have found to have° a friend,   *be*
And I cast down when atomies° do climb."   *tiniest creatures*
The King replied but thus, "Peace, peevish bee,
Th' art bound to serve the Time,[3] the Time not thee."

QUEEN ELIZABETH

DOCUMENTS ON THE WAR (1599)

The Queen Majesty's Proclamation Declaring Her Princely Resolution in Sending Over of Her Army into the Realm of Ireland[†]

By the Queen
   Although our actions and carriage in the whole course of our government,
ever since it pleased God to call us to the succession of this crown (being
truly considered), may as evidently manifest to all our subjects as our conscience doth clearly witness it to ourself how earnestly we have affected the
peace and tranquility of the people of our dominions and how much we
have preferred clemency before any other respect as a virtue both agreeable
to our natural disposition, the sincerity of the religion which we profess,
and always esteemed by us the greatest surety to our royal state, when our
subjects' hearts are assured to us by the bond of love rather than by forced
obedience; notwithstanding, it hath fallen out to our great discontentation
that this our gracious intention in the whole scope of our government hath
not wrought in all men's minds a like effect nor brought forth everywhere
that fruit of obedience which we expected, and namely in our kingdom and
people of Ireland, where (as oftentimes heretofore, so now especially of late
years) divers of our subjects, both of the better sort and of the meaner
(abusing our lenity to their advantage), have unnaturally and without all

2. Was a dependent on Time (here personified); he spent his time at Court seeking advancement.
   Elsewhere in the poem, "the Time" is used as if it were a title, like "the King."
3. Hence, to be what we call a "time-server," or useless parasite, at Court.
† Copy text: Queen Elizabeth, *The Queenes Maiesties proclamation declaring her princely resolution
   in sending ouer of her army into the realme of Ireland* (London: Christopher Barker, 1599; STC
   14146), single broadsheet.

ground or cause offered by us forgotten their allegiance and (rebelliously taking arms) have committed many bloody and violent outrages upon our loyal subjects. And though their own consciences can bear them witness that, both by us and by our ministers there, more ways have been attempted to reclaim them by clemency (for avoiding of bloodshed) than is usual with princes that have so good means to reduce them by other means, yet have we not thereof reaped those fruits which so great a grace hath deserved, if there had been in them any sense of religion, duty, or common humanity.

This is therefore the cause that after so long patience we have been compelled to take resolution to reduce that kingdom to obedience (which by the laws of God and nature is due unto us) by using an extraordinary power and force against them, assuring ourselves so much in the justice of our cause as we shall find the same success (which ever[1] it is the pleasure of God to give to princes' rights) against unnatural rebellions.

Wherein notwithstanding, because we do conceive that all our people which are at this present actors in this rebellion are not of one kind, nor carried into it with one mind, but some out of sense they have of hard measures heretofore offered them by some of our ministers, some for fear of power and might which their adverse sects and factions have grown unto by advantage of this loose time, and some for want of protection and defense against the wicked and barbarous rebels, and many inveigled with superstitious impressions wrought in them by the cunning of seditious priests and seminaries[2] (crept into them from foreign parts, suborned by those that are our enemies), and a great part out of a strong opinion put into them by the heads of this rebellion that we intended an utter extirpation and rooting out of that nation and conquest of the country, we have therefore thought it good and answerable to that justice and clemency (which we profess to be with us in account above all other royal virtues) to accompany our army, which we send thither, with this signification to our subjects: that we are not ignorant of the divers causes that have misled them into these unnatural actions, and that we both can and will make distinction of their offences. And for their better comfort touching the apprehension of conquest, wherewith the capital and unnatural traitors do seek to harden the hearts of those that have less offended us, thereby hoping to bind them faster to run their desperate fortune, we do profess hereby to the world that we are so far from any such purpose, as the very name of conquest in this case seemeth so absurd to us as we cannot imagine upon what ground it could enter into any man's conceit[3] that our actions (tending only to reduce a number of unnatural and barbarous rebels and to root out the capital heads of the most notorious traitors) should need any such title of conquest when we have in that our kingdom (to our great contentment) the best part of our nobility, the people of all our good towns, and divers of our subjects so assured in their loyalty to us as they give us no suspicion of falling from their duties.

Of which our true and princely meaning: we require all our subjects there in general to take comfort and such as for any cause are revolted from their duty to bethink themselves betimes of the extreme misery whereinto they shall throw themselves, if by persisting in this rebellion they give us cause to

---

1. Always.
2. Jesuits trained at seminaries in Douai and Rome, who were sent into Ireland to minister to the people there and to help bring the British Isles back to the Catholic fold.
3. Thought.

use against them the last but worst of all remedies, the sword, which for repairing of our honor, the safety of the rest of our people, and the assurance of the course of our justice, we are both forced and so resolved to do to all that shall not with all expedition, penitency, and humility prostrate themselves to our mercy, as their only way to redeem themselves from the calamities and confusions whereof their own hearts cannot but feel (beforehand) the horror.

For confirmation of all which resolutions, as well how to proceed with the grieved and humbled hearts as with the obstinate and obdurate, we have made choice of such a person[4] to be in that realm the minister both of our justice and mercy, whose valor, wisdom, and success in other public actions which we have committed unto him and the force of our good subjects, with which he is now and shall be furnished, as it may be just terror to the wicked in making them see before their eyes the short and desperate end of these their barbarous and unnatural courses, so may this our election of a person of his place and rank every way, both in our counsels and in our kingdom, sufficiently assure our dutiful subjects there of the great care we have of their preservation, of the abundance of our clemency and gracious disposition to those that shall deserve mercy, and of our resolution to make the obstinate enemies to God and traitors to our crown and dignity to feel our powerful arm.

Given at her Majesty's manor of Richmond, the last day of March 1599, in the one and fortieth year of her Highness's reign.

God save the Queen.

Letter to Essex in Ireland (July 19, 1599)[†]

19mo Julii. From her Majesty to the Lord Lieutenant.

We have perceived by your letters to our Council brought by Henry Carey that you are arrived at Dublin after your journey into Munster, where though it seemeth by the words of your letter that you had spent divers days in taking an account of all that have passed since you left that place, yet have you in this dispatch given us small light either when or in what order you intend particularly to proceed to the northern action.[1] Wherein, if you compare the time that is run on and the excessive charges that is spent with the effects of anything wrought by this voyage (howsoever we may remain satisfied with your own particular cares and travails of body and mind), yet you must needs think that we that have the eyes of foreign princes upon our actions and have the hearts of people to comfort and cherish—who groan under the burden of continual levies and impositions which are occasioned by these late actions—can little please ourself hitherto with anything that hath been effected.

For what can be more true (if things be rightly examined) than that your two months' journey hath brought in never a capital rebel against whom it had been worthy to have adventured one thousand men; for of their two

---

4. Robert Devereux, Earl of Essex.

† Copy text: *Elizabeth I: Collected Works*, ed. Leah S. Marcus, Janel Mueller, and Mary Beth Rose (Chicago and London: University of Chicago Press, 2000), 390–94. Reprinted by permission of the University of Chicago Press. Copyright © 2000 by the University of Chicago.

1. Elizabeth wished Essex to proceed to Ulster, home of the rebel Hugh O'Neill, second Earl of Tyrone; *Henry Carey*: younger son of the late Henry Carey, Lord Hunsdon, Elizabeth's Lord Chamberlain, and brother to George Carey, current Lord Hunsdon and Lord Chamberlain.

coming-in that were brought unto you by Ormond (namely Mountgarrett and Cahir), whereupon ensued the taking of Cahir Castle,[2] full well do we know that you would long since have scorned to have allowed it for any great matter in others to have taken an Irish hold from a rabble of rogues with such force as you had and with the help of the cannon, which were always able in Ireland to make his passage where it pleased. And therefore, more than that, you have now learned upon our expenses, by knowledge of the country, that those things are true which we have hertofore told you. If you would have believed us, how far different things would prove from your expectations! There is little public benefit made to us of any things happened in this action which the President[3] with any convenient addition to his numbers by you might not have effected, either now or hereafter, in a time more seasonable, when it should less have hindered the other enterprise on which depends our greatest expectation.

Whereas we will add this one thing that doth more displease us than any charge or expense that happens, which is that it must be the Queen of England's fortune (who hath holden down the greatest enemy she had) to make a base bush kern[4] to be accounted so famous a rebel as to be a person against whom so many thousands of foot and horse, besides the force of all the nobility of that kingdom, must be thought too little to be employed. For we must now remember unto you that our cousin of Ormond, by his own relation when you arrived, assured us that he had delivered you a charge of a kingdom without either town maritime,[5] or island, or hold possessed by the traitors. But we did ever think that Tyrone would please himself to see such a portion of our fair army, and led by the person of our General, to be harassed out and adventured in encountering those base rogues who were no way strengthened by foreign armies, but only by such of his offal as he was content to spare and let slip from himself, whiles he hath lived at his pleasure, hath spoiled all where our army should come, and preserved for himself what he thought necessary. Little do you know how he hath blazed in foreign parts the defeats of regiments, the death of captains, and loss of men of quality in every corner, and how little he seemeth to value their power who use it so as it is like to spend itself!

It is therefore apparent that all places require not one and the selfsame knowledge, and that drafts and surprises would have found better successes than public and notorious marches, though where the rebel attends you with greater forces, it is necessary that you carry our army in the form you use. But it doth sound hardly in the ears of the world that, in a time when there is a question to save a kingdom and in a country where experience giveth so great advantage to all enterprises, regiments should be committed to young gentlemen that rather desire to do well than know how to perform it, a matter wherein we must note that you have made both us and our Council so great strangers as to this day we know but by reports who

---

2. The Anglo-Irish Thomas Butler, tenth Earl of Ormond and Lord Deputy of Ireland, and his kinsmen: Richard Butler, third Viscount Mountgarret, married to the eldest daughter of rebel leader Hugh O'Neill; and Thomas Butler, baron of Cahir, married to Mountgarret's sister. After they had made their submission, Cahir's younger brother unsuccessfully sought to defend Cahir Castle, the family stronghold in Leinster, against Essex's forces [Marcus, Mueller, and Rose's note].
3. Sir Thomas Norris, brother of Sir John Norris and Lord President of Munster after his brother's death.
4. Peasant.
5. Seacoast town.

they be that spend our treasure and carry places of note in our army. Wherein you know we did by our instructions direct you as soon as you should be arrived, seeing you used reasons why it could not be done so conveniently beforehand.

These things we would pass over but that we see your pen flatters you with phrases—that here you are deceived, that you are disgraced from hence in your friends' fortune, that poor Ireland suffers in you—still exclaiming against the effects of your own causes. For if it be not enough that you have all and more than that which was agreed on before you went concerning public service, but that you must by your voluntary actions there in particular things (which you know full well are contrary to our will and liking) raise an opinion that there is any person that dare displease us, either by experience of our former toleration or with a conceit to avoid blame by distinctions, then must we not hide from you, how much soever we do esteem you for those good things which are in you, but that our honor hath dwelt too long with us to leave the point now uncleared that, whosoever it be that you do clad with any honor or place[6] (wherein the world may read the least suspicion of neglect or contempt of our commands), we will never make dainty to set on such shadows as shall quickly eclipse any of these lusters.

And therefore, although by your letter we found your purpose to go northward, on which depends the main good of our service and which we expected long since should have been performed, yet because we do hear it bruited (besides the words of your letter written with your own hand, which carries some such sense) that you who allege such weakness in our army by being traveled with you and find so great and importunate affairs to digest at Dublin, will yet engage yourself personally in Offaly,[7] being our lieutenant, when you have there so many inferiors able enough to victual a fort or seek revenge of these that have lately prospered against our forces. And when we call to mind how far the sun hath run his course, what dependeth upon the timely plantation of garrisons in the north, and how great a scandal it would be to our honor to leave that proud rebel unassaulted when we have with so great an expectation of our enemies engaged ourself so far in this action, so as without that be done, all these former courses will prove like *via navis in mare*,[8] besides that our power, which hitherto hath been dreaded by potent enemies, will now even be held contemptible amongst our rebels, we must now plainly charge you, according to the duty you owe us, so to unite soundness of judgment to the zeal you have to do us service, and with all speed to pass thither in such order as the axe may be put to the root of that tree which hath been the treasonable stock from whence so many poisoned plants and grafts have been derived. By which proceedings of yours we may neither have cause to repent our employment of yourself for omitting these opportunities to shorten the war, nor receive in the eye of the world imputation of too much weakness in ourself to being a work without better foresight.

What would be the end of our excessive charge, the adventure of our people's lives, and the holding-up of our own greatness against a wretch

6. Essex made many battlefield grants of knighthood; *any person*: that is, Essex himself; *blame by distinctions*: with a thought to avoid blame by claiming to be an exception to usual rules of obedience.
7. A central Irish county.
8. "A ship's path in the sea," which quickly fades from sight.

whom we have raised from the dust[9] and who could never prosper if the charges we have been put to were orderly employed? For the matter of Southampton,[1] it is strange to us that his continuance or displacing should work so great an alteration either in yourself (valuing our commandments as you ought) or in the disposition of our army, where all the commanders cannot be ignorant that we not only not allowed of your desire to him, but did expressly forbid it. And being such a one whose counsel can be of so little and experience of less use, yea, such a one as, were he not lately fastened to yourself by an accident wherein for our usage of yours we deserve thanks,[2] you would have used many of your old, lively arguments against him for any such ability or commandment. It is therefore strange to us that, we knowing his worth by your report and you our disposition from ourself in this point, will dare thus to value your own pleasing in things unnecessary, and think by your private arguments to carry for your own glory a matter wherein our pleasure to the contrary is made notorious. And where you say further that divers or the most of the voluntary gentlemen are so discouraged thereby as they begin to desire passports and prepare to return, we cannot as yet be persuaded but that the love of our service and the duty which they owe us have been as strong motives to these their travails and hazards as any affection to the Earl of Southampton or any other. If it prove otherwise, which we will not so much wrong as to suspect, we shall have the less cause either to acknowledge or reward it.

At the Court at Greenwich the nineteenth of July, 1599.

SIR JOHN HARINGTON

ON THE IRISH CAMPAIGN, THE FALL OF ESSEX, AND THE QUEEN (c. 1599–1618)

From a Letter to Robert Markham (1606)[†]

[*The Queen's anger upon the return of Essex and Harington from Ireland*]

My good cousin,

Herewith you will have my journal, with our history during our march against the Irish rebels. I did not intend any eyes should have seen this discourse but my own children's. Yet, alas, it happened otherwise, for the Queen did so ask and, I may say, demand my account, that I could not withhold showing it; and I, even now, almost tremble to rehearse her Highness's

---

9. In 1562 Elizabeth had offered the young Hugh O'Neill protection and education in England after the murder of his father. Before assuming the earldom of Tyrone, he had served under Sir Henry Sidney in Ireland.
1. Against the Queen's explicit wishes, Essex had attempted to make Henry Wriothesley, Earl of Southampton, his Master of Horse. Southampton had been in disfavor with the Queen since his secret marriage in 1598 with Essex's cousin, Elizabeth Vernon, one of the Queen's maids of honor.
2. The Queen deserves thanks for not prosecuting Essex's cousin, Elizabeth Vernon.
† Copy text: Sir John Harington, *Nugae antiquae: being a miscellaneous collection of original papers in prose and verse written during the reigns of Henry VIII, Edward VI, Queen Mary, Elizabeth, and King James: by Sir John Harington, Knt.*, ed. Henry Harington, 3 vols. (London: Vernor and Hood, Poultry, and Cuthell and Martin, 1804), 1.354–57.

displeasure hereat. She swore, by God's Son, we were all idle knaves, and the Lord Deputy[1] worse, for wasting our time and her commands in such wise as my journal doth write of. I could have told her Highness of such difficulties, straits, and annoyance as did not appear therein to her eyes nor, I found, could not be brought to her ear, for her choler did outrun all reason, though I did meet it at a second hand, for what show she gave at first to my Lord Deputy at his return was far more grievous, as will appear in good time. I marvel to think what strange humors do conspire to patch up the natures of some minds. The elements do seem to strive which shall conquer and rise above the other. In good sooth, our late Queen did enfold them all together. I bless her memory, for all her goodness to me and my family; and now will I show you what strange temperament she did sometime put forth.

Her mind was oft-time like the gentle air that cometh from the westerly point in a summer's morn: 'twas sweet and refreshing to all around her. Her speech did win all affections, and her subjects did try to show all love to her commands. For she would say her state did require her to command what she knew her people would willingly do from their own love to her. Herein did she show her wisdom fully; for who did choose to lose her confidence, or who would withhold a show of love and obedience, when their sovereign said it was their own choice and not her compulsion? Surely she did play well her tables[2] to gain obedience thus without constraint. Again, she could put forth such alterations, when obedience was lacking, as left no doubtings whose daughter she was.

I say this was plain on the Lord Deputy's coming home, when I did come into her presence. She chafed much, walked fastly to and fro, looked with discomposure in her visage; and, I remember, she catched my girdle when I kneeled to her and swore, "By God's Son, I am no Queen. That *man* is above me. Who gave him command to come here so soon? I did send him on other business." It was long before more gracious discourse did fall to my hearing. But I was then put out of my trouble and bid, "Go home." I did not stay to be bidden twice. If all the Irish rebels had been at my heels, I should not have had better speed, for I did now flee from one whom I both loved and feared, too.[3]

* * *

I have now passed my storms and wish for a quiet harbor to lay up my bark,[4] for I grow old and infirm. I see few friends and hope I have no enemies. So now adieu, good cousin, and read my tale which I penned of our marches, ambuscades, culverins,[5] and such-like matters, which, if it give you no more pleasure in the reading than it did me in the enduring, I must think it a sorry tale truly.

I rest your loving cousin,
JOHN HARINGTON

Send me Petrarch[6] by my man, at his return.

1. The Earl of Essex.
2. Play her cards well.
3. A subsequent section of the letter describing the Queen's character is included in Part Eleven of this anthology.
4. Small boat.
5. Cannons; *penned*: in the journal; *ambuscades*: ambushes.
6. An edition of works by the Italian poet and humanist Petrarch (Francesco Petrarca).

From a Letter to Sir Anthony Standen
(February 1600)†

[*Harington's reconciliation with the Queen*]

Sir,

It is not a lake of Lethe that makes us forget our friends, but it is the lack of good messengers. For who will write when his letters shall be opened by the way and construed at pleasure, or rather displeasure?[1] Some used this in Ireland that perhaps have repented it since in England.[2] I came to Court in the very heat and height of all displeasures. After I had been there but an hour, I was threatened with the Fleet.[3] I answered poetically that, coming so late from the land-service, I hoped that I should not be pressed[4] to serve in her Majesty's fleet in Fleet Street. After three days, every man wondered to see me at liberty. But though, in conscience, there was neither rhyme nor reason to punish me for going to see Tyrone, yet if my rhyme had not been better liked of than my reason (I mean when I gave the young Baron of Dungannon an Ariosto), I think I had lain by the heels[5] for it. But I had this good fortune, that, after four or five days, the Queen had talked of me and twice talked to me, though very briefly. At last she gave me a full and gracious audience in the withdrawing chamber at Whitehall,[6] where herself being accuser, judge, and witness, I was cleared and graciously dismissed. What should I say? I seemed to myself, for the time, like St. Paul, rapt up[7] in the third heaven, where he heard words not to be uttered by men; for neither must I utter what I then heard. Until I come to heaven, I shall never come before a statelier judge again, nor one that can temper majesty, wisdom, learning, choler, and favor better than her Highness did at that time. In the discourse, you were not unspoken of her. You shall hear ere long, but not by writing, for I will send a man.

✼   ✼   ✼

You wonder I write nothing of *one*.[8] Believe me, I hear nothing; but *he* is where he was, and I think must be, till these great businesses be concluded. Let this suffice from a private country knight that lives among clouted shoes in his frieze[9] jacket and galoshes and who envies not the great commanders of Ireland, but hereby commends himself to them.

Your true friend,

JOHN HARINGTON

Kelston, near Bath,
February 20, 1600

---

† Copy text: *Nugae Antiquae*, 1.309–11.
1. Read for the servant's entertainment and his master's displeasure; here the mischief led to rumors of his return that reached London before he did.
2. Essex came to London so that he could make his case about the botched Irish campaign directly to the Queen rather than address her through messengers; *this*: this practice of avoiding the use of letters.
3. A prison in Fleet Street.
4. Enlisted by force.
5. Been fettered in irons; *Tyrone*: Hugh O'Neill, Earl of Tyrone, the leader of the Irish rebellion. On Harington's unauthorized visit to him, see Historical Background in this section; *Ariosto*: a copy of Harington's translation of Ariosto's *Orlando Furioso*. Tyrone was also, at this time, Baron of Dungannon.
6. A royal palace in London.
7. Lifted up by God, as recounted in 2 Corinthians 12.2–4.
8. Essex, then under house arrest.
9. Coarse cloth made of wool.

From Brief Notes and Remembrances
(late autumn 1600)†

[*Essex's final appeals to the Queen for mercy*]

What perils have I escaped! I was entrusted by Essex, whom I did adventure to visit, with a message to the Queen's Majesty setting forth his contrition and sore grievance for his many offenses. I was right glad to hear such contrition and labored to effect this matter, but ere I could bear these tidings (which I was well advised to do), the Earl's petition reached her hand,[1] and I fear her displeasure too, but herein I bore no part. I was much encouraged to go through this friendly part on many sides, but I said charity did begin at home and should always sail with a fair wind, or it was not likely to be a prosperous voyage. I had nearly been wracked on the Essex coast[2] in my last venture, as I told the Queen, had it not been for the sweet calm of her special forgiveness. I have heard much on both hands, but the wiser he who reporteth nothing hereof. Did either know what I know either have said, it would not work much to contentment or good liking.

It resteth with me in opinion that ambition thwarted in its career doth speedily lead on to madness; herein I am strengthened by what I learn in my Lord of Essex, who shifteth from sorrow and repentance to rage and rebellion so suddenly, as well proveth him devoid of good reason or right mind. In my last discourse, he uttered strange words bordering on such strange designs that made me hasten forth and leave his presence. Thank heaven! I am safe at home, and if I go in such troubles again, I deserve the gallows for a meddling fool. His speeches of the Queen becometh no man who hath *mens sana in corpore sano*.[3] He hath ill advisors, and much evil hath sprung from this source. The Queen knoweth well how to humble the haughty spirit; the haughty spirit knoweth not how to yield, and the man's soul seemeth tossed to and fro, like the waves of a troubled sea.[4]

From Epigrams (ca. 1589–1602)‡

Of the Earl of Essex

Great Essex, now of late, incurréd hath
His mistress' indignation and her wrath;
And that in him she chiefly disalloweth:
She sent him north, he bent him to the south.[1]
5   Then what shall Essex do? Let him henceforth
Bend all his wits, his power, and courage north.

---

† Copy text: *Nugae Antiquae*, 1.178–79.
1. Probably Essex's suit in the fall of 1600 to be allowed to retain his license to levy duties on sweet wines, which was his primary source of income and was needed to stave off bankruptcy.
2. A pun on the Earl's name and that of a region in eastern England.
3. A sound mind in a healthy body.
4. An allusion to the state of a double-minded person in the New Testament Epistle of James 1.6.
‡ Copy text: Sir John Harington, *The most elegant and witty epigrams of Sir Iohn Harrington, Knight* (London: G.P. for Iohn Budge, 1618; STC 12776), I4r–v, E8r–E8v, K7r.
1. On Essex's refusal to attack the Irish rebels in the north and his hasty trip south to England, where he incurred the Queen's wrath, see introduction.

Of Misacmos's Success in a Suit

Misacmos[2] hath long time a suitor been,
To serve in some near place about the Queen,
In which his friends, to work his better speed,
Do tell her Highness, as 'tis true indeed,
5 That he's a man well born and better bred,
In humane studies seen, in stories read,
Adding unto an industry° not small,   *diligence*
Pleasant conceit° and memory withal.   *wit; disposition*
And chiefly that he hath been from his youth
10 A zealous searcher of Eternal Truth.
Now never wonder he his suit doth miss:
What I have told you, that the reason is.

The Author to Queen Elizabeth, in Praise of Her Reading

Forever dear, forever dreaded Prince,
You read a verse of mine a little° since,   *little while*
And so pronounced each word, and every letter,
Your gracious reading graced my verse the better.
5 Sith° then your Highness doth, by gift exceeding,   *Since*
Make what you read the better in your reading,
Let my poor Muse your pains thus far importune
To leave to read my verse and read my fortune.

QUEEN ELIZABETH

Proclamation on the Seizure of the Earls of Essex, Rutland, and Southampton for Rebellion (1601)[†]

By the Queen
Whereas the Earl of Essex, accompanied with the Earls of Rutland and
Southampton and divers other their complices, gentlemen of birth and
quality, knowing themselves to be discovered in divers treasonable actions
into which they have heretofore entered (as well in our realm of Ireland,
where some of them had laid plots with the traitor Tyrone, as in this our
realm of England) did upon Sunday, being the eighth of this month, in the
morning not only imprison our Keeper of our Great Seal of England, our
Chief Justice of England, and others both of our nobility and Council that
were sent in our name to his house to persuade the said Earl to lay open
any his petitions or complaints, with promise (if he would disperse his disordered company in his house) that all his just requests should be heard
and graciously considered; but also did (after strait order given by him to
murder our said counselors and others whensoever they should offer to stir

---

2. Harington's pseudonym, meaning "hater of filth." Though Elizabeth was the poet's godmother, she
never entrusted him with a major position at Court.
† Copy text: Queen Elizabeth, *By the Queene. Whereas the Earle of Essex, accompanied with the Ear-
les of Rutland & Southampton.* . . . (London: Robert Barker, 1601; *STC* 8279), single broadsheet.

out of that place) traitorously issue into our city of London in arms, with great numbers, and there, breaking out into open action of rebellion, devised and divulged base and foolish lies that their lives were sought, spreading out divers strange and seditious inventions to have drawn our people to their party with purpose to attempt traitorous actions, both against our person and state, and to expose (as it now appeareth) our city and people with their goods to the spoil of a number of needy and desperate persons, their adherents continuing still in arms and killing divers of our subjects after many proclamations of rebellion made by our King of Heralds.[1]

Forasmuch as, notwithstanding (God be thanked) they have found themselves deceived of their expectation (being now all apprehended and within our Tower of London, as well the three principal traitorous Earls of Essex, Rutland, and Southampton, as divers others of the principal gentlemen their confederates), our good subjects of our city and elsewhere having showed themselves so constant and unmoveable from their duties towards us, as not any one of them of any note (that we can yet hear of) did offer to assist the said Earl and his associates, we have been contented, in regard of the comfort that we take, to find by so notorious evidence the loyal disposition of our people (whereof we never doubted), not only to make known to all our said subjects of our city and elsewhere in how thankful part we do accept both their loyal persisting in their duty and stay from following the false persuasions of the traitors, but to promise on our part that, whensoever we shall have cause to show it, they shall find us more careful over them than for ourselves. And hereby also, in regard of our gracious meaning towards our good people, to admonish them that, seeing this open act was so sudden as it cannot yet be thoroughly looked into how far it stretched and how many hearts it hath corrupted, but that it is to be presumed by the common example of the manner of proceeding of all rebels in like actions that it was not without instruments and ministers dispersed in divers places to provoke the minds of our people to like of their attempts with calumniating[2] our government and our principal servants and ministers thereof, that they shall do well (and so we charge them) to give diligent heed in all places to the conversation of persons not well known for their good behavior and to the speeches of any that shall give out slanderous and undutiful words or rumors against us and our government; and they that be in authority to lay hold on such spreaders of rumors, and such as be not in authority to advertise those thereof that have authority to the end that, by the apprehension of such dangerous instruments, both the drift and purpose of evil-minded persons may be discovered, their designs prevented, and our people conserved in such peace and tranquility as heretofore by God's favor we have maintained and do hope still to continue amongst them.

Given at our palace of Westminster the ninth day of February 1601, in the three and fortieth year of our reign.

God save the Queen.

---

1. Thomas Cecil, Lord Burghley, son of Elizabeth's longtime counselor; *Earls of Rutland and Southampton*: Roger Manners, fifth Earl of Rutland, and Henry Wriothesley, third Earl of Southampton. Both were young soldiers who had risen through Essex's patronage, and both were in disgrace, Rutland for his part in the Irish debacle of 1599 and Southampton for impregnating and secretly marrying a Maid of Honor; *complices*: accomplices; *Tyrone*: in 1599, Essex had negotiated with the Irish rebel, the Earl of Tyrone, without authorization; *keeper of our Great Seal of England*: Sir Thomas Egerton; *Chief Justice of England*: Sir John Popham; *strait*: strict.
2. Falsely accusing of misconduct.

THE QUEEN IN HER FINAL GLORY

By the turn of the century, Elizabeth enjoyed a level of love and reverence among her subjects that few English monarchs had ever attained. Yet problems and conflicts remained, and one of the most pressing led to the last of the Queen's great speeches. Late in the reign, a crisis arose over the abuse of royal monopolies. Often bestowed on courtiers as a reward for their service, these granted the right to tax various commodities, including common ones such as salt and glass bottles. Essex, for example, enjoyed a monopoly to tax sweet wines. As can be imagined, such arrangements—and the people who benefited from them—were widely resented. When Elizabeth's last Parliament met in 1601, members called on the Queen to undertake reform, and she responded by issuing a proclamation correcting the worst abuses. In gratitude, Sir John Croke, the speaker of the House of Commons, and about 140 members of Parliament came to Whitehall Palace to thank the Queen, and she responded with what became known as her "Golden Speech." Her repeated assurances of love for her subjects, care for their welfare, devotion to God, and commitment to impartial justice were just what the occasion called for, and the government rushed an official version into print. A fuller, far more lucid and eloquent version was preserved, however, by Haywood Townshend, one of the members of Parliament who attended the speech, and it probably comes closest to what Elizabeth actually said.

Late in the reign, while Elizabeth was dealing with the ongoing war with Spain, a depleted treasury, and a major rebellion in Ireland, Mary Sidney Herbert, Countess of Pembroke, wrote a poem in her honor that sought to turn her mind to pleasanter things. Serving as a dedication to the metrical version of the Psalms that Mary and her brother Philip had composed, the poem was part of a handsomely bound manuscript presented to the Queen. Beginning with an apology for turning Elizabeth's attention to something as apparently unimportant as poetry, the Countess went on to compare Elizabeth's virtues and accomplishments with those of King David. Both loved poetry and song; both came to the throne through adversity; and both gained renown as godly and victorious rulers. The poem ends with an attack on the Queen's enemies as a new race of Philistines and a celebration of England as a new Israel.

The translations themselves continue the Protestant tradition of rendering the Psalms into verse, though the Sidneys greatly expanded the usual range of metrical possibilities. In a display of remarkable virtuosity, the Countess gave each of the 107 psalms that she translated its own form. Each verse of Psalm 72, for instance, is composed of a pentameter quatrain (four lines of five strong beats each, rhyming ABAB) followed by a complex sestet (six lines rhyming CCD EED, where each triplet has two lines with two strong beats followed by a third with three). Comparison with the popular prose translation in the Geneva Bible reveals the skill required to carry out such a delicate and complicated scheme.

Less studiously crafted, though similarly refined, were three New Year's letters by Francis Bacon that were written to accompany gifts to the Queen. It was customary for members of the Court to exchange presents with her on New Year's Day, and many were designed to convey special meaning. Once, after displeasing the Queen by challenging the Earl of Oxford to a duel over a dispute on a tennis court, young Philip Sidney had offered her a piece of costly jewelry in the shape of a whip to convey the message that, if he should ever misbehave again, she should whip him. Detailed lists of such gifts survive, as do some of the notes that accompanied them. The three by Bacon—who later gained renown as an essayist and proponent of empirical science—were of special elegance and wit. Though he had long sought a position in the government, the Queen had never granted his wish, and his consequent lack of income gave ironic bite to his repeated protestations that he was unable to buy her a suitable present.

Though the annual round of rituals and entertainments continued unabated in Elizabeth's final years, the question of her advanced age could not be avoided. The anonymous "Ode of Cynthia," which concluded Francis Davison's famous anthology of Elizabethan verse *A Poetical Rhapsody,* glanced at the issue only to deny it, treating her, as other poems of the period often did, as altogether beyond the reach of time. As a note following the text suggests, even in her late sixties, to her people she was still the Queen of the May. John Davies's "Verses of the Queen" display a similar disregard for her mortality. Drawing paradoxical comparisons between her and the Virgin Mary, the poet first imagines her heart as a celestial "globe" from which Christ, the "light of the world," shines down on the kingdom. He then treats her as the bride of Christ and finally as the mother of Christ's children, ten thousand of them having been given new birth through the Protestant Queen. As at the first virgin birth, angels gather to sing to the people "peace, goodwill to men."

QUEEN ELIZABETH

The Golden Speech (November 30, 1601)

[*The Townshend version*][†]

Master Speaker, we have heard your declaration and perceive your care of our state by falling into the consideration of a grateful acknowledgment of such benefits as you have received,[1] and that your coming is to present thanks unto us, which I accept with no less joy than your loves can have desire to offer such a present.

I do assure you there is no prince that loveth his subjects better or whose love can countervail[2] our love. There is no jewel, be it of never so rich a price, which I set before this jewel, I mean your love. For I do more esteem of it than of any treasure or riches, for that we know how to prize, but love and thanks I count unvaluable.[3]

And though God hath raised me high, yet this I count the glory of my crown, that I have reigned with your loves. This makes me that I do not so much rejoice that God hath made me to be a Queen as to be a Queen over so thankful a people. Therefore, I have cause to wish nothing more than to content the subjects, and that is a duty which I owe; neither do I desire to live longer days than that I may see your prosperity, and that's my only desire.

And as I am that person that still (yet under God) hath delivered you, so I trust (by the almighty power of God) that I still shall be His instrument to preserve you from envy, peril, dishonor, shame, tyranny, and oppression, partly by means of your intended helps,[4] which we take very acceptably because it manifests the largeness of your loves and loyalty to your Sovereign.

Of myself I must say this: I was never any greedy, scraping grasper, nor a strait, fast-holding[5] prince, nor yet a waster. My heart was never set on

---

† Copy text: Hayward Townshend, *Historical collections, or, An exact account of the proceedings of the four last parliaments of Q. Elizabeth* (London: T. Basset, W. Crooke, and W. Cademan, 1680; Wing T1991), 263–66.
1. Elizabeth notes that, rather than coming to complain, the members of Parliament are grateful for the proclamation against monopolies. *Master Speaker*: Sir John Croke; the Speaker, who directed the debates, was nominated by the Queen but elected by the House of Commons at the beginning of each session.
2. Match.
3. Beyond price.
4. The subsidy to cover royal expenses to be approved by Parliament.
5. Strict and miserly.

worldly goods but only for my subjects' good. What you do bestow on me, I will not hoard it up but receive it to bestow on you again. Yea, my own proprieties[6] I count yours and to be expended for your good, and your eyes shall see the bestowing of all for your good. Therefore render unto them[7] from me, I beseech you, Master Speaker, such thanks as you imagine my heart yieldeth but my tongue cannot express.

(*Note: all this while we kneeled, whereupon her Majesty said:*)

Master Speaker, I would wish you and the rest to stand up, for I shall yet trouble you with longer speech.

(*So we all stood up and she went on with her speech, saying:*)

Master Speaker, you give me thanks, but I doubt me that I have more cause to thank you all than you me, and I charge you to thank them of the Lower House from me, for had I not received a knowledge[8] from you, I might have fallen into the lapse of an error only for lack of true information.

Since I was Queen, yet did I never put my pen unto any grant but that upon pretext and semblance made unto me it was both good and beneficial to the subject in general,[9] though a private profit to some of my ancient servants who had deserved well at my hands. But the contrary being found by experience, I am exceedingly beholding to such subjects as would move the same at the first. And I am not so simple to suppose but that there are some of the Lower House whom these grievances never touched, and for them I think they spake out of zeal for their countries[1] and not out of spleen or malevolent affection as being parties grieved. And I take it exceeding gratefully from them because it gives us[2] to know that no respects or interests had moved them other than the minds they bear to suffer no diminution of our honor and our subjects' loves unto us, the zeal of which affection, tending to ease my people and knit their hearts unto me, I embrace with a princely care. For above all earthly treasure, I esteem my people's love, more than which I desire not to merit.

That my grants should be grievous to my people and oppressions privileged under color[3] of our patents, our kingly dignity shall not suffer it. Yea when I heard it, I could give no rest unto my thoughts until I had reformed it. Shall they think to escape unpunished that have thus oppressed you and have been respectless of their duty and regardless[4] of our honor? No, Master Speaker, I assure you were it not more for conscience-sake than for any glory or increase of love that I desire, these errors, troubles, vexations, and oppressions done by these varlets and lewd persons (not worthy the name of subjects) should not escape without condign[5] punishment. But I perceive they dealt with me like physicians who, administering a drug, make it more acceptable by giving it a good, aromatical savor, or when they give pills do gild[6] them all over.

I have ever used to set the Last Judgment Day before my eyes, as so to rule as I shall be judged to answer before a higher Judge, to whose judgment seat

6. Possessions.
7. Members of the House of Commons.
8. Information; *doubt me:* fear.
9. All the citizens; *pretext and semblance:* advice and argument.
1. The counties they represent.
2. The royal plural.
3. Under the authority; *grants:* the monopolies.
4. Without regard; *respectless:* without respect.
5. Well-deserved; *lewd:* wicked.
6. Sugarcoat.

I do appeal, that never thought was cherished in my heart that tended not to my peoples' good, And now if my kingly bounty have been abused and my grants turned to the hurt of my people, contrary to my will and meaning, or if any in authority under me have neglected or perverted what I have committed to them, I hope God will not lay their culps[7] and offences to my charge who, though there were danger in repealing our grants, yet what danger would I not rather incur for your good than I would suffer them still to continue?

I know the title of a king is a glorious title, but assure yourself that the shining glory of princely authority hath not so dazzled the eyes of our understanding but that we well know and remember that we also are to yield an account of our actions before the great Judge.

To be a king and wear a crown is a thing more glorious to them that see it than it is pleasing to them that bear it. For myself, I was never so much enticed with the glorious name of a king or royal authority of a queen as delighted that God had made me His instrument to maintain His truth and glory and to defend this kingdom, as I said, from peril, dishonor, tyranny, and oppression.

There will never queen sit in my seat with more zeal to my country, care for my subjects, and that sooner with willingness will venture her life for your good and safety than myself, for it is not my desire to live nor reign longer than my life and reign shall be for your good. And though you have had and may have many princes more mighty and wise sitting in this state, yet you never had or shall have any that will be more careful[8] and loving.

Shall I ascribe anything to myself and my sexly[9] weakness? I were not worthy to live then, and of all most unworthy of the great mercies I have had from God, who hath ever yet given me a heart which never yet feared foreign or home enemy. I speak it to give God the praise as a testimony before you and not to attribute anything to myself; for I, O Lord, what am I whom practices and perils past should not fear?[1] or what can I do?

(*These words she spake with a great emphasis:*)

That I should speak for[2] any glory, God forbid.

This, Master Speaker, I pray you deliver to the House, to whom heartily commend me, and so I commit you all to your best fortunes and further counsels. And I pray you, Master Comptroller, Master Secretary,[3] and you of my Council, that before these gentlemen depart into their countries you bring them all to kiss my hand.

[*The official version*][†]

Her Majesty's most princely answer, delivered by herself at the Court at Whitehall on the last day of November, 1601, when the speaker of the Lower House of Parliament (assisted with the greatest part of the knights and burgesses) had presented their humble thanks for her free and gracious favor in preventing and reforming of sundry grievances by abuse of many grants, commonly called monopolies, the same being taken verbatim in writing by A.B.[1] as near as he could possibly set it down.

7. Sins.
8. Full of care; *in this state*: on this throne.
9. Pertaining to my (female) sex.
1. Frighten.
2. Claim.
3. Parliamentary officials.
† Copy text: Queen Elizabeth, *Her Maiesties most princelie answere, deliuered by her selfe at the court at VVhite-hall* (London: [R. Barker], 1601; STC 7578), A3r–A5v.
1. Probably Anthony Blagrave, a member of Parliament.

Master Speaker,

We perceive by you, whom we did constitute the mouth of our Lower House, how with even consent they are fallen into the due consideration of the precious gift of thankfulness, most usually least esteemed where it is best deserved. And therefore we charge you tell them how acceptable such sacrifice is worthily received of a loving king, who doubteth much whether the given thanks can be of more poise than the owed is to them[2] and suppose that they have done more for us than they themselves believe. And this is our reason: who keeps their sovereign from the lapse of error (in which, by ignorance and not by intent, they might have fallen) what thank they deserve we know, though you may guess. And as nothing is more dear to us than the loving conservation of our subjects' hearts, what an undeserved doubt might we have incurred if the abusers of our liberality, the thrallers of our people, the wringers of the poor had not been told us! Which, ere our heart or hand should agree unto, we wish we had neither and do thank you the more, supposing that such griefs touch not some amongst you in particular.[3] We trust there resides, in their conceits of us, no such simple cares of their good whom we so dearly prize, that our hand should pass aught that might injure any, though they doubt not it is lawful for our kingly state to grant gifts of sundry sorts of whom we make election,[4] either for service done or merit to be deserved, as being for a king to make choice on whom to bestow benefits, more to one than another.

You must not beguile yourselves nor wrong us to think that the glossing luster of a glistering glory of a king's title may so extol us that we think all is lawful what we list,[5] not caring what we do. Lord, how far should you be off from our conceits! For our part, we vow unto you that we suppose physicians' aromatical savors, which in the top of their potion they deceive the patient with, or gilded drugs that they cover their bittersweet with, are not more beguilers of senses than the vaunting boast of a kingly name may deceive the ignorant of such an office.[6] I grant that such a prince as cares but for the dignity, nor passes[7] not how the reins be guided (so he rule), to such a one it may seem an easy business. But you are cumbered (I dare assure) with no such prince, but such a one as looks how to give account afore another tribunal seat than this world affords and that hopes that, if we discharge with conscience what He bids, will not lay to our charge the fault that our substitutes (not being our crime) fall in.

We think ourselves most fortunately born under such a star as we have been enabled by God's power to have saved you under our reign from foreign foes, from tyrants' rule, and from your own ruin and do confess that we pass not so much to be a Queen as to be a Queen of such subjects, for whom (God is witness, without boast or vaunt) we would willingly lose our life ere see such to perish. I bless God He hath given me never this fault of fear, for He knows best whether ever fear possessed me, for all my dangers. I know it is His gift, and not to hide His glory I say it. For were it not for

---

2. Than the thanks I owe to them; *poise*: importance.
3. Elizabeth wryly suggests that no one in Parliament was supporting changes to regulate monopolies in order to reap personal benefits, but only for the common good.
4. Choose; *conceits*: thoughts; *aught*: anything.
5. Desire; *glossing*: superficial.
6. As a sweet taste disguises bitter medicine, so the name of "king" disguises the difficulty of the kingly office; *gilded*: sugarcoated.
7. Regards.

conscience and for your sake, I would willingly yield another my place, so great is my pride in reigning as she that wisheth no longer to be than best and most[8] would have me so. You know our presence cannot assist[9] each action but must distribute in sundry sorts to divers kinds our commands. If they (as the greatest number be commonly the worst) should (as I doubt not but some do) abuse their charge, annoy[1] whom they should help, and dishonor their King, whom they should serve, yet we verily believe that all you will (in your best judgment) discharge us from such guilt. Thus we commend us to your constant faith and yourselves to your best fortunes.

MARY SIDNEY HERBERT, COUNTESS OF PEMBROKE

From the Sidney Psalms (1593–1600)

[Even Now That Care] (ca. 1599)[†]

Even now that care which on thy crown attends
And with thy happy greatness daily grows
Tells me, thrice-sacred Queen, my muse offends°   *stumbles*
And of° respect to thee the line outgoes.°   *out of / overreaches*
One instant° will, or willing can, she lose,   *moment*
5 I say not reading but receiving rhymes,
On whom in chief dependeth to dispose
What Europe acts in these most active times?[1]

Yet dare I so, as humbleness may dare,
Cherish some hope they shall acceptance find,
10 Not weighing less thy state, lighter thy care,
But knowing more thy grace, abler thy mind.
What heav'nly pow'rs thee highest throne assigned,
Assigned thee goodness suiting that degree°   *rank*
And by thy strength thy burden so defined,
15 To others toil[2] is exercise to thee.

Cares, though still great, cannot be greatest still;°   *always*
Business must ebb, though leisure never flow.
Then these,[3] the posts° of Duty and Goodwill   *messengers*
20 Shall press to offer what their senders owe,
Which once in two, now in one subject go,[4]

8. Best and largest number of my people; *be*: be ruler.
9. Perform.
1. Cause trouble for.
† Copy text: Mary Sidney Herbert, *Selected Works of Mary Sidney Herbert, Countess of Pembroke*, ed. Margaret P. Hannay, Noel J. Kinnamon, and Michael G. Brennan (Tempe, AZ: Arizona Center for Medieval and Renaissance Studies, 2005), 159–63. Copyright Arizona Board of Regents for Arizona State University. Reprinted with permission. This dedicatory poem to Queen Elizabeth is found only in the Tixall Manuscript of the Sidney Psalms.
1. Will the Queen be able to spare any time even receiving such a poem (rhymes) when she has duties to attend to as head of state in troubled times? [Hannay, Kinnamon, and Brennan's note].
2. That which to others is toil.
3. The Psalms themselves.
4. The two subjects of the Queen were her brother Sir Philip Sidney, now dead, and herself.

The poorer left, the richer reft° away,   taken
Who better might (oh, "might": ah, word of woe!)
Have giv'n for me what I for him defray.[5]

25 How can I name whom[6] sighing signs extend,
And not unstop my tears' eternal spring?
But he did warp, I weaved this web to end;[7]
The stuff° not ours, our work no curious thing,   original material
Wherein yet well we thought the Psalmist King°   David
30 Now English denizened,° though Hebrew born,[8]   made a countryman
Would to thy music undispleaséd sing,
Oft having worse without repining worn.[9]

And I the cloth in both our names present,
A livery robe to be bestowed by thee;[1]
35 Small parcel of the undischargéd rent
From which no pains nor payments can us free.
And yet enough to cause our neighbors see
We will our best, though scanted° in our will;   restricted
And those nigh fields where sown thy favors be
40 Unwealthy do not else unworthy till.[2]

For in our work what bring we but thine own?
What English is, by many names is thine.
There humble laurels, in thy shadows grown,
To garland others would themselves repine.[3]
45 Thy breast the cabinet,° thy seat the shrine,   private study
Where Muses hang their vowéd memories;
Where wit, where art, where all that is divine
Conceivéd best and best defended lies,

Which if men did not (as they do) confess
50 And wronging worlds[4] would otherwise consent,
Yet here who minds° so meet° a patroness   knows / worthy
For author's state or writing's argument?[5]
A king° should only to a queen be sent: David
God's lovéd choice unto His chosen love,[6]
55 Devotion to devotion's president,[7]
What all applaud to her whom none reprove.

5. Pay out as partial settlement of the debt to the Queen [Hannay, Kinnamon, and Brennan's note].
6. Sir Philip Sidney.
7. Her brother laid down the initial threads on the loom (the warp), and Pembroke completed the weaving by running the woof, or cross threads; of the 150 Psalms, Pembroke wrote 107.
8. The psalms, though written in Hebrew, sound natural in English.
9. An allusion to earlier and inferior metrical psalms in English [Hannay, Kinnamon, and Brennan's note].
1. A court uniform Elizabeth can give to others.
2. The conceit of this stanza casts Pembroke and her brother as poor tenants of the Queen. Although they till their fields diligently, they produce only a small revenue.
3. The laurels would rather remain in Elizabeth's shadow than adorn the brow of another.
4. Perhaps a reference to non-Protestant countries. But "worlds" may be a scribal error for "words": thus, even if men did not confess and wronging words did not consent, she would still be best patroness [Hannay, Kinnamon, and Brennan's note].
5. Elizabeth is a worthy patron for poems ("writing's argument") derived from a kingly author (David).
6. The psalms of David, the man after God's own heart, are sent to Elizabeth, who herself is loved by God.
7. An allusion to Elizabeth as supreme governor of the English Church.

And who sees aught° but sees how justly square°   *anything / perfectly fitted*
His haughty° ditties to thy glorious days?   *lofty*
How well beseeming thee his triumphs are?
60 His hope, his zeal, his prayer, plaint,° and praise,   *complaint*
Needless° thy person to their height to raise,   *Need not*
Less need to bend them down to thy degree;[8]
These holy garments each good soul assays,°   *tries on*
Some sorting all, all sort to none but thee.

65 For ev'n thy rule is painted° in his reign: *foreshadowed*
Both clear in right, both nigh by wrong oppressed;[9]
And each at length (man crossing God in vain)
Possessed of place,° and each in peace possessed.   *rank*
Proud Philistines[1] did interrupt his rest,
70 The foes of heav'n no less have been thy foes;
He with great conquest, thou with greater blest;
Thou sure to win, and he secure to lose.°   *unable to lose*

Thus hand in hand with him thy glories walk;
But who can trace them where alone they go?
75 Of thee two hemispheres[2] on honor talk,
And lands and seas thy trophies jointly show;
The very winds did on thy party° blow,   *behalf*
And rocks in arms thy foe men eft° defy.[3]   *afterwards*
But soft, my Muse, thy pitch is earthly low;
80 Forbear this heav'n, where only eagles fly.

Kings on a queen enforced their states to lay,°   *wait*
Mainlands for empire waiting on an isle;
Men drawn by worth a woman to obey
One moving all, herself unmoved the while;[4]
85 Truth's restitution, vanity's exile,
Wealth sprung of want, war held without annoy
Let subject be of some inspired style,
Till then the object of her subjects' joy.[5]

Thy utmost° can but offer to her° sight   *greatest effort / Elizabeth's*
90 Her handmaid's° task, which most her will endears;[6]   *Pembroke's*
And pray unto° thy pains life from that Light°   *for / God*
Which lively lightsome° Court and kingdom cheers.   *radiant*
What wish she° may (far past her living peers   *Elizabeth*
And rival still to Judah's faithful King,

---

8. Since David's psalms are so suited to the Queen, she need not be raised up to them nor they lowered to her.
9. Both David and Elizabeth possessed a clear right to rule, and both were wrongfully opposed.
1. The Philistines were the traditional enemies of King David.
2. Those containing England and Virginia.
3. A reference to the storm that shipwrecked the Armada and the rocks, standing like armored knights, that destroyed much of the Spanish fleet.
4. Pembroke compares Elizabeth to the "unmoved mover," a classic definition of God.
5. Until Elizabeth's achievements become the subject of a lofty, inspired poem, they remain a joy to her own subjects.
6. Pembroke most delights in the task of writing poems for the Queen's eyes.

more years

95   In more° than he and more triumphant years)[7]
     Sing what God doth and do what men may sing.

Psalm 72[†]

Teach the king's son, who king himself shall be,[1]
     Thy judgments, Lord, Thy justice make him learn:
To rule Thy realm as justice shall decree
     And poor men's right in judgment to discern.
5   Then fearless peace
                     With rich increase
          The mountains proud shall fill,
                     And justice shall
                     Make plenty fall
10   On ev'ry humble hill.

Make him the weak support, th' oppressed relieve,
     Supply the poor, the quarrel-pickers quail:
So ageless ages shall Thee reverence give,
     Till eyes of heav'n, the sun and moon, shall fail,
15   And Thou again
                     Shalt blessings rain,
          Which down shall mildly flow,
                     As showers thrown
                     On meads° new mown   *meadows*
20   Whereby they freshly grow.

During his rule the just shal aye° be green   *always*
     And peaceful plenty join with plenteous peace.
While of sad night the many-forméd queen,°   *moon*
     Decreas'd, shall grow and grown again, decrease.
25   From sea to sea
                     He shall survey
          All kingdoms as his own,
                     And from the trace
                     Of Physons race[2]
30   As far as land is known.

The desert-dwellers at his beck shall bend;
     His foes them suppliant at his feet shall fling.
The kings of Tharsis homage-gifts shall send,
     So Seba, Saba, ev'ry island king,[3]
35   Nay all, ev'n all
                     Shall prostrate fall,
          That crowns and scepters wear.

---

7. May Elizabeth outlast and outshine her fellow monarchs, as well as David himself, in both length of life and glorious achievements.
† Copy text: Mary Sidney Herbert, *The Psalms of Sir Philip Sidney and the Countess of Pembroke*, ed. and intro. J. C. A. Rathmell ([New York]: New York University Press, 1963), 165–67.
1. Traditionally the psalm is understood to be penned by David for his son Solomon.
2. The course of the Euphrates River.
3. Tarshish, Sheba, and Seba were all countries associated with King Solomon's international fame.

And all that stand
   At their command
40   That crowns and scepters bear.

For he shall hear the poor when they complain
   And lend them help, who helpless are oppressed.
His mercy shall the needy sort sustain;
   His force shall free their lives that live distressed.
45   From hidden sleight,
         From open might,
   He shall their souls redeem;
         His tender eyes
         Shall highly prize
50   And dear their blood esteem.

So shall he long, so shall he happy live;
   Health shall abound, and wealth shall never want.
They gold to him, Arabia gold, shall give,
   Which scantness dear, and dearness maketh scant.[4]
55   They still shall pray
         That still he may
   So live and flourish so.
         Without his praise
         No nights, no days
60   Shall passport have to go.[5]

Look how the woods, where interlacéd trees
   Spread friendly arms each other to embrace,
Join at the head, though distant at the knees,
   Waving with wind and lording on° the place.   *over*
65   So woods of corn
         By mountains born
   Shall on their shoulders wave,[6]
         And men shall pass
         The numbrous° grass,   *dense*
70   Such store each town shall have.[7]

Look how the sun, so shall his name remain;[8]
   As that in light, so this in glory one,°   *is one*
All glories that, at this all lights shall stain,°   *lose their luster*
   Nor that shall fail nor this be overthrown.
75   The dwellers all
         Of earthly ball
   In him shall hold them blest.
         As one that is

---

4. The scarcity of Arabian gold makes it costly, and its costliness makes it scarce.
5. Neither night nor day will have leave to neglect the King's praises.
6. Grain will stand so thickly in the fields that it will look like a forest.
7. There will be such abundance of grain in each town that men will pass by fields without harvesting them.
8. As the sun endures, so shall the King's name.

Of perfect bliss
A pattern to the rest.

O God who art, from whom all beings be;
Eternal Lord, whom Jacob's stock adore,
And wondrous works are done by only Thee.
Blesséd be Thou, most blesséd evermore,
80   And let Thy name,
Thy glorious fame,
No end of blessing know.
Let all this round
Thy honor sound,
85   So Lord, O be it so.

ANONYMOUS

From the Geneva Bible[†]

Psalm 72

He prayeth for the prosperous estate of the kingdom of Solomon, who was
the figure of Christ; under whom shall be righteousness, peace, and felicity; unto whom all kings and all nations shall do homage; whose name and
power shall endure forever; and in whom all nations shall be blessed.

A Psalm of Solomon[1]

1 Give Thy judgments to the King, O God, and Thy righteousness to
the king's son.[2]
2 Then shall he judge Thy people in righteousness and Thy poor with
equity.
3 The mountains[3] and the hills shall bring peace to the people by justice.
4 He shall judge[4] the poor of the people; he shall save the children of
the needy and shall subdue the oppressor.
5 They shall fear[5] Thee as long as the sun and moon endureth, from
generation to generation.
6 He shall come[6] down like the rain upon the mown grass and as the
showers that water the earth.
7 In his days shall the righteous flourish and abundance of peace shall
be so long as the moon endureth.

---

† Copy text: *The Bible and Holy Scriptures conteyned in the olde and newe Testament* (Geneva:
Rouland Hall, 1560; STC 2093), Rr1v–Rr2r. Unless otherwise indicated, the following footnotes
are the marginal comments from the Geneva Bible.
1. Composed by David as touching the reign of his son Solomon.
2. To wit, to his posterity; *Give Thy judgments*: endue the King with the spirit of wisdom and justice
that he reign not as do the worldly tyrants.
3. When justice reigneth, even the places most barren shall be enriched with Thy blessings.
4. He showeth wherefore the sword is committed to kings: to wit, to defend the innocent and suppress the wicked.
5. The people shall embrace Thy true religion when Thou givest a king that ruleth according to Thy
word.
6. As this is true in all godly kings, so is it chiefly verified in Christ, who with His heavenly dew maketh
His Church ever to flourish.

8 His dominion shall be also from sea[7] to sea and from the river unto the ends of the land.

9 They that dwell in the wilderness shall kneel before him and his enemies shall lick the dust.

10 The kings of Tarshish and of the isles shall bring presents; the kings of Sheba[8] and Seba shall bring gifts.

11 Yea, all kings shall worship him; all nations shall serve him.

12 For he shall deliver the poor when he crieth, the needy also, and him that hath no helper.

13 He shall be merciful to the poor and needy and shall preserve the souls of the poor.

14 He shall redeem their souls from deceit and violence, and dear[9] shall their blood be in his sight.

15 Yea, he shall live, and unto him shall they give of the gold[1] of Sheba; they shall also pray for him continually and daily bless him.

16 An handful of corn shall be sown in the earth, even in the top of the mountains, and the fruit[2] thereof shall shake like the trees of Lebanon, and the children shall flourish out of the city like the grass of the earth.

17 His name shall be forever; his name shall endure as long as the sun. All nations shall bless[3] him and be blessed in him.

18 Blessed be the Lord God, even the God of Israel, which only doth wondrous[4] things.

19 And blessed be His glorious name forever, and let all the earth be filled with His glory. So be it, even so be it.

FRANCIS BACON

Three Letters Accompanying New Year's Gifts to the Queen (ca. 1594–1602)[†]

Letter 1

It may please your Majesty,
According to the ceremony of the time, I would not forget, in all humbleness, to present your Majesty with a small New Year's Gift: nothing to my

---

7. That is, from the Red Sea to the sea called Syriacum [the Mediterranean Sea] and from Euphrates forward, meaning that Christ's kingdom should be large and universal.
8. That is, of Arabia, that rich country, whereof Sheba was a part bordering upon Ethiopia; *kings of Tarshish*: of Sicily and of all other countries beyond the sea, which he meaneth by the isles.
9. Though tyrants pass [hesitate] not to shed blood, yet this godly King shall preserve his subjects from all kind of wrong.
1. God will both prosper his life and also make the people most willing to obey him.
2. Under such a king shall be most great plenty, both of fruit and also of the increase of mankind.
3. They shall pray to God for his continuance and know that God doth prosper them for his sake.
4. He confesseth that except God miraculously preserve His people, that neither the King nor the kingdom can continue.
† Copy text: Sir Francis Bacon, *Resuscitatio, or, Bringing into publick light severall pieces of the works, civil, historical, philosophical, & theological, hitherto sleeping, of the Right Honourable Francis Bacon, Baron of Verulam, Viscount Saint Alban*, 2 vols. (London: William Lee, 1657; Wing B319), 2.3–4, 99.

mind.[1] And therefore to supply[2] it, I can but pray to God to give your Majesty His New Year's Gift, that is, a new year that shall be as no year to your body, and as a year with two harvests to your coffers, and every other way prosperous and gladsome. And so I remain.[3]

Letter 2

Most excellent sovereign Mistress,
The only New Year's gift which I can give your Majesty is that which God hath given to me, which is a mind in all humbleness to wait upon your commandments and business, wherein I would to God that I were hooded,[4] that I saw less, or that I could perform more. For now I am like a hawk that bates when I see occasion of service but cannot fly because I am tied to another's fist.[5] But meanwhile, I continue my presumption of making to your Majesty my poor oblation[6] of a garment, as unworthy the wearing as his service that sends it. But the approach of your excellent person may give worth to both, which is all the happiness I aspire unto.

Letter 3

It may please your most excellent Majesty,
I presume, according to the ceremony and good manner of the time and my accustomed duty, in all humbleness to present your Majesty with a simple gift, almost as far from answering my mind as sorting with[7] your greatness and therewith wish that we may continue to reckon on (and ever) your Majesty's happy years of reign. And they that reckon upon any other hopes I would they might reckon short[8] and to their cost. And so craving pardon most humbly, I commend your Majesty to the preservation of the divine goodness.

ANONYMOUS

Ode of Cynthia (1602)[†]

The ancient readers of heaven's book[1]
Which with curious eye did look
    Into Nature's story

---

1. Nothing I think satisfactory.
2. Add to.
3. Copy text omits closings and signatures. Presumably, the letter ended with some such phrase as "Your humble servant, Francis Bacon."
4. Hawks were kept hooded to calm them when out of their cages but not hunting.
5. Bacon blamed his failure to advance at Court on his powerful kinsmen, the Cecils, who did little to support him after he fell into disfavor for opposing the Queen in a key Parliamentary vote; *bates*: beats its wings impatiently.
6. Offering.
7. Being suitable to; *answering*: satisfying.
8. Count on too few years; *hopes*: in the late years of Elizabeth's reign, some at Court began to ingratiate themselves with her likely successor, James VI of Scotland.
† Copy text: *A poetical rapsody containing, diuerse sonnets, odes, elegies, madrigalls, and other poesies*, ed. Francis Davison (London: Iohn Baily, 1602; STC 6373), L7v.
1. God was thought to reveal Himself through the Bible and the "book" of Nature.

All things under Cynthia took
5   To be transitory.[2]

This the learnéd only knew,
But now all men find it true;
    Cynthia is descended,
With bright beams, and heavenly hue,
10   And lesser stars[3] attended.

Lands and seas she rules below,
Where things change, and ebb, and flow,
    Spring, wax old, and perish;
Only Time, which all doth mow,
15   Her alone doth cherish.

Time's young Hours attend her still
And her eyes and cheeks do fill
    With fresh youth and beauty.
All her lovers old do grow,
20   But° their hearts; they do not so,   *Except*
    In their love and duty.

JOHN DAVIES

Verses of the Queen (1602)[†]

A virgin° once a glorious star[1] did bear,   *Mary*
Like to the Sun[2] enclosed in globe of glass;
A virgin's heart is now the golden sphere
Whence to this earth that influence[3] doth pass.
5   He° shines on her and she on Him again,   *The Son*
Reflecting love all earthly stars doth stain.[4]

He whilome° took a stable for His cell,   *once*
Thrise happy cell in which a god hath been,
But He will now in prince's palace dwell
10   And weds Himself to rare Eliza Queen.
Come, wise men, come, present your gifts divine;
Here stands the star that makes your star to shine.[5]

---

2. Everything within the orbit of the moon was said to be mutable, everything beyond it unchanging.
3. The lords and ladies of her Court.
† Copy text: Codrington Library, All Souls College, Oxford University, MS 155 (Yelverton), fol. 12r. Used with permission.
1. Jesus, seen as the Morning Star whose coming announces the dawn of a new age (Revelation 22.16).
2. Christ, regarded as the light to the world, with a pun on "Son" for the Son of God. See John 1.1–9.
3. Influence of Christ, compared to the astrological influence of the sun on affairs on earth.
4. Since God is love (1 John 4.16), and Christ is God, the Queen reflects love itself in reflecting the light of Christ. Stars seem dark by contrast.
5. With Christ's coming to the English royal palace, compare the original revelation of Christ to the wise men in Matthew 2.1–12. According to scripture, the star of Bethlehem and the rest of the material world were created by Christ (Colossians 1.12–17).

This sacred nymph, because no mortal wight°   *creature*
Deserved to link with her in chains of love,
15 Unto the God of souls her faith hath plight
And vowed herself to Him without remove.
Thus doth this bride ten thousand children breed
And virgin's milk the Church of God doth feed.

To see this birth did angels sweetly sing;[6]
20 Now sings that nest of nightingales again.
Joy, peace, goodwill to men they bring;
Of forty-five years thus tuning they remain.[7]
Long may they tune that sweet and pleasant song,
And long may she, our angel, sing among.°   *among them*

25   For Zion's[8] sake, preserve from death
Our noble Queen Elizabeth. Amen.

ELIZABETH'S DECLINE AND DEATH

Early intimations that all was not well with Elizabeth may be found in Sir John Harington's letter to Lady Mary Harington, his wife, in December 1602, roughly three months before the Queen died. Already evident were the fretfulness, the dwelling on unpleasant memories, and the loss of delight in living that characterized her last days. Though the Queen rebounded after Harington's visit, the lack of will to live returned and seems to have been the most important cause of her death. By mid-March, she had stopped eating and bathing, refusing to undress or to go to bed and unable to sleep. Standing for long periods, she would only consent to lie down on cushions that servants laid out on the floor around her when she was too weak to stand. It was with great difficulty, "what by fair means, what by force," that Charles Howard, now Earl of Nottingham, finally managed to get her into bed on March 22, two days before she died.

As we can see from a letter to King James by Henry Percy, Earl of Northumberland, preparations to bring the King of Scotland to power upon the Queen's death were by that time well advanced. Those hoping for positions in the new government were already lining up to win his good opinion. Such a man was Robert Carey, whose account of the Queen's last sickness and death is the most detailed that has come down to us. Brother of George Carey, Lord Hunsdon, the Queen's Chamberlain, Carey was also a kinsman of the Queen. His ready access to her chambers allowed him to speak with her and to observe her decline. He was also, as it happened, responsible for security in northern England, along the border with Scotland, and in that role, he had cultivated a relationship with James VI. Eager to impress the King, Carey laid plans to ride northward as fast as humanly possible to convey news of Elizabeth's death. Having reserved relay horses along the four-hundred-mile route from London to Edinburgh, he was able to make the arduous journey, most of it over very rough roads, in just three days. On March 24 alone, he rode 155 miles, a record never again equaled. His hopes were not disappointed. At the end of his grueling ride, he found a receptive king, who in gratitude for his efforts granted him an office in the new government.

More disturbing than Carey's account of Elizabeth's last days is Elizabeth Southwell's "True Relation of What Succeeded at the Sickness and Death of

---

6. At Christ's birth, angels sang "peace in earth, and towards men good will" (Luke 2.14).
7. They continue to sing the tune throughout her forty-five year reign.
8. England and its (Protestant) people, seen figuratively as the "new Zion," or New Jerusalem, foretold in the Book of Revelation 19–22.

Elizabeth's funeral procession.

Queen Elizabeth." A distant relative of the Queen, Southwell was just a teen-ager when she witnessed her mistress's death, but she was well placed to observe the event. Her mother was a Lady of the Bedchamber; her grandmother was Katherine Carey Howard, granddaughter of Anne Boleyn's sister Mary; and her grandfather was the Lord Admiral, Charles Howard. Though there is no evidence to contradict the main outlines of her account, some regard it as suspect because it was first published by Robert Parsons, the Jesuit apologist, in a work denying the legitimacy of Elizabeth's reign. Southwell probably gave him her account in 1607 while they were both in Italy, where she had gone as part of an elaborate plot to disguised herself as a page, elope with Robert Dudley, the bastard son of the Earl of Leicester, and declare herself a Catholic.

SIR JOHN HARINGTON

Letter to Lady Mary Harington (December 27, 1602)[†]

Sweet Mall,

I herewith send thee, what I would God none did know, some ill bodings of the realm and its welfare. Our dear Queen, my royal godmother and this state's natural mother, doth now bear show of human infirmity, too fast for that evil which we shall get by her death and too slow for that good which she shall get by her releasement from pains and misery.

Dear Mall, how shall I speak what I have seen or what I have felt? Thy good silence in these matters emboldens my pen. For (thanks to the sweet god of silence) thy lips do not wanton out of discretion's path like the many gossiping dames we could name, who lose their husband's fast-hold in good friends rather than hold fast their own tongues.[1] Now I will trust thee with great assurance, and whilst thou dost brood over thy young ones in the chamber, thou shalt read the doings of thy grieving mate in the Court.

I find some less mindful of what they are soon to lose than of what they may perchance hereafter get. Now, on my own part, I cannot blot from my memory's table[2] the goodness of our Sovereign Lady to me, even (I will say)

---

† Copy text: Sir John Harington, *Nugae antiquae: being a miscellaneous collection of original papers in prose and verse written during the reigns of Henry VIII, Edward VI, Queen Mary, Elizabeth, and King James: by Sir John Harington, Knt. . . .* , ed. Henry Harington, 3 vols. (London: Vernor and Hood, Poultry, and Cuthell and Martin, 1804), 1.320–24.
1. Lose their chance to gossip; *fast-hold*: stronghold.
2. Board where school lessons were written.

before born: her affection to my mother, who waited in Privy Chamber; her bettering the state of my father's fortune (which I have, alas, so much worsted); her watchings over my youth; her liking to my free speech and admiration of my little learning and poesy, which I did so much cultivate on her command, have rooted such love, such dutiful remembrance of her princely virtues, that to turn askant from her condition with tearless eyes would strain and foul the spring and fount of gratitude.

It was not many days since I was bidden to her presence. I blessed the happy moment, and found her in most pitiable state. She bade the Archbishop[3] ask me if I had seen Tyrone. I replied, with reverence, that I had seen him with the Lord Deputy.[4] She looked up, with much choler and grief in her countenance, and said, "Oh, now it mindeth me that you was *one* who saw this man *elsewhere*,"[5] and hereat, she dropped a tear, and smote her bosom. She held in her hand a golden cup, which she often put to her lips, but in sooth, her heart seemeth too full to lack more filling. This sight moved me to think on what passed in Ireland, and I trust she did not less think on *some*[6] who were busier there than myself. She gave me a message to the Lord Deputy[7] and bade me come to the chamber at seven o'clock. Hereat some who were about her did marvel, as I do not hold so high place as those she did not choose to do her commands. Dear Mall, if I get no profit, I shall get some envy, and this business may turn to some account with the Lord Deputy.[8]

Her Majesty inquired of some matters which I had written, and as she was pleased to note my fanciful brain, I was not unheedful to feed her humor and read some verses, whereat she smiled once and was pleased to say, "When thou dost feel creeping Time at thy gate, these fooleries will please thee less; I am past my relish for such matters. Thou seest my bodily meat doth not suit me well: I have eaten but one ill-tasted cake since yesternight." She rated most grievously at noon at some who minded[9] not to bring up certain matters of account. Several men have been sent to and, when ready at hand, her Highness hath dismissed in anger; but who, dearest Mall, shall say that "your Highness hath forgotten?"

I was honored at dinner with the Archbishop and several of the church pastors, where I did find more corporeal than spiritual refreshment, and though our ill state at Court may, in some sort, overcast the countenance of these apostolical messengers, yet were some of them well anointed with the oil of gladness on Tuesday past. Hereof thou shalt in some sort partake. My Lord of Salisbury had seisen his tenant's corn and hay, with sundry husbandry matters,[1] for matters of money due to his Lordship's estate. Hereat the aggrieved man made suit to the Bishop and requested longer time and restitution of his goods.

"Go, go," saith the Bishop, "I hear ill report of thy living, and thou canst not crave mercy; thou comest not to church service and hast not received

---

3. John Whitgift.
4. The Earl of Essex.
5. Harington had met the Earl of Tyrone while accompanying Sir William Warren to a parley in 1599. Elizabeth here has more recent events in mind, but recalls her former wrath that her godson was present at negotiations that she had not authorized.
6. Essex, whose execution still grieved the Queen.
7. The current Lord Deputy of Ireland, Lord Mountjoy.
8. That is, advance Harington in Mountjoy's estimation.
9. Remembered; *rated*: berated.
1. Items needed in farming; *Lord of Salisbury*: Henry Cotton, Bishop of Salisbury; *seisen*: confiscated.

confirmation.[2] I command thee to attend my ordinance[3] and be confirmed in thy faith at Easter next coming."

"I crave your Lordship's forgiveness," quoth the man. "In good sooth I durst not come there, for as your Lordship hath lain your hand on all my goods, I think it full meet to take care of my head!"[4]

Such was part of our discourse at dinner. So thou seest, sweet Mall, although the Bishop's hand was heavy, our peasant's head was not weak, and his Lordship said he would forego his payment.

Next month I will see thy sweet face and kiss my boys and maids, which I pray thee not to omit on my account. Send me up, by my man Combe, my Petrarch. Adieu, sweet Mall.

I am thine ever loving,
JOHN HARINGTON

HENRY PERCY, EARL OF NORTHUMBERLAND

From a Letter to King James on Elizabeth's Decline (March 17, 1603)[†]

Sir,

According your commandment, I have forborne to present you with my letters, which now causes of importance moves me to, and I have deferred it this long because I was willing to see what likelihood of event[1] it would come to. Her Majesty hath been evil[2] now almost one month. In the twelve first days it was kept secret under a misprision, taking the cause to be the displeasure she took at Arabella, the motions of taking in Tyrone, and the death of her old acquaintance the Lady Nottingham.[3] Those that were nearest her did imagine these to be the reasons. More days told us it was an indisposition of body. Sickness was not in any manner discerned; her sleep and stomach[4] only bereft her, so as for a twenty days she slept very little. Since, she is grown very weak, yet sometimes gives us comfort of recovery; a few hours after, threatens us with despair of her well doing. Physic she will not take any, and the physicians conclude that, if this continue, she must

---

2. Church attendance and confirmation were required by law in England; those who refused were usually Catholics, and they were subject to heavy fines.
3. Heed my decree.
4. If convicted of converting others to Catholicism, or having been converted themselves, recusants could be executed for treason.
† Copy text: *Correspondence of James VI of Scotland with Sir Robert Cecil and Others in England During the Reign of Queen Elizabeth*, ed. John Bruce (London: Camden Society, 1861), 72–74.
1. Newsworthy outcome.
2. Ill.
3. Katherine Howard, Countess of Nottingham, eldest daughter of Henry Carey, first Baron Hunsdon. Having served among Elizabeth's attendants for nearly half a century, she was very close to the Queen; *misprision*: mistaken notion; *Arabella*: Lady Arabella Stuart, daughter of Charles Stuart, Earl of Lennox, and Elizabeth Cavendish. As first cousin of James VI of Scotland and the granddaughter of Elizabeth Hardwick Talbot, Countess of Shrewsbury, who was a first cousin of Queen Elizabeth, Arabella rivaled James in her legal claim to the English crown; in fact, since he was not born in England, many regarded her claim as superior. In 1602, she proposed a marriage to another serious claimant to the throne, a grandson of Edward Seymour, first Earl of Hertford. When Elizabeth discovered that such a dynastically significant marriage was being proposed behind her back, she was furious and sent agents to question Arabella; *Tyrone*: Lord Mountjoy's ending of the Irish rebellion and the treaty with the Earl of Tyrone.
4. Desire for food.

needs fall into a distemper, not a frenzy[5] but rather into a dullness and a lethargy.

This accident hath made all the whole nation look about them. Men talks freely of your Majesty's right, and all in general gives you a great allowance. The affections of many are discovered to be wholly devoted to your service. Every one, almost, embraces you, for which we that are your true servants are glad of.***

In the meantime, order is given for pressing[6] of all such rogues as might be apt to stir, and [they] are sent unto the Low Countries. The city of London is commanded to keep strong watch lest discontented persons might make any head there. The two presidents[7] in their governments have the like charge, and withal to have an eye to the papists. Some recusants of greatest note are committed and commanded, but not with any manner of rigor.[8] ***

In all this likelihood of so mighty a change, not one man hath stirred saving Sir Edward Baynham, a wild and free-speaking youth, who braving it and protesting that he would lose his life, and so would 40,000 Catholics more, ere your Majesty should come in, this man is committed to prison and, I assure your Majesty, condemned by all of them, or the most part, that are Catholic affected, unless it be by some of them that are puritan papists that thirst after a Spanish title.[9] * * *

Now, sir, matters standing thus, I have no more to say than that I wish you to be ready in as strong a manner as you can (with as little show of moving as you may) to help your servants if we find opposition. The doubt that I have ordinarily[1] propounded is fear of your entrance in hostile manner, which would give an impression of disaster to the people. I must still rest upon the text of my first letters, in which I think I shall not much have erred, and that was that your Majesty would come in with all peace, with all joy and gladness to us all, and free from all opposition.

I have labored in your vineyard with all the industry my poor under-standing would give me leave. If it shall happen, or please God to take from us our mistress, you shall have instantly word, and I think news of her departure will be no sooner with your Majesty than word of your being pro-claimed among us will overtake it. I speak it confidently, and therefore I hope your Majesty will pardon my rich[2] thoughts, which are devoted with eagerness to your Majesty's service and my country's good.

NORTHUMBERLAND

---

5. Violent disorder; *Physic*: medicine; *distemper*: illness of mind or body.
6. Impressing into military service.
7. Unclear, but probably the mayors of London and Westminster.
8. Harsh treatment; *committed . . . commanded*: committed to prison and commanded not to cause trouble.
9. Papists of the purest sort, who want to curry favor with the Spanish government; *come in*: enter England from Scotland.
1. Regularly.
2. Abundant.

ROBERT CAREY

From Memoirs of Robert Carey (ca. 1626)[†]

[*The Queen's Last Sickness and Death*]

When I came to Court,[1] I found the Queen ill disposed, and she kept her inner lodging; yet she, hearing of my arrival, sent for me. I found her in one of her withdrawing chambers, sitting low upon her cushions. She called me to her. I kissed her hand and told her it was my chiefest happiness to see her in safety and in health, which I wished might long continue. She took me by the hand and wrung it hard and said, "No, Robin, I am not well," and then discoursed with me of her indisposition and that her heart had been sad and heavy for ten or twelve days, and in her discourse she fetched not so few as forty or fifty great sighs. I was grieved at the first to see her in this plight, for in all my lifetime before I never knew her fetch a sigh but[2] when the Queen of Scots was beheaded. Then, upon my knowledge, she shed many tears and sighs, manifesting her innocence, that she never gave consent to the death of that Queen.

I used the best words I could to persuade her from this melancholy humor, but I found by her it was too deep rooted in her heart and hardly to be removed. This was upon a Saturday night, and she gave command that the great closet[3] should be prepared for her to go to chapel the next morning. The next day, all things being in a readiness, we long expected[4] her coming. After eleven o'clock, one of the grooms came out and bade make ready for the private closet; she would not go to the great. There we stayed[5] long for her coming, but at the last she had cushions laid for her in the privy chamber hard by the closet door, and there she heard service.

From that day forwards she grew worse and worse. She remained upon her cushions four days and nights at the least. All about her could not persuade her either to take any sustenance or go to bed.

I, hearing that neither the physicians nor none about her could persuade her to take any course for her safety, feared her death would soon after ensue. I could not but think in what a wretched estate I should be left, most of my livelihood depending on her life. And hereupon, I bethought myself with what grace and favor I was ever received by the King of Scots, whensoever I was sent to him. I did assure myself it was neither unjust nor unhonest for me to do for myself,[6] if God at that time should call her to His mercy. Hereupon, I wrote to the King of Scots (knowing him to be the right heir to the crown of England) and certified him in what state her Majesty was. I desired him not to stir from Edinburgh; if of that sickness she should die, I would be the first man that should bring him news of it.

† Copy text: Robert Carey, *Memoirs of Robert Cary, Earl of Monmouth,* ed. G. H. Powell (London: Alexander Moring, De la More Press, 1905), 70–79. Since Carey's original manuscript is now lost, modern editions all derive from *Memoirs of the Life of Robert Carey, Baron of Leppington and Earl of Monmouth* (London: R. and J. Dodsley, 1759), a second edition of the same year, and Thomas Birch's independently published transcription of the material on Elizabeth's death in *An Historical View of Negotiations Between the Courts of England, France, and Brussels* (London: A. Miller, 1749).
1. Apparently in early March 1603.
2. Except.
3. Largest of her private rooms.
4. Waited for.
5. Waited.
6. Do what was in my own interest.

The Queen grew worse and worse because she would be so, none about her being able to persuade her to go to bed. My Lord Admiral was sent for, who by reason of my sister's death, that was his wife,[7] had absented himself some fortnight from Court. What by fair means, what by force, he got her to bed. There was no hope of her recovery because she refused all remedies.

On Wednesday, the twenty-third of March, she grew speechless. That afternoon, by signs, she called for her Council, and by putting her hand to her head when the King of Scots was named to succeed her, they all knew he was the man she desired should reign after her.

About six at night she made signs for the Archbishop[8] and her chaplains to come to her, at which time I went in with them and sat upon my knees, full of tears to see that heavy sight. Her Majesty lay upon her back, with one hand in the bed and the other without. The Bishop kneeled down by her and examined her first of her faith, and she so punctually answered all his several questions, by lifting up her eyes and holding up her hand, as it was a comfort to all the beholders. Then the good man told her plainly what she was, and what she was to come to; and though she had been long a great queen here upon earth, yet shortly she was to yield an account of her stewardship to the King of kings. After this he began to pray, and all that were by did answer him.[9] After he had continued long in prayer, till the old man's knees were weary, he blessed her and meant to rise and leave her. The Queen made a sign with her hand. My sister Scrope,[1] knowing her meaning, told the Bishop the Queen desired he would pray still. He did so for a long half hour after and then thought to leave her. The second time she made sign to have him continue in prayer. He did so for half an hour more, with earnest cries to God for her soul's health, which he uttered with that fervency of spirit as the Queen to all our sight much rejoiced thereat and gave testimony to us all of her Christian and comfortable end. By this time it grew late, and everyone departed, all but her women that attended her.

This, that I heard with my ears and did see with my eyes, I thought it my duty to set down and to affirm it for a truth, upon the faith of a Christian, because I know there have been many false lies reported of the end and death of that good lady.

I went to my lodging and left word with one in the Cofferer's chamber to call me if that night it was thought she would die, and gave the porter an angel[2] to let me in at any time when I called. Between one and two of the clock on Thursday morning, he that I left in the Cofferer's chamber brought me word the Queen was dead. I rose and made all the haste to the gate to get in. There I was answered I could not enter, the lords of the Council having been with him and commanded him that none should go in or out but by warrant from them. At the very instant, one of the Council (the Controller)[3] asked whether I was at the gate. I said yes. He said to me, if I pleased, he would let me in. I desired to know how the Queen did. He answered, "Pretty well." I bade him goodnight. He replied and said, "Sir, if you will come in, I will give you my word and credit you shall go out again at your own pleasure."

---

7. Katherine Howard, eldest daughter of Henry Carey, first Lord Hunsdon; *Lord Admiral*: Charles Howard, Earl of Nottingham.
8. John Whitgift.
9. Give the prescribed responses in the liturgy for the Visitation of the Sick.
1. Philadelphia Carey Scrope, second daughter of Lord Hunsdon.
2. Gold coin; *Cofferer's*: treasurer of the royal household, Sir Henry Cock.
3. Steward who managed the Queen's household, Sir Edward Wotton.

Upon his word I entered the gate and came up to the Cofferer's chamber, where I found all the ladies weeping bitterly. He led me from thence to the Privy Chamber, where all the Council was assembled. There I was caught hold of and assured I should not go for Scotland till their pleasures were farther known. I told them I came of purpose to that end. From thence they all went to the Secretary's chamber,[4] and as they went, they gave a special command to the porters that none should go out of the gates but such servants as they should send to prepare their coaches and horses for London. There was I left in the midst of the Court to think my own thoughts till they had done counsel. I went to my brother's chamber, who was in bed, having been overwatched[5] many nights before. I got him up with all speed, and when the Council's men were going out of the gate, my brother thrust to the gate. The porter, knowing him to be a great officer, let him out. I pressed after him and was stayed by the porter. My brother said angrily to the porter, "Let him out, I will answer for him." Whereupon I was suffered to pass, which I was not a little glad of.

I got to horse and rode to the Knight Marshal's lodging by Charing Cross, and there stayed till the lords came to Whitehall Garden.[6] I stayed there till it was nine o'clock in the morning, and hearing that all the lords were in the old orchard at Whitehall, I sent the Marshal to tell them that I had stayed all that while to know their pleasures and that I would attend them if they would command me any service. They were very glad when they heard I was not gone and desired the Marshal to send for me and I should with all speed be dispatched for Scotland. The Marshal believed them and sent Sir Arthur Savage for me. I made haste to them. One of the Council (my Lord of Banbury that now is)[7] whispered the Marshal in the ear and told him, if I came, they would stay me and send some other in my stead. The Marshal got from them and met me coming to them between the two gates. He bade me be gone, for he had learned for certain that, if I came to them, they would betray me.

I returned and took horse between nine and ten o'clock and that night rode to Doncaster. The Friday night I came to my own house at Witherington and presently took order with my deputies to see the borders kept in quiet, which they had much to do, and gave order the next morning the King of Scotland should be proclaimed King of England, et cetera,[8] at Morpeth and Alnwick. Very early on Saturday I took horse for Edinburgh and came to Norham about twelve at noon, so that I might well have been with the King at supper time; but I got a great fall by the way, and my horse with one of his heels gave me a great blow on the head that made me shed much blood. It made me so weak that I was forced to ride a soft pace after, so that the King was newly gone to bed by the time that I knocked at the gate.[9]

I was quickly let in and carried[1] up to the King's chamber. I kneeled by him and saluted him by his title of England, Scotland, France, and Ireland.

4. That of Sir Robert Cecil.
5. Kept sleepless by his duties; *brother's*: that of George Carey, Lord Hunsdon, who as Lord Chamberlain managed Elizabeth's private quarters.
6. Garden of Whitehall Palace on the Thames in London; *Knight Marshal's*: judicial official responsible for keeping order in the royal household.
7. William Knollys, Controller before Wotton.
8. Copy text: and. Birch's transcription of 1749 reads "etc." to indicate the omission of other royal titles; *Witherington*: town in northern England; *much to do*: as High Commissioner for the Province of York, Carey was responsible for keeping order along the Scottish border.
9. At the royal palace of Holyrood House; *soft*: slow.
1. Led.

He gave me his hand to kiss and bade me welcome. After he had long discoursed of the manner of the Queen's sickness and of her death, he asked what letters I had from the Council. I told him none and acquainted him how narrowly I escaped from them. And yet I had brought him a blue ring from a fair lady that I hoped would give him assurance of the truth that I had reported.[2] He took it and looked upon it, and said, "It is enough: I know by this you are a true messenger." Then he committed me to the charge of my Lord Home[3] and gave straight command that I should want nothing. He sent for his chirurgeons[4] to attend me, and when I kissed his hand at my departure, he said to me these gracious words: "I know you have lost a near kinswoman and a loving mistress, but take here my hand. I will be as good a master to you and will requite this service with honor and reward."

So I left him that night, and went with my Lord Home to my lodging, where I had all things fitting for so weary a man as I was. After my head was dressed, I took leave of my Lord and many others that attended me and went to my rest.

The next morning by ten o'clock, my Lord Home was sent to me from the King to know how I had rested, and withal said that his Majesty commanded him to know of me what it was that I desired most that he should do for me; bade me ask, and it should be granted. I desired my Lord to say to his Majesty from me that I had no reason to importune him for any suit, for that[5] I had not as yet done him any service; but my humble request to his Majesty was to admit me a gentleman of his bedchamber, and hereafter, I knew, if his Majesty saw me worthy, I should not want to taste of his bounty. My Lord returned this answer, that he[6] sent me word back, with all his heart, I should have my request. And the next time I came to Court (which was some four days after, at night), I was called into his bedchamber and there, by my Lord of Richmond in his[7] presence, I was sworn one of the gentlemen of his bedchamber, and presently I helped to take off his clothes and stayed till he was in bed. After this, there came daily gentlemen and noblemen from our court, and the King set down a fixed day[8] for his departure towards London.

ELIZABETH SOUTHWELL

A True Relation of What Succeeded at the Sickness and Death of Queen Elizabeth" (1607)[†]

Her Majesty being in very good health, one day Sir John Stanhope, being the Vice Chamberlain and Secretary Cecil's dependent and familiar, came and presented her Majesty with a piece of gold of the bigness of an angel,

---

2. Carey, Birch, and others report that the King had made an arrangement with Carey's sister Philadelphia that, whenever Elizabeth should die, she should send back a sapphire ring that James had sent to her for the purpose. Prevented from seeing her brother when he stopped at Richmond Palace on his way to Scotland, she threw the ring to him from a window.
3. Alexander, first Earl of Home.
4. Doctors.
5. Because.
6. The King.
7. The King's; *Lord of Richmond*: Ludovick Stuart, second Duke of Lennox, elevated to Earl of Richmond in James I's reign.
8. He left on April 5, 1603.
† Copy text: Catherine Loomis, ed., "Elizabeth Southwell's Manuscript Account of the Death of Queen Elizabeth [with Text]," *English Literary Renaissance* 26.3 (Autumn 1996): 484–87. Reprinted by permission of Blackwell Publishing.

full of characters, which he said a old woman in Wales bequeathed her on her death bed, and thereupon he discoursed how the said old woman by virtue of the same lived to the age of 120 years and, being in that age having all her body withered and consumed and wanting nature to nourish,[1] she died, commanding that said piece of gold to be carefully sent her Majesty, alleging further that, as long as the said old woman wore it upon her body, she could not die. The Queen, upon the confidence she had hereof, took the said gold and wore it about her neck.

Now though she fell not suddenly sick, yet daily decreased of her rest and feeding and within fifteen days fell downright sick, and the cause being wondered at by my Lady Scrope[2] (with whom she was very private and confident, being her near kinswoman), her Majesty told her, commanding her to conceal the same, she saw one night in her bed her body exceeding lean and fearful in a light of fire. For the which, the next day she desired to see a true[3] looking glass (which in twenty years before she had not seen but only such a one which of purpose was made to deceive her sight), which glass being brought her, she fell presently exclaiming at all those which had so much commended her and took it so offensively that all those which had before flattered her durst not come in her sight. Now falling into extremity, she sat two days and three nights upon her stool,[4] ready dressed, and could never be brought by any of her Council to go to bed or eat or drink. Only my Lord Admiral[5] one time persuaded her to drink some broth; for any of the rest, she would not answer them to any question, but said softly to my Lord Admiral's earnest persuasions that, if he knew what she had seen in her bed, he would not persuade her as he did, and Secretary Cecil, overhearing her, asked if her Majesty had seen any spirits, to which she say she scorned to answer him to so idle a question. Then he told her how, to content the people, her Majesty must go to bed. To which she smiled, wonderfully contemning[6] him, saying that the word "must" was not to be used to princes. Thereupon said, "Little man, little man, if your father had lived, ye durst not have said so much. But thou knowest I must die and that maketh thee so presumptuous." And presently commanding him and the rest to depart her chamber, willing my Lord Admiral to stay, to whom she shook her head and with a pitiful voice said, "My Lord, I am tied with a chain of iron about my neck." He alleging her wonted[7] courage to her, she replied, "I am tied and the case is altered with me."

Then two Ladies waiting on her in her chamber discovered in the bottom of her chair the queen of hearts with a nail of iron knocked through the forehead of it, the which the Ladies durst not pull out remembering that the like thing was used to the Old Lady of Sussex[8] and proved afterwards for a witchcraft, for the which certain were hanged as instruments of the same. The Lady Elizabeth Guildford, then waiting on the Queen and leaving her asleep

1. Lacking the natural ability to get stronger; *Vice Chamberlain*: the Vice-Chamberlain assisted the Lord Chamberlain in supervising the daily Court routine; *Secretary Cecil*: Robert Cecil, son of William Cecil, Lord Burghley, and now Elizabeth's Secretary of State; *dependent and familiar*: intimate friend, but also demonic associate; *gold . . . angel*: a gold coin with the emblem of St. Michael lancing a dragon.
2. Philadelphia Scrope, a Lady of the Bedchamber and Southwell's great-aunt.
3. Accurate.
4. Possibly her privy stool [Loomis's note].
5. Charles Howard, Earl of Nottingham, and Southwell's grandfather.
6. Scorning or treating with contempt.
7. Accustomed.
8. Scholars have not identified this person.

in her privy chamber, met her as she thought three or four chambers off, fearing she would 'a' been displeased that she left her alone, came towards her to excuse herself, and she vanished away, and, when she returned into the same chamber where she left her, found her asleep as before.

So growing past recovery (having kept her bed fifteen days, besides three days she sat upon her stool and one day being pulled up by force stood on her feet fifteen hours), the Council sent to her the Bishop of Canterbury and other of her prelates, upon sight of whom she was much offended, cholericly rating them, bidding them be packing, saying she was no atheist but knew full well that they were [illegible] hedge-priests⁹ and took it for an indignity that they should speak to her.

Now being given over¹ by all and at her last gasp keeping still her sense in everything and giving ever when she spake apt answers, though she spake very seldom, having then a sore throat, she desired to wash it that she might answer more freely to what the Council demanded, which was to know whom she would have king. But they, seeing her throat troubled her so much, desired her to hold up her finger when they named whom liked her,² whereupon they named the King of France, the King of Scotland, at which she never stirred. They named my Lord Beauchamp,³ whereto she said, "I will have no rascal's son in my seat but [illegible] one worthy to be a king." Hereupon instantly she died.

Then the Council went forth and reported she meant the King of Scots. Whereupon they went to London to proclaim him, leaving her body with charge not to be opened,⁴ such being her desire. But Cecil, having given a secret warrant to the surgeons, they opened her, which the rest of the Council afterwards passed it over, though they meant it not so. Now her body being cered up was brought to Whitehall, where being watched every night by six several ladies (myself that night there watching as one of them), being all about the body, which was fast nailed up in a board coffin with leaves of lead covered with velvet, her body and head break with such a crack that spleeted the wood, lead, and cerecloth.⁵ Whereupon the next day she was fain to be new trimmed up. Whereupon they gave their verdicts that if she had not been opened, the breath of her body would 'a' been much worse. But no man durst speak it publicly for displeasing Secretary Cecil.

Her Majesty understood that Secretary Cecil had given forth to the people that she was mad and therefore in her sickness did many times say to him, "Cecil, know I am not mad. You must not think to make Queen Jane⁶ of me," and although many reports by Cecil's means were spread how she was distracted, myself nor any that were about her could ever perceive her speeches, so well applied, proceeded from a distracted mind.

9. Uneducated priests of inferior status; *Bishop of Canterbury*: John Whitgift, the Archbishop of Canterbury; *rating*: scolding.
1. Despaired of.
2. Whom she liked.
3. Edward Seymour, Baron Beauchamp, the son of Katherine Grey (sister to Lady Jane Grey) and Edward Seymour, Earl of Hertford (son of Edward Seymour, Duke of Somerset). Elizabeth sent Beauchamp's parents to the Tower for marrying without her permission and refused to recognize his claim to the throne, despite the fact that Henry VIII had named the Grey sisters as next in the royal succession following his own children.
4. Disemboweled in preparation for embalming.
5. A winding sheet for the corpse; *cered up*: wrapped in cerecloth for burial; *spleeted*: split.
6. Probably a reference to Lady Jane Grey and her ill-fated and "mad" attempt to become queen.

ENGLAND IN MOURNING

Upon the Queen's death, writers of every class and background wrote tributes. The playwright Thomas Dekker, a close observer of London life, provided one of the most imaginative in a work entitled *The Wonderful Year*. It progressed from a highly literary account of the death of the Queen through the period of national mourning to the coronation of King James and the terrible plague that subsequently ravaged the city. Depicting Elizabeth's death as the beginning of a storm sent by the Destinies to trouble paradise, it describes the favor that the gods had bestowed on England, their call to Elizabeth to join them in heaven, and the sorrows that followed. The contrast between the lofty mythology with which the work begins and the grimly, even brutally, realistic descriptions of the plague makes the death of Elizabeth seem an event of apocalyptic proportions.

Thomas Newton's elegy for the Queen, *Atropoïon Delion, or the Death of Delia*, plays on the ancient association between Cynthia and the island of Delos, particularly its dominant mountain Cynthus, from which the goddess takes her name. An Anglican priest, Newton was best known for his translations of Cicero and of various classical and religious works, including *Seneca's Ten Tragedies*. Appropriately, he cast his elegy for the Queen in quasi-dramatic form, including speeches by such figures as Chastity, Time, the World, and Death as well as angels and the Fates. Like other poems in the volume, the speech of Fame included here takes the form of a love sonnet. The anonymous elegy "A Mournful Ditty, Entitled Elizabeth's Loss" is a song with a refrain that addresses those who grieve for her, from the peers of the kingdom to the ladies of her chamber, ordinary Englishmen, musicians, poets, virgins, and water nymphs. The poem is at heart religious, praising her because "In spite of Spain's proud Pope," she risked her life to bring benefits to God's people and to preserve the Gospel.

Like Newton's *Death of Delia*, Henry Petowe's work *Eliza's Funeral* included a series of sonnets brought together to compose a single elegy. It was followed by an account of the funeral, giving the order of the dignitaries who marched in the procession. The three stanzas reprinted here are remarkable for their eerie depiction of Queen's hearse, passing through London on its way to Westminster Abbey, where her body was interred beside the tomb of her grandfather, Henry VII. Multitudes of black-clad mourners appear as sudden clouds, darkening the landscape. As the queen's effigy comes into view, lying splendidly arrayed upon the hearse, it is as if the sun has come out after a storm.

THOMAS DEKKER

From The Wonderful Year (1603)[†]

[*The Sickness and Death of Queen Elizabeth*]

Vortumnus, being attired in his accustomed habit of changeable silk, had newly passed through the first and principal court-gate of heaven; to whom, for a farewell and to show how dutiful he was in his office, Janus (that bears two faces under one hood) made a very mannerly low leg[1] and, because he was the only porter at that gate, presented unto this king of the months all the New Year's gifts, which were more in number and more

---

[†] 1 Copy text: Thomas Dekker, *The vvonderfull yeare* (London: Thomas Creede, 1603, STC 6535.5), B1r–B2v, B4r–B4v.
1. A formal bow; *Vortumnus . . . heaven*: an image for the beginning of the New Year, which at this time in England occurred in March rather than January.

worth than those that are given to the Great Turk or the emperor of Persia. On went Vortumnus in his lusty progress: Priapus, Flora, the Dryads, and Hamadryads, with all the wooden[2] rabble of those that dressed orchards and gardens, perfuming all the ways that he went with the sweet odors that breathed from flowers, herbs, and trees, which now began to peep out of prison, by virtue of which excellent airs the sky got a most clear complexion, looked smug and smooth, and had not so much as a wart sticking on her face. The sun likewise was freshly and very richly appareled in cloth of gold like a bridegroom, and instead of gilded rosemary, the horns of the Ram (being the sign of that celestial bride-house where he lay, to be married to the spring) were not like your common horns parcel-gilt[3] but double double-gilt, with the liquid gold that melted from his beams, for joy whereof the lark sung at his window every morning, the nightingale every night. The cuckoo, like a single sole fiddler that reels from tavern to tavern, plied it all the day long. Lambs frisked up and down in the valleys; kids and goats leapt to and fro on the mountains; shepherds sat piping, country wenches singing; lovers made sonnets for their lasses, whilst they made garlands for their lovers. And as the country was frolic, so was the city merry. Olive trees (which grow nowhere but in the garden of peace) stood, as common as beech does at midsummer, at every man's door; branches of palm[4] were in every man's hand. Streets were full of people, people full of joy. Every house seemed to have a Lord of Misrule[5] in it, in every house there was so much jollity. No screech-owl frighted the silly countryman at midnight, nor any drum the citizen at noonday, but all was more calm than a still water, all hushed, as if the spheres[6] had been playing in consort. In conclusion, heaven looked like a palace and the great hall of the earth like a paradise.

But O the short-lived felicity of man! O world, of what slight and thin stuff is thy happiness! Just in the midst of this jocund holiday, a storm rises in the west. Westward, from the top of a rich mount,[7] descended a hideous tempest that shook cedars, terrified the tallest pines, and cleft in sunder even the hardest hearts of oak. And if such great trees were shaken, what think you became of the tender eglantine[8] and humble hawthorn? They could not, doubtless, but droop; they could not choose but die with the terror. The element (taking the Destinies' part, who indeed set abroach[9] this mischief) scowled on the earth and (filling her high forehead full of black wrinkles, tumbling long up and down like a great-bellied wife, her sighs being whirlwinds and her groans thunder) at length she fell in labor and was delivered of a pale, meager, weak child named Sickness, whom Death, with a pestilence, would needs take upon him to nurse, and did so. This starveling, being come to his full growth, had an office given him for nothing, and that's a wonder in this age. Death made him his herald, attired him like a courtier, and in his name charged him to go into the privy chamber of the English queen to summon her to appear in the Star Chamber[1] of heaven.

2. Woodland
3. Partly gilded; *rosemary*: flower worn at weddings; *Ram*: Aries, sign of the zodiac associated with the beginning of spring.
4. Symbols of honor, in springtime associated with Palm Sunday.
5. Master of Revelry, who presided on festive occasions.
6. Crystal spheres thought to hold up the sun, moon, and stars and to make music as they revolved.
7. A pun. The Queen died at Richmond Palace.
8. Wild rose.
9. Unleashed; *element*: the sky.
1. Judicial court that ruled in the Queen's name.

The summons made her start but, having an invincible spirit, did not amaze her. Yet whom would not the certain news of parting from a kingdom amaze? But she knew where to find a richer, and therefore lightly regarded the loss of this, and thereupon made ready for that heavenly coronation, being (which was most strange) most dutiful to obey that had so many years so powerfully commanded. She obeyed Death's messenger and yielded her body to the hands of Death himself. She died, resigning her scepter to posterity and her soul to immortality.

To report of her death, like a thunderclap, was able to kill thousands; it took away hearts from millions. For having brought up, even under her wing, a nation that was almost begotten and born under her, that never shouted any other *Ave* than for her name, never saw the face of any prince but herself, never understood what that strange outlandish word "change" signified,[2] how was it possible but that her sickness should throw abroad an universal fear and her death an astonishment? She was the courtier's treasure, therefore he had cause to mourn; the lawyer's sword of justice, he might well faint; the merchant's patroness, he had reason to look pale; the citizen's mother, he might best lament; the shepherd's goddess, and should not he droop? Only the soldier, who had walked a long time upon wooden legs and was not able to give arms, though he were a gentleman, had bristled up the quills of his stiff porcupine mustachio and swore by no beggars that now was the hour come for him to bestir his stumps.[3] Usurers and brokers, that are the Devil's ingles and dwell in the Long Lane[4] of hell, quaked like aspen leaves at his oaths. Those that before were the only cut-throats in London now stood in fear of no other death. But my Signor Soldado was deceived; the tragedy went not forward.[5]

Never did the English nation behold so much black worn as there was at her funeral. It was then but put on to try if it were fit, for the great day of mourning was set down in the book of heaven to be held afterwards.[6] That was but the dumb-show;[7] the tragical act hath been playing ever since. Her hearse, as it was borne, seemed to be an island swimming in water, for round about it there rained showers of tears. About her deathbed none, for her departure was so sudden and so strange that men knew not how to weep because they had never been taught to shed tears of that making.[8] They that durst not speak their sorrows whispered them; they that durst not whisper sent them forth in sighs. O what an earthquake is the alteration of a state! Look from the Chamber of Presence to the farmer's cottage, and you shall find nothing but distraction.[9] The whole kingdom seems a wilderness, and the people in it are transformed to wild men.

* * *

2. Elizabeth's motto was "*Semper eadem*" ("Always the same"); *Ave*: Latin "Hail," the first of the angel's words to Mary at the annunciation, which Catholics recited over their Rosary beads. Since England was now Protestant, people no longer said the Rosary.
3. Elizabeth's dislike of war did not please her soldiers, but it kept her from money-lenders until late in her reign; *give arms*: present his weapons for inspection by a superior officer; *swore . . . beggars*: a weak oath.
4. Street in Aldersgate where moneylenders lived; *Devil's ingles*: boy prostitutes.
5. Spanish forces at war with England hoped that, because the Queen had long refused to name a successor, civil war would break out after her death. The hope proved vain. *Signor Soldado*: Sir Soldier (Spanish).
6. Once the plague struck later in the year, mourning clothes became common.
7. Pantomimes used in plays of the period to foreshadow disaster.
8. To avoid alarm, the Privy Council withheld news of the Queen's sickness.

She came in with the fall of the leaf and went away in the spring, her life (which was dedicated to virginity) both beginning and closing up a miraculous maiden circle, for she was born upon a Lady Eve and died upon a Lady Eve, her nativity and death being memorable by this wonder; the first and last years of her reign by this, that a Lee was Lord Mayor when she came to the crown and a Lee Lord Mayor when she departed from it.[1] Three places are made famous by her for three things: Greenwich for her birth, Richmond for her death, Whitehall for her funeral. Upon her removing from whence (to lend our tiring prose a breathing time), stay and look upon these epigrams, being composed,

I. Upon the Queen's Last Remove, Being Dead

> The Queen's removed in solemn sort,
> Yet this was strange and seldom seen:
> The Queen used to remove the Court,
> But now the Court removed the Queen.

II. Upon Her Bringing by Water to Whitehall

> The Queen was brought by water to Whitehall.
> At every stroke, the oars tears let fall.
> More clung about the barge; fish under water
> Wept out their eyes of pearl and swam blind after.
> 5   I think the bargemen might with easier thighs[2]
> Have rowed her thither in her people's eyes.
> For howsoe'er, thus much my thoughts have scanned:
> S' had come by water had she come by land.[3]

III. Upon Her Lying Dead at Whitehall

> The Queen lies now at Whitehall dead
> And now at Whitehall living.
> To make this rough objection even:
> Dead at Whitehall at Westminster
> 5   But living at White Hall in heaven.

THOMAS NEWTON

From Atropoïon Delion, or the Death of Delia (1603)[†]

FAMA:° Bright heavens, you that enjoy our Delia's soul,   *Fame*
    And Death, with death that caused our ladies mourn,

---

9. Derangement.
1. Thomas Leigh was elected Lord Mayor of London in 1558; Robert Lee was elected Lord Mayor of London in 1602. The term of the office began and ended in the fall; *Lady Eve*: September 7, the Queen's birthday, was the day before the feast commemorating the birth of the Virgin Mary; March 24, the day she died, was the day before Lady's Day, the Feast of the Annuciation.
2. Less strained thighs; in rowing, the legs impart much of the force.
3. The people's tears caused such a flood that the bargemen might have rowed their boat through it.
† Copy text: Thomas Newton, *Atopoïon Delion, or, The death of Delia with the teares of her funerall. A poeticall excusiue discourse of our late Eliza* (London: W. Iohnes, 1603: STC 18513.5), B1v–B2r.

That did the wisdom of our lords control
And strived against all Cynthus'[1] power in scorn,
5   Know this:[2] that Fame immortal is on earth,
As you in heaven, and will not loose° her so.   *release*
You have her substance; I, a god beneath,
Will keep the substance of her life to show.[3]
I have her shape drawn in as lively dye°   *colors*
10   As if my Delia were herself in being,
And that's her Delia's self unto my eye;
I need no other's Delia for my seeing.
And yet methinks she's[4] not in heaven assigned,
So plain I keep her trophy° in my mind.   *memorial*

15   I have in writing golden pens to praise her
In dateless volumes of the silver air;
The very style so lofty high shall raise her
That Time shall be too short to tear her hair.[5]
Wherein shall first her chastity be writ
20   As pure in picture as itself was pure;
Next her religion, love, her art and wit
So fair that Delia's life may still endure.
Then, Cynthus, think thou hast thy Delia ever:
The heavens do keep her soul, thou keep'st her life,
25   Which life (I vow) from thee shall never sever,
Nor subject be to Fate's Atropian[6] knife.
Take this to wipe thy bleared eyes again;
Her life is thine, though heaven her soul contain.

ANONYMOUS

A Mournful Ditty, Entitled Elizabeth's Loss (1603)†

To a pleasant new tune

Farewell, farewell, farewell, brave England's joy;
Gone is thy friend that kept thee from annoy.
Lament, lament, lament, you English peers,
Lament your loss, possessed so many years.

5   Gone is thy queen, the paragon of Time,
On whom grim Death hath spread his fatal line.
Lament, lament, etc.

---

1. Mountain on the island of Delos, birthplace of Apollo and Diana (or Cynthia).
2. Fame reminds the Heavens and Death that he is immortal.
3. The poem preserves her image.
4. Copy text: she.
5. The poet will elevate her above the destructive malice of Time.
6. Of the three Fates, Atropos was the one who cut the thread of life.
† Copy text: *A mournfull dittie, entituled Elizabeths losse, together with a welcome for King Iames* (London: T[homas] P[avier], 1603; *STC* 7589), single broadsheet.

Gone is that gem which God and man did love;
She hath us left to dwell in heaven above.
10   Lament, lament, etc.

You gallant ladies of her princely train,
Lament your loss, your love, your hope and gain.
Lament, lament, etc.

Weep, wring your hands, all clad in mourning weeds;°   *garments*
15 Show forth your love in tongue, in heart and deeds.
Lament, lament, etc.

Full four and forty years, four months, seven days,
She did maintain this realm in peace always.
Lament, lament, etc.

20 In spite of Spain's proud Pope[1] and all the rout,
Who lion-like ran ranging round about.[2]
Lament, lament, etc.

With traitorous plots to slay her royal Grace,
Her realm, her laws and Gospel to deface.
25 Lament, lament, etc.

Yet, time and tide,° God still was her defense,   *season*
Till for Himself from us He took her hence.
Lament, lament, etc.

We need not to rehearse what care, what grief
30 She still° endured, and all for our relief.   *continually*
Lament, lament, etc.

We need not to rehearse what benefits
You all enjoyed, what pleasures and what gifts.
Lament, lament, etc.

35 You virgins all, bewail your virgin queen,
That phoenix rare on earth but seldom seen.
Lament, lament, etc.

With angel's wings she pierced the starry sky
When death, grim death, hath shut her mortal eye.
40 Lament, lament, etc.

You nymphs that sing and bathe in fountains clear,
Come lend your help to sing in mournful cheer.°   *countenance*
Lament, lament, etc.

---

1. The Pope was under the sway of the powerful Philip II of Spain throughout much of Elizabeth's reign.
2. An allusion to Satan, said to prowl like a hungry lion "to and fro in the earth" (1 Peter 5.8; Job 1.7).

All you that do profess sweet music's art,
45   Lay all aside, your viol, lute, and harp.
Lament, lament, etc.

Mourn organs, flutes, mourn sackbuts[3] with sad sound;
Mourn trumpets shrill, mourn cornets mute and round.
Lament, lament, etc.

50   You poets all, brave Shakespeare, Jonson, Greene,[4]
Bestow your time to write for England's queen.
Lament, lament, etc.

Return your songs and sonnets and your lays[5]
To set forth sweet Elizabeth's praise.
55   Lament, lament, etc.

In fine,° all you that loyal hearts possess,   *conclusion*
With roses sweet bedeck her princely hearse.
Lament, lament, etc.

Bedeck that hearse sprung from[6] that famous king,
60   King Henry the Eighth, whose fame on earth doth ring.
Lament, lament, etc.

Now is the time that we must all forget
Thy sacred name, O sweet Elizabeth.
Lament, lament, etc.

65   Praying for King James, as erst° we prayed for thee,   *once*
In all submissive love and loyalty.
Lament, lament, etc.

Beseeching God to bless his Majesty
With earthly peace and heaven's felicity.
70   Lament, lament, etc.

And make his reign more prosperous here on earth
Than was the reign of late Elizabeth.
Lament, lament, etc.

Wherefore all you that, subjects true, bear names,[7]
75   Still pray with me and say "God save King James!"
Lament, lament, lament, you English peers,
Lament your loss, enjoyed so many years.

---

3. Instrument similar to a trombone.
4. The author seems unaware that Robert Greene, writer of pamphlets, plays, and romances, had died years earlier.
5. Short lyric or narrative poem.
6. That hearse carrying one sprung from.
7. The last stanza is addressed to Peers of the Realm, noblemen with aristocratic titles (or "names").

HENRY PETOWE

From Eliza's Funeral (1603)[†]

From *A Few April Drops Showered on the Hearse of Dead Eliza*

Gaze, greedy eye; note what thou dost behold:
Our horizon is of a perfect hue,
As clear as crystal, and the day not old.
Yet thousand blacks present them to thy view.
5   Three thousand and odd hundred clouds appear[1]
Upon the earthly element below
As black as night, trampling the lower sphere,
As by degrees from place to place they go.
They pass away; O whither pass they then?
10   Into a further climate out of sight.
Like clouds they were, but yet like clouded men,
Whose presence turned the day to sable night.
  They vanish thence; note what was after seen,
  The lively picture of a late-dead queen,[2]

15   Who, like to Phoebus in his golden car,
Was the bright eye of the obscuréd day.
And though her glorious progress was not far,
Yet like the smiling sun this semblance lay,
Drawn in a jetty° chariot veiled with black,   *black*
20   By four fair palfreys that did hang the head,
As if their lady mistress they did lack
And they but drew the figure° of the dead.   *only drew the effigy*
O ye spectators which did view that sight,
Say, if you truly say, could you refrain
25   To shed a sea of tears in Death's despite,
That reft° her hence, whom Art brought back again?   *seized*
  He that knew her, and had Eliza seen,
  Would swear that figure were fair England's Queen.

Fair England's Queen, even to the life, though dead.
30   Speak if I write not true, did you not cry?
Cry forth amain° and say her princely head   *vehemently*
Lay on a pillow of a crimson dye
Like a sweet beauty in a harmless slumber.
She is not dead; no sure it cannot be.
35   Thus with unlikely hopes the vulgar number°   *common multitude*
Flatter themselves (O sweet-lived flattery).
Indeed, a man of judgment would have thought
(Had he not known her dead but seen her so,

---

† Copy text: H[enry] P[etowe], *Elizabetha quasi viuens Eliza's funerall. A fevve Aprill drops, showred on the hearse of dead Eliza. Or The funerall teares af* [sic] *a true hearted subiect* (London: M. Lawe, 1603; STC 19804), B2r–B3r.
1. Dim forms of the mourners.
2. An effigy of Elizabeth, borne on her casket.

Triumphant drawn in robes so richly wrought,
40 Crown on her head, in hand her scepter, too),
     At this rare sight he would have sworn and said,
     "To Parliament rides this sweet slumbering Maid."

EULOGIES AND THE END OF AN AGE

In the years just before and after the death of the Queen, great changes occurred in the balance of power between England, Ireland, and powers on the Continent. With Philip II dead, Tyrone's Rebellion at an end, and a friendly Henry IV on the throne in France, the world of the new English monarch, James I, was a very different place than that of his predecessor. In 1604, shortly after his accession, Spain ended its long and fruitless war with England, thus bringing to an end the long-standing military alliance between England and the Protestant provinces of the Netherlands. It is not surprising, then, that many authors saw the passing of Elizabeth as the end of one age and the dawning of another.

William Shakespeare and Michael Drayton reflected on the contrast in love sonnets that are remarkable for looking outward from their own private affairs to those of the world around them. Since both realms are uncertain and fleeting, the poets seek consolation at the end of the poem, Drayton by asserting his unchanging constancy to his beloved and Shakespeare by seeking solace in thinking of the

Elizabeth's tomb.

immortality that great poetry bestows on him and his lover. In Drayton's later poem *The Muses' Elysium*, which served as an introduction to a longer pastoral work published in 1631, the poet looks back from greater distance. Recalling the peaceful days when Spenser and others first celebrated the Queen as the shepherdess Eliza, Drayton describes England as an ideal pastoral world called Elyzium, withdrawn from destructive forces of time and resembling the Elysian Fields, where the souls of the blessed go to live a life of peace and harmony after death.

The poem "Gone is Elizabeth," by an anonymous lady-in-waiting, is not so finely wrought as those of Shakespeare or Drayton, but its simple expressions of love and respect for a dead mistress are all the more moving for their plainness. In remarkably few lines, it praises the Queen's love of her servants, her care for her people, her lasting attainments abroad, and the virtues for which she will be remembered.

Lady Diana Primrose's nostalgic eulogy, *A Chain of Pearl, or A Memorial of Queen Elizabeth*, is more reflective and elevated. Little is known about its author, though circumstantial evidence suggests that she was the wife or daughter of Gilbert Primrose, the minister of a French Protestant church. Employing the Queen's favorite item of jewelry, a chain of the pearls, as a symbol of the virtues that marked her life, the poem calls to mind the biblical parable of the Pearl of Great Price (Matthew 13.46), in which the kingdom of God is likened to a gem so precious that one should be willing to sell everything one has to obtain it. The poem suggests that, as a model of womanly virtue, Elizabeth is similarly precious. In working its way from one pearl on the chain to the next, the poet reminisces about the adversities that marked the Queen's life and the qualities that allowed her to triumph over them, from persecutions under Mary Tudor to the many invasion and assassination attempts later in the century. The great enemies of the poem are the King of Spain and the Pope, and the heroes are the Protestants of the British Isles and Europe, whom the Queen defended. Primrose's stress on the virtue of fortitude—which, in this period, was not commonly attributed to women—is striking, as is the claim (echoed by Drayton and others) that Elizabeth's reign was England's Golden Age, a time when the Muses and the Graces reigned. The poem is perhaps the best summation that has come down to us of the qualities that made "good Queen Bess" the object of such veneration in the ages that followed.

WILLIAM SHAKESPEARE

Sonnet 107 [Not Mine Own Fears, nor the Prophetic Soul] (ca. 1603)[†]

Not mine own fears, nor the prophetic soul
Of the wide world, dreaming on things to come,
Can yet the lease° of my true love control,   term
Supposed as forfeit to a confinèd doom.[1]
5 The mortal moon° hath her eclipse endured,[2]   Elizabeth
And the sad augurs mock their own presage.[3]

[†] Copy text: William Shakespeare, *Shake-speares sonnets Never before imprinted* (London: T[homas] T[horpe], 1609; *STC* 22353), G3r.
1. Thought of as a lease that has to be given up for legal reasons on a particular date.
2. Since there is no way to date the sonnet, some have suggested that it was written after the defeat of the Spanish Armada in 1588 (since the ships were sent in a formation shaped like a crescent moon), and others have thought that it was inspired by a lunar eclipse. The most common interpretation, however, is that it was written after the death of the Queen, referred to here in her guise as Cynthia, goddess of the moon.
3. The sad prophets laugh at their earlier forecasts (since many thought she would die or be killed long before).

Incertainties now crown themselves assured,[4]
And peace proclaims olives of endless age.[5]
Now with the drops° of this most balmy time,   *dew*
10 My love looks fresh, and Death to me subscribes,°   *surrenders*
Since, spite° of him, I'll live in this poor rhyme,   *in spite*
While he insults o'er dull and speechless tribes.[6]
    And thou in this shall find thy monument
    When tyrants' crests and tombs of brass are spent.°   *wasted away*

MICHAEL DRAYTON

Sonnet 51 [Calling to Mind, Since First My Love Begun] (1605)[†]

Calling to mind,[1] since first my love begun,
Th' incertain times oft varying in their course,
How things still° unexpectedly have run,   *always*
As please the Fates by their resistless force,
5 Lastly,[2] mine eyes amazedly have seen
Essex' great fall, Tyrone his peace to gain,[3]
The quiet end of that long-living queen,°   *Elizabeth*
This king's fair entrance,[4] and our peace with Spain,
We and the Dutch at length ourselves to sever.
10 Thus the world doth (and evermore shall) reel.
Yet to my goddess am I constant ever,
Howe'er blind Fortune turn her giddy wheel.
    Though heaven and earth prove both to me untrue,
    Yet am I still inviolate to you.

MICHAEL DRAYTON

From The Muses' Elyzium (1630)[‡]

The Description of Elyzium[1]

A paradise on earth is found,
Though far from vulgar sight,

4. Good consequences, formerly uncertain, now seem assured in the reign of her newly crowned successor.
5. After the Queen died, James I swiftly negotiated a treaty ending England's long war with Spain.
6. Boasts of his power over races that are dull and cannot gain immortality through writing poetry.
† Copy text: Michael Drayton, *Poems: by Michaell Draiton Esquire* (London: N. Ling, 1605; *STC* 7216), Cc5v.
1. Copy text: Calling mind.
2. Last of all the uncertain times since he fell in love.
3. On the unexpected changes mentioned here and in the lines following, see introduction.
4. Though James I was crowned July 11, 1603, his ceremonial entrance into London was delayed by fear of plague until March 15, 1604.
‡ Copy text: Michael Drayton, *The Muses Elizium lately discouered, by a new way ouer Parnassus* (London: Iohn Waterson, 1630; *STC* 7210), B1r–B2v.
1. A pun on the names "Elizabeth" and "Elysian," referring to the fields of the blessed in the classical underworld.

Which with those pleasures doth abound
That it Elyzium hight,°   *is called*

5   Where, in delights that never fade,
The Muses lulléd be,
And sit at pleasure in the shade
Of many a stately tree,

Which no rough tempest makes to reel
10   Nor their straight bodies bows.
Their lofty tops do never feel
The weight of winter's snows.

In groves that evermore are green,
No falling leaf is there,
15   But Philomel² (of birds the queen)
In music spends the year.

The merle,° upon her myrtle perch,   *blackbird*
There to the mavis° sings,   *song thrush*
Who, from the top of some curled birch,
20   Those notes redoubled rings.

There daisies damask³ every place
Nor once their beauties lose,
That when proud Phoebus hides his face,
Themselves they scorn to close.

25   The pansy and the violet here,
As seeming to descend
Both from one root, a very pair,
For sweetness yet contend,

And pointing to a pink⁴ to tell
30   Which bears it,° it° is loath   *the sweet scent / the pink*
To judge it; but replies, for smell,
That it excels them both;

Wherewith displeased they hang their heads,
So angry soon they grow,
35   And from their odoriferous beds
Their sweets at it they throw.

The winter here a summer is,
No waste is made by time,
Nor doth the autumn ever miss
40   The blossoms of the prime.⁵

2. The nightingale, with reference to the myth of Philomela.
3. Ornament the ground, as if on a tapestry.
4. Low plant with fragrant pink or white blossoms.
5. Nor does autumn ever lack fruit because spring frost spoiled the blossoms.

The flower that July forth doth bring
In April here is seen;
The primrose that puts on° the spring   *brings*
In July decks each green.°   *grassy area*

45 The sweets for sovereignty contend
And so abundant be,
That to the very earth they lend
And° bark of every tree.   *And to the*

Rills° rising out of every bank   *Brooks*
50 In wild meanders° strain,   *winding courses*
And playing many a wanton° prank   *naughty*
Upon the speckled plain,

In gambols⁶ and lascivious gyres°   *voluptuous turnings*
Their time they still° bestow,   *continually*
55 Nor to their fountains none retires,
Nor on their course will go,

Those brooks with lilies bravely decked,
So proud and wanton made
That they their courses quite neglect,
60 And seem as though they stayed

Fair Flora in her state to view,
Which through those lilies looks,
Or as those lilies leaned to show
Their beauties to the brooks,

65 That° Phoebus, in his lofty race,   *So that*
Oft lays aside his beams
And comes to cool his glowing face
In these delicious streams.

Oft spreading vines climb up the cleves,°   *cliffs*
70 Whose ripened clusters there
Their purple liquid drop, which drives°   *prolongs*
A vintage° through the year.   *harvest of wine*

Those cleves whose craggy sides are clad
With trees of sundry suits,⁷
75 Which make continual summer glad,
Even bending with their fruits,

Some ripening, ready some to fall,
Some blossomed, some to bloom,
Like gorgeous hangings on the wall
80 Of some rich princely room:

6. Youthful bounds or leaps.
7. Liveries, species of foliage.

Pomegranates, lemons, citrons, so
Their laded branches bow,
Their leaves in number that outgo
Nor roomth° will them allow.   *space, room*

85 There in perpetual summer's shade,
Apollo's prophets[8] sit,
Among the flowers that never fade,
But flourish like their wit,

To whom the nymphs upon their lyres,
90 Tune many a curious lay,[9]
And with their most melodious choirs
Make short the longest day.

The thrice three virgins,[1] heavenly clear,
Their trembling timbrels° sound,   *tambourines*
95 Whilst the three comely Graces there
Dance many a dainty round.

Decay nor age there nothing knows;
There is continual youth,
As time on plant or creatures grows,
100 So still their strength renew'th.

The poets' paradise this is,
To which but few can come,
The Muses' only bower of bliss,[2]
Their dear Elyzium.

105 Here happy souls (their blessed bowers,
Free from the rude resort
Of beastly people) spend the hours,
In harmless mirth and sport.

Then on to the Elyzian plains
110 Apollo doth invite you,
Where he provides with pastoral strains,
In nymphals[3] to delight you.

8. Pastoral poets, seen as inspired by the god of music, prophecy, poetry, and healing.
9. Brief lyric, narrative poem, or romance.
1. The nine Muses.
2. An allusion to Spenser's *Faerie Queene* Book 2, cantos 11–12, where a corrupt bower of the same name is ruled by a lustful witch named Acrasia. Drayton's bower is more temperately ruled by the Virgin Queen.
3. Pastoral poems represented as the songs of nymphs.

ANONYMOUS

Gone is Elizabeth (1612)[†]

A short and sweet sonnet made by one of the Maids of Honor upon the death of Queen Elizabeth, which she sewed upon a sampler in red silk.

To a new tune or to "Phillida Flouts Me."

Gone is Elizabeth
    whom we have loved so dear;
She our kind Mistress was
    full four and forty year.
5 England she governed well,
    not to be blamed.
Flanders she succored still°   *always*
    and Ireland tamed.
France she befriended,
10   Spain she hath foiled,
Papists rejected,
    and the Pope spoiled.
To princes powerful,
    to the world virtuous,
15 To her foes merciful,
    to subjects gracious.
Her soul is in heaven,
    the world keeps her glory,
Subjects her good deeds,
20   and so ends my story.

LADY DIANA PRIMROSE

A Chain of Pearl, or
A Memorial of Queen Elizabeth (1630)[‡]

The First Pearl: Religion

The goodliest pearl in fair Eliza's chain
Is true religion, which did chiefly gain
A royal luster to the rest and tied
The hearts of all to her when Mary died.
5 And though she found the realm infected much
With superstition and abuses, such
As (in all human judgment) could not be

---

† Copy text: Richard Johnson, *A crovvne garland of goulden roses* (London: Iohn Wright, 1612; *STC* 14672), C4r–C4v.

‡ Copy text: Lady Diana Primrose, *A chaine of pearle. Or A memoriall of the peerles graces, and heroick vertues of Queene Elizabeth, of glorious memory* (London: Thomas Paine, 1630; *STC* 20388), B1r–C2v.

Reformed without domestic mutiny
And great hostility from Spain and France,
10   Yet she, undaunted, bravely did advance
Christ's glorious ensign,[1] maugre° all the fears   *despite*
Or dangers which appeared, and for ten years[2]
She swayed the scepter with a lady's hand,
Not urging any Romist in the land
15   By sharp edicts the temple to frequent,
Or to partake the holy sacrament.[3]
But factious Romanists, not thus content,
Their agents to their Holy Father sent,
Desiring him by solemn bull proclaim
20   Elizabeth an heretic and name
Some other sovereign, which might erect°   *establish*
Their masking° Mass and hence forthwith eject   *theatrical*
The Evangelical profession,[4]
Which flourished under her protection.
25   The Pope to this petition condescends
And soon his leaden bull to England sends,
Which by one Felton on the Bishop's gate
Of London was affixed;[5] but the State
For that high treason punished him with death,
30   That would dethrone his Queen, Elizabeth.
Yet was this ball of wildfire[6] working still
In many Romanists which had a will
The present state and government to change,
That they in all idolatry[7] might range.
35   And hence it came that great Northumberland,
Associate with Earl of Westmoreland
And many more, their banners did display
In open field, hoping to win the day.[8]
Against these rebels, noble Sussex[9] went
40   And soon their bloody purpose did prevent.
Westmoreland fled, Northumberland did die
For that foul crime and deep disloyalty,
Having engaged thousands in that cause,
After which time, the Queen made stricter laws
45   Against recusants,[1] and with lion's heart
She banged the Pope and took the Gospel's part.

1. Battle flag.
2. From her Religious Settlement in 1559 to the rebellion of the Northern Earls in 1569.
3. Though church attendance was mandatory after the Settlement, the fine for noncompliance was small and taking communion was not required.
4. Protestant profession of faith.
5. In 1570, the Pope issued a bull excommunicating Elizabeth for heresy, depriving her of her "pretended" title to the crown, and commanding her subjects not to obey on pain of excommunication (see above, Part Three). One John Felton nailed a copy to the garden gate of the Bishop of London's palace.
6. Flaming ball of pitch used in warfare.
7. For giving reverence to images of saints and other holy objects, Protestants accused Catholics of worshipping idols.
8. A reference to the rebellion of 1569, led by Thomas Percy, Earl of Northumberland, and Charles Neville, Earl of Westmoreland.
9. Thomas Radcliff, Earl of Suffolk, who defeated the rebels.
1. English Catholics who refused to conform to the Protestant state religion.

The Pope, perceiving that his bull was baited[2]
In such rude sort and all his hopes defeated,
Cries out to Spain for help, who takes occasion
50 Thereby t' attempt the conquest of this nation.[3]
But such sage counselors Eliza had
As, though both Spain and Rome were almost mad
For grief and anger, yet they still did fail
And against England never could prevail.

The Second Pearl: Chastity

55 The next fair pearl that comes in order here
Is chastity, wherein she had no peer
'Mongst all the noble princesses which then
In Europe were the royal anadem.[4]
And though for beauty she an angel was
60 And all our sex did therein far surpass,
Yet did her pure, unspotted chastity
Her heavenly beauty rarely° beautify.   *exceptionally*
How many kings and princes did aspire
To win her love? In whom, that vestal[5] fire
65 Still flaming, never would she condescend
To Hymen's rites, though much she did commend
That brave French Monsieur,[6] who did hope to carry
The Golden Fleece[7] and fair Eliza marry.
Yea, Spanish Philip, husband to her sister,
70 Was her first suitor and the first that missed her.
And though he promised that the Pope by bull
Should license it, she held it but a gull,°   *cunning lie*
For how can Pope with God's own law dispense?[8]
Was it not time such popes to cudgel hence?
75 Thus her impregnable virginity
Throughout the world her fame did dignify.
            And this may be a document to all
The pearl of chastity not to let fall
Into the filthy dirt of foul desires,
80 Which Satan kindles with his hell-bred fires;
For whether it be termed virginal
In virgins, or in wives styled conjugal,
Or vidual[9] in widows, God respects

2. In the sport of "baiting" bulls, the animals were forced to fend off attacks by dogs.
3. Though Philip II considered overthrowing Elizabeth as early as 1569, an invasion was not under-
    taken until 1588.
4. Floral wreath worn like a crown. Each princess is imagined as a flower.
5. A reference to the virgins who tended the ever-burning flame in the temple of Vesta.
6. The Duke of Anjou, who actively courted Elizabeth in the years 1578–82.
7. An allusion to the story of Jason and the Argonauts.
8. To marry the husband of her dead sister Mary was, many thought, forbidden by the Bible (see
    Leviticus 21.21). It was certainly against church law and would have required a bull (or "license")
    from the Pope dispensing with legal objections.
9. Appropriate to widows.

All equally[1] and all alike affects.°   *loves*
85   And here I may not silent overpass
That noble lady of the Court[2] which was
Solicited by Taxis, that great Don,
Ambassador for Spain,[3] when she° was gone,   *Elizabeth*
Who to obtain his will gave her a chain
90 Of most rare orient pearl, hoping to gain
That worthy lady to his lust; but she,
That well perceived his Spanish policy,°   *cunning*
His fair chain kept but his foul offer scorned,
That sought thereby her husband to have horned.[4]
95 Taxis, repulsed, sent to her for his chain,
But as a trophy she did it retain,
      Which noble precedent may all excite
To keep this pearl, which is so orient bright.[5]

The Third Pearl: Prudence

How prudent was her government appeared
100 By her wise counsels, by the which she steered
In the most dangerous times that ever were
Since king or queen did crown in England wear.
Her choice of famous councilors did show
That she did all the rules of prudence know.
105 For though her wit and spirit were divine,
Counsels (she knew) were best, where more combine
That for experience and deep policy[6]
Are well approved, whose fidelity
Retains them in the bonds of loyal love
110 And no great pensions from their prince can move.
Thus ruled she prudently with all her power,
With Argus' eyes foreseeing every hour
All dangers imminent, lest any harms
Should us befall by Spanish arts or arms.
115   This gift in her was much more eminent
In that it is so rarely incident
To our weak sex and, as a precious stone
Deep set in gold shines fairer than alone
Or set in lead, so did all graces shine
120 In her more gloriously, because divine:
For kings are gods, and queens are goddesses

---

1. Chastity here includes virginity, virtuous abstinence among widows, and the proper expression of sexuality in marriage. Many Protestants rejected what they saw as the inappropriate Catholic veneration of virginity in priests and nuns and in the Virgin Mary.
2. Katherine Howard, Countess of Suffolk, who in 1599 became a Lady of the Privy Chamber to Elizabeth. After 1603, she was also Keeper of the Jewels to Queen Anne. Beautiful and vivacious, she served Robert Cecil, Earl of Salisbury and Secretary of State to James I, as a convenient go-between with the Spanish Ambassador.
3. Juan de Taxis, who in 1604 urged the Spanish government to meet Lady Suffolk's demands for jewelry and a pension as the price for her influence with Salisbury. Lady Primrose impugns his personal motives in the transaction.
4. Made a cuckold, for which the common symbol was horns on the man's brow.
5. Brilliant, like the sun rising in the east.
6. Political wisdom; the term was used positively and negatively in this period.

On earth, whose sacred virtues best expresses
Their true divinity, wherein if we
Them imitate, 'tis our felicity.
125 This pearl of prudence, then, we all should prize
Most highly, for it doth indeed comprise
All moral virtues, which are resident
In that blest soul where this is president.

The Fourth Pearl: Temperance

The golden bridle of Bellerophon
130 Is temperance, by which our passion
And appetite we conquer and subdue
To reason's regiment; else may we rue
Our yielding to men's Siren blandishments,
Which are attended with so foul events.
135   This pearl in her was so conspicuous
As that the King her brother° still did use   *Edward VI*
To style her his sweet Sister Temperance,
By which her much admired self-governance
Her passions still° she checked, and still she made   *continually*
140 The world astonished that so undismayed
She did with equal tenor still proceed
In one fair course, not shaken as a reed
But built upon the rock of temperance;
Not dazed with fear, not 'mazed with any chance;°   *unexpected problem*
145 Not with vain hope (as with an empty spoon)
Fed or allured to cast beyond the moon;[7]
Not with rash anger too precipitate;
Not fond° to love nor too, too prone to hate;   *foolish*
Not charmed with parasites or Sirens' songs,
150 Whose hearts are poisoned, though their sugared tongues
Swear, vow, and promise all fidelity
When they are brewing deepest villainy;
Not led to vain or too profuse expense,
Pretending thereby state magnificence;
155 Not spending on these momentary pleasures
Her precious time, but deeming her best treasures
Her subjects' love, which she so well preserved,
By sweet and mild demeanor, as it served
To guard her surer than an army royal,
160 So true their loves were to her, and so loyal.
O Golden Age! O blest and happy years!
O music sweeter than that of the spheres[8]
When prince and people mutually agree
In sacred concord and sweet symphony!

---

7. Proverbial expression meaning to attempt something beyond one's means.
8. Crystal spheres in which astral bodies such as the sun and stars were thought to be embedded.

The Fifth Pearl: Clemency

165 Her royal clemency comes next in view,
The virtue which in her did most renew
The image of her Maker, who in that
Exceeds Himself and doth commiserate°   *pity*
His very rebels,[9] lending them the light
170 Of sun and moon and all those diamonds bright.
So did Eliza cast her golden rays
Of clemency on those which many ways
Transgressed her laws, and sought to undermine
The Church and state, and did with Spain combine.°   *conspire*
175 And though by rigor of law she might,
Not wronging them, have taken all her right,
Yet her innate and princely clemency
Moved her to pardon their delinquency
Which sought her gracious mercy, and repented
180 Their misdemeanors, and their crimes lamented.
So doth the kingly lion with his foe,
Which once prostrate, he scorns to work his woe.
So did this virtue's sacred oriflamme[1]
Immortalize our great Eliza's name.

The Sixth Pearl: Justice

185 Her justice next appears, which did support
Her crown and was her kingdom's strongest fort.
For should not laws be executed well
And malefactors curbed, a very hell
Of all confusion and disorder would
190 Among all states ensue. Here to unfold
The exemplary penalties of those
Which to the realm were known and mortal foes,
And, as some putrid members, pared away
Lest their transcendent villainy should sway
195 Others to like disloyalty, would ask
A larger volume and would be a task
Unfit for feminine hands, which rather love
To write of pleasing subjects than approve
The most deservéd slaughtering of any,
200 Which justly cannot argue tyranny.
For though the Pope have lately sent from Rome
Strange books and pictures painting out the doom
Of his pretended martyrs[2] as that they
Were baited in bears' skins, and made a prey
205 To wild beasts, and had boots with boiling lead

9. That is, those who turn away from God.
1. Banner around which others rally.
2. Such cruelties are described in *A Brief History of the Glorious Martyrdom of Twelve Reverend Priests* (1584), by Cardinal William Allen, principal organizer of papal attempts to return England to the Catholic fold. Many recusants were, in fact, tortured and executed for treason after 1580, when Allen sent Jesuit priests secretly into England and several Catholic assassination plots against the Queen were discovered.

Drawn on their legs and horns nailed to their head,
Yet all our British world knows these are fables,
Chimeras, phantasms, dreams, and very baubles°   *toys*
For fools to play with, and right goblin sprites,
210   Wherewith our nurses oft their babes affrights.
His Holiness these martyrdoms may add
To the *Golden Legend*,[3] for they are as mad
That first invented them as he that writ
That brainless book, and yet some credit it,
215   For cruelty and fond credulity
Are the main pillars of Rome's hierarchy.

The Seventh Pearl: Fortitude

This goodly pearl is that rare fortitude
Wherewith this sacred princess was endued.
Witness her brave, undaunted look when Parry[4]
220   Was fully bent she should by him miscarry.
The wretch confessed that her great Majesty
With strange amazement did him terrify.
So heavenly graceful and so full of awe
Was that majestic queen, which when some saw,
225   They thought an angel did appear. She shone
So bright as none else could her paragon.°   *match*
But that which doth beyond all admiration
Illustrate her, and in her this whole nation,
Is that heroic march of hers and speech
230   At Tilbury,[5] where she did all beseech
Bravely to fight for England, telling them
That what their fortune was should hers be then
And that with full resolve she thither came
Ready to win or quite to lose the game.
235   Which words, delivered in most princely sort,
Did animate the army and report
To all the world her magnanimity,[6]
Whose haughty courage naught° could terrify.   *nothing*
Well did she show great Henry was her sire,
240   Whom Europe did for valor most admire
'Mongst all the warlike princes which were then
Enthronized with regal diadem.°   *crown*

The Eighth Pearl: Science

Among the virtues intellectual
The van° is led by that we science[7] call,   *vanguard*
245   A pearl more precious than th' Egyptian Queen°   *Cleopatra*

3. Medieval collection of saints lives.
4. Dr. William Parry, who in 1584 was executed for conspiring to assassinate the Queen. On the myth
   that he confronted her and she faced him down, preventing the killing, see Heywood's *If You Know
   Not Me* in Part Six.
5. See accounts of Elizabeth's speech to the troops there in Part Seven.
6. Greatness of soul, regarded in this period as the master virtue that includes all the others.
7. Intellectual virtue gained by study of the Liberal Arts.

Quaffed off[8] to Anthony; of more esteem
Than Indian gold or most resplendent gems,
Which ravish us with their translucent beams.
How many arts and sciences did deck
250 This heroina, who still° had at beck[9]   *always*
The Muses and the Graces when that she
Gave audience in state and majesty?
Then did the goddess Eloquence inspire
Her royal breast; Apollo with his lyre
255 Ne'er made such music; on her sacred lips
Angels enthroned most heavenly manna[1] sips.
Then might you see her nectar-flowing vein[2]
Surround the hearers, in which sugared stream
She able was to drown a world of men
260 And, drowned, with sweetness to revive again.
Alasco, the ambassador Polonian,[3]
Who perorated like a mere Slavonian
And in rude rambling rhetoric did roll,[4]
She did with Attic eloquence[5] control.
265 Her speeches to our academians:
Well showed she knew among Athenians
How to deliver such well-tuned words
As with such places punctually[6] accords.
But with what oratory ravishments
270 Did she imparadise her parliaments?
Her last most princely speech[7] doth verify
How highly she did England dignify,
Her loyal commons[8] how did she embrace,
And entertain with a most royal grace.

The Ninth Pearl: Patience

275 Now come we her rare patience to display
Which, as with purest gold, did pave her way
To England's crown, for when her sister[9] ruled,
She was with many great afflictions schooled;
Yet all the while her mot° was *Tamquam ovis*,[1]   *motto*
280 Nor could her enemies prove ought amiss

8. Drank as a toast.
9. At her command.
1. Miraculous bread supplied by God to sustain the ancient Israelites during their wanderings in the Sinai Desert after their departure from Egypt (Exodus 16.15–35).
2. Way of speaking.
3. Albert Laski, a Polish royal official who visited the Court and Oxford University in 1583.
4. Recite rapidly or in deep, rolling tones.
5. Ancient Greek style based on shorter, tighter sentences than the expansive and complex Ciceronian style popular in the 1580s. Attic style became the fashion in the seventeenth century.
6. In every detail.
7. The so-called Golden Speech of 1601, reprinted above in Part Nine.
8. Members of the House of Commons.
9. Mary Tudor, who in 1554–58 imprisoned Elizabeth in the Tower on suspicion of treason and then confined her to the royal palaces at Woodstock and Hatfield.
1. Her witty saying was "As a sheep." On the road to prison at Woodstock in 1554, Elizabeth used the Latin phrase as coded warning to her servants that she expected to be assassinated on the way by henchmen of her sister, Mary I. The Princess was quoting the Vulgate Latin of Psalm 44.11 and perhaps also alluding to Isaiah 53.7, "He is brought as a sheep to the slaughter," which was widely interpreted as a prophecy of the death of Christ, with whom she identified in her persecution.

In her, although they thirsted for her blood,
Reputing it, once shed, their sovereign good.
Sometime in prison this sweet saint was pent,
Then hastily away she thence was sent
285 To places more remote, and all her friends
Debarred access, and none but such attends
As ready were, with poison or with knife,
To sacrifice this sacred princess' life
At bloody Bonner's beck or Gardiner's nod,[2]
290 Had they not been prevented by that God
Who did Susanna from the elders free
And at the last gave her her liberty.
Thus by her patient bearing of the cross[3]
She reaped greatest gain from greatest loss,
295 For he that loseth his blest liberty
Hath found a very hell of misery.
By many crosses thus she got the crown,
To England's glory and her great renown.

The Tenth Pearl: Bounty

As rose and lily challenge chiefest place
300 For milk-white luster and for purple grace,[4]
So England's rose and lily had no peer
For princely bounty shining everywhere.
This made her fame with golden wings to fly
About the world, above the starry sky,
305 Witness France, Portugal, Virginia,
Germany, Scotland, Ireland, Belgia,°   *Belgium*
Whose provinces and princes found her aid
On all occasions, which sore dismayed
Spain's king,° whose European monarchy   *Philip II*
310 Could never thrive during her sovereignty;
So did she beat him with her distaff,[5] so
By sea and land she him did overthrow.
Yea, so that tyrant on his knees she brought
That of brave England peace he begged and thought
315 Himself most happy, that by begging so
Preserved all Spain from beggary and woe.[6]
     Here all amazed my Muse sets up her rest,
     Adoring her was° so divinely blest.   *who was*

At nos horrifico cinefactam te prope busto
Insatiabiliter deflebimus eternumque.[7]

2. In Mary's reign, Edmund Bonner (Bishop of London) and Stephen Gardiner (Bishop of Winchester) were instrumental in burning Protestants for heresy.
3. Fulfillment of Christ's command to believers to share in his suffering for the sake of the gospel (Matthew 16.24).
4. White symbolizes purity and virginity, red royalty and love.
5. Used by women in spinning thread and by the Fates in determining destiny.
6. Peace with Spain was concluded shortly after Elizabeth's death.
7. But we shall mourn, inconsolably and without ceasing, for you who have been reduced to ashes on the dreadful pyre (Lucretius, *De Rerum Natura*, 3.906–7; source identified by James A. Arieti in private correspondence).

Part Ten: Lingering Images of the Queen

HISTORICAL BACKGROUND

In the last half of Elizabeth's reign, a group of well-educated and unusually gifted poets created new and dazzling images of her. Among these writers—known in their own day as the "new poets"—were a number whose work has appeared in earlier parts of this Norton Critical Edition, including Edmund Spenser, Sir Walter Ralegh, Sir Philip Sidney, John Davies, Michael Drayton, and Mary Sidney Herbert, Countess of Pembroke. So accomplished were they that their representations have lingered on, shaping impressions of Elizabeth down to our own day.

Though most of the new poets were militantly Protestant, they relied less on biblical figures for the Queen than had earlier poets, preferring to draw on classical mythology and a variety of more recent sources, including love lyrics, folk tales, pastoral eclogues, and chivalric romances. The qualities that set their work apart from that of earlier Elizabethan poets are their range of sources and learned allusion, their poetic delicacy and skill, and their tendency to treat the aging Queen as if she were forever young, elevating and idealizing her to such an extent that she transcends the limits of human nature. As earlier selections in this collection have shown, poets such as Spenser, Sidney, Ralegh, and Lyly sometimes criticized her or her policies, but Ralegh kept his prison poems to himself, and the others couched their criticisms in ambiguous allegories or suggestive but inconclusive parallels between fictional characters and the Queen. Many works by the new poets go to the opposite extreme, virtually deifying Elizabeth, treating her as if she were as lithe and ageless as the goddess Diana, as wise as Minerva, or as just as Astraea. Other works portray her as the Fairy Queen, ethereal, mysterious, and wise, or as God's viceroy on earth, ruling with mercy and justice but also inspiring wonder and fear. To be sure, less elevated images also had their place. Elizabeth frequently appeared as a shepherdess or as a chaste and distant lady of the sort common in sonnet sequences of the day. Even these depictions, however, set her apart, stressing her beauty and purity or celebrating her capacity to live in harmony with the ideal order of nature.

Although the troubles of the last two decades of Elizabeth's reign sometimes came up in the work of these poets, the divisions and shortcomings of the government rarely did, and it is not difficult to understand why. With nationalism growing and religious emotion at its height, Protestant poets bent on promoting the English cause against hostile forces on the Continent were hardly inclined to present the regime in an unfavorable light, at least openly. Those who wrote against the Queen's policies too boldly faced censorship by the government, which employed the Stationer's Company to watch over the London book trade, calling in and destroying any publication that might undermine the

551

authority of the state. Harsh laws were also in place to punish anyone who dishonored the monarch, even in private conversation.

Yet it would be a mistake to overemphasize the role of censorship, nationalism, Protestant zeal, or any other indirect cause in shaping the lofty images of Elizabeth. Her constant travels to mingle with her subjects moved them. Her evident commitment to protect their peace and well being—even, as a long succession of would-be assassins had shown, at the cost of her own life—earned their love and respect. Few other English monarchs have gained such devotion from their subjects as she did. So deep is the adulation in many of the works of the "new poets" that it is tempting to speak, as Sir Roy Strong has done, of a "cult of Elizabeth." Though writers may have flattered her as she aged or used her image for their own political purposes, there is no mistaking the veneration that she often inspired in them.

A QUEEN OF MANY GUISES

Cult-like devotion to the aging Queen appears in its most popular forms in Thomas Dekker's play *Old Fortunatus*, which was selected for performance before the Queen in the Christmas playing season of 1599. In preparing for his first command performance, the young playwright rewrote much of the script, adding a prologue that paid tribute to the Queen under many of the guises that writers of the latter part of the reign had invented for her. Perpetuating the fiction that Eliza was not only "still bright, still one, still divine," but was also still youthful and "flourishing in May," the poem moves toward an apotheosis in which she appears as a goddess in a temple, the object of breathless adoration by two aged "pilgrims." That one is an Englishman and the other a stranger from Cyprus, the locale of the play, suggests the extent to which her reputation has gone out into the world. Many of the representations of her in Dekker's prologue call to mind the poetry of Spenser, in which Elizabeth also appears as the shepherdess Eliza, the chaste huntress Belphoebe (or Diana), and the just goddess Astraea.

Like Dekker's Prologue, Sir Walter Ralegh's poem "Now We Have Present Made" rehearses a number of the neoclassical figures that rose to the fore in poems on Elizabeth written during the latter half of her reign: "Cynthia, Phoebe, Flora, / Diana, and Aurora." Apparently intended to accompany a gift, the poem ends on a note of sorrow at the cost that love of such a woman exacts from the lover.

THOMAS DEKKER

From Old Fortunatus (1600)[†]

The Prologue at Court

    Enter two old men.
1ST OLD MAN: Are you then traveling to the temple of Eliza?
2ND OLD MAN: Even to her temple are my feeble limbs traveling. Some call
    her Pandora, some Gloriana, some Cynthia, some Delphoebe, some

---

† Copy text: Thomas Dekker, *The pleasant comedie of old Fortunatus As it was plaied before the Queenes Maiestie this Christmas* (London: William Aspley, 1600; STC 6715), A1v–A2r.

Astraea, all by several names to express several loves; yet all those names make but one celestial body, as all those loves meet to create but one soul.[1]

1ST OLD MAN: I am one of her own country, and we adore her by the name of Eliza.[2]

2ND OLD MAN: Blessed name, happy country. Your Eliza makes your land Elysium.[3] But what do you offer?

1ST OLD MAN: That which all true subjects should: when I was young, an armed hand; now I am crooked, an upright heart. But what offer you?

2ND OLD MAN: That which all strangers do: two eyes struck blind with admiration, two lips proud to sound her glory, two hands held up full of prayers and praises. What not, that may express love? What not, that may make her beloved?

1ST OLD MAN: How long is't since you last beheld her?

2ND OLD MAN: A just[4] year. Yet that year hath seemed to me but one day because her glory hath been my hourly contemplation, and yet that year hath seemed to me more than twice seven years[5] because so long I have been absent from her. Come, therefore, good father, let's go faster, lest we come too late, for see, the tapers of the night[6] are already lighted and stand brightly burning in their starry candlesticks. See how gloriously the moon shines upon us.

    Both kneel.[7]

1ST OLD MAN: Peace, fool. Tremble and kneel. The moon, say'st thou?
Our eyes are dazzled by Eliza's beams.
See (if at least thou dare see) where she sits.
This is the great Pantheon[8] of our goddess,
And all those faces which thine eyes thought stars
Are nymphs attending on her deity.
Prithee begin, for I want° power to speak.   *lack*

2ND OLD MAN: No, no, speak thou. I want words to begin.   *Weeps.*

1ST OLD MAN: Alack, what shall I do? Com'st thou with me,
And weep'st now thou behold'st this majesty?

2ND OLD MAN: Great landlady° of hearts, pardon me.   *owner, ruler*

1ST OLD MAN: Blame not mine eyes, good father, in these tears.

2ND OLD MAN: My pure love shines, as thine doth in thy fears.

---

1. Love for the Queen unites the people as one soul; *Delphoebe*: Belphoebe ("beautiful Phoebe"), goddess of the moon; *celestial body*: Elizabeth's "body politic" (or official role as an embodiment of the entire state), as distinct from her personal "body natural." All the deities listed here have contributed their special gifts to make her a "celestial," or godlike, ruler.
2. Common pastoral name for the Queen.
3. Resting place in the afterlife for those favored by the gods, described variously as a pleasant meadow in Hades or the "Islands of the Blessed" in the mythical, world-encompassing sea current Oceanus.
4. Complete. Since *Old Fortunatus* was staged for the annual Christmas Revels at Court, when plays were frequent, the actor playing the old man may well have performed before the Queen the year before.
5. Perhaps an allusion to Genesis 29.1–30, where Jacob must serve fourteen years before receiving his beloved wife Rachael.
6. The stars.
7. As the pilgrims kneel to their goddess, they shift from prose to verse.
8. Temple in ancient Rome where all deities from throughout the empire were worshipped.

I weep for joy to see so many heads
Of prudent ladies, clothed in the livery
Of silver-handed age for serving you,
Whilst in your eyes youth's glory doth renew:
I weep for joy to see the sun look old,[9]
To see the moon mad at her often change,[1]
To see the stars only by night to shine,
Whilst you are still° bright, still one, still divine.   *always*
I weep for joy to see the world decay
Yet see Eliza flourishing like May.
O pardon me, your pilgrim. I have measured
Many a mile to find you and have brought
Old Fortunatus and his family,
With other Cypriots,[2] my poor countrymen,
To pay a whole year's tribute. O vouchsafe,
Dread Queen of Fairies,[3] with your gracious eyes
T' accept theirs and our humble sacrifice.
IST OLD MAN: Now I'll beg for thee too, and yet I need not.
Her sacred hand hath evermore been known
As soon held out to strangers as her own.
2ND OLD MAN: Thou dost encourage me. I'll fetch them[4] in.
They have no princely gifts; we are all poor.
Our offerings are true hearts. Who can wish more?   *Exeunt.*

SIR WALTER RALEGH

Now We Have Present Made (ca. 1582–87)[†]

Now we have present made
To Cynthia, Phoebe, Flora,
Diana, and Aurora,
Beauty that cannot fade,

5   A flower of love's own planting,
A pattern kept by Nature
For beauty, form, and stature
When she° would frame a darling.   *Nature*

She° as the valley of Peru[1]   *Elizabeth*
10   Whose summer ever lasteth,
Time conquering, all she mast'reth
By being alway new.

9. By comparison with the ever-young Queen.
1. By comparison with Elizabeth, whose personal motto was *Semper eadem* ("Always the same").
2. The play is partly set in Cyprus.
3. After the publication of Spenser's *Faerie Queene* (1590), a common literary figure for the Queen.
4. Others in his family.
† Copy text: Sir *Walter Ralegh, The Poems of Sir Walter Ralegh: A Historical Edition,* ed. Michael Rudick (Tempe: Arizona Center for Medieval and Renaissance Studies, Renaissance English Texts Society, 1999), 46–47. Copyright Arizona Board of Regents for Arizona State University. Reprinted with permission.
1. Ralegh was, as an explorer, fascinated with the New World.

As elemental fire
Whose food and flame consumes not,[2]
15   Or as the passion ends not
Of virtue's true desire,

So her celestial frame
And quintessential[3] mind,
Which heavens together bind,
20   Shall ever be the same.[4]

Then to her servants leave her
Love, nature, and perfection.
Princes of world's affection
Or praises but deceive her.[5]

25   If Love° could find a quill   *Cupid*
Drawn from an angel's wing,
Or did the Muses sing
That pretty wanton's° will,   *Cupid's*

Perchance he could indite°   *compose a poem*
30   To please all other sense.
But love's and woe's expense°   *costs to the lover*
Sorrows can only write.

ELIZABETH AS SHEPHERDESS

The image of the Queen as a shepherdess was first popularized by Edmund
Spenser's *Shepherd's Calendar*. Like other writers influenced by Philip and
Mary Sidney, with whom he was acquainted, Spenser was committed to
creating a national literature for England worthy of comparison with that of
Renaissance Italy or France. Though a shepherdess might seem an odd
choice to represent the Queen in such a project, England was a nation of
sheep farmers, and both the Bible and the pastorals of Virgil (Spenser's model
throughout his career) employed shepherds as figures for rulers. The genre of
pastoral had also been developed to reveal the excesses of royal courts by
offering a contrasting ideal of life lived in simplicity, humility, and harmony
with nature.

    The *Calendar* was remarkable in its day, both for its learning and skill and for
the elegance of its presentation. The volume contained twelve eclogues, one for
each month of the year. Each took the form of an exchange or a debate between
shepherds, which they carried on in poetry and song. Each eclogue was preceded by an original woodcut representing the month in question and the shepherds involved and followed by a cryptic "emblem" or saying. Each was also
supplied with headnotes and a running commentary by a scholar identified only

---

2. Fire as one of the four irreducible elements of which everything was thought to be made. Unlike
    ordinary fire, it needed nothing else to feed on and was not consumed by the process of burning.
3. In medieval philosophy, the "fifth essence" was the purest, most perfect of substances, the stuff of
    the unchanging heavenly bodies.
4. An allusion to Elizabeth's motto *Semper eadem* ("Always the same").
5. Princes who render to her worldly affection or praises only deceive her, missing her celestial
    worth.

as E.K. (possibly Edward Kirke, one of the poet's friends from his days at Cambridge University). The result was a learned edition of the sort usually reserved for celebrated poets of the past. Since Spenser was young, of humble origins, and largely unknown at the time, the book was a clever and audacious means of self-promotion.

The portrait of "Eliza, Queen of shepherds all," in the "April" eclogue reinforces the poet's claims to literary stature by offering the Queen both praise and a subtle, indirect critique. Sung by the shepherd Hobbinol for his friend Thenot, the eclogue calls to mind a song composed in earlier days by Colin Clout, the best poet in their circle. At the time, Colin had revered Eliza, calling her "my goddess" and representing her as an angelic figure who stands over all the orders of creation, from Apollo and Diana to the Muses and the Graces and so down to the forest nymphs and the mortal women who attend on her. The song ends with a call to the daughters of the shepherds to gather around Eliza and deck her with springtime flowers, which, in the symbolism of the day, represented her many admirable qualities. In the simple tableau of Eliza seated on the grass among her attendants, the poet was making sweeping claims, not only about the Queen's merits, but also about her divine and human authority.

The eclogue in which Colin's lyric is embedded is not, however, as sunny and laudatory as the song itself. Beginning and ending with references to Colin's later feelings of grief and loss, the conversation between Thenot and Hobbinol leaves the impression that the happiest days of Eliza's reign are past. Some critics identify the mysterious woman Rosalind, who has rejected Colin and caused his grief, with Elizabeth as well. Since Colin is Spenser's own literary name for himself, and since the eclogues were published in the fall of 1579 at the height of the French marriage negotiations, it may be that the prospect of a Catholic Duke becoming King of England was one cause of the poet's distress. Spenser's name does not appear on the title page of the *Calendar*, and the opening dedication to Philip Sidney concedes that the book was "begot with blame" and brought forth in "jeopardy." Along with passages of court satire elsewhere in the *Calendar*, the dark frame of "April" may have led the poet to hide his identity, for he signed the dedication simply "Immeritô" (one without merit).

Though mixed in its responses to the Queen, Spenser's "April" set the standard for subsequent pastorals that were more wholeheartedly laudatory. Michael Drayton's lyric "Rowland's Song in Praise of the Fairest Beta" presents a similar tableau of the Queen seated among her female attendants, shaming the sun by her glory and wearing symbolic flowers. For Drayton, writing in the early 1590s, dangers were still present: late in the poem, "stormy winds" threaten the flock and the shepherds are called on to be watchful so that they may crush "that foul, sev'n-headed beast," a common Protestant figure for the papacy in Rome. Yet the danger does not lie in the desires of the Queen herself, as it had in Spenser's "April," and the future is promising. Drayton ends with a vision of England's "large empire" stretching "her arms from east unto the west."

Even further removed from a sense of peril is the "Dialogue Between Two Shepherds" by Mary Sidney Herbert, Countess of Pembroke, which was written in 1599. It employs a traditional pastoral singing match as a source of comic relief, pitting two shepherds, Thenot and Piers, against one another in a debate over the Queen's merits. Though Thenot praises Elizabeth in extravagant terms, Piers accuses him of lying since, on every point that his companion has raised, even higher forms of praise are appropriate. The dialogue was apparently written for presentation at Wilton, the Countess's rural estate, during the summer progress of 1599. Since news of a possible Spanish invasion led the Queen to cancel most of the journey and return to London, however, it is unlikely that she ever heard Thenot and Piers discuss the proper way to praise a queen. It is a shame, since the Countess's easy playfulness was an elegant solution to a problem that frequently plagued the Queen's arrival at households unused to her presence: how to put her and everyone else at their ease.

EDMUND SPENSER

From THE SHEPHERD'S CALENDAR (1579)†

To His Book[1]

Go, little book, thy self present
As child whose parent is unkent,[2]
To him° that is the president[3]   *Sidney*
Of noblesse° and of chivalry.   *nobility*
5   And if that Envy bark at thee,
As sure it will, for succor flee
Under the shadow of his wing,
And askéd who thee forth did bring,
A shepherd's swain[4] say did thee sing
10 All as his straying flock he fed.
And when his Honor has thee read,°   *perused; identified*
Crave pardon for my hardihead.°   *audacity*
But if that any ask thy name,
Say thou wert base begot with blame;
15 For thy° thereof thou takest shame.   *For that reason*
And when thou art past jeopardy,
Come tell me what was said of me,
And I will send more after thee.

IMMERITÔ[5]

*   *   *

April

Aegloga Quarta[6]

Argument[7]

This eclogue is purposely intended to the honor and praise of our most gracious sovereign, Queen Elizabeth. The speakers herein be Hobbinoll and Thenot, two shepherds, the which Hobbinoll, being before mentioned greatly to have loved Colin, is here set forth more largely, complaining him

---

† Copy text: Edmund Spenser, *The shepheardes calender conteyning tvvelue aeglogues proportionable to the twelue monethes* (London: Hugh Singleton, 1579; STC 23089), ¶1v, C3v–D4r.
1. A poem of dedication to Sir Philip Sidney.
2. Little known; unidentified; untaught.
3. One who presides over; precedent.
4. Country laborer; lover; servant to a knight. Though Spenser pretends to be a rustic, he was highly educated and served as secretary to Sidney's uncle, Robert Dudley, Earl of Leicester.
5. One without merit. On the reason that the poet concealed his identity, see Elizabeth as Shepherdress on previous page.
6. Fourth eclogue.
7. Summary.

Elizabeth as Eliza in Spenser's "April" eclogue.

of that boy's great misadventure in love, whereby his mind was alienate and withdrawn not only from him, who most loved him, but also from all former delights and studies, as well in pleasant piping as conning,[8] rhyming, and singing and other his laudable exercises. Whereby he taketh occasion, for proof of his more excellency and skill in poetry, to record a song which the said Colin sometime[9] made in honor of her Majesty, whom abruptly he termeth Elisa.

Thenot.[1]

	Tell me, good Hobbinoll, what gars thee greet?°	*makes thee weep*
	What? Hath some wolf thy tender lambs ytorn?[2]	
	Or is thy bagpipe broke, that sounds so sweet?	
	Or art thou of thy lovéd lass forlorn?°	*abandoned*
5	Or been thine eyes attempered° to the year,	*attuned*
	Quenching the gasping furrows' thirst with rain?	
	Like April shower, so streams the trickling tears	
	Adown thy cheek to quench thy thirsty pain.	

Hobbinoll.

	Nor this nor that so much doth make me mourn,	
10	But for° the lad whom long I loved so dear	*But because*
	Now loves a lass that all his love doth scorn.	
	He, plunged in pain, his tresséd° locks doth tear.	*braided*
	Shepherd's delights he doth them all forswear,	
	His pleasant pipe, which made us merriment,	

---

8. Memorizing; *before*: earlier in the *Calendar*; *set forth more largely*: presented at greater length.
9. Once.
1. The copy text here gives the names of both shepherds who participate in the eclogue.
2. Archaic form of "torn." Spenser makes the eclogues seem old and rustic by using old-fashioned words such as "yclad" (clothed) and "yblent" (blinded), and "forswonk" (exhausted).

15 He willfully hath broke, and doth forbear
His wonted songs, wherein he all outwent.°[3]   *surpassed*

Thenot.

What is he for a lad° you so lament?   *What kind of boy is he*
Is love such pinching pain to them that prove?°   *experience it*
And hath he skill to make[4] so excellent
20 Yet hath so little skill to bridle love?

Hobbinoll.

Colin thou kenst,° the southern shepherd's[5] boy;   *know*
Him love hath wounded with a deadly dart.
Whilom° on him was all my care and joy,   *once*
Forcing with gifts to win his wanton° heart.   *lustful, undisciplined*

25 But now from me his madding mind is start°   *run away*
And woos the widow's daughter of the glen.[6]
So now fair Rosalind hath bred his smart;
So now his friend is changéd for a frenne.°   *to a stranger, enemy*

Thenot.

But if his ditties been so trimly dight,[7]
30 I pray thee, Hobbinoll, record° some one,   *sing*
The whiles our flocks do graze about in sight
And we close shrouded in this shade alone.

Hobbinoll.

Contented I. Then will I sing his lay°   *song*
Of fair Elisa, Queen of shepherds all,[8]
35 Which once he made as by a spring he lay
And tuned it unto the water's fall.[9]

"Ye dainty nymphs that in this blessed brook
       do bathe your breast,
Forsake your wat'ry bowers and hither look
40   at my request;

---

3. In pastoral, the shepherd's pipe is a figure for the poet's art and its role in influencing the surrounding culture.
4. E. K.: "To rhyme and versify; for in this word "making" our old English poets were wont to comprehend all the skill of poetry, according to the Greek *poiein*, make, whence cometh the name of poets."
5. E. K. identifies Colin's master as "some southern nobleman," but since Spenser refers to himself as "Colin," the "southern shepherd" may be his patron in 1579, the Earl of Leicester, or perhaps Bishop John Young, another early employer of the poet.
6. E. K.: "He calleth Rosalind 'the Widow's daughter of the glen'" because it is well known "that she is a gentlewoman of no mean house, nor endued with any vulgar and common gifts," but "such indeed as need neither Colin be ashamed to have her made known by his verses, nor Hobbinol be grieved that so she should be commended to immortality for her rare and singular virtues."
7. Songs be so neatly crafted.
8. E. K.: "In all this song is not to be respected what the worthiness of her Majesty deserveth, nor what to the highness of a prince is agreeable, but what is most comely for the meanness of a shepherd's wit or [either] to conceive or to utter. And therefore he calleth her Elisa, * * * a shepherd's daughter."
9. In each of Colin's stanzas, the long first and third lines overflow into shorter lines that follow, and the long fifth and sixth lines lead to a quick, tripping couplet and then a more expansive final line. The pattern suggests the alternate pooling, rushing, and subsiding of falling water during the spring runoff.

And eke° you Virgins[1] that on Parnasse dwell,   *also*
Whence floweth Helicon,[2] the learnéd well,
    Help me to blaze
    Her worthy praise,
45 Which in her sex° doth all excel.   *gender*

"Of fair Elisa be your silver song,
    that blessed wight;°   *person*
The flower of virgins, may she flourish long
    in princely plight.°   *state*
50 For she is Syrinx' daughter[3] without spot,
Which Pan, the shepherd's god, of her begot.
    So sprung her grace
    Of heavenly race,
No mortal blemish may her blot.

55 "See, where she sits upon the grassy green
    (O seemly sight),
Yclad in scarlet, like a maiden Queen,
    And ermines white.
Upon her head a crimson coronet,[4]
60 With damask roses° and daffadillies set;   *pink roses*
    Bay° leaves between   *laurel*
    And primroses green
Embellish the sweet violet.[5]

"Tell me, have ye seen her angelic face,
65   like Phoebe fair?
Her heavenly havior,° her princely grace   *estate; deportment*
    can you well compare?
The red rose meddled° with the white yfere,°   *mingled / together*
In either cheek depeincten° lively cheer.   *depict*
70   Her modest eye,
    Her majesty,
Where have you seen the like, but there?

"I saw Phoebus thrust out his golden head
    upon her to gaze,

1. The Muses.
2. Like Parnassus, a mountain in central Greece associated with Apollo and the Muses. Helicon was not a "well" but the site of the springs Hippocrene and Aganippe, regarded as fonts of poetic inspiration.
3. E. K.: "[Spenser] could devise no parents in his judgement so worthy for [Elizabeth] as Pan, the shepherd's god, and his best beloved Syrinx, so that by Pan is here meant the most famous and victorious King, her Highness's father." Pan often denotes "kings and mighty potentates and, in some place, Christ himself, who is the very Pan and god of shepherds."
4. The gown and coronet (or small crown) suggest, not the mature Queen of 1579, but the princess of the 1540s and 1550s, whose most famous portrait (at Windsor Castle) depicts her in scarlet. The crimson roses in the coronet were associated with Venus, the Virgin Mary, and the goddess Isis—all favored by poets as figures for Elizabeth. On the flower symbolism of "April," see Brooks-Davies, *Selected Shorter Poems*. The spotted white fur of the ermine symbolized purity and was a personal emblem of the Queen.
5. The pink rose was an emblem of the Tudor monarchs. If Spenser distinguished "daffadillies" from "daffadowndillies," he probably meant by the former the white flower asphodel, symbol of virgin purity. On the symbolism of daffadowndillies, see note below on lines 136–44. E. K. terms bay leaves "the sign of honor and victory" and "eke of famous poets." Violets symbolized modesty and primroses the "greenness" of youth, another reminder that the eclogue represents Elizabeth as a young princess.

75 But when he saw how broad her beams did spread,
          it did him amaze.
    He blushed to see another Sun below,
    Ne° durst again his fiery face out show.   *Nor*
          Let him, if he dare,
80   His brightness compare
    With hers to have the overthrow.°   *victory over her*

    "Show thyself, Cynthia, with thy silver rays,
          and be not abashed.
    When she the beams of her beauty displays,
85   O how art thou dashed?
    But I will not match her with Latona's seed;
    Such folly great sorrow to Niobe did breed.
          Now she is a stone
          And makes daily moan,
90 Warning all other to take heed.

    "Pan may be proud that ever he begot
          such a bellibone[6]
    And Syrinx rejoice that ever was her lot
          to bear such an one.
95 Soon as my younglings cryen for the dam,
    To her will I offer a milk-white lamb.
          She is my goddess plain
          And I her shepherd's swain,
    Albe forswonk° and forswat° I am.   *Although exhausted / bathed in sweat*

100 "I see Calliopê speed her to the place
          Where my goddess shines,
    And after her the other Muses trace
          with their violins.
    Been they not bay branches which they do bear,
105 All for Elisa in her hand to wear?
          So sweetly they play
          And sing all the way
    That it a heaven is to hear.

    "Lo, how finely the Graces can it foot
110   to the instrument:
    They dancen deftly and singen soot°   *sweetly*
          in their merriment.
    Wants not a fourth Grace to make the dance even?
    Let that room° to my Lady be yeven.°   *place / given*
115   She shall be a Grace,
          To fill the fourth place
    And reign with the rest in heaven.

---

6. Fair and virtuous maid.

"And whither runs this bevy of ladies bright,
  rangéd in a row?
120 They been all Ladies of the Lake[7] behight,°   *called*
   that unto her go.
Chloris,[8] that is the chiefest nymph of all,
Of olive branches bears a coronal.°   *circlet about the head*
   Olives been for peace;[9]
125   When wars do surcease,°   *cease*
Such for a princess been principal.°   *most important*

"Ye shepherds' daughters that dwell on the green,
  hie you° there apace.   *hasten*
Let none come there but that virgins been
130   to adorn her Grace.
And when you come whereas° she is in place,   *where*
See that your rudeness° do not you disgrace: *lack of refinement*
  Bind your fillets° fast   *hair bands*
  And gird in your waist,
135 For more finesse, with a tawdry lace.[1]

"Bring hither the pink and purple columbine
  With gillyflowers;
Bring coronations and sops-in-wine,
  worn of paramours.°   *lovers*
140 Strow me the ground with daffadowndillies,°   *daffodils*
And cowslips, and kingcups,° and lovéd lilies.   *buttercups*
  The pretty pawnce°   *pansy*
  And the chevisance
Shall match with the fair flower delice.[2]

145 "Now rise up, Elisa, decked as thou art
  in royal array.
And now ye dainty damsels may depart,
  each one her way;
I fear I have troubled your troupes° too long. *companies of singers*
150 Let Dame Eliza[3] thank you for her song.
  And if you come hether°   *here*
  When damsons° I gether,   *small, black plums*
I will part them all you among."

7. E. K.: "Ladies of the lake be nymphs. For it was an old opinion amongst ancient heathen that of every spring and fountain was a goddess the sovereign," an opinion fostered by "fine fablers and loud liars," such as the authors of works about King Arthur.
8. E. K.: "The name of a nymph (and signifieth greenness), of whom is said that Zephyrus, the western wind, being in love with her and coveting her to wife, gave her for a dowry the chiefdom and sovereignty of all flowers and green herbs growing on earth." See Ovid, *Fasti*, 5.183–374.
9. Elizabeth was known for her reluctance to entangle England in Continental wars.
1. Lace sold at country fairs, named for St. Audrey, who renounced jewels for necklaces made of cloth.
2. As Brooks-Davies points out in his notes on these lines, pinks were associated with perfection and purple with royalty. Gillyflowers, sops-in-wine, and coronations (all kinds of carnation) are shaped like crowns and, like kingcups, symbolized royalty. The fleur-de-lise represented the French royal family and also Juno, Queen of Heaven. Columbines and carnations implied love, as did daffodils, cowslips, and buttercups (because yellow is Venus's color). Lilies symbolized purity, pansies thought. "Chevisance" represented "achievement." Though "match with the fair flower delice" might suggest Elizabeth as a suitable mate for Anjou, "match with" also meant "to encounter as an adversary."
3. Since the Queen of Shepherds was Elisa, the change of name to Eliza pointed directly to Elizabeth.

Thenot.

And was thilk° same song of Colin's own making?   *this*
155 Ah, foolish boy that is with love yblent;°   *blinded*
Great pity is he be in such taking,°   *so taken*
For nought caren that been so lewdly bent.[4]

Hobbinoll.

Sicker° I hold him for a greater fon[5]   *Certainly*
That loves the thing he cannot purchase.[6]
160 But let us homeward, for night draweth on
And twinkling stars the daylight hence chase.

Thenot's emblem:[7]
O quam te memorem virgo?[8]

Hobbinoll's emblem:
O dea certe.[9]

MICHAEL DRAYTON

Rowland's Song in Praise of the Fairest Beta (1594)[†]

O thou fair silver Thames,[1] O clearest crystal flood,
Beta alone the Phoenix is of all thy watery brood.
The Queen of Virgins only she,
And thou the Queen of Floods shalt be.[2]
5 Let all thy nymphs be joyful then to see this happy day;
Thy Beta now alone shall be the subject of my lay.[3]

With dainty and delightsome strains of sweetest virelayes,[4]
Come, lovely shepherds, sit we down and chant our Beta's praise,
And let us sing so rare a verse,
10 Our Beta's praises to rehearse,
That little birds shall silent be to hear poor shepherds sing,
And rivers backward bend their course and flow unto the spring.

---

4. They care for nothing who are so bent on their own folly.
5. French for "fool." Hobbinoll may mean that Colin (like Anjou) was a fool to desire a virgin so far above him.
6. Colin was poor, and so (for a prince) was Anjou, who continually pressed Elizabeth for money for the Dutch wars.
7. Literally, something "thrown in" as an added ornament. Each eclogue ends with pithy phrases that require the reader to puzzle out their relation to what has come before.
8. "By what name, maiden, shall I remember you?"
9. "Certainly a goddess." Thenot and Hobbinoll take lines from *Aeneid* 1.327–28, where Aeneas has just spoken with Venus, his mother, who came to him disguised as young girl. After she turned away and vanished, he realized who she was. E. K. suggests the meaning that "Eliza is no whit inferior to the majesty of [the goddess]."
†   Copy text: Michael Drayton, *Idea the shepheards garland. Fashioned in nine eglogs. Rowlands sacrifice to the nine Muses* (London: Thomas Woodcocke, 1593; STC 7202), C4r–D1r (Eclog 3, lines 49–120).
1. The river that flows through the city of London, past the seat of government in Westminster.
2. An allusion to growing English sea power after the defeat of the Spanish Armada in 1588.
3. Short lyric poem, meant to be sung.
4. A song, originally consisting of short lines arranged in stanzas with only two rhymes, the end-rhyme of one stanza being the chief one of the next.

Range all thy swans, fair Thames, together on a rank,° *in a line*
And place them duly, one by one, upon thy stately bank.
15 Then set together all agood,° *in good harmony*
Recording° to the silver flood, *Warbling*
And crave the tuneful nightingale to help you with her lay,
The ouzel and the throstlecock,[5] chief music of our May.

O see what troupes of nymphs been sporting on the strands,° *bank*
20 And they been blesséd nymphs of peace, with olives in
   their hands.
How merrily the Muses sing,
That all the flowery meadows ring,
And Beta sits upon the bank in purple and in pall,[6]
And she the Queen of Muses is and wears the coronal.° *small crown*

25 Trim up her golden tresses with Apollo's sacred tree,[7]
O happy sight unto all those that love and honor thee.
The blesséd angels have prepared
A glorious crown for thy reward,
Not such a golden crown as haughty Caesar wears,
30 But such a glittering starry crown as Ariadne bears.

Make her a goodly chapelet° of azured columbine, *wreath or necklace*
And wreath about her coronet with sweetest eglantine.° *wild rose*
Bedeck our Beta all with lilies
And the dainty daffodillies,
35 With roses damask,° white and red, and fairest flower delice, *pink*
With cowslips of Jerusalem and cloves of paradise.[8]

O thou fair torch of heav'n,° the day's most dearest light, *the sun*
And thou bright-shining Cynthia, the glory of the night,
You stars, the eyes of heav'n,
40 And thou the gliding levin,° *lightening*
And thou, O gorgeous Iris, with all strange colors dyed,
When she° streams forth her rays, then dashed is all your *Elizabeth*
   pride.

See how the day stands still, admiring of her face,
And Time, lo,° stretcheth forth her arms thy Beta to embrace. *behold*
45 The Sirens sing sweet lays,
The Tritons sound her praise.
Go pass on Thames and hie° thee fast unto the ocean sea,[9] *run*
And let thy billows there proclaim thy Beta's holy-day.[1]

---

5. The blackbird and the male thrush.
6. Her royal rank is suggested by her dark red robes of pall, a rich, heavy cloth reserved for such garments.
7. The laurel, symbol of victory and excellence in poetry.
8. Symbol of love. Other flowers in the stanza carry symbolic associations: eglantine (or sweetbriar rose) and daffodils with love; lilies with purity; damask roses with the House of Tudor, which reconciled the red rose of Lancaster with the white rose of York at the end of the Wars of the Roses; the fleur-de-lis with the French crown, to which English royalty continued to lay claim because of medieval holdings there; and cowslips and sweet-smelling cloves with the love and pleasures of the heavenly Jerusalem.
9. The sea-river or current named for the god Oceanus was thought to encircle the globe.
1. Holiday, with its original meaning of a day reserved as holy because of its association with a religious figure.

And water thou the blesséd root of that green olive tree,[2]
50 With whose sweet shadow all thy banks with peace preservéd be;
Laurel for poets and conquerors
And myrtle for love's paramours,
That fame may be thy fruit, the boughs preserved by peace,
And let the mournful cypress[3] die, now storms and tempest
    cease.

55 We'll strew the shore with pearl where Beta walks alone,
And we will pave her princely bower with richest Indian stone,
Perfume the air and make it sweet;
For such a goddess it is meet.
For if her eyes for purity contend with Titan's light,°   *light of the sun*
60 No marvel then although they so do dazzle human sight.

Sound out your trumpets, then, from London's stately towers,
To beat the stormy winds aback and calm the raging showers.
Set to° the cornet and the flute,   *Sound*
The orpharion[4] and the lute,
65 And tune the tabor° and the pipe to the sweet violins,   *small drum*
And move the thunder in the air with lowest clarions.°   *narrow trumpets*

Beta, long may thine altars smoke with yearly sacrifice,
And long thy sacred temples may their Sabbaths solemnize.
Thy shepherds watch by day and night,
70 Thy maids attend the holy light,
And thy large empire stretch her arms from east unto the west,
And thou under thy feet mayst tread that foul, sev'n-headed beast.[5]

MARY SIDNEY HERBERT,
COUNTESS OF PEMBROKE

A Dialogue Between Two Shepherds, Thenot and Piers, in Praise of Astraea (ca. 1599)[†]

THEN: I sing divine Astraea's[1] praise.
        O Muses, help my wits to raise,
           And heave my verses higher.
PIERS: Thou need'st the truth but plainly tell,

---

2. Symbol of peace and salvation (see Genesis 8.6–12).
3. Tree associated with death and mourning.
4. Large lute-like instrument with six to nine pairs of strings.
5. The beast on which the Whore of Babylon rides in the Book of Revelation, Chapter 17. Since Rome was built on seven hills, many Protestants interpreted the beast as the Roman Catholic Church. In later editions, Drayton substituted the line "And Albion on the Apennines advance her conquering crest," where Albion is England and the Apennines are mountains in central Italy.
† Copy text: Mary Sidney Herbert, *A Poetical Rapsody*, ed. Francis Davison (London: Iohn Baily, 1602; STC 6373), B5r–B6r. A headnote reads "Made by the excellent lady, the lady Mary, Countess of Pembroke, at the Queen's Majesty's being at her house at   , Anno 15 " (place and date blank, probably because the visit was cancelled).
1. Elizabeth was commonly represented as Astraea, goddess of justice.

5

           Which much I doubt thou canst not well,
              Thou art so oft a liar.

THEN.   If in my song no more I show
           Than heaven and earth and sea do know,
              Then truly I have spoken.

10   PIERS.   Sufficeth not no more to name,
           But being no less, the like, the same,
              Else laws of truth be broken.[2]

THEN.   Then say she is so good, so fair,
           With all the earth she may compare,
15   Not Momus' self denying.

   PIERS.   Compare may think where likeness holds;[3]
           Naught like to her the earth enfolds.
              I looked to find you lying.

THEN.   Astraea sees with Wisdom's sight;
20   Astraea works by Virtue's might,
             And jointly both do stay° in her,   *abide*

   PIERS.   Nay, take from them her hand, her mind,
           The one is lame, the other blind.
              Shall still your lying stain her?°   *dim her excellence*

25   THEN.   Soon as Astraea shows her face,
           Straight every ill avoids the place
              And every good aboundeth.

   PIERS.   Nay, long before her face doth show,
           The last doth come, the first doth go.
30   How loud this lie resoundeth!

THEN.   Astraea is our chiefest joy,
           Our chiefest guard against annoy,
              Our chiefest wealth, our treasure.

   PIERS.   Where chiefest are, three others be,
35   To us none else but only she.
              When will thou speak in measure?

THEN.   Astraea may be justly said
           A field in flowery robe arrayed,
              In season freshly springing.

40   PIERS.   That spring endures but shortest time,
           This never leaves Astraea's clime.[4]
              Thou liest instead of singing.

THEN.   As heavenly light that guides the day,
           Right so doth shine[5] each lovely ray
45   That from Astraea flyeth.

---

2. We leave this riddle and others in the poem to the reader's ingenuity.
3. One who compares may question where your likeness holds true.
4. Astraea was said to have lived on the earth during the Golden Age, when all the year was springlike.
5. Copy text: thine.

PIERS.   Nay, darkness oft that light° enclouds;   *the sun*
         Astraea's beams no darkness shrouds.
         How loudly Thenot lieth!

THEN.   Astraea rightly term I may,
50   A manly palm, a maiden bay,[6]
         Her verdure° never dying.   *springlike vitality*
PIERS.   Palm oft is crooked, bay is low,
         She still° upright, still high doth grow.   *always*
         Good Thenot, leave thy lying.

55 THEN. Then Piers, of friendship tell me why,
         My meaning true, my words should lie
         And strive in vain to raise her?
PIERS.   Words from conceit° do only rise;   *thought*
         About conceit her honor flies.[7]
60   But° silence, naught° can praise her.   *Except / nothing*

ELIZABETH AS PETRARCHAN MISTRESS

Even before the sonnet craze of the 1590s, Elizabeth was idealized as a
modern-day Laura, the unattainable but otherwise largely unknown beauty who
was the object of obsessive desire in the *Rime sparse* (or "scattered rhymes") of
the Italian poet Petrarch. In the two centuries since the poems were first published, the features of the Petrarchan mistress had become conventional. Her
hair was like filaments of gold, her eyes like stars (or suns), her cheeks like
roses, her lips like rubies, and her breasts like bowls of purest alabaster. To the
extent that poets exercised originality, it was in adapting old elements to new
effects. The standard blazon describing the lady from head to foot, for example,
usually began with her eyes, lingered over her face, and then wandered downward. Poets had options, though, as to where to direct their gaze, and some
were more daring than others. The aim was not to capture the appearance of a
living, breathing woman so much as to reflect on an ideal, and the subject was
not so much the lady herself as the inward torments of loving and desiring her
without response. Tormented by fire and ice, the lover felt both ennobled and
enslaved, lifted to heaven and consigned to hell.

From the time of Sir Christopher Hatton's first love letters to the Queen in
the 1570s, courtiers had adopted Petrarchan conventions in addressing Elizabeth. For some, the aim was simply to flatter her and gain her attention. For
others, however, something more complex was involved. As an unmarried
queen, living and working in close quarters with men unused to being ruled by
a woman, Elizabeth needed a code of manners and expectations to keep them
in line. As high-spirited courtiers with a sense of their own importance, they, in
turn, needed a way to enjoy a sense of personal intimacy without calling her
honor into question. Petrarch provided a way to satisfy both needs. Just as
Laura had remained religious, chaste, and independent, so did the Queen. Just
as Petrarch had devoted his life to an unattainable woman, so did the courtiers
who addressed love poems to Elizabeth.

It would be a mistake to press the Petrarchan analogy too far. With her most
intimate favorites, such as Leicester, Ralegh, and Essex, her actions more closely

6. Palm and bay (or laurel) leaves symbolize highest honor.
7. Her honor eludes our ability to conceive.

Caricature of the Petrarchan mistress.

resembled those of a lady in the older tradition of Courtly Love. Far from being cruel or distant, she was constantly in the company of such favorites, encouraging and returning their love and, in the process, forming them, advancing them, and sending them off to serve and defend her state. Accounts of the Accession-Day tilts suggest just how thoroughly such ideals of Courtly Love and chivalry influenced the Queen and the rituals of her Court. Yet even with her most intimate courtiers, the language and conventions of Petrarchan love were also commonly invoked (as in the poems of Ralegh in Parts Six and Eight).

Of lyrics written mainly in the Petrarchan mode, George Puttenham's "Riddle of the Princess Paragon" is among the earliest and the most daring. Depicting Elizabeth as the Fairy Queen, standing naked before the poet's gaze, it is a good example of the freedom to innovate still possible in time worn conventions such as the blazon. Less daring, and less favorable to Elizabeth, was Philip Sidney's song "Now Was Our Heav'nly Vault Deprived of the Light." Written in 1579 or 1580, shortly after Puttenham's poem, it stressed the frustration at the heart of the Petrarchan tradition. Midway through his long pastoral romance, the Old *Arcadia,* Sidney presents a song composed by the melancholy character Philisides, whose name in Greek means "star lover." Since Sidney's name for himself in his later sonnet sequence *Astrophil and Stella* was "Astrophil," which had the same meaning, and since "Philisides" echoes the sound of his own name, the song seems to reflect the poet's own unhappiness at a time when he was stymied in his attempts to gain a major position at Court.

The poem turns on rejection. In an incident resembling the origin of the Trojan War, the goddesses Venus and Diana appoint Philisides to decide which of them is worthiest. He, however, bestows the honor on a woman named Mira ("Wonderful"), on the grounds that she combines the beauty of Venus with the chastity of Diana. The angry goddesses then foretell the fire of desire and the ashes of despair that Mira will inflict on him by rejecting his suits. Several women have been suggested as real-life counterparts to Mira. Since the incident is an adaptation of the Judgment of Paris, and since Elizabeth was a usual subject of such adaptations, it seems likely, however, that Sidney had the Queen in mind. Just as he withdraw from Court in the years 1579–80, when the poem was written, so did Philisides draw back from Mira. He reports that, "having been not only refused all comfort but new quarrels picked against me, I did resolve by perpetual absence to choke mine own dear fortunes."

Although Henry Constable's later sonnet "To the Queen" begins with typical Petrarchan images of her beauty, it too takes an unusual turn. Accusing the Queen of provoking in him the mortal sins of envy and pride, so condemning him to hell, the poet finds himself torn between revering her as an angel and denouncing her as a devil. He resolves his difficulty by invoking the Catholic doctrine of purgatory, seeing Elizabeth as an angel sent to set him ablaze with desire in order to burn away the impurities in his soul. The poem invites comparison with another work that mingles the erotic and the religious, John Lyly's "Ditty" from the Cowdray Entertainment of 1591. In glorifying the Queen, Lyly attributes to her a similarly violent power that only God has, namely to destroy sinful mortals simply by allowing them to gaze directly upon her face.

GEORGE PUTTENHAM

From Partheniads (1579)[†]

Partheniad 7, Euterpê.[1] [A riddle of the princess paragon]

I saw march in a meadow green
A fairer wight° than Fairy Queen,   creature
And as I would approach her near,
Her head is shown like crystal clear.
5 Of silver was her forehead high,
Her brows two bows of ebony.
Her tresses trussed were to behold,
Frizzled° and fine as fringe of gold.   *Tightly curled*
Her eyes, God wot° what stuff they are,   *knows*
10 I durst be sworn each is a star
As clear and bright as to guide
The pilot in his winter tide.
Two lips wrought out of ruby rock,
Like leaves to shut and to unlock,
15 As portal door in prince's chamber;
A golden tongue in mouth of amber,
That oft is heard, but none it seeth;
Without, a guard of ivory teeth,
Even arrayed, and richly, all
20 In scarlet or in fine coral.
Her cheek, her chin, her neck, her nose,
This was a lily, that was a rose.

† Copy text: British Library MS Cotton Vespasian E.VIII, fol. 171r–72v.
1. Each Partheniad has a marginal heading giving its number in the manuscript and the Muse that inspired it. Euterpê is the Muse of Music.

Her hand so white as whale's bone,
Her finger tipped with cassidone.[2]
25 Her bosom, sleek as Paris plaster,
Held up two bowls of alabaster;
Each bias° was a little cherry   *raised part (nipple)*
Or, as I think, a strawberry.
A slender greve,° swifter than roe;°   *leg / deer*
30 A pretty foot to trip and go,
But of a solemn pace pardie[3]
And marching with a majesty.
Her body, shaped as straight as shaft,
Disclosed each limb withouten craft,°   *dissembling, hiding*
35 Save shadowed all, as I could guess,
Under a veil of silk cypress.[4]
From top to toe ye might her see
Timbered and tall as cedar tree,
Whose stately turf[5] exceedeth far
40 All that in frith° and forest are.   *unused pasture*
This marked I well, but lo, anon
Methought, all like a lump of stone
(The stone that doth the steel enchant
The dreadful rock of adamant,[6]
45 And works the ship, as authors speak,
In salt sea many a woeful wreak°),   *harm*
Her heart was hid, none might it see.
Marble or flint folk ween° it be.   *think*
Not flint I trow° (I am a liar)   *believe*
50 But siderite° that feels no fire.   *lodestone*
Now rede° aright and do not miss   *decide*
What jolly[7] dame this lady is.

The assoil.[8]

This flesh and blood, this head, members and heart,
These lively looks, graces, and beauty sheen,°   *resplendent*
55 Make but one mass, by nature and by art
Rare to the earth, rath° to the world seen.   *unexpected*
Would ye fain know her name and see your part?
Hie,° and behold awhile the maiden Queen.   *Hasten*

Partheniad 8, Thalia. [The assoil at large, moralized in three dizains[9]]

A head harbor° of all counsel and wit,   *abode*
Where Science[1] dwells, making a lively sprite°   *spirit*

2. Chalcedony, a translucent white stone.
3. Certainly (literally, "by God").
4. Cobweb lawn, a transparent fabric.
5. Grassy area, metaphor for England.
6. Lodestone, said to have sufficient magnetic attraction to drag ships under.
7. Lively, delightful; fair, amorous; brave, spirited.
8. A riddle or enigma that requires readers to discover its meaning for themselves.
9. Poems of ten lines each; *Thalia*: the Muse of Comedy, a genre that, like the poem, has to do with desire and marriage; *at large*: at length.
1. Knowledge acquired by study.

And Dame Discourse (as in her castle) sit,
Scanning causes by mind and by foresight.
5 A cheer° where Love and Majesty do reign,   *countenance*
Both mild and stern, having some secret might
Twixt hope and dread, in woe and with delight,
Man's heart in hold° and eye for to detain,   *confinement*
Feeding the one with sight in sweet desire,
10 Daunting th' other, by danger,[2] to aspire.

Affable grace, speech eloquent and wise,
Stately presence such as becometh one
Who seems to rule realms by her looks alone
And hath what else Dame Nature could devise
15 To frame a face and corsage° paragon,   *body*
Such as these blessed sprites of paradise°   *angels*
Are wont° to assume, or such as lovers ween   *accustomed*
They see sometimes in sleep and dainty dream,
In female form a goddess and no queen,
20 Fitter to rule a world than a realm.

A constant mind, a courage° chaste and cold,   *disposition*
Where love lodgeth not nor love hath any powers;
Not Venus' brands° nor Cupid can take hold,   *firebrands*
Nor speech prevail, tears, plaint, purple,[3] or gold,
25 Honor n' empire, nor youth in all his flowers.
This wot° ye all full well if I do lie.   *know*
Kings and kings' peers, who have sought far and nigh
(But all in vain) to be her paramours,°   *lovers*
Since two Capets, three Caesars assayed,[4]
30 And bid° repulse of the great Briton[5] maid.   *invited*

SIR PHILIP SIDNEY

From the Old Arcadia (ca. 1579–80)[†]

Now Was Our Heav'nly Vault Deprived of the Light

Now was our heav'nly vault deprivéd of the light
With sun's depart; and now the darkness of the night
Did light those beamy stars, which greater light did dark.°   *darken*
Now each thing that enjoyed that fiery, quick'ning spark
5 (Which life is called) were moved their spirits to repose,
And wanting use of eyes, their eyes began to close.

2. Threat of her power.
3. Color of royalty.
4. In the past, two from the French royal house of Capet (Henry, Duke of Anjou, and his brother, François, Duke of Alençon and later Anjou.) and three imperial heirs (Philip II and his son Don Carlos, descendents of Charles V, and Archduke Charles, son of Ferdinand I) attempted to marry her.
5. British.
† Copy text: Sir Philip Sidney, *The Covntesse of Pembrokes Arcadia* (London: William Ponsonbie, 1590; STC 22539a), Mm8v–Nn3v.

A silence sweet each-where° with one consent[1] embraced   *everywhere*
(A music sweet to one in careful musing[2] placed),
And Mother Earth, now clad in mourning weeds, did breathe
10   A dull desire to kiss the image of our death,[3]
When I, disgracéd wretch, not wretched then, did give
My senses such relief as they which quiet live,
Whose brains broil not in woes nor breasts with beatings ache,
With nature's praise are wont° in safest home to take.   *accustomed*
15   Far from my thoughts was aught° whereto their minds aspire   *anything*
Who under courtly pomps° do hatch a base desire.   *displays*
Free all my powers were from those captiving snares
Which heav'nly purest gifts defile in muddy cares.
Ne° could my soul itself accuse of such a fault   *Nor*
20   As tender conscience might with furious pangs assault.
But like the feeble flower (whose stalk cannot sustain
His weighty top) his top doth downward[4] drooping lean,
Or as the silly[5] bird in well acquainted nest
Doth hide his head with cares but only how° to rest,   *so as*
25   So I, in simple course and unentangled mind,
Did suffer drowsy lids mine eyes, then clear, to blind,
And laying down my head did Nature's rule observe,
Which senses up doth shut, the senses to preserve.
They first their use forgot, then fancies lost their force,
30   Till deadly sleep at length possessed my living corse.°   *corpse*
A living corse I lay; but ah, my wakeful mind
(Which, made of heav'nly stuff, no mortal change doth blind)
Flew up with clear° wings, of fleshly bondage free,   *unencumbered*
And having placed my thoughts, my thoughts thus placéd me.
35   Methought, nay sure I was, I was in fairest wood
Of Samothea[6] land, a land which whilom° stood   *once*
An honor to the world, while honor was their end
And while their line of years they did in virtue spend.
But there I was, and there my calmy° thoughts I fed   *tranquil*
40   On Nature's sweet repast, as healthful senses led.
Her gifts my study was, her beauties were my sport;
My work her works to know, her dwelling my resort:
Those lamps of heav'nly fire to fixéd motion bound,
The ever-turning spheres,[7] the never-moving ground,
45   What essence dest'ny hath, if fortune be or no,
Whence our immortal souls to mortal earth do flow,
What life it is, and how that all these lives do gather,
With outward maker's force, or like an inward father.

---

1. With pun on "concent," meaning a harmony of sounds; see "sweet music" in the next line.
2. Musing filled with cares.
3. Welcome sleep.
4. Copy text: his top downward. Manuscripts show this to be a printer's error.
5. Humble, simple-minded, weak.
6. Archaic name for Britain.
7. Crystal spheres in which it was thought that astral bodies such as the sun and moon were embedded.

Such thoughts, methought, I thought and strained my single°   *solitary*
     mind,
50 Then void of nearer cares, the depth of things to find.
    When lo, with hugest noise (such noise a tower makes
    When it blown down with wind[8] a fall of ruin takes,
    Or such a noise it was as highest thunders send
    Or cannons thunder-like, all shot together, lend),
55 The moon asunder rent,[9] whereout with sudden fall
    (More swift than falcon's stoop° to feeding falconer's call)   *sudden drop*
    There came a chariot fair, by doves and sparrows[1] guided,
60 Whose storm-like course stayed not till hard by me it bided.°   *stopped*
    I, wretch, astonished was and thought the deathful doom[2]
    Of heaven, of earth, of hell, of time and place was come.
    But straight there issued forth two ladies (ladies sure
    They seemed to me) on whom did wait a virgin pure.
65 Strange were the ladies' weeds,° yet more unfit than strange: *clothes*
    The first[3] with clothes tucked up as nymphs in woods do range,
    Tucked up even with the knees, with bow and arrows pressed.[4]
    Her right arm naked was, discovered° was her breast,[5]   *uncovered*
    But heavy was her pace, and such a meager cheer,[6]
70 As little hunting mind (God knows) did there appear.
    The other[7] had, with art more than our women know,
    (As stuff meant for the sale) set out to glaring show
    A wanton woman's face, and with curled knots had twined
    Her hair, which, by the help of painter's cunning, shined.
75 When I such guests did see come out of such a house,
    The mountains great with child, I thought, brought forth a mouse.
    But walking forth, the first thus to the second said,
    "Venus, come on." Said she, "Diane, you are obeyed."
    Those names abashed me much when those great names I heard,
80 Although their fame (me seemed) from truth had greatly jarred.
    As I thus musing stood, Diana called to her
    The waiting nymph,[8] a nymph that did excel as far
    All things that erst° I saw as orient pearls exceed   *at first*
    That which their mother hight or else their silly seed,[9]
85 Indeed a perfect hue, indeed a sweet concent°   *harmony*
    Of all those Graces' gifts the heav'ns have ever lent.
    And so she was attired as one that did not prize
    Too much her peerless parts, nor yet could them despise.
    But called, she came apace, a pace wherein did move

---

8. Some manuscripts: blown up with mine.
9. Here, some manuscripts insert the following: (O gods, O pardon me, / That forced with grief reveals what grievéd eyes did see) / The moon asunder rent; whereat.
1. Birds associated with Venus.
2. The Last Judgment.
3. The Goddess Diana, known as a huntress.
4. The bow and quiver pressed her clothes against her body.
5. She had removed garments that might hinder her shooting.
6. Her face showed little pleasure.
7. Venus.
8. The young woman attending on them.
9. Humble seed pearls; *That . . . hight*: that which is called mother-of-pearl.

90   The band of beauties all, the little world of love.
     And bending humbled eyes (O eyes, the sun of sight),
     She waited mistress' will, who thus disclosed her sprite:[1]
     "Sweet Mira mine," quoth she, "the pleasure of my mind,
     In whom of all my rules the perfect proof I find,
95   To only thee thou seest we grant this special grace
     Us to attend, in this most private time and place.
     Be silent, therefore now, and so be silent still°   *always*
     Of that° thou seest; close up in secret knot thy will."   *that which*
     She answered was with look and well performed behest,
100 And Mira I admired; her shape sank in my breast.
     But thus with ireful eyes and face that shook with spite,
     Diana did begin: "What moved me to invite
     Your presence, sister dear, first to my moony sphere
     And hither now, vouchsafe to take with willing ear.[2]
105 I know full well you know what discord long hath reigned
     Betwixt us two. How much that discord foul hath stained
     Both our estates while each the other did deprave,°   *defame*
     Proof speaks too much to us that feeling trial° have.   *experience*
     Our names are quite forgot, our temples are defaced;
110 Our off'rings spoiled, our priests[3] from priesthood are displaced.
     Is this the fruit of strife? Those thousand churches high,
     Those thousand altars fair now in the dust to lie?
     In mortal minds, our minds but planets' names preserve;
     No knee once bowed, forsooth, for them they say we serve.
115 Are we their servants grown? No doubt a noble stay:[4]
     Celestial pow'rs to worms, Jove's children serve to clay.
     But such they say we be. This praise our discord bred,
     While we for mutual spite a striving passion fed.
     But let us wiser be, and what foul discord brake,
120 So much more strong again let fastest° concord make.   *closest*
     Our years do it require; you see we both do feel
     The weak'ning work of Time's forever-whirling wheel.
     Although we be divine, our grandsire Saturn is
     With age's force decayed, yet once the heav'n was his.
125 And now before we seek by wise Apollo's skill
     Our young years to renew (for so he saith he will),
     Let us a perfect peace between us two resolve,
     Which, lest the ruinous want° of government dissolve,   *lack*
     Let one the princess be, to her the other yield,
130 For vain equality is but contentious field.
     And let her° have the gifts that should in both remain.[5]   *the winner*
     In her let beauty both and chasteness fully reign,

---

1. Spirit, inner feelings.
2. Listen carefully to what led me to invite you, dear sister, first to my lunar sphere and then to the place where we now are.
3. Copy text: priest.
4. Final state.
5. Let her have the attributes that should still be present in each of us.

So as,° if I prevail, you give your gifts to me;   *So that*
If you, on you I lay what in my office be.
135 Now resteth only this: which of us two is she
To whom precédence shall of both accorded be.
For that (so that you like), hereby doth lie a youth"
(She beckoned unto me) "as yet of spotless truth,
Who may this doubt discern;° for better wit than lot[6]   *question resolve*
140 Becometh us; in us Fortune determines not.
This crown of amber fair" (an amber crown she held)
"To worthiest[7] let him give, when both he hath beheld,
And be it as he saith." Venus was glad to hear
Such proffer made, which she well showed with smiling cheer,
145 As though she were the same as when by Paris' doom°   *judgment*
She had chief goddesses in beauty overcome,
And smirkly thus 'gan say, "I never sought debate,
Diana dear; my mind to love and not to hate
Was ever apt; but you my pastimes did despise.
150 I never spited you, but thought you over-wise.
Now° kindness proffered is, none kinder is than I,   *Now that*
And so most ready am this mean° of peace to try.   *middle way*
And let him be our judge; the lad doth please me well."
Thus both did come to me, and both began to tell
155 (For both together spake, each loath to be behind)
That they by solemn oath their deities would bind
To stand unto my will; their will they made me know.
I that was first aghast when first I saw their show,°   *appearance*
Now bolder waxed, waxed proud, that I such sway must bear,
160 For near acquaintance doth diminish reverent fear.
And having bound them fast by Styx° they should obey   *river of hell*
To all what I decreed, did thus my verdict say:
"How ill both you can rule well hath your discord taught;
Ne yet, for aught° I see, your beauties merit aught.   *anything*
165 To yonder nymph, therefore" (to Mira I did point)
"The crown above you both forever I appoint."
I would have spoken out,° but out they both did cry,   *further*
"Fie, fie, what have we done? Ungodly rebel, fie.
But now we needs must yield to that° our oaths require."   *that which*
170 "Yet thou shalt not go free," quoth Venus. "Such a fire
Her beauty kindle shall within thy foolish mind
That thou full oft shalt wish thy judging eyes were blind."
"Nay, then," Diana said, "the chasteness I will give,
In ashes of despair (though burnt), shall make thee live."
175 "Nay, thou," said both, "shalt see such beams shine in her face
That thou shalt never dare seek help of wretched case."[8]
And with that curséd curse away to heav'n they fled,
First having all their gifts upon fair Mira spread.

6. Better human reason than casting lots.
7. In the original Judgment of Paris, which Diana lost, the prize was an orb bearing the inscription "To the most beautiful."
8. Relief from your erotic desire.

The rest I cannot tell, for therewithal I waked
180 And found with deadly fear that all my sinews shaked.
Was it a dream? O dream, how hast thou wrought in me
That I things erst° unseen should first in dreaming see?   *until now*
And thou, O traitor sleep, made for to be our rest,
How hast thou framed the pain wherewith I am oppressed?
185 O coward Cupid, thus dost thou thy honor keep,
Unarmed, alas, unwares° to take a man asleep?   *stealthily*

HENRY CONSTABLE

To the Queen, Touching the Cruel Effects of Her Perfections (ca. 1589)[†]

Most sacred Prince, why should I thee thus praise
Which both of sin and sorrow cause hast been?
Proud hast thou made thy land of such a queen,
Thy neighbors envious of thy happy days.[1]

5   Who never saw the sunshine of thy rays
An everlasting night his life doth ween,°   *believe*
And he whose eyes thy eyes but once have seen
A thousand signs of burning thoughts bewrays.°   *betrays*

Thus sin thou caused, envy, I mean, and pride;
10   Thus fire and darkness do proceed from thee,
The very pains which men in hell abide.

Oh no, not hell, but purgatory this,
Whose souls some say by angels punished be,
For thou art she from whom this torment is.

JOHN LYLY

"A Ditty" from an Entertainment at Cowdray (1591)[‡]

Behold her locks like wires of beaten gold,
    Her eyes like stars that twinkle in the sky,
Her heav'nly face not framed of earthly mold,
    Her voice that sounds Apollo's melody,

---

† Copy text: Henry Constable, *The Poems of Henry Constable*, ed. Joan Grundy (Liverpool: Liverpool University Press, 1960), 138. Used with permission.
1. Pride and envy are the worst of the Seven Deadly Sins.
‡ Copy text: John Lyly, *The speeches and honorable entertainment giuen to the Queenes Maiestie in progresse, at Cowdrey in Sussex, by the right honorable the Lord Montacute. 1591* (London: Thomas Scarlet, 1591; STC 3907.7), A4r–A4v.

5   The miracle of time, the world's story,
     Fortune's queen, Love's treasure, Nature's glory.

   No flattering hope she likes, blind Fortune's bait,
     Nor shadows of delight, fond fancy's glass,°   *mirror*
   Nor charms that do enchant, false art's deceit,
10   Nor fading joys, which time makes swiftly pass,
   But chaste desires, which beateth all these down.
   A goddess' look is worth a monarch's crown.

   Goddess and monarch of this[1] happy isle,
     Vouchsafe this bow,[2] which is an huntress' part.
15 Your eyes are arrows, though they seem to smile,
     Which never glanced but galled° the stateliest hart.[3]   *wounded*
   Strike one, strike all, for none at all can fly.
   They gaze you in the face, although they die.

ELIZABETH AS GODDESS OF THE MOON

After the French marriage negotiations of 1578–82, when it became clear that Elizabeth was unlikely to marry, more and more poets began to represent her as the virgin goddess Diana. Traditionally associated with the moon in all its temperate and distant beauty, Diana went by more than one name, including Cynthia, Phoebe, and Belphoebe (or "beautiful Phoebe"). To writers eager for fresh angles, she was also readily conflated with other ancient moon goddesses: Luna, Selênê, and even Hecate, Queen of the Underworld. Though Spenser, Ralegh, and Lyly had the greatest impact in making imagery of the moon goddess popular, others followed their lead, including writers as various as George Peele, George Chapman, Richard Barnfield, and Ben Jonson.

Because the moon is gentler than the sun and, in its crescent phase, takes the shape of a bow, Diana was also associated with archery and with pleasures of evening after the heat of the day. Sir Walter Ralegh's delicate lyric "Praised be Diana's Fair and Harmless Light" draws on these associations, beginning with imagery of a peaceful, moonlit night and moving to a depiction of Elizabeth pursuing one of her favorite pastimes: hunting deer with her courtiers and maids of honor. The poem ends with more exalted associations. Just as the moon controls the tides, Elizabeth and her navy now govern the seas. As the moon (in the astrological theories of the day) occupies the lowest of the celestial spheres surrounding the earth, conveying light and influence downward from the higher bodies (the sun, the planets, and the stars), the Queen serves as a mediator between the immutable heavens and the mutable order of her kingdom. And as the moon remains beautiful, pure, and unchanging throughout its endless cycles, Elizabeth remains ever the same, despite the harsh vicissitudes of life.

The most famous depiction of Elizabeth as the goddess of the moon is perhaps Spenser's Belphoebe in *The Faerie Queene*. In the poet's prefatory letter to Ralegh, he announces his intention to represent the Queen in at least two ways. As Queen

1. Copy text: his.
2. Grant me sight of your face. In Petrarchan love conventions, the lady's eyebrows are bows and the eye beams flashing from her eyes are arrows, which pass through the beholder's eyes into his heart, carrying with them the image of the beloved. This festers, causing love-sickness and, potentially, death.
3. Male deer, with pun on heart.

of England, the "head" to the "body" of her state, she is to appear in the guise of Gloriana, the Fairy Queen. As a private person, she is to appear as Belphoebe. One of Spenser's signal achievements was to bring the character to life, enduing her not only with the mythic stature of a goddess but also with the feelings and reactions of a mortal woman. When she first enters the poem in Book 2, a cowardly braggart named Braggadoccio has just stolen the horse of one of Spenser's principal heroes, Sir Guyon, and has set out to impersonate a knight. He is accompanied by a fawning sidekick, Trompart, whose role (as his name suggests) is to trumpet his friend's supposed virtues and so conceal Braggadoccio's tendencies to thievery and cowardice. As Belphoebe comes across the pair while she and her maidens are out hunting in the forest, however, the braggart's true character proves impossible to conceal. Some critics see in him a sly, half-concealed representation of the Duke of Anjou served by his emissary Jean de Samier.

In drawing parallels between Elizabeth and Cynthia, no poem displays more learning or ingenuity than George Chapman's *Hymnus in Cynthiam*. Conflating the various moon goddesses in Greek and Roman mythology, he allows them to mingle in a dazzling profusion of images and associations. Immutable but ever changing, ancient but endlessly new, Cynthia represented for Chapman the power of fate itself, the force that moves the tides, controls the earth, and governs the underworld. She could incite war and bring peace, excite hope and plunge the earth into darkness, purge the world of impure desire and defy death by rising again. She was all that is beautiful, majestic, wise—and wisely feared. The fascination of the poem lay in its deft juggling of three intentions: to depict the moon itself in all its power over earthly life, to celebrate its associations in classical myth, and to glorify the Queen as a power worthy of similar veneration. It was flattery, of course, but flattery of strange beauty. Richard Barnfield's *Cynthia*, by contrast, was designed to be simpler, adapting the myth of the Judgment of Paris. It invites comparison with the Masque of the Gods in the Norwich entertainments (printed above in Part Five), George Peele's *Arraignment of Paris* (in Part Six), and Sidney's myth of Mira (in Part Ten), as well as with a well-known 1569 portrait by George Gower entitled "Elizabeth and the Three Goddesses."

So prevalent had associations between the moon and Elizabeth become by the 1590s that, though the anonymous poem "My Thoughts Are Winged with Hopes" has no provable connection with Elizabeth, its employment of the figure could hardly have failed to call her to mind. Sometimes attributed to Ralegh, it mingles praise with complaint, seeing in Cynthia both changeability and beauty. More positive about the Queen, though not about her court, was Ben Jonson's "Hymn" to Cynthia. It was originally sung as part of a satiric play entitled *Cynthia's Revels*, which, among other things, lampooned common varieties of fools and parasites at Court. In contrast to them, Cynthia appears as celestially elevated, pure, and majestic as poetic skill can convey.

SIR WALTER RALEGH

Praised be Diana's Fair and Harmless Light
(ca. 1582–87)[†]

Praised be Diana's fair and harmless light;
Praised be the dews wherewith she moists the ground;

---

† Copy text: *The phoenix nest Built vp wjth the most rare and refined workes of noble men, woorthy knights, gallant gentlemen, masters of arts, and braue schollers*, ed. R. S. (London: Iohn Iackson, 1593; STC 21516), K3r.

Praised be her beams, the glory of the night;
Praised be her power, by which all powers abound.

5   Praised be her nymphs, with whom she decks the woods;
Praised be her knights, in whom true honor lives;
Praised be that force by which she moves the floods;°   *tides*
Let that Diana shine which all these gives.

In heaven, Queen she is among the spheres;
10   In aye,° she mistress-like makes all things pure;   *perpetuity*
Eternity in her oft change she bears;[1]
She beauty is, by her the fair endure.[2]

Time wears her not, she doth his chariot guide;
Mortality below her orb is placed;[3]
15   By her the virtue of the stars down slide;[4]
In her is virtue's perfect image cast.

A knowledge pure it is her worth to know;
With Circes let them dwell that think not so.

EDMUND SPENSER

From The Faerie Queene, Book 2 (1596)[†]

[*Braggadoccio and Trompart encounter Belphoebe*]

Eft° through the thick° they heard one rudely rush,   *Afterward / thicket*
With noise whereof he° from his lofty steed   *Braggadoccio*
Down fell to ground and crept into a bush
To hide his coward head from dying dread.
5   But Trompart stoutly stayed to taken heed
Of what might hap. Eftsoon° there steppéd forth   *Soon after*
A goodly lady clad in hunter's weed,
That seemed to be a woman of great worth
And, by her stately portance,° borne of heavenly birth.   *bearing*

10   Her face so fair as flesh it seeméd not
But heavenly portrait of bright angel's hue,
Clear as the sky, withouten blame or blot,
Through goodly mixture of complexions' dew;[1]
And in her cheeks the vermeil red did show

---

1. The moon's cycle of changes goes on forever, as will the Queen's nature in heaven.
2. As a goddess, she is not simply beautiful; she is beauty itself, embodied in beautiful people.
3. In Ptolemaic cosmology accepted in this period, all things below the sphere of the moon were seen as mutable, all above immutable.
4. The influence of higher astral bodies—the sun, planets, and stars—was thought to pass through the sphere of the moon to earth, where it influenced human destinies.
† Copy text: Edmund Spenser, *The faerie qveene Disposed into twelve bookes, fashioning XII. morall vertues* (London: William Ponsonbie, 1596; STC 23082), P1v–P5r (2.3.21–46).
1. Humors or spirits in the blood, thought to appear in the skin of the face (like "dew"). When the humors are rightly mixed, the complexion is fair and clear.

15   Like roses in a bed of lilies shed,
      The which ambrosial[2] odors from them threw
      And gazers' sense with double pleasure fed,
    Able to heal the sick and to revive the dead.

    In her fair eyes two living lamps did flame,
20   Kindled above at th' heavenly Maker's light,
      And darted fiery beams out of the same,[3]
      So passing persant[4] and so wondrous bright,
      That quite bereaved° the rash beholder's sight.   *took away*
      In them the blinded god° his lustful fire   *Cupid*
25   To kindle oft assayed,° but had no might;   *attempted*
      For with dread majesty and awful ire
    She broke his wanton darts and quenchéd base desire.

    Her ivory forehead, full of bounty brave,
      Like a broad table° did itself dispread   *memorial tablet*
30   For Love his lofty triumphs to engrave
      And write the battles of his great godhead.
      All good and honor might therein be read,
      For there their dwelling was. And when she spake,
      Sweet words, like dropping honey, she did shed,
35   And twixt the pearls and rubins[5] softly brake
    A silver sound that heavenly music seemed to make.

    Upon her eyelids many Graces sate,°   *sat*
      Under the shadow of her even brows,
      Working belgards° and amorous retrait,[6]   *loving looks*
40   And every one her with a grace endows,
      And every one with meekness to her bows.
      So glorious mirror of celestial grace
      And sovereign monument of mortal vows,
      How shall frail pen descrive° her heavenly face,   *write down*
45   For fear through want of skill her beauty to disgrace?

    So fair, and thousand thousand times more fair
      She seemed, when she presented was to sight,
      And was yclad, for heat of scorching air,
      All in a silken camis° lily white,   *light dress*
50   Purfled upon° with many a folded plight,°   *Adorned / pleat*
      Which all above besprinkled was throughout
      With golden aigulets,° that glistered bright   *spangles*
      Like twinkling stars, and all the skirt about
    Was hemmed with golden fringe.[7]

---

2. Fragrant, like the oil used to anoint the gods.
3. It was thought that eyes emit light (the eye beams) as well as take it in.
4. Surpassingly penetrating.
5. Between her teeth and lips (rubies).
6. Portraiture.
7. A half-line, which is quite rare in *The Faerie Queene*.

55 Below her ham[8] her weed° did somewhat train,°   garment / trail
        And her straight legs most bravely were embailed°   encompassed
        In gilden buskins° of costly cordwain,[9]   gilded boots
        All barred with golden bends,° which were entailed°   bands / engraved
        With curious antics[1] and full fair aumailed°   enameled
60   Before they fastened were under her knee
        In a rich jewel, and therein entrailed
        The ends of all their knots, that none might see
How they within their foldings close enwrappéd be.

    Like two fair marble pillars they were seen,
65   Which do the temple of the gods support,
        Whom all the people deck with garlands green
        And honor in their festival resort.
        Those same with stately grace and princely port°   bearing
        She taught to tread, when she herself would grace,
70   But with the woody nymphs when she did play,
        Or when the flying libbard° she did chase,   leopard
She could them nimbly move and after fly apace.[2]

    And in her hand a sharp boar-spear she held,
        And at her back a bow and quiver gay,
75   Stuffed with steel-headed darts, wherewith she quelled
        The savage beasts in her victorious play,
        Knit with a golden baldric,° which forelay   strap
        Athwart her snowy breast and did divide
        Her dainty paps,[3] which like young fruit in May
80   Now little 'gan to swell and, being tied,°   bound up
Through her thin weed their places only signified.

    Her yellow locks crisped, like golden wire,
        About her shoulders weren loosely shed,
        And when the wind amongst them did inspire,
85   They waved like a pennon° wide dispread   slender flag
        And low behind her back were scatteréd;
        And whether art it were or heedless hap,°   accident
        As through the flow'ring forest rash she fled,
        In her rude hairs sweet flowers themselves did lap
90 And flourishing fresh leaves and blossoms did enwrap.

    Such as Diana, by the sandy shore
        Of swift Eurotas or on Cynthus[4] green,
        Where all the nymphs have her unwares forlore,°   unexpectedly lost
        Wandreth alone with bow and arrows keen

8. Thigh, or perhaps back of the knee.
9. Spanish leather.
1. Grotesque forms of plants or animals.
2. Fly after them swiftly.
3. Breasts.
4. Mountain on the island of Delos, birthplace of Apollo and Diana; *Eurotas*: river that flows through Sparta in southern Greece.

95   To seek her game;[5] or as that famous Queen
     Of Amazons,° whom Pyrrhus[6] did destroy   *Penthesilea*
     The day that first of Priam she was seen,
     Did show herself in great triumphant joy
    To succor the weak state of sad afflicted Troy.

100 Such whenas heartless Trompart her did view,
     He was dismayéd in his coward mind,
     And doubted whether he himself should show,
     Or fly away, or bide alone behind.
     Both fear and hope he in her face did find,
105   When she at last him spying thus bespake:
     "Hail, groom. Didst not thou see a bleeding hind,
     Whose right haunch erst° my steadfast arrow strake?   *not long ago*
    If thou didst, tell me, that I may her overtake."

    Wherewith revived, this answer forth he threw:
110   "O goddess (for such I thee take to be,
     For neither doth thy face terrestrial show°   *appear*
     Nor voice sound mortal), I avow to thee
     Such wounded beast as that I did not see
     Sith erst into this forest wild I came.
115   But mote° thy goodlihead° forgive it me   *might / excellence*
     To weet° which of the gods I shall thee name,   *know*
    That unto thee due worship I may rightly frame."

    To whom she thus;° but ere her words ensued,   *addressed herself*
     Unto the bush her eye did sudden glance
120   In which vain Braggadocchio was mewed°   *hidden*
     And saw it stir. She left her piercing lance
     And towards 'gan a deadly shaft advance,[7]
     In mind to mark° the beast. At which sad stour,°   *aim at / danger*
     Trompart forth stepped to stay the mortal chance,
125   Out crying, "O whatever heav'nly pow'r
    Or earthly wight° thou be, withhold this deadly hour.   *creature*

    "O stay thy hand, for yonder is no game
     For thy fierce arrows them to exercise,
     But lo, my lord, my liege, whose warlike name,
130   Is far renowned through many bold emprise,°   *enterprise*
     And now in shade he shrouded yonder lies."
     She stayed. With that he crawled out of his nest,
     Forth creeping on his caitiff° hands and thighs   *vile*
     And, standing stoutly up, his lofty crest
135 Did fiercely shake and rouse, as coming late from rest.

    As fearful fowl that long in secret cave
     For dread of soaring hawk herself hath hid,

---

5. The simile echoes the *Aeneid*, 1.498–99.
6. According to Homer, Achilles, not his son Pyrrhus, killed Penthesilea.
7. Began to aim a deadly arrow toward him.

Not caring how, her silly life to save,
She, her gay painted plumes disorderéd,
140   Seeing at last herself from danger rid,
Peeps forth and soon renews her native pride;
She gins her feathers foul disfiguréd
Proudly to prune and set° on every side,   *preen*
So shakes off shame, ne thinks how erst° she did her hide.   *at first*

145   So when her goodly visage he beheld,
He 'gan himself to vaunt;° but when he viewed   *bear himself proudly*
Those deadly tools which in her hand she held,
Soon into other fits[8] he was transmewed,°   *transmuted*
Till she to him her gracious speech renewed:
150   "All hail, Sir Knight, and well may thee befall,[9]
As all the like° which honor have pursued   *such knights*
Through deeds of arms and prowess martial.
All virtue merits praise, but such the most of all."

To whom he thus: "O fairest under sky,
155   True be thy words and worthy of thy praise,
That warlike feats dost highest glorify.
Therein have I spent all my youthly days,
And many battles fought, and many frays
Throughout the world, whereso they might be found,
160   Endeavoring my dreaded name to raise
Above the moon,[1] that fame may it resound
In her eternal trump with laurel garland[2] crowned.

"But what art thou, O Lady, which dost range
In this wild forest, where no pleasure is,
165   And dost not it for joyous Court exchange,
Amongst thine equal peers, where happy bliss
And all delight does reign much more than this?
There thou mayst love, and dearly lovéd be,
And swim in pleasure, which thou here dost miss.
170   There mayst thou best be seen, and best mayst see.
The wood is fit for beasts, the Court is fit for thee."

"Who so in pomp of proud estate," quoth she,
"Does swim and bathes himself in courtly bliss,
Does waste his days in dark obscurity
175   And in oblivion ever buried is.
Where ease abounds, it's eath° to do amiss.   *easy*
But who° his limbs with labors and his mind   *whoever*
Behaves with cares cannot so easy miss.
Abroad in arms, at home in studious kind,°   *kind of pursuit*
180   Who seeks with painful toil shall Honor soonest find.

8. Sudden moods.
9. Fortune befall you.
1. Beyond the moon, everything was thought to be unchanging.
2. Symbol of highest honor.

"In woods, in waves, in wars she wonts° to dwell   *is accustomed*
    And will be found with peril and with pain,
    Ne can the man that moulds in idle cell,[3]
    Unto her happy mansión attain.
185   Before her gate high God did sweat ordain[4]
    And wakeful watches ever to abide,
    But easy is the way and passage plain
    To Pleasure's palace; it may soon be spied,
And day and night her doors to all stand open wide.[5]

190   "In Prince's court . . ." The rest she would have said
    But that the foolish man, filled with delight
    Of her sweet words that all his sense dismayed°   *overpowered*
    And with her wondrous beauty ravished quite,
    'Gan burn in filthy lust and, leaping light,
195   Thought in his bastard arms her to embrace.
    With that she, swerving back, her javelin bright
    Against him bent° and fiercely did menace,   *turned*
So turnéd her about and fled away apace.°   *swiftly*

Which when the peasant saw, amazed he stood
200   And grievéd at her flight, yet durst he not
    Pursue her steps through wild unknowén wood.
    Besides, he feared her wrath and threatened shot
    Whiles in the bush he lay, not yet forgot,
    Ne cared he greatly for her presence vain
205   But turning said to Trompart, "What foul blot
    Is this to knight, that lady should again
Depart to woods untouched and leave so proud disdain?"

"Perdie,"° said Trompart, "let her pass at will,   *By God*
    Lest by her presence danger mote° befall.   *might*
210   For who can tell (and sure I fear it ill)
    But that she is some pow'r celestial?
    For whiles she spake, her great words did appall
    My feeble courage and my heart oppress,
    That yet I quake and tremble over all."
215   "And I," said Braggadocchio, "thought no less,
When first I heard her horn sound with such ghastliness.

"For from my mother's womb this grace I have
    Me given by eternal destiny,
    That earthly thing may not my courage brave
220   Dismay with fear or cause one foot to fly,
    But either hellish fiends, or pow'rs on high,
    Which was the cause, when erst that horn I heard,
    Weening° it had been thunder in the sky,   *Thinking*

3. Becomes worthless though idleness, like a hermit or monk in his cell.
4. See Genesis 3.19.
5. See Matthew 7.13–14. Elsewhere in the poem, the witch Acrasia (regarded by some as a figure for Mary, Queen of Scots) keeps such an open, idle court.

    I hid myself from it as one affeared,°   *afraid*
225 But when I other knew, myself I boldly reared.

    "But now, for fear of worse that may betide,
       Let us soon hence depart." They soon agree;
       So to his steed he got and 'gan to ride
       As one unfit therefore, that all might see
230   He had not trainéd been in chivalry.
       Which well that valiant courser° did discern,   *warhorse*
       For he despised to tread in due degree[6]
       But chaffed and foamed, with courage fierce and stern,
    And to be eased of that base burden still did earn.°   *yearn*

GEORGE CHAPMAN

From Hymnus in Cynthiam (1594)[†]

    Nature's bright eyesight[1] and the night's fair soul,
    That with thy triple forehead[2] dost control
    Earth, seas, and hell, and art in dignity
    The greatest and swiftest planet in the sky,
5   Peaceful, and warlike, and the power of fate,
    In perfect circle of whose sacred state
    The circles of our hopes are compassed,[3]
    All wisdom, beauty, majesty, and dread
    Wrought in the speaking portrait[4] of thy face:
10   Great Cynthia, rise out of the Latmian palace,[5]
    Wash thy bright body in th'Atlantic streams,
    Put on those robes that are most rich in beams,
    And in thy all-ill-purging purity
    (As if the shady Cytheron[6] did fry
15   In sightful fury of a solemn fire)
    Ascend thy chariot, and make earth admire
    Thy old swift changes, made a young fixed prime.[7]
    O let thy beauty scorch the wings of Time,
    That fluttering he may fall before thine eyes
20   And beat himself to death before he rise.
    And as Heaven's genial parts[8] were cut away

---

6. Go forward in appropriate submission to its master.
† Copy text: George Chapman, Σκὶα Νυκτὸσ: *The shaddovv of night containing two poeticall hymnes, deuised by G. C. Gent.* (London: William Ponsonby, 1594; STC 4990), C2v–C4r.
1. The moon, treated as the "eye of heaven."
2. Cynthia was sometimes equated with Hecate, goddess of Hades (or hell), who was often portrayed with three heads facing in different directions.
3. The circle (here formed by the full moon) symbolized perfection and fulfillment.
4. According to a famous saying that Plutarch attributes to Simonides of Ceos, "poetry is a speaking picture, painting a silent poetry" (*On the Fame of the Athenians,* 3).
5. Mount Latmos in modern Turkey, home of Endymion, with whom the moon goddess spent each night.
6. Island associated with Venus, here portrayed as fiery with desire at the sight of Cynthia.
7. Though old, the Queen is regarded as ageless, like the moon, which continually returns to its prime.
8. Reproductive organs of the god Uranus, cut off by his son Saturn and thought to be composed of "prime" or "universal" matter, the undifferentiated stuff that gave rise to all forms of matter in the world.

By Saturn's hands with adamantine[9] Harpy,
Only to show that, since it was composed
Of universal matter, it enclosed
25 No power to procreate another heaven,[1]
So since that adamantine[2] power is given
To thy chaste hands to cut off all desire
Of fleshly sports and quench to° Cupid's fire,   *quench*
Let it approve:° no change shall take thee hence   *serve as proof*
30 Nor thy throne bear another inference.[3]
For if the envious forehead of the earth
Lour on thy age and claim thee as her birth,[4]
Tapers nor torches nor the forests burning,
Soul-winging music nor tear-stilling° mourning   *distilling*
35 (Used of old Romans and rude Macedons°   *Greeks*
In thy most sad and black discessions°)   *eclipses*
We know can nothing° further thy recall   *in no way*
When Night's dark robes (whose objects blind us all)
Shall celebrate thy change's funeral.[5]

                    *   *   *

40   The pureness of thy never-tainted life,
Scorning the subject title of a wife;
Thy body not composéd in thy birth,
Of such condenséd matter as the earth;
Thy shunning faithless men's society,
45 Betaking thee to hounds and archery,
To deserts and inaccessible hills,[6]
Abhorring pleasure in earth's common ills,
Commit most willing rapes on all our hearts
And make us tremble, lest thy sovereign parts°   *capacities*
50 (The whole preservers of our happiness)
Should yield to change, eclipse, or heaviness.
And as thy changes happen by the sight,
Near or far distance,° of thy father's light,   *distant*
Who (set in absolute remotion°) reaves°   *arising / deprives*
55 Thy face of light and thee all darkened leaves,[7]
So for thy absence, to the shade of death
Our souls fly mourning, wingéd with our breath.

---

9. Adamant was a mythical mineral of supreme hardness, often equated with diamond.
1. Presumably because heaven was not made of the same sort of matter as earth.
2. Adamant was thought to prevent the natural attraction of a lodestone for iron, just as the chastity of Elizabeth (and Cynthia) quenched desire in others.
3. Elizabeth's motto was *Semper eadem* ("Always the same"). Since the Queen is unchanging, she cannot die and her throne will never have to bear another inferred (lit., "brought in") as a successor. Chapman also puns on "inference" as a means for "approving" a conclusion.
4. The image of the moon setting as if it were being buried in the earth seems to counter the claim that Elizabeth is immortal, but as the remainder of the poem suggests, she, like Cynthia, will rise again.
5. The end of her cycle of waxing and waning.
6. Elizabeth, like Cynthia, was fond of hunting and archery.
7. Just as the moon seems dim when the sun is near but bright when it is distant, Elizabeth was hardly seen while her father lived but appears brilliantly now that he is dead. Chapman here follows the tradition that the moon goddess is the daughter, not the sister, of the sun god Apollo.

Then set thy crystal and imperial throne
(Girt in thy chaste and never loosing zone[8])
Gainst Europe's sun[9] directly opposite,
60 And give him darkness that doth threat thy light.

RICHARD BARNFIELD

From Cynthia (1595)[†]

To His Mistress[1]

Bright star of beauty, fairest fair alive,
Rare precedent° of peerless chastity   *Foremost example*
In whom the Muses and the Graces strive
Which shall possess the chiefest part of thee,
5 O let these simple lines accepted be,
    Which here I offer at thy sacred shrine,
    Sacred because sweet beauty is divine.

And though I cannot please each curious ear
With sugared notes of heavenly harmony,
10 Yet if my love shall to thyself appear,
No other muse I will invoke but thee.
And if thou wilt my fair Thalia be,
    I'll sing sweet hymns and praises to thy name
    In that clear temple of eternal fame.

15 But ah, alas, how can mine infant muse,
That never heard of Helicon[2] before,
Perform my promise past when they[3] refuse
Poor shepherd's plaints? Yet will I still adore
Thy sacred name, although I write no more.
20   Yet hope I shall, if this accepted be.
    If not, in silence sleep eternally.

Cynthia

Now was the welkin° all enveloped   *vault of the heavens*
    With dusky mantle of the sable night,
    And Cynthia, lifting up her drooping head,
    Blushed at the beauty of her borrowed light°   *borrowed from the sun*
5   When sleep now summoned every mortal wight.°   *being*

---

8. Belt, referring to orbit of the moon and to a cincture about the Queen's waist, seen as a symbol of her chastity.
9. An allusion to Philip II's royal emblem, which depicted the sun-god in his chariot, bringing light to the world. When the poem was written, England was at war with Spain.
† Copy text: Richard Barnfield, *Cynthia. VVith certaine sonnets, and the legend of Cassandra* (London: Humfrey Lownes, 1595; STC 1484), A4v–B5v.
1. A prologue, addressed to the Queen.
2. Mountain in central Greece sacred to the Muses.
3. Refers to "each curious ear" in the preceding stanza.

Then lo,° methought° I saw, or seemed to see,   *behold / I thought*
An heavenly creature like an angel bright
That in great haste came pacing towards me.
Was never mortal eye beheld so fair a she.

10 "Thou lazy man," quoth she, "what mak'st thou° here,   *are you doing*
Lulled in the lap of honor's enemy?[4]
I here command thee now for to appear
By virtue of love's mickle° majesty   *great*
In yonder wood." Which with her finger she
15 Out-pointing had no sooner turned her face,
And leaving me to muse what she should be,
Yvanishéd into some other place.
But straight, methought, I saw a rout° of heavenly race.   *company*

Down in a dale, hard° by a forest side,   *close*
20 Under the shadow of a lofty pine
Not far from whence a trickling stream did glide,
Did Nature by her secret art combine
A pleasant arbor of a spreading vine,
Wherein Art strove with Nature to compare,[5]
25 That made it rather seem a thing divine,
Being situate all in the open air.
A fairer ne'er was seen, if any seen so fair.

There might one see, and yet not see indeed,[6]
Fresh Flora flourishing in chiefest prime,[7]
30 Arrayéd in all gay and gorgeous weed,°   *attire (with pun)*
The primrose and sweet-smelling eglantine°   *wild rose*
As fitted best, beguiling so the time.
And ever as she went, she strewed the place,
Red roses mixed with daffodillies fine
35 For gods and goddesses that in like case°   *situation*
In this same order sat with ill-beseeming grace.°   *ungracious looks*

First, in a royal chair of massy° gold   *solid*
Barred all about with plates of burning steel
Sat Jupiter, most glorious to behold,
40 And in his hand was placéd Fortune's wheel,
The which he often turned and oft did reel.
And next to him, in grief and jealousy
(If sight may censure° what the heart doth feel),   *judge*
In sad lament was placéd Mercury,
45 That dying seemed to weep, and weeping seemed to die.

On th' other side, above the other twain,
Delighting as it seemed to sit alone,

4. That is, in darkness.
5. Though artificial, the arbor was comparable to a natural glade.
6. Because it was a vision.
7. At the height of springtime ("chiefest prime"), one might see Flora's effects, though not the goddess herself. For the symbolic meaning of the flowers in the staza, see Spenser's "April" eclogue above (in Part Ten), lines 60-63.

Sat Mulciber,° in pride and high disdain,   *Vulcan*
Mounted on high upon a stately throne,
50   And even with that I heard a deadly groan.
Musing at this, and such an uncouth sight,
Not knowing what should make that piteous moan,
I saw three Furies all in armor dight,°   *arrayed*
With every one a lamp and every one a light.

55   I deeméd so, nor was I much deceived,
For pouréd forth in sensual delight
There might I see, of senses quite bereaved,
King Priam's son that Alexander[8] hight,°   *was called*
Wrapped in the mantle of eternal night.°   *the darkness of Hades*
60   And under him, awaiting for his fall,
Sat Shame, here Death, and there sat fell Despite,°   *Contempt*
That with their horror did his heart appall.
Thus was his bliss to bale, his honey turned to gall.

In which delight feeding mine hungry eye,
65   Of two great goddesses[9] a sight I had,
And after them, in wondrous jollity
(As one that inly joyed, so was she glad),
The Queen of Love,° full royally yclad°   *Venus / dressed*
In glist'ring gold and peerless precious stone,
70   There might I spy and her companion bad,
Proud Paris, nephew to Laomedon,
That afterward did cause the death of many a one.

By this[1] the foremost° melting all in tears   *Juno*
And raining down resolvéd pearls in showers
75   'Gan to approach the place of heavenly feres,°   *companions*
And with her weeping watering all their bowers,
Throwing sweet odors on those fading flowers,
At length she them bespake thus mournfully:
"High Jove," quoth she, "and ye celestial powers
80   That here in judgment sit twixt her° and me,   *Venus*
Now listen for a while and judge with equity.[2]

"Sporting ourselves today, as we were wont
(I mean, I,° Pallas, and the Queen of Love),   *Juno*
Intending with Diana for to hunt
85   On Ida[3] mountain top our skill to prove,
A golden ball was trindled° from above,   *rolled*
And on the rind was writ this poesy,
Pulcherimae,[4] for which a while we strove,

8. Alexander is more commonly called Paris.
9. Juno and Minerva (later in the poem called Pallas).
1. At this (the sight of Venus with Alexander).
2. Juno's formal complaint against Venus's conduct continues until line 113.
3. Mountain where Alexander was raised.
4. For the most beautiful.

Each saying she was fairest of the three,
90 When lo, a shepherd's swain[5] not far away we see.

"I spied him first, and spying thus bespake,
    'Shall yonder swain unfold the mystery?'
    'Agreed,' quoth Venus, 'and by Stygian lake,[6]
    To whom he gives the ball so shall it be.'
95 'Nor from his censure will I fly,' quoth she,
    (Pointing to Pallas)[7] 'though I lose the goal.'
    Thus, every one yplaced in her degree,[8]
    The shepherd comes, whose partial eyes 'gan roll,
And on our beauties looked, and of our beauties stole.

100 "I promised wealth, Minerva promised wit
    (She promised wit to him that was unwise),
    But he, fond fool, had soon refuséd it,
    And minding to bestow that glorious prize
    On Venus, that with pleasure might suffice
105 His greedy mind in loose lasciviousness,
    Upon a sudden, wanting° good advice,   *lacking*
    'Hold here,' quoth he. 'This golden ball possess,
Which Paris gives to thee for meed° of worthiness.'   *reward*

"Thus have I showed the sum of all my suit,
110 And as a plaintiff here appeal to thee
    And to the rest,[9] whose folly I impute
    To filthy lust and partiality
    That made him judge amiss." "And so do we,"
    Quoth Pallas. Venus: "Nor will I gainsay,
115 Although it's mine by right, yet willingly,
    I here disclaim my title and obey."
When silence being made, Jove thus began to say:

"Thou, Venus, art my darling; thou my dear,
    Minerva; thee° my sister and my wife,   *Juno*
120 So that of all a due respect I bear,
    Assigned as one to end this doubtful strife
    Touching your form, your fame, your love, your life.
    Beauty is vain, much like a gloomy° light,   *dim*
    And, wanting° wit, is counted but a trife,°   *lacking / trifle*
125 Especially when honor's put to flight.
Thus of a lovely soon becomes a loathly sight.

"Wit without wealth is bad, yet counted good.   *thought just as good*
    Wealth wanting wisdom's worse, yet deemed as well,°

---

5. Paris, represented as a shepherd's servant.
6. Pool in the classical underworld formed by the river Styx.
7. Juno points to Pallas as she quotes her words.
8. Ordered according to rank.
9. The rest of the gods hearing the case, who had often proved vulnerable to the erotic desire represented by Venus.

From whence (for ay°) doth flow, as from a flood,   *forever*
130   A pleasant poison and a heavenly hell,
       Where mortal men do covet still to dwell.
       Yet one there is to virtue so inclined
       That, as for majesty, she bears the bell,[1]
       So, in the truth, who tries° her princely mind   *examines*
135 Both wisdom, beauty, wealth, and all in her shall find.

       In western world, amidst the ocean main,
       In complete virtue shining like the sun
       In great renown, a maiden queen doth reign,
       Whose royal race, in ruin first begun,[2]
140   Till heav'n's bright lamps° dissolve shall ne'er be done,   *the stars*
       In whose fair eyes love linked with virtues been
       In everlasting peace and union,
       Which sweet consort° in her full well beseem,°   *harmony / are fitting*
Of bounty and of beauty fairest Fairy Queen.[3]

145 And to conclude, the gifts in her yfound
       Are all so noble, royal, and so rare,
       That more and more in her they do abound,
       In her, most peerless prince without compare,
       Endowing still her mind with virtuous care,
150   That through the world (so wide), the flying fame
       (And name that Envy's self cannot impair)
       Is blown of this fair queen, this gorgeous dame,
Fame borrowing all men's mouths to royalize the same."

       And with this sentence Jupiter did end.
155   "This is the prick,"[4] quoth he, "this is the praise,
       To whom this° as a present I will send,   *the golden ball*
       That shameth Cynthia in her silver rays,
       If so you three this deed do not displease."
       Then one, and all, and every one of them:
160   "To her that is the honor of her days,
       A second Judith in Jerusalem,[5]
To her we send this pearl,[6] this jewel, and this gem."

       Then called he up the wingéd Mercury,
       The mighty messenger of gods enrolled,°   *assigned as*
165   And bade him hither° hastily to hie,°   *to England / run*
       Whom tended by her nymphs he should behold
       Like pearls ycouched° all in shining gold.   *set*
       And ev'n with that, from pleasant slumbering sleep,

1. The leader of the sheep was given a bell so that the wanderings of the flock could be tracked, even at night.
2. A reference to the defeat of the Britons (Elizabeth's Tudor ancestors) by the Anglo-Saxons.
3. After publication of Spenser's *Faerie Queene*, a common figure for Elizabeth.
4. The target at which all others aim.
5. To many Protestants, the English were the new Chosen People and London the new Jerusalem.
6. Elizabeth's favorite jewel was the pearl, symbol of the Kingdom of God.

Desiring much these wonders to unfold,°   *recount*
170   I, wakening when Aurora 'gan to peep,
Deprived so soon of my sweet dream 'gan almost weep.

The Conclusion

Thus, sacred virgin, Muse of Chastity,°   *Elizabeth*
This difference is betwixt the moon and thee:
She shines by night, but thou by day dost shine;
175   She monthly changeth, thou dost ne'er decline.
And as the sun to her doth lend his light,
So he by thee is only made so bright.
Yet neither sun nor moon thou canst be named
Because thy light hath both their beauties shamed.
180   Then, since an heav'nly name doth thee befall,
Thou Virgo[7] art (if any sign at all).

Finis.

ANONYMOUS

My Thoughts Are Winged with Hopes (1597)[†]

My Thoughts are winged with[1] Hopes, my Hopes with Love.
Mount, Love, unto the Moon in clearest night
And say, as she doth in the heavens move,
In earth so wanes and waxeth my delight.
5   And whisper this but softly in her ears:
     Hope oft doth hang the head, and trust shed tears.

And you, my Thoughts, that some mistrust do carry,
If for mistrust my mistress do you blame,
Say, though you alter, yet you do not vary,
10   As she doth change and yet remain the same.[2]
Distrust doth enter hearts, but not infect,°   *cause disease*
     And love is sweetest seasoned with suspect.°   *suspicion*

If she for this with clouds do mask her eyes
And make the heavens dark with her disdain,
15   With windy sighs disperse them in the skies,
Or with thy tears dissolve them into rain.
Thoughts, Hopes, and Love, return to me no more
     Till Cynthia shine as she hath done before.

---

7. The constellation identified with Astraea, goddess of justice.
† Copy text: John Dowland, *The first booke of songes or ayres of fowre partes with tableture for the lute* (London: Peter Short, 1597; STC 7091), B1v–B2r. The song is printed with musical score.
1. Carried swiftly by.
2. Though the moon changes in appearance, in its essence it remains the same.

BEN JONSON

"Hymn" to Cynthia (1601)†

[Hesperus¹ sings:]

Queen and huntress,² chaste, and fair,
Now the sun is laid to sleep;
Seated in thy silver chair,
State in wonted° manner keep.   *accustomed*
5 Hesperus entreats thy light,
Goddess excellently bright.

Earth, let not thy envious shade
Dare itself to interpose;
Cynthia's shining orb was made
10 Heaven to clear when day did close.
Bless us then with wishéd sight,
Goddess excellently bright.

Lay thy bow of pearl apart
And thy crystal-shining quiver;
15 Give unto the flying hart°   *escaping deer (with pun)*
Space to breathe, how short soever.
Thou that mak'st a day of night,
Goddess excellently bright.

ELIZABETH AS THE FAIRY QUEEN

When Edmund Spenser's *Faerie Queene* was first published, it included seven "commendatory verses" by various authors. Two were by the poet's friend Sir Walter Ralegh, who had arranged an audience with Queen Elizabeth at which Spenser read from his great romance. Ralegh's sonnet "A Vision upon This Conceit of the Fairy Queen" compares Gloriana, the central figure in the work, with Petrarch's Laura. Here, however, Laura lies forgotten in her tomb, supplanted by Spenser's Fairy Queen as the most celebrated subject of love poetry of the day.

Spenser himself followed a much less obvious strategy, never actually representing Gloriana, though his romance is ostensibly about her. She is mentioned only in flashbacks, mostly in scenes where she sends the various heroes of the book out on their quests. Besides these, the most important representation of Gloriana in *The Faerie Queene* appears in a story told by the central hero, Prince Arthur. Having fallen in love with her in a dream, he set out to find her, encountering all sorts of adventures on the quest but never her. The dream of Gloriana as a queen who is as unattainable as she is erotically enticing thus hangs over the entire work. A dedicatory letter from Spenser to Ralegh explains that Arthur is destined to fulfill his quest and marry her. In the unfinished epic that has come down to us, however, that goal still lies in the future, apparently to be fulfilled in the concluding book.

† Copy text: Ben Jonson, *The fountaine of selfe-loue. Or Cynthias reuels* (London: Walter Burre, 1601; *STC* 14773), K1v (5.1.1–18).
1. The character in the play who sings the song is named after the planet Venus, seen at dawn as the "morning star."
2. Elizabeth, like the goddess Diana, was famous for her love of hunting.

It may be that the prolonged quest is a figure for the painfully slow process of bringing about the marriage between the Queen and her people that Elizabeth herself claimed to have consummated when she first came to the throne. If so, Spenser saw many impediments to be overcome before the kingdom was truly united behind her. Much the same point is made in another vision in the poem, that of the Red Cross Knight in Book 1, who catches sight of Gloriana's city of Cleopolis from the Hill of Contemplation in the episode where he learns his true identity, that of St. George, Patron Saint of England. Although he gazes longingly toward Cleopolis and toward his more distant home, the Heavenly Jerusalem, he never reaches either in the poem as Spenser left it at his death.

A final glimpse of Spenser's feelings toward his Fairy Queen may be found in his sonnet sequence *Amoretti*. In recounting his successful courtship of his second wife, Elizabeth Boyle, the poet recalls her initial aloofness and cruelty, depicting her as a Petrarchan lady. Later, however, as she gradually warms to his attentions, she steps out of her traditional role and accepts him. Sonnets 74 and 80 celebrate this last stage in the wooing with reference to the other Petrarchan lady whom Spenser courted in the 1590s, Queen Elizabeth. With her, he seems to have had less success, for the proem to Book 4 of *The Faerie Queene* suggests trouble at Court over his publication of the first three books some years earlier. By the time he came to write the last complete part of his romance (Book 6, the Legend of Courtesy), he had stopped including figures of Elizabeth in the action entirely. Just when one would expect the virtues of the Court to be most central, he turned instead to those of the world of ordinary people, taking common shepherds as illustrations of the life well lived. It is hard not to suppose that, when the poet died three years later, he was no longer as enchanted by his Fairy Queen as he once had been.

SIR WALTER RALEGH

A Vision upon This Conceit of the Fairy Queen (1590)[†]

Methought I saw the grave where Laura[1] lay,
Within that temple where the vestal flame[2]
Was wont to burn, and passing by that way
To see that buried dust of living fame,
5   Whose tomb fair Love and fairer Virtue kept,
All suddenly I saw the Fairy Queen,
At whose approach the soul of Petrarch wept,
And from thenceforth those graces[3] were not seen,
For they this queen attended, in whose stead
10   Oblivion laid him down on Laura's hearse.
Hereat[4] the hardest stones were seen to bleed,
And groans of buried ghosts the heavens did pierce,
     Where Homer's sprite° did tremble all for grief   *spirit*
     And cursed th' access of that celestial thief.[5]

†   Copy text: Sir Walter Ralegh, commendatory sonnet in Edmund Spenser, *The faerie qveene Disposed into twelue books, fashioning XII. morall vertues* (London: William Ponsonbie, 1590; STC 23081), Pp3v.
1. The chaste and distant lady idealized in Petrarch's *Rime* (or *Canzonieri*).
2. The sacred fire in the ancient Roman Temple of Vesta, which was tended by priestesses pledged to lifelong virginity. Laura was not a virgin but the wife of another man.
3. That is, Love and Virtue.
4. At the publication of *The Faerie Queene*.
5. Spenser's Gloriana, Queen of the Fairies, who, according to Ralegh, has stolen not only Laura's glory, but also Homer's, since Spenser's epic is greater than his; *th'access*: accession to the throne.

EDMUND SPENSER

From The Faerie Queene, Book 1 (1596)†

[*Prince Arthur's vision of Gloriana*]

   "Well worthy imp,"° said then the lady gent,[1]   *offspring*
     "And pupil fit for such a tutor's hand.[2]
     But what adventure, or what high intent,
     Hath brought you hither into fairyland
5   Aread,° Prince Arthur, crown of martial band?"[3]   *Make known*
     "Full hard it is," quoth he, "to read aright
     The course of heavenly cause or understand
     The secret meaning of th' eternal might
That rules men's ways and rules the thoughts of living wight.°   *being*

10 "For whether He through fatal deep foresight
     Me hither sent for cause to me unguessed,
     Or that fresh bleeding wound which day and night
     Whilom° doth rankle in my riven breast,   *At times*
     With forcéd fury° following His behest,   *ungovernable passion*
15   Me hither brought by ways yet never found
     You to have helped, I hold myself yet blest."
     "Ah, courteous knight," quoth she, "what secret wound
Could ever find[4] to grieve the gentlest heart on ground?"°   *earth*

   "Dear Dame," quoth he, "you sleeping sparks awake
20   Which, troubled once, into huge flames will grow,
     Ne° ever will their fervent fury slake   *Nor*
     Till living moisture into smoke do flow
     And wasted life do lie in ashes low.
     Yet sithens° silence lesseneth not my fire,   *since*
25   But told it flames and hidden it does glow,
     I will reveal what you so much desire.
Ah Love, lay down thy bow the whiles I may respire.[5]

   "It was in freshest flower of youthly years,
     When courage first does creep in manly chest,
30   Then first the coal of kindly° heat appears   *natural*
     To kindle love in every living breast;
     But me had warned old Timon's wise behest[6]
     Those creeping flames by reason to subdue
     Before their rage grew to so great unrest

---

† Copy text: Edmund Spenser, *The faerie qveene Disposed into twelue bookes, fashioning XII. morall vertues* (London: William Ponsonbie, 1596; STC 23082), H5v–H7r and K4v–K5v (1.9.6–16 and 1.10.55–61).
1. Noble lady, Una, the heroine of Book 1. Arthur has just came to assist her in a time of trouble.
2. Arthur was educated by the magician Merlin.
3. Most honored of knights.
4. Find the way.
5. While I catch my breath.
6. Old Timon's wise behest had warned me.

35   As miserable lovers use to rue,
      Which still wax° old in woe whiles woe still waxeth new.   *grow*

      That idle name of love and lover's life
          As loss of time and virtue's enemy
          I ever scorned and joyed to stir up strife
40   In middest of their mournful tragedy,
          Ay wont° to laugh when them I heard to cry   *Always accustomed*
          And blow the fire which them to ashes brent.°   *burnt*
          Their god° himself, grieved at my liberty,   *Cupid*
          Shot many a dart at me with fierce intent,
45   But I them warded all with wary government.°   *self-control*

      But all in vain; no fort can be so strong,
          Ne fleshly breast can arméd be so sound,
          But will at last be won with batt'ry long
          Or unawares at disadvantage found.
50   Nothing is sure that grows on earthly ground,
          And who° most trusts in arm of fleshly might   *he who*
          And boasts in beauty's chain not to be bound
          Doth soonest fall in disadvent'rous° fight   *unfortunate*
      And yields his caitiff° neck to victor's most despite.[7]   *captive*

55   Ensample make of him,[8] your hapless° joy,   *luckless*
          And of myself now mated,[9] as ye see,
          Whose prouder vaunt° that proud avenging boy°   *boast / Cupid*
          Did soon pluck down and curbed my liberty.
          For on a day, pricked forth with jollity[1]
60   Of looser[2] life and heat of hardiment,°   *boldness*
          Ranging the forest wide on courser° free,   *war horse*
          The fields, the floods, the heavens with one consent
      Did seem to laugh at me and favor mine intent.

      Fore-wearied with my sports, I did alight
65   From lofty steed and down to sleep me laid;[3]
          The verdant grass my couch did goodly dight,°   *adorn*
          And pillow was my helmet fair displayed.
          Whiles every sense the humor sweet embayed[4]
          And slumbering soft my heart did steal away,
70   Me seeméd[5] by my side a royal maid
          Her dainty limbs full softly down did lay;
      So fair a creature yet saw never sunny day.

7. Utmost disdain.
8. Una's defender in the main quest of Book 1, the Red Cross Knight. Supposing that Una has
   betrayed him with another man, he for a time becomes emotionally involved with the enchantress
   Duessa.
9. Overthrown; also paired with a mate and checkmated by a queen.
1. Spurred forth by high spirits, erotic desire, or presumption. "Pricked" is also a sexual pun.
2. More free or wanton.
3. The dream vision of the Fairy Queen is based on Chaucer's *Canterbury Tales*, "The Tale of Sir
   Thopas," 778–96.
4. While sweet spirits in the blood suffused every sense.
5. It seemed to me that.

Most goodly glee and lovely blandishment°   *allurement*
   She to me made, and bade me love her dear,
75 For dearly sure her love was to me bent,
   As when just° time expired should appear.   *due*
   But whether dreams delude or true it were,
   Was never heart so ravished with delight,
   Ne living man like words did ever hear
80 As she to me delivered all that night,
And at her parting said she Queen of Fairies hight.°   *was called*

When I awoke, and found her place devoid,
   And naught but pressèd grass where she had lyen,
   I sorrowed all so much as erst° I joyed   *at first*
85 And washed all her place with watery eyen.°   *eyes*
   From that day forth I loved that face divine;
   From that day forth I cast in careful mind[6]
   To seek her out with labor and long tine°   *affliction*
   And never vow° to rest till her I find.   *vow never*
90 Nine months I seek in vain, yet nill° that vow unbind."   *will not*

Thus as he spoke, his visage waxèd pale,
   And change of hue great passion did bewray,°   *reveal*
   Yet still he strove to cloak his inward bale°   *suffering*
   And hide the smoke that did his fire display,
95 Till gentle Una thus to him 'gan say,
   "O happy Queen of Fairies, that hast found
   'Mongst many one that with his prowess may
   Defend thine honor and thy foes confound.
True loves are often sown but seldom grow on ground."

[The Red Cross Knight's vision of the New Jerusalem and of Gloriana's city of Cleopolis]

From thence, far off he[7] unto him did show
   A little path that was both steep and long,
   Which to a goodly city led his view,
   Whose walls and towers were builded high and strong
   Of pearl and precious stone,[8] that earthly tongue
5 Cannot describe nor wit of man can tell,
   Too high a ditty for my simple song.
   The City of the Great King[9] hight it° well,   *it was called*
Wherein eternal peace and happiness doth dwell.

10 As he thereon stood gazing, he might see
   The blessèd angels to and fro descend

---

6. Sought with a mind full of cares.
7. The allegorical figure Contemplation, who in Canto 10 briefly serves as guide to Red Cross, the hero of Book 1.
8. See the scriptural descriptions of the New Jerusalem (Revelation 21.10–22:5; Hebrews 12.22–24).
9. That is, city of the Christ (Psalm 48.2).

From highest heav'n[1] in gladsome company
And with great joy into that city wend,
As commonly as friend does with his friend,[2]
15   Whereat he wondered much and gan enquire
What stately building durst so high extend
Her lofty towers unto the starry sphere
And what unknown nation there empeopled° were.   *made citizens*

20   "Fair knight," quoth he,° "Jerusalem that is,   *Contemplation*
The New Jerusalem that God has built
For those to dwell in that are chosen His,
His Chosen People,[3] purged from sinful guilt
With piteous blood, which cruelly was spilt
25   On cursed tree,° of that unspotted Lamb   *the cross*
That for the sins of all the world was kilt.[4]
Now are they saints[5] all in that city sam,°   *together*
More dear unto their God than younglings to their dam."[6]

"Till now," said then the knight, "I weenéd° well   *believed*
30   That great Cleopolis,[7] where I have been,
In which that fairest Faery Queen[8] doth dwell,
The fairest city was that might be seen,
And that bright tower all built of crystal clean,
Panthea,[9] seemed the brightest thing that was.
35   But now by proof all otherwise I ween,
For this great city that does far surpass,
And this bright angel's tower quite dims that tower of glass."[1]

"Most true," then said the holy agéd man,
"Yet is Cleopolis for earthly fame
40   The fairest piece that eye beholden can
And well beseems all knights of noble name,
That covet in th' immortal book of fame
To be eternized, that same to haunt
And doen their service to that sovereign dame,°   *the Fairy Queen*
45   That glory does to them for guerdon graunt,°   *grant for reward*
For she is heav'nly born and heav'n may justly vaunt.°   *boast*

1. See Jacob's dream-vision of the ladder from earth to heaven (Genesis 28.12). See also John 1.51, in which Christ prophesies that his disciples will one day see the heavens open and angels ascend and descend upon him.
2. Moses's intimacy with God is described in similar terms (Exodus 33.11).
3. See 1 Peter 2.9; Revelation 17.14.
4. Killed. Jesus Christ is the promised sacrificial lamb, whose death on the cross atoned for the sins of the world (John 1.29; Hebrews 1.3–4; 1 Peter 1.17–21 and 2.24).
5. Whereas Catholics tended to regard as saints those canonized by the Church, Protestants used the term of all those redeemed through faith.
6. Young lambs to their mother.
7. City of Glory. In the poet's general allegorical intention, this is the community of righteous fame sought by all Christian knights. In his particular intention, it is London or Westminster.
8. Spenser allegorizes Elizabeth in a number of characters, depending on the royal function he has in mind. The Fairy Queen represents her as a monarch and a figure for earthly glory.
9. Greek for "All sight," a reference to the fact that it is built of glass and so allows clear vision of the surrounding world. The New Jerusalem is also said to be "clear as crystal" (Revelation 21.11).
1. See 1 Corinthians 13.12: "For now [on earth] we see through a glass darkly."

"And thou fair imp,° sprung out from English race,   *offspring*
  How ever now accounted elfin's son,[2]
  Well worthy dost thy service for her grace
50 To aid a virgin desolate foredone.[3]
  But when thou famous victory hast won
  And high amongst all knights hast hung thy shield,
  Thenceforth the suit° of earthly conquest shun   *pursuit*
  And wash thy hands from guilt of bloody field,
55 For blood can naught° but sin, and wars but sorrows, yield.   *nothing*

"Then seek this path, that I to thee presage,
  Which after all to heaven shall thee send.
  Then peaceably to thy painful pilgrimage
  To yonder same Jerusalem do bend,°   *turn your steps*
60 Where is for thee ordained a blessèd end;
  For thou amongst those saints whom thou doest see
  Shalt be a saint and thine own nation's friend
  And patron. Thou Saint George shalt callèd be,
Saint George of merry England, the sign[4] of victory.

From Amoretti (1595)[†]

Sonnet 74 [Most Happy Letters Framed by Skillful Trade]

Most happy letters framed by skillful trade°   *method*
  With which that happy name was first designed,
  The which three times[1] thrise happy hath me made
  With gifts of body, fortune, and of mind.
5 The first my being to me gave by kind,°   *nature*
  From mother's womb derived by due descent.
  The second is my sovereign queen most kind,
  That honor and large riches to me lent.
The third my love, my life's last ornament,
10 By whom my spirit out of dust was raised[2]
  To speak her praise and glory excellent,
  Of all alive most worthy to be praised.
Ye three Elizabeths forever live
That three such graces[3] did unto me give.

2. Regarded as an elf's son. Red Cross was stolen by fairies at his birth and raised in ignorance of his true lineage. In this episode, Contemplation tells him for the first time his true name of George, his English parentage, and his destiny to destroy the dragon afflicting Una's kingdom and become the Patron Saint of England.
3. Una ("one"), figure of the one true (Protestant) English Church and of Elizabeth as its defender following the harsh reign of her Catholic sister Mary. The dragon afflicting Una and her parents is, in one of its allegorical meanings, the Catholic Church.
4. Symbol. The Tudors displayed the red cross of St. George on their battle flags.
† Copy text: Edmund Spenser, *Amoretti and Epithalamion* (London: William Ponsonby, 1595; STC 23076), E6v, F1v.
1. The poet's mother, wife, and queen were all named Elizabeth.
2. A restoration of order in the original ingredients of human life, spirit and dust (Genesis 2.7).
3. Life, riches, and love. "Grace" here means "gift," though there is a suggestion that the three ladies are themselves gifts of the goddesses known as the Graces.

Sonnet 80 [After So Long a Race As I Have Run]

After so long a race as I have run
  Through fairy land, which those six books compile,
  Give leave to rest me, being half fordone,°   *exhausted*
  And gather to myself new breath awhile.
Then as a steed refreshéd after toil,
  Out of my prison I will break anew
  And stoutly will that second work[4] assoil,°   *discharge*
5   With strong endeavor and attention due.
Till then give leave to me in pleasant mew[5]
  To sport my muse and sing my love's sweet praise,
  The contemplation of whose heavenly hue°   *form*
  My spirit to an higher pitch[6] will raise.
10   But let her praises yet be low and mean,
  Fit for the handmaid of the Fairy Queen.

ELIZABETH AS THE GODDESS OF JUSTICE

The mythic figure of Astraea held special fascination for late Elizabethan poets. As the goddess of justice and one of the deities who presided over the unspoiled world at the beginning of time, she represented everything good that had been lost in subsequent ages. According to the most influential collection of classical myths of the day, Ovid's *Metamorphoses*, the Golden Age had been one in which food was plentiful and peace reigned. In the Silver Age, people began to till the ground and build houses, and in the Ages of Bronze and Iron, they had become increasingly possessive and violent, devising weapons of war to seize what they wanted. As injustice grew, Astraea departed from the earth and was transformed by Jupiter into the constellation Virgo. Since legend had it that she would return to usher in a new Golden Age, it was natural to associate the relative peace, justice, and prosperity of Elizabeth's reign with that return.

In George Peele's *Descensus Astraea*, a pageant written for the inauguration of William Webb as Mayor of London in 1591, this tradition was invoked to celebrate both the government of the Mayor and that of the Queen he served. By contrast, Spenser's "Legend of Justice" in *The Faerie Queene* was more guarded in its assessment. Set in the Age of Stone, it depicts a time so far declined from the world's first perfection that little goodness remains. Since astronomers first wrote of the stars and planets, the skies themselves have altered, with the signs of the zodiac shifting their places in the night sky and exerting disordered influences on the earth. In consequence, everything has gone awry. Animals now kill one another, and what people used to call vice is now called virtue.

In recounting all that has gone wrong, Spenser brings in the myth of Astraea, suggesting that, before she departed for heaven, she selected a young man, Sir Artegall, to be her knight and restore order on the earth. Book 5, which is

---

4. The writing of the remaining six books in Spenser's original plan. After the first six books, he lived to complete only a short fragment of Book 7.
5. Cage where birds were confined for breeding or fattening.
6. Height. In falconry, the altitude to which a bird soars before swooping down on its prey.

devoted to his quest, begins with the history of the world's decline and of the goddess's early training of Artegall, who represents the English government in its attempts to establish a just order in Ireland and other troubled places. The world of Book 5 remains, however, a violent and treacherous place. If the dawn of a new Golden Age has occurred, it is only in its first light, and Astraea's return has not yet come to pass.

For John Davies, the state of the contemporary world was little better, at least in his epigrams, where the language was so acerbic and sexually suggestive that the poems were called in by church authorities and burned. In his later volume *Hymns of Astraea,* the image of the age was more elevated. Depicting all creation standing in wonder at England's queen, the work begins by asserting what Spenser never does, namely that Elizabeth has brought back the Golden Age. Order has been restored to the birds, the flowers, and even the sun, presiding over the months of seedtime and harvest, which all proclaim her glory. The collection ends by praising the Queen for her outward form and goodness as well as for her heart and mind. In a final, cocky poem entitled "To Envy," Davies casts scorn on other poets who have written about the Queen, boasting of his own poem that "The pomp of coronation / Hath not such power her fame to spread." Despite the virtuosity required to write so many acrostics spelling out "Elisabetha Regina" in a complex rhyme scheme, the poems achieve a remarkable sense of ease and delicacy.

GEORGE PEELE

From Descensus Astraeae (1591)[†]

The Presenter's Speech:

See, lovely lords, and you, my Lord,° behold	*the Mayor*
How Time hath turned his restless wheel about	
And made the silver moon and heaven's bright eye	
Gallop the zodiac[1] and end the year,	
5 Whose revolution now begets anew	
The days that have created° and confirmed	*raised to office*
A worthy governor for London's good,	
To underbear,° under his sovereign's sway,	*lend support to*
Unpartial justice' beam, and weaved a web[2]	
10 For your content and her command in all.	
You citizens of this metapolis,°	*metropolis*
Whose honor and whose oath to gratulate,°	*celebrate*
Lordings,° behold what emblem[3] I present:	*Gentlemen*

Astraea, daughter of the immortal Jove,
15 Great Jove, defender of this ancient town,
Descended of the Trojan Brutus' line,

[†] Copy text: George Peele, *Descensus Astraeae, the Device of a Pageant, borne before M. William Web, Lord Maior of the Citie of London* (London: William Wright, [1591]; STC 19532), A2r–A4v.

1. Hasten the annual procession of constellations in the night sky.
2. One of the poet's several puns on the Lord Mayor's name; *justice' beam:* the part of the scales of justice from which the weighing pans are suspended.
3. Pictorial representation of a concept (here, justice), usually with verses to suggest (or riddle about) the meaning.

Offspring of that courageous conquering king,[4]
Whose pure renown hath pierced the world's large ears
In golden scrolls, rolling about the heavens,
20 Celestial sacred nymph, that tends her flock
With watchful eyes and keeps this fount in peace,
Guarded with Graces and with gracious trains,°   *followers*
Virtues divine and gifts incomparable,
Nor lets blind superstitious Ignorance
25 Corrupt so pure a spring. O happy times,
That do beget such calm and quiet days,
Where sheep and shepherd breathe in such content.
Honor attends her throne; in her bright eyes
Sits Majesty; Virtue and Steadfastness
30 Possess her heart; sweet Mercy sways her sword;
Her champion,[5] armed with resolution,
Sits at her feet to chastise malcontents
That threat her honor's wrack;° and Time and Kind°   *ruin / Nature*
Produce her years to make them numberless,
35 While Fortune, for her service and her sake,
With golden hands doth strengthen and enrich
The web that they for fair Astraea weave.
Long may she live, long may she govern us
In peace triumphant, fortunate in wars,
40 Our fair Astraea, our Pandora fair,
Our fair Eliza, or Zabeta fair;
Sweet Cynthia's darling, beauteous Cypria's° peer;   *Venus's*
As dear to England and true English hearts
As Pompey to the citizens of Rome;
45 As merciful as Caesar in his might;
As mighty as the Macedonian king,°   *Alexander the Great*
Or Trojan Hector, terror to the Greeks.
Goddess, live long, whose honors we advance,
Strengthen thy neighbors, propagate thine own.
50 Guide well thy helm; lay thine anointed hand
To build the temple of triumphant Truth,
That while thy subjects draw their peace from thee,
Thy friends with aid of arms may succored be.

Astraea, *with her sheep hook on the top of the pageant*[6]
Feed on, my flock, among the gladsome green,
55 Where heav'nly nectar[7] flows above the banks.
Such pastures are not common to be seen.
Pay to immortal Jove immortal thanks,
For what is good from heav'n's high throne doth fall,
And heav'n's great Architect be praised for all.

4. That is, Brutus.
5. Until 1591, Sir Henry Lee.
6. Temporary stage.
7. Drink of the gods.

EDMUND SPENSER

From The Faerie Queene, Book 5 (1596)†

Proem

So oft as I with state of present time
    The image of the antique° world compare,   *ancient*
    Whenas man's age was in his freshest prime°   *springtime*
    And the first blossom of fair virtue bare,°   *bore*
5   Such odds° I find twixt those and these which are   *differences*
    As that, through long continuance of his course,
    Me seems° the world is run quite out of square   *It seems to me*
    From the first point of his appointed source[1]
And, being once amiss, grows daily worse and worse.

10 For from the Golden Age that first was named,
    It's now at erst become a stony one,[2]
    And men themselves, the which at first were framed
    Of earthly mould[3] and form'd of flesh and bone,
    Are now transformed into hardest stone,
15   Such as behind their backs (so backward bred)[4]
    Were thrown by Pyrrha and Deucalion,
    And if than those may any worse be read,°   *thought*
They into that ere long will be degenderéd.°   *degenerated*

Let none then blame me if, in discipline
20   Of virtue and of civil uses' lore,[5]
    I do not form them to the common line
    Of present days,[6] which are corrupted sore,
    But to the antique use° which was of yore,   *custom*
    When good was only for itself desired,
25   And all men sought their own, and none no more;
    When justice was not for most meed outhired,[7]
But simple truth did reign and was of all admired.

For that which all men then did virtue call
    Is now called vice; and that which vice was hight°   *named*
30   Is now hight virtue and so used of all.
    Right now is wrong, and wrong that was is right,
    As all things else in time are changéd quite.
    Ne° wonder, for the heavens' revolution   *Nor*
    Is wandered far from where it first was pight,°   *placed*

---

† Copy text: Edmund Spenser, *The faerie qveene Disposed into twelue bookes, fashioning XII. morall vertues* (London: VVilliam Ponsonbie, 1596; STC 23082), M4r–M7v (5.proem and 5.1.1–12).
1. Like a building out of square, the world has shifted since it was first created and is no longer sound.
2. To Ovid's account of the decline of the world through the Ages of Gold, Silver, Bronze, and Iron (*Metamorphoses*, 1.395–415), Spenser adds a final Age of Stone; *at erst*: for the first time.
3. Soil. See Genesis 2.7; 3.19.
4. Raised so backwardly.
5. Teaching about civil customs.
6. Set their foundation along the line commonly accepted today.
7. Sold to the highest bidder.

35   And so do make contrary constitution
Of all this lower world, toward his° dissolution.[8]   *leading to its*

For who so list° into the heavens look   *wishes*
    And search the courses of the rolling spheres,[9]
    Shall find that, from the point where they first took
40   Their setting forth, in these few thousand years[1]
    They all are wandered much; that plain appears.
    For that same golden fleecy Ram,° which bore   *Aries*
    Phrixus and Helle from their stepdame's° fears,   *Ino's*
    Hath now forgot where he was placed of yore
45 And shouldered hath the Bull,° which fair Europa bore.   *Taurus*

And eke the Bull hath with his bow-bent horn
    So hardly° butted those two twins of Jove[2]   *forcefully*
    That they have crushed the Crab° and quite him borne   *Cancer*
    Into the great Nemean lion's° grove.   *Leo's*
50   So now all range and do at random rove
    Out of their proper places far away,
    And all this world with them amiss do move
    And all his creatures from their course astray,
Till they arrive at their last ruinous decay.

55 Ne is that same great glorious lamp of light°   *the sun*
    That doth illumine all these lesser fires[3]
    In better case, ne keeps his course more right,
    But is miscarried with the other spheres.
    For since the term of fourteen hundred years
60   That learnéd Ptolomy his height did take,
    He is declinéd from that mark of theirs
    Nigh thirty minutes° to the Southern Lake,[4]   *half a degree*
That° makes me fear in time he will us quite forsake.   *Which*

And if to those Egyptian wizards old
65   Which in star-rede° were wont° have best insight   *lore / accustomed*
    Faith may be given, it is by them told
    That, since the time they first took the sun's height,
    Four times his place he shifted hath in sight
    And twice hath risen where he now doth west°   *set in the west*
70   And wested twice where he ought rise aright.

---

8. Two changes in the heavens were thought to have harmful influences on earth: "precession," or
the gradual change in the position of the constellations of the zodiac in relation to the positions
first assigned them, and "trepidation," or the shift over a 7000-year cycle of the sun's path through
the zodiac. Together, these gave the impression that the constellations were wandering into one
another's assigned spaces. Spenser links such changes with the widespread belief that the world
had become so corrupt that its end and the Last Judgment were near.
9. The transparent, concentric spheres in which the heavenly bodies were thought to be embedded.
1. Counting the generations in scripture from Adam to Christ led to the view that the world was about
6000 years old.
2. The Gemini, Castor and Pollux.
3. The moon, planets, and stars, thought to reflect light from the sun.
4. Ocean in the southern hemisphere.

But most is Mars amiss of all the rest,
And next to him old Saturn, that was wont be best.

For during Saturn's ancient reign,[5] it's said
  That all the world with goodness did abound;
75 All lovéd virtue, no man was afraid
  Of force, ne fraud in wight° was to be found.   *any person*
  No war was known, no dreadful trumpet's sound,
  Peace universal reigned 'mongst men and beasts,
  And all things freely grew out of the ground.
80 Justice sat high, adored with solemn feasts,
And to all people did divide° her dread behests.   *distribute*

Most sacred virtue she of all the rest,
  Resembling God in His imperial might,
  Whose sovereign power is herein most expressed
85 That both to good and bad He dealeth right
  And all His works with justice hath bedight.°   *adorned*
  That power He also doth to princes lend
  And makes them like Himself in glorious sight,
  To sit in His own seat His cause to end
90 And rule His people right, as He doth recommend.[6]

Dread sovereign goddess, that dost highest sit
  In seat of judgment in th'Almighty's place
  And with magnific might and wondrous wit
  Dost to thy people righteous doom aread,°   *judgment declare*
95 That furthest nations fills with awful dread,
  Pardon the boldness of thy basest thrall,°   *servant*
  That dare discourse of so divine a rede°   *subject*
  As thy great justice, praiséd over all,
The instrument whereof lo here thy Artegall.[7]

Canto I.

[Astraea instructs Artegall in justice
and abandons the earth]

100 Though virtue then were held in highest price°   *esteem*
  In those old times of which I do entreat,
  Yet then likewise the wicked seed of vice
  Began to spring which shortly grew full great,
  And with their boughs the gentle° plants did beat.   *noble*
105 But evermore some of the virtuous race
  Rose up, inspired with heroic heat,
  That cropped the branches of the sient base°   *ignoble root*
And with strong hand their fruitful rankness° did deface.   *fecundity*

5. The Golden Age. For a description, see Ovid, *Metamorphoses*, 1.89–112.
6. Spenser stresses Positive Law based on Elizabeth's divine right to rule, rather than Common Law based on judges' right to establish legal precedent.
7. Half brother of Prince Arthur and hero of Book 5, the Legend of Justice. In the historical allegory, he represents the English government.

Such first was Bacchus, that with furious might
110   All th' East, before untamed, did overrun
      And wrong represséd and established right,
      Which lawless men had formerly fordone.°   *done away with*
      There justice first her princely rule begun.
      Next Hercules his like ensample showed,
115   Who all the West with equal conquest won
      And monstrous tyrants with his club subdued,
The club of justice dread with kingly power endued.

      And such was he of whom I have to tell,
      The champion of true justice, Artegall,
120   Whom (as ye lately mote° remember well)   *might*
      An hard adventure, which did then befall,
      Into redoubted° peril forth did call;   *dreaded*
      That was to succor a distresséd dame,
      Whom a strong tyrant did unjustly thrall°   *enthrall*
125   And from the heritage which she did claim
Did with strong hand withhold. Grantorto[8] was his name.

Wherefore the lady, which Eirena[9] hight,°   *was called*
      Did to the Fairy Queen her way address,
      To whom complaining her afflicted plight,
130   She her besought of gracious redress.
      That sovereign queen, that mighty emperess,
      Whose glory is to aid all suppliants poor
      And of weak princes to be patroness,
      Chose Artegall to right her to restore,
135 For that° to her he seemed best skilled in righteous lore.   *Because*

For Artegall in justice was upbrought,
      Even from the cradle of his infancy,
      And all the depth of rightful doom° was taught   *judgment*
      By faire Astraea with great industry,
140   Whilst here on earth she livéd mortally.
      For till the world from his perfection fell
      Into all filth and foul iniquity,
      Astraea here 'mongst earthly men did dwell
And in the rules of justice them instructed well.[1]

145 Whiles through the world she walkéd in this sort,°   *manner*
      Upon a day she found this gentle° child   *noble*
      Amongst his peers playing his childish sport,
      Whom seeing fit and with no crime defiled,
      She did allure with gifts and speeches mild
150   To wend° with her. So thence him far she brought   *go*
      Into a cave, from company exiled,

---

8. A figure for Philip II of Spain in his military intervention in Ireland on behalf of the Pope.
9. A pun on the Gaelic name for Ireland (Éire) and the Greek word for peace (*eirênê*). Eirena repre-
    sents the Irish who remained loyal subjects of Elizabeth.
1. See Ovid's *Metamorphoses*, 1.149–50.

In which she nursled° him till years he raught[2]   *trained*
And all the discipline of justice there him taught.

There she him taught to weigh both right and wrong
155   In equal balance with due recompense
    And equity[3] to measure out along,
    According to the line of consciénce,
    When so it needs with rigor to dispense.
    Of all the which, for want° there of mankind,   *lack*
160   She causéd him to make° experience   *gain*
    Upon wild beasts, which she in woods did find
With wrongful power oppressing others of their kind.

Thus she him trained and thus she him taught
    In all the skill of deeming° wrong and right,   *distinguishing*
165   Until the ripeness of man's years he raught,
    That even wild beasts did fear his awful sight,
    And men admired his overruling might,
    Ne any lived on ground that durst withstand
    His dreadful hest,° much less him match in fight   *command*
170   Or bide° the horror of his wreakful° hand   *abide / avenging*
When so he list° in wrath lift up his steely brand.°   *willed / sword*

Which steely brand, to make him dreaded more,
    She gave unto him, gotten by her sleight°   *close*
    And earnest search, where it was kept in store
175   In Jove's eternal house, unwist of wight°   *unknown to anyone*
    Since he himself it used in that great fight
    Against the Titans that whilom° rebelled   *once*
    'Gainst highest heaven. Chrysaor it was hight,
    Chrysaor that all other swords excelled,
180 Well proved in that same day when Jove those giants quelled.

For of most perfect metal it was made,
    Tempered with adamant[4] amongst the same
    And garnished all with gold upon the blade
    In goodly wise, whereof it took his° name,[5]   *its*
185   And was of no less virtue° than of fame.   *excellence*
    For there no substance was so firm and hard
    But it would pierce or cleave, where so° it came,   *wherever*
    Ne any armor could his dint out ward,°   *fend off its blow*
But wheresoever it did light it throughly shard.°   *completely sheared*

190 Now when the world with sin 'gan to abound,
    Astraea, loathing longer here to space°   *roam*
    'Mongst wicked men in whom no truth she found,

2. Reached maturity.
3. A corrective to legal justice that returns to general principles in order to give clemency in cases
   involving special circumstances not taken into account by those who framed the laws.
4. Mythical substance of supreme strength.
5. Chrysaor is Greek for "golden sword."

Returned to heaven, whence she derived her race,
Where she hath now an everlasting place
195 'Mongst those twelve signs[6] which nightly we do see
The heav'ns bright-shining baldric to enchase[7]
And is the Virgin, sixth in her degree,[8]
And next herself her righteous balance hanging be.[9]

But when she parted hence, she left her groom,
200 An iron man which did on her attend
Always to execute her steadfast doom,°   *judgment*
And willéd him with Artegall to wend
And do whatever thing he did intend.
His name was Talus,[1] made of iron mould,°   *material*
205 Immoveable, resistless, without end,°   *ceaseless*
Who in his hand an iron flail did hold
With which he threshed out falsehood and did truth unfold.

JOHN DAVIES

From Hymns of Astraea (1599)[†]

HYMN 1

Of Astraea

E arly, before the day doth spring,
L et us awake, my Muse, and sing.
I t is no time to slumber;
S o many joys this time doth bring
5 A s time will fail to number.
B ut whereto shall we bend our lays?°   *poems*
E v'n up to heav'n again to raise°   *lift up in song*
T he maid which, thence descended,
H ath brought again the golden days
10 A nd all the world amended.[1]

R udeness itself she doth refine,
E v'n like an alchemist[2] divine,
G ross times of iron turning
I nto the purest form of gold,

---

6. The signs of the zodiac, where she appears as Virgo.
7. To adorn the brightly shining belt of the zodiac as it encompasses the earth.
8. Sixth sign of the zodiac.
9. The seventh sign, Libra, shaped like the scales of distributive justice.
1. Talus represents the executive arm of government, responsible for investigating offenses and enforcing laws.
† Copy text: John Davies, *Hymnes of Astraea, in acrosticke verse* (London: I.S., 1599; STC 6351), A2r–A3r, A4v–B2r, B3v–B4r, C1r–C1v, C3r, C4v–D2v.
1. Astraea as Virgo is associated with Virgil's prophecy that a Virgin will come to bring back the peace and justice of the Golden Age (*Eclogues* 4).
2. One who, through rudimentary chemistry and magic, aimed to produce precious metals out of common ones.

15 N ot to corrupt° till heav'n wax old   *tarnish*
    A nd be refined with burning.³

HYMN 2

To Astraea

E ternal virgin, goddess true,
L et me presume to sing to you.
I ove,⁴ even great Jove, hath leisure
S ometimes to hear the vulgar crew°   *ordinary mortals*
5 A nd hears them oft with pleasure.
B lessed Astraea, I in part
E njoy the blessings you impart,
T he peace, the milk and honey,⁵
H umanity, and civil art,
10 A richer dower° than money.   *dowry*

R ight glad am I that now I live,
E v'n in these days whereto you give
G reat happiness and glory.
I f after you I should be born,
15 N o doubt I should my birthday scorn,
A dmiring your sweet story.

HYMN 3

To the Spring

E arth now is green, and heav'n is blue;
L ively Spring which makes all new,
I olly° Spring doth enter.   *Jolly*
S weet young sunbeams do subdue
5 A ngry, agéd Winter.
B lasts are mild, and seas are calm;
E very meadow flows with balm;
T he earth wears all her riches;
H armonious birds sing such a psalm
10 A s ear and heart bewitches.

R eserve, sweet Spring, this nymph° of ours   *Elizabeth*
E ternal garlands of thy flowers,
G reen garlands never wasting.
I n her shall last our state's fair spring,
15 N ow and forever flourishing,
A s long as heav'n is lasting.

---

3. At the Second Coming of Christ, the old heaven and earth will be burned and new ones created (Revelation 19–22).
4. In Elizabethan spelling, the letter *i* is often used for a *j*.
5. In the Bible, the land promised to God's Chosen People flows with "milk and honey" and wine (Deuteronomy 31.20; Joel 3.12–21).

HYMN 6

To the Nightingale

E very night from ev'n till morn
L ove's chorister amid the thorn
I s now so sweet a singer,
S o sweet as for her song I scorn
5 A pollo's voice and finger.[6]
B ut, Nightingale, since you delight
E ver to watch the starry night,
T o° all the stars of heaven   *Compared to*
H eav'n never had a star so bright
10 A s now to earth is given.

R oyal Astraea makes our day
E ternal with her beams, nor may
G ross darkness overcome her.
I now perceive why some do write
15 N o country hath so short a night
A s England hath in summer.[7]

HYMN 7

To the Rose

E ye of the garden, queen of flowers,
L ove's cup, wherein he nectar pours,
I ngendred first of nectar;[8]
S weet nurse-child of the spring's young hours,
5 A nd beauty's fair character;°   *symbol*
B est jewel that the earth doth wear,
E v'n when the brave young sun draws near,
T o her hoat° love pretending,   *promised*
H imself likewise like form doth bear
10 A t rising and descending.[9]

R ose of the Queen of Love beloved,
E ngland's great kings divinely moved
G ave roses in their banner.[1]
I t showed that beauty's Rose indeed,
15 N ow in this age should them succeed,
A nd reign in more sweet manner.[2]

6. Apollo, god of music, is often portrayed playing a lyre.
7. Because of England's northerly location, its summer nights are short.
8. Engendered first of the mythical drink of the gods.
9. When rising and setting, the sun takes on the red hues of the rose and is cooler, hence more chaste.
1. A reference to the flowers symbolic of the houses of Lancaster and York in the fifteenth-century Wars of the Roses.
2. Elizabeth was much loved for keeping peace among rival factions of the recent past.

HYMN 8

To All the Princes of Europe

E urope, the earth's sweet paradise,
L et all thy kings that would be wise,
I n politic devotion
S ail hither to observe her eyes
5　A nd mark her heav'nly motion.
B rave princes of this civil age,
E nter into this pilgrimage.
T his saint's tongue is an oracle;
H er eye hath made a prince a page
10　A nd works each day a miracle.

R aise but your looks to her and see
E v'n the true beams of majesty.
G reat princes, mark her duly.
I f all the world you do survey,
15　N o forehead spreads so bright a ray
A nd notes a prince so truly.

HYMN 9

To Flora

E mpress of flowers, tell where away
L ies your sweet court this merry May?
I n Greenwich[3] garden alleys,
S ince there the heav'nly powers do play
5　A nd haunt no other valleys.
B eauty, Virtue, Majesty,
E loquent Muses, three times three,
T he new fresh Hours and Graces
H ave pleasure in this place to be
10　A bove all other places.

R oses and lilies did them draw,
E re they divine Astraea saw;
G ay flowers they sought for pleasure.
I nstead of gathering crowns of flowers,
15　N ow gather they Astraea's dowers°　　　　　　　　*dowries, gifts*
A nd bear to heaven that treasure.

HYMN 12

To Her Picture

E xtreme was his audacity,
L ittle his skill that finished thee.
I am ashamed and sorry

---

3. Royal palace on the River Thames below London.

S o dull her counterfeit should be,
5 A nd she so full of glory.
B ut here° are colors red and white,   *in this hymn*
E ach line and each proportion right;
T hese lines, this red and whiteness,
H ave wanting° yet a life and light,   *Though lacking*
10 A majesty and brightness.

R ude counterfeit, I then did err,
E v'n° now, when I would needs infer[1]   *Just*
G reat boldness in thy maker.
I did mistake, he was not bold,
15 N or durst° his eyes her eyes behold,   *dared*
A nd this made him mistake her.

HYMN 13

Of Her Mind

E arth, now adieu; my ravished thought,
L ifted to heav'n, sets thee at naught.[5]
I nfinite is my longing
S ecrets of angels to be taught
5 A nd things to heav'n belonging.
B rought down from heav'n of angels' kind,
E ven now do I admire her mind.
T his is my contemplation:
H er clear sweet spirit, which is refined
10 A bove humane° creation.   *human*

R ich sunbeam of th' eternal light,
E xcellent soul, how shall I write?
G ood angels, make me able;
I cannot see but by your eye,
15 N or, but by your tongue, signify
A thing so admirable.

HYMN 15

Of Her Wit

E ye of that mind, most quick and clear,
L ike heaven's eye,° which from his sphere[6]   *the sun*
I nto all things pryeth,
S ees through all things everywhere
5 A nd all their natures tryeth.°   *puts to the test*
B right image of an angel's wit,
E xceeding sharp and swift like it,

---

4. When I, lacking a better explanation, inferred.
5. Regards thee as of little value.
6. In Ptolemaic astronomy, the sun, moon, planets, and stars were thought to be embedded in rotating crystal spheres.

T hings instantly discerning,[7]
H aving a nature infinite,
10 A nd yet increased by learning,

R ebound upon thyself thy light;[8]
E njoy thine own sweet precious sight.[9]
G ive us but some reflection;
I t is enough for us if we,
15 N ow in her° speech, now policy,   *the reflection's*
A dmire thine° high perfection.   *Elizabeth's own*

HYMN 16

Of Her Will

E ver well-affected Will,
L oving goodness, loathing ill,
I nestimable treasure,
S ince such a power hath power to spill°   *overturn, ruin*
5 A nd save us at her pleasure,
B e thou our law, sweet Will, and say
E v'n what thou wilt, we will obey
T his law, if I could read it.
H erein would I spend night and day
10 A nd study still to plead it.[1]

R oyal Free Will, and only° free,   *alone*
E ach other will is slave to thee;
G lad is each will to serve thee.
I n thee such princely power is seen
15 N o spirit but takes thee for her queen
A nd thinks she must observe° thee.   *follow*

HYMN 19

Of the Organs of Her Mind

E clipsed she is, and her bright rays
L ie under veils,[2] yet many ways
I s her fair form[3] revealed.
S he díversely herself conveys
5 A nd cannot be concealed.
B y instruments[4] her powers appear
E xceedingly well tuned and clear.

---

7. Angels are said to have intellect in the strict sense: the ability to discern the truth immediately, without reasoning it out.
8. Eyes were thought to take in light and also to emit it as "eyebeams."
9. Since the Queen's mind is angelic, it can delight only in things of similar perfection, such as her own form.
1. Davies was a lawyer.
2. Her body.
3. Not her outward shape but her inward organization, which is a function of her mind.
4. A pun, suggesting bodily instruments that carry out her will and musical instruments that express her inward state.

T his lute[5] is still in measure,°   *always in harmony*
H olds still in tune, even like a sphere,[6]
10 A nd yields the world sweet pleasure.

R esolve me, Muse, how this thing is,
E ver a body like to this
G ave heav'n to earthly creature?
I am but fond° this doubt to make;   *foolish*
15 N o doubt the angels bodies take
A bove our common nature.

HYMN 22

Of Her Wisdom

E agle-eyed Wisdom, life's lodestar,[7]
L ooking near on things afar,
I ove's best beloved daughter[8]
S hows to her° spirit all things that are,   *Elizabeth's*
5 A s Jove himself hath taught her.
B y this straight rule she rectifies
E ach thought that in her heart doth rise.
T his is her clear true mirror,
H er looking glass, wherein she spies
10 A ll forms of truth and error.

R ight princely virtue, fit to reign,
E nthronized in her spirit remain,
G uiding our fortunes ever.
I f we this star once cease to see,
15 N o doubt our state will shipwrecked be,
A nd torn and sunk forever.

HYMN 23

Of Her Justice

E xiled Astraea is come again.
L o, here she doth all things maintain
I n number, weight, and measure.
S he rules us with delightful pain,°   *care*
5 A nd we obey with pleasure.
B y love she rules more than by law;
E v'n her great mercy breedeth awe.
T his° is her sword[9] and scepter;   *Love*
H erewith she hearts did ever draw,
10 A nd this guard ever kept her.

---

5. The Queen's favorite instrument, treated as a metaphor for the Queen herself.
6. The crystal spheres in which the astral bodies were said to be embedded made tones as they revolved.
7. The Pole Star, used in navigation; *E agle-eyed Wisdom*: Jove, the god of wisdom, was associated with the eagle.
8. Minerva, who was engendered in the mind of Jove without a mother.
9. Elizabeth kept at the foot of her throne a rusty sword, symbolic of her reluctance to use military force.

R eward doth sit in her right hand;
E ach virtue thence takes her garlánd
G athered in honor's garden.
I n her left hand (wherein should be
15 N aught but the sword) sits clemency
A nd conquers vice with pardon.

HYMN 24

Of Her Magnanimity

E ven as her state, so is her mind
L ifted above the vulgar kind.
I t treads proud Fortune under.
S un-like it sits above the wind,
5 A bove the storms and thunder.
B rave spirit, large heart, admiring naught,°   *wondering at nothing*
E steeming each thing as it ought,
T hat swelleth not nor shrinketh,
H onor is always in her thought,
10 A nd of great things she thinketh.

R ocks, pillars, and heav'n's axle-tree[1]
E xemplify her constancy.
G reat changes never change her.
I n her sex fears are wont° to rise;   *accustomed*
15 N ature permits, virtue denies[2]
A nd scorns the face of danger.

HYMN 25

Of Her Moderation

E mpress of kingdoms though she be,
L arger is her sovereignty
I f she herself do govern.
S ubject unto herself is she,
5 A nd of herself true sovereign.
B eauty's crown though she do wear,
E xalted into Fortune's chair,
T hroned like the Queen of Pleasure,
H er virtues still possess her ear
10 A nd counsel her to measure.°   *moderate desire*

R eason, if she incarnate were,
E v'n Reason's self, could never bear
G reatness with moderation.
I n her,° one temper still is seen;   *Elizabeth*
15 N o liberty claims she as Queen,
A nd shows no alteration.[3]

1. In Ptolemaic astronomy, all the crystal spheres are supported on a single axis.
2. Her nature as a woman permits fear, but her virtue prevents it.
3. A reference to the Queen's motto, *Semper eadem* ("Always the same").

HYMN 26

To Envy

E nvy, go weep. My Muse and I
L augh thee to scorn. Thy feeble eye
I s dazzled with the glory
S hining in this gay poesy[4]
5   A nd little golden story.
B ehold how my proud quill doth shed
E ternal nectar on her head.
T he pomp of coronation
H ath not such power her fame to spread
10   A s this my admiration.

R espect my pen as free and frank,
E xpecting not reward nor thank;
G reat wonder only moves it.
I never made it mercenary,
15   N or should my Muse this burden carry
A s hired, but that° she loves it.   *because*

Finis.

ELIZABETH AS THE VIRGIN QUEEN

Of all the attributes that captured poets' imaginations in the last half of Elizabeth's reign, none was more important than her virginity. A central element in the myths of Cynthia and Astraea, it became so associated with her that the American state founded in her honor was named simply Virginia, and over the space of four centuries, books, films, plays, and an opera about her have taken the title *The Virgin Queen*.

The stress on her virginity first became pronounced in the late 1570s, when concern that Elizabeth would marry the Duke of Anjou led opponents to praise her for her own long-expressed inclination to remain single. Once the crisis had passed, there were other reasons to celebrate her celibacy. In an age when rule by women was rare, it struck many as a wonder that a queen should govern so long and so successfully without a husband. Lingering veneration for virginity as a sign of religious purity and devotion also played a part. Though associated with Roman Catholicism, such veneration had its roots in passages of the New Testament and so continued to influence Protestants of the day, as did special reverence for the Virgin Mary. Though Reformers rejected her elevated status in the late-medieval Church as a mediator between Christ and His people, Mary was still very much revered as the mother of Christ and a model of faithfulness and obedience, leading Protestant writers to draw comparisons between her and the Queen.

However we explain the phenomenon, poets tended to see the Queen as a prodigy. In comparing her with other monarchs, George Puttenham's Fourth *Partheniad* treats her as wonder of nature—a woman possessing a lion's heart, an angel's face, and a serpent's head. Although the last detail was meant to suggest wisdom rather than evil, the image is nonetheless unset-

---

4. Poetry, with a pun on "posy" (bouquet of flowers).

tling, suggesting as it does that she was not "as other women are." Although Fulke Greville's Sonnet 81 from the sequence *Caelica* is more conventional, it too sets her apart from other human beings by suggesting that she has taken over the role of the goddess Fortuna, raising some people up and casting others down.

Shakespeare's famous allusion to Elizabeth in *A Midsummer Night's Dream* also treats her as a prodigy. Titania, Queen of the Fairies, resembles Spenser's Fairy Queen in combining beauty and grace with lofty independence and preternatural power. Unlike Gloriana, however, Titania is married, and she is no match for the wiles of her husband, Oberon. After quarreling with him over who will raise the orphaned child of an Indian attendant, she separates from him, and he conceives a plan to punish her and bring her back. With the help of his mischievous henchman Puck, he employs a flower struck by one of Cupid's arrows that the god fired fruitlessly at Elizabeth, described as a "fair vestal throned by west." Once Oberon daubs Titania's eyes with juice from the flower, its magical effects cause her to fall in love with Bottom, an Athenian tradesman whose head Puck has magically transformed into that of an ass. The compliment paid Elizabeth by contrasting her invulnerability to Cupid with the plight of the doting Titania suggests that England was well off in being ruled by a woman who is able to quench desire "in the chaste beams of the wat'ry moon." Like the poems of Puttenham and Greville, however, the passage also sets her apart as a wonder. The reunions and marriages that end the play suggest that it is more natural to fall in love and marry than to remain a virgin.

Less concerned with her virginity as such and more with her sanctity and justice is the last of several representations of Elizabeth in Spenser's *Faerie Queene*. Late in Book 5, Prince Arthur joins forces with Artegall to restore justice in Ireland and Belgium. As the two men pause for the night at the court of Mercilla, they find the Queen enthroned among her people. Raised on a dais and surmounted with a royal canopy, she resembles God seated upon His judgment seat in the Book of Revelation. Despite such suggestions of the Queen's divine authority, however, all is not well in her kingdom. The dangerous witch Duessa (representing Mary Stuart) is still a threat, though she will be tried and executed later in the episode. The Blatant Beast (a figure for the envy and the personal attacks that destroy the reputations of rulers and their councilors) is still at large and proves impossible to control. Perhaps most notable of all, the bad poet Malefont (who represents poets who undermine the state) stands in Mercilla's Court with his tongue unmercifully nailed to a pillar. However much Spenser may have idealized Elizabeth in the figure of Mercilla, he took pains to make clear that the age was still a stony one, its monarchs still limited in their power to bring order, and its poets still in danger should they speak of the Queen too critically.

The anonymous elegy *"Britanniae Lachrimae"* offers a fitting final memorial to England's virgin queen. Though the poet praises her as the "daughter of war," he reserves his highest honor for her as the "mother of peace." In his concluding line, which is perhaps the most famous in all the poems that seek to assess the Queen's stature in the great scheme of things, he compares her with the Virgin Mary, concluding that Elizabeth is "In earth the first, in heav'n the second maid."

GEORGE PUTTENHAM

From Partheniads (1579)[†]

Partheniad 4, Thalia [That her Majesty surmounteth all the princesses of our time in wisdom, beauty, and magnanimity,[1] and is a thing very admirable in nature]

Whom Princes serve, and realms obey,
And greatest of Briton° kings begot,   *British*
She came abroad° ev'n yesterday,   *outside*
When such as saw her knew her not,
5   For one would ween° that, stood afar,   *think*
She were as other women are.

In truth it fares much otherwise,
For whilst they think they see a queen,
It comes to pass ye can devise
10   No stranger sight for to be seen;
Such error falls° in feeble eye   *occurs*
That cannot view her steadfastly.[2]

How so, alas? Forsooth° it is,   *True*
Nature, that seldom works amiss,
15   In woman's breast by passing° art   *surpassing*
Hath harbored safe the lion's heart[3]
And featly fixed,[4] with all good grace,
The serpent's head[5] and angel's face.

FULKE GREVILLE, BARON BROOKE

From Caelica (ca. 1590s)[†]

Sonnet 81 [Under a Throne I Saw a Virgin Sit]

Under a throne I saw a virgin sit,
The red and white rose quartered in her face,[1]

[†] Copy text: British Library MS Cotton Vespasian E.VIII, fol. 170r.
1. Aristotle's master virtue, greatness of soul, which comprises all the other virtues; *Thalia*: each Partheniad (literally, "poem on a virgin") has a marginal heading giving its number in the manuscript and the Muse that inspired it, in this case, Thalia, Muse of Comedy.
2. Without turning away, as from a dazzling light.
3. An allusion to Richard I, the Lionhearted, first English king to use a lion in his coat of arms, and to Henry VIII, who favored it as an emblem. Elizabeth boasted that she had inherited the "heart and stomach of a king."
4. Cleverly joined together.
5. An emblem of wisdom. See Matthew 10.16: "Be ye therefore wise as serpents and innocent [harmless] as doves." The well-known Rainbow Portrait of Elizabeth draws on the same symbolism when it includes an embroidered serpent on her sleeve. In the Queen's coat of arms, a golden dragon (a serpent representing her Tudor ancestors, who were said to descend from King Arthur's father, Uther Pendragon) faces a rampant lion (symbol of the English monarchy).
[‡] Copy text: Fulke Greville, Lord Brooke, *Certaine learned and elegant workes of the right honorable Fvlke Lord Brooke, written in his youth, and familiar exercise with Sir Philip Sidney* (London: Henry Seyle, 1633; STC 12361), Ii2v.
1. Elizabeth's grandfather ended the Wars of the Roses by uniting the house of Lancaster (the red rose) with that of York (the white). The poet imagines Elizabeth's face as a coat of arms, with roses in its sections ("quartered").

Star of the North[2] and, for true guards to it,
Princes, church, states, all pointing out her Grace.[3]
5   The homage done her was not born of Wit;
Wisdom admired, Zeal took Ambition's place,[4]
State° in her eyes taught Order how to fit   *Majesty*
And fix Confusion's unobserving race.°   *people*
        Fortune can here claim nothing truly great
10   But that this princely creature is her seat.°[5]   *place of residence*

WILLIAM SHAKESPEARE

From A Midsummer Night's Dream (ca. 1595–96)[†]

[*Oberon demands Titania's Indian boy, then lays a plot
involving a magic flower*]

OBERON: Give me that boy,[1] and I will go with thee.
QUEEN:[2]   Not for thy fairy kingdom. Fairies, away.
   We'll chide downright, if I longer stay. *Exeunt*
OBERON: Well, go thy way. Thou shalt not from this grove
5   Till I torment thee for this injury.
   My gentle Puck, come hither. Thou rememb'rest
   Since° once I sat upon a promontory   *When*
   And heard a mermaid on a dolphin's back
   Uttering such dulcet and harmonious breath
10   That the rude sea grew civil at her song
   And certain stars shot madly from their spheres
   To hear the sea-maid's music?
PUCK: I remember.
OBERON: That very time I saw (but thou couldst not),
   Flying between the cold moon and the earth
15   Cupid, all armed. A certain aim he took
   At a fair vestal, throned by° west,   *in the*
   And loosed his love-shaft smartly from his bow
   As° it should pierce a hundred thousand hearts;   *As if*
   But I might see young Cupid's fiery shaft
20   Quenched in the chaste beams of the wat'ry moon,
   And the imperial vot'ress[3] passed on,
   In maiden meditation, fancy free.
   Yet marked I where the bolt of Cupid fell.
   It fell upon a little western flower,

2. Pole Star, used by others in setting their course and visible to Catholic Europe from the south.
3. Graciousness and also the unmerited gift of God's favor that, as Protestants liked to stress, brings salvation.
4. Religious zeal replaced ambition as the motive for serving the Queen.
5. As the seat of the goddess Fortune's government, Elizabeth controls destiny in the world around her.
†   Copy text: William Shakespeare, *A Midsommer nights dreame* (London: Thomas Fisher, 1600; STC 22302), C1r–C1v (2.1.143–85).
1. The orphaned child of Titania's deceased Indian servant.
2. Titania, Queen of the Fairies.
3. Woman devoted to a religious life.

25   Before milk-white, now purple with love's wound,
    And maidens call it love-in-idleness.[4]
    Fetch me that flow'r, the herb I showed thee once.
    The juice of it, on sleeping eyelids laid,
    Will make or man or woman madly dote
30   Upon the next live creature that it sees.
    Fetch me this herb, and be thou here again
    Ere the leviathan[5] can swim a league.
PUCK: I'll put a girdle round about the earth
    In forty minutes.
OBERON: Having once this juice,
35   I'll watch Titania when she is asleep
    And drop the liquor of it in her eyes.
    The next thing then she, waking, looks upon
    (Be it on lion, bear, or wolf, or bull,
    On meddling monkey, or on busy ape)
    She shall pursue it with the soul of love.
40   And ere I take this charm from off her sight
    (As I can take it with another herb),
    I'll make her render up her page to me.

EDMUND SPENSER

From The Faerie Queene, Book 5 (1596)[†]

[Prince Arthur and Artegall enter the Court and behold Mercilla]

There they, alighting, by that damsel were
    Directed in and showéd all the sight,[1]
    Whose porch, that most magnific did appear,
    Stood open wide to all men day and night,[2]
    Yet warded° well by one of mickle° might   *guarded / great*
5   That sat thereby, with giantlike resemblance,[3]
    To keep out guile, and malice, and despite,°   *spitefulness*
    That under show oftimes of feignéd semblance
Are wont[4] in princes' courts to work great scathe and hindrance.°   *harm*

His name was Awe, by whom they passing in
    Went up the hall, that was a large, wide room,
10   All full of people making troublous din
    And wondrous noise, as if that there were some°   *someone*
    Which unto them was dealing righteous doom.°   *judgment*

---

4. Popular name for the pansy.
5. Sea monster in Hebrew scripture (see, for example, Job 41; Psalm 74.14; Isaiah 27.1).
† Copy text: Edmund Spenser, *The faerie qveene Disposed into twelue bookes, fashioning XII. morall vertues* (London: William Ponsonbie, 1596; STC 23082), T7v–V1v (5.9.22–35).
1. Arthur and his half-brother Artegall (the Knight of Justice and hero of Book V) have just rescued Samient (an emissary of Mercilla), who has brought them to Court.
2. The same is said of the New Jerusalem (Isaiah 60.11).
3. The entrance resembles that of Elizabeth's palace at Hampton Court, and her porter was indeed a giant, being 8'6" tall.
4. Accustomed.

15　　By whom they passing through the thickest press,
　　　　The marshal of the hall to them did come.
　　　　His name hight° Order who, commanding peace,　　　　*He was called*
　　Them guided through the throng, that did their clamors cease.

　　They ceased their clamors upon them to gaze;
20　　　　Whom seeing all in armor bright as day,
　　　　Strange there to see, it did them much amaze
　　　　And with unwonted terror half affray,°　　　　*frighten*
　　　　For never saw they there the like array,
　　　　Ne° ever was the name of war there spoken,　　　　*Nor*
25　　　　But joyous peace and quietness alway,
　　　　Dealing just judgments that mote° not be broken　　　　*might*
　　For any bribes or threats of any to be wroken.°　　　　*carried out*

　　There, as they entered at the screen,[5] they saw
　　　　Someone whose tongue was for his trespass vile
30　　　　Nailed to a post, adjudgéd so by law,
　　　　For that therewith he falsely did revile
　　　　And foul blaspheme that queen for forgéd guile,
　　　　Both with bold speeches, which he blazéd° had,　　　　*published*
　　　　And with lewd° poems, which he did compile;　　　　*vulgar*
35　　　　For the bold title of a poet bad
　　He on himself had ta'en and railing rhymes had sprad.°　　　　*spread*

　　Thus there he stood, whilst high over his head
　　　　There written was the purport of his sin
　　　　In ciphers strange, that few could rightly read:
40　　　　BON FONS,[6] but "Bon" that once had written been,
　　　　Was 'raced out, and "Mal" was now put in.[7]
　　　　So now "Malfont" was plainly to be read,
　　　　Either for th' evil which he did therein
　　　　Or that he likened was to a wellhead
45　　Of evil words and wicked slanders by him shed.

　　They passing by were guided by degree[8]
　　　　Unto the presence[9] of that gracious Queen,
　　　　Who sat on high that she might all men see
　　　　And might of all men royally be seen
50　　　　Upon a throne of gold full bright and sheen,[1]
　　　　Adornéd all with gems of endless price,°　　　　*infinite value*
　　　　As either might for wealth have gotten been
　　　　Or could be framed by workman's rare device,°　　　　*artistry*
　　And all embossed with lions and with fleur-de-lis.[2]

5. Room divider with a door.
6. Good fountain.
7. Was erased and "Bad" was written in.
8. Guided up the steps of a raised dais.
9. They are now in the Presence Chamber, where visitors were received.
1. Shiny. The throne resembles the mercy-seat of God (Exodus 25.17).
2. Symbols of the English and French monarchies, to both of which Elizabeth had legal claims.

55 All over her a cloth of state[3] was spread,
  Not of rich tissue,° nor of cloth of gold,   *transparent fabric*
  Nor of ought else that may be richest read,°   *thought*
  But like a cloud,[4] as likest may be told,
  That her broad spreading wings did wide unfold,
60   Whose skirts were bordered with bright sunny beams,
  Glist'ring like gold, amongst the plights° enrolled,   *pleats*
  And here and there shooting forth silver streams,
'Mongst which crept little angels through the glittering gleams.

Seemed those little angels did uphold
65   The cloth of state,[5] and on their purpled wings
  Did bear the pendants through their nimbless° bold.   *nimbleness*
  Besides, a thousand more of such as sings
  Hymns to high God and carols heavenly things
  Encompasséd the throne on which she sate,°   *sat*
70   She angel-like, the heir of ancient kings
  And mighty conquerors, in royal state,
Whilst kings and kesars° at her feet did them prostrate.   *emperors*

Thus she did sit in sovereign majesty,
  Holding a scepter in her royal hand,
75   The sacred pledge of peace and clemency,
  With which high God had blest her happy land
  Maugre° so many foes which did withstand.   *Despite*
  But at her feet her sword was likewise laid,
  Whose long rest rusted the bright steely brand;°   *blade*
80   Yet whenas° foes enforced or friends sought aid,   *whenever*
She could it sternly draw, that all the world dismayed.[6]

And round about, before her feet there sate
  A bevy of fair virgins clad in white,
  That goodly seemed t' adorn her royal state,
85   All lovely daughters of high Jove, that hight
  Litae, by him begot in love's delight
  Upon the righteous Themis.[7] Those they say
  Upon Jove's judgment seat wait day and night,
  And when in wrath he threats the world's decay,
90 They do his anger calm and cruel vengeance stay.

They also do by his divine permission
  Upon the thrones of mortal princes tend,
  And often treat° for pardon and remission   *entreat*
  To suppliants, through frailty which offend.

---

3. Canopy symbolizing royal authority.
4. A detail recalling the cloud of glory that surrounds God and will surround Christ at His Second Coming (Exodus 24.15–18; Psalm 97.2; Matthew 24.30).
5. Another parallel with the mercy seat of God, which had cherubim on either side covering the throne with their wings (Exodus 25.18–22).
6. Elizabeth refers to such a rusty sword and her capacity to wield it if need be in her 1570 poem "The Doubt of Future Foes" (included in Part Three).
7. The mother of the Litae is not specified in ancient myth. Themis is mother of the Hours.

95   Those did upon Mercilla's throne attend:
    Just Dicê, wise Eunomia, mild Eirênê,[8]
    And them amongst, her glory to commend,
    Sat goodly Temperance in garments clean,
And sacred Reverence, yborn of heavenly strain.°   *lineage*

100 Thus did she sit in royal rich estate,
    Admired of many, honoréd of all,
    Whilst underneath her feet, there as she sate,
    An huge great lion lay, that mote° appall   *might*
    An hardy courage like captived thrall,
105   With a strong iron chain and collar bound,
    That once he could not move nor quitch[9] at all.
    Yet did he murmur with rebellion's sound,
And softly roin,° when savage choler 'gan redound.[1]   *growl*

So sitting high in dreaded sovereignty,
110   Those two strange knights were to her presence brought;
    Who bowing low before her Majesty,
    Did to her mild obeisance,° as they ought,   *homage*
    And meekest boon° that they imagine mought,°   *favor / might*
    To whom she eke° inclining her withal,   *also*
115   As a fair stoop[2] of her high soaring thought,
    A cheerful countenance on them let fall
Yet tempered with some majesty imperial.

ANONYMOUS

Britanniae Lachrimae (1603)[†]

Weep, little isle, and for thy mistress' death
Swim in a double sea of brackish water.
Weep, little world, weep for great Elizabeth:
Daughter of war, for Mars himself begat her,
5 Mother of peace, for she bore the latter.
She was and is (what can there more be said?)
In earth the first, in heav'n the second maid.[1]

---

8. Peace; *Dicê:* Justice; *Eunomia:* Good Order. Following Renaissance sources, Spenser treats these figures as Litae, though they are in fact a combination of Homer's Litae (*Iliad* 9.502–12) and Hesiod's Hours (*Theogony* 901–2).
9. Stir against her.
1. Began to well up.
2. Swift descent of a falcon.
† Copy text: British Museum MS Additional 4712, fol. 94bv.
1. Mary, mother of Christ, stands first among the virgins in heaven.

COMMENTARY AND CRITICISM

Part Eleven: Remembering Elizabeth: Early Accounts of the Queen (1577–1848)

AN EARLY CHRONICLE

When Raphael Holinshed's *Chronicles of England, Scotland, and Ireland* appeared in 1577, it joined a growing group of published works intended to elevate the role of England in the world and to promote the use of the English language for learned books at home. Starting with the earliest kings of Britain, Holinshed concludes with a narrative of Queen Elizabeth written in the usual chronicler's style of a year-by-year account of public events. The chronicle ranges over many subjects, juxtaposing money and monstrosities, sermons and civil wars, Turks and translators, pikemen and poems. The emphasis on England's public affairs means that in this early history there are few insights into Elizabeth's character and almost none of the personal anecdotes that delighted later writers. Holinshed simply honors the Queen for her godly rule and for her justice, mercy, and statesmanship. He concludes with a list of writers who flourished in the peace and prosperity that characterized much of her reign, though he also includes stark reminders of ongoing religious conflicts. The excerpts below include a description of the capture, enforced recantation, and burning of Dutch Anabaptists, the forerunners of the modern-day Amish and Mennonites.

RAPHAEL HOLINSHED

From The Chronicles of England, Scotland, and Ireland (1577)†

On Wednesday, the three and twentieth of November [1558], the Queen's Majesty removed from Hatfield unto the Charter House in London, where she lodged in the Lord North's house, in which removing and coming thus to the city it might well appear how comfortable her presence was to them that went to receive her on the way and likewise to the great multitudes of people that came abroad to see her Grace, showing their rejoicing hearts in countenance and words with hearty prayers for her Majesty's prosperous estate and preservation, which no doubt were acceptable to God, as by the sequel of things it may certainly be believed, sith[1] his Divine Majesty hath

---

† Copy text: Raphael Holinshed, *The laste volume of the Chronicles of England, Scotlande, and Irelande* (London: Iohn Harrison, 1577; *STC* 13568), 2:1785, 1816, 1860, 1862, 1871–72, 1874.

1. Since; *removed from Hatfield*: left her estate northeast of London in preparation for her coronation; *Charter House*: a former Carthusian monastery; *Lord North's*: Edward, first Baron North.

so directed her doings that, if ever the commonwealth of this land hath flourished, it may rightly be said that in her most happy reign it hath been most flourishing in peace, quietness, and due administration of justice, mixed with merciful clemency, so as those which cannot content themselves with the present state of things under her rule, no doubt they are such factious creatures as will not rest satisfied with any kind of government, be it never so just and commendable. From the which sort of men the Lord deliver her royal Majesty and all her true and loving subjects, and preserve her in long life, to all our comforts, and continue her in such happy proceedings as she hath begun to the end.

*   *   *

This year [1562] in England were many monstrous births: in March a mare brought forth a foal with one body and two heads and, as it were, a long tail growing out between the two heads. Also a sow farrowed a pig with four legs, like to the arms of a man-child with hands and fingers, etc.[2]

*   *   *

The ninth of November [1571], a sermon was preached in Paul's Church at London by Master William Foulkes of Cambridge to give thanks to Almighty God for the victory which of His merciful clemency it had pleased Him to grant to the Christians in the Levant Seas[3] against the common enemies of our faith, the Turks, the seventh of October last past. His theme was taken out of the sixtieth psalm of David's Psalter, the fourth verse.[4] There were present at this sermon the Lord Mayor of London, Sir William Allen, with the aldermen and crafts in their liveries[5] and in the evening there were bonfires made through the city with banqueting and great rejoicing, as good cause there was for a victory of so great importance to the whole state of the Christian commonwealth.

*   *   *

The five and twentieth and six and twentieth of March [1572], by the commandment of the Queen's Majesty's Council, the citizens of London assembling at their several halls, the masters collected and chose out the most likely and active persons of every their companies to the number of three thousand, whom they appointed to be pikemen and shot.[6] The pikemen were forthwith armed in fair corslets and other furniture according thereunto; the gunners had every of them his caliver with the furniture and morions[7] on their heads. To these were appointed divers valiant captains who, to train them up in warlike feats, mustered them thrice every week, sometimes in the artillery yard teaching the gunners to handle their pieces, sometimes at the Miles End and in Saint George's field[8] teaching them to skirmish. In the which skirmishing on the Miles End the tenth of April, one

---

2. Such monstrosities were often described in illustrated broadsides that drew moral examples from their appearance.
3. Mediterranean Sea. The Battle of Lepanto ended attempts by the Ottoman Turks to conquer parts of Christian Europe.
4. "But now Thou hast given a banner to them that fear Thee, that it may be displayed because of Thy truth."
5. Official uniforms; *crafts*: guildsmen.
6. Gunners; *halls*: guildhalls; *masters . . . chose out*: throughout her reign, the Queen relied on private citizens to muster and train the soldiers who could be called upon to defend England.
7. Helmets; *corslets*: body armor; *furniture*: military equipment; *caliver*: a light musket.
8. Open areas in Southwark, near the King's Bench Prison in Southeast London.

of the gunners of the goldsmith's company was shot in the side with a piece of a scouring stick[9] left in one of the calivers, whereof he died and was buried the twelfth of April in Saint Paul's churchyard. All the gunners marching from the Miles End in battle ray[1] shot off their calivers at his grave. On May Day they mustered at Greenwich before the Queen's Majesty, where they showed many warlike feats but were much hindered by the weather, which was all day showering.[2] They returned that night to London and were discharged on the next morrow.

* * *

On Easter day [1575], which was the third of April, about nine of the clock in the forenoon was disclosed a congregation of Anabaptists, Dutchmen, in a house without the bars of Aldergate at London, whereof twenty-seven were taken and sent to prison; and some of them, bearing faggots, recanted at Paul's Cross[3] on the tenth of May, in form as followeth:

Whereas I, *** being seduced by the devil, the spirit of error, and by false teachers, his ministers, have fallen into certain most detestable and damnable heresies, namely

1. That Christ took not flesh of the substance of the blessed virgin Mary;
2. That infants of the faithful ought not to be baptized;
3. That a Christian man may not be a magistrate or bear the sword or office of authority;
4. That it is not lawful for a Christian to take an oath;

now by the grace of God and through conference with good and learned ministers of Christ's Church, I do understand and acknowledge the same to be most damnable and detestable heresies and do ask God here before His Church mercy for my said former errors and do forsake them, recant and renounce them, and abjure them from the bottom of my heart * * *.

And further I confess that the whole doctrine and religion established and published in this realm of England, as also that which is received and preached in the Dutch Church here in this city,[4] is sound, true, and according to the Word of God, whereunto in all things I submit myself and will most gladly be a member of the said Dutch Church, from henceforth utterly abandoning and forsaking all and every Anabaptistical error.

* * *

The twenty-first of May, being Whitsuneven, one man and ten women Anabaptists, Dutch, were in the consistory of Paul's condemned to be burnt in Smithfield, but after great pains taken with them,[5] only one woman was

---

9. A stick attached to a small piece of cloth used to extinguish stray embers in the barrel of a musket.
1. Array.
2. Rain caused the black powder muskets to misfire.
3. A cross in the churchyard of St. Paul's Cathedral, where sermons were delivered and public statements were proclaimed. *Anabaptists*: literally, "again-baptists," so called for their practice of rebaptizing adults who had been baptized as infants. They were predecessors of the Mennonites, the Amish, and other related groups that oppose infant baptism and have traditions of pacifism and disengagement from the world and its governing institutions. In the sixteenth century, they were persecuted by Roman Catholics and Protestants alike; *faggots*: wood for their own burning for heresy.
4. London was home to a number of foreign-language churches, attended by exiles from the Continent.
5. Churchmen generally undertook long interrogations and arguments to persuade heretics of their errors before punishing them; *Whitsuneven*: the eve of Whitsun (White Sunday), or Pentecost, the seventh Sunday after Easter; *Smithfield*: field near the meat market in London, where heretics were put to death.

converted; the other were banished [from] the land. * * * The twenty-second of July, two Dutchmen, Anabaptists, were burnt in Smithfield, who died in great horror, with roaring and crying.

* * *

But now to observe the order which hitherto I have followed in mentioning of such writers of our nation as lived in the days of other princes,[6] I have thought good to write also the names of some of those that have flourished in the time of the peaceable reign of our sovereign lady, Queen Elizabeth, whose happy state with long life the Lord maintain. Of which writers as there are many (some departed and others yet living), so the great number of works, treatises, poesies, translations, and pamphlets by them published to the world may fully witness the flourishing state of the Muses in these days of peace, in the which learning is both cherished and the studious enjoy their wished quietness, the better to encourage them to utter their talents.[7]

RECOLLECTIONS BY THOSE WHO KNEW THE QUEEN

Early accounts of Elizabeth and her reign were often by people who had known her. Sir John Harington's reminiscences of the Queen, which were written to a friend three years after her death, are among the most amusing and well-known glimpses of her behind the scenes. As her godson and one of her favorites, Harington saw her in private more regularly than most men of his modest rank. He also had a gift for capturing her personality, and even her way of speaking, in brief but revealing anecdotes. His letter brings out her relentless powers of personal observation, her sternness when she perceived that her courtiers were not being candid with her, and her method of lying in wait while they convicted themselves and then rounding on them. In considering her angry reactions to ladies-in-waiting who dallied with men or wore dresses that rivaled her own, it is well to remember that clothing was an accepted symbol of rank and that for a servant in her private chamber to become romantically involved left her open to pressures to advance causes other than the Queen's. Harington's conclusion suggests both the fear and the affection that she inspired in those who knew her best.

Less personal is the retrospective written by Sir Francis Bacon, later Viscount St. Alban, which he entitled *The Felicity of Queen Elizabeth and Her Times*. Bacon, the son of Sir Nicholas Bacon (Lord Keeper of the Great Seal) and Anne Cooke (one of the redoubtable and well-educated Cooke sisters whose father had been a tutor to Edward VI), had enjoyed access to the Court of Elizabeth from his earliest years. He was the nephew of William Cecil, Lord Burghley, who helped him obtain his first official position as a translator during the Duke of Anjou's visit to London in 1580, when Bacon was only nineteen years old. His subsequent relations with the Queen, however, were rocky; although she appreciated his legal expertise, he frequently supported unpopular positions in Parliament. Under James I, Bacon rose to become Attorney General, Lord Keeper, and finally Chancellor, although he was later deposed. In 1608, just five years after Elizabeth's death, he wrote *In felicem memoriam Reginae Elizabethae*, a defense of Elizabeth's person and policies, which was translated into English

---

6. In the earlier sections of the *Chronicles*.
7. There follows a list of more than 175 writers.

in 1651. It is not so much a personal memoir as an evaluation of her character. A moderate Puritan himself, Bacon argued that Elizabeth was a godly and virtuous queen, both in her private and public lives, and defended her injunctions against Roman Catholics as necessary to the preservation of England's stability and peace.

SIR JOHN HARINGTON

From Reminiscences of the Queen from a Letter to Robert Markham (1606)[†]

Her Highness was wont to sooth her ruffled temper with reading every morning when she had been stirred to passion at the Council or other matters had overthrown her gracious disposition. She did much admire Seneca's wholesome advisings, when the soul's quiet was flown away, and I saw much of her translating thereof. By art and nature together so blended, it was difficult to find her right humor at any time. Her wisest men and best counselors were oft sore troubled to know her will in matters of state, so covertly did she pass her judgment as seemed to leave all to their discreet management; and, when the business did turn to better advantage, she did most cunningly commit the good issue to her own honor and understanding, but, when aught fell out contrary to her will and intent, the Council were in great strait[1] to defend their own acting and not blemish the Queen's good judgment. Herein her wise men did oft lack more wisdom, and the Lord Treasurer[2] would oft shed a plenty of tears on any miscarriage, well knowing the difficult part was not so much to mend the matter itself as his mistress's humor. And yet he did most share her favor and goodwill, and to his opinion she would oft-time submit her own pleasure in great matters. She did keep him till late at night in discoursing alone and then call out another at his departure and try the depth of all around her sometime. Walsingham had his turn, and each displayed their wit in private.

On the morrow, every one did come forth in her presence and discourse at large, and if any had dissembled with her or stood not well to her advisings before, she did not let go unheeded and sometimes not unpunished. Sir Christopher Hatton was wont to say, "The Queen did fish for men's souls and had so sweet a bait, that no one could escape her network." In truth, I am sure her speech was such as none could refuse to take delight in when frowardness[3] did not stand in the way. I have seen her smile, sooth[4] with great semblance of good liking to all around, and cause every one to open his most inward thought to her when, on a sudden, she would ponder in private on what had passed, write down all their opinions, draw them out as occasion required, and sometime disprove to their faces what had been

---

† Copy text: *Nugae antiquae: being a miscellaneous collection of original papers in prose and verse written during the reigns of Henry VIII, Edward VI, Queen Mary, Elizabeth, and King James: by Sir John Harington, Knt. . . . ,* ed. Henry Harington (London: Vernor and Hood, Poultry, and Cuthell and Martin, 1804), 357–63. For the remainder of the letter, see Part Nine.
1. Difficulty.
2. William Cecil, Lord Burghley.
3. Obstinacy.
4. Truly.

delivered a month before. Hence she knew every one's part and by thus *fishing*, as Hatton said, she caught many poor fish, who little knew what snare was laid for them.

I will now tell you more of her Majesty's discretion and wonder-working to those about her, touching their minds and opinions. She did oft ask the ladies around her chamber if they loved to think of marriage. And the wise ones did conceal well their liking hereto, as knowing the Queen's judgment in this matter. Sir Matthew Arundel's fair cousin,[5] not knowing so deeply as her fellows, was asked one day hereof and simply said she had thought much about marriage, if her father did consent to the man she loved.

"You seem honest, i' faith," said the Queen. "I will sue for you to your father."

The damsel was not displeased hereat, and, when Sir Robert[6] came to Court, the Queen asked him hereon and pressed his consenting, if the match was discreet. Sir Robert, much astonied[7] at this news, said he never heard his daughter had liking to any man and wanted to gain knowledge of her affection, but would give free consent to what was most pleasing to her Highness's will and advice.

"Then I will do the rest," saith the Queen.

The lady was called in, and the Queen told her father had given his free consent.

"Then," replied the lady, "I shall be happy and please your Grace."

"So thou shalt, but not to be a fool and marry. I have his consent given to me, and I vow thou shalt never get it into thy possession; so, go to thy business. I see thou art a bold one, to own thy foolishness so readily.[8]

I could relate many pleasant tales of her Majesty's outwitting the wittiest ones, for few knew how to aim their shaft against her cunning. We did all love her, for she said she loved us, and much wisdom she showed in this matter. She did well temper herself towards all at home and put at variance those abroad, by which means she had more quiet than her neighbors. I need not praise her frugality,[9] but I will tell a story that fell out when I was a boy. She did love rich clothing, but often chid those that bought more finery than became their state.[1] It happened that Lady M. Howard was possessed of a rich border[2] powdered with gold and pearl and a velvet suit belonging thereto, which moved many to envy, nor did it please the Queen, who thought it exceeded her own. One day the Queen did send privately and got the lady's rich vesture, which she put on herself and came forth the chamber among the ladies. The kirtle[3] and border was far too short for her Majesty's height, and she asked everyone how they liked her new-fancied suit. At length, she asked the owner herself if it was not made too short and ill becoming, which the poor lady did presently consent to.

---

5. The Arundel family, derived from Cornish gentry, held offices at Court and in Parliament in this period.
6. The young woman's father.
7. Stunned, amazed.
8. The Queen's opposition was probably more to the lady's entertainment of a wooer behind her father's back than to the marriage *per se*. Though Elizabeth preferred that her ladies-in-waiting not disrupt their service by marrying and occasionally opposed them unaccountably, she also allowed many to marry with her blessing.
9. Harington frequently complained of the Queen's lack of open-handedness toward him.
1. Status.
2. Piece of ornamental clothwork.
3. Gown.

"Why, then, if it become not me as being too short, I am minded it shall never become thee, as being too fine; so it fitteth neither well."

This sharp rebuke abashed the lady, and she never adorned her herewith any more. I believe the vestment was laid up till after the Queen's death.

As I did bear so much love toward her Majesty, I know not well how to stop my tales of her virtues and sometimes her faults, for *nemo nascitur sine,*[4] saith the poet, but even her errors seem great marks of surprising endowments. When she smiled, it was a pure sunshine, that every one did choose to bask in, if they could; but anon came a storm from a sudden gathering of clouds, and the thunder fell in wondrous manner on all alike. I never did find greater show of understanding and learning than she was blest with, and whoever liveth longer than I can, will look back and become *laudator temporis acti.*[5] Yet, too, will I praise the present times, or I should be unmindful of many favors received from many hands.

Now will I try to stop and give your patience a breathing time from my history, but the subject of the letter will excuse my tedious reciting. I write from wonder and affection.

FRANCIS BACON

From The Felicity of Queen Elizabeth and Her Times (1608)[†]

In her religion she was pious, constant, moderate, and could not away with[1] innovations. Her piety chiefly appeared in her works and actions, but it was also seen in the ordinary course and conversation of her life: she was seldom absent from prayers in her closet or at sermons and solemn service abroad; diligent in reading the Scriptures; well versed in the Fathers[2] and above all in St Augustine; upon diverse occasions she composed sundry prayers. When she mentioned God (though in common talk) added for the most part of Creator, casting, as I have often observed, her face and eyes into a reverend form of humility.[3] And whereat some have published that she put off the thought of mortality nor could abide to hear of old age or death, it is most untrue. For many years before her end, she was not nice[4] often and with much grace to call herself "old woman" and used to discourse of her tomb and what inscription would most please her, saying she delighted not in long titles or shadows of glory: a line or two would be enough for her memory, which in few words should only express her name in her virginity, the time of her reign, the restoring of religion, and establishment of peace. True it is that being once importuned to declare her successor whilst she was yet in her full strength, not unfit to bear children,

4. No one is born without them.
5. Praiser of the deeds of those days.
† Copy text: Francis Bacon, *The felicity of Queen Elizabeth and her times with other things* (London: George Latham, 1651; Wing B297), 23–31, 36–41.
1. Was not moved by.
2. Ancient and medieval theologians; *conversation*: daily activities; *abroad*: in public.
3. Elizabeth did not casually use God's name, but honored him as Creator even in her ordinary speech; *though*: even; *Creator*: she generally said "Creator God."
4. Reluctant.

she would not endure her winding sheet[5] to be spread before her eyes; and yet not long before her death, sitting pensive and (as it were) musing of mortality, as one came and told her that diverse places stood too long vacant in the state, she rose up somewhat offended and said she knew well enough that her place would not stand an instant empty.

Her moderation may perchance be doubted in matter of religion, considering the severity of those laws she made against the papists, but herein we will produce such only things whereof we have certain knowledge and made diligent search. Out of all question, the meaning of this Princess's mind was this: neither to offer violence to the consciences of men nor to suffer her state to be disquieted under pretext of conscience, out of which foundation she judged, first of all, that the toleration of two religions in one hot heart-burning people, who from difference in mind might break out into blows, might be of pernicious consequence to the state. Thereupon, at her entrance upon the crown, when all things were full of suspicion, she used the power of the law and committed some of the busiest and most factious prelates for the rest of their coat.[6] So far was she from vexing them with severe inquisitions that she winked at their faults and took them into her protection. This was the first state of things, and although the interdiction of Pius V[7] might have stirred up her anger and made her resolve of a sharper course, yet she departed not from her nature and changed little from her mildness. For, like a most wise and heroical lady, secure of her people's love and that the popish faction could not stir at home without far assistance, she passed[8] little for the claps of the Pope's thunder.

But about the three and twentieth of her reign, things received an alteration, which change of time was not complotted by design[9] but recorded in public acts and cut, as it were, in brass for perpetuity. Till that year, no great or heavy punishment was laid upon her popish subjects by the laws precedent,[1] but now the vast projects and ambitions of Spain for subduing of this kingdom began to be detected, whereof a principal part was that a newfangled faction should be raised in the bowels of this state, which should not only be ready to receive a foreign invader, but also (under pretence of the Roman religion and power of the Pope's Bull) should absolve her subjects from their faith and allegiance and prepare their spirits for dangerous innovations. About that time, Ireland was assaulted with open arms, scandalous libels were cast out against the fame and government of the Queen, and all things seemed to swell up in presage[2] of greater emotions.

* * *

In the beginning of her reign, when prisoners (as the manner is) were released for a boon of her new inauguration, a certain courtier, who by custom had taken up a boldness of speech and jestingly waited for her as she went to chapel, when (either of himself or set on by wiser men) he put

---

5. Funeral shroud, used metaphorically to mean her future death.
6. Elizabeth committed to prison only her most outspoken religious critics as a warning to others of their stripe.
7. The Bull excommunicating her in 1570 (see Part Three).
8. Cared; *far*: foreign.
9. A secret conspiracy; *three and twentieth . . . reign*: 1580, the year in which the Jesuits began their campaign to reconvert England to Roman Catholicism.
1. Previous laws.
2. Prophecy; *of the Queen*: copy text: and the Queen.

an humble petition, crying out aloud withal that yet there remained four or five honest prisoners who were unjustly detained, beseeching her Majesty to set them at liberty: and they were the four evangelists and Saint Paul the Apostle, who had been long shut up in a strange language, as in a prison, and kept from conversing among the people.[3] To whom she wisely answered that full inquiry should be made of themselves[4] whether they would be revealed, yea or no. Whereby she put off a sudden question with a suspended answer and still reserved the interest of things[5] in her own freedom and decision.

In which business she proceeded not by pieces or with trepidation, but in a grave and settled order: first, calling the synods to conference and the states to Parliament, and then within compass of one year so reformed ecclesiastical affairs that till her dying day she departed not a whit from the constitution[6] then determined. Yea, ever after, her custom was to warn almost every Parliament when it sat that nothing should be changed in the rite and discipline of the Church. And thus far concerning religion.

Now to leave these sadder things: if any man should think it a lightness that she suffered herself to be courted and wooed and refused not to be seen upon the scene of Love, even beyond the condition of her age, this (if it be gently construed) wanted[7] not also a share in admiration. For it soundeth unlike those old stories of a maiden queen living in Elysian Islands, from whose Court none was debarred that used fair accostment and no lasciviousness in love; but if it be severely scanned,[8] then greater is the wonder. For albeit that we often see that a state is loosened by the looseness of the prince, yet these delights she used with such a curb that they little dimmed her fame, less her majesty, and softened the vigor and dispensation of her state nothing at all.

But to shut up[9] my discourse, the Prince was certainly good and virtuous, and so she desired to seem. She hated vices and took the way to fame by that of honor. Whilst I am upon her virtues, I cannot forget one passage: when letters were written to her ambassadors in France to deliver some private message to the Queen Mother then of Valois wherein her secretary[1] (as it were) to curry favor had inserted this clause, that the ambassador should say they two were two such queens so versed in sovereign arts and seen in politic affairs as no kings nor men in the world went beyond them, she misliked the association and commanded it to be blotted out, saying the arts she had learned were of a better stamp and the principles of a far higher nature whereby she ruled her people.

She was not puffed up with the length of her reign, although she was long a queen. For if any had told her fitly in discourse that the world would

---

3. Prohibitions against the English Bible and the Book of Common Prayer had been instituted by Elizabeth's predecessor, her sister Mary Tudor, and were among the laws Protestants were most eager to see overturned; *her Majesty:* copy text: he Majesty; *strange language:* Latin.
4. The four gospel writers (Matthew, Mark, Luke, and John) and St. Paul.
5. Issue in question.
6. The acts of Parliament that established the Elizabethan Settlement of 1559, which charted a moderate Protestant course for the English Church; *synods:* groups composed of church officials; *states:* estates; members of the Upper and Lower Houses of Parliament.
7. Lacked; *sadder:* more serious; *even beyond the condition of her age:* even when she was old; *gently:* generously.
8. Carefully analyzed; *Elysian Islands:* the Isles of the Blessed in the ancient underworld; *accostment:* approach.
9. Conclude.
1. Probably William Cecil, Lord Burghley. *Queen Mother . . . Valois:* Catherine de Medici, infamous in England for such acts as the St. Bartholomew's Day massacre.

have taken notice of her admirable parts, though she had lived in some mean estate, she would have been well pleased with such insinuations,[2] so much she desired that her virtue should stand alone, unbeholding to her fortune for praise.

EARLY HISTORIES AND BIOGRAPHIES

While seventeenth-century writers were publishing personal recollections and evaluations of the Queen, they were also beginning more careful histories of the reign based on a new model of history. Rather than chronicling year by year, which had long been customary in England, they began to produce works that were not bound to the amassing of annual details on various subjects, from earthquakes and misshapen births to royal decrees, but that traced religious, military, and political developments over longer intervals.

A leader in the development of new forms of historical writing was William Camden, the headmaster of Westminster Grammar School in London, who published the first topographical survey of Britain in 1586. Between 1608 and 1617, he worked on *The History of the Life and Reign of Queen Elizabeth*, which he wrote in Latin. It was the first complete biography of Elizabeth, and it was begun at the request of William Cecil, Lord Burghley, who gave Camden access to his private papers. The full English translation, running to over 300 pages, was finally published in 1630, after Camden's death. Camden was a careful historian, but he also enjoyed reporting personal anecdotes from the Queen's life. His partisanship of Burghley shows through, particularly in the slighting remarks made of Leicester, Walsingham, and others with whom Cecil sometimes found himself at odds.

Another man with an interest in new forms of historical writing was Sir Robert Naunton. He served James I and his son, Charles I, but as a serious Protestant found himself out of step with much of the politics in the Stuart Court. In 1634, during the final months of his life, he completed his only book, *Fragmenta Regalia*, which looks back with some nostalgia at the Court of Elizabeth. Naunton particularly disliked the ways in which the Stuart monarchs relied on and rewarded favorite courtiers. By contrast, Naunton points out that Elizabeth judiciously managed her

The Illustrious and most Renowned Princess ELIZABETH late QVEENE of ENGLAND

Elizabeth enthroned.

2. Statements.

councilors and rewarded them appropriately, although he acknowledges her well-known penchant for frugality. The excerpt that follows includes an anecdote about the Earl of Leicester's presumption and the Queen's famous put-down of him in her response, as well as praise of Elizabeth's amiable relations with Parliament and the wise "Parliament men" who served her and the nation.

In 1599, Sir John Hayward, a lawyer and historian, had published a biography of Henry IV that already moved away from the sequential chronicle style of Holinshed and other early historians to emphasize the role that character and personal behavior played in causing events within the public realm. Elizabeth suspected the biography of fueling the ambitions of Robert Devereux, Earl of Essex, to whom it was dedicated, and she remanded Hayward to the Tower of London, where he remained until her death. On his release, however, Hayward joined the Court of James I and may have become a tutor to his son Henry, Prince of Wales. It was Henry, apparently, who encouraged Hayward to continue his psychological portraits and he did so with one entitled *The Beginning of the Reign of Queen Elizabeth*.

WILLIAM CAMDEN

From The History of the Life and Reign of . . . Elizabeth, Late Queen of England (1617)†

[In 1562,] the war now growing hot in France between the princes of the blood[1] and the Guises, both sides seeking (as I said) the cloak and color of religion as the foundation of their party, Queen Elizabeth began to fear lest England would also be involved in the fire of her neighbor's war. For she had heard that the Guises, to the end to allure Antoine of Bourbon, King of Navarre, to their party had secretly offered unto him the kingdom of Navarre and the marriage of the Queen of Scots, together with the kingdom of England in dowry, and that by the help of the King of Spain's wealth and the Bishop of Rome's authority who would dissolve the marriage of Navarre with his heretical wife[2] and withal depose Queen Elizabeth from her crown for heresy. Hereupon she sent thither Sir Henry Sidney,[3] a man of most approved note, to learn these things more certainly and persuade the heads of the parties to peace. But the matter was now grown to that pass that they stopped their ears on both sides against peace. Sidney, returning out of France, was presently sent to the Queen of Scots that the interview which she had desired with Queen Elizabeth in England might be put off till the next year following or till the French war were pacified.[4]

*   *   *

[In 1564], the Queen went in progress to take the pleasures of the country and visited the University of Cambridge, one of the eyes of Britain, where being with all kinds of honor received by the students and delighted with

---

† Copy text: William Camden, *The historie of the life and reigne of . . . Elizabeth, late Queene of England* (London: Benjamin Fisher, 1630; STC 4500.5), 1:59, 72; 2:62–63, 115; 4:16–17.
1. Heirs of the royal Valois line.
2. Jeanne d'Albret, a Protestant princess and heiress of Navarre; *kingdom of Navarre*: area of France that he ruled by virtue of his marriage.
3. The father of Sir Philip Sidney and Mary Sidney Herbert, Countess of Pembroke.
4. Elizabeth and Mary Stuart never met for their face-to-face interview.

comedies, tragedies, and scholastical disputations, she surveyed every college and, in a Latin oration, acknowledged their love and kindness, commending their multiplicity of learning, exhorting them to bend their whole mind and cogitations to the study of good letters, whereof she promised to deserve well.

* * *

Whether I should make mention of the frantic opinion of Peter Burchet I know not, who had persuaded himself that it was lawful to kill such as opposed the truth of the Gospel.[5] So far had the error of this opinion transported him that [in 1573] he drew his dagger upon Hawkins, that famous navigator, in the open street and wounded him, supposing him to be Hatton, who was then in great grace with the Queen and of her Privy Council, whom he had heard to be one that opposed the innovators.[6] The Queen was so extraordinarily incensed with this fact that she commanded the man to be presently executed by martial or camp law until she was informed by the wiser sort that martial law was not to be used but in camps or in turbulent times, but at home and in time of peace, the proceeding must be by form of judiciary process. Being therefore indicted, he affirmed that that which he had done was consonant to the Holy Scriptures and therefore lawful. Whereupon being to be condemned of heresy, he promised to renounce his opinion, but yet he shifted i[t] off and would not. Then being cast into the Tower of London, he slew one of his keepers with a billet,[7] which he snatched up out of the chimney and knocked him on the head, for which he was condemned of murder, had his right hand cut off and nailed to the gallows, and then was hanged, he making resistance without any words.

* * *

[Sir Francis Drake] returned with a prosperous gale into England the third of November in the year 1580, to the haven of Plymouth, from whence he had set forth, having sailed round about the world in the space of three years or thereabouts to the great admiration of all men and without any crime laid to his charge by his adversaries other than this: that he had put Doughty to death, that he had left a Portuguese whom he had taken upon the coast of Africa to the cruelty of the Spaniards at Aquatulco,[8] and had inhumanely set that negress maid on shore in an island after she was gotten with child in his ship.

The Queen received him graciously and laid up his wealth by way of sequestration[9] that it might be forthcoming if the Spaniard should demand it. His ship she caused to be drawn up into a little creek near Deptford upon the Thames for a monument of his so lucky sailing round about the world (where the carcass thereof is yet to be seen). And in it, being consecrated for a memorial with great ceremony, she was banqueted and honored Drake with the dignity of knighthood. At which time a bridge of planks by which they came aboard the ship sunk under the press of people and fell down

5. See also Strickland's account below.
6. The emerging Puritan party; *Hawkins*: Sir John Hawkins, later treasurer of the Navy and a rear admiral during the Spanish Armada, who undertook trade voyages to the Americas in the 1560s. *Hatton*: Christopher Hatton, who was beginning his ascent at Court.
7. Piece of firewood.
8. Now named Huatulco, in Oaxaca, Mexico; *Doughty*: Thomas Doughty, executed for mutiny at Port St. Julian, near the Magellan Straits.
9. In the Tower of London.

with an hundred men upon it, who notwithstanding had none of them any harm, so as that ship may seem to have been built under a lucky planet.

*   *   *

[In 1590], Queen Elizabeth, who had always made peace the sum of her cogitations and therefore had never cast away the cares of war lest she should be surprised at unawares by the Spaniard, in the very beginning of the spring maketh levies[1] of men in England and in the south part of Ireland [and made many large military expenditures]. * * * Insomuch as very many admired whence this wealth came to supply these turns,[2] seeing she was in no man's debt (as almost all other princes were) and was able to defend herself and hers without foreign helps, which not one of her neighbor kings could do.

But the truth is she, being providently frugal, scarcely spent anything but for the maintenance of her royal honor, the defense of her kingdom, or the relieving of her neighbors. And Burghley, Lord Treasurer, looked narrowly into those which had the charge of customs and imposts (by whose avarice many things were under-hand embezzled, and through their negligence much was not exacted), especially after such time as the Queen (being not long before informed by one Caermarden, a diligent and subtle fellow, of the mysteries of the farmers of her customs) had caused Sir Thomas Smith, Customer[3] (as they call him), who had bought or farmed her customs for £14,000 a year of English money, to pay from thenceforth £42,000, contributing no small sum of money in recompense for so gainful a bargain so many years, and afterwards to pay £50,000 for the same, although the Lord Treasurer, Leicester, and Walsingham labored to the contrary, opposed themselves against Caermarden, commanded the gentlemen of the Privy Chamber not to let him in, yea and expostulated with the Queen as if this would tend to the disgrace of her and her Council, if she should harken to the accusations of so silly an informer. But she answered that it was the duty of a prince to hold the highest in equal right with the lowest; that such as accuse magistrates and councilors rashly are to be punished, they which accuse them justly to be heard; that she was Queen of the lowest as well as of the greatest; neither would she stop her ears against them, nor endure that the farmers of the customs should, like horse leaches, suck themselves fat with the goods of the commonwealth whilst the poor treasury waxeth lean, nor that the treasury should abound with the spoils of poor men.

Certainly she ever detested extortions and all bitterness in exacting extraordinary contributions, which the former kings sweetened with the flattering names of "the people's liberality," "benevolence," and "friendly grant" and other such like. The taxing of living creatures by the poll,[4] propounded in Edward VI's reign, she would not suffer to be once named. Besides, the people always gave subsidies cheerfully and, though the taxation by sessment[5] seemed greater than in old time, yet was there no rough manner of taxing used. Insomuch as those subsidies were rather voluntary, without inquiry or any constraint, and always less than the estates of the realm[6] thought them. Yea, she commanded it to be referred to the estates of the

1. Taxes; *cares of*: concerns about.
2. Various public works.
3. One who collects customs; *imposts*: customs levied on imports; *farmers*: collectors.
4. A flat head-tax.
5. Assessment.
6. Parliament, with its three estates: commoners, clergy, and nobility.

realm that the rich might pay more and the poorer sort might be spared, which was once done in the reign of Richard II, but it failed of success. For casting up the accounts, they found that the subsidies would be very small if men of mean estates, whereof there was the greatest number (whom we call the poundmen), should pay less than they were wont.[7]

SIR ROBERT NAUNTON

From Fragmenta Regalia, or Observations on the Late Queen Elizabeth (1634)[†]

She was of personage tall, of hair and complexion fair, and therewith well-favored but high nosed, of limbs and feature neat and (which added to the luster of those exterior graces) of stately and majestic comportment, participating in this more of her father than mother, who was of an inferior allay, plausible or (as the French hath it) more debonair and affable, virtues which might well suit with majesty and which descending, as hereditary to the daughter, did render her of a more sweeter temper and endeared her more to the love and liking of the people, who gave her the name and fame of a most gracious and popular prince, the atrocity of her father's nature being rebated in hers by the mother's sweeter inclinations, for to take (and that no more than the character)[1] out of his own mouth, he never spared man in his anger nor woman in his lust.

If we search further into her intellectuals and abilities, the whole course of her government deciphers them to the admiration of posterity, for it was full of magnanimity tempered with justice and piety and, to speak truly, noted but with one act or taint, all her deprivations[2] either of life or liberty being legal and necessitated. She was learned (her sex and the time considered) beyond common belief, for letters about this time, and somewhat before, began to be of esteem and in fashion, the former ages being overcast with the mists and fogs of the Roman ignorance,[3] and it was the maxim that overruled the foregoing times that ignorance was the mother of devotion.

Her wars were a long time more, in the auxiliary part, in assistance of foreign princes and states than by invasion of any, till common policy advised it for a safer way to strike first and broad than at home to expect the war,[4] in all which she was felicious and victorious.

The change and alteration of religion upon the instant of her accession (the smoke and fire of her sister's martyrdoms scarcely quenched) was none of her least remarkable accounts. But the support and establishment thereof, with the means of her subsistence amidst so powerful enemies abroad and those many domestic practices were (methinks) works of inspiration and of

---

7. Accustomed to do.
† Copy text: Robert Naunton, *Fragmenta regalia, or, Observations on the late Queen Elizabeth, her times and favorits* ([London: s.n.], 1641; Wing N250), 4–9.
1. The actual words; *allay*: alloy; as Naunton notes earlier, Anne Bolyen, though a gentlewoman, was not descended from royalty; *plausible*: praiseworthy.
2. Punishments involving taking something away; *deciphers*: reveals.
3. Protestants accused Roman Catholics of promoting ignorance by keeping people illiterate and withholding from them vernacular translations of the Bible.
4. She attacked Spanish ports before the Armada set sail; *broad*: abroad; *expect*: anticipate.

no human providence, which on her sister's departure she most religiously acknowledged, ascribing the glory of her deliverance to God alone, so she received the news both of the Queen's death and her proclamation by the general consent of the House and the public suffrage of the people, whereat, falling on her knees (after a good time of respiration) she uttered this verse of the Psalms, "*A Domino factum est istud, et est mirabile in oculis nostris*," which we find to this day on the stamp of her gold, with this on her silver: "*Posui Deum adjutorem meum*."[5]

* * *

The principal note of her reign will be that she ruled much by faction and parties, which herself both made, upheld, and weakened as her own great judgment advised, for I disassent[6] from the common received opinion that my Lord of Leicester was absolute and above all in her grace, and though I come somewhat short of the knowledge of those times, yet (that I might not rove and shoot at random) I know it from assured intelligence that it was not so, for proof whereof (among many that I could present) I will both relate a short and therein a known truth. And it was thus: Bowyer, a gentleman of the Black Rod, being charged by her express command to look precisely to all admissions into the Privy Chamber one day stayed[7] a very gay captain and a follower of my Lord of Leicester from entrance, for that he was neither well known nor a sworn servant to the Queen, at which repulse the gentleman, bearing high on my Lord's favor, told him he might perchance procure him a discharge. Leicester, coming into the contestation, said publicly (which was none of his wont) that he[8] was a knave and should not continue long in his office, and so, turning about to go in to the Queen, Bowyer (who was a bold gentleman and well-beloved) stepped before him and fell at her Majesty's feet, related the story, and humbly craves her Grace's pleasure and whether my Lord of Leicester was King or her Majesty Queen.

Whereunto she replied, with her wonted oath, "God's death, my lord, I have wished you well, but my favor is not so locked up for you that others shall not partake hereof, for I have many servants unto whom I have and will at my pleasure bequeath my favor, and likewise resume the same, and if you think to rule here, I will take a course to see you forthcoming.[9] I will have here but one mistress and no master, and look that no ill happen to him,[1] lest it be severely required at your hands," which so quelled my Lord of Leicester that his feigned humility was long after one of his best virtues.

* * *

We are naturally prone to applaud the times behind us and to vilify the present, for the current of her fame carries it to this day, how royally and victoriously she lived and died, without the grievance and grudge of the

---

5. "I have chosen God for my helper." Agnes Strickland notes that these sentences were used on Mary's coins, Elizabeth turning them to her own use at this time (3:103); *House*: Parliament; *respiration*: respite; *A Domino . . . in oculis nostris*: "This was the Lord's doing, and it is marvelous in our eyes" (Psalm 118.23).
6. Dissent.
7. Stopped; *gentleman . . . Black Rod*: an usher, or doorkeeper, whose symbol of office was a black rod topped by a golden lion.
8. Bowyer; *which . . . wont*: which was not his business.
9. Leaving the Court.
1. Bowyer.

people, yet that truth may appear without retraction from the honor of so great a princess. * * * For I believe no prince living that was so tender of honor and so exactly stood for the preservation of sovereignty, that was so great a courtier of her people, yea of the commons,[2] and that stooped and descended lower in presenting her person to the public view, as she passed in her progresses and perambulations and in the ejaculation of her prayers on her people. And truly, though much may be given in praise of her magnanimity and therewith comply with her Parliaments, and for all that come off at last with honor and profit, yet must we ascribe some part of the commendation to the wisdoms of the times and the choice of Parliament men, for I find not that they were at any time given to any violent or pertinacious[3] dispute, elections being made of grave and discreet persons, not factious and ambitious of fame, such as came not to the House with a malevolent spirit of contention but with a preparation to consult on the public good, rather to comply than contest with her Majesty. * * * So that the Queen and her Parliaments had ever the good fortune to depart in love and on reciprocal terms.

SIR JOHN HAYWARD

From The Beginning of the Reign of Queen Elizabeth (1636)[†]

Now if ever any person had either the gift or the skill to win the hearts of people, it was this Queen, and if ever she did express the same, it was at that present,[1] in coupling mildness with majesty as she did and in stately stooping to the meanest sort. All her faculties were in motion, and every motion seemed a well guided action: her eye was set upon one, her ear listened to another, her judgment ran upon a third, to a fourth she addressed her speech. Her spirit seemed to be everywhere and yet so entire in herself as it seemed to be nowhere else. Some she commended, some she pitied, some she thanked, at others she pleasantly and wittily jested, contemning[2] no person, neglecting no office, and generally casting forth such courteous countenance, gestures, and speeches that thereupon the people again redoubled the testimonies of their joy and, afterwards, raising everything to the highest strain, filled the ears of all men with immoderate extolling their Prince.

She was a lady upon whom Nature had bestowed and well placed many of her fairest favors: of stature mean,[3] slender, straight, and amiably composed; of such state in her carriage as every motion of her seemed to bear majesty. Her hair was inclined to pale yellow, her forehead large and fair (a seemly seat for princely grace), her eyes lively and sweet but short-sighted,

---

2. Common people.
3. Stubborn; *comply with*: include.
† Copy text: John Hayward, *The life and reigne of King Edward the Sixth with the beginning of the reigne of Queene Elizabeth* (London: Iohn Partridge, 1636; STC 12999), 448–54.
1. During her coronation procession.
2. Disdaining.
3. Average height.

her nose somewhat rising in the midst, the whole compass of her countenance somewhat long but yet of admirable beauty, not so much in that which is termed the flower of youth as in a most delightful composition of majesty and modesty in equal mixture. But without good qualities of mind, the gifts of nature are like painted flowers, without either virtue or sap; yea, sometimes they grow horrid and loathsome.

Now her virtues were such as might suffice to make an Ethiopian beautiful, which the more a man can know and understand, the more he shall admire and love. In life, she was most innocent; in desires, moderate; in purpose, just; of spirit, above credit and almost capacity of her sex;[4] of divine wit, as well for depth of judgment as for quick conceit and speedy expedition; of eloquence, as sweet in the utterance, so ready and easy to come to the utterance; of wonderful knowledge both in learning and affairs, skillful not only in the Latin and Greek but in diverse other foreign languages. None knew better the hardest art of all others, that is, of commanding men. She was religious, magnanimous, merciful and just, respective of the honor of others and exceeding tender in the touch[5] of her own. She was lovely and loving, the two principal bands of duty and obedience. She was very ripe and measured in council and experience, as well not to let go occasions as not to take them when they were green. She maintained justice at home and arms abroad, with great wisdom and authority in either place. Her majesty seemed to all to shine through courtesy, but as she was not easy[6] to receive any to especial grace, so was she most constant to those whom she received and of great judgment to know to what point of greatness men were fit to be advanced. She was rather liberal than magnificent, making good choice of the receivers, and for this cause was thought weak[7] by some against the desire of money. But it is certain that beside the want[8] of treasure which she found, her continual affairs in Scotland, France, the Low Countries, and in Ireland, did occasion great provision of money, which could not be better supplied than by cutting off either excessive or unnecessary expense at home.

Excellent Queen! What do my words but wrong thy worth? What do I but gild gold? What but show sun with a candle, in attempting to praise thee, whose honor doth fly over the whole world upon the two wings of Magnanimity and Justice, whose perfection shall much dim the luster of all others that shall be of thy sex?

ANTIQUARIAN BIOGRAPHIES

In the late seventeenth century, as the reign of Elizabeth passed further into memory, a new kind of biography emerged. Higher literacy rates, lower costs for books, and an expanding market for retrospectives on England's past led to biographies designed for wide appeal, one of which was written by Edmund Bohun, a religious and political controversialist famous for his irascible temperament and his adoption of unpopular positions. Such friends as he did not drive away

---

4. Beyond belief and almost possibility for a woman.
5. Quick to take offense at any disparagement of her honor.
6. Quick.
7. Parsimonious; *rather . . . magnificent*: more generous than extravagant.
8. Lack.

with his attacks on religious dissenters deserted him over his view that William and Mary deserved to rule England following their defeat of James II in the "Glorious Revolution" of 1688 simply because they had conquered their opponents. In 1693, he lost his post as Licenser of the Press for approving publication of a book that propounded that view. His *Character of Queen Elizabeth*, which appeared in the same year, may have been written as an escape to an age less turbulent than his own. Not only is it the fullest account of the Queen and her reign to appear in the seventeenth century, but it is also one of the most personal and entertaining. Balancing glimpses of the splendors of her surroundings at Court with more prosaic details about her daily routine and her interactions with servants and the common people, it brings out her human qualities, such as her dislike of seeing her reflection in the mirror as she aged, her fondness for small animals and birds, her tendency to fly into sudden rages, and her delight in ceremonial display. The influence of Bohun's depiction of Elizabeth is evident in the work of later biographers, including Ballard and Strickland.

As the Enlightenment, with its interest in cause and effect within the human and natural world, widened its effect in the eighteenth century, it led to the development of antiquarian interests among men outside the university, who collected documents and artifacts from former ages and published what they had found for educated readers of the day. George Ballard, a tailor by trade and an amateur historian, spent some fifteen years researching the intellectual achievements of over sixty women who lived between 1400 and 1733. In a period when women were generally praised for their noble birth, piety, or beauty, Ballard sought instead to refurbish the reputations of those who had been wrongfully excluded from the "republic of letters," noting incredulously that many women "who were really possessed of a great share of learning" had been "passed by in silence by our greatest biographers" (53). His appreciation of Queen Elizabeth follows her progress from her earliest instruction by Katherine Champernowne and William Grindal through to her final acts of devotion and prayer upon her deathbed. The following excerpts from *Memoirs of Several Ladies of Great Britain* recount her education during her adolescence and her return to her studies once she became Queen of England.

In the second half of the nineteenth century, the antiquarian movement continued to produce popular biographies of rulers such as Elizabeth even as serious academic study was beginning to undertake new and more systematic searches of state archives, personal papers, and other documents. *Lives of the Queens of England*, written by Agnes Strickland and her elder sister Elizabeth, was one of the most popular of the many Victorian collections of biographies. Written in accessible prose, the multiple volumes were well researched—the authors, after some difficulty, having obtained permission to work with the archival papers—and they remain a landmark of their genre.

The following excerpts from *Lives of the Queens of England* describe Queen Elizabeth at work, at leisure, and among her people. Although Strickland admired Elizabeth, she was not above criticizing her, as in her retelling of Camden's account of Peter Burchet. Nor was she pleased at the Queen's abiding interest in the occult arts, which brought her into repeated contact with the alchemist, astrologer, and mathematician Dr. John Dee, who influenced the thinking of a number of great men at Court. Strickland records with distaste a meeting at Dee's country home at Mortlake in 1575, where he delighted the Queen by reflecting her image in a mirror thought to have magic powers. But Strickland, unlike Naunton, also passes judgment on Elizabeth's councilors, frequently calling them to account for poor advice or bad behavior.

EDMUND BOHUN

From The Character of Queen Elizabeth (1693)†

[In old age,] time was able to make no change in her as to her majesty, her princely speech and carriage. Her mind was high, her manners as regular, and the course of her life the same it had ever been. She was, however, so displeased to see her beauty wear off and her body decline from its former luster that she made herself a little ridiculous by her taking too much notice of it. If she happened by accident to cast her eye upon a true looking glass, she would be strangely transported and offended, because it did not still show her what she had been. The courtiers who knew her humor, if she were to pass through any of the ladies' chambers that waited on her, presently conveyed away all the looking-glasses, and sometimes for haste broke them. To please and flatter her, they would also frequently admire her beauty and pretend, in her greatest age and deformity, she was still handsome and lovely. She was strangely pleased to hear the beauty of her face, the sweetness of her voice, the majesty and *décence*[1] of her countenance still admired by others, and this gave occasion to many unworthy strokes of flattery and examples of adulation.

* * *

She loved a prudent and moderate habit in her private apartment and conversation[2] with her own servants, but when she appeared in public, she was ever richly adorned with the most valuable clothes, set off again with much gold and jewels of inestimable value, and on such occasions, she ever wore high shoes that she might seem taller than indeed she was. The first day of the Parliament, she would appear in a robe embroidered with pearls, the royal crown upon her head, the golden ball in her left hand and the scepter in her right, and as she never failed then of the loud acclamations of her people, so she was ever pleased with it, and went to the House in a kind of triumph, with all the ensigns[3] of majesty. There was at such times so great a concourse of the people to see and salute the queen that many were trodden down and some have been lamed.

* * *

In the furniture[4] of her royal palaces, she ever affected magnificence and an extraordinary splendor. She adorned the galleries with excellent pictures done by the best artists; the walls she covered with rich tapestries. She was a true lover of jewels and pearls, all sorts of precious stones, plate (plain, bossed of gold and silver, and gilt); rich beds, fine coaches and chariots,[5] Persian and Indian carpets, statues, medals, etc, which she would purchase

---

† Copy text: Edmund Bohun, *The Character of Queen Elizabeth, or, A full and clear account of her policies, and the methods of her government both in church and state her virtue and defects, together with the characters of her principal ministers of state, and the greatest part of the affairs and events that happened in her times* (London: Ric. Chiswell, 1693; Wing B3448), 302–3, 339, 341–42, 345–46, 348–51, 354–56, 376.
1. Propriety (French).
2. Living arrangements; *habit*: attire.
3. Symbols; *golden ball*: royal orb, with cross on top, symbol of monarchy; *House*: House of Parliament.
4. Furnishings.
5. Carriages; *plate*: metal vessels and utensils; *bossed*: ornamented; *gilt*: gold plated.

at great prices. * * * She had caused her naval victories obtained against the Spaniards to be represented in excellent tapestries and laid up amongst the richest pieces of her wardrobe.

* * *

The coming of the Duke of Alençon[6] into England opened a way to a more free way of living and relaxed very much the old severe form of discipline. The Queen danced often then and omitted no sort of recreation, pleasant conversation, or variety of delights for his satisfaction. * * * There were then acted comedies and tragedies with much cost and splendor, from whence proceeded in after-times an unrefrainable desire of frequenting these divertisements, so that there was afterwards a greater concourse at the theater than at the sermon. When these things had once been entertained, the courtiers were never more to be reclaimed from them, and they could not be satiated or wearied with them. But when Alençon was once dismissed and gone, the Queen herself left off these divertisements and betook herself, as before, to the care of her kingdom, and by her own example and severe corrections, she as heartily endeavored to reduce her nobility to their old, severe way of living and the former, provident way of clothing.

* * *

In the summer, she for the most part lived in the country. * * * In her progress, she was the most easy to be approached. Private persons and magistrates, men and women, country people and children, came joyfully and without any fear to wait upon her and see her. Her ears were then open to the complaints of the afflicted and of those that had been any way injured. She would not suffer the meanest of her people to be shut out from the places where she resided, but the greatest and the least were then in a manner leveled.

* * *

She spent her winter in London in the procuring the safety of her people and that of her allies and confederates. Before day every morning, she heard the petitions of those that had any business with her, and calling her Secretaries of State and Masters of Requests, she caused the orders of Council, proclamations, patents, and all other papers relating to the public to be read which were then depending,[7] and gave such order in each affair as she thought fit, which was set down in short notes, either by her self or her secretaries. As often as anything happened that was difficult, she called her great and wise men to her, and proposing the diversity of opinions, she very attentively considered and weighed on which side the strongest reason lay, ever preferring that way which seemed most to promote the public safety and welfare.

* * *

She loved little dogs, singing birds, parrots, and apes; and when she was in private, she would recreate herself with various discourses, a game at chess, dancing, or singing. Then she would retire into her bedchamber,

6. Known in this volume by his later title, Duke of Anjou.
7. Pending approval; *Secretaries . . . Requests*: Court officials who dealt with petitions to the monarch for relief; *patents*: documents conferring some privilege, right, office, or benefit.

where she was attended by married ladies of the nobility. * * * She would seldom suffer any to wait upon her there, except Leicester, Hatton, Essex, Nottingham,[8] and Sir Walter Ralegh, who were more intimately conversant with her than any other of the courtiers.

* * *

She was subject to be vehemently transported with anger, and when she was so, she would show it by her voice, her countenance, and her hand. She would chide her familiar servants so loud that they that stood afar off might sometimes hear her voice, and it was reported that for small offences, she would strike her Maids of Honor with her hand. But then her anger was short, and very innocent, and she learned from Zenophon's book of the institution of Cyrus[9] the method of curbing and correcting this unruly and uneasy passion.

* * *

When the report had once spread the news of her death in the city of London, an incredible sorrow and lamentation, both of the citizens and strangers, was observed, which spread itself to all the neighbor nations as the fame of her death was communicated to them. But none more heartily deplored this loss than the Hollanders[1] who were thereby deprived of the author of their fortunes, the defender of their liberty, and the preserver of their peace and safety. A prince she was that would refuse no labor, no expense, no hazard, how great soever it were, that the Protestants might live in peace and enjoy their liberty; and this and the many good offices she had done to them and all the neighbor nations had made her name so venerable that it was no easy task for the magistrates at home or abroad to keep the common people in any bounds in this their outrageous sorrows.

GEORGE BALLARD

From Memoirs of Several Ladies
of Great Britain (1752)[†]

[In 1549,] having lost King Henry, her father, and her valuable tutor at the same time, she was exceedingly fortunate and happy in those who succeeded, for King Edward, her brother, loved her extremely, usually called her his "Lady Temper,"[1] and countenanced and encouraged her in her studies more than could be expected from so young a prince. And she was now no longer apprehensive of her father's furious jealousy in regard to her principles in religion and could without the least restraint read such books of divinity as she and her tutors thought proper.

---

8. Charles, Lord Howard of Effingham, Earl of Nottingham, commander of English naval forces at the defeat of the Spanish Armada; *any to wait*: any men to attend.
9. *Cyropaedia,* a book by the ancient Greek author Xenophon on the education of King Cyrus; *very innocent*: without any serious harm.
1. Dutch Protestants.
† Copy text: George Ballard, *Memoirs of Several Ladies of Great Britain* (Oxford: W. Jackson, 1752), 214, 215–16, 218, 219–20.
1. Temperance; *tutor*: William Grindal, who died in 1548.

In order to supply herself with another preceptor, she sent to the celebrated Master Roger Ascham, who at her pressing importunity left Cambridge, came up to her at Cheshunt, and well supplied the place of her
former tutor.[2] She now pursued her studies with great ardor and read with
peculiar[3] attention many of the best Greek and Latin historians, philosophers, and orators. Her great diligence and ingenuity pleased her new and
learned tutor so much that he speaks of it with the highest satisfaction in
a letter to his friend Sturmius.[4]

*   *   *

Being thus prepared by skill in very many languages, philosophy, etc., she
was by the learned Dr. Grindal, professor of divinity,[5] initiated in the study
of theology, which she pursued with uncommon application and industry.
She read over Melancthon's *Commonplaces*, and (as Mr. Bohun[6] observes)
gained very much by an exact and accurate perusal of the sacred writings.
There were innumerable sentences in the New Testament and the oracles
of the prophets which she had treasured up in her memory and which she
would upon occasion mention, and she attended the offices of religion and
piety with great devotion and care. She often addressed her devoutest prayers
to God and implored His assistance for the obtaining of a chaste heart, a pure
and unspotted life, and a steady and constant soul. Thus did her studies run
in a calm and regular course all the happy but short reign of her excellent
brother, and thus did she by her sincere piety and devotion obtain such a
share of truly Christian fortitude, patience, and resignation as firmly supported her under the long, great, and many afflictions and calamities which
befell her in the cruel reign of the succeeding princess.[7]

*   *   *

After a long interruption of her beloved studies, when she had by her
great wisdom settled the perplexed affairs of her kingdom, I find, in the year
1563, she was then renewing them with great intentness under the care
and inspection of her schoolmaster Master Ascham, who was so transported
with his royal mistress's diligence and progress in literature that he tells the
young gentlemen of England it was their shame that one maid should go
beyond them all in excellency of learning and knowledge of divers tongues.[8]

*   *   *

She herself read over Cicero, Pliny, Livy, and others with so much care
that she became (as Mr. Bohun observes) the mistress of an even, beautiful, pure, unmixed, and truly princely style, in which she could speak with
elegance and facility. As she became thus eloquent and well furnished with

2. William Grindal; *preceptor*: teacher; *Master Roger Ascham*: Ascham served as Elizabeth's tutor from
   1548 to 1550, later became Latin secretary to Edward VI, and wrote of Elizabeth's intellectual
   prowess in the posthumously published *Schoolmaster* (see selection in Part One).
3. Particular.
4. Johann Sturm, a German humanist and educator.
5. Ballard here circles back to Elizabeth's earlier studies with Grindal.
6. Edmund Bohun, author of *The Character of Queen Elizabeth* (see above); *Commonplaces*: the *Loci
   Commune* or *Theological Common Places* of Philipp Melancthon, a Lutheran theologian, was one
   of the most popular Protestant theology textbooks of the sixteenth century. The 1535 edition was
   dedicated to Elizabeth's father, Henry VIII.
7. Her sister, Mary Tudor.
8. See selection in Part One; *renewing . . . Master Ascham*: there is no corroborating evidence that
   Ascham continued to tutor Elizabeth after her accession to the throne.

knowledge by the means of this language, so upon all occasions she was ready to express her love and esteem for the Latin tongue. In this language, she did not make it her business, whilst she was reading the best Latin authors, to furnish her memory only with grammatical observations or a plenty of elegant phrases, which might help to adorn her style or exalt her reputation for learning, but she treasured up those precepts very carefully which were useful for the government of her life or for the managing her private affairs or those of the state well and wisely. To this end she particularly read Livy's *History*, Tacitus's *Annals*, the acts of Tiberius the Emperor, and all Seneca's works. She likewise made many observations for the regulation of manners, the equal administration of justice, and the allaying [of] human passions, that nothing might be done by her angrily, proudly, injuriously, and beyond the rules of civility. There was not one remarkable story or expression in all the works of Thucydides and Xenophon pertaining to the government of life or manners or to the ordering of public affairs but she had it by heart.

She was as great an admirer of philosophy as of eloquence and history, by which she attained the knowledge of many excellent things and that civil prudence or policy which is so absolutely necessary for all princes. And besides all that civil prudence and the knowledge of governing by which the public utility is acquired and improved, she drew from the ancient and most noble philosophers all those precepts which they have set down for the gaining of moral prudence and virtue. Her greatest care was spent in the cultivating these two beautiful parts of philosophy. * * * The divine Plato, that illustrious light of Greece, was made more noble by the hands of this heroic princess, and Aristotle, the prince of the philosophers, was read by her; also Xenophon's *Cyrus*, a piece not writ with the truth of an historian, but to represent the lively image of a just and moderate prince, accomplished with all those endowments which the great Socrates had set forth for the living well and happy.

AGNES STRICKLAND

From Lives of the Queens of England (1848)[†]

[In 1572], Elizabeth kept her Maundy[1] at Greenwich. The palace hall was prepared with a long table on each side, with benches, carpets, and cushions, and a cross-table at the upper end, where the chaplain stood. Thirty-nine poor women, being the same number as the years of her Majesty's age at that time, March 19, 1572, entered and were seated on the forms. Then the yeoman of the laundry came with a fair towel and a silver basin filled with warm water and sweet flowers and washed all their feet, one after the other; he likewise made a cross a little above the toes and kissed each foot after drying it. The sub-almoner[2] performed the same ceremony and the

---

† Copy text: Agnes Strickland, *Lives of the Queens of England, from the Norman Conquest*, revised and augmented edition (London: Bell and Daldy, 1866), 3:258–59, 290–91, 191, 348–50, 441–42, 446.
1. The ceremony of washing the feet of poor persons on Maundy Thursday, the day before Good Friday, in imitation of Christ's washing of his disciples feet (John 13).
2. Almoners and sub-almoners distributed alms on behalf of their employers.

Queen's almoner also. Then her Majesty entered the hall and went to a *prie-dieu*[3] and cushion, placed in the space between the two tables, and remained during prayers and singing and while the Gospel was read how Christ washed his apostles' feet. Then came in a procession of thirty-nine of the Queen's maids of honor and gentlewomen, each carrying a silver basin with warm water, spring-flowers, and sweet herbs, having aprons and towels withal. Then her Majesty, kneeling down on the cushion placed for the purpose, proceeded to wash, in turn, one of the feet of each of the poor women and wiped them with the assistance of the fair basin-bearers. Moreover she crossed and kissed them as the others had done. Then, beginning with the first, she gave each sufficient broadcloth for a gown and a pair of shoes, a wooden platter (wherein was half a side of salmon), as much ling, six red herrings, two manchets,[4] and a mazer or wooden cup full of claret. All these things she gave separately. Then each of her ladies delivered to her Majesty the towel and apron used in the ablution, and she gave each of the poor women one apiece. This was the conclusion of the ladies' official duty of the Maundy. * * * After taking her ease on her cushion of state and listening awhile to the choir, her Majesty withdrew, for it was near sunset.

* * *

Soon after Elizabeth's return from her Kentish progress [in 1573], the following strange circumstance occurred: a crazy fanatic named Peter Burchet, having persuaded himself by the misapplication of certain Scripture texts that it was lawful to kill all who opposed the Gospel—that is to say, those who took a different view of church government from the sect to which he belonged—wounded the famous naval commander Hawkins[5] with his dagger, mistaking him for Sir Christopher Hatton, whom he intended to dispatch as an enemy of the Puritans. The Queen was so much incensed at this outrage that she ordered justice to be done on Burchet in the summary way of martial law and directed her secretary to bring the commission to her after dinner for her signature. Sussex,[6] her Lord Chamberlain, wrote in great haste to Burghley to apprize him of her Majesty's intention and that he and all her lords in waiting were in consternation at the royal mandate. "What will become of this act after dinner," says he, "your Lordship shall hear tonight." Her prudent counselors succeeded, finally, in convincing her Majesty that the ceremony of a trial was necessary before an Englishman could be executed for any offence whatsoever. It appears almost incredible that Elizabeth, after reigning sixteen years, should require to be enlightened on this point and to be informed that martial law was only used in times of open rebellion.

* * *

That she was a believer in the occult sciences and an encourager of those who practiced the forbidden arts of divination and transmutation[7] no one who

---

3. Praying desk, with a stand to hold a prayerbook and a bench on which to kneel.
4. Loaves of wheat bread; *ling*: small codfish.
5. Sir John Hawkins; *strange circumstance*: see also Camden's account above.
6. Thomas Radcliffe, third Earl of Sussex.
7. The process by which alchemists sought to change baser metals into precious ones, like gold and silver.

has read the diary of her pet conjuror, Dr. Dee, can doubt. It is probable that he was an instrument used by her to practice on the credulity of other princes,[8] and that, through his agency, she was enabled to penetrate into many secret plots and associations in her own realm, but she placed apparently an absurd reliance on his predictions herself. She even condescended with her whole Court and Privy Council to visit him one day at Mortlake [in 1575], when it was her gracious intention to have examined his library and entered into further conference, but notwithstanding that his wife[9] had only been buried four hours, she contented herself with a peep into his magic mirror, which he brought to her. "Her Majesty," says Dee, "being taken down from her horse by the Earl of Leicester, Master of the Horse, at the church wall at Mortlake, did see some of the properties of that glass, to her Majesty's great contentment and delight."[1]

* * *

The unjust detention of Mary, Queen of Scots, in an English prison had for fifteen years proved a source of personal misery to Elizabeth and a perpetual incentive to crime. The worst passions of the human heart—jealousy, hatred, and revenge—were kept in a constant state of excitement by the confederacies that were formed in her dominions in behalf of the captive heiress of the crown. Her ministers pursued a systematic course of espionage and treachery in order to discover the friends of the unfortunate Mary and, when discovered, omitted no means, however base, by which they might be brought under the penalty of treason. The sacrifice of human life was appalling, the violation of all moral and divine restrictions of conscience more melancholy still. Scaffolds streamed with blood; the pestilential jails were crowded with victims, the greater portion of whom died of fever or famine, unpitied and unrecorded save in the annals of private families.

* * *

But while plots, real and pretended, threatening the life of the Queen agitated the public mind from day to day, it had become customary for groups of the populace to throw themselves on their knees in the dirt by the wayside whenever she rode out and pray for her preservation, invoking blessings on her head and confusion to the papists with the utmost power of their voices. A scene of this kind once interrupted an important political dialogue, which the Maiden Queen was holding with the French ambassador Mauvissière, as he rode by her side from Hampton Court to London in November 1583. She was in the act of discussing the plots of the Jesuits, "when," says he, "just at this moment many people, in large companies, met her by the way and, kneeling on the ground, with divers sorts of prayers wished her a thousand blessings and that the evil-disposed who meant to harm her might be discovered and punished as they deserved. She frequently stopped to thank them for the affection they manifested for her. She and I being alone amidst her retinue mounted on

8. Prince Albert Laski of Poland visited Dee while at Court in 1583 and invited him to his palace near Cracow, hoping that he would produce the "philosopher's stone," which was thought to have the power of transmutation. Nothing, of course, came of the experiment.
9. Katherine, his first wife, who died shortly before the Queen's arrival.
1. *The Private Diary of Dr. Dee*, ed. James O. Halliwell (London: Camden Society, 1842) [Strickland's note, revised].

goodly horses, she observed to me that she saw clearly that she was not disliked by all."

*   *   *

She frequently spent the winter in London and (according to the witness of a contemporary who has written much in her praise)[2] led no idle life. Before day, every morning, she transacted business with her Secretaries of State and Masters of Requests. She caused the orders in Council, proclamations, and all other papers relating to public affairs, to be read and gave such orders as she thought fit on each, which were set down in short notes either by herself or her secretaries. If she met with anything perplexing, she sent for her most sagacious councilors and debated the matter with them, carefully weighing the arguments on each side till she was able to come to a correct decision. When wearied with her morning work, she would take a walk in her garden if the sun shone, but if the weather were wet or windy, she paced her long galleries in company with some of the most learned gentlemen of her Court, with whom she was wont[3] to discuss intellectual topics. There was scarcely a day in which she did not devote some portion of her time to reading history or some other important study. She would commonly have some learned man with her, or at hand, to assist her, whose labor and talent she would well reward.

She ate very little and in her declining life became still more abstemious. She seldom drank anything but common beer, fearing the use of wine, lest it should cloud her faculties. She strictly observed all the fast-days and then allowed no meat to be served up. When she dined in public, she ordered her table to be served with the greatest magnificence and the side-tables to be adorned with costly plate, taking great pride in displaying her treasures, especially when she entertained the foreign ambassadors. Her nobles then waited upon her very reverentially. The cupbearer never presented the cup without much ceremony, always kneeling when he gave or took it; but this was by no means remarkable, as she was always served on the knee. Songs and music were heard during the banquet. If she dined in private, she generally in summer reposed herself for a short time on an Indian couch, curiously and richly covered, but in the winter she omitted her noon sleep.

At supper she would relax herself with her friends and attendants and endeavor to draw them into merry and pleasant discourse. After supper she would sometimes listen to a song or a lesson or two played on the lute. She would then admit Tarlton,[4] a famous comedian, and other persons of the kind, to divert her with stories of the town and any droll occurrences that befell but would express her displeasure if any uncourteous personality were used towards anyone present or the bounds of modesty transgressed. Tarlton, however, either from the natural presumption of his character or suborned by Burghley, took the liberty of aiming his sarcastic shafts at two of the men most distinguished by the favor of royalty. First, he glanced at Ralegh's influence with the Queen and then, unawed by her Majesty's frown, went on to reflect on the over-great power and riches of the Earl of Leicester, which was received with such unbounded applause by all present that Elizabeth,

---

2. Strickland here references Bohun (see above).
3. Accustomed.
4. Richard Tarlton, a founding member of the Queen's Men acting company; references to Yorick in Shakespeare's *Hamlet* may allude to Tarlton.

though she affected to hear it with unconcern, was inwardly so deeply offended that she forbade Tarlton and the rest of her jesters from coming near her table anymore.

✳   ✳   ✳

It is a pleasure to be able to call attention, with deserved praise, to one instance of true magnanimity on the part of Queen Elizabeth. Among the attendants of Mary, Queen of Scots, was a Scotchwoman named Margaret Lambrun whose husband had also been in the service of that unfortunate Queen, to whom he was so greatly attached that his death was attributed to his excessive grief for the tragic fate of his royal mistress. Margaret, on this bereavement, took the desperate resolution of revenging the death of both on Queen Elizabeth. For this purpose she put on male apparel and, assuming the name of Anthony Sparke, proceeded to the English Court, carrying a brace of loaded pistols concealed about her at all times, intending to shoot Queen Elizabeth with one and to evade punishment by destroying herself with the other.

One day, when her Majesty was walking in the garden, Margaret endeavored to force her way through the crowd to approach close enough to the royal person to perpetrate her design, but in her agitation she dropped one of the pistols. This being observed by the yeomen of the guards, she was instantly seized, but when they were about to hurry her away to prison, Elizabeth, not suspecting the sex of the intended assassin, said she would examine the prisoner herself. When Margaret was brought before her, she asked her name and country and what had incited her to such a crime. Margaret undauntedly acknowledged who she was and what she had intended. The Queen heard her with unruffled calmness and granted her a full and unconditional pardon. The President of the Council protested that so daring an offender ought to be punished, whereupon Margaret, with the characteristic caution of her country, implored her Majesty to extend her goodness one degree further by granting her a safe-conduct with permission to retire to France. This request was graciously complied with by the Queen who, in this instance, chose to obey the impulse of her own feelings rather than the stern promptings of her minister.[5]

---

5. Strickland cites as source for the anecdote Michael Adams's *The new, complete, and general biographical dictionary: or, universal, historical, and literary repository of human knowledge: memoirs of the lives of the most eminent persons of every nation in the world* (London: Alex Hogg, 1793).

ABBREVIATIONS USED IN THE NOTES

Additional — British Library, Additional Manuscripts.

APC — *Acts of the Privy Council of England*, ed. John Roche Dasent *et al.*, new series, 46 vols. (London, 1890–1964).

BL — British Library, London.

BM — British Museum, London.

CP — Cecil Papers, Hatfield House, Hertfordshire.

CSP Domestic — *Calendar of State Papers, Domestic Series, of the reigns of Edward VI, Mary, Elizabeth, 1547–1625*, ed. Robert Lemon and Mary Anne Everett Green, 12 vols. (London, 1856–72).

CSP Foreign — *Calendar of State Papers, Foreign. Elizabeth I*, ed. J. Stevenson *et al.*, 23 vols. (London, 1863–1950).

CSP Rome — *Calendar of State Papers, relating to English affairs, in the Vatican Archives and Library*, ed. J. M. Rigg, 2 vols. (London, 1916–26).

CSP Scotland — *Calendar of State Papers, relating to Scotland and Mary, Queen of Scots, 1547–1603, preserved in the Public Record Office, the British Museum, and elsewhere in England*, ed. Joseph Bain, William K. Boyd, and J. D. Mackie, 13 vols. (Edinburgh: H. M. General Register House, 1898–1969).

CSP Spanish — *Calendar of the Letters and State Papers relating to English affairs, preserved principally in the archives of Simancas*, ed. M. A. S. Hume, 4 vols. (London, 1892–99).

CSP Venice — *Calendar of State Papers and Manuscripts relating to English affairs, existing in the archives and collections of Venice, and in other libraries of Northern Italy*, ed. Rawden Brown *et al.*, 38 vols. (London, 1864–1947).

HMC — *Historical Manuscripts Commission*.

LPL — Lambeth Palace Library, London.

MS — Manuscript.

NA — National Archives, London (formerly the Public Record Office).

NRO — Northamptonshire Record Office, Northamptonshire.

PRO — Public Record Office.

SP — State Papers, National Archives.

Part Twelve: Modern Scholarship and Criticism

ELIZABETH'S STRATEGIES FOR RULE

J. E. NEALE

The Affability of Their Prince[†]

* * *

At Court there were regular spectacles to which it was easy for any gentleman to get access. Each Sunday there was a ceremonial procession through the rooms of the Palace to the Chapel, and the Presence Chamber was usually crowded with spectators to many of whom Elizabeth would say a few gracious words as she passed along. Lord Herbert of Cherbury, as a young man, came to Court on such an occasion, at the end of the reign. 'As soon as she saw me,' he tells, 'she stopped, and swearing her usual oath, "God's death!", demanded, "Who is this?" Everybody there present looked upon me, but no man knew me until Sir James Croft, a Pensioner, finding the Queen stayed, returned back and told who I was, and that I had married Sir William Herbert of St. Julian's daughter. The Queen hereupon looked attentively upon me, and swearing again her ordinary oath, said, "It is a pity he was married so young," and thereupon gave her hand to kiss twice, both times gently clapping me on the cheek'.

While the Queen was at service in the Chapel, the spectators could watch the ceremonial laying of dinner in the Presence Chamber, to the accompaniment of trumpets and kettledrums. The articles—table-cloth, salt-cellar, etc., as well as food—were brought in by attendants preceded by an usher with his rod, all of whom knelt three times before the Cloth of State, on entering and retiring. A lady-taster gave each attendant a morsel of the dish that he bore, this being the assay; and then, when everything was ready, a number of the Queen's maids appeared and solemnly carried the food into an inner, private apartment, for it was rarely, and only on great festival or state occasions, that Elizabeth actually fed in the Presence Chamber, before spectators. She was abstemious over food and drink.

In the Presence Chamber Elizabeth graced the general body of courtiers with her presence at various entertainments, including dancing, of which she was fond; in the Privy Chamber she talked or played cards or chess with councillors and the privileged great having access there; in her Withdrawing

[†] From *Queen Elizabeth I* (London: Jonathan Cape, 1958), pp. 212–19. Reprinted by permission of Dr. Stella Tristram.

Chambers she became, so far as she could, a private person, and in addition to her ladies, passed the time with a very small intimate circle, who from one point of view were personal friends, but from the point of view of those without were 'favourites'. All monarchs had 'favourites'. How could it be otherwise? The anomaly in Elizabeth's reign was the difference in sex, and this was emphasized by the romantic note which the language of intimacy assumed. It betokened neither a lustful disposition, nor a callous heart; and though the amorous way in which men addressed her may seem highly suspicious, the staggering promiscuity of Elizabeth's 'love' mocks at such fond credulity. Sir Thomas Heneage sent her a bodkin and pendant with the message, *Amat iste sine fine*—'This man loves you without end'. She sent him answer that as these were his words to her, so hers to him were, 'I love *sine fine*', giving him 'ten thousand millions of thanks' and promising to wear his pendant on that ear 'that should not hearken to anything that should anyways hurt him that sent it'. 'Knowing that her Sanguine—presumably a nickname—was far in the cold north country where no butterflies were', she sent him a mother-of-pearl butterfly to play with. The quality of the 'love' may be gauged by the fact that she told him to hasten back to his wife and bring her to Court.

All Elizabeth's close friends seem to have received nicknames. Leicester was her 'Eyes', and ornamented his letters with a pair of eyes. Christopher Hatton, who was entering the fortunate circle of intimates in the late 'sixties, was her 'Lids', and employed a cipher which may have been a crude representation of eyelids. 'Adieu, most sweet Lady', he ended a letter. And then, with a play on the initials of *Elizabetha Regina*, went on 'All and EveR yours, your most happy bondman, Lids'. Later he became her 'Mutton', or 'Bell-wether'. On one occasion, fearing that Sir Walter Raleigh, nicknamed 'Water', was displacing him from Elizabeth's affections, he sent her what one imagines was a sweet, reproachful letter along with some 'tokens', including a diminutive bucket, signifying Raleigh. She sent a verbal answer, 'that if Princes were like Gods (as they should be) they would suffer no element so to abound as to breed confusion'. The beasts of the field were 'so dear unto her that she had bounded her banks so sure as no water or floods could be able ever to overthrow them'; and for better assurance unto him that he should fear no drowning, she sent him a bird—a dove—'that, together with the rainbow, brought the good tidings and the covenant that there should be no more destruction by water'. Further, she willed him to remember she was a Shepherd, and then he might think 'how dear her Sheep was unto her'. The dark-featured Walsingham was her 'Moor'. Burghley was her 'Spirit'. 'Sir Spirit', she wrote to him playfully, when he was in one of his blue moods, 'I doubt I do nickname you, for those of your kind (they say) have no sense; but I have of late seen an *ecce signum*, that if an ass kick you, you feel it too soon. I will recant you from being my spirit, if ever I perceive that you disdain not such a feeling. Serve God, fear the King, and be a good fellow to the rest'. Don't be 'so silly a soul', she went on, 'as not to regard her trust, who puts it in you. God bless you, and long may you last. *Omnino*, E.R.'

It is difficult to convey a proper appreciation of this amazing Queen, so keenly intelligent, so effervescing, so intimate, so imperious and regal. She intoxicated Court and country, keyed her realm to the intensity of her own spirit. No one but a woman could have done it, and no woman without her superlative gifts could have attempted it without disaster. In part instinctive, it was also conscious and deliberate. 'Her mind', wrote her witty godson, Sir John Harington, 'was oftime like the gentle air that cometh from the west-erly point in a summer's morn; 'twas sweet and refreshing to all around. Her speech did win all affections, and her subjects did try to show all love to her commands; for she would say, "Her state did require her to command, what she knew her people would willingly do from their own love to her" . . . Surely she did play well her tables to gain obedience thus, without con-straint. Again, she could put forth such alterations, when obedience was lacking, as left no doubtings whose daughter she was'. Harington tells how she would covertly search out the minds of her councillors, talking to Burghley till late at night, and then calling in another councillor, and so on; and afterwards compare their real thoughts with their utterances in council. 'Sir Christopher Hatton was wont to say, "The Queen did fish for men's souls, and had so sweet a bait that no one could escape her network" . . . I have seen her smile—sooth, with great semblance of good liking to all around—and cause everyone to open his most inward thought to her; when, on a sudden, she would ponder in private on what had passed, write down all their opinions, draw them out as occasion required, and some-times disprove to their faces what had been delivered a month before. . . . She caught many poor fish, who little knew what snare was laid for them'.

Elizabeth was exceedingly human, and was always letting impulse break through regal formality, which she regarded as made for her, not she for it. Glowing postscripts scribbled at the foot of formal letters to convey her grat-itude or remind a distant servant of her affection: there were numerous touches of this kind, and we know their miraculous healing power. Or she might scribble a political letter, unbeknown to her officials as she did to Sir Henry Sidney in Ireland in 1565. 'Harry', it began; and went on in her most euphuistic style, like the utterance of some oracle, ending, 'Let this memo-rial be only committed to Vulcan's base keeping, without any longer abode than the leisure of the reading thereof, yea, and with no mention made thereof to any other wight. I charge you, as I may command you. Seem not to have had but Secretary's letters from me. Your loving mistress, Elizabeth R.' Fortunately, Penshurst and not Vulcan kept the letter. Or she might inter-rupt a speech or sermon. At the end of one parliament, when the Speaker had made a long-winded speech and Lord Keeper Bacon was rivalling him in the answer, Elizabeth told him to cease. In his text of the speech Bacon writes: 'Hereafter followeth that I intended to have said if I had not been countermanded'. In contrast, at the beginning of another parliament, after confirming the election of a new Speaker and listening to his happy and elo-quent oration, as she passed she pulled off her glove and gave him her hand to kiss, and using a figure of archery, said, 'You, sir, you are welcome to the butts, sir', and laid both her hands about his neck, and stayed a good space, and so most graciously departed; and in her Privy Chamber after, amongst her ladies, said, 'she was sorry she knew him no sooner.'

Preachers who overstepped discretion, sometimes found themselves sharply pulled up. Nowell, Dean of St. Paul's, preaching a Lenten sermon before a large congregation at Court in 1565, inveighed against a recent Catholic book dedicated to the Queen, and then went on to attack images and idolatry, an attack which in the circumstances was palpably meant for the crucifix in the royal Chapel. 'Do not talk about that', Elizabeth called out; and as he went on, not hearing her, 'Leave that', she cried, raising her voice, 'it has nothing to do with your subject, and the matter is now threadbare'. In 1596, when Elizabeth was in her sixty-third year—the grand climacteric, very much feared in those days—Bishop Rudd, encouraged by previous praise and Whitgift's report that 'the Queen now is grown weary of the vanities of wit and eloquence wherewith her youth was formerly affected, and plain sermons which come home to her heart please her the best', chose for his Lenten sermon the text, 'O teach us to number our days, that we may incline our hearts unto wisdom'. Having spoken a while of some sacred and mystical numbers, as 3 for the Trinity, 3 times 3 for the heavenly Hierarchy, 7 for the Sabbath, and 7 times 7 for a Jubilee, he came to 7 times 9 for the grand climacterical year, and Elizabeth seeing the trend of his sermon grew troubled. The Bishop noticed this, and tried to save himself by treating of some more plausible numbers, as 666 making Latinus, 'with which, he said, he could prove the Pope to be Antichrist', and also of the fatal number 88. But at the end of the service, the Queen opened the window of her closet and told him plainly that 'he should have kept his arithmetic for himself'. 'I see', said she, 'the greatest clerks are not the wisest men': a pertinent saying, for it was the height of folly to play on the fears that were entertained about her death.

In the sorrows of others the Queen was a woman. When the Earl of Huntingdon died she had the news kept from his wife and moved suddenly to Whitehall in order to break the blow by her own ministration of comfort. When Lady Norris lost a son in Ireland, 'My own Crow', she wrote to her, 'Harm not yourself for bootless help, but show a good example to comfort your dolorous yoke-fellow. . . .' And when two years later the same service took the lives of two more sons, she wrote to both father and mother: 'We couple you together from desire that all the comfort we wish you may reach you both in this bitter accident. We were loth to write at all, lest we should give you fresh occasion of sorrow, but could not forbear, knowing your past resolution in like mishaps, and your religious obedience to Him whose strokes are unavoidable. We propose ourselves as an example, our loss being no less than yours'. In 1595, when the Earl of Hertford took steps to set aside the declaration of invalidity against his marriage with Lady Catherine Grey and was imprisoned in the Tower for his dangerous action, Elizabeth wrote to his second wife, who was distraught with anxiety. 'Good Francke,' she began, and bade her not to think the crime 'more pernicious and malicious than an act of lewd and proud contempt against our own direct prohibition'. 'It is far from our desire to pick out faults in such as he. Being slow to rigour towards the meanest, we will use no more severity than is requisite for others' caution in like cases, and than shall stand with honour and necessity. . . . For a farewell, you are to observe this rule, that seeing griefs and troubles make haste enough, unsent for, to surprise us, there can be no folly greater than by fearing that which is not, or by over grieving for that which needs not, to overthrow the health of mind and body'.

Another very human glimpse of the Queen is in a note which she sent to her godson Harington, then a boy, accompanying a copy of her speech to the Parliament of 1576: 'Boy Jack, I have made a clerk write fair my poor words for thine use, as it cannot be such striplings have entrance into parliament assembly as yet. Ponder them in thy hours of leisure, and play with them till they enter thy understanding; so shalt thou hereafter, perchance, find some good fruits hereof when thy godmother is out of remembrance;

and I do this, because thy father was ready to serve and love us in trouble and thrall'—a reference to the days of her sister, Mary.

Elizabeth's courtiers and advisers found her humours difficult. She had foibles: good health was one. Most of her life she enjoyed remarkable health and hated to be ill or even thought ill. In 1577 she several times commanded Leicester to write to Burghley, then at Buxton, asking him to send her some of the medicinal water from there. When it arrived, she mistrusted 'it will not be of the goodness here it is there'; though the truth was that she had been told people were talking of it, 'as though her Majesty had had some sore leg'; and she was half angry with Leicester now for writing to Burghley! In 1578 a tooth was giving her pain, and needed to come out, but because the Queen 'doth not or will not so think', her physicians were afraid to tell her. In 1597 she had 'a desperate ache' in her right thumb, but the gout it *could* not be, it *dare* not be; in fact, she had no ache, but she would not sign letters!

A person of such vivacity and wilfulness was in the nature of things trying at times. Her eyes were everywhere, faults were numerous, and she was exacting. Efficiency she would have, or know the reason why. And her very freedom with those around her called for sharp tugs on the rein to remind them that she was mistress. When Lord Hunsdon, her cousin, took advantage—as others did—and overstayed his leave from his post at Berwick, his son wrote to him that Elizabeth 'grew into a great rage, beginning with, "God's wounds! that she would set you by the feet, and send another in your place if you dallied with her thus, for she would not be thus dallied withal."' But when all is said of her passionate outbursts, they were usually little more than flashes of summer lightning. Sir John Harington, whose freshest memories were of her last years, when worry fretted her temper, says: 'When she smiled, it was a pure sunshine that everyone did choose to bask in if they could; but anon came a storm from a sudden gathering of clouds, and the thunder fell in wondrous manner on all alike'.

DAVID LOADES

The Great Queen[†]

At the end of a recent, and exhaustive, study of Elizabeth's reign, the author concluded that she merited the title, not of 'the Great', but of 'the Fortunate'.[1] This prompts two immediate thoughts; if by 'fortunate' is meant lucky, then no one is consistently lucky for nearly fifty years; secondly, she had lived over a third of her life before she became queen. Was she equally fortunate during her formative years? Fortune is also not quite the same as luck. Luck is random, but fortune can be earned. It can be interpreted as divine favour, or as an instinctive capacity to judge situations and people correctly. In the latter sense it is distinct from rational calculation, or even the exercise of conscious will, and can also be described as wisdom. Elizabeth was fortunate in the sense of being wise. She was not always right, and her mistakes sometimes had serious consequences, but she had every reason

---

† From *Elizabeth I* (London: Hambledon and London, 2003), pp. 303–19. Reprinted by permission of Hambledon Continuum, a Continuum imprint.
1. Wallace MacCaffrey, *Elizabeth I: War and Politics, 1588–1603* (London, 1992), p. 574.

to feel, at the end of her life, that she could render a good account of her stewardship.

Her sister Mary spoke with unwonted shrewdness when she declared that there were certain respects in which Elizabeth resembled her mother.[2] What the queen probably had in mind was a proclivity for heresy, but there was a lot more to it than that. Anne Boleyn had made a career out of her sexual allure. It had brought both triumph and disaster, and her daughter had inherited much of that appeal. What Elizabeth knew of her mother's history, or which version of it, we do not know. She must, however, have realised that Edward believed his stepmother to have been a witch and a whore; otherwise he would have had no cause to exclude his younger half-sister from the succession in 1553 on the grounds of bastardy. Anne's marriage to Henry had not been dissolved on the grounds of adultery, or even incest, which was alleged to have been committed after Elizabeth was born, but on a technical pretext arising from the fact that the king was con-vinced that he had been deceived (or even bewitched) into the union in the first place.[3] To believe that both Mary and Elizabeth were illegitimate, as Edward clearly did, was to follow the strict line of his father's reasoning, who had rejected both his first two marriages and their offspring. On securing the throne, Mary immediately corrected the record in respect of herself. This was easy to do, because the canon law had supported her throughout, and all that was necessary was to rescind judgements in the same way in which they had been made, and by the same authority. She had claimed the crown as Henry's legitimate daughter, and to her the Succession Act of 1543 was irrelevant. No such straightforward solution was available to Elizabeth. She also had herself declared legitimate on coming to the throne, and as she was the last of Henry's children there was little point in challenging that. As, however, she never tried to invalidate Mary's reign retrospectively (and did not allow anyone else to do so), her claim had to rest on the statute. It was that Act, and that alone, which provided legal protection against the Scottish line.[4]

Consequently, although we are told that Elizabeth 'gloried' in her father, she was equally aware of her mother. Whichever version of the story she accepted, it had many implications for herself. In 1547, when it was rumoured that she was with child by the lord admiral, it was also whispered that she was behaving exactly like her mother. Elizabeth was far too sharp not to have heard those voices. She learned, almost as soon as it was possible to do so, that sex was a dangerous game. It was also both exhilarating and useful. To be reassured of her physical attractiveness did as much for her confidence as it would for any young woman. Unfortunately for her, her early twenties, when these instincts were at their strongest, and the skills most highly developed, were years of acute danger and psychological pres-sure. She kept herself under tight control, affecting a puritanical simplicity, and survived.[5] The slightest relaxation in that austere demeanour would

2. *CSP, Spanish*, xi, p. 393. This had been in the context of a discussion on excluding her from the succession.
3. E. W. Ives, *Anne Boleyn* (London, 1986), pp. 393–95.
4. Mary was undoubtedly the legitimate granddaughter of Margaret Tudor, and had been excluded only on the dubious grounds that she had been born outside the realm. On the other hand the statute which had passed her over was both valid and lawful.
5. A number of observers commented upon her simple style of dress; a marked contrast with her image as queen.

certainly have been exploited by those who were only too anxious to discredit her, if more direct attacks were frustrated.

When she came to the throne, that sort of constraint disappeared; but it was replaced by others. It was then that she discovered, or first displayed, those arts of coquetry for which her mother had been famous. Courtly love was essentially the art of man-management, and that was above all what a ruling queen needed. Anne had succeeded brilliantly while she was playing to a sympathetic audience, but not when she had only a husband to please. Husbands were tricky creatures to manage, not least because of the over-whelming strength of their position in law and custom. When that husband was also a king the difficulties were compounded. Anne had failed to adjust, with fatal consequences.[6]

All this Elizabeth knew, but there is no evidence to suggest how it affected her behaviour. Many years later, probably in the 1580s, she wrote:

> When I was fair and young, favour graced me,
> Of many was I sought their mistress for to be,
> But I did scorn them all, and answered them therefore,
> Go, go, go, seek some otherwhere,
> Importune me no more . . .
> Then spake fair Venus' son, that proud victorious boy,
> And said Fine Dame, since that you be so coy,
> I will so pluck your plumes that you shall say no more
> Go, go, go, seek some otherwhere,
> Importune me no more.[7]

Perhaps it was a voice of poignant regret for lost love; but more likely it was a conventional trope. Neither during the dangerous years of her sister's reign, nor after she had ascended the throne herself, did Elizabeth enjoy the freedom to be a 'mistress', even in the conventional courtly sense. This caused her great personal distress and frustration, because she was by nature an emotional, even a passionate woman; but it had its compensations. Above all, by remaining unattainable, she was able to stay in control. The 'belle dame sans merci' is a dominant figure, whose lovers serve her without reward, and who is untouched by their service and devotion.

The need to stay in control was indeed the key to most of Elizabeth's behaviour, both as a queen and as a woman. It was contrary to nature, even, as some thought, to the will of God, that a woman should exercise rule over men.[8] But the Fairie Queen, by whatever name she went, was an image of power. Moreover no man denied, except at his peril, that a woman unwed had the disposition of her own body, and to intrude upon that sovereignty was both a sin and a crime. So the queen's virginity became a symbol not only of her integrity but also of her power.[9] Marriage meant compromise and a surrender of autonomy. Elizabeth did not know how to resolve that problem, and her uncertainty undermined every negotiation. It was not

---

6. Ives, *Anne Boleyn*, pp. 358–82.
7. There are a number of versions of this poem, which are discussed in *Elizabeth I: Collected Works*, eds. Leah S. Marcus, Janel Mueller, and Mary Beth Rose (Chicago, 2000), pp. 303–4.
8. The most extreme expression of this view was in John Knox, *The First Blast of the Trumpet against the Monstrous Regiment of Women* (Geneva, 1558). This had been aimed at Mary Tudor and Mary of Guise, the queen regent of Scotland, but Knox became *persona non grata* in England as a consequence.
9. On this point see particularly Philippa Berry, *Of Chastity and Power* (London, 1989), esp. pp. 111–33.

simply that she was acting the part of a reluctant bride, whilst manoeuvring for political advantage. Always there was an instinctive calculation as to whether the political and personal advantages would outweigh the price to be paid. That issue was never prejudged, and the balance might change from day to day, resulting in exchanges of bewildering complexity.[1]

Eventually, as each courtship developed, the queen concluded that she did not wish to compromise her independence. As long as a negotiation continued, she was a woman who had to be wooed; had a conclusion ever been reached, that freedom would have disappeared, and her position would have become defined and constrained. Her half-sister Mary had pursued marriage with a single-minded determination, not because she knew how to resolve these contradictions, but because she believed them to be less important than the securing of the succession.[2] Elizabeth lacked that singleness of purpose, and remained famously a *femme seule*. Eventually this was put to political advantage, not because the Virgin Queen could take the place of the Virgin Mary, but because the integrity of the queen's body became a symbol for the integrity of her realm. When in 1588 she rhetorically juxtaposed the body of a weak and feeble woman with her 'foul scorn' that the prince of Parma should seek to invade her realm, the imagery was quite deliberate.[3] Whether (or when) Elizabeth herself chose to use her body in this metaphorical fashion we do not know; it was always quite consistent with the imagery of marriage to the kingdom, which she had adopted from the beginning.

The queen rejected anything that smacked of submission, whether sexual or political. She had, no less than Mary, a powerful sense of vocation. Just as Mary had believed that God had called her to her high office in order to restore His own honour and true worship, Elizabeth also believed in her divine calling. The two women differed, however, in one fundamental respect. Mary remained unswerving in her conviction that God intended her to fulfil His will by becoming a wife and mother, and by acting as a channel and vehicle for her husband and son. Elizabeth believed her calling to be personal and unique. Whether she chose to marry or not, it was she and she alone who was responsible for the rule of her kingdom. In a sense, by choosing her God had absolved her from the limitations of womanhood. This did not make her, in human terms, any less a woman; but it did mean that to surrender any aspect of the responsibilities which had been given her would mean failing in her duty. Mary had no difficulty in accepting conventional gender limitations, but could not come to terms with the bitter disappointments of childlessness and a failed marriage. Elizabeth rejected gender limitation and then had to struggle, not only with a sense of personal deprivation but also with the endless problems created by dealing with men who did not see the world with her eyes.

Her constant prevarication and changes of mind have to be seen in this light. She could have simply made a decision, after proper consultation, and then left it to her ministers or other servants to carry it out. That was what her council (at first) expected her to do. In their own minds they

---

1. For a detailed exposition of all these shifts and changes, see Susan Doran, *Monarchy and Matrimony: The Courtships of Elizabeth I* (London, 1996) passim.
2. The imperial ambassadors reported this as her opinion on 2 August 1553, *CSP Spanish*, xi, pp. 129–34.
3. In her Tilbury speech, *Elizabeth I: Collected Works*, pp. 325–26.

would have glossed that expectation with the thought that women did not really understand the details of diplomacy, or ecclesiastical administration, or military deployment, or whatever was in question. Elizabeth had no time for such thoughts; so she intervened constantly. She stopped voyages that were on the point of sailing, and even tried to call them back; she authorised agreements with the Dutch or with Henry IV, and then went back on them because she thought an extra ounce of advantage could be extracted.[4] She sent clear signals to the duke of Anjou that she would marry him, then changed her mind, and left him fuming about women's inconstancy. By acting in this apparently irresponsible manner she not only kept everyone on their toes, she also made it abundantly clear that she could not be bypassed or taken for granted. Her political grasp was formidable. Although that did not make her prevarications any easier to bear, it did mean that they were never gratuitous.

Elizabeth's whole style of rule was pragmatic and free from preconceptions. It was not that she had no strategic aims, but they were broad and simple. God had entrusted her with three things: a realm to defend; a church to lead in the true way; and a people to protect, both against foreign enemies and against themselves. The second of these aims was pursued in a manner very different from the other two; and anyone tempted to believe that Elizabeth was congenitally incapable of decisive action or long-term consistency should consider her ecclesiastical policy. At the beginning of her reign, and against the best worldly advice, she created a Protestant establishment, which she then defended with tenacity and ingenuity for over forty years. It was her church, her thank offering to God, and she was utterly determined to keep it that way, against both papist assault and radical subversion. Her notoriously low opinion of the clergy who staffed that church was not caused (usually) by contempt for their learning or diligence, but by suspicion that, given the chance, they would reimpose a sacerdotal regime.[5] Protestant clergy did not claim the *potestas ordinis*, but they were set apart by their ordination and given a function which she, as a woman, could not share. It was therefore essential to keep them under firm control and to assert her authority over bishops and archbishops, such as Grindal, whose own sense of duty made them too independent, or even defiant. How dare they! She would decide what their duty was, because God had given that authority to her.[6] It was an issue of control.

By contrast, neither her foreign nor her secular domestic policies were so determined. There the queen was not predisposed to any particular strategy. Whereas Mary had been quite clear that England's best interests would be served by a Habsburg alliance, or even dependency, Elizabeth was uncommitted. She inherited a war with France, and in those circumstances the continuation of the Habsburg alliance was mere common sense: hence good relations with Philip II, and the Austrian marriage negotiations. Yet any hint of dependency was ruled out, and the war was quickly concluded.

4. For one typical example of such tactics, see MacCaffrey, *War and Politics*, pp. 156–62.
5. She was particularly suspicious of convocation for that reason; W. P. Haugaard, *Elizabeth and the English Reformation: The Struggle for a Stable Settlement of Religion* (Cambridge, 1970).
6. So, of course, had the Act of Supremacy, which had declared 'that it be established and enacted by the authority aforesaid that such jurisdictions, privileges [etc] for reformation, order and correction of all manner of errors, heresies, schisms[,] abuses, offences, contempts and enormities, shall forever by authority of this present parliament be united and annexed to the Imperial Crown of this realm.' *Statutes of the Realm*, iv, pt 2, pp. 350–55.

Thereafter Elizabeth's priority was clear. England's interests, including her own, took precedence over every other consideration. This led directly to the endless convolutions and short-term shifts that every historian of Elizabethan foreign policy has charted. As the storms of ideological conflict rose in Europe, engulfing England's nearest neighbours, France and the Netherlands, the queen struggled to keep her realm in peace, and to avoid commitment. She disliked rebels on principle, fearing that such ideas could prove infectious, yet self-interest dictated that she should support them; first in Scotland, then in France and finally in the Low Countries. In every case the negotiations were a complicated dance as the queen, her advisers, and the potential allies advanced, retreated, spun, disengaged and re-engaged. Elizabeth's aim was always to do as little as possible for as long as possible; and she took advantage of every shift in the circumstances to achieve this, with baffling displays of indecisiveness and inconsistency.

The trouble with examining these negotiations in detail is that the wood cannot be seen for the trees. The observer inevitably becomes bogged down in short-term shifts, and in the anger and frustration that they caused.[7] Walsingham, Norris, Sadler, even Cecil, regularly threw up their hands in despair at having to deal with such displays of feminine inconstancy. Yet it is worth noticing how often these negotiations succeeded in achieving the desired objectives, and usually at minimal cost. The queen empowered her delegates, but frequently intervened herself. In a case like the treaty of Edinburgh (1560), where the chief credit is always given to Cecil, he knew perfectly well that he could not conclude an agreement against her wishes, or independent of them.[8]

Elizabeth, however, often had her own reasons for not wanting to make her control obvious; and she regularly reserved a position from which it was possible to disown mistakes. The growth of English piracy, particularly at the expense of Spain, between 1565 and 1580 is an obvious case in point. Elizabeth could, and occasionally did, forbid these adventurers to set out, which suggests that those who did go went with her explicit or implicit approval. Foreign complaints, however, were regularly met with bland surprise or assumed concern, and referred to the admiralty court, as not being political issues.[9] Even when the queen's own ships were involved, she could point out that the voyages had no official status, because instructions had not been issued. Even when a commitment had been made, she was at pains to limit it. It was because the earl of Leicester exceeded his orders in accepting the governorship of the Low Countries that she became so angry with him. Leicester himself appears to have believed that his commission entitled him to use his own discretion in such matters, but that was never Elizabeth's intention. She could not tell him how to fight a battle, but she could keep him on a short political lead, and that she had every intention of doing. She may have wished it to appear that he had freedom to act, so that she could disown him if he made an error; but woe betide him if he made any major decision on that assumption.[1]

---

7. Cecil's frustration over the Scottish situation in 1560 even prompted him to offer his resignation; Conyers Read, *Mr Secretary Cecil and Queen Elizabeth* (London, 1955), p. 161.
8. Ibid., 135–72.
9. N. A. M. Rodger, *The Safeguard of the Sea* (London, 1997), pp. 199–200.
1. MacCaffrey, *Making of Policy*, pp. 348–53.

Norris in Brittany and Mountjoy in Ireland were given more freedom, precisely because they were not major political figures but professional soldiers doing a job which even Elizabeth did not profess to understand.[2] Essex, however, fell into the same category as Leicester; and it was his cavalier treatment of his instructions, rather than his failure in the field, which brought him into disfavour. It was Essex who inadvertently exposed the weakness in this carefully crafted system of management. Angered and baffled as they often were, Elizabeth's servants usually accepted that it was not their business to penetrate her arcane ways. William Davison was deeply distressed when he was made a scapegoat for the execution of Mary Queen of Scots; a case in which the queen, having been forced to make a decision, was anxious to evade the responsibility. He did not run away to Spain, however, or conspire with the queen's enemies. Essex, on the other hand, could not accept that it was his function to be picked up and dropped at the whim of a woman, even one old enough to be his mother. He glossed his disaffection with hatred of Robert Cecil, but he knew perfectly well that it was Elizabeth who was responsible for his disgrace.[3] She misjudged his proud and volatile disposition, and it was the bid to escape from her control that brought him to the block.

Essex was an extreme case; but we can see in many aspects of her government how suspicious Elizabeth was of those who might, or might think that they could, act independently or upon the basis of some authority other than her own. Woe betide the preacher who told her that she was misinterpreting the will of God. Woe betide also that nobleman or great gentleman who believed that his status entitled him to flout the law. As Lord Buckhurst told the earl of Salisbury in 1592:

> Your Lordship must remember that in the policy of this Common wealth, we are not over ready to add encrease of power and countenance to such great personages as you are. And when in the country you dwell in you will needes enter in a warr with the inferiors therein, we thinke it both justice, equity and wisdom to take care that the weaker part be not put down by the mightier.[4]

Neither Elizabeth nor her council was particularly concerned by the constant aristocratic feuds over land or honour, which occasionally erupted into violence.[5] Homicide was not tolerated, but even then pardons could be obtained at a price. These feuds might be a threat to local order, but they were not a challenge to the queen's authority. The intimidation of juries, or the bullying of those unable to protect themselves, were challenges, however, and the court of Star Chamber was quick to call such offenders to account.[6] It might not always be clear to those on the receiving end when a sheriff or a justice of the peace was acting in an official capacity and when in a private one, but a degree of latitude in that respect was part of his bargain with the crown, and the line between acceptable and unacceptable behaviour was often a fine one. Nevertheless, as Buckhurst's observation makes clear, every man was expected to be accountable for the authority

2. E.g., J. S. Nolan, *Sir John Norreys and the Elizabethan Military World* (Exeter, 1997), pp. 177–79.
3. L. B. Smith, *Treason in Tudor England: Politics and Paranoia* (London, 1986), pp. 235–36.
4. Longleat, MS 114 A, iv, fol. 66; Lawrence Stone, *Crisis of the Aristocracy* (Oxford, 1965), p. 237.
5. Ibid., pp. 234–40.
6. Ibid.

that he exercised. There was nothing particularly new about this; both Henry VIII and Mary had called noblemen to account for committing common felonies;[7] but Elizabeth's attitude to her nobility resembled that of her grandfather more closely than either her father or her sister. She created no dukes or marquises, and very few earls; most of her new creations were barons, and she got very upset if her field commanders dubbed too many knights, as Essex did in France. Nor, with the exception of Leicester and Essex, were noblemen used any longer as field commanders; and the days when they were expected to go to war at the head of their own retinues were over.[8] Typically, noblemen were lords lieutenant, commanding men raised and armed by public authority—that is, the authority of the queen.

By the same token, parliament was supposed to provide a service; useful, indeed essential, but not expected to show initiative. Elizabeth was quite happy for noblemen to exercise their patronage in the House of Commons, but not at all happy if they tried to put pressure upon her by that means. Similarly, she was happy to receive petitions from the House of Commons, but not to bargain with the members over issues of policy. Debates over her marriage, the succession, the government of the church and the fate of Mary Queen of Scots, were all ruled out of order at one time or another. Elizabeth nevertheless knew that the Commons, like the gentry that it represented, could be led but not driven; and it was because she knew this that she refused to put issues of principle to the test. Her prerogatives were *arcana imperii*, to be neither questioned nor defined. It was a balancing act. She knew perfectly well that she could not govern effectively without what she chose to describe as the 'love' of her subjects; but she also knew that that love constrained her own freedom of action.[9] She never admitted this publicly, but she developed political antennae that enabled her to avoid most of these obstacles without apparently noticing their existence.

Elizabeth had no grand ambitions, as her father had done, either for 'honour' in the military sense or for territorial expansion. It was a lack of such ambition that made her intervention in Scotland at the beginning of her reign acceptable.[1] It was a lapse from that principle which brought her to grief in France in 1563. She had no desire to be the leader of Protestant Europe, but she had no option but to accept the pope as a declared enemy after 1570. She did not make alliances with Protestants such as the Huguenots or the Dutch because they were Protestants (although some of her council took that view), but because they were curbs upon the power of Spain. Elizabeth would happily have avoided conflict with Philip II if she could have done so, and wriggled like an eel for years to preserve the peace; but the logic of both their positions made that eventually impossible. She was innocent of any ambition to convert Spaniards to the truth of the gospel, but perfectly well aware that they did not share a similar restraint. Unless she defended her kingdom by all the means at her disposal, both its religion and its independence would be destroyed. The fact that her subjects

---

7. Lord Dacre of the South was hanged in 1541 for murdering a witness to a poaching expedition; and Lord Stourton was hanged in 1556 for imprisoning and murdering two private enemies.
8. For a discussion of the way in which the musters were organised, see L. O. Boynton, *The Elizabethan Militia* (London, 1967).
9. Judith Richards, 'Love and a Female Monarch: The Case of Elizabeth Tudor', *Journal of British Studies*, 38 (1999), pp. 133–60.
1. Cecil was very careful to renounce any territorial or jurisdictional ambition in respect of Scotland, in spite of his conviction that England possessed an imperial authority over its neighbour.

also knew that, and entirely supported her efforts, was one of the great bonds between them. Any enemy of Philip thus became, actively or passively, an ally. Much as she may have deplored Henry IV's conversion, he was still an ally where it mattered. The same was true of the sultan. After years of privileged and profitable trading with the Ottoman empire, she wrote to Mohammed III in 1601:

> Most high and most puissant prince; It is no small contentment to us that the amity we have with so high and renowned a prince as you, is by our neighbour princes and their subjects so well known that when they have need to ask any favour or kindness from you, they implore our mediation as the readiest way to obtain their desires.[2]

The French believed that Elizabeth had incited the sultan to war against the emperor, and Philip II had similarly supported the Persians against the Turks.

The queen was not directly involved with Frobisher's explorations, or with the Roanoake venture, although she was interested in both, but she was an active participant in many of the ventures and expeditions which brought about the diversification of English trade during her reign, and created the springboard for the great expansion of the following century.[3] Her role in this promotion was one of the most positive features of her reign, as well as one of the most neglected in conventional assessments. Elizabeth did not share John Dee's vision of a British empire, but she was impressed by it; and convinced to the point of believing that England's future strength and prosperity lay in its commerce. Both Hawkins and Drake should be counted among her favourites. Good relations with the sultan, and with the tsar of all the Russias, to say nothing of Drake's circumnavigation of the world, spelled out a global ambition which the queen herself had neither the time nor the resources to realise; but it was a legacy to her successors.

Elizabeth was not easily frightened, but her early experiences had made her apprehensive of danger. The traumatic experiences of 1547 and 1554 were never entirely erased from her mind. Then she had feared dishonour more than death, and that remained with her, although the nature of the dishonour changed. Her physical courage was perfect. When James I feared assassination, he took refuge in padded mattresses and other undignified expedients.[4] Elizabeth was similarly threatened for years, but would allow no additional precautions, and never curtailed her exposure to her people. Greatly as they feared for her safety, her people found her courage an inspiration. The dishonour which she feared as queen was not sexual assault in the common sense, but a theft of her authority which was also related to gender. If a king was weak, his male subordinates would exploit him, but a woman might be exploited simply because she was a woman. The language and imagery of power were profoundly masculine.[5] A woman's honour was sexual and private; a man's honour was military and public. So Elizabeth

---

2. *Elizabeth I: Collected Works*, pp. 400–2.
3. D. Loades, *England's Maritime Empire: Seapower, Commerce and Policy*, 1490–1690 (London, 2000), pp. 79–108.
4. Or is alleged to have done so, his horror of violence arising, it was claimed, from his mother having witnessed the murder of David Rizzio while carrying him. D. H. Willson, *King James the VI and I* (London, 1956).
5. J. N. King, *Tudor Royal Iconography: Literature and Art in an Age of Religious Crisis* (Princeton, New Jersey, 1989); Sydney Anglo, *Images of Tudor Kingship* (London, 1992).

faced two problems: she had to lead and dominate men who were accustomed to think of women as inferior creatures and she had to find an imagery of power that was both effective and feminine. Her father had been an imposing figure, and her brother had made a somewhat feeble attempt to imitate his pose, but that was not a road open to Elizabeth.[6] At first she was the aloof, mysterious beauty of the courtly love tradition, later the magnificent unattainable Virgin, Gloriana.

In a sense this imagery was brilliantly successful, and it dictated the language of courtly discourse throughout the reign. But it was only half the battle, because practical men were quite accustomed to humouring their women with such language, while leaving them virtually no control over their own lives. Her councillors might also play the courtier, but when it came to business they were hardheaded. It was in council, not in public display, that Elizabeth faced her longest and toughest battles. Fortunately she was extremely intelligent and had a barrister's ability to grasp a brief. She could not be outfaced in debate, and her knowledge was often superior to that of her advisers. Like other women in managerial situations, she felt vulnerable; vulnerable when confronted by male bonding, and vulnerable to that patronising attitude which was instinctive to men in such a position. When Mary had felt similarly threatened she had yelled at her council; to no effect, as she admitted.[7] Elizabeth shouted at her courtiers and ladies, and occasionally boxed their ears, but she did not shout at her council. Instead she delayed decisions, recycled ideas, reopened closed issues, changed her mind, and indulged in irrelevant rhetoric. No doubt her indecisiveness was often genuine, but it was also a control mechanism. Except in routine matters, her council could not act until she had made up her mind; so she kept them waiting, dancing with frustration and impatience. She did the same thing with foreign envoys, particularly if they wanted some favour from her. Sometimes these tactics worked in an objective fashion: they won valuable time, or allowed contentious issues to resolve themselves. Sometimes they did not work, and valuable opportunities were allowed to slip away. They were only ever partly aimed at the substantive issues; partly they were aimed at the councillors themselves, and some of them probably realised this. Other than Essex, no one who worked closely with the queen was ever alienated by this behaviour, however cross it made them in the short term. Of course they attributed it to her gender, and they were right; but they never found a way to circumvent it, and eventually it just became an accepted fact of political life.

As a young woman Elizabeth had been thought beautiful; she was also an intellectual, and brilliantly educated. Apart from a Welsh great grandfather, she was entirely and self-consciously English. The first propaganda piece of the reign, published within days of her accession, had made that very point, describing the new queen as a

> Prince (as ye wot all) of no mingled blood, of Spaniard or stranger, but borne mere Englishe here amongst us, and therefore most natural unto us. Of education brought up and induct in all vertuous qualities and Godlye learnynge, specially (that may be the most comfort and

---

6. There is a well-known portrait of Edward, imitating his father's hand-on-hip posture, by Willem Scrots. Jennifer Loach, *Edward VI* (London, 1999), plate 7.
7. D. Loades, *The Reign of Mary Tudor* (London, 1991), pp. 196–202.

ioy to us all) in the sincere knowledge and following of God's holy word.[8]

The author was, of course, a Protestant, and concerned to condemn Mary at least as much as to praise Elizabeth, but his description of the queen as 'mere Englishe' struck a responsive chord in all sections of society. Mary had been half Spanish by blood, and her husband was wholly Spanish; so that, although she never set foot outside England, she was vulnerable to the criticism that both her antecedents and her priorities were alien.[9] Elizabeth was quick to seize the opportunity that this perception created. In responding to the first of many petitions for her to marry, in February 1559, she said:

> Reproach me no more that I have no children; for every one of you, and as many as are English, are my children and kinsfolk, of whom, so long as I am not deprived and God shall preserve me, you cannot charge me, without offence, to be destitute.[1]

It was a consistent theme, and it was well judged to catch the mood of her people. As Feria observed even before her coronation, Elizabeth loved the plaudits of the crowd, and it was a characteristic that stayed with her to the end. Up to a point this was sheer vanity; she loved flattery, and did not mind much who provided it. It was also partly a consequence of her lurking insecurity. Flattery was a form of reassurance; even if she did not merit it, she was able to exact it like a kind of tribute. In later life, when she was no longer beautiful, she was no less English, and the adulation of her subjects could persuade her that God was in His heaven and all was right with the world. As parliament constantly reminded her after 1570, her life had become synonymous with her kingdom's welfare—and even its very survival. She not only knew how to talk to her subjects, she knew what gestures to make and which symbols to invoke. Richard Mulcaster's *The Passage of our most dread Sovereign Lady* is the only source for her famous coronation entry, so we cannot be sure that it is an accurate description; but we can be sure at least that it represented what the queen wanted to be believed—and that is almost the same thing for this purpose.[2]

Whether Elizabeth was equally good at listening is another matter. It would be hard to point to any aspect of her policy which was clearly influenced by public opinion; and when her subjects spoke through their representatives in the House of Commons, she was quick to tell them to mind their own business. Her policies became more obviously popular as the reign progressed. In 1560 her church settlement pleased very few, but, as Catholicism became increasingly associated with foreign interference and plots against her life, Protestantism gradually became part of the fabric of national identity. The war with Spain was popular, as was the execution of Mary Queen of Scots, while the failure of the Armada convinced all but the most sceptical that God approved of the queen of England.[3]

---

8. *A Speciall Grace Appointed to Have Been Said after a Banket at York*, November 1558 (STC, 7599), sigs Aiii verso–Aiv.
9. 'The Queen is a Spaniard at heart. She loves another realm better than this' etc.; Loades, *Reign of Mary*, pp. 186–88.
1. *Elizabeth I: Collected Works*, pp. 56–58.
2. *The Passage of Our Most Dread Sovereign Lady, Queen Elizabeth, through the City of London* (1559), in A. F. Pollard, *Tudor Tracts* (London, 1903), pp. 365–95; Richards, 'Love and a Female Monarch'.
3. MacCaffrey, *War and Politics*, p. 3.

Elizabeth herself did little to improve the lives of most of her subjects, but there were no disturbances to equal those of 1549 or 1536. Justice was well administered in the sense that it was not widely perverted by private interests; and the council's tight control over the commissions of the peace was largely responsible for that. The crisis of her brother's reign had demonstrated the danger of ignoring what might be called the 'yeoman officers' in the interests of the gentry. Elizabethan England was a 'gentry commonwealth', and that was by the queen's deliberate choice, but enough was done to protect the interests of constables and churchwardens to prevent them from becoming disaffected as a group—either from the justices or from the crown. Consequently, although real wages continued to decline until almost the end of the reign, disaffection was successfully contained to local agrarian riots of the kind that were endemic in early modern Europe.[4]

Elizabeth's regular progresses were, and were designed to be, occasions for loyal demonstrations. Although these could be orchestrated up to a point, large-scale popular enthusiasm could not be simulated, and was recorded by disinterested observers as well as royal propagandists.[5] The courtly literature of flattery was large, subtle and frequently replicated. Some of the finest 'courtly makers' of Renaissance Europe attended upon Elizabeth and the whole image which she bequeathed to posterity reflected that fact.[6] There was also a more homely version of the same thing:

> Her faithful soldiers great and small
> as each one stood within his place,
> upon their knees began to fall
> desiring God to 'save her Grace!'
> for joy whereof, her eyes were filled
> that water down distilled,
> 'LORD bless you all, my friends!' she said,
> 'but do not kneel so much to me!'[7]

Her public utterances may have been calculated, but she had a charisma that transcended the court, and indeed was probably stronger among those who were not regularly exposed to her uncertain temper. It is hard to say whether this had any tangible effect upon her government; but the combination of a country at war with a great enemy, discovering its identity and fired by loyalty to such a ruler, certainly conferred a sense of purpose. That in turn helped to keep the peace during years of plague, harvest failure and high inflation which could easily have destabilised a less popular regime.

Intellect, image and sexuality are the three defining words that come to mind when attempting any assessment of Elizabeth; but she possessed other qualities. She was a fine scholar and linguist, and a competent poet. Many of her letters are elaborate and latinate to the point of incomprehensibility, but her style was much admired and imitated at the time. She

---

4. Peter Clark, *English Provincial Society from the Reformation to the Revolution* (Brighton, 1977).
5. 'The great rejoycing of the said parish and the country thereabouts' is recorded in the Lewshall parish register in the Bury St Edmunds Record Office; Zillah Dovey, *An Elizabethan Progress* (Stroud, 1996), p. 47.
6. Blair Worden, *The Sound of Virtue: Philip Sidney's Arcadia and Elizabethan Politics* (New Haven, 1996).
7. 'The Queens Visiting of the Camp at Tilbury', T. Delony, 10 August 1588; A. F. Pollard, *Tudor Tracts* (London, 1903), p. 494.

had a good ear for music, and was a capable performer upon the virginals, although she does not appear to have inherited either her father's singing voice or his talent for composition. The fact that she protected Catholic musicians such as Byrd and Tallis tells its own story. She danced with enthusiasm, was a good horsewoman, and hunted and hawked with the best. Unlike Mary Queen of Scots, she seems not to have been a needle-woman, except as a child; but then she did not have the advantage of Mary's enforced leisure. She also had that endearing characteristic, a sense of humour, and often addressed her familiars by affectionate nicknames. The best known is 'Eyes' for Robert Dudley, but when she wrote to her old friend and servant Margery Norris to condole with her on the death of her son, she scribbled at the head of an otherwise somewhat formal letter 'Mine own Crow, harm not yourself for bootless help, but show a good example to comfort your dolorous yokefellow'.[8] More intriguingly, when writing to Lord Mountjoy about the affairs of Ireland in December 1600, she started her letter 'Mistress Kitchenmaid', and proceeded to observe 'that you with your frying pan and other kitchen stuff have brought to their last home more rebels, and passed greater breakneck places than those that promised more and did less'.[9] Clearly she was in a good mood that day, and had picked up a reference in one of Mountjoy's own letters to his task in Ireland being like that of a kitchen wench.

Elizabeth also kept jesters. There was nothing surprising in that, because it was an old custom, and her father's elderly retainer Will Somers was still in her service at the very beginning of her reign.[1] He was succeeded by one Jack Greene, and then by Richard Tarlton. These were clowns and mimics, whose repertoire was probably not very sophisticated. Of the latter it was written:

> When Tarlton clowned it in a pleasant vaine
> With conceits did good opinions gaine,
> Upon the stage his merry humours shop.
> Clownes knew the Clowne by his great clownish slop.[2]

This suggests comic capers and outlandish costume rather than sharp verbal sallies; the rustic rather than the courtier. This may have been because more pointed humour frequently sailed too close to the wind. Elizabeth enjoyed a romp and a coarse joke or innuendo, but any witticism designed to deflate her dignity was not well taken; and John Pace, the earl of Leices-ter's fool, was banned from her presence for his 'bitter' jibes.[3] It would appear that while the queen enjoyed laughing at other people, she was not particularly good at laughing at herself. She did not, apparently, indulge in the common contemporary practice of keeping 'innocents', or freaks, although two mysterious young women feature in the records who may have been something of the kind. The first was known as Ippolyta the Tartarian, described in 1564 as 'oure deare and wellbeloved woman', and the second was Tomasina de Paris. Both were made clothing allowances

8. Lady Norris was apparently dark complexioned; *Elizabeth I: Collected Works*, p. 389.
9. Ibid., p. 399.
1. John Southworth, *Fools and Jesters at the English Court* (Stroud, 1998), p. 107.
2. *The Letting of Humours Blood in the Head-Vaine* (1600), epigram 30, sig. C 2 verso.
3. Southworth, *Fools and Jesters*, p. 110.

over a number of years, and Tomasina appears to have been a dwarf; but the nature of the service they provided is nowhere described.[4] They are unlikely to have been jesters in the ordinary sense, and whether they were supposed to be a source of humour is not known. Tarlton, in contrast was a famous comedian who also appeared on the public stage, and was remembered with affection years after his death. But just what he did that contributed so much to Elizabeth's sense of well-being is nowhere recorded.

In spite of her occasional tantrums, the queen was a loyal friend, and the turnover of her servants, both at court and council, was very slow and almost entirely natural. Her fatal break with the earl of Essex was altogether exceptional. The fact that she never married does not mean that she either was, or felt herself to be, lonely or unloved. She may have felt frustrated as a woman, but she was devoid of self-pity, and as a monarch felt confident that she had discharged the trust that God had bestowed upon her.

Elizabeth was that rare creature, a genuinely independent woman. However gratifying an orthodox sexual relationship might have been, it would have meant sacrificing that independence; and probably the independence of her kingdom by which both she and her subjects set such store. It is unlikely that she ever made a decision of principle not to marry; but every time that a particular decision about a courtship had to be made, the price of consummation was always too great. We do not know when she passed the menopause, although she must have known herself and her physicians would have had a pretty shrewd idea. As long as marriage was on the political agenda, it was a state secret of great delicacy; then quite suddenly it no longer mattered. She was a woman forced by genetic accident (or the will of God) to do a man's job, and to manage men. No other woman in England held a public office above the parochial level. Mary had set some useful legal precedents, but her whole style of government had been a warning rather than an example.[5] Consequently Elizabeth was forced to improvise, to make up the rules as she went along. She used her sexuality, her acute brain and her sense of theatre to develop a unique method of management. She never ceased to feel vulnerable, however, which was why her control could be more than a little obsessive, and her tactics for maintaining it so devious. The motto attributed to Philip II, 'Time and I against the World', could well have been applied to Elizabeth, whose instinct was always to avoid both action and commitment for as long as possible. She also knew when her options had run out, as the treaties of Edinburgh and Nonsuch demonstrate.

In no issue of foreign policy could her prevarication and indecisiveness be said to have led to disastrous consequences for her country. On the international stage there was no better survivor. At home her achievement can only be judged with hindsight. A combination of good sense and longevity settled the church, and it was no fault of hers that confessional issues became so divisive forty years after her death. She gave her country pride, and set its commercial development on a course that was eventually to be spectacularly successful; for that she deserves more credit than she is usually given.

4. Janet Arnold, *Queen Elizabeth's Wardrobe Unlock'd* (London, 1988), pp. 107–8.
5. Mary was generally felt to have surrendered her kingdom's interests to her husband—particularly in going to war with France in 1557.

She failed to deal with two issues of crucial importance which were to derail the regimes of her successors. Having encouraged the gentry to adopt a higher and higher profile in government, she failed to find a satisfactory definition of the constitutional relationship between crown, lords and commons, although several models were offered to her by William Cecil in the course of the reign. By refusing to define it she protected her prerogative from formal limitation, but left it vulnerable to attack, as was already becoming apparent before she died. Secondly, she conspicuously failed to tackle the problem of inadequate revenue. By muddling along, and improvising from hand to mouth, she managed to survive; but the consequence was that nobody faced the fact that the crown needed a regular and substantial taxation income, even to conduct its normal peacetime operations, never mind to wage war. It was as much ignorance as extravagance or ill-will that caused the financial crises of the early Stuarts; and for that ignorance Elizabeth was to blame. Her inability to act promptly and decisively was thus more damaging at home than it was abroad. It was caused directly by her fear that parliament, and particularly the House of Commons, would be empowered to exercise a measure of control which she believed should belong to herself alone.

Elizabeth chose for herself the motto *Semper Eadem* ('Always the Same') and in most respects that consistency served her well, both as a person and as a ruler. It also meant an unwillingness, even an inability, to embrace change. It could be said that she was so concerned to remain in charge of the ship, and to avoid the icebergs of Spanish and papal hostility, that she failed to spot the other unobtrusive rocks lying in her path. She was not on the bridge when the ship went down. When she died, the theatrical displays of mourning were accompanied by audible sighs of relief. It would be good to have a king again after fifty years of female rule. Kings were creatures defined by ancient custom; but queens, however loved and admired, were unpredictable.

James I was a foreigner, but he spoke the same language and shared the same religion. He was also an experienced ruler with two healthy sons to guarantee the succession. As he began to make mistakes, however, the more the subtle virtues of the old queen began to be appreciated. The new king did not know how to talk to his subjects, and he misunderstood their prejudices, being in a sense too intellectual to be intelligent. He overestimated both the wealth of his new kingdom (or at least the accessibility of that wealth) and the powers of his office. As a stranger, he had no sense for the obstacles that might lie in his path, and blundered into them repeatedly. His foreign policy particularly baffled and offended those who, for over a generation, had regarded Spain as an evil enemy. By comparison 'Good Queen Bess' seemed a model of straightforward patriotism.

Charles I was a great deal worse. If James had not known how to talk to his subjects, at least he had tried. Charles never felt called upon to make any such effort. Where Elizabeth's court had been dignified but accessible, and James's had been scandalous and turbulent, Charles's was refined and esoteric. Handicapped by a speech impediment and by natural reticence, he could communicate effectively only with a small and narrow circle of friends. His belief in the divine nature of his office was probably not very different from Elizabeth's, but he completely lacked her pragmatism. Because of her dubious legitimacy, she could not appeal to the simple certainties of Divine Right. Charles, on the other hand, saw no reason to equivocate, or even to watch where he was putting his feet. Elizabeth may not have appeared to listen, but she knew her way around. Charles was like a man steering by compass, but without the benefit of either a map or a knowledge of the ground. It is not surprising that nostalgia had created a powerful myth by 1640.

Elizabeth was unique. Her myth depended less upon substantive success than upon her gender. Samuel Johnson observed that a woman preaching was like a dog walking on its hind legs, remarkable for the feat rather than its quality. Similarly what was surprising about Elizabeth as a ruler was not that she was always a brilliant success, but that she was a success at all. Those who followed her also contributed to her reputation, both directly and indirectly: directly by making mistakes that she had avoided, and indirectly by treating her memory with respect. Her reputation was also partly fortuitous, in that it depended upon developments for which she was only partly responsible. There is a good case for crediting her with the diversification and expansion of trade, and also with the growth of London as a financial centre; but her responsibility for the great flowering of English literature, drama and music was less direct. She was a discriminating patron, but not a hugely generous one, and it is difficult to say how much her courtiers owed in this respect to her example. In culture as in politics, history has credited her with other people's achievements. But it was because she caught the English imagination that this happened. As Lytton Strachey observed:

> While the Spanish ambassador declared that ten thousand devils possessed her, the ordinary Englishmen saw in King Hal's full blooded daughter a queen after their own heart. She swore, she spat, she struck with her fist when she was angry; she roared with laughter when she was amused.

An exaggeration, of course, but a testimony to a durable achievement, as well as to what the English appreciated in a ruler.

NATALIE MEARS

[Queenship and Political Discourse][†]

A series of meetings in 1579 provides a lens for reconstructing not only the process of Elizabethan counselling but also for understanding the wider structure of policy-making. At the end of March 1579, Lord Burghley, the earls of Leicester and Sussex, Sir Francis Walsingham, Dr Thomas Wilson (the two principal secretaries) and Lord Hunsdon (one of Elizabeth's cousins, governor of Berwick and warden of the East March) were appointed by Elizabeth to discuss Francis, duke of Anjou's offer of marriage. Their meetings began on 27 March and continued to around 3 April.[1] According to Gilbert Talbot, writing to his father, the earl of Shrewsbury, the meetings

---

† From *Queenship and Political Discourse in the Elizabethan Realms* (Cambridge: Cambridge University Press, 2005), pp. 33–36, 47–56, 69–70. Reprinted with the permission of Cambridge University Press.
1. Digest of Marriage proceedings 1570–Nov. 1579, CP148, fo. 74v.

began at eight o'clock in the morning and continued until dinner, after which the councillors conferred with Elizabeth and then reconvened for further deliberation.[2] Councillors presented their individual opinions to Elizabeth on 13 April.[3] On 3 and 4 May, Elizabeth ordered the privy council to discuss three articles for the marriage treaty which had previously been referred or denied but were now resubmitted by Jean de Simier, Anjou's agent.[4] A long lull in organised discussions followed until 4 October, when selected councillors reconvened for further debate.[5] A larger group met two days later on the 6th, deciding 'to require hir Majesty, to shew hir own mynd . . . that the resolutions might not be to the Contrary,'[6] Elizabeth's reaction—bursting into tears and then railing at them for not making a 'universal request' for her marriage—prompted a further meeting after which councillors 'offred to hir Majesty all our services in furderance of this Marriadg, if so it should lyk hir' on the 8th.[7]

Talbot perceived the meetings between 27 March and c.3 April as conducted by the privy council acting at less than its full strength but, though all attendees were councillors, the meetings can not be mapped onto those of the privy council as recorded in the council's registers.[8] According to both the first council register (1540) and Sir Julius Caesar, Chancellor of the Exchequer (1606–14), writing in 1625, the purpose of the registers was to act as a point of reference, recording the council's actions and copies of its letters, rather than the substance of debates.[9] Crucially, however, no privy council meetings are recorded at all between 26 and 30 March. Letters from the council were subscribed by a group of councillors on the 29th but this does not match the attendance of the conferences on the marriage: for instance, Leicester did not subscribe but Sir Francis Knolly did. A meeting occurred on 31 March but attendance was not recorded and so it cannot be mapped onto the marriage debates.[1] On 4 October, councillors selected to discuss the marriage—Burghley, Sussex, Leicester, Hunsdon, Walsingham, Wilson and Sir Christopher Hatton (vice-chamberlain)—met at Westminster while the privy council met at Greenwich. Attendance was also different: Sussex and Leicester did not attend the privy council meeting, while Knollys (treasurer of the Chamber), Sir Thomas Bromley (the Lord Chancellor), and the earls of Lincoln and Arundel did.[2] Likewise, Wilson's absence from the

2. Gilbert Talbot to the earl of Shrewsbury, 4 Apr. 1579, LPL, Talbot Papers 3197, fo. 307r.

3. The remedyes sought for to preserve hir Maty and the state in peace, if she shall not marry, 13 Apr. 1579, CP148, fos. 39r–41v.

4. The councillors were Lord Burghley, Lord Chancellor Bromley, the earls of Lincoln, Sussex, Leicester and Warwick, Lord Hunsdon, Sir Francis Knollys, Sir James Croft, Sir Christopher Hatton, Thomas Wilson and Sir Walter Mildmay. The articles were that Anjou be crowned king, have joint authority with Elizabeth in patronage and have an annual income of £40,000 during his lifetime. CP148, fo. 75v.

5. An ordre how to procede to the discussion of the Questions moved concerning the Queens Mariadg with Monsieur Aniou, 2 Oct. 1579, CP148, fos. 47r–54v; Notes on the marriage and succession, 4 Oct. 1579, CP148, fo. 58r.

6. The Anjou marriage, 6 Oct. 1579, Hatfield, CP140, fos. 6r–7v; At the counsell board at Greenwich, 6 Oct, 1579, NRO, Fitzwilliam (Milton) Political 111, fos. 14r–16v; The summe & principall heades of a Conference at westminister touching Queene Elizabethes mariag, 4 Oct. 1579, Additional 4149, fos. 104r–105v; Minute by Lord Burghley on the marriage, 6 Oct. 1579, CP148, fo. 59r.

7. Messadg accorded to be delyvered to hir Majesty, 7–8 Oct. 1579, CP148, fos. 64r–65v.

8. LPL, Talbot Papers 3197, fo. 307r.

9. Proceedings and ordinances of the privy council of England, 10 Richard II–33 Henry VIII, ed. H. Nicolas (7 vols., London, 1834–7), VII, p. 4; Notes concerning the Priuate Counsell, 31 Oct. 1625, Additional 34324, fos. 238r-239v.

1. APC, XI, pp. 87–92.

2. Poin[t]s to state considered vpon by the Counselle at Grenwiche, 6 Oct. 1579, Additional 4149, fos. 104r–105v; APC, IX, p. 276.

privy council meeting on 6 October suggests that the meeting to debate the marriage operated separately from the privy council's proceedings.[3]

Two other points are also suggestive. First, the council's clerks were not used as secretaries; this role was assumed by Burghley. Clerks could be asked to leave the council chamber: in 1541, William Paget was asked to leave when the council, meeting with the Chief Justices and 'other of the King's learned counsel', discussed Lord Dacre's case (though they talked so loudly he could hear them between two closed doors).[4] Stephen Alford has also shown how, in the 1560s, there was a close working relationship between Burghley and one of the clerks, Bernard Hampton, which blurred the lines between council business and Burghley's own.[5] However, the absence of the council's clerks could also suggest the meetings in March, April and October operated separately from those of the privy council. This is rendered more likely by the clear distinction Elizabeth made between the roles of the two groups on 3 May: the select group were to examine the marriage as a resolution to the problems raised by the succession and Catholic conspiracy, the privy council only specific articles in the marriage treaty. Though Burghley attempted to open up the debate on the marriage as a whole in the privy council, Elizabeth's message was clear: she did not want the privy council to debate policy, only elements for its realisation.[6]

This distinction in roles suggests a conscious organisation of counselling in which the privy council did not take the leading advisory role. The group of selected councillors acted as a probouleutic group,[7] conducting the primary examination and discussion of policy. If Talbot's broad description can be believed, they did not initially present Elizabeth with one piece of advice * * * but consulted with her on a daily basis.[8] Individual opinions were offered on 13 April and, more controversially, 7 October: Elizabeth's anger in October may have been a delaying tactic because, unresolved on the marriage, she could not 'shew to us [the councillors] any inclination of hir mynd'.[9] In contrast, the privy council was used to examine issues at a secondary stage: specific (albeit important) elements for the implementation of policy. Even when probouleutic discussion was opened up to a larger number of individuals—as on 6 October—meetings continued to operate independently of the privy council.

Restricting probouleutic debate to a small group of personally selected councillors was particularly appropriate for an issue—Elizabeth's marriage—which she defined as one of the *arcana imperii* ('mysteries of state') reserved for her own judgement and on which she had sought to restrict debate in council, parliament and public debate since her accession. Indeed, the circumscription of counsel in the spring of 1579 ran alongside orders Elizabeth issued to limit uninformed debate, rumour, gossip and opinion within and

3. *APC*, IX, p. 276.
4. William Paget to Sir Thomas Wriothesley, 27 June 1541, *Letters and Papers, Foreign and Domestic, Henry VIII*, ed. J. S. Brewer *et al*. (22 vols., London, 1864–1932), XVI, p. 450.
5. Michael Barraclough Pulman, *Elizabethan privy council in the fifteen-seventies* (Berkeley and Los Angeles, CA, 1971), p. 52; Stephen Alford, *The Early Elizabethan polity: William Cecil and the British succession crisis, 1558–1569* (Cambridge, 1998), pp. 11, 32, 57, 66, 125–6, 168, 173, 178, 207, 213–14.
6. Reports as to the conferences with Simier, 3–4 May 1579, CP148 fos. 42r–43v.
7. A council that engages in preliminary debate [*Editors*].
8. LPL, Talbot Papers 3197, fo. 307.
9. Message from the Council on the marriage, 7–8 Oct. 1579, CP148, fo. 64v. I have examined this episode in more detail in Natalie Mears, '"The personal rule" of Elizabeth I': marriage, succession anc Catholic conspiracy, c. 1578–1582 (Ph.D. thesis, St. Andrews, 1999), ch. 3.

beyond the court.[1] Similar examples of probouleutic groups can also be found for negotiations with the Archduke Charles of Austria in 1567, Henry, duke of Anjou in 1571 and in the later stages of negotiations with Francis, duke of Anjou, in April 1581.[2] * * *

* * *

The Nature of Elizabethan Counsel and Elizabeth's Role in Policy-Making

Elizabethan counselling was therefore neither institutionalised nor conciliar, as Pulman argued, but informal and dynamic. Elizabeth took an active role in organising, managing and seeking counsel, constructing probouleutic groups or consulting with individuals on an *ad hoc* basis. * * *

The active role played by Elizabeth and the use of informal and non-institutionalised methods were also characteristic of other stages of policy-making: information gathering and decision-making. Elizabeth received information directly and indirectly through letters that she read herself or asked others to summarise; she also asked counsellors to summarise the contents of letters they received from agents and ambassadors.[3] On 9 August 1581, Burghley delivered Walsingham's letters from France to the queen, 'shewinge her also that I had others directed to my self. But she said she would firste reade her owne'. Having done so, Elizabeth demanded that Burghley report the contents of his letters, provoking a dispute because he argued it was too long and detailed for him to condense. Elizabeth eventually conceded to hear the entire letter.[4] She also received information informally, through court gossip.[5] The receipt of information, and ensuing debate, was subject to Elizabeth's schedule and health: on 6 February 1568, she read only two of Sussex's letters from the Imperial court about the negotiations for the marriage with the Archduke Charles because they arrived just as she was going out hunting and she did not want 'to lose the day's pleasure'.[6] In November 1572, Leicester had to wait before discussing Mar's death with her because, at six o'clock, she 'was at her wonted repose'.[7] In 1578, a 'payne . . . in her face' prevented consultation on the Netherlands.[8]

Elizabeth also took the lead role in decision-making. In April 1571 she decided that Walsingham should only deliver to Charles IX and Catherine de Médici her answers to the French articles for the marriage treaty with Henry, duke of Anjou, and not additional articles proposed by the English. Upon 'some late intelligence brought thence', she believed that if she stuck

1. LPL, Talbot Papers 3197, fo. 307r.
2. Elizabeth to the earl of Sussex [draft], 12 Dec. 1567, SP70/95, fos. 133r–133v; Burghley to Sir Francis Walsingham, 3 May 1571, DWL, Morrice D, p. 275; same to same, 5 June 1571, DWL, Morrice D, p. 285; Elizabeth to same, 8 June 1571, DWL, Morrice D, pp. 288–9; same to same, 9 July 1571, DWL, Morrice D, pp. 298–9; the earl of Leicester to same, [15 Aug. 1571], DWL, Morrice D, p. 339; [Journal des Négociations des commissaires et Ambassadeurs français du 24 avril au 1er mai 1581], Discours envoyé au Roy et a Monseigneur son frere avec la depesche de Messre le Prince Dauphine et aultres Commissaires, du XXVe d'avril 1581, PRO31/3/28, fos. 285r–287v.
3. Harleian 6991, fo. 23r; Harleian 6265, fo. 52r–52v; CP7, fo. 57; Walsingham to Bowes, [27 Feb.] 1583, SP52/31/45; Cotton Galba C.9, fo. 83r.
4. Harleian 6265, fo. 52r–52v.
5. Cotton Galba C. 9, fo. 79v.
6. De Silva to Philip II, 7 Feb. 1568, CSP Spanish, II, p. 6.
7. CP7, fo. 57r.
8. Walsingham to Hatton, 9 Oct. 1578, Additional 15891, fo. 49v. See also Cecil to Throckmorton, 20 Aug. 1567, SP59/14, fo. 49r.

fast to her answers on Anjou's free exercise of religion, they would be accepted.[9] On hearing that Lennox had seized possession of Dumbarton castle in August 1580, she immediately dispatched Robert Bowes to James VI's court to seek Lennox's surrender of the castle and ordered Hunsdon to prepare troops along the border to force surrender militarily if Bowes's mission failed.[1] Decision-making could be painfully slow and subject to Elizabeth's vacillation: characteristically, having slept on her bellicose instructions to Bowes in 1580, she revoked the final clause the following day,[2] * * * but it can be noted here that it was not always because she was pathologically indecisive or financially stingy.[3] She did find it difficult to resolve personal questions, like marriage, but issues central to the agenda also raised practical and politically sensitive problems. In 1580, Elizabeth considered that any hasty offer of military assistance would bring the Scots more quickly into a civil war and that Lennox would seize the king, take him to Dumbarton whence he would either remove him to France or call in foreign aid.[4] Proposals to resolve the succession politically that included Mary's exclusion from the English succession and a tripartite agreement (with France and Scotland) condoning her deposition and preventing her restoration to the Scottish crown were also problematic: to condone Mary's deposition was to sanction precisely the behaviour that Spain, France and the Papacy were perceived to be engineering against her.[5]

The active role Elizabeth played in policy-making, her use of probouleutic groups, informal and extra-conciliar counselling and the ways her actions intersected with those of other political actors raise two immediate issues central to our understanding of the structure of Elizabethan court politics. First, they demonstrate that counsel was polymorphic and policy-making interactive. Elizabeth not only managed and organised counselling on an informal and dynamic basis but counsellors adopted similar methods. Combined with pervasive humanist-classical concepts of citizenship—to argue in the law courts, debate in public assemblies and counsel a monarch—and attitudes towards female monarchy, this meant the line between Elizabeth actively seeking counsel and receiving unsolicited advice was increasingly blurred. Second, they undermine the importance of the privy council as the principal advisory and policy-making body. In effect, they demand a new paradigm for policy-making be reconstructed, conceived in terms of the networks of individuals active in policy-making, either directly through interaction with Elizabeth or with key counsellors and actors.

Elizabeth's Network of Counsellors and Agents

Burghley, Leicester, Sussex, Walsingham, Hatton, Wilson, Throckmorton, Heneage and Randolph were at the core of Elizabeth's network, followed by

9. Burghley to Walsingham, 19 Apr. 1571, DWL, Morrice D, pp. 250–1.
1. Bowes to Walsingham, 22 Aug. 1580, SP52/28/70, fo. 135r–135v; same to Burghley and Walsingham, 27 Aug. 1580, SP52/28/72, fo. 139r–139v; Walsingham to Leicester, 31 Aug. 1580, Cotton Caligula C. 3, fos. 614r–615; same to Bowes, 31 Aug. 1580, SP52/28/76, fos. 147r–148v. See also Burghley to Leicester, 12 Jan. 1586, Cotton Galba C.9, fo. 16v.
2. Walsingham to Bowes, 1 Sept. 1580, SP52/28/77, fo. 149r. See also Burghley to Walsingham, 5 June 1571, DWL, Morrice D, p. 284.
3. Keith M. Brown, 'The price of friendship: the "well-affected" and English economic clientage in Scotland before 1603', in Roger A. Mason (ed.), Scotland and England 1286–1815 (Edinburgh, 1987), pp. 139–62.
4. SP52/28/77, fo. 149r.
5. Degrees, 1577, Cotton Caligula C. 3, fo. 543r–543v.

outer rings formed by others like Killigrew, Somers, Stafford and Gresham. Yet, the informal and dynamic nature of counselling in particular raises questions about how a new paradigm for Elizabethan court politics can be reconstructed beyond this. Counselling is a key focus because it enables us to see the interaction between individuals, but as already noted, the line between Elizabeth seeking counsel and receiving unsolicited advice was indistinct. Compounded further by the fact that counsel was an ongoing process, it questions whether the paradigm should be defined only in terms of individuals from whom Elizabeth actively sought advice. There is also a secondary question of whether her acceptance of counsel should act as a barometer of an individual's importance.

In sketching an outline of the paradigm (focusing on representative individuals, rather than providing a definitive list), I have privileged active consultation with individuals, as well as secretarial duties. These were areas of direct interaction with Elizabeth that suggest a degree of intimacy and trust. Offering unsolicited advice has been incorporated if there are signs of solicited consultation with Elizabeth too: Killigrew, Somers and Stafford provide examples. The acceptance of counsel is not used as a standard: Elizabeth's active role in policy-making, her attitudes towards monarchical power and counsel and her personal understanding of the problems she faced make this less acceptable. After all, the central characteristic of the structure of Elizabethan policy-making outlined above is precisely her active role.

Forming an extra, peripheral dimension to the inner core of probouleutic and *ad hoc* counsellors were the Lord Keeper, Sir Nicholas Bacon, Sir Francis Knollys, the earls of Lincoln and Ormond and Lord Hunsdon. Bacon, Knollys and Lincoln had all been regular members of probouleutic debate in the 1560s (as far as evidence attests) and active in *ad hoc* counselling or consultation.[6] But Bacon was not selected for probouleutic debate after 1572 (he died in 1579) and neither Knollys nor Lincoln after 1576, though Lincoln was part of the delegation (with Burghley, Sussex and Leicester) to inform Simier of the queen's and privy council's answers to the three treaty articles he had resubmitted for further consideration in May 1579.[7] Both Bacon and Knollys, however, continued to offer advice to Elizabeth informally in letters, either directly or through one of the secretaries.[8]

Hunsdon's only definite appearance in probouleutic debates occurred in 1579, though he also attended (with Randolph) the dinner organised by Burghley for Dunfermline in July 1578 and was selected, with Walsingham, to interview the Scottish ambassador in May 1583.[9] As governor of Berwick, Anglo-Scottish relations were his particular field of expertise and he offered advice from at least 1575 (on the dispute between Sir John Forster, warden of the Middle March, and Sir John Carmichael, keeper of

6. Cotton Caligula B. 10, fos. 301r–308r; Cotton Caligula B. 10, fos. 358r–359v; Cotton Caligula C. 2, fos. 63r–65v; Cotton Caligula C. 3, fos. 92r–93v; DWL, Morrice D, pp. 308–9, 339; Robert Tittler, *Nicholas Bacon: the making of a Tudor statesman* (Athens, OH, 1976), pp. 139–43; Alford, *Early Elizabethan polity*, pp. 78–9, 140–2, quoting SP63/18, fo. 62v; Knollys to Cecil, 2 June 1568, Cotton Caligula C. 1, fo. 119r; Harleian 6991, fo. 17r.
7. SP70/137, fos. 25r–26v; Answer made by the lordes Treasorer, Admirall . . . , 4 May 1579, CP148, fo. 44r.
8. Sir Nicholas Bacon to Elizabeth, 15 Sept. 1577, Additional 15891, fo. 4r–4v; Tittler, *Bacon*, pp. 178–80, 183–4; Sir Francis Knollys to Wilson, Harleian 6992, fo. 89r.
9. Burghley to Randolph, 21 July 1578, Harleian 6992, fo. 104r; SP52/31/17.

Liddesdale).[1] Ormond's position was distinctive. A favourite, nearly comparable to Leicester and Hatton, the earl does not appear to have been active in policy-making but he did exploit his access to Elizabeth to advance or defend his own family's and clientele's interests, particularly against the Lord Deputies, like Sir Henry Sidney and Sir John Perrot, whose attempts to establish personal authority in Ireland conflicted with Ormond's own.[2]

Orbiting at a further remove were the wider groups of agents, ambassadors as well as officials who held posts in England, Wales and Ireland. Even here, however, it seems possible to make a tentative sketch of how the lines of Elizabeth's main network extended into this wider group. For instance, Thomas Sackville, Lord Buckhurst, Sir Henry Norris and Fulke Greville seem to have been favoured by Elizabeth, while Dr Valentine Dale was not. Buckhurst was appointed a special ambassador to France to negotiate the match with Henry, duke of Anjou; Norris (resident ambassador of France, 1566–71) acknowledged he was inexperienced and relied heavily on one of his secretaries, John Barnaby, yet he and his wife were close friends of Elizabeth's.[3] Greville accompanied Duke John Casimir, son of the Elector Palatine who had led English forces in support of the Dutch the previous year, back to Germany in 1579 and Francis, duke of Anjou to Antwerp in 1581; he was also special ambassador to the Netherlands in 1582 charged with enquiring into William of Orange's recovery from a recent assassination attempt. In contrast, though Valentine Dale was appointed to replace Walsingham as resident ambassador to France in 1573, Elizabeth cavilled at her own choice: he was 'but a simple man & she liketh not that he shoulde deale in them [the marriage negotiations]'.[4]

Thomas Leighton and Robert Bowes provide additional lenses for defining the network at this level. Like Killigrew and Stafford, Leighton was employed on sensitive diplomatic missions: in 1568, he carried Elizabeth's letters to Mary Stuart; in 1574, he was sent to France ostensibly to commiserate on Charles IX's poor health but really to remonstrate with Catherine de Médici for Francis, duke of Anjou's imprisonment at Vincennes.[5] He made contact with Anjou and conveyed his requests for English aid to escape, actions which were only nullified by Charles IX's death and Anjou's subsequent transferral to the Louvre.[6] Bowes had an intensive period of activity as an envoy or ambassador to Scotland between 1577 and 1583, during which he was involved in negotiations (often with Randolph) to strengthen Anglo-Scottish amity after Morton's fall in 1578 and secure his release, and Lennox's removal from power, in 1581. Yet neither had a central role in counselling: there is no evidence that Leighton offered advice,

1. Cotton Caligula C. 5, fo. 42r–42v; Hunsdon to Burghley, 19 Aug. 1578, Cotton Caligula C. 5, fo. 129r; Harleian 6999, fo. 138r–138v; Harleian MS 6999, fo. 165r; Hunsdon to Walsingham, 26 June 1581, Harleian MS 6999, fos. 211r–212r.
2. Ciaran Brady, 'Political women and reform in Tudor Ireland', in Margaret MacCurtain and Mary O'Dowd (eds.), *Women in early modern Ireland* (Edinburgh, 1991), pp. 85–6; John Dudley to Leicester, 29 Mar. 1566, SP15/13, fo. 8r.
3. Mark Taviner, 'Robert Beale' and the Elizabethan polity (Ph.D. thesis, St. Andrews, 2000), pp. 74–8, 87; Leicester to Hatton, 11 Sept. 1582, Additional 15891, fos. 72v–73r; Elizabeth to Lady Norris, 22 Sept. 1597, Folger, Folger MS V.b.214, fo. 68r.
4. Harleian 6991, fo. 19r.
5. Hasler, II, pp. 458–9; Conyers Read, *Mr. Secretary Walsingham and the policy of Queen Elizabeth*, (3 vols., Oxford, 1925), I, pp. 282–3, 362–5. He was also dispatched twice to the Netherlands in December 1577–February 1578 to threaten Don John with full English intervention if he did not enter into peace negotiations and to France in 1588 to urge Henry III to proclaim Guise a traitor, to back the Huguenots and offer English aid in 1588. See Read, *Walsingham*, III, pp. 214–15.
6. Read, *Walsingham*, I, pp. 282–3, 362–5.

while Bowes's advice—specifically on challenging Lennox's ascendancy in 1580–1 and restoring Anglo-Scottish amity in 1582—was made either at the request of the privy council or his own initiative.[7] Moreover, his advice on the need to use force against Lennox in 1581 was ultimately overruled by Randolph's.[8] Important in the diplomatic network, Leighton and Bowes appeared to operate on the periphery of Elizabeth's inner networks. Similar examples—those who were frequently employed as special agents and ambassadors—are Thomas Wilkes, Daniel Rogers and Thomas Bodley.[9]

Elizabeth's network was male-dominated but not exclusively male. Parallel to the inner ring of counsellors was a group of female intimates often holding feed or unfeed privy chamber posts.[1] They included Frances Newton, Lady Cobham; Elizabeth Fitzgerald, countess of Lincoln; Elizabeth Brooke, marchioness of Northampton; Anne, countess of Warwick; Mary Shelton, Lady Scudamore; Lady Mary Sidney; Elizabeth, Lady Carew; Bridget Skipworth-Cave; Blanche Parry; Lady Dorothy Stafford; and her daughter, Elizabeth, Lady Drury.[2] Even more than secondary male figures, evidence of their political activity is fragmentary, but evidence points to them acting in two crucial ways: as barometers of the queen's moods or channels of communication, even for her most trusted advisers, and as negotiators in marriage diplomacy, especially in the 1560s. In a memorandum of 1559, the Spanish ambassador, the Count of Feria, identified Elizabeth Brooke, marchioness of Northampton as 'in high favour with the queen [and] has served His Majesty when opportunity has occurred'; she was cultivated by both de Quadra and Guzman de Silva, successive Spanish ambassadors.[3] Lady Cobham, the countess of Lincoln and Mary Sidney were all in contact with Feria's wife, Jane Dormer, one of Mary I's most trusted ladies-in-waiting.[4] In August 1571, Elizabeth told Lady Drury that the earl of Rutland should return from France knowing that she was in correspondence with him and

7. Cotton Caligula C. 5, fo. 129r; Bowes to Walsingham, 10 May 1580, SP52/28/20, fo. 43r; Privy council to Burghley and Walsingham, 13 Sept. 1580, Cotton Caligula C. 6, fos. 80r–81v; Bowes to Walsingham, 7 Sept. 1582, in *The correspondence of Robert Bowes of Aske*, ed. John Stevenson (Surtees Society, 14; London, 1842), pp. 180–1.

8. SP52/29/1; Harleian 6999, fo. 138r–138v; Huntingdon to Walsingham, 2 Apr. 1581, Harleian 6999, fo. 152r.

9. Wilkes was special agent or ambassador to Spain 1577–8, the Netherlands in 1578, 1582 and 1586, as well as to France and the Netherlands in the 1590s. Rogers was agent (1576–8, 1578–9) and special ambassador (1578) to the Low Countries and had audiences with Casimir (1576 and 1578–9), the Elector Palatine (1577, 1578–9) and the Landgrave of Hesse (1577); and was special ambassador to the Emperor in 1580 (during which time he was imprisoned) and Denmark, 1587–8. (See also J. A. van Dorsten, *Poets, patrons and professors: Sir Philip Sidney, Daniel Rogers, and the Leiden humanists* [Leiden and Oxford, 1962], pp. 9–75.) Bodley was one of Stafford's secretaries during his residency in France and then agent; he was special ambassador to Denmark and the duke of Brunswick in 1585 and Denmark again in 1588. Both Wilkes and Bodley were also English representatives on the Dutch council of state in the late 1580s and early 1590s. See Gary M. Bell, *A Handlist of British diplomatic representatives 1509–1688* (Royal Historical Society, 16; London, 1990), passim.

1. The wages of the ladies and others of the Privie Chamber and bedchamber, 22 May 1589, Lansdowne 59/22, fo. 43r–43v which includes the dates of warrants (or letters patent) for appointments; Payments of money to the Ladies and Gentlemen of the Privy Chamber, 1579, Lansdowne 104/18, fo. 41r. See also Lansdowne 29/68, fo. 161r–161v (1580), Lansdowne 34/30, fo. 76r–76v (1582).

2. De Silva to Philip II, 8 Oct. 1565, *CSP Spanish*, I, pp. 487–8; *Russia at the close of the sixteenth century, comprising the treatise 'Of the Russe Common Wealth' by Dr Giles Fletcher, and the travels of Sir Jerome Horsey, knt*, ed. Edward A. Bond (Hakluyt Society; London, 1856), pp. 233–4; Mendoza to Philip II, 27 Jan. 1582, *CSP Spanish*, III, p. 274; Merton, 'Women who served', pp. 96–7.

3. Bishop de Quadra to Philip II, 13 Sept. 1561, *CSP Spanish*, I, p. 214; Memorandum of the count of Feria, 1559, ibid., p. 36; de Silva to the duchess of Parma, 23 Sept. 1564, ibid., p. 381. The marchioness never held an official post in the privy chamber but was a long-standing intimate of Elizabeth's.

4. *CSP Spanish*, I, p. 214; bishop of Aquila to the duchess of Parma, 7 Sept. 1559, ibid., p. 96; Merton, 'Women who served', pp. 166–7; *CSP Spanish*, I, p. 454.

would inform him.[5] Lady Cobham and Lady Stafford asked Sussex, the Lord Chamberlain, to request Lady Scudamore to return to court, though it is unclear from Sussex's letter whether they were acting on Elizabeth's command.[6] A letter appointing Sir Edward York to a command of infantry in Ireland was delivered by the countess of Warwick's messenger on the Signet Office's behalf.[7] Even the likes of Leicester, Burghley and Heneage maintained contacts with privy chamber women.[8] In April 1587, Lady Cobham made use of her intimacy with Elizabeth to try and smooth Burghley's return to court in the aftermath of Mary's execution: she advised him 'to hasten your commynge hether' and promised to deliver a letter to Elizabeth.[9] Lady Scudamore was an intermediary for Heneage.[1] Indeed, Robert Beale's 'Instructions for a Principall Secretarie . . . for Sir Edwarde Wotton' (1592) explicitly acknowledged the importance of privy chamber women in facilitating the Principal Secretary's duties: 'Learne before your accesse her majesties disposicion by some in the Privie Chamber, with whom you must keepe credit: for that will stande yow in much steede'.[2]

In 1559, Mary Sidney acted as Elizabeth's go-between with de Quadra in the Archduke Charles's marriage negotiations until de Quadra tried to force Elizabeth's hand on accepting Charles's visit and to bind her to accepting his proposal: Elizabeth retreated from the negotiations and denied anyone had commission from her to deal with the ambassadors. 'I am obliged to complain of somebody in this matter, and have complained of Lady Sidney only, although in good truth she is no more to blame than I am, as I have said privately.'[3] Male members of the privy chamber also played political roles: John Tamworth (gentleman of the privy chamber and keeper of the privy purse, 1559) was special ambassador to Mary in 1565; Charles Howard (gentleman of the privy chamber, 1558) and George Howard (gentleman usher from c.1558) were special ambassadors to France in 1559.[4]

✳   ✳   ✳

✳ ✳ ✳ [P]olitical debate was not restricted to, nor monopolised by, Elizabeth's inner ring of counsellors. ✳ ✳ ✳ Activity was not confined to men. Women in and without the privy chamber met and corresponded with each other and with men and discussed political events and issues.[5] For instance,

---

5. Elizabeth Stafford to the earl of Rutland, 16 Aug. 1571, *HMC Rutland*, I, pp. 95–6.
6. Sussex to Lady Scudamore, n.d., Additional 11042, fo. 131r.
7. Merton, 'Women who served', pp. 183–4.
8. Taviner, 'Robert Beale', pp. 243–4; Lady Cobham to Burghley, 10 Apr. 1587, SP12/200/20, fo. 38r; same to same, 15 June 1584, SP12/171/25, fo. 43r; Cecil to Heneage, 30 July 1570, *HMC Finch*, I, p. 10; SP15/13, fos. 7r, 8r–8v; John Dudley to Leicester, 29 Mar. 1566, SP15/13, fo. 11r–11v. Leicester's sister, Mary Sidney, and sister-in-law, the countess of Warwick, were unfeed members of the privy chamber and Elizabeth's intimates.
9. SP12/200/20, fo. 38r; SP12/171/25, fo. 43r. See also Merton, 'Women who served', pp. 168–9.
1. W. Poyntz to Heneage, 4 July 1583, *HMC Finch*, I, pp. 24–5; same to same, 23 July 1583, ibid., p. 25.
2. 'Instructions for a Principall Secretaries obserued by R. B. for Sir Edwarde Wotton A. D. 1592', Additional 48149, fo. 8r.
3. *CSP Spanish*, I, p. 95; de Quadra to the Emperor, 2 Oct. 1559, ibid., pp. 98–9; same to same, 16 Oct. 1559, ibid., p. 101; same to Philip II, 13 Nov. 1559, ibid., pp. 111–13; same to same, 18 Nov. 1559, ibid., p. 115. For a more detailed discussion of this episode see Naralie Mears, 'Politics in the Elizabethan privy chamber: Lady Mary Sidney and Kat Ashley', in Daybell (ed.), *Women and politics in early modern England*, pp. 67–82.
4. Subsidy roll (royal household), assessment, 18 Elizabeth [1575–6], NA, E179/69/93, m. 2.
5. Cotton Galba C. 9, fo. 79v; Poyntz to Heneage, 4 July 1583, *HMC Finch*, 1, pp. 24–5; same to Lady Anne Heneage, 23 July 1583, ibid., pp. 25–6; same to same, 9 Apr. 1586, ibid., pp. 26–7; Elizabeth Finch to same, 27 Apr. [1589?], ibid., p. 28; SP12/171/25, fo. 43; Elizabeth Stafford to Rutland, 16 Aug. 1571, *HMC Rutland*, I, pp. 95–6; Lady Savage to same, 28 Jan. 1576, Ibid., p. 107; Eleanor Bridges to same, Jan. 1576, ibid., p. 107; Rauf Rabbards to Lady Knyvett, 19 Oct. 1599, BL, Egerton MS 2714, fo. 29r; same to same, 24 July 1600, BL, Egerton MS 2714, fo. 73r.

George Blyth, one of Burghley's secretaries and, from 1574, a member of the Council of the North, informed the countess of Huntingdon of Henry III's entry into France.[6] The countess of Warwick supplied troops for Leicester's Netherlands expedition and was involved in Irish affairs in the 1580s and 1590s.[7] The countess of Sussex and Lady Anne Fitzwilliam played small diplomatic roles while their husbands were Lord Deputies of Ireland: the countess developed contacts with Shane O'Neill, chieftain of the O'Neills of Tyrone in Ulster, while Lady Fitzwilliam was active at court defending Fitzwilliam's position and pressing for men, money and munitions.[8] Eleanor Butler, countess of Desmond, was a major diplomatic force in Anglo-Irish politics, acting as an intermediary between her husband and Dublin to persuade him to accept 'composition'; her role was fundamental to the decision to restore Desmond in 1574.[9] Though wondering why her experience had not taught her more patience, Burghley described Heneage's wife, Anne (daughter of Sir Nicholas Poyntz) as a 'courtyar': her 'grete stomack were meter for the Court than for Essex'.[1]

In other words, Elizabethan politics was truly 'court politics'. Counselling and policy-making were conducted primarily by the queen and a group of personal intimates, either in specially selected probouleutic groups or informally and *ad hoc*. Personal relationships could be articulated by appointment to the privy council, but it was household office that was more important: it demonstrated, or facilitated, one's personal relationship with the queen. The principal institutional focus was the Chamber, extending to the rest of the royal household (the privy chamber, the Stables), but this was always less significant than the network that was formed by Elizabeth's counsellors, intimates and favoured agents and ambassadors. Elizabethan politics was also truly 'court politics' in that debate often spilled out beyond the boundaries of Elizabeth's network to members of the court. * * *

THE VIRGIN MONARCH

SUSAN DORAN

Why Did Elizabeth Not Marry?[†]

Elizabeth I's virginity has been her most famous attribute since the late sixteenth century. This is understandable, not least because her chastity was celebrated from the 1580s onwards in art, poetry, and drama. But her unmarried state has also attracted criticism. During the first decade of the reign, marriage and childbirth provided the only hope of securing a clear and unchallenged Protestant line of succession to the English throne and of averting the danger of civil war on the queen's death. During the 1570s,

6. George Blythe to the countess of Huntingdon, 20 June 1574, Additional 46367, fo. 54v.
7. Sherley to Leicester, 21 Mar. 1586, Cotton MS Galba C. 9, fo. 139v; Merton, 'Women who served', pp. 183–6.
8. Brady, 'Political women', pp. 82–3.
9. Ibid., pp. 79–80. Also significant were some of the Irish women, including Agnes Campbell (Turlough Luineach O'Neill's wife) and Grace O'Malley: ibid., pp. 80–1.
1. *HMC Finch*, I, p. 6.
† From *Dissing Elizabeth: Negative Representations of Gloriana*. Ed. Julia M. Walker (Durham: Duke University Press, 1998), pp. 30–44, 50–59. Copyright, 1998, Duke University Press. All rights reserved. Used by permission of the publisher.

when Elizabeth was in her forties and unlikely to bear a child, the country needed her marriage to a powerful prince in order to seal an alliance which might bring an end to its increasingly dangerous isolation in Europe. Yet, despite these considerations, Elizabeth rejected the hand of at least a dozen suitors, including King Philip II of Spain, King Eric XIV of Sweden, King Charles IX of France and his two brothers, Henry and Francis, and an Austrian archduke. By this action, or rather nonaction, she appeared to be betraying her dynasty, her religion, and her realm, especially as she also refused to designate a successor. It was behavior seemingly at variance with her reputation as a monarch traditionally praised for her dedication to national unity and the national interest.

Elizabeth was exhorted to marry time and time again in the early part of the reign. The Privy Council as a body called on her to take a husband in late December 1559 as part of its advice for dealing with the dangers posed by Mary Stuart.[1] In 1559, 1563, 1566, and 1576 her parliaments sent her petitions urging marriage as a way to resolve the succession. Sometime around 1560, Matthew Parker, the archbishop of Canterbury, Edmund Grindal, the bishop of London, and Richard Cox of Ely "thought it our parts for our pastoral office, to be solicitous in that cause which all your loving subjects so daily sigh for and morningly in their prayers desire to appear to their eyes," for they could not "but fear that this continued sterility in your Highness' person to be a token of God's displeasure towards us."[2] During her summer progress of 1565, the Recorder of Coventry greeted her with an oration which included the wish that "like as you are a mother to your kingdom . . . so you may, by God's goodness and justice, be a natural mother, and, having blest issue of your princely body, may live to see your children's children unto the third and fourth generation."

More oblique petitions were also addressed to the queen. Court masques were performed before her in the mid-1560s which focused on the theme of the superiority of marriage over celibacy. In most of them, the goddess Diana representing virginity was trounced by Venus or Juno, the goddess of marriage.[3] As a New Year's gift for 1560, the diplomat Sir Thomas Challoner presented and dedicated to the queen a book in praise of Henry VIII, which ended with the plea that she "bestow the bonds of your modesty on a husband. . . . For then a little Henry will play in the palace for us."[4]

As time went on and childbirth became less likely, Elizabeth's councillors viewed her marriage as a necessary preliminary to a league with the French king. Thus, when the earl of Sussex listed seven advantages to a match with Henry III of France's brother, Francis duke of Alençon, in August 1578, only one related to the possibility of producing an heir, and this was the last one he mentioned; the remainder concerned the beneficial effects that would arise from a dynastic alliance with the house of France.[5]

1. Petition of the Privy Council drafted by Cecil 28 December 1559, Public Record Office, SP 12/7, fol. 186 (hereafter abbreviated as PRO). To be accurate, the concern here was as much Mary's present claim to the throne as the succession.
2. J. Bruce, ed., *Correspondence of Matthew Parker, Archbishop of Canterbury* (Cambridge: Parker Society, 1853), 129–32.
3. Susan Doran, "Juno versus Diana: The Treatment of Elizabeth's Marriage in Plays and Entertainments, 1561–1581," *Historical Journal* 38 (1995): 257–74.
4. J. B. Gabel and C. C. Schlam, eds., *Thomas Chaloner's "In Laudem Henrici Octavi"* (Lawrence, Kan.: Coronado Press, 1979). I would like to thank Dr. Jonathan Woolfson for this reference.
5. "Notes taken out of a letter from the earl of Sussex 28 August 1578," cited in J. Payne Collier, "The Egerton Papers," *Camden Society* 12 (London: Royal Historical Society, 1840): 74–75.

These petitions and recommendations were always courteous but they often contained a critical note. The 1566 parliamentary petition on the marriage and succession implicitly censured the queen for lack of action despite her promise to marry during the previous session, thereby prompting Elizabeth to reprimand both Houses with the words: "A strange ordere of petycyoners, that wyll make a request and cannot be otherwyse asserteynyde but by the prince's worde, and yet wyll not beleve yt when yt ys spoken."[6] The masques presented before the queen also implied criticism, leading Elizabeth to exclaim after one performance, "This is all against me."[7]

Historians and biographers have always argued that Elizabeth made a conscious decision to reject her subjects' appeals and remain unwed out of personal or political considerations: either an implacable hostility to matrimony or a determination to rule alone. Biographers in particular have focused on the psychological explanations. Some have detected in Elizabeth an antipathy to marriage stemming from an emotional block to any kind of change or an almost pathological inability to make a decision. Others, however, have turned to more complex motives, and have tried to explore the depths of Elizabeth's psyche to discover a cause of her "choice" to remain single.[8] It is certainly easy to find in her childhood experiences a ready explanation for an irrational aversion to marriage. After all, her mother, Anne Boleyn, was executed by her father on a charge of adultery before Elizabeth had reached her third year; Anne's supplanter, Jane Seymour, died soon after giving birth to Prince Edward in 1538; and in 1542, a third stepmother, Catherine Howard, was also executed for adultery. No wonder that some writers have claimed that these early traumas naturally led the young Elizabeth to associate sexual relations with death and develop a hysterical reaction against marriage. They propose, furthermore, that this association was reinforced by the experiences of her troubled adolescence, when she fell victim to the lustful advances and political ambitions of Lord Thomas Seymour, a maternal uncle of the new king, Edward VI. If Elizabeth had been the victim of a degree of sexual abuse and especially if she had found Seymour's advances exciting or even enjoyable, it seems reasonable to infer that she might well have internalized intense guilt at the death in childbirth of Catherine and the execution of Seymour.[9]

According to some historians, these childhood experiences had another important effect in that they taught Elizabeth that "maleness mattered" and left her with a "masculine identification"; after all, had she been born a boy, her mother would not have been destroyed while she herself would have retained her father's affections. As a result, argues Larissa J. Taylor-Smither, Elizabeth came to value and adopt the masculine qualities of dominance,

6. T. E. Hartley, ed., *Proceedings in the Parliaments of Elizabeth I* (Leicester: Leicester University Press, 1981), 147.

7. *Calendus State Papers Spanish, 1558–67*, 404 (hereafter abbreviated *Cal. S. P. Span, 1558–67*).

8. For hostility to change see Paul Johnson, *Elizabeth I: A Study in Power and Intellect* (London: Weidenfeld and Nicolson, 1974), 112, and for her irresolution see Jaspar Ridley, *Elizabeth I* (London: Constable, 1987), 214. For more complex psychological explanations see L. J. Taylor-Smither, "Elizabeth I: A Psychological Profile," *Sixteenth Century Journal* 15 (1984): 47–70.

9. Alison Plowden, *Marriage with My Kingdom: The Courtships of Elizabeth I* (London: Macmillan, 1977), 160.

aggression, and fearlessness, which made it impossible for her to assume the subservient role expected of a wife in the sixteenth century.[1]

Psychological theories such as these have proved extremely popular, because they seem to explain not only why Elizabeth did not marry, but also why she appeared to have such an implacable hatred of matrimony in general. Her attempt to curb clerical marriage, her opposition to the marriages of her courtiers and ladies-in-waiting, and her fury when she discovered that their clandestine marriages had taken place despite her wishes, seem to be more readily understandable in the light of some pathological disorder. The uncontrollable rages Elizabeth frequently displayed on such occasions (as when she broke the finger of Mary Shelton on discovering her secret marriage to James Scudamore) only seem to make sense if we accept that her behavior was clinically hysterical and the result of unconscious anxieties stemming from childhood disturbance.

Nonetheless, this kind of psychological speculation is suspect, since it is based on unproved models of human behavior and inadequate evidence. There is no factual information at all to indicate how the deaths of her mother and stepmothers affected the young princess, and it could equally well be argued that their emotional impact was slight. Queen Anne was a very remote figure in Elizabeth's early childhood; the young princess had, moreover, stable surrogate mothers in the persons of Lady Bryan and then Katherine Champernowne, later to be Mrs. Ashley. Attitudes to parenthood and death in the sixteenth century were in any event quite different from those of today, and it is ahistorical to transpose late-twentieth-century sensibilities to the past. Furthermore, in adult life Elizabeth showed herself capable of forming relationships with male courtiers and advisors on a range of levels of intimacy, which suggests that she was not the emotionally stunted woman depicted by many biographers. Finally, Elizabeth's hostility to the marriages of her subjects had their own specific explanations. Antipathy to clerical marriage stemmed from the queen's religious conservatism, while her anger at the secret weddings of her ladies and courtiers often had a political cause. In general terms, she wanted her privy chamber to be apolitical and consequently required her ladies to be free from loyalties to a husband and his kin.[2] By marrying, her ladies were risking their political neutrality; furthermore, when they married secretly (often of necessity), they were demonstrating to their mistress their untrustworthiness and divided loyalties.

For this reason, other historians have generally discarded psychological explanations and tended instead to see Elizabeth's decision to remain unwed as the deliberate, rational response of an intelligent woman to the practical problems of being a female ruler. Marriage, they argued, would inevitably have jeopardized Elizabeth's authority, since sixteenth-century patriarchal society believed that a wife should always defer to her husband when making decisions, given that women were naturally inferior to men and that God had ordained female subordination to men in all private relationships. Accordingly, an unmarried Elizabeth would have been expected to hand over power to her husband or at the very least to follow his wishes

1. Taylor-Smither, "Elizabeth I," 47–70.
2. Pam Wright, "A Change in Direction: The Ramifications of a Female Household, 1558–1603," in *The English Court from the Wars of the Roses to the Civil War*, by David Starkey et al. (Harlow: Longman, 1987), 159, 168.

over policy.[3] Her refusal to risk this loss of control has been praised by some feminist writers, but others have denounced it. Allison Heisch, for example, complained that Elizabeth represented the typical token woman who accepted "male notions of how the world was or should be organised" and who reinforced rather than eroded "those systems which oppress and exclude women."[4]

It is a mistake, however, to assume that Elizabeth believed that she could deal with the issue of her gender only by remaining celibate, and had to remain unmarried because she did not wish to share her rule with a husband. In his treatise *"An Harborowe for Faithfull and Trewe Subiectes"* (which was written in 1559 as an answer to John Knox's *First Blast of the Trumpet Against the Monstruous Regiment of Women*, the most famous work denying the legitimacy of gynecocracy), John Aylmer, later to be bishop of London, argued against those who said that a married queen regnant should always display uxorial subordination in line with God's law and defer to her husband on all matters of state:

> Yea say you, God hath appoynted her to be subject to her husband . . . therefore she maye not be the heade. I graunte that, so farre as perteining to the bandes of mariage, and the offices of a wife, she must be a subjecte; but as a Magistrate she maye be her husbande's head. . . . Whie may not the woman be the husbande's inferiour in matters of wedlock, and his head in the guiding of the commonwelth.[5]

Aylmer saw a queen regnant as two persons, one private and one public. As a wife she would be subordinate to her husband in private affairs, but as a magistrate she would be dominant and could command and even punish her husband if he broke the law. Since her obligations as a wife would not take precedence over her regal responsibility, Elizabeth could thus retain her powers when married.

There were few practical obstacles to this political theory. It was in the obvious interests of all Elizabeth's advisors and servants to exclude her husband from power. The means to do so, moreover, were at hand in the marriage-treaty of Mary I and Philip of Spain, which had fixed clear limits on the king's political power in England, barring him from policy-making and patronage. Consequently, Elizabeth's councillors agreed that any marriage contract negotiated for the queen should be based on this 1553 treaty; as Sir Nicholas Bacon explained, this would ensure that her husband "shall not intermeddell with any parte of the governement of the realme to move

---

3. Joel Hurstfield, *Elizabeth I and the Unity of England* (London: English Universities Press, 1960), 40; Paula Louise Scalingi, "The Scepter or the Distaff: The Question of Female Sovereignty, 1515–1607," *The Historian* 42 (1978): 59–75; Mortimer Levine, "The Place of Women in Tudor Government," in *Tudor Rule and Revolution: Essays for G. R. Elton from His American Friends*, ed. D. J. Guth and J. W. McKenna (Cambridge: Cambridge University Press, 1982), 109–23; Constance Jordan, "Women's Rule in Sixteenth-Century British Political Thought," *Renaissance Quarterly* 40 (1987): 421–51; Patricia-Ann Lee, "A Bodye Politique to Governe: Aylmer, Knox, and the Debate on Queenship," *The Historian* 52 (1990): 242–61.

4. Allison Heisch, "Queen Elizabeth and the Persistence of Patrimony," *Feminist Review* 4 (1980): 45–56. Susan Bassnett, on the other hand, praises Elizabeth's virginity as a feminist statement in *Elizabeth I: A Feminist Perspective* (Oxford: Berg, 1988), 124–25, 128.

5. Quoted in Carole Levin, *The Heart and Stomach of a King: Elizabeth I and the Politics of Sex and Power* (Philadelphia: University of Pennsylvania Press, 1994), 43. For further discussion of Aylmer's tracts and other writings justifying female rule, see also Amanda Shepherd, *Gender and Authority in Sixteenth-Century England* (Keele, Staffordshire: Keele University Press, 1994).

any suspection."[6] The experience of the previous reign was also a reassuring precedent; Mary had not been a weak, dependent woman who had allowed power and authority to slip from her hands into those of her husband. For one thing, she placed difficulties in the way of Philip's playing an effective role in government by denying him a personal patrimony in England, which would allow him to build up an independent patronage base.[7] For another, she made little attempt to push his coronation through Parliament, an investiture which would have enhanced his status as king. Furthermore, all the court rituals and ceremonies of the reign asserted Mary's role as sovereign and emphasized that Philip was merely her consort: her throne was larger than his and placed at a higher level; she was served off gold while he was served off silver.[8] The treaty itself was upheld in every detail. Philip had to pay the total costs of his huge household, and, even when it came to the war against France, the Privy Council did not automatically approve England's participation on the side of Spain but only agreed entry after the French-backed raid on Scarborough Castle. The Marian precedent, therefore, did not suggest that it was necessary for Elizabeth to remain unmarried in order to rule rather than reign.

But some historians argue, in addition, that the decision to remain a virgin gave Elizabeth opportunities to play a role and develop an image, which could help her in a more general way to overcome the obstacle of her gender in asserting her rule.[9] It is often said that she fashioned for herself a public persona as a virginal goddess, which would give her a special mystique as a female ruler and allow her to command the respect and awe reserved for kings. In courtly pageantry she acted out the roles of the *bel dame* of medieval chivalry or the Petrarchan mistress of Renaissance poetry, who was beloved and served by male courtiers without any loss to their honor. In this way, the queen could keep in line male courtiers chafing at the obligation to obey a female monarch. Similarly, through the image of the Virgin Queen she was able to present herself as no ordinary woman, but as an exceptional woman whose purity made her worthy of devotion, even adoration. Her virginity allowed her to be cast in portraits and literature as the moon goddesses, Diana, Phoebe, and Cynthia, as well as Astraea, the virgin who in Virgil's poetry had once presided over the Golden Age and would return again to restore it. Her virginity also enabled her to exploit the

6. "A discourse of the queen's marriage with the duke of Anjou, drawn out by the Lord Keeper," 1570, in "Egerton Papers," *Camden Society* 12 (London: Royal Historical Society, 1857).

7. D. M. Loades, "Philip II and the Government of England," in *Law and Government under the Tudors,* ed. C. Cross, D. M. Loades, and J. J. Scarisbrick (Cambridge: Cambridge University Press, 1988), 177–94.

8. Sarah Duncon of Yale University, who is working on Philip II as king of England, shared some of her ideas with me, in particular how courtly ritual inversed the traditional gender roles of king and consort during the reign of Mary I. The example of the silver and gold plate comes from D. M. Loades, *The Reign of Mary Tudor: Politics, Government, and Religion in England, 1553–58,* 2nd ed. (Harlow: Longman, 1991), 170.

9. Interest in the portrayal of Elizabeth as the Virgin Queen has grown in recent years, largely thanks to the work of scholars of literature during the 1980s and 1990s. See for example: Stephen Greenblatt, *Renaissance Self-Fashioning: From More to Shakespeare* (Chicago: University of Chicago Press, 1980), 166–68; David Norbrook, *Poetry and Politics in the English Renaissance* (London: Routledge and Kegan Paul, 1984); Louis A. Montrose, "'Shaping Fantasies': Figurations of Gender and Power in Elizabethan Culture," in *Representing the Renaissance,* ed. Stephen Greenblatt (Berkeley: University of California Press, 1988), 31–64; Philippa Berry, *Of Chastity and Power: Elizabethan Literature and the Unmarried Queen* (London: Routledge, 1989); Susan Frye, *Elizabeth I: The Competition for Representation* (Oxford: Oxford University Press, 1993); Helen Hackett, *Virgin Mother, Maiden Queen: Elizabeth I and the Cult of the Virgin Queen* (London: Macmillan, 1995).

coincidence of her birth date, 7 September, with the feast of the Nativity of the Virgin Mary and claim a symbolic kinship with the mother of Christ. These public personae were obviously incompatible with marriage. Quite simply, as Christopher Haigh has explained so succinctly, "how could she admit that she was just the same as the rest, and submit herself to a husband? . . . Elizabeth had refused to be a mere woman, and was not going to be a mere wife."[1]

Elizabeth, however, did not have to remain unmarried and chaste to appear exceptional to her subjects, nor did she need to develop the secular cult of the Virgin to create for herself a special mystique. Instead, she could and did derive a special status as a female monarch by emphasizing her position as the instrument of God's purpose and identifying herself with providential figures in the Bible. Most Protestant publicists described Elizabeth in this fashion. In his treatise of 1559, Aylmer asserted that God had ordained Elizabeth to rule, as a special woman, when he provided for no male heir through the succession: "It is a plain argument that for some secret purpose he [God] myndeth the female should reign and governe."[2] John Calvin too believed that Elizabeth's accession was "ordained by the peculiar providence of God"; although accepting the contemporary assumption that female rule was a "deviation from the original and proper order of nature," he acknowledged that "there were occasionally women," like Elizabeth, who "were raised up by divine authority" to be queen in order to become "the nursing mothers of the church."[3] In John Jewel's *Apology of the Church of England* of 1562 and John Foxe's *Acts and Monuments* of the following year, the authors argued that all the signs of Scripture and history confirmed the providential nature of the queen's rule. Both elitist poetry and popular verses expressed the same argument. From Edmund Spenser's *Faerie Queene* came the lines:

> But vertuous women wisely understand
> That they were borne to base humilitie
> Unlesse the heavens they lift to lawfull soveraintie.[4]

Meanwhile, the verse of the Protestant balladeer John Awdelay proclaimed:

> Up, said this God with voice not strange,
> Elizabeth, thys realme nowe guyde,
> My wyll in thee doo not thou hyde.[5]

Elizabeth also liked to project herself in this providential mold; in her parliamentary rhetoric, for example, she frequently described herself as a woman raised by Providence to be a monarch, one who was thus exceptional in nature, quite unlike other women.[6] The image of the Virgin

---

1. Christopher Haigh, *Elizabeth I: Profile in Power* (London: Longman, 1988), 16.
2. According to Levine, "The Place of Women," 112–13, despite Aylmer's acceptance of the legitimacy of gynecocracy, modern feminists would find his views insulting as he shared his contemporaries' misogynist prejudices.
3. Hastings Robinson ed., *The Zurich Letters*, 2nd ser. (Cambridge: Parker Society, 1845), 2:35.
4. Edmund Spenser, *The Faerie Queene*, ed. A. C. Hamilton (London: Longman, 1977), 5.5.25 (p. 562).
5. Elkin Calhoun Wilson, *England's Eliza* (Cambridge, Mass.: Harvard University Press, 1939), 8.
6. Allison Heisch, "Queen Elizabeth I: Parliamentary Rhetoric and the Exercise of Power," *Signs* 1 (1975): 31–55.

Queen, in fact, appeared relatively late in Elizabeth's reign. Early royal portraits which deployed emblems of virginity were clearly presenting a marriageable queen rather than one whose power rested on her celibacy. A change began to take place only after 1578. The entertainments performed before the queen at Norwich in the summer of 1578 were possibly the first attempt to lay stress on Elizabeth's special status as a virgin queen, and this was soon followed by a series of some seven Sieve Portraits painted between 1579 and about 1583 in which the queen was depicted holding a sieve, the symbol of Tuccia, a Roman Vestal Virgin, who when accused of breaking her vestal vows had proved her virginity by carrying water in a sieve from the River Tiber back to the temple without spilling a drop. The appearance of this imagery coincided with the unpopular matrimonial negotiations, which had opened with Francis duke of Alençon in the summer of 1578 and were to continue until the end of 1581. Elizabeth herself did not construct it; the patrons of these early representations of the Virgin Queen were some of her subjects who opposed the French match.

* * *

Indeed, at no time during the first half of the reign did Elizabeth rule out the prospect of marriage in her public statements. Certainly her answers to petitions from her House of Commons were often ambivalent, even perhaps obscure, yet they always admitted the possibility of marriage. On 10 February 1559 Elizabeth promised the MPs that if "it may please God to enclyne my heart to an other kynd of life, ye may well assure your selves my meaning is not to do or determyne anie thinge wherwith the realme may or shall have iuste cause to be discontented."[7] In 1563, she told the Speaker: "Yf anie thinke I never meant to trade that [single] lief, they be deceaved; but yf I may hereafter bende my minde thereunto the rather for fullfillinge your request I shalbe therwith very well content."[8] In 1566, she was more direct: "And therefore I saye ageyn, I wyll marrye assone as I can convenyentlye, yf Gd take not hym awaye with whom I mynde to marrye, or my self, or els sum othere great lette happen. . . . And I hope to have chylderne, otherwyse I wolde never marrie."[9]

* * *

Of course it was in Elizabeth's interests to leave open the possibility that she might one day wed, but it is doubtful that her public statements were merely cynical gestures to silence her parliamentary critics or encourage matrimonial suits for diplomatic gain. In the 1560s, she well knew that marriage and childbirth provided the best route for resolving the thorny issue of the succession. Although there were Protestant claimants in the persons of Catherine and Mary Grey, the granddaughters of Henry VIII's younger sister Mary Tudor, the Roman Catholic Mary Stuart, who had descended from Henry VIII's elder sister Margaret, had the best title by

7. For the speech of Elizabeth to the House of Commons see Hartley, *Proceedings*, 1:44–45. A fuller discussion of the two speeches can be found in Frances Teague, "Queen Elizabeth in Her Speeches" in *Gloriana's Face: Women, Public and Private, in the English Renaissance*, ed. S. P. Cerasano and Marion Wynne-Davies (Detroit: Wayne State University Press, 1992), 63–78.
8. Hartley, *Proceedings*, 112.
9. Ibid., 147.

right of heredity.[1] Mary Stuart's claim, moreover, was strengthened during the 1560s by the disgrace of the Grey sisters, caused by the illicit union of Catherine to the earl of Hertford in 1561, the bastardization of their two sons, and the misalliance in 1566 of the dwarfish Mary to a lowly servant of the court, who was reputed to be over six feet tall. As Elizabeth consistently refused to name her heir, and was especially unwilling to exclude Mary Stuart from the throne, a move which might have satisfied her Protestant subjects, she was in no position to reject matrimony as a way of solving the succession problem. Whatever her personal preferences, such freedom of action was not open to her.

On two occasions, moreover, Elizabeth showed a strong interest in marrying. First, after the death of Lord Robert Dudley's wife in September 1560, most contemporary observers believed that she was seriously contemplating marriage to her favorite. Then in 1579, she demonstrated a resolution to wed the duke of Alençon; marriage to him was an essential plank in her foreign policy and she was also attracted to his person during his visit to England in the summer of that year. Furthermore, in response to intense pressure from her councillors and parliaments, she showed a readiness to marry two other suitors, though admittedly without the enthusiasm displayed during the Dudley and later Alençon courtships. In the mid-1560s she agreed to open negotiations with the Archduke Charles of Austria as a way to secure a Habsburg alliance and resolve the succession problem. From late 1570 through to the autumn of 1571 she encouraged matrimonial negotiations with Henry duke of Anjou (then heir to the French throne and later in 1574 to become Henry III) in the hope that a betrothal might provide the foundation for an Anglo-French alliance which would protect the realm against Spain. * * *

Finding an explanation for Elizabeth's single status in her own personal preference for the single life is therefore unsatisfactory. To understand why all her courtships came to nothing, eyes have to be turned away from the character and gender of the queen, and be directed instead on the matrimonial suits themselves, especially on the sticking-points in the attempts to conclude a marriage contract and on the political tactics employed by the opponents of the various matches to bring about their ultimate failure. With this new focus, the role of the Privy Council rather than the attitude of the queen emerges as crucial to the outcome of the courtships. It is therefore inappropriate to level criticism or blame at Elizabeth for remaining unwed, as far too many historians and biographers have done.

Had Elizabeth's council ever united behind any one of her suitors, she would have found great difficulty in rejecting his proposal; likewise, without strong conciliar backing Elizabeth would not or could not marry a particular candidate. In the case of those men whom she had no particular wish to wed, opposition from within the council allowed her to elude their suits. Thus, it had required concerted conciliar pressure to force her into negotiations for a marriage with the Archduke Charles, and it was only when a significant number of councillors spoke out against accepting Habsburg demands for a private Mass in November 1567 that she felt able to bring the courtship to an end. Similarly, in April 1572 she was able to slip out of the negotiations for a marriage alliance with Francis duke of Alençon on the

---

1. For the legal claims of the Greys and Mary Stuart, see Mortimer Levine, *Tudor Dynastic Problems, 1460–1571* (New York: Barnes and Noble, 1973), 99–101.

grounds that her council was divided over whether or not to accept the French terms on religion. * * *

At other times, however, when Elizabeth appeared to be close to accepting the hand of her favored suitors, first Robert Dudley in the early 1560s and then Francis of Alençon in 1579, the active opposition of some leading councillors convinced her that it would be definitely unwise and perhaps disastrous to proceed with the match. During the course of these courtships she attracted sufficient expressions of disrespect to cause her great concern. Rumors abounded about the propriety of her behavior with both suitors, while questions were raised about the wisdom of her choice of consort. She was all too aware that both Wyatt's Rebellion in Mary I's reign and Mary Stuart's deposition in 1567 had occurred when a queen regnant insisted upon taking a husband against the wishes of her important subjects. Elizabeth was far too cautious and politically adept to make the same mistake. There is every reason to suppose that had her councillors overwhelmingly supported either Dudley in late 1560 or Alençon she would have gone ahead with the wedding.

But why could no suitor ever command the overwhelming support of her councillors? As far as most of the early matrimonial candidates were concerned, the answer is that there was little to recommend any of them. Philip II, who presented his suit in early 1559, was worthy of the queen in terms of dignity and descent, but unacceptable in England as the man held responsible (admittedly most unfairly) for the loss of Calais and the persecution of Protestants during the previous reign. Marriage to him, moreover, was clearly incompatible with the radical changes in religion favored by the queen and her new council. The three younger sons of Henry II were clearly out of the question at the beginning of the reign because of their extreme youth. Even in 1564, when Charles IX was of marriageable age and a suitor for the queen's hand, he was only fourteen to the queen's thirty-one years. While Elizabeth herself was worried that she would look ridiculous at the wedding, like a mother taking her child to the altar, her councillors were more concerned that the young king would be unable to consummate the marriage for several years and that the match would thus fail to resolve immediately the succession problem.[2]

Almost all the remaining early candidates were thought simply not good enough for a reigning monarch. Most were of relatively inferior status—European dukes who were not of royal blood; the duke of Savoy, moreover, had lost his territories to the French, while the duke of Holstein was a mercenary. Even King Eric XIV of Sweden was not a respected monarch in England, for he was the son of a usurper and his throne was elective. The disparagement involved in marrying any one of these men was not insignificant for a queen who had been pronounced a bastard and whose title to the throne was challenged by Mary Stuart and her allies. * * *

The Austrian Archduke Charles was probably the most suitable candidate to appear during the first couple of years of the reign, but even he could command little vocal support among Elizabeth's advisors in 1559 when Emperor Ferdinand first offered his son to the queen. Perhaps they were distracted by other political problems or bemused by the variety and number of Elizabeth's

---

2. PRO, SP 31/3/26, fol. 32; Hector de la Ferrière-Percy and Comte Baguenault de Puchesse, eds., *Lettres de Catherine de Médicis* (Paris, 1880–1909), 2:306.

suitors. Perhaps too they were in no great rush for the queen to marry, but were content to consolidate their own positions before a foreign consort appeared in England. Hence there was no great pressure on the queen to choose the archduke, or indeed any other of her foreign suitors before 1561.

In the minds of most contemporaries, Robert Dudley was also considered a suitor who was not good enough for the queen. As William Cecil rightly noted: "Nothing is increased by Marriadg of hym either in Riches, Estimation, Power."[3] It was often said that the nobility despised him as a "new man," whose father and grandfather had been attainted for treason, and that they considered the queen's marriage to a commoner as disparagement.[4] Again, such thoughts went beyond the social elitism that was undoubtedly present; Elizabeth's child might well have to compete for the throne against Mary Stuart or any son she might have, and would be at a disadvantage with only one grandparent of royal blood, especially as some Catholics persisted in questioning whether Henry VIII had indeed fathered Elizabeth. The queen's deep affection for Dudley, however, outweighed these obstacles, while his own abilities as a self-publicist and politician helped him gradually to win over many initial opponents of his suit, including the duke of Norfolk and the earl of Pembroke, both of whom petitioned the queen to marry her favorite at a meeting of the Knights of the Garter in April 1562.[5] As a result, Dudley was considered a serious candidate by contemporaries until the mid-1560s and beyond.

Dudley's main handicap in courting the queen was the mysterious death of his wife. Although the coroner's court judged Amy Robsart's fall down the staircase at Cumnor Place to be "death by misadventure," many clearly believed otherwise. Consequently, Elizabeth had good reason to fear that her marriage to Dudley would damage both their reputations: giving credibility to the rumors that she and Dudley had long been lovers, confirming the suspicions that her favorite had conspired to bring about his first wife's death, and implicating her in the murder.[6] Councillors like Cecil and royal servants like Sir Nicholas Throckmorton who opposed the marriage played on her anxiety that a Dudley marriage would impugn her honor, by bringing to her attention the scurrilous comments circulating both at home and abroad about her relationship with her favorite. Calumnies spread in England—that the queen was either pregnant or had borne a child—were brought before the Privy Council, while "dishonorable and naughty reaportes" at the French court were reported home by Throckmorton: "One laugheth at us, an other threatneth, an other revileth her Majestie, and some let not to say what religion is this, that a subject shall kill his wief, and the prince not onely beare withall but marry with him."[7]

Although these concerns about the queen's reputation stimulated opposition to Dudley's suit, hostility to the match also owed much to political self-interest. Most of Elizabeth's councillors and nobles distrusted Dudley as a

3. "De matrimonia Reginae Angliae cum extero principe," April 1566, in Samuel Haynes, *William Cecil's State Papers* (London, 1740), 444.
4. Victor Von Klarwill, *Queen Elizabeth and Some Foreigners* (London: John Lane, 1928), 189–90.
5. 1 May 1562, Archivo General de Simancas, (hereafter abbreviated to AGS), E 8340/234, fol. 158v BL, Additional MS 48023, fol. 363.
6. 29 October 1560, PRO, SP 70/19, fol. 411; 17 November 1560, Philip Yorke, ed., *Hardwicke State Papers* (1778), 1:145.
7. PRO, SP/12/13, no. 21;29 October 1560, Throckmorton to Chamberlain, PRO, SP 70/19, fol. 132; 10 October 1560, Throckmorton to Northampton, PRO, SP 70/19, fol. 39.

potential faction leader who would promote his own men and take revenge on the enemies of his father, the late duke of Northumberland.[8] * * *

* * *

Obviously, Elizabeth's marriage was a divisive issue in the council and at court; but to what extent, if any, did it create, reflect, or exacerbate "factional" struggles involving Cecil, Leicester, and the Howards? Simon Adams has consistently argued that faction played no part in the politics of the Elizabethan court before the 1590s. He questions the very existence of faction. * * *

* * *

Nonetheless, it would be a mistake to conclude that the absence of "faction" in a narrowly defined sense meant that harmony always prevailed in political life. Between 1558 and 1581 personal antagonisms, political rivalries, and policy differences were at least as much a feature of the court scene as cooperation and consensus. Disagreements over the question of the queen's marriage and foreign policy exacerbated personal conflicts among courtiers and councillors, which could easily get out of hand and disrupt political stability. In late 1560 the threat of an armed conflict between Dudley and the earls of Arundel and Pembroke shook the court, while an affray broke out between the retinues of Dudley and Pembroke.[9] In 1562 a meeting of the Knights of the Garter around the time of St. George's Day was disrupted when Arundel and Northampton stormed out in protest after a petition in favor of Dudley's marrying the queen was approved.[1] In January 1566 rival followers of the Howards and Leicester wore distinctive colors to show their group loyalty; four months later "hard words and challenges to fight were exchanged" between Sussex and Leicester, and the queen was forced to intercede between them.[2] In 1579 the divisions generated by the Alençon matrimonial project nearly resulted in a "palace revolution" when Leicester and Walsingham were banished from court and the queen considered bringing some Catholics onto the council. Nor were these disputes always confined to the court. Both the 1563 and 1566 parliaments were affected by divisions within the council on the marriage and succession, while in 1579 preachers and polemicists brought a wider public into the debate on the Alençon marriage.

There is little evidence that Elizabeth encouraged these disputes and divisions by pursuing a "divide and rule" policy which gave her "freedom of action" and turned her into "an umpire to whose judgement the contenders would always have to bow."[3] Too much weight has been placed on the report of the Jacobean Sir Robert Naunton that Elizabeth made and unmade factions "as her own great judgement advised."[4] On the contrary, she usually encouraged rival politicians to work together to formulate and execute policy, and attempted to calm down passions which arose from their

8. J. H. Pollen, ed., "Papal Negotiations with Mary, Queen of Scots during Her Reign in Scotland, 1561–1567," *Scottish Historical Society* 37 (1901): 61.
9. Haynes, *Cecil's State Papers*, 365; J. Gough Nichols, ed., "The Diary of Henry Machyn," *Camden Society*, 43 (London: Camden Society, 1848), 252.
1. BL, Additional MS 48023, fol. 363; 1 May 1562, AGS, E 8340/234, fol. 158v.
2. *Cal. S. P. Span.* 1558–67, 511, 560–61, 565.
3. Wallace T. MacCaffrey, *Elizabeth I* (London: Edward Arnold, 1993), 360.
4. Quoted in P. Collinson, "The Monarchical Republic of Queen Elizabeth I," in *Elizabethan Essays* (London: Hambledon Press, 1994), 41.

disputes. Thus Cecil was brought into the negotiations with de Quadra and Dudley in 1562 concerning England's representation at the Council of Trent, a move which in the event allowed her secretary to outmaneuver both queen and favorite. In 1571 she left the day-to-day negotiations with the French to be handled by Leicester and Burghley in tandem. In October 1579 she tried to obtain the consent of the whole council collectively to the Alençon match; only later did she seek out councillors' individual written views as a way of breaking down the opposition to her plans.[5] On the whole, then, Elizabeth preferred "consensus" politics to "divide and rule"; and the divisions at her court over her courtships were a mark of political failure, not a means for securing freedom of action. Indeed, the marriage issue demonstrates that Elizabeth had less control over politics and policy-making than is usually appreciated; she was unable to impose her will on her council or suppress criticisms of her policies in the court and country.

The courtships were undoubtedly damaging to Elizabeth's reputation both at home and abroad. In the first place, slanders were widely spread about her sexual immorality. During the Dudley courtship "she showed herself so affectionate to him" that gossip questioned or denied her chastity. At the French court in 1571, Henry of Anjou labeled her a whore and eight years later the papal nuncio in Paris accused her of having borne Dudley's illegitimate children. As late as 1590 two Essex villagers declared that Elizabeth and Dudley had stuffed their illegitimate offspring up a chimney.[6] Such allegations suggest that Elizabethan propaganda in the form of her representation as the Virgin Queen had only a limited success. During the Dudley, Archduke Charles, and Alençon courtships, holes were also driven into her carefully constructed image as a wise ruler and Protestant heroine. On each occasion, opponents queried her political judgment in choosing such an unsuitable husband and warned of the danger to religion if the match went ahead. In 1561 tales were spread, and at least one sermon preached, that Elizabeth had promised "to turn Catholic at the instance of Lord Robert" in order to win Spanish support for the match.[7] In the mid-1560s and 1579 fears were expressed that Elizabeth's toleration of the Mass would threaten England's covenant with God and provoke divine vengeance.

On the other hand, the matrimonial negotiations reveal to historians Elizabeth's great strength as a ruler. Like all successful heads of state she had a highly developed instinct for survival: a sensitivity to public opinion and an awareness of what was politically possible. She listened and acted upon calls to marry but ultimately turned down suits which proved unpopular or divisive. Only briefly during 1579 did her political intuition falter, but even then she soon recovered and stepped back from the brink of the disaster which would surely have accompanied the Alençon marriage. Aware of her own limitations, therefore, she listened to counsel, rejected controversial matches, and in the event remained single.

5. *Cal. S. P. Span.* 1558–67, 186–91; Dudley Digges, ed., *The Compleat Ambassador* (London, 1665), 111; Fénélon, *Correspondance Diplomatique* (Paris, 1838–40), 4:59, 93; William Murdin, *Lord Burghley's State Papers* (London, 1759), 322–42.
6. Von Klarwill, *Queen Elizabeth*, 113–14. I. Cloulas, *Correspondance du Nonce en France, Anselmo Dandino (1578–1581)*, Acta Nuntiaturae Gallicae 8 (Paris, 1979), 516; Joel Samaha, "Gleanings from Local Criminal Court Records: Sedition amongst the 'Inarticulate' in Elizabethan Essex," *Journal of Social History* 8 (1975): 69.
7. 5 May 1561, de Quadra to Philip II, AGS, E 815, fol. 5, translated in *Cal. S. P. Span.* 1558–67, 199–203.

Queen Elizabeth as Defender of the Faith.

THE QUEEN'S RELIGIOUS POSITION

PATRICK COLLINSON

Windows in a Woman's Soul[†]

Dr Samuel Johnson claimed to have read a book about Iceland which included a chapter on snakes consisting of a single sentence: 'There are no snakes to be found anywhere in the island.' Some historians have treated this subject with almost equal brevity. Surely there *are* no questions; there

† From "Windows in a Woman's Soul: Questions about the Religion of Queen Elizabeth," *Elizabethan Essays*. Ed. Patrick Collinson (London: The Hambledon Press, 2003), pp. 87–118. Reprinted by permission of Hambledon Continuum, a Continuum imprint.

is no religion to be found in the lady. A. F. Pollard's verdict on Queen Elizabeth's religion was that 'it can hardly be doubted that she was sceptical or indifferent'. Moreover, she was 'almost as devoid of a moral sense as she was of religious temperament'.[1] Among historians in the Protestant-Secularist-Whiggish tradition, to acknowledge the *politique* in Elizabeth was intended as a compliment. Pollard's pupil, Sir John Neale, suspicious as he was of most of the more or less apocryphal 'sayings' attributed to her, nevertheless liked to quote with admiration the rhetorical question she was supposed on one occasion to have put: why couldn't the king of Spain allow his subjects to go to the Devil in their own way?[2] One could do business with such a woman. Catholic writers, well into our own century, have indicted Elizabeth of actual atheism. Christopher Hollis boldly asserted in the year that I was born that while 'possessed of a certain talent in the production of conventional religious phraseology', she was 'certainly an atheist in practice. Religion did not at all influence her conduct.'[3]

Yet in 1550 the Protestant Bishop John Hooper had assured the Swiss reformer Bullinger that the young Edward VI's sister, 'the daughter of the late King by queen Ann', was 'inflamed with the same zeal for the religion of Christ', that is, a zeal equal to that of her royal brother. 'She not only knows what the true religion is, but has acquired such proficiency in Greek and Latin that she is able to defend it . . .'[4]

Later, when in the tenth year of her reign the great English pulpit Bible known as the Bishops' Bible was published, its title page bore a fetching but regal engraved portrait, the work of Franciscus Hogenberg, embellished with the motto: 'Non me pudet Evangelii Christi. Virtus enim Dei est ad salutem Omni credenti Rom. 1°', rendered on the title-page of the New Testament for non-Latinists as 'I am not ashamed of the Gospel of Christ, because it is the power of God unto salvation to all that beleve': a text with deeply emotional resonances for anyone brought up in the modern evangelical tradition and hard to relate to a Tudor monarch, certainly a sentiment antithetical to the *politique* position. (But the same text had been made an emblem by or on behalf of Henry VIII.)[5] In 1585, Elizabeth told parliament:

> I am supposed to have many studies . . . And yet, amidst my many volumes, I hope God's book hath not been my seldomest lectures; in which we find that which by reason (for my part) we ought to believe—that, seeing so great wickedness and griefs in the world, in which we

1. A. F. Pollard, *The History of England from the Accession of Edward VI to the Death of Elizabeth (1547–1603)*, The Political History of England, vi (1910), pp. 179–80.
2. J. E. Neale, 'The Sayings of Queen Elizabeth', reviewing Frederick Chamberlin's book of that title (1923), in his *Essays in Elizabethan History* (1958), pp. 85–112. I have forgotten where, and indeed whether, Sir John Neale published his endorsement of the alleged remark about the king of Spain and the Devil. But I often heard him quote it in conversation.
3. Christopher Hollis, *The Monstrous Regiment* (1929), pp. 28–30.
4. Bishop John Hooper to Bullinger, 5 February 1550, *Original Letters Relative to the English Reformation*, ed. H. Robinson, i, Parker Society (Cambridge, 1846), p. 76.
5. It occurs in Holbein's engraved title-page for Coverdale's Bible. The engraved portraits of Elizabeth in the 1568 Bishops' Bible are attributed to Franciscus Hogenberg by A.M. Hind in *Engraving in England in the Sixteenth and Seventeenth Centuries*, i (Cambridge, 1952), p. 65. However, Margaret Aston notes that Remigius Hogenberg, brother of Franciscus, was in Archbishop Parker's employ. Dr Aston also notes that the portraits are absent from the 1574 and all subsequent editions of the Bishops' Bible. She attributes their suppression to 'the conviction of some contemporary purists that portraiture was an inherently idolatrous act': Margaret Aston, 'The *Bishops' Bible* Illustrations', in *The Church and the Arts*, Studies in Church History, 28, ed. Diana Wood (Oxford, 1992), pp. 267–85.

live but as wayfaring pilgrims, we must suppose that God would never have made us but for a better place and of more comfort than we find here.[6]

In a tiny sextodecimo New Testament preserved in the Bodleian Library, Elizabeth has inscribed with her own hand in the flyleaf: 'I walke many times in the pleasaunt fieldes of the holye scriptures, Where I plucke up the goodlie greene herbes of sentences by pruning: Eate the[m] by reading: Chawe the[m] by musing': a conceit attributed to St Augustine.[7]

So suddenly the whole island appears to be alive with snakes. But were they real snakes? Was Elizabeth really religious? Dealing as we are with a woman of such accomplished and rarely relaxed artifice, not to say prevarication, the question cannot be answered. And what did it mean, in the circumstances of Elizabethan England, indeed in any circumstances, to be 'really religious'? We may assume (and the assumption will not be further discussed) that Elizabeth was conventionally religious in the sense that she attended with regularity to her religious duties and heard in her time many hundreds of sermons.[8] We can say no less, and no more, of the vast majority of her subjects, which is a grave embarrassment to the Elizabethan religious historian. Religious conformity has, if not no history, a most elusive history.

However, the question put by the late Neville Williams was legitimately as well as neatly posed: was there no window into her own soul?[9] Williams has supplied our title, with a little help from the nineteenth-century historian J. A. Froude, talking about Erasmus. You will best see the sixteenth century as it really was, said Froude, if you look at it through the eyes of Erasmus (meaning his letters).[1] But what do you see if you look back through the eyes of Erasmus into his mind and inner being, in any of the famous portraits? Elizabeth, said Francis Bacon, was reluctant to look into her subjects' souls. If we dared to make spiritual eye contact, scrutinising her own soul, what might we see?

II

One tiny window exists in the form of an exquisite little book of private devotions in five languages (English, French, Italian, Latin, Greek) measuring exactly three inches by two, enriched by Hilliard miniatures of the queen and her suitor François duc d'Anjou and so fabricated (one assumes) in about 1578 or 1579: a precious little thing now sadly lost (or at least misplaced), but fortunately not before a limited number of facsimiles had been published.[2] * * * Dr Christopher Haigh has endorsed the firm evidence it

6. J. E. Neale, *Elizabeth I and her Parliaments, 1584–1601* (1957), p. 100.
7. Quoted by John N, King, *Tudor Royal Iconography: Literature and Art in an Age of Religious Crisis* (Princeton, 1989), p. 109.
8. Her reactions to some of these were reported by Sir John Harington in the little book known (from its mid seventeenth-century title) as *A briefe view of the state of the Church of England*. See Patrick Collinson, 'If Constantine, Then Also Theodosius: St Ambrose and the Integrity of the Elizabethan *Ecclesia Anglicana*', in my *Godly People: Essays on English Protestantism and Puritanism* (1983), pp. 119–20.
9. Neville Williams, *Elizabeth Queen of England* (1967), p. 79.
1. J. A. Froude, *Life and Letters of Erasmus* (1900), p. 431.
2. BL, MS FACS 218. J. W. Whitehead exhibited the MS at the Fine Art Society in 1902, after which it was 'lost to sight'. Forty copies of the facsimile were printed in 1893, with notes by Whitehead on its saleroom history.

appears to provide of Elizabeth's religious sincerity, and equally of her essential and unwavering Protestantism.[3] Dr Haigh concedes that the prayers were a piece of image-making, perhaps even for the queen's own private purposes, Elizabeth as she would have liked God to have seen her, rather than as she actually was. 'But her self-image was as patroness of the Gospel and she took her religious duties seriously.' 'There can be little doubt of Elizabeth's Protestantism.'

One does not have to be a radical deconstructionist to have one's doubts about these readings of this text, or to consider other possibilities. The little collection of prayers with their Hilliard miniatures evidently had some connection with the Anjou marriage negotiations which, if they had come to fruition, would have struck a damaging if not fatal blow at the Protestant cause in the perception of very many of the queen's Protestant subjects.[4] Moreover we cannot be sure that this book of devotions contains a *self*-image of Elizabeth. It has been widely assumed that the queen wrote the prayers herself and there has even been speculation about the hands in which they are written, whether any or all of them were her own. They are certainly very royal and in the first person— 'drawing my blood from kings . . . placing me a Sovereign Princess over thy people of England'—but so are other prayers which we can be confident she did *not* compose herself but which were placed in her hand and mouth, whole collections of 'right godlie Psalmes, fruitfull Praiers, and comfortable Meditations to be said of our most vertuous and deere Soveraigne Ladie Elizabeth'.[5] But let us by all means allow that the dignity and restraint of that tiny book of private devotions places it in a different class and makes it very probable that these were Queen Elizabeth's own prayers.

✻   ✻   ✻

III

At first glance, another precious relic of Elizabeth's religiosity may appear to open wider that elusive window on her emergent soul. A second glance may suggest conventions so stilted as to tell us very little. Whereas a third proves surprisingly and intriguingly informative. I refer to Elizabeth's translation into English prose of the *Miroir de l'âme pechereuse*, a mystical religious poem composed by Marguerite d'Angoulême, queen of Navarre, the 'Pearl of the Valois', sister of one king of France and grandmother of another. The *Miroir* was printed several times between its composition in 1530–1 and Princess Elizabeth's prose rendering, which was executed in 1545 at the age of eleven and presented to her step-mother, Queen Catherine Parr, as a New Year's gift. The original copy survives in the Bodleian Library, bound and embroidered by the princess herself, in a

---

3. William P. Haugaard, 'Elizabeth Tudor's *Book of Devotions*: A Neglected Clue to the Queen's Life and Character', *Sixteenth-Century Journal*, 12 (1981), pp. 79–105; Christopher Haigh, *Elizabeth I* (1988), pp. 27–8.
4. *John Stubbs's 'Gaping Gulf'*, ed. L. E. Berry (Charlottesville, VA, 1968); W. T. MacCaffrey, 'The Anjou Match and the Making of Elizabethan Foreign Policy', in *The English Commonwealth, 1547–1640: Essays on Politics and Society Presented to Joel Hurstfield*, ed. Peter Clark et al. (Leicester, 1979), pp. 59–75.
5. Thomas Bentley, *The Monument of Matrones* (1582), p. 253.

rather over-worked version of what was already her favourite style in the crafting of books.[6]

The backcloth to Elizabeth's translation of Marguerite d'Angoulême concerns the Renaissance chapter in the perennial *querelle des femmes* which Ruth Kelso has investigated in the 891 titles on noblewomen written between 1400 and 1600 which fed into her *Doctrine for the Lady of the Renaissance*.[7] This 'lady' exemplified such gender-specific virtues as modesty, humility, constancy, temperance, pity. This was as much as to say that such women were more naturally religious than men, or at least had a higher quality of religiosity attributed to them. These qualities were non-assertive, but were compatible with the acquisition of an advanced philological and rhetorical education, expressing itself, typically, in literary works of translation rather than in original composition. The Tudor educators, Grindall, Aylmer, Ascham, seem to have found aristocratic girls perfect recipients for their pedagogical programmes of double translation, in and out of the ancient languages. Such were the female Greys, especially Lady Jane, Cookes, especially Lady Ann (Bacon), and Tudors, especially Elizabeth.[8]

The cultivated, pious Renaissance lady also related, with increasing frequency and consistency, to an entourage or coterie of similar ladies, some of them grouping themselves around a great and suitably talented patroness. * * *

Marguerite d'Angoulême's *Miroir* might seem a suitable text for a young woman reared in this tradition to concern herself with, but this would be on a very superficial reading. The opening words (in Elizabeth's translation) 'Is there any hell so profounde that is sufficient to punish the tenth parte of my synnes?' sets the scene for a sombre mood of self-accusation from which the soul emerges only through a series of passionate encounters with the Trinitarian Godhead, conceived according to the metaphors of familial relationship. God is addressed as father by the soul as daughter; but also by the soul employing the holy title of Mother of God—with due apologies to the Virgin for usurping her title. God then calls the soul 'sister' and speaks of 'the fraternitie that thou hast towards me'. 'And likewise thou dost

---

6. *Le miroir de l'âme pechereuse* was printed at Alençon in 1531, Paris in 1533, Geneva in 1539 and Toulouse in 1552. There is a critical edition of the 1531 text, ed. Joseph L. Allaire (Munich, 1972). Princess Elizabeth's translation, to which she gave the title *The glasse of the synnefull soule*, was printed in facsimile from the original MS by Percy W. Ames in 1897. A more recent edition from Oxford, Bodleian Library, MS Cherry 36, is in *Annales Academica Scientiarum Fennicae Dissertationes Litterarum*, 22 (Helsinki, 1979). On this entire subject I have been helped immeasurably by the work of the late Dr Heather Vose of Perth, Western Australia, in her unpublished University of Western Australia Ph.D. thesis 'Marguerite d'Angoulême: A Study in Sixteenth-Century Spirituality Based on her 1521–1524 Correspondence with Guillaume Briçonnet' (1985); and her article, 'Marguerite of Navarre: that "Righte English Woman"', *Sixteenth-Century Journal*, 16 (1985), pp. 315–33. Ames (*The Mirror*, pp. 30–1) suggests that Elizabeth received the text from her mother, who he thought might have been in Marguerite's service as duchesse d'Alençon. Hugh Richmond, *Shakespeare Studies*, 12 (1979), 49–63, thought it possible that Ann Boleyn carried the *Miroir* to the scaffold. Retha Warnicke, *Women of the English Renaissance and Reformation* (1983), p. 95, preferred the theory that it was Queen Catherine Parr who made the original available to Elizabeth. However Dr Vose ('Marguerite d'Angoulême', p. 114) believes that Elizabeth had access to it through her father, who is known to have received a copy. Anne Lake Prescott (see n. 9 below) is 'fairly confident' that Elizabeth worked from the Geneva edition of 1539.
7. Ruth Kelso, *Doctrine for the Lady of the Renaissance* (Urbana, IL, 1956).
8. See several of the studies collected in Margaret P. Hannay, ed., *Silent but for the Word: Tudor Women as Patrons, Translators and Writers of Religious Works* (Kent, OH, 1985), with extensive references supplied to other literature. See also John N. King, 'The Godly Woman in Elizabethan Iconography', *Renaissance Quarterly*, 38 (1985), pp. 41–84, and 'The "Godly" Queens', in his *Tudor Royal Iconography*, pp. 182–266.

call me wife'. 'Rise up my spouse' (Canticles, chapter 2). 'Therefore shall i say with loving faith, thou art mijn and i am thine. Thou doest call me love and faire spouse, if so it be, suche hast thou made me.' 'O my father, brother, childe and spouse.' Here, in the context of a religion anchored to the words 'Our Father', are reasons more compelling than many often given for the so often observed religious propensity of women, whose lives within our culture are structured by family relationships to a greater extent than those of men, or are commonly supposed to be so structured. Such gender-related and generational confusions and elisions were standard to the repertoire, especially of Marian piety.

Nevertheless, these were deep waters into which to plunge a prepubescent eleven-year old: a psychological shark pool. According to Anne Lake Prescott's reading of the text, the young Elizabeth knew what she was doing, to the extent of indulging in wilful mistranslations which perhaps uniquely reveal the psyche of a child whose mother had been executed for adultery in her infancy, and whose father was remote and uncaring.[9] It was odd to put such a text into her hands. But there were good bread and butter reasons. Marguerite d'Angoulême had always been on good terms with Henry VIII and at this very time was playing a constructive part in the diplomacy designed to end the last of his wars. The late Dr Heather Vose writes of 'the wide and worldly setting for her lively Christian faith'. (One is reminded of Elizabeth's great grandmother, the Lady Margaret Beaufort.) If Wolsey had had his way, or so according to Shakespeare, Marguerite might have been Elizabeth's mother, or, indeed, her step grandmother, since there had been plans to marry her to Henry VII.[1] Of course the princess's teacher, Roger Ascham, would have regarded her work on the *Miroir* as a simple exercise in translation, as with the scriptural passages in four languages (Latin, Greek, French, Italian) which she later added to it, or, her other labour of love (or duty), the prayers and meditations translated from the English of Catherine Parr into Latin, French and Italian and dedicated to her father, another New Year's gift.[2]

But the *Miroir* in the hands of its translator was explosive material to which she reacted in curious ways. Where Marguerite had written 'père, fille, o bieneureux lignaige', speaking of the father's love for the daughter, Elizabeth translated *père* as 'mother': further gender confusion and surely a Freudian if not a deliberate mistake. Where Marguerite compares divine mercy to a father's forgiveness of his child—'si père a eu de son enfant mercy'—Elizabeth omits the line altogether. And then, most curiously of all, where Marguerite writes of husbands who put adulterous wives to death (that was near the bone), Elizabeth reverses the genders and makes the husband die the death: 'Assez en est, qui pour venger leur tort, / Par les juges les on faict mettre à mort.' Elizabeth rendered this: 'There be inoughe of them, wiche for to avenge their wronge, did cause the judges to condemne hym to dye.' She then crossed out 'hym' and wrote 'them' above it. So 'hym' may have been intended as 'hem', which is to say, them. This is all splendidly speculative, but Prof. Prescott believes that Elizabeth is (perhaps

9. Anne Lake Prescott, 'The Pearl of the Valois and Elizabeth I: Marguerite de Navarre's *Miroir* and Tudor England', in Hannay, ed., *Silent but for the Word*, pp. 61–91.
1. Vose, 'Marguerite d'Angoulême', pp. i, 96, 103.
2. BL, MS Royal 7.D.X. The MS is bound in an embroidered cover, doubtless Elizabeth's own handiwork, with the title beginning 'precationes seu meditationes'. It is dated from Hertford 30 December 1545 and dedicated to Henry VIII by 'Elizabeta Maiest. s. humillissime filia'.

subliminally?) turning Marguerite's poem into an 'impassioned evocation of God as a great king and judge who is kind to daughters and does not execute adulterous wives'.[3] In her 1579 prayers (if they were hers), Elizabeth asks Christ the Son to let her love him 'for thy promises as my father'.[4]

* * *

* * * [I]n 1548, shortly before his return from his first period of exile, Bale published at Wesel the first printed edition of Elizabeth's *Miroir*, now called *A godly medytacyon of the christen sowle*.[5] This publication in effect hi-jacked Elizabeth's juvenile exercise for the Protestant cause; and with it Elizabeth herself, who was made to collude in a typically vituperative attack on the 'Romyshe clergye ymagenynge to exalte themselves above the lewde layte [i.e., laity]', and on the images themselves. How curious that the British Library copy of this tract should once have belonged to the mid seventeenth-century East Anglian iconoclast, William Dowsing![6] But this is also ironical given the views of the mature Elizabeth on the subject of religious images.[7] It is instructive to note how Bale has subtly converted into the key of godly, Protestant edification the tone of Elizabeth's discourse. Where Elizabeth, addressing the reader, wrote 'if thou doest rede thys whole worke', Bale has: 'If thu [sic] do throughly reade thys worke (dere frynde in the lorde).'

So little relating to this subject is certain. It is possible, as Bale implies, that Elizabeth herself had a copy of her translation sent to him overseas, together with some additional matter, scriptural texts rendered in Latin, Greek, French and Italian, 'whyche she wrote first with her owne hande'.[8] But it is more likely that Bale's copy reached him from other ladies in the super-aristocratic, crypto-Protestant entourage of the late 1540s: perhaps from the duchess of Richmond whose patronage Bale enjoyed as soon as he set foot back in England, who was also the patron of the martyrologist John Foxe.[9]

Bale included in his preface to *A godly medytacyon* a catalogue of queens and princesses, some mythical or semi-mythical, who had served as rulers in their own right or as queens regent, which suggests that his motive in this publication may have been to favour and advance the claims of Queen Catherine Parr to a kind of regency in the early months of Edward VI's reign, in which case events overtook him, for Catherine would soon be dead. But his flattery of Princess Elizabeth for her extraordinary philological prowess and model piety was significant, and especially in that he almost approximated her to the recent Protestant martyr, Anne Askew, herself a kind of hanger-on to the evangelical-aristocratic-female connection, a sprat intended to catch the mackerel of the queen, no less. After extolling Askew as 'Christes myghty member' who had 'strongly troden downe the head of the serpent', Bale spoke of what 'other noble women' had achieved

---

3. Prescott, 'Pearl of the Valois and Elizabeth I', pp. 69–71.
4. Haugaard, 'Elizabeth Tudor's *Book of Devotions*', p. 86.
5. The full title of this text (STC no. 17320) is *A godly medytacyon of the Christen sowle concerninge a love towardes God and hys Christe, compiled in Frenche by Lady Margaret queene of Navere and aptely translated into Englysh by the ryght vertuous lady Elyzabeth doughter to Kynge Henri the viii.* A substantially different edition also appeared in 1548 (not included in the *Short-Title Catalogue*, but see British Library, C.38.c.57), *A godly meditacion of the inwarde love of the soule.* Yet another version would later appear in Bentley's *Monument of matrones.*
6. BL, C.12.d.l. The title-page bears Dowsing's signature.
7. See pp. 704–7 below.
8. *A godly medytacyon*, epistle, fol. 41.
9. King, 'Patronage and Piety', in *Silent but for the Word*, pp. 51–2.

and would achieve. 'Marke thys present boke for one, whose translacyon was the worke of her whyche was but a babe at the doynge therof.'[1]

* * * And we are carried forwards to the woodcut adorning Bale's edition of Elizabeth's *Miroir*, where the princess is seen, Bible in hand, kneeling at Christ's feet in the posture of a Magdalene.[2]

This was to tap a rich vein of scriptural and especially of apocalyptic imagery and metaphor, all destined in the dimensions of gender and generational inversion very like those explored by Marguerite d'Angoulême to be united with Christ as spouse, but also as the fruit of their wombs. These were the emblems of the Bride of Canticles, the Woman Who Feareth the Lord of Proverbs 31, and, most significantly and prophetically, the Woman Who Flees into the Wilderness who becomes the Woman Clothed With the Sun, the Woman of Revelation 12. Such emblems had both a general and a more particular application. Generally, and in the spirit both of the Protestant emphasis on the priesthood (or ministry) of all believers and of Erasmian educational aspirations, they appropriated to godly womankind in general, and as an emblem of the status and experience of all Christians, the exemplary qualities hitherto attributed only to special women, saints, above all to the Virgin Mary. The point is made by the women who are prominent among the throng of faithful and obedient subjects at the foot of the prodigious woodcut which forms the title-page of Henry VIII's Great Bible of 1539; and equally by the centrally positioned, essentially emblematic woman[3] who sits, Bible open on her lap, at the preacher's feet in John Foxe's picture of Bishop Hugh Latimer preaching before Edward VI. More particularly, first Mary Tudor, and then, more famously and enduringly, Elizabeth Tudor would be credited with the traditional *persona* and roles of the Virgin.[2]

Given the emphasis often and justifiably placed on the mysoginistic chauvinism of the Protestant reformers, it is necessary to insist on the gynophilia which, at one level, characterises these texts. * * * Foxe's handling of the threat to Queen Catherine Parr from the conservative faction at court makes an especially piquant parody. Catherine wittily outwitted her adversaries by obediently submitting to her lord and master; perhaps with fingers crossed, tongue in cheek and winking eye.[4] It is possible, of course, and a suspicious feminist historian might well make this point, that the apparent gynophilia was patriarchally motivated, a device for subordinating women by emphasising the submissive qualities characteristic of their piety.

Princess Elizabeth was never depicted as a scold. And yet she was the principal inheritor (both beneficiary and victim) of this well-established tradition of apotheotic gynophilia. This is especially apparent in the narrative inserted by Foxe as a kind of appendix to the 1563 of his Book of Martyrs, or *Acts and Monuments*, a narrative which I believe to be in form a sort of fiction, even an early form of the novel: 'The Miraculous Preservation of the Lady Elizabeth, now Queen of England, From Extreme Calamity and Danger of Life; in the Time of Queen Mary, Her Sister'. As a kind of preface to this romantic tale, 'we all Englishmen' are exhorted to give thanks for 'so good, godly and virtuous a queen; such a chosen instrument of [God's]

---

1. *A godly medytacyon*, fos. 46–7 r.
2. The woodcut appears in Part One, p. 18 [*Editors' note*].
3. John Bale, *The image of both churches* (Antwerp, ?1545) (STC no. 1296.5); *A godly medytacyon*; King, 'The Godly Woman'.
4. *The Acts and Monuments of John Foxe*, ed. S. R. Cattley, v (1838), pp. 553–61.

clemency, so virtuosly natured, so godly disposed, . . . as amends and recompense, now to be made to England, for the cruel days that were before.'[5]

The account of Elizabeth's tribulations which follows, in the Tower and at Woodstock, was later embellished in such secondary and derivative works as Thomas Heywood's *Englands Elizabeth* and in his play *If You Know Not Me You Know Nobody*. In *Englands Elizabeth*, the trivial episode of an accidental fire at Woodstock is enlarged until it becomes all one with the fires of Smithfield: 'the whole Kingdom was then enflamed with *Bonfires* of Gods Saints'. A humble, prostrate prayer is put into the princess's mouth: 'Lady Elizabeths prayer in the midst of her sorrow'. 'Thus did shee both devoutly and religiously make use of all afflictions imposed upon her . . .' In the play, Elizabeth awakens from sleep to find a Bible miraculously placed in her hand by an angel and open at the text: 'Whoso putteth his trust in the Lord shall not be confounded.'

> My saviour thankes, on thee my hope I build,
> Thou lov'st poore Innocents, and art their shield.[6]

In Protestant England, Elizabeth's Stuart successors were at a considerable disadvantage in not being able to claim to have undergone such experiences. What Foxe and these poets and dramatists do not tell us about Elizabeth 'in the time of Queen Mary her sister' was that she conformed outwardly to her sister's religion and regularly heard mass. Mary would not have done the opposite thing and have heard Protestant prayers. In later years it would not be proposed that Elizabeth's various Catholic suitors should abandon the practice of their own religion. So what Elizabeth was in religion, in 1559, was not as transparent as her apologists and mythmakers would have us believe.

IV

With Elizabeth on the throne, as Deborah, some adjustment was necessary to convert the godly woman as sinful, dependent, meek and ripe for martyrdom, if active active only in prayer and meditation, into the historically, even biblically, less familiar figure of the female ruler in her own right, something the Scottish reformer John Knox regarded as simply unnatural, a 'monstrous regiment'. But remarkably little was done by publicists to alter the fundamental image of the female as penitent, ever aware of her sins and infirmities, hanging upon God as her strength and redemption. The apotheosis of this tradition arrived with the publication in 1582 of an extraordinarily ambitious literary undertaking, a vast compilation of prayers, meditations, role models, all written by or for or relating to women. This was Thomas Bentley's *The Monument of Matrones*, 'to remaine unto women as one entire and godlie monument of praier, precepts and examples'.[7] * * *

* * *

5. Ibid., viii (1839), 600–25; this passage at p. 601.
6. Thomas Heywood, *Englands Elizabeth: her life and troubles during her minoritie, from the Cradle to the Crowne* (1631), pp. 166–7, 169, 175; idem, *If You Know Not Me You Know Nobody*, part I, Malone Society Reprint (Oxford, 1934), scene xiv, lines 1047–67.
7. Thomas Bentley, *The Monument of Matrones: conteining seven severall lamps of virginilie, or distinct treatises: whereof the first five concerne praier and meditation: the other two last, precepes and examples* (1582) (STC nos. 1892–4).

* * * The title-page announces that the collection was 'compiled for the necessarie use of both sexes'. But, on the face of it, the enterprise was primarily intended to both flatter and admonish the queen, who dominates under every conceivable literary device and pretext. Besides sundry extensive collections of prayers which the queen either allegedly used or should use, Bentley reprints her translation of Marguerite d'Angoulême, called here *The Queenes meditation*, invents spiritual acrostics from the letters of her name, and composes 'The King's Heast or Gods familiar speech to the Queene',[8] addressed as 'Daughter'; with the queen's ecstatic 'selfe-talke with God' in response, beginning 'Rabboni'.[9] There is a special liturgy for November 17th, 'commonlie called The Queenes daie', to be celebrated by 'Mother and Daughter'.[1]

It was only a year since the French marriage negotiations had been finally broken off, and this was perhaps the earliest unrestrained celebration of Elizabeth's perpetual virginity. One of the prayers put into the queen's mouth by Bentley ends by asking that she may

> in the purenesse of my virginitie, and holinesse of mine innocencie, be presented to the Lambe my sovereigne Lord and onlie God, my heavenlie Bridegroom and spirituall spouse, my everlasting King deere Christ, and onlie sweet saviour Jesus, there to see the Sainets, and to be a Sainct, and with all the holie Patriarches, Judges, Kings and Queens, yea with all Archangells, Angels, saints, martyrs, confessors, Virgins, and the whole companie of thy celestiall and blessed spirits, to reyne with him over spirituall powers and principalities for ever, and to sing the sugred songs of my wedding-daie to my perpetuall ioie, and thine eternall praise.[2]

* * *

V

The essential point is that in Bentley's monstrous text Elizabeth was being fashioned (to use a term made fashionable by Professor Stephen Greenblatt) and almost marketed as a commodity.[3] The product was doubtless consistent with the queen's perception and presentation of herself and was consequently a piece of what Greenblatt calls *self*-fashioning, but it does little to lift the blinds on those opaque windows into her soul; and takes us not very far in determining whether the queen in her natural self was a convinced and devoutly Protestant Christian (and what kind of a Protestant), and whether that impinged perceptibly upon her public self, and policy.

As reported at the outset, the view has recently prevailed that Elizabeth was indeed a sincere and committed Protestant. Dr Haigh has already been quoted.[4] Professor Norman Jones, whose deconstruction work on Sir John Neale's interpretation of the parliamentary settlement of religion will probably stand, concludes that Elizabeth in 1559 knew what kind of religious settlement she wanted and got it, after overcoming objections and resistance, which were confined to conservative, Catholic objections and resistance,

---

8. Bentley, *Monument*, pp. 306ff.
9. Ibid., pp. 320ff.
1. Ibid., pp. 686ff.
2. Ibid., p. 272.
3. Stephen Greenblatt, *Renaissance Self-Fashioning: From More to Shakespeare* (Chicago, 1980).
4. Haigh, *Elizabeth I*, pp. 27–46.

mainly in the House of Lords. That may well be in substance correct. But to go further, as Jones does, and suggest that the queen was 'as Protestant as Jewel, Grindal or Cox' is to go too far, and to exclude the distinct possibility (however hard to establish from evidence) that the queen who made the settlement was manipulated and constrained, if not inside the parliament then outside it, in her own court and household.[5] Winthrop Hudson seems to be of the same doubtful persuasion. His book on the Elizabethan Settlement dismisses as evidentially unfounded suggestions that Elizabeth favoured the late Henrician position, or Lutheranism, or, as vaguely consistent with Lutheranism, the 1549 Prayer Book. He concludes that she was a Protestant leaning, like most of her first bishops, towards the Swiss confessions and the Zwinglian model of 'pure' religion, her own position on the confessional spectrum accurately indicated by the 1559 Prayer Book.[6]

It is necessary to consider evidence to the contrary. Evidence of Elizabeth's religious conservatism and of the consequent strains in her relations with her more unreservedly Protestant bishops hardly constitutes news. Much of it has provided the most familiar themes of Elizabethan ecclesiastical history. But its interpretation leaves room for significant differences. Some historians may choose to interpret the evidence in its entirety as examples of rational public policy. The queen could not afford to alienate the religious sensibilities of a nation which was still widely and deeply addicted to the old ways, not least in its aristocratic and politically powerful upper levels, still less to offend gratuitously foreign Catholic powers. Dr Haigh writes: 'Elizabeth's liturgical conservatism, her enforcement of clerical conformity, her reluctance to support Protestant rebels abroad, her restraint of Protestant preaching, and her moderation of the persecution of Catholics, all suggest a determination not to drive the Catholics into outright opposition.[7] This may well be what her policies and actions most plausibly suggest. Her personal preferences (it must again be said) are all but inaccessible. And yet her religious conservatism was so consistently manifested, applied with such apparent conviction, that it is hard to believe that it went against the grain of her own beliefs and tastes. * * * It remains possible that the Elizabethan compromise of Protestantism was a concession not only to the conservative prejudices of Elizabeth's subjects but to her own feelings.

Most of the episodes which found Elizabeth more or less publicly at odds with more advanced Protestant opinion are well known: a story central to any discussion of the Elizabethan Injunctions, Articles and Homilies, as well as to the particular matter of the ornaments rubric of the Prayer Book, that tiny Trojan horse out of which, in a sense, all the subsequent contention between conformists and nonconformist Puritans presently poured.[8] It makes sense to regard as concessions to the old religion the rules about surplices and square caps and even more the injunction which required the use

5. Norman L. Jones, *Faith By Statute: Parliament and the Settlement of Religion 1559* (1982). The quoted remark is at p. 9.
6. Winthrop S. Hudson, *The Cambridge Connection and the Elizabethan Settlement of 1559* (Durham, NC, 1980), esp. pp. 90–9, 131–7. A forthcoming study by Dr Roger Bowens of the music of the Chapel Royal in 1559 calls in question the Jones-Hudson interpretation of the religious settlement.
7. Haigh, *Elizabeth I*, p. 36.
8. R. W. Dixon, *History of the Church of England from the Abolition of the Roman Jurisdiction* (1902), v and vi; Patrick Collinson, *The Elizabethan Puritan Movement* (1967); idem, *Archbishop Grindal, 1519–1583: The Struggle for a Reformed Church* (1979); W. P. Haugaard, *Elizabeth and the English Reformation: The Struggle for a Stable Settlement of Religion* (Cambridge, 1968); John H. Primus, *The Vestments Controversy: An Historical Study of the Earliest Tensions within the Church of England in the Reigns of Edward VI and Elizabeth* (Kampen, 1960).

at communion not of plain baker's bread (as the Prayer Book prescribed) but wafers somewhat resembling the old hosts or 'singing cakes'. It would matter to an unreconstructed Catholic that he should receive his maker in a still familiar form from a celebrant vested like some kind of priest. The absence from the Injunctions of any specific order to remove stone altars and replace them with plain wooden tables can be explained in the same way. The case only has to be turned upside down to account for the insistence of Grindal and other bishops that altars must indeed be eradicated: Bishop Ridley, Bishop Latimer, Bishop Hooper and Mr Bradford had all gone to the stake as witnesses against the doctrine of which the stone altar was a symbol. 'So that by re-edifying of altars we shall also seem to join with the adversaries that burned those good men in condemning some part of their doctrine.' On this issue Elizabeth appears to have climbed down.[9]

The related issue of the cross as an emotive Christian symbol and focal point of vision in worship brings us closer to the queen's own convictions and is harder to square with a purely *politique* explanation for her conservatism. The 1559 Injunctions had called for the removal from all churches of 'things superstitious', specifying monuments of feigned miracles, pilgrimages, idolatry and superstition. Apparently it had not occurred to Elizabeth that crosses were included in that catalogue. Indeed, if Bishop Sandys is to be believed, writing to Peter Martyr on 1 April 1560, 'the queen's majesty considered it not contrary to the word of God, nay, rather for the advantage of the church, that the image of Christ crucified, together with Mary and John, should be placed as heretofore, in some conspicuous part of the church, where they might more readily be seen by all the people'.[1] As Margaret Aston has recently remarked: 'This passage speaks volumes for Elizabeth's religious position.'[2] Protestants—the Protestants' sort of Protestants—felt very differently about the cross, whether used as a bodily gesture (for example, after sneezing) or as personal adornment or as street furniture, and above all in the form of the great 'rood' with its flanking imagery in a commanding position above the heads of the worshipping congregation. To considerable extent these 'idols' were understood to be included among the 'monuments of superstition' condemned in the Injunctions and were removed from many, perhaps most parish churches in or soon after the Royal Visitation of the summer of 1559. When, some years later, the suffragan bishop of Dover and future dean of Canterbury Richard Rogers found the rood still standing in Kentish church of which he was rector, he was so indignant that in expostulating with a leading parishioner he swore 'by God's soul!'—a scandalous story which immediately went the round of Kentish hostelries, forcing the bishop to take action for slanderous defamation.[3]

But that oath would not have troubled Elizabeth Tudor in the least. An old friend of her youth later remonstrated with her for her habit of using oaths a great deal stronger than 'by God's soul'. 'Your gratious M[ajesty] in your anger hath used to sweare, sometime by that abhominable Idoll the Masse, and often and grievouslie by God, and by Christ, and by manie parts of his glorified bodie, and by Saints, faith, troth, and other forbidden things.'[4]

9. Collinson, *Grindal*, pp. 100–1. The Injunctions can be found in H. Gee and W. Hardy, ed., *Documents Illustrative of English Church History* (1896), pp. 417–67.
1. Sandys to Peter Martyr, 1 April 1560, *Zurich Letters*, ed. Hastings Robinson, i, Parker Society (Cambridge, 1842), pp. 73–4.
2. Margaret Aston, *England's Iconoclasts*, i, *Laws against Images* (Oxford, 1988), p. 303
3. Patrick Collinson, *The Birthpangs of Protestant England: Religious and Cultural Change in the Sixteenth and Seventeenth Centuries* (1988), p. 52.
4. *The Seconde Parte of a Register*, ed. Albert Peel (Cambridge, 1915), ii, pp. 53–4.

Trivial it may seem, but this (by no means the only evidence of Elizabeth's use of the old catholic oaths) opens not a mere window but a whole wall on the queen's soul. There were no Protestant oaths. The Puritan who dared to rebuke the queen for her swearing and accused her of wholesale backsliding from true religion ('but halflie by your Majesty hath God been honoured, his Church reformed and established') had known her in early days, when she had lived with Catherine Parr. He had found his wife in that household, and his reminiscences about those good old days have the stamp of authenticity. He recalled how Elizabeth had said that she would one day walk down by the river and visit his old and ailing mother, who 'joyed then not a little to hear of your godly study and virtuous inclination'. But later he had heard that she was 'so marvellously altered in mind, manners and manie things, that there was no hope of any such reformation . . . as was before hoped for'.[5]

We must return to the issue of the cross. There seems little doubt that the reinstatement of a cross and candlesticks in the royal chapel in the autumn of 1559 was a calculated retort to the unauthorised holocaust of roods and rood imagery in the Visitation of the previous summer; little doubt either, given the alarmed reaction of the newly elected bishops, that she also intended to signal in this way that the crosses should be restored, throughout the country. That was how her action was interpreted in the precincts of Canterbury Cathedral. In the event that retrograde measure, which would have been utterly damaging to the credit of the newly appointed bishops, was headed off by spirited acts of protest which included an episcopal letter accompanying a short treatise, 'Reasons Against Images in Churches': 'We beseech your Highness most humbly not to strain us any further . . . We pray your Majesty also not to be offended with this our plainness and liberty, which all good and Christian princes have ever taken in good part at the hands of godly bishops.'[6]

But in the Chapel Royal the cross remained, to provoke a whole series of teacup storms for years to come, including a verbal attack from the pulpit in the queen's presence, a major literary engagement with the Catholic writer John Martial who (no doubt embarrassingly) came to the queen's defence on the issue, and a whole succession of temerarious iconoclastic attacks on the offensive idol, smashing it, burning it, treading it under foot. One of these incidents involved the queen's fool, apparently instigated by Protestant courtiers. Elizabeth fought back, shouting down the dean of St Paul's in the pulpit and regularly repairing the work of the inonoclasts. A similar battle was fought in the public thoroughfares of London where the great cross of Cheapside was more than once saved from destruction by the queen's personal intervention.[7] The biblical precedent and *topos* for the strongly negative feelings entertained towards the image of the cross among 'godly' Protestants was the act of King Hezekiah who in his general purge of idolatry broke in pieces the brazen serpent which Moses had lifted up in the wilderness. Like that serpent, the cross in its original erection was a living, saving force, but preserved

5. Ibid.
6. Collinson, *Grindal*, pp. 97–9; Collinson, *Birthpangs* p. 52; Haugaard, *Elizabeth and the English Reformation*, pp. 185–200.
7. Aston, *England's Iconoclasts*, i, pp. 310–14; Patrick Collinson, 'If Constantine, Then Also Theodosius', in *Godly People*, pp. 130–1. For the literary exchanges, see *An Answer to John Martial's Treatise of the Cross by James Calfhill*, ed. R. Gibbings, Parker Society (Cambridge, 1846).

as a kind of museum piece and idol, dead and corrupting. It appears that Queen Elizabeth did not like to be compared to King Hezekiah.[8]

So while the symbolism of the royal chapel furnishings may have served a diplomatic purpose, in the perception of foreign Catholic governments, it is hard not to believe that Elizabeth was personally addicted to her little cross, impossible to accept the contrary: that she tolerated it with barely concealed distaste for thirty years, as a mere political necessity. The cross still stood on her altar in 1586.

✻ ✻ ✻

Elizabeth's unusually deep prejudice against clerical marriage is notorious. It was an odd and eclectic kind of Protestantism which was consistent with such views. When they were first shared with Matthew Parker, himself a married man (but destined to be the last married archbishop of Canterbury for well over a century), the primate's reaction was one of utter consternation: 'I was in an horror to hear such words to come from her mild nature and Christianly learned conscience.' 'We have cause all to be utterly discomforted and discouraged.'[9]

It was equally an odd sort of Protestant who nursed a negative prejudice against the preaching ministry and wished it to be reduced to a bare, skeletal, ancillary service. ✻ ✻ ✻ There may have been good reasons why Elizabeth thought that three or four preachers were sufficient for a shire.[1] But it is hard to reconcile that opinion with the reputation otherwise attributed to her of a godly evangelical Protestant, not ashamed of that Gospel of Christ which is the power of God unto salvation. Archbishop Grindal, no less dismayed than his predecessor had been when confronting the queen on clerical marriage, found this hard to stomach: 'Alas, Madam! is the scripture more plain in any one thing, than that the Gospel of Christ should be plentifully preached; and that plenty of labourers should be sent into the Lord's harvest; which, being great and large, standeth in need, not of a few, but many workmen.' 'But God forbid, Madam, that you should . . . any way go about to diminish the preaching of Christ's gospel: for that would ruinate all together at the length.'[2] Grindal knew that the queen preferred the authorised Homilies to the unpredictability of preaching. That was why she had taken some trouble with the text presented to her in 1563. But he told her that if every parish could be provided with a preaching pastor, 'which is rather to be wished then hoped for', there would be no need to read homilies. But, until then, 'better half a loaf than no bread'. Elizabeth was not persuaded. Eight years later she told a number of bishops that there was more learning in one of those homilies than in twenty of some of their sermons.[3]

---

8. This [is] brilliantly expounded in a monograph by Margaret Aston, *The King's Bed-Post* (Cambridge University Press, 1993).

9. Parker to Cecil, 1561, *Parker Correspondence*, pp. 156–7.

1. A view attributed to the queen by Archbishop Grindal in his famous letter of 20 December 1576; presumably uttered in one of the interviews known to have preceded its composition. See *Remains of Edmund Grindal*, ed. W. Nicholson, Parker Society (Cambridge, 1843), p. 379. Elizabeth's negative attitude to preaching comes through strongly in the conversation recorded on the occasion of the presentation of the clerical subsidy in February 1585, Neale, *Elizabeth I and her Parliaments, 1584–1601*, pp. 69–71.

2. *Remains of Grindal*, pp. 378, 382; Collinson, *Grindal*, pp. 239–45.

3. *Remains of Grindal*, pp. 382–3; Neale, *Elizabeth I and her Parliaments, 1584–1601*, p. 70.

VI

It was rare and unusual for Elizabeth's conservative religious prejudices to be attacked with such vehement directness as Archbishop Grindal used in his famous but fatal letter; or William Fuller in his 'Book to the Queen' which contained those strictures against swearing already quoted; or Dean Alexander Nowell when he preached against the cross in the royal chapel; and for understandable reasons. Grindal's effective career was abruptly terminated. After his unfortunate sermon, Archbishop Parker took Nowell home to dinner 'for pure pity'. 'He was utterly dismayed.'[4]

More often, covert and tactful ways and means were found to instruct the queen's conscience. This returns us to the prayers and pious ejaculations put into her mouth which it is tempting but not always safe to read as first-hand evidence not only of Elizabeth's religious beliefs and opinions but of the depth and quality of her spirituality. When Alexander Nowell was accused of flattery in his court sermons (the attack on the cross was not in his usual style), he replied that 'he had no other way to instruct the queen what she should be but by commending her'.[5]

Bentley's *Monument of Matrones* represented a variant of this strategy, although it cut closer to the bone by making Elizabeth confess, profusely, indeed with prolixity, her many sins. This she may not have been in the least reluctant to do, but surely not in the full public light of day, for all her female subjects to read. Bentley's texts also underline in the very words placed in the queen's mouth, or in the mouth of God as he addresses her, that her office is a public office and a solemn trust, held in subordination to God and for the sole purpose of advancing his kingdom and conserving the souls and bodies of the people committed to her charge. In a prayer which in Bentley's third 'lamp' immediately follows Theodore Beza's paraphrase of Psalm 18 ('The Lord is my rock and my fortress') Elizabeth is made to call herself God's handmaid, 'a subject and servant to thy most high and sacred Maiestie, and a child depending alone and wholie upon thy divine and fatherlie providence for all things.'

> And that I remembering whose minister I am may first above all things in a perfect zeale of thy house, and love of thy people, ever seeke thy honour and glorie, and studie continuallie to preserve thy people committed to my charge, in wealth, peace or godlinesse.

> Lastlie, O most mightie God, looke what remaineth yet of the happie building, enlarging and finishing of thy Church, and to the establishing and planting of thy Religion perfectlie therein, according to the prescript rule of thy blessed word and full discharge of my dutie . . . [6]

This last passage is redolent of the evangelical ecclesiology of 'edification', the very hallmark of the puritan reading of St Paul.[7]

There is no 'or else' in these petitions; no suggestion of 'if not, remove me from this place'. So there is less of the politics of Old Testament prophecy, less menace, than we find, for example, in a memorandum drawn up by the bishops at the time of the 1572 parliament, which threatened the queen with

4. *Parker Correspondence*, p. 235.
5. Ralph Churton, *The Life of Alexander Nowell* (Oxford, 1809), p. 92.
6. Bentley, *Monument*, pp. 253–71.
7. John S. Coolidge, *The Pauline Renaissance in England: Puritanism and the Bible* (Oxford, 1970).

divine displeasure and even divine deposition if she failed to execute Mary queen of Scots, citing the precedent of King Saul who lost his throne for the sin of sparing the life of Agag.[8] But trained sniffer dogs ought nevertheless to be able to pick up the scent of a kind of resistance doctrine in Bentley's prayers and meditations. In the section called 'The Kings Heast or Gods familiar speech to the Queene', God tells her: 'Beware therefore that yee abuse not this authoritie given unto you by me, under certaine lawes and conditions . . . For be you sure that I have placed you in this seate upon this condition.'[9] I am reminded of the great parliament man Thomas Norton who wrote to his son (from his imprisonment in the Tower): 'I have no dealing with the queen but as with the image of God', which at first sight looks like a piece of divine-right absolutism but in fact is anything but; and of the earl of Huntingdon's brother, Sir Francis Hastings, who made this note at a sermon: 'Obedience, what it is, it is due unto the Lorde only.'[1]

There was a note of conditionality, an implied threat, in Bentley's ostensibly flattering text, as none would have known better than Elizabeth herself. It was not difficult in the sixteenth century for any woman, royal or not, to pass, in one or two false moves on the chauvinistic snakes and ladders board, from the shining emblem of the Woman Clothed with the Sun to its antitype, the Whore of Babylon, those contrasted images pictured side by side in Bale's *Image of both churches*, the whore seductive and curvaceous, sexy and sexist. Patterns of godly and faithful womanhood were always balanced and opposed by their opposites, seductresses, harlots, female tyrants, according to the all-pervading rhetorical repertoire of binary opposition.[2] Any royal lady was liable, by putting a moral, religious or political foot wrong, to find herself newly type-cast as Jezebel, as in their times were Mary Tudor, Mary of Guise, Catherine de Medicis and Mary queen of Scots; and eventually Elizabeth herself, on the catholic continent, after the execution of Mary Stuart, in the polemical poem published at Antwerp, *De Jezebelis*.[3]

So, since Elizabeth understood such matters perfectly well, it is likely that she was as conscious of this protestant factor as of the need to conciliate Catholicism. If the one factor helps to account for her religious conservatism, the other may explain the fulsomeness of her widely acclaimed evangelical piety. If Paris was worth a mass to Henry of Navarre, a secure place in the hearts of Elizabeth's protestant subjects was worth Bentley's *Monument of Matrones*.

But if we were able to strip off both these layers, open all the Chinese boxes and Russian dolls, what should we find inside? Are there, after all, any snakes in Iceland?

8. *Proceedings in the Parliament of Elizabeth I*, i, *1558–1581*, ed. T. E. Hartley (Leicester, 1981), pp. 274–82.
9. Bentley, *Monument*, p. 309.
1. BL, MS Add. 48023, fol. 33 r; Huntington Library, MS HA Religious Box 1 (9).
2. King, *Tudor Royal Iconography*, p. 183.
3. The Antwerp text attacked Elizabeth in the following extreme terms:

> Batarde incestueuse, et paillard publique
> Perfide, deloyale, et fille de ta soeur.

Bentley might have been glad to use such language with respect to other 'Jezebels'. Readers of his *Monument* (p. 35) read: 'There is not a more wicked head than the head of a serpent: and there is no wrath above the wrath of a woman. . . . It were better to dwell with a Lion and a Dragon, then to keep house with a wicked woman.' But nothing is quite what it seems. These were texts from the book of Ecclesiastes and the young Princess Elizabeth had copied them out 'with her owne hande', or so according to John Bale who incorporated her scriptural texts into his edition of *A godly medytacyon of the christen sowle*, which Bentley reprinted.

THE POEMS AND SPEECHES OF ELIZABETH

ILONA BELL

Elizabeth Tudor: Poet[†]

During her lifetime and in the decades following her death Elizabeth I was celebrated as a most excellent poet. Not only did George Puttenham dedicate *The Art of English Poesie* to Elizabeth, but he addressed her throughout, quoting her poems, mixing encomium with instruction, assuming that she would actually enjoy reading and using his three-hundred page tome: "my most Honored and Gracious: if I should seeme to offer you this my deuise for a discipline and not a delight, I might well be reputed . . . the most arrogant and injurious: your selfe being alreadie, of any that I know in our time, the most excellent Poet" (21). No doubt this was an extravagant courtly compliment, crafted to win Elizabeth's patronage, but it may not have been as incredible as it seems today because Puttenham's treatise and many of Elizabeth's poems were written during the drab age of English poetry, before Sidney, Spenser, Shakespeare, and Donne raised it to such magnificent heights.[1]

Elizabeth I reigned over the English poetic imagination far longer than she reigned over the realm. Elizabeth was still being lauded as a great poet long after she was in a position to reward anyone—when worms had tried her long-preserved virginity and her quaint honor turned to dust. "Before many, or most, I may iustly and without flatterie preferre the famous Queene *Elizabeth*," John Heywood wrote in *Gunaikeion*. "Of whose pleasant Fancies, and ingenious Ditties, I haue seene some, and heard of many" (398). By the middle of the twentieth-century Elizabeth's reputation as a poet had declined precipitously. When Leicester Bradner published *The Poems of Elizabeth I* in 1963, he excluded "When I was fair and young" on the grounds that he did not believe Elizabeth could have written such a fine poem. By the end of the twentieth century Elizabeth was the subject of more historical, biographical, and artistic productions than anyone except Abraham Lincoln. Yet literary scholars were more interested in how the Elizabethans represented their queen than in how Elizabeth represented herself. Elizabeth's reputation as a writer and poet is now in recovery. I hope this essay will help spark further interest in Elizabeth Tudor as poet, for the work of analyzing, annotating, and reevaluating her poems and their significance has just begun.[2]

Like most Elizabethan lyric poetry, Elizabeth Tudor's poems were written not for print but for a private manuscript audience, but that only increased their value, as Heywood reveals when he boasts that "I haue seene some, and heard of many." Elizabeth may have written additional poems that were not signed or preserved, as Puttenham's fulsome tribute

† From *Images of Elizabeth I: A Quadricentennial Celebration*. Ed. Donald Stump and Carole Levin. Special issue, *Explorations in Renaissance Culture* 30.1 (Summer 2004): 1–22. Reprinted by permission of *Explorations in Renaissance Culture*.

1. For an illuminating account of the drab age of English poetry, and Elizabeth's place in it, see May's introduction to *Courtier Poets*.
2. Thanks to the editorial labors of Bradner, Marcus, Mueller, Rose, and May, we are now in a much better position to study the language, textual variants, dates, and historical circumstances of Elizabeth's writing. The best study to date of Elizabeth's poetry is Summit, "The Arte of a Ladies Penne.'"

to her seems to suggest: "the Queene our soueraigne Lady, whose learned, delicate, noble Muse, easily surmounteth all the rest that haue written before her time or since, for sence, sweetnesse and subtillitie, be it in Ode, Elegie, Epigram, or any other kinde of poeme Heroick or Lyricke, wherein it shall please her Maiestie to employ her pen" (77). This is often cited as evidence that Elizabeth wrote more poems in more genres than surviving manuscripts indicate, but that is not what Puttenham meant. His mid-sentence shift to the future tense—"wherein it *shall* please her Maiestie to employ her pen"—reveals that this list is not a compendium of Eliza-beth's collected works; rather it is an advertisement for the kinds of poems Elizabeth would be able to write if she chose to apply her proven poetic skills to the genres set forth in Puttenham's treatise.

Elizabeth's English poems are short, ranging from two to thirty-two lines. The poems that have survived are occasional poems or posies designed to be circulated in manuscript, recited in person, sent as mes-sages, or left where they would be seen by someone known to the Queen. Elizabeth wrote both the first and second half of poem-and-answer sets. She wrote a posie in her French Psalter. She wrote a lover's complaint and a response to a lover's complaint, thereby helping to transform the mono-logic male voice of Petrarchan poetry into a characteristically Elizabethan lyric dialogue of courtship.[3] Since she wrote courtly lyrics and occasional verse, the original, private lyric situation was deeply embedded in the poem's language and is still an intrinsic part of its meaning and purpose.

Elizabeth discovered the power of poetry even before her accession to the throne, when, defenseless and suspected of treason, she wrote an epi-gram "with her diamond in a glass window" at Woodstock. Elizabeth had been imprisoned in the Tower of London for two months following Wyatt's plot to assassinate Queen Mary. When the government failed to find any evidence proving Elizabeth's direct involvement, she was sent to Wood-stock Castle where she was held for eleven months under the ever-vigilant custody of Sir Henry Bedingfield. Bedingfield, a precise and conscientious man, was afraid to make even the smallest decision without approval from the Queen or the Privy Council. Fortunately, he kept a record of all cor-respondence to and fro. Upon arriving at Woodstock, Bedingfield was instructed by Mary not to allow Elizabeth to have "conference wth anye suspected p[er]son oute off his heryng, nor that she dooe by eny menes eyther receyve or sende eny message, l[ett]^{re}, or token" (Manning 158). Bedingfield asked how he was to know who was "suspected." The Council responded that he "must forsee that nooe p[er]sons suspecte have anye conference wth hyr at all; and yet to p[er]mitte such straungers whom [he] shall thynke honeste and not suspicious . . . to speke wth hyr In yor heryng onlye" (Manning 164). That was no help; Bedingfield responded that he had no idea how to "foresee" or "perceive" who was "suspect" or who was "honest." The council resolved the problem by deciding that Elizabeth should not be allowed to see or communicate with anyone without special permission. The decision shaped Elizabeth's day-to-day existence, and severely curtailed her power to defend herself.

Locked up inside a decrepit, drafty old castle, allowed to walk in the small private garden but refused permission to wander in the park or to

---

3. See Bell, *Elizabethan Women and the Poetry of Courtship*, especially 108–13, and Marotti, *Manu-script, Print, and the English Renaissance Lyric.*

study with her tutor, unable to see anyone but Bedingfield without special permission, these were the conditions under which Elizabeth carved the epigram with a diamond on a window at Woodstock:

> Much suspected by me,
> Nothing proved can be.
> *Quod* Elizabeth the prisoner.[4]

This two line couplet, with a total of twelve syllables, is about as short as an epigram can be. The brevity and compactness of the poem is central to its meaning for it shows how much Elizabeth's life and words were circumscribed by the role she had been assigned, the role of prisoner and suspected traitor. Of course, the traditional challenge of an epigram, and to some extent any lyric, is to see "what man can say / In a little," as Ben Jonson's lovely little "Epitaph on Elizabeth, L.H" avers. In some ways, Elizabeth's challenge was just the opposite, to show how little could be made out of anything she was prepared to speak or write. The terse poetic diction epitomizes what the poem asserts: Elizabeth's opponents can only elicit what she chooses to speak.

The oppressive constraints of Elizabeth's incarceration and the ominously unresolved charges against her pervade the poem. The passive construction captures Elizabeth's situation: as prisoner, her only recourse is constant vigilance and continued resistance. The rhythm and syntax focus attention on the first word of each line, "Much" and "Nothing," suggesting that "much" had been made of "nothing." By inverting the standard iambic rhythm, the trochaic lines convey symbolically or subliminally the disruption of the social order. Yet the trochaic rhythm also suggests—as does the poem itself—that Elizabeth is poised, ready to take the first step to exonerate herself.[5] The Woodstock epigram provides only the barest facts. It does not say Elizabeth has done nothing; it only says that nothing can be proven. If "by" is taken in the older sense of "concerning," the couplet declares that although much is suspected *about* or concerning Elizabeth, nothing can be proven against her. She could still be condemned and executed without due cause, but, the poem implies, such an injustice would only heighten hostility to the regime. If "by me" is read as the implied subject of the passive verb "suspected," the lines contain a second meaning: Elizabeth's accusers are also suspected by her. The two meanings coexist, complicating and reinforcing each other.

But why engrave the poem on a window? First of all, Elizabeth's access to writing materials was carefully controlled because the Council had repeatedly warned Bedingfield to take every precaution to prevent Elizabeth from sending tokens, letters, or messages to her friends and supporters. The window and diamond were there, ready to be used, and Elizabeth was clever enough to make them a symbolic part of the poem's meaning. Elizabeth could see herself reflected and represented in the window, which could so easily shatter under pressure but did not, and in the

---

4. Elizabeth's writing is quoted from *Elizabeth I: Collected Works* unless noted otherwise.
5. Elizabeth continued to lobby for permission to write to Mary and the Privy Council, clearly believing that her rhetorical skills would convince them of her innocence. When Mary responded coldly to Elizabeth's first letter, and Bedingfield refused to forward her pleas to the Council, Elizabeth complained that she was worse off than a common prisoner at Newgate.

diamond, one of the few remaining vestiges of her privileged status, valuable now not for its beauty or net worth but for its hard core and sharp edges. The multi-faceted form of the diamond symbolizes the hermeneutic challenge the poem poses: Elizabeth's epigram, like her situation, looks totally different depending on one's point of view.

Elizabeth's words would have been easily legible from within, but the indefinite pronouns, cryptic diction, and ambiguous syntax could only be fully understood by those who were willing to see the situation from Elizabeth's point of view. When seen from outside the letters were reversed, but the epigram was short enough to be deciphered and remembered by anyone who cared enough to do so. The mirror text invites Elizabeth's foes to pause and consider how they would feel if the situation were reversed. To Elizabeth's supporters, it says, be vigilant and patient, the situation may soon be reversed.

The epigram served a number of different functions. First of all, it provided consolation for Elizabeth herself, and reminded her, every time she looked out the window, that constant vigilance was required if she was to avoid incriminating herself. Second, it was a message to her accusers, warning them not to confuse suspicion with proof. Third, I think, it was a message to Elizabeth's supporters. Elizabeth's old ally Thomas Parry had taken up lodging at a local inn where he managed Elizabeth's finances, arranged provisions for the castle, and received visits from scores of Elizabeth's supporters.[6] Although no one was allowed to visit Elizabeth, Parry was permitted to bring funds to the kitchen staff and to send servants bearing provisions. The epigram was a way of informing her friends that she was safe, that the Marian government had no evidence against her, and that her allies must be exceedingly careful not to say or do anything to incriminate her. Finally, the epigram addressed posterity. If Elizabeth had been executed, it would have become an emblem of her innocent martyrdom. When she was finally released, it became a famous emblem of her ability to outwit and outbrave her enemies.[7] The final line, "*Quod* Elizabeth the prisoner," could have been added when the poem was later copied onto the wall where it was seen and transcribed by visitors to England in the 1590s, but I think it was written by Elizabeth herself because it frames and recasts the epigram, much as the signature frames and recasts the posie written in the book at Windsor which we shall examine shortly. By writing the poem, Elizabeth reconstructs the situation, giving it a form and meaning of her own. Just as the artful doubleness of "Much suspected by me" enables Elizabeth to transform herself from the object of others' designs to the critic and judge of their actions, the narrative frame turns her from a helpless victim to a character in a narrative that she herself constructs and enacts. By choosing poetic language that is as artfully evasive as it is bluntly assertive, Elizabeth outmaneuvered her interrogators, thwarted her enemies, and gained a measure of control over her situation.

---

6. For information about Woodstock Castle, see Thurley, *Royal Palaces*; and Dunlop, *Palaces and Progresses of Elizabeth I*. Elizabeth was lodged in the gatehouse rather than the castle, so her window would have been more easily visible from without.

7. Visitors began to make pilgrimages to the site during Elizabeth's reign, and, Dunlop reports, "[r]ight into the eighteenth century, sightseers could remember this room, retaining the name of 'Queen Elizabeth's Chamber'" (15).

Elizabeth also wrote another, somewhat longer epigram while imprisoned at Woodstock:

> O Fortune, thy wresting, wavering state
> Hath fraught with cares my troubled wit,
> Whose witness this present prison late
> Could bear, where once was joy flown quite.
> Thou causedst the guilty to be loosed
> From lands where innocents were enclosed,
> And caused the guiltless to be reserved,
> And freed those that death had well deserved.
> But all herein can be naught wrought,
> So God grant to my foes as they have thought.
>   *Finis*. Elisabetha a prisoner, 1555

The poem begins with a direct expression of personal feeling, "Hath
fraught with cares my troubled wit," but here too the focus is less on physical suffering than mental constraint. The first four lines offer a terse but
surprisingly powerful glimpse of Elizabeth's distress, but it is only a glimpse,
not a full-fledged narrative, because she is not soliciting pity, she is
demanding justice. Elizabeth finds solace in the thought that Woodstock
Castle bears witness to a long line of injustice that traces its history back
to an originary moment, "where *once* was joy flown quite" (my emphasis).
The original Woodstock castle was built by Henry II to conceal and confine his mistress, Rosamond Clifford. The medieval castle had been
destroyed by Elizabethan times, but Rosamond's story was well known,
and it was widely believed that Henry's wife discovered the underground
labyrinth leading to Rosamond's apartment and poisoned her. The vague-
ness of the reference ("Where once was joy flown quite") protects Elizabeth from any direct association with Rosamond's sexual dishonor while
expressing sympathy with her plight, much as the other Woodstock epigram protects Elizabeth from any direct association with Wyatt's political
dishonor while leaving open the possibility that he and his actions were
justified.[8]

Elizabeth's final couplet imagines that Woodstock's history of releasing
the guilty and restraining the innocent "can be" reversed, if fortune's random acts are overturned by God's justice. The final rhymes, "wrought" and
"thought," strengthened by the internal rhyme, "naught wrought," echo
and imagine a release from the constraint that "Hath *fraught* with cares
my troubled wit" (my emphasis). The conclusion, "So God grant," provides
a much-anticipated answer to the prayer the poem itself constitutes. The
liberation the final couplet foresees could take a number of different
forms, depending on how one interprets the words, "all herein can be
naught wrought." All that remain imprisoned "herein," i.e., "here in"
Woodstock Castle, can be made "naught" if God grants her foes what they
want: the opportunity to convict and execute her. From the perspective of

---

8. The variant, "bands," confirmed by Waldstein's accompanying Latin translation, meaning chains,
   seems to make more literal sense, but I prefer the "lands" because it extends the injustice from the
   grounds of Woodstock itself to all the "lands" of England where the "guilty" executioners of Mary's
   will were free to wreak their vengeance upon "innocent" Protestants.

eternity, that would be a welcome liberation because it would free Elizabeth's troubled wit from the cares of this world, retrospectively giving a
more positive spin to the previous line, "And freed those that death had
well deserved." "[A]ll herein can be naught wrought" could also mean, all
I've said "here in" the poem will be turned to "naught" if God grants my
foes what they have "thought," i.e., if God does to my foes what they have
thought about doing to me. In that case, Elizabeth will be released, her
opponents will be "naught" as will the poem's argument, for it will no
longer be true that the guilty are "freed" while the "guiltless" are "reserved"
in prison. By warning her enemies that God will punish them for treating
her unjustly, Elizabeth exercises some measure of control over her fate,
much as she would later warn the members of her first parliament that
they could not force her to marry because her decisions were guided by
God, "who hath hitherto therein preserved and led me by the hand" (57).

A final, even more veiled epigrammatic turn suggests that if God grants
what her foes have thought—if the treason plots she has been accused of
should come to pass—then her foes will be rendered "naught," Elizabeth
will be crowned queen, and everything her foes "wrought" will be undone.
Highly conscious that anything she writes or says "can be" used against
her, Elizabeth can only prophesy her foes' defeat by concealing it, as an
amphibolous subtext, beneath the more obvious image of her own destruction. As it draws to a close, the poem makes a self-reflexive move, meditat-
ing on its own enigmatic form: since her foes have "caused the guiltless to
be reserved" (in the sense of close-mouthed), Elizabeth remains as tersely
self-protective as she is morally outspoken, using the epigram's twists and
turns both to protest her bondage and to have her say without giving her
foes anything to hold against her. With that, the ending takes its final epigrammatic turn, recapitulating the message of the other Woodstock epigram: "But all herein can be naught wrought." If "naught" can be made of
"all" that is written "herein," then "Nothing proved can be."[9]

The moral discrimination, incisive verbal wit, enigmatic multiplicity of
meaning, and self-reflexive form developed in the two Woodstock epigrams became a hallmark of Elizabeth's poetic style—and her prose style
as well. They recur in poem #4 where the concrete physical images of the
opening lines pose deeper questions of perception, judgment, trust, and
the process of interpretation itself:

> No crooked leg, no bleared eye,
> No part deformèd out of kind,
> Nor yet so ugly half can be
> As is the inward, suspicious mind.
>   Your loving mistress, *Elizabeth*[1]

Compared, for example, to Ben Johnson's epigrams, this language sounds
generalized and impersonal. The initial physical traits provide a foil for the
final moral judgment, but the poem does not deny the importance of physical attraction or repulsion. Rather the final epigrammatic twist declares

---

9. The version printed in *Collected Works* has the two-line epigram following the signature of the
   longer epigram; clearly, they are closely related but discrete compositions.
1. As Steven May pointed out to me, *Collected Works* mistakenly prints the signature as Elizabeth R.

that mental and moral ugliness are far worse. Yet despite the generalizing diction, Elizabeth clearly intended the poem for a particular person because the autograph text, written in her French psalter, is signed, "your loving mistress, Elizabeth." The puzzling disjunction between the impersonal judgment and the intimate signature constitutes the poem's primary interpretive crux. The signature complicates the poem substantially, making it not only trenchant but also conciliatory. "Mistress" meant both lady-love and a woman with power over someone else; hence the signature reminds Elizabeth's private lyric audience that she has the power to decide whether he is attractive or repugnant to her, and whether she is, and will continue to be, his "loving mistress." The signature reveals, moveover, that the epigram was written to and for someone Elizabeth cares about so deeply and knows so intimately that she can read—and sway—his inward mind.

By hiding the posie at the end of the psalter rather than inscribing it on the opening pages, Elizabeth made it into a secret missive.[2] As was characteristic of posies, she discreetly omitted the name of her private lyric audience, or any identifiable references to his person, so that if anyone else happened to come upon the poem, it would seem like an abstract, ethical speculation on the relative importance of body and mind rather than a judgment of a specific person. But if Elizabeth showed her private lyric audience the poem, or more likely if she sent him the psalter with a hint to look at the final pages, the words would almost certainly have contained a more pointed, private reference to events, or thoughts and feelings, known to them both—to some sort of unspecified tension or disagreement between them. Elizabeth clearly wanted to reassure him that she was still his "loving mistress," even as she felt compelled to warn him that his thoughts and actions could easily destroy her good opinion of him.

The editors of Elizabeth's *Collected Works* suggest that "[t]his may be the 'obscure sentence' referred to by Burghley as written by the Queen in "'a book at Windsor' when she was 'much offended with the earl of Leicester' in August 1565."[3] That seems likely for a number of reasons. First, the epigram or posie is in fact a single sentence. Second, it *was* actually written by Elizabeth in a book, a French psalter, that is still extant in the Royal Library at Windsor Castle.[4] Third, the handwriting suggests an early date (Doran, *Elizabeth* 201), and Dudley is one of the few people the youthful

2. Puttenham explains that posies, or short epigrams, were extremely fashionable—"made as it were vpon a table, or in a windowe, or vpon the wall or mantell of a chimney in some place of common resort, where it was allowed euery man might come," but also "put in paper and in bookes, and vsed as ordinarie missives" (68).

3. Marcus, Mueller, Rose, and Doran all believe the epigram was written in the first part of Elizabeth's reign. May thinks the poem was written while Elizabeth was still princess because the signature ends with a knot (similar to the one her father used in his signature). According to May, there are no extant examples of this signature after Elizabeth became queen when she signed her letters Elizabeth R. We cannot know for certain that Elizabeth stopped using the knotted signature because, as Susan Doran commented in response to my query, virtually all of the extant autograph letters written while Elizabeth was queen are official correspondence. Most of her more intimate letters to Leicester have disappeared; the ones printed in *Collected Works* are copies and thus lack a signature. As Carol Levin suggested, Elizabeth may have chosen the more intimate signature on this particular occasion, using a knot instead of an R for Regina, to strike a more reassuring and less regal note. Although Starkey provides a wonderfully detailed account of Elizabeth's early years, I could not find a situation before her coronation that fits the poem's complex mixture of tones and concerns.

4. The possibility that Elizabeth gave Dudley (or whomever the poem was addressed to) the psalter is strengthened by the fact that the book, acquired by the Royal Library, has not been at Windsor Castle since Elizabeth's day.

Elizabeth loved and chastised in this way. Burghley's journal entry is also a single rather obscure sentence, but the actual wording contains a valuable clue to the function the epigram may have served: "The Queen Majesty semed to be much offended with the Erle of Lecester, and so she wrote an obscure sentence in a Book at Wyndsor" (Burghley 2: 760). The logical connective, "and so she wrote," suggests that Elizabeth wrote the "obscure sentence" because she had been, and still "seemed to be," much offended with Robert Dudley, the Earl of Leicester. But are the epigram and the "obscure sentence" one and the same?[5] Do the events Burghley cites match, and shed light on, the Windsor epigram? More importantly, what role might the poem have played in the historical drama unfolding at Windsor Castle in August 1565?

Burghley's journal entry offers no further information, but the reports of the Spanish ambassador, Don Diego Guzmán De Silva, provide a detailed account of what was happening at the time.[6] The Queen arrived at Windsor on 10 August 1565, more preoccupied than ever with perturbing questions of courtship and marriage. To Elizabeth's great consternation, Mary Queen of Scots had recently married Darnley, a decision as rash as it was disastrous. While the court anxiously awaited news from Scotland, Elizabeth was being actively courted by several suitors of her own.[7] The French ambassador was pressing for an immediate answer to a marriage proposal from Charles IX. The sister of the King of Sweden was on her way to England, presumably to urge Elizabeth to reconsider her brother's suit. Elizabeth thought the French match would make her look ridiculous because Charles was only fourteen years old, and she showed little interest in reviving the Swedish courtship. She was much more attentive to the Austrian envoy, Adam von Swetkowich, Baron von Mitterburg, who had been sent to England to negotiate a marriage contract between Elizabeth and Archduke Charles (*Calendar Simancas* 1: 456). "She will have no lack of husbands," de Silva commented laconically (*Calendar Simancas* 1: 445). But in mid July Emperor Maximilian sent an uncompromising letter, demanding that Elizabeth rather than Charles should provide a dowry, declaring that Charles' household expenses must be paid by the English treasury, asking for certain political prerogatives, and most problematic of all, insisting that Charles must be allowed to practice his Catholic religion. Meanwhile, Robert Dudley, the Earl of Leicester, began jockeying to see whether Elizabeth might still be persuaded to marry him. While doing everything he could to support the Archduke's suit, de Silva believed that Elizabeth would marry Robert Dudley or no one.

5. The psalter was exhibited at the National Maritime Museum, and this page is reproduced in the catalogue (Doran, *Elizabeth* 201). Natalie Mears, who wrote the commentary, thought that Elizabeth may have written the poem "to Robert Cecil who was a hunchback," but the logic of the poem suggests that the private lyric audience had an inward, suspicious mind not a deformed body.

6. This is the first journal entry for August, and atypically, the day is not noted. The second entry is dated August 10. De Silva reports that the Queen arrived at Windsor from Richmond on August 8. If Burghley wrote his journal entries singly, in sequence, that would mean Elizabeth wrote the obscure sentence on August 9, but Burghley may have made several entries at one sitting, omitting the date because he did not know exactly when Elizabeth wrote the obscure sentence. De Silva first mentions the tiff between Elizabeth and Dudley on August 27. On September 3 he writes again, having learned: "[t]he real ground of the dispute between Lord Robert and Heneage" (*Calendar Simancas* 1: 472). It could easily have taken de Silva two to three weeks to find out what happened.

7. For an invaluable account of the financial, religious, and political issues surrounding Dudley's and Charles's courtships, see Doran, *Monarchy and Matrimony* 40–98.

On one level, the Windsor epigram explores the difficult judgments that courtship and courtiership entail. While the English and Austrian governments were trying to hammer out a marriage agreement, Elizabeth was pondering what qualities were important in a potential husband. She repeatedly assured Parliament that she would never make a match that was detrimental to the country (as her cousin Mary, Queen of Scots had just done), but she also insisted from the start of her reign that she would not be compelled to marry for pragmatic reasons alone. Indeed, she went so far as to take a vow that she would marry no man whom she had not seen.[8] True to her word, in August 1565 Elizabeth refused to make a commitment to marry the Archduke—even if the religious, financial, and political differences could be resolved—until he came to England, so they could find out, as she put it, "whether they will be mutually satisfied personally." Sexual attractiveness and physical deformity may have been on Elizabeth's mind because she had been told that Charles "had a head bigger than the Earl of Bedford's" (*Calendar Simancas* 1: 72). She was much relieved to learn that his head was not, in the words of the epigram, "a part deformed out of kind." On July 13 de Silva reported that "we spoke of the archduke's person, his age, his good parts, and she evidently felt pleasure in dwelling upon the subject" (*Calendar Simancas* 1: 448). Elizabeth may also have been thinking about misshapen body parts and marriage because Jane Grey's sister Mary, whom de Silva described as "little, crookbacked, and very ugly," was living at Windsor when, on August 20, it "came out that she had married a gentleman named Keyes. . . . They say the Queen is very much annoyed and grieved thereat. They are in prison" (*Calendar Simancas* 1: 468).

Relations between Elizabeth and Dudley were strained during the entire month of August. Towards the end of July, de Silva noted that Dudley "seems lately to be rather more alone than usual, and the Queen appears to display a certain coolness towards him. She has begun to smile on a gentleman of her chamber named Heneage, which has attracted a great deal of attention" (*Calendar Simancas* 1: 454). Dudley became increasingly jealous, and an argument broke out between the two men. Meanwhile, Throckmorton urged Dudley to find out whether he was still a lively candidate for the Queen's hand by pretending that he had fallen in love with one of the ladies of the court and observing Elizabeth's response when he then requested permission to return to his own lodgings. Dudley began ostentatiously flirting with the Viscountess of Hereford, "one of the best-looking ladies of the court," according to de Silva. "The queen was in a great temper and upbraided him" for fighting with Heneage and flirting with the Viscountess (*Calendar Simancas* 1: 472). Heneage was sent away, and Robert returned to his own apartments where he remained for three days while Cecil and Sussex sought to bring about a reconciliation. At the beginning of September de Silva wrote that "Robert and the Queen shed tears, and he has returned to his former favor" (*Calendar Simancas* 1: 472).

The reference to the "inward, suspicious mind" would have struck Dudley with particular force. By flirting with the Viscountess and fighting with

---

8. For a more detailed discussion of Elizabeth's vow and its ramifications, see my essay, "Elizabeth I—Always Her Own Free Woman."

Heneage, Dudley had not only displayed an "inward, suspicious mind," but he had made himself "suspicious" to Elizabeth. ("Suspicious" means not only open to or deserving of suspicion but also disposed to suspect evil, mistrustful.) Indeed, his whole life had been clouded by suspicions. To begin with (since the word "kind" could refer to birth or family), "No part deformed out of kind" refers to lingering feelings that Dudley's honor was tainted because both his father and grandfather had been attainted for treason. Then too, Dudley, like Elizabeth herself, had been imprisoned in the Tower of London on suspicion of treason. But even more to the point, suspicions about Dudley's mind and character were the principal reason Elizabeth had not married him. After Amy Robsart's death in 1560, rumors that Dudley had his wife killed so that he could wed the Queen were so rampant and far-reaching that Elizabeth decided she simply could not marry him, even though she was physically attracted to him and seemed to love him. By 1565 the gossip had subsided, but many of Elizabeth's subjects and allies continued to harbor their own inward suspicions about Dudley's mind and character.

There is also good reason to associate the "inward, suspicious mind" with Elizabeth herself since the very word "suspicious" alludes to and builds upon the key term in the Woodstock epigram, "Much suspected by me, / Nothing proved can be." While at Woodstock, Elizabeth outwitted her foes by countering their suspicions with inward suspicions of her own. The Windsor epigram confronts Elizabeth's fear of being plagued by the inward suspicious thoughts that both tormented and protected her at Woodstock and that recurred, to her consternation, whenever she faced a potential betrayal.[9] By writing the Windsor epigram and suggesting that Dudley (or whoever the poem was intended for) was the object of her suspicion, Elizabeth was expressing her own suspicious or mistrustful thoughts. That's precisely what makes this brief little posie at once so multi-faceted a piece of writing and so intriguing an outward and visible sign of Elizabeth's inward preoccupations. But, one might well ask, was it fair for Elizabeth to admonish her private lyric audience for a quality of mind that she herself shared, and that her own behavior may well have provoked? If Dudley's schemes incited Elizabeth's suspicions, she had herself given him good reason to be suspicious: after all, she had been showering attention on Heneage and encouraging the Archduke to come to England to meet her. Upon learning that Dudley had been trying to provoke her jealousy by flirting with the Viscountess, Elizabeth "was in a great temper and upbraided him." Their reconciliation, complete with tears (or "bleared eyes") on both sides, reaffirmed their mutual affection. As de Silva's account illustrates, Elizabeth herself had behaved badly, but she was not wont to apologize. If, as the signature suggests, Elizabeth wrote the epigram to confront and work through her anger, the implicit acknowledgement—both to herself and to her private lyric audience—that her own inward, suspicious mind had led her to behave in an "ugly" way probably helped bring about a reconciliation.

Since the poem neither attributes "the inward, suspicious mind" to any particular individual nor addresses the private lyric audience directly,

9. Given the verbal similarities and the knotted signature, it is tempting to think that this epigram was also written when Elizabeth was at Woodstock; however, the only Psalter she had was in Latin (Manning 161), and she was not allowed to communicate with anyone whom she would have addressed as "Your loving mistress."

Elizabeth may have originally written the poem about Dudley but not for Dudley; however, it seems more likely that she was thinking about how it would strike him because the abstract language is a tactful way of admonishing him without criticizing him directly. The choice of the penultimate verb, "nor yet so ugly half can be," suggests that "the inward, suspicious mind" is a danger to beware, a condition, unlike a crooked leg or a deformed body part, that "can be" resisted if it cannot be entirely avoided. While the poem raises objections that "can be" made in the past or future, its formal structure, when read along with the "loving" signature, implies that Elizabeth is no longer as "offended" as she "seemed to be" before writing the epigram. In the autograph copy the rhyme words appear at the beginning of lines 2 and 3, and in the middle of line 4. Elizabeth was not a professional scribe. Perhaps she simply miscalculated the space needed, but the result is interesting nonetheless. Like the mirror text written on the window at Windsor, the outer deformity of the apparently unrhymed lines conceals an internal pattern that the poem invites the reader to discover. Despite appearances, there is an inner harmony that secretly links Elizabeth and her private lyric audience together, much as the internal rhymes transform the four and a half line sentence into a quatrain.

Although questions about the signature and the date remain, the remarkably close correlation between the language of the poem, events at Windsor in August 1565, and Elizabeth's ongoing concerns about Dudley, make it highly likely that this was indeed the obscure sentence Elizabeth wrote in a book at Windsor. If Elizabeth wrote the poem in her French psalter when she "semed to be much offended" with Leicester as Burghley notes, the pointed critique of the epigram's final lines, tempered by the loving signature, could have been a pivotal intervention in the historical situation: a way of telling Dudley (without recommencing the quarrel) that his attempts to manipulate and deceive her by pretending to be in love with the Viscountess of Hereford were uglier than any sort of physical deformity, but that she was ready to forgive him as long as he didn't make it a regular habit of mind. If so, the epigram would have served a dual function: at once gentle admonition and tacit apology, it offered a face-saving rhetorical strategy that made reconciliation possible.

When we reconsider the epigram as a whole, the apparent dichotomy between physical and mental traits becomes a continuum that interrogates the very distinctions upon which the poem rests. This larger hermeneutical challenge pivots on the word "ugly" which alludes back to the physical deformity of the previous images, even as it anticipates the morally offensive loathsomeness of "the inward, suspicious mind." The "bleared eye" refers initially to someone whose eyes are inflamed with infection or swollen with tears; upon rereading, the "bleared eye" also refers proleptically to someone who is mentally blinded or deceived by mistrust (as both Dudley and Elizabeth were temporarily). Similarly, "[n]o part deformed out of kind" evokes, first of all, a body part twisted out of its natural shape, but in retrospect, it also describes a part of one's mind or character that is "deformed out of kind"—deformed as a result of birth, or family, or a manner that is natural or habitual to a person, or an obsession with a single part of a much larger problem—a mind haunted by the kind of anxieties that troubled both Dudley and Elizabeth in August 1565 and throughout their courtship. Even "[t]he crooked leg" begins to look less straightforward, embodying the twisted movements of an "inward, suspicious mind," suggesting that the gestures of obeisance (for crooking the leg was a synonym for bowing) are marred by his inward suspicions.[1] The penultimate line suggests that the distinction between body and mind is a matter of magnitude rather than kind: "[t]he inward, suspicious mind" is related to but much worse than any of those previous traits because it encompasses them all, perverting all one's actions and distorting all one's perceptions, even at times causing physical ailments. As the literal and figurative meanings merge, the "bleared eye" begins to perceive—even as it comes to symbolize—just how easily the process of perception, judgment, and interpretation "can be" distorted by distrust and deceit. Thus even if the epigram is rooted in events at Windsor in August 1565, it transcends them.

The exchange of lyrics between Walter Ralegh and the Queen provides another example, probably the best example, of the way in which Elizabeth's poetry moves from historically situated lyric dialogue, designed to resolve a private disagreement or misunderstanding, to literary and intellectual critique. The dialogue begins with Ralegh's lyric to the Queen in which he fashions himself as a noble knight errant, the allegorical figure of sorrow, who has searched the heavens and earth, armed with sighs and tears, trying to rescue his "Love," his "princess," his "true fancie's mistress," from "fortunes hands."[2] Ralegh's lyric is so carefully veiled in allegorical abstractions that it is impossible to know, on the basis of the poem alone, exactly what provoked his complaint that "Fortune hath taken thee way . . . Fortune hath taken all by takinge thee." These huge and rather vague claims take on real weight when we remember that Ralegh was an ordinary gentleman who became an extraordinarily wealthy and powerful courtier due to the Queen's personal favor. Based on the date of the manuscript, May argues convincingly that the poetic exchange almost certainly took place in the first half of 1587 when Ralegh's position as Elizabeth's preeminent favorite was challenged by the rise of the Earl of Essex.[3] But whatever the exact circumstances, Ralegh's poem is courtly, coterie verse, addressed directly to the Queen, written in the hope of regaining Elizabeth's favor.

Ralegh's poetic persuasion had its desired effect, for Elizabeth's lyric response reassures him of her continuing affection and regard:

> Ah silly pugg, wert thou so sore afrayd?
> Mourne not my Wat, nor be thou so dismaid;
> It passeth fickle fortune's powre and skill
> To force my harte to thinke thee any ill.

The intimate, teasing banter, the opening question which invites an answering response, the affectionate terms of endearment, "pugg" and "Wat" (Elizabeth's pet name for Walt), and the reference to "my harte," instantly

---

1. I am grateful to Donald Stump for suggesting this alternative reading.
2. I quote May's carefully edited text of this poetic exchange (*Elizabethan Courtier Poets* 318–19) because the version of Elizabeth's response selected by the editors of the *Collected Works* is missing a line.
3. For further information see the introduction to May's *Elizabethan Courtier Poets*. As Tennenhouse explains, "the poetic fiction presumes that the lover is a victim through the accident of birth or class, and not through some fault or error on his part" (240).

dissolve the distance Ralegh bemoans, implying that the lyric dialogue is part of an intimate conversation that predated Ralegh's complaint and that will continue after Elizabeth's reply. The adjective "silly" has an intriguing range of sympathetic and critical meanings (deserving of pity; defenseless; weak, sick; lacking in judgment; weak or deficient in intellect; foolish; poor; of humble rank) which encapsulate Elizabeth's complex response to Ralegh's poetic plea.

Ralegh has traditionally occupied a more important place in English literary tradition than Elizabeth, so it is not surprising that his poem has received more attention and regard than hers, and perhaps that is appropriate since he originated the lyric form and argument that Elizabeth adopted and recast. Stephen Greenblatt, who finds "something vast and heroic in [Ralegh's] sorrow," does not take Elizabeth's poem seriously. "From heroic love and despair," Greenblatt writes, "we descend to reassuring but demeaning pleasantries" (58). I don't think Greenblatt does Elizabeth's poem justice, for "[t]he question that he frames in all but words / Is what to make a diminished thing" (Frost, "The Oven Bird" lines 13–14). Instead, I want to argue that Elizabeth's deflationary rhetoric constitutes a witty and withering but nonetheless affectionate critique of Ralegh's conventional poetic persona, disingenuous rhetoric, and contradictory reasoning.

The very fact that Elizabeth takes the trouble to match Ralegh's poem, thought for thought, quatrain for quatrain, is a tribute not only to his place in her imagination and regard but also to the seriousness which she accorded his rhetorical strategies and lyric form.[4] Elizabeth reuses in order to interrogate many of Ralegh's rhymes. Yet the initial rhyme words, "afrayd" and "dismaid," do not appear in Ralegh's poem; they disclose what Ralegh hoped to conceal. His poetic complaint is motivated not by the elevated Petrarchan sentiments of his opening couplet ("My live's Joy and my sowle's heaven above") or the heroic suffering Greenblatt admires in the following stanzas ("Ded to all Joyes, I onlie Live to woe") but by much less noble and impressive emotions: fear and dismay.

Alluding to the Woodstock epigram on fortune, Ralegh attributes his loss of favor not to Elizabeth herself but to Fortune, that blind goddess whose arbitrary acts neither recognize nor reward "vertue right." Elizabeth reminds Ralegh that her earlier epigram resisted fortune's power and prayed God to punish the guilty and free the innocent: "No fortune base, thou saist, shall alter thee; / And may so blind a wretch then conquer me? / No, no, my pug, though fortune weare not blind / Assure thie selfe she could not rule my mind." The blunt, straightforward diction, softened by the endearing reassurances ("my pug," "assure thyself"), asserts Elizabeth's powerful independence of mind and reminds Ralegh that his rise at court was due not to fortune but to Elizabeth's appreciative recognition of his intelligence and wit.

To show that her thoughts and actions are no more controlled by "fickle fortune's powre" than her feelings and attitudes are controlled by Ralegh's words, Elizabeth offers a detailed and thoughtful critique of Ralegh's logic.

---

4. May comments, "Elizabeth's response, carefully coordinated with Ralegh's lines, develops its own remarkably tender, coaxing tone" (122). I agree that Elizabeth is at once attentive and "tender," but I think the tone is more trenchant than "coaxing."

By wallowing in self-pitying pride ("And onlie love the sorrowe Due to me") and pledging allegiance to sorrow ("Sorrowe hencefourth that shall my princess bee"), Ralegh betrayed his own initial protestations of love and loyalty to Elizabeth ("my Love," "my princess"). Worse yet, having described Elizabeth as "my live's Joy," Ralegh's lyric takes an invidious pleasure in proclaiming Elizabeth's subjection to fortune: "And onlie Joy that fortune conquers kings, / Fortune that rules on earth and earthlie things." From Elizabeth's point of view, this is not only disingenuous, it is also insulting and "silly" or foolish. Ralegh concludes his poem by boldly proclaiming, "No fortune base shall ever alter me"; but as Elizabeth's reply implies, fortune has already altered him, turning his witty, incisive intelligence to self-pitying fear and irrational despair.

The heart of Elizabeth's poem is a discriminating, measured critique of fortune's power which implies that Ralegh's logic—both his initial premises and his conclusion—is pretentious, dishonest, and internally inconsistent. Here, as in the Woodstock epigram, Elizabeth carefully weighs the extent and limits of fortune's power:

> Fortune I grant *somtimes* doth conquer kings,
> And rules and raignes on earth and earthlie things,
> But never thinke that fortune can beare sway,
> If vertue watche and will her not obay. (my emphasis)

Elizabeth's active verbs give vertue the power Ralegh denied it. While Ralegh's poetic persona wallows in self-pity and refuses to take responsibility for his situation, his imagery and rhetoric offer an implicit critique of Elizabeth's wisdom and judgment: "With wisdome's eyes had but blind fortune seen," Ralegh claims, "Then had my love my love for ever bin." When you stop to think about it, this is really presumptuous, as Elizabeth's response pointedly reminds Ralegh. Just because she is "Thie Love, thie Joy," that doesn't mean *he* is *her* love or joy. As a courtly poet addressing a private female lyric audience, he cannot control her response to his poem. As a courtier addressing his Queen, he is certainly free, if he wishes, to declare his love for her in poetry; however, it behooves him to remember, poetry of courtship, whether amorous or political, depends for its success upon an answering response.

Having begun with a series of questions, Elizabeth ends with a series of imperatives that urge Ralegh to show some spirit and wit: "Plucke up thie hart, suppresse thie brackish teares." Elizabeth's directive speech acts command their own answers, for she is undoubtedly in a position of power over Ralegh. Her poem culminates in a performative speech act: "The lesse afrayde the better shalt thou spead." Elizabeth clearly has the power to make it so by saying so. Her playful, teasing language not only laughs at Ralegh's self-aggrandizing, self-indulgent sorrow, it also offers an astute literary critique of his conventional Petrarchizing: "But must thou neads sowre sorrowe's servant be, / If that to try thie mistris jest with thee."[5] Elizabeth's impatience with "sowre sorrow" and her offer to "jest with thee"

---

5. The awkward demonstrative pronoun "that" alludes to the key moment in Ralegh's argument—"And onlie Joy that fortune conquers king"—where a syntactical sleight of hand transforms joy from a noun to a verb, betraying Ralegh's own initial claim that Elizabeth herself is "my live's Joy."

suggests that Ralegh could make both his courtship and his poetry more effective if he replaced his weary, woebegone abstractions with some fresh imagery, colloquial diction, and incisive, spirited wit.

As we have learned from the Woodstock epigrams, Elizabeth's poems are generally written not only to clarify and articulate her own thoughts and feelings but also to make an impact: to shape or alter the immediate situation; to inform and sway the private lyric audience. Even when Elizabeth was as powerless as a future monarch could be, she realized that poetry "can be" a means of action. When she became queen, poetry became not only admonitory but also performative and efficacious, for she was clearly in a position to make it so by saying so. Throughout her reign, Elizabeth I continued to write poetry, or to deploy the rhetorical strategies of poetry, whenever the situation demanded not only blunt assertion but also inference, discrimination, deft persuasion, and discreet intervention. Elizabeth's poems expose and conceal, threaten and cajole, edify and deride, placate and stonewall. They not only reflect the private circumstances that comprise the poem's dramatic situation; they also assess and alter the historical situation. Elizabeth developed rhetorical strategies in her poetry which she then translated into other, more explicitly political modes of speech and writing. The prophecies and warnings developed in the Woodstock epigrams reappear in her early parliamentary speeches, even as they find their way into later proclamations directed against Catholic insurgents. In her public speeches as in her private negotiations with foreign ambassadors, courtiers, and suitors, whenever she was faced with a particularly nettlesome political situation, Elizabeth used the rhetorical figures described in Puttenham's *Art of English Poesie*: "*Enigma*, or the Riddle," when "[w]e dissemble againe vnder couert and darke speaches"; *Amphibologia*, "the *ambiguous*, or figure of sence incertaine"; "the Courtly figure *Allegoria*, which is when we speake one thing and thinke another" (196–98, 267, 196).

Although the letters, speeches, and prayers far outnumber the fifteen poems contained in *Elizabeth I: Collected Works*,[6] the significance of Elizabeth's poetry far outweighs its volume. Elizabeth wrote poems that are more masterful and intricate than they may seem, and she encouraged or inspired her subjects to write some of the most powerful, complex, witty, and multifaceted poetry in the English language. Like many of the greatest Elizabethan lyrics, Elizabeth's poems move from enigmatic epigrams, coded posies, and witty self-dramatizations to abstract meditations on fortune, justice, and the very process of interpretation itself. Even in the few short poems examined here, Elizabeth mastered many of poetic tropes and rhetorical strategies that were later used so brilliantly by Sidney, Spenser, Shakespeare, and Donne: sharp, colloquial speech and deeply personal feeling; epigrammatic wit and ironic critique; enigmatic ambiguity, multiplicity of meaning, and veiled references intended to mean different things to different members of her private lyric audience; abstract moral judgment and hermeneutical self-reflexiveness. Perhaps that is why, when Mary Sidney dedicated the Sidney psalter "To the Thrice-Sacred Queen Elizabeth," she posed her ultimate tribute as a rhetorical question: "For in

---

6. This tally does not include the twenty-seven stanzas written in French around 1590, which may or may not be a translation.

our worke what bring wee but thine owne?" By then, the answer was self-evident: "What English is, by many names is thine." Elizabethan English was the Queen's English.

Works Cited

Bell, Ilona. *Elizabethan Women and the Poetry of Courtship*. Cambridge: Cambridge UP, 1998.

———. "Elizabeth I—Always Her Own Free Woman." *Political Rhetoric, Power, and Renaissance Women*. Ed. Carole Levin and Patricia A. Sullivan. Albany: State U of New York P, 1995. 57–82.

Bradner, Leicester. *The Poems of Elizabeth I*. Providence: Brown UP, 1964.

Burghley, William Cecil. *A Collection of State Papers . . . 1542 to 1598*. Ed. Samuel Haynes. 2 vols. London: W. Bowyer, 1740–59. Rpt. Ann Arbor: U of Michigan P, 1991.

Calendar of Letters and State Papers Relating to English Affairs Preserved Principally in the Archives of Simancas. Ed. Martin A. S. Hume. 4 vols. London: Her Majesty's Stationery Office, 1892–99. Rpt. Nendeln/Liechtenstein: Kraus, 1971.

Doran, Susan. *Monarchy and Matrimony: the Courtships of Elizabeth I*. London: Routledge, 1996.

———, ed. *Elizabeth: The Exhibition at the National Maritime Museum*. London: Chatto & Windus, 2003.

Dunlop, Ian. *Palaces and Progresses of Elizabeth I*. New Haven: Yale UP, 1993.

Elizabeth I. *Collected Works*. Ed. Leah S. Marcus, Janel Mueller, and Mary Beth Rose. Chicago: U Chicago P, 2000.

Frost, Robert. "The Oven Bird." *The Poetry of Robert Frost*. Ed. Edward Conery Lathem. New York: Hold, 1969. 119–20.

Greenblatt, Stephen. *Sir Walter Ralegh: The Renaissance Man and His Roles*. New Haven: Yale UP, 1973.

Heywood, John. *Gunaikeion*. London, 1624.

Manning, C. R., ed. "State Papers Relating to the Custody of the Princess Elizabeth at Woodstock in 1554." *Norfolk Archaeology* 4 (1855): 133–231.

Marotti, Arthur F. *Manuscript, Print, and the English Renaissance Lyric*. Ithaca, NY: Cornell UP, 1995.

May, Steven. *The Elizabethan Courtier Poets: The Poems and Their Contexts*. Columbia: U of Missouri P, 1991.

Puttenham, George. *The Arte of English Poesie*. Kent, OH: Kent State UP, 1970.

Sidney, Mary. *The Triumph of Death, and Other Unpublished and Uncollected Poems*. Ed. G. F. Waller. Elizabethan & Renaissance Studies 65. Salzburg, Austria: Institut für Englische Sprache und Literatur, U of Saltzburg, 1977.

Starkey, David. *Elizabeth: The Struggle for the Throne*. New York: Harper Collins, 2001.

Summit, Jennifer. "'The Arte of a Ladies Penne': Elizabeth I and the Poetics of Queenship." *The Mysteries of Elizabeth*. Ed. Kirby Farrell and Kathleen Swaim. Amherst: U of Massachusetts P, 2003. 67–96.

Tennenhouse, Leonard. "Sir Walter Ralegh and the Literature of Client-age." *Patronage in the Renaissance*. Ed. Guy Fitch Lytle and Stephen Orgel. Princeton: Princeton UP, 1981. 235–58.

Thurley, Simon. *The Royal Palaces of Tudor England*. New Haven: Yale UP, 1993.

GEORGE P. RICE, JR.

The Speaker and the Speeches[†]

> She shall be, to the happiness of England,
> An aged princess; many days shall see her,
> And yet no day without a deed to crown it.
> —Shakespeare, *King Henry*, VIII, iii

*   *   *

The very great majority of [Elizabeth's] utterances was intended for an immediate audience and is exemplified by talks opening or closing sessions of Parliament; one, the "State of the Nation" speech of 1569, was designed to be read throughout the country by many individual speakers, in the queen's name. Several of the addresses are those of a monarch advising with her senate, proposing or disposing the ordinary business of rulership. A few, however, were delivered upon occasions of great pith and moment— the Tilbury speech of 1588 and the Golden Speech of 1601. Still others were ceremonial in content and purpose, spoken to groups of citizens or university students. A third classification includes remarks between Eliza-beth and foreign diplomats, conducted by the discussion method.

It is impossible to assess the accuracy of most of the talks. There are many for which more than one version is available. Occasionally an address was preserved verbatim by being recorded in the notes of a collector like John Stow, who reported Elizabeth's speech to Parliament when it rose in 1585, or by the chaplain of the Earl of Essex who jotted down [a] version of the Tilbury speech * * *. There are instances, too, of copies being made from a printed version in the hands of a court personage. Although a system of short-hand was known, there is no evidence that the several clerks of the Com-mons were able to produce identical accounts of the minutes of that House. It is reasonable to assume that complete accuracy even for the most reliable of the versions offered here cannot be established. They are probably most accurate for the general ideas, less so for the broad rhetoric, and least so for the precise phraseology of her diction. Contemporary accounts do afford, however, a general sense of the spoken style of the period.

How were the queen's speeches prepared? To what extent did they rep-resent her ideas and her choice of language? Did she encourage assistance from her advisors with regard to composition and delivery? Here again very little certainty can be established, though probabilities suggest them-selves. It is known that Elizabeth wrote some of her state papers in her own hand. For example, one collection of her correspondence with James

† From *The Public Speaking of Queen Elizabeth* (New York: AMS Press, 1966), pp. 42–59. Reprinted by permission of Columbia University Press.

VI shows thirty-two letters so indited; six others are signed by the queen, but are written in another hand. No drafts of speeches in Elizabeth's own hand are known to this writer. Common sense would dictate that the topics of speeches dealing with important state affairs would receive careful consideration by the queen and Cecil. The employment of an amanuensis was common; Elizabeth undoubtedly had the services of such a person. Thomas Windebank, clerk of the signet in 1568 and of the privy seal in 1598, assisted the queen as copyist for her translation of Boethius during 1593. It is altogether likely that he and others like him took Elizabeth's dictation on state papers and for speeches; such drafts, in whole or in part, would then have passed along to Cecil for final checking. The latter's approving initials are found on the lower right-hand corner of certain state papers which survive. A few of the queen's addresses, in some scholarly opinion, were written *in toto* by Cecil for Elizabeth's delivery. A few were, of course, impromptu, and occasionally in a foreign tongue, as exemplified by her Latin rebuke to de Ialines in 1597; others were read by the queen, seated, either from notes or a manuscript.

Usually the audiences which heard Elizabeth were fairly intelligent; their reactions ranged from strongly critical (when they heard her in Parliament on marriage and succession) to awe and admiration (when she spoke at the universities). Large groups of illiterate hearers were exceptional and were found only in the background of civic occasions or during an emergency such as that of 1588. The size of the audiences varied very greatly. Most of the speeches in Parliament were delivered to the combined Houses; these taken together did not number much over five hundred, but to this must be added hundreds of spectators. Groups at Oxford and Cambridge were larger; when Elizabeth delivered her Latin farewell to Oxford in 1566, some eighteen hundred persons were in attendance. Over fifteen thousand troops were in camp at Tilbury in 1588 when she spoke there, though only a small proportion of them must have been able to hear her. Sometimes the audience consisted of a score or so of members of the privy council; often her diplomatic conversations were conducted in dialogue with ambassadors, with only a few attendants on hand.

The overwhelming majority of the formal speeches were in English or in Latin; there is a reference to a brief talk in Greek at Oxford, where the Greek professor had greeted the royal visitor in that tongue and had received her thanks in the same language, but no version of a verbatim report has been found by the writer. There are numerous references to the queen's fondness for French and Italian, of which Maitland's reports are evidence, and it is noted by him that on occasion of conversations with foreigners Elizabeth raised her voice above normal pitch as though to assure herself of hearers beyond her immediate circle.

The queen's estimate of what she owed to her station manifested itself by the pomp and circumstance which surrounded a royal procession to Parliament on Tuesday, January 12, 1562, at eleven o'clock in the morning. She was preceded by nobles, guards, and judges, the trumpets she liked so well sounding loudly. Elizabeth herself rode on horseback, richly garbed. When the assemblage reached the Parliament room, the lord chancellor took his place to the right of the vacant throne reserved for the later appearance of the queen. In front of him sat the spiritual lords and directly before them but still to Elizabeth's right were the places of the judges. Temporal lords were seated on the south side to the left of the throne. Immediately to its left was the station of William Cecil in his official capacity of principal secretary to the queen. Marquesses, earls, and barons were ranged before him in that order from the throne. Before the monarch's chair was the woolsack and farther away but in a line with the throne were the masters in chancery. Far off in the distance the several clerks sat at their tables to record proceedings, a situation which did not contribute to accuracy of the reports when a speaker's voice was low or muffled. The speaker of the House of Commons, the serjeant-at-arms of that body, "black-rod," and the members of the lower house crowded together just outside the bar. When all was in readiness, Queen Elizabeth emerged from her privy chamber and entered the room to seat herself in the accustomed place. Three or four ladies placed themselves near her. Parliament was ready to begin.

It is no exaggeration to say that the mature Elizabeth brought to the rostrum the happy combination of natural endowment and careful training needed for success in public speaking. She possessed high intelligence, disciplined firmly by able professors such as Ascham and Grindal. Ascham believed her intellectual abilities equaled the best at the universities. The queen herself set a high premium on the extent of her learning. "I am supposed," she told Parliament in 1585, "to have many studies, but most Philosophical. I must yield this to be true, that I suppose few, that be no Professors, have read more." Professor Neale, among modern scholars, judged she had a "remarkable precocity of intellect."

The preparatory studies of the Princess Elizabeth were pursued with industry and discrimination and emphasized in particular the province of rhetoric and its classical antecedents. A letter of Ascham to his friend Sturm, dated April 4, 1550, from St. John's, affords authoritative insight into her accomplishments at sixteen. She could speak French and Italian with facility equal almost to her English and wrote accurately and easily in Latin, moderately so in Greek. She was, moreover, a skillful musician upon lute and virginals, and wrote a fine hand. In the company of her chief tutor she read almost all of Cicero and the greater part of Livy. Translation from the Greek Testament was a regular part of her morning's schedule of studies. Her readings in eloquence included selections from the orations of Isocrates and from the tragedies of Sophocles. Elizabeth had also looked into St. Ciprian and the "Commonplaces" of Melancthon during the years 1548–49. Her Cambridge professor noted that "she likes a style that grows out of the subject" and that she was fond of "modest metaphors." It was during these years, then, that she laid the solid foundations of her linguistic skills, especially Latin, and developed the taste for reading which made history her favorite subject. Nor did her interest in reading and translation of classical authors halt when she became monarch. The youthful rendering of *Mirror of a Guilty Soul* had companions which were the result of more mature occupations. At a late age, she translated Boethius' *De Consolatione*, Sallust's *De Belle Jugurthino*, and the larger portion of Horace's *De Arte Poetica*, together with a little treatise of Plutarch's *De Curiositate*. She essayed similar tasks with parts of Seneca's *Epistles*, Cicero, a play of Euripides, two orations of Isocrates, translated from Greek to Latin a comment on Plato, and the *Meditations* of the Queen of Navarre which she turned from French into English. There was also a dialogue from the Greek of Xenophon. In all of these pursuits it seems likely that Ascham's famous "double translation" method was used. Competent scholarship finds much fault with the taste and accuracy of Elizabeth's work as a translator, but the wonder is that with manifold cares of state she found time and inclination to do so much with foreign tongues.

This study has produced no evidence that Elizabeth ever received instruction in delivery. Ascham, however, was interested in what today is called voice and diction. It is possible that he applied some of his precepts to her training. In the *Scholemaster* he had recommended that speaking should be "not troubled, mangled, and halfed, but sound, whole, full, and able to do [its] office; as a Tongue, not stammering, or over hardly drawing forth words, but plain and ready to deliver the meaning of the mind."

*   *   *

A foreign observer noted that Elizabeth spoke with her voice pitched high and at a rapid rate of speed. Willcock suggests that personal peculiarities in pronunciation are sometimes preserved in spellings found in letters and other documents. Upon this ground it may be supposed that Elizabeth's speech was characterized by saying "sojer" for "soldier," "summat" for "somewhat," "swarve" for "swerve," "skars" for "scarce," "wacking" for "waking," and "vacabond" for "vagabond."

An examination of the texts will indicate that Elizabeth's public utterance was marked by logical reasoning through close argumentation. She had the faculty of determining the status of a particular controversy, as she demonstrated in the discussions with Maitland in 1561, and of sticking to it with great tenacity. She was quick to adjust to situations of which she was a part and able to identify herself with her audience in a speedy and effective manner. One may cite her gracious conduct toward the lord mayor of London and his fellow citizens in 1558, her winning ways with the students at Oxford in 1566, and the considerate and skillful handling of the parliamentarians during her valedictory of November, 1601. She displayed, moreover, a remarkable consistency of design in her addresses. She wanted peace and security with honor for her people; this idea recurs again and again, and in speeches of all types. Whatever contributed to this end found favor with her and what opposed it was frowned upon. She spoke primarily from a sense of duty, realizing that occasions make demands necessary. The subject matter of many of her speeches to Parliament was unpopular to the listeners, but this consideration never deterred the queen from saying what she believed needed to be said. Even in lighter moments at the universities she was really meeting the popular expectation and demand when she rose to say a few words, although she must have taken some personal delight on such occasions. The ideas expressed in the speeches reflected the queen's state of mind sincerely in the very great majority of instances. The basic theses referred to are repeated over and over again. With one or two well-remembered exceptions, such as the unfulfilled promises to the students at Oxford and to the troops at Tilbury, the queen's words were forerunners of her actions on such great concerns as marriage, succession, war and peace, domestic repose, education, prerogative, and the like. Certain broad principles of public conduct found expression in her speeches, some of them exceedingly revealing and personal to the speaker. Englishmen knew Elizabeth felt that the good ruler lives for his people, that peace and prosperity were the goals needful for the common good, that she wanted their love and loyalty, that glory achieved through foreign conquest was far from her design, that she would defend their island home to the last man and ship.

When one applies the three traditional tests to determine the integrity of her ideas, he concludes that her intellectual resources in terms of native capacity and excellence of training were outstanding; he realizes that a combination of nature and nurture enabled her to demonstrate the logic of her arguments in formal Parliamentary speech as well as in the cut-and-thrust of conversation pieces; he becomes aware that her practical wisdom was exemplary. Few projects involving prestige, men, or money were begun without being thoroughly explored.

The bases of Elizabeth's propositions in argument were rooted deeply in the accepted intellectual and emotional sanctions of her countrymen. She stressed love of country, loyalty, reverence for religion, obedience, the wisdom of the ancestors, respect for precedent, and freedom from foreign oppression. The evidence cited for specific support of these contentions was drawn from history, both classical and contemporary, personal experience, and a fund of well-developed common sense. There are few references to the Bible or to the classics. Elizabeth's fondness for deductive reasoning is revealed, but she did not neglect pains to assure that examples were adequate to the inferences drawn from them, as in speeches of 1561, 1564, and 1566. She used definition sparingly but effectively, as demonstrated in 1588 in the speech to the troops: "I know I have but the body of a weak and feeble woman, but I have the heart and stomach of a king." That she possessed a highly developed ability to use comparison and contrast is indicated in the speech of 1561; in it she also uses some of the "modest metaphor" mentioned by Ascham. Her facts are generally, but not always, dependable. Statistics have little place, save for occasional references to the budget. The queen supports her contentions with tersely stated arguments and amplifies them with skillful exposition, though the role of exposition is subordinate to that of argument in most cases. The seriousness of purpose of most of the speeches prevented the display of that wit and humor so characteristic of Elizabeth in private conversations. With the exception of some well-timed humor in the speech at Oxford in 1566, the reader will search in vain for evidences of attempts to move an audience to laughter.

A functional appraisal of her ideas rests upon three considerations. How accurate and powerful were her conceptions in terms of their utility to the society she headed? Elizabeth gauged well the insular point of view of her people and estimated accurately the relation of her resources to the part England had to play on the stage of European politics. She was accurate in her appraisal of her own role, too. She knew what her people wanted and, when she could, she provided it for them. Since her insight enabled her to voice with great fidelity the aspirations of her countrymen, it is to be expected that the wisdom and general popularity of her ideas gained acceptance most of the time. The verdict of history has supported the judgments of Elizabeth in so far as they were concerned with the maintenance of the state; it has also shown her lack of foresight in her design to perpetuate the autocratic control she exemplified so well for so long. The political and social fabric of England was changed during Elizabeth's tenure of office without her being fully aware of the process and what it portended.

What value is assigned to emotional appeal in the queen's talks? It seems reasonable to judge that Elizabeth's emphasis upon logical argument leaves to pathetic proof an important but subordinate position. She was the teacher and leader of her people; she was not often called upon to win support by stirring their emotions. Her attitude was authoritative, her words those of a person who had only to command in order to be obeyed. Yet the strong nature of Elizabeth was not without expression of an emotional sort in some of her addresses. She assessed wisely the expectations of the men who heard her at the universities, at Tilbury, and at her farewell to power. But these were the exceptional utterances. An analysis of her emotional mode of persuasion shows little awareness of need to adapt to the age levels of varying audiences or of their sex. On the other hand it does show her mastery of the subject under discussion, her desire to awaken audience awareness of the common political, social, and religious bonds which united speaker and hearers. A keen sense of the tone and temper of particular occasions is manifested; even in full maturity, there is modest self-appraisal in speeches to the students on her second visit to Oxford. In general, the most direct adaptation of pathetic proof is found in the exordium and in the peroration of a particular speech. There is no evidence of simulated passion. Motivation of audience moved along traditional channels: self-preservation, respect for personal rights and property, power, reputation, affections and sentiments, and curiosity. Men are moved by appeals to patriotism, fear, social responsibility, expediency, personal loyalty to the queen as the embodiment of national aspirations. It would seem that Elizabeth regarded emotion as auxiliary to the process of persuasion by the manner in which she relates new beliefs to old beliefs already held and accepted. For example, in 1566 she asserts that religion is a strong bond between her and the subject. Again she is proudly English and hence declares her right to share a common national heritage.

Ethical proof in discourse is shown by the moral character of the speaker, by her good will toward the audiences, and by the practical wisdom embodied in her suggestions. On all of these counts Elizabeth rates superior rank. The public character of the queen is exemplary. Her speeches indicate a desire to show herself as she really is, neither better nor worse in learning, wisdom, or ambition than the facts warrant. There is a consistent effort to reveal good-will toward particular audiences and toward Englishmen in general. Beginning with her assertion of 1558 that "no will in me can lack" to do good, she proceeds to utilize every opportunity to declare her benevolence toward the subject. The practical wisdom of Elizabeth is revealed in scores of ways: the careful planning of policy, the selection of wise and honest counselors, the cautious scrutiny of the budget, the insight with which she balances one probability against another in the realm of international affairs, her systematic examination of the qualifications of potential consorts.

There is manifest also an intelligent awareness of the importance of association of speaker with what is virtuous and elevated. Her name and office are associated with "the safety and quietness of you all." God is with her and watches over England. Elizabeth acquires also the advantage of modest praise bestowed upon herself and her cause. "I will be as good to you as ever queen was to her people." And this rhetorical device is reversed with telling effect upon her enemies. As she grew older, the queen called upon authority derived from her years and successful experience. There is finally her ability to meet the standard tests of practical wisdom: she is fundamentally a woman of common sense; she acts with tact and moderation in submitting demands to her Parliament; she is ready with merited praise and alert to take the sting out of criticism with affectionate reminders of her love of the realm and its people.

Ready insight into Elizabeth's rules for governorship can be achieved by exploring the intellectual and emotional sanctions invoked between 1558 and 1601: the safety and peace of the realm is the prime concern of the monarch; divine guidance assists the righteous ruler in her official duties; the common welfare takes precedence over every other concern of the queen, including her personal aims and desires; there must be good will between the queen and her people and it should be evidenced by both sides in suitable fashion and upon frequent occasions; the nation is the "husband" of the queen and the ring she wears is proof of this relation; treaties between England and other states must be mutually beneficial if they are to be observed; a ruler must be governed by the highest ethical considerations originating from obedience to divine and natural laws; English policy is one of peaceful expansion, but the implications of the Mosaic law will not be forgotten; laws must be upheld; a prince's word is sacred and must never be in doubt; the law must be administered by due process without favor to persons or interests; a proper prince admires wholesome learning and does his best to recognize and reward it within the bounds of his realm; wise men avoid undue praise for reasons of modesty and in order to avoid the evil consequences of flattery; dissimulation is an evil which ought to be avoided in intercourse between persons and states; it is not wise to examine all actions too closely for the purpose of finding fault; goods and ships of neutral nations may be seized if they are known to be carrying cargo for enemies of the state; all benefits come from the hand of God and the queen is His regent on earth; she is charged with the ultimate task of rendering Him an accounting of her purposes and actions; the rules governing the conduct of monarchs and of private persons differ; rulers of states are very much in the public eye and must control their actions accordingly; the preservation of personal and national honor is worth every sacrifice; the administration of justice is an exalted responsibility; unnecessary strife among nations is foolish and should not be countenanced; the responsibilities of kingship are great and sometimes onerous; the privileges of a queen should be exercised freely and without criticism.

Elizabeth was sometimes an auditor and now and then a participant in rhetorical games and exercises intended for instruction and amusement. She was fond of a game called "Questions and Answers." Once, as judge, she decided against Leicester on the topic, "Which was the more difficult to erase from the mind, an evil opinion created by a wicked informer, or jealousy." At the universities or in discussions at court she was called upon to listen to serious philosophical disputation, controversial or suasory, sometimes in Latin. Among these propositions were the following: "An licent in Christiana respublica dissimulare in causa religionis";[1] "An disseniones

---

1. Whether it be lawful in a Christian commonwealth to feign in the cause of religion.

ciuium sint respublicae utiles";[2] "An, ob mundi senectam, homines minus-
sunt heroici nunc quam olim";[3] and "An anima cuiusuis praestantior anima
alterius."[4]

Enough reports of her casual conversation remain to stamp Elizabeth as
a witty and gracious speaker who could be winning and tactful or cutting
and satiric at will. When she was at Oxford in 1566, she greeted the aged
canon of Christ Church with, "We have heard of you before, but now we
know you." But to the presumptuous Polish ambassador who aroused her
invective in 1597, these words were spoken: "And concerning yourself, you
seem unto me to have read many books, but books of princes' affairs you
have not attained unto, and are further ignorant what is convenient
between them." She closed with the blunt instruction to "take your rest."
A long conversation on a difficult matter such as the status of Mary with
regard to the succession showed Elizabeth to advantage as a debater in
1561. There in the cut-and-thrust of question, answer, objection, and
weighing of evidence, she displays a keen mind, a quick alertness to raise
the vital issue, a persistence in pursuing it to the logical conclusion, and a
remarkable facility to make the most of argument favoring her point of
view.

Elizabeth's high position, her personal popularity, and the chivalrous
deportment of courtiers, scholars, and officials generally toward her combined to elicit praise of her speeches to the degree one might expect. It is
too much to hope that some critic-judge in the audience ever went home
and put on paper his sincere reaction to a royal speech, in terms of the
rhetorical and psychological devices used during delivery, together with a
composite opinion solicited from representative citizens who listened. It
was apparently a practice of the queen to appear somewhat coy at times
and to make it necessary for her courtiers to plead with her for a speech.
It took the combined efforts of the Spanish ambassador, Leicester, and
Cecil to get the Oxford speech in 1566. The speech at Tilbury in 1588 was
"saluted with Cries, with Shoutes, with all Tokens of Love, of Obedience,
of Readinesse and Willingnesse to fight for her."

Elizabeth, it may well be assumed, pleased her audiences and she generally said what they wanted to hear and said it in a way they understood.
She had a fine sense of timing, would look over her audience carefully
before speaking, and surrounded herself, especially for parliamentary
addresses, with all the panoply of power.

In the early years of her rule Elizabeth did not like to speak publicly;
inclination, sex, and tradition were all against it, and so it fell frequently to
the lot of Nicholas Bacon to speak in her stead. She told Parliament in
1566 that she "had not been used, nor love to do it in such open Assemblies; yet now remembring, that commonly Princes' own words be better
printed in the hearers memory, than those spoken by her Command," she
did speak with increasing effectiveness and frequency. Although Coke
might please her by quoting a queenly opinion during his speakership of the
Commons in 1593, Elizabeth did not hesitate to indicate with brutal
bluntness when a speaker or his views did not please her. She seems to have
been in an impatient mood during the 1592 visit to Oxford. Dr. Westphaling,

2. Whether the disagreements of citizens are useful to the state.
3. Whether, on account of the age of the world, men be less heroic now than formerly.
4. Whether the soul of one man be more excellent than the soul of another.

bishop of Hereford, had made a tedious oration at the end of the disputations and the queen had sent twice to him to cut short his remarks. The
unfortunate clergyman could or would not do so, and the queen left without giving her own address. And Thomas Smith, orator of the University,
was informed when he, too, offended by speaking too long on the heroic
qualities of mankind. Too much adulation in speech also displeased her.
An arbitrary attitude was displayed toward discussion in Parliament at times.
In 1566 the speaker of the Commons, presiding over debate on the question of marriage and succession among his colleagues, received a special
command from her to discontinue the debate. Again, in 1571 the presiding
officer of the Commons interrupted proceedings to recite orders from the
queen to act and speak more briefly. Penalties for incurring her wrath could
be severe. Freedom of speech among the people and even within the
precincts of the Parliament meant speaking on topics and along lines
approved by the queen and her advisers. To her it did not imply the right to
talk freely and sincerely on whatever subject came to mind. It would take
another half century of struggle between royalist prerogative and Parliamentary privilege before the Commons could make good such claims.

The ultimate judgment on Elizabeth as a public speaker is that she used
speech as a useful tool in government for informative rather than per-
suasive ends. On one or two occasions, such as the Spanish invasion and
the final meeting with her Parliament, Elizabeth rose to heights of eloquence. She alone in England possessed on these occasions the requirements for the greatest and highest use of the art: complete freedom of
utterance, the existence of a political crisis of magnitude, audiences
which were responsive and, in Parliament, intellectually alert, and finally,
she had the good fortune to be born in an age in which the development
of the English language favored good speaking and writing. Her speeches
stress ethical rather than intellectual accountability toward her hearers.
She brought to her task an exceptional educational background and a
tremendous grasp of what was going on around her. Her concept of herself as speaker was predominantly that of a user of a social tool rather
than a stylist who addressed herself alike to contemporary audience and
to posterity. She was close to her audience in feeling and sympathies; she
was very English; she exemplified great personal force and vigor. That she
possessed what is today called a good understanding of the psychology of
public speaking is beyond debate. Her intellectual and emotional sanctions are those of her time and achieved, as she intended, a wide range of
acceptance among her people. Her themes were those for which taste and
cultivation had fitted her to address with at least ordinary success. She
had the assistance of able men as advisors as to the lines of action she
might propose. In the discussions and speeches relating to her potential
marriage, at least, she shows herself an intellectual person as well as an
emotional woman at grips with a problem in the various stages of its
development and solution. Her ultimate attitude toward her audience is
that of the benevolent despot who is confident in her own political powers and acumen. Expediency in the great majority of the speeches is the
important factor. Her success is limited by her time: the difficulty of communication, the low educational level of the masses of the people, the
infrequent Parliaments; by her own imperial isolation from many of
those who might have useful criticisms to make; by dangerous trends

which called for secrecy or for prompt action without the benefit of extended public discussion. She is fully conscious of the force and direction of public opinion and makes definite attempts to mold it, and even adapts herself to it at times when it appears to be stronger than she had originally supposed. Her style is intensely personal though on a plain level, with the exception of the two great orations upon which her reputation as a speaker rests primarily. Serious preoccupation with the cares of state did not often allow her leisure to prepare speeches as she might have wished. Thus, her public speaking was largely incidental and lacked in its architectonics the polish which her fine learning and well-developed discernment might have provided in happier circumstances.

In sum, the chief value in Elizabeth's speeches is historical rather than personal; they are informative to a degree in what they do *not* say as well as in what is said. But he who reads her verbal fencing with Maitland knows that he is in contact with an able forensic speaker; when he reads the Tilbury and Golden Speeches, he realizes that on those two occasions Elizabeth represented herself at her royal best and through them added luster to the annals of English eloquence.

THE PROGRESSES AND ENTERTAINMENTS

J. E. NEALE

[The Annual Round of Entertainments]†

* * * No Prince has been a greater courtier of the people, nor any actress known better how to move her audience to transports of love and admiration. Save for a fleeting crisis like that over Dudley, Elizabeth's mind was ever fixed on popular favour, at first as an art of government, and later as a profound emotional satisfaction.

The opportunities of showing herself to the people were numerous, for the Court was constantly on the move. Greenwich, Whitehall, Richmond, Hampton Court, Windsor: there was not a year but the Queen could often be seen, like some very human and approachable goddess with her train, going by river or road from one of these palaces to another, or visiting other royal houses or private homes in the near neighbourhood of London. The City was afforded an annual autumn spectacle on the return of the Court to Whitehall, where Christmas was ordinarily kept. It became a ceremonial occasion, when Mayor, Aldermen, and Citizens in their rich finery met the splendid royal procession, and to mutual greetings of 'God save your Grace!', 'God save my people!' welcomed their sovereign back to town. In 1570, after the Northern Rebellion, the anniversary of Elizabeth's accession, November 17th, which had before then been celebrated with ringing of bells, was made a day of national thanksgiving and festival, and continued throughout the reign to be one of the great days of the year. It was revived in James I's reign, as Elizabeth's name came to connote the peak of national greatness, retained much of its emotional significance for a hundred years after that, and still left its traces during another century.

† From *Queen Elizabeth I* (London: Jonathan Cape, 1958), pp. 205–206.

On this day young courtiers displayed their manhood and wit before thousands of spectators, running at tilt in the tilt-yard at Westminster, with all the pageantry and extravagant devices, part of the romance between them and their Queen. After that, preparations were made for the plays and masks that marked the high season of festivity, the twelve days from Christmas on.

Londoners, naturally, had the lion's share of Elizabeth's favours. She kept them bewitched, for it was a secret of power to hold this key to the kingdom. But for those who could not come to City or Court, there were the annual royal progresses. These were the Queen's summer holidays, when, combining business with pleasure, she took the Court on a month's or two months' perambulation through the country, staying at some royal manor or claiming the ready hospitality of the gentry or towns. She loved them, as she had reason to do, for they satisfied her healthy desire for activity and change of air and surroundings, and offered supreme opportunities to her genius in winning the hearts of the people; and if they allowed little or no respite from the business of being Queen, that was no disadvantage, for her work was the very breath of life, and she never seemed to lose her gusto for it.

* * *

MARY HILL COLE

[Politics on Summer Progress]†

Every spring and summer of her 44 years as queen, Elizabeth I insisted that her court go with her on "progress," a series of royal visits to towns and aristocratic homes in southern England. Between 1558 and 1603, her visits to over 400 individual and civic hosts provided the only direct contact most people had with a monarch who made popularity a cornerstone of her reign. These visits gave the queen a public stage on which to present herself as the people's sovereign and to interact with her subjects in a calculated attempt to keep their support. While all Renaissance monarchs of necessity traveled, the progresses of Elizabeth were both emblematic of her rule and intrinsic to her ability to govern. These visits provided the settings in which Elizabeth crafted her royal authority. In their expression of her role as sovereign queen, the progresses reflected the strengths and limitations of Elizabeth's personal monarchy.

The progresses of Elizabeth I reveal much about the queen's agenda, her priorities, and her character. During four decades, the queen committed her financial resources to the maintenance of the court on progress. That these funds came from a fiscally conservative monarch, not known for largesse, heightened the significance of this royal investment: in Elizabeth's judgment, the burdens of travel were worth its rewards. The heart of the progresses was the blend of politics, socializing, and ceremony that enabled the queen to accomplish royal business on the move while

† From *The Portable Queen: Elizabeth I and the Politics of Ceremony* (Amherst: University of Massachusetts Press, 1999), pp. 1–5. Copyright © 1999 by the University of Massachusetts Press and *The Portable Queen* by Mary Hill Cole.

satisfying the needs of those courtiers, townspeople, and country residents who welcomed her into their communities. These groups, always changing in their membership and motives, pursued their own local and individual agendas within the larger national arena created by the traveling court now suddenly available to them. For hosts, royal visits became occasions to fan local pride and woo favors from their powerful, momentarily accessible guests. At the center of the crowd was a female sovereign who embraced the visit's turmoil and pageantry for the flexibility they offered. For the queen, these progresses satisfied her needs—personal and political—by creating ceremonially rich moments of dialogue that advanced royal goals and diminished ministerial interference. No wonder she kept moving.

Through her intentional wanderings, the queen made conscious choices about her destinations that reflected her perception of the political and diplomatic scene. Her progresses brought the queen into the homes of both her favorite courtiers and those in disgrace, such as the duke of Norfolk, for whom the private visit might erase past indiscretions and return them to favor. Trusted ministers and old friends had their privileged position marked by frequent or lavish royal visits. Elizabeth recognized that the power of her queenly presence and the symbolism attached to the crown made the progresses useful in matters related to her prerogative. The queen saw such issues—the succession, marriage, war, diplomacy, and religion—as properly belonging to her, and traveling provided occasions for her to communicate her views on these matters. Her military duty to defend the kingdom, which her fellow kings fulfilled in invasions, battles, and wars, Elizabeth carried out by crafting bellicose ceremonies that expressed England's power. Visiting ports such as Bristol, Southampton, Portsmouth, and Dover let her inspect the defenses in the fortified towns. These civic visits, with their martial pageants and mock battles, conveyed an impression of English military strength to foreign rulers. Standing on English soil, she fought her international battles.

In matters of religion as well as war, the progresses helped the queen exert her prerogative. In her travels, Elizabeth encouraged religious conformity by setting the correct example and then pressuring her subjects to abandon their resistance to the established church. The vestments controversy, for example, drew the queen to the two universities, where her presence brought the scholars, at least temporarily, into outward conformity. One of her steps against unlicensed preaching involved visits to Bristol and Canterbury so that the wayward people could see their religious governor in all her royal splendor and thereafter mend their ways. Bolder methods characterized her visit to Ipswich, where the angry queen issued a ringing denunciation of women residing on the cathedral grounds and demanded obedience to her injunctions to vacate. But she proved willing to tolerate occasional Puritan activity when the controversy threatened the local stability. In East Anglia in 1578, for example, her concern for religious conformity yielded to her concern for harmony, and she turned the religious issue into a political one that she could finesse. By publicly rewarding her conformist hosts, no matter how marginal or nominal their obedience, and by reversing the anti-Puritan policies of the bishop, the queen recognized that peace in the counties was worth some increased Puritan activity. Even recusant hosts entertained the queen, as Elizabeth chose to validate their loyalty and by example to draw them into conformity with her national church. Her progresses reminded observers and participants of the ceremonial authority of the queen in matters of religion.

Thus, in a variety of ways Elizabeth made her progresses part of a government that existed as an extension of her royal authority. Beyond the matters of royal prerogative, her travels brought the people into contact—visual, physical, or indirect—with their monarch in an overt solicitation of their support. Her public entertainments, speeches in welcoming towns, and open travel through the countryside allowed people to form an impression of Elizabeth as accessible and successful. As propaganda, the progresses fostered an appealing image of the queen that won her the goodwill so necessary to her longevity and success as a monarch. This image was often more important than the reality: the demonstrable popularity of Elizabeth, the sense that she had a secure tenure, carried her through the rough spells that came more frequently in her later years. Her popularity implied a consensus, real or imaginary, which in turn created a base of support for the last Tudor.

The extensive participation of her hosts in the progresses indicated how central to her rule was this interaction with hundreds of her subjects. Increased access to the queen enabled hosts to solicit favors and enhance their local prestige through such occasions of hospitality. In her later years, as her ministers and household grew reluctant to suffer the inconvenience of travel and dissatisfied courtiers and hosts looked with self-interest toward the arrival of the next monarch, willingness to entertain the queen waned, but Elizabeth still could make a progress if she chose. Compared to hosts in the 1570s, later reluctant hosts had become more vocal about their feelings, but the queen always had hosts ready to open their doors as she made her last long journeys in the 1590s. The tradition of hospitality and the opportunity for rewards created a general willingness among hosts to entertain the queen, who continued through her reign to see progresses as central to her government and to her dominance of the court.

The progresses enabled Elizabeth to learn about local concerns and offered her subjects opportunities to solicit the queen. The civic visits in particular brought the queen face to face with petitioners who voiced grievances to their sovereign. Local officials asked the queen for help in strengthening the civic economy, especially the harbors, markets, and industries, as well as in adjudicating local disputes. A royal visit fed civic pride and, her hosts hoped, civic prosperity. The energetic receptions from the towns matched the queen's pleasure in visiting those communities so important to her governance.

*   *   *

This study, then, places the progresses in the sixteenth-century world of politics and images, where the queen and her hosts exchanged ceremonial messages that advanced their own agendas. People who entertained the queen sought favors or turned that access itself into a statement about their status and reputation in the locality. For Elizabeth, going on progress reiterated her central position in the country and in the court. The constant disruption of court life inherent in her progresses generated a climate of chaos, I would suggest, whose effect was to keep the queen at the center of everyone's attention, as courtiers and hosts focused on welcoming, entertaining, and petitioning her. Elizabeth's travels inconvenienced every member of the court and hurt her treasury, but as queen she found power in the turmoil of an itinerant court and in a ceremonial dialogue with her subjects.

* * *

ZILLAH DOVEY

[Managing the Royal Entourage]†

The Queen enjoyed her summer expeditions. She and her Court were used to moving up and down the Thames—they shifted regularly between the palaces of Greenwich, Whitehall, Richmond, Hampton Court, Oatlands and Windsor—and the mechanics of removal were matters of routine. Furnishings, hangings and so on were regularly taken down, brushed and aired and put up somewhere else; then the rooms vacated could be cleaned. But in the summer the Queen like to get away from London and show herself to her people. Progresses were primarily an exercise in image-making. To establish and maintain her personal popularity among her people was one of the Queen's major—and successful—policies. As the Spanish ambassador reported in 1568, 'She was received everywhere with great acclamations and signs of joy as is customary in this country whereat she was exceedingly pleased.'[1] Wherever she went the church bells were rung and crowds gathered. To the ordinary people, though not always to her Council and courtiers, she was accessible and patient. She could, said Thomas Churchyard, always an admirer, 'draw the hearts of the people after hyr wheresoever she travels'.

So Elizabeth made a summer progress whenever she could, which meant in almost every year until the end of the 1570s. She travelled less often and less far as she got older and times more dangerous, but she went off again in the last four years of her life. In 1600, when she was sixty-seven and her ministers tried to dissuade her from moving on from the palace of Nonsuch, she retorted that the old could stay behind if they wished, the young and able would go with her,[2] and in what was to be her last summer, two years later, it was reported that 'notwithstanding her earnest affection to go her Progress', out of compassion for her entourage, she had agreed to take heed of the unseasonable weather.[3]

In the course of her long reign she covered a good deal of southern England, sometimes staying within the Home Counties but often travelling as far as Southampton, Bristol, Worcester, Warwick and Stafford. Such journeys served not only to give many people a once-in-a-lifetime chance to catch a glimpse of their sovereign but also to show the Queen herself

† From *An Elizabethan Progress: The Queen's Journey into East Anglia, 1578* (Gloucester: Sutton, 1996), pp. 1–6. Reprinted by permission of Zillah Dovey and Sutton Publishing Ltd.
1. *Calendar of Spanish State Papers*, ed. Martin A. S. Hume (London, HMSO, 1894), vol. II: *Elizabeth 1568–79*, pp. 50–1.
2. Arthur Collins, *Letters and Memorials of State* (2 vols, London, T. Osborne, 1756), p. 210.
3. Edmund Lodge, *Illustrations of British History, Biography and Manners* (3 vols, London, 1791), vol. III, p. 135.

something of the more distant parts of her realm. However, that said, she never went to the south-west or further north than Stafford—or out of England.

With her had to go her Court, the environment in which she lived and worked wherever she was. The basic necessities of her life, and of course of all those who went with her, were the responsibility of the Lord Steward, the chief officer of the Household. He was in charge of the expenditure through the Treasurer of the Household, the Controller and the Cofferer (who made up the 'Board of Greencloth') and their Clerks of the Counting House, all of whom travelled with the Queen. The services needed to maintain the Court were provided by twenty Household departments, each with its particular job—the bakehouse, the larder, the spicery, the kitchen, the cellar, the buttery, the laundry and so on. When the Court moved, all of these went too. The other, external, side of the Queen's life, her handsome lifestyle, was headed by the Lord Chamberlain. With the Vice-Chamberlain and the Treasurer of the Chamber, he was responsible for the Chamber. His staff of ushers, grooms and pages looked after her accommodation, her wardrobe (with her ladies and her maids), her entertainments and her travels. Her guards, her chaplains and the court musicians were also Chamber personnel. All these too had work to do wherever the Queen might be.

Also during a progress affairs of state had to continue as usual; it was by no means a holiday. The Queen with her Council constituted the government of the country and where she was they had to be. The Council consisted of between seventeen and twenty chief officers of state and of the Court, and a varying but limited number of these moved between palaces or across the country with her. Their business had to be conducted on the wing, their meetings held as necessary wherever they and she happened to be. The Queen was rarely present; on all subjects of sufficient importance her views would be sought and reported by one or other of the councillors. Their decisions were recorded and submitted for her approval. Then instructions would be sent to ambassadors abroad or to local authorities at home, sheriffs of counties, Justices of the Peace or others who had commissions to carry out particular assignments. The Council met frequently and a steady stream of visitors, messengers and couriers flowed to and fro, however temporary their bases. It is remarkable how rarely letters from Council members mentioned their travels; usually the only indication is the superscription 'from the Court at' such and such a place or, often, 'from the house of' so and so. Everyone involved was accustomed to this peripatetic way of conducting affairs.

Nevertheless, for her ministers and officials and their servants, progresses must have been uncomfortable and inconvenient. They involved a considerable effort in organization and administration, even if the procedures were more or less established routine. A great many arrangements had to be made in advance, but plans also had to be flexible and were often altered because of the Queen's inclinations, the weather or, most importantly, the plague. When finally they set off, for most of the several hundred people who accompanied the Queen, the great Court and state officials, all with their own staff, working and living conditions were considerably less satisfactory than in their quarters in and around the royal palaces.

Travelling was difficult and slow even on the main highways, and cross-country roads were little more than tracks made by use. In 1555 the maintenance of the roads had become the responsibility of each parish, but they were required to work on them only four, later six, days a year. At best they cut down the undergrowth and filled in the pot-holes with stones, and the results were patchy and unreliable. Complaints about poor conditions continued to the end of the century. Even in 1607 there was no attempt at drainage. There were few hedges or fences, so roads could change course to avoid obstacles.

A man on horseback was the fastest form of travel, changing horses at intervals on the way (royal couriers had warrants to commandeer horses). Even so, on a long journey he would cover little more than 4 miles an hour. Goods went by packhorse or wagon. Coaches had come into use in the mid-sixteenth century but, though the Queen did sometimes use one on progress, they were uncomfortable on good and impossible on the many bad roads. Similarly a litter carried by men or horses was suitable only for the town or city.

Mostly, the Queen and her retinue rode, but they were preceded or accompanied by an immense baggage train, between 200 and 300 two-or four-wheeled carts drawn by teams of six horses, carrying everything necessary for the Queen, the Court and the Council—bedding, furniture, hangings, clothing, plate and kitchen equipment, documents and office requirements. The main body moved 10 to 12 miles a day.

The Queen went from house to house, in the Home Counties sometimes staying in a palace of her own but more often in the houses of her subjects, from national figures to local gentlemen. Her usual practice was to arrive before supper, towards the end of the afternoon or in the early evening, and to leave after dinner in the late morning. Alternatively, on a longer stage, the start might be earlier and she would stop for dinner at another house—or perhaps, if none was suitable, a picnic—on the way. The ministers and courtiers who travelled with her were lodged in other houses in the neighbourhood. Inevitably, there were disputes over their accommodation, which could not always be appropriate for the status of everyone. The rest of the officials and their servants put up wherever they could, in inns or even in the tents which were always carried to provide stabling for the horses and housing for their keepers. When stationary, the whole train was scattered over a considerable distance.

Naturally, the Queen gave the final word, but the planning of a progress was left to the Privy Council, which included the major officers of the Court. Two of these, the Lord Chamberlain and the Vice-Chamberlain, were responsible for the detailed preparation and the day-to-day management.

Early in the year likely houses where the Queen might stay along the route were inspected by Court officers, who reported on their suitability or otherwise, looking particularly at the outlook and surroundings and whether there was plague in the area. The Queen's lodging places were selected for their comfort and convenience (the houses where she stopped for dinner were not inspected in the same way). According to feudal tradition, the sovereign, from whom in principle all manors were ultimately held, retained the right to occupy any subject's house, so the Chamber officers simply took over wherever it was thought best for the Queen to stay; the owners, if they were not rich or important figures, were disregarded.

Later, other officers, the harbingers, went ahead looking for lodgings for the Court and Council and their staff.

Finally, the Queen's 'gestes', itineraries in the form of lists of lodgings, were published at Court (without precise dates) and copies sent to mayors of towns and Lord-Lieutenants of counties, who had to confirm that there was no plague in their areas. Towns and villages were ordered to provide stocks of food, fuel and fodder, which would then be bought up by the Purveyors, who organized all the regular supplies for the Royal Household. A Yeoman Purveyor and his deputy were assigned to an area with a Royal Commission 'to take up and provide for us and our name for the only provision of our household in all places.'[4] The commission went on to refer to 'our reasonable prices', which were fixed by the Queen's Clerk of the Market, who also checked the local weights and measures to see that the Purveyors were not cheated. The system was unpopular and the Purveyors were frequently accused of corruption; areas which were regularly visited by the Queen could be exempted. Similarly, although the Queen's stables never held less than 220 horses, transport could, when needed, be commandeered by the Yeoman Cart-taker and his three grooms, who were supposed to pay 2*d* a mile.

Nearer the time, prospective hosts were told the approximate date of the Queen's arrival. What they were expected to provide varied according to their circumstances; for minor country gentlemen of modest means, it would be only a clean, empty house, the family having moved out at least from the main rooms. Supplies would be provided through the purveyance system or paid for by the Counting House, though no doubt the machinery of reimbursement moved slowly. The Queen herself was unwilling to cause her subjects too much expense, though naturally more was expected of the wealthy and ambitious, who were anxious to display their loyalty.

A few days before the Queen was due to arrive, a team of eight to ten men would come to make arrangements for the Queen's accommodation. They were led by a Gentleman Usher, whose regular job was the management of the Queen's public rooms and control of all who entered and left. A little later an officer of the Wardrobe of Robes with a smaller team would come 'to make reddye the office of Her Majesty's roabes'. They all came, whether the Queen was staying several days or stopping for dinner, the length of their stay varying according to the expected length of hers. If she was to stay for her usual two nights, the ushers normally took six days and the Robes men three. If she was coming only for dinner, the ushers would stay two days and the Robes one. On progress the ushers created appropriately furnished rooms to match those in her palaces: an audience or presence chamber which was open to anyone with a right to be at Court (everyone, however important, had to have permission both to come to Court and to leave) and was where entertainments were held; a privy chamber, where the less public business took place; and a withdrawing chamber or bedchamber, which was private to all but the Queen's ladies

---

4. Allegra Woodworth, 'Purveyance for the Royal Household in the Reign of Queen Elizabeth', *Transactions of the American Philosophical Society* new series, XXXV, 1 (1945) p. 28.

and a few favoured courtiers. Each room or suite of rooms led into the next and the doors between them were guarded.

A good deal of careful planning had to be done before the ushers set off. Each had to arrive at a house in good time to get all ready, stay until the Queen left, then take down and pack up everything his team had brought and move on. There had therefore to be several teams on the road. While the Queen was at one house, attended by one team, another would have gone ahead to prepare the next stopping place. Often a single team worked on two houses, one where she would be staying and another about half-way to the next, where she would have dinner on the day she left. They would then move on to another house, which the Queen was due to reach some days later. The Wardrobe officers followed a similar, though less regular, leapfrogging pattern.

At least in the main stopping places, there also had to be a room where the Council could meet and an adjoining one for their clerks, who brought the 'paper pennes inke waxe and other necessaries' for their work. In the royal palaces and perhaps in some other great houses, the Keeper of the Counsell Chamber also saw that it was embellished with 'bowes' (branches) and flowers.

There might also be a visit by the Controller of Works, who was responsible for the maintenance of the royal palaces and would carry out work on other people's houses as well, such as improving the door locks, if necessary.

Other officers from the Jewel House at the Tower of London brought silver plate for use at the Queen's table and to ornament the rooms she would use. Finally, the Court officers had to be supplied with money to meet their running costs and some of their clerks would bring the coin from the City of London. In spite of all the hospitality received on its travels, the Court on progress added £2,000 a year to its usual budget. Changes of plan en route added particularly to the cost, requiring supplies and staff to be redirected and relocated.

In areas where a regular royal mail service was not normally in place, special arrangements had to be made for the Council and Court to receive and dispatch their reports and instructions. Post horses were stationed every 10 miles or so along a route and were ridden from one post to the next by the courier, the horses being returned to their bases by a postboy. On routes with permanent, as distinct from ad hoc, arrangements, the letters would be carried from post to post by a rider stationed at each point who would hand over the packet to the next man and return to his own base.

All these people arriving with their horses—at least two each—had to be fed and housed while they carried out the Queen's business.

The owners of the great houses where the Queen stayed two or three days gave lavish feasts and entertainments, sometimes going to enormous lengths to provide spectacular 'shows'—and there was always a personal present for the Queen, as well as gifts for courtiers and officials. The costs were enormous and a visit could make or break a man's political career. No wonder the prospect was likely to cause anxiety, particularly among the less eminent gentlemen, even if the Queen was coming only for dinner in the middle of the day or staying for one night.

For the towns where the Queen stayed, a visit brought honour and opportunity but also demanded expenditure of both effort and money.

There were formal occasions with loyal greetings by the mayor and cor-
poration or the guilds, feasts and entertainments. The streets were
cleaned, buildings were painted, new civic gowns were made. Shows and
pageants were arranged; on some occasions, they were master-minded by
professionals sent on ahead by the Lord Chamberlain. The Queen was
always presented with a gift, frequently including cash in gold. In all it was
an expensive occasion.

   The incidental costs could be high too, with an invasion by a large number of officials, servants and hangers-on looking for gifts, bribes, and board
and lodging. Property could be damaged and objects disappear. An even
greater burden might be brought by the invaders from London in the
shape of the plague. London had by far the largest, most densely housed
population in the country and outbreaks of plague there were common.
They caused the law courts to be adjourned thirty-five times during Elizabeth's reign. The Court made every effort to safeguard the Queen's
health, but they could not protect everyone who came into contact with
their vast and varied train.

THE QUEEN'S PORTRAITS

SIR ROY STRONG

[Depicting Gloriana][†]

'For the face, I graunt, I might well blushe to offer, but the mynde I shall
never be ashamed to present'.
                              The Lady Elizabeth to her brother, Edward VI,
                   in answer to his request for her portrait, probably 1547[1]

Every visitor to Windsor Castle is familiar with the portrait of Queen Elizabeth I as a princess. Painted probably in 1546–7 for her brother Edward
VI, it depicts her as a young girl of about fourteen years of age. The pallor
of her complexion is relieved only by her fair auburn hair and her eyes,
which still possess a childlike innocence. Her dress is of simple and unos-
tentatious cut, her jewels but few; it is a picture of Elizabeth as the young
and virtuous bluestocking of whom her tutor Roger Ascham was so justly
proud. No less well known is the great canvas, painted probably in 1592,
in the National Portrait Gallery and called the 'Ditchley' portrait. The
cheeks once filled with the bloom of youth have become sunken and
rouged; the eyes have the penetration of one for whom life has been an
unceasing battle of wits; the lips are thin and mean; the face wrinkled,
almost haggard, in appearance; in short the young girl has become the
great Queen whose genius has guided victoriously the destinies of a
people for over thirty years. The painter of the first saw her as a slip of a
girl, whose future role was to be the King's sister and who would certainly
be expected to marry a foreign prince. The painter of the second approaches
her awestruck as he struggled to depict someone who had become an

† From *Gloriana: The Portraits of Queen Elizabeth I* (London: Thames & Hudson, 1987), pp. 9–45.
   Reprinted by permission of the Random House Group Ltd.
1. Janet Arnold, 'The "Pictur" of Elizabeth I When Princess', *The Burlington Magazine*, CXXIII, 1981,
   p. 303.

unmarried ruler of legendary fame, a visionary figure towering above her realm of England, an image of almost cosmic power. In a span of forty years an individual has been transposed into a symbol. To place side by side these two portraits is to pose visually the problem of the portraits of Queen Elizabeth I.

*   *   *

Portrait production

> There is no evidence that Elizabeth had much taste for painting; but she loved pictures of herself.
>
> Horace Walpole, 'Anecdotes of Painting'[2]

Any study of the portraits of Queen Elizabeth I must begin by asking why they were needed in the first place. These images of Gloriana have both a European and an English dimension, for royal portraiture is one aspect of the alliance of art and power that was of such profound significance in the Renaissance and Baroque periods. Other manifestations of that alliance include the deliberate development of state festivals in glorification of rulers, the evolution of the palace as an architectural complex and the patronage of humanist poets and historiographers to sing a dynasty's praises. It was partly by consciously cultivating all these, and thus intensifying the mystique of monarchy, that the houses of Valois, Habsburg and Tudor consolidated their sway over France, Spain, the Holy Roman Empire and England during the sixteenth century. That intensification escalated as the century drew to its close, with rulers assuming more and more of a messianic role in an age which had witnessed the breakdown of the universal Church and the advent of religious division, the discovery of the New World and the shattering of the old cosmology. Portraiture was one aspect of this massive expansion of the Idea of Monarchy, involving the dissemination a ruler's image in paint, stone, print and metal throughout the realm on a scale unheard of since Classical antiquity.

All of this came late to England, on the fringes of Europe. It began initially with the production of sets of kings and queens, c. 1515–20 designed to emphasize the legitimacy of the Tudor right to the throne.[3] This tentative interest in royal portraiture, in the main under French influence, did not assume a major role until the advent of the Reformation in the 1530s, which led to the first deliberately orchestrated propaganda programme designed to build up the crown in the face of the break with the Universal Church.[4] In terms of the royal likeness that moment was summed up in one artist and one image, Hans Holbein's full-length portrait of Henry VIII, conceived as part of the monumental wall painting celebrating the Tudor dynasty which adorned the King's Privy Chamber in Whitehall Palace in 1537. This portrait continued to be manufactured in all sizes throughout the sixteenth century and for the first time we have evidence of the production of the royal portrait, on almost factory lines, as a symbol of political loyalty. That precedent was followed both by Edward VI, whose official likeness was the work of William Scrots, and Mary I, whose

2. H. Walpole, *Anecdotes of Painting in England*, ed. R. M. Wornum, London, 1862, i. 150.
3. Roy Strong, *The English Renaissance Miniature*, London, 1983, p. 27.
4. See the same author's *Holbein and Henry VIII*, London, 1967.

unofficial court painter was Hans Eworth. When Elizabeth I succeeded her sister in 1558 she inherited a working tradition, but in her case it was to have one fundamental difference: she was never to have a court painter well paid by the crown and hence be able to sustain government control over her own image. This was a marked contrast to the French system where the Valois appointed a *peintre du roi* who had the sole right to manufacture the royal portrait. Hence the kings of France were never to run into the difficulties which perpetually beset the Elizabethan government when it came to controlling the depiction of their queen.

The saga of these problems begins in 1563 with a draft proclamation preserved amongst the State Papers.[5] Although there is no evidence that this was ever put into effect, it is a fundamental document which carried within it a considerable amount of information concerning the mechanics of Tudor state portraiture. The proclamation was designed to counter the production of debased images of the Queen until 'some speciall person that shall be by hir allowed shall have first fynished a portraicture thereof, after which fynished, hir Majesty will be content that all other payntors, or grauors . . . Shall and maye at ther plesures follow the sayd patron or first portraictur'. It is, therefore, quite specific as to the method of disseminating the royal likeness. A portrait was completed which was in some manner circulated or exhibited, so that all concerned in the production of portraits of the Queen might copy it. One may conclude that in this way pattern drawings found their way into the great portrait workshops. There was nothing new in this. It was the reassertion of a system which had previously been in operation—certainly in the reign of her sister, whose portraiture can be reduced to two patterns by Hans Eworth and Anthonis Mor.[6]

This ideal liaison between the court and the artists in the manufacture of the Queen's portraits, in strict accordance with official images or patterns, did not, in practice, work. Sir Walter Raleigh, in the introduction to his *History of the World*, records how at one period in her reign Elizabeth caused all portraits of her made by unskilful 'common Painters' to be cast into the fire.[7] Raleigh is, no doubt, alluding to the action of the Privy Council in July 1596, ordering public officers to aid the Queen's Serjeant Painter in seeking out unseemly portraits which were to her 'great offence' and therefore to be defaced and no more portraits produced except as approved by the Serjeant Painter.[8] The latter was George Gower, a descendant of the Gower family of Stettenham, in Yorkshire. He had held the post since 1581, when he was at the height of his career as a fashionable portrait painter, but he died in the August of that same year, 1596. This event was followed by a vacuum of almost two years, until June 1598, when the Painter to the Navy, Leonard Fryer, was appointed his successor.[9] In the light of this, it is difficult to speculate as to how far the Privy Council's

5. PRO, SP 12/31, no. 25. Imperfect transcripts are in *Archaeologia*, ii, 1773, pp. 169–70 and F. M. O'Donoghue, *A Descriptive and Classified Catalogue of Portraits of Queen Elizabeth*, London, 1984, pp. ix–x. See also Sir Henry Hake, 'The English Historic Portrait, Document and Myth', *British Academy Lecture*, 1943, pp. 8, 19.
6. Roy Strong, *Tudor and Jacobean Portraits*, National Portrait Gallery Catalogue, London, HMSO, 1969, I, pp. 211–13.
7. Sir Walter Raleigh, *The History of the World*, London, 1687 edn, p. x.
8. *Acts of the Privy Council*, ed. J. R. Dasent, xxvi, 69.
9. E. Auerbach, *Tudor Artists*, London, 1954, p. 147.

instructions were carried out. Richard Haydocke's fulmination against 'disproportioned and unseemelie Counterfeites' of royal and noble persons, in the preface to his translation of Lomazzo's *Trattato*,[1] reveals that the problem was no nearer solution in 1598. From this we may at least conclude that the demand for the royal likeness had by the nineties far outstripped the number that could be produced by competent artists and in line with government thinking, with the consequent manufacture of debased images of the Queen by hack artists. This abuse was a problem never satisfactorily solved under Elizabeth.

The draft proclamation of 1563 represents the first of a succession of attempts to control royal portraiture. It was designed to ensure that the copying of the official pattern was to be strictly limited to those artists who had been licensed by 'the hed officers' of the places where they lived. This solution, as far as we know, was not adopted. Over a decade passes, until November 1575, when the Painter Stainers' Company petitioned the Queen in respect of the spread of shoddy workmanship by those never trained in the art of painting, 'as well as counterfeyting of your Majesties picture and the pictures of noble men and others . . .'.[2] This was followed in July 1578 by a further petition, this time to the Lord Treasurer, Burghley,[3] and finally by a charter from the Queen herself and the establishment of a Book of Ordinances (1581), full of reforming zeal. It was hoped to eliminate unskilful painters of portraits by a renewed insistence upon the seven years' apprenticeship. Furthermore, artists were not to wander 'in and about' the streets selling portraits as they had been doing, but each finished picture was to be endorsed with the mark of the house.[4] The Painter Stainers' Company was trying to establish something of a monopoly in the field of picture-making, a venture in which they were doomed to failure, for the court often bestowed its patronage on visiting foreigners who, as far as it can be ascertained, worked outside the restrictions of the Company.

Between the Painter Stainers' Ordinances and the Privy Council order of 1596, only one attempt was made to solve the problem. This took the form of a draft patent drawn up by Gower, the Serjeant Painter, in 1584 to gain the total monopoly for himself in the production of every kind of image of Elizabeth except that in limning, which was assigned to Nicholas Hilliard. It was to cover painting on wood or canvas, engraving and woodcuts and the right to print them.[5] The patent failed to materialize but provided a pointer that the answer to the problem of the control of royal portraiture lay, not in the dissemination of patterns to London portrait studios, but in the establishment of a single court painter whose workshop was large enough to sustain the production of the royal image *en masse* at a high level. The ultimate solution, in a word, was Van Dyck.

1. P. Lomazzo, *A Tracte Containing the Artes of curious Paintinge, Carvinge, Building . . .* , trans. R. Haydocke, Oxford, 1598, Preface.
2. BL Lansdowne MS XX, no. 9. Transcript in W. A. D. Englefield, *The History of the Painter-Stainers Company of London*, London, 1923, pp. 56–7.
3. *Ibid.*, pp. 51–9.
4. *Ibid.*, pp. 60 ff.
5. BM Cotton Charter IV. 26. Transcript in F. Madden, 'Portrait Painters of Queen Elizabeth', *Notes and Queries*, series i, vi, 1852, 238. For a recent interpretation of this see Strong, *Renaissance Miniature*, 1983, pp. 84–5.

The 1563 proclamation reveals that the Queen urgently needed to sit for her portrait. As our knowledge of Elizabethan painting has enlarged it has become evident that the Queen must have sat with a remarkable regularity. The art of limning presupposes an *ad vivum* encounter which means that miniatures of her by Levina Teerlinc and Nicholas Hilliard were the result of sittings, except in instances where several versions survive.[6] Her encounter with Isaac Oliver gives us the greatest portrait ever painted of her as she approached old age and a unique example of a pattern for studio use in the production of repetitions. We have documentary evidence that she sat for Federigo Zuccaro in 1575, Cornelius Ketel in 1578 and a French painter in 1581. She probably sat to George Gower for the 'Armada' portrait and Marcus Gheeraerts the Younger's 'Ditchley' portrait is inconceivable without a sitting. That and the Oliver miniature were arguably the last and painters were kept at arm's length during the closing decade, deliberately avoiding any record of the physical decay of the sovereign in the interests of the state, promoting instead a fabricated Mask of Youth.

There is only one account of Queen Elizabeth actually sitting for her portrait, and that is by Hilliard, in his 'Treatise concerning the Arte of Limning'. This remains a document of unique importance in the understanding of the portraits' aesthetic. He had learned, he records, a great deal in his conversations with her, and when she had first sat for her portrait, presumably about 1572, she had inquired why the Italians, the best painters, did not use shadow in their work. In this she showed a total ignorance of Italian art but the knowledge of her limner was equally limited. Hilliard replied that shadow was used only by painters whose pictures possessed a 'grosser line', a feature which ill-became the art of limning. 'Heer,' he says, 'her Majestie conseued the reason, and therfor chosse her place to sit in for that porposse in the open ally of a goodly garden, where no tree was neere, nor any shadowe at all. . . .'.[7] The Queen's view coincided exactly with Hilliard's use of an even frontal light. When Elizabeth early in the 1590s tried to come to terms with the *chiaroscuro* of Oliver it was a disaster and the resulting pattern remained unmultiplied. Even the *chiaroscuro* in Gheeraerts' 'Ditchley' portrait is noticeably softened and smoothed out in the numerous versions produced by his studio. The same censorship applied even more to engravings. Evelyn, in his *Sculptura*, records that 'vile *copies* multiplyed from an ill Painting' were called in and furnished the cooks at Essex House for several years 'with *Peels* for the use of their Ovens'.[8]

The pattern process is important, in that it explains how so many different hands could produce the same face mask. No particular pattern was the exclusive monopoly of a single studio, and several may have been producing the same type simultaneously. The pattern became a studio lay figure which was periodically reversed or reattired. No certain pattern drawing of Queen Elizabeth has survived,[9] but the process is illustrated well enough by the portrait pattern of John Fisher, Bishop of Rochester, now in the National Portrait Gallery.[1] The cut-out head is covered with

6. See *ibid.*, and Roy Strong and J. M. Mussell, *Artists of the Tudor Court*, Victoria and Albert Museum Extribition Catalogue, 1983.
7. *A Treatise Concerninge the Arte of Limning by Nicholas Hilliard*, ed. R. K. R. Thornton and T. G. Cain, Carcanet Press, 1981, p. 87.
8. J. Evelyn, *Sculptura*, ed. C. F. Bell, Oxford, 1906, p. 25.
9. For a borderline case see Strong, *Tudor and Jacobean Portraits*, 1969, I, pp. 107–8 (2825).
1. *Ibid.*, pp. 119–20 (2821).

pin-pricks following the main lines of the features, so that it could be applied to panel or canvas and a tracing made by means of rubbing coloured chalk through the holes. It is a process familiar through the Holbein drawings of members of the court of Henry VIII. Around this head the artist, with the help of his apprentices and assistants, would build up the portrait. In the case of the Queen, pattern books were probably drawn upon, for the lace, for example, and the recurrence of certain dresses and jewels suggests that drawings of these too were available. For the more elaborate of the allegorical portraits, the artists must have worked in close collaboration with the poet or writer who drew up the iconographic schema. The whole process was a piecemeal one, although by the end of the reign, under the impact of what must have been a vast expansion in the portrait market, organized production would seem to have replaced the isolated artist working, perhaps, with only one or two apprentices.

The 1563 proclamation states that 'all sortes of subiectes and people both noble and meane' wished to procure the Queen's portrait for exhibition in their houses. How, may we ask, was this demand satisfied? Studios must certainly have kept a stock of royal portraits; the Painter Stainers' Ordinances show that this had even degenerated into hawking portraits of the Queen about the streets. It was more customary, however, for royal portraits to be commissioned. In the household accounts of Sir Thomas Egerton for 1597 there is a payment of £9.10s. for a portrait of Elizabeth by William Segar, Somerset Herald,[2] and in 1598–9 Hilliard agreed to paint 'a faire picture in greate' for the Goldsmiths' Company.[3] Most light is shed by the correspondence of one Charles Bradshawe with his master, William More of Loseley Park.[4] The letters, on internal evidence, can be dated to the years 1572–6.[5] They begin with Bradshawe collecting four pictures from a 'Master Wanslee' of Lambeth, after which he had gone to the house of the Lord Admiral, the Earl of Lincoln, to discover that the painter there had made the portraits of More and his wife larger than the ones he had just collected, and that of the Queen larger still. He inquires of More whether they should all be made the same size, and further reports that 'the Quense picktur . . . hath a great Dell of labor about it in Juellse and Flaunders worke'. He next writes to say that the portrait of the Queen remains unfinished and that the painter 'sayth it lacketh A Fortnites worcke'. The last letter reports the dispatch of the artist together with the portraits of the Mores to Loseley, but nothing more is heard of Elizabeth's picture. An artist who was of such status as to be in the household of one of the great dignitaries of the court is worthy of notice for he is likely to have been the poet-painter Lucas de Heere. He had fled to England in 1567 to escape the reign of terror Alva had inaugurated in the Netherlands, and Van Mander records that Lucas had been in the service of Lincoln, painting a great costume gallery in his house. De Heere returned to the Netherlands towards the end of 1576, soon after the Pacification of

2. D. Piper, 'The 1590 Lumley Inventory: Hilliard, Segar and the Earl of Essex', *The Burlington Magazine*, XCIX, 1957, p. 300.
3. E. Auerbach, 'More Light on Nicholas Hilliard', *The Burlington Magazine*, XCI, 1949, p. 168.
4. *HMC VIIth Report*, p. 667.
5. Edward Fiennes, Lord Clinton, was created Earl of Lincoln in 1572 and Master More was knighted in 1576. Miss Auerbach's dating 1572–85 is, therefore, not quite accurate nor, it should be noticed, is her acceptance of the published sequence of the letters or the association of 'Master Wanslee' with the painter in Lincoln's service ('Portraits of Elizabeth I', 198 and note 18). On the latter the letters are quite specific.

Ghent, so that he may well prove the painter of the More-Bradshawe correspondence.

These letters are the nearest approach to a backstage view of the artist in his studio in Elizabethan England. How exactly the large ones which had sprung up by the end of the reign were organized, it is impossible to say. Almost complete mystery surrounds, for instance, the workings of the Gheer-aerts and De Critz studios, which must surely have been the most productive by 1603. It is, moreover, difficult to deduce with certainty the techniques of portrait production, as one is able to, for instance, from examples of the great seventeenth-century workshops of say Van Dyck or Lely, where a gradual decadence overtakes portraits as they get farther and farther away from the original. All of this goes back to the absence throughout the reign of a court painter. In the early Tudor period William Scrots had followed Lucas Hornebolte as King's painter. No successor was appointed. Hilliard never held any official office. Gower became Serjeant Painter, and the bulk of his work lay in the maintenance of decorative painting in the royal palaces. This explains why, unlike the Valois court where royal portraiture was vigorously controlled by a succession of *peintres du roi*, Elizabeth's, in sharp contrast, emerges as such an episodic, uneven and, at times, contradictory saga.

The Queen in her Portraits

> Sir Christopher Hatton and another knight made challenge whoe should present the truest picture of hir Majestie to the Queene. One caused a flattering picture to be drawne; the other presented a glas, wherein the Queene sawe hir selfe, the truest picture that might be.
> *Diary of John Manningham*[6]

There are remarkably few descriptions of Queen Elizabeth I. These begin in 1557 with Giovanni Michiel's report to the Venetian Doge and Senate on the Princess Elizabeth's features at the age of twenty-three: 'her face is comely rather than handsome, but she is tall and well formed, with a good skin, although swarthy; she has fine eyes.'[7] This is followed by a vacuum of nearly forty years until 1596, when an Italian visitor, Francesco Gradenigo, describes her as 'short, and ruddy in complexion; very strongly built'.[8] Monsieur de Maisse, an agent of Henri IV's, refers to her in 1597 as looking old, her face being long and thin, her teeth yellow and decayed, but her 'figure is fair and tall and graceful in whatever she does'.[9] Paul Hentzner's oft-quoted description of the Queen at Greenwich in 1598 remains the most detailed contemporary account: 'her face oblong, fair but wrinkled; her eyes small, yet black and pleasant; her nose a little hooked, her lips narrow . . . her hair . . . an auburn colour, but false . . .'.[1] It is a description which one fancies harmonizes with the 'Ditchley' portrait and with Oliver's pattern miniature in the Victoria and Albert Museum.

Giovanni Michiel records in 1557 that above all the Princess Elizabeth

---

6. *Diary of John Manningham*, ed. J. Bruce, Camden Society, 1868, pp. 130–31.
7. *Relazione* of 13 May 1557, CSP *Venetian*, 1556–7, p. 1058; an earlier notice in CSP *Venetian*, 1534–54, p. 539, does not describe her in detail.
8. Letter of Francesco Gradenigo, CSP *Venetian*, 1592–1603, p. 239.
9. *A Journal of all that was accomplished by M. de Maisse*, ed. G. B. Harrison and R. A. Jones, London, 1931, pp. 25–6.
1. W. B. Rye, *England as seen by Foreigners in the Days of Elizabeth and James I*, London, 1865, p. 104.

had a beautiful hand, of which she made great display. De Maurier, in his *Memoirs of Holland*, describes how his father had watched the English Queen take off and draw on her gloves while giving audience,[2] a mannerism of which the ever-observant De Maisse took note: 'she drew off her glove and showed me her hand, which is very long and more than mine by three broad fingers. It was formerly very beautiful but it is now very thin, although the skin is still most fair.'[3] It is this vanity which may account for some of the curious poses in her portraits, where she holds one hand before her breast clasping gloves or a symbolic jewel.

De Maisse states that 'When anyone speaks of her beauty she says that she was never beautiful, although she had that reputation thirty years ago. Nevertheless,' he continues, 'she speaks of her beauty as often as she can.'[4] This was in 1597 and gives a fair impression of Elizabeth's extreme sensitivity over her personal appearance and her awareness and fear of its decay. In her portraits it is reflected in a policy of deliberate rejuvenation. This may not have reflected vanity so much as a genuine fear of the dangers inherent in dwelling on the physical mortality of the sovereign while the succession was unsettled. As a result, sometime about 1594 a government decision was taken that the official image of the Queen in her final years was to be of a legendary beauty, ageless and unfading. Such a vision contained within it an element of truth for, through the politic handling of her wardrobe and the expertise of her tirewomen, the Queen could still appear to the outside world something of a goddess. An envoy from the Duke of Württemberg states in 1592 that despite her age she could 'in grace and beauty vie with a maiden of sixteen years'[5] and an observer at the Twelfth Night Revels for 1594 muses that she appeared as beautiful to his old sight as ever he had seen her.[6] Even in her sixty-sixth year she seeemed surprisingly to one German visitor no more than a girl of twenty.[7]

The portraits are also a record of Elizabeth's famous wardrobe.[8] When in 1577 Don John of Austria granted audience to Dr Wilson, the English agent, he was shown Fulke Greville's miniature of the Queen, at the sight of which he was 'moche pleased'. He inquired whether Elizabeth dressed in the Spanish manner, to which Wilson answered that the Queen used 'diverse attires, italian, spanyshe and frenshe, as occasion served'. Don John bade the doctor send him a portrait of her dressed in the style of the court of Spain as soon as he had returned to England.[9] This conversation harks back nearly fifteen years to Sir James Melville's visit to Elizabeth, then about thirty, when on successive days she wore dresses of the different nations, in response to which Melville wisely expressed his preference for the Italian, in which the Queen displayed

2. L. Aubery, Seigneur de Maurier, *Mémoires pour servir à l'Histoire de Hollande*, Paris, 1680, p. 256 and pp. 255–6 on her desire to be praised for her beauty.
3. De Maisse, *Journal*, p. 59.
4. *Ibid.*, p. 38.
5. V. von Klarwill, *Queen Elizabeth and Some Foreigners*, London, 1928, p. 349.
6. T. Birch, *Memoirs of the Reign of Queen Elizabeth*, London, 1754, i. 146.
7. *Thomas Platter's Travels in England*, 1599, trans. C. Williams, London, 1937, p. 192.
8. The best account of Queen Elizabeth's dresses is to be found in H. Norris, *Costume and Fashion*, London, 1938, iii, *The Tudors*, ii. 484–98, 602–16; some attempt is also made in F. M. Kelly, 'Queen Elizabeth and her Dresses', *Connoisseur*, CXIII, 1944, 71–8. [A full-length study by Janet Arnold is now standard: *Queen Elizabeth's Wardrobe Unlock'd* (Leeds, 1988) [*Editors' note*].]
9. Kervyn de Lettenhove, *Relations Politiques des Pays-Bas et de l'Angleterre*, Brussels, 1890, ix. 336; *CSP Foreign, 1575–7*, p. 596.
1. *Memoirs of Sir James Melvile*, ed. G. Scott, London, 1752, p. 98.

her fair hair, 'curled in appearance naturally', confined with a caul and bon-
net.[1] Dress played an important part in sixteenth-century life, and its significance in the portraits should not be overlooked.[2] It could reflect
political alignment. When in January 1582 the full-length of Elizabeth
painted for Catherine de' Medici was displayed at the Valois court, the
ladies marvelled at the size of the pearls on her dress and noted with satisfaction that she was attired all over in the French fashion.[3] This was during a period when negotiations for the Anjou match were at their climax.
The 'Armada' portrait depicts her dressed entirely in the manner of the
French court under the last Valois, in fashions which are familiar from the
Bal du Duc de Joyeuse in the Louvre. There is also the possibility of colour
symbolism. Black and white were Elizabeth's personal colours and were
worn, for example, by her champions in the tiltyard and by dancers in court
masques.[4] One fancies that some of the more elaborate of her allegorical
pictures, such as the 'Sieve' portrait at Siena or the 'Ermine' portrait at Hatfield, in which she wears black relieved only by a little white, may be a
reflection of this. In the last years of her reign white—the colour of purity
and chastity—was widely adopted at court in deference to the Queen. The
'Ditchley' portrait is the most significant statement on the cult of white.

As for their Use

> . . . the common pictures of that Queen . . . show her in the midst, or lat-
> ter end of her government, where she appears all set out in gaudy attire;
> whereas her habit, as well as her face, was very different when she first was
> Queen.

The Rev. John Strype,
the historian, to Ralph Thoresby, 7 October 1708

Knowledge of portraits in contemporary English collections is scanty,
although most families of substance would probably have owned a portrait
of the Queen, and prominent nobles used her image as the focal point of the
great portrait collections which it became fashionable to assemble. Sir
Edward Hoby, Constable of Queenborough Castle, made her picture the
culmination of a series of portraits of the Constables of the Castle from the
reign of Edward III onwards.[5] Lord Lumley, whose collection may have
exceeded that of the Queen, possessed in 1590 one of her 'as she was
comyng first to the Crowne' and a second 'as she was the XXXth yeare of the
Reigne' (i.e. 1588). The somewhat obscure entries in the Hatfield inventó-
ries of 1611–12 hint that the Cecils may have had three or more.[6] In retro-

---

2. She is traditionally said to have sat for her portrait holding a pair of perfumed gloves which the
   Earl of Oxford brought back from Italy; John Nichols ed., *The Progresses and Public Processions of
   Queen Elizabeth, et al.* London, 1823, iii. 660.
3. Cobham to Walsingham, 22 January 1581/2, PRO, SP 78/7, no. 12.
4. *CSP Spanish, 1558–67*, p. 368.
5. E. K. Waterhouse, *Painting in Britain 1530–1790*, London, 1953, p. 25; cf. Leicester inventory in
   George Vertue, *Notebooks*, Oxford, 1930–1955, ii. 74; iv. 121.
6. L. Cust, 'The Lumley Inventories', *Walpole Society*, 1918, vi. 22. There was also (p. 15) a bust of
   her in the Great Hall (repr. p. vii) but it is not identical with that formerly at Lumley and now in
   the National Portrait Gallery, Roy Strong, *Portraits of Elizabeth*, Oxford, 1963, p. 145 (1). Hatfield
   House, Salisbury MS, Boxes A, B and D (inventories). There were three at Hardwick in 1601; Lord
   Hawkesbury, *Catalogue of the Pictures at Hardwick Hall*, 1903, pp. 40–41; two are recorded in the
   1575 inventory of Lambeth Palace; see W. Sandys, 'Copy of the Inventory of Archbishop Parker's
   Goods', *Archaeologia*, XXX, 1844, 11, 12. Leicester owned five; see C. L. Kingsford, 'Essex House,
   formerly Leicester House, and Exeter Inn', *Archaeologia*, LXIII, 1923, 46, 47, 49–50; *Notes and
   Queries*, 3rd series, 11, 1862, 224–5.

spect, this trend may be summed up by Sanderson in his *Graphice* (1658), where he states that whereas in time past loyalty had been expressed by displaying the royal arms, now it was done by the royal portrait.[7] This interchangeability of royal arms and portraits, it should be noted in parenthesis, is an important line of thought, as our study of the theory will reveal.

Portraits of Elizabeth also found their way into collections abroad.[8] An amazed Fynes Moryson records seeing Elizabeth's picture in the Palazzo Signoria in Florence in 1594.[9] On inquiry he was told that the Grand Duke esteemed the Queen for her many virtues. The Grand Duke Ferdinand was anti-Spanish and supported the armies of the Huguenot Henri IV. Most portraits, however, reached the Continent in the way of diplomatic gifts, or in connection with the numerous marriage negotiations which cover twenty or more years of the reign. These references, scattered through the diplomatic correspondence, begin in 1561 with an exchange of portraits between Elizabeth and Mary, Queen of Scots, then Queen of France. 'You know I have sent mine to the Queen, my good sister, according to my promise', Mary complained to the English ambassador, 'but have not received hers.'[1] Elizabeth was reluctant and remained so until a year later the whole matter rose to the surface again in the negotiations attending the proposed meeting of the two queens. Mary dispatched hers, followed by a heart-shaped diamond and some effusive verses by Buchanan.[2] The English Queen's reactions were less enthusiastic, but eventually, towards the end of July 1562, her picture arrived in Scotland. Randolphe, the English ambassador, on being asked whether it resembled his mistress, replied that Mary would 'be judge therof her self', to which the Scottish Queen answered 'let God be my wytnes, I honor her in my harte, and love her as my dere and naturall syster'.[3] That same 15 July that Randolphe wrote the report of his poignant audience, the English court decided to abandon the project of the interview for that year. An abortive attempt to stage the meeting in 1563 ended in failure.

Four years pass, until the summer of 1567, when an embassy bore the Queen's picture to the imperial court. The match with the Archduke Charles had been revived; never before had negotiations for the Queen's hand seemed so near completion. The embassy, ostensibly carrying the Order of the Garter to the Emperor, was a splendid one headed by the Earl of Sussex. It stopped first at Brussels, where Sussex and his company were received by the Emperor's aunt, Margaret of Parma, Regent of the Netherlands. Sussex's reception at the magnificent Burgundian court was the occasion for one of the most important pieces of evidence we have concerning the early portraits of the Queen. He reports that Margaret had:

> . . . harde so moche of Your Majestie by the Conte of Stolborg as she desired moche to see your picture, which with some travell she recovered, and for that it was drawn in blacke with a hoode and a

7. W. Sanderson, *Graphice*, London, 1658, pp. 26–7.
8. Catherine de' Medici possessed two: 'Ung petit portraict de la royne d'Angleterre enchassé d'ébène' and 'Ung autre portraict de la royne de Angleterre', E. Bonnaffé, *Inventaire des Meubles de Catherine de Medicis en 1589*, Paris, 1874, pp. 92, 128.
9. Fynes Moryson, *An Itinerary*, Glasgow, 1907, i. 322.
1. Throckmorton and Bedford to the Queen, 26 February 1560/61, P. Fraser Tytler, *On the Portraits of Mary, Queen of Scots*, 1845, p. 20.
2. *CSP Scotland, 1547–63*, pp. 603–6, see G. Buchanan, *Franciscanus et Fratres*, 1594, pp. 117–18, 177.
3. *CSP Scotland, 1547–63*, p. 588, which mentions the indisposition of the artist as the cause of the delay, pp. 608, 638–40.

cornet which she perceived was not the attire Your Majestie now used to were, she desired me, if I had your picture, that she might see it, for that I shold do her great pleasure to shewe her the picture of her whose persone she honored and loved so moche.[4]

I answered at the first that the picture commonly made to be solde did nothinge resemble Your Majestie, and forbare to answer her request untill she so earnestly pressed me as I coulde not denye the havinge of your picture, which she sawe with the Duchesse of Askott and the Countesse of Mansfelde and certen other lordes and ladyes, in whose presens Mons[r] de Maldingham affirmed it to be so like unto you as ther lacked but speche, and that he sewe Your Majestie when he toke his leave in the same attyre. The Regent with the rest affirmed they sawe thereby as moche as they had harde of your person and wis-shed they might also see and heare them selfes that they harde by oth-ers of your qualities, affirminge ther was onely one fault in you, which was with all these great giftes of God to live sole without a husbande.

Sussex is providing us with the story behind the 1563 draft proclamation, of the circulation of portraits of the Queen, attired in a French hood and a black dress, which 'did nothinge resemble' her. It certainly sheds light on Catherine de' Medici's comment three years before: 'After what everyone tells me of her beauty, and after the paintings that I have seen, I must declare that she did not have good painters.'[5] The portrait which the ambassadors were carrying to Vienna would seem to have been an *ad vivum* likeness, a true record of the features and attire of the young Queen.

By 1570 the Habsburg alliance had been abandoned in favour of a match with the French royal house. In December of that year Elizabeth declared that she would marry the Duke of Anjou, the future Henri III, and the courts indulged in an exchange of portraits. This began in March 1571 with a portrait of Elizabeth being presented to Monsieur to testify to 'the bewtie and favour' of the Queen.[6] On 3 July the Queen Mother, Catherine de' Medici dispatched a study of Anjou's face in crayons, the first of two portraits by Clouet of the future bridegroom. Catherine further wanted a new portrait of Elizabeth *en petit volume* like the one she already possessed of the Earl of Leicester. This must refer to a miniature by either Levina Teerlinc or the young Nicholas Hilliard. The picture she already had depicted Elizabeth *tout en plat*, which failed to do justice to her *si bonne grace*.[7] Elizabeth finally sent her portrait to Catherine but the delay was so great that by that time the match with Anjou had collapsed and his brother Francis, Duke of Alençon, had succeeded as the prospective bridegroom. When, however, the Queen beheld the latter's age in the inscription on his portrait, she said, it was just half of hers—nineteen to thirty-eight—and that she feared being so much his senior.[8] An abortive

---

4. Lettenhove, *Relations Politiques*, iv. 470; CSP *Foreign, 1566–8*, p. 272. I am indebted to the late Dame Frances Yates for this reference.
5. G. Lebel, 'British-French Artistic Relations in the XVI Century', *Gazette des Beaux-Arts*, XXXII, 1948, p. 278.
6. Buckhurst to the Queen, 16 March 1570/71, PRO, SP 70/117, f. 270[v].
7. *Correspondance Diplomatique de Bertrand de Salignac de la Mothe Fénélon*, Paris and London, 1840, vii. 229–31; Elizabeth's comments on the portrait, iv. 186–7; see also *Les Mémoires de Monsieur le Duc de Nevers*, Paris, 1665, i. 543.
8. Quoted A. Strickland, *Life of Queen Elizabeth*, Everyman edn., p. 326.

attempt to revive the match 'upon view of the portraiture brought by Randolphe' in 1574 ended in failure.[9]

A lull of some four years ushers a somewhat more mature Alençon, now successor to his brother's title of Anjou, on to the scene as the last of a long line of official suitors. The proceedings were prefaced by the usual exchange of portraits, both full-lengths.[1] When the French commissioners came over to treat, in May 1581, they brought with them the Queen Mother's own portrait painter, who executed a full-length of Elizabeth dressed in the French manner.[2] He remains anonymous, but he was evidently accustomed to move with some assurance in court society, for on receiving the commissioners it was reported that the Queen engaged in conversation with the painter, angling for a compliment by saying that he must depict her with a veil over her face.[3] Undated letters in the Hatfield collection reveal the ecstasy with which Anjou received each portrait: 'Je garde vostre belle pinture, qui ne se seperera j'ames de moy que par la fin de mes os.'[4] The Duke died in 1584, and Elizabeth finally came off the marriage market, making her exit in full mourning as Anjou's 'widow'.

In her declining years portraits went abroad as diplomatic gifts.[5] Sometime about 1594 she sent her picture to Henri IV's sister, Catherine de Navarre. The portrait was intercepted by Henri, who wrote to the Queen that the blame lay with her, for he had been unable to resist such great beauty. He is loth to part with it, he writes, for it is infused with some divine spirit, and he entreats her that he might be allowed to keep it.[6] We may fancy that it was some poetical Hilliardesque rendering of the Queen which had evoked the chivalry of Henri IV.

Limnings or miniatures of the Queen begin as no more than occasional pieces. Levina Teerlinc, who was not only a limner but also a Gentlewoman of the Privy Chamber, presented Elizabeth annually with a miniature of herself. These belong to a period when the miniature was still an object kept in a box, to the end that it might occasionally be perused. Sir James Melville, ambassador of Mary Queen of Scots, describes in his *Memoirs* how Elizabeth had taken him 'to her bed-chamber, and opened a little cabinet, wherein were divers little pictures wrapt within paper, and their names written with her own hand upon the papers. Upon the first she took up was written, "My lord's picture". I held the candle . . . and found

9. *CSP Foreign, 1572–4*, pp. 464–5; Strickland, *Queen Elizabeth*, p. 365; La Mothe, *Correspondance*, vi. 23, 26.
1. Dispatch of 6 November 1578, *CSP Venetian, 1558–80*, p. 587.
2. See above, p. 754 [*Editors' note*].
3. Martin S. Hume, *The Courtships of Queen Elizabeth*, London, 1904 edn, p. 240.
4. Undated letter, *c*. 1579, *HMC Hatfield*, ii. 237, 478. See also Fremyn's letter to Walsingham (9 April 1582) recording that Anjou was 'very happy and joyous at the portrait which her Majesty has sent him', *CSP Foreign, 1581–2*, p. 618.
5. In 1583 a portrait was presented to Frederick II of Denmark, *26th Report of the Deputy Keeper of the Public Records*, Appendix II, p. 56. See Auerbach, 'Portraits of Elizabeth I', p. 193, note 16. In 1587 the young Elector Palatine entreated for her portrait, *CSP Foreign, 1587–8*, p. 198. In 1598 the Muscovy Company presented the Tzar on behalf of the Queen with 'A gilt goblet bearing a stone in which a likeness of the Queen had been carved', T. Goldberg, *English Silver in the State Armoury Museum in the Moscow Kremlin*, 1954, p. 442. I am indebted to the late C. Oman for this reference.
6. *Recueil des Lettres Missives de Henri IV*, ed. M. B. de Xivrey, Paris, 1848, iv. 292–4. The letter dates from about 1594.

it to be the Earl of Leicester's picture.'[7] This was succeeded in the seventies by the fashion for carrying miniatures within jewelled lockets about the person, and from about 1585 onwards there ensued the heyday of the royal portrait miniature. That year's diplomatic correspondence contains an entreaty by a German agent for a miniature of her to wear around his neck,[8] besides a report from Lord Willoughby d'Eresby that the King of Denmark continually wore her picture within a tablet of gold.[9] Both Sir Henry Unton and Sir Robert Cecil[1] made great play in the last decade of the reign of displaying the Queen's portrait to the amorous Henri IV. On the former occasion there occurred an extraordinary incident, when Unton produced his miniature to prove that he served 'a farr more excellent Mistress' than any of Henri IV's 'and yet did her Picture come farr short of the Perfection of her Beauty'.

> As you love me (sayd he) shew it me, if you have it about you. I made some Difficultie; yett, upon his Importunity, offred it unto his Viewe verie seacretly, houlding it still in my Hande: he beheald it with Passion and Admiration, saying, that I had Reason, *Je me rends*, protesting, that he never had seene the like; so, with great Reverence, he kissed it twice or thrice, I detayning it still in my Hand.

In the end Unton was prevailed upon to part with his miniature which, he reported to Queen Elizabeth, had had more effect than all his wasted eloquence.

Documentary evidence concerning royal miniatures at home is less profuse. They, like the cameos, were highly prized as costly jewels. One such belonged to that flower of chivalry, Sir Henry Lee, a jewel known as 'the Queenes pickture', which, along with other of his possessions, was to cause a great deal of trouble to his old mistress, Anne Vavasour.[2] It was not the picture which made these items costly—the average price charged by Hilliard for a miniature was three pounds—but the setting. Lord Zouche wrote to Sir Robert Cecil in June 1598, on receiving a miniature of the Queen, that he held it to be the fairest picture in Europe: 'I would I could have as rich a box to keep it in as I esteem the favour great.'[3] This establishes that the gift of a miniature did not include a frame, a greater expense falling on the receiver. The bejewelled lockets, the rich 'boxes', were even more ephemeral than the miniatures which they contained, and only isolated examples survive. These include the celebrated 'Drake' and 'Armada' Jewels, besides that in the Victoria and Albert Museum. In each instance the case becomes a vehicle for a personal apotheosis of the sovereign in terms of allegory, symbol and motto.

'I give unto my nephew, Mr. Nicholas Bacon . . . my achate [agate] with Queene Elizabeth's picture in it, and the chaine of achate it hangs at of

---

7. *The Memoirs of Sir James Melvile*, ed. cit., pp. 96–7.
8. *CSP Foreign, 1584–5*, p. 616. See also *Correspondence of Robert Dudley, Earl of Leycester*, ed. J. Bruce, Camden Society, 1844, p. 245 for request to bestow 'her picture in a tablett', presumably a miniature, on Count Hohenloe in 1586.
9. *CSP Foreign, 1585–6*, p. 218.
1. *HMC Hatfield*, viii. 94; H. Murdin, *State Papers*, London, 1759, pp. 718–19.
2. E. K. Chambers, *Sir Henry Lee*, Oxford, 1936, pp. 314, 309.
3. *HMC Hatfield*, viii. 208.

thirty beads', wrote Sir Edmund Bacon in his will dated 1648.[4] A number of these cameos survive, some of exquisite workmanship, which accounts for the high esteem in which they were held, even in the middle of the seventeenth century.[5] The actual wearing of the royal image in cameo form was, however, specifically an Elizabethan development. The Renaissance predilection for the cameo was in imitation and emulation of the antique and the wearing of the Queen's portrait in this manner would appear to have sprung from just such an intellectual framework. It is likely that the fashion was inspired by a passage in which Pliny describes how the Roman emperors wore cameo portraits as part of their personal insignia. Cameo portraits of Elizabeth are referred to from about 1580 onwards. During a masque staged as part of the fetes for Christmas 1582, Elizabeth was presented with a rich jewel of gold set with diamonds together with her own 'phisnamy' in agate.[6] Four years later we find the Earl of Rutland expending the sum of eighty pounds on a 'brooch of her Majesties picture in an aggatt sett with 53 diamondes'[7] and in the 1587 list of royal jewels there is her portrait within 'a Tablett of golde with an Agath grauen'.[8] The same year there is a payment for an onyx portrait of her *'au vif'* to one Thomas Papillon in the accounts of the court of Navarre. Simultaneously they can be discerned in portraits of members of the court.[9] Sir Christopher Hatton, Sir Thomas Heneage, Sir Francis Walsingham, and several others indulged in such ostentation. Even Lord Burghley in the last portrait he ever sat for, as a tired white-bearded old man seated in a chair, wears a cameo of his sovereign in his hat.

Engravings and woodcuts were undoubtedly one of the most influential of all portrait forms of expression. The Bible frontispieces depicting the Queen supported by the Virtues must have been seen by almost every subject. This to a lesser extent would also be true of the woodcut letter C in John Foxe's *Actes and Monuments*, to be seen in many cathedrals and churches throughout the land, in which Elizabeth attended by the estates of the realm holds in her right hand the sword of justice. In spite of the researches of A. M. Hind, much remains to be done on the history of engraving in Tudor England.[1] This is especially true of the mechanics of the trade: how the portraits were engraved, the sources available to the artists, how far the subject-matter was deliberately organized as visual

4. *Bury Wills and Inventories*, ed. S. Tymms, Camden Society, 1850, p. 217. Cf. the will of Thomas Sackville, Earl of Dorset, 11 August 1607, where he bequeathed as an heirloom 'one picture of our late famous Queen Elizabeth, being cut out of an agate, with excellent similitude, oval fashion, and set in gold, with 26 rubyes about the circle of it, and one orient pearle pendant to the same', Walpole, *Anecdotes*, i. 189, note 2. On the progress of 1573 Archbishop Parker presented Elizabeth with a salt cellar which had 'two rich achats therein curiouslie carued, the one with the queenes image and the other with saint George killing the dragon . . .', H. Holinshed, *Chronicles*, London 1697, p. 240.

5. *The Diary of John Evelyn*, ed. E. S. de Beer, Oxford, 1955, iii. 79–80; Evelyn, *Sculptura*, p. 61; same author's *Numismata*, London, 1697, p. 240.

6. Nichols, *Progresses*, ii. 389.

7. *The Ancestor*, i, 1902, 35.

8. BL Royal Appendix 68, f. 7. I am indebted to Mr C. Blair for drawing my attention to the following entry in the Inventory of Garderobe of Robes, 27 July, 42 Elizabeth; a jewel of diamonds and rubies 'with her Majesties picture graven within a Garnett' (PRO, LR 2/121); 'an Armelet of fold . . . with a Ruby in the middest thereof cut with her Majesties picture' (New Year's Gift, 1588; BL Additional MS 5751A, f. 218ʳ–18ᵛ).

9. An attempt to assemble these is made in the Earl of Ilchester, 'Cameos of Queen Elizabeth and Their Reproduction in Contemporary Portraits', *Connoisseur*, LXIII, 1922, pp. 65–72.

1. A. M. Hind, *Engraving in England in the 16th and 17th Centuries*, Cambridge, 1952. More work needs to be done on the relationship of the engravings to contemporary paintings.

propaganda, and how the engravings were sold and distributed. As far as it concerns the Elizabeth portraits, book illustration accounts for most of the woodcuts and engravings, and it is not until the nineties that single cult images were produced for separate sale. Some of these give testimony that they were cult images in every sense of the word. An impression of William Rogers' *Eliza Triumphans* at Exeter is brilliantly coloured and much worn, and the impression of a related version, once in the possession of the French church, Soho Square, is surrounded by printers' lace and other decoration, much in the same way that an engraving of the Virgin would be adorned in a Catholic country.[2]

There is no doubt that in the 1580s Hilliard must have produced some of the designs for these woodcuts which he could even have executed himself.[3] Oliver was certainly used as the source for Crispin van de Passe's famous posthumous engraving of the Queen and, by implication, must also have been the source for at least one of William Rogers' most celebrated images.[4] More interesting is the action of the Privy Council in August 1600 ordering the calling in of engravings of Essex and other noblemen:

> There is of late a use brought up to engrave in brasse pictures of noblemen and other persons and then sell them printed in paper sett forth oftentimes with verses and other circumstances not fytt to be used. Because this custome doth growe common and indeed [it] is not meete such publique setting forth of anie pictures but of her most excellent Majesty should be permytted yf the same be well done, we have for divers good respects thought good to praie your Grace [i.e. the Archbishop of Canterbury] that you will give direction that hereafter no personage of any noblemann or other person shal be ingraven and printed to be putt to sale publiquely, and those prints that are already made to be called in, unless your Lordship shall first be made acquainted with the same, and thincke meete to allow them.[5]

In this order we are witnessing the breakdown of the cult of Elizabeth. By 1600 the royal image was having to share the stage with that of other heroes, Essex, Cumberland, Nottingham and Mountjoy.

As a footnote to this, it should not be forgotten that abroad portraits were circulated to defame the Queen. Sir Edward Stafford, the English ambassador in France, reported with alarm from Paris in November 1583 that licentious pictures of Elizabeth and Anjou had been publicly exhibited in the city.[6] The pictures were immediately suppressed and no further outbreaks occurred until 1587, when news reached Paris of the execution of the Queen of Scots. This was followed by Catholic propagandists displaying hideous portraits of Elizabeth in reply to which Huguenots set up

2. *Ibid.*, I, pl. 139 (b); Joel Hurstfield, *The Elizabethan Nation*, BBC Publications, 1964, p. 57.
3. Strong, *Renaissance Miniature*, 1983, p. 89.
4. *Ibid.*, pp. 157–9.
5. *Acts of the Privy Council, 1599–1600*, pp. 619–20. See Richard C. McCoy, '"A dangerous image": the Earl of Essex and Elizabethan Chivalry', *Journal of Medieval and Renaissance Studies*, XIII, 2, 1983, pp. 313–29.
6. Stafford to Walsingham, 17 November 1583, describes it as 'a fowle picture of the Queen's majesty sett vpp she beinge on horsback her left hande holdinge the brydell of the horse, with her right hande pullynge vpp her clothes shewinge her hindparte . . . vnder ytt was a picture of Monsieur . . . in his best apparell havynge vppon his fiste a hawke which continually bayted and koulde never make her sytt styll', PRO, SP 78/10, no. 79. The pictures were less licentious than Stafford believed, same to same, 19 November, *ibid.*, no. 82.

pictures of her in all her magnificence, accompanied by laudatory verses.[7]
Familiar as we are with the cult images of the *Diva Elizabetha*, it is easy to
forget that abroad she was not only written about but depicted as the
Jezebel of the North, the scourge of Catholic martyrs.

Ruler Image and Holy Image

> But ever at Pyrochles when he smitt,
> (Who Guyons shield cast ever him before,
> Whereon the Faery Queenes pourtract was writt,)
> His hand relented and the stroke forbore,
> And his deare hart the picture gan adore . . .
>   *Spenser, 'The Faerie Queene'*[8]

In September 1598 Queen Elizabeth was entertained by her new Master
of Requests, Sir Julius Caesar, at his house at Mitcham. The occasion was
graced by costly gifts and splendid revelry, in the midst of which a dialogue
between a poet, a painter and a musician was most prominent. The
Queen[9] encountered an artist who was engaged in painting her portrait
and holding the following conversation with a poet:

> But how thinkst thow it possible to shadowe her picture?
> As possible as for thee to number her prayses.
> Yet haue I the odds; for though I cannot expresse all her worth, yet
> so much as I can, as shall make all men wonder.
> That is as much as if I should drawe the forehead, and never finish
> the face. To bee possessd with this in thy head, *that she is a Virgin;
> that affections wayte uppon her trayne in fetters; that there was no
> vertue singuler in those kinges that meete not all in her to make one
> only absolute*, and not by art in the highest strayne to amplifie the
> rarenes and happines, is as if sondrye of my colors should lye in sev-
> erall shells, and I make no vse by my art.[1]

This dialogue suggests that the Queen's painters, like her poets, were concerned with depicting her as an object of worship. John Davies, in his lyri-
cal *Hymnes to Astraea*, written to honour the anniversary of the Queen's
accession in 1599, further suggests the difficulties with which the artist
had to contend in portraying the royal image:

TO HER PICTURE

> E xtreame was his Audacitie
> L ittle his skill, that finisht thee;
> I am asham'd and Sorry,
> S o dull her counterfait should be,
> A nd she so full of glory.
>
> B ut here are colours red and white,
> E ach lyne, and each proportion right;

---

7. J. Hooper Grew, *Elisabeth d'Angleterre, la Reine Vierge dans la Littérature Française*, Paris, 1932,
   pp. 38–9.
8. Spenser, *Faerie Queene*, II. viii. 43, 11. 1–5.
9. *Queen Elizabeth's Entertainment at Mitcham*, ed. L. Hotson, Yale UP, 1953, pp. 20–28.
1. *Ibid.*, p. 25. Vertue records a portrait of Queen Elizabeth in the possession of the descendants of
   Sir Julius Caesar, *Notebooks*, i. 101.

T hese Lynes, this red, and whitenesse,
H ave wanting yet a life and light,
A Majestie, and brightnesse.

R ude counterfaith, I then did erre,
E ven now, when I would needes inferre
G reat boldnesse in thy maker:
I did mistake, he was not bold;
N or durst his eyes her eyes behold:
A nd this made him mistake her.[2]

Such a topos was a standard one and part of the stock-in-trade of the Renaissance court poet. None the less, it would be true to say that the Elizabethan royal portrait painter was concerned, not with portraying a
likeness in the sense in which we should understand it, but with transforming a 'Rude counterfeit' into an image 'full of glory', an icon calculated
to evoke in the eyes of the beholder those principles for which the Queen
and her government stood.

How effective were the portraits of Elizabeth I? In retrospect one can
gauge their impact by the fact that it has taken a century of scholarship to
re-establish her likeness for almost the first fifty years of her life. This is a
sure indication of the success of the spectacular bejewelled icons of the last
twenty years of her reign, recording her past the age of fifty, which managed
to totally obliterate any memory and ultimately any recognition of those early
portraits in which she appears as something approximating to a human being.
We can sense that already happening by the 1630s, when Van der Doort cata-
logues a miniature of the Queen by Levina Teerlinc from the 1560s in the
collection of Charles I and writes 'supposed to have bin Queene Elizabeth
before shee came to the Crowne'.[3] The process reaches its culmination at the
close of the eighteenth century in Horace Walpole's unforgettable criterion
for identifying her portrait. * * * It also accounts for the mass mislabelling of
pictures as her in the nineteenth century.

When it comes to measuring their effectiveness as a political tool in
their own age we are on much less certain ground. What can be said is that
due both to the variety of media and to the length of her reign, her image
must have been more widely disseminated than that of any previous monarch. And more of her subjects would have seen one of these than the
woman herself. Elizabeth was essentially a Home Counties ruler. She only
travelled as far east as Norwich, as far west as Bristol, and no further north
than Oxford. The images produced after 1580 must have reinforced the
concept of the monarch as a being sacred and set apart, whose very jewels embodied the glory and the riches of the kingdom. In an age when the
portrait was still a novelty pertaining only to a narrow section of society,
the revelatory nature of these royal images cannot be overestimated. That
this was so can be substantiated by an approach first through the Renaissance concept of the dynastic portrait and secondly, and crucially, through
a study of the unique role that they came to occupy in a Protestant country which had rejected other forms of holy image as idolatry.

2. *The Poems of Sir John Davies*, ed. Robert Krueger, Oxford, 1975, pp. 77–8.
3. Oliver Millar, 'Abraham van der Doort's Catalogue of the Collection of Charles I', *Walpole Society*,
   XXVII, 1960, p. 113 (no. 42).

The primary purpose of a state portrait was, of course, not to portray an individual as such, but to invoke through that person's image the abstract principles of their rule.[4] The ceremonial portrait in the sixteenth century was to a great extent made possible through the imperial revival of the Emperor Charles V, whose alliance with Titian can be said to have established the Renaissance state portrait and its conventions as an art form. For the theoretical background of the cult images of Elizabeth-Virgo, it is necessary to read the Mannerist treatises on painting. These define the aim of the portrait as the immortalization of the great and virtuous; it is the humanist appeal to antiquity—the role of images as visual *exempla*. Ludovico Dolce, for example, explains that, just as religious images awakened the mind to devotion, so representations of good and virtuous men should bestir the beholder to imitation and emulation.[5] The relationship of the religious to the secular image in the sixteenth century was a close one, so close that Paolo Lomazzo in his *Trattato dell' Arte de la Pittura* (1584), our chief source for Mannerist art theories on the portrait, made no clear distinction between the two.[6] For Lomazzo, the religious image was aligned to secular portraiture in such a way that it seeemed to partake of the same qualities. Like Dolce, he was preoccupied with the ethical 'effects' of the ruler portrait, behind which loomed statues of Egyptian, Greek and Roman kings and emperors and their 'effects' on the people of antiquity. The painter, moreover, was not to imitate but to perfect nature; to depict a ruler accompanied by the full panoply of state, so that his degree should never be in question, and posed in a majestic and grave manner, even though by nature he lacked those graces. In short, for the Renaissance neo-platonist the portrait painter was concerned with the ruler, not as an individual, but as the embodiment of the 'Idea' of kingship.

Lomazzo has relevance to our study because he was the only continental theorist with whom we can be sure that the Elizabethans were at least acquainted. In 1598 there appeared Richard Haydocke's translation of the first five books of the *Trattato*, and although Lomazzo's main discussion on the portrait occurs in book six, Haydocke's translation contains at least one important passage in connection with the portrait. The original section on proportion, which Vitruvius calls 'Eurythmy', reads as follows:

> The further importance of this beauty and majesty of the body is seen more clearly in the divine cult than in anything else, for it is a marvellous thing how piety, religion, and reverence for God and the saints are increased in our minds by the majesty and beauty of sacred images, caused by the presence in them of Eurythmy.[7]

Compare this with the corresponding passage in Haydocke:

> But if we shall enter into further consideration of this beauty, it will appear most evidently, in things appertaining to *Ciuile dicipline*. For it is strange to consider, what effects of piety, reverence and religion,

---

4. A useful introduction is M. Jenkins, *The State Portrait, Its Origin and Evolution*, Monographs on Archaeology and Fine Arts, iii, 1947.
5. *Ibid.*, pp. 4–5; cf. for England More, *Utopia*, ed. J. H. Lupton, Oxford, 1895, p. 233, where 'the ymages of notable men' are to be set up in the market place 'that the glory and renowme of the auncetors may sturre and provoke theire posteritie to vertue'. Also W. Segar, *Honor Military and Civill*, London, 1602, pp. 254–6.
6. P. Lomazzo, *Trattato dell' Arte de la Pittura*, Milan, 1584, pp. 430–38.
7. Translation quoted from Jenkins, *State Portrait*, p. 6.

are stirred vp in mens mindes, by meanes of this sutable comelinesse of apte proportion.[8]

This case of the substitution of 'Ciuile dicipline' for *culto divino*, to which Miss Jenkins drew attention, is important evidence for developments in the use of images in a Protestant country. The sacred images of Christ, the Virgin, and saints had been cast out of the churches as so much rubbish, while in their place we see the meteoric rise of the sacred images of the *Diva Elizabetha*.

Haydocke's Lomazzo would suggest that England was an artistic backwater and that the Elizabeth portraits stand apart from their contemporaries on the Continent. This, to a great extent, is true, for it may be argued that the Elizabethan state portrait is a magnificent—one is almost tempted to say a deliberate—archaism. The royal portrait painters are still working in the tradition of the high Middle Ages, the face of *divina majestas,* as illustrated, for example, by the portrait of Richard II in Westminster Abbey, or by other portraits of medieval kings and emperors.[9] The remote and expressionless mask with its calm and never-ending vision, the face of *divina majestas*, of the God-ordained ruler of the Middle Ages, lives on and is indeed, through the Elizabeth-cult, revitalized in the hieratic icon-like images of the Virgin Queen. The medieval ruler image cult is reinforced and extended by the exponents of the monarch by Divine Right. In this sense the Elizabeth portraits stand at the end of a long tradition of sacred royal portraiture: the cult images of Roman and Byzantine emperors and of the medieval French kings[1]—holy images classed in legislation along with images of Christ, the Virgin, and saints.[2] Behind the cult of the royal image and its insular peculiarities in Elizabethan England extend the wider horizons of the Renaissance ruler image cult which in France, for example, could lead to the wax effigy of a deceased king making an *entrée* into Paris and having whole banquets served to it.[3]

Our journey ends with the incomparable John Jewel, Bishop of Salisbury and unrivalled exponent of the Anglican *via media*, and his successor in the endless pamphlet warfare with Rome, Thomas Bilson. For an understanding of the theory of Elizabethan state portraiture, it is to these Anglican theologians that we turn. Elizabethan state portraiture becomes yet one more facet of that vast struggle concerning images which divided the reformed and the Roman Churches.[4] Bishop Jewel in his famous *Apology*, the official one for the Anglican theological position, praised the early Christian emperors who had swept images out of churches and regarded the Tudor policy of image destruction as a resurgence of an imperial iconoclast tradition personified particularly by the Greek iconoclast emperors. He agreed, however, with his opponent, the Catholic Harding, that the

---

8. Haydocke, *Tracte*, p. 26; quoted by Jenkins, *State Portrait*, p. 6.
9. H. P. L'Orange, *Apotheosis in Ancient Portraiture*, Oslo, 1947, pp. 110–26.
1. L. Bréhier and P. Battifol, *Les Survivances du culte impérial romain*, Paris, 1920, pp. 59–65. More can be learnt by approaching the Elizabeth portraits through Greek, Roman and medieval ruler images than from the more conventional framework of English art history. See also H. P. L'Orange's studies *Apotheosis in Ancient Portraiture, op. cit.*, and *Studies in the Iconography of Cosmic Kingship in the Ancient World*, Oslo, 1953.
2. E. H. Kantorowicz, *The King's Two Bodies*, Princeton UP, 1957, p. 425 and note 371.
3. R. E. Giesey, *The Royal Funeral Ceremony in Renaissance France*, Geneva, 1960, pp. 145 ff. Giesey does not attempt to relate this to the context of sixteenth-century theories concerning ruler images.
4. On which see John Phillips, *The Reformation of Images: Destruction of Art in England, 1535–1660*, University of California Press, 1973, pp. 119 ff.

original purpose of religious images had been to instruct the simple and ignorant, but said that painters, like poets, are liars and that God had banished painters from Israel in the same way that Plato had exiled poets from his Republic. Jewel admitted that images and pictures produced powerful 'effects': 'I grant,' he writes, 'images do oftentimes vehemently move the mind diuersly to sundrie affections',[5] but that this made them all the more unmeet for use in churches. Where Jewel and his opponent Harding failed to agree was over the traditional Catholic distinction between *latria*, due only to the Trinity, and *doulia*, an inferior reverence or devotion, paid to holy images.[6] Jewel, in contrast, will admit neither, and maintained that images were worshipped, taking his stand, along with all other iconoclasts, on the second commandment. Sanders, another Catholic polemicist, taunted Jewel by saying, 'Breake if you dare the Image of the Queenes Maiestie, or Armes of the Realme . . . or token belonging to the honorable Knights of the Garter.'[7] Sanders was touching upon the pathetic weakness of the Anglican position.

A large part of Thomas Bilson's work is devoted to an exposition of the Anglican stance over images, accompanied by the usual paraphernalia of the Old Testament, the Fathers and the example of the emperors. A Jesuit, Philander, states that 'if images of Princes may be reuerenced, & idolatry not committed, much more the image of God'.[8] Theophilus, the Christian, answers—and here begins a series of passages of crucial interest:

> Earthly similitudes of your making, may not controule the heauenly precepts of Gods owne giuing. The images of Princes may not wel be despited or abused, least it be taken as a signe of a malicious hart against the Prince, but bowing the knee or lifting vp the hand to the image of a Prince is flat & ineuitable idolatrie.[9]

Further on, the Jesuit again persists:

> May wee not giue some reuerence to the Image of Christ, though he be in heauen; as well as you doe to the thrones and letters of Princes, when themselves be not present?[1]

Theophilus replies that reverence paid to the vacant throne and to the royal seal was no argument that images should be used for religious purposes, for the sanctity of these objects arose from God's ordinance to 'honour the king'.[2] Homage to a ruler's sceptre, seal,[3] sword, image, or other token was tribute, not to the objects, but to the absent power of which they were but emanations. The respect paid to coats of arms or images which

5. *The Works of John Jewel*, Parker Society, ed. J. Ayre, 1947, ii. 651–68, 662.
6. *Ibid.*, pp. 666–8. Cf. John Bridges, *The Supremacie of Christian Princes . . .* , London, 1573, pp. 490–95, where he violently attacks the scholastic subtleties over image adoration; and William Fulke, *A Defence . . . against the Cavils of Gregory Martin*, ed. C. H. Hartshorne, Parker Society, 1843, pp. 179–216.
7. Nicholas Sanders, *A Treatise on the Images of Christ and his saints . . .* , Louvain, 1567, p. 109; see T. Veech, *Dr. Nicholas Sanders and English Reformation*, Louvain, 1935, p. 185.
8. T. Bilson, *The True Difference betweene Christian Subiection and Vnchristian Rebellion*, Oxford, 1585, pp. 547–80.
9. *Ibid.*, p. 552.
1. *Ibid.*, p. 557.
2. The old text—*Cujus est haec imago? Caesaris, inquiunt. Ergo reddite quae sunt Caesaris Caesari*— of the ruler image, is of course cited: see *The Catechism of Thomas Brecon*, Parker Society, ed. J. Ayre, 1844, pp. 68–73; *Early Writings of John Hooper*, Parker Society, ed. S. Carr, 1843, pp. 44–5.
3. Bale argues that reverence may be done to seals 'without sin', *Select Works of John Bale*, ed. H. Christmas, Parker Society, 1849, pp. 94–9.

princes set up 'is accepted as rendred to their owne persons, when they can not otherwise be present in the place to receiue it. . . .'[4] It is a line of thought which stretches back to the image of the new Emperor being borne into the provinces of the Roman Empire, where it was honoured as though the divine ruler himself were present. The Anglican position was thus a somewhat peculiar one, for on the one hand the use of religious images was denounced as popish superstition, while on the other, the sacred nature of the royal portrait image was to be maintained. In the latter they were successful to a degree which would suggest that the royal portrait filled the vacuum left by the pre-Reformation image cult. The passion for wearing the royal image as a kind of talisman makes the Elizabeth-cult draw to itself mysterious traditions.

In the discussion of the theory the interchangeability of the arms, seal, and other royal attributes is of immense importance. It provides yet another key towards the comprehension of the Queen's portraits. They become one of a series of material objects which were universally regarded as emanations of royal power. In this way, for instance, the royal arms erected in churches[5] as manifestations of the royal governorship of the *Ecclesia Anglicana* become 'portraits' of the Queen. The Tudor cult of royalist symbols offers a striking parallel with the Byzantine Empire under the iconoclast emperors, where there was likewise a deliberate 'increase of a profane imperial art which was meant to replace religious art in the public buildings and places'.[6]

The theologians have provided us with the ideological background of the Elizabeth portraits, and we have examined the primitive notions that linger behind even the most sophisticated of the Mannerist art treatises. The royal image was desirable for its good 'effects', but because it partook in some mysterious way of the nature of the sitter it was also potentially dangerous. Throughout the reign efforts were made to dispose of the Queen by stabbing, burning, or otherwise destroying her image. All these attempts were foiled, but the alarm that they always engendered in government circles supports to a considerable degree our contention concerning the nature of the portrait image in Elizabethan England. Those cases concerning pierced wax images were out and out black magic, of which the *cause-célèbre* was that of 1578–9, when three images—one supposed to represent the Queen—were found pierced with hog's bristles.[7] One of the models for Hilliard's Great Seal was used in this way, being found embedded in poison. 'I cannot conceive', it was related, 'he can have a good meaning that will place the picture of her Majesty's sacred person with such poison as hath endangered the apothecary's man that did but put it to his tongue.'[8]

4. Bilson, *True Difference*, p. 561. Cf. Raleigh's presentation to the natives of Guiana of gold coins 'with her Majesties picture to weare' with the promise that they would henceforth be her subjects (R. Hakluyt, *The Principal Navigations Voyages Traffiques & Discoueries*, London, 1927, vii. 336).
5. See H. M. Cautley, *Royal Arms and Commandments in our Churches*, Ipswich, 1934, pp. 28–42; S. J. Wearing and P. Millican, 'Post Reformation Royal Arms in Norfolk Churches', *Norfolk Record Society*, xvii, 1944, 7ff.
6. G. B. Ladner, 'Origin and Significance of the Byzantine Iconoclast Controversy', *Mediaeval Studies*, ii, 1940, 136; see also the same author's 'The Concept of the Image in the Greek Fathers and the Byzantine Iconoclastic Controversy', *Dumbarton Oaks Papers*, vii, 1953, 20–22; A. Grabar, *L'Empereur dans l'Art Byzantin*, Publications de la Faculté de l'Université de Strasbourg, lxxv, Paris, 1936, 167ff.
7. On this aspect see G. L. Kittredge, *Witchcraft in Old and New England*, Harvard UP, 1929, pp. 87–8; C. F. Smith, *John Dee*, London, 1909, pp. 19–20.
8. *HMC Hatfield*, xi, pp. 404, 405–6.

But even eliminating witchcraft proper, it is clear that it was a common-place that maliciously to attack or deface a portrait of the Queen would somehow affect her. In 1591 a religious maniac called Hacket expressed his hatred of Elizabeth by defacing the royal arms and stabbing a panel portrait of her through the breast.[9] Two years later O'Rourke, the Irish rebel, caused a wooden image of her to be trailed daily through the streets while boys hurled stones at it.[1] In France under the Catholic League Elizabeth's por-trait was publicly consigned to the flames[2] and even, it was reported in 1590 to Sir Thomas Heneage, hung up upon a gallows from which it was rescued by some patriotic Englishman.[3] It gives a strange edge to our study of the portraits of Queen Elizabeth I to know that to her enemies they were symbols of the *civitas diaboli* of Protestantism and as such to be hurled into the fire.

Between the ecstasy of love and adoration engendered by the Queen's portraits on the one side, and the bitterness and turmoil they evidently evoked on the other, it is possible for us to relive some of the vital issues of the age. It has been said that in the case of the portraits of Queen Eliz-abeth I 'The Common principles by which the historian of painting is accustomed to judge Western portraiture of the Renaissance do not apply.'[4] Is this, in fact, true? If Elizabeth had married or died before 1580 it would certainly not be. There is little in her portraiture before that date which is in any way extraordinary or different from, say, that of her sister, Mary. An examination of her portraits sequentially, however, pinpoints the year when those 'common principles' ceased to apply. It happened some twenty years into the reign, in 1579, when it became virtually certain that Elizabeth would never marry, when confrontation with the might of Cath-olic Spain became inevitable and when the imperialistic and maritime aspirations of the *magus* Dr John Dee were taken up by government. In that year the first elaborately allegorical portrait of the Queen was painted. Up until then complex symbolic representations of her had been confined to those who were religious exiles from the Netherlands. It is understand-able that to such exiles Elizabeth appeared a major heroine, far more so than was the case with her own people who needed the war with Spain for the cult to be generated. Joris Hoefnagel's *Queen Elizabeth I and the Three Goddesses* (1569) and Lucas de Heere's *The Allegory of the Tudor Succes-sion* (1572?) are celebrations of her by exiles to whom England was a haven from religious persecution. Neither picture is a vehicle for native imperial aspirations. Those came only in 1579 in George Gower's awkward presentation of Elizabeth as a Roman Vestal to whom, for the first time, the globe is given as an attribute. In a wider perspective this deliberate cre-ation of a cult can be paralleled in the celebration of the monarch's Acces-sion Day.[5] Although we have evidence of a sporadic observance after 1570 in the wake of the papal bull of excommunication, it was not until 1576 that government stepped in and issued an official form of service, one which was revised two years later, when it assumed a far more laudatory tone. Exactly the same is true of the Accession Day Tilts. Once again there

9. W. Camden, *The History of Princess Elizabeth*, London, 1688 edn, pp. 451–4.
1. *HMC VIth Report*, p. 336; *Carew MSS, 1589–1600*, p. 76.
2. J. Foxe, *Actes and Monuments*, London, 1641 edn, III, Continuation, p. 76.
3. *HMC Hatfield*, iv, p. 77.
4. Waterhouse, *Paintings in Britain*, p. 23.
5. Spenser, *Faerie Queene*, dedication.

is evidence of some form of fête at court as early as 1572 but there is none for the gigantic tournament devised for the eyes of the general public in the tiltyard at Whitehall before 1581. The fundamental ingredients of what we now call the cult of the Virgin Queen, including visual panegyric, therefore, were put together very rapidly in the years immediately before and after 1580. And as research progresses it becomes clearer that there was more deliberate orchestration from the centre than was thought twenty-five years ago.

In the two and a half decades that followed, these initial statements were merely elaborated and expanded to messianic proportions, as England triumphed over the Armada and the Queen assumed the status of an immortal. The portraits produced during this period take on an impenetrable mask which looks back across the centuries to the holy countenance of majesty of the Byzantine and the medieval emperors and shares with them a common debt to sacred imperialism. The Elizabeth of these portraits is 'the most high, mightie, and magnificent Empresse, renowned for Pietie, Vertue, and all gratious government'.[6] The symbolism of her state portraits is that of the virtue, peace and justice of an imperial golden age—not just for England alone—but, in the hands of the poets and visionaries, for the whole world. The discrepancy between the poetic dream of the peace and justice of empire embodied in the state portraits of the Queen and the grim realities of the political scene offers material for reflection on the enormous gap between idea and reality in the Elizabethan world.

The Creation of a Legend

> Finally, there is the roof of this room: it is most beautifully decorated with astronomical figures, and in one part of it there is a picture of the Queen being received into Heaven.
>
> Description of the Paradise Chamber, Hampton Court, 1600[7]

Three days after the death of the Queen on 24 March 1603, Dr King preached at Whitehall. He referred to Elizabeth in the following terms:

> Soe there are two excellent women, one that bare Christ and an other that blessed Christ; to these may wee joyne a thrid that bare and blessed him both. She [i.e. Elizabeth] bare him in hir heart as a wombe, she conceived him in fayth, shee brought him forth in aboundaunce of good workes. . . .[8]

Elizabeth is soberly hailed as a second Virgin giving birth to the Gospel of Christ. This alarming apotheosis was to be the keynote of the seventeenth-century cult of 'Saint' Elizabeth; she was, as several books and poems state: 'In earth the first, in heaven the second Maid.'[9] She looms, a portent in the skies, arrayed in the attributes of the Virgin as the Woman of the Apocalypse; clouds billow about her and she is haloed by a circle of

---

6. *The Diary of Baron Waldstein. A Traveller in Elizabethan England*, trans. G. W. Groos, London, 1981, p. 151.
7. *Diary of John Manningham*, p. 152.
8. Lewis Bayly, *The Practise of Pietie*, London, 1613, pp. 534–5; T. Fuller, *The Holy State*, London, 1642, p. 318.
9. T. Fuller, *The Church History of Britain*, Oxford, 1845 edn, v, p. 258.

stars within a glory. Angels descend from the heavens bearing diadems to proclaim her victory and Time and Death are rendered impotent in her presence. Thomas Fuller, the church historian, moreover, records that when she had exchanged her earthly for a heavenly crown, representations of her tomb were erected in numerous churches.[1]

> This was she that in despight of death
> Lives still ador'd . . . [2]

chants one set of verses beneath such a picture. In a country which had rejected images as idolatry such a development was extraordinary. To trace Elizabeth's portraits through the seventeenth century is, therefore, to witness this final and staggering apotheosis, for as the popularity of Stuart rule declines, Elizabeth is transformed into a ruler of a vanished golden age.

Iconographically, English royal portraiture was to live off the Elizabeth inheritance for some years, for the stock themes and poses recur again and again. James I holds up the Garter badge, clasps the globe of the world and is accompanied by the sword of justice and the Bible, much in the same way as his predecessor had been. The stiff icon-like portraits of James and his consort, Anne of Denmark, re-echo back to the state images of the *Diva Elizabetha*. In him the imperial theme was to be intensified in his role as Emperor of Great Britain. Royal iconography was only radically changed in one way, namely by the advent of a family, a welcome contrast after half a century of rule by a virgin queen. More important was the resumption by the crown of the patronage of the arts and in the years after 1620 the isolationist icon-manufacture could no longer resist the impact of artists from abroad, beginning in 1617 with Paul van Somer, soon to be followed by Van Dyck. These sounded the death knell of the Elizabethan aesthetic which had contributed so much to the ethos of the Queen's portraits, one in which the standard ingredients of Renaissance painting, *chiaroscuro* and both linear and aerial perspective had yet to be received or understood. This is a fundamental fact which explains much of the curious intensity of these images, for their aesthetic is wholly medieval, painting as outline and colour. It is the marriage of this archaism to the imagery of Renaissance rulership which makes these portraits utterly unique. Into them pour the attributes of sacred empire as it was revived by the Emperor Charles V, the imagery of Petrarch's *Trionfi*, the new-fangled fashion for emblems and *imprese*, Protestant propaganda and the subtleties of neo-platonic allegory. Viewed in this light one can understand why these images of a single unmarried female ruler should have retained their hypnotic hold upon the imagination, because locked within them are most of the fundamental patriotic myths that have sustained an island people for over three centuries. In the portraits of Elizabeth Tudor we witness their creation.

---

1. J. Prince, *The Worthies of Devon*, London, 1810 edn, p. 246; cf. the verses beneath that in St Saviour's Southwark, Nichols, *Progresses*, iii, 660.
2. See Lucy Gent, *Picture and Poetry 1560–1620*, Leamington Spa, 1981.

Elizabeth in Literature

JOHN N. KING

[Representing the Virgin Queen]†

✳   ✳   ✳

The Origins of a Myth

Modern scholarship has transmitted a frequently cited report by William Camden that supports the widespread view that the queen chose a life of perpetual virginity. He indicates that at the outset of her reign Elizabeth rejected advice that she settle the succession by marrying and bearing an heir to the throne. She spoke in response to a 1559 petition from the House of Commons urging her to choose a husband on the ground that "nothing can be more repugnant to the common good, than to see a Princesse, who by marriage may preserve the Common-wealth in peace, to leade a single life, like a Vestal Nunne."[1] According to the tradition established by Elizabeth's first historian, this speech provided the earliest sign that the queen would flout patriarchal convention through a deliberate decision to remain unwed:

> And therefore it is, that I have made choyce of this kinde of life, which is most free, and agreeable for such humane affaires as may tend to his [God's] service . . . and this is that I thought, then that I was a private person. But when the publique charge of governing the Kingdome came upon mee, it seemed unto mee an inconsiderate folly, to draw upon my selfe the cares which might proceede of marriage. To conclude, I am already bound unto an Husband, which is the Kingdome of England. . . . (And therwithall, stretching out her hand, shee shewed them the Ring with which she was given in marriage, and inaugurated to her Kingdome, in expresse and solemne terms.) And reproch mee so no more, (quoth shee) that I have no children: for every one of you, and as many are English, are my Children. . . . Lastly, this may be sufficient, both for my memorie, and honour of my Name, if when I have expired my last breath, this may be inscribed upon my Tombe:

> Here lyes interr'd ELIZABETH,
> A virgin pure untill her Death.[2]

---

† From "Queen Elizabeth I: Representations of the Virgin Queen," *Renaissance Quarterly* 43.1 (Spring 1990): 30–74. Reprinted by permission of the Renaissance Society of America. This essay was prepared with the support of a National Endowment for the Humanities Senior Residential Fellowship at the Folger Shakespeare Library and a Roger C. Schmutz research grant from Bates College. I have profited from conversations with Andrew Gurr, Patricia Harris, Peter Lake, Peter Lindenbaum, Jeanne Roberts, Lois Schwoerer, and other readers and staff members at the Folger Library. James Bednarz has offered helpful advice, and William Watterson has provided good counsel back in Maine. An initial version of this essay was written before publication of Roy Strong, *Gloriana: The Portraits of Queen Elizabeth I* (1987), rev. ed. of *Portraits of Queen Elizabeth I* (Oxford, 1963). My text has been revised in light of Strong's findings.

1. Camden, *Annales: The True and Royall History of the Famous Empresse Elizabeth, Queene of England, France, and Ireland, etc. True Faith's Defendresse of Divine Renowne and Happy Memory* (1625), bk. 1, 26, trans. from *Annales rerum Anglicarum et Hibernicarum, regnante Elizabeth* (1615).
2. Ibid., 27–29.

The youthful queen's "prophecy" was borne out at the approach of her death, according to Camden, when she ordered that the "Ring, wherewith shee had beene joyned as it were in marriage to her kingdome at her inauguration, and she had never after taken off, to be filed off from her finger, for that it was so growne into the flesh, that it could not be drawne off." This action "was taken as a sad presage" of the coming dissolution of her "marriage with her kingdome."[3]

Camden's account provides every indication that Elizabeth skillfully manipulated political language and imagery by adapting a patriarchal vocabulary whereby kings governed as "fathers" of their people and as "husbands" of the country.[4] She was known to style herself as the virgin mother of her people. Accounts based on Camden's interpretation argue that Elizabeth's invocation of divine authority as an external and universal source of power supported her effort to validate royal sovereignty and to deny its limitation by male subjects.[5] Louis Montrose therefore concludes that she refused "to enact the female paradigm desired by . . . [her] advisors: to become the medium through which power, authority, and legitimacy are passed between generations of men."[6]

As appealing as Camden's view may be, it begs quite a few questions. The absence of the queen's reported epitaph upon her tomb need not be too troublesome, because James I established her naturalistic funerary monument at Westminster Abbey in 1606 as a counterpart to the flattering memorial that vindicates his own mother, Mary, Queen of Scots.[7] But what about the analogy that Camden draws between the queen's marriage to England as her husband and the tradition that nuns are betrothed to Christ the Bridegroom? Is it a simple coincidence? How authoritative is Camden's historical testimony, which appeared in print more than half a century after the events described and midway through her successor's reign? Did the queen actually speak the words that her first historian attributes to her?

Scholars have tended to accept at face value Camden's declaration that he has inaugurated a historiographical method that makes unprejudiced use of manuscript "monuments." In actual fact, it is difficult to track down his sources because he omits citations. His use of Tacitus as the

3. Idem, *The Historie of the Most Renowned and Victorious Princesse Elizabeth, Late Queene of England*, trans. R. N[orton]. (London, 1630), 222. This edition contains the account of the last half of the reign in bk. 4 of Camden's *Annales*, which had been published posthumously in 1627 as *Tomus alter annalium rerum Anglicarum, et Hibernicarum*. The concluding section of the present essay explains why *Annales rerum Anglicarum et Hibernicarum* and the English translation of 1625 end after Camden's account of the trial and execution of Mary, Queen of Scots.
4. See Marie Axton, *The Queen's Two Bodies: Drama and the Elizabethan Succession* (London, 1977), 133–34.
5. See Elkin Wilson, *England's Eliza* (Cambridge, MA, 1939), 6 (note) and 61; Lacey Baldwin Smith, *Elizabeth Tudor: Portrait of a Queen* (Boston, 1975), 120, 122; Axton, 38–39. Compare the aligned use of Camden's testimony in Leonard Tennenhouse, *Power on Display: The Politics of Shakespeare's Genres* (London, 1986), 22. Although Yates (*Astraea: The Imperial Theme in the Sixteenth Century* [London and Boston, 1975]) claims that "from the very beginning of her reign the Virgo-Astraea symbol was used of Elizabeth," I have discovered no examples between 1558 and 1569. Yates, 59, cites the unverified testimony of Camden's *Remains* (1674) that the figure was in use "'in the beginning of her late Majesties Reign.'"
6. Louis Adrian Montrose, "The Elizabethan Subject and the Spenserian Text, in *Literary Theory / Renaissance Texts*, ed. Patricia Parker and David Quint (Baltimore, 1986), 310.
7. J[odocus] C[rull], *The Antiquities of St. Peters, or the Abbey Church of Westminster* (London, 1711), 93; Edward Brayley, *The History and Antiquities of the Abbey Church of St. Peter, Westminster*, vol. 1 (London, 1818), pt. 2, 65.

model for compiling a work in the annals format might suggest the need for caution in assessing his "objectivity," because of the Roman author's commitment to moralizing history, his habit of silently harmonizing conflicting sources, and his invention of speeches in a rhetoric appropriate to the character and style of historical personages. Camden himself acknowledges that he views Tacitus as a model for moralized exemplary history because the Roman author declares that the "principall office" of compiling annals "is to take care, that Vertue be not obscured, and by the relation of evill words or deeds, to propose the feare of infamie, with posteritie." Camden informs the reader that his testimony is drawn from the archives of his patron, William Cecil, Lord Burghley, who, shortly before his death, "willed me to compile a *Historie of Q. Elizabeths* Raigne from the beginning." Camden acknowledges the manifest point that Cecil's goal of providing "for the propagation of the Queenes honour"[8] was not disinterested, because a flattering view of the queen would necessarily reflect glory on the man who served as her chief minister throughout four decades.

The preservation of a transcript of the queen's speech among the Cecil papers makes it possible to assess Camden's accuracy.[9] Examination of the Cecil manuscript reveals an entirely new set of problems, however, because Camden (or an unnamed intermediary) falsified the contemporary record of the queen's speech.[1] This falsification offers one indication that Camden transmits a hagiographical account that may be less accurate as a portrayal of the Tudor queen than it is of Jacobean patronage and politics. After all, the historian admits that he turned away from this project in dismay at its arduous nature until James I returned him to the task. The concluding section of the present essay explains how the *Annales* came to enshrine a posthumous myth of Elizabeth as a perpetual virgin, one that has passed into modern scholarship through many retellings. Camden's version of events provides a Jacobean representation of Elizabeth as a virgin queen, one that followed in sequence upon her earlier celebration, first as a marriageable maiden, and second as a mythically youthful object of courtly desire. An awareness of the anachronistic processes at work in the first history of Elizabeth's reign throws light on these earlier phases of Elizabethan iconography and demonstrates how the entire Gloriana cult was defined by the practicalities of Elizabethan *and Jacobean* politics. Differentiation among the different "cults" of the Virgin Queen demonstrates how the royal image was fashioned dynamically by

8. Camden, 1625, sigs. [b7–8].
9. British Library, MS Lansdowne 94, fol. 29. Transcribed in T. E. Hartley, ed., *Proceedings in the Parliaments of Elizabeth I* (Leicester, 1981), 1:44–45; the textual introduction lists many contemporary manuscript and printed copies.
1. George P. Rice, Jr., transcribes both versions of the queen's speech in *The Public Speaking of Queen Elizabeth: Selections from Her Official Address* (New York, 1951), with the undocumented claim that the Camden variation represents a "second, much shorter, and obviously superior version" (114–18). With rare skepticism, John E. Neale acknowledges Camden's version of the queen's address in *Elizabeth I and Her Parliaments*, vol. 1 (London, 1953), 47 n. 3, where he remarks: "I know of no text from which he could have made it, and it does not correspond with the Queen's description. I have therefore ignored it." On the contrary, Louis Montrose, 309, makes the unsubstantiated claim that the Camden transcript is drawn from "official records."
2. See Herbert Thurston, in *The Catholic Encyclopedia*, vol. 13 (New York, 1912), 60, s. v. "Rings." The wedding ring was also attributed to St. Catherine, whose cult had a strong following in medieval England, as the bride of Christ.

Elizabeth and her government from above, and by her apologists and suppliants from below.

The "Cult" of the Marriageable Virgin

Within months of her accession to the throne, Elizabeth acknowledged to a parliamentary delegation the desirability of marriage. The transcript of "The Ansuere of th[e] Quenes highnes to th[e] peticion proponed [i.e., set forth] unto hir by th[e] Lower howse Concerning[e] hir mariage" in MS Lansdowne 94 contains a version of her 10 February 1559 address that differs in many respects from the Camden variation. In all likelihood this very clean copy was transcribed at the behest of Cecil or someone close to the man who served as chief secretary of state throughout most of the queen's reign. Cecil's collected papers provide what may be the most complete and reliable contemporary account of Elizabethan state events. Because neither MS Lansdowne 94 nor the profuse contemporary documentary record refers to a queenly vow to remain a chaste virgin married to her realm, one may presume that this promise is a later addition. The absence of contemporary reference to the regal display of the coronation ring suggests that this histrionic gesture is an apocryphal embellishment, one possibly modeled on the custom that nuns wear rings commemorating their vow of celibacy and wedding to Christ.[2] The version of the speech that Camden attributes to the parliamentary delegation establishes an iconographical link between the alleged unacceptability of Elizabeth's behavior and that of a "Vestal Nunne," but this reference is absent from contemporary Elizabethan documents for this Parliament.[3]

The manuscript version of the queen's speech records no vow of perpetual virginity; indeed, any such vow would have violated the official disapproval of all vows, including that of celibacy, by the Church of England, of which Elizabeth served as Supreme Governor. * * * The conditional nature of her promise that she *would* be content, *should* she remain unmarried, to have on her tomb the inscription "that a Queen having raigned such a tyme, lyved and dyed a virgin" is lost sight of in Camden's hindsight view of this epitaph as a self-fulfilling prophecy. Words that she spoke in 1559 might have undergone embellishment in an oral tradition that resulted in the legendary account in Camden's *Annales.* * * *

During the 1560s and 1570s virtually everyone assumed that Elizabeth would marry. * * * [I]ndeed, her portraits were sent abroad in 1567, 1571–74, and 1578–81 in connection with marriage negotiations.[4] Although she had no want of suitors, each one had personal or political liabilities. Thus a renewal of the English marital alliance with Spain

---

3. Camden, 1625, bk. 1, 26. What appears to be the earliest printed account of the parliamentary petition and the queen's answer is in *Grafton's Abridgement of the Chronicles of Englande*, 3d ed. (London, 1570), sigs. Z3ᵛ–4ᵛ. Richard Grafton, who sat as a member of several parliaments, claims to provide an eyewitness account, "as nere as I could beare the same away," of the queen's address to the parliamentary delegation at Whitehall Palace. Holinshed's *Chronicles* and the second edition of John Stow's *Annales* (1592) agree almost completely with MS Lansdowne 94, fol. 29, and Grafton. John Nichols provides the same speech in *Progresses and Public Processions of Queen Elizabeth*, vol. 1 (London, 1823), 63–65. Neale quotes extensive extracts; 1953, 47–50.

4. Strong, 1987, 22–24.

through marriage to her sister's widower, Philip II, was never seriously entertained. Her well-known refusal to wed a man she had never met may have reflected the disastrous influence of the flattering portraits that were made for use during the negotiations leading up to the marriage of Henry VIII and Anne of Cleves. Elizabeth's declaration in a letter of 25 February 1560 to Eric, King of Sweden, that she was determined "not to marry an absent husband"[5] surely reflects her memory of the ill effect of the prolonged absenteeism of Philip of Spain during her sister's reign; this objection implies the corollary fear that a married queen must depart with her husband "out of her own native country and sweet soil of England."[6] Archduke Charles of Austria offered the best possibility for a diplomatically successful marriage, but his Catholicism and Hapsburg lineage represented stumbling blocks for the English who regarded the queen as the nation's only hope for preserving political independence and the Protestant settlement in religion. Elizabeth's interest in Robert Dudley, Master of the Queen's Horse (later Earl of Leicester), incurred no opposition on religious or nationalistic grounds, but the queen refused to marry her own subject. Furthermore, he was a married man who made domestic political enemies. The death of his wife in 1560 under mysterious circumstances dashed any real hope that the queen might achieve a true love match.[7]

During an age of early menopause and a high rate of death in childbed, Elizabeth's advancement into her fourth decade fueled anxiety that the House of Tudor would die with the queen.[8] Her own statements indicate that during her thirties and forties she fashioned a public identity as an unmarried ruler who is eligible, indeed eager, for marriage to a politically *appropriate* husband. Elizabeth's reply to a 1563 petition from her second parliament therefore argued that she was no less capable of childbirth than Saint Elizabeth, to whom God sent offspring despite her advanced years (Lk. 1:5–25).[9] Even though she may have been the saint's namesake, this scriptural comparison was not distinctively Elizabethan because apologists for Mary Tudor used the same precedent to declare that providential intervention would produce a royal heir when she was close to forty, a very old age for bearing children during the sixteenth century.[1]

Continuing agitation in favor of a royal marriage caused Elizabeth to go on record for a third time on 5 November 1566 in response to a petition from her second parliament that she marry and settle the succession. This reply follows along the lines of the first, except that the queen explic-

5. Elizabeth I, *The Letters of Queen Elizabeth I* (New York, 1935), 31.
6. John Stubbs, *John Stubbs's "Gaping Gulf" with Letters and Other Relevant Documents*, ed. Lloyd E. Berry (Charlottesville, 1968), 49.
7. Neale provides a useful account of the "marriage problem" even though he minimizes the queen's commitment to wedlock (*Queen Elizabeth* [London, 1934], 76–90). See also Smith, 118–25. From the age of fifteen, Elizabeth's letters record her awareness of the political complications of courtship and marriage (Elizabeth 1, 1935, 9–11). Axton, 11–25, considers the succession debate in light of the Elizabethan adaptation of the theory of the king's two bodies.
8. Forty was the average age at menopause according to Lawrence Stone, *The Family, Sex and Marriage in England 1500–1800* (New York, 1977), 63 and n. 48.
9. Neale, 1953, 110. Minutes in the queen's own hand concerning her reply to Parliament are preserved in MS Landsdowne 94, fol. 30.
1. John N. King, *Tudor Royal Iconography: Literature and Art in an Age of Religious Crisis* (Princeton, NJ, 1989), 216.

itly vows to marry despite her personal inclination toward a celibate life. Her elaboration that the sole reason for marriage is her wish to bear children acknowledges the political expediency of producing heirs to perpetuate her dynasty; it accords further with the orthodox view that the chief purpose of wedlock is "the procreation of children."[2] Once again the queen acknowledges the political difficulties attendant upon this issue, this time mentioning the probability that the most earnest proponents of marriage are those most likely to object to her choice of a husband. At the same time, she takes strenuous exception to the expression of doubt concerning the sincerity of her intention to take a husband. In actual fact, neither the privy council nor parliament ever agreed on the appropriateness of any of the queen's many suitors. In her promise to marry and in her awareness of the problematic nature of her choice, the speech accords with the queen's actions during the 1560s and 1570s. According to a contemporary manuscript, these are the words that she delivered in 1566 to a delegation made up of thirty members from each of the two houses:

> I dyd send theym aunswere by my counseyle I wolde marrye (althowghe of myne own dysposycion I was not enclyned thereunto), but that was not accepted nor credyted, althowghe spoken by theyre Prynce. And yet I usede so many wordes that I coulde saye no more. And were yt not nowe I had spoken those wordes, I wold never speke theyme ageyne. I wyll never breke the worde of a prynce spoken in publyke place, for my honour sake. And therefore I saye ageyn, I wyll marrye assone as I can convenyentlye, yf God take not hym awaye with whom I mynde to marrye, or my self, or els sum othere great lette happen. I can saye no more except the partie were presente. And I hope to have chylderne, otherwyse I wolde never marrie. . . . But theye (I thynke) that movythe the same wylbe as redy to myslyke hym with whom I shall marrie as theye are nowe to move yt, and then yt wyll apere they nothynge mente yt. I thowght theye wold have byn rathere redye to have geven me thankes then to have made anye newe requeste for the same. There hathe byn some that have or [i.e., ere] thys sayde unto me they never requyred more then that theye myght ones here me saye I wold marrie. Well, there was never so great a treason but myght be coveryde undere as fayre a pretence.[3]

Political concerns of the kind stated by the queen shaped the representation of her virginity in the iconography of the first half of her reign. Maidenly chastity was a necessary attribute of her claim to be a legitimate and marriageable queen. The straightforward virginity symbolism of Elizabeth's early images differs from the esoteric iconography of the virgin goddess—Cynthia or Venus-Virgo—that emerged in the 1580s and flowered during her final decade. The *Coronation Portrait* in which the queen wears the regalia of investiture typifies the early phase as do related miniatures by

2. John E Booty, ed., *The Book of Common Prayer 1559: The Elizabethan Prayer Book* (Charlottesville, 1976), 290.
3. From a copy of the speech in Cambridge University Library MS Gg.iii. 34, fols. 208–12; transcribed in Hartley, 145–49. A fragment of the draft in the queen's own hand, with an endorsement by Cecil, is preserved in Public Record Office, State Papers Domestic, Elizabeth 41/5. Modernized texts are in Elizabeth I, 1951, 77–81; and Neale, 1953, 146–50.

Nicholas Hilliard (ca. 1600). Although the portrait was painted on a panel close to the time of her death (ca. 1600–10), its depiction of the queen's youthful features is modeled on a lost original painted ca. 1559. Her facial appearance is in line with the anachronistic "mask of youth" characteristic of her last years. Possibly this portrait was used as a funerary image. It is noteworthy that Elizabeth's long hair flows down onto her shoulders in the style of an intact virgin.[4]

Because of the close ties between the English establishment and the Inns of the Court, where many members of the royal court, privy council, and parliament received their legal education, it was a natural move to dramatize questions concerning royal marriage and succession in revels and entertainments staged by lawyers. Although a royal proclamation of 16 May 1559 forbade discussion of religion and politics in the popular drama, dramatic performances at the royal court and the Inns of the Courts were excluded from the prohibition. *Gorboduc* is a case in point, because Thomas Norton, a prominent member of the House of Commons, and Thomas Sackville, later Earl of Dorset, designed the play to reflect upon the dangers attendant upon a realm where the royal succession remains unsettled. Although the work was written for only a single production at the Inner Temple on Epiphany, 6 January 1562, the work was revived before Elizabeth at Whitehall Palace twelve days later. Along with other revels and entertainments during this season, it takes a position critical of the queen on the controversial political issues of royal marriage and succession.[5]

✳   ✳   ✳

The last great flurry of excitement over Elizabeth's professed desire to marry began in 1579, when Alençon arrived in England to court her during the final interval when she was still remotely capable of bearing an heir. The queen's taking of the initiative late in the wooing suggests that she had every intention of wedding the duke, despite her personal distaste for marriage and despite the opposition of powerful Protestant lords on the privy council who believed that the choice of a husband who was both an heir to a foreign throne and a Catholic would threaten England's religious settlement and its political autonomy.[6] Her own letters specify that the chief stumbling block to marriage was the Catholicism of the younger brother of the king of France. At the height of the controversy over the proposed match, she wrote that she wished to wed should he modify his "public exercise of the Roman Religion."[7]

4. London, National Portrait Gallery, no. 5175. See Strong, 1987, 41, 125–28, 147, 163–64, 178, and fig. 157.
5. Axton, 38–41; David Bevington, *Tudor Drama and Politics: A Critical Approach to Topical Meaning* (Cambridge, MA, 1968), 141–47.
6. Wallace T. MacCaffrey, *Queen Elizabeth and the Making of Policy, 1572–1588* (Princeton, NJ, 1981), 254–66. On the prolific literature in opposition to the Alençon match, see Doris Adler, "Imaginary Toads in Real Gardens," *English Literary Renaissance* 11 (1981):235–60.
7. Elizabeth I, 1935, 136. In 1581 Walsingham counseled that if she meant to marry, she should make haste (ibid., 149). Articles that Alençon proposed on 16 June 1579 for governing the marriage were annotated with Elizabeth's replies on the following day (MS Lansdowne 94, fols. 58–60). For Cecil's "satisfaction," scriptural and legal precedents were compiled to support an affirmative answer to the question of "Whether a Protestant may marye with a Papyste" (MS Lansdowne 94, fols. 62–69).

Spenser's *Shepheardes Calender* evokes the political milieu of the Alençon courtship. The assumption that the queen remained eligible and interested in marriage well into her forties underlies the inclusion of a transparent allusion to the earl of Leicester in the "October" eclogue. Piers's appeal that Cuddie devote himself to epic poetry includes an aside on the queen's love for the great noble that seems to nominate him as a candidate for her hand in marriage:

> Whither thou list in fayre *Elisa* rest,
> Or if thee please in bigger notes to sing,
> Advaunce the worthy whome shee loveth best,
> That first the white beare to the stake did bring. (ll. 45–47)[8]

The prominence of this allusion to the Dudley device of the staked bear places Spenser in the camp of the Protestant progressives who opposed the Alençon match, even though Leicester's secret marriage during the previous year excluded him as a potential mate for the queen.[9] Further indication of the poet's interest in this topic is provided by the presumable composition of part of *Mother Hubberds Tale* at about this time, given the likely satire directed against Alençon and his agent, Jean de Simier, in the form of the Ape. The connection of that poem to the *Calender* may be noted in Spenser's 1591 description of the *Tale* as a work "composed in the raw conceipt of my youth" and in its affinity with the satirical mode of his ecclesiastical eclogues.[1]

The appearance of the *Calender* during the immediate aftermath of the political explosion triggered by the publication of the most notorious appeal that Elizabeth spurn a foreign marriage, John Stubbs's *Discoverie of a Gaping Gulf whereinto England is like to be Swallowed by an other French mariage* (August 1579), may account for Spenser's last-minute alteration of the *Calender's* dedication from Leicester to his nephew, Sir Philip Sidney.[2] Whereas the queen's anger over the appearance of this tract gave the earl every reason to distance himself from the anti-Alençon faction, Sidney went on record against the French marital alliance in a letter that he sent directly to the queen.

Even though the writings of Stubbs and Sidney document the existence of broadly-based opposition to the Alençon match, they never argue against the desirability of marriage as such; indeed, they assume that Elizabeth will marry and bear children. The fact that no one adopts the rhetorical strategy of reminding the queen of a 1559 vow to live out her life like a celibate nun wedded to England provides yet another proof that Camden (or an unknown intermediary) invented that apocryphal story. Sidney presumably wrote his letter "Touching Her Marriage with Monsieur" after the appearance of Stubbs's *Discoverie of a Gaping Gulf* because he often

8. Spenserian references are to *The Works of Edmund Spenser: A Variorum Edition*, ed. Edwin A. Greenlaw, C. G. Osgood, F. M. Padelford, et al. (Baltimore, 1932–57), 10 vols. in 11.
9. David Norbrook, *Poetry and Politics in the English Renaissance* (London, 1984), 86–87.
1. Edwin A. Greenlaw, *Studies in Spenser's Historical Allegory* (Baltimore, 1932), 119; Spenser, Vol. 7, Pt. 2, 105.
2. William A. Ringler, Jr., "Spenser, Shakespeare, Honor, and Worship," *Renaissance News* 14 (1961):159–61. The dedication was changed from Dudley to Sidney after E. K. dated his epistle to Gabriel Harvey on 10 April 1579, by which time Spenser's composition must have been virtually complete.

follows the tract in argument and phraseology; manuscript copies of his letter were in circulation at about the time that Spenser's *Calender* went to press in late 1579. Although Sidney ennumerates Alençon's liabilities both as a foreigner and as a Roman Catholic, he nevertheless assumes that the queen will choose a more appropriate husband and bear children who will be "the perfect mirror to your posterity."[3] According to tradition, Sidney withdrew to his sister's estate to escape the queen's wrath.[4] Sidney's unpublished advice incurred no punishment, but Stubbs suffered the penalty of the loss of his right hand for publically challenging the queen's prerogative concerning her potential marriage.

Unlike Sidney, who remains discreetly silent about the queen's age and vulnerability to fatal complications in a pregnancy, Stubbs explicitly raises the danger of death in childbirth. His acknowledgment of the queen's real age and mortality lacks Sidney's courtly delicacy: "If it may please her Majesty to call her faithfulest wise physicians and to adjure them by their conscience towards God, their loyalty to her, and faith to the whole land to say their knowledge simply . . . how exceedingly dangerous they find it by their learning for Her Majesty at these years to have her first child, yea, how fearful the expectation of death is to mother and child; I fear to say what will be their answer." Stubbs's witty reference to "her natural body" as "her very self or self self, as I may say" suggests mockery of the legal fiction of the queen's "two bodies." Furthermore, his use of bestial imagery to compare the proposed marital union to "contrary couplings together . . . [like] the uneven yoking together of the clean ox to the unclean ass" could only draw the queen's wrath.[5] By lodging strictures based upon biblical injunctions against "unnatural" acts (Dt. 22:10), Stubbs evokes the widespread association between Roman Catholicism and sexual uncleanliness; Protestants widely assumed that devotion to Roman "idolatry" constituted "spiritual fornication" (Rev. 2:14, 17:2). Prejudice of this kind flared up against French Catholics after the St. Bartholomew Massacre (1572).

If it was not until after the failure of this last effort at marriage, one third of the way through Elizabeth's reign, that the patriotic cult of an unmarried virgin queen who would remain ever wedded to her nation took hold in officially-sponsored propaganda, in poetry of praise generated outside of the royal court, and in the popular imagination, how are we to interpret the celebration of Eliza as the "flowre of Virgins" and "a mayden Queene" in Spenser's "April" eclogue (11. 48, 57)? It is important to note that Hobbinol sings the lay to Eliza in the place of Colin Clout, who no longer sings this song of praise. The absence of Colin, Spenser's pastoral surrogate, distances the poet from this blason. Eliza's portrait obviously fuses classical mythology and Christian iconography associated with yet another virgin queen, Mary:

---

3. *Miscellaneous Prose of Sir Philip Sidney,* ed. Katherine Duncan-Jones and Jan Van Dorsten (Oxford, 1973), 57, ll. 7–8. Cecil preserved an anonymous letter written close in time to Sidney's composition that reviews the problem and urges the queen to marry (MS Lansdowne 94, fols. 70–71).
4. Andrew Weiner, *Sir Philip Sidney and the Poetics of Protestantism: A Study of Contexts* (Minneapolis, 1978), 22. Duncan-Jones and Van Dorsten challenge this view in Sidney, 34–37.
5. Stubbs, 9, 51, 68.

> For shee is *Syrinx* daughter without spotte,
> Which *Pan* the shepheards God of her begot:
>> So sprong her grace
>> Of heavenly race,
> No mortall blemishe may her blotte. (ll. 50–54)

The "argument" explains that the eclogue "is purposely intended to the honor and prayse of our most gracious sovereigne, Queene Elizabeth," just as Eliza's company of virgins (nymphs, muses, graces, and shepherds' daughters) idealizes the sociology of the privy chamber, where the queen surrounded herself with attendant maidens whom she watched over like a jealous mother. The naturalistic representation of Eliza in the eclogue's woodcut illustration is devoid of the esoteric symbolism often found in Elizabeth's later portraits, although muses playing upon their musical instruments do attend her.

Even though this eclogue was "a seminal work in creating the image of the Virgin Queen,"[6] a French marriage was still regarded as a distinct possibility, indeed a threat, in the eyes of Protestant progressives, until *after* the entry of the *Calender* in the Stationers' Register on 5 December 1579. The "April" eclogue's floral imagery indicates that Eliza is the "goddess of love and procreation as well as goddess of chastity and virginity."[7] Spenser alludes to the Ovidian account that Syrinx preserved her virginity when her flight from Pan, the Arcadian fertility god, resulted in her transformation into a reed-bed (*Meta.* ll. 688–712). In a paradoxical rewriting of the classical myth, Syrinx fails to evade Pan; indeed, she conceives of Eliza by means of an insemination vaguely aligned with the virgin birth of Christ. Nevertheless, the Mariological tag "without spotte" refers to Eliza's virginity, not that of her mother, and she clearly derives her "heavenly race" from her father. We should not look for tight one-to-one correspondences because Spenser situates this eclogue within a complicated symbolic matrix. After all, it is ultimately the poet who makes Eliza spotless because the progeny of Syrinx are songs.[8] E. K.'s gloss on line 50 recognizes Spenser's synthesis of Christian and classical imagery by noting that Christ "is the verye Pan and god of Shepheardes."[9] The comment that Pan also refers to "the most famous and victorious King, her highnesse Father, late of worthy memorye K. Henry the eyght" reflects the icononographical inconsistency of Colin Clout's song.

What E. K. leaves unstated is more significant historically than his explanation of the Pan reference, because Syrinx must refer to Anne Boleyn, the mother of the queen who was executed on grounds of adultery during Elizabeth's infancy. Soon after Anne's death and Henry's remarriage to Jane Seymour in 1536, Princess Elizabeth was declared

---

6. Norbrook, 1984, 84.

7. Patrick Cullen, *Spenser, Marvell, and Renaissance Pastoral* (Cambridge, MA, 1970), 116. Anne Lake Prescott has commented to me that Eliza's scarlet attire is appropriate to a "mayden Queene" (1. 57) who remains marriageable.

8. Thomas H. Cain, *Praise in "The Faerie Queen"* (Lincoln, NE, 1978), 16–17; David Lee Miller, *The Poem's Two Bodies: The Poetics of the 1590 "Faerie Queene"* (Princeton, NJ, 1988), 95, 238. See also n. 2, page 786 below.

9. On the Christianization of Pan, see D. C. Allen, *Mysteriously Meant: The Rediscovery of Pagan Symbolism and Allegorical Interpretation in the Renaissance* (Baltimore, 1970), 245–46.

illegitimate in order to clear the way for the accession of the male heir expected of her father's third wife. When Elizabeth acceded to the throne long after her father's death, she did so as the bastardized daughter for whose sake her father had rejected papal authority. The recovery of personal and political legitimacy was therefore always a matter of concern to the queen, whose legalism disconcerted her counselors and parliament when it extended even to defense of the claim of Mary, Queen of Scots, "as heir presumptive to the Tudor throne."[1] The emphasis of the "April" eclogue on Eliza's purity runs counter to long-standing Catholic allegations concerning Elizabeth's bastardy.[2]

The witty mythologization of Elizabeth's birth constitutes a flattering rewriting of the historical record, one that glosses over the chronic succession crisis that England had experienced because of her inability and that of her entire dynasty to perpetuate a sturdy line of male—or female— heirs to the throne. Colin Clout's blason declares:

> *Pan* may be proud, that ever he begot
>   such a Bellibone,
> And *Syrinx* rejoyse, that ever was her lot
>   to beare such an one. (ll. 91–94)

According to this view, both Henry VIII and Anne Boleyn could take satisfaction for having produced such a splendid heir to the throne. Poetic diction suggests further that Elizabeth may yet continue the Tudor line if the choice of words is aligned with Perigot's love-smitten praise of "the bouncing Bellibone" in the "August" eclogue, whose green skirt and floral crown are clearly appropriate to a nubile maiden (ll. 61–112). Although the "April" eclogue's mythic view of dynastic history crumbles under a literal interpretation, it succeeds on a figurative level due to the syncretic combination of pagan myth with a trope of scriptural pastoral (the Good Shepherd), whereby both father *and daughter* receive homage as Christ-like monarchs. It is debatable, however, whether celebration of a king deeply implicated in dynastic chaos is appropriate to a poem dedicated to praising Queen Elizabeth.

The delicate ambiguity of Spenser's praise of queenly virginity may be noted in the "April" eclogue's very early comparison of Elizabeth to Cynthia, goddess of the moon, in her guise as Phoebe, the twin sister of Phoebus Apollo: "Tell me, have ye seene her angelick face, / Like *Phoebe* fayre?" (ll. 64–65). This astronomical figure highlights the political power of the queen's femininity when Eliza outshines the sun-god, Phoebus, who "blusht" in amazement "to see another Sunne belowe" (l. 77). This imagery is androgynous because Elizabeth's lunar qualities as both a woman and a queen are overlaid with the solar symbolism that iconographical tradition accorded to kings as males. The singer identifies Eliza's moonlike qualities with the queen's dominant aspect:

1. Smith, 64–65. See also Norman L. Jones, "Elizabeth's First Year: The Conception and Birth of the Elizabethan Political World," in Christopher Haigh, ed., *The Reign of Elizabeth I* (London, 1984), 28.
2. Norbrook, 1984, 85.

> Shew thy selfe *Cynthia* with thy silver rayes,
>   and be not abasht:
> When shee the beames of her beauty displayes,
>   O how art thou dasht? (ll. 82–85)

Having introduced this complicated astronomical conceit, Spenser ostentatiously denies its appropriateness to queenly iconography by employing *occupatio*, a rhetorical device that emphasizes something by seeming to omit it: "But I will not match her with *Latonaes* seede, / Such follie great sorow to *Niobe* did breede" (ll. 86–87). Having introduced the possibility of lauding Eliza as a new Cynthia, the singer immediately retreats from that simile in a manner that is inconsistent with an interpretation of Elizabeth's virginity as a permanent condition.

Spenser's homage to Eliza as a virgin queen is poised at a liminal moment in the development of Elizabethan iconography. He shares Sidney's realization that ambiguity is the appropriate posture for one to assume in praising or advising a queen whose own image and desires are ambiguous. The "April" eclogue enhances the queen's standing as an eligible woman at virtually the last moment when she is still remotely capable of marriage and child-bearing, on the one hand, but it praises her in a manner that may be understood as an appeal that she retain her unwedded state, on the other hand. Colin's blason praises a marriageable queen who is on the verge of a decision to remain unmarried. Virgilian emblems spoken by Thenot and Hobbinol highlight the transitional standing of Colin's lay to Eliza. E. K. interprets them as words spoken "in the person of Aeneas to his mother Venus, appearing to him in the likenesse of one of Dianaes damosells: being there most divinely set forth." Although these words, "O quam te memorem virgo?" and "O dea certe" ("By what name should I call thee, O maiden?" and "O goddess surely!") were to become famous as a "prophetic" compliment to the perpetual innocence of Elizabeth as Venus-Virgo, the *Calender*'s publication during the marriage controversy creates a delicate ambiguity about whether the phrase emphasizes Elizabeth's virginity, her potential maternity, or both qualities. The Graces who appear in the eclogue may accompany Venus (or Athena, or the muses), but not Diana. The potential fusion of chastity and erotic love afforded by this early application of the Venus-Virgo figure would soon be forgotten.[3]

The eclogue's involvement with questions of dynastic politics and succession is made manifest by E. K. 's interpretation of Colin's description of Eliza's cheeks, where the "Redde rose medled with the White yfere" (l. 68), as a figure for "the uniting of the two principall houses of Lancaster and of Yorke: by whose longe discord and deadly debate, this realm many yeares was sore traveiled, and almost cleane decayed. Til the famous Henry the seventh, of the line of Lancaster, taking to wife the most vertuous Princesse Elisabeth, daughter to the fourth Edward of the house of Yorke, begat the most royal Henry the eyght aforesayde, in whom was the firste union of the Whyte Rose and the Redde." This gloss corresponds to a well-known dynastic image, the

---

3. *Aeneid*, 1.327–28, in Virgil, *Eclogues, Georgics, and Aeneid*, vol. 1, ed. and trans. H. Rushton Fairclough (Cambridge, MA, 1940); *Variorum*, 7, pt. 1, 41, 45, 287–88. According to Virgil, Venus appears as a nymph, possibly a votaress of Diana. On a contemporary application of the Venus-Virgo figure to Elizabeth, see King, 259, 261.

Tudor rose arbor designed for the title page of a work published soon after the *Calender*, the first edition of John Stow's *Chronicles of England, from Brute unto this present yeare of Christ 1580*. This figure is modeled ultimately upon the Tree of Jesse, the genealogy of Jesus as the scion of the royal House of David, which was reapplied during the Middle Ages in praise of Christian kings. The Tree of Jesse had already undergone adaptation for purposes of dynastic praise in the title page border for Edward Halle's *Unyon of the twoo noble and illustre famelies of Lancastre and Yorke* (1550), in which Henry VIII occupies the place of honor as a Christlike king. The Stow border constitutes a reconfiguration of a conventional dynastic image in which the marriage of Henry VII and "Elizabeth daughter to Kinge Edward the fourth" unites the houses of York and Lancaster in the form of their second son and heir.[4] Interpretation of the Stow title page is ambiguous, however, like that of the "April" eclogue. Would Elizabeth be the last bud upon the rose arbor? Or, flanked by sterile offshoots, Edward VI and Mary I, is she still capable of perpetuating her line? The liminality of both of these "texts" disappears in a poem attributed to the queen, "On Monsieur's Departure," that employs Petrarchan vocabulary to lament the dashing of her hope to marry when Alençon made his final departure from England in 1582:

> I grieve and dare not show my discontent,
> I love and yet am forced to seem to hate,
> I do, yet dare not say I ever meant,
> I seem stark mute but inwardly do prate.
> I am and not, I freeze and yet am burned,
> Since from myself another self is turned.[5]

The Cult of the Virgin Goddess

Emerging during the tortuous negotiations that marked the last phase of the Alençon courtship (1579–83), the best-known face of the Elizabethan image made it possible to argue for the first time that by reigning as England's perpetually virgin queen, Elizabeth could escape the political compromises necessitated by the marriages of her kindred monarchs, Mary I and Mary, Queen of Scots. After the danger of foreign Catholic entanglement had subsided, progressive Protestants could acclaim "this virgin queen with all the greater enthusiasm, and her virginity became a symbol of national independence." That this change coincided with increased emphasis on classical mythology in royalist panegyrics may be noted in Thomas Blenerhasset's *A Revelation of the True Minerva* (1582) and George Peele's *The Araygnement of Paris* (1584), a "pastorall" performed before Queen Elizabeth by the children of the Chapel Royal.[6]

This iconographical shift is clearly evident in royal portraiture, which begins to incorporate esoteric virginity symbols into arcane allegories that may be impenetrable to casual observers. Thus the mundane utensil held by the queen in the "Sieve" portraits (1579–83) celebrates her standing as

4. See Michael O'Connell, *Mirror and Veil: The Historical Dimension of Spenser's "Faerie Queene"* (Chapel Hill, 1977), 6–7.
5. *The Poems of Queen Elizabeth I*, ed. Leicester Bradner (Providence, RI, 1964), 5. He expresses doubt concerning the accuracy of this attribution (xiii), but see Caldwell, 22 n. 1.
6. Norbrook, 1978, 58.

a latter-day Vestal Virgin, whose maiden state is essential to the imperialistic program proposed by John Dee. Roy Strong concludes that these paintings "must be seen as statements against the [Alençon] marriage by means of a deliberate intensification of the mystique of chastity as an attribute essential to the success of her rule."[7] In the *Ermine Portrait* (1585), the queen captivates the ermine of chastity, which stands transfixed without a tether but with a royal crown about its neck. After Isaac Oliver's disastrous experiment with naturalistic portraiture of the queen as an aging woman (ca. 1592), authorized images shifted to the anachronistic "Mask of Youth" that appears in paintings of the queen until her death. It may be noted in the convoluted *Rainbow Portrait* (ca. 1600–03), which depicts the preternaturally youthful queen with the shoulder–length hair of a marriageable virgin.[8]

Praise of Elizabeth as Cynthia (or Diana, or Belphoebe, or any one of a number of other variants) became indelibly imprinted during the last half of the reign. Marie Axton notes that as the queen "grew older and hope for offspring faded, Diana or Cynthia as a public image found reluctant acceptance."[9] Unlike the *Princely Pleasures at Kenelworth Castle* and the "April" eclogue, in which unambiguous praise of Zabeta or Eliza as Cynthia had not yet won a place, the emergence of the queenly moon-cult typifies the increasing Petrarchism and Platonism of royal circles, where courtiers paid homage to Elizabeth as an ever-youthful yet unapproachable object of desire.[1] The cult originated in Giordano Bruno's praise of Elizabeth during his mid-1580s residence in England, according to Roy Strong, who concludes that it "must have become public" by the end of the decade. Her status as "Cynthia, Queen of Seas and Lands" further alludes to John Dee's claim for England's status as an imperialistic military and naval power, which was voiced with increased stridency following the destruction of the Spanish Armada. Thus jeweled crescent moons symbolic of Diana appear in the queen's hair in miniatures by Nicholas Hilliard (ca. 1586–1603) and at the apex of the headpiece in the *Rainbow Portrait*.[2] The queen actually appears as crescent-crowned Diana in a portrait in which she bears bow and arrows and holds the tether of a hunting dog.[3]

---

7. Strong, 1987, 94–99, 107.
8. Ibid., 112–14, 130–33, 142–47; Yates, 215. Louis Montrose, 315, proposes that the presence of a virgin-knot in the *Armada Portrait* (ca. 1588) "suggests a causal relationship between her sanctified chastity and the providential destruction of the Spanish Catholic invaders" without exploring the alternative possibility that this jeweled bow is no more than a straightforward symbol of the kind that appears throughout Elizabeth's pre- and post-Armada portraiture. His daring view is based upon analogy to his interpretation of Henry VIII's codpiece in the Holbein cartoon of *Henry VIII with Henry VII*, which argues for the presence of political symbolism in "the king's phallic self-assertion" (312–14). Here again, Montrose neglects the alternative possibility that this appendage is no more than an item of conventional attire. Codpieces appear with some frequency in portraits of Renaissance royalty, nobility, and commoners.
9. Axton, 60.
1. Leonard Forster notes that it is after the failure of the Alençon negotiations that "the icon of Elizabeth as Laura begins to take shape" in *The Icy Fire: Five Studies in European Petrarchism* (Cambridge, 1969), 135.
2. Strong, 1987, 91–93, 124–27, 146–50. For an opposed view that the Cynthia cult predated the Alençon courtship, see Ray Waddington, *The Mind's Empire: Myth and Form in George Chapman's Narrative Poems* (Baltimore, 1974), 78–79.
3. Lawrence G. Holland, *Catalogue of the Pictures at Hatfield House* (privately printed, 1891), no. 51, attributed to Cornelius (or Henrik) Vroom and cited, 36, in an inventory of 1611 as "a portrait of her late majesty." Ill. Mandell Creighton, *Queen Elizabeth* (Edinburgh, 1896), facing 76.

The apotheosis of the queen as Cynthia was complete by the time that boy actors from St. Paul's School performed John Lyly's *Endimion: The Man in the Moone* at the royal court on Candlemas 1588. Her cult image is clearly apparent in a fiction showing (paradoxically) her love for a mortal. Although it cannot be proved that this elaborate play contains a detailed program of topical allegory, queenly symbolism differentiates between the celestial state of the moon goddess and the mortality of her subjects, who are associated with Tellus (the earth). The goddess herself is significantly absent during the first two acts, which dramatize the condition of the love-sick shepherd, Endimion. Eumenides explains that his companion's desire is incapable of satisfaction because "there was never any so peevish to imagin the Moone eyther capable of affection, or shape of a Mistris: for as impossible it is to make love fit to her humor which no man knoweth, as a coate to her forme, which continueth not in one bignesse whilst she is measuring."[4] (Her inconstancy and variable form refer to the waxing and waning of the moon.) Although this viewpoint might seem critical of the unending virginity of the queen, the play "apotheosizes a queen for whom marriage is unthinkable," and whose courtiers may now direct toward her "harmonious, platonic affection without rivalry for special favor."[5] One critic concludes that Endimion's adoration dramatizes the "proper worship of the ideal courtier for his monarch." Cynthia's manifestation of truth, justice, mercy, and peace in the concluding act, after her kiss releases Endimion from the enchantment of sleep, accords with the attribution of all virtue to the queen in her later iconography.[6] The goddess herself proclaims that this mythic act of noblesse oblige manifests virginal innocence, in accordance with her own comment that "my mouth hath beene heere tofore as untouched as my thoughts" (5.1.20–21). The direct appeal for royal favor in the epilogue makes explicit the identification between the queen as a member of the audience and the boy playing her role as the moon goddess: "but if your Highnes vouchsafe with your favorable beames to glaunce upon us, we shall not only stoope, but with all humilitie, lay both our handes and heartes at your Majesties feete."

The place of Sir Walter Ralegh as a major disseminator of the moon-cult may be noted in his nocturnal portrait (1588),[7] which depicts the ability of feminine Luna to govern the male. The device of the crescent moon in the upper left corner compliments the queen as the goddess controlling Ralegh's tides in a nautical conceit that presumably refers to the importance of his own maritime skills in advancing Elizabethan imperialism. This symbolic image defines the courtier's relationship to the queen as Cynthia, who in turn gave him the punning nickname of "Water." His wearing Elizabeth's colors of black and white affiliates him with the Virgin Queen as a nighttime figure who is ever alluring and changeable, but the motto *Amor et Virtute* reaffirms the innocent chastity of his love. Several years later, Ralegh lamented the loss of the intimate and protected relationship that he once enjoyed as the queen's favorite in "The 11th: and last booke of the

4. *The Complete Works of John Lyly*, ed. R. Warwick Bond (Oxford, 1902), 1.1.19–23.
5. Bevington, 178–81.
6. Peter Saccio, *The Court Comedies of John Lyly: A Study in Allegorical Dramaturgy* (Princeton, NJ, 1969), 173–77, 184–85. See also G. K. Hunter, *John Lyly: The Humanist as Courtier* (London, 1962), 184–93, 237–41.
7. Strong, 1987, 127, fig. 135.

Ocean to Scinthia" (ca. 1592): "What stormes so great but Cinthias beames apeased? / What rage so feirce that love could not allay?"[8] George Chapman's celebration of the cult of the Moon Queen in *The Shadow of Night* (1594), which includes his "Hymnus in Noctem" and "Hymnus in Cynthiam," is aligned with Ralegh's views and those of their originators, John Dee and Giordano Bruno. The ascendancy of the powerful Elizabethan moon over the European sun through the grand conceit of a solar eclipse may allude in particular to the outcome of the Alençon courtship a decade earlier. Surely it lodges a general claim to English imperialistic triumph late in the queen's reign:

> Then set thy Christall, and Imperiall throne,
> (Girt in thy chast, and never-loosing zone)
> Gainst Europs Sunne directly opposit,
> And give him darknesse, that doth threat thy light.[9]

The Faerie Queene's dedicatory "Letter to Ralegh" (23 January 1589/90) declares that Spenser models the name Belphoebe on "your owne excellent conceipt of Cynthia, (Phoebe and Cynthia being both names of Diana)." When the narrator praises Elizabeth as the enshrinement of chastity at the outset of the "Legend of Chastity," he indicates that the most perfect representation of the queen's image, "in living colours, and right hew," is to be found in the "sweet verse" of Ralegh, "In which a gracious servant pictured / His *Cynthia*, his heavens fairest light" (3.proem.4). Spenser presumably refers to a lost section of the fragmentary manuscript of *Ocean to Cynthia* that predated Ralegh's disgrace.

The androgynous conceit that fuses solar and lunar qualities in the "April" eclogue is akin to some queenly images in the *Faerie Queene*, where the concealment of Una's brilliant whiteness beneath a "black stole" (1.1.4) suggests a lunar image that is a witty variation of the figure of the Woman Clothed with the Sun, who has "the moon . . . under her feet" (Rev. 12:1). Una wears Elizabeth's personal colors of black and white in the manner of Ralegh's nocturnal portrait. The subordination of the masculine sun to the feminine moon in Britomart's dream at Isis Church raises the intriguing possibility that Elizabeth's crescent moon imagery may derive from Isis as well as Cynthia. In Britomart's vision the Crocodile, that is Osiris or the sun, submits as a consort to Isis, who "doth the Moone portend." The "rich Mitres shaped like the Moone" worn by the priests of Isis correspond to the moon devices that appear in the queen's portraiture during her last decade (5.7.4). The Egyptian fertility goddess shares the queen's androgynous nature, and the history of her search for the dead Osiris, whom Typhon had dismembered, makes her look like a type for Elizabeth in her restless quest for a spouse. Although Isis recovers the rest of her husband's body, she never finds his phallus, a lost member that forever eludes her.[1]

8. *The Poems of Sir Walter Ralegh*, ed. Agnes M. C. Latham (London, 1951), 29, ll. 118–19.
9. "Hymnus in Cynthiam," *The Poems of George Chapman*, ed. Phyllis Bartlett (New York, 1941), ll. 116–119. See Yates, 76–77; and Waddington, 73–74.
1. *Plutarch's Moralia*, ed. and trans. Frank C. Babbitt (Cambridge, MA, 1969), 5:358.18, 365.36, 371–72.51. I am indebted to William Watterson concerning the importance of the Isis imagery.

Belphoebe personifies Elizabeth's private capacity as a woman according to the "Letter to Ralegh." Her portrayal is problematic, however,
because it tends to identify chastity with perpetual virginity, even though
Spenser characteristically associates that virtue with the consummation of
love in marriage. Belphoebe's status as the elder sister of Amoret, the twin
who is destined for marriage to Scudamour, might appear to elevate the
celibate life above wedded love in the mythic account of their birth, but
Amoret participates equally in their virgin birth by Chrysogone:[2] "Pure and
unspotted from all loathly crime, / That is ingenerate in fleshly slime"
(3.6.3). It looks as if Spenser has cleaved the virginal and fertile sides of
Eliza into two characters, one remote and divine and the other approachable and worldly. The anomalous aspect of Belphoebe's virginity invites the
reader, almost automatically, to equate her unmarried state with that of
Elizabeth, whose private capacity as woman rather than queen is "fashioned" in the chaste huntress (3.proem.5). Nevertheless, the queenly
nubility of Britomart and Gloriana makes it difficult to accept Belphoebe
as any *more* representative of Elizabeth than those other queenly figures
or to assimilate the huntress into an unequivocal sanction of Elizabeth's
status as a virgin queen. Indeed, the "paradoxical doubleness" of the
huntress combines attributes of Venus and Diana in a complicated symbolic depiction of the queen.[3]

Although Belphoebe is a strong woman who conquers enemies and
hunts, Spenser passes her over to make the female knight, Britomart, his
chief personification of chastity. Her commitment to heterosexual love
contrasts sharply with Belphoebe's celibacy. While the "martiall Mayd"
(3.2.9) matches Belphoebe's militance in defending her virginity against
an inappropriate suit like that of Malecasta, that she is destined to marry
Artegall is never in question. This "Magnificke Virgin" is clearly labeled
as a type for Elizabeth by her name ("martial Britoness"), by her dream at
Isis Church, and by the maidenliness and chastity that she shares with
the queen. As a member of the blood royal and Tudor ancestress, she
shares many of the queen's attributes. Like Elizabeth, she is the heir to a
"Crowne" and a giver of "royall gifts of gold and silver wrought" (5.7.21–24).
When Britomart removes her helmet, the reader learns that she wears her
hair long in the manner of a marriageable virgin, a style similar to the one
that Elizabeth maintained as an aged queen according to the *Rainbow
Portrait*. The presence of this symbolic detail indicates that the knight's
appearance is analogous to the "Mask of Youth" found in so many other
portraits made during Elizabeth's last decade of life:

> Her golden locks, that were in tramels gay
> Upbounden, did them selves adowne display,

---

2. See Thomas P. Roche, *The Kindly Flame: A Study of the Third and Fourth Books of Spenser's "Faerie
Queene"* (Princeton, NJ, 1964), 103. In an otherwise astute analysis, David Lee Miller identifies the
births of Belphoebe and Amoret, and before them Eliza, as types of the Immaculate Conception (95,
235–36, 238–40). Surely the allusion is to the virgin birth of Christ rather than to the Immaculate
Conception whereby St. Anne bore the Virgin Mary. Furthermore, it is debatable whether the
explicit comments that Pan "begot" (i.e., procreated) Eliza define a virginal conception ("April," ll.
51, 91). See n. 8, p. 779 above, and related text.

3. O'Connell, 100–103. On some of the cautiously negative touches in Spenser's portrayal of
Belphoebe or Elizabeth, see Judith H. Anderson, "'In living colours and right hew': The Queen of
Spenser's Central Books," in *Poetic Traditions of the English Renaissance*, ed. Maynard Mack and
George deForest Lord (New Haven, 1982), 47–66; and Miller, 6, 100, 233, and passim.

And raught unto her heeles; like sunny beames,
That in a cloud their light did long time stay,
That vapour vaded, shew their golden gleames,
And through the persant aire shoote forth their azure streames. (3.9.20)

* * *

BIBLIOGRAPHY

Adler, Doris. "Imaginary Toads in Real Gardens." *English Literary Renaissance* 11 (1981):235–60.

Allen, D. C. *Mysteriously Meant: The Rediscovery of Pagan Symbolism and Allegorical Interpretation in the Renaissance.* Baltimore, 1970.

Anderson, Judith H. "'In living colours and right hew': The Queen of Spenser's Central Books." In *Poetic Traditions of the English Renaissance,* ed. Maynard Mack and George deForest Lord, 47–66. New Haven, 1982.

Axton, Marie. *The Queen's Two Bodies: Drama and the Elizabethan Succession.* London, 1977.

Bergeron, David M. *English Civic Pageantry, 1558–1642.* Columbia, SC, 1971.

Bevington, David. *Tudor Drama and Politics: A Critical Approach to Topical Meaning.* Cambridge, MA, 1968.

Booty, John E., ed. *The Book of Common Prayer 1559: The Elizabethan Prayer Book,* Charlottesville, 1976.

Brayley, Edward. *The History and Antiquities of the Abbey Church of St. Peter, Westminster.* London, 1818–23. 2 vols.

Cain, Thomas H. *Praise in "The Faerie Queene"* (Lincoln, NE, 1978).

Caldwell, Ellen M. "John Lyly's *Gallathea*: A New Rhetoric of Love for the Virgin Queen." *English Literary Renaissance* 17 (1987):22–40.

Camden, William. *Annales rerum Anglicarum et Hibernicarum, regnante Elizabeth.* London, 1615. Books 1–3.

———. *Tomus alter annalium rerum Anglicarum, et Hibernicarum* [Book 4]. London, 1627.

———. *Annales: The True and Royall History of the Famous Empresse Elizabeth, Queene of England, France, and Ireland, etc. True Faith's Defendresse of Divine Renowne and Happy Memory* [trans. of Books 1–3]. London, 1625.

———. *The Historie of the Most Renowned and Victorious Princesse Elizabeth, Late Queene of England,* trans. R. N[orton]. London, 1630.

Chapman, George. *The Poems of George Chapman,* ed. Phyllis Bartlett. New York, 1941.

Churchyard, Thomas. *A Discourse of the Queenes Majesties Entertainement in Suffolk and Norffolk.* London, 1578.

Creighton, Mandell. *Queen Elizabeth.* Edinburgh, 1896.

C[rull], J[odocus]. *The Antiquities of St. Peters, or the Abbey Church of Westminster.* London, 1711.

Cullen, Patrick. *Spenser, Marvell, and Renaissance Pastoral.* Cambridge, MA, 1970.

Elizabeth I. *The Letters of Queen Elizabeth,* ed. and trans. G. B. Harrison. London, 1935.

———. *The Poems of Queen Elizabeth I,* ed. Leicester Bradner. Providence, RI, 1964.

———. *The Public Speaking of Queen Elizabeth: Selections from Her Official Addresses,* ed. George P. Rice, Jr. New York, 1951.

Forster, Leonard. *The Icy Fire: Five Studies in European Petrarchism.* Cambridge, 1969.

Foxe, John. *Actes and Monuments.* London, 1563.

Gascoigne, George. *Complete Works,* ed. John W. Cunliffe. Cambridge, 1907–10. 2 vols.

Grafton, Richard. *Grafton's Abridgement of the Chronicles of Englande.* 3d ed. London, 1570.

Greenblatt, Stephen. *Renaissance Self-Fashioning: From More to Shakespeare.* Chicago, 1980.

Greenlaw, Edwin A. *Studies in Spenser's Historical Allegory.* Baltimore, 1932.

Haigh, Christopher, ed. *The Reign of Elizabeth I.* London, 1984.

Hartley, T. E., ed. *Proceedings in the Parliaments of Elizabeth I.* Leicester, 1981. 2 vols.

Helgerson, Richard. *Self-Crowned Laureates: Spenser, Jonson, Milton and the Literary System.* Berkeley and Los Angeles, 1983.

Heywood, Thomas. *If You Know Not Me, You Know No Bodie: Or, The Troubles of Queene Elizabeth,* ed. Madeleine Doran. Malone Society Reprints. Oxford, 1935. 2 vols.

Hill, Christopher. *The Century of Revolution, 1603–1714.* Rev. ed. London, 1980.

Holinshed, Raphael. *Chronicles.* London, 1577. 2 vols.

Holland, Lawrence G. *Catalogue of the Pictures at Hatfield House.* London, 1891.

Hunter, G. K. *John Lyly: The Humanist as Courtier.* London, 1962.

Jones, Norman L. "Elizabeth's First Year: The Conception and Birth of the Elizabethan Political World." In *The Reign of Elizabeth I,* ed. Christopher Haigh, 27–53. London, 1984.

King, John N. *Tudor Royal Iconography: Literature and Art in an Age of Religious Crisis.* Princeton, NJ, 1989.

Levine, Mortimer. "The Place of Women in Tudor Government." In *Tudor Rule and Revolution: Essays for G. R. Elton from his American Friends,* ed. D. J. Guth and J. W. McKenna, 109–23. Cambridge, 1982.

Limon, Jerzy. *Dangerous Matter: English Drama and Politics, 1623/24.* Cambridge, 1986.

Lyly, John. *The Complete Works of John Lyly,* ed. R. Warwick Bond. Oxford, 1902. 3 vols.

MacCaffrey, Wallace T. *Queen Elizabeth and the Making of Policy, 1572–1588.* Princeton, NJ, 1981.

Miller, David Lee. *The Poem's Two Bodies: The Poetics of the 1590 "Faerie Queene."* Princeton, NJ, 1988.

Montrose, Louis Adrian. "The Elizabethan Subject and the Spenserian Text." In *Literary Theory / Renaissance Texts,* ed. Patricia Parker and David Quint, 303–40. Baltimore, 1986.

Neale, John E. *Elizabeth I and Her Parliaments.* Vol. 1. London, 1953.

———. *Queen Elizabeth.* London, 1934.

Nichols, John, ed. *Progresses and Public Processions of Queen Elizabeth.* London, 1823. 3 vols.

Norbrook, David. "Panegyric of the Monarch and Its Social Context under Elizabeth I and James I." Unpub. diss. Oxford University, 1978.

———. *Poetry and Politics in the English Renaissance.* London, 1984.

O'Connell, Michael. *Mirror and Veil: The Historical Dimension of Spenser's "Faerie Queene."* Chapel Hill, 1977.

Parry, Graham. *The Golden Age Restor'd: The Culture of the Stuart Court, 1603–42.* Manchester, 1981.

Patterson, Annabel. *Censorship and Interpretation: The Conditions of Writing and Reading in Early Modern England.* Madison, WI, 1984.

Plutarch. *Plutarch's Moralia,* ed. and trans. Frank C. Babbitt. Loeb Classical Library. Cambridge, MA, 1969. 16 vols.

Quilligan, Maureen. *Milton's Spenser: The Politics of Reading.* Ithaca, NY, 1983.

Ralegh, Sir Walter. *The Poems of Sir Walter Ralegh,* ed. Agnes M. C. Latham. London, 1951.

Ringler, William A., Jr. "Spenser, Shakespeare, Honor, and Worship." *Renaissance News* 14 (1961):159–61.

Roche, Thomas P., Jr. *The Kindly Flame: A Study of the Third and Fourth Books of Spenser's "Faerie Queene."* Princeton, NJ, 1964.

Saccio, Peter. *The Court Comedies of John Lyly: A Study in Allegorical Dramaturgy.* Princeton, NJ, 1969.

Sharpe, Kevin. "The Foundation of the Chairs of History at Oxford and Cambridge: An Episode in Jacobean Politics." *History of the Universities* 2 (1982):127–52.

Shepherd, Simon. *Amazons and Warrior Women: Varieties of Feminism in Seventeenth-Century Drama.* New York, 1981.

Sidney, Sir Philip. *Miscellaneous Prose of Sir Philip Sidney,* ed. Katherine Duncan-Jones and Jan Van Dorsten. Oxford, 1973.

Smith, Lacey Baldwin. *Elizabeth Tudor: Portrait of a Queen.* Boston, 1975.

Spenser, Edmund. *The Works of Edmund Spenser: A Variorum Edition,* ed. Edwin A. Greenlaw, C. G. Osgood, F. M. Padelford, et al. Baltimore, 1932–57. 10 vols. in 11.

Spikes, Judith Doolin. "The Jacobean History Play and the Myth of the Elect Nation." *Renaissance Drama* 8 (1977):117–49.

Stone, Lawrence. *The Family, Sex and Marriage in England 1500–1800.* New York, 1977.

Stow, John. *Annales.* London, 1592.

Stubbs, John. *John Stubbs's "Gaping Gulf with Letters and Other Relevant Documents* ed. Lloyd E. Berry. Charlottesville, 1968.

Strong, Roy. *The Cult of Elizabeth: Elizabethan Portraiture and Pageantry.* London, 1977.

———. *Gloriana: The Portraits of Queen Elizabeth I.* London, 1987.

———. *Portraits of Queen Elizabeth I.* Oxford, 1963.

Tennenhouse, Leonard. *Power on Display: The Politics of Shakespeare's Genres.* London, 1986.

Thurston, Herbert. "Rings." In *The Catholic Encyclopedia,* vol. 13, 60. New York, 1912.

Trevor-Roper, Hugh. *Queen Elizabeth's First Historian: William Camden and the Beginnings of English "Civil History."* London, 1971.

Virgil. *Eclogues, Georgics, and Aeneid,* ed. and trans. H. Rushton Fairclough. Loeb Classical Library. 2 vols. Cambridge, MA, 1940.

Waddington, Ray. *The Mind's Empire: Myth and Form in George Chapman's Narrative Poems.* Baltimore, 1974.

Weiner, Andrew. *Sir Philip Sidney and the Poetics of Protestantism: A Study of Contexts.* Minneapolis, 1978.

Wells, Robin H. *Spenser's "Faerie Queene and the Cult of Elizabeth.* London, 1983.

Wilson, Elkin. *England's Eliza.* Cambridge, MA, 1939.

Yates, Frances. "Queen Elizabeth as Astraea." *Journal of the Warburg and Courtauld Institutes* 10 (1947):27–82. Rpt. in idem, *Astraea: The Imperial Theme in the Sixteenth Century.* London, 1975.

JEFFREY KNAPP

[Empress of England and America][†]

> I was minded also to have sent you some English verses: or Rhymes, for a farewell: but by my Troth, I have no spare time in the world, to think on such Toys.
>
> —Spenser, *Two Other, Very Commendable Letters* (1580)

Of the traditional explanations for England's literary Renaissance—the Reformation, the rediscovery of the classics, the rise of nationalism and of individualism, the discovery of America—the causal account most implausible on the face of it, and perhaps for that reason least often cited in this century, is the notion that the discovery of America somehow spurred the English to write. The nineteenth-century British historian and chauvinist James Froude considered Renaissance exploration and Renaissance literature such correlative triumphs that he could describe the major Elizabethan collection of travel narratives, Richard Hakluyt's *Principal Navigations* (1589; 1598–1600), as "the Prose Epic of the modern English nation."[1] But with the demise of the modern English empire that helped excite Froude's enthusiasm, his grand view of epic-making Elizabethan explorers has managed to survive in large part only on the strength of prestige now borrowed from the literature that the explorers supposedly helped to inspire. No contemporary historian, that is, would be led to claim, as the literary critics Cleanth Brooks, R. W. B. Lewis, and Robert Penn Warren have done, that "it was the English who were first seized by the epochal idea of colonization, and . . . they were the first successful colonizers" (*American Literature* 1:3). For the English were in fact remarkably slow to colonize America, and their first attempts were dismal failures. As Howard Mumford Jones points out, comparing English to Spanish colonial efforts, "When in 1585 a forlorn little band of Englishmen were trying to stick it out on Roanoke Island, three hundred poets were competing for a prize in Mexico City" (*O Strange New World*, 85).

---

† From *An Empire Nowhere: England, America, and Literature from Utopia to The Tempest* (Berkeley: University of California Press, 1992), pp. 1–7, 12–17. Reprinted by permission of the University of California Press.

1. "England's Forgotten Worthies," 446. For Froude, the relation between the voyagers and the literature is causal in a surprisingly direct way. "We wonder at the grandeur, the moral majesty of some of Shakespeare's characters," writes Froude, but in fact "the men whom he draws were such men as he saw and knew" (445)—preeminently, Froude's essay implies, "the Elizabethan navigators," who were not merely heroic but "full for the most part with large kindness, wisdom, gentleness, and beauty" (462).

Only after the death of Elizabeth did an English colony in America succeed—Jamestown—but then for many years it too seemed on shaky ground. The ineptitude of even Jacobean colonialism appeared to many Jacobean colonialists themselves strikingly exemplified by the Virginia Company's decision early in the history of Jamestown to apply there something like the feudalist "surrender and regrant" policy instituted in Ireland during the 1540s: as Nicholas Canny explains, "The essence of the scheme was that the ruling [Irish] chieftains should surrender the lands of their lordships to the king and receive them back as a fief from the crown."[2] Accordingly, the company's agent Captain Christopher Newport arrived in Virginia with the ceremonial appurtenances necessary both to "crown" the Indian cacique Powhatan and to astound him with English sophistication.[3] Yet, as Captain John Smith (1612) reports the ceremony, the coronation so little impressed Powhatan that the English were forced in the end to apply a comically literal form of pressure simply in order to get the crown on his head:

> All things being fit for the day of his coronation, the presents were brought up, his bason, ewer, bed and furniture set up, his scarlet cloak and apparel (with much ado) put on him (being persuaded by Namontack they would do him no hurt). But a foul trouble there was to make him kneel to receive his crown, he neither knowing the majesty, nor meaning of a Crown, nor bending of the knee, endured so many persuasions, examples, and instructions, as tired them all. At last by leaning hard on his shoulders, he a little stooped, and Newport put the Crown on his head. (*Works* 1:237)

Though he finds it ludicrous, Smith also thinks the coronation worse than a waste of time and effort, and his influential editor Samuel Purchas (1625) agrees: "Smith and Newport," he writes,

> may by their examples teach the just course to be taken with such [the Indians]: the one breeding awe and dread, without Spanish or Panic terror, the other disgraced in seeking to grace with offices of humanity, those which are graceless. Neither doth it become us to use Savages with savageness, nor yet with too humane usage, but in a middle path (medio tutissimus ibis) to go and do so that they may admire and fear us, as those whom God, Religion, Civility, and Art, have made so far superior.[4]

When, in an earlier complaint about the coronation, Smith suggests what this via media might be, he still sounds far from the heroic exertions that Froude leads us to expect: Smith says of Powhatan that "we had his favor much better, only for a poor piece of Copper, till this stately

---

2. *Elizabethan Conquest*, 33; for more on the policy, see 32–34, 48–50, 62–63, 105, and 113. The anonymous writer of "Of the Voyage for Guiana" similarly recommends that the English have "the Inga of Manoa [i.e., of El Dorado] by the consent of his Lords and Casiques surrender the ensigns of his Empire to her Majesty to be returned to him again to be holden in chief of the Crown of England" (Raleigh, *Discoverie*, 146).

3. Throughout this study, I use the terms *savage* and *Indian*, rather than *Native American* or *Amerindian*, in order to emphasize that I am describing English conceptions of Native Americans, not Native Americans as they were in fact.

4. *Pilgrimes* 18:497–98; quoted in Smith, *Works* 1:237 n. 9. In every text I cite, excluding titles and Spenser's poetry, I have modernized spelling (and silently corrected obvious typographical errors). Even in the case of titles and Spenser, I have changed *i* to *j* and *u* to *v*.

kind of soliciting made him so much overvalue himself" (*Works* 1:234).
Purchas again comments, "Children are pleased with toys and awed with
rods; and this course of toys & fears hath always best prospered with wild
Indians either to do them, or to make them good to us or themselves."[5]
"Toys & fears": Smith's histories often present the second incentive as
less an alternative to the first than a way to continue the trade in trifles
even after the Indians grow unwilling; but ideally toys were supposed to
help the enlightened English put all fears aside. As Smith reports at the
beginning of his first narrative, *A True Relation* (1608), the original
encounter between Indians and the Jamestown settlers ends in battle,
but the second results in the Indians "kindly entreating us, dancing and
feasting us with strawberries, Mulberries, Bread, Fish, and other their
Country provisions whereof we had plenty: for which Captain Newport
kindly requited their least favors with Bells, Pins, Needles, beads or
Glasses, which so contented them that his liberality made them follow
us from place to place, and ever kindly to respect us" (*Works* 1:27–29).

The Spanish—successful settlers in America more than a century before
the English—had of course practiced trifling with the Indians from the
time of Columbus's first voyage. Yet, as Purchas's reference to "Spanish or
Panic terror" shows, the English generally considered Spanish colonialism
far better characterized by its "more than barbarous and savage endless
cruelties";[6] while at least until the massacre of Jamestown settlers in 1622,
English colonialism argued itself specially inclined to benignity and thus
specially dedicated to trifling.[7] Theoretically, the avoidance of war was only
the first benefit that trifling was supposed to bring. If the English colonist
required Indian land, trifles were seen as the way both to smooth and to
justify possession: "Every soul which god hath sealed for himself he hath
done it with the print of charity and Compassion, and therefore even every
foot of Land which we shall take unto our use, we will bargain and buy of
them for copper, hatchets, and such like commodities, for which they will
even sell them-selves."[8] If Indians themselves were needed, then, as this
passage suggests, trifling and not torture would best obtain their labor:
listing the expenses that the English should expect in running a Guianan
gold mine—reputedly the sort of enterprise that, in Spanish hands, always
began with enslavement and ended with genocide—Raleigh (c. 1613) is
careful to specify the price of "Hatchets knives hats shirts and other trifles

---

5. *Pilgrimes* 18:494; quoted in Smith, *Works* 1:234 n. 2. For another angry reference by Smith to the
coronation, see 2:189.
   In a broadside publicizing the coronation, the Virginia Company ("Considering . . . ," 1609)
declares that Powhatan "hath granted Freedom of Trade and Commerce to our English people,"
"witnessing the same by accepting a Copper Crown presented unto him, in the name of King *James*,
and set upon his head by Captain *Newport*." Cf. *True Declaration*, 11. The specification that the
crown was copper would seem to indicate that the company believed the coronation was itself a
sophisticatedly trifling action. As later pronouncements from the company show, it came still closer
to Smith's position; cf., e.g., the references to the Indians "glutted with our trifles" in Barbour,
Jamestown Voyages 2:266 and *True Declaration*, 40.
6. Hakluyt, "Discourse," 263; for an introduction to the "black legend" of Spanish atrocities in the
New World, see Maltby, *Black Legend*.
7. Writing for the Virginia Company after the massacre, Edward Waterhouse (1622) explicitly recommends the adoption of Spanish colonial methods, which include the use of "Mastiffs to tear"
the Indians (*Declaration*, 24). In his essay "Of Plantations" (1625), also published after the massacre, Bacon too rejects trifling, but only because he believes it is not benign enough: he advises
that "if you *Plant*, where Savages are, do not only entertain them with Trifles, and Gingles; But use
them justly, and graciously, with sufficient Guard nevertheless" (*Essayes*, 108).
8. Strachey, *Historie*, 26; cf. Smith, *Works* 3:276.

for the Indians whom we must wage, to carry baskets from the Mine to the River side."[9] The repeated failures of England and the continuing success of Spain in America, however, suggest a less optimistic view of this colonial theory and practice: that, whether by necessity or choice, England's relation to the New World was essentially a frivolous one.

Yet if England's colonial trifling makes the discovery of America seem an unlikely source of inspiration for a burgeoning English literature, neither on closer inspection do the other traditional sources for England's literary Renaissance look especially capable of having taught English literature an expansive lesson.[1] After all, the Reformation meant a break with Catholic Europe, and England became a "nation" only as it also lost its possessions on the continent. England's troubled colonialism, in other words, seems only to complete a larger picture of national isolation, in the light of which even the classics might have appeared chastening: for their rediscovery gave new life to an old image of England that uncannily reflected its modern plight—an island whose inhabitants were *penitus toto divisos orbe* (Virgil, *Eclogues* 1), wholly divided from all the world.

The strange truth about this apparently depressing picture of an England as other-worldly as the New World, however, is that the English themselves loved to highlight it. Particularly after the advent of a virgin queen able to keep the English as true believers "not walking any more according to this world, but in the fruits of the Spirit,"[2] the English could see their island as much excluding the world as being excluded by it. What would otherwise have appeared dispiriting tokens of England's weakness—its littleness, its circumscription by enemies, its female monarch—could signify instead England's abjuration of material or worldly means to power and its extraordinary reliance on God: "Whosoever will humble himself shall be exalted" (Matthew 23.12). The exceptional confidence of English colonialists in both the practical and ethical utility of trifling, then, could reflect a more general faith that the power of little England, other-worldly in both its origins and its aims, would be vindicated through the conquest of a New World—achieved by means of littleness. "God hath chosen the weak things of the world, to confound the mighty things" (1 Corinthians 1.27).

To no other group in England did this conception of England's powerful immateriality more appeal than to its poets. From classical times poetry as well had been relegated to the status of a trifle; and an English poetry had been considered almost a contradiction in terms. This classical animus did not fade with the dawn of some fresh literary individualism during the Renaissance, but itself seemed rediscovered: rather than extol their new good fortune, Tudor writers far more often lamented the "scorn and derision" (Puttenham, *English Poesie*, 18) into which literature had recently fallen. Indeed, the self-consuming grievance expressed by the poet Drummond of Hawthornden early in the next century (c. 1620) seems to show the Renaissance poet as having only internalized the prevailing derogatory view of his work: "Great men in this age either respect

9. Quoted in Strathmann, "Raleigh," 265; cf. Strachey, *Historie*, 93.
1. For an exceptional instance of skepticism regarding the standard explanations for the Renaissance, see the first chapter of C. S. Lewis's *English Literature in the Sixteenth Century*.
2. From the prayer concluding the epistle to the reader in the Geneva Bible (°°°4v). Unless otherwise noted, I quote the Geneva version throughout.

not our toys at all; or, if they do, because they *are* toys, esteem them only worthy the kiss of their hand."[3] Yet the contemporary idealization of England as itself a kind of toy located value precisely in apparent deficiency; and, as the nation increasingly celebrated its unworldliness, England's literary writers more confidently presented themselves as superior to the worldly standards that had placed literature (especially English literature) so low. In fact, by emphasizing their reputed immateriality rather than denying it, many poets came to see themselves as peculiarly equipped to recognize the value of their little nation, to epitomize by seeming contrast England's spiritual greatness, even to help direct England in its other-worldly course. It is this perceived identity of interest, I will argue—the increasingly equated paradoxicality of national sublimity on the one hand and of poetical sublimity on the other—that in large part accounts not only for the literary boom in Renaissance England but also for another otherwise curious feature of the times: around 1580, at the height of the enthusiasm generated by Frobisher's three voyages and Drake's circumnavigation, "we find no policy-maker in the Queen's circle equal in his patronage of imperialism to Sir Christopher Hatton, whose greatest influence with Elizabeth was in the areas of entertainment; no London merchant to compete with the poets, Edward Dyer, Richard Willes, George Gascoigne, and Thomas Churchyard."[4] In Tudor England, it seems, the cause of a New World empire depended on not only the colonist's trifling beads but also the poet's trifling books.

For some Tudor writers, moreover, the poet was capable of promoting empire when abroad as well as when at home. In his *Apology for Poetry* (c. 1582), Sir Philip Sidney, for instance, maintains that the only way to civilize "the most barbarous and simple Indians" will be by "the sweet delights of poetry" (9–10). His rationales are both historical and theoretical. According to Sidney, the apparent fable about the first poet Orpheus, that he was "listened to by beasts," actually represents an historical truth disguised, that Orpheus moved "stony and beastly people" (7); as George Puttenham (1589) explains, "by his discreet and wholesome lessons uttered in harmony and with melodious instruments, he brought the rude and savage people to a more civil and orderly life" (*English Poesie*, 6).[5] But what gave Orpheus such rhetorical power? Of all the arts, Sidney maintains, poetry best inspires virtue by "being the most familiar to teach it, and most princely to move towards it" (*Apology*, 41), a claim anticipated in his earlier discussion of Aesop, "whose pretty allegories, stealing under the formal tales of beasts, make many more beastly than beasts begin to hear the sound of virtue from these dumb speakers" (30); for Sidney, in other words, poetry alone can elevate its lowly, even savage auditors because poetry alone looks commensurately, and therefore invitingly, low too. Hoping to prove his point, Sidney both begins and ends the *Apology* with just such an accommodating self-debasement, first by bemoaning the fact that, "in these my not old years and idlest times," he has "(I know not by what mischance) . . . slipped into the

3. Quoted in Masson, *Drummond*, 120, cited (though misascribed) in Sheavyn, *Literary Profession*, 157–58; my emphasis.
4. Parker, *Books*, 94; for the central role in Tudor colonial advocacy of what Parker calls a "literary-nationalist tradition" (82), see Parker, passim.
5. Sidney and Puttenham are drawing on Horace in *De Arte Poetica*, ll. 391–401; for other Tudor references to this allegory in a literary-critical context, see Smith, *Elizabethan* 1:74, 231, 234, and 297.

title of a poet" (5); and finally by apologizing for the "triflingness" of his *Apology*, which he now labels an "ink-wasting toy" (87). Like Sidney, the English literary writers most prominently associated with the New World would also represent English colonialism as an extension of the poet's ideal mastery, but a mastery that could thus be realized only through the medium of toys.[6]

In order both to demonstrate this claim and to grasp its significance—to show how England's literary Renaissance arose in large part from circumstances that fortuitously encouraged the conjunction of separate traditions about unworldly poetry and unworldly England, and then how this conflation of "trifles" helped motivate a peculiarly otherworldly expansionism—my book will focus precisely on the literary "New World" texts of Renaissance England. These texts—notably More's *Utopia* (1516), Spenser's *Faerie Queene* (1590–96), and Shakespeare's *Tempest* (1611)—prove more closely related than critics have so far allowed, revolving as they do around three interlocking issues: the problem of an island empire; colonialism as a special solution to the problem; and poetry as a special model of both problem and solution. The most striking similarity among these works, however, is their setting: in each case they combine otherworldly poetry and nation, and then direct them both toward the New World, only by placing England, poetry, and America—or rather by *dis*placing them—Nowhere. Such a displacement could seem ironic, a product of skepticism regarding American ventures; and I will indeed maintain that the seemingly providential separation of England from the Catholic world during the sixteenth century helped make many of the English more isolationist, more absorbed in their island as the trifling material index of England's spiritual power. But the purpose of Nowhere for More, Spenser, and Shakespeare, I will argue, is rather to turn the English into imperialists by differentiating their other-worldly potentiality from their other-worldly island: each writer imagines the more appropriate setting for England's immaterial value to be a literary no-place that helps the English reader see the limitations of a material investment in little England alone. Nonetheless, Nowhere represents as much a constraint on these writers as a release. Faced with the inescapable negativity of a power signified only by material lack, along with the increasing difficulty of arguing that England's materially small island has no essential relation to its ideally grand destiny, these writers also have little choice but to confine their expansionism to an indirection variously conceived as unworldliness, superstition, error, incapacity, introversion, distraction, or disgrace—modes of contrary idealization that I subsume under the larger rubric, again, of trifling. The supreme irony of this shadowy indirection for Spenser in particular is that his contemporaries generally take his otherworldy poetry to represent a sublime defense of the insularism he deplores.

*   *   *

While one would expect her enemies to portray her as a personification of English weakness, it comes as something of a surprise that Elizabeth, like the trifling poet, herself repeatedly emphasized her apparent

---

6. For the literary-theoretical topos of Orphic power turned into a colonialist topos, see, e.g., Parmenius, *De Navigatione*, 178–92; Raleigh, "Observations," 33–34 (which expands Botero, *Cities*, 2); and Barbour, *Jamestown Voyages* 1:233; and Lescarbot, *Nova Francia*, 186. George Chapman (1596) expects to see "a world of Savages fall tame" before Raleigh's adventurers in Guiana "as if each man were an *Orpheus*" ("De Guiana," ll. 165–66).

insufficiency. Over considerable opposition, especially during the first two decades of her reign, she also refused to ease England's embarrassment by ceding at least part of her power to a husband; and so the English were forced to accommodate a ruler who seemed to underscore not merely the weakness of the nation but its virginal isolation. By the time of the Armada, however, even other Europeans could see Elizabeth's virginity as divinely inspired, a sign and source of her island's unyielding integrity. If England, pure and insular, came increasingly to define itself in opposition to papist and imperial Spain, the articulation of this difference turned increasingly on the virgin queen who kept England a world apart.[7] Compared to Elizabeth's motto *Semper eadem* (Always the same), for instance, the impresa of the Spanish king, *Non sufficit orbis* (The world does not suffice), seemed to the Elizabethans to express an insatiability that, unlike Alexander's, had indeed found new worlds to conquer: as one Elizabethan tract claims, "even the *Spaniards* themselves do not forbear to report that by a certain celestial constitution, the monarchy of the whole world is due unto them, having as an earnest penny thereof, through their own power and might, conquered a new world to our ancestors heretofore unknown" (Marnix, *Exhortation*, 17). And yet, as I have begun to show, the English generally considered Philip's "lustful desire, and ambitious thoughts" (Keymis, *Second Voyage*, 484) too short-sighted to complete so massive an undertaking: though Philip would like the world to be "wholly *Spain*," says William Warner (1592), the merely worldly power of "*Indian* Gold" or "pope-buld [i.e., built and bulled] hopes" (*Albions England* 9:48) will ultimately fail him.[8] The true-believing English were, of course, not impervious to a little insatiability themselves: in unpublished notes, Hakluyt (1580), for instance, recommends seizing Spanish gold shipments by "taking the straights of Magellan," and like Raleigh in Guiana exaggeratedly predicts that the "Treasure and such great Spoils as shall upon this enterprise be taken upon the sudden shall be able to work wonderful effects and to carry the world etc." (Taylor, *Original Writings* 1:163–64). But Hakluyt found that his insular readers could only with the greatest difficulty be convinced to pursue more than piratical ventures in search of American

7. Fulke Greville (c. 1604–1614) claims that Sidney became interested in another rivalry, between little England and equally little Holland: "they without any native commodities (art and diligence excepted) making themselves masters of wealth in all nations; we, again, . . . exporting our substantial riches to import a superfluous mass of trifles" (*Dedication*, 84). But the belief that Holland was using littleness rather than being used by it gained currency primarily with the Jacobeans, beginning, e.g., with Greville's "Treatise of Monarchy," 414–16. For a short bibliography of Jacobean works on Holland as a mercantile and possibly colonial power, see Shammas, "English Commercial Development," 167 and 172.

8. Warner also mentions Philip's impresa here; for other invidious references to it, see Lea, *Answer*, 25 and Keeler, *Voyage*, 245. Hakluyt is at times less optimistic than Warner about the limitations of Spanish gold: in his "Discourse" he says that Martyr "truly prognosticated" when he declared to the young Charles V that from America "shall instruments be prepared for you whereby all the world shall be under your obeisance" (244–45, quoting Eden, *Decades*, 64). Hakluyt later quotes Oviedo: "God hath given you these Indies . . . to the intent that your Majesty should be the universal and only monarch of the world" (311–12). The most famous expression of this belief appears in Ariosto (1532), who moves from an account of the discovery of America to an apocalyptic prediction concerning Charles:

> God means to grant him all this earthly Isle,
> And under this wise Prince his dear anointed,
> One shepherd and one flock he hath appointed.
> (*Orlando Furioso* 15.22–26;
> trans. Harington 15.14–18)

gold; and their reluctance to settle even those parts of America unoccu-
pied by Spain, along with the apparent lack of gold there, helped keep
colonial policy in line with the already compelling orthodox view that England shared the restraint, and therefore the sublimer power, of its
queen. "Greater than *Alexander* she was," maintains Richard Niccols in
his elegy for Elizabeth (1603), "for the world which he subdued by force,
she conquered by love" (*Expicedium*, A3v). In other words, seemingly
incapable of material coercion by virtue of her gender and her island
nation, Elizabeth could both claim and be accorded the only means of
power traditionally granted to trifling woman, which her virginity could
then idealize into something "greater" than mere "force"[9]—a "love" conquering yet chaste, an immaterial expansiveness that enabled the English not only to value the strength in Elizabeth's material weakness but
to picture her conquests as sacrificing neither her own nor England's
purity.

In such propaganda as the entertainment at Elvetham (1591), Elizabeth's charms could in fact be imagined as enabling England to command
America's riches without the English even having to travel there: the sea-
god Nereus, come to pay homage to the queen, declares that

> with me came gold breasted India,
> Who, daunted at your sight, leapt to the shore,
> And sprinkling endless treasure on this Isle,
> Left me with this jewel to present your Grace.
>   (Nichols, *Progresses* 3:112)

In one respect—the implicit comparison with Spain—this passage makes
a familiar claim: the uncoercive imperialism that Elizabeth sponsors will
in the end win more treasure in America than will Philip's barbarous
tyranny there. Yet a later entertainment more fully betrays the limitations
inherent in so literally ascribing England's trifling powers to the mere
"sight" of Elizabeth. Alluding to an Indian prince whom Raleigh had just
brought back from Guiana, the "Device Made by the Earl of Essex for the
Entertainment of Her Majesty" (1595) presents another (or perhaps even
the same) Guianan to Elizabeth, and tells her that, though the prince has
been blind from birth, an Indian prophecy has foretold that he will ultimately "expel the Castilians" from his land. First, however, he must learn
to see, and an oracle has explained where he can find his cure:

> Seated between the Old World and the New
> A land there is no other land may touch,
> Where reigns a Queen in peace and honor true;
> Stories or fables do describe no such.
>   (Bacon, *Works* 3:388)

Hence the prince has traveled to virginal England and queen, where his
cure, yet also his transformation, instantly begins: "Your Majesty's sacred
presence hath wrought the strangest innovation that ever was in the world.

---

9. For a fine recent discussion of this old chestnut about Elizabeth, see Montrose, "Shaping
Fantasies."

You have here before you Seeing Love, a Prince indeed, but of greater territories than all the Indies" (389). Like the Elvetham entertainment, the
"Device" manages, then, to celebrate the miraculously expansive strength
of Elizabeth's isolated "presence"; but if the foreign territories that Elizabeth sways turn out to be far greater than even Guiana, they also end up
looking like no territories in particular: the "Device" makes Elizabeth
imperial only at the expense of the actual expansionism that the Guianan-
turned-Cupid seemed originally intended to advance.[1]

If any of her subjects helped Elizabeth to represent herself as a conqueror more benign and therefore more powerful than the king of Spain,
it was Spenser, the most "Elizabethan" poet by virtue not only of his singular attention to the queen but of the pension that the queen granted to
no other writer. In fact, Spenser's own career seemed itself to demonstrate
how an English "trifle" like Elizabeth could come to wield such authority:
though born the son of an artisan, Spenser by the time of his death could
be hailed as the English Virgil, "our principal poet."[2] In an important recent
study, Richard Helgerson has argued that Spenser rose to such "laureate"
rank by resisting the "pressure . . . to define himself and his work" in the
self-dismissive terms of "amateur" poets (Self-Crowned, 67). But as I have
already begun to show, both the amateur and the laureate poet in Renaissance England were able to find value in poetry precisely as trifling; and
Spenser the laureate was only more, not less, committed than the amateur
to the self-dismissive pose. Consistently presenting himself as the unworthy poet and lover of Elizabeth and England, Spenser argued that the sublimity of each was best revealed in contrast to his own "meanness," as in a
sonnet addressed to yet another lesser Elizabeth, his future wife Elizabeth
Boyle:

> To all those happy blessings which ye have,
>   with plenteous hand by heaven upon you thrown,
>   this one disparagement they to you gave,
>   that ye your love lent to so meane a one:
> Yee whose high worths surpassing paragon,
>   could not on earth have found one fit for mate,
>   ne but in heaven matchable to none,
>   why did ye stoup unto so lowly state?
> But ye thereby much greater glory gate,
>   then had ye sorted with a princes pere:
>   for now your light doth more it selfe dilate,
>   and in my darknesse greater doth appeare.
> Yet since your light hath once enlumind me,
>   with my reflex yours shall encreased be.
>   (Amoretti, sonnet 66)

As this passage first admits, however, what Spenser elsewhere calls his
dark conceits (V 1:167) could at the same time appear to obscure the

---

1. See Bacon, Works 8:387–88, for the critical debate concerning the relation of the entertainment
   to Raleigh. The inability of scholars to decide whether the entertainment supports or derides
   Raleigh reflects my point.
2. Chamberlain, Letters, 1:64–65; for Spenser matched with Virgil in his own lifetime, see, e.g., Wells,
   Spenser Allusions, 7, 29, 36, 41, 60, and 63.

ideals he celebrates, making them not only hard to see but hard to see apart from the "meane" poetry shadowing them. And indeed, like the cult that developed around the figure of the queen, the extraordinarily high regard in which "lowly" Spenser came to be held could just as well seem to reflect England's increasing complacence about its own inconsequence. Nothing makes England's love for Spenser appear more of a "disparagement" for the nation than the contrast between Spenser and his Iberian counterparts. Where an epic like Ercilla's *Araucana* (1569–90), an account of Spain's war with the Araucanan Indians, commits itself so thoroughly to the actual events of the Conquest as to be prefaced by Ercilla's assertion that he began writing his poem in the Araucanan battlefield (1.121), Spenser's *Faerie Queene* (1590–96) derives, according to a dedicatory sonnet (V 3:194),[3] from the "savadge soyle" only of Ireland, not the New World; the epic was composed by "a rustick Muse," not an heroic one; and she has chosen to represent not Indians but fairies.

I will argue, however, that Spenser welcomes such apparently invidious comparisons: he intends his fairy poem to look both trifling and epic at once, because he wants to stress that the real sinews of war consist not of worldly Spanish gold but of otherworldly English virtues. Yet, just as he deplores Spanish materialism, so Spenser also condemns England's cultish absorption in the queen's literal "presence." He wants England to recognize the real power that the "sight" of Elizabeth's weak body should contrastingly highlight—what Spenser's friend Gabriel Harvey calls "her Empiring spright" (V 3:187). So persistently, indeed, does Spenser attack the insularist admirers of Elizabeth that, with increasing boldness, he tries to displace the queen in England's eyes with the more errant representative trifles of both his poetry and himself. By requiring his readers to envision Elizabeth only through the conspicuously trifling mirror of a superstitious and immaterial no-place, Fairyland, Spenser hopes that his poetical *Queene* will conversely reflect a more extensive field for Elizabeth than her virginal body or virginal island; while, in his self-portrayals, he refuses to limit himself even to the excursive identity of a colonist, an identity he acknowledges, in a characteristically indirect and dismissive way, by the punning name of his pastoral, not heroic, persona, Colin.[4] Yet the polemical necessity of emphasizing first his literal distance from Elizabeth's island and second his incommensurability to any particular elsewhere he might settle increasingly forces Spenser to associate his representative otherworldliness less with the vast and uncolonized New World than with the island neighboring England that he himself helped occupy, Ireland. Spenser's allegorical trifling, in other words, ultimately proves as incapable of escaping the little, insular otherworlds that paradoxically suggest English power as is the supposedly literal-minded cult of Elizabeth—so incapable, in fact, that when later writers like Cowley and

---

3. V is Knapp's abbreviation for the Variorum Edition of Spenser's Works [*Editors' note*].
4. For the possibility of the pun, see Richard Stanyhurst in his "Description of Ireland" (1577) on a community within the English Pale: "But Fingall especially from time to time hath been so addicted to all the points of husbandry, as that they are nicknamed by their neighbors, for their continual drudgery, Collonnes, of the Latin word Coloni, whereunto the clipt English word clown seemeth to be answerable" (4). Cf. Jonson's *Tale of a Tub* (acted 1633) 1.3.30–47; the editors' note (*Jonson* 9:280); and a Jamestown figure, George Percy, who spells *colony* "Colline" ("Trewe Relacyon," 267). Colin Clout is, of course, not even a husbandman: his mere association with coloni-alism will become a feature of the red-cross knight's identity.

Addison reexamine the fairy empire that Elizabeth and Spenser helped create, it will appear to them truly unconnected not just to America but also to a now imperial England. For these writers, the otherworldly English potentiality that Spenser's poetry would shadow has come to seem an empire merely—yet also sublimely—poetical.

Bibliography

PRIMARY SOURCES

Ariosto, Ludovico. *Orlando Furioso.* 1516, 1521, 1532. Trans. Sir John Harinton. 1591. *Ariosto's* Orlando Furioso, ed. R. McNulty. Oxford: Oxford University Press, 1972.

Bacon, Sir Francis. *The Essayes or Counsels, Civill and Morall.* 1597–1625. Ed. Michael Kiernan. Cambridge, Mass.: Harvard University Press, 1985.

———. *Works.* Ed. James Spedding, Robert Leslie Ellis, and Douglas Denn Heath. 14 vols. London, 1858–74.

Barbour, Philip, ed. *The Jamestown Voyages under the First Charter, 1606–1609.* 2 vols. Hakluyt Soc., 2nd ser., vols. 136–37. London, 1969.

The Bible. [Geneva Version.] Geneva, 1560.

Botero, Giovanni. *A Treatise, Concerning the Causes of the Magnificencie and Greatnes of Cities.* 1589. Trans. Robert Peterson. London, 1606.

Chamberlain, John. *The Letters of John Chamerlain.* Ed. Norman E. McClure. 2 vols. Philadelphia: American Philosophical Soc., 1939.

Chapman, George. *The Poems.* Ed. Phyllis Bartlett. 1941. Reprint. New York: Russell & Russell, 1962.

Eden, Richard, trans. *The Decades of the New World or West India.* 1555. Trans. of Peter Martyr [Pietro Martire d'Anghiera], *De Orge Novo* (1511–30). In *The First Three English Books on America,* ed. Edward Arber. Birmingham, 1885.

Ercilla y Zuniga, Alonso de. *La Araucana.* 1569–1590. Ed. Marcos A. Morinigo and Isaias Lerner. 2 vols. Madrid: Clasicos Castalia, 1979.

Greville, Fulke, Lord Brooke. *A Dedication to Sir Philip Sidney.* (Written 1604–14.) In *Prose Works,* ed. John Gouws. Oxford: Clarendon, 1986.

———. "A Treatise of Monarchy." (Written c. 1599–1604, with later revisions.) In *The Remains,* ed. G. A. Wilkes. Oxford: Oxford University Press, 1965.

Hakluyt, Richard. "Discourse of Western Planting" ["A Particuler Discourse Concerninge the Greate Necessitie and Manifolde Comodyties That Are Like to Growe to This Realme of Englande byu the Westerne Discoveries Lately Attempted"] MS, 1584. In *The Original Writings and Correspondence of the Two Richard Hakluyts,* ed. Eva G. R. Taylor, 2:211–326. Hakluyt Soc., 2nd ser., vol. 77. London, 1935.

Jonson, Benjamin. *Ben Jonson.* Ed. C. H. Herford and Percy and Evelyn Simpson. 11 vols. Oxford: Oxford University Press, 1925–52.

Keeler, Mary Frear, ed. *Sir Francis Drake's West Indian Voyage, 1585–86.* Hakluyt Soc., 2nd ser., vol. 149. London, 1981.

Keymis, Lawrence. *A Relation of the Second Voyage to Guiana.* 1596. In *The Principal Navigations,* ed. Richard Hakluyt, 10:441–501. Reprint. Glasgow: MacLehose, 1905.

[Lea], I[ames]. *The Birth, Purpose and Mortall Wound of the Romish Holie League*. London, 1589.

Lescarbot, Marc. *Nova Francia: Or the Description of That Part of New France, which is One Continent with Virginia*. 1609. Trans. P. Erondelle from *Histoire de la Nouvelle France*. 1609. Ed. H. P. Biggar. New York: Harper, 1928.

[Marnix van Sant Aldegonde, Philips van.] *A Pithie, and Most Earnest Exhortation, Concerning the Estate of Christiandome*. Antwerp [London], 1583.

Niccols, Richard. *Expicedium*. London, 1603.

Nichols, John, ed. *The Progresses and Public Processions of Queen Elizabeth*. 3 vols. London, 1823.

Parmenius, Stephen. *De Navigatione*. 1582. In *The New Found Land of Stephen Parmenius*, trans. and ed. D. B. Quinn and Neil Cheshire. Toronto: University of Toronto Press, 1972.

Percy, George. "A Trewe Relacyon of the Procedeinges . . . in Virginia from . . . 1609 untill . . . 1612." MS. In *Tyler's Quarterly Historical and Genealogical Magazine* 3 (1922): 260–82.

Purchas, Samuel. *Hakluytus Posthumus, or Purchas His Pilgrimes*. 4 vols. 1625. Reprinted in 20 vols. Glasgow: MacLehose, 1905–6.

[Puttenham, George.] *The Arte of English Poesie*. 1589. Ed. Gladys Doidge Willcock and Alice Walker. 1936. Reprint. Cambridge: Cambridge University Press, 1970.

Ralegh, Sir Walter. *The Discoverie of the Large, Rich, and Bewtifull Empyre of Guiana*. 1596. Ed. V. T. Harlow. London: Argonaut, 1928.

———. "Observations Concerning the Causes of the Magnificency and Opulency of Cities." In *Sir Walter Raleigh's Sceptick [and Other Works]*, 33–58. London, 1651.

Sidney, Sir Philip. *An Apology for Poetry*. 1595. (Written c. 1580–82.) Ed. Forrest G. Robinson. Indianapolis: Bobbs-Merrill, 1970.

Smith, G. Gregory, ed. *Elizabethan Critical Essays*. 2 vols. London: Oxford University Press, 1904.

Smith, John. *Complete Works*. Ed. Philip L. Barbour. 3 vols. Chapel Hill: University of North Carolina Press, 1986.

Spenser, Edmund. *Works: A Variorum Edition*. Ed. Edwin Greenlaw et al. 9 vols., index, and *A Life of Edmund Spenser* by Alexander Judson. Baltimore: Johns Hopkins University Press, 1932–57.

Stanyhurst, Richard. "Description of Ireland." 1577. In *Holinshed's Chronicles*, by Raphael Holinshed et al., vol. 6. Reprint. London, 1808.

Strachey William. "The Historie of Travell into Virginia Britania." MS, 1612. Ed. Louis B. Wright and Virginia Freund. Hakluyt Soc., 2nd ser., vol. 103. London, 1953.

Taylor, Eva G. R., ed. *The Original Writings and Correspondence of the Two Richard Hakluyts*. Hakluyt Soc., 2nd ser., vols. 76–77. London, 1935.

A True Declaration of the Estate of the Colonie in Virginia. London, 1610.

Virginia Company. Broadside. "Considering there is no publicke action, [etc.]." [London, 1609?]

Warner, William. *Albions England*. London, 1586–1606.

Waterhouse, Edward. *A Declaration of the State of the Colony and Affaires in Virginia*. London, 1622.

Wells, William, ed. *Spenser Allusions in the Sixteenth and Seventeenth Centuries.* Compiled by Ray Heffner, Dorothy E. Mason [and] Frederick M. Padelford. Chapel Hill, University of North Carolina Press, 1972.

SECONDARY SOURCES

Brooks, Cleanth, R. W. B. Lewis, and Robert Penn Warren, eds. *American Literature: The Makers and the Making.* 4 vols. New York: St. Martin's Press, 1973–74.
Canny, Nicholas. *The Elizabethan Conquest of Ireland: A Pattern Established, 1565–76,* Hassocks: Harvester Press, 1976.
Froude, James Anthony. "England's Forgotten Worthies." 1852. In *Short Studies on Great Subjects,* 1:443–501. 1867. Reprint. London, 1888.
Helgerson, Richard. *Self-Crowned Laureates: Spenser, Jonson, Milton, and the Literary System.* Berkeley: University of California Press, 1983.
Jones, Howard Mumford. *O Strange New World. American Culture: The Formative Years.* 1952. Reprint. New York: Viking, 1964.
Lewis, C. S. *English Literature in the Sixteenth Century, Excluding Drama.* Oxford: Clarendon, 1954.
Maltby, William S. *The Black Legend in England.* Durham: Duke University Press, 1971.
Masson, David. *Drummond of Hawthornden: The Story of His Life and Writings.* London, 1873.
Montrose, Louis Adrian. "'Shaping Fantasies': Figurations of Gender and Power in Elizabethan Culture." *Representations* 2 (1983): 61–94.
Parker, John. *Books to Build an Empire: A Bibliographical History of English Overseas Interests to 1620.* Amsterdam: N. Israel, 1965.
Shammas, Carol. "English Commercial Development and American Colonization, 1560–1620." In *The Westward Enterprise,* ed. K. R. Andrews et al., 151–47. Liverpool: Liverpool University Press, 1979.
Strathmann, Ernest A. "Ralegh Plans His Last Voyage." *The Mariner's Mirror* 50 (1964): 261–70.

FRANCES A. YATES

[England's Astraea]†

Queen Elizabeth as Astraea[1]

It would seem that from the very beginning of her reign the Virgo-Astraea symbol was used of Elizabeth.[2] We read in Camden that 'In the beginning of her late Majesties Reign, one upon happy hope conceived, made an half

---

† From *Astraea: The Imperial Theme in the Sixteenth Century* by Frances A. Yates (London: Routledge & Kegan Paul, 1975), pp. 59, 74, 76, 80. (Copyright © the Estate of Dame Frances Yates, 1975); reproduced by kind permission of PFD on behalf of the Estate of Dame Frances Yates.
1. Warburg drew attention in a note to the use of Astraea as a name for Elizabeth (see A. Warburg, *Gesammelte Schriften,* Leipzig-Berlin, 1932, I, p. 415).
2. E. C. Wilson, *England's Eliza,* Cambridge, Mass., 1939, is a useful survey of imagery used of Queen Elizabeth by the poets.

of the Zodiack, with *Virgo*, rising, adding JAM REDIT ET VIRGO. . . .'[3] But the use of the image was at its height in the years following the Armada.

The play *Histrio-Mastix* (1589?) contains pageant-like scenes in glorification of Elizabeth's reign. Peace, Bacchus, Ceres, and Plenty enter at one door, bearing the cornucopiae, and Poverty and her attendants vanish by the other door. After speeches in praise of Peace, Astraea enters 'Ushered by Fame, supported by Fortitude and Religion, followed by Virginity and Artes'. Peace does obeisance to Astraea for her justice and virginity and the latter then 'mounts unto the throne'. A note in the margin explains that Astraea represents Queen Elizabeth, and she is hailed by the following paean:[4]

> Mount, Emperesse, whose praise for Peace shall mount,
> Whose glory which thy solid vertues wonne,
> Shall honour Europe whilst there shines a Sunne.
> Crown'd with Heavens inward beauties, worlds applause
> Thron'd and repos'd within the loving feare
> Of thy adoring Subjects: live as long
> As Time hath life, and Fame a worthy tongue!
> Still breath our glory, the worlds *Empresse,*
> *Religions* Gardian, *Peaces* patronesse!
> Now flourish Arts, the Queene of *Peace* doth raigne;
> Vertue triumph, now she doth sway the stemme,
> Who gives to Vertue honours Diadem.
> All sing Paens to her sacred worth,
> Which none but Angels tongues can warble forth:
> Yet sing, for though we cannot light the Sunne,
> Yet utmost might hath kinde acceptance wonne.

> Song.
> Religion, Arts and Merchandise
> triumph, triumph:
> Astraea rules, whose gracious eyes
> triumph, triumph.
> O're *Vices* conquest whose desires
> triumph, triumph:
> Whose all to chiefest good aspires,
> then all triumph.

Here we have Elizabeth-Astraea as the empress of the world, guardian of religion, patroness of peace, restorer of virtue; she is hailed with a Roman triumph which extols the wealth and prosperity which her golden age have brought.

George Peele's *Descensus Astraeae*, a pageant given to welcome a new lord mayor of London in 1591, brings out strongly the reforming side of Astraea's mission. The presenter of the pageant describes it as an emblem of Elizabeth as Astraea 'descended of the Trojan British line'. At the top of

3. W. Camden, *Remains,* London, 1674 ed., p. 466.
4. *The School of Shakespeare,* ed. R. Simpson, New York, 1878, II, pp. 84–7; cf. Wilson, *op. cit.,* pp. 109–10.

the pageant Astraea appeared as a shepherdess, with her sheep-hook, speaking these words:[5]

> Feed on, my flock among the gladsome green
> Where heavenly nectar flows above the banks . . .

She is opposed by Superstition, a Friar, and Ignorance, a Priest, who attempts in vain to poison the fountain from which her flock is drinking. One of the Graces thus describes Astraea:[6]

> Whilom, when Saturn's golden reign did cease,
>   And iron age had kindled cruel wars,
> Envy in wrath perturbing common peace,
>   Engendering canker'd hate and bloody jars;
> Lo, then Olympus' king, the thundering Jove,
>   Raught hence this gracious nymph Astraea fair:
> Now once again he sends her from above,
>   Descended through the sweet transparent air;
> And here she sits in beauty fresh and sheen,
> Shadowing the person of a peerless queen.

Peele clearly associates the return of the virgin of the golden age with reformation in religion. She is the shepherdess of her people's souls, guarding them with her sheep-hook. She is exercising that supreme pastorship and authority in things spiritual at which the Catholic Harding protested and which Jewel defended on the ground of the authority of emperors to judge ecclesiastical causes. Her golden age is the age of purified religion. She is the simple shepherdess, contrasting with the superstitious friar and the ignorant priest. It is in a somewhat similarly controversial vein than an anonymous poet lamented after Elizabeth's death that:[7]

> Righteous *Astraea* from the earth is banish't.
> And from our sight the morning star is vanish't
> Which did to us a radiant light remaine,
> But was a comet to the eye of *Spaine:*
> From whose chaste beames so bright a beautie shin'de,
> That all their whorish eyes were stricken blinde.

Peele was a purveyor of both town and court pageantry and in both spheres the Astraea image holds good. In a poem which reflects one of the Accession Day tilts, held in 1595, Peele urges Clio to bring the Muses to Elizabeth-Astraea's court:[8]

> Conduct thy learnèd company to court,
> Eliza's court, Astraea's earthly heaven;

---

5. George Peele, *Works*, ed. A. H. Bullen, London, 1888, I, p. 363.
6. *Ibid.*, p. 364.
7. John Lane, *An Elegie upon the death of the high and renowned Princesse, our late Soueraigne Elizabeth*, Fugitive Tracts, second series, no. 2, London, 1875.
8. *Anglorum Feriae*; Peele, *Works*, ed. cit., II, p. 343.

There take survey of England's emperess,
And in her praise tune your heroic songs . . .

And after his description of the tilt, and of the devices and accoutrements of the knights, he concludes on the same note:[9]

Long may they run in honour of the day!
Long may she live to do them honour's right,
To grace their sports and them as she hath done,
England's Astraea, Albion's shining sun!

In a very similar poem, describing the Accession Day tilt of 1591,[1] we know that Peele's allusions to Elizabeth as a Vestal Virgin related to an elaborate presentation of the Temple of Vesta erected for the occasion.[2] Very possibly his references to the queen as Astraea in the 1595 Accession Day poem may also refer to some visual presentation of the Astraea theme on that occasion.[3]

✳   ✳   ✳

Richard Barnfield's *Cynthia* (1595) is based on a theme quite common in Elizabethan literature, which found visual expression in the picture at Hampton Court, which is dated 1569. It consists of a revised Judgment of Paris in which the golden apple is awarded to neither Juno, Venus, nor Minerva, but to the Virgin Queen, a goddess who excels them all. Barnfield's poem, which shows throughout the influence of Spenser, describes Elizabeth as a 'Fairy Queen' reigning in peace and union amidst the ocean. To this sacred virgin Jove (not Paris) awards the golden ball, and it is as Virgo that she receives this distinction:[4]

Thus, sacred Virgin, Muse of chastitie,
This difference is betwixt the Moone and thee:
Shee shines by Night; but thou by Day do'st shine:
Shee monthly changeth; thou dost nere decline:

9. *Ibid.,* pp. 354–5.
1. *Polyhymnia; ibid.,* pp. 287 ff.
2. The pavilion 'made of white Taffeta . . . being in proportion like unto the sacred Temple of the Virgins Vestall' erected for this occasion is described by Sir W. Segar, *Honor, military and civill,* London, 1602, Bk III, ch. 54. See E. K. Chambers, *Sir Henry Lee,* Oxford, 1936, pp. 135 ff.
3. The prevalence of the Virgo idea in the *imprese* reported by Camden rather supports the notion that this may have been a leading theme at one or some of the Accession Day tilts. For example: 'A very good invention was that to shew his stay and support by a Virgin Prince, who presented in his shield, the Zodiack with the characters only of *Leo and Virgo,* and this word, HIS EGO PRAESIDIIS' (Camden, *Remains, ed cit.,* pp. 460–1).
   'The Star called *Spica Virginis,* one of the fifteen which are accounted to be of the first magnitude among the Astronomers, with a scrole inwritten, MIHI VITA SPICA VIRGINIS, declared thereby haply, that had that Star in the Ascendant at his Nativity, or rather that he lived by the gracious favour of a Virgin Prince' (*ibid.,* p. 461).
   'It may be doubtful whether he affected his Sovereign or Justice more zealously, which made a man hovering in the Air, with FEROR AD ASTRAEAM' (*ibid.,* p. 462).
   Possibly the jewel of a woman 'called virtute or virgo' with compasses in one hand, a garland in the other, and standing on a rainbow may have been a representation of some 'Virgo' *impresa* (the jewel is described in John Nichols, *The Progresses of Queen Elizabeth,* London, 1823, II, p. 79).
4. R. Barnfield, *Poems,* ed. E. Arber, 1896, pp. 54–5. Other examples of Judgments of Paris in which the prize is awarded to Elizabeth are, Francis Sabie, *Pan's Pipe,* 1595; George Peele, *Arraignment of Paris,* 1584. Cf. Wilson, *op. cit.,* pp. 147, 431.
   The award to the mysterious 'Avisa' of a place above Juno, Minerva, or Venus (*Willobie His Avisa,* 1594, ed. G. B. Harrison, London, 1926, pp. 23 ff.) ought to be placed in the context of all these Judgments of Paris.

> Yet neither Sun, nor Moone, thou canst be named,
> Because thy light hath both their beauties shamed:
> Then, since an heauenly Name doth thee befall,
> Thou Virgo art: (if any Signe at all).

Here Virgo, whilst still remembering her connection with the sign, has become even more than the 'Zodiac's joy' or the 'Planets' chief delight'. She is a being greater than the sun and moon.

*   *   *

The attribution to Elizabeth of all the virtues was a commonplace which fits very easily into the Astraea theme, for Justice is an imperial virtue, and also the virtue which is theoretically supposed to include all the others. When Astraea comes again she brings with her, not only Justice, but all other banished virtues, as Ariosto says. The portrait of Elizabeth in Dover Town Hall shows, behind the queen, a column on which can be seen the three theological and the four cardinal virtues; Faith, Hope, Charity, Justice, Fortitude, Temperance, Prudence. The central position is held by Justice with the sword, and this virtue seems to be wearing a dress similar to that of Elizabeth herself. Perhaps one may imagine that this might be a picture of the Virgin Queen as Astraea-Justice, including all the virtues.

*   *   *

It is by now already apparent that the elucidation of Astraea as a name for Elizabeth throws beams of illumination upon many of her other epithets and aspects. This can be still further emphasized by turning to Sir John Davies of Hereford's *Hymnes to Astraea*.

The hymns to Astraea are a series of twenty-six fifteen-lined poems; in each poem the first letters of each line, when read downwards, spell the words ELISABETHA REGINA. This is a very near formulation of Astraea-worship in its relation to Eliza-worship, and the various poems bring out various aspects of the cult.

The first is merely the general statement, that Elizabeth Regina is the Virgin of the golden age returned to earth:[5]

> E arly before the day doth spring
> L et us awake my Muse, and sing;
> I t is no time to slumber,
> S o many ioyes this time doth bring,
> A s Time will faile to number.
>
> B ut whereto shall we bend our layes?
> E uen vp to Heauen, againe to raise
> T he Mayd, which thence descended;
> H ath brought againe the golden dayes,
> A nd all the world amended.
>
> R udenesse it selfe she doth refine,
> E uen like an Alychymist diuine;

5. Sir John Davies, *Complete Poems*, ed. A. B. Grosart, London, 1876, I, p. 129.

G rosse times of yron turning
I nto the purest forme of gold;
N ot to corrupt, till heauen waxe old,
A nd be refined with burning.

It is, on the whole, a courtly interpretation of the theme. Astraea has refined the rude manners of the age of iron and ushered in a more civilized epoch.

One side of the Astraea theme upon which we have not hitherto touched comes out very clearly in these hymns, namely her relation to Spring. In the golden age, Spring eternal reigned, and the virgin of the golden age brings Spring with her:[6]

E arth now is greene, and heauen is blew,
L iuely Spring which makes all new,
I olly Spring doth enter;
S weete yong sun-beames doe subdue
A ngry, agèd Winter.

B lasts are milde, and seas are calme,
E uery meadow flowes with balme,
T he Earth wears all her riches;
H armonious birdes sing such a psalme,
A s eare and heart bewitches.

R eserue (sweet Spring) this Nymph of ours,
E ternall garlands of thy flowers,
G reene garlands neuer wasting;
I n her shall last our *State's* faire Spring,
N ow and for euer flourishing,
A s long as Heauen is lasting.

Two of the other poems also relate to Elizabeth-Astraea as Spring; one is addressed to her as May, where she is called 'May of Maiestie'; and another to her as Flora, 'Empresse of Flowers'.

That Virgo can represent the Spring might seem at first sight something of an anomaly, for, as we know, she is an autumnal sign, bearing corn in her hand. The cornucopiae overflowing with fruitful abundance and *ubertas rerum* would seem to be more properly her own than the flowers of Spring. It is, however, the conflation of Virgo the sign of autumn with Astraea the virgin of the golden age which brings about this seeming anomaly, for in the eternal spring of the golden age flowers and fruits grew together at the same time: 'Then spring was everlasting, and gentle zephyrs with warm breath played with the flowers that sprang unplanted. Anon the earth, untilled, brought forth her stores of grain. . . .'[7] Astraea's spring is not the ordinary season but the eternal spring of the golden age. This is very clearly brought out by Sir Philip Sidney's sister, Mary, Countess of Pembroke, in her poem entitled *Dialogue between two shepherds Thenot*

6. *Ibid.*, I, p. 131.
7. Ovid, *Metamorphoses*, I, 107–10.

and Piers, in praise of Astraea, written in honour of the queen's visit to Wilton. Thenot's compliments to Astraea are contradicted by Piers, yet the contradiction always turns out to be an even greater compliment. Thus Thenot says:[8]

> Astraea may be justly said,
> A field in flowery robe arrayed,
>   In Season freshly springing.

to which Piers replies:

> That Spring endures but shortest time,
> This never leaves Astraea's clime,
>   Thou liest instead of singing.

The Astraea-Elizabeth garlanded with spring flowers of Davies's poem represents 'our State', the state of England renewed in a golden age, a *renovatio temporum* which the poet hopes will last for ever. She is here the state virgin, the 'Renaissance' princess, centre of a newly refined court.

Her aspect as the representative of the virtues is not forgotten in these hymns, which tell of her moral virtue in the control of her passions ('Of the passions of her heart', XX);[9] of her innumerable intellectual virtues which no mathematician can count ('Of the innumerable virtues of her minde', XXI);[1] of her wisdom, ('Right princely vertue fit to reaigne', XXII);[2] and above all, of her justice:[3]

> Of her Justice
> E xil'd *Astraea* is come againe,
> L o here she doth all things maintaine
> I n *number, weight,* and *measure*;
> S he rules vs with delightfull paine,
> A nd we obey with pleasure.
>
> B y *Loue* she rules more then by *Law,*
> E uen her great mercy breedeth awe;
> T his is her sword and scepter:
> H erewith she hearts did euer draw,
> A nd this guard euer kept her.
>
> R eward doth sit at her right-hand,
> E ach vertue thence taks her garland
> G ather'd in Honor's garden;
> I n her left hand (wherein should be
> N ought but the sword) sits Clemency
> A nd conquers Vice with pardon.

8. *A Dialogue betweene two Shepheards, Thenot, and Piers, in praise of* Astraea, *made by the excellent Lady, the Lady Mary Countesse of Pembroke, at the Queenes Maiesties being at her house,* reprinted in *A Poetical Rhapsody,* ed. H. C. Rollins, Cambridge, Mass., 1931, I, pp. 15 ff.
9. Davies, *ed. cit.,* I, p. 148.
1. *Ibid.,* p. 149.
2. *Ibid.,* p. 150.
3. *Ibid.,* p. 151.

The justice of Astraea is here tempered with mercy, and she appears in this poem as a combination of the imperial virtues of Justitia and Clementia.

The hymns to Astraea as a whole cover nearly all the points included in the cult of the imperial virgin. There is an engraving of Queen Elizabeth which shows her in a glory and with a crown of stars encircling her head. In its original version it was accompanied by verses by Sir John Davies,[4] and so is perhaps a representation of her under that poet's favourite image, as the starry virgin of the golden age returned to earth. The contrast between the crudity of this representation and the accomplished poetic imagery which flows from Sir John's pen, is typical of the strange gap in quality between the visual arts and the literature of the period.

Spenser and Astraea

Spenser is the Virgil of the Elizabethan golden age, and the *Faerie Queene* its great epic poem. Here, if anywhere, we should expect to find Astraea enshrined, and here in fact we do find her, not only under that name but under many names. The concept of Elizabeth as the imperial virgin is the lynch-pin of the poem; it is the Prime Mover, round which its whole elaborate universe of moral allegory revolves.

The ground-plan of the *Faerie Queene*, as Spenser explained in his letter to Raleigh, was that it should present in an allegorical framework every virtue, both public and private. Of the projected twelve books on the private virtues we have only six and part of a seventh; whilst the section on the public virtues, which would probably also have had twelve parts, is non-existent. All these virtues were summed up in the queen, or rather in the 'most high Mightie and Magnificent *Empresse*' to use the words of the dedication. Gloriana, the fairy queen, represented, so Spenser informs Raleigh, Queen Elizabeth in her public character as the just and righteous ruler; whereas Belphoebe was Elizabeth in her private character as a most beautiful and virtuous lady. The combination Gloriana-Belphoebe is Elizabeth as all the virtues, public and private. Belphoebe, the queen as private virtue, symbolized above all her chastity; Gloriana—the queen as public virtue—symbolized the glory of her just government. Elizabeth is implored by Spenser not to refuse[5]

> In mirrors more than one her self to see,
> But either Gloriana let her choose
> Or in Belphoebe fashioned to be:
> In th' one her rule, in th' other her rare chastity.

4. See Freeman M. O'Donoghue, *A Descriptive and Classified Catalogue of Portraits of Queen Elizabeth*, London, 1894, p. 62; Roy Strong, *Portraits of Queen Elizabeth I*, Oxford, 1963, Posthumous portraits, 9. The picture was engraved by F. Delaram, and the verses accompanying it by Sir John Davies are as follows:

> Lo here her type, who was of late,
>   the Propp of Belgia, Stay of France:
> Spaine's Foyle, Faith's Shield, and Queen of State;
>   of Armes and Learning, Fate and Chance:
> In briefe; of women, neere was seene,
>   so great a Prince, so good a Queene.

    Reduced in size and with the inscription cut off, this engraving became the frontispiece to Camden's *Annales, or the Historie of the Most Renowned and Victorious Princess Elizabeth*, London, 1630. It also appears in Nichols, *op. cit.* (See O'Donoghue, *op. cit.*, pp. 62–3; Strong, *op. cit.*, Posthumous portraits, 16.)

5. *Faerie Queene*, BK III, v; Edmund Spenser, *Works: A Variorum Edition*, eds. Edwin Greenlaw *et al.*, Baltimore, 1932–57, III, p. 2.

Belphoebe-Gloriana is the Virgin-Ruler, religiously adored for her virginity and her justice.

The historical framework of the poem also brings out the theme of the advent of a just, imperial virgin. The British virgin whose advent is prophesied to Britomart by Merlin (in that prophecy which is a transference to Elizabeth of the prophecy of the *Orlando furioso*) is to be a descendant of Britomart and Artegal, the representatives of the virtues of Chastity and Justice. And she comes of an 'imperial' Trojan line. The descent of Gloriana from the Trojan Brut is the theme of the tenth canto of Book I, and the story is told by Merlin to Britomart in Book III when he foresees that out of her 'ancient Trojan blood' will spring a line of kings and 'sacred Emperors' culminating in the royal virgin Elizabeth.

Thus the dominant themes in Spenser's glorification of Elizabeth correspond to the leading characteristics of Astraea.

As might be expected, Spenser's most open treatment of Virgo-Astraea in relation to Elizabeth comes in the fifth book which treats of Justice. The book opens with a lament for the golden age:[6]

> For during *Saturnes* ancient reigne it's sayd,
>   That all the world with goodness did abound:
>   And loued vertue, no man was affrayd
>   Of force, ne fraud in wight was to be found:
>   No warre was known, no dreadful trumpets sound,
>   Peace universall rayn'd mongst men and beasts,
>   And all things freely grew out of the ground:
> Iustice sate high ador'd with solemne feasts,
> And to all people did diuide her dred beheasts.

> Most sacred vertue she of all the rest,
>   Resembling God in his imperiall might;
>   Whose soueraine powre is herein most exprest,
>   That both to good and bad he dealeth right,
>   And all his workes with Iustice hath bedight.
>   That powre he also doth to Princes lend,
>   And makes them like himselfe in glorious sight,
> And rule his people right, as he doth recommend.

This paean in honour of Astraea-Justice is the corner-stone of the poem, for it lays down the 'imperialist' theory of the divine right of kings. Justice is the key virtue, the most sacred of all, for it reflects the 'imperiall might' of God which he 'lends' to princes, giving them a divine right, like his own. Spenser now naturally turns to the just goddess who reigns in England:[7]

---

6. Bk V, introduction, ix, x; *Works, ed. cit.*, V, p. 3. Cf. also the stanza quoted above, p. 31.
    Another allusion to Saturn and Virgo is probably to be found in Bk III, XI, xliii, where we are told that Saturn loved Erigone (another name for Virgo). This has been regarded as a mythological mistake on Spenser's part (*Works, ed. cit.*, III, p. 296).
7. *Ibid.*, Bk V, introduction, xi; *Works, ed. cit.*, V, p. 4.
    The last lines of this stanza state that Artegal is the instrument of Elizabeth's justice; and a little later (Bk V, I, v; *Works, ed. cit.*, V, p. 6) we are told that Artegal was instructed in justice in his infancy, 'By faire *Astraea*, with great industrie . . . .' It clearly follows from these two statements that Elizabeth is Astraea.
    Spenser does not make the crude statement that Astraea and the golden age have automatically returned with Elizabeth. His is the loftier conception that Elizabeth is the celestial justice for which Artegal, and her other knights, have to fight in the wicked world.

> Dread Souerayne Goddesse, that doest highest sit
> In seate of iudgement, in the'Almighties stead,
> And with magnificke might and wondrous wit
> Doest to thy people righteous doome aread . . .

It is a vision of the enthroned imperial virgin.

Other visions of, and names for, the queen in the poem embody differ-ent aspects of the theme. In this same fifth book on Justice there is a pic-ture of the queen as Mercilla. She is seated on a high throne. Little angels hold back the cloth of state; in her hand she holds the sceptre; at her feet is the sword of justice.[8] Here the queen represents justice tempered with mercy, hence the name Mercilla. Spenser's Mercilla is, in fact, Elizabeth as Justitia-Clementia, both imperial virtues.

The title-page of the Bishops' Bible of 1569 (Plate 10b),[9] shows Justice and Mercy holding the crown over the enthroned queen's head. If we turn back to one of Sir John Davies's hymns, we learn that 'exil'd Astraea' when she returns as Elizabeth rules by mercy, and that

> In her left hand (wherein should be
> Nought but the sword) sits Clemency . . .

And the portrait of Elizabeth, attributed to Marcus Geeraerts, in a flowery robe with the sword of justice at her feet and what appears to be an olive-branch in her right hand[1] might be a representation of the queen as Justitia-Clementia, or Astraea-Mercilla.[2]

One of the most striking of all the names used by Spenser in this poem is that of Una, the One, the heroine of the first book which is dedicated to Holiness, or pure religion. Philosophical emphasis on the One may here be combined with idealist politics and connected with the imperial theme of the One sovereign ruler under whom Justice is the most powerful in the world and the peace and unity of the golden age return to mankind. Una is descended of a royal lineage. Her ancestors were[3]

> Ancient Kings and Queenes, that had of yore
> Their scepters stretcht from East to Westerne shore,
> And all the world in their subjection held;
> Till that infernal feende with foule vprore
> Forwasted all their land, and them expeld:
> Whom to auenge, she had this Knight from far compeld.

Una can lay claim to a world empire (she is always called a 'royal virgin') and it is the mission of the Red Cross Knight to restore her to her heritage.

---

8. *Ibid.*, Bk V, viii, xvii ff.; ix, xxvii ff.: *Works, ed. cit.*, V, pp. 93 ff., 108 ff. Attendant on Mercilla are 'Just *Dice*, wise *Eunome*, myld *Eirene*,' Justice, Order, and Peace, the three daughters of Jove, according to Hesiod.
9. O'Donoghue, *op. cit.*, p. 39; Strong, *op. cit.*, Woodcuts, 70.
1. O'Donoghue, *op. cit.*, p.12; Strong, *op. cit.*, Paintings, 85. It is perhaps too fanciful to suggest that the little dog by the sword might indicate that this is Astraea under her name of Erigone, daugh-ter of Icarus, whose little dog symbolized her piety to her father's memory.
2. See the cover of this Norton Critical Edition [*Editors' note*].
3. *Ibid.*, Bk I, I, v; *Works, ed. cit.*, I, p. 6.

He is, however, temporarily seduced from her allegiance by another lady, also daughter of an emperor, who, in contrast to the simplicity and humility of Una's bearing, is proudly and richly attired:[4]

> A goodly lady clad in scarlot red,
> Purfled with gold and pearl of rich assay,
> And like a *Persian* mitre on her hed
> She wore, with crownes and owches garnished . . .

This lady was of light reputation, and entertained her lover all the way with 'mirth and wanton play', in marked contrast to the gravity and seriousness of Una.

It is generally admitted that the false Duessa stands in Spenser's eyes for the scarlet woman of Rome and false religion; whilst Una is the purity of reformed religion. But the full significance of the contrast now comes out more clearly. Both are emperors' daughters; both make a universal claim. Duessa wears a 'Persian mitre';[5] Una a royal crown. Duessa and Una symbolize the story of impure papal religion and pure imperial religion. Una is the royal virgin of the golden age of pure religion and imperial reform; she is the One Virgin whose crown reverses the tiara.

There is yet another side to Spenser's Astraea, by which she becomes approximated to the Renaissance vision of beauty, of the celestial Venus.

In the sixth book of the *Faerie Queene*, that devoted to the legend of Sir Calidore, or the virtue of Courtesy, the knight comes upon a little wooded hill, said to be the haunt of Venus, and there he sees the Three Graces, and a hundred other naked maidens, dancing around a 'faire one' in the centre. She is crowned with a rosy garland, and the damsels as they dance throw flowers and sweet odours upon her. These nymphs and graces, as they move in solemn yet sweet attendance on the 'faire one', are rather strangely compared to stars moving round the constellation of Ariadne's Crown (*Corona borealis*):[6]

> Looke how the Crowne, which *Ariadne* wore
> Vpon her yuory forehead that same day,
> That *Theseus* her vnto his bridale bore,
> When the bold *Centaures* made that bloudy fray
> With the fierce *Lapithes* which did them dismay;
> Being now placed in the firmament,
> Through the bright heauen doth her beames display,
> And is vnto the starres an ornament,
> Which round about her move in order excellent.

---

4. *Ibid.*, Bk I, II, xiii; *Works*, I, p. 22.
5. Jewel refers to the 'Persian' pride of the Bishop of Rome; cf. *Works*, Parker Society (Cambridge, 1847), IV, pp. 81, 104.
    M. Y. Hughes ('England's Eliza and Spenser's Medina', *Journ. of Eng. and Germ. Philol.*, 1944, pp. 1–15) suggests that in the name Medina, Spenser alludes to Elizabeth's *via media* in religious policy. This interesting interpretation need not conflict with the above; the imperialist religious policy was always conciliatory in theory.
6. *Faerie Queene*, Bk VI, X, xiii–xiv; *Works, ed. cit.*, VI, p. 117.

> Such was the beauty of this goodly band,
>> Whose sundry parts were here too long to tell;
> But she that in the midst of them did stand,
> Seem'd all the rest in beauty to excell,
> Crown'd with a rosie girlond, that right well
> Did her beseeme. And euer, as the crew
> About her daunst, sweet flowers, that far did smell,
> And fragrant odours they vppon her threw;
> But most of all, those three[7] did her with gifts endew.

Through the comparison with Ariadne's Crown, the Venus of this vision can be connected with Virgo-Astraea. Ariadne, like Astraea, was a maiden who became a constellation. When deserted by Theseus, she was loved and crowned by Bacchus and found a place in heaven, not very far from Virgo, as the group of stars known as the Northern Crown. Several classical writers, including Lucian,[8] and above all, Manilius, seem to identify Virgo with Ariadne.

Manilius introduces Ariadne's Crown in association with Erigone (his name for Virgo) and then describes Erigone surrounded and crowned with flowers of many hues and painting the grassy meadows on a wooded hill with all the colours of Spring. This love of flowers and of sweetly mingled odours in those born under her symbolizes their love of elegance and of all the gentler arts and graces of life.[9] Spenser has fused this flowery Virgo, associated with Ariadne's Crown, with Venus and the Graces,[1] and thereby creates a vision eminently suited to the knight who represents the virtue of Courtesy. And there can be no doubt that this Virgo-Ariadne was also Elizabeth-Virgo when we learn from William Camden that:[2]

> Sir Henry Lea upon some Astrological consideration, used to her late Majesties honour, the whole constellation of Ariadnes Crown, culminant in her Nativity, with this word: CAELUMQUE SOLUMQUE BEAVIT.

The picture of Elizabeth seen by Sir Calidore represents her as a vision of celestial beauty, decked with all the flowers and scents of the civilizing arts and graces of a Renaissance court. There was no Elizabethan Botticelli to give this vision an enduring place in art, but Spenser's is an intensely visual imagination, and he invests the fierce anti-papal Virgo of the Protestant theologians with the gentle elegance of Neoplatonic allegory.[3]

❊ ❊ ❊

---

7. The Three Graces.
8. Lucian, *Deor. conc.*, LXXIV, 51; Propertius, III, 17, 6 ff. For other references and a discussion of the whole point see Franz Boll, *Sphaera*, Leipzig, 1903, p. 276.
9. Manilius, *Astronomicon*, V, 251–69. Cf. Sir John Davies on Astraea as Flora, *op. cit.*, p. 137.
1. In the preceding stanzas the vision is that of a medieval Realm of Venus, which, in the stanzas quoted, melts into reminiscences of the Manilius passage on Ariadne-Virgo. There were precedents for the affiliation of Virgo to Venus (see Cumont's article on the Zodiac, in *Dictionaire des antiquetés grecques et romaines*, ed. C. Daremberg and S. Saglio (Paris, 1875–1917).
2. *Remains, ed. cit.*, p. 470; cf. Chambers, *Sir Henry Lee*, p. 141
3. We have seen how the Elizabethan theologians can regard Dante, Petrarch, Savonarola, Ficino, Pico della Mirandola, as supporters of their imperial reform. A poet like Spenser would therefore feel justified in drawing for his glorification of the imperial Virgo upon those Florentine philosophical, poetic, and religious currents which were also the inspiration of Botticelli.

Astraea; the Imperial Moon; and the Virgin Mary

Astraea is a symbol which links easily with other symbols used of the queen. The suggestion made at the beginning of this study that Astraea as a name for the queen might prove an Ariadne's thread to guide us through Elizabethan symbolism as a whole has already been found to have some substance in it and might be carried still further.

Take, for example, the moon symbolism. The goddess of the moon under various names—Diana, Cynthia, Belphoebe—is the most popular of all the figures employed by Elizabeth's adorers, and in the minds of certain poets the Cynthian cult appears to take on some kind of esoteric philosophical significance.

Our studies have reminded us that the moon is the symbol of empire, and the sun of papacy. The virgin of imperial reform who withstood the claims of the Papacy might therefore well become a chaste moon-goddess shedding the beams of pure religion from her royal throne. Moreover, the imperial cult has constantly drawn to itself a philosophical justification: the ideal ruler is always the Philosopher King. The so-called Elizabethan 'School of Night', with its worship of Cynthia and its devotion to intellectual contemplation,[4] might have been drawing on the 'imperialist' tradition, not only in the political, but also in the religious, philosophical, and poetic sense.

To work this suggestion out fully would require a separate study; here there is not space to support it by quotation from more than one poem. In George Chapman's *Hymnus in Cynthiam*, which may be fairly said to be the quintessence of the Cynthian cult, Elizabeth-Cynthia is thus adjured:[5]

> Then set thy Christall, and Imperiall throne,
> (Girt in thy chast, and neuer-loosing zone)
> Gainst Europs Sunne directly opposit,
> And giue him darkness, that doth threat thy light.

Here, under the image of an eclipse, the imperial moon is set up against the sun of Europe, in the kind of antithesis which we are accustomed to see visualized in the crown versus the tiara. And later in the same poem we find what appears to be a description of a moon device, beginning with these lines:[6]

> Forme then, twixt two superior pillers framd
> This tender building, Pax Imperij named . . .

One is reminded of the two columns of Charles V's imperial device, and they here frame a 'Pax Imperii' symbolized by the moon. To these quotations it would be possible to add others in support of a theory that the contemplative world of night and moonshine, in which some intellectual Elizabethan poets seem to find their spiritual home, might be a Ghibelline world, ruled by a moon of imperial reform.

---

4. The existence of a 'School of Night', of which Raleigh, Chapman, and others were members and which was opposed by Shakespeare, the Earl of Southampton and others, is based, perhaps rather insecurely, on a phrase in *Love's Labour's Lost*. See my *A study of Love's Labour's Lost*, Cambridge, 1936, pp. 89 ff.; M. C. Bradbrook, *The School of Night*, Cambridge, 1936.
5. George Chapman, *Poems*, ed. P. B. Bartlett, New York and London, 1941, p. 33.
6. *Ibid.*, p. 35.

Another virgin image frequently used of Elizabeth is that the 'Vestal Virgin'. The interesting 'Sieve' portraits of the queen, which portray her as the Vestal Virgin Tuccia bearing her attribute, the sieve, are a reference to this image. The Roman and religious connotations of vestal virginity need little elaboration.[7] It is as a vestal virgin that Elizabeth swims into our ken in one of the very few certain allusions to her by Shakespeare, as 'a fair Vestal, throned by the West'.[8] The 'imperial' character of this vestal is emphasized, and it is perhaps no accident that she appears in *A Midsummer Night's Dream*—a play bathed from beginning to end in moonlight.

The symbols used of Elizabeth are not always virgin symbols. In her capacity as the just and peaceful ruler she brings wealth and plenty to her people, and can be hailed as Ceres, a mother-goddess:[9]

> Mater Eliza, meae, dum viverat alma, parentis,
> Dives eram, placidae Pacis alumna, Ceres . . .

lamented a university poet at her death. But it will be remembered that the just virgin of the golden age carries corn and is compared to Ceres. She is a virgin yet her influences are fruitful, and so also are Eliza's. This applies not only in the material but also in the spiritual sphere, where we find Jewel describing Elizabeth as the nursing mother of the church in England.[1]

The notion of a fruitful virgin in relation to the virgin queen brings in the most daring comparison of all. Many of the symbols of this virgin—for example the Rose (the Tudor Rose, badge of union, of peace, of mystic empire), the Star, the Moon, the Phoenix, the Ermine,[2] the Pearl[3]—were also symbols of the Virgin Mary. There is a good deal of evidence that some Elizabethans did not flinch from such a comparison. A song in John Dowland's *Second Book of Airs* gives this advice:[4]

---

7. John Florio in his *First Fruites* (London, 1578, dialogue 28), shortly after celebrating the virtues of Elizabeth, laments the pure golden age of imperial Rome in terms of Vestal virginity: 'O golden worlde . . . then was chastitie knowen in the Temple of Vesta. Then the Emperours dyd frequent the Chappel of Iupiter, then Lust durst not come to the Court of Cesar, then abstinence walked through the markette in euerye Cittye, then the worlde was chaste, then the world dyd triumph, but nowe euery thyng goeth contrary. Certis it is a lamentable thyng, to consider the state of this world.' Florio probably has in mind here Petrarch's *Trionfo della Castità* (in which Tuccia is mentioned).

   In view of the Elizabethan interpretation of Petrarch as a Protestant ally in the fight with the Whore of Babylon the *Trionfo della Castità* might be a useful guide to Elizabeth symbolism. Another figure, besides the chaste Tuccia, who occurs in that poem is the chaste 'Judit ebrea', slayer of the tyrant Holofernes. Judith is a name often used of Elizabeth.

   For the use of the Judith story in Protestant and Catholic controversy, see E. Purdie, *The Story of Judith in German and English Literature*, Paris, 1927.
8. *A Midsummer Night's Dream*, II, 158.
9. *Oxonienses academiae Funebre Officium in memoriam honoratissimam serenissimae et beatissimae Elizabethae*, Oxford, 1603, sig. S 4 v.; cf. Wilson, p. 381.
1. Addressing Elizabeth, Jewel can call her 'now the only nurse and mother of the church of God within these your majesty's most noble dominions,' expressing the hope that she may live to be 'an old mother in Israel' (*Works*, III, p. 118).

   This aspect of the queen, as the source of spiritual nourishment to her church, may account for her appropriation of the sacred 'Pelican' symbol.
2. The ermine is a symbol of chastity and of the Virgin Mary. Its appearance in the portrait of Elizabeth at Hatfield House, in close proximity to the sword of state, makes of that picture a variation on the just virgin theme.
3. The pearl as a symbol of Elizabeth, for which there is plenty of literary material, ought to be fully worked out. It may have something to do with the marked predominance of pearl jewellery in the portraits.
4. *Shorter Elizabeth Poems*, ed. A. H. Bullen, in *An English Garner*, IV, (1904, rpt. New York: Cooper Square, 1964), 107; cf. Wilson, *op. cit.*, p. 206. (On this and the preceding pages, Wilson discusses the analogies between the Elizabeth cult and the worship of the Virgin.) This poem has been attributed to Sir Henry Lee, see E. K. Chambers, *Sir Henry Lee*, pp. 142–3.

When others sing *Venite exultemus!*
Stand by and turn to *Noli emulari!*
For *Quare fremuerant* use *Oremus!*
Vivat Eliza! for an *Ave Mari!*

'Long live Eliza !' instead of 'Hail Mary' ! The startling suggestion makes one begin to ask oneself whether the cult of the virgin queen, was, perhaps half-unconsciously, intended to take the place of the cult of the Virgin, one of the most abiding characteristics of the ancient faith. There is an engraving of the queen, with her device of the Phoenix, below which is written 'This Maiden-Queen Elizabeth came into this world, the Eve of the Nativity of the blessed virgin Mary; and died on the Eve of the Annunciation of the virgin Mary, 1602.' This statement is accompanied by the following couplet:[5]

She was, She is (what can there more be said?)
In earth the first, in heaven the second Maid.

This staggering remark seems to imply that the defunct Queen Elizabeth is now a second Blessed Virgin in heaven. What more can there be said indeed? * * * To emphasize the worship of 'diva Elizabetta', the imperial virgin, in place of that of the Queen of Heaven, to carry her gorgeously arrayed through street and countryside that she might show her divine Justice and Clemency to the people, was a way by which the virgin of the imperial reform might draw ancient allegiances to herself. The bejewelled and painted images of the Virgin Mary had been cast out of churches and monasteries, but another bejewelled and painted image was set up at court, and went in progress through the land for her worshippers to adore. The cult of the Virgin was regarded as one of the chief abuses of the unreformed church,[6] but it would be, perhaps, extravagant to suggest that, in a Christian country, the worship of the state Virgo was deliberately intended to take its place.

These strange tones and colourings in the Elizabeth symbolism can, perhaps, once again be best understood by reference to Astraea-Virgo. That many-sided figure also had affinities with moon-cults—with Astarte or Isis; she also, though not the Virgin Mary, was an echo of her. Queen Elizabeth as a symbol draws to herself a mysterious tradition.

❊   ❊   ❊

CRITICIZING ELIZABETH

CAROLE LEVIN

[Royal Wanton and Whore]†

Elizabeth's contemporary, Henry IV of France, was known for his sense of humor. Henry, originally a Protestant, had converted to Catholicism in

---

5. O'Donoghue, *op. cit.*, p. 79.
6. Cf. Jewel's controversy with the Catholic Harding. Jewel reproaches the Catholics with worshipping the Virgin Mary as 'lady of angels', 'queen of heaven' and 'God's most faithful fellow'; this, says Jewel, is to make 'a creature equal in fellowship with God' (*Works*, III, p. 121).
† From *"The Heart and Stomach of a King": Elizabeth I and the Politics of Sex and Power* (Philadelphia: University of Pennsylvania Press, 1994), 66–90. Reprinted by permission of the University of Pennsylvania Press.

1593 when it was clear that the French country as a whole would never accept a Protestant king. On that occasion he claimed that "Paris is well worth a mass." In the 1590s Henry is supposed to have joked to a Scottish marquis that there were three questions that would never be resolved: the first was, how valiant was Maurice of Orange (a leader in the Dutch resistance against the Spanish) who had never fought a battle; the second was, what was Henry IV's own religion; and the third was "whether Queen Elizabeth was a maid or no."[1] The three topics jokingly mentioned by Henry IV deal with some of the most important facets of the Renaissance princely persona: courage on the battlefield, which often had to do with how honorable a ruler was seen to be; religion, and serving as a religious figure for the people; and the sexuality of the monarch and the reputation for chaste behavior. The first two issues Henry discussed he applied to male monarchs, while the last, sexuality, the French king mentioned as of most concern for the woman ruler. For Elizabeth, however, presenting herself as a courageous leader and a religious figure were as important as the way she dealt with questions surrounding her sexuality. In both these areas gender played a significant role in how Elizabeth both presented herself to, and was perceived by, her people. But the questions about her sexuality were those asked the most intensely throughout her reign. Perceptions of gender and role expectation influenced Elizabeth's public and private images in terms of courage, religion, and, most especially, sexuality, and the ways these images were shaped reflected the insecurity caused by female rule, especially that of a woman who refused to marry yet had many suitors and favorites.[2]

Beliefs about Elizabeth's sexual behavior disturbed many of her own subjects as well as foreigners, but this concern was expressed in terms quite different from those involving the sexuality of a male monarch. While questions, comments, and gossip about Elizabeth's sexual behavior had begun long before she became queen,[3] attention to her behavior intensified once she ascended the throne, and continued throughout her reign, even when she was in her sixties. Nor did it end with her death. This solicitude over Elizabeth's sexual capacity was a means for the people to express their

1. Francis Osborne, *Osborne's Works*, 8th ed. (London: Printed for R.D., 1682), 383–84. In the early seventeenth century Henry Clifford gives a slightly different version of this story. He writes, "The queen when she came to the crown was full twenty-five years of age, a gracious lady and gallant of aspect. Yet she would not be persuaded to marry, but would have it written on her tomb that she lived and died a virgin. King Henry the Fourth of France merrily said the world would never believe this, or would the many favourites she had." Henry Clifford, *The Life of Jane Dormer, Duchess of Feria*, ed. Joseph Stevenson (London: Burns and Oates, 1887), 96. Clifford, of course, is writing from a hostile Catholic perspective.

2. As Jean Wilson puts it, "The most important fact about Elizabeth I was her sex." *Entertainments for Elizabeth I*, (Woodbridge: Brewer, 1982), 3. Other particularly significant studies that consider the question of Elizabeth and gender are by Leah Marcus, Louis Montrose, Frances Yates, John King, and Allison Heisch. Also interesting is Larissa J. Taylor-Smither "Elizabeth I: A psychological Profile," *Sixteenth Century Journal* XV, 1 (1984), 47–72, in looking at gender issues in terms of Elizabeth's psychological development and how that affected her rule.

3. Speaking of Elizabeth while a princess, Henry Clifford, writing early in the next century, says, "In King Edward's time what passed between the Lord Admiral, Sir Thomas Seymour, and her Dr. Latimer preached in a sermon, and was a chief cause that the Parliament condemned the Admiral. There was a bruit of a child born and miserably destroyed, but could not be discovered whose it was; only the report of the midwife, who was brought from her house blindfold thither, and so returned; saw nothing in the house while she was there, but candlelight; only she said, it was the child of a very fair young lady, who was then between fifteen and sixteen years of age. If it were so, it was the judgment of God unto the Admiral; and upon her, to make her ever after incapable of children." *The Life of Jane Dormer, Duchess of Feria*, 86–87.

concern over a female monarch, and also a way of expressing the hope she would fulfill her womanly function, and have a child—a son who would reverse the dangerous precedent of a woman ruler. Especially in the last two decades of the reign, when Elizabeth was too old to marry and have a child, the rumors served as a focus for discontent and fear for the succession. Elizabeth was deeply loved by her subjects but her refusal to follow the feminine gender expectations of passivity and acquiescence, her refusal to consider the need of a named heir, caused great fear. Every time the queen was ill the fear over the succession intensified. Comments, questions, and hypotheses about the queen's health and about her sexuality became intertwined as the reign progressed. People wondered if there were some problem about Elizabeth's health that made her refuse to marry and have a child. But if she were to die without a named successor the country could be left in chaos.

By not marrying, Elizabeth also refused the most obvious function of being a queen, that of bearing a child. Nor would she name a successor as Parliament begged her to do, since Elizabeth was convinced this would increase, rather than ease, both the political tension and her personal danger. Until her execution in 1587 Mary Stuart would have been the most logical heir by right of primogeniture. She was, however, Catholic. After she was forced to abdicate the throne of Scotland in 1568 and fled to England the situation became even more problematic for Elizabeth. Elizabeth kept Mary as an enforced "guest," whose freedoms were more and more limited as Mary conspired to have Elizabeth assassinated and herself placed on the throne of England. Elizabeth feared any named successor would be the focus of all potential dissatisfaction. Instead Elizabeth tried to calm fears with vague promises and hoped the future would somehow take care of itself and provide a peaceful succession. She responded to a Parliamentary petition on the succession in 1563 with the statement:

> [I] say and pray, that I may linger here in this vale of misery for comfort, wherein I have witness of my study and travail for your surety: and I cannot . . . end my life, without I see some foundation of your surety after my gravestone.[4]

While time proved her right, the risk to England was horrifying if she should die without a clear successor. As well as believing it was better for the country not to have a named heir, Elizabeth knew it was better for herself. She said in 1561, "Think you that I could love my winding sheet?" Leah Marcus also convincingly suggests that Henry VIII's obsessions and difficulties begetting a male heir and Mary's false pregnancies would have made Elizabeth wary about marriage as a solution to providing a male heir. Why create a situation where failure was such a possibility and which would have so many other risks connected with it?[5]

Elizabeth was effective at conveying her love for her people and encouraging their love for her. Yet many of the English still had great difficulty with the concept of a woman ruler. Elizabeth could not always control the way people responded to her. Together with the love and respect she

4. G. W. Prothero, ed., *Select Statutes and Other Constitutional Documents Illustrative of the Reigns of Elizabeth and James I*, 4th ed. (Oxford: at the Clarendon Press, 1913), 109.
5. Christopher Haigh, *Elizabeth I: Profile in Power* (London: Longman, 1988), 19; Leah Marcus, "Erasing the Stigma of Daughterhood: Mary I, Elizabeth I, and Henry VIII," in *Daughters and Fathers*, eds. Lynda E. Boose and Betty S. Flowers (Baltimore; Johns Hopkins University Press, 1989), 406.

inspired, one discovers expressions of hostility towards her as an unmarried female ruler whose position transcended the traditional role allotted to women in English Renaissance society. This hostility was expressed in the many rumors that circulated about Elizabeth.

Rumors could be very dangerous and damaging to a monarch's reputation. While this is true of all monarchs, it was especially the case for women in power, and the rumors were so often ones suggesting sexual improprieties. For a woman, her only source of honor is her sexual "credit." Losing it, particularly for a woman in the public sphere, could be devastating.[6] Catherine de Medici made a declaration of this danger during the marriage negotiations between Elizabeth and the Duke of Anjou in 1572, carefully explaining to the English that the future Henry III had not broken off the negotiations because of slanders he had heard about Elizabeth, but rather because of his religious scruples. Catherine repeated to the English envoy Thomas Smith for Elizabeth's benefit a discussion she had had with her son about Elizabeth's reputation.

> And I told him it is all the hurt that evil men can do to Noble Women and Princes, to spread abroad lies and dishonorable tales of them, and that we of all Princes that be women are subject to be slandered wrongfully of them that be our adversaries, other hurt they cannot do to us.[7]

Francis Bacon once wrote that rumors and treasons were siblings, a view that certainly suggests why Elizabeth's government took the rumors about her so seriously. The 1559 Parliament made it treason for anyone not only by "open preaching express words or sayings" to "maliciously, advisedly, and directly say . . . that the Queen's Majesty that now is, during her life, is not or ought not to be Queen of this realm," but also simply to "hold opinion" of this view. Spreading gossip about Elizabeth's claim, even agreeing with gossip, was perceived as very dangerous. The treason act of 1571 reaffirmed this definition of treason. Many of the people arrested in the reign of Elizabeth had gossiped about the queen in malicious ways. There was also a law against sedition that was passed in 1554 in the reign of Mary; Parliament made this law even more stringent in 1581.[8]

During Elizabeth's reign the records of the Privy Council are filled with examples of people charged with the crime of slandering the queen. Over and over again people were arrested for "lewd words" spoken against Elizabeth. For example, at the very beginning of the reign, 1558, a "lewde, Malycious fellowe of Assheforth," was to be examined to determine "whither he uttred the trayterous wordes, or no . . . agaynst the Quenes Hieghnes." The next year the Privy Council sent a letter to "the Keper of the Kinges Benche to kepe in saf warde one Byrche, a priest, that hath uttred lewde wordes of the Quenes Majestie." In 1564 Lord Cobham was asked to investigate "certaine lewde sedytious woordes spoken by some of

---

6. Linda Woodbridge, *Women in the English Renaissance: Literature and the Nature of Womankind, 1540–1620* (Urbana and Chicago: University of Illinois Press, 1984), 53.

7. Dudley Digges, *The Compleat Ambassador* (London, 1655), 196.

8. Lacey Bladwin Smith, *Treason in Tudor England: Politics and Paranoia* (Princeton, NJ: Princeton University Press, 1986), 137; Prothero, *Select Statutes*, 23; William Camden, *The History of the Most Renowned and Victorious Princess Elizabeth* (London, 1688), 28; Haigh, *Elizabeth I*, 18; Joel Samaha, "Gleanings from Local Criminal-Court Records; Sedition Amongst the 'Inarticulate' in Elizabethan Essex," *Journal of Social History* 8 (Summer, 1975), 64–65.

Tenterden in Kent against the Quenes Majestie . . . that they may be all apprehended and committed." In 1580 Vicar John Pullyver stated that "some did saie that we had no quene," and was placed in the pillory. Some who were found guilty of uttering lewd words were ordered to be put in the pillory and also have their ears cropped or ordered on "the nexte markett daye"—so that there might be maximum publicity—to be put in the pillory "with a paper on his hed having thies words written in great letters therin, 'for lewd and slaunderous wordes' and so suffer him stande all the market tyme." Public humiliation was used frequently in Tudor England not only as punishment but in the hopes it would also serve as a public deterrent. Letters from the Council went out to other counties where "lewd and sedicious wordes" were reported, ordering investigation and punishment. People accused included vicars, tailors, laborers, and gentlemen.[9]

And the court as well as the country was a place where rumors spread easily, especially when the ruler was a young unmarried woman who refused to follow advice. At the beginning of Elizabeth's reign Sir Thomas Chaloner wrote a very concerned letter to Cecil on this issue. "As I count the Slaunder most false, so a yong Princesse canne not be to ware. . . . This delaye of rype tyme for Maryage, besides the Losse of the Realme . . . mynistreth Matter to theis lewde Towngs to descant apon, and breedith Contempt." The belief that women are gossips, are most interested in love affairs, and are quick to spread rumors also intensified gender expectations about the spreading of rumors at Elizabeth's court. Referring to the possibility of the marriage of Mary Stuart and the Duke of Norfolk in 1569, Camden wrote: "Soon after the Rumour of this Marriage came more clearly to Queen Elizabeth's ears, by means of the Women of the Court, who do quickly smell out Love-matters." In 1564 de Silva wrote to Philip about watching a comedy with Elizabeth. Comedies, he observed, generally deal with marriage. Elizabeth then led the talk to the question of marriage between Don Carlos and Mary Stuart. De Silva denied it, claiming that "It is no new thing for great princes to be the subjects of gossip." "So true is that," replied the queen, "that they said in London the other day that the King my brother, was sending an Ambassador to treat of the marriage of the Prince with me!"[1]

* * * Elizabeth presented herself to her people as an icon of virginity, a Virgin Queen, to bring her people through the break with the Catholic Church and the worship of the Virgin Mary. Elizabeth and her government deliberately took over the symbolism and prestige of the suppressed Marian cult in order to foster a cult of the Virgin Queen. This proved a powerful resource for Elizabeth in dealing with the political problems of her regime.

People did not, however, regard Elizabeth solely as a Virgin Queen. They were also intrigued by her imagined and real sexuality, a speculation that

9. *Acts of the Privy Council (APC)*, ed. John Roche Dasent, New Series (London: HMSO, 1890–1943), VII, 31, 71, 92, 94, 180, 299; Samaha, "Gleanings from Local Criminal-Court Records," 68; *Calendar of the Assize Records; Essex Indictments, Elizabeth I*, ed. J. S. Cockburn (London: Her Majesty's Stationery Office, 1978), 203. I am in no way suggesting that Elizabeth was unique in the seditious words said about her. Particularly at the time of the Divorce, the records are filled with seditous comments about Henry VIII.

1. 6 December 1559, William Murdin and Samuel Haynes, ed., *A Collection of State Papers Relating to Affairs in the Reign of Queen Elizabeth from 1542 to 1596 left by William Cecil, Lord Burghley* (London: William Bowyer, 1740–1759), I, 212; Camden, *The History of the Most Renowned and Victorious Princess Elizabeth*, 1688 ed., 129; *CSP, Spain*, I, 368.

echoed some late medieval questions about the Virgin Mary. People talked about Elizabeth's love affairs, speculating on the one hand, about the number of illegitimate children she had, and, wondering, on the other, whether she had a physical deformity that kept her from consumating a physical relationship. These rumors served the dual purpose of allowing people to openly speculate about the succession of a male heir, while denigrating Elizabeth in a typically misogynist way—by dismissing her as a whore.

The interest in Elizabeth's sexuality was undoubtedly heightened by the many courtships in which Elizabeth was involved. While Elizabeth proclaimed that she hated these negotiations, as we have seen, many believed otherwise. While the previous chapter concerned itself with the official courtships of Elizabeth and responses to them, this chapter instead concentrates on the rumors that she took lovers and had illegitimate children. Her love not only of marriage offers but of the accoutrements of courtship worked to encourage this perception. While it is extremely unlikely that she had any intention of actually satisfying her courtiers, she loved their claims of adoration. As Jonathan Goldberg suggests, "Courting was a metaphor for the desire for power and authority, a metaphor enacted and lived."[2]

In the first years of her reign, Elizabeth was seen everywhere with Robert Dudley, whom she eventually created Earl of Leicester. The Dudley family was one that had been been intimately connected with the Tudors for two generations, a connection that had previously led to disastrous setbacks for the Dudley family. Robert's grandfather, Edmund, had ruthlessly squeezed money out of the populace for Henry VII; the young Henry VIII had him executed at the beginning of his reign as a way to court popularity. Robert's father John, Duke of Northumberland, had attempted the coup to place Lady Jane Grey on the throne in 1553 as a means to continue the power he had assumed in the reign of the boy king, Edward. When the plot failed John Dudley was one of the few that Mary immediately had executed. Robert and Elizabeth had known each other since childhood and Elizabeth clearly cared deeply for him. Their friendship may have been further strengthened while both were in the Tower during Mary's reign. Upon becoming queen, Elizabeth sent Robert Dudley to the astrologer/magician John Dee, his old tutor, to discover the most auspicious day for her coronation. Almost immediately she made Dudley her Master of the Horse, the man who chose the horses for her official processions and rode with her, and so had close access to her. She showered him with other gifts and honors.[3] Within a few months of Elizabeth's accession the foreign ambassadors' letters home were filled with references to the close friendship of Robert and the new queen. The Spanish Ambassador, the Count de Feria, wrote to Philip in April 1559 that "during the last few days Lord Robert has come so much into favour that he does whatever he likes with affairs and it is even said that her Majesty visits him in his chamber day and night."[4]

2. Jonathan Goldberg, *Endlesse Worke: Spenser and the Structures of Discourse* (Baltimore and London: Johns Hopkins University Press, 1981), 152.

3. Useful modern studies of Robert Dudley include Alan Haynes, *White Bear: Robert Dudley, the Elizabethan Earl of Leicester* (London: Peter Owen, 1987); Alan Kendall, *Robert Dudley, Earl of Leicester* (London: Cassell, 1980); Eleanor Rosenberg, *Leicester, Patron of Letters* (New York: Columbia University Press, 1958); Derek Wilson, *Sweet Robin: A Biography of Robert Dudley, Earl of Leicester* (London: Hamilton, 1981). On the relationship between Elizabeth and Robert Dudley see Milton Waldman, *Elizabeth and Leicester* (London: Collins, 1944) and Elizabeth Jerkins, *Elizabeth and Leicester* (New York: Coward–McCann, 1962).

4. *CSP, Spain*, I, 57–58.

Unfortunately (from his point of view), as we know, at the time Elizabeth became queen Dudley was already married. Many people suggested that Robert was simply waiting for Amy to die so that he might marry the queen. Paolo Tiepolo, the Venetian ambassador in Brussels, heard from England that Elizabeth "evinces such affection and inclination [toward Robert] that many persons believe that if his wife, who has been ailing some time, were perchance to die, the Queen might easily take him for her husband."[5] We know that Amy's mysterious death made Dudley's courtship of Elizabeth far more problematic. Whenever Dudley was mentioned as a potential marriage partner for the queen, people were bound to bring up the rumor that he had murdered his wife.

Whatever the truth, the scurrilous comments about Elizabeth and Robert Dudley disturbed many people. Thomas Lever wrote to Francis Knollys and William Cecil on September 17, 1560 about "the grevous and dangerous suspition, and muttering" in Coventry about Amy's death. Unless these suspicions were allayed, the "displeasure of God, the dishonor of the Quene, and the Danger of the whole Realme is to be feared." The next January de Quadra wrote to Philip about certain preachers who spoke about Amy's death in a way that harmed the queen's honor. The other courts of Europe were rife with gleeful gossip. Mary Stuart, still queen of France and without yet a scandal to touch her, said that "the Queen of English is going to marry her horsekeeper." Sir Nicholas Throckmorton, the English Ambassador, wrote from Paris that the French gossip about Elizabeth's morals made him wish he were dead. "The bruits be so brim, and so maliciously reported here, touching the marriage of the Lord Robert, and the death of his wife. . . . We begin already to be in derision and hatred, for the bruit only." Throckmorton added, "One laugheth at us, another threateneth, another revileth the Queen. Some let not to say, what religion is this that a subject shall kill his wife, and the Prince not only bear withal but marry with him?" Throckmorton begged William Cecil to discover some method to prevent the marriage. If the queen married Dudley, he predicted, "God and religion will be out of estimation; the Queen discredited, condemned, and neglected; and the country ruined and made prey."[6]

So strong was the belief that Elizabeth would marry Dudley that in November of 1560 de Quadra reported to Philip that the marriage had already taken place. "Cecil has given way to Robert, who they say was married to the Queen in the presence of his brother and two ladies of the chamber." Whether to marry Dudley or not must have caused Elizabeth great anguish. In the same month Elizabeth's servant R. J. Jones wrote to Throckmorton in Paris that "the Queen's Majesty looketh not so hearty and well as she did, by a great deal; and surely the matter of my Lord Robert doth much perplex her." Despite such stories and all her soul-searching, Elizabeth never did marry Robert Dudley, no matter how close she may have felt toward him and how long and intensely he courted her. It was not really until 1575, after he had grandly feted the queen at Kenilworth, that Dudley finally and completely recognized that she would never marry him. In what some saw as a bizarre twist, in 1564 Elizabeth did propose Dudley as

---

5. 4 May 1559, *CSP, Venice*, 81.
6. Murdin and Haynes, *Collection of State Papers*, I, 362; 22 January 1561, *CSP, Spain*, I, 179; Philip Yorke, earl of Hardwicke, *Miscellaneous State Papers: From 1501–1726* (London, 1778), I, 121–23, 163; *CSP, Foreign, 1560–1561*, 348, 377.

a marriage partner for the then-widowed Mary Stuart before the Scottish queen married her second husband, Henry Stuart, Lord Darnley. It was to make Dudley a more acceptable suitor that Elizabeth made him Earl of Leicester. But even at this solemn ceremony Elizabeth tickled his neck. People were on occasion shocked by the affection she showed to him. Yet when Katherine Ashley, Elizabeth's closest confidante when she was in her teens and then one of the ladies of the queen's bed chamber, "covertly commended Leicester unto her for a husband, [Elizabeth] answered in a passion: 'Dost thou think me so unlike myself, and so unmindful of my Royal Majesty, that I would prefer my servant, whom I myself have raised, before the greatest princes of Christendom, in choosing of an husband.'" And when Elizabeth thought she was dying of smallpox in October 1562 she solemnly swore that, though she loved Lord Robert dearly, God was her witness that nothing improper had happened between them, that there was no dishonor to their relationship. She asked, however, that if she died not only should Dudley be made the protector of the realm but his man servant should be given a large salary, which does suggest there were aspects of her relationship with Dudley that she did not want exposed.[7]

Elizabeth's bout with smallpox intensified the already existing fear of a lack of a successor felt by her councillors and the people. What would happen if the queen were to die with no child and no established succession? To add to the sense of popular horror, about the same time that Elizabeth was ill a monstrosity was found in the Lincoln's Inn Fields—"a certaine image of wax, with a great pin struck into it about the brest of it." If Elizabeth's illness was caused by magic how even more helpless her councillors were. They sent urgent messages to John Dee, begging him to "prevent the mischeife," or at least so Dee himself later claimed. Such fear might well engender not only pressure on Elizabeth to marry and name a successor, but also rumors about her that expressed in a more latent fashion some of that fear. Throughout her reign any illness of Elizabeth caused panic and consternation on the part of her councillors. Gossip about the queen's health, which must have heightened the tension even more, was as intense as the gossip about her sexuality, and often intertwined with it. The Venetian envoy reported in June of 1559, "Before leaving London her Majesty was blooded from one foot and from one arm, but what her infirmity is, is not known. Many persons say things which I should not dare write." In March 1561 the Venetian ambassador to Philip II wrote back to Venice that "I am informed on good authority that the Queen of England has become indisposed, and that the physicians greatly fear her malady to be dropsy." Six months later de Quadra was mentioning similar rumors. "What is most important now, as I am informed, is that the Queen is becoming dropsical and has already began to swell extraordinarily. I have been advised of this by three different sources and by a person who had the opportunity of being an eye witness. To all appearance she is falling away, and is extremely thin and the colour of a corpse."[8]

<hr />

7. Of course her statement of the relationship in 1562 does not cover what went on between Dudley and Elizabeth after the smallpox scare. *CSP, Spain*, I, 178; Hardwick, *Miscellaneous State Papers*, I, 167; John Nichols, *The Progresses and Public Processions of Queen Elizabeth* (London: J. Nichols and Son, 1823; rpt. New York: Burt Franklin, n.d.), I, xxxiii; II, 617; *CSP, Spanish*, I, 263.

8. John Dee, *The Comendious Rehearsall*, ed. James Crossley, Remains Historical and Literary, 24 (Manchester: The Chetham Society, 1851), 21; *CSP, Venice*, VII, 105, 301–2; *CSP, Spanish*, I, 214.

De Quadra's successor, Guzman de Silva, wrote to Philip II in August 1564 that Elizabeth was returning to London from her progress sooner than planned. "She is much in fear of falling ill, which I do not wonder at if they tell her the prophecies that are current about her short life. Everybody is talking of them." In 1571 Cecil again expressed panic over Elizabeth becoming ill in a letter to Francis Walsingham. "This bearer . . . can also tell you of a sudden alarm given to me, specially yesternight, by her Majestie, being suddenly sick in her stomach, and as suddenly relieved by a vomit. You must think such a matter would drive men to the end of their wits, but God is the stay of all that put their trust in him." In 1572 the Earl of Shrewsbury wrote to Cecil, "Five weeks are passed since I had any advertisements from your Lordship, which I think is long; and now especially that it is spoken the Queen's Majesty has been lately sick . . . and as yet no certainty is heard of her Majesty's recovery or perfect health. You may be sure it is no little grief or discomfort to me." News of the queen's health peppered letters to and from Court. The next year Leicester wrote to Shrewsbury, "This is all the news presently worth the writing, save the good and perfect health of her Majesty." Leicester echoed this statement in 1578 as well. "The best news I can write your Lordship is of her Majesty's good and perfect health, which God long continue." There was great concern in 1580. Thomas Bawdewn wrote to the Earl of Shrewsbury, "The Queen our Sovereign, being persuaded by her physicians, did enter into a bath on Sunday last; and, either by taking cold, or by some other accident, did presently fall sick, and so did continue two days together, but now is very well recovered again." And Shrewsbury ended a letter to Walsingham, "Thus, with my daily prayer for the Queen's Majesty's long life and good health, I take my leave." Elizabeth's request to make Robert Dudley protector of the realm would not in any way have reassured her councillors, and their relief must have been enormous that in 1562 they were not called upon to either keep—or break—that promise.[9]

That Elizabeth wanted Dudley to be protector suggests how important he was to her at least at that moment, and one can certainly imagine that their relationship was close, romantic, complex, and ambiguous, and may well have had some sort of sexual component, yet Elizabeth's statement in 1562 (and the way she behaved throughout her reign) makes it doubtful that they were lovers in the traditional sense.[1] What is more important than the possible relationship between Elizabeth and Dudley is the widespread belief about the nature of their relationship. The gossip about the two continued throughout the reign and was carefully gathered up by worried government officials. A generation earlier rumors and scandal about Elizabeth's mother helped to destroy Anne Boleyn.[2]

Implicit in these comments and speculations, which we find in the public records, is a definite thread of malice—the sense that Elizabeth, this unmarried woman of questionable morals, had no business ruling. In

9. *CSP, Spain*, I, 274; Digges, *The Compleat Ambassador*, 146; Edmund Lodge, *Illustrations of British History* (London, 1838), I, 550–51; II, 25, 41, 94, 174.
1. I would, however, disagree with Elizabeth Jenkins, in her otherwise excellent and intuitive study of Elizabeth and Robert Dudley, when she suggests that one way we know they were not lovers is that Elizabeth was never emotionally yielding to Robert in the way a woman would be after she had slept with her lover. This point seems to suggest more about Jenkins' 1950s values than a real historical analysis.
2. See Retha Warnicke, *The Rise and Fall of Anne Boleyn* (Cambridge: Cambridge University Press, 1989) for a full discussion of this issue.

1560 there were several reports that Elizabeth was pregnant. For instance, Mother Anne Dowe was committed to jail for "openly asserting that the Queen was with child by Robt. Duddeley." Mother Dowe had come in one morning to a tailor's shop, saying that there were things going on that no one should speak about—which she immediately proceeded to do. She told the astonished tailor that Lord Robert had given the queen a child. When the tailor responded, "Why she hath no child yet!" Mother Dowe replied, "He hath put one to the making." Three years later Edmund Baxter openly expressed the not uncommon view that Elizabeth's reputed unchastity disqualified her as a monarch, something that had never been said of her father or any other heterosexual male ruler. Baxter's reported words were: "that Lord Robert kept her Majesty, and that she was a naughty woman, and could not rule her realm, and that justice was not being administered." His wife added that when she saw the queen at Ipswich "she looked like one lately come out of child-bed." Though the ability to administer justice should have nothing to do with Elizabeth's sexual behavior, in these subjects' minds, and it was far from an unusual perspective, they were inextricably linked. Even the most private sin would have impact in public rule, and this was particularly the case for a sexual sin. Corruption to the body of the monarch would reflect the corrupting of the whole realm, the body politic. By being called unchaste, Elizabeth was also being charged with not being a good ruler in a way that was directly connected with her sex, especially since the concept of honor and its relation to behavior was markedly different for women and for men in the sixteenth century. For males, honor had to do with keeping one's word and with not being shamed on the battlefield. Women preserved their honor not only through their actual chastity but also by maintaining the reputation of chaste behavior. For a woman to be thought unchaste, even if it were untrue, was a loss of honor. In accusing the queen of sexual improprieties, people were charging her with dishonorable behavior in a way that would not be the case in a similar rumor about a king.[3]

Moreover, accusations of behaving as a "lewd woman," or being called "whore," were among the principal terms of abuse used against women on all social levels of society. By calling their monarch a whore, these people were identifying Elizabeth's gender as the most salient aspect of her entity as ruler.[4] There are parallels to the reaction of the Scottish people toward Mary Stuart, except that Mary's weakness in handling government and her behavior with Darnley and Bothwell were such she was forced to abdicate and fled Scotland after a short reign. The rumors and hostile denigrations

3. *CSP, Domestic Eliz.*, XIII, 157; Elizabeth Jenkins, *Elizabeth the Great* (London: Gollancz, 1958), 96; F. G. Emmison, *Elizabethan Life: Vol. 1, Disorder* (Chelmsford: Essex Country Council, 1971), 41; *CSP, Dom. Addenda, Eliz.*, XI, 534; Patricia Meyer Spacks, *Gossip* (Chicago: University of Chicago Press, 1985), 32; Lawrence Stone, *Family, Sex, and Marriage* (New York: Harper and Row, 1977), 503–4. For a very useful discussion of women's honor and sexuality, particularly as it affected Elizabeth's mother, Anne Boleyn, see Warnicke, *The Rise and Fall of Anne Boleyn*. For a discussion of the impact of Protestantism on the concept of honor, see also Mervyn James, *English Politics and the Conception of Honour, 1485–1642* (Cambridge: Cambridge University Press, 1986). It is also useful to look at proverbs about women in the Renaissance to see the linking of sexual misconduct and generally dishonorable behavior. Morris Palmer Tilley, *A Dictionary of the Proverbs in England in the Sixteenth and Seventeenth Centuries* (Ann Arbor: University of Michigan Press, 1950), 741–49.
4. J. A. Sharpe, *Defamation and Sexual Slander in Early Modern England: The Church Courts at York* (York: Borthwick Institute of Historical Research, 1980).

of Elizabeth never put the English queen at such risk, nor was she ever personally such a target as Mary was. In August 1562, while Mary was walking with Sir Henry Sidney, the day before he was to depart back to England, a Captain Hepburn "presented her grace a byll," which contained "as ribbalde verses as anye dyvleshe wytte coulde invent, and under them drawne with a penne the secreate members both of men and women in as monstrous a sort as nothynge coulde be more shamefullye dyvisede." Jenny Wormald points out how "profoundly humiliating and insulting" it was for Mary to not only be "the object of scandal spread about her, but the personal recipient of a direct gesture," and argues no one would have dared hand such a paper to Elizabeth. After Darnley's murder and her marriage to Bothwell, a rebellion forced Mary off the throne. As she was taken back to Edinburgh as a prisoner in June 1567 people cried out, "burn the whore! . . . burn her, burn her, she is not worthy to live, kill her, drown her."[5]

The English never yelled "burn the whore" at Elizabeth, but they did feel free to speculate about her lovers and supposed bastards. The gossip of Mother Ann Dowe and the Baxters may be more comprehensible than the later rumors, since in the 1560s Elizabeth was young, unmarried, and indiscreet in some people's eyes with her public displays of affection for Robert Dudley. Elizabeth herself responded to the various rumors that surrounded her. In 1564 she told the Spanish Ambassador, Guzman de Silva, a man with whom she shared a number of confidences:

> They charge me with a good many things in my own country and elsewhere, and, amongst others, that I show more favour to Robert than is fitting; speaking of me as they might speak of an immodest woman. . . . I have shown favour, although not so much as he deserves, but God knows how great a slander it is, and a time will come when the world will know it. My life is in the open, and I have so many witnesses that I cannot understand how so bad a judgement can have been formed of me.[6]

Two years later, when Elizabeth was upset with Dudley, or at least wished de Silva to believe she was so he would encourage the prospective marriage with the Archduke Charles, she complained to de Silva about Robert's ingratitude, "after she had shown him so much kindness and favour, that even her honour had suffered for the sake of honouring him." William Cecil for one did not have this "bad a judgement," and believed in the virtue of his queen. But he too was well aware of what was being said, and how her honor had suffered. In a letter to his close associate Thomas Smith in March 1566 he wrote: "Briefly I affirm, that the Quene's Majesty may be, by malicious tongs, not well reported, but in truth she herself is blameless, and hath no spot of evil intent."[7] De Silva also came to believe in the virtue of the queen he observed so closely. He wrote in 1564 to the Duchess of

---

5. *CSP, Scotland*, I, 646; Jenny Wormald, *Mary Queen of Scots: A Study in Failure* (London: George Philip, 1988), 145; *CSP, Foreign*, 1566–68, 256; Patrick Collinson, *The English Captivity of Mary Queen of Scots* (Sheffield: Sheffield History Pamphlets, 1987), 5. After the Ridofi Plot of 1572, and even more in the 1580s, Protestants in Parliament did all they could to encourage the image of Mary Stuart as an adulterous murderer as a justification for having her killed to safeguard Elizabeth. Collinson, *The English Captivity of Mary Queen of Scots*, 7–8. Elizabeth, of course, refused to listen to this argument for the nearly nineteen years of Mary's presence in England.

6. *CSP, Spain*, I, 387.

7. *CSP, Spain*, I, 592; Thomas Wright, ed., *Queen Elizabeth and Her Times* (London, 1838), I, 225.

Parma about Elizabeth that "she bears herself toward [Robert] in a way that together with other things that can be better imagined than described make me doubt sometimes whether Robert's position is so irregular as many think. It is nothing for princes to hear evil, even without giving any cause of it."[8]

Yet the gossip about Elizabeth's behavior continued. De Silva heard rumors that Dudley slept with the queen on New Year's day, 1566.[9] In 1570 a man named Marshame was condemned to lose both his ears or else pay a fine of a hundred pounds for saying that Elizabeth had two children by Robert Dudley. Two years later, during the investigations of the Ridolfi Plot, further comments about Elizabeth and her lovers were divulged. Keneln Berney confessed that a confederate, Mather, a supporter of the Duke of Norfolk, had intended to kill the queen, for "yf she weare not kylled, or made awaye, ther was no Waye but Deathe with the Duke." Berney claimed that Mather had described Elizabeth as "so vyle a Woman . . . that desyrethe nothinge but to fede her owne lewd fantasye." The way she would do it would be to ignore the worthwhile nobililty in favor of "Daunsers . . . [who] please her delycate Eye," such men as Dudley and Sir Christopher Hatton. Mather claimed these men "had more recourse to Her Majesty in her Privy Chamber than reason would suffer if she were so virtuous and well-inclined as some [noiseth] her!" According to Berney, Mather had "other suche vyle Words as I ame ashamed to speake, much more to wrytt." Mather asked for mercy, "I confesse further, of mislanguage in seeking to praise the Queen of Scottes, and to slander your Royall Persone. . . . I wholly remit my Cause to your Majestie's Mercie, who beinge a Mirror of Clemencie, will of your Majestie's Graciousnes, deale herein." But despite Elizabeth's reputation for leniency, both Berney and Mather were executed for their part in the Ridolfi Plot, soon after the death of Norfolk.[1] In 1572 Robert Blosse was brought before the Record of London, William Fleetwood, for spreading rumors that Elizabeth had four children by Robert Dudley. That same year Matthew Parker, Archbishop of Canterbury, wrote a very concerned letter to William Cecil about the "most shamefull words against" Elizabeth spoken by a man brought before the mayor of Dover. What the man said about Elizabeth and both Dudley and Sir Christopher Hatton was "a matter so horrible" that Parker would not put it on paper, but instead, he wrote, wished only to speak of it to Cecil when he had the chance.[2]

By 1570 sexual rumors mentioned not only Dudley but Sir Christopher Hatton as well, making Elizabeth even more a whore in the eyes of those who spread these stories. Hatton, like Dudley, had risen to prominence because of Elizabeth's affection for him. Hatton was seven years younger than the queen, and had first captured her attention by his graceful dancing in a court masque. Some people believed that Hatton's rise to power came from his charm rather than his ability. Mather's contemptuous comment about Elizabeth's favor to Hatton is an example of a stereotypical view

---

8. *CSP, Spain*, I, 381.
9. *CSP, Spain*, I, 520–21.
1. Murdin and Haynes, *Collection of State Papers*, II, 203, 204, 208.
2. Wright, ed., *Queen Elizabeth and Her Times*, I, 374, 440–41; John Strype, *Annals of the Reformation* (Oxford, 1824), II, Part 2, 503. I am indebted to Dennis Moore for the reference to Blosse in Strype. Robert Blosse also spread rumors that Edward VI was still alive, and fifteen years later actually claimed to be Edward VI.

of a powerful woman—that she could be dazzled by a man's dancing and give him a responsible place. MacCaffrey argues that "Leicester and Hatton were advanced to high office and a share in the royal confidence solely because of their private attraction for the Queen. . . . .To promote them from personal intimacy to public eminence was a risky business for any ruler, all the more so for a woman."[3]

In 1564 Hatton had become a gentleman pensioner. Eventually he gained positions of real stature. In 1578 he became Vice-Chamberlain of the queen's household. Nine years later he became the Lord Chancellor. Hatton's letters to Elizabeth express deep feelings for her, but also a fear that they are not reciprocated on the same level. In 1573 he wrote to her, "Would God I were with you but for one hour. My wits are overwrought with thoughts. I find myself amazed. Bear with me, my most dear sweet lady. Passion overcometh me. I can write no more. Love me; for I love you. . . . Live forever. . . . Ten thousand thousand farewells. He speaketh it that most dearly loveth you." Yet Hatton was also aware that his position did not make him an appropriate consort to the queen. In 1580, during the negotiations for Elizabeth to marry Alençon, Hatton wrote to Thomas Heneage, sending him a ring for Elizabeth that she should wear for good health and referring to the differing status of himself and the French prince. Hatton spoke of his feelings for "Our mistress, whom through choice I love no less than he that by the greatness of a kingly birth and fortune is most fit to have her. I am likewise bold to commend my most humble duty by this letter and ring, which hath the virtue to expel infectious airs, and is, as is telled to me, to be wearen betwixt the sweet dugs,— the chaste nest of more pure constancy." Hatton's reference to Elizabeth's dugs—her breasts—suggest some level of at least emotional intimacy, though they are described as "chaste." Hatton's supposed influence over Elizabeth led to an assassination attempt in 1573 by a fanatic Puritan, though Peter Burchet mistook Sir John Hawkins for Hatton on the London streets; luckily Hawkins was not hurt seriously. Elizabeth's fury at this attack, and her concern over Hatton when he was ill, certainly fanned rumors that he was her lover. And the stories persisted.[4]

In the 1560s and 1570s the rumors of Elizabeth's pregnancies and illegitimate children continued to crop up, especially among hostile foreign Catholics. Writing in 1564, Luis Roman, the secretary to the former Spanish Ambassador de Quadra, commented on plans for Elizabeth to go to the North of England. "Some say she is pregnant and is going away to lie in." A decade later Antonio de Guaras, acting Spanish agent in London, reported that there would be a marriage between the son of Catherine Grey and "a daughter of Leicester and the Queen . . . who, it is said, is kept hidden, although there are bishops to witness that she is legitimate." In December of 1575 Nicholas Ormanetto, Bishop of Padua and Nuncio in Spain, heard the rumor that Elizabeth had a daughter. He suspected that Sir Henry Cobham, whom Elizabeth had sent to Spain to negotiate with Philip II, spread the rumors. "I am assured that he has let it be known that the pretended Queene has a daughter, thirteen years of age, and that she

3. Wallace MacCaffrey, *War and Politics, 1588–1603* (Princeton: Princeton University Press, 1992), 457.
4. Nicholas Harris Nicholas, *Memoirs of the Life and Times of Sir Christopher Hatton* (London: R. Bentlye, 1847), 26, 155.

would bestow her in marriage on someone acceptable to his Catholic Majesty. I have heard talk before of this daughter, but the English here say that they know nought of such matter." The pope took the possibility of Elizabeth having a marriageable daughter seriously and saw it as a way to "bring the realm back to the Catholic faith" without the hazards of war. In 1578 there were rumors on the continent that Alençon, the French king's younger brother, would marry, not Elizabeth, but her niece or daughter. It is interesting and revealing that the pope and some of the Spanish not only took seriously the idea that Elizabeth had a child, but despite her probable illegitimacy (if she had in fact existed), they were willing to consider negotiating a marriage. For Catholics, after all, Elizabeth herself was not legitimate and was still the ruler of England. Seemingly they were willing to overlook these technicalities if England could thus be brought back to the Catholic faith.[5]

But some Catholics were less forgiving. Cardinal William Allen also used these stories in his 1588 *Admonition to the Nobility and People of England*, a propaganda tract to gain support for Philip II's proposed invasion. Allen argues that Elizabeth was damaged even from her birth, since she was "an incestuous bastard, begotten and born in sin." Not only was Henry married to Catherine of Aragon at the time, but more shockingly, Allen implies that Anne Boleyn was Henry's own daughter since "he did before unnaturally know and kepe both the said Anne's mother and sister." Elizabeth proves herself the true daughter of such parents by how she acts as queen. "She sells laws, licences, dispensations, pardons, &c., for money and bribes, with which she enriches her poor cousins and favourites." The chief favorite is Dudley, whom "she took up first to serve her filthy lust." Allen repeats every damaging comment about Dudley that he can. "To have more freedom and interest, he caused his own wife to be murdered, as afterwarde, for the accomplishment of his like brutish pleasures with another noble dame, it is openly known he made away with her husband." But, according to Allen, Dudley is not Elizabeth's only lover, and the older she gets, the more debased is her court. With "divers others, she hath abused her bodie against God's lawes, to the disgrace of princely majestie, and the whole nation's reproache, by unspeakable and incredible variety of luste . . . shamfully she hath defiled her person and cuntry, and made her court as a trappe, by this damnable and detestable art to intangle in sinne, and overthrowe the yonger sorte of her nobilitye and gentlemen of the lande." Elizabeth's behavior has made her "notorious to the worlde . . . [with] the whole worlde deriding our effeminate dastardie, that have suffered such a creature almost thirty years together to raigne both over our bodies and soules." Allen explains that the reason Elizabeth never married is "because she cannot confine herself to one man." He describes how she has "unlawfule, longe concealed, or fained issue," and claims that "she forced the very parliament to give consent to a law, that none should be named for her successor, savinge the natural, that is to saie, bastard-borne child of her owne bodie."[6] Allen's attack on Elizabeth's rule

5. *CSP, Spain*, I, 362, II, 491; *CSP, Rome*, 1572–78, 238, 250.
6. John Lingard, *The History of England* (London, 1883), VI, 706–8. These stories were current in such works as *Leicester's Commonwealth*, published 1584. That work, however, saw Elizabeth as his victim, rather than as evil in her own right. During the time of the Divorce there were some rumors that Henry had years earlier had an affair with Anne Boleyn's mother. He denied it but admitted her sister Mary had previously been his mistress.

is centered around her supposed sexual behavior. His claim that she took lovers demonstrates how her female identity and the beliefs about appropriate womanly behavior determined the attacks on her monarchy. Such an attack on a king—that he had lovers and was thus unfit to rule and somehow monstrous—would be laughable, unless, of course, the king's lovers, like Elizabeth's, were male. Allen's tract, the most inflammatory of all his works, was a great embarrassment once the Armada failed. Most copies were destroyed, but the scandal invoked continued to be repeated.

Of course there was no child born of her body, but the rumors of illegitimate children eventually brought forth someone who did claim to be her child. In 1587 a young Englishman in pilgrim's garb was arrested in the north of Spain on suspicion of being a spy. He was sent to Madrid where Philip II's English secretary, Sir Francis Englefield, examined him. The young man claimed to be Arthur Dudley, the illegitimate son of Robert Dudley and the queen. His first name is an interesting choice—the Tudors had attempted throughout the century to demonstrate strong ties to the King Arthur legend, and Henry VII had named his eldest son Arthur. It was only his premature death that had allowed Henry VIII to become the heir. James V of Scotland (son of Henry VIII's older sister, Margaret) also named his son Arthur; this boy too died in his youth and so did not ascend the throne. "Arthur Dudley" gave Englefield a detailed account of his childhood in the household of Robert Southern, who had told the boy his real identity on his deathbed.[7] Dudley described meetings he had had with important members of Elizabeth's government before he finally successfully fled the country in the mid-1580s to wander the continent in the company of disaffected English and Elizabeth's enemies. Arthur Dudley proposed to Englefield that Philip II take him under his protection and utilize him in the coming attack on England. Though at first inclined to believe Dudley's story, Englefield came to believe that Dudley was actually "a simple instrument in the hands of Elizabeth herself." Englefield suggested to the Spanish king, "I am of the opinion that he should not be allowed to get away, but should be kept very secure to prevent his escape. It is true his claim at present amounts to nothing, but . . . it cannot be doubted that France and the English heretics, or some other party, might turn it to their own advantage." Alarmingly for Dudley, Philip added the notation to the letter that it would be "safest to make sure of [Dudley's] person until we know more about it."[8]

Though Dudley's story has enough plausible details to suggest that he had been well coached, its basic premise is impossible. We know that Elizabeth was seriously ill in 1562 with smallpox; this was not a cover for her having given birth to a child. And, as Martin Hume pointed out, "It is. . . . beyond belief that a boy in the condition represented would have been allowed to run about the world at his own free will." Hume believes that Dudley was a spy who used this story to try and gain access and to save himself when caught. Elizabeth Jenkins adds that he may well have been willing to spy for either side. After Philip's notation, "Arthur Dudley"

7. For more on this story, see Ettwell A. B. Barnard, *Evesham and a Reputed Son of Queen Elizabeth* (Evesham: published by the author, 1926).
8. *CSP, Spain*, IV, 101–12. Martin Hume suggests, "The poor foolish young man [was] apparently under the impression that King Philip was an amiable altruist, who would help him to a crown for the sake of his *beaux yeux*." *The Courtships of Queen Elizabeth* (London: Nash & Grayson, 1926), 341.

disappears from the records, certainly kept safe by the Spanish, never to be heard from again.[9]

The rumors about Elizabeth's illegitimate children became even more intense in the last two decades of Elizabeth's reign, as did attacks on her rule. By the late 1570s and early 1580s Elizabeth, already in her late forties, was playing out the final marriage negotiations of her reign with the young Duke of Alençon. Critics such as John Stubbs outraged the queen by arguing against the marriage in part on the grounds that Elizabeth was now too old to bear a child. And Elizabeth still refused to name a successor. At Court people worried desperately about her health, and reassurances became even more intense.[1] In the countryside, these worries took on a different form. The rumors about her illicit children, often coupled with the suggestion that these children had also been destroyed, reflect on another level the fears over the succession and the antagonism toward a queen who refused to provide for her people's future. In 1577 Mary Clere, an Ingatestone spinster, declared Elizabeth was base born and Mary Stuart had a better claim to the throne. She was brought to trial and executed. Soon after, Randall Duckworth, a laborer in the village of Bradwell, stated that "this is no good government which we now live under and it was merry England when there was better government and if the queen die there will be a change." He was made to stand in the pillory with a paper on his head.[2]

In 1580 an Essex laborer, Thomas Playfere, stated that Elizabeth had two children by Lord Robert; he had himself seen them when they had been shipped out at Rye in two of the queen's best ships. The next year Henry Hawkins explained Elizabeth's frequent progresses throughout the countryside as a way for her to leave court and have her illegitimate children by Dudley—five all told. Said Hawkins of the queen, "She never goethe in progress but to be delivered." At the end of the decade, in 1589, Thomas Wendon claimed that "Parson Wylton spake openly in church . . . that the Queen's Majesty was an arrant whore" since "the Queen is a dancer, and Wylton said that all dancers are whores."[3]

The next year a widow named Dionisia Deryck claimed that Elizabeth "hath already had as many children as I, and that two of them were yet alive, one a man child and the other a maiden child, and the others were burned." We do not know exactly how many that was meant to be since the records do not state how many times Deryck herself had given birth. The father of the queen's children, claimed Deryck, was Dudley, who had "wrapped them up in the embers which was in the chamber where they were born." The same year Robert Gardner or Garner told a similar story; Leicester "had four children by the Queen's Majesty, whereof three were

9. Hume, *Courtships*, 345; Jenkins, *Elizabeth and Leicester*, 334.
1. John Stubbs, *Gaping Gulf*, ed. Lloyd E. Berry (Charlottesville: Folger Shakespeare Library, 1968), 51. John Stanhope wrote to Lord Talbot in December 1589, "The Queen is so well as I assure you." The next year he wrote again, "The Queen for health is wondrous well." At the end of the year Stanhope wrote "God be thanked she is in better health this winter than I have seen her before." In September of 1602 Fulke Greville wrote to the Countess of Shrewsbury, "The best news I can yet write your Ladyship of the Queen's health and disposition of body, which I assure you is excellent good, and I have not seen her every way better disposed these many years." Lodge, *Illustrations of British History*, II, 386, 422, 433, 582.
2. Samaha, "Gleanings from Local Criminal-Court Records," 68–69.
3. Louis A. Montrose, "The Elizabethan Subject and the Spenserian Text," in *Literary Theory/Renaissance Texts*, ed. Patricia Parker, David Quint (Baltimore: Johns Hopkins University Press, 1986), 311; Emmison, *Elizabethan Life*, 42–43; *Calendar of Assize Records: Essex*, 195; *CSP, Domestic Eliz.*, CXLVIII, 12; Samaha, "Gleanings from Local Criminal-Court Records," 69.

daughters alive, and the fourth a son that was burnt." Both Deryck and Gardner stood in the pillory for their indiscreet comments.[4]

In 1598 Edward Fraunces, of Melbury Osmond in Dorsetshire, attempted to seduce Elizabeth Baylie by telling her the queen had three bastards by noblemen at court, two sons and a daughter. Why should not Baylie have a sexual relationship without marriage, he asked her, when "the best in England, i.e. the Queen, had done so." Elizabeth Baylie's refusal made Fraunces angry not only with her but with the woman he had urged on her as a model. He called the queen "base born," and he added, "that the land had been happy if Her Majesty had been cut off twenty years since, so that some noble prince might have reigned in her stead." Elizabeth Baylie testified about this conversation before the magistrates, as did some of her neighbors. Frauncis attempted to bribe the witnesses, offering the men twice the money he offered the women. The witnesses, however, were outraged enough by his slander of the queen to refuse. Fraunces further amplified his misogyny when he attempted to discredit Baylie's testimony with the statement that "women are base creatures and of no credit."[5]

There are several more reports of infanticide in 1601. The most interesting version is from Hugh Broughton, who again wove together the themes of Elizabeth's lack of chastity, hostility toward her rule, and destruction of the potential heir. According to Broughton, a midwife was taken to a secret chamber where she was told to save the mother (Elizabeth, of course) at whatever cost to the child. The midwife was too skilled; she saved them both.

> And after [delivering] . . . a daughter, [the midwife] was brought to another chamber where there was a very great fire of coals, into which she was commanded to cast the child, and so it was burnt. This midwife was rewarded with a handful of gold, and at her departure, one came to her with a cup of wine, and said, Thou whore, drink before thou goest from hence, and she drank, and was sent back to her house, where within six days after she died of poison, but revealed this before her death.[6]

By this time the story has become absurdly melodramatic. If one wanted to keep someone from revealing information, one surely would not use a poison that took six days to take effect.

In Playfere's story of 1580, the children were shipped away. Closer to the end of the reign, in the rumors spread by Deryck, Gardner, and Broughton, the children are actually destroyed. Elizabeth had therefore not only dishonored herself by being a whore, but had destroyed, literally burned up, her succession. Gardner, for example, insisted that although Elizabeth's supposed daughters survived, the son, the potential king, died horribly. We cannot simply label these stories of Elizabeth's sexual misconduct as male discomfort at female rule, since women also participated in this gossip.

There is another possible example illustrating the difficulty many English people early in Elizabeth's reign had in accepting her refusal to follow the traditional role of a woman as wife and mother. In these years there were

4. Emmison, *Elizabethan Life*, 42; Samaha, "Gleanings from Local Criminal-Court Records," 69.
5. *CSP, Domestic Eliz.*, CCLXIX, #22, 136–37; G. B. Harrison, ed., *The Elizabethan Journals* (New York: Macmillan Co., 1939), II, 51.
6. *CSP, Domestic Eliz.*, CCLXXIX, #48, 24.

a larger number of reported monstrous births than earlier in the century. Stories of monsters were immensely popular throughout the sixteenth and seventeenth centuries. It seems as if childbirth, and the fear around it, were on the minds of many people. It is possible that for some people having as ruler an unmarried woman who refused to have a child or name an heir was unnatural and frightening. Especially with the religious situation causing such uncertainty, they may have believed that the only progeny possible from such an unnatural situation was monstrous. There were at least a dozen broadsides describing these monstrous births in the 1560s, five in the year 1562 alone.[7]

The rumors about Elizabeth's illegitimate children and the use of these rumors to discredit her continued after her death. In 1609 *Pruritanus*, a Catholic book in Latin published in France and smuggled into England, caused James I's government a great deal of concern. The book was highly critical of Henry VIII, Elizabeth, and James. Of Elizabeth it said that, though she styled herself head of the Church and a Virgin, she was an immodest woman who had given births to sons and daughters. It claimed that Elizabeth prostituted herself with men of many backgrounds and nationalities, "even with blackamoors." The book repeated the rumor already circulated by William Allen, that Henry VIII had had an affair with Anne Boleyn's mother, and thus Anne was actually his own daughter, making Elizabeth the child of incest.[8]

From a very different perspective and a half century after Elizabeth's death, Francis Osborne referred to stories that "she had a son bred in the state of Venice, and a daughter, I know not where nor when." Osborne, however, dismissed these stories as "fitter for a romance than a history." Wistfully, he added that after considering the straits to which Elizabeth's successors, the Stuarts, had brought England, he wished that she had left "the smallest chip of that incomparable instrument of honour, peace, and safety." Osborne did not care if such a child were legitimate or illegitimate.[9]

At the same time that some people were whispering about just how many illegitimate children Elizabeth had, others were doubting whether she was capable of conceiving a child or of even consumating a sexual relationship. The Spanish Ambassador, de Feria, told Philip II, "for a reason they have given me, I understand she will not bear children." His successor, de Quadra, believed the same. "It is the common opinion confirmed by certain

---

7. Katherine Park and Lorraine J. Daston, "Unnatural Conceptions: The Study of Monsters in Sixteenth- and Seventeenth-Century France and England," *Past and Present* 92 (1981), 20–54; Joseph Lilly, ed., *A Collection of Seventy-Nine Black-Letter Ballads and Broadsides, printed in the reign of Queen Elizabeth between the year 1559 and 1597* (London: Joseph Lilly, 1867), xvi. A further bizarre account that reflects some gender confusion occurred in 1583. The Spanish Ambassador de Mendoza reported in a letter: "I cannot help mentioning a very strange thing that has happened in this country, as I am assured by very trustworthy persons. In a place called Beaumaris, in the province of Chester, there is a hermaphrodite, who has hitherto chosen to dress as a man, and as such, was married and had children. A few months ago, however, he changed his functions and is now pregnant. It seems contrary to nature that he should both conceive and engender as well." *CSP, Spain*, III, 475. John Neale also notes the monstrous births of 1562, but argues they were perceived as Protestant omens against a proposed meeting between Elizabeth and Mary Stuart. *Queen Elizabeth I* (Garden City: Anchor Books, 1957), 115–16.
8. G. B. Harrison, *A Second Jacobean Journal* (Ann Arbor: University of Michigan Press, 1958), 143–44.
9. Francis Osborne, *Historical Memories on the Reigns of Queen Elizabeth and King James* (London: Francis Grismond, 1658), 384. The belief that Elizabeth had children continued in the centuries after her death. In 1850 a correspondent to *Notes and Queries* Stated "there s a current belief in Ireland that the family of Mapother, in Roscommon, is descended from Queen Elizabeth." II, 60 (December 21, 1850), 500.

physicians, that this woman is unhealthy and it is believed that she will not bear children." Early in her reign, foreign ambassadors bribed the women of Elizabeth's bedchamber for intimate information about her life, and their reports home are filled with such details as Elizabeth's light and irregular periods. The Venetian Ambassador heard that she had been bled in the foot in an attempt to correct this problem. Later the Nuncio in France heard rumors that Elizabeth flowed from "an issue in one of her legs" since "she has hardly ever had the purgations proper to all women." One of Elizabeth's physicians, Dr. Robert Huicke, apparently encouraged Elizabeth's desire not to marry, which greatly angered members of Parliament. Camden reported that the 1566 Parliament "cursed Huic, the Queen's Physician, as a Disswader of her marriage for I know not what womanish Impotency." Elizabeth probably felt comfortable with Huicke's advice; he was eventually appointed chief physician to the queen. Elizabeth may well have had some fears of pregnancy. Camden certainly believed this. "The perils by conception and child-bearing, objected by the physicians and her gentlewomen for some private reasons, did many times run in her mind, and very much deter her from thoughts of marrying."[1]

There were also rumors that Elizabeth had an impediment that would prohibit regular sexual relations and thus make conception impossible. Mary Stuart referred to these rumors in a vitriolic letter she wrote to Elizabeth (which William Cecil apparently suppressed). Claiming Bess of Hardwick, the Countess of Shrewsbury, as her source, Mary Stuart wrote, "she says, moreover, that indubitably you are not like other women, and it is folly to advance the notion of your marriage with the Duke of [Alençon], seeing that such a conjugal union would never be consummated." This opinion was probably widespread. After Elizabeth's death, Ben Jonson made a similar remark, suggesting that Elizabeth had a membrane that made her incapable of intercourse, though despite that "for her delight she tryed many." At the time of the proposed marriage to Alençon, Jonson claimed, a French surgeon "took in hand to cut it, yett fear stayed her." These statements suggest that one way to minimize the power of a woman such as Elizabeth was to describe her as "different from other women," less than them in the most fundamental sense of the ability to be wife and mother. In 1566, however, the queen's physician assured the French ambassador if Elizabeth married the French king she would have ten children at least, although how much this was based on any real diagnosis and how much on wishful thinking is another question. William Cecil always assumed that Elizabeth would be able to produce a child.[2]

By being "wed to England," as she so often claimed, Elizabeth could present yet another image to her subjects, that of a mother.[3] The many

---

1. Jenkins, *Elizabeth the Great*, 77; *CSP, Spain*, I, 63; *CSP, Venice*, I, 105; *CSP, Rome*, II, 363; Camden, *The History of the Most Renowned and Victorious Princess Elizabeth*, 1688 ed., 83, 269; *Dictionary of National Biography*, ed. Leslie Stephen and Sidney Lee (London, 1885–1901), X, 192–93.

2. Quoted in Stefan Zweig, *Mary Queen of Scots and the Isles* (New York: Viking Press, 1935), 299. The original letter appears in French in Murdin and Haynes, ed., *A Collection of State Papers*, 558–59. I have used Zweig's translation. David Laing, ed., *Notes of Ben Jonson's Conversations with William Drummond* (London: Printed for the Shakespeare Society, 1842), 23; *CSP, Spain*, I, 569.

3. Elizabeth is not the only one to put it in those terms. De Feria wrote to Philip II at the very beginning of her reign that Elizabeth "is very much wedded to the people." *CSP, Spain*, I, 4. In analyzing Elizabeth's parliamentary rhetoric, Allison Heisch points out that, throughout her reign, Elizabeth "pictures and presents herself as a loving and yet virginal mother." "Queen Elizabeth I and the Persistence of Patriarchy," *Feminist Review* 4 (1980), 32.

godchildren she sponsored encouraged the concept that all the English were in some sense her children.[4] At the very beginning of her reign, when the House of Common beseeched the queen to marry, Elizabeth had responded,

> And doe not upbraid me with miserable lacke of children: for every-one of you, and as many as are Englishmen, are children, and kinsmen to me; of whom if God deprive me not . . . I cannot without injury be accounted Barren.[5]

In a letter to his wife Sir John Harington referred to Elizabeth when he feared that she was dying as "our deare Queene, my royale godmother, and this state's natural mother." John Jewel, bishop of Salisbury, in 1567, referred to Elizabeth as "the only nurse and mother of the church of God." In 1578 a person representing the city of Norwich told Elizabeth in a pageant to celebrate her coming: "Thou art my joy next [to] God, I have no other, My Princesse and my peerlesse Queene, my loving Nurse and Mother." This image was repeated throughout the week of Elizabeth's stay, and when she left she was told, "Farewell, oh Queene, farewell, oh Mother dere." Yet Elizabeth's self-presentation as mother was not always successful. In 1566 one member of the House of Commons, Paul Wentworth, Peter's younger brother, suggested that if Elizabeth did not designate a successor "she may be reckoned of, not as a Nurse, not as a Mother of Countrye, but as a Step-mother, nay as a Parricide of her Countrey, which had rather that England, which now breathed with her Breath, should expire together with her than survive her." The concern over the succession was rational; had Elizabeth died in the first decade of her reign the problems for the country could have been horrific—disrupted succession and religious civil war. The way the anger is expressed here, however, may suggest not just a subject to his sovereign, but a child disappointed by his mother and rejecting her.[6]

By not marrying, by being both no-one's mother and everyone's, and by presenting herself as both a virgin to be revered and a sensuous woman to be adored, Elizabeth exerted a strong psychological hold on her subjects.

4. Louis A. Montrose, "Shaping Fantasies: Figurations of Gender and Power in Elizabethan Culture," *Representations* 1 (1983), 78.

5. Camden, *The History of the Most Renowned and Victorious Princess Elizabeth*, 1688 ed., 27. In 1563 she told her Parliament, "I assure you all, that thoughe, after my death, you may have many stepdames yet shall you never [have] a more naturall mother than I meane to be unto you all." John Harington, *Nugae Antiquae*, ed. Henry Harington and Thomas Park (London, 1804), I, 83.

6. Norman Egbert McClure, ed., *The Letters and Epigrams of Sir John Harington* (Philadelphia: University of Pennsylvania Press, 1930), 96; John Ayre, *The Works of John Jewel* (Cambridge: Cambridge University Press, 1845–50), III, 118; Nichols, *The Progresses and Public Processions of Queen Elizabeth*, II, 146, 165; Camden, *The History of the Most Renowned and Victorious Princess Elizabeth*, 1688 ed., 84–85. The image of Elizabeth as nurse is a common one. See, for example, a speech in her honor at Cambridge, 1578. She was thanked for what she did "particularly to the two Universities, which were kept by her as by a Nurse in quietness to be nourished in piety, and all other learning." Nichols, *Progress*, II, 110. In 1588 Anthony Marten, keeper of the royal library at Westminster, described Elizabeth as "sent from above, to nurse and protect the true Christian commonwealth." "An Exhortation to stirre the Minds of all Her Majesty's faithfull Subjects, to defend their Countrey, in this dangerous Time, from the Invasion of Enemies" (London: John Windet, 1588) in *The Harleian Miscellany*, ed. William Oldys and Thomas Park (London: John White and John Murray, 1808), I, 174. In his ground-breaking article on gender and power in Elizabethan England, Louis Montrose argues that "by fashioning herself into a singular combination of Maiden, Matron, and Mother, the queen transformed the normal domestic life-cycle of an Elizabethan female into what was at once a social paradox and a religious mystery." "Shaping Fantasies," 80.

In 1600 a sailor, Abraham Edwards, was arrested for sending the queen passionate love letters and drawing a dagger in her presence. Officials were convinced that though apparently mad, "greatly distracted" Edwards had no wish to harm the queen, rather that he was "transported with a humour of love." Described as "very bare and in pitiful case," Edwards was placed in Bedlam. In the seventeenth century, Francis Osborne advised his son about the dangers of passionate attachments; he described the "voluptuous death" of a tailor, who "whined away" for love of Elizabeth.[7]

Certainly there were rumors about male monarchs as well. As de Silva said to Elizabeth in 1564, "It is no new thing for great princes to be the subjects of gossip."[8] During the reign of Henry VIII there were many prophecies contending the king would die. In late 1537 people in Kent, Sussex, Northamptonshire, Berkshire, and Oxfordshire were repeating rumors that Henry VIII was dead. Those the authorities were convinced were the worst scandalmongers were put in the pillory. The next year Norfolk was filled with rumors that Henry was dead after Mabel Brigge performed a black fast, also known as a "Saint Trinian's Fast," against him. Henry lived another eight years but Brigge was executed for treason. At about the same time there were also rumors that Henry would impose a "horn tax" on every head of cattle; this rumor especially concerned authorities who were afraid it might lead to an uprising.[9] In 1590, William Cecil's grandson and namesake wrote to Lord Talbot that Philip II was dead, adding for good measure that before his death "he had sent to the Pope to obtain licence to marry his own daughter." Philip did not die until 1598 and, though he had a penchant for marrying cousins, his marriage plans were not as bizarre as Cecil indicated.[1]

And many of the rumors spread about Elizabeth did not have to do with her sexuality. During Elizabeth's reign a wide variety of rumors about her spread throughout Europe. In 1576 the Venetian envoy had to assure those back in Venice that Elizabeth was well and in good health since the city was rife with rumors that she was dead. At the time of the Armada some people believed that England had been "subdued, the Quene taken and sent prisoner over the Alpes to Rome, where, barefoote, she should make her humble reconciliation." Don Barnardino de Mendoza, the Spanish Ambassador who had been expelled from England and was now in residence in Paris, so believed this that he entered "into our Ladie Church, (Notre Dame) advancing his rapier in his right hande, and with a loud voice cried, 'Victorie! victorie!' and it was forthwith bruted, that England was vanquished. But the next day, when truth was knowne of the Armada's overthrowe. . . . Mendoza, being much dismayed, obscured himself, not daring to shewe his face." But the rumors about her sexuality were particularly intense and widespread, suggesting they resonated far more than other rumors.

---

7. *Calendar of the Manuscripts of the . . . Marquess of Salisbury* (London, 1883–1976) X, 172–73. One can see how much of a psychological pull a female monarch has even to this day. The incident with Edwards is eerily reminiscent of the case of Michael Fagin, who broke into the second Elizabeth's bedchamber, also professing love. Fagin was also perceived as having "serious personal problems and . . . suicidal tendencies." *Time*, August 2, 1982; Osborne, *Works*, 54.
8. *CSP, Spain*, I, 368.
9. George Lyman Kittredge, *Witchcraft in Old and New England* (Cambridge, MA: Harvard University Press, 1929), 129; Jasper Ridley, *Henry VIII: The Politics of Tyranny* (New York: Fromm International, 1986), 306–7; Carolly Erickson, *Great Harry* (New York: Summit Books, 1980), 266.
1. Lodge, *Illustrations of British History*, II, 413.

Coupled with the concerns and rumors over her health they express some of the terror over a future for which she had not provided her country.[2]

Though the way Elizabeth behaved may have fostered these rumors they might well have surfaced even if she had not enjoyed and encouraged the ritual of courtship and favorites. Her sister Mary I in no way mirrored this behavior; she was the epitome of virgin and then chaste wife. Moreover, she was clearly infertile in her reign. Her marriage to Philip yielded only a false pregnancy that ended in humiliation and despair. Despite this a rumor surfaced during her reign that she had an illegitimate child by Stephen Gardiner, the bishop of Winchester, a most improbable combination. Here as well this rumor represented both denigration of the queen and wish fulfillment.[3]

The belief in Elizabeth's lovers, in her illegitimate children, and the sexual interest in her suggest how significant and complex gender constructions and sexual issues were in the minds of Elizabeth's subjects and the important part they played in shaping the way English men and women regarded their queen. Though there were often comments about the personal lives of male monarchs, they were of a different nature, and served very different functions. With a king, the need for an heir was equally important, but it was the *wife* of the king who was there to produce the heir, and, as Henry VIII demonstrated all too clearly, if the wife did not adequately perform this role, if she did not have healthy sons, she could always be replaced. With Elizabeth, the question of the queen marrying and producing an heir was much more serious, since she herself was both ruler and potential producer of the heir. Elizabeth's councillors and Parliament felt a deep need to insure the legitimate succession in order to safeguard the peace of the nation. In the Parliament of 1559, one member maintained that "nothing can be more contrary to the public [interest] than that such a Princess, in whose marriage is comprehended the safety and peace of the Commonwealth, should live unmarried, and as it were a Vestal Virgin." But perhaps there were also other more obscure motivations behind the repeated behests to Elizabeth to marry. This nation of men at times found it both frustrating and degrading to serve a female, especially one not under the control of any man. William Cecil, for one, prayed that "God send our mistress a husband, and by time a son, that we may hope our posterity shall have a masculine succession."[4]

Elizabeth was queen to a people unused to female rule, a people who were just getting over the dislocation of the break with the Catholic Church. Elizabeth, unmarried and refusing to name an heir, was both Virgin and Mother; queen and prince. The very real adoration most of her people felt for Elizabeth made her even more the focus for their distress. The gossip about Elizabeth allowed her subjects to express their ambiguous feelings about her anomalous position in a patriarchal culture as a female ruler who took the unprecedented step of refusing to assume the roles traditionally allotted to women as wives and mothers. Instead, Elizabeth ruled with great

2. *CSP, Venice*, VII, 557; Stowe cited in Wright, *Queen Elizabeth and Her Times*, II, 381.

3. John Strype, *Memorials of the Reverend Father in God, Thomas Cranmer*, (Oxford: Oxford University Press, 1840), 456. In the seventeenth century, Lady Eleanor Davies was convinced that her second husband, Sir Archibald Douglas, was the true oldest son of James I. *The New Jerusalem at Hand* (London, 1649), 11; *The Lady Eleanor Douglas, Dowager, Her Jubiles Pleas or Appeal* (London, 1650), 2–3. I am indebted to Esther Cope for this reference.

4. Camden, *The History of the Most Renowned and Victorious Princess Elizabeth*, 1688 ed., 26; Montrose, "Shaping Fantasies," 80; *Miscellaneous State Papers*, I, 174.

success—establishing a broadly based religious policy and a long peace as well as presiding over spectacular cultural developments. Elizabeth was not only politically astute but truly loved her subjects and revelled in their love for her. Yet with all her varied self-presentations, she was still an unmarried woman instead of a king. She could not overcome either her sex or the decision she made not to provide England with a king-consort and an heir of her body or to name any other successor. The comments about her sexuality were one way for her people to come to express their ambivalent feelings about her position as ruler, and also to come to terms with it.

DONALD STUMP

[Protestant Voices of Dissent]†

I

It is a curious fact that so many of the best and most familiar poems written in praise of Queen Elizabeth idealize her as if she were a pagan goddess. Though she is sometimes represented in such figures as a shepherdess, a courtly or Petrarchan mistress, or the queen of the fairies, she is best known in the guise of classical deities, particularly Astraea, Diana, and the moon goddess Cynthia (or Belphoebe). Since Elizabeth was arguably most important to her subjects as a defender of the Protestant Reformation, both in England and on the Continent, it is strange that so little of the best work about her—most of it written in the last two decades of her reign—draws its analogs from biblical, or even distinctly Christian, sources.[1]

This is especially puzzling since, until the early 1580s, she was commonly compared with, or urged to follow the example of, great figures from the Old Testament. In exhorting and representing Elizabeth, writers frequently invoked biblical women such as Eve,[2] Sara,[3] Dinah,[4] Deborah,[5] Esther,[6] Huldah,[7] Judith,[8] Susannah[9]—and even Jael.[1] They also employed

---

†   Reprinted, with revisions, from "Abandoning the Old Testament: Shifting Paradigms for Elizabeth, 1578–82," *Images of Elizabeth I: A Quadricentennial Celebration*. Ed. Donald Stump and Carole Levin. Special issue, *Explorations in Renaissance Culture* 30 (Summer 2004): 89–109.

1.   Studies by Roy Strong, John King, Helen Hackett, and others who have analyzed images of the Queen in relation to specific periods and incidents in her reign have not treated this anomaly in any detail. E. C. Wilson's early discussion treats the imagery involving classical goddesses as a logical extension of the veneration afforded her as the Defender of the Faith, but does not consider the clash with prevailing religious sensibilities that such figures entailed (57–60).

2.   Stubbs, A2ʳ. Since the mass of surviving material from Elizabeth's reign is enormous, my citations of scriptural references can only be representative, not exhaustive. The sources that I draw on include E. C. Wilson's *England's Eliza*, John Nichols's *Progresses and Public Processions of Queen Elizabeth*, and E. K. Chambers's *Elizabethan Stage*, as well as the indexes in collected works of prominent Elizabethan literary figures and a good deal of material that Susan Felch and I have reviewed in compiling this Norton Critical Edition.

3.   Bentley 288.

4.   Stubbs A3ᵛ (implicit).

5.   Mulcaster D3ʳ–D4ʳ; Grafton, f.179ʳ, Knox 6: 50; Calvin 34–35; Aylmer B3ᵛ, D2ᵛ–D3ʳ, O4r; Hales qtd. Foxe 8: 678; Griffin qtd. Nichols 1: 316; Humphrey qtd. Nichols 1: 597; "Meditation" C4ʳ; Garter and Goldingham C1ᵛ–C2ʳ; Lyly 2: 209–10; Bentley 262, 272.

6.   Hake, *Commemoration* A7ʳ; Garter and Goldingham C2ʳ–C2ᵛ; Bentley 262.

7.   Calvin 34–35.

8.   Aylmer B3ᵛ, O4r; Hales qtd. Foxe 8: 676 (implicit); Garter and Goldingham C2ʳ, Bentley 262, 272.

9.   Hake, *Commemoration* A8ʳ; Munday rpt. Morfill 2: 187.

1.   "Meditation" C4ʳ; Humphrey qtd. Nichols 1: 597; Bentley 262, 272.

a long list of male figures, including Adam,[2] Abel,[3] Joseph,[4] Moses,[5] Joshua,[6] Gideon,[7] Samuel,[8] David,[9] Solomon,[1] Zerubabel,[2] Elijah,[3] Jonah,[4] Daniel,[5] Nehemiah,[6] and the reformer kings of Judah: Asa, Hezekiah, Josiah, and others.[7]

By the early 1580s, however, the Old Testament heroes and heroines were rapidly going out of fashion at court. In works as various as royal entertainments, welcoming speeches, poems for special occasions, devotional works, and polemical tracts, such figures were rarely held up for comparison to, or emulation by, the Queen. Between 1558 and 1582, I have found about twenty such works containing well over a hundred references to exemplary Old Testament figures. Between 1583 and 1603, however, I have located only five works containing a total of six references.[8] My scan has not been exhaustive. I have not attempted, for example, to examine parliamentary acts or petitions, government documents, the routine correspondence of officials or churchmen (which are too numerous to survey), or the prescribed liturgies of the English Church or the mass of sermons delivered at Court (which, by their very nature, turn to scripture in offering exempla). Alexandra Walsham's recent examination of a number of such works, as well as many more that were not composed for the attention of the Queen or the court, suggests that comparisons with the Old Testament heroes and heroines were still fairly common among militant Protestants in the country at large.[9] My rather extensive search of literature connected more directly with the court reveals, however, a dramatic falling off in their use there. By the mid 1580s, aspiring young writers addressing the Queen or seeking to catch her eye in that arena were rarely comparing her with Old Testament figures, and in consequence, her public image was becoming less overtly implicated in the religious turmoils of the day.

All this was happening, moreover, precisely when the Catholic threat to England was greatest and Protestant zeal was at its height. The period saw the harshest anti-Catholic measures of Elizabeth's reign. Following the covert arrival of the Jesuits leaders William Campion and Robert Parsons

2. Hales qtd. Foxe 8: 675; Stubbs, A2^{r}.
3. Bentley 705.
4. "Oration of the Minister of the Dutch Church" qtd. Garter and Goldingham D1^{v}–D2^{r}; Bentley 262, 271, 721.
5. Aylmer 14^{v}–K1^{r}, Hales qtd. Foxe 8: 675–76 (implicit); *Geneva Bible* *.*3^{r}; Hake, *Commemoration* Avr^{r} (implicit); "Meditation" B7^{r}, C1^{r}, C2^{v}, C4^{r}; Bentley 262, 271, 706, 724.
6. Aylmer P4^{r}–P4^{v}; "Meditation" C4^{r}; Stubbs B1^{r}; Bentley 262, 271–72.
7. Aylmer B3^{r}; Stubbs F1^{r}.
8. Bentley 262, 268, 687.
9. Aylmer B3^{v}, O4^{r}; O4^{v}, Hales qtd. Foxe 8: 677–78; Humphrey qtd. Nichols 1: 597, 598; "Meditation" B7^{r}, C2^{r}, C4^{r}; Oration of the Mayor of Norwich qtd. Garter and Goldingham B1^{v}; Stubbs A7^{v}; Bentley 262, 270, 272, 288, 292, 306, 687, 706, 709, 712, 716, 721, 725, 726, 728; Beza rpt. Bentley 306, 349, 350.
1. Hales qtd. Foxe 8: 678, 679; *Geneva Bible* *.*4^{r}; "Meditation" C2^{r}, C4^{r}–C4^{v}; Sanford A3^{v}; Stubbs B8^{r}; Bentley 262, 272, 279, 709.
2. *Geneva Bible* *.*2^{r}; Bentley 298.
3. "Meditation" C3^{r}.
4. Stubbs C2^{r}; Bentley 262.
5. Elizabeth's prayer before coronation qtd. Mulcaster E4^{r}–E4^{v}; Munday rpt. Morfill 2: 187.
6. Stubbs B1^{v}, Humphrey qtd. Nichols 1: 597.
7. Hales qtd. Foxe 8: 676 (implicit); *Geneva Bible* *.*2^{r}–*.* 4^{r}, "Meditation" C3^{r}; Stubbs B1^{r}; Bentley 272, 687.
8. Hake, "Oration" qtd. Nichols 2: 465 (Moses implicitly, David), 468 (Moses); Stockwood B3^{v}–B4^{r}; Spenser 3.4.2; Mary Sidney 2: 102–4. I do not include elegies or memorials written after the Queen's death because such works typically reprise images from throughout a person's career.
9. Walsham, 143–56.

in 1580, the repression accelerated steadily through the discovery of the Throckmorton and Babington assassination plots against Elizabeth in 1584 and 1586, the execution of Mary Stuart in 1587, and the invasion of the Spanish Armada in 1588. Despite this crescendo in Protestant fervor, however, writing about the Queen centered on the court in the last two decades of the reign is oddly silent on the Old Testament figures that Protestants were once so fond of citing.

This fact is all the more surprising when one considers the affiliations of the poets who set the fashions in poetic representations of the Queen during this period. Most of the "new poets" of the generation of Spenser, Sidney, and Ralegh were closely associated with the most aggressively Protestant faction in the government and might have been expected to draw on a full range of scriptural materials. In fact, they did little to slow the abandonment of Old Testament paradigms and much to hasten it. Two major genres that the so-called "new poets" adapted and pressed into service to the Queen—the courtly or Petrarchan love lyric and the pastoral—were by their very nature not well suited to represent Elizabeth as a prophetic figure or as a militant Defender of the Faith against Catholic forces on the Continent. Neither was Sidney's influential pastoral romance, *Arcadia*. Spenser's representations of the Queen as Una and Mercilla in *The Faerie Queene* served the purpose better, but they were exceptional by any standard and did not draw on the usual Old Testament paradigms invoked in the first half of the reign. After 1582, one occasionally encounters ballads, poems, sermons, or religious works written for a popular audience in which Elizabeth is figured as Moses, Esther, Judith, or Deborah,[1] but such comparisons rarely appear in the work of writers addressing themselves to the Queen or the court.

Elizabeth herself seems to have led the way in the shift against such biblical comparisons. Study of her *Collected Works* reveals that, in the first half of her reign, from 1558 to 1582, she alludes to exemplary Old Testament figures twenty-three times in eleven different pieces of her writing.[2] In the second half of her reign, however, the numbers have dropped to a mere six times in three works. In the later years, in fact, she mentions only three male figures (Solomon, Jacob, and Joseph) and never names the biblical heroines at all.[3] Since the volume of *Collected Works* contains only a fraction of the Queen's correspondence, my counts are not, of course, exhaustive, but they are suggestive. Particularly revealing are her prayers, where we might expect such references to abound. In those that she composed between 1558 and 1582, we find eighteen references to fifteen different biblical figures who are treated in a favorable light, including the women Deborah, Judith, Esther, and Susannah. From 1582 to the Queen's death, by contrast, not a single biblical figure is mentioned. To be sure, prayers from that period are fewer and occupy only half the space, and as the editors point out, they are more personal. Yet it is still striking that they do not invoke a single Old Testament paradigm.

Nothing shows the trend more clearly than the prologue to Thomas Dekker's *Old Fortunatus*. By 1599, when the play was staged before the

---

1. Besides the examples cited by Walsham, see Wilson 36–37, 43–44, and 148 and Vennar rpt. Nichols 3: 541.
2. Elizabeth I 55, 142, 145–56, 147, 149, 155, 156, 157, 159 (Daniel implicitly?), and 245.
3. Elizabeth I 198, 371, 411.

Queen, it was possible to rattle off her most common literary names without mentioning any that are scriptural, or even distinctively Christian. The Queen is celebrated as a goddess enshrined in a pagan temple. As the two old men who speak the prologue travel toward London to join in her cultic adoration, one asks, "Are you then traveling to the temple of Eliza?" and the other replies, "Euen to her temple are my feeble limmes trauelling. Some cal her Pandora: some Gloriana, some Cynthia: some Delphoebe, some Astraea: all by seuerall names to expresse seuerall loues . . ." (sig. A1ᵛ).

The question, then, is why the Queen and her court should have set aside the Old Testament paradigms in the 1580s and 1590s. Part of the explanation is undoubtedly that they were following a larger shift in fashions brought about by the rise of Humanism earlier in the century. The growing influence of classical figures in royal iconography during the sixteenth century is evident not only in England but also on the Continent. In the early 1580s, moreover, the generation of English writers coming into prominence had been educated under the uniform grammar-school curriculum established in the early 1560s. They included such prominent figures as Ralegh, the Sidneys, Spenser, Lyly, and Peele, all heavily steeped in the classics. Since the Queen herself was proficient in Latin, wrote personal prayers in Greek, and loved the literature and philosophy of pagan antiquity, works derived from the classics were welcome at court.

Another spur to the proliferation of non-scriptural paradigms was the growing popularity of foundation myths based on chronicle accounts of England as Troynovant and on romance representations of King Arthur as a national hero. Elizabeth, like her father, favored works based on these myths, which conveniently sidestepped questions of Tudor legitimacy by tracing the family's Welsh lineage back through King Arthur to the earliest race of Briton kings. Spenser's *Faerie Queene* provides the most elaborate literary representation of this mythic pedigree (2.10.5–68; 3.3.22–50, 9.38–51). In an age of conflict with the Habsburg Empire and the Roman Catholic Church, it did not hurt that such a lineage was neither Roman nor Anglo-Saxon, having its origins in the ancient Trojan Brutus, grandson of Aeneas. The Tudors were thus said to derive from a mythic line as glorious and ancient as that of the founders of Rome and the Empire. In the troubled decades of the 1580s and 1590s, court writers and entertainers buttressed their Queen's authority by transforming such foundation myths into elaborate and stylized rituals of tiltyard chivalry and quasi-medieval courtly love (Hackett 78–80, 83–87; Strong, *Gloriana* 91–93 and *Cult* 121–62). Not only did such works lend a comforting sense of antiquity and legitimacy to the monarchy, but they also introduced a tantalizing element of erotic play, quasi-religious homage, and masculine competition for favor into the life of the aging Virgin Queen. It is no coincidence that the extraordinary elaboration and ritualization of the Accession Day Tilts as the preeminent festival of the Elizabethan court took place after the collapse of the French marriage negotiations in the early 1580s, when foreign suitors no longer courted Elizabeth (Strong 133).

It seems to me, however, that the Protestant fervor of the period was too strong for the triumph of Humanist education or the cultivation of Tudor mythology to have been more than contributing factors in the great paradigm shift at court that I have been describing. Most of the "new poets" were committed to an aggressive, Protestant agenda, and their grammar-school curriculum included study of the Bible and the Church Fathers as well as the "ancients." Although their reading in the classics, English chronicle history, and Arthurian romance gave them court-approved alternatives to the conventional Old Testament paradigms of the 1560s and 1570s, it offered them no compelling reason to pursue those alternatives as exclusively as they did in the 1580s and 1590s. Before the great shift, writers such as Aylmer, Griffin, and the authors of the Norwich pageants had mingled biblical material with classical precedents or the "matter of Britain," and one wonders why the new generation of Protestant writers did not adopt that mixed mode as well. They were not, heaven knows, squeamish about mingling material from more than one culture or epoch. Nothing, moreover, in the nature of these alternative paradigms explains the suddenness with which they supplanted the heroines and heroes of the Old Testament.

I would argue, then, for other, less obvious explanations in addition to the long-term trends favoring classical Humanism and Tudor mythmaking. First there was the loss of favor at court suffered by forward Protestants during the controversies over nonconformity and popular "prophesyings" in the 1570s. Then there was the Queen's harsh response to the Protestant outcry over her desire to marry the Catholic Duke of Anjou at the end of the decade. And finally, there was her compelling need to inspire awe in both her subjects and her foreign enemies in the perilous decades that followed. It was the excessive rhetoric of Bible-thumping favored by forward Protestants, I believe, and their campaign against the French Duke that initially brought the Old Testament paradigms into bad odor at court. Heightened international tensions and the outbreak of war with Spain in the 1580s, however, followed by military, economic, and political malaise in the 1590s, assured the ultimate ascendancy of neoclassical and quasi-medieval figures for the Queen.

II

In the 1570s, Elizabeth faced an increasingly disaffected group of radical Protestants clamoring for religious reform and for a crackdown on English Catholics. Roused by the Rebellion of the Northern Earls and the threat of Spanish invasion in 1569, by the papal bull excommunicating Elizabeth and inviting her overthrow in 1570, and by the Ridolfi assassination plot against her in 1571, many forward Protestants were scandalized that the Queen continued to temporize with her Catholic subjects and refused to turn Westminster into Geneva. She, in turn, was eager to maintain the 1559 settlement establishing the order of the English Church and to avoid turning England into the France of the Civil Wars (MacCaffrey, *Elizabeth I* 310–23). By 1576, she was also growing increasingly impatient over her largely unsuccessful attempts to reign in nonconformity, limit the number of preachers stirring up the populace, and crack down effectually on the popular Protestant social and religious gatherings known as "prophesyings," which combined bible study and doctrinal debate with instruction in the art of preaching. In 1576, when the Archbishop of Canterbury, Edmund Grindal, tried to protect such meetings from government interference, the simmering conflict between the Queen and her most aggressively Protestant subjects came to a head. Angrily suspending Grindal from all but the most routine administrative functions of his office, the Queen set a course of markedly colder and more confrontational relations with the faction that he represented (MacCaffrey, *Elizabeth I* 319–22).

In the decade before the shift away from Old Testament paradigms took place, then, a deep rift was opening between militant Protestants and their Queen. We see it as early as 1570, when Edward Dering, a fellow of Christ's College Cambridge and a reader at St. Paul's Cathedral in London, set out to lecture her about her responsibilities as a monarch, telling her bluntly that her court was corrupt, that she herself was subject to lingering Catholic influences, and that she would soon feel the wrath of God if she did not change her ways. For our purposes, the point to note is that Dering packed his sermon with examples of kings and godly leaders of Israel who took a hard line against idolatry and corruption. Citing roughly 125 passages from scripture, all noted in the margins of the printed text, he marshaled a veritable army of witnesses against the Queen. The main charges were that she had failed to put down Catholic elements in England; had allowed dicing, swearing, pleasure-seeking, and worldliness at her court; and had ignored abuses in the training of ministers and the filling of church benefices. Dering's use of scripture is both patronizing and tedious, taking on at times the irritable tone of an exasperated schoolmaster:

> The Lorde open the Queenes Maiesties eyes, that she may looke to this charge: Otherwise if we liued neuer so peaceably vnder her, yet when the Lorde shall come to aske accompte of her stewardshippe . . . , then shee will be founde eating and drinking with sinners. But because we are so dull of hearing, that a little teaching of our duetie is not sufficient for vs, I will shewe out of the scriptures somewhat more plainly if ought may bee playner, what is the duetie of a Prince.   (A8ʳ)

In one particularly offensive passage, the intrepid preacher warned the Queen against popish superstition, remnants of which he saw in the cross and candles on the altar in the royal chapel. Ostentatiously assuming the mantle of Jeremiah, he began by defending "prophets" in the Protestant camp who spoke openly against corruption, then turned to the queen's own failings:

> be not cruell vnto Gods anoynted, and doe his Prophetes no harme. I neede not seeke farre for offences, whereat Gods people are greeued, euen round about this Chapell I see a great manye, and God in his good tyme shall roote them out. If you haue said somtyme of yourselfe: *Tamquam ouis*, as a sheepe appointed to be slayne, take hede you heare not now of the Prophet . . . as an vntamed & vnruly Heiffer.   (A5ʳ)

Part of the sting in this attack lay in Dering's implicit comparison of the pious young Elizabeth of the 1550s with the monarch seated before him in 1570. The image of the "sheep appointed to be slain" echoes John Foxe's account of the two-word message sent by the Queen to her servants as she was being taken to captivity at Woodstock after Wyatt's Rebellion: "Tamquam ovis," which called to mind the unjust condemnation of Christ (Foxe 8: 615; Acts 8:32).[4] That a fellow Protestant like Dering should call Elizabeth to repentance by invoking Jeremiah's characterization of Ephraim as an "unruly heifer," in need of chastisement by the Lord (Jer. 31:18), was a sign of the times. Dering's warning that objects in her chapel were

---

4. My thanks to Susan Felch for pointing out this connection.

offenses against "Gods people" and that God would "roote them out" came perilously close to accusing the Queen of idolatry. Having heard herself thus boldly reproved, she responded by depriving Dering of his license to preach (*Dictionary of National Biography* 5: 844).

Between early signs of trouble such as this and the storm of Protestant opposition that broke over Elizabeth during the French marriage negotiations of 1579, the Old Testament paradigms were increasingly employed in ways that she would have found offensive. Sometimes resistance to her initiatives was explicit, as in John Stubbs's pamphlet *The Discoverie of a Gaping Gvlf whereinto England is Like to Be Swallowed by an Other French Mariage, if the Lord forbid not the banes, by letting her Maiestie See the Sin and Punishment Thereof.* In one memorable passage, Stubbs compared the Queen with Eve, England with Eden, Anjou with Satan, and the French with carriers of disease—first the bodily infection of syphilis and now, in Anjou, also the mental disease of "atheism":

> Because this infection spreeds it selfe after an other maner from the first, they haue sent us hither not Satan in body of a serpent, but the old serpent in shape of a man, whose sting is in his mouth, and who doth his endeuour to seduce our Eue, that she and we may lose this Englishe Paradise.   (A2ʳ)

The remainder of the pamphlet treated the Queen as a naive woman in need of better advisors to govern her, lest "this Englishe Paradise" come to ruin. For passages like this and for attacks on Anjou's character, Elizabeth exacted her famous punishment on Stubbs and his publisher, pursuing legal measures to have their right hands chopped off.

Even when the forward Protestants were not so explicit in their opposition, they often invoked the Old Testament heroes and heroines in ways that the Queen would have found offensive. Her prolonged struggle with them turned on a matter more basic than reform of the church or nuptial alliances with the French. The underlying issue was royal authority, which Elizabeth and her ministers were concerned to defend at all costs. Following mainly Calvinist teachings on women's rule, forward Protestants hesitated to concede that her authority stood on as firm a foundation, or might be exercised as independently, as that of English kings.

Consider, for example, Richard Mulcaster's account of the Coronation pageants of 1559, which reached their climax in a prolonged comparison between Elizabeth and Deborah. By having the biblical figure appear "apparelled in parliament robes, with a sceptre in her hand, as a Queen crowned with an open crowne" (D3ᵛ), the authors not only highlighted the limitations that the parliamentary system placed on Elizabeth's power, but they also withheld from her the closed, or imperial, crown that she would claim as rightfully hers in later years. By surrounding the pageant Deborah with six councilors, "two representing the nobilite, two the clergie, and two the comminaltye," the writers also suggested that her rule should be guided by men. Mulcaster records that "before these personages was written in a table *Debora with her estates consulting for the good gouernement of Israel*" (D3ᵛ), Needless to say, no such consultations are found in the original story of Deborah. As Michelle Osherow points out, moreover (111–19), nothing in the pageant suggests Deborah's extraordinary attainments as a ruler: her successes as judge and prophet to her people, as their supreme leader in war, or as the composer and singer of their great victory song, a role first played by Moses and Miriam (Judges 4–5; Exod. 15). Elizabeth, of course, lived to rival Deborah in all these roles, including that of singer, which she fulfilled upon the defeat of the Armada (Elizabeth I 410–11). The forward Protestants who crafted her coronation pageants were not prepared for a Queen capable of emulating Deborah in so many ways.

Other ostensibly encomiastic invocations of the Old Testament heroines by forward Protestants show the same tendency to underestimate and constrain Elizabeth. Consider Edward Hake's poem *A Commemoration of the Most Prosperous and Peaceable Reign of our Gracious and Dear Sovereign Lady Elizabeth*, which was written to celebrate the Queen's Accession Day in 1575. The poem begins by exalting Elizabeth, claiming that "of all that ever came / From Englishe loynes to royall Seate: / I say, none worthy more / Amongst the race of Englishe kings" (A7ᵛ–A8ʳ). Yet Hake continually circumscribes Elizabeth's role in ways that remind us of the Coronation pageants. Among the biblical heroines, it is not the commanding figure of Deborah that he invokes but Susannah, who was saved from unjust condemnation by a wise judge, and Esther, who saved Israel by listening to the advice of an astute uncle and by relying on the authority of her husband, King Ahasuerus. Hake writes of the "virgin Queene" Elizabeth,

> Is hand of fleshe her firmest force? is frowning face her swaye?
> Doth subtile drifts drawe forth her peace, or vaunting glory? Nay:
> Of fleshe, the feeblest sexe by kinde: of face not Iunoes faere,
> But mylde Susanna in her lookes and Hester in her cheere.   (A8ʳ)

From one of "the feeblest sexe by kind," Hake did not expect military might or prophetic speech, or even Juno's regal demeanor. In his view, Elizabeth's "swaye" depended on "mylde" looks and the sort of "cheere" characteristic of Esther, notable for courage, humility and obedience rather than for command. That Elizabeth did well to be suspicious of such biblical comparisons was made clear in the rest of the poem. Hake continually suggested an underlying distrust of her abilities by stressing the importance of her council and urging her to heed the wisdom of the Protestant preachers pressing her for religious reform. Hake prays, "let her (Lorde) so loue to heare thy godly Preachers voyce, / That shee reiecte not what they teache, but take the best in choyce. / Let pompous state be unto her no stoppe of dew regarde / Ne let the faults of faythlesse mates, at any time be sparde" (Bivᵛ). In urging her to take instruction from the very preachers she was cracking down on, and in warning her against surrounding herself with "pompous state," Hake was taking a line very like that of Dering, though sweetened with a syrup of praise.

We see the same constraints on royal authority at work when he writes of his countrymen that "With them doth liue a louing Queene who like a mother raignes, / And like a chosen sacred Imp immortall glory gaines" (A7ᵛ). From Elizabeth's perspective, the speech was insidious in two respects. One was that she was being cast as "mother" to her people, a metaphor popular among forward Protestants[5] but not, as Mary Beth Rose

---

5. Along with the numerous examples cited by Hackett (255n.33), see Stubbs C7ᵛ; Bentley 272, 276; Beza qtd. Bentley 307.

has shown, with the Queen herself after her early years on the throne (1077–79). The difficulty with such language was that it limited her role to that of a nurturer. In selecting the four main qualities for which the Queen was to be praised, Hake fell back on traditional "feminine" attributes: "Truth, mercy, peace, and loue" (A8^v–B2^r). The abilities to discern the will of God, to judge the nation, and to command its armies as Deborah had done are not among those that Hake chooses to stress.

The other difficulty with Hake's characterization of the Queen was that it treated her as a "chosen sacred Imp." If she was indeed the imp, or offspring, of a royal line and had come to the throne by due succession, why, one wonders, did Hake stress the claim that she was "sacred" and "chosen"? As later passages in the work make clear, his respect for her authority had less to do with her royal lineage than with his belief in her divine election. In Calvinist political theory, God sometimes brings women to rule states, but in doing so, He violates the usual order of nature. Only in exceptional circumstances—generally when the men in a state have failed to uphold their responsibilities—do such aberrations have divine warrant (Calvin 34–35; see Stump 403–15). We find the same emphasis on divine election in works by other forward Protestants of the period, from Knox's early letter to the Queen on women's rule (6: 50) to Theodore Beza's *King's Heast, or Gods familiar speech to the Qveene*, written two decades later (qtd. Bentley 309–11), to Edmund Spenser's 1596 *Faerie Queene*, where the poet, though far more open to women's participation in public affairs than Calvin, nonetheless denies their right to rule "Vnlesse the heauens them lift to lawfull soueraintie" (5.5.25).

While the role of divinely ordained exception was one that Elizabeth sometimes allowed herself to be cast in, it afforded, as she well knew, a precarious form of legitimacy. If her subjects should ever come to doubt that God was with her—as Dering, Stubbs and many other forward Protestants had begun to do in the 1570s—then the basis for her authority would have evaporated. As a woman, she could count on obedience from her most ardently Calvinist subjects only in so far as she could avoid crossing them in matters of religion, and that was not easy to do. Should she disappoint them, little remained as a firm basis for requiring their allegiance—not English tradition (which had hardly any precedents for women's rule), nor the Act of Succession of 1544, nor even, as Calvin presented the case, the dictates of natural law.

It seems to me, then, that the Queen's own tendency to shy away from paradigms such as Deborah and Judith in her later writings is entirely understandable. Such figures were being employed against her, not only by hectoring, self-appointed prophets, but also by more supportive Protestants who insisted on celebrating her reign in ways that undercut the very earthly basis of her authority.[6] And if the insistently scriptural rhetoric of the forward Protestants had gradually become a stench in the nostrils of the Queen, it must also have begun to smell worrisome to many of the male writers connected with her court. Reactions to it go a long way toward explaining the paradigm shift that we have been examining.

6. Walsham also notes in the works that she has studied the same tendency to praise in order to exhort and to accept Elizabeth's authority only so long as the writers deem her to be a special instrument of divine providence to further the reform of the church (148–50). See also McLaren 237–38.

Yet puzzles remain. Why, for example, was the shift so sudden? And why did it take place right around 1580? Though her quarrel with people like Dering and Archbishop Grindal started well before that time, we still find biblical figures being fairly widely invoked in the late 1570s and early 1580s. Why, moreover, did the declining popularity of Old Testament paradigms extend even to women such as Deborah, Judith, and Esther, who had proved so useful in court literature early in the reign? Such compelling images might, one supposes, still have been employed in royal iconography so long as they were not part of a Protestant tirade. The Bible and its conceptions of public and private virtue were, after all, still the dominant ideals of English society. To understand this last and most surprising stage in the retreat from such figures at court, we must turn our attention to a sudden and far-reaching shift in international strategy, namely the Queen's decision in 1578 to pursue serious marriage negotiations with that widely hated Frenchman, the Duke of Anjou.

III

At a time when Elizabeth was warming to the prospect of a union with the Catholic Duke, the biblical paradigms posed rhetorical problems—ones so serious, in fact, that they placed the poets who employed them in personal danger. When Protestant writers of the earlier decades of the reign had compared Elizabeth with the Old Testament heroines, the rhetorical advantages had been obvious. Judith and Esther had used their appeal as women to preserve their people from foreign attack, much as Elizabeth had used her wiles as an attractive candidate for marriage to keep the major Catholic powers on the Continent divided and at bay. Susannah hadn't saved anybody but herself, of course, but she was useful in Protestant propaganda all the same, since she, like the Queen, was a godly woman imperiled by cunning and corrupt enemies. Deborah was even more useful to English writers, since she had governed God's Chosen People long and well and defended true religion against an idolatrous foreign enemy.

   In the first two decades of Elizabeth's reign, the foreign enemy that had offered the greatest threat to God's Chosen People in England was, of course, France. Made especially dangerous in the 1560s by ties with Mary, Queen of Scots, and in the 1570s by the machinations of the Pope, who had excommunicated Elizabeth and was actively encouraging her overthrow, the powerful House of Guise lay somewhere behind many of Elizabeth's most serious problems in this period. England had been at war with France as recently as 1557, and Elizabeth renewed hostilities by sending English expeditionary forces to attack the French in Scotland during the winter of 1559–60. In the 1560s, she deployed regular troops to France to aid the Huguenots during the First War of Religion and permitted involvement by English volunteers in the Third (Ridley 159–60). In this historical context, the biblical heroines—who had all stood up for godliness and justice against irreligious oppressors—did nicely as literary paradigms for the Queen.

   Once Elizabeth had successfully thwarted the French threat of the 1560s and early 1570s, however, such comparisons became problematic. As early as the mid-1570s, Spain had replaced France as the primary threat to England and the Reformation, and Elizabeth felt compelled to counter Philip II by aligning England more closely with France. Accordingly, in the period from April to June of 1578, she renewed marriage negotiations with Anjou, subsequently taking strong measures to suppress the rising tide of Protestant reaction against the match (MacCaffrey, *Making of Policy* 243–66). As we know from her treatment of Stubbs and his publisher, to criticize the Queen on this point was dangerous. Since comparisons between Elizabeth and the Old Testament heroines had been popularized during a time when English polemics were directed primarily against France, it is not surprising that they should have passed so quickly out of use when the winds shifted in France's favor. Protestant poets hoping for favor and advancement at Court did well to mind their metaphors, for they were precisely the faction being most closely watched by the Queen.

Signs of the impact of the French marriage negotiations are apparent in a number of works. In Lyly's *Euphues and His England*, for example—a work published in 1580—we find mention of Deborah, but only in passing. In an otherwise neoclassical passage on Elizabeth as a proponent of peace and England as "a new Israel, [God's] chosen and peculiar people," the author proclaims that the Temple of Janus "is now removed from Rome to England"; its door has not opened for twenty years, which is "more to be meruayled at, then the regiment of Debora, who ruled twentie yeares with religion, or Semyramis that gouerned long with power, or Zenobia that reigned six yeares in prosperitie" (2: 205, 209–10). The biblical note is sounded ever so lightly. Similarly, Edmund Spenser mentions Deborah in *The Faerie Queene*, invoking her in a passage celebrating the prowess of his heroine Britomart, a fictive ancestor of Elizabeth who, elsewhere in the romance, sometimes serves as an allegorical analog to her. Here, however, the biblical heroine is tucked in among the Amazons Penthisilea and Camilla in a celebration of women's "warlike feates." No direct connection with Elizabeth is made (3.4.2).

The tendency to soften or deflect reactions to such biblical references is nowhere seen more clearly than in the series of pageants and poems presented during the summer progress of 1578 and printed by the publisher Henry Bynneman as *The Joyfull Receyving of the Queene's most Excellent Majestie into hir Highnesse Citie of Norwich.*[7] Written just two months after Elizabeth's interest in a French marriage had flared again after several years of dormancy, and just a year before the appearance of Spenser's *Shepheardes Calender*, which was the first major work published by the "new poets," the Norwich poems came at a notable turning point in the political and literary climate of the age. The part of the entertainments that is of most interest for our purposes is the second welcoming pageant, by Bernard Garter (sigs. C1^r–C3^v; rpt. Nichols 2: 145–50). The printed account mentions in passing what I take to be a central point, namely that Garter's poems were read to the Queen in the presence of three ambassadors from France (E1^r). Since Norwich was known as a hotbed of Protestant agitation (King 48), both the author of the pageant and the town fathers who commissioned it faced an interesting rhetorical dilemma. If, in praising Elizabeth, they employed the usual biblical comparisons found in earlier Protestant works of this sort, they risked offending the French ambassadors and, with them, the Queen. If, however, they silenced their objections against the French marriage, they would seem to their fellow townsmen

---

7. Rpt. Nichols 2: 136–78. The portion of the entertainments by Thomas Churchyard appeared as *A Discourse of the Queenes . . . Entertainment in Suffolk and Norfolk*, rpt. Nichols 2: 179–213.

little better than cowards and toadies. As one might expect, they chose a middle ground, invoking the names of Deborah, Judith, and Esther, but doing their level best to deflect the royal anger that their pageant might otherwise provoke.

As the published text remarks, the poems were presented on a "Stage . . . replenished with fiue personages appareled like women. The first was, the City of Norwich: the second Debora: the third Judeth: the fourth Esther: the fifthe Martia, sometime Queene of Englande" (C1r). The sequence of speakers was, I think, carefully planned to lead Elizabeth gently into, then out of, the Protestant polemics that occupied the three central speeches of the entertainment.

The first speaker, the female persona of Norwich itself, flattered Elizabeth, calling her, as Protestants were wont to do, "my louing nurse and mother." Then, as if Garter feared that the Queen would dislike the pageant, he asked her not to take offence at what was to follow: "Graunt then (oh gracious soueraigne Queene) this only my request, / That that which shal be done in me, be construed to the best" (C1v). There was reason to worry.

The next speech was delivered by Deborah and drew a series of parallels between her life and that of Elizabeth. After telling of her "appointment" by God as a Judge in Israel and of her defeat of the foreign forces arrayed against her, she asserted that God had called Elizabeth to play a similar role in England: "So mightie prince, that puisaunt Lord, hath plaste thee here to be" (C1v). Details of phrasing point up other similarities between the two rulers. For instance, Deborah had ruled Israel "twenty winters long," just as, in 1578 when the entertainment was performed, Elizabeth had also ruled for twenty years. Deborah heightened the comparison, first by calling the ancient Israelites God's "elect," as if they were good English Protestants, and then by charging their enemies with unjust aggression and treachery. Of her enemy, King Jabin, she remarked, "His force was great, his fraude was more," and the ending of the speech included a direct appeal to Elizabeth to stand firm against her own foreign enemies:

> So mightie prince, that puisaunt Lord, hath plaste thee here to be,
> The rule of this triumphant Realme alone belongeth to thee.
> Continue as thou hast begon, weede out the wicked route,
> Vpholde the simple, meeke, and good, pull downe the proud
>   & stoute.
> Thus shalt thou liue and raigne in rest, and mightie God
>   shalt please.   (C1v–C2r)

With the French ambassadors in the audience, this was dangerous stuff indeed. Since Elizabeth had only recently embarked on her new policy of concerted opposition to Spain, the war of "twenty winters" waged against a foreign enemy could only be interpreted as her long struggle with France. Similarly, the observation that "rule of his triumphant Realme *alone* belongeth to thee" and the admonition to "Continue *as thou hast begon*" (my emphasis) sound suspiciously like advice not to marry but to remain a virgin and to stand up to the King of France and his warlike brother Anjou, as Deborah had stood up to Jabin and his military commander Sisera. The final set of admonitions, beginning "weede out the wicked route," suggest a vigorous campaign against Catholicism on all fronts, both foreign and domestic.

Unwelcome polemics of a similar sort characterized the speeches of Judith and Esther, with the latter warning the Queen against foreign enemies who "haue skill, / As well by fraude as force to finde their pray" and who hide their tyrannical intentions in "smiling lookes" (C2ʳ). For the Protestants of Norwich, the "smiling lookes" may have called to mind the Queen's new friends, the French ambassadors, who courted her so assiduously and were entertained so warmly during the summer of 1578.

As if to head off an angry reaction by the Queen and her guests, Garter quickly dropped his Protestant polemics after Esther's speech, retreating for the remainder of the pageant into the safer language of pagan myth. The last speech, spoken by Martia, the only queen regnant to govern England prior to Mary Tudor and Elizabeth, painted an elaborate word picture of the end of the world, when Apollo would exalt Elizabeth over all other monarchs on the ground that she combined the virtues of Pallas, the Muses, Venus, Mercury, and Juno. By lapsing into pagan myth and puffs of flattery, the poet was, I suspect, intent on taking some of the edge off his earlier Protestant polemics. Since the subsequent entertainments were largely neoclassical rather than Biblical in nature, and were not pointedly hostile to the French,[8] the Queen may have been pleased that her Protestant subjects in Norwich had been as civil in their remonstrances as anyone had a right to expect. It seems unlikely, however, that either she or her foreign guests overlooked the political subtext of the second welcoming pageant.

IV

It would be simplistic, of course, to suppose that the changes I have been examining were the only ones at work in the shift away from the Old Testament paradigms. I suspect, for example, that the Kenilworth Pageants of 1575 were an early factor in their decline. Fashioned almost exclusively from neoclassical myth and Arthurian legend, the entertainments were the most dazzling and elaborate of the reign. Since they were commissioned by the Earl of Leicester—the Queen's favorite, leader of the forward Protestant faction at court, and one of England's most influential literary patrons—their impact on other writers must have been substantial. That Leicester and his principal writer, George Gascoigne, shied away from biblical allusions may be an early indication that the Queen was growing impatient with tendentious uses of scriptural figures.

Another phenomenon that deserves fuller scrutiny is the advent of the celebration of Elizabeth as an ever-virgin queen (King 58–65; Hackett 95–127). After the French marriage scheme foundered in the winter of 1580–81, it became increasingly awkward to praise the aging Elizabeth with comparisons to Judith, the enticing widow who tempted an enemy commander by plying him with wine in his tent; to Esther, the concubine who became the wife of an Eastern potentate; to Susannah, the vulnerable young woman falsely accused of adultery; or even to Deborah, the faithful wife of Lappidoth. Writers were happy to ascribe to Elizabeth youthful beauty and allure, even when she was old; but they had good reason to

---

8. Goldingham's "Masque of the God's" ended with a scene in which Cupid gave the Queen a golden arrow to shoot "at King or Caesar" as she thought fit (E3ᵛ).

avoid comparing her with feminine analogs who had been married, widowed, or sexually abused.

Of even greater importance during the 1580s and 1590s, I suspect, was England's precarious position in the world. The Old Testament heroines and heroes had won temporary victories for their people in a long and ultimately unsuccessful struggle against two deadly perils: religious division at home and hostile force abroad. In the second half of Elizabeth's reign, which was mired in religious strife and war with Spain, England faced just these perils. The Queen's response seems to have been to rouse her troops and calm her people by distracting them from their vulnerability. She dazzled them with images of strength. We see this new resolve in her portraits, where she allowed herself to be transformed from the relatively modest and stolid figure of the early years into an icon of serene opulence and power. In the Armada Portrait of 1588, she appeared to her people as a supremely victorious monarch, with her hand resting confidently on the globe and the closed, imperial crown placed securely at her side. In the Ditchley Portrait of three years later, she hovered as an enormous, almost angelic figure over a map of the British Isles, which rested safely at her feet. In the Rainbow Portrait of 1600, painted when she was nearing death, she appeared as a youthful sun goddess, radiating light to the world.

Much had changed from the heady early days of the reign, when a young Elizabeth had rallied her people to defend the English Reformation against their Catholic enemies in France. Her most threatening foreign rival was now Spain, and her most influential domestic opposition the forward Protestants. In such a climate, royal imagery involving classical goddesses and pastoral shepherdesses, Petrarchan mistresses and medieval fairies, had the advantage of transporting Elizabeth to fictive realms far removed from the dangers and entanglements that dogged her in reality. That such chaste and distant figures attracted "new poets" such as Peele, Lyly, Ralegh, and Spenser showed not only their desire for symbols of national independence and imperial might but also for royal paradigms safely removed from threats of assassination, insurrection, and invasion. In the end, younger Protestant writers of the 1580s and 1590s may have turned from Biblical narrative to classical myth and Arthurian legend for much the same reasons that Bernard Garter did in writing the ending of the second Norwich pageant. To drop the scriptural paradigms offered a welcome relief from unwelcome realities, and to invoke them risked the displeasure of the Queen.

Works Cited

Aylmer, John. *An Harborowe for Faithfvll and Trewe Subjects.* London, 1559.

Bentley, Thomas. *The Monument for Matrones.* London, 1582.

Calvin, John. "Letter XV," to Sir William Cecil, 1559. *The Zurich Letters,* 22nd ser. Tr. Hastings Robinson. Cambridge: Cambridge UP, 1845. 34–35.

Dekker, Thomas, *The Pleasant Comedie of Old Fortunatus.* London, 1600.

Dering, Edward. "A Sermon preached before the Queens Maiestie the .25. daye of Februarie . . . , 1569 [new style 1570]." *Two Godly Sermons,* by Edward Dering. London, 1590.

Dictionary of National Biography. Ed. Sir Leslie Stephen and Sidney Lee. 63 vols. London: Smith, Elder, 1885–1901.

Elizabeth I. *Collected Works.* Ed. Leah S. Marcus, Janel Mueller, and Mary Beth Rose. Chicago: U of Chicago P, 2000.

Foxe, John. *The Acts and Monuments.* Ed. George Townsend 8. vols. London, 1843–49. Rpt. New York: AMS, 1965.

Garter, Bernard, and William Goldinham. *The Ioyfvll Receyuing of the Queenes most excellent Maiestie into hir Highnesse Citie of Norwich.* London, [1578.]

The Geneva Bible, A Facsimile of the 1560 Edition. Ed. Lloyd E. Berry. Madison: U of Wisconsin P, 1969.

Grafton, Richard. *Graftons Abridgement of the Chronicles of Englande.* London, 1570.

Griffin, Mr. "Triste absti letum," 1572. Rpt. Nichols 1: 316–17.

Hackett, Helen. *Virgin Mother, Maiden Queen: Elizabeth I and the Cult of the Virgin Mary.* New York: St. Martin's, 1995.

Hake, Edward. *A Commemoration of the Most Prosperous and Peaceable Raigne of our Gratious and Deere Soueraigne Lady Elizabeth.* London, 1575.

———. "An Oration . . . upon the Queenes . . . Birth-day [Sept. 7, 1586]." Nichols 2: 461–81.

Hales, John. "An Oration . . . to the Queen's Majesty; and delivered to her Majesty by a certain Nobleman, at her first Entrance to her Reign." Qtd. Foxe 8: 673–79.

Humphrey, Lawrence. Oration to the Queen at Woodstock, 1575. *The Progresses and Public Processions of Queen Elizabeth.* Rpt Nichols 1: 583–99.

King, John N. "Queen Elizabeth I: Representations of the Virgin Queen." *Renaissance Quarterly* 53 (Spring 1990): 30–74.

Knox, John. Letter to Elizabeth, 1559. *The Works of John Knox.* Ed. David Laing. 6 vols. Edinburgh: J. Thin, 1854–95.

Lyly, John. *Euphues and His England* (1580). *The Complete Works of John Lyly.* Ed. R. Warwick Bond. 3 vols. Oxford, 1902.

MacCaffrey, Wallace T. *Elizabeth I.* London: Edward Arnold, 1993.

———. *Queen Elizabeth and the Making of Policy, 1572–1588.* Princeton: Princeton UP, 1981.

McLaren, Anne. *Political Culture in the Reign of Elizabseth I: Queen and Commonwealth, 1558–1585.* Cambridge: Cambridge UP, 1999.

"A Meditation wherein the godly English geueth thankes to God for the Queenes Maiesties prosperous gouernment hitherto." Qtd. Hake, *Comemoration.* B6ᵛ–C4ᵛ.

Mulcaster, Richard. *The Passage of Our Most Drad Souereigne Lady Quene Elizabeth Through the Citie of London to Westminster, the Daye before Her Coronacion.* London, 1559.

Munday, Anthony. "A Dialogue betweene a Christian and Consolation" (1582). Rpt. *Ballads from Manuscripts.* Ed. W. R. Morfill. 2 vols. Hertford: Ballad Society, Stephen Austin & Sons, 1868–73. 2: 187–88.

Nichols, John, ed. *The Progresses and Public Processions of Queen Elizabeth.* 3 vols. London, 1823.

Osherow, Michele. "'Give Ear O' Princes': Deborah, Elizabeth and the Right Word." *Images of Elizabeth I: A Quadricentennial Celebration.* Ed.

Donald Stump and Carole Levin. Special issue, *Explorations in Renais-sance Culture* 30 (Summer 2004): 111–19.

Ridley, Jasper. *Elizabeth I: The Shrewdness of Virtue*. New York: Fromm International, 1989.

Rose, Mary Beth. "The Gendering of Authority in the Public Speeches of Elizabeth I." *PMLA: Publications of the Modern Language Association* 115.5 (October 2000): 1077–82.

Sanford, James. Preface. *Houres of Recreation, or Afterdinners, Which May Aptly be Called the Garden of Pleasure*, by Ludovico Guicciardini. Tr. James Sanford. London, 1576.

Sidney, Mary, Countess of Pembroke. *Collected Works*. Ed. Margaret P. Hannay, Noel J. Kinnamon, and Michael G. Brennan. 2 vols. Oxford: Clarendon, 1998.

Spenser, Edmund. *The Faerie Queene*. London, 1590.

Stump, Donald. "A Slow Return to Eden: Spenser and Women's Rule." *English Literary Renaissance* 29 (1999): 401–21.

Strong, Roy. *The Cult of Elizabeth: Elizabethan Portraiture and Pageantry*. London: Thames & Hudson, 1977.

———. *Gloriana: The Portraits of Queen Elizabeth I*. London: Thames & Hudson, 1987.

Stockwood, John. Epistle Dedicatory. *A Right Godly and Learned Discourse upon the Booke of Ester*, by Johannes Brenz. Trans. John Stockwood. London, 1584.

Stubbs, John. *The Discoverie of a Gaping Gvlf*. London, 1579.

Wilson, E. C. *England's Eliza*. Cambridge: Harvard UP, 1939.

Vennar, Richard. *The Right Way to Heaven, and the True Testimonie of a Faithfull and Loyall Subject*. London, 1601. Rpt. Nichols 3: 532–43.

Walsham, Alexandra. "'A Very Deborah?' The Myth of Elizabeth I as a Providential Monarch." *The Myth of Elizabeth*. Ed. Susan Doran and Thomas S. Freeman. Houndmills, Eng.: Palgrave Macmillan, 2003. 143–68.

THE QUEEN ON FILM

THOMAS BETTERIDGE

A Queen for All Seasons[†]

In 1912 Sarah Bernhardt was the first actor to portray Elizabeth I on the big screen in a film entitled *The Loves of the Queen* (1912). Despite its age this film anticipates many of the key issues that reappear in latter films depicting Elizabeth I. Bernhardt's Elizabeth is a woman torn between her duty as a queen and her love for the earl of Essex. The film opens with Essex bringing news of the Armada's defeat to the English camp at Tilbury. It then moves to court and becomes a complicated story of personal and political intrigue. Essex's fate is sealed when the husband of his lover, the countess of Nottingham, finds out about their relationship and gets Essex sent to Ireland. After 11 years away Essex returns to the court. Nottingham, however,

---

[†] From *The Myth of Elizabeth*. Ed. Susan Doran and Thomas S. Freeman (Houndsmills, Eng.: Palgrave Macmillan, 2003), 242–59. Reprinted by permission.

tricks the queen into thinking Essex is a traitor. After his trial and execution Elizabeth pays Essex one last visit as he lies in state, discovers that she has been deceived and dies of melancholy.

The Loves of the Queen also anticipates many later films in its emphasis on Elizabeth's court. Indeed, the film takes place almost entirely within the confines of the royal apartments. This confinement motif is made explicit when after the queen's death, the curtains over the court's windows are pulled back for the first time. The placing of Elizabeth within an enclosed court is a trope that is repeated in the 1939 *The Private Lives of Elizabeth and Essex* and also in the recent film *Elizabeth* (1998). In *The Loves of the Queen* the outside world intrudes only rarely, as when early in the film Essex introduces William Shakespeare to the queen. A far more significant breaching of the boundaries of the court, however, takes place later when a female soothsayer enters to prophesise Essex's downfall. The film emphasises her non-courtly status by showing her being refused entry into the court. It is only when the countess of Nottingham intervenes that the soothsayer can get past the guards and reach the queen. It is noteworthy that the person who facilitates the soothsayer's entrance is a woman since in *The Loves of the Queen* the most important and significant relationships the queen has, apart from that with Essex, is with other women, the soothsayer and the countess of Nottingham. Indeed the scene when the queen and countess comfort each other over Essex's death is one of the few moments in this film when two characters physically interact. Their grief brings them together as they hold each other, sharing their tears, hugs and sighs. Despite its complete disregard for the facts of the past—for example the length of time that Essex spends in Ireland—*The Loves of the Queen* is a historical film. It explicitly claims to be portraying truths about the past. In these terms it is like all other cinematic versions of Elizabeth I and her reign. Indeed *The Loves of the Queen* even includes a shot of a letter that explicitly claims to have been written by the historical Essex.

In this essay I am going to start by focusing on the two themes that I have begun to discuss in this introduction, gender and history. I will then analyse three Elizabeth films in detail *Fire over England* (1937), *The Private Lives of Elizabeth and Essex* (1939) and *Elizabeth* (1998).

Elizabethan myth-making commenced from the moment that Henry VIII's second child came to the throne. In part this was simply an invariable aspect of Tudor kingship; however, it was also a product of the problems of legitimacy that surrounded Elizabeth's succession. In particular, the political implications of the new queen's gender were, as is well known, a constant source of debate. Was Elizabeth the exception that proved the rule, the Virgin Queen who managed to transcend the limitations of her gender? Or was she a painted Jezebel, one of a monstrous regime of female princes whose rule was inevitably corrupted by their femininity? These two options, Jezebel or Virgin Queen, are constantly produced and reflected upon in cinematic versions of Elizabeth. For example, in *Mary, Queen of Scots* (1971) the viewer is given the choice between a 'real' woman—Mary played by Vanessa Redgrave—who constantly and disastrously puts her female desires before the needs of her kingship—and Glenda Jackson's Elizabeth—who wins as a ruler but is clearly depicted in this film as failing as a woman.

Gender and history

Cinema has always emphasised Elizabeth I's gender. The tensions caused by a woman occupying the masculine role of monarch have allowed, and indeed incited, filmmakers to use Elizabeth as a reason to reflect upon the relationship between gender, in particular femininity, and power. These reflections have, however, tended to take relatively predictable forms. In particular, they are invariably structured around such basic binary oppositions as duty versus womanhood, public role versus private desires and denial versus desire. The repetition of these themes, however, does not preclude variation; for example, while in *Fire Over England* Elizabeth is depicted as being able to control her female desires, in *The Private Lives of Elizabeth and Essex* she is represented as being entirely at their mercy.

Almost all cinematic portrayals of Elizabeth include scenes depicting the queen breaking mirrors or dressing. What is invariably being represented at these moments is the way in which Elizabeth's status as monarch and woman means she is trapped in a constant state of performance. The smashing of the mirrors reflects the extent to which being caught in this trap has a price—the denial of the true or proper pleasures of femininity. This emphasis on the performative status of Elizabeth's gender implies that the other women in these films are not performing and that their gender and sexuality are non-performative and given.[1] This aspect of cinematic representations of Elizabeth is often stressed by filmmakers through the creation of plots in which normative versions of femininity and heterosexuality are contrasted to Elizabeth. For example, in the 1998 film *Elizabeth* the performative nature of the identity which the queen takes on at the end of the film is emphasised against her earlier 'true' femininity. The fiction which this film asks us to accept as one of its central motifs is that before Elizabeth adopts the role of the Virgin Queen there is a part of her—her sexuality expressed in her relationship with Dudley—that escapes the performative requirements of queenship and, at a more ideological level, of gender itself. In early films centred around male protagonists the performative and therefore aberrant nature of the queen's gender is marked against romantic sub-plots. For example in *The Sea Hawk* (1940) there is a romance between Cynthia (Olivia de Havilland) and Captain Thorpe (Errol Flynn). Elizabeth, of course, finds Captain Thorpe attractive and is represented as vicariously enjoying the relationship between him and de Havilland. This pleasure is essential to the way in which this film deals with the issue of Elizabeth's gender since it allows her to be constructed as a normal woman—that is she desires Errol Flynn—but one whose duty prevents her from directly indulging these desires. Elizabeth's vicarious involvement in this romance is underscored by the name of de Havilland's character, Cynthia, being one of the Virgin Queen's historical poetic titles.[2] The portrayal of gender in *The Sea Hawk*, as in the recent film *Elizabeth*, is fundamentally conservative. In these films proper or normative feminine desire leads naturally to heterosexual closure. This excludes Elizabeth who is left with the implicitly aberrant and certainly non-natural performative aspects of

---

1. On gender as performance, see Judith Butler, *Gender Trouble* (New York, 1990).
2. The importance of the name of the Olivia de Havilland character, Cynthia, being one of Elizabeth's poetic titles was pointed out to me by Tom Freeman.

femininity which *The Sea Hawk* and *Elizabeth* imply are antithetical to heterosexuality.

Cinema's interest in Elizabeth's gender is also reflected in the way in which it has represented her court. Indeed, it is possible to divide films that depict Elizabeth on the basis of their symbolic construction of her court. On one side there are those films that choose to emphasise the court, physically and symbolically, as a place of containment and formality, *The Private Lives of Elizabeth and Essex* and *Elizabeth*. On the other, for example, *The Sea Hawk* and *Fire over England*, are those which focus upon Elizabeth's ability to transgress the court's limits and cross into other cultural spaces. It is also important to note that the Elizabethan court as represented on screen is often portrayed as an inherently feminine space.[3] This aspect of cinematic representations of Elizabeth becomes particularly noticeable when one compares the way in which the English court is imagined in other historical films. In *The Private Life of Henry VIII* (1933) the court is marked by a similar formality, and appears to contain the same gossiping women, as Elizabeth's court in *The Private Lives of Elizabeth and Essex*. However in *The Private Life of Henry VIII* the court's atmosphere is constantly disrupted, its formality ignored and its rules torn up by Charles Laughton's Henry. In *The Private Lives of Elizabeth and Essex* Elizabeth is depicted as being a victim of her court's formality. Her gender means she is unable to reject or dominate the court; instead Bette Davis's Elizabeth is caught within a feminine space that reflects back her lack of masculine power and purpose. In *The Private Life of Henry VIII* Henry's rejection of court etiquette is used to stress his boisterous masculine nature. Laughton's Henry is not dominated by his court; rather, he takes it into hand and makes it the stage upon which he performs. One can see a similar gendered difference in the representation of the English court in *The Madness of King George* (1994) and *Elizabeth*. In the latter the court is a place where the boundary between public and private is unstable and fraught. In *The Madness of King George* the problem with the court is that it has no private space—even in the royal bedchamber formal titles are used. Elizabeth's gender gives cinematic portrayals of her court, and in particular the way in which the relationship between the court's public and private aspects is depicted, an inflection lacking in other historical films.

As one watches 'Elizabethan' films one is constantly being incited to enjoy the voyeuristic pleasure of the slowly opened door and the illicitly lifted tapestry; the fear but also the excitement of tip-toeing down darkened forbidden passageways.[4] Cinematic representations of Elizabeth's court also tend to develop through the use of gendered space a clear distinction between the formal, sterile enclosed space of the court and the open, informal world of the street, park or high seas; places where uncomplicated mas-

3. These differences are, moreover, complicated by the way in which space occupies a privileged place in the production of gender. Sue Best comments that: 'In an extraordinary array of contexts, space is conceived as a woman. This is particularly noticeable in relation to the "bounded" spatial entities which are seen as the context of, and for, human habitation'. Sue Best, 'Sexualising Space', in Elizabeth Grosz and Elspeth Probyn, eds, *Sexy Bodies: The Strange Carnalities of Feminism* (London, 1995), 181–194, at p. 181.
4. The idea of space as symbolically feminine can be related directly to the cinematic representation of Elizabeth's court in terms of the close relationship between film and architecture. Indeed, the portrayal of Elizabeth I's court on film is a perfect illustration of the similarities between film and architecture in terms of their production of gendered space. See Giuliana Bruno, 'Site-seeing: Architecture and the Moving Image', *Wide Angle* 19:4 (1997), 8–24, especially pp. 9 and 20.

culinity holds uncontested sway. For example, *The Private Lives of Elizabeth and Essex* consistently represents those male courtiers who can happily exist at the court as being less then masculine. This is particularly noticeable in the case of Sir Walter Raleigh who, although invariably viewed in history as a decidedly masculine figure, is portrayed, rather uneasily by Vincent Price, as an effeminate dandy. Poor old Essex/Errol is, of course, pure masculinity. Whenever he enters the court there is an upsurge of energy, conflict and action. At the end of these periodic moments of excitement, however, the court reverts to its previous feminine state; Bette Davis, her ladies in waiting, her courtiers (and the viewers) hang around gossiping, muttering and plotting. They mimic action by such petty acts as breaking the palace's mirrors or dressing in fancy armour; all the time waiting for the show to start again and for the court's all pervasive and oppressive feminine atmosphere to be lifted by the return of Essex.

Films that focus on Elizabeth also appear to be particularly sensitive to the relationship between the cinema and history. For example, Shekhar Kapur's recent film *Elizabeth* asks in numerous ways to be viewed as historical; its opening credits contain a terse account of the events of the years proceeding the events depicted in the film and its costume and set designs consistently refer to the past. However, while *Elizabeth* is purportedly historical, it is also almost entirely unencumbered by any reference to the real history of Elizabeth's reign. Kapur's film almost entirely departs from the historical record and in the process, presumably unwittingly, produces an understanding of Elizabeth's reign that is genuinely historical since its basic outline and tropes, the lone virgin protecting her pure land against the wiles of treacherous European papists, can be found in numerous Elizabethan works. It is also noticeable that the Eurosceptic English press focused their criticism of *Elizabeth* on the way that it depicted her as engaged in a full sexual relationship with Dudley. This may be because, while they were happy to accept the film's representations of Europeans as inherently treacherous, violent and transsexual, they were concerned to protect the honour of Elizabeth/England.[5]

Kapur's *Elizabeth* also illustrates the extent to which changes in cinema's depiction of the Virgin Queen during the last century have kept pace with developments in the way academics have understood Elizabeth's reign. Sarah Bernhardt's Elizabeth is similar to the ways in which Elizabeth was portrayed in histories written in the early twentieth century. For example, Arthur D. Innes, in *England Under the Tudors* (1911), claims that all Elizabeth's faults as a ruler were related to her femininity. He criticises her for being vain, capricious and constantly needing to be flattered.[6] Elizabeth as she appears in the films of the 1930s and 1940s, with the important exception of Davis's portrayal, could be drawn directly from the pages of Whig history. Glenda Jackson's various incarnations of the Virgin Queen appear to be clearly based on the work of G. R. Elton. In particular, films like *Mary, Queen of Scots*, and the television series *Elizabeth R*, reproduce Elton's emphasis on politics and the court. In the former case the tensions that the

---

5. In this example contemporary concerns not only shaped the film's production but also its reception. The point about the way in which the right-wing English press commented on the *Elizabeth* film was suggested to me by Andrew Higson.

6. Arthur D. Innes, *England Under the Tudors* (New York, 1911), 427.

film depicts between the two models of femininity offered by Redgrave's Mary and Jackson's Elizabeth can be related directly to Elton's view of these two queens. In his seminal work *England under the Tudors* Elton suggested that Elizabeth was 'the most masculine of all the female sovereigns of history'.[7] He was more critical of Mary, arguing that 'whatever excuses one might make for the women none can be made for the queen'.[8] It is precisely this dichotomy between Elizabeth the successful queen but flawed woman and Mary the hopeless ruler but real woman worthy of male protection that *Mary, Queen of Scots* depicts. Finally, the most recent Elizabeth film focuses on precisely those aspects of Elizabeth's reign that have recently occupied revisionist historians and literary critics—its conflict-ridden nature, the queen's chastity and the Elizabethan court as a site of cultural production.

These similarities between history's and cinema's Elizabeths can be accounted for in a number of ways. Perhaps filmmakers are doing far more research than seems to find its way into their films. Perhaps historians are more influenced by what is going on in popular culture than they would perhaps want to admit. I would suggest, however, that there are two more interesting reasons for these similarities. It is important to note that cinematic representations of Elizabeth relate directly to the way the status of women has changed during the twentieth century. This is perhaps most obvious in the cases of Jackson's career woman Elizabeth who is a product of liberal humanist feminism and Cate Blanchett's post-feminist girl-power queen taking control of her life through media manipulation. Clearly, one can see reflected in historical and cinematic versions of Elizabeth I social and cultural changes that transcend the different conditions of their production. I would also suggest, however, that the similarities between history's and cinema's Elizabeths can be traced directly back to the figure of Elizabeth Tudor herself. It is perhaps a sad reflection on history and film that neither have managed to transcend the conflict between good ruler/bad woman that one finds in Elizabethan responses to the last Tudor monarch. Perhaps the truth is that the persistence of Elizabeth's iconic status is a testament to the power of the myth, the extent to which we, historians and filmmakers, are still under her spell.[9]

Fire over England (1937)

Fire over England is one of a number of films released before the outbreak of the Second World War that sought to draw a direct parallel between the sixteenth-century conflict between Spain and England and the struggle against Fascism. In this film a young Englishman, Michael, played by Laurence Olivier in full matinee-idol splendour, has to learn how to channel his bravery and hatred of oppression through proper—namely English—channels. *Fire over England* is an explicitly political film. It creates an absolute

---

7. G. R. Elton, *England under the Tudors* (London, 1972), 262.
8. Ibid., 292.
9. Elizabeth's continuing potency seems to me to be the only possible explanation for Judi Dench's Oscar for her performance as Elizabeth in *Shakespeare in Love* (1998). Would a performance, albeit an excellent one, lasting only a few moments have been worthy of an Oscar were it not for the power of the figure being portrayed? Was the Oscar really for Dench or for that greatest of Elizabethan actors—Elizabeth herself?

distinction between Spain and England over a range of registers. In Spain Philip II is depicted as ruling alone, while in England the viewer is constantly shown Elizabeth in debate with her ministers. In particular, the film contrasts the possibility of productive debate and disagreement in England with the silence and fear of the Spanish polity. In this context the film implicitly relates Elizabeth's gender to the emergence of a collective democratic polity. Flora Robson's Elizabeth has power but it is represented as being deployed through traditionally feminine traits. She persuades, cajoles and seduces her subjects into doing her bidding. In the process the film depicts her rule as consensual. Philip is silent and brooding—a man of commands and orders.

When Michael returns from captivity in Spain, he is obsessed with the need to fight Spanish tyranny. He tells the privy council that, 'Spain is horror'. Significantly, one of the central arguments of the film is that while the English rulers need to find a way of using Michael's passion, he also has to learn from them. In particular, Michael has to be prepared to bring his extreme political beliefs under control so that they can be of use to the commonwealth. It is the example of Elizabeth and the sacrifices her queenship demands of her as a woman that teach Michael to control his feelings. He learns that he has a duty to harness his beliefs to the good of the cause. Having learnt this important lesson, Michael agrees to be sent back to Spain on a spy mission. When Cynthia, Burghley's daughter, played by Vivian Leigh, tries to persuade him not to go by telling him that, 'Everyone has the right to be happy', he replies, 'Everyone. Yes. That is why we can't be'. In effect, he has to follow Elizabeth's lead. He too has to place duty before personal happiness. Michael also, however, has to reproduce Elizabeth's adoption of disguises. He, like his queen, has to play a role in order to fight Spain.

Fire over England deploys the tensions implicit in the figure of Elizabeth in order to critique Spanish models of gender and space. In Spain Philip II's courtiers are depicted as scared feminine men. When Michael during his spy mission proposes a singing competition, the Spanish men sing a light, complicated song while Michael's one is rough and masculine—or at least this is how it is perceived by the Spanish woman who hears it. In *Fire over England* it is Philip's court that is represented as being feminine. In particular, the terror he inspires in his courtiers emasculates them. It makes them unable to speak their minds. The Spanish court is a place of unspoken tensions, extreme formality; a place where treason and danger lurk behind every arras. Elizabeth's court, however, is represented as relatively informal. Certainly, there are grand state occasions and the audience does get its fix of passageways and dark corners. However, what is made implicit in *Fire over England* is that secrecy and plotting is a product of Spanish aggression and not Elizabeth's gender. The femininity of the Elizabethan court in this film is presented more as a product of outside or external pressures than the queen's gender. Indeed, Robson's Elizabeth is often portrayed as leaving the confines of the court and more importantly, since one can leave the court but still take it with one, is shown on a number of occasions talking directly to her people. Elizabeth's gender in *Fire over England* is depicted as a source of strength. It has personal costs for the queen—although the film goes out of its way to suggest that such costs are the sort that everyone has to bear in the fight against tyranny.

Fire over England embodies a positive model of the past in arguing that its lessons are relevant to the present. Indeed, the basic narrative motivation of this film is the desire to collapse the present into the past. As a member of its audience, one is constantly being asked to draw parallels between Michael's story and the present. This reflects the confidence of the filmmakers in their audience's ability to understand properly the political message of the film. *Fire over England* is committed to the anti-elitist populist model of history discussed by Sue Harper in her study *Picturing the Past: The Rise and Fall of the British Costume Film.*[1] In particular, it constantly incites its audience to make political and historical connections between Michael's words and the state of 1930s Europe. For example, when Michael claims that 'Spain is a land of ghosts', or later when he is in Spain and proposes a toast to the 'prudent' people of Spain 'who think as the State thinks', it is clear what parallels we as an audience are expected to draw.

Fire over England does not ignore the tensions caused by Elizabeth I's gender. However, like the dominant Whig history of the period, it is more concerned with the clash of ideas and political systems personified in Elizabeth and Philip. England in this film is depicted as being on the brink of greatness. The implication of *Fire over England* is that the coming struggle with Fascism will return England to a historical moment when it first took on a transnational or European role. Although Robson's Elizabeth is consistently shown having to put her duty and public life before her needs and desires as a woman, the film's insistence that this kind of sacrifice is common in a time of emergency and the way in which it refuses to make this act of denial the meaning of Elizabeth's queenship reflects its political agenda. It, like Robson's Elizabeth, has no time to waste on these matters—there is, or was, tyranny to fight.

The Private Lives of Elizabeth and Essex (1939)

The Private Lives of Elizabeth and Essex can be seen as a direct response to *Fire over England*. At one level it is a radically a- (almost anti-) political film. Although it opens with the usual historical titles, its first substantial piece of dialogue is a conversation between the court's women, including Olivia de Havilland, over Essex's attractiveness. This opening sequence immediately sets up the film's main focus, the problems caused by Elizabeth's gender. In particular, de Havilland's character complains that it is easy for the queen to win Essex's love because she can command it. The idea of a female ruler being able to command love, to collapse her public and private roles in order to benefit the latter, reverses the relationship between these two worlds as constructed in *Fire over England*. In *The Private Lives of Elizabeth and Essex* the world of politics is consistently upstaged by the queen's private relationship with Essex. Indeed, it is noticeable that in this film the external threat is represented by the Irish who are depicted as the victims of English incompetence and violence.

Bette Davis's Elizabeth is obsessed with the problems the queenship causes her as a woman. There is an extended mirror-smashing scene in this film, at the end of which the queen tells one of her ladies in waiting that

---

1. Sue Harper, *Picturing the Past: The Rise and Fall of the British Costume Film* (London, 1994).

'To be a queen is to be less than human'. She goes on to describe herself as 'An empty glittering husk', before stating that a queen 'must give up all a woman finds most dear'. This scene illustrates perfectly the way in which Elizabeth as a figure can be deployed by filmmakers to sustain a conservative version of femininity. At a simple level what is being implied here is that what is most dear for a woman is a family, husband and children. The suggestion that Davis's queen is 'an empty husk', however, reflects the way in which this film consistently insists on the unnaturalness of Elizabeth's position. The queen is a husk because she is all performance—and she has all the mirrors in the palace removed because they remind her of this fact. At the same time, however, the audience knows that Elizabeth does have private or deep feelings. Why do these not fill her? Not stop her being empty?

The key word to notice here is, however, 'glittering'. Davis's Elizabeth may be empty but she is still desirable. In a sense this is the whole problem with this film. Essex and Elizabeth, and the audience, are caught in a desire filled cul-de-sac—Elizabeth's court. Teresa de Lauretis has argued that the basic principle of narrative is the movement of the masculine subject through a feminine space.[2] Certainly, in *The Private Lives of Elizabeth and Essex* Errol Flynn is constantly moving through the feminine space of Elizabeth's court, taking the audience with him, in a search for Elizabeth the woman. Ultimately, however, this search is bound to fail and for this reason the film is marked by narrative failure. Moreover, this failure is inevitable since the only way for it to be avoided would be for Errol and Bette to end up married. Instead, the film concludes with Essex going to his death while Elizabeth is left caught in a darkened, restricted feminine space. The glittering queen's desirability is undermined and degraded because it is never productive or fulfilled.

Throughout *The Private Lives of Elizabeth and Essex* one is invited to view Elizabeth as an object of desire. At the film's opening, and later in other formal court settings, Elizabeth is presented to the audience through a long shot so that the details of her appearance and presence only slowly come into definition. Before this shot, however, we have heard the queen's voice—it is only now that we get to see her in full glittering (or perhaps empty) glory. We—the audience and Essex—see Elizabeth as an object of desire, but each time we move towards fulfilling our desire we are thwarted by the queen's aberrant gender. It is almost as though Davis's Elizabeth has an excess of the feminine. Certainly, her court is full of hopeless feminised men who are, of course, no match for Essex. Equally, however, he simply cannot live in this world of treachery, deceit and flattery.

Elizabeth and Essex battle away throughout the film but nothing changes, nothing really happens. Early in the film, after she has banished Essex for turning his back on her, Elizabeth addresses his portrait and tells it: 'Robert, I don't know which I hate the most. You for making me love you or myself for needing you so much.' Essex and Elizabeth are in this film stuck in a parodic heterosexual relationship which is caught forever in the condition of seduction but never of consummation. It is Elizabeth's aberrant gender that creates this sterile situation (although one could represent

2. Teresa de Lauretis, 'Desire in Narrative', in Susana Onega and José Ángel García Landa, eds, *Narratology* (London, 1996), 262–72, especially p. 265.

this condition in a more positive way if one wished). Her court, like herself, is suffused with an excessive, emasculating femininity, over which she has no control. It is a kind of monstrous feminine machine or more accurately labyrinth from which there is clearly no escape. While the audience desires narrative closure in terms of escape from this monstrous space, at the film's end we are given nothing—consumption, closure, satisfaction are all denied as the audience is left with the empty husk of its desires.

This failure of closure is not, however, simply a product of the representation of gender in *The Private Lives of Elizabeth and Essex*. History is also a site of sterility in this film. This is primarily due to the asymmetrical way in which the historical enters the film. Renée Pigeon has recently discussed the implications of Bette Davis's insistence that she be made up to be a historically accurate depiction of the queen. Pigeon comments that:

> despite an ostensible desire for historical accuracy, Davis' Elizabeth becomes instead a bizarre and exotic figure, posing a choice for Flynn's Essex between this strange, be-wigged woman, who constantly bemoans her age yet doesn't appear truly old, and the fresh, young girl played by Olivia de Havilland.[3]

Davis's make-up marks her out as historical and grotesque. Unlike Essex/Flynn and Cynthia/Havilland, Elizabeth in this film is trapped in history. The falseness of the relationship between Essex and Elizabeth, its non-productive performative nature, is marked by the contrast between Davis (false historical woman) and Havilland (true natural woman). *The Private Lives of Elizabeth and Essex* embodies a conservative version of history in which the truth of such categories as gender transcends history and is located in nature. Davis's Elizabeth is, however, caught behind the ghastly painted mask of history.

Elizabeth (1998)

Obviously, the recent film *Elizabeth* is a profoundly post-modern piece of cinema. It indulges its audience's desire to find or label the post-modern. It has pastiche, is self-referential, nostalgic and sceptical. It also constructs gender as, at one level, a matter of performance. Indeed, the film's end when Elizabeth has to take control by inflicting upon herself a brutal makeover can be seen as an enactment of Judith Butler's ideas concerning the performativity of gender norms.

Elizabeth's most clearly post-modern element is, however, the way its narrative structure is explicit and circular. The film opens by announcing that its central object will be Elizabeth—the queen, a historical figure, an object to be studied and analysed. The film then shows its audience the process by which this Elizabeth—with a capital E—comes into being. It shows how elizabeth becomes Elizabeth. At the end of the film the audience are presented with Elizabeth the media-icon and it is clearly to this figure that the film's title refers. At one level, therefore, this is a film about the production

3. Renée Pigeon, 'Gloriana Goes to Hollywood: Elizabeth I on Film, 1937–1940', in William F. Gentrup, ed., *Reinventing the Middle Ages and the Renaissance: Constructions of the Medieval and Early Modern Periods*, Amazon Studies in the Middle Ages and the Renaissance, 1 (Turnhout, 1998), 107–21, at p. 117.

of a film. It tells the story of how an object becomes the fit subject of cinema and in the process recounts the grounds of its own existence. This is perhaps the real reason why Howard and his supporters are punished—not only because they are traitors but also because they have been gazing on the wrong object. Their distorted, corrupt and false gaze endangers the film itself and for this they have to be punished.

At the same time *Elizabeth* narrates the emergence of a female subject. It is only at the end of the film that Elizabeth hears her father's call and becomes the Elizabeth of history. Before this moment the film implies that she is unsure who she is. Indeed, Cate Blanchett's Elizabeth clearly fits into the Bette Davis/Sarah Bernhardt tradition of Elizabeths in that she is depicted as being constantly torn between her desires as a woman and her role as a queen. The end of the film suggests that not only are these two sides of Elizabeth's life incompatible, but that Elizabeth must empty out her personal desires in order to become a fit receptacle for the public desires of her subjects. This is, potentially, a deeply conservative conclusion. It rests on the assumption that a woman's private desires are naturally centred on heterosexuality and cannot be political. Indeed, the implication of this ending is that the new Elizabeth is a kind of freak. Her rejection of the 'natural joys' of heterosexuality, and in particular her relationship with Dudley, mark her out as non-natural, and performative; a glittering but empty husk, designed simply to incite desiring gazes from her subjects.

It is important to note some of the historical choices being made in this film, and in particular its opening scenes. The reign of Elizabeth's elder sister Mary I is defined on the basis of her childlessness. Her inner court is represented as dark, foreign and feminine. It is full of drapes, enclosed and enclosing. It incites the viewer's curiosity through its oddness, its darkness, while at the same time frustrating it. Kathy Burke's Mary is a hysterical unattractive woman. Her tightly controlled hair contrasting with her emotional instability signifying a woman in conflict with herself. She is accompanied by a person of restricted growth indicating the unnaturalness and aberrant nature of the Marian regime. This film constructs a clear symbolic difference between the courts of Mary and Elizabeth. Mary's court is a sterile place in which an overtly feminine inner space is separated from an entirely masculine outer court. On the other hand, Cate Blanchett's Elizabeth is located in these opening scenes in the countryside, among nature and colour. Her hair, in direct contrast to Mary's is long and unkempt signifying femininity, naturalness, openness and, by implication, feminine weakness. To stress the contrast between these two female rulers further the film depicts Elizabeth's court as a place where gender functions properly—that is on the basis of heterosexuality; under the benign gaze of the sexually available woman, the sexes mix in joyous harmony.

A key element in the opening sequence of *Elizabeth* is the burning of the three Protestant martyrs, Bishops Hugh Latimer and Nicholas Ridley and an unnamed woman. Obviously, this is a largely fictitious version of a famous historical event. In particular, there was no woman martyr burned alongside Latimer and Ridley. The female martyr's presence in this scene allows the film to create a parallel between the treatment she receives at her death with Elizabeth's self-administered make-over at the film's conclusion. It is clearly significant that there is an emphasis in the film's opening sequence on the physical violence the female martyr suffers at the hands of her male captors. At the end of the film Elizabeth makes herself into an object to be consumed—here the audience is shown a person being forced to become just such an object. This is important since the gender of these two figures is fundamental to the kind of objects they become. The woman martyr, like Elizabeth at the end of the film, is depicted as being made into an object for an—or the—audience's voyeuristic, implicitly masculine gaze. This mythical martyr can be seen as representing the voyeurism of history unencumbered by the need to be factual, to take account of the notations of the past.[4] Her presence indicates the extent to which Kapur's film consistently places the need to entertain, indeed to indulge its audience's voyeurism, above any concern with historical accuracy. This is perhaps not a problem. *Elizabeth* is after all a film. However, one wonders at what stage an event needs to be sufficiently shocking or horrific for it not to be open to this kind of post-modern appropriation?

Elizabeth is, however, not simply a film about the production of gender. It is a history film since it claims at one level to be based upon past events and people. In representing the burning of martyrs as unpopular and Mary's court as foreign, it is giving cinematic expression to a Protestant view of the past. In particular, Kapur's film reproduces an understanding of Mary Tudor's reign that can be found in the work of Robert Crowley and John Foxe. These committed Protestants related Mary's false or failed pregnancies to a view of the Catholic Mass as a moment of inherently failed liminality in order to create an image of the reign of Mary as being sterile and disordered; as being marked by an excess of femininity that could not give birth or be creative because it was locked into the falseness and unnaturalness of Catholicism. It could be argued that the way in which *Elizabeth* reproduces a Protestant version of the relationship between Mary's and Elizabeth's reigns is unimportant. However, to do so would be to ignore the extent to which there are still people for whom Foxe's history is the truth. Ian Paisley's writings, and in particular *The Battle of the Reformation: Why It Must Be Fought Today* and *Three Great Reformers*, consistently deploy tropes identical to those found in Foxe and, more surprisingly, *Elizabeth* in order to construct the difference between Catholicism and Protestantism in gender specific terms.

Elizabeth's status as a historical film is not simply a product of its claim to represent real historical figures and events, although in scenes like that depicting Elizabeth's coronation it certainly makes this claim with verve. It is also a history film because it reflects on the place of history within films about Elizabeth I. The ending of Kapur's film takes on its true meaning when viewed in relation to *The Private Lives of Elizabeth and Essex* and *Fire over England*. In the latter Elizabeth's gender, and in particular the way that the queen sacrifices her pleasures as a woman for the good of the cause, is held up as an example to the film's hero. This possibility, the idea that the meaning of Elizabeth is not entirely determined or restricted by her gender, is rejected in *Elizabeth*. It is Davis's Elizabeth, a woman stunted and trapped by the conflict between her gender and her public role, who is the precursor to Blanchett's Virgin Queen. And it is the emergence of this

---

4. This female martyr could also be seen as representing the other 300 martyrs burnt during Mary's reign, and therefore as a symbol of Catholic cruelty.

Elizabeth that concludes Kapur's *Elizabeth* in a moment that exemplifies the lack of ambition and parochialism of most post-modern historical texts.

Conclusion

Cinematic representations of Elizabeth I constantly play with the tensions between her public and private sides, between her gender and her queenship. In doing so they seem to reflect, no doubt in a partial and distorting fashion, historical truths about her reign and the myths that surround it. This is despite the fact that all the films which depict Elizabeth I take liberties, often major, with what actually happened in her reign. However, it is perhaps the myth of Elizabeth that these films reproduce and not the facts of her reign. Indeed cinema has tended to reproduce many of the tropes found in Elizabethan apologists for, and critics of, Elizabeth Tudor. This suggests that either they were very forward looking, which seems unlikely, or that our culture's ways of making sense of strong women have not moved on much since the sixteenth century. Bette Davis's, Cate Blanchett's and Flora Robson's Elizabeths are all nothing like the real Queen Elizabeth—but, then, is this not also true of Foxe's, Camden's and Aylmer's Elizabeths?

Selected Bibliography

• Indicates items included or excerpted in this Norton Critical Edition.

GENERAL STUDIES AND REFERENCE WORKS

The Book of Common Prayer, 1559: The Elizabethan Prayer Book. Ed. John E. Booty. Charlottesville, VA: Folger Shakespeare Library, U of Virginia P, 1976.

Collins, Arthur, ed. *Letters and Memorials of State, in the Reigns of Queen Mary, Queen Elizabeth, King James, King Charles the First, Part of the Reign of King Charles the Second, and Oliver's Usurpation.* 2 vols. London: T. Osborne, 1746.

Dictionary of Literary Biography. Detroit, MI: Gale Research Co., 1978–

Early English Books, 1475–1640, Selected from Pollard and Redgrave's Short-Title Catalogue. Ann Arbor, MI: Xerox University Microfilms, [1937?–] (microfilm and online resource).

Geneva Bible. Ed. Lloyd E. Berry. Madison: U of Wisconsin P, 1969.

Geoffrey of Monmouth. *The History of the Kings of Britain.* Trans. Lewis Thorpe. London: Folio Society, 1969.

Kinney, Arthur F. *Elizabethan Backgrounds: Historical Documents of the Age of Elizabeth.* 2nd ed. Hamden, CT: Shoe String, 1975.

———. *Titled Elizabethans: A Directory of Elizabethan State and Church Officers and Knights, with Peers of England, Scotland, and Ireland, 1558–1603.* Hamden, CT: Archon, 1973.

Oxford Classical Dictionary. 3rd ed. Ed. Simon Hornblower and Antony Spawforth. Oxford: Oxford UP, 2003.

Oxford Companion to Classical Literature. Comp. and ed. Sir Paul Harvey. Oxford: Clarendon, 1966.

Oxford Companion to English Literature. 5th ed. Ed. Margaret Drabble. Oxford: Oxford UP, 1985.

Oxford Dictionary of National Biography. Ed. H. C. G. Matthew and Brian Harrison. Oxford: Oxford UP, 2004– (printed and online resource).

Oxford English Dictionary, 2nd ed. Ed. J. A. Simpson and E. S. C. Weiner. 20 vols. Oxford: Clarendon, 1989 (printed and online resource).

Ruoff, James E. *Crowell's Handbook of Elizabethan and Stuart Literature.* New York: Crowell, 1975.

Seneca. *Moral Essays.* Trans. John W. Basore. 3 vols. Cambridge, MA: Harvard UP, 1935.

Short-Title Catalogue of Books Printed in England, Scotland, and Ireland and of English Books Printed Abroad 1475–1640. 2nd ed. Comp. W.A. Jackson, F. S. Ferguson, and Katharine F. Pantzer; A. W. Pollard and G. R. Redgrave. 3 vols. London: Bibliographical Society, 1976–91.

Short-Title Catalogue of Books Printed in England, Scotland, Ireland, Wales, and British America and of English Books Printed in Other Countries 1641–1700. 2nd ed. Comp. Donald Wing. 3 vols. New York: Modern Language Association, 1982–94.

Thurley, Simon. *The Royal Palaces of Tudor England.* New Haven: Yale UP, 1993.

Wagner, John A. *Historical Dictionary of the Elizabethan World: Britain, Ireland, Europe, and America.* Phoenix: Oryx, 1999.

Whiting, Bartlett Jere, and Helen Wescott Whiting. *Proverbs, Sentences, and Proverbial Phrases from English Writings Mainly before 1500.* Cambridge, MA: Harvard UP, 1968.

THE LIFE OF QUEEN ELIZABETH

Adler, Doris. "Imaginary Toads in Real Gardens." *English Literary Renaissance [ELR]* 2 (1981): 235–60.

Arnold, Janet. *Queen Elizabeth's Wardrobe Unlock'd.* Leeds: Maney, 1988.

Bassnett, Susan. *Elizabeth I: A Feminist Perspective.* Oxford: Berg, 1988.

Bell, Ilona. "Elizabeth I—Always Her Own Free Woman." *Political Rhetoric, Power, and Renaissance Women.* Ed. Carole Levin and Patricia A. Sullivan. Albany: State U of New York P, 1995. 57–82.

Cavanagh, Sheila. "The Bad Seed: Princess Elizabeth and the Seymour Incident." *Dissing Elizabeth: Negative Representations of Gloriana.* Ed. Julia Walker. Durham: Duke UP, 1998. 9–29.

Coch, Christine. "'Mother of my Contreye': Elizabeth I and Tudor Constructions of Motherhood." *ELR* 26 (1996): 423–51.

Cole, Mary Hill. "Maternal Memory: Elizabeth Tudor's Anne Boleyn." *Images of Elizabeth I: A Quadricentennial Celebration.* Ed. Donald Stump and Carole Levin. Special issue, *Explorations in Renaissance Culture* 30 (Summer 2004): 41–55.

Collinson, Patrick. *Elizabeth I.* Oxford: Oxford UP, 2007.

Doran, Susan. *Monarchy and Matrimony: The Courtships of Elizabeth I*. London: Routledge, 1996.
———. *Queen Elizabeth I*. New York: New York UP, 2003.
• ———."Why Did Elizabeth Not Marry?" *Dissing Elizabeth: Negative Representations of Gloriana*. Ed. Julia Walker. Durham, NC: Duke UP, 1998. 30–59.
Dunlop, Ian. *Palaces and Progresses of Elizabeth I*. New Haven: Yale UP, 1993.
Dunn, Jane. *Elizabeth and Mary: Cousins, Rivals, Queens*. New York: Knopf, 2004.
Farrell, Kirby, and Kathleen Swaim, eds. *The Mysteries of Elizabeth I: Selections from "English Literary Renaissance."* Amherst: U of Massachusetts P, 2003.
Guy, John, ed. *The Reign of Elizabeth I: Court and Culture in the Last Decade*. Cambridge: Cambridge UP, 1995.
———. *Tudor England*. Oxford and New York: Oxford UP, 1990.
Haigh, Christopher. *Elizabeth I: Profile in Power*. London: Longman, 1988.
———, ed. *The Reign of Elizabeth I*. Athens: U of Georgia P, 1985.
Hibbert, Christopher. *The Virgin Queen*. Cambridge, MA: Perseus, 1991.
Hulse, Clark. *Elizabeth I: Ruler and Legend*. Urbana: Newberry Library, U of Illinois P, 2003.
Jenkins, Elizabeth. *Elizabeth the Great*. London: Gollancz, 1958.
Johnson, Paul. *Elizabeth I: A Study in Power and Intellect*. New York: Holt, Rinehart & Winston, 1974.
Lee, Stephen J. *Reign of Elizabeth I*. Abingdon, Oxon: Routledge, 2007.
• Levin, Carole. *The Heart and Stomach of a King: Elizabeth I and the Politics of Sex and Power*. Philadelphia: U of Pennsylvania P, 1994.
———. *The Reign of Elizabeth I*. New York: Palgrave, 2002.
Levin, Carole, and Patricia A. Sullivan, eds. *Political Rhetoric, Power, and Renaissance Women*. Albany: State U of New York P, 1995.
Levin, Carole, Jo Eldridge Carney, and Debra Barrett-Graves, eds. *Elizabeth I: Always Her Own Free Woman*. Burlington, VT: Ashgate, 2003.
• Loades, David. *Elizabeth I*. London: Hambledon & London, 2003.
MacCaffrey, Wallace T. *Elizabeth I*. London: Edward Arnold, 1993.
Mulstein, Anka. *Elizabeth I and Mary Stuart: The Perils of Marriage*. Trans. John Brownjohn. London: Haus, 2007.
• Neale, J. E. *Queen Elizabeth I*. London: Jonathan Cape, 1934; 1pt. 1958.
Orlin, Lena. "The Fictional Families of Elizabeth I." *Political Rhetoric, Power, and Renaissance Women*. Ed. Carole Levin and Patricia A. Sullivan. Albany, NY: SU of New York P, 1995, 85–109.
Perry, Maria. *The Word of a Prince*. Woodbridge, Suffolk: Boydell, 1990.
Picard, Liza. *Elizabeth's London: Everyday Life in Elizabethan London*. New York: St. Martin's, 2004.
Plowden, Alison. *Elizabeth I*. Stroud, Eng.: Sutton, 2004.
———. *Marriage with My Kingdom: The Courtships of Elizabeth I*. London: Macmillan, 1977.
———. *The Young Elizabeth: The First Twenty-Five Years of Elizabeth I*. Stroud, Eng.: Sutton, 1999.
Ridley, Jasper. *Elizabeth I: The Shrewdness of Virtue*. New York: Fromm International, 1989.
Ross, Josephine. *The Men Who Would be King: Suitors to Queen Elizabeth I*. London: Phoenix, 2005.
Smither, L. J. "Elizabeth I: A Psychological Profile." *Sixteenth Century Journal* 15 (1984): 47–72.
Somerset, Anne. *Elizabeth I*. London: Weidenfeld & Nicolson, 1991.
Starkey, David. *Elizabeth: The Struggle for the Throne*. London: Perennial, 2000.
Stump, Donald, and Carole Levin, eds. *Images of Elizabeth I: A Quadricentennial Celebration*. Special issue, *Explorations in Renaissance Culture* 30 (Summer 2004).
Walker, Julia, ed. *Dissing Elizabeth: Negative Representations of Gloriana*. Durham: Duke UP, 1998.
Watkins, Susan. *In Public and in Private: Elizabeth I and Her World*. London: Thames & Hudson, 1998.
Weir, Alison. *The Life of Elizabeth I*. New York: Ballantine, 1998.
Williams, Penry. *The Later Tudors: England 1547–1603*. Oxford: Clarendon P, 1995.
Ziegler, Georgianna, ed. *Elizabeth I: Then and Now*. Seattle: U of Washington P, 2003.

WRITINGS BY QUEEN ELIZABETH

• Bell, Ilona. "Elizabeth Tudor: Poet." *Images of Elizabeth I: A Quadricentennial Celebration*. Ed. Donald Stump and Carole Levin. Special issue, *Explorations in Renaissance Culture* 30 (Summer 2004): 1–22.
Benkert, Lysbeth. "Translation as Image-Making: Elizabeth I's Translation of Boethius's *Consolation of Philosophy*." *Early Modern Literary Studies* 6.3 (January 2001): 2.1–20.
Bradner, Leicester, ed. *The Poems of Elizabeth I*. Providence: Brown UP, 1964.
Bruce, John, ed. *Letters of Queen Elizabeth and King James VI of Scotland*. London: Camden Society, 1849. Rpt. New York: AMS, 1968.
Frye, Susan. "The Myth of Elizabeth at Tilbury." *Sixteenth Century Journal* 23 (1992): 95–114.
Green, Janet M. "'I My Self': Queen Elizabeth I's Oration at Tilbury Camp." *Sixteenth Century Journal* 28 (1997): 421–45.
Harrison, G. B., ed. *The Letters of Queen Elizabeth I*. New York: Funk & Wagnalls, 1935, 1968.
Heisch, Allison. "Queen Elizabeth I: Parliamentary Rhetoric and the Exercise of Power." *Signs* 1.1 (1975): 31–55.
———. *Queen Elizabeth I: Political Speeches and Parliamentary Addresses, 1558–1601*. Madison: U of Wisconsin P, 1994.
Herman, Peter C., ed. *Reading Monarch's Writing: The Poetry of Henry VIII, Mary Stuart, Elizabeth I, and James VI/I*. Tempe: Arizona Center for Medieval and Renaissance Studies, 2002.

Hopkins, Lisa. *Writing Renaissance Queens: Texts by and about Elizabeth I and Mary, Queen of Scots.* Newark: U of Delaware P, 2002.

Kinney, Arthur F. *Elizabethan Backgrounds: Historical Documents of the Age of Elizabeth.* 2nd ed. Hamden, CT: Shoe String, 1975.

• Marcus, Leah S., Janel Mueller, and Mary Beth Rose, eds. *Elizabeth I, Collected Works.* Chicago: U of Chicago P, 2000.

May, Steven W., ed. *Elizabeth I: Selected Works.* Washington Square, 2004.

May, Steven W. "Queen Elizabeth to Her Subjects: The Tilbury and Golden Speeches." *Images of Elizabeth I: A Quadricentennial Celebration.* Ed. Donald Stump and Carole Levin. Special issue, *Explorations in Renaissance Culture* 30 (Summer 2004): 23–39.

• Mueller, Janel, and Leah S. Marcus. *Elizabeth I, Autograph Compositions and Foreign Language Originals.* Chicago: U of Chicago P, 2003.

Mueller, Janel. "Textualism, Contextualism, and the Writings of Queen Elizabeth I." *English Studies and History.* Ed. David Robertson. Tampere, Finland: U of Tampere P, 1994. 11–38.

Perry, Maria. *The Word of a Prince.* Woodbridge, Eng.: Boydell, 1995.

Prescott, Anne Lake. "The Pearl of the Valois and Elizabeth I: Marguerite de Navarre's *Miroir* and Tudor England." *Silent but for the Word: Tudor Women as Patrons, Translators and Writers of Religious Works.* Ed. Margaret Patterson Hannay. Kent, OH: Kent State UP, 1985. 61–76.

Prior, Felix, ed. *Elizabeth I: Her Life in Letters.* Berkeley: U of California P, 2003.

• Rice, George P., ed. *The Public Speaking of Queen Elizabeth: Selections from Her Official Addresses.* New York: Columbia UP, 1951.

Rose, Mary Beth. "The Gendering of Authority in the Public Speeches of Elizabeth I." *PMLA* 115 (2000): 1077–82.

Shell, Marc. *Elizabeth's Glass; With The Glass of the Sinful Soul (1544) by Elizabeth I and Epistle Dedicatory and Conclusion by John Bale.* Lincoln: U of Nebraska P, 1993.

Summit, Jennifer. " 'The Arte of a Ladies Penne': Elizabeth I and the Poetics of Queenship." *The Mysteries of Elizabeth.* Ed. Kirby Farrell and Kathleen Swaim. Amherst: U of Massachusetts P, 2003. 67–96.

Teague, Frances. "Elizabeth I: Queen of England." *Women Writers of the Renaissance and Reformation.* Ed. Katharine M. Wilson. Athens: U of Georgia P, 1987. 522–47.

———. "Queen Elizabeth in Her Speeches." *Gloriana's Face.* Ed. S. P. Cerasano and Marion Wynne-Davies. Detroit: Wayne State UP, 1992. 67–69.

ELIZABETH'S COURT AND GOVERNMENT

Adams, Simon. "Eliza Enthroned? The Court and Its Politics." *The Reign of Elizabeth I.* Ed. Christopher Haigh (London: Macmillan, 1985). 55–77.

Adams, Simon. *Leicester and the Court: Essays on Elizabethan Politics.* Manchester: Manchester UP, 2002.

Alford, Stephen. *The Early Elizabethan Polity: William Cecil and the British Succession Crisis, 1558–1569.* Cambridge: Cambridge UP, 1998.

Berbard, G. W., ed. *The Tudor Nobility.* Manchester: Manchester UP, 1992.

Bossy, John. *Under the Molehill: An Elizabethan Spy Story.* New Haven: Yale UP, 2001.

Brennan, Michael G. *The Sidneys of Penshurst and the Monarchy, 1500–1700.* Burlington, VT: Ashgate, 2006.

Brigden, Susan. *New Worlds, Lost Worlds: The Rule of the Tudors, 1485–1603.* New York: Viking, 2001.

Brimacombe, Peter. *All the Queen's Men: The World of Elizabeth I.* New York: St. Martin's, 2000.

Brooks, Eric St. John. *Sir Christopher Hatton: Queen Elizabeth's Favourite.* London: Jonathan Cape, 1946.

Budiansky, Stephen. *Her Majesty's Spymaster: Elizabeth I, Sir Francis Walsingham, and the Birth of Modern Espionage.* New York: Viking, 2005.

Chambers, E. K. *Sir Henry Lee: An Elizabethan Portrait.* Oxford: Clarendon, 1936.

Coleman, Christopher, and David Starkey, eds. *Revolution Reassessed: Revisions in the History of the Tudor Government and Administration.* Oxford: Clarendon, 1986.

Collinson, Patrick. "The Monarchial Republic of Queen Elizabeth I." *Elizabethan Essays.* By Patrick Collinson. London: Humbledon, 1994. Rpt. *Elizabethans.* Hambledon & London, 2003. 31–57.

Coote, Stephen. *A Play of Passion: The Life of Sir Walter Ralegh.* London: Macmillan, 1993.

Croft, Pauline, ed. *Patronage, Culture, and Power: The Early Cecils.* New Haven: Paul Mellon Centre for Studies in British Art, Yale Center for British Art, Yale UP, 2002.

Dean, D. M. *Law-Making and Society in Late Elizabethan England: The Parliament of England, 1584–1601.* Cambridge: Cambridge UP, 1996.

Edwards, Philip. *Sir Walter Ralegh.* Folcroft, PA: Folcroft Library, 1976.

Elton, G. R. *The Parliament of England 1559–1581.* Cambridge: Cambridge UP, 1986.

Graves, Michael A. R. *Burghley: William Cecil, Lord Burghley.* London: Longman, 1998.

———. *Elizabethan Parliaments, 1559–1601.* 2d ed. London: Longman, 1996.

Greenblatt, Stephen. *Sir Walter Ralegh: The Renaissance Man and His Roles.* New Haven: Yale UP, 1973.

Gristwood, Sarah. *Elizabeth and Leicester: Power, Passion, and Politics.* New York: Viking, 2007.

Guth, Delloyd J., and John W. McKenna, ed. *Tudor Rule and Revolution.* Cambridge: Cambridge UP, 1982.

Guy, J. A., ed. *The Reign of Elizabeth I: Court and Culture in the Last Decade.* Cambridge: Cambridge UP, 1995.

————. *The Tudor Monarchy.* London: Arnold, 1997.

Hammer, Paul E. J. *The Polarisation of Elizabethan Politics: The Political Career of Robert Devereux, 2nd Earl of Essex, 1585–1597.* Cambridge: Cambridge UP, 1999.

Handover, P. M. *The Second Cecil: The Rise to Power, 1563–1604, of Sir Robert Cecil, Late First Earl of Salisbury.* London: Eyre & Spottiswoode, 1959.

Harrison, G. B. *The Life and Death of Robert Devereux, Earl of Essex.* Folcroft, PA: Folcroft Library, 1973.

Hartley, T. E. *Elizabeth's Parliaments: Queen, Lords, and Commons 1559–1601.* Manchester: Manchester UP, 1992.

Haynes, Alan. *Invisible Power: The Elizabethan Secret Services, 1570–1603.* New York: St. Martin's, 1992.

————. *Robert Cecil, Earl of Salisbury, 1563–1612: Servant of Two Sovereigns.* London: Owen, 1989.

————. *The White Bear: Robert Dudley, the Elizabethan Earl of Leicester.* London: Owen, 1987.

Hopkins, Lisa. *Queen Elizabeth I and Her Court.* London: Vision, 1990.

Howarth, David. *The Voyage of the Armada: The Spanish Story.* London: Collins, 1981.

Hume, Martin A. S. *The Great Lord Burghley: A Study in Elizabethan Statecraft.* London: Nisbet, 1898. Rpt. New York: Haskell House, 1968.

Hurtsfield, Joel. *Freedom, Corruption, and Government in Elizabethan England.* Cambridge: Harvard UP, 1973.

Ives, Eric W. *Faction in Tudor England.* London: Historical Association, 1979.

Jones, Gareth. *The Gentry and the Elizabethan State.* Swansea: C. Davies, 1977.

Jones, J. Gwynfor. *Wales and the Tudor State: Government, Religious Change, and the Social Order, 1534–1603.* Cardiff: U of Wales P, 1989.

MacCaffrey, Wallace T. *Queen Elizabeth and the Making of Policy, 1572–1588.* Princeton: Princeton UP, 1981.

McDiarmid, John F. *The Monarchical Republic of Early Modern England: Essays in Response to Patrick Collinson.* Burlington, VT: Ashgate, 2007.

McLaren, A. N. *Political Culture in the Reign of Elizabeth I: Queen and Commonwealth 1558–1585.* Cambridge: Cambridge UP, 1999.

• Mears, Natalie. *Queenship and Political Discourse in the Elizabethan Realms.* Cambridge: Cambridge UP, 2005.

Neale, J. E. *Elizabeth I and Her Parliaments 1584–1601.* 2 vols. London: Jonathan Cape, 1954, 1957.

Oosterhoff, F. G. *Leicester and the Netherlands, 1586–1587.* Utrecht: HES, 1988.

Peltonen, Markku. *Classical Humanism and Republicanism in English Political Thought 1570–1640.* Cambridge: Cambridge UP, 1995.

Pullman, Michael. *The Elizabethan Privy Council in the Fifteen-Seventies.* Berkeley: U of California P, 1971.

Read, Conyers. *Lord Burghley and Queen Elizabeth.* London: Jonathan Cape, 1960.

————. *Mr. Secretary Cecil and Queen Elizabeth.* New York: Knopf, 1961.

————. *Mr. Secretary Walsingham and the Policy of Queen Elizabeth.* 3 vols. Oxford: Clarendon, 1925.

Rosenbert, Eleanor. *Leicester, Patron of Letters.* New York: Columbia UP, 1955.

Trevelyan, Raleigh. *Sir Walter Raleigh.* London: Allen Lane, 2002.

Vines, Alice Gilmore. *Neither Fire nor Steel: Sir Christopher Hatton.* Chicago: Nelson-Hall, 1978.

Waldman, Milton. *Elizabeth and Leicester.* 4th ed. London: Collins, 1946.

Williams, Neville. *All the Queen's Men: Elizabeth I and Her Courtiers.* London: Weidenfeld & Nicolson, 1972.

Williams, Penry. *The Tudor Regime.* Oxford: Oxford UP, 1995.

Wilson, Derek. *Sweet Robin: A Biography of Robert Dudley, Earl of Leicester, 1533–1588.* London: Hamilton, 1981.

Wilson, Violet A. *Queen Elizabeth's Maids of Honour and Ladies of the Privy Chamber.* London: John Lane, 1922.

Winton, John. *Sir Walter Raleigh.* London: Joseph, 1975.

Wright, Pam. "A Change of Direction: The Ramifications of a Female Household, 1558–1603." *The English Court: From the War of the Roses to the Civil War.* Ed. David Starkey. London: Longman, 1987. 147–72.

ELIZABETH'S RELIGIOUS VIEWS AND RELATIONS WITH PROTESTANTS AND CATHOLICS

Aston, Margaret. *England's Iconoclasts.* Oxford: Clarendon P, 1988.

Boyer, Allen D. *Sir Edward Coke and the Elizabethan Age.* Stanford: Stanford UP, 2003.

Brook, V. J. K. *A Life of Archbishop Parker.* Oxford: Clarendon, 1962.

Capp, Bernard. "The Political Dimension of Apocalyptic Thought." *The Apocalypse in English Renaissance Thought and Literature: Patterns, Antecedents, and Repercussions.* Ed. C.A. Patrides and Joseph Wittreich. Ithaca: Cornell UP, 1984. 93–124.

Carlson, Leland H., and Albert Peel, eds. *Elizabethan Non-Conformist Texts.* 4 vols. London: Allen & Unwin, 1951–53.

Collinson, Patrick. *Archbishop Grindal, 1519–1583: The Struggle for a Reformed Church.* Berkeley: U of California P, 1979.

————. *The Elizabethan Puritan Movement.* Berkeley: U of California P, 1967.

———. *From Cranmer to Sancroft*. London: Hambledon Continuum, 2006.

• ———. "Windows in a Woman's Soul: Questions about the Religion of Queen Elizabeth I." *Elizabethan Essays*. By Patrick Collinson. London: Hambledon, 1994. Rpt. *Elizabethans*. Hambledon & London, 2003. 87–118.

Cross, Claire. *The Royal Supremacy in the Elizabethan Church*. London: Allen & Unwin, 1969.

Dickins, A. G. *The English Reformation*. 2nd ed. University Park: Pennsylvania State UP, 1989.

Doran, Susan. *Elizabeth I and Religion, 1558–1603*. London and New York: Routledge, 1994.

———. *Princes, Pastors, and People: The Church and Religion in England, 1500–1700*. London and New York: Routledge, 2003.

Duffy, Eamon. *The Stripping of the Altars: Traditional Religion in England, 1400–1580*. 2d ed. New Haven: Yale UP, 2005.

Fincham, Kenneth, and Peter Lake. *Religious Politics in Post-Reformation England: Essays in Honour of Nicholas Tyacke*. Woodbridge: Boydell, 2006.

McGinnis, Timothy Scott. *George Gifford and the Reformation of the Common Sort: Puritan Priorities on Elizabethan Religious Life*. Kirksville, MO: Truman State UP, 2005.

Greaves, Richard L. *Society and Religion in Elizabethan England*. Minneapolis: U of Minnesota P, 1981.

Gregory, Brad S. *Salvation at Stake: Christian Martyrdom in Early Modern Europe*. Cambridge, MA: Harvard UP, 1999.

Haugaard, William P. *Elizabeth and the English Reformation: The Struggle for a Stable Settlement of Religion*. London: Cambridge UP, 1968.

Holmes, Peter. *Resistance and Compromise: The Political Thought of the Elizabethan Catholics*. Cambridge: Cambridge UP, 1982.

Jones, Norman. *Faith by Statute: Parliament and the Settlement of Religion 1559*. London: Royal Historical Society, 1982.

King, John N. *Voices of the English Reformation: A Sourcebook*. Philadelphia: U of Pennsylvania P, 2004.

Knapp, Jeffrey. *Shakespeare's Tribe: Church, Nation, and Theater in Renaissance England*. Chicago: U of Chicago P, 2002.

Lake, Peter. *Moderate Puritans and the Elizabethan Church*. Cambridge: Cambridge UP, 1982.

———. "The Significance of the Elizabethan Identification of the Pope as Antichrist." *Journal of Ecclesiastical History* 31 (1980): 161–78.

Maltby, Judith D. *Prayer Book and People in Elizabethan and Early Stuart England*. Cambridge: Cambridge UP, 1998.

Marotti, Arthur F. *Religious Ideology and Cultural Fantasy: Catholic and Anti-Catholic Discourses in Early Modern England*. Notre Dame: U of Notre Dame P, 2005.

McCullough, Peter E. *Sermons at Court: Politics and Religion in Elizabethan and Jacobean Preaching*. Cambridge: Cambridge UP, 1998.

Monta, Susannah Brietz. *Martyrdom and Literature in Early Modern England*. Cambridge: Cambridge UP, 2005.

Morey, Adrian. *The Catholic Subjects of Elizabeth I*. Totowa, NJ: Rowman & Littlefield, 1978.

Pearson, Andrew Forest Scott. *Thomas Cartwright and Elizabethan Puritanism*. Cambridge: Cambridge, UP, 1925.

Perry, Edith Weir. *Under Four Tudors, Being the Story of Matthew Parker*. London: Allen & Unwin, 1964.

Plowden, Alison. *Danger to Elizabeth: The Catholics under Elizabeth I*. London: Macmillan, 1973.

Pollen, John Hungerford. *The English Catholics in the Reign of Queen Elizabeth: A Study of Their Politics, Civil Life, and Government, 1558–1580*. London: Longmans, Green, 1920. Rpt. New York: Burt Franklin, 1971.

Pritchard, Arnold. *Catholic Loyalism in Elizabethan England*. Chapel Hill: U of North Carolina P, 1979.

Southern, A. C. *Elizabethan Recusant Prose, 1559–1582*. London and Glasgow: Sands & Co., [1950].

Targoff, Ramie. *Common Prayer: The Language of Public Devotion in Early Modern England*. Chicago: U of Chicago P, 2001.

Thorpe, Malcolm. "William Cecil and the Antichrist: A Study of Anti-Catholic Ideology." *Politics, Religion, and Diplomacy in Early Modern Europe: Essays in Honor of Lemar Jensen*. Ed. Malcom Thorp and Arthur J. Slavin. Kirksville, MO: Sixteenth Century Journal Publications, 1994. 289–304.

Tyacke, Nicholas. *Aspects of English Protestantism, c. 1530–1700*. Manchester: Manchester UP, 2001.

Yates, Frances A. *The Occult Philosophy in the Elizabethan Age*. London: Routledge & Kegan Paul, 1979.

Wenig, Scott A. *Straightening the Altars: The Ecclesiastical Vision and Pastoral Achievements of the Progressive Bishops under Elizabeth I, 1559–1579*. New York: Peter Lang, 2000.

ELIZABETH'S FOREIGN POLICY AND ROLE IN EXPLORATION AND COLONIZATION

Berleth, Richard J. *The Twilight Lords: Elizabeth I and the Plunder of Ireland*. Lanham, MD: Roberts Rinehart, 2002.

Coote, Stephen. *Drake: The Life and Legend of an Elizabethan Hero*. New York: Simon & Schuster, 2003.

Dop, Jan Albert. *Eliza's Knights: Soldiers, Poets and Puritans in the Netherlands, 1572–1586*. Alblasserdam: Remak, 1981.

Doran, Susan. *Elizabeth I and Foreign Policy, 1558–1603.* London: Routledge, 2000.
———. *England and Europe, 1485–1603.* London and New York: Longman, 1986.
Doran, Susan, and Glenn Richardson, eds. *Tudor England and Its Neighbors.* New York: Palgrave Macmillan, 2005.
Falls, Cyril. *Elizabeth's Irish Wars.* New York: Barnes & Noble, 1970.
Hammer, Paul E. J. *Elizabeth's Wars: War, Government, and Society in Tudor England, 1544–1604.* New York: Palgrave Macmillan, 2003.
Hazlewood, Nick. *The Queen's Slave Trader: John Hawkyns, Elizabeth I, and the Trafficking in Human Souls.* New York: William Morrow, 2004.
Kelsey, Harry. *Sir Francis Drake: The Queen's Pirate.* New Haven: Yale UP, 1998.
———. *Sir John Hawkins: Queen Elizabeth's Slave Trader.* New Haven: Yale UP, 2003.
Lievsay, John L. *The Elizabethan Image of Italy.* Ithaca, NY: Folger Shakespeare Library, Cornell UP, 1964.
Mason, Roger A., ed. *Scots and Britons: Scottish Political Thought and the Union of 1603.* Cambridge: Cambridge UP, 1994.
Mattingly, Garrett. *The Armada.* Boston: Houghton Mifflin, 1959.
Miller, Shannon. *Invested with Meaning: The Raleigh Circle in the New World.* Philadelphia: U of Pennsylvania P, 1998.
Milton, Giles. *Big Chief Elizabeth: The Adventures and Fate of the First English Colonists in America.* New York: Farrar, Straus & Giroux, 2000.
Moran, Michael G. *Inventing Virginia: Sir Walter Raleigh and the Rhetoric of Colonization, 1584–1590.* New York: Peter Lang, 2007.
Nolan, John S. *Sir John Norreys and the Elizabethan Military World.* Exeter, Eng.: U of Exeter P, 1997.
Oosterhoff, F. G. *Leicester and the Netherlands, 1586–1587.* Utrecht: HES, 1988.
Patterson, Benton Rain. *With the Heart of a King: Elizabeth I of England, Philip II of Spain, and the Fight for a Nation's Soul and Crown.* New York: St. Martin's, 2007.
Ronald, Susan. *The Pirate Queen: Queen Elizabeth I, Her Merchant Adventures, and the Dawn of Empire.* New York: HarperCollins, 2007.
Warren, John. *Elizabeth I: Religion and Foreign Affairs.* 2nd ed. London: Hodder & Stoughton, 2002.
Watkins, John. "Elizabeth Through Venetian Eyes." *Images of Elizabeth I: A Quadricentennial Celebration.* Ed. Donald Stump and Carole Levin. Special issue, *Explorations in Renaissance Culture* 30 (Summer 2004): 121–38.
Wernham, R. B. *The Making of Elizabethan Foreign Policy 1558–1603.* Berkeley: U of California P, 1980.
Whitehead, Bertrand T. *Brags and Boasts: Propaganda in the Year of the Armada.* Stroud, Eng.: Sutton, 1994.
Whitfield, Peter. *Sir Francis Drake.* New York: New York UP, 2004.
Wilson, Derek. *The World Encompassed: Drake's Great Voyage 1577–1580.* London: Hamilton, 1977.
Yungblut, Laura Hunt. *Strangers Settled Here Amongst Us: Policies, Perceptions, and the Presence of Aliens in Elizabethan England.* London: Routledge, 1996.

PORTRAITS AND IMAGES OF THE QUEEN

Portraits, etchings, woodcuts, and other representations of Elizabeth are readily available on the World Wide Web.

Doebler, Bettie Anne. "Venus-Humanitas: An Iconic Elizabeth." *Journal of European Studies.* 12.4 (1982): 233–48.
Doran, Susan, ed. *Elizabeth: The Exhibition at the National Maritime Museum.* Curator and intro. David Starkey. London: Chatto & Windus, 2003.
———. "Virginity, Divinity and Power: The Portraits of Elizabeth I." In *The Myth of Elizabeth.* Ed. Susan Doran and Thomas S. Freeman. Basingstoke, Eng.: Palgrave Macmillan, 2003. 171–99.
Erler, Mary C. "Sir John Davies and the Rainbow Portrait of Queen Elizabeth." *Modern Philology* 84 (1987): 359–71.
Gittings, Claire. *The National Portrait Gallery Book of Elizabeth I.* London: Scala, 2006.
Graziani, René. "The 'Rainbow Portrait' of Queen Elizabeth I and Its Religious Symbolism." *Journal of the Warburg and Courtauld Institutes* 35 (1972): 247–59.
Havens, Earle, Stephen Parks, and James Mooney. *Gloriana: Monuments and Memorials of the Reign of Queen Elizabeth I.* New Haven, CT: Elizabethan Club, Yale University, 2006.
Hulse, Clark. *Elizabeth I: Ruler and Legend.* Urbana: Newberry Library, U of Illinois P, 2003.
King, John N. *Tudor Royal Iconography: Literature and Art in an Age of Religious Crisis.* Princeton: Princeton UP, 1989.
Levin, Carole. "Power, Politics and Sexuality: Images of Elizabeth I." *The Politics of Gender in Early Modern Europe.* Ed. Jean R. Brink, Allison P. Coudert, and Maryanne C. Horowitz. Kirksville, MO: Sixteenth Century Journal Publications, 1989. 95–110.
Pomeroy, Elizabeth W. *Reading the Portraits of Queen Elizabeth I.* Hamden, CT: Archon, 1989.
Strong, Roy. *The Cult of Elizabeth: Elizabethan Portraiture and Pageantry.* London: Thames & Hudson, 1977.

• ———. *Gloriana: The Portraits of Queen Elizabeth I*. London: Thames & Hudson, 1987.
———. *The Tudor and Stuart Monarchy: Pageantry, Painting, Iconography*. 3 vols. Woodbridge, Eng.: Boydell, 1995–98.

WRITINGS FOR AND ABOUT QUEEN ELIZABETH

General Studies

Anglo, Sydney. *Spectacle, Pageantry, and Early Tudor Policy*. Oxford: Clarendon, 1969.
Archer, Jayne Elisabeth, Elizabeth Goldring, and Sarah Knight, ed. *The Progresses, Pageants, and Entertainments of Queen Elizabeth I*. Oxford: Oxford UP, 2007.
Axton, Marie. "The Tudor Masque and Elizabethan Court Drama." *English Drama: Forms and Development*. Ed. Marie Axton and Raymond Williams. Cambridge: Cambridge UP, 1977.
———. *The Queen's Two Bodies: Drama and the Elizabethan Succession*. London: Royal Historical Society, 1977.
Bates, Catherine. *The Rhetoric of Courtship in Elizabethan Language and Literature*. Cambridge: Cambridge UP, 1992.
Bell, Ilona. *Elizabethan Women and the Poetry of Courtship*. Cambridge: Cambridge UP, 1998.
Benson, Pamela Joseph. *The Invention of the Renaissance Woman: The Challenge of Female Independence in the Literature and Thought of Italy and England*. University Park, PA: Pennsylvania State UP, 1992.
Bergeron, David M. *English Civic Pageantry, 1558–1642*. Columbia: U of South Carolina P, 1971.
Bevington, David. *Tudor Drama and Politics: A Critical Approach to Topical Meaning*. Cambridge: Harvard UP, 1968.
Cerasano, S. P., and Marion Wynne-Davies, ed. *Gloriana's Face: Women, Public and Private, in the English Renaissance*. Detroit: Wayne State UP, 1992.
Chambers, E. K. *The Elizabethan Stage*. 4 vols. Oxford: Clarendon, 1923.
• Cole, Mary Hill. *The Portable Queen: Elizabeth I and the Politics of Ceremony*. Amherst: U of Massachusetts P, 1999.
Collinson, Patrick. "William Camden and the Anti-Myth of Elizabeth: Setting the Mould?" *The Myth of Elizabeth*. Ed. Susan Doran and Thomas S. Freeman. Basingstoke, Eng.: Palgrave Macmillan, 2003. 79–98.
Durning, Louise, ed. *Queen Elizabeth's Book of Oxford*. Trans. Sarah Knight. Oxford: Oxford UP, 2006.
Frye, Susan. *Elizabeth I: The Competition for Representation*. New York: Oxford UP, 1993.
Hackett, Helen. *Virgin Mother, Maiden Queen: Elizabeth I and the Cult of the Virgin Mary*. New York: St. Martin's, 1995.
Hadfield, Andrew. *Literature, Politics and National Identity: Reformation to Renaissance*. Cambridge: Cambridge UP, 1994.
Helgerson, Richard. *Forms of Nationhood: The Elizabethan Writing of England*. Chicago: U of Chicago P, 1992.
Jansohn, Christa, ed. *Queen Elizabeth I: Past and Present*. Münster, Ger.: LIT, 2004.
• King, John N. "Queen Elizabeth I: Representations of the Virgin Queen." *Renaissance Quarterly* 43 (1990): 30–74.
———. *Tudor Royal Iconography: Literature and Art in an Age of Religious Crisis*. Princeton: Princeton UP, 1989.
• Knapp, Jeffrey. *An Empire Nowhere: England, America, and Literature from "Utopia" to the "Tempest."* Berkeley: U of California P, 1992.
Leahy, William. *Elizabethan Triumphal Processions*. Aldershot, Eng.: Ashgate, 2005.
May, Stephen W. *The Elizabethan Courtier Poets: The Poems and Their Contexts*. Columbia, MO: U of Missouri P, 1991.
McClure, Peter, and Robin Headlam Wells. "Elizabeth I as a Second Virgin Mary." *Renaissance Studies* 4 (1990): 38–70.
McCoy, Richard C. *The Rites of Knighthood*. Berkeley: U of California P, 1989.
Montrose, Louis A. *The Subject of Elizabeth: Authority, Gender, and Representation*. Chicago: U of Chicago P, 2006.
Morinin, Massimiliano. *Tudor Translation in Theory and Practice*. Burlington, VT: Ashgagte, 2006.
• Nichols, John. *The Progresses and Public Processions of Queen Elizabeth*. 3 vols. London: John Nichols & Son, 1823. Rpt. New York: Burt Franklin, 1961.
Norbrook, David. *Poetry and Politics in the English Renaissance*. London: Routledge & Kegan Paul, 1984.
Osborne, June. *Entertaining Elizabeth I: The Progresses and Great Houses of Her Time*. London: Bishopsgate, 1989.
• Stump, Donald. "Abandoning the Old Testament: Shifting Paradigms for Elizabeth, 1578–82." *Images of Elizabeth I: A Quadricentennial Celebration*. Ed. Donald Stump and Carole Levin. Special issue, *Explorations in Renaissance Culture* 30 (Summer 2004): 89–109.
Wickham, Glynne. *Early English Stages, 1300–1660*. 2nd ed. 4 vols. London: Routledge, 1980.
Wilson, Elkin Calhoun. *England's Eliza*. Cambridge, MA: Harvard UP, 1939.
Wilson, Jean. *Entertainments for Elizabeth I*. Woodbridge: D.S. Brewer, 1980.
• Yates, Frances A. *Astraea: The Imperial Theme in the Sixteenth Century*. Part II, Chap. 1. London: Routledge, 1975.

Individual Authors

For information on writers not listed, see the *Oxford Dictionary of National Biography*, the *Dictionary of Literary Biography* (cited above under "General Reference Works"), or general works on the Queen's life and reign.

Cardinal William Allen
Southern, A. G. *Elizabethan Recusant Prose, 1559–1582*. London: Sands, 1950.

James Aske
Frye, Susan. "The Myth of Elizabeth at Tilbury." *Sixteenth Century Journal* 23 (1992): 95–114.
Green, Janet M. "'I My Self': Queen Elizabeth I's Oration at Tilbury Camp." *Sixteenth Century Journal* 28 (1997): 421–45.

John Aylmer
Benson, Pamela Joseph. *The Invention of the Renaissance Woman: The Challenge of Female Independence in the Literature and Thought of Italy and England*. University Park, PA: Pennsylvania State UP, 1992.
Lee, Patricia-Ann. "A Bodye Politique to Governe: Aylmer, Knox, and the Debate on Queenship." *Historian* 52 (1990): 242–61.

Sir Francis Bacon
Hammer, Paul E. J. "Upstaging the Queen: The Earl of Essex, Francis Bacon, and the Accession Day Celebrations of 1595." *The Politics of the Stuart Court Masque*. Ed. David Bevington, Peter Holbrook, and Leah Marcus. Cambridge: Cambridge UP, 1998, 41–66.

John Bale
Kastan, David S. "An Early English Metrical Psalm: Elizabeth's or John Bale's? *Notes and Queries* 21 (1974): 505–505.
Kesselring, Krista. "Representations of Women in Tudor Historiography: John Bale and the Rhetoric of Exemplarity." *Renaissance and Reformation/Renaissance et Réforme* 22.2 (1998): 41–61.
Shell, Marc. *Elizabeth's Glass; With The Glass of the Sinful Soul (1544) by Elizabeth I and Epistle Dedicatory and Conclusion by John Bale*. Lincoln: U of Nebraska P, 1993.

Richard Barnfield
Borris, Kenneth, and George Klawitter, eds. *The Affectionate Shepherd: Celebrating Richard Barnfield*. Selinsgrove, PA: Susquehanna UP, 2001.
Klawitter, George, ed. *Richard Barnfield: The Complete Poems*. Selinsgrove, PA: Susquehanna UP, 1990.

Thomas Bentley
Atkinson, Colin B. and Jo B. Atkinson, "The Identity and Life of Thomas Bentley, Compiler of *The Monument of Matrones* (1582)," *Sixteenth Century Journal* 31 (2000): 323–48.
————., eds. *The Monument of Matrones*, Series III, Part One of The Early Modern Englishwoman: A Facsimile Library of Essential Works—Essential Works for the Study of Early Modern Women. Burlington, VT: Ashgate, 2005.
Felch, Susan M. "The Development of the English Prayer Book." *Worship in Medieval and Early Modern Europe: Change and Continuity in Religious Practice*. Ed. Karin Maag and John D. Witvliet. Notre Dame: U of Notre Dame P, 2004, 132–161.
King, John. "Thomas Bentley's Monument of Matrons: The Earliest Anthology of English Women's Texts." *Strong Voices, Weak History: Early Women Writers and Canons in England, France, and Italy*. Ed. Pamela J. Benson and Victoria Kirkham. Ann Arbor: U of Michigan P, 2004, 216–38.

William Birch
Livingston, Carole Rose. *British Broadside Ballads of the Sixteenth Century: A Catalogue of the Extant Sheets and an Essay*. New York: Garland, 1991.

Adam Blackwood
Lewis, Jayne Elizabeth, ed. *The Trial of Mary Queen of Scots: A Brief History with Documents*. Boston: Bedford, St. Martin's, 1999.

Thomas Blenerhasset
Schulze, Ivan L. "Blenerhasset's *A Revelation*, Spenser's *Shepheardes Calender*, and the Kenilworth Pageants." *ELH* 11.2 (1944): 85–91.

Robert Carey
Mares, F. H., ed. *The Memoirs of Robert Carey*. Oxford: Clarendon, 1972.

William Cecil, Lord Burghley
Beckingsale, B. W. *Burghley: Tudor Statesman, 1520–1598*. London: Macmillan: 1967.

George Chapman
Bartlett, Phyllis Brooks, ed. *The Poems of George Chapman*. New York: Russell & Russell, 1962.

Henry Constable
Grundy, Joan. *The Poems of Henry Constable*. Liverpool: Liverpool UP, 1960.

Sir John Davies
Erler, Mary C. "Sir John Davies and the Rainbow Portrait of Queen Elizabeth." *Modern Philology* 84 (1987): 359–71.
Krueger, Robert, ed. *The Poems of Sir John Davies*. Oxford: Clarendon, 1975.
Sanderson, James L. *Sir John Davies*. Boston: Twayne, 1975.

Thomas Dekker
Pendry, E. D., ed. *Thomas Dekker: The Wonderful Year; The Gull's Horn-Book; Penny-Wise, Pound-Foolish; English Villainies Discovered by Lantern and Candlelight; and Selected Writings*. Cambridge: Harvard UP, 1968.
Price, George R. *Thomas Dekker*. Boston: Twayne, 1969.

Thomas Deloney
Wright, Eugene P. *Thomas Deloney*. Boston: Twane, 1981.

Edward Dering
Christian, Margaret. "Elizabeth's Preachers and the Government of Women: Defining and Correcting a Queen." *Sixteenth Century Journal*. 24.3 (1993): 561–76.
Collinson, Patrick. "A Mirror of Elizabethan Puritanism: The Life and Letters of 'Godly Master Dering'." *Godly People: Essays on English Protestantism and Puritanism*. Ed. Patrick Collinson. London: Hambledon Press, 1983. 288–324.
Freeman, Thomas S. "Providence and Prescription: The Account of Elizabeth in Foxe's Book of Martyrs." *The Myth of Elizabeth*. Ed. Susan Doran and Thomas S. Freeman. Basingstoke, Eng.: Palgrave Macmillan, 2003. 27–55.

Edward De Vere, Earl of Oxford
May, Steven W. "The Poems of Edward De Vere, Seventeenth Earl of Oxford and of Robert Devereux, Second Earl of Essex," *Studies in Philology* 77.5 (1980): 5–42, 67–83.

Robert Devereux, Earl of Essex
May, Steven W. "The Poems of Edward De Vere, Seventeenth Earl of Oxford and of Robert Devereux, Second Earl of Essex," *Studies in Philology* 77.5 (1980): 43–64, 84–114.

Michael Drayton
Brink, Jean R. *Michael Drayton Revisited*. Boston: Twayne, 1990.
Hardin, Richard F. *Michael Drayton and the Passing of Elizabethan England*. Lawrence: UP of Kansas, 1973.
Hebel, J. William, ed. *The Works of Michael Drayton*. 5 vols. Oxford: Shakespeare Head P, 1931–61.

William Elderton
Livingston, Carole Rose. British Broadside Ballads of the Sixteenth Century: A Catalogue of the Extant Sheets and an Essay. New York: Garland, 1991.

Elvetham Pageants
Boyle, Harry H. "Elizabeth's Entertainment at Elvetham: War Policy in Pageantry." *Studies in Philology* 68 (1971): 146–66.
Kinney, Arthur F., ed. *The Honorable Entertainment Given to the Queen's Majesty in Progress, at Elvetham in Hampshire*. Renaissance Drama: An Anthology of Plays and Entertainments. Oxford: Blackwell, 1999. 139–54.
Suerbaum, Ulrich. "Performing Royalty. The Entertainment at Elvetham and the Cult of Elisa." *Word and Action in Drama*. Ed. Günter Ahrends, Stephan Kohl, Joachim Kornelius, and Gerd Stratmann. Trier: Wissenschaftlicher, 1994. 53–64.

Richard Fletcher
McCullough, Peter E. "Out of Egypt: Richard Fletcher's Sermon before Elizabeth I after the Execution of Mary Queen of Scots." *Dissing Elizabeth: Negative Representations of Gloriana*. Ed. Julia M. Walker. Durham, NC: Duke UP, 1998. 118–49.

John Foxe

Freeman, Thomas S. "Providence and Prescription: The Account of Elizabeth in Foxe's Book of Martyrs." *The Myth of Elizabeth.* Ed. Susan Doran and Thomas S. Freeman. Basingstoke, Eng.: Palgrave Macmillan, 2003. 27–55.

John Foxe. *Acts and Monuments [. . .]. The Variorum Edition.* [online]. (hriOnline, Sheffield 2004). Available from: www.hrionline.ac.uk/foxe/.

King, John N. *Foxe's Book of Martyrs and Early Modern Print Culture.* Cambridge: Cambridge UP, 2006.

Levin, Carole. "John Foxe and the Responsibilities of Queenship." *Women in the Middle Ages and the Renaissance: Literary and Historical Perspectives.* Ed. Mary Beth Rose. Syracuse: Syracuse UP, 1986. 113–31.

Loades, David, ed. *John Foxe: An Historical Perspective.* Aldershot, Eng.: Ashgate, 1999.

Bernard Garter and William Goldingham

• Dovey, Zillah. *An Elizabethan Progress: The Queen's Progress into East Anglia, 1578.* Gloucester: Sutton, 1996.

Purdy, Mary M. "Political Propaganda in Ballad and Masque." *If By Your Art: Testament to Percival Hunt.* Ed. Agnes Lynch Starrett. Pittsburgh, 1948, 264–93.

George Gascoigne

Hamrick, Stephen. " 'Set in Portraiture': George Gascoigne, Queen Elizabeth, and Adapting the Royal Image," *Early Modern Literature Studies* 11.1 (2005): 54 paragraphs.

Hazard, Mary E. " 'A magnificent Lord': Leicester, Kenilworth, and Transformations in the Idea of Magnificence." *Cahiers Élisabéthains* 31 (1987): 11–35.

Nash, Ilana. " 'A Subject without Subjection': Robert Dudley, Earl of Leicester, and *The Princely Pleasures at Kenelworth Castle.*" *Comitatus* 25 (1994): 81–102.

Prouty, Charles. "George Gascoigne, The Noble Arte of Venerie, and Queen Elizabeth at Kenilworth." *Joseph Quincy Adams Memorial Studies.* Ed. James G. McManaway, Giles E. Dawson, and Edwin E. Willoughby. Washington: Folger Shakespeare Library, 1948. 639–64.

———. *George Gascoigne: Elizabethan Courtier, Soldier, and Poet.* New York: Columbia UP, 1942.

David Gwyn

Shaaber, M. A. "David Gwyn's Verses." *Papers of the Bibliographical Society of America* 66 (1972): 293–96.

Edward Hake

Wilson, Luke. "Edward Hake." In *Sixteenth Century British Nondramatic Writers,* 2nd Ser. Ed. David A. Richardson. Detroit: Gale, 1994. 171–76.

Sir John Harington

Craig, D. H. *Sir John Harington.* Boston: Twayne, 1985.

Feinberg, Nona. *Elizabeth, Her Poets, and the Creation of the Courtly Manner: A Study of Sir John Harington, Sir Philip Sydney, and John Lyly.* New York: Garland, 1988.

McClure, Norman Egbert, ed. *Letters and Epigrams of Sir John Harington, Together with "The Prayse of Private Life."* Foreword by Felix E. Schelling. New York: Octagon, 1977, c. 1930.

Scott-Warren, Jason. *Sir John Harington and the Book as Gift.* Oxford: Oxford UP, 2001.

Richard Harvey

Whitehead, Bertrand T. *Brags and Boasts: Propaganda in the Year of the Armada.* Stroud, Eng.: Sutton, 1994.

Mary Sidney Herbert, Countess of Pembroke

Erler, Mary C. "Davies's Astraea and Other Contexts of the Countess of Pembroke's 'A Dialogue.' " *SEL: Studies in English Literature, 1500–1900* 30 (1990): 41–61.

Hannay, Margaret P. " 'Doo What Men May Sing': Mary Sidney and the Tradition of Admonitory Dedication." *Silent but for the Word: Tudor Women as Patrons, Translators and Writers of Religious Works.* Ed. Margaret Patterson Hannay. Kent, OH: Kent State UP, 1985. 149–165.

Hannay, Margaret P., Noel J. Kinnaman, and Michael G. Brennan, ed. *Mary Sidney, Countess of Pembroke: Collected Works.* 2 vols. Oxford: Clarendon, 1998.

———, ed. *Selected Works of Mary Sidney Herbert, Countess of Pembroke.* Tempe: Arizona Center for Medieval and Renaissance Studies, 2005.

Thomas Heywood

Grant, Teresa. "Drama Queen: Staging Elizabeth in *If You Know Not Me You Know Nobody.*" *The Myth of Elizabeth.* Ed. Susan Doran and Thomas S. Freeman. Basingstoke, Eng.: Palgrave Macmillan, 2003. 120–42.

Howard, Jean E. "Staging the Absent Woman: The Theatrical Evocation of Elizabeth Tudor in Heywood's *If You Know Not Me, You Know Nobody,* Part I." *Women Players in England, 1500–1650: Beyond the All-Male Stage.* Ed. Pamela Allen Brown and Peter Parolin. Burlington, VT: Ashgate, 2005. 263–80.

Mehl, Dieter. "The Late Queen on the Public Stage: Thomas Heywood's *If You Know Not Me You Know Nobody*, Parts I and II." *Queen Elizabeth I: Past and Present.* Ed. Christa Jansohn. Münster, Germany: LIT, 2004. 153–72.

Ziegler, Georgianna. "England's Savior: Elizabeth I in the Writings of Thomas Heywood." *Renaissance Papers* (1980): 29–37.

André Hurault, Sieur De Maisse

Harrison, G. B., and R. A. Jones, eds. and trans. *De Maisse; a Journal of All That Was Accomplished by Monsieur de Maisse.* London: Nonesuch Press, 1931. 22–26.

James VI/I

Allinson, Rayne. "Queen Elizabeth I and the 'Nomination' of the Young Prince of Scotland." *Notes and Queries* 53 (2006): 425–27.

Ben Jonson

Wilkes, G. A. *Cynthia's Revels. The Complete Plays of Ben Jonson.* Vol. 2. Oxford: Clarendon, 1981. 1–117.

John Knox

Felch, Susan M. "The Rhetoric of Biblical Authority: John Knox and the Question of Women." *Sixteenth Century Journal* 26 (1995): 807–24.

Hansen, Melanie. "The Word and the Throne: John Knox's *The First Blast of the Trumpet against the Monstrous Regiment of Women.*" *Voicing Women: Gender and Sexuality in Early Modern Writing.* Ed. Kate Chedgzoy, Melanie Hansen, and Suzanne Trill. Pittsburgh: Duquesne UP, 11–24.

Healey, Robert M. "Waiting for Deborah: John Knox and Four Ruling Queens." *Sixteenth Century Journal* 25.2 (1994): 371–86.

Lee, Patricia-Ann. "A Bodye Politique to Governe: Aylmer, Knox, and the Debate on Queenship." *Historian* 52 (1990): 242–61.

Robert Laneham (pseud.)

Laneham, Robert. *A Letter.* Ed. R. J. P. Kuin. Leiden: E. J. Brill, 1983.

Scott, David. "William Patten and the Authorship of 'Robert Laneham's *Letter.*'" *English Literary Renaissance* 7 (1977): 297–306.

Anne Vaughan Lock

Collinson, Patrick. "The Role of Women in the English Reformation Illustrated by the Life and Friendships of Anne Locke." *Godly People: Essays on English Protestantism and Puritanism.* Ed. Patrick Collinson. London: Hambledon Press, 1983. 273–87.

• Felch, Susan M. *The Collected Works of Anne Vaughan Lock.* Medieval & Renaissance Texts & Studies, vol. 185. Renaissance English Text Society, vol. 21. Tempe, AZ: Arizona Center for Medieval and Renaissance Studies, 1999.

———. "Curing the Soul: Anne Lock's Authorial Medicine." *Reformation* 2 (1997): 7–38.

Hannay, Margaret P. "'Unlock my lipps': the *Miserere mei Dei* of Anne Vaughan Lok and Mary Sidney Herbert, Countess of Pembroke." *Privileging Gender in Early Modern England.* Ed. Jean R. Brink. Kirksville, MO: Sixteenth Century Journal Publishers, 1993. 19–36.

Woods, Susanne. "Anne Lock and Aemilia Lanyer: A Tradition of Protestant Women Speaking." *Form and Reform in Renaissance England: Essays in Honor of Barbara Kiefer Lewalski.* Ed. Amy Boesky and Mary Thomas Crane. Newark: U of Delaware P, 1999.

Henry Lok

Roche, Thomas P. *Petrarch and the English Sonnet Sequence.* New York: AMS, 1989.

John Lyly

Bond, R. Warwick, ed. *The Complete Works of John Lyly.* 3 vols. Oxford: Clarendon, 1902.

Pincombe, Michael, ed. *The Plays of John Lyly: Eros and Eliza.* New York: Manchester UP, 1996.

Vanhoutte, Jacqueline. "A Strange Hatred of Marriage: John Lyly, Elizabeth I, and the Ends of Comedy." *The Single Woman in Medieval and Early Modern England: Her Life and Representation.* Ed. Laurel Amtower and Dorothea Kehler. Tempe, AZ: Arizona Center for Medieval and Renaissance Studies, 2003. 97–115.

Christopher Marlowe

Stump, Donald. "Marlowe's Travesty of Virgil: *Dido* and Elizabethan Dreams of Empire." *Comparative Drama* 34 (Spring 2000): 79–107.

Williams, Deanne. "Dido, Queen of England." *English Literary History* 73 (2006): 31–59.

Richard Mulcaster

Breitenberg, Mark. "'. . . the hole matter opened': Iconic Representation and Interpretation in 'The Quenes Majesties Passage.'" *Criticism* 28 (1986): 1–25.

Hoak, Dale. "Tudor Deborah? The Coronation of Elizabeth I, Parliament, and the Problem of

Female Rule." *John Foxe and his World*. Ed. Christopher Highley and John N. King. Aldershot: Ashgate, 2002. 73–88.

Kinney, Arthur F., ed. *The Queen's Majesty's Passage. Renaissance Drama: An Anthology of Plays and Entertainments*. Oxford: Blackwell, 1999. 17–34.

Leahy, William. "Propaganda or a Record of Events? Richard Mulcaster's *The Passage of Our Most Drad Soveraigne Lady Quene Elyzabeth through the Citie of London to Westminster the Daye before Her Corunacion." Early Modern Literary Studies* 9.1 (2003): 20 paragraphs.

Logan, Sandra. "Making History: The Rhetorical and Historical Occasion of Elizabeth Tudor's Coronation Entry." *Journal of Medieval and Early Modern Literary Studies* 31 (2001): 251–82.

Warkentin, Germaine, ed. *The Queen's Majesty's Passage and Related Documents*. By Richard Mulcaster, et al. Toronto: Center for Reformation and Renaissance Studies, 2004.

Thomas Norton

Shaw, Barry. "Thomas Norton's 'Devices' for a Godly Realm: An Elizabethan Vision for the Future," *Sixteenth Century Journal* 22.3 (1991): 495–509.

"Peddler's Tale"

Colthorpe, Marion, "A Pedlar's Tale to Queen Elizabeth I," *Records of Early English Drama* 10.2 (1985): 1–5.

George Peele

Braunmuller, A. R. *George Peele*. Boston: Twayne, 1983.

Horne, David H., ed. *The Life and Minor Works of George Peele*. New Haven: Yale UP, 1952.

Lady Diana Primrose

McBride, Kari Boyd. "Diana Primrose." *Seventeenth-Century British Nondramatic Poets*. 2nd. Ser. Ed. M. Thomas Hester. Detroit: Gale, 1993, 222–26.

Wynne-Davies, Marion, ed. *Women Poets of the Renaissance*. London: J. M. Dent, 1998. 229–38, 328–37, 364–66.

Grorge Puttenham

Gim, Lisa. "Blasoning 'the princesse Paragon': The Workings of George Puttenham's 'False semblant' in His *Partheniades* to Queen Elizabeth." *Modern Language Studies* 28.3 (1998): 75–89.

Sir Walter Ralegh

Latham, Agnes M. C. *The Poems of Sir Walter Ralegh*. London: Routledge & Kegan Paul, 1951.

May, Steven W. *Sir Walter Ralegh*. Boston: Twayne, 1989.

• Rudick, Michael. *The Poems of Sir Walter Ralegh: A Historical Edition*. Tempe: Arizona Center for Medieval and Renaissance Studies, Renaissance Early English Text Society, 1999.

Stillman, Robert E. "'Words Cannot Knytt': Language and Desire in Ralegh's 'The Ocean to Cynthia'." *SEL: Studies in English Literature, 1500–1900* 27 (1987): 35–51.

James Sanford

Felch, Susan M. "'Noble Gentlewomen Famous for Their Learning.'" *ANQ: A Quarterly Journal of Short Articles, Notes, and Reviews* 16.2 (2003): 14–19.

Jane Seager

Malay, Jessica L. "Jane Seager's Sibylline Poems: Maidenly Negotiations Through Elizabethan Gift Exchange [with text]." *English Literary Renaissance* 36.2 (2006): 173–88.

William Shakespeare

Richmond, Hugh Macrae. "Elizabeth I in Shakespeare's Henry VIII." *Queen Elizabeth I: Past and Present*. Ed. Christa Jansohn. Münster, Germany: LIT, 2004. 45–58.

Sir Philip Sidney

Duncan-Jones, Katherine. *Sir Philip Sidney, Courtier Poet*. New Haven: Yale UP, 1991.

Moore, Dennis. "Philisides and Mira: Autobiographical Allegory in the Old *Arcadia." Spenser Studies* 3 (1982): 125–37.

Quilligan, Maureen. "Sidney and His Queen." *The Historical Renaissance: New Essays on Tudor and Stuart Literature and Culture*. Ed. Heather Dubrow and Richard Strier. Chicago: U of Chicago P, 1988. 171–96.

Van Dorsten, Jan [Adrianus]. "Recollections: Sidney's Ister Bank Poem." *Between Dream and Nature: Essays on Utopia and Dystopia*. Ed. Dominic Baker-Smith and C. C. Barfoot. Amsterdam: Rodopi, 1987. 47–60.

Elizabeth Southwell

• Loomis, Catherine. "Elizabeth Southwell's Manuscript Account of the Death of Queen Elizabeth." *English Literary Renaissance* 26.3 (1996): 482–509.

Edmund Spenser
Brooks-Davies, Douglas. *Edmund Spenser: Selected Shorter Poems*. London: Longman, 1995.
Cain, Thomas H. *Praise in "The Faerie Queene."* Lincoln: U of Nebraska P, 1978.
Greenlaw, Edwin, Charles Grosvenor Osgood, Frederick Morgan Padelford, eds. *The Works of Edmund Spenser: A Variorum Edition*. 11 vols. Baltimore: Johns Hopkins UP, 1935–57.
Hamilton, A. C., Hiroshi Yamaschita, and Toshiyuki Suzuki, eds. *Edmund Spenser: The Faerie Queene*. Harlow, Eng.: Longman, 2001.
McLane, Paul E. *Spenser's "Shepheardes Calender": A Study in Elizabethan Allegory*. Notre Dame: U of Notre Dame P, 1961.
Montrose, Louis A. "'Eliza, Queene of Shepheardes' and the Pastoral of Power." *English Literary Renaissance* 10 (1980): 153–82.
Oram, William. "Spenser in Search of an Audience: The Kathleen Williams Lecture for 2004." *Spenser Studies* 20 (2005): 23–47.
Oram, William A., *et al.*, eds. *The Yale Edition of the Shorter Poems of Edmund Spenser*. New Haven: Yale UP, 1989.
Stump, Donald. "Isis Versus Mercilla: The Allegorical Shrines in Spenser's Legend of Justice." *Spenser Studies* 3 (1982): 87–98.
———. "The Two Deaths of Mary Stuart: Historical Allegory in Spenser's Book of Justice." *Spenser Studies* 9 (1991): 81–105.
Walker, Julia M. "From Allegory to Icon: Teaching Britomart with the Elizabeth Portraits." *Approaches to Teaching Spenser's "Faerie Queene."* Ed. David Lee Miller and Alexander Dunlop. New York: MLA, 1994. 106–116.
Wells, Robin Headlam. *Spenser's "Faerie Queene" and the Cult of Elizabeth*. London: Croom Helm, 1983.

Mary Stuart
Phillips, James Emerson. *Images of a Queen: Mary Stuart in Sixteenth-Century Literature*. Berkeley: U of California P, 1964.

John Stubbs
Bell, Ilona. "'Soueraigne Lord of Lordly Lady of This Land': Elizabeth, Stubbs, and the *Gaping Gulf*." *Dissing Elizabeth: Negative Representations of Gloriana*. Ed. Julia M. Walker. Durham, NC: Duke UP, 1998. 99–117.
Stubbs, John. *The Gaping Gulf; with Letters and Other Relevant Documents*. Ed. Lloyd E. Berry. Charlottesville: U of Virginia P, 1968.

Elizabeth Tyrwhit
Felch, Susan M., ed. *Elizabeth Tyrwhit's Morning and Evening Prayers*. Burlington, VT: Ashgate. 2008.

William Whittingham
Gribben, Crawford. "Deconstructing the Geneva Bible: The Search for a Puritan Poetic." *Literature and Theology* 14.1 (2000): 1–16.

Robert Wyngfield
Lewis, Jayne Elizabeth, ed. *The Trial of Mary Queen of Scots: A Brief History with Documents*. Boston: Bedford, St. Martin's, 1999.

ELIZABETH'S LATER RECEPTION AND INFLUENCE

Abbott, Reginald. "Rough with Rubies: Virginia Woolf and the Virgin Queen." *Virginia Woolf: Reading the Renaissance*. Ed. Sally Greene. Athens, OH: Ohio UP, 1999. 65–88.
• Betteridge, Thomas. "A Queen for All Seasons." *The Myth of Elizabeth*. Ed. Susan Doran and Thomas S. Freeman. Houndmills, Eng.: Palgrave Macmillan, 2003. 243–59.
Dobson, Michael, and Nicola J. Watson. *England's Elizabeth: An Afterlife in Fame and Fantasy*. Oxford: Oxford UP, 2002.
Doran, Susan, and Freeman, Thomas S. *The Myth of Elizabeth*. Basingstoke, Eng.: Palgrave Macmillan, 2003.
Hageman, Elizabeth H., and Katherine Conway, eds. *Resurrecting Elizabeth I in Seventeenth-Century England*. Madison, NJ: Fairleigh Dickinson UP, 2007.
Lee, Christopher. *1603: The Death of Queen Elizabeth, the Return of the Black Plague, the Rise of Shakespeare, Piracy, Witchcraft, & the Birth of the Stuart Era*. New York: St. Martin's, 2003.
Perry, Curtis. "The Citizen Politics of Nostalgia: Queen Elizabeth in Early Jacobean London." *Journal of Medieval and Renaissance Studies* 23 (1993): 89–111.
Pigeon, Renée. "'No Man's Elizabeth': The Virgin Queen in Recent Films." *Retrovisions: Reinventing the Past in Film and Fiction*. Ed. Deborah Cartmell, I. Q. Hunter, and Imelda Whelehan. London, England: Pluto, 2001. 8–24.
Rozett, Martha Tuck. *Constructing a World: Shakespeare's England and the New Historical Fiction*. Albany: State U of New York P, 2003.
van den Berg, Sara. "The Passing of the Elizabethan Court." *Ben Jonson Journal* 1 (1994): 31–61.
Walker, Julia. *The Elizabethan Icon, 1603–2003*. New York: Palgrave Macmillan, 2004.

Watkins, John. *Representing Elizabeth in Stuart England: Literature, History, Sovereignty.* Cambridge and New York: Cambridge UP, 2002.

SELECTED FILMS ABOUT ELIZABETH AND HER REIGN

Black Adder II. Dir. Mandie Fletcher. Perf. Miranda Richardson. BBC Television, 1986.
The Body of the Queen. Episode 7. *A History of Britain.* Pres. and Dir. Simon Schama. BBC/History Channel, 2000.
Elizabeth. Dir. Steven Clarke and Mark Fielder. Pres. David Starkey. BBC/Channel 4, 2001.
Elizabeth. Dir. Shekar Kapur. Perf. Cate Blanchett, Geoffrey Rush. Polygram Entertainment/-Channel Four Films/ Working Title, 1998.
Elizabeth I. Dir. Sue Hayes. Satel Documentary Production for A&E Network, 1996.
Elizabeth I. Dir: Tom Hooper. Perf. Helen Mirren, Jeremy Irons. HBO Films, 2005.
Elizabeth I—The Virgin Queen. Dir. Coky Giedroyc. Perf. Anne-Marie Duff, Tara Fitzgerald. Masterpiece Theatre/WGBH, 2005.
Elizabeth R. Dir. Donald McWhinnie, Claude Whatham, and Herbert Wise. Perf. Glenda Jackson, Ronald Hines. BBC Video, 1971.
Elizabeth Rex. Dir. Barbara Willis Sweete. Perf. Diane D'Aquila. Rhombus Media/CBC Home Video, 2002.
Fire Over England. Dir. William K. Howard. Perf. Laurence Olivier, Vivien Leigh, Flora Robson. Home Vision Entertainment, 1937.
Orlando. Dir. Sally Potter. Perf. Tilda Swinton, Quentin Crisp. Sony, 1993.
Private Lives of Elizabeth and Essex. Dir. Michael Curtiz. Perf. Bette Davis, Errol Flynn. Warner Home Video, 1939.
Queen Elizabeth. Dir. Louis Mercanton. Perf. Sarah Bernhardt. Grapevine Video, 1912.
Roberto Devereux. Dir. Tito Capobianco. Perf. Beverly Sills. VAI, 1975.
Shakespeare in Love. Dir. John Madden. Perf. Gwyneth Paltrow, Judi Dench. Miramax, 1998.
Sea Hawk. Dir. Michael Curtiz. Perf. Errol Flynn, Flora Robson. MGM/UA, 1940.
Virgin Queen, The. Dir. Henry Koster. Perf. Bette Davis, Richard Todd. Twentieth Century Fox, 1955.
Young Bess. Dir. George Sidney. Perf. Jean Simmons, Stewart Granger. MGM/UA, 1953.

Glossary of Names

The following names are from the Bible, Classical history, and Classical myth. Within entries in the glossary, boldface type indicates names that appear elsewhere in the listing.

Abel: see **Cain**.

Abiathar: see **Absalom**.

Abner: see **Joab**.

Abraham: father of the Jewish nation through his son Isaac, whose mother was **Sarah**.

Absalom: son of King **David**, who aspired to the throne of Israel and led a rebellion with the help, among others, of **Abiathar** the priest.

Achates: see **Aeneas**.

Achilles: Greek warrior who defeated Hector to win the Trojan war. He was slain when **Paris**, the cause of the war, shot an arrow into his only vulnerable spot, his heel.

Adam: the first human, created out of the dust of the ground and animated by the breath of God; in the biblical account, the name refers both to male and female (Genesis 1) and to the first man (Genesis 2).

Aeneas: hero of the Trojan war who later won and broke the heart of **Dido**, queen of Carthage. With his son **Ascanius**, his friend **Achates**, and his companions **Sergestus**, **Ilioneus**, and **Cloanthus**, he founded Rome. His great-grandson, **Brutus**, is said to have established Troynovant (New Troy), later known as London.

Aeolus: god of the winds.

Ahab: king of Israel known for corruption under the influence of his wife **Jezebel**, who worshipped the god **Baal**. When **Naboth** refused to sell Ahab his vineyard, and thus his birthright, Jezebel arranged his death and seized the property, leading the prophet **Elijah** to curse her. After persecuting him, she died at the hands of **Jehu**, and the dogs devoured her body.

Ahaz: king of Israel who made his son pass through fire in a heathen ritual.

Aholiab: along with the architect **Bezaleel**, one of the builders of the ancient Jewish Tabernacle.

Ajax: the largest and strongest of the Greek warriors who besieged Troy.

Alcibiades: Athenian politician and guardian of Pericles, the great ruler of the city.

Alexander the Great: king of Macedonia who conquered vast territories in Asia Minor, North Africa, and parts of India, bringing Greek domination and culture to all but the last of these areas.

Amazons: a tribe of women famous in classical literature for their disdain of marriage, refusal to be subject to men, and prowess as warriors. See also **Penthesilea** and **Camilla**.

Anna: see **Dido**.

Antaeus: a giant, the son of **Poseidon** and the earth goddess Ge. In wrestling with **Hercules**, he rose up stronger from every fall because he was given strength by his mother. Hercules killed him by holding him up and crushing him.

Antichrist: the great enemy of Christians, prophesied in the New Testament to appear in the last days and often identified in this period with the Pope or his servants.

Antiochus Epiphanes: Seleucid king who sacrificed a pig on the high altar at the temple in Jerusalem, thus igniting the revolt of the Maccabees.

Aphrodite: see **Venus**.

Apollo (Phoebus):   god of poetry, music, archery, healing, care of flocks, and prophecy. He is associated with the sun and enlightened principles of justice, morality, philosophy, and religion.

Argus (Argos):   herdsman with eyes over all his body. When **Jupiter** turned his human lover Io into a heifer to conceal her, his wife **Juno** set Argus to guard her from his advances. When Jupiter's servant **Mercury** devised a way to kill Argus, Juno honored the herdsman by placing his eyes in the tail feathers of the peacock.

Ariadne: daughter of **Pasiphae** and Minos, the king of Crete, who required of Athens a yearly human sacrifice to the **Minotaur**, a monster who lived at the heart of a labyrinth. Ariadne aided **Theseus** in killing the monster and ending the tribute by providing him with a thread to guide him out of the monster's lair. On his return to Athens, Theseus abandoned Ariadne on the island of Naxos, where she married **Bacchus**.

Aries: see **Mars**.

Aristotle: Greek philosopher and student of Plato. He was the tutor to **Alexander the Great**.

Artemis: see **Cynthia**.

Artemisia: female counselor to **Xerxes I**, who urged him not to fight the Greeks in the battle of Salamis in the fifth century B.C.E.

Arthur: legendary king of England and founder of the order of knights known as the Round Table. The Tudor monarchs liked to derive their Welsh lineage from the royal line of Arthur and his mythic ancestors.

Asa: king of Judah who removed male cult prostitutes and altars to foreign gods. As a religious reformer he was sometimes compared to Elizabeth.

Ascanius: see **Aeneas**.

Aspasia: fifth-century consort of the Athenian politician Pericles, often criticized for her public influence.

Astraea: virgin goddess of justice, the daughter of **Jupiter** and **Themis**. After the Ages of Gold and Silver, she withdrew to heaven at the beginning of the Iron Age, when human violence and injustice become intolerable. She is identified with the constellation **Virgo**, which provided her name (Greek, "starry maid"). In her own day, Elizabeth was commonly associated with Astraea.

Athalia: queen of Judah; daughter of **Jezebel** and **Ahab**. In the ninth century B.C.E., she usurped the throne of Judah by killing all the heirs except the infant **Joash**, who was rescued by the priest **Jehoida**.

Athena: see **Minerva**.

Atropos: see **Fates**.

Aurelian: see **Zenobia**.

Aureola: see **Fairy Queen**.

Aurora: goddess of the dawn, daughter of the giant Hyperion and mother of Memnon, for whose death at the hands of **Achilles**, her tears fall each day as the morning dew. Since Elizabeth was seen as bringing in a new day for England, she was sometimes associated with Aurora.

Baal: god of the Phoenicians and Canaanites, worshipped in opposition to Jehovah in the period of the Judges and Kings of Israel and Judah. Used by sixteenth-century Protestants as a symbol for Roman Catholic practices that they thought idolatrous.

Babylon: city-state that conquered the kingdom of Judah in the sixth century B.C.E., destroying the temple and instigating the seventy-year "Babylonian Captivity." In the Book of Revelation, it is the city of the **Antichrist** and the source of persecution against the true church. Early modern Protestants often identified it with the Roman Catholic Church.

Bacchus (Dionysus): god of wine, music, and dramatic poetry. His female adherents, known as Bacchae, held secret woodland religious rites involving drinking, ecstatic dancing, and the tearing and eating of raw flesh. He was celebrated as a bringer of justice to uncivilized peoples.

Balaam: reluctant prophet who took money from Balak, King of Moab, to curse Israel but was rebuked by God, who sent an angel to frighten his donkey, leading the beast to complain in human speech.

Barak: see **Deborah**.

Bashan: the kingdom of Og, formerly known for its giants, conquered by the Israelites under the leadership of Moses.

Beelzebub: see **Satan**.

Belinus (Belin): king of Britain, elder son of Dunvallo. Geoffrey of Monmouth records the legend that, after warring with his brother **Brennius**, they joined forces to conquer Gaul, Rome, and parts of Germany.

Bellerophon: son of Glaucus who, on a visit to King Proteus, temperately rejected the adulterous advances of the Queen, Anteia. When Bellerophon attempted to ride his winged horse, Pegasus, to heaven, **Jupiter** sent a gadfly to sting the steed and cause him to buck his expert rider off.

Bellona: goddess of war.

Belphoebe: see **Cynthia**.

Bezaleel: see **Aholiab**.

Boadicia: legendary Queen of England, based on the first-century Queen Boudicca, wife of Prasutagus (Arviragus), King of the Iceni, who rebelled against the Romans. Her daughter **Voadicia** also led successful attacks during the insurrection.

Brennius: see **Belinius**.

Brutus: great-grandson of **Aeneas** and legendary first king of Britain, who founded Troynovant (New Troy), later known as London.

Caesar (Gaius Julius): Roman general, politician, and dictator of the first century B.C.E., whose histories of the Gallic and Roman civil wars provided models of classic historiography.

Caesar Augustus (Gaius Julius Caesar Octavianus): First Roman Emperor, who defeated Marc Antony to rule alone and rebuild Rome after a time of civil war. He ushered in its Golden Age, a long period of peace and plenty marked by literary, cultural, and civic achievements.

Cain: eldest son of **Adam** and Eve, who killed his brother **Abel** when the latter offered a more suitable sacrifice to God. As the primeval murderer, he was branded and exiled but not put to death. He was seen as the progenitor of those who opposed the people of God.

Calliopê: see **Muses**.

Camilla: maiden warrior who fought on the side of Turnus in **Virgil**'s *Aeneid*. Often treated as an **Amazon**, she is renowned for her swiftness of foot.

Cancer: astrological sign associated with the constellation known as the Crab.

Cassius (Gaius Cassius Longinus): distinguished Roman senator and military commander who conspired with the Roman Brutus to assassinate **Caesar**.

Castor and Pollux: twin gods associated with the astrological sign **Gemini**, which appears in the spring and indicates good sailing weather.

Cerberus: the three-headed dog who guarded the entrance to Hades.

Ceres: see **Proserpina**.

Chimera: fire-breathing monster, pictured either as having a lion's head, a goat's body, and a serpent's tail or else as having the heads of a lion, a goat, and a serpent. It was killed by **Bellerophon**.

Cicero (Marcus Tullius Cicero, or Tully):   orator and statesman of the first century B.C.E. valued for his literary style and his political wisdom.

Circe: enchantress who held **Ulysses** captive on the island of Calypso, where men, in their desire for her, were turned into beasts.

Cleobulina: female Greek poet who composed enigmas in hexameter verse.

Clio: see **Muses**.

Cloanthus: see **Aeneas**.

Clotho: see **Fates**.

Corinna: female Greek lyric poet who flourished in the fifth century B.C.E.

Cornelia: daughter of the Roman general **Scipio Africanus Major**, she is known for educating her sons, the Gracchi brothers, in Greek culture prior to their rebellion against the rulers of Rome in second century B.C.E.

Croesus: legendary king of Lydia, known for his fabulous riches. The Greek historian Herodotus records an exchange about wealth between Croesus and the Athenian wiseman Solon.

Cronus: see **Saturn**.

Cupid (Eros):   god of erotic desire. The son of **Mercury** and **Venus** and husband of Psyche, he is commonly represented armed with a bow and two sorts of arrows: one tipped with lead that arouses lust, and the other tipped with gold that causes love.

Cynthia (Artemis, Diana, Phoebe):   Diana is the virgin goddess of the moon, daughter of **Jupiter** and Leto and sister of **Apollo**. A patron of wildlife, virgins, and the very young, she is also associated with women and childbirth because of correlations between the lunar cycle and menstruation. She is often portrayed as a huntress accompanied by a band of nymphs. The name Cynthia—popular in comparisons between the moon goddess and the Queen in the Elizabethan period—comes from Cynthus, a mountain in the Greek island of Delos associated with Artemis. **Phoebe** ("bright one") was originally a Titaness and the grandmother of Artemis, but the two are often confused, as are Cynthia, **Hecatê**, and **Selênê**.

Daniel: prophet in Judah and Babylon, best known for his visions and for his delivery from King Darius's den of lions.

David: second king of Israel, father of **Solomon**, and ancestor of Jesus. As a singer and player of the harp, he is said to have written many of the biblical Psalms. He is celebrated as a paragon of kings, skillful and courageous in defeating Goliath and Israel's other enemies and godly in ruling his people. His chief lapse was adultery with Bathsheba and involvement in her husband's death. Assisted by his general **Joab**, he survived rebellions led by **Abner**, **Sheba**, and his own son, **Absalom**. His love of poetry, skill in ruling, long reign, and success in overcoming rebels made him a frequent subject of literary comparisons with Elizabeth.

Deborah: biblical judge and prophet of Israel. With **Barak**, she defeated a superior army commanded by **Sisera**, a Canaanite in the service of King Jabin. Afterwards, she composed a famous victory song. Elizabethans saw parallels with their own militant Queen, who likewise defeated a great invading power (the Spanish Armada) and devised a song about the victory.

Dedalus: Athenian inventor. He devised the figure of a cow in which **Pasiphae** mated with a bull and conceived the **Minotaur**, after which he built the Labyrinth to contain the monster. He also created wings so that he and his son, **Icarus**, could fly.

Demosthenes: fourth-century B.C.E. Greek statesman and orator who attempted to mobilize the Athenians against Philip II of Macedon and his son, **Alexander the Great.**

Destinies: see **Fates.**

Deucalion: son of **Prometheus** and ancestor of the Hellenic peoples of Greece. When **Zeus** sent a flood to destroy sinful mankind, Deucalion built a boat to save himself and his wife **Pyrrha.** Afterward, an oracle told them to throw "the bones of their mother" (the earth) over their shoulders. The stones then turned into men and women.

Diana (Diane): see **Cynthia.**

Dido: legendary founder and queen of the ancient empire of Carthage. She was celebrated for her wise rule. According to **Virgil's** *Aeneid,* having fallen in love with **Aeneas,** she burned herself alive after he obeyed a divine decree that he leave Carthage to found Rome. Her sister was **Anna.** Elizabethans associated Dido with Elizabeth, whom they saw as founder of a new empire that set itself apart from Rome. At the time of the French marriage negotiations in the late 1570s, they played on Dido's tragic love affair in warning against the match.

Diogenes: fourth-century B.C.E. Greek cynic who promoted an austere lifestyle.

Dionysus: see **Bacchus.**

Diotima: legendary priestess and teacher of **Socrates.** Her views of love are recorded in **Plato's** *Symposium.*

Dryads (Hamadryads): nymphs of trees.

Dunvallo Molmutius (Dunwallo): legendary king of Cornwall, who conquered neighboring rulers to become the first King of all Britain. According to Geoffrey of Monmouth, he established the Molmutine Laws and his sons **Belinus** and **Brennius** conquered Gaul and Rome.

Elijah (Elia): biblical prophet who confronted **Ahab** and **Jezebel** and whose name led to witty comparisons with Eli[zabeth].

Elisha: biblical prophet and successor of **Elijah,** whose name was also elided with that of Eliza[beth].

Elizabeth: mother of **John the Baptist** and wife of the priest **Zechariah,** who lost his ability to speak for nine months when he doubted the angel's announcement that he would have a son. His canticle, recorded in Luke 1, was sung during Morning Prayer. Elizabeth was cousin to the Virgin **Mary** and welcomed her during their pregnancies.

Endymion: shepherd of extraordinary beauty who asked the gods that he be allowed to sleep forever and never age. He was loved by Selênê (or **Cynthia**), the moon goddess, who returned every night to embrace him as he slept.

Ephraim: younger son of the Hebrew patriarch **Joseph.** With his brother Manasseh, he founded the tribe of Joseph, one of the twelve tribes of Israel.

Erinna: Greek poet and friend of **Sappho.** She flourished around 600 B.C.E.

Esau: see **Jacob.**

Esther (Hester): Hebrew wife of the Persian emperor Ahasuerus (or Xerxes). Following the advice of her uncle **Mordecai,** she foiled a plot by the royal councilor **Haman** to destroy her people. The event is commemorated in the Old Testament Book of Esther and in the Jewish festival of Purim. As queen and saviour of her people, Elizabeth was sometimes compared to her.

Eurialus: see **Nisus.**

Europa: daughter of Agênôr, King of Tyre on the eastern end of the Mediterranean. **Jupiter,** who desired her, came to her in the form of a bull so gentle that she climbed on its back. The continent of Europe bears her name, and the constellation **Taurus** is named for the bull.

Eve: first woman, created by God from the rib of **Adam**.

Fabius (Quintus Fabius Maximus Rullianus): successful Roman general of the fourth-century C.E. condemned for failing to obey orders.

Fairy Queen (Aureola, Gloriana, Titania): in medieval romance and folklore, an immortal figure with wings and magical powers, visualized both as human-sized and tiny. In some sources, she is the wife of **Oberon**. Her various names mean "halo of light" (**Aureola**), "glory" (**Gloriana**), and "female Titan" (**Titania**). All of them were used of Elizabeth, who was often depicted as the Fairy Queen.

Fates: three sisters, the daughters of Night (or of **Jupiter** and **Themis**), who decide at birth each person's allotment of years. In spinning the thread of life and bringing it to an end, **Clotho** holds the distaff, **Lachesis** draws it off, and **Atropos** cuts it.

Faunus (Pan): woodland god of flocks and shepherds, represented with the lower body and horns of a goat. When he sought to rape the nymph **Syrinx**, she prayed to the gods for help and was transformed into the musical pipe with which he is associated. The terror of being left alone in wild places, known as Panic fear, was said to be his doing.

Flora: Roman goddess of fertility and flowering plants.

Fortune: goddess of change and luck, often represented turning a wheel that raises some people up to worldly prosperity and fame and carries others down to ruin.

Furies: primordial beings who avenge crime, particularly between kin. Their names are Alecto, Megaera, and Tisiphone. Generated by the blood of the mutilated **Uranus**, they are often represented as winged women wreathed with snakes.

Galba (Servius Sulpicius Galba): Roman emperor who succeeded Nero. He was known for his military prowess and his willingness to stand against the corrupt system of bribing soldiers to secure their loyalty. He was overthrown in consequence.

Gemini: see **Castor and Pollux**.

Gideon: biblical judge of Israel who defeated a vastly superior Midianite army with a band of 300 soldiers.

Gloriana: see **Fairy Queen**.

Gorgons: winged female monsters with hideous faces and snakes in their hair, whose gaze turned mortals to stone.

Graces: in Greek mythology, personifications of loveliness and charm of the sort seen in flowers and the young. Usually said to be daughters of **Zeus** and **Hera**, the best known are Euphrosynê ("joy"), Aglaia ("radiance"), and Thalia ("flowering").

Gurgunt (Gurguntius): legendary British king, son of **Belinus** and founder of the city of Norwich. According to Geoffrey of Monmouth, he pillaged Denmark after its king (**Gutlack**) refused to pay him tribute.

Gutlack: see **Gurgunt**.

Haggai: see **Zerubbabel**.

Hamadryads: see **Dryads**.

Haman: see **Esther**.

Hamor: Hivite prince whose son, Shechem, raped Dinah, the only daughter of the biblical patriarch **Jacob**.

Harpy: a monster known for its rapacity and filth, which combined the head and body of a woman with the wings and claws of a bird. It served as an instrument of divine vengeance.

Hecatê: patron goddess of the underworld, the moon, and women, who is sometimes regarded as having the power to control fate. Often confused with **Diana** and other lunar goddesses, she is the goddess of crossroads, often portrayed with three heads facing in different directions.

Hector: son of **Priam** and **Hecuba** and greatest of the Trojan heroes. In **Homer**'s *Iliad*, Achilles kills him in the climactic battle of the Trojan War.

Hecuba: wife of King **Priam** of Troy and mother of **Hector, Paris**, and many other sons. She revenged the murder of her son **Polydorus** by pricking out the eyes of his killer, **Polymestor**.

Helen: see **Paris**.

Helios: see **Phaeton**.

Hellê: see **Phrixus**.

Hengist: legendary Germanic conqueror of England. According to Geoffrey of Monmouth, he and his brother Horsa were the first Saxons to arrive in the British Isles.

Hera: see **Juno**.

Heracles: see **Hercules**.

Hercules (Heracles): greatest of the Greek heroes, the son of **Jupiter** and the mortal woman Alcmenê. Hated by **Juno**, he won immortality by performing for her twelve labors requiring superhuman strength. His slaughter of the great Nemean Lion is called to mind by the constellation **Leo**, supposed to have the lion's shape.

Hero: priestess of Aphrodite at Sestos, a city on the Hellespont, the strait between modern-day Turkey and Greece. Beloved of **Leander**, who lived in Abydos on the other side, she guided him each night with a torch as he swam to visit her. When he drowned in a storm, she cast herself into the sea.

Herod: see **Mary**.

Hesiod: Greek writer of the seventh century B.C.E., author of *Theogony* and *Works and Days*.

Hesperus: son of Eos and personification of the evening star, **Venus**.

Hester: see **Esther**.

Hezekiah: king of Judah who restored the Temple and was miraculously rescued from Sennacherib, King of Assyria. He was famous for tearing down the brass serpent made by Moses during the exodus from Egypt. His religious zeal was often compared to that of Elizabeth in her reform of the English Church.

Hippolytus: son of **Theseus** and Antiope, whose stepmother, **Phaedra**, fell in love with him, leading to his eventual death.

Hiram: king of Tyre who sent cedar wood and craftsmen to Jerusalem to assist Solomon in building the first Temple in Jerusalem. Also the name of the craftsman who made metal implements for the Temple.

Holofernes: see **Judith**.

Homer: blind Greek poet thought to have lived sometime between the seventh and ninth centuries B.C.E. He is reputed to be the author of two epics, the *Iliad* and the *Odyssey*.

Hortensius: Roman orator of the first century C.E., whose daughter, Hortensia, gave an important speech against taxation of women without representation.

Hours (Seasons): three daughters of **Jupiter** and **Themis** (Spring, Summer, and Winter), who preside over the changes of the seasons. In Hesiod, they are identified differently, as Justice, Good Order, and Peace.

Huldah: prophetess during the reign of King **Josiah** of Judah.

Hymen (Hymeneus): the god of marriage.

Icarus: son of **Dedalus**, who devised wings so that he could fly. When Icarus disobeyed his father and flew too close to the sun, the wax in his wings melted and he plunged to his death in the sea.

Ilioneus: see **Aeneas**.

Ino: see **Phrixus**.

Iphigenia: daughter of Agamemnon and Clytemnestra, sacrificed by her father in return for the favorable wind needed to drive his ships to Asia so that the Greeks could fight the Trojan War. She was seen as an early example of a virgin martyr.

Iris: goddess of the rainbow and messenger of the gods, particularly **Juno**.

Isis: wife of **Osiris**, Egyptian god of the underworld and the son of Keb (Earth) and Nut (Sky). Osiris is patron of law, science, writing, and the arts. Isis, who is tangentially connected with the constellation **Virgo** and with the moon, was said to rule with him, bringing justice to the poor. Both were also worshipped in Greece and Rome.

Israel: the name given to **Jacob** when he returned to Canaan after fleeing Esau. Also the name of the entire Hebrew nation until its division under Rehoboam and **Jeroboam**. Thereafter, the name designates the ten northern tribes.

Ishbosheth: see **Joab**.

Jabin: see **Deborah**.

Jacob: second son of the biblical patriarch Isaac by his wife Rebecca. By cajoling and tricking his elder twin, **Esau**, he received the birthright and blessing usually reserved for the firstborn son. Later, by tricking his father-in-law Laban, he gained great wealth. As the father of the patriarchs who founded the twelve tribes of **Israel**, his name sometimes denotes the nation as a whole.

Jael: Kenite woman who killed the Canaanite general **Sisera** following the defeat of his army by **Deborah** and **Barak**. After luring the exhausted general into her tent to drink milk and rest, she drove a tent peg through his temple as he slept.

James: see **John**.

Janus: Roman god of beginnings (of the month, of the new year, and so on), often represented with two heads, looking inward and outward at a gate. The doors of his temple stood open in time of war and closed in time of peace.

Jason: mythic leader of the Argonauts (men of the ship *Argo*, including **Hercules** and Orpheus), who sailed from Thessaly to Colchis on the Black Sea to bring back the golden fleece of a legendary winged ram. Aided by the local king's treacherous daughter Medea, Jason performed heroic tasks, including planting dragon's teeth that turned into soldiers. He escaped to Greece with her and the fleece.

Jehoida: see **Joash**.

Jehoshaphat: king of Judah and the son of **Asa**, who began well but later made an alliance with the ungodly kings of the northern kingdom of Israel.

Jehu: king of Israel chosen by **Elijah** the prophet to destroy the evil house of King **Ahab** and Queen **Jezebel**.

Jeremiah: biblical prophet of the southern kingdom of Judah, often persecuted for his unpopular pronouncements and known as the "weeping prophet" for his lamentations.

Jeroboam: first king of the northern kingdom of Israel after its division from the southern kingdom of Judah. Jeroboam established an alternative form of worship, which included the creation of golden calves, to prevent his subjects from journeying to the temple in Jerusalem. As the progenitor of the faithless northern kings, he is often referred to by the epithet "Jeroboam, the son of Nebat, who caused Israel to sin."

Jesus Syriac: Jesus ben Sira, author of the apocryphal book of Ecclesiasticus, written in the second century B.C.E.

Jezebel: Phoenician wife of **Ahab**, King of Israel. She is known for her corrupting influence. When **Naboth** refused to sell a vineyard to Ahab, she brought about the innocent man's death. Seeking to establish the worship of **Baal**, she also contended with the Hebrew prophets **Elijah** and **Elisha** and was ultimately killed by **Jehu**.

Joab: son of Zeruiah, sister to King **David**, and the general of his uncle's army. Joab was instrumental in defeating three rebellions: those of **Sheba**, of **Absalom**, and of **Ishbosheth**, the son of **Saul** (whose forces were commanded by **Abner**).

Joash: king of Judah rescued from death by the priest **Jehoida**, who protected him until he could reclaim the throne from his grandmother, **Athalia**.

John: beloved disciple of Christ, known with his brother **James** as the "sons of thunder" and reputed to be author of the fourth Gospel as well as the Book of Revelation (or Apocalypse).

John the Baptist: see **Elizabeth**.

Jonah: Israelite prophet who refused to go to Nineveh and who, after being cast into the sea, was swallowed by a great fish. He is emblematic of both reluctant prophets and the death and resurrection of Christ.

Joseph (Josephus, patriarch):   a son of **Jacob**, he was sold by his brothers into slavery in Egypt. He later became **Pharoah**'s chief minister and saved his own family and many others by storing grain in response to a dream foretelling a great famine.

Joseph (husband of Mary):   see **Mary**.

Joshua: leader chosen by **Moses** to bring the Israelites into the Promised Land and drive out other peoples.

Josiah: king of Judah who restored the Temple, recovered the Law of **Moses,** and suppressed the worship of foreign gods. As a child king, he is often cited as a precedent for the young Protestant King Edward VI, Elizabeth's brother.

Jove: see **Jupiter**.

Judah: fourth son of **Jacob** and progenitor of the tribe of Israel that bears his name. From his line came **David** and ultimately Jesus. After the division of the kingdom, the name denotes the southern areas occupied by the tribes of Judah and Benjamin, including Jerusalem.

Judas: the disciple who betrayed Jesus for thirty pieces of silver.

Jude: author of an epistle in the New Testament that warns against heresies and rebellions.

Judith: heroine of the apocryphal Book of Judith. When the Persian commander **Holofernes** attacked Israel, Judith visited his tent by night, got him drunk, and cut off his head, after which Israel (under the leadership of Uzziah) routed his army. Because of her leadership and courage in opposing a powerful enemy, Judith was sometimes employed as a literary figure for Queen Elizabeth.

Juno (Hera):   wife of **Jupiter** and Queen of the Gods. As patron of queens and of women generally, she is associated with hearth and home, marriage and childbirth. Because one of her temples contained the Roman mint, she is also associated with money. Her bird is the peacock. Before Elizabeth became too old to marry, she was frequently compared with Juno.

Jupiter (Jove, Zeus):   ruler of the Olympian gods, associated with light, the sky, thunderbolts, victory, justice, and the order in the state. His tree is the oak and his bird the eagle, symbol of the rulers of Rome.

Justinus (Marcus Junianus):   Roman historian of the second or third century C.E., best known for his abridgement of the *Philippic History* of Trogus Pompeius.

Korah: see **Moses**.

Laban: see **Jacob**.

Lachesis: see **Fates**.

Laelius: friend of **Scipio Africanus** and military commander under him. His daughter Laelia is said to have been her father's equal in rhetorical skill.

Laomedon: treacherous king of Troy, who brought suffering on the city by cheating **Apollo** and the sea god **Poseidon** of payment for building its great walls and by defrauding **Hercules** after he defended it from a sea monster.

Latona: see **Niobe**.

Leander: see **Hero**.

Leo (Nemean Lion):   see **Hercules**.

Litae: aged daughters of **Zeus** who, according to **Homer**, follow his exiled daughter Atê ("folly" or "madness" and its attendant disorder), seeking to heal what she has harmed. Since they are lame, however, they cannot keep up with her.

Livy (Titus Livius):   first-century Roman historian who emphasized character and morality rather than politics; his style was widely admired and copied in the sixteenth century.

Lot: nephew of the patriarch **Abraham**, who chose to live in the city of Sodom and, with his two daughters, was rescued by an angel when God destroyed Sodom and its neighboring town, Gomorrah, with fire.

Lucifer: see **Satan**.

Luna: see **Cynthia**.

Manoah: see **Samson**.

Marcia (Martia):   legendary English queen who ruled as regent after the death of Guithelin, son of **Gurgunt**. According to Geoffrey of Monmouth, she wrote the code of laws known as the *Lex Martiana*.

Marcus Terentius: see **Varro**.

Mars (Aries):   god of war, the son of **Jupiter** and **Juno**. He had an illicit affair with **Venus**, wife of the lame god **Vulcan**.

Martia: see **Marcia**.

Mary: mother of Jesus and wife of **Joseph**. She conceived Jesus as a virgin by means of the Holy Spririt. After the child was born, Joseph took the young family into Egypt after an angel warned him that **Herod**, the ruler of Palestine, was planning to murder the infant.

Masinissa: a Numidian raised in Carthage who, in the third century C.E., joined the Romans in their attack on the north African city.

Melchizedek: priestly king who blessed **Abraham**, gave him bread and wine, and received tithes from him. Considered to be a prefiguring of Christ.

Meleager: one of the **Jason**'s celebrated seamen, the Argonauts. He is famous for slaying the Calydonian boar.

Melpomenê: see **Muses**.

Mercury (Hermes):   herald and messenger of the gods, and so associated with eloquence. He is the son of **Jupiter** and Maia and the patron deity of sleep and dreams, merchants and thieves.

Minerva (Pallas, Athena):   virgin goddess of wisdom and war and daughter of **Jupiter** and Metis. As the patron deity of ancient Athens and of Greek cities in general, she is associated with urban arts such as spinning and weaving. She is represented in armor, with a Gorgon's head on her shield. Queen Elizabeth was often compared with her.

Minotaur: a monster that was half man, half bull, the offspring of **Pasiphae**, Queen of Crete, and a bull sent by **Poseidon** to be a sacrifice. King Minos, the husband of Pasiphae, later required Athens to send him an annual tribute of young maidens, who were shut up with the monster in a labyrinth devised by **Dedalus**.

Mordecai: see **Esther**.

Moses: biblical prophet raised by the **Pharoah**'s daughter. He subsequently led the Israelites from bondage in Egypt to the borders of the Promised Land. He also organized the Israelites, received the Ten Commandments on Mount Sinai, and withstood the rebellion of **Korah** and his fellow conspirators.

Muses: nine sister goddesses, the patrons of the liberal arts and of major genres of poetry. They are **Calliopê** (epic), **Clio** (history), Erato (lyric), Euterpê (music), **Melpomenê** (tragedy), Polymnia (sacred verse), **Terpsichorê** (dancing), **Thalia** (comedy), and Urania (astronomy). Some Renaissance mythographers treat them as daughters of **Apollo**, though they are usually said to be offspring of **Jupiter**.

Naboth: see **Jezebel**.

Neaera: sea nymph who, according to **Homer**, bore to the sun-god **Helios** two daughters, Phaethusa and Lampetia. They guarded the god's sacred cattle on the island of Thrinacia.

Neptune (Poseidon):   god of the sea. As **Poseidon**, he was revered by Greek sailors, and as Neptune he was associated with horses and celebrated in Rome at the Neptunalia celebrated at the Campus Martius. His symbol is the trident, or three-pointed spear. He was frequently invoked as a patron of England, particularly after the defeat of the Armada, when the English navy began to alter the balance of power in Europe.

Nereids: see **Nereus**.

Nereus: benevolent and wise Greek god of the Mediterranean known as the Old Man of the Sea. Son of Gaia and Pontus, he educated **Venus** and fathered the fifty Mediterranean sea nymphs known as **nereids**, among them **Thetis** and Galatea. He has the power of prophecy, but only when physically constrained, and because he, like **Proteus**, is a shape-shifter, he is difficult to capture.

Nestor: aged Greek hero, king of Pylos, celebrated by **Homer** for his wisdom.

Nicanor: son of Patroclus, sent by Ptolemy to crush the Jewish insurrection led by the Maccabees.

Niobe: daughter of Tantalus and wife of King Amphion of Thebes. When she boasted that her family of fourteen was larger than that of **Latona**, the giantess commanded her children, **Apollo** and **Diana**, to slay them, and Niobe turned to stone in grief.

Nisus: Trojan warrior who, in **Virgil**'s *Aeneid*, loses his life trying to save his friend **Eurialus** in battle.

Noah: biblical patriarch who saved his family and the animals and birds from the great flood described in the Book of Genesis.

Nymphs: minor goddesses associated with streams, lakes, hills, woods, the sea, and other natural sites.

Oberon: see **Fairy Queen**.

Oceanus (Ocean):   son of **Uranus** and Gaia and one of the **Titans**. With his wife Tethys, he engendered the gods, the rivers of the world, and the nymphs known as oceanids. The "Ocean sea" was regarded as a great river encircling the earth.

Odysseus: see **Ulysses**.

Onesimus: the runaway slave of **Philemon** in the New Testament, who returned to his master after meeting Saint Paul and being converted to Christianity.

Osiris: see **Isis**.

Otho: leader who overthrew the Roman Emperor Galba in the first century C.E.

Pallas: see **Minerva**.

Pan: see **Faunus**.

Pandora: in Greek myth, the first woman, who was created by Zeus, given the breath of life by **Athena**, and endowed with charms by all the gods (hence, her name, which means "all gifts"). When she married **Prometheus**'s brother Epimetheus, she brought with her a box that, when opened, released all the evils that afflict human beings, leaving only Hope behind. Elizabeth was sometimes compared with Pandora because of her many gifts and graces.

Paris (Alexander):   son of King **Priam** of Troy and his wife **Hecuba**. In the so-called Judgment of Paris, he was asked to decide who was the most fair: **Juno**, **Minerva**, or **Venus**. The prize was a golden orb devised by Atê, the Goddess of Discord. He chose Venus because she had bribed him with the promise of the Greek queen **Helen**, the most beautiful woman in the world. When he later abducted Helen, the Greeks made war on Troy and destroyed it. The Elizabethans often adapted the story so that the orb was awarded to Elizabeth.

Pasiphae: the daughter of **Helios** and wife of Minos, King of Crete. When Minos refused to kill a bull sent by Poseidon as a sacrifice, Pasiphae fell in love with it and persuaded **Dedalus** to devise a figure of a cow in which she could be concealed to mate with it. She later gave birth to the half-bull, half-man **Minotaur**.

Paul: apostle to the Gentiles, who was converted to Christianity after seeing a bright light and being struck blind on the road to Damascus.

Peleus: see **Thetis**.

Penelope: faithful wife of Odysseus (or **Ulysses**). She was besieged by suitors when he failed to return from the Trojan War. Promising to remarry when she had completed a shroud for her father-in-law, she secretly unraveled it each night for ten years, until Odysseus returned and killed all the suitors.

Penthesilea: queen of the **Amazons**, who fought for Troy in the Trojan War and was killed by **Achilles**. She and another Amazon queen, **Camilla,** were sometimes compared with Elizabeth to stress the Queen's courage and prowess.

Persephonê: see **Proserpina**.

Peter: disciple who denied knowing Christ at his trial but who later became a leader in the early Christian church and, by tradition, was crucified upside down in Rome.

Phaedra: see **Hippolytus**.

Phaeton: son of the sun god **Helios** (or Phoebus **Apollo**) and Clymene. Having asked his father to allow him to drive the team that draws the sun across the sky, he got his wish but lost control, swooping dangerously close to the earth. To prevent disaster, **Jupiter** destroyed him with a thunderbolt.

Pharaoh: title of the ancient Egyptian kings. Two Pharoahs are particularly important in the Old Testament. One is the king who refused to allow **Moses** and the Israelites to leave Egypt until God had sent ten plagues, killing all firstborn sons and livestock in the land. The other is the king who elevated the patriarch **Joseph** to power.

Philemon (in classical myth):   poor man who, with his wife Baucis, offered warm hospitality to **Jupiter** and **Mercury** when the two gods visited the earth disguised as mortals. The rich, who were not so hospitable, were destroyed in a deluge, but the old couple was saved and their home made a temple.

Philemon (in the New Testament):   see **Onesimus**.

Philomela: sister of **Procne** and daughter of Pandion, legendary king of Athens. Sexually defiled by Procne's husband Tereus, she had her tongue cut out to prevent her from reporting the crime. By weaving a tapestry about it, she informed her sister, who avenged the act by killing her son Itys and serving his flesh to Tereus. Philomela was then transformed into a nightingale, Procne into a swallow, and Tereus into a hoopoe.

Phoebe: see **Cynthia**.

Phoebus: see **Apollo**.

Phoenix: mythic bird said to rise to new life from the ashes of its own funeral pyre. The phoenix was a common symbol for Queen Elizabeth because, though in danger of execution for treason during the reign of Mary Tudor, she resurrected her political career and ascended the throne.

Phrixus: son of Athamas and brother of **Hellê**. Afflicted by his stepmother **Ino**, he and his sister fled from their native Thebes to modern-day Turkey, borne on the back of a ram with wings and golden fleece. Hellê fell from its back, landing on the channel later named for her, the Hellespont. Her brother arrived safely in Colchis, sacrificed the ram, and hung up its fleece in the temple, with a dragon to guard it. **Jason** led an expedition to seize the fleece.

Pilate (Pontius Pilate): Roman governor of Palestine who ordered Jesus to be crucified, against the advice of his wife.

Plato: Greek philosopher of the fourth century B.C.E. who wrote down the dialogues of his master, **Socrates**.

Pliny the Elder: Roman scholar of the first century C.E., whose most important work was his *Natural History*.

Pollux: see **Castor and Pollux**.

Polydorus: see **Hecuba**.

Polymestor: see **Hecuba**.

Pomona: goddess of fruit.

Pompey the Great: Roman general who served with Caesar and Crassus in the ruling coalition known as the First Triumvirate and was later defeated by Caesar.

Pontius Pilate: see **Pilate**.

Poseidon: see **Neptune**.

Praxilla: Greek lyric poet of the fifth century B.C.E.

Priam: king of Ancient Troy, the husband of **Hecuba** and father of the **Hector**, **Paris**, and many other children. He and Hecuba died at the hand of **Achilles's** son **Pyrrhus**.

Priapus: god of fertility of gardens and herds.

Procne: see **Philomela**.

Prometheus: son of the **Titans**. He made humans out of clay and gave them the gift of fire from Mount Olympus, for which theft he was punished by **Zeus** to be chained to a rock in the Caucasus, where each day his liver was eaten by a vulture.

Proserpina (Persephonê): daughter of **Jupiter** and **Ceres**. She represents the annual cycle of planting, growth, and death in crops. Seized by Hades and taken to be his bride in the underworld, she was forced to stay because she had eaten some of his pomegranate seeds. Her mother, who sought her throughout the earth, was allowed to spend six months each year with her during the growing season.

Proteus: the son of **Poseidon** and the herdsman of seals. When held down, he could be compelled to foretell the future, but since he was a shape-changer, he was difficult to capture.

Pyrrha: see **Duecalion**.

Publius Cornelius: see **Tacitus**.

Publius Vergilius Maro: see **Virgil**.

Pyrrhus (Neoptolemus): son of **Achilles**. After his father's death, he was brought to Troy by Odysseus (or **Ulysses**) as a necessary condition to Greek victory. He fought bravely there, ultimately killing King **Priam** and Queen **Hecuba**.

Pythia: the **Sibyl**, or priestess of **Apollo**, at Delphi, whose inspired utterances were preserved in hexameter verse.

Saba: see **Sheba, Queen of**.

Samson: son of **Manoah** and one of the judges of Israel. He was known for his physical strength, which he lost when Delilah, a Philistine woman, learned that his power resided in his long hair and had it shaved off.

Samuel: prophet and priest of God, called as a young boy to serve the priest Eli. He later anointed **Saul**, the first king of Israel, and **David**, the second king.

Sappho: Greek woman poet born in the seventh century B.C.E. on the island of Lesbos. Her celebrations of homoerotic love between women led to the use of the term "Lesbian."

Sarah: see **Abraham**.

Satan (Beelzebub, Lucifer):   the Devil, called in scripture the father of lies and "the Adversary." Sometimes represented as a lion prowling for prey, he is identified with the Serpent in the Book of Genesis and with Lucifer, known as the angel of light or the Son of the Morning.

Saturn (Cronus):   husband of Ops and god of agriculture, who reigned over the universal peace and plenty of the Age of Gold. He came to power by overthrowing and castrating his father, **Uranus**, and was in turn overthrown when his son **Zeus** became the supreme Olympian god. Elizabeth's reign was often characterized, both in her own day and later, as a return to the Golden Age.

Saul: see **David**.

Scipio Africanus: Roman hero who conquered Spain and defeated Hannibal, ruler of Carthage.

Seasons: see **Hours**.

Selênê: see **Cynthia**.

Seneca: Roman philosopher and (it was thought in the Renaissance) author of a number of tragedies based on Greek models. He was a proponent of the view that people should discipline themselves to be impassive to misfortune and suffering, regarding the inner peace and reason of the soul as of paramount concern.

Sergestus: see **Aeneas**.

Sheba, Queen of: see **Solomon**.

Sheba (rebel):   see **David**.

Sibyls: Greek prophetesses. At the temple of **Apollo** at Delphi and elsewhere, they replied in poetic riddles to questions put to the god through them. A prophecy by the Cumaean Sibyl in **Virgil**'s Fourth *Eclogue* was later interpreted as a revelation of the coming of Christ, giving her an honored place in some Christian works of art and literature.

Sinon: Greek soldier who persuaded the Trojans to admit the wooden horse into Troy.

Sirens: mythical beings, often represented with bodies of birds and the heads of women, who were said to sing so beautifully that they lured sailors to destruction on rocky shores.

Sisera: see **Deborah, Jael**.

Socrates: Greek philosopher who lived in the fifth century B.C.E. and was unjustly made to drink hemlock for corrupting the youth of Athens. His dialogues were written down by his student, **Plato**.

Solomon: king of Judah famous for his wisdom and wealth, for his many foreign wives, and for his building of the first Jewish temple. The preeminence of Israel over neighboring states in his day is suggested by the account of the visit of the **Queen of Sheba**. Because of his wisdom and his construction of the house of God, Solomon was frequently compared with Elizabeth.

Susannah: a virtuous woman falsely accused of adultery; her story is recorded in the apocryphal additions to the book of Daniel. Occasionally, Elizabeth was compared with her because of her virtue in the face of false accusations.

Sylvanus: Roman god of forests, groves and meadows. He protects herds and cattle and is associated with **Faunus**.

Syrinx: see **Faunus.**

Tacitus (Publius Cornelius): first-century orator, politician, and historian who recorded the decline of Roman political freedoms. He was admired for his prose style.

Taurus: see **Europa.**

Telesilla: Greek female poet of the fifth century B.C.E., who, by arming slaves, women, and old men, saved Argos from the Spartans.

Tellus: god of the earth.

Terpsicorê: see **Muses.**

Thalia: see **Muses.**

Themis: see **Hours.**

Theseus: Greek hero, son of Aegeus and Aethra, whose many adventures included resisting Medea, conquering the **Minotaur**, marrying the **Amazon** princess Hipppolyta, and helping Pirithous rescue **Persephonê** from Hades.

Thetis: one of the **Nereids**, or sea nymphs. Beloved of **Zeus** and **Poseidon**, she was nonetheless wedded to a mortal, **Peleus**, King of Phthia, because of a prophecy that her son would be mightier than his father. The son was **Achilles.**

Thucydides: Greek general and historian of the fifth century B.C.E. He wrote the *History of the Peloponnesian War.*

Tiberius: second Roman emperor, who lived in the first century B.C.E.

Titans: race of twelve giants, the offspring of **Saturn** and Ge. They rebelled against **Jupiter** and were subdued. The sun god (Sol), who is one of their ancestors, is also called **Titan.**

Titania: see **Fairy Queen.**

Titus Livius: see **Livy.**

Tobias: son of Tobit and Anna, who is miraculously protected when he journeys to Media to regain the family fortune. Their story is told in the apocryphal Book of Tobit.

Triton: sea god with the upper body of a man and the tail of a fish. The son of **Neptune** and Amphitrite, he is often represented blowing a conch shell. In some accounts, there are several such mermen.

Tully: see **Cicero.**

Ulysses (Odysseus): Greek hero of the Trojan war, known for his cunning and strength; his adventurous ten-year journey home to **Penelope** in Ithaca is recorded in **Homer**'s *Odyssey.*

Uranus: see **Saturn.**

Uzziah: see **Judith.**

Varro (Marcus Terentius): Roman orator who flourished in the second century B.C.E.

Venus (Aphrodite): goddess of love, the mother of **Cupid** and wife of **Vulcan**. Her bird is the dove. On her adulterous love affair with **Mars**, see **Vulcan**. Elizabeth's beauty and cultivation of idealized love relationships with her poets and courtiers led to comparisons between her and the goddess, particularly the chaste and virtuous form of the goddess known as Venus Urania.

Vesta: goddess of the hearth, worshipped with an ever-burning flame in a temple central to the state religion in ancient Rome. The Vestal Virgins who served there took vows, on pain of death, not to engage in sexual relations. Elizabeth's virginity invited literary associations with the Roman goddess and her priestesses.

Virgil (Publius Vergilius Maro): Roman author and favorite of the emperor Augustus Caesar. He was famous for his pastoral *Eclogues*, his epic *The Aeneid*, and his agricultural poem *The Georgics.*

Virgo: see **Astraea, Isis.**

Voadicia: see **Boadicia.**

Vortumnus: Roman god of the changing seasons. He is the husband of **Pomona.**

Vulcan: god of fire and blacksmith to the gods, famous for making Jupiter's thunderbolts and things of beauty such as **Achilles**'s shield. The son of **Jupiter** and **Juno,** he was lame from birth. His wife **Venus** cheated on him with **Mars.** When he learned of the affair, he devised a net to catch them in the act and expose them to the ridicule of the gods.

Whore of Babylon: figure in the Book of Revelation representing pride, immorality, worldly wealth, and corruption, particularly that of ancient Rome and, in this period, the Roman Catholic Church and female rulers associated with it, such as Mary Tudor, Mary Stuart, and Catherine de Medici. She is pictured in scarlet robes and elaborate jewelry, riding on a beast with seven heads (representing the seven hills of Rome) and ten horns and holding a golden cup from which she drinks the blood of the saints. At the end of the world, she will fall in battle against the Lamb of God, or Christ.

Xenophon: fifth-century B.C.E. Greek historian whose work *Anabasis* on the Persian king Cyrus influenced subsequent Latin literature.

Xerxes I: fifth-century B.C.E. Persian king, who built a bridge across the Hellespont in his war against the Greeks, but was defeated at the Battle of Salamis.

Zechariah: see **Elizabeth.**

Zenobia: queen of Egypt as well as Syria and much of Asia Minor, said to be descended from **Dido** and from Cleopatra and Mark Antony; she fought Rome but was defeated by the emperor **Aurelian** in the third century C.E.

Zerubbabel: descendent of the kingly line of the tribe of **Judah** who supervised the rebuilding of the temple after the return of the Jews from captivity in Babylon.

Zeus: see **Jupiter.**